Nineteenth-Century Literature Criticism

Guide to Gale Literary Criticism Series

For criticism on	Consult these Gale series
Authors now living or who died after December 31, 1959	*CONTEMPORARY LITERARY CRITICISM (CLC)*
Authors who died between 1900 and 1959	*TWENTIETH-CENTURY LITERARY CRITICISM (TCLC)*
Authors who died between 1800 and 1899	*NINETEENTH-CENTURY LITERATURE CRITICISM (NCLC)*
Authors who died between 1400 and 1799	*LITERATURE CRITICISM FROM 1400 TO 1800 (LC)* *SHAKESPEAREAN CRITICISM (SC)*
Authors who died before 1400	*CLASSICAL AND MEDIEVAL LITERATURE CRITICISM (CMLC)*
Black writers of the past two hundred years	*BLACK LITERATURE CRITICISM (BLC)*
Authors of books for children and young adults	*CHILDREN'S LITERATURE REVIEW (CLR)*
Dramatists	*DRAMA CRITICISM (DC)*
Hispanic writers of the late nineteenth and twentieth centuries	*HISPANIC LITERATURE CRITICISM (HLC)*
Native North American writers and orators of the eighteenth, nineteenth, and twentieth centuries	*NATIVE NORTH AMERICAN LITERATURE (NNAL)*
Poets	*POETRY CRITICISM (PC)*
Short story writers	*SHORT STORY CRITICISM (SSC)*
Major authors from the Renaissance to the present	*WORLD LITERATURE CRITICISM, 1500 TO THE PRESENT (WLC)*

ISSN 0732-1864

Volume 64

Nineteenth-Century Literature Criticism

Topics Volume

Excerpts from Criticism of Various
Topics in Nineteenth-Century Literature,
including Literary and Critical Movements,
Prominent Themes and Genres, Anniversary
Celebrations, and Surveys of National Literatures

Gerald R. Barterian
Denise Evans

Editors

GALE

DETROIT · NEW YORK · TORONTO · LONDON

STAFF

Gerald R. Barterian and Denise Evans, *Editors*

Jelena Krstović, Marie Lazzari, *Contributing Editors*

Amy K. Crook, *Associate Editor*

Aarti D. Stephens, *Managing Editor*

Susan M. Trosky, *Permissions Manager*
Kimberly F. Smilay, *Permissions Specialist*
Sarah Chesney, *Permissions Associate*
Steve Cusack, Kelly A. Quin, *Permissions Assistants*

Victoria B. Cariappa, *Research Manager*
Julia C. Daniel, Tamara C. Nott,
Tracie A. Richardson, Cheryl L. Warnock, *Research Associates*
Jeffrey Daniels, Talitha Jean, *Research Assistants*

Mary Beth Trimper, *Production Director*
Deborah L. Milliken, *Production Assistant*

Christi Fuson, *Macintosh Artist*
Randy Bassett, *Image Database Supervisor*
Robert Duncan, Michael Logusz, *Imaging Specialists*
Pamela A. Reed, *Photography Coordinator*

This book is printed on acid-free paper that meets the minimum requirements of American National Standard for Information Sciences—Permanence Paper for Printed Library Materials, ANSI Z39.48-1984.

Library of Congress Catalog Card Number 84-643008
ISBN 0-7876-1247-2
ISSN 0732-1864
Printed in the United States of America

10 9 8 7 6 5 4 3 2 1

Contents

Preface

Since its inception in 1981, *Nineteenth-Century Literature Criticism* has been a valuable resource for students and librarians seeking critical commentary on writers of this transitional period in world history. Designated an "Outstanding Reference Source" by the American Library Association with the publication of its first volume, *NCLC* has since been purchased by over 6,000 school, public, and university libraries. The series has covered more than 300 authors representing 29 nationalities and over 17,000 titles. No other reference source has surveyed the critical reaction to nineteenth-century authors and literature as thoroughly as *NCLC*.

Scope of the Series

NCLC is designed to introduce students and advanced readers to the authors of the nineteenth century, and to the most significant interpretations of these authors' works. The great poets, novelists, short story writers, playwrights, and philosophers of this period are frequently studied in high school and college literature courses. By organizing and reprinting commentary written on these authors, *NCLC* helps students develop valuable insight into literary history, promotes a better understanding of the texts, and sparks ideas for papers and assignments. Each entry in *NCLC* presents a comprehensive survey of an author's career or an individual work of literature and provides the user with a multiplicity of interpretations and assessments. Such variety allows students to pursue their own interests; furthermore, it fosters an awareness that literature is dynamic and responsive to many different opinions.

Every fourth volume of *NCLC* is devoted to literary topics that cannot be covered under the author approach used in the rest of the series. Such topics include literary movements, prominent themes in nineteenth-century literature, literary reaction to political and historical events, significant eras in literary history, prominent literary anniversaries, and the literatures of cultures that are often overlooked by English-speaking readers.

NCLC continues the survey of criticism of world literature begun by Gale's *Contemporary Literary Criticism (CLC)* and *Twentieth-Century Literary Criticism (TCLC)*, both of which excerpt and reprint commentary on authors of the twentieth century. For additional information about *TCLC, CLC,* and Gale's other criticism series, users should consult the Guide to Gale Literary Criticism Series preceding the title page in this volume.

Coverage

Each volume of *NCLC* is carefully compiled to present:

- criticism of authors, or literary topics, representing a variety of genres and nationalities
- both major and lesser-known writers and literary works of the period
- 5-8 authors or 4-6 topics per volume
- individual entries that survey critical response to an author's work or a topic in literary history, including early criticism to reflect initial reactions, later criticism to represent any rise or decline in reputation, and current retrospective analyses.

Organization

An author entry consists of the following elements: author heading, biographical and critical introduction, list of principal works, excerpts of criticism (each preceded by a bibliographic citation and an annotation), and a bibliography of further reading.

- The **Author Heading** consists of the name under which the author most commonly wrote, followed by birth and death dates. If an author wrote consistently under a pseudonym, the pseudonym will be listed in the author heading and the real name given in parentheses on the first line of the biographical and critical introduction. Also located at the beginning of the introduction to the author entry are any name variations under which an author wrote, including transliterated forms for an author whose language uses a nonroman alphabet.

- The **Biographical and Critical Introduction** outlines the author's life and career, as well as the critical issues surrounding his or her work. References are provided to past volumes of *NCLC* in which further information about the author may be found.

- Most *NCLC* entries include a **Portrait** of the author. Many entries also contain reproductions of materials pertinent to an author's career, including manuscript pages, title pages, dust jackets, letters, and drawings, as well as photographs of important people, places, and events in an author's life.

- The list of **Principal Works** is chronological by date of first publication and identifies the genre of each work. In the case of foreign authors with both foreign-language publications and English translations, the English-language version is given in brackets. Unless otherwise indicated, dramas are dated by first performance, not first publication.

- **Criticism** in each author entry is arranged chronologically to provide a perspective on changes in critical evaluation over the years. All titles of works by the author featured in the entry are printed in boldface type to enable the user to easily locate discussion of particular works. Also for purposes of easier identification, the critic's name and the publication date of the essay are given at the beginning of each piece of criticism. Unsigned criticism is preceded by the title of the journal in which it appeared. Publication information (such as publisher names and book prices) and some parenthetical numerical references (such as page and line references to specific editions of works) have been deleted at the editors' discretion to provide smoother reading of the text. Footnotes that appear with previously published pieces of criticism are reprinted at the end of each essay or excerpt. In the case of excerpted criticism, only those footnotes that pertain to the excerpted text are included.

- A complete **Bibliographic Citation** provides original publication information for each piece of criticism.

- Critical excerpts are prefaced by **Annotations** providing the reader with a summary of the critical intent of the piece. Also included, when appropriate, is information about the critic's reputation, individual approach to literary criticism, and particular expertise in an author's works, as well as information about the relative importance of the critical excerpt. In some cases, the annotations cross-reference excerpts by critics who discuss each other's commentary.

- An annotated list of **Further Reading** appearing at the end of each entry suggests secondary sources on the author. In some cases it includes essays for which the editors could not obtain reprint rights.

Cumulative Indexes

- Each volume of *NCLC* contains a cumulative **Author Index** listing all authors who have appeared in Gale's Literary Criticism Series, along with cross-references to such biographical series as *Contemporary Authors* and *Dictionary of Literary Biography*. Useful for locating authors within the various series, this index is particularly valuable for those authors who are identified with a certain period but who, because of their death dates, are placed in another, or for those authors whose careers span two periods. For example, Fyodor Dostoevsky is found in *NCLC,* yet Leo Tolstoy, another major nineteenth-century Russian novelist, is found in *TCLC* because he died after 1899.

- Each *NCLC* volume includes a cumulative **Nationality Index** which lists all authors who have appeared in *NCLC*, arranged alphabetically under their respective nationalities.

- Each new volume in Gale's Literary Criticism Series includes a cumulative **Topic Index**, which lists all literary topics treated in *NCLC, TCLC, LC 1400-1800*, and the *CLC* Yearbook.

- Each new volume of *NCLC*, with the exception of the Topics volumes, contains a **Title Index** listing the titles of all literary works discussed in the volume. In response to numerous suggestions from librarians, Gale has also produced a **Special Paperbound Edition** of the *NCLC* title index. This annual cumulation lists all titles discussed in the series since its inception. Additional copies of the index are available on request. Librarians and patrons have welcomed this separate index: it saves shelf space, is easy to use, and is recyclable upon receipt of the following year's cumulation. Titles discussed in the Topics volume entries are not included in the *NCLC* cumulative index.

Citing *Nineteenth-Century Literature Criticism*

When writing papers, students who quote directly from any volume in Gale's Literary Criticism Series may use the following general forms to footnote reprinted criticism. The first example pertains to material drawn from periodicals, the second to material reprinted from books:

[1]T.S. Eliot, "John Donne," *The Nation and Athenaeum*, 33 (9 June 1923), 321-32; excerpted and reprinted in *Literature Criticism from 1400-1800,* Vol. 10, ed. James E. Person, Jr. (Detroit: Gale Research, 1989), pp. 28-9.

[2]Clara G. Stillman, *Samuel Butler: A Mid-Victorian Modern* (Viking Press, 1932); excerpted and reprinted in *Twentieth-Century Literary Criticism,* Vol. 33, ed. Paula Kepos (Detroit: Gale Research, 1989), pp. 43-5.

Suggestions Are Welcome

In response to suggestions, several features have been added to *NCLC* since the series began, including annotations to excerpted criticism, a cumulative index to authors in all Gale literary criticism series, entries devoted to criticism on a single work by a major author, more illustrations, and a title index listing all literary works discussed in the series.

Readers who wish to suggest authors, single works, or topics to appear in future volumes, or who have other suggestions, are cordially invited to write: The Editors, *Nineteenth-Century Literature Criticism,* 835 Penobscot Bldg., 645 Griswold St., Detroit, MI 48226-4094; call toll-free at 1-800-347-GALE; or fax to 1-313-961-6599.

Acknowledgments

The editors wish to thank the copyright holders of the excerpted criticism included in this volume and the permissions managers of many book and magazine publishing companies for assisting us in securing reproduction rights. We are also grateful to the staffs of the Detroit Public Library, the Library of Congress, the University of Detroit Mercy Library, Wayne State University Purdy/Kresge Library Complex, and the University of Michigan Libraries for making their resources available to us. Following is a list of the copyright holders who have granted us permission to reproduce material in this volume of *NCLC*. Every effort has been made to trace copyright, but if omissions have been made, please let us know.

COPYRIGHTED EXCERPTS IN *NCLC,* VOLUME 64, WERE REPRODUCED FROM THE FOLLOWING PERIODICALS:

American Imago, v. 45, Summer, 1988. Copyright (c) 1988 by The Johns Hopkins University Press. Reproduced by permission of The Johns Hopkins University Press.—*American Literature*, v. 65, September, 1993. Copyright (c) 1993 Duke University Press, Durham, NC. Reproduced with permission.—*American Quarterly*, v. 37, Winter 1985. Copyright (c) 1985 by John Hopkins University Press. Reproduced by permission of The Johns Hopkins University Press.—*Ameriksastudien/American Studies (Amst)*, v. 26, 1981 for "Autobiographical Works by Native Americans" by Bernd C. Peyer. Reproduced by permission of the author.—*Eire-Ireland*, v. 7, Winter 1972 for "Love and Famine, Family and Country in Trollope's Castle Richmond" by Hugh L. Hennedy. Copyright (c) 1972 by the Irish American Cultural Institute. Reproduced by permission of the publisher.—*ELH*, v.53, Summer, 1986. Copyright (c) 1986 by The Johns Hopkins University Press. Reproduced by permission.—*The Mississippi Valley Historical Review*, v. XLVII, September 1960 for "Some Themes of Counter-Subversion: An Analysis of Anti-Masonic, Anti-Catholic, and Anti-Mormon Literature" by David Brion Davis. Copyright Organization of American Historians, 1960. Reproduced by permission.—*PMLA*, v. 111, January, 1996. Copyright (c) 1996 by the Modern Language Association of America. Reproduced by permission of the Modern Language Association of America.—*Representations*, v. 34, Spring, 1991 for "The Uses of Male Hysteria: Medical and Literary Discourse in Nineteenth-Century France" by Jan Goldstein. Copyright (c) The Regents of the University of California. Reproduced by permission of the publisher and the author.—*Studies in American Indian Literature*, v. 4, Summer/Fall 1992 for "An Indian, An American" by Erik Peterson. Reproduced by permission of the author.—*Studies in Romanticism*, v. 23, Winter, 1974. Reproduced by permission.—*Studies in the Novel*, v. XXV, Summer, 1993. Copyright 1993 by North Texas State University. Reproduced by permission of the publisher.

COPYRIGHTED EXCERPTS IN *NCLC,* VOLUME 64, WERE REPRODUCED FROM THE FOLLOWING BOOKS:

Bataille, Gretchen M. and Kathleen Mullen Sands. From *American Indian Women: Telling Their Lives*. University of Nebraska Press, 1984. Copyright (c) The University of Nebraska Press 1984. Reproduced by permission.—Brumble, H. David, III. From *American Indian Autobiography*. The University of California Press, 1988. Copyright (c) 1988 The Regents of the University of California. All rights reserved. Reproduced by permission of the publisher and the author.—Canfield, Gae Whitney. From *Sarah Winnemucca of the Northern Paiutes*. University of Oklahoma Press, 1983. Copyright (c) 1983 by the University of Oklahoma Press, Norman. Reproduced by permission.—Ender, Evelyne. From *Sexing the Mind: Nineteenth-Century Fictions of Hysteria*. Cornell University Press, 1995. Cornell University Press, 1995. Copyright (c) 1995 by Cornell University. All rights reserved. Reproduced by permission of the publisher, Cornell University Press. All additional uses of this material—including, but not limited to, photocopying and reprinting—are prohibited without the prior written approval of Cornell University Press.—Ender, Evelyne. From *Sexing the Mind: Nineteenth-Century Fictions of Hysteria*. Cornell University Press, 1995. Copyright (c) 1995 by Cornell University. All rights reserved. Reproduced by permission of the publisher, Cornell University Press. All additional uses of this material-including, but not limited to, photocopying and reprinting-are prohibited without the prior written approval of Cornell University Press.—Franchot, Jenny. From *Roads to Rome: The Antebellum Protestant Encounter with Catholicism*. The University of California Press, 1994. Copyright (c) 1994 The Regents of the University of California. All rights reserved. Reproduced by permission of the publisher and the author.—Georgi-Findlay, Brigitte. From *New Voices in Native American Literary Criticism*. Edited by Arnold Krupat. Smithsonian Institution Press, 1993. Copyright (c) 1993 by the Smithsonian Institution. All rights reserved. Reproduced by

PHOTOGRAPHS AND ILLUSTRATIONS APPEARING IN *NCLC*, VOLUME 64, WERE RECEIVED FROM THE FOLLOWING SOURCES:

during the 1840's famine, photograph. Illustrated London News/Corbis. Reproduced by permission.—Trollope, Anthony, photograph. The Bettman Archive. Reproduced by permission.—"View of 'Black Hawk Pointe'" a lithograph by J. E. Dillingham, photograph. Library of Congress/Corbis. Reproduced by permission.—Winnemucca, (The Giver), photograph. National Archives and Records Administration.

Catholicism in Nineteenth-Century American Literature

INTRODUCTION

Insofar as the American colonies were settled and the nation founded predominantly by Protestants, the culture of America in the nineteenth century was mainly characterized by the Protestant spirit. Despite a period of toleration immediately following the Revolutionary War when Protestant-Catholic relations were cordial, anti-Catholicism broke out in the early nineteenth century and took on a definite shape and direction with the nativist movement, which waged war against Mormonism, the Masonic Order, and Catholicism. Historians offer various explanations for the phenomenon of nativism occurring at that point in American history as well as for its vast sweep and special virulence. But it is generally agreed that it was a convergence of the political ideals and religious beliefs by which most Americans defined themselves, and the sudden and dramatic increase in the sheer number of Catholic immigrants that produced nativism and, particularly, anti-Catholicism. The Roman Catholic Church seemed to nativists the antithesis of America's democratic ideals—the Roman Church was conspicuously hierarchical and authoritarian and so, it was assumed, politically anti-democratic. Its belief in celibacy for clergy made it appear anti-social; its rites were mystical and, therefore, ran counter to the purely ethical religion and natural theology prevalent in the Protestant churches of the nineteenth century; and the highly cultured and learned Roman Magesterium clashed with strong egalitarian instincts, especially during the era of Jacksonian democracy.

The movement spawned some mob violence, the most famous being the burning of the Ursuline convent in Charlestown, Massachusetts, in the mid-1830s. But nativism was largely an ideological movement that produced vast quantities of published material alleging vicious depredations on the part of the Roman Catholic Church, as well as seditiousness, superstitions, and perversions of Christian belief and virtue. The persistent focus of this literature was on the convents as the element of Catholicism to be feared the most, because it was believed that they would enslave and corrupt free and wholesome American womanhood. It was the widely-read nativist anti-Catholic tract *Awful Disclosures* (1836) by Maria Monk, a young Ursuline nun, that incited the burning of the convent she had fled (and later voluntarily sought to return to) in Charlestown. Many other similar, popular exposés, like Rebecca Reed's *Six Months in a Convent* (1835) were published in New York, Philadelphia, and Boston. Convents, it is generally agreed, were the main target of nativist attacks on Catholicism because, as closed societies, they appealed at once to prurience and to popular suspicions of what appeared to be "foreign" and not generally understood. Besides the exposés, many articles, tracts, and books were published which advanced theological and historical arguments attacking papal authority, priestly celibacy, the confessional, and the veneration of saints, among other issues.

In response, the Catholic press produced a large number of works in which the Catholic faith was defended and Protestantism, in turn, was attacked. Catholics also countered by attempting to undo the libel against convent life and to discredit the false accounts of "renegades" like Maria Monk. In addition, the Catholic Church reacted by drawing the theological lines between itself and Protestantism more emphatically. Its most effective line of defense was the parish school: many school texts were published, along with a growing number of devotional guides for the average Catholic, which stressed the exclusivity of the "one holy, catholic, and apostolic Church." Much less strident than the Protestant assault, the Catholic response aimed to persuade rather than revile by showing the weaknesses of Protestantism's intellectual positions, which it frankly disdained as historically disingenuous and theologically simplistic. One of the most prolific and vociferous of the nineteenth-century Catholic writers was Orestes Brownson, a lay convert, who asserted that the logic of Protestantism, which kept it in perpetual revolt, would also lead inevitably to atheism. Much of the Catholic argument was devoted to the Reformation of the sixteenth century; here, in the Catholic view, lay the root cause of the present religious, moral, and civil decay, for Protestants had rejected the religious and moral authority of the church.

The Catholic novel, too, was a means of defending and propagating the faith. In the thirty-six years between 1829 and 1865 almost fifty specifically pro-Catholic novels were written (largely by priests of varying skill) and published. Unlike many of its Protestant counterparts, the Catholic novel propagandized not with sensational gothic tales of kidnapping, seduction, and rapine, but with mannered, sentimental romances illustrating the way good Catholics lived and practiced their religion. Because of the difficult task of at once disproving Protestantism and converting Protestants to Catholicism, Catholic fiction became, on the one hand, excessively sentimental in its attempt to appeal to the prevailing tastes of novel readers, and, on the other hand, too abstract and discursive. Either tendency, as Orestes Brownson, who was also a critic and novelist, pointed out, rendered a work less effective. A few Catholic writers of this period approached their task by deemphasizing the more exclusive forms of Catholicism and emphasizing their common American patriotic sentiments.

Just as the Catholic response to rampant anti-Catholicism reached high tide around mid-century, the public image of Catholics suddenly turned favorable. The more strident anti-Catholicism that decried all priests and other religious orders as demonic gave way to a view of them as exemplars of Christian virtue. This change is evident in the treatment of the role of the nun in fiction from the middle to the end of the nineteenth century: depicted before 1860 as a demonic perpetrator of the "evils" of Catholicism, between 1860 and 1870 she was described as a woman of supreme, unworldly virtue, and finally, in the last three decades of the century, she became simply a good woman whose antiquated religion rendered her incompetent to do the good she desires.

The Catholic novel changed accordingly after 1860. Becoming more and more the occupation of lay writers, it was transformed from a thinly-veiled apologetic treatise to a more thoroughly literary product that had largely assimilated and affirmed American culture. This secularization was already a tendency in Catholic fiction before 1850, and Orestes Brownson, who saw the novel as the most effective mode of apologetics, severely criticized the trend in his reviews as dangerous to Catholic integrity. But after 1850 the tendency became the rule, one which even Brownson found all but irresistible. By the end of the century, anti-Catholicism remained but was submerged under a broad civil tolerance effected by an increasingly secularized American society.

REPRESENTATIVE WORKS

Anonymous
An Apology for the Conversion of Stephen Cleveland Blythe, To the Faith of the Catholic, Apostolic, and Roman Church (treatise) 1815
"The Priest—the Wife—the Family" (essay) 1846, published in *United States Magazine* 17
Pope or President? Startling Disclosures of Romanism as Revealed by Its Own Writers (treatise) 1859

Edward Beecher
The Papal Conspiracy Exposed, and Protestantism Defended in the Light of Reason, History and Scripture (treatise) 1855

George Bourne
Lorette. The History of Louise, Daughter of a Canadian Nun: Exhibiting the Interior of Female Convents (novel) 1833

Orestes Brownson
Charles Elwood; or, The Infidel Converted (novel) 1840
"Novel-Writing and Novel-Reading" (essay) 1848
The Spirit-Rapper: An Autobiography (novel) 1854
"Rome or Reason" (essay) 1867, published in *The Works of Orestes A. Brownson*

Charles James Cannon
Father Felix: A Tale (novel) 1845
"Catholic Literature in the United States" (essay) 1854, published in *Metropolitan* 2

Norwood Damon
The Chronicles of Mount Benedict. A Tale of the Ursuline Convent—The Quasi Production of Mary Magdalen (satire) 1837

Anna Hanson Dorsey
The Student of Blenheim Forest; or, The Trials of a Convert (novel) 1846
The Oriental Pear; or, The Catholic Immigrants (novel) 1848
Conscience; or, The Trial of May Brooke, An American Catholic Tale (novel) 1864

Theodore Dwight
Open Convents: or, Nunneries and Popish Seminaries Dangerous to the Morals, and Degrading to the Character of a Republican Community (treatise) 1836
"Female Convents" (essay) 1837, published in *The Christian Examiner* 19

Charles W. Frothingham
The Convent's Doom: A Tale of Charlestown in 1834 (novel) 1854

Jedidiah Vincent Huntington
Alban. A Tale of the New World (novel) 1853
Blonde and Brunette or The Gotham Arcady (novel) 1858

[Mary Anne Ursula Moffat] Mother Mary Edmund St. George
An Answer to Six Months in a Convent Exposing Its Falsehoods and Manifold Absurdities by the Lady Superior (essay) 1835

Maria Monk
Awful Disclosures of the Hotel Dieu Nunnery of Montreal (exposé) 1836

Charles Constantine Pise
Father Rowland: An American Tale (novel) 1829
Zenosius; or, The Pilgrim Convert (novel) 1845

Hugh Quigley

The Cross and the Shamrock; or, An Irish-American Catholic Tale of Real Life; or, How to Defend the Faith (novel) 1853

Profit and Loss: A Story of the Life of the Genteel Irish-Americans, Illustrative of Godless Education (novel) 1873

Rebecca Theresa Reed

Six Months in a Convent; or, The Narrative of Rebecca Theresa Reed (exposé) 1835

John T. Roddan

John O'Brien; or, The Orphan of Boston, A Tale of Real Life (novel) 1850

OVERVIEWS

Barbara Welter

SOURCE: "From Maria Monk to Paul Blanshard: A Century of Protestant Anti-Catholicism," in *Uncivil Religion: Interreligious Hostility in America*, edited by Robert N. Bellah and Frederick E. Greenspahn, The Crossroad Publishing Company, 1987, pp. 43-71.

[*In the following excerpt, Welter summarizes some of the enduring themes of the nativist crusade of nineteenth-century America, and illustrates some of its institutional arguments by focusing on the popular anti-Catholic tract* Awful Disclosures, *by Maria Monk.*]

American historians are willing to spare few of our cherished illusions. George Washington's cherry tree and Thomas Jefferson's family life have vanished with our lost passenger pigeons. It is, therefore, not surprising that our boast to be a nation dedicated to religious freedom has also been refuted.

When the Statue of Liberty, symbol of a safe harbor for tempest-tossed souls, was completed in 1886, its symbolic lamp was dimmed by the prior publication of Josiah Strong's *Our Country*, a best seller extolling undiluted Anglo-Saxon racial and religious purity.[1] The Haymarket Riot, which John Higham termed "the most important single incident in late nineteenth-century nativism,"[2] occurred in the same year. It was, however, only one incident in a very long line of nativist hostilities, of which those involving Roman Catholics and Protestants were perhaps closest to the original concept of what well-ordered religious hostility should be about in this new Jerusalem.

The origins of this conflict and its linear growth on this continent have been well traced in several monographs, and I do not intend to repeat the chronology of these tensions from colonial times to the present.[3] I should like only to recapitulate some of the enduring themes in this most Christian crusade, especially those most appropriate to the New World, and then focus on two texts written more than a century apart in order to illustrate some of the peculiarly institutional arguments.

Maria Monk's *Awful Disclosures of the Hotel Dieu Nunnery of Montreal* was a best seller in 1836, and Paul Blanshard's *American Freedom and Catholic Power* achieved the same status in 1949. I suggest that the themes and even the language—metaphor, invective, connotative adjectives—are remarkably similar. Best sellers rarely demonstrate great literary imagination or intellectual rigor, but they do show what a large segment of the Republic wants to be told at a given time. When books are reprinted over and over, as has been the case with Monk's work, they reveal at the very least attitudes and ideas that appeal to many generations.

Historians of nativism—Ray Allen Billington, John Kane, John Higham, David Brion Davis, Richard Hofstadter, and Sydney Ahlstrom among them—uniformly denounce and categorically deny the objective reality of this anti-Catholic prose. The writers of these inflammatory tracts are dismissed as "hatemongers," "fanatics," and, most damning of all to the healthy historical mind, "paranoids."[4] I should like to suggest, if only as a kind of devil's advocate for popular culture, that these popular writings be reexamined, not as embarrassing blots on the national copybook of rights or as the ravings of a lunatic fringe of un-American Americans. I suggest that these two documents (and others in the same vein) be taken seriously as the expression of serious concern on the part of perfectly rational Americans.

Consensus is a way of dealing with controversies, not of denying them. The inflamed rhetoric of the anti-Catholic tracts, like the actual conflagration of anti-Catholic mobs, sprang from deep concern for values and for a way of life based on that most fragile value of all, personal liberty. Paranoids may be persecuted or, more often, may remember a time when they were persecuted. When anguish translates into hate literature and mob violence, it may reflect a passionate although inarticulate commitment to a genuinely endangered specific. Popular delusions and the madness of crowds are not hallucinatory in origin, however illusory in accomplishment. When there is widespread fear, as Mrs. Willy Loman might have defended her class, "Attention must be paid."

The litany of Protestant grievances against Catholics is a long and bitter one, as long and bitter as its reverse would be. Any list of grievances in any national catalogue of collected injustices tends to run to many

Publication of Maria Monk's Awful Disclosures of the Hotel Dieu Nunnery of Montreal *(1836) created a storm of controversy.*

pages, incorporating many varieties of experience, religious and political. To recite them, or even to list them all, sounds perilously like "How do I not love you? . . . . Let me count the ways." In this particular litany it might include: "We dislike your men (priests), your women (nuns) and your children (Boy Scouts), and a few institutions; we dislike the arrogance and elitism of claiming to be the 'one, holy, catholic and apostolic church'; we dislike the reliance on authority, rather than on individual judgment; we dislike the substitution of a parochial for a public school system; we find celibacy unwholesome and perverse for the clergy (indeed, for practically anyone); we oppose inflexible social rules masquerading as immutable natural laws; we oppose censorship in books; we prefer to read the Bible for ourselves and scorn official interpretation; we deplore the level of taste in architecture, statuary, and hymns; we shudder at the superstition surrounding the Virgin and the saints; and we deplore intransigence in the face of progressive reform, especially in temperance and women's rights." Now, although the most casual perusal of Puritan doctrine and law would find equal or greater violations of all the above without leaving the boundaries of Massachusetts, that does not deny the fact that Protestants believed themselves to

be the upholders of these yeoman, self-evident truths, which they believed Catholics opposed.

Catholics have historically responded to these accusations with such helpful arguments as: "You do not understand, and because you are not a member of the One True Church there is not a prayer that you ever could understand," or, "Only certain benighted ethnic or social groups believe that," or, "Have you stopped burning your witches lately?" Historians and liberal Protestants have been equally quick to deny any lingering validity on their side of the controversy. They metaphorically stuff Maria Monk and Paul Blanshard into the closet, saying soothingly to liberal Catholics, "We know that you, like us, have nothing to do with the clods who read bad books and burn convents. That's un-American and frightfully low, but neither side can be responsible for its 'crazies.'" This argument is both anti-historical and evasive.

When historians actually address themselves to the question of why the unenlightened Protestant has gotten these ideas so firmly fixed, they respond with a litany of their own:

> the English anti-Catholic tradition dates back at least to the Armada;

> it was intensified by an anti-Irish bias dating at least to Cromwell and extending, with all its ugly stereotypical ramifications, across the ocean;

> American Protestantism has been quick to refer to its honorable scars from Reformation Wars, even though the Reformation predated the founding of this country;

> the anti-Catholic rhetoric of the Puritans was intensified by popular books and sermons (John Foxe's *Book of Martyrs* was, after all, one of the few books a Protestant child could read on Sunday);

> the Quebec Act of 1774 had galvanized Americans into revolutionary action as they saw the spread of American Protestantism checked;

> France and Spain, which represented continual threats to American independence, were identified with moral decadence and woeful disregard of the work ethic;

> the large influx of Catholics to American cities represented what one historian refers to as a "disruption of America's agrarian dream,"[5] and those same immigrants posed an economic threat to American labor and an overburdening of very modest social-welfare agencies;

a "Protestant frontier thesis" saw winning the West as a religious rather than a territorial race, with "Presbyterians and Jesuits" as a more sober version of "Cowboys and Indians";

the gradual loss of status and prestige by American Protestants called forth a "backlash" which was expressed in the historical terms most familiar to the threatened group, namely, Reformation rhetoric.[6]

Seeking to explain the persistence of the anti-Catholic bias, David Brion Davis sees the nineteenth-century stereotyped Catholic as the "precise antitheses of American ideals, an inverted image of Jacksonian democracy."[7] Since the Jacksonian "ideals" were, in fact, largely composed of mythful thinking, constantly challenged by internal and external events, they were all the more in need of a countervailing demonic force. John William Ward argues that the need for a hero was so strong that if the age had not in fact produced Andrew Jackson, it would have invented him.[8] A similar need for an anti-hero produces the inverse of that thesis: If the age had not produced Catholics, it would have invented them as the necessary negative image of the proposed national virtue. This early Republic nationalism culminated in the most widely publicized burst of anti-Catholic violence, the burning of the Ursuline convent in Charlestown, Massachusetts, and the publication of that remarkable nativist tract, *The Awful Disclosures* of Maria Monk.[9]

The period before the American Civil War saw the "Beast of Rome" invading even this new Eden, as a series of highly visible conversions brought Americans from well-known American families (Sophia Dana Ripley, for example) and the "Seeker for Truth," Orestes Brownson, into the Catholic church. The Paulist Fathers were founded by another such convert, Isaac Hecker, for the avowed purpose of bringing the United States into the "True Church."[10] Hecker's visionary prose added to the bombastic transcendentalism of Brownson suggested to many Americans that Protestantism was being attacked for being too permissive, too secular, and too democratic. Since Protestants themselves were split over recent liberal changes in theology and society, this was a very palpable hit. Lyman Beecher went full tilt against the pernicious influence of convents in general and the Ursuline convent in particular, starting in 1830 when the convent had already been successfully educating young women for a dozen years.[11]

Besides the traditional Protestantism at war with the more relaxed tenets of Unitarians, the "New Light" versus the "Old Light," and other quasi-theological controversies, there was the persistent class structure, denied by both church and state and equally pervasive in both institutions. To the lower-class bricklayers in Charlestown, the Ursuline convent represented luxury

and mystery. The vagaries of heterodox and orthodox were mere puffs of smoke compared to the concrete fury generated by the flight of a young woman, Elizabeth Harrison, from the convent in 1834. Here was something a man could protest with all his strength and be proud in the blow he was striking for free American womanhood. The young Ursuline nun subsequently repented of her decision and asked Bishop Fenwick to allow her to return to her convent, but by this time all of Boston was involved. The selectmen were invited to tour the convent in order to put the more lascivious rumors to rest, but they were embroiled in a separate controversy with the bishop over a Catholic cemetery and dragged their feet. By the time they had their tour and published their report guaranteeing Miss Harrison's freedom and safety, a mob had burned the building, to the cheers of a large crowd.[12]

The persistent focus on convents as the most feared element in Catholic life involved more than just maintaining the female as scapegoat or even than substituting sexual for political issues in order to make the latter seem more threatening. This was a period in which American women, consistently described by themselves and foreign observers as the "free female in a free country" and "uniquely blessed among women in Christian lands," were beginning to exert themselves. Most Americans hoped to combine the traditional roles for women with a belief that these roles were carried out in the New World in such a way as to make them part of democratic life, liberty, and happiness. The existence of groups of women in convents was both a persistent threat and a frightening alternative to the cult of domesticity.

The prospectus of the school run by the Ursulines differed almost not at all from those of similar "female seminaries" of the period, and there is no evidence of overt religious proselytizing. In fact, it would appear that at this school, as well as in similar schools staffed by Roman Catholic Sisters, the curriculum was highly traditional and ornamental. In many parts of the country these convent schools were eagerly prized because they taught the rather raw young women at least some of the graces associated with civility, gentility, and the dubious values of young ladyism. Since it was widely believed that it took three generations to turn a young man into a gentleman but only one to make the woman into a lady, this crash course in social mobility was all the more prized.[13]

Americans' fascination for convents—illustrated in the twentieth century by the popularity of *The Nun's Story*[14]—was explained by one nineteenth-century British visitor, Frederick Marryat, as a national feeling that nothing must be kept veiled, an inherent commitment to freedom of information and open covenants openly arrived at. "Americans," he wrote in 1839, "cannot bear anything like a secret—that's *unconstitutional*."[15] In the absence of knowledge, they constructed their own fantasies, aided by a small but lurid literature of "ex-priest" and "ex-nun" autobiographies.[16] What went on after the Portress closed the heavy doors to those mysterious buildings surrounded by high walls? What mysterious sounds, smells, ceremonies took place in an atmosphere that, for many Protestants, literally reeked with incense and with sin? Simplicity in church liturgy and architecture, along with services in the vernacular, were identified with the vigor and strength of the country. Would not these virtues be eroded, smothered in the images, obscured by the Latin, shrouded by the very mysteries and authorities from which Protestants had presumably fled in escaping to America?

The most popular tale of all was that constructed by Maria Monk and presented to the public in 1836. (Monk's work is a sort of revenant of anti-Catholicism, most recently wafted through the country in the wake of John F. Kennedy's presidential campaign.) Although refutations appeared almost immediately, challenging both her authorship and her sanity (in a published interview with her mother it was revealed that a slate pencil had entered Maria's head as a child and she was never the same since), nature in this case proved no match for art.[17] And in this particular art the public most definitely knew what they wanted. Interestingly enough, however, although there certainly was the requisite discussion of hanky-panky in the confessional and elsewhere, the majority of the pages were devoted to a diatribe against Catholics because of their resistance to democracy, rather than their immorality.[18] The focus of attack was the complete authority that the priests had over the nuns and that the Mother Superior exercised over her charges. No matter how repugnant the act required might be, blind obedience replaced reason or independent judgment. Unspeakable humiliation was sanctioned in the name of obedience to authority. It is of interest that "breaking the will," a staple mandate in child-rearing manuals, was under attack in this period, and the parental authority formerly invested in the rod was being replaced by a "dominion of love and reason."[19]

The traditional mainspring of Protestant conviction, the independent reading of the Bible, was a long-standing matter of controversy between the two religions. Monk solemnly averred that she was not allowed to read the Bible and indeed never had, although a few chapters of scripture had been read aloud in her presence. When she asked her superiors why Catholics did not read the New Testament, she was told, "Because the mind of man is too limited and weak to understand what God has written."[20] The young women systematically became automatons, until they could say to their priests (not their God), "Not my will, but thine be done." Instead of encouraging a nation of sturdy yeoman, pulling their forelocks to no man, the network of

Catholic clergy demanded a subservience based not on Jefferson's "elite of virtue and intellect," but on the hierarchy of religion. Superstition was rampant, and the Blessed Virgin was a terrible role model for the American girl. At a time when what William James dubbed "the religion of positive thinking" was replacing the negativism of earlier years, such acts of penance as putting a pin through one's cheek or disciplining the flesh with a whip brought new revulsion.[21] The grim enthusiasms of Cotton Mather and Jonathan Edwards might have produced equal consternation if offered to this new generation, but the "mortification of the flesh" once so much a part of Puritan life was identified with the negative aspects of Catholicism.

One of the things most noticeable about Monk's book is the specificity of her charges. The reader is given detailed descriptions of the layout of the convent, the room for *accouchement* so conveniently placed next to the room where the priests strangled the babies after first baptizing them to secure "their everlasting happiness."[22] If these details were so accurately drawn, the overall theme of obedience and authoritarianism replacing independent thought and democratic process seemed equally true. These were the same Americans who, according to amazed travelers' accounts, let their hired girls sit at the dinner table and declined to respect titles or degrees. Samuel F. B. Morse, painter and inventor, allegedly became an ardent anti-Catholic when a soldier in Rome knocked off his hat as a religious procession was passing.[23]

The fragility of democracy seemed real, and the tightrope between European reaction and European revolution was difficult for Americans to walk during the tumultuous years before the Civil War. The threat from Catholicism was even more serious, since it combined the outer threat of external rule—the pope and his "guards"—with the inner threat of subversion, especially of the minds and wills of young women, future mothers of democratic men. Protestantism consistently defined itself as the liberator of women. This was the primary theme used to recruit women missionaries, urging them to volunteer in order to bring their benighted heathen sisters the blessings American Protestantism had conferred on women.

As the missionary movement increased in energy and numbers during the nineteenth century, it was often defined as a "war" between Catholics and Protestants for the dominion of the earth. One of its early themes was the impending millennium, which could take place only if the world was converted. This was interpreted as meaning not only the required baptism of the "heathen," but also the reconversion of what Protestants termed "nominal Christians" or Roman Catholics. This passion resulted eventually in a plaque that adorns the walls of the Vatican to this day, announcing the coming of the American Baptists in 1870 on their mission of "conversion."

The rivalry on the mission field usually consisted in harmless attempts on the part of the Protestants to harass their boards and their congregations by demanding more money or missionaries. Roman Catholic nuns were allegedly drawing away prospective women converts in China by dint of their beautiful embroidery. A call went out for Protestant girls with similar skills—a call not well heeded, it might be said. The popularity of the Catholic priest Father Damien resulted in the demand for a "Protestant leper," which was partially met through the work of Mary Reed, although stories about her never achieved the virtual cult of Damien. The Catholic Indian saint Catherine Tegawitha was responded to with a call for a Protestant Indian saint. Duly converted and duly dead, Henrietta Brown, young and pious though she was, somehow never captured the public imagination as did the "Lily of the Mohawks." At a more virulent level, however, Protestants charged that the Whitman Massacre, which occurred in Oregon in 1847, was the result of the Jesuits inciting "their" Indians to remove the threat of a Protestant Northwest.[24]

Violence was the exception, not the rule, even during the demonstrations and confrontations of the school Bible controversy and other rock-throwing, name-calling incidents. Rather than consider these well-documented incidents, let me instead point to the permeation of cultural anti-Catholicism in virtually every area of American popular culture.

What my colleague John Cuddihy has called "Protestant taste" became the measure of American taste—other religions were, by definition, lower on the aesthetic ranking and fell short of approved literary and artistic standards.[25] A brief examination of the children's literature popular from the mid-nineteenth to the mid-twentieth century is replete with examples of almost offhand anti-Catholicism, often associated with convents. Although there is nothing as avowedly polemical as the work of the English writer "Charlotte Elizabeth," the Elsie Dinsmore series by Martha Finley and the numerous works of "Pansy" are imbued with the principles of Protestantism and of Chautauqua.[26] A "convent" is the threat with which a wicked adult attempts to control an innocent child.

There are no comparably popular books of Catholic literature preaching against Protestants, at least not until the twentieth century, but one vivid example of Catholic retaliation, even if it never reached the bestseller list, is the 1874 work purporting to be the autobiography of Lizzie St. John Eckel.[27] This earnest work was entitled *Maria Monk's Daughter* and told of the career of the former nun's illegitimate child. (There is a parallel here, perhaps a case of nature imitating art again, in which the sequel to the best seller *Charlotte Temple* is the story of her illegitimate daughter, who lives a life of Christian piety and self-denial as redemp-

tion for her mother's sin.) Maria Monk's daughter had nothing good to say for her parent, who left her to fend for herself after her birth in 1837. A passion for self-improvement ("I had always been fond of studying encyclopedias"[28]) kept her mind alive through the drudgery of menial employment. When at the age of thirty she visited a convent for the first time, she shrieked aloud a prayer for enlightenment. As she listened in wonder to the happy laughter of the nuns, "a moral light" illumined her soul and she quickly joined the Roman Catholic Church.[29] The church became her real mother, "for it was she who took me by the hand and raised me out of the abyss of spiritual misery, into which the faults of my parents had helped to plunge me."[30] Her mother's book is specifically repudiated: "In my heart of hearts I *am sure* that my mother's book is a lie."[31] But this is only the penultimate conclusion. The real meaning of her work she saves for the final page, where she addresses her book "to the hearts of those women who consider themselves strong-minded. . . . Could they only see themselves as they are in the sight of God, they would find themselves to be the weakest of their weak sex. For the truly strong-minded woman is she who strives to conquer herself, and by charity and humility to assist Christ in establishing His kingdom on earth . . . not she who seeks to take the position which God had assigned on this earth to men"; the most important truth for woman is to realize that she cannot escape "the law of suffering."[32]

In a similar vein, Orestes Brownson used the presumed model of the Blessed Virgin to speak against the woman's movement. Catholic females, "trained up in the love and imitation of her virtues . . . are trained to be wives and mothers, or holy virgins, spouses of Jesus Christ."[33] He identified the demand for the vote with "hostility to the marriage law, and the cares and drudgery of maternity and human life."[34] It is not surprising that with friends like these the Catholic Church had its enemies among the ranks of the women's movement, although even Elizabeth Cady Stanton (who claimed to dislike Catholics, Protestants, and Jews as equally inimical to woman's progress) had a grudging admiration for the communal kitchens of convent life.[35] In its feminist category, the *Dictionary of Notable American Women* (whose deaths occurred before 1950) lists only three born Catholics, two of whom lost their faith, and one Catholic convert.[36]

The anti-Catholicism of popular literature was also present in the etiquette manuals where "Bridget" was assumed to be a slothful, drunken, and immoral person, the heritage of her Irish nationality and Catholic religion. The Protestant housewife, although she was told to let her servants attend their own church, was also told to force them to attend family prayers, to give them copies of the Bible ("which they have never been allowed to read") and to equate civil order with Protestantism, in the home and on the streets.[37] Similarly, in the literature of the philanthropic organizations of the nineteenth century, the "fallen" woman was to be rehabilitated through conversion to Protestantism. The "lady visitors" of such organizations as the Magdalen Society reserved their highest praise for the reclamation of the "lamb that had strayed," in which renouncing her former religion was synonymous with renouncing her former way of life.[38] Even when such factors as class, ethnicity, and gender were specified, religion had a kind of moral override as the significant differentiating factor between virtue and vice. . . .

Notes

[1] Josiah Strong, *Our Country: Its Possible Future and Its Present Crisis* (rev. ed., New York: American Home Missionary Society, 1891). The publisher claimed that by the time of this edition more than 140,000 volumes had been printed. The fifth chapter (pp. 46-52) deals with the "Conflict of Romanism with the Fundamental Principle of our Government."

[2] John Higham, *Strangers in the Land: Patterns of American Nativism 1860-1925* (original edition 1963; reprinted Westport, CT: Greenwood Press, 1980) p. 54.

[3] John Higham identifies four major periods of "virulent" nativism: the late 1790's, the 1850's, 1886 through 1896, and the years following World War I. Basic histories of religion in the United States, especially Sydney E. Ahlstrom's A *Religious History of the American People* (New Haven: Yale University Press, 1972); Winthrop S. Hudson's *Religion in America* (2d ed., New York: Charles Scribner's, 1973); and William Warren Sweet's *The Story of Religion in America* (2nd ed., New York: Harper & Row, 1950), also discuss manifestations of anti-Catholicism as do the histories of the Roman Catholic Church in America. See, for example, Thomas T. McAvoy, C.S.C., *A History of the Catholic Church in the United States* (Notre Dame, IN: Notre Dame University Press, 1969); John Tracy Ellis, *American Catholicism* (Chicago: University of Chicago Press, 1956); Andrew M. Greeley, *The Catholic Experience* (New York: Doubleday & Co., 1967); and the treatise that was itself virtually a primary source for these tensions, John D. Gilmary Shea, *History of the Catholic Church in the United States 1843-1866* (New York: J. G. Shea, 1892), and its companion volume *Our Faith and Its Defenders* (2 vols., New York: Office of Catholic Publishing, 1894).

Eighteenth century manifestations are described by Thomas More Brown, "The Image of the Beast: Anti-Papal Rhetoric in Colonial America." in *Conspiracy: The Fear of Subversion in American History,* ed. Richard D. Curry and Thomas M. Brown (New York:

Holt, Rinehart and Winston, 1972) 1-20. See also J. Higham, *Strangers in the Land;* Carlton Beals, *Brass-Knuckle Crusade: The Great Know-Nothing Conspiracy* (New York: Hastings House, 1960); Reuben Maury, *The Wars of the Godly* (New York: R. M. McBride & Co., 1928); Gustavus Myers, *History of Bigotry in the United States* (New York: Random House, 1945); Seymour Mandelbaum, *The Social Setting of Intolerance* (Chicago: Scott, Forsman, 1964); Harry Carmen, "Some Aspects of the Know-Nothing Movement Reconsidered," *South Atlantic Quarterly* 39 (1940) 213-34; Donald L. Kinzer, *An Episode in Anti-Catholicism: The American Protective Association* (Seattle: University of Washington Press, 1964); and especially Ray Allen Billington, *The Protestant Crusade 1800-1860: A Story of the Origins of American Nativism* (New York: The Macmillan Company, 1938).

Catholic responses include a series of monographs based on dissertations at the Catholic University of America and published by its press, for example, Marie Fell, *The Foundation of Nativism in American Textbooks, 1783-1860* (Washington, DC: Catholic University of America Press, 1941); Agnes McGann, *Nativism in Kentucky to 1860* (Washington, DC: Catholic University of America Press, 1944); Carroll J. Noonan, *Nativism in Connecticut 1829-1860* (Washington, DC: Catholic University of America Press, 1938); and Evangeline Thomas, *Nativism in the Old Northwest 1850-60* (Washington, DC: Catholic University of America Press, 1936). Other Catholic presentations include Dorothy Dohen, *Nativism and American Catholicism* (New York: Sheed and Ward, 1967); and Robert Francis Hueston, *The Catholic Press and Nativism 1840-60* (New York: Arno Press, 1976)

[4] See S. Ahlstrom, *A Religious History of the American People;* R. A. Billington, *The Protestant Crusade;* and J. Higham, *Strangers in the Land;* as well as David Brion Davis, "Some Themes of Countersubversion: An Analysis of Anti-Masonic, Anti-Catholic and Anti-Mormon Literature," *Mississippi Valley Historical Review* 47 (1960) 205-24, and his introduction and notes to *Fear of Conspiracy* (Ithaca, NY: Cornell University Press, 1971); Richard Hofstadter, *The Paranoid Style in American Politics* (New York: Knopf, 1965); and John J. Kane, *Catholic-Protestant Conflicts in America* (Chicago: Regnery, 1955). In a rare display of unanimity, these sources all treat nativism as an aberration. They disagree only as to whether its source is primarily religious or ethnic; most of the Protestant historians accept the latter interpretation, and the Catholic historians the former. In a paper delivered at the April 1978 meeting of the Organization of American Historians, Stanley Coben offered a bio-historical theory, equating "nativism" with the behavior of lizards with brain lesions.

[5] S. Ahlstrom, *A Religious History of the American People,* p. 556.

[6] See the Catholic historians cited in note 3 and J. Kane in *Catholic-Protestant Conflicts,* especially pp. 1-14 ("A Hundred Years of Anti-Catholicism"). Also Theodore Roemer, *The Catholic Church in the United States* (St. Louis: B. Herder, 1957), especially pp. 50-75; Anson Phelps Stokes and Leo Pfeffer, *Church and State in the United States* (rev. ed., New York: Harper & Row, 1964); Jerome G. Kerwin, *The Catholic Viewpoint on Church and State* (Garden City, NY: Hanover House, 1959); and Richard J. Regan, S.J., *American Pluralism and the Catholic Conscience* (New York: Macmillan, 1963); as well as the documents in Thomas McAvoy, *Roman Catholicism and the American Way of Life* (Notre Dame: Notre Dame University Press, 1960).

[7] D. B. Davis, "Some Themes of Countersubversion," p. 208.

[8] John William Ward, *Andrew Jackson: Symbol for an Age* (New York: Oxford University Press, 1955).

[9] *Awful Disclosures of the Hotel Dieu Nunnery of Montreal* (New York: Howe & Bates, 1836). In his introduction to the facsimile edition published by Archon Books (Hamden, CT: 1962), Ray Allen Billington claims that "in all the long, sad saga of man's mistreatment of man, few books have played such a malicious role" (p. 1).

[10] Elwyn A. Smith, *Religious Liberty in the United States* (Philadelphia: Fortress Press, 1972) 85-209. For a nineteenth-century tract on conversion, see Charles Constantine Pise, *Letters to Ada* (New York: Harper, 1834). For the conversion experience, see Peter Hardeman Burnett, *The Path Which Led a Protestant Lawyer to the Catholic Church* (New York: D. Appleton and Co., 1860); Levi Silliman Ives, *The Trials of a Mind in Its Progress to Catholicism: A Letter to Old Friends* (Boston: Patrick Donahoe, 1854). The best source for Orestes Brownson is "The Seeker" himself, in the twenty volumes of his works. The works which most reflect Isaac Thomas Hecker's spirit are *Aspirations of Nature* (New York: J. P. Kirker, 1857), *The Catholic Church in the United States: Its Rise, Relations with the Republic, Growth, and Future Prospects* (New York: Catholic Publication Society, 1879), and *The Church and the Age* (New York: Catholic Book Exchange, 1896). In his 1879 volume, Hecker asserted, "There is scarcely an American family, distinguished either by its ancestry, or its social position, which today has not one or more representatives among the converts to the Catholic Church" (p. 7). Archbishop John Ireland said that Hecker "assumed that the American people are naturally Catholic" (Introduction to Walter Elliott's *Life of Father Hecker* [2nd ed., New York: Columbus Press, 1894] p. xi). The French translation of Elliott's biography was one cause of the "Americanism" controversy of the 1880s and 90s. Good

biographies of Hecker are Vincent Holden, *The Yankee Paul: Isaac Thomas Hecker* (Milwaukee, WI: Bruce Publishing Co., 1958); and Joseph McSorley, *Father Hecker and His Friends* (St. Louis, MO: B. Herder, 1952). See also John Arina, *An American Experience of God: The Spirituality of Isaac Hecker* (New York/Ramsay, NJ: Paulist Press, 1981) and *Hecker Studies: Essays on the Thought of Isaac Hecker* (New York/Ramsay, NJ: Paulist Press, 1983). Edward J. Mannix's attempt to explain the phenomenon of conversion to the Roman Catholic Church (*The American Convert Movement* [New York: Devin-Adair Co., 1923]) lacks historical perspective.

[11] Lyman Beecher, *A Plea for the West* (2nd ed., Cincinnati: Truman & Smith, 1835). Beecher believed it plain that "in the province of God" the United States was "destined" to lead the way in the moral and political emancipation of the world" and "equally plain that the religious and political destiny of our nation is to be decided in the West" (p. 11). His idea that the West was to be "won" for Protestantism is responsible for his particular resentment of Catholic educational and missionary enterprises.

[12] The social and historical background of the burning of the Ursuline Convent (Mount St. Benedict) at Charlestown is described in S. Ahlstrom, *A Religious History of the American People,* pp. 560-61; and R.A. Billington, *The Protestant Crusade,* pp. 71-75. Contemporary documents include *Papers of the Vigilance Committee,* 15 December 1834-January 1835 (Boston: *Municipal Proceedings,* 1835); James T. Austin, *Argument of James T. Austin, Attorney General, before the Supreme Judicial Court in Middlesex on the Case of John R. Buzzell, charged with being concerned in destroying the Ursuline Convent in Charlestown* (Boston: Ford and Damrell, 1834); and *The Charlestown Convent . . .* (Boston: New England News Co., 1870). Its publication date notwithstanding, this latter, valuable volume is "compiled from authentic sources," as promised. Later historical treatments include Mrs. Louisa (Goddard) Whitney, *The Burning of the Convent . . . As Remembered by One of the Pupils* (Boston: J. B. Osgood, 1877), and Carmine A. Prioli, "The Ursuline Outrage," *American Heritage* 33 (February/March 1982) 101-5.

A very popular American novel based on the Charlestown fire was Justin Jones, *The Nun of St. Ursula or The Burning of the Convent, a Romance of Mt. Benedict,* written under the pseudonym of Harry Hazel (Boston: F. Gleason, 1845). His *The Convent's Doom* and *The Haunted Convent* were published together in a fifth edition in 1854 (Boston: Graves & Weston).

[13] Ursuline work in the United States is discussed in P. W. Browne, "The Oldest Institutions of Learning for

Women in North America," *Catholic Education Review* 30 (1932) 87-99; and Ettie Madeline Vogel, "The Ursuline Nuns in America," *American Catholic Historical Society of Philadelphia, Proceedings* 1 (1887) 214-43. There is no single monograph for the larger role of nuns in American society; see, for example, Elizabeth Kolmer, A.S.C., "Catholic Women Religious and Women's History," in *Women in American Religion,* ed. Janet Wilson James (Philadelphia: University of Pennsylvania Press, 1980) 127-40. Mary Ewens covers more limited topics in *The Role of the Nun in Nineteenth-Century America* (New York: Arno Press, 1978), which is largely a study of fictional sources, and "The Leadership of Nuns in Immigrant Catholicism," in *Women and Religion in America,* ed. Rosemary Radford Ruether and Rosemary Skinner Keller (New York: Harper & Row, 1981) vol. I (19th Century) 101-7. See also Ellen Ryan Jolly, *Nuns of the Battlefield* (Providence: Providence Visitors Press, 1927).

For a comparison of the curriculum at the Ursuline Convent (given in the appendix to *The Charlestown Convent* [n. 12 above]) see the catalogues of such contemporary institutions as Boston's Monitorial Female Seminary (1812) and Pittsfield's Young Ladies' Institute (1842). James Frothingham Hunnewell provides a general discussion of the area itself in *A Century of Town Life: A History of Charlestown, Mass. 1775-1887* (Boston: Little, Brown and Co., 1888).

One of the main charges of the anti-convent literature was that even with the best intentions—which the writers were unlikely to concede to them—the nuns could not help but proselytize. See, for example, the very influential work of Timothy Dwight, who insists that "by every artful measure which they can adopt (and they are the most artful of all human beings), by every insinuation, every captivating ceremony which can be presented to the youthful mind and the excited imagination, they steal upon their fancies, and by sly but dangerous artifices gradually attach them to the most destructive system of faith and morals which the history of the Christian world has ever known (*Open Convents* [New York: Van Nostrand and Dwight, 1936] 128-29). Dwight also suggests that the convents were inferior in science, mathematics, and, of course, religious teaching. *The Know-Nothing Almanac* for 1856 also suggests deficiency in subject matter as well as in ideology when it denounces convent education because "even if they teach French, or some other frivolous or secondary branch better than other schools near them, they teach none of the grand and indispensable sciences thoroughly and correctly, if at all" (*The Know-Nothing Almanac or True American's Manual* [New York, 1856]). To these charges, the defenders of the convents responded that since the majority of the young women were Protestants, *a priori* the convent became a "Protestant" convent. See the testimony of Samuel K. Williams, editor of *The Daily Advertiser,* who sent four daughters to the Ursuline Convent, in *The Charlestown Convent,* pp. 90-91.

[14] Kathyrn Cavarly Hulme, *The Nun's Story* (Boston: Little, Brown, 1956); this best-seller was made into a popular movie starring Audrey Hepburn.

[15] Quoted in Dan Herr, *Through Other Eyes* (Westminster, MD: Newman Press, 1965) 44. The travelers that Herr quotes are generally favorable to American Catholicism. Alexis de Tocqueville felt Catholicism had been "erroneously" identified as the enemy of democracy (p. 30). Alexander MacKay believed that both in St. Louis and New Orleans there were excellent seminaries for young ladies and "not a few of those who attend them become converts to the church" (p. 55). Harriet Martineau's 1837 statement that "The Catholic religion is modified by the spirit of the time in America; and its professors are not a set of men who can be priest-ridden to any fatal extent" was used to refute anti-Catholic charges of undue clerical interest (J. T. Ellis, *American Catholicism,* p. 73). A more critical view is noted in Max Berger, "The Irish Immigrant and American Nativism As Seen by British Visitors, 1830-60," *Pennsylvania Magazine* 70 (1946) 146-60. Andrew Greeley dismisses this evidence by saying that "Most of the foreign visitors, alas, did not know what they were talking about" (*The American Catholic: A Social Portrait* [New York: Basic Books: 1977] 48).

[16] Ex-priest autobiographies began to be popular during the 1830s and had successive waves of popularity during the nineteenth century. The addition of "former priest of Rome" to an author's name seemed to give the required verisimilitude. William Hogan, who signed all his literature as "formerly Roman Catholic Priest," wrote *A Synopsis of Popery As It Is* (Boston: Saxon and Kelt, 1845). Hogan felt that, insofar as women were concerned, Catholicism should be compared to Mormonism for the perversion of the sexual ethic (D. B. Davis, *Fear of Conspiracy,* pp. 100-101); Vincent Philip Mayerhoffer had similar lurid tales to tell of the confessional (*Twelve Years a Roman Catholic Priest* [Toronto: Rowsell & Ellis, 1861]). The most widely published priestly recusant of the nineteenth century was Charles Pascal Chiniquy. His autobiographical work *Fifty Years in the Church of Rome* (New York: F. H. Revell Co., 1886) was a straightforward tale of increasing disillusionment with anti-democratic and jesuitical pressures. But his *The Priest, the Woman and the Confessional* (St. Anne, IL, 1884) was highly sensational. Chiniquy asked the inflammatory rhetorical question, "Do American men know what their wives tell the priests in the Confessional?" This putative tableau—the American wife telling her priest unmentionable sins—is invoked many times in the anti-Catholic literature; see, for example, Rev. Isaac J. Lansing, *Romanism and the Republic* (Boston: W. Kellaway, 1889).

Ex-nun books captured the public imagination infinitely more than did those tales of former priests. Although the genre can be traced to Diderot and eighteenth-century French anti-Catholicism, the first to receive wide circulation was Rebecca Reed's *Six Months in a Convent* (Boston: Russell, Odiorne and Metcalfe, 1835) which purported to be the story of an "inmate" of Charlestown's Ursuline Convent on Mt. Benedict for six months in 1831-32. Reed was the "simple Protestant girl" whose testimony was to be refuted by a series of persons, including the Mother Superior of her convent. According to her editors, Reed had written her story of misery at Mt. Benedict before the burning of the convent. Her supporters saw her as a Protestant Jeanne d'Arc, who had "escaped from Catholic superstition, in order to maintain the infalliable purity of a secret community of foreign females, who have introduced among us for the imitation of the daughters of republicans, the ascetic austerities of a religious discipline destructive of all domestic and social relations" (p. 6). The young woman did not wish to publish her story; it was "committed to the press" only after "a long, deliberate and . . . prayerful consideration" (p. 11). According to the "preliminary suggestions for candid readers" which served as a preface, the purpose of publication was to deter Protestants from educating their daughters in convents. The editor was indignant at the "humiliations" practiced by the nuns, "unsuitable for the daughters of a republic," especially the humiliations of one sister who, presumably because of her rustic simplicity of speech, was frequently forced to kiss the floor in penance. "As a test of humility," Reed herself was forced to eat the Mother Superior's apple parings. This volume charged no gross impurities (which may account for its being less popular than Maria Monk's *Disclosures*), but stressed the priests' and nuns' economic rapacity and their alien need of subservience and "austerities," equally repugnant to the American temper. Reed's work was answered by a pamphlet written by Mother Mary Edmund St. George (originally Mary Ursula Moffat), exposing its falsehoods and manifold absurdities (*An Answer to Six Months in a Convent* [Boston: J. H. Eastburn, 1835]). The "Lady Superior" started by repeating the claim of Reed's publishers that no "innocent young Protestant girl" could make up such a story, which she refuted by saying, "If they had any recollection of the history of mankind, they would see that nothing was more easy." The Superior claimed that Reed came from desperately poor parents, that she was too lazy to work in a way "commensurate with her humble origins," and that she was "artful, suspicious, and a double dealer" whom the Superior had long recognized as "a romantic and ignorant girl" (pp. xxxvii and 12). She refuted most of the specific charges, pointed out that the "flighty and unsteady" girl had no real vocation, and that the nuns could not only "laugh very heartily at recreation" but that they read the Bible too (pp. 19 and

31). Reed's final rejoinder was in her *Supplement to Six Months in a Convent* (Boston: Russell, Odiorne and Co., 1835).

Reed was called upon to testify at the trial of the men accused of burning down the convent and was described as "a delicate looking creature" whose "deportment on the stand was modest and pensive." The trial reporter commented on the spectators' "great curiosity" "to see the Convent ladies in the court room." Although the writer was very much opposed to the burning, he made much of the appearance of Mother St. George who, in contrast to Reed, was "a woman of masculine appearance and character, high-tempered, resolute, defiant, with stubborn imperious will." Lending credence to the general air of strangeness and mystery, she arrived wearing a veil, "which she declined to remove, until it was suggested by the court that this would be necessary in order to understand her testimony, then she unveiled" (*The Charlestown Convent*, pp. 42, 80, and 35). The final document in the Reed case was a refutation of Mother St. George's refutation, which, as its subtitle promised, "was a vindication of Miss Reed" (*Review of the Lady Superior's Reply to Six Months in a Convent* [Boston: W. Peirce and Webster and Southard, 1835]).

Other "escaped nun" narratives, such as Rosamund Culbertson's *Rosamund* (New York: Leavitt, Lord & Co., 1836), followed Monk's *Awful Disclosures*. This work had an introduction by Samuel B. Smith, "late a priest," and so was doubly authentic. Located in Cuba, an exotic touch, it tells the "sufferings of an American female under the popish priests. Josephine M. Bunkley's *The Testimony of an Escaped Novice from the Sisterhood of St. Joseph, Emmetsburg, Maryland* (New York: Harper, 1855) may be the volume advertised as *The Escaped Nun or Confessions of a Sister of Charity* in the 1855 *Know-Nothing Almanac*. The Mother House of the Sisters of Charity of St. Joseph, founded by Mother Elizabeth Seton, is at Emmitsburg, Maryland, and a misplaced "i" or "e" is of no great moment in these rather freewheeling narratives. The *Almanac* quoted a review from the *Boston Daily Times* according to which *The Escaped Nun* was expected "to exceed *Uncle Tom's Cabin* in its circulation, and it certainly should do so, for it is far beyond the latter, in a literary point of view" (p. 49). Other examples of this genre were by Edith O'Gorman (*The Trials and Persecution of Miss Edith O'Gorman* [Hartford: Connecticut Publishing Co., 1871]), who claimed to have escaped from St. Joseph's Convent in Hudson City, New York, and Julia Wright (*Secrets of the Convent and Confessional* [New York: National Publishing Co., 1872]), who concentrated primarily on the unfortunate nature of papal infallibility (which had been announced as doctrine in 1870) and its incompatibility with republican institutions.

[17] See "Interviews of Maria Monk with Her Opponents Held in This City on Wednesday, August 17th," Printed for the Author, presumably Ms. Monk (New York, 1836); and W. W. Sleigh, *An Expose of Maria Monk's Pretended Abduction and Conveyance to the Catholic Asylum in Philadelphia by Six Priests on the Night of August 15, 1837* (Philadelphia: T.K. and P.G. Collins, 1837). "The True History of Maria Monk," an "expose" by William L. Stone which appeared in the *New York Commercial Advertiser* on 8 October 1836, has been reprinted by the Paulist Press.

[18] Thus even though through their vows nuns and priests opposed a "normal" domestic life, subservience and the lack of intellectual autonomy were the primary thrust of the argument against convents. This was emphasized in the many stories of "abduction" and imprisonment—the outward sign of the inward bondage. See, for example, Hiram Mattison's *The Abduction of Mary Ann Smith by the Roman Catholics and Her Imprisonment in a Nunnery for Being a Protestant* (Jersey City, NJ, 1868).

In his diatribes against papism, Robert J. Breckinridge interjects several case studies, of which he claims personal knowledge, of women being held against their will in the Carmelite Convent in Baltimore. One of them, "for the last nineteen years a prisoner called Sister Isabella," actually managed to escape but was forcibly returned by a priest (*Papism in the XIX. Century in the United States, being Select Contributions to the Papal Controversy, during 1835-40* [Baltimore: D. Owen & Son, 1841] 235-38). He points out that the Catholic authorities have responded in the same way to all the criticism ("Milly McPherson was mad," "Miss Harrison was mad," "Miss Reed was mad") and wonders at the possiblity of so many deranged young females in the same kind of institution at a given time. His conclusion is that they were driven mad by being kept by priests "in a prison for women" (p. 236).

The importance of woman's free will and her ability to exert it for her religion meant that she could, if her cause was righteous enough, defy male authority. A good deal of popular literature is devoted to this theme. See, for example, Barbara Welter, "Defenders of the Faith: Women Novelists of Religious Controversy in the Nineteenth Century," in B. Welter, *Dimity Convictions: The American Woman in the Nineteenth Century* (Athens, OH: Ohio University Press, 1976) 103-29; and also such nativist fiction as that in William H. Ryder, *Our Country or The American Parlor Keepsake* (Boston. J. M. Usher, 1854), of which "The Heretic Wife: A Tale of Our Own Times" (pp. 104-25) is a good example: Mary Lee, a Protestant, is married to a wealthy, delightful Roman Catholic, Harry Stratton. Although he loves his wife, Harry is worked upon by his church, in the persons of a drunken Irish priest

and a "wily young Jesuit" who perjures himself, claiming to have been Mary's lover. As a result, she is divorced by her husband and rejected by her family before she dies of a broken heart.

[19] Some examples of child-rearing manuals are John C. Abbot, *The Mother at Home* (Boston, 1833); Lydia Child, *The Mother's Book* (Boston, 1831), and *Hints and Sketches by an American Mother* (New York, 1839). See also Anne L. Kuhn, *The Mother's Role in Childhood Education: New England Concepts* (New Haven: Yale University Press, 1947); Robert Sunley, "Early Nineteenth-Century Literature on Child Rearing," in *Childhood in Contemporary Cultures,* ed. Margaret Mead and Martha Wolfenstein (Chicago: University of Chicago Press, 1955) 150-67; and Philip Greven, *The Protestant Temperament: Patterns of Child-Rearing, Religious Experience and the Self in Early America* (New York: Alfred A. Knopf, 1977).

[20] M. Monk, *Awful Disclosures,* p. 18.

[21] Chapters 4 and 5 of William James' *The Varieties of Religious Experience: A Study in Human Nature* (orig. ed. 1902; reprinted New York: Modern Library, 1929) are the "Religion of Healthy-Mindedness" (pp. 77-114). James had definite views on the distinctive differences between Protestantism and Catholicism: "The two will never understand each other—their centres of energy are too different. Rigorous truth and human nature's intricacies are always in need of a mutual interpreter" (p. 450).

[22] M. Monk, *Awful Disclosures,* pp. 49 and 69.

[23] Samuel F. B. Morse, *Foreign Conspiracies against the Liberties of the United States* (New York: Leavitt, Lord & Co., 1835); this was originally published as a series of lectures in the *New York Observer* under the name "Brutus." While admitting that some critics believed that these inflammatory articles were responsible for the burning of the Ursuline Convent, Morse's biographer, Carleton Mabee, says that Morse had nothing against Catholic religious practices. Morse objected purely on the grounds of their incompatibility with the free will and independence required in a democracy (*American Leonardo: A Life of Samuel F.B. Morse* [New York: Knopf, 1943] 164). G. Myers, however, is less generous in his assessment: " . . . a strange mixture of pliancy to new ideas in the realm of invention and imperviousness to any fresh ideas in the religious or social field" (*History of Bigotry,* p. 160).

[24] For the rivalry between Catholic and Protestant missionaries see Barbara Welter, "She Hath Done What She Could: Protestant Women's Missionary Careers in Nineteenth Century America," in *Women in American Religion,* ed. J. W. James, pp. 111-26.

[25] John Murray Cuddihy, *No Offense: Civil Religion and Protestant Taste* (New York: Seabury Press, 1978). The question of taste and its related matter of caste, in which religions are ranked socially, has been explored by Digby Baltzell, *The Protestant Establishment: Aristocracy and Caste in America* (New York: Random House, 1964). Twentieth-century Catholics discussed the "taste" associated in the public mind with the church more freely. See, for example, *Catholicism in America: A Series of Articles from The Commonweal* (New York: Harcourt, Brace and Co., 1954), especially Walter Kerr's article on "Movies" (pp. 209-17). He remarks, "Bad taste is not one of the seven deadly sins. . . . The Church in this country has permitted itself to become identified with the well-meaning second rate" (p. 209).

[26] Martha Finley and Isabella Macdonald Alden (writing as "Pansy") both used the convent to symbolize punishment and repression, a particular threat to the spiritual life and physical health of young women. The former's *Elsie Dinsmore* was published in 1867 and had twenty-seven sequels; the latter's work sold over a thousand copies annually from 1870 to 1919. See Paul R. Messbarger, "Isabella Macdonald Alden," in Edward T. James et al., eds., *Notable American Women 1607-1950: A Biographical Dictionary* (Cambridge, MA: Belknap Press, 1971) 1:31-33.

The permeation of English literature with anti-Catholicism is discussed in Edward Hutton, *Catholicism and English Literature* (Folcroft, PA: Folcroft Press, 1969); and Edward Norman, *Anti-Catholicism in Victorian England* (London: Allen & Unwin, 1968). Three English women novelists who wrote prolifically against the Catholic Church and were particularly opposed to the influence of Catholicism on women were very popular in the United States. "Charlotte Elizabeth" (Charlotte Browne Tonna) is typified in *The Convent Bell and Other Poems* (New York: S. J. Taylor & Co., 1845). The Presbyterian Board published prose works such as *The English Martyrology* (Philadelphia: Presbyterian Board of Publications, 1843) and *The Female Martyrs of the English Revolution* (1844). Martha Butt Sherwood's collected works, virtually all on anti-Catholic themes, were published in a special American edition of fifteen volumes in 1855. *The Nun*, published in America in 1834, ends with the pious hope, "trusting that those things respecting the Roman Catholic Church which I have faithfully recorded may tend to fill the inhabitants of this Protestant land with a sense of that gratitude to God who has liberated this country from the slavery of this great apostasy whose name is Mystery" (quoted in G. Myers, *History of Bigotry*, p. 149). The third is Catherine Sinclair, whose *Beatrice, or The Unknown Relatives* had its fourteenth edition in 1853 (New York: DeWitt & Davenport). The preface to this edition gave "the object of this narrative" as the portrayal for "consideration of young girls" of the "enlightened happiness derived from the religion of England, founded on the Bible, contrasted with the misery arising from the superstition of Italy." One of Mrs. Sinclair's prose works that was well received in the United States was *The Priest and the Curate* (London: R. Bentley, 1853), which had the diary of a wholesome Anglican curate on one side of the page and that of a bigoted, venal priest on the other, making the most of the contrasts.

[27] Lizzie St. John Eckel, *Maria Monk's Daughter: An Autobiography* (New York: Published for the author by U.S. Publishing Co., 1874). It is hard to know how much of this long autobiography has any claim to truth. It is taken as historical statement by Leo L. Twinem in *Maria Monk's Daughter of Sharon and Amenia: The Story of Lizzie St. John Eckel Harper and Her Church on the Hill* (Flushing, NY: Privately printed, 1932). Twinem accepts her birth as Monk's second child in 1838 and thinks she died between October 1916 and October 1917. He quotes a review from *Brownson's Quarterly* which may have said it all: "her book bears on every page the stamp of rare genius. No novel is more entertaining" (p. 31). She later published *St. Peter's Bride* (New York: G. W. Carleton and Co., 1878), which is an attempt to discuss the church-state controversy as a dialogue between St. Peter (the Church) and his Bride (the State). She concludes that the match is hopeless and walks away.

[28] Lizzie St. John Eckel, *Maria Monk's Daughter*, p. 95.

[29] Ibid., p. 232.

[30] Ibid., p. 602.

[31] Ibid., p. 597.

[32] Ibid., pp. 603-4.

[33] Orestes A. Brownson, "The Worship of Mary," in *The Works of Orestes A. Brownson*, ed. Henry F. Brownson (Detroit: T. Nourse, 1882-1907) 8:83. For biographies (which do not discuss his feelings about women) see Arthur M. Schlesinger, *Orestes A. Brownson: A Pilgrim's Progress* (Boston: Little Brown & Co., 1939); and Theodore Maynard, *Orestes Brownson: Yankee, Radical, Catholic* (New York: Macmillan Co., 1943.)

[34] Orestes A. Brownson, "Spiritism and Spiritists," in *The Works of Orestes A. Brownson*, 9:346.

[35] Theodore Stanton and Harriot Stanton Blatch, eds., *Elizabeth Cady Stanton as Revealed in Her Letters, Diary and Reminiscences* (New York: Harper & Brothers, 1922) 2:195; and Elizabeth Cady Stanton, *Eighty Years and More: Reminiscences 1815-1897* (T. Fisher Unwin, 1898; reprinted New York: Schocken Books,

1971) 347, see also pp. 376-93 and her *The Woman's Bible,* originally published in two parts in 1896 and 1898 (reprinted New York: Arno Press, 1972).

[36] Edward T. James et al., eds., *Notable American Women,* 3:715-16. The Catholics are Mathide Franziska Giesler Anneke, Kate Kennedy, and Hortense Sparks Malsch Ward; Mary Nichols is the convert.

[37] See, for example, Sarah Josepha Hale, *Manners or Happy Homes and Good Society* (Boston, 1868); Eliza Leslie, *The Ladies Guide to True Politeness and Perfect Manners* (Philadelphia, 1864); and Mary Elizabeth Wilson Sherwood, *Manners and Social Usages* (New York, 1884) as examples of the mentor literature.

[38] See, for example, *Reports of the Magdalen Society of Philadelphia* (1800) and *The Magdalen Society of New York* (1813). The latter eventually became Inwood House, a home for unmarried mothers; see Annette K. Baxter and Barbara Welter, *Inwood House: One Hundred and Fifty Years of Service to Women* (New York: Inwood House, 1980). . . .

POLEMICAL LITERATURE

David Brion Davis

SOURCE: "Some Themes of Counter-Subversion: An Analysis of Anti-Masonic, Anti-Catholic, and Anti-Mormon Literature," in *From Homicide to Slavery: Studies in American Culture,* Oxford University Press, 1986, pp. 137-154.

[*In this essay, originally published in 1960, Davis analyzes various themes of anti-Catholic, anti-Masonic, and anti-Mormon literature in nineteenth-century America, suggesting that it tended to subvert the established order it claimed to protect by liberating certain irrational impulses against an imagined enemy.*]

During the second quarter of the nineteenth century, when danger of foreign invasion appeared increasingly remote, Americans were told by various respected leaders that Freemasons had infiltrated the government and had seized control of the courts, that Mormons were undermining political and economic freedom in the West, and that Roman Catholic priests, receiving instructions from Rome, had made frightening progress in a plot to subject the nation to popish despotism. This fear of internal subversion was channeled into a number of powerful counter movements which attracted wide public support. The literature produced by these movements evoked images of a great Ameri-

can enemy that closely resembled traditional European stereotypes of conspiracy and subversion. In Europe, however, the idea of subversion implied a threat to the established order—to the king, the church, or the ruling aristocracy—rather than to ideals or a way of life. If free Americans borrowed their images of subversion from frightened kings and uneasy aristocrats, these images had to be shaped and blended to fit American conditions. The movements would have to come from the people, and the themes of counter-subversion would be likely to reflect their fears, prejudices, hopes, and perhaps even unconscious desires.

There are obvious dangers in treating such reactions against imagined subversion as part of a single tendency or spirit of an age.[1] Anti-Catholicism was nourished by ethnic conflict and uneasiness over immigration in the expanding cities of the Northeast; anti-Mormonism arose largely from a contest for economic and political power between western settlers and a group that voluntarily withdrew from society and claimed the undivided allegiance of its members.[2] Anti-Masonry, on the other hand, was directed against a group thoroughly integrated in American society and did not reflect a clear division of economic, religious, or political interests.[3] Moreover, anti-Masonry gained power in the late 1820's and soon spent its energies as it became absorbed in national politics; anti-Catholicism reached its maximum force in national politics a full generation later;[4] anti-Mormonism, though increasing in intensity in the 1850's, became an important national issue only after the Civil War.[5] These movements seem even more widely separated when we note that Freemasonry was traditionally associated with anti-Catholicism and that Mormonism itself absorbed considerable anti-Masonic and anti-Catholic sentiment.[6]

Despite such obvious differences, there were certain similarities in these campaigns against subversion. All three gained widespread support in the northeastern states within the space of a generation; anti-Masonry and anti-Catholicism resulted in the sudden emergence of separate political parties; and in 1856 the new Republican party explicitly condemned the Mormons' most controversial institution. The movements of counter-subversion differed markedly in historical origin, but as the image of an un-American conspiracy took form in the nativist press, in sensational exposés, in the countless fantasies of treason and mysterious criminality, the lines separating Mason, Catholic, and Mormon became almost indistinguishable.

The similar pattern of Masonic, Catholic, and Mormon subversion was frequently noticed by alarmist writers. The *Anti-Masonic Review* informed its readers in 1829 that whether one looked at Jesuitism or Freemasonry, "the organization, the power, and the secret operation, are the same; except that Freemasonry is much the more secret and complicated of the two."[7] William

Hogan, an ex-priest and vitriolic anti-Catholic, compared the menace of Catholicism with that of Mormonism.[8] And many later anti-Mormon writers agreed with Josiah Strong that Brigham Young "out-popes the Roman" and described the Mormon hierarchy as being similar to the Catholic. It was probably not accidental that Samuel F. B. Morse analyzed the Catholic conspiracy in essentially the same terms his father had used in exposing the Society of the Illuminati, supposedly a radical branch of Freemasonry,[9] or that writers of sensational fiction in the 1840's and 1850's depicted an atheistic and unprincipled Catholic Church obviously modeled on Charles Brockden Brown's earlier fictional version of the Illuminati.[10]

If Masons, Catholics, and Mormons bore little resemblance to one another in actuality, as imagined enemies they merged into a nearly common stereotype. Behind specious professions of philanthropy or religious sentiment, nativists[11] discerned a group of unscrupulous leaders plotting to subvert the American social order. Though rank-and-file members were not individually evil, they were blinded and corrupted by a persuasive ideology that justified treason and gross immorality in the interest of the subversive group. Trapped in the meshes of a machine-like organization, deluded by a false sense of loyalty and moral obligation, these dupes followed orders like professional soldiers and labored unknowingly to abolish free society, to enslave their fellow men, and to overthrow divine principles of law and justice. Should an occasional member free himself from bondage to superstition and fraudulent authority, he could still be disciplined by the threat of death or dreadful tortures. There were no limits to the ambitious designs of leaders equipped with such organizations. According to nativist prophets, they chose to subvert American society because control of America meant control of the world's destiny.

Some of these beliefs were common in earlier and later European interpretations of conspiracy. American images of Masonic, Catholic, and Mormon subversion were no doubt a compound of traditional myths concerning Jacobite agents, scheming Jesuits, and fanatical heretics, and of dark legends involving the Holy Vehm and Rosicrucians. What distinguished the stereotypes of Mason, Catholic, and Mormon was the way in which they were seen to embody those traits that were precise antitheses of American ideals. The subversive group was essentially an inverted image of Jacksonian democracy and the cult of the common man; as such it not only challenged the dominant values but stimulated those suppressed needs and yearnings that are unfulfilled in a mobile, rootless, and individualistic society. It was therefore both frightening and fascinating.

It is well known that expansion and material progress in the Jacksonian era evoked a fervid optimism and that nationalists became intoxicated with visions of America's millennial glory. The simultaneous growth of prosperity and social democracy seemed to prove that Providence would bless a nation that allowed her citizens maximum liberty. When each individual was left free to pursue happiness in his own way, unhampered by the tyranny of custom or special privilege, justice and well-being would inevitably emerge. But if a doctrine of laissez-faire individualism seemed to promise material expansion and prosperity, it also raised disturbing problems. As one early anti-Mormon writer expressed it: What was to prevent liberty and popular sovereignty from sweeping away "the old landmarks of Christendom, and the glorious old common law of our fathers"? How was the individual to preserve a sense of continuity with the past, or identify himself with a given cause or tradition? What, indeed, was to ensure a common loyalty and a fundamental unity among the people?

Such questions acquired a special urgency as economic growth intensified mobility, destroyed old ways of life, and transformed traditional symbols of status and prestige. Though most Americans took pride in their material progress, they also expressed a yearning for reassurance and security, for unity in some cause transcending individual self-interest. This need for meaningful group activity was filled in part by religious revivals, reform movements, and a proliferation of fraternal orders and associations. In politics Americans tended to assume the posture of what Marvin Meyers has termed "venturesome conservatives," mitigating their acquisitive impulses by an appeal for unity against extraneous forces that allegedly threatened a noble heritage of republican ideals. Without abandoning a belief in progress through laissez-faire individualism, the Jacksonians achieved a sense of unity and righteousness by styling themselves as restorers of tradition.[12] Perhaps no theme is so evident in the Jacksonian era as the strained attempt to provide America with a glorious heritage and a noble destiny. With only a loose and often ephemeral attachment to places and institutions, many Americans felt a compelling need to articulate their loyalties, to prove their faith, and to demonstrate their allegiance to certain ideals and institutions. By so doing they acquired a sense of self-identity and personal direction in an otherwise rootless and shifting environment.

But was abstract nationalism sufficient to reassure a nation strained by sectional conflict, divided by an increasing number of sects and associations, and perplexed by the unexpected consequences of rapid growth? One might desire to protect the Republic against her enemies, to preserve the glorious traditions of the Founders, and to help insure continued expansion and prosperity, but first it was necessary to discover an enemy by distinguishing subversion from simple diversity. If Freemasons seemed to predomi-

The Beecher family, 1855.

nate in the economic and political life of a given area, was one's joining them shrewd business judgment or a betrayal of republican tradition?[13] Should Maryland citizens heed the warnings of anti-Masonic itinerants, or conclude that anti-Masonry was itself a conspiracy hatched by scheming Yankees?[14] Were Roman Catholics plotting to destroy public schools and a free press, the twin guardians of American democracy, or were they exercising democratic rights of self-expression and self-protection?[15] Did equality of opportunity and equality before the law mean that Americans should accept the land claims of Mormons or tolerate as jurors men who "swear that they have wrought miracles and supernatural cures"? Or should one agree with the Reverend Finis Ewing that "the 'Mormons' are the common enemies of mankind and ought to be destroyed"?[16]

Few men questioned traditional beliefs in freedom of conscience and the right of association. Yet what was to prevent "all the errors and worn out theories of the Old World, of schisms in the early Church, the monkish age and the rationalistic period," from flourishing in such salubrious air?[17] Nativists often praised the work of benevolent societies, but they were disturbed by the

thought that monstrous conspiracies might also "show kindness and patriotism, when it is necessary for their better concealment; and oftentimes do much good for the sole purpose of getting a better opportunity to do evil."[18] When confronted by so many sects and associations, how was the patriot to distinguish the loyal from the disloyal? It was clear that mere disagreement over theology or economic policy was invalid as a test, since honest men disputed over the significance of baptism or the wisdom of protective tariffs. But neither could one rely on expression of allegiance to common democratic principles, since subversives would cunningly profess to believe in freedom and toleration of dissent as long as they remained a powerless minority.

As nativists studied this troubling question, they discovered that most groups and denominations claimed only a partial loyalty from their members, freely subordinating themselves to the higher and more abstract demands of the Constitution, Christianity, and American public opinion. Moreover, they openly exposed their objects and activities to public scrutiny and exercised little discrimination in enlisting members. Some groups, however, dominated a larger portion of their members' lives, demanded unlimited allegiance as a condition of membership, and excluded certain activities from the gaze of a curious public.

Of all governments, said Richard Rush, ours was the one with most to fear from secret societies, since popular sovereignty by its very nature required perfect freedom of public inquiry and judgment.[19] In a virtuous republic why should anyone fear publicity or desire to conceal activities, unless those activities were somehow contrary to the public interest? When no one could be quite sure what the public interest was, and when no one could take for granted a secure and well-defined place in the social order, it was most difficult to acknowledge legitimate spheres of privacy. Most Americans of the Jacksonian era appeared willing to tolerate diversity and even eccentricity, but when they saw themselves excluded and even barred from witnessing certain proceedings, they imagined a "mystic power" conspiring to enslave them.

Readers might be amused by the first exposure of Masonic ritual, since they learned that pompous and dignified citizens, who had once impressed non-Masons with allusions to high degrees and elaborate ceremonies, had in actuality been forced to stand blindfolded and clad in ridiculous garb, with a long rope noosed around their necks. But genuine anti-Masons were not content with simple ridicule. Since intelligent and distinguished men had been members of the fraternity, "it must have in its interior something more than the usual revelations of its mysteries declare."[20] Surely leading citizens would not meet at night and undergo degrading and humiliating initiations just for the sake of novelty. The alleged murder of William Morgan raised an astonishing public furor because it supposedly revealed the inner secret of Freemasonry. Perverted by a false ideology, Masons had renounced all obligations to the general public, to the laws of the land, and even to the command of God. Hence they threatened not a particular party's program or a denomination's creed, but stood opposed to all justice, democracy, and religion.[21]

The distinguishing mark of Masonic, Catholic, and Mormon conspiracies was a secrecy that cloaked the members' unconditional loyalty to an autonomous body. Since the organizations had corrupted the private moral judgment of their members, Americans could not rely on the ordinary forces of progress to spread truth and enlightenment among their ranks. Yet the affairs of such organizations were not outside the jurisdiction of democratic government, for no body politic could be asked to tolerate a power that was designed to destroy it.[22] Once the true nature of subversive groups was thoroughly understood, the alternatives were as clear as life and death. How could democracy and Catholicism coexist when, as Edward Beecher warned, "The systems are diametrically opposed: one must and will exterminate the other"?[23] Because Freemasons had so deeply penetrated state and national governments, only drastic remedies could restore the nation to its democratic purity.[24] And later, Americans faced an "irrepressible conflict" with Mormonism, for it was said that either free institutions or Mormon despotism must ultimately annihilate the other.[25]

We may well ask why nativists magnified the division between unpopular minorities and the American public, so that Masons, Catholics, and Mormons seemed so menacing that they could not be accorded the usual rights and privileges of a free society. Obviously the literature of counter-subversion reflected concrete rivalries and conflicts of interest between competing groups but it is important to note that the subversive bore no racial or ethnic stigma and was not even accused of inherent depravity.[26] Since group membership was a matter of intellectual and emotional loyalty, no *physical* barrier prevented a Mason, Catholic, or Mormon from apostatizing and joining the dominant in-group, providing always that he escaped assassination from his previous masters. This suggests that counter-subversion was more than a rationale for group rivalry and was related to the general problem of ideological unity and diversity in a free society. When a "system of delusion" insulated members of a group from the unifying and disciplining force of public opinion, there was no authority to command an allegiance to common principles. This was why oaths of loyalty assumed great importance for nativists. Though the ex-Catholic William Hogan stated repeatedly that Jesuit spies respected no oaths except those to the Church, he inconsistently told Masons and Odd Fellows that they could prevent infiltration by requiring new members to swear they were not Catholics.[27] It was precisely the absence of distinguishing outward traits that made the enemy so dangerous, and true loyalty so difficult to prove.

When the images of different enemies conform to a similar pattern, it is highly probable that this pattern reflects important tensions within a given culture. The themes of nativist literature suggest that its authors simplified problems of personal insecurity and bewildering social change by trying to unite Americans of diverse political, religious, and economic interests against a common enemy. Just as revivalists sought to stimulate Christian fellowship by awakening men to the horrors of sin, so nativists used apocalyptic images to ignite human passions, destroy selfish indifference, and join patriots in a cohesive brotherhood. Such themes were only faintly secularized. When God saw his "lov'd Columbia" imperiled by the hideous monster of Freemasonry, He realized that only a martyr's blood could rouse the hearts of the people and save them from bondage to the Prince of Darkness. By having God will Morgan's death, this anti-Mason showed he was more concerned with national virtue and unity than with Freemasonry, which was only a providential instrument for testing republican strength.[28]

Similarly, for the anti-Catholic "this brilliant new world" was once "young and beautiful; it abounded in all the luxuries of nature; it promised all that was desirable to man." But the Roman Church, seeing "these irresistible temptations, thirsting with avarice and yearning for the reestablishment of her falling greatness, soon commenced pouring in among its unsuspecting people hoardes of Jesuits and other friars." If Americans were to continue their narrow pursuit of self-interest, oblivious to the "Popish colleges, and nunneries, and monastic institutions," indifferent to manifold signs of corruption and decay, how could the nation expect "that the moral breezes of heaven should breathe upon her, and restore to her again that strong and healthy constitution, which her ancestors have left to her sons"?[29] The theme of an Adamic fall from paradise was horrifying, but it was used to inspire determined action and thus unity. If Methodists were "criminally indifferent" to the Mormon question, and if "avaricious merchants, soulless corporations, and a subsidized press" ignored Mormon iniquities, there was all the more reason that the *"will of the people* must prevail."[30]

Without explicitly rejecting the philosophy of laissez-faire individualism, with its toleration of dissent and innovation, nativist literature conveyed a sense of common dedication to a noble cause and sacred tradition. Though the nation had begun with the blessings of God and with the noblest institutions known to man, the people had somehow become selfish and complacent, divided by petty disputes, and insensitive to signs of danger. In his sermons attacking such self-interest, such indifference to public concerns, and such a lack of devotion to common ideals and sentiments, the nativist revealed the true source of his anguish. Indeed, he seemed at times to recognize an almost beneficent side to subversive organizations, since they joined the nation in a glorious crusade and thus kept it from moral and social disintegration.

The exposure of subversion was a means of promoting unity, but it also served to clarify national values and provide the individual ego with a sense of high moral sanction and imputed righteousness. Nativists identified themselves repeatedly with a strangely incoherent tradition in which images of Pilgrims, Minute Men, Founding Fathers, and true Christians appeared in a confusing montage. Opposed to this heritage of stability and perfect integrity, to this society founded on the highest principles of divine and natural law, were organizations formed by the grossest frauds and impostures, and based on the wickedest impulses of human nature. Bitterly refuting Masonic claims to ancient tradition and Christian sanction, anti-Masons charged that the Order was of recent origin, that it

was shaped by Jews, Jesuits, and French atheists as an engine for spreading infidelity, and that it was employed by kings and aristocrats to undermine republican institutions.[31] If the illustrious Franklin and Washington had been duped by Masonry, this only proved how treacherous was its appeal and how subtly persuasive were its pretensions.[32] Though the Catholic Church had an undeniable claim to tradition, nativists argued that it had originated in stupendous frauds and forgeries "in comparison with which the forgeries of Mormonism are completely thrown into the shade."[33] Yet anti-Mormons saw an even more sinister conspiracy based on the "shrewd cunning" of Joseph Smith, who convinced gullible souls that he conversed with angels and received direct revelations from the Lord.[34]

By emphasizing the fraudulent character of their opponents' claims, nativists sought to establish the legitimacy and just authority of American institutions. Masonic rituals, Roman Catholic sacraments, and Mormon revelations were preposterous hoaxes used to delude naïve or superstitious minds; but public schools, a free press, and jury trials were eternally valid prerequisites for a free and virtuous society.

Moreover, the finest values of an enlightened nation stood out in bold relief when contrasted with the corrupting tendencies of subversive groups. Perversion of the sexual instinct seemed inevitably to accompany religious error.[35] Deprived of the tender affections of normal married love, shut off from the elevating sentiments of fatherhood, Catholic priests looked on women only as insensitive objects for the gratification of their frustrated desires.[36] In similar fashion polygamy struck at the heart of a morality based on the inspiring influence of woman's affections: "It renders man coarse, tyrannical, brutal, and heartless. It deals death to all sentiments of true manhood. It enslaves and ruins woman. It crucifies every God-given feeling of her nature."[37] Some anti-Mormons concluded that plural marriage could only have been established among foreigners who had never learned to respect women. But the more common explanation was that the false ideology of Mormonism had deadened the moral sense and liberated man's wild sexual impulse from the normal restraints of civilization. Such degradation of women and corruption of man served to highlight the importance of democratic marriage, a respect for women, and careful cultivation of the finer sensibilities.[38]

But if nativist literature was a medium for articulating common values and exhorting individuals to transcend self-interest and join in a dedicated union against evil, it also performed a more subtle function. Why, we may ask, did nativist literature dwell so persistently on themes of brutal sadism and sexual immorality? Why did its authors describe sin in such minute details, endowing even the worst offenses of their enemies with a certain fascinating appeal?

Freemasons, it was said, could commit any crime and indulge any passion when "upon the square," and Catholics and Mormons were even less inhibited by internal moral restraints. Nativists expressed horror over this freedom from conscience and conventional morality, but they could not conceal a throbbing note of envy. What was it like to be a member of a cohesive brotherhood that casually abrogated the laws of God and man, enforcing unity and obedience with dark and mysterious powers? As nativists speculated on this question, they projected their own fears and desires into a fantasy of licentious orgies and fearful punishments.

Such a projection of forbidden desires can be seen in the exaggeration of the stereotyped enemy's powers, which made him appear at times as a virtual superman. Catholics and Mormon leaders, never hindered by conscience or respect for traditional morality, were curiously superior to ordinary Americans in cunning, in exercising power over others, and especially in captivating gullible women.[39] It was an ancient theme of anti-Catholic literature that friars and priests were somehow more potent and sexually attractive than married laymen, and were thus astonishingly successful at seducing supposedly virtuous wives.[40] Americans were cautioned repeatedly that no priest recognized Protestant marriages as valid, and might consider any wife legitimate prey.[41] Furthermore, priests had access to the pornographic teachings of Dens and Liguori, sinister names that aroused the curiosity of anti-Catholics, and hence learned subtle techniques of seduction perfected over the centuries. Speaking with the authority of an ex-priest, William Hogan described the shocking result: "I have seen husbands unsuspiciously and hospitably entertaining the very priest who seduced their wives in the confessional, and was the parent of some of the children who sat at the same table with them, each of the wives unconscious of the other's guilt, and the husbands of both, not even suspecting them."[42] Such blatant immorality was horrifying, but everyone was apparently happy in this domestic scene, and we may suspect that the image was not entirely repugnant to husbands who, despite their respect for the Lord's Commandments, occasionally coveted their neighbors' wives.

The literature of counter-subversion could also embody the somewhat different projective fantasies of women. Ann Eliza Young dramatized her seduction by the Prophet Brigham, whose almost superhuman powers enchanted her and paralyzed her will. Though she submitted finally only because her parents were in danger of being ruined by the Church, she clearly indicated that it was an exciting privilege to be pursued by a Great Man.[43] When Anti-Mormons claimed that Joseph Smith and other prominent Saints knew the mysteries of Animal Magnetism, or were endowed with the highest degree of "amativeness" in their phrenological makeup, this did not detract from their covert appeal.[44] In a ridiculous fantasy written by Maria Ward, such alluring qualities were extended even to Mormon women. Many bold-hearted girls could doubtless identify themselves with Anna Bradish, a fearless Amazon of a creature, who rode like a man, killed without compunction, and had no pity for weak women who failed to look out for themselves. Tall, elegant, and "intellectual," Anna was attractive enough to arouse the insatiable desires of Brigham Young, though she ultimately rejected him and renounced Mormonism.[45]

While nativists affirmed their faith in Protestant monogamy, they obviously took pleasure in imagining the variety of sexual experience supposedly available to their enemies. By picturing themselves exposed to similar temptations, they assumed they could know how priests and Mormons actually sinned.[46] Imagine, said innumerable anti-Catholic writers, a beautiful young woman kneeling before an ardent young priest in a deserted room. As she confesses, he leans over, looking into her eyes, until their heads are nearly touching. Day after day she reveals to him her innermost secrets, secrets she would not think of unveiling to her parents, her dearest friends, or even her suitor. By skillful questioning the priest fills her mind with immodest and even sensual ideas, "until this wretch has worked up her passions to a tension almost snapping, and then becomes his easy prey." How could any man resist such provocative temptations, and how could any girl's virtue withstand such a test?[47]

We should recall that this literature was written in a period of increasing anxiety and uncertainty over sexual values and the proper role of woman. As ministers and journalists pointed with alarm at the spread of prostitution, the incidence of divorce, and the lax and hypocritical morality of the growing cities, a discussion of licentious subversives offered a convenient means for the projection of guilt as well as desire. The sins of individuals, or of the nation as a whole, could be pushed off upon the shoulders of the enemy and there punished in righteous anger.[48]

Specific instances of such projection are not difficult to find. John C. Bennett, whom the Mormons expelled from the Church as a result of his flagrant sexual immorality, invented the fantasy of "The Mormon Seraglio" which persisted in later anti-Mormon writings. According to Bennett, the Mormons maintained secret orders of beautiful prostitutes who were mostly reserved for various officials of the Church. He claimed, moreover, that any wife refusing to accept polygamy might be forced to join the lowest order and thus become available to any Mormon who desired her.[49]

Another example of projection can be seen in the letters of a young lieutenant who stopped in Utah in 1854 on his way to California. Convinced that Mormon women could be easily seduced, the lieutenant wrote frankly of his amorous adventures with a married woman. "Everyone has got one," he wrote with obvious pride, "except the Colonel and Major. The Doctor has got three—mother and two daughters. The mother cooks for him and the daughters sleep with him." But though he described Utah as "a great country," the lieutenant waxes indignant over polygamy, which he condemned as self-righteously as any anti-Mormon minister: "To see one man openly parading half a dozen or more women to church . . . is the devil according to my ideas of morality virtue and decency."[50]

If the consciences of many Americans were troubled by the growth of red light districts in major cities, they could divert their attention to the "legalized brothels" called nunneries, for which no one was responsible but lecherous Catholic priests. If others were disturbed by the moral implications of divorce, they could point in horror at the Mormon elder who took his quota of wives all at once. The literature of counter-subversion could thus serve the double purpose of vicariously fulfilling repressed desires, and of releasing the tension and guilt arising from rapid social change and conflicting values.

Though the enemy's sexual freedom might at first seem enticing, it was always made repugnant in the end by associations with perversion or brutal cruelty. Both Catholics and Mormons were accused of practicing nearly every form of incest.[51] The persistent emphasis on this theme might indicate deep-rooted feelings of fear and guilt, but it also helped demonstrate, on a more objective level, the loathsome consequences of unrestrained lust. Sheer brutality and a delight in human suffering were supposed to be the even more horrible results of sexual depravity. Masons disemboweled or slit the throats of their victims; Catholics cut unborn infants from their mothers' wombs and threw them to the dogs before their parents' eyes; Mormons raped and lashed recalcitrant women, or seared their mouths with red-hot irons.[52] This obsession with details of sadism, which reached pathological proportions in much of the literature, showed a furious determination to purge the enemy of every admirable quality. The imagined enemy might serve at first as an outlet for forbidden desires, but nativist authors escaped from guilt by finally making him an agent of unmitigated aggression. In such a role the subversive seemed to deserve both righteous anger and the most terrible punishments.

The nativist escape from guilt was more clearly revealed in the themes of confession and conversion. For most American Protestants the crucial step in anyone's life was a profession of true faith resulting from a genuine religious experience. Only when a man became conscious of his inner guilt, when he struggled against the temptations of Satan, could he prepare his soul for the infusion of the regenerative spirit. Those most deeply involved in sin often made the most dramatic conversions. It is not surprising that conversion to nativism followed the same pattern, since nativists sought unity and moral certainty in the regenerative spirit of nationalism. Men who had been associated in some way with un-American conspiracies were not only capable of spectacular confessions of guilt, but were best equipped to expose the insidious work of supposedly harmless organizations. Even those who lacked such an exciting history of corruption usually made some confession of guilt, though it might involve only a previous indifference to subversive groups. Like ardent Christians, nativists searched in their own experiences for the meanings of sin, delusion, awakening to truth, and liberation from spiritual bondage. These personal confessions proved that one had recognized and conquered evil, and also served as ritual cleansings preparatory to full acceptance in a group of dedicated patriots.

Anti-Masons were perhaps the ones most given to confessions of guilt and most alert to subtle distinctions of loyalty and disloyalty. Many leaders of this movement, expressing guilt over their own "shameful experience and knowledge" of Masonry, felt a compelling obligation to exhort their former associates to "come out, and be separate from masonic abominations."[53] Even when an anti-Mason could say with John Quincy Adams that "I am not, never was, and never shall be a Freemason," he would often admit that he had once admired the Order, or had even considered applying for admission.[54]

Since a willingness to sacrifice oneself was an unmistakable sign of loyalty and virtue, ex-Masons gloried in exaggerating the dangers they faced and the harm that their revelations supposedly inflicted on the enemy. In contrast to hardened Freemasons, who refused to answer questions in court concerning their fraternal associations, the seceders claimed to reveal the inmost secrets of the Order, and by so doing to risk property, reputation, and life.[55] Once the ex-Mason had dared to speak the truth, his character would surely be maligned, his motives impugned, and his life threatened. But, he declared, even if he shared the fate of the illustrious Morgan, he would die knowing that he had done his duty.

Such self-dramatization reached extravagant heights in the ranting confessions of many apostate Catholics and Mormons. Maria Monk and her various imitators told of shocking encounters with sin in its most sensational forms, of bondage to vice and supersition, and of melodramatic escapes from popish despotism. A host of "ex-Mormon wives" described their gradual recognition of Mormon frauds and iniquities, the anguish and misery of plural marriage, and their breathtaking flights over deserts or mountains. The female apostate was especially vulnerable to vengeful retaliation, since she could easily be kidnapped by crafty priests and nuns, or dreadfully punished by Brigham Young's Destroying Angels.[56] At the very least, her reputation could be smirched by foul lies and insinuations. But her willingness to risk honor and life for the sake of her country and for the dignity of all womankind was eloquent proof of her redemption. What man could be assured of so noble a role?

The apostate's pose sometimes assumed paranoid dimensions. William Hogan warned that only the former priest could properly gauge the Catholic threat to American liberties and saw himself as providentially appointed to save his Protestant countrymen. "For twenty years," he wrote, "I have warned them of approaching danger, but their politicians were deaf, and their Protestant theologians remained religiously coiled up in fancied security, overrating their own powers and undervaluing that of Papists." Pursued by vengeful Jesuits, denounced and calumniated for alleged crimes, Hogan pictured himself single-handedly defending American freedom: "No one, before me, dared to encounter their scurrilous abuse. I resolved to silence them; and I have done so. The very mention of my name is a terror to them now." After surviving the worst of Catholic persecution, Hogan claimed to have at last aroused his countrymen and to have reduced the hierarchy to abject terror.[57]

As the nativist searched for participation in a noble cause, for unity in a group sanctioned by tradition and authority, he professed a belief in democracy and equal rights. Yet in his very zeal for freedom he curiously assumed many of the characteristics of the imagined enemy. By condemning the subversive's fanatical allegiance to an ideology, he affirmed a similarly uncritical acceptance of a different ideology; by attacking the subversive's intolerance of dissent, he worked to eliminate dissent and diversity of opinion; by censuring the subversive for alleged licentiousness, he engaged in sensual fantasies; by criticizing the subversive's loyalty to an organization, he sought to prove his unconditional loyalty to the established order. The nativist moved even father in the direction of his enemies when he formed tightly-knit societies and parties which were often secret and which subordinated the individual to the single purpose of the group. Though the nativists generally agreed that the worst evil of subversives was their subordination of means to ends, they themselves recommended the most radical means to purge the nation of troublesome groups and to enforce unquestioned loyalty to the state.

In his image of an evil group conspiring against the nation's welfare, and in his vision of a glorious millennium that was to dawn after the enemy's defeat, the nativist found satisfaction for many desires. His own interests became legitimate and dignified by fusion with the national interest, and various opponents became loosely associated with the un-American conspiracy. Thus Freemasonry in New York State was linked in the nativist mind with economic and political interests that were thought to discriminate against certain groups and regions; southerners imagined a union of abolitionists and Catholics to promote unrest and rebellion among slaves; gentile businessmen in Utah merged anti-Mormonism with plans for exploiting mines and lands.

Then too the nativist could style himself as a restorer of the past, as a defender of a stable order against disturbing changes, and at the same time proclaim his faith in future progress. By focusing his attention on the imaginary threat of a secret conspiracy, he found an outlet for many irrational impulses, yet professed his loyalty to the ideals of equal rights and government by law. He paid lip service to the doctrine of laissez-faire individualism, but preached selfless dedication to a transcendent cause. The imposing threat of subversion justified a group loyalty and subordination of the individual that would otherwise have been unacceptable. In a rootless environment shaken by bewildering social change the nativist found unity and meaning by conspiring against imaginary conspiracies.

Notes

[1] For an alternative to the method followed in this article, see John Higham's perceptive essay, "Another Look at Nativism," *Catholic Historical Review* (Washington), XLIV (July, 1958), 147-58. Higham rejects the ideological approach to nativism and stresses the importance of concrete ethnic tensions, "status rivalries," and face-to-face conflicts in explaining prejudice. Though much can be said for this sociological emphasis, as opposed to a search for irrational myths and stereotypes, the method suggested by Higham can easily lead to a simple "stimulus-response" view of prejudice. Awareness of actual conflicts in status and self-interest should not obscure the social and psychological functions of nativism, nor distract attention from themes that may reflect fundamental tensions within a culture.

[2] For a brilliant analysis of Mormon-Gentile conflict, see Thomas F. O'Dea, *The Mormons* (Chicago, 1958).

[3] Freemasons were blamed for various unrelated economic and political grievances, but anti-Masonry showed no uniform division according to class, occupation, or political affliction. See Charles McCarthy, "The Anti-Masonic Party," American Historical Association, *Annual Report for the Year 1902*. Vol. I (Washington, 1903), 370-73, 406-408. I am also indebted to Lorman A. Ratner, whose "Antimasonry in

New York State: A Study in Pre-Civil War Reform" (M.A. thesis, Cornell University, 1958) substantiates this conclusion.

[4] For a detailed analysis of the issues and development of anti-Catholicism, see Ray A. Billington, *The Protestant Crusade, 1800-1860* (New York, 1938).

[5] It should be noted, however, that national attention was attracted by the Mountain Meadows Massacre and by Albert Sidney Johnston's punitive expedition to Utah.

[6] For anti-Catholic references in *The Book of Mormon,* see I Nephi 13:4-9; II Nephi 6:12, 28:18. Parallels between Masons and the "Gadianton robbers" have been frequently discussed.

[7] *Anti-Masonic Review and Magazine* (New York), II (October, 1829), 225-34. It was even claimed that Jesuits had been protected by Frederick the Great because they were mostly Freemasons and shared the same diabolical designs. See *Free Masonry: A Poem. In Three Cantos, Accompanied with Notes. Illustrative of the History Policy, Principles, &c. of the Masonic Institution; Shewing the Coincidence of Its Spirit and Design with Ancient Jesuitism. . . . By a Citizen of Massachusetts* (Leicester, Mass., 1830), 134.

[8] William Hogan, *Popery! As It Was and as It Is. Also, Auricular Confession: and Popish Nunneries,* two books in one edition (Hartford, 1855), 32-33.

[9] Jedidah Morse, *A Sermon Preached at Charleston, November 29, 1798, on the Anniversary Thanksgiving in Massachusetts* (Boston, 1799); Vernon Stauffer, *The New England Clergy and the Bavarian Illuminati* (New York, 1918), 98-99, 233, 246-48.

[10] In Ned Buntline's *The G'hals of New York* (New York, 1850) the Jesuits seem to be connected with all secret conspiracies, and their American leader, Father Kerwin, is probably modeled on Brown's Carwin. George Lippard admired Brown, dedicated a novel to him, and was also fascinated by secret societies and diabolical plots to enslave America. In *New York: Its Upper Ten and Lower Million* (New York, 1853), the Catholic leaders are Illuminati-like atheists who plan revolutions, manipulate public opinion, and stop at no crime in their lust for wealth and power. These amoral supermen were clearly inspired by such characters as Brown's Ormond, as well as by the anti-Catholic writings of Eugène Sue and others.

[11] Though the term "nativist" is usually limited to opponents of immigration, it is used here to include anti-Masons and anti-Mormons. This seems justified in view of the fact that these alarmists saw themselves as defenders of native traditions and identified Masonry and Mormonism with forces alien to American life.

[12] For a lucid and provocative discussion of this "restoration theme," see Marvin Meyers, *The Jacksonian Persuasion* (Stanford, 1957), 162-64.

[13] Hiram B. Hopkins, *Renunciation of Free Masonry* (Boston, 1830), 4-7.

[14] Jacob Lefever of Hagerstown appealed to regional loyalty and urged citizens of Maryland to forget their differences and unite against "foreign influence" from an area notorious for its "tricks and frauds." *Free-Masonry Unmasked: or Minutes of the Trial of a Suit in the Court of Common Pleas of Adams County, Wherein Thaddeus Stevens, Esq. Was Plaintiff, and Jacob Lefever, Defendant* (Gettysburg, 1833), pp. xiii-xiv.

[15] *The Cloven Foot: or Popery Aiming at Political Supremacy in the United States, by the Rector of Oldenwold* (New York, 1855), 170-79.

[16] William Mulder and A. Russell Mortensen (eds.), *Among the Mormons: Historic Accounts by Contemporary Observers* (New York, 1958), 76-79. The quotation is from the minutes of an anti-Mormon meeting in Jackson County, Missouri, July 20, 1833.

[17] John H. Beadle, *Life in Utah: or, the Mysteries and Crimes of Mormonism* (Philadelphia, [1872]), 5.

[18] *Anti-Masonic Review,* I (December, 1828), 3-4.

[19] Letter of May 4, 1831, printed in *The Anti-Masonic Almanac, for the Year 1832,* ed. by Edward Giddins (Utica, 1831), 29-30.

[20] *Anti-Masonic Review,* I (December, 1828), 6-7; Lebbeus Armstrong, *Masonry Proved to Be a Work of Darkness, Repugnant to the Christian Religion; and Inimical to a Republican Government* (New York, 1830), 16.

[21] *The Anti-Masonic Almanack, for the Year 1828: Calculated for the Horizon of Rochester, N.Y. by Edward Giddins* (Rochester, 1827), entry for November and December, 1828; Armstrong, *Masonry,* 14.

[22] Hogan, *Popery,* 32-33.

[23] Edward Beecher, *The Papal Conspiracy Exposed, and Protestantism Defended, in the Light of Reason, History, and Scripture* (Boston, 1855), 29.

[24] *Anti-Masonic Review,* I (February, 1829), 71.

[25] Mulder and Mortensen (eds.), *Among the Mormons,* 407; Jennie Anderson Froiseth (ed.), *The Women of Mormonism: or, the Story of Polygamy as Told by the Victims Themselves* (Detroit, 1881-1882), 367-68.

[26] It is true that anti-Catholics sometimes stressed the inferiority of lower-class immigrants and that anti-Mormons occasionally claimed that Mormon converts were made among the most degraded and ignorant classes of Europe. This theme increased in importance toward the end of the century, but it seldom implied that Catholics and Mormons were physically incapable of being liberated and joined to the dominant group. Racism was not an original or an essential part of the counter-subversive's ideology. Even when Mormons were attacked for coarseness, credulity, and vulgarity, these traits were usually thought to be the product of their beliefs and institutions. See Mrs. B. G. Ferris, "Life among the Mormons," *Putnam's Monthly Magazine* (New York), VI (August, October, 1855), 144, 376-77.

[27] Hogan, *Popery,* 35.

[28] *Free Masonry: A Poem,* 55-58.

[29] Hogan, *Popery,* 7-8; *Auricular Confession,* 264-65.

[30] Froiseth (ed.), *Women of Mormonism,* 285-87, 291-92.

[31] *Free Masonry: A Poem,* 29-37; *Anti-Masonic Review,* I (June, 1829), 203-207. The charge was often repeated that higher degrees of Freemasonry were created by the "school of Voltaire" and introduced to America by Jewish immigrants. Masonry was also seen as an "auxiliary to British foreign policy."

[32] This question was most troubling to anti-Masons. Though some tried to side-step the issue by quoting Washington against "self-created societies," as if he had been referring to the Masons, others flatly declared that Washington had been hoodwinked, just as distinguished jurists had once been deluded by a belief in witchcraft. Of course Washington had been unaware of Masonic iniquities, but he had lent his name to the cause and had thus served as a decoy for the ensnarement of others. See *Free Masonry: A Poem,* 38; *Anti-Masonic Review,* I (January, 1829), 49, 54; *The Anti-Masonic Almanac, for the Year of the Christian Era 1830* (Rochester, 1829), 32.

[33] Beecher, *Papal Conspiracy Exposed,* 391.

[34] Beadle, *Life in Utah,* 30-34.

[35] *Ibid.,* 332-33. According to Beadle, religious error and sexual perversion were related "because the same constitution of mind and temperament which gives rise to one, powerfully predisposes toward the other."

[36] *Cloven Foot,* 294-95.

[37] Froiseth (ed.), *Women of Mormonism,* 113.

[38] Though Horace Greeley was moderate in his judgment of Mormonism, he wrote: "I joyfully trust that the genius of the Nineteenth Century tends to a solution of the problem of Woman's sphere and destiny radically different from this." Quoted in Mulder and Mortensen (eds.), *Among the Mormons,* 328.

[39] It should be noted the Freemasons were rarely accused of sexual crimes, owing perhaps to their greater degree of integration within American society, and to their conformity to the dominant pattern of monogamy. They were sometimes attacked, however, for excluding women from their Order, and for swearing not to violate the chastity of wives, sisters, and daughters of fellow Masons. Why, anti-Masons asked, was such an oath not extended to include *all* women? David Bernard, *Light on Masonry: A Collection of all the Most Important Documents on the Subject* (Utica, 1829), 62 n.

[40] Anthony Gavin, *A Master-Key to Popery, Giving a Full Account of All the Customs of the Priests and Friars, and the Rites and Ceremonies of Popish Religion* (n.p., 1812), 70-72. Such traditional works of European anti-Catholicism were frequently reprinted and imitated in America.

[41] *Cloven Foot,* 224. The Mormons were also alleged to regard the wives of infidels "lawful prey to any believer who can win them." Beadle, *Life in Utah,* 233.

[42] Hogan, *Auricular Confession,* 289.

[43] Ann Eliza Young, *Wife No. 19: or, the Story of a Life in Bondage, Being a Complete. Exposé of Mormonism* (Hartford, 1875), 433, 440-41, 453.

[44] Maria Ward, *Female Life among the Mormons: A Narrative of Many Years' Personal Experience, By the Wife of a Mormon Elder, Recently Returned from Utah* (New York, 1857), 24; Beadle, *Life in Utah,* 339.

[45] Ward, *Female Life among the Mormons,* 68, 106, 374.

[46] The Mormons, for instance, were imagined to engage in the most licentious practices in the Endowment House ceremonies. See Nelson W. Green (ed.), *Fifteen Years among the Mormons: Being the Narrative of Mrs. Mary Ettie V. Smith* (New York, 1857), 44-51.

[47] Hogan, *Auricular Confession,* 254-55; *Cloven Foot,* 301-304.

[48] This point is ably discussed by Kimball Young, *Isn't One Wife Enough?* (New York, 1954), 26-27.

[49] *Ibid.,* 311.

[50] Quoted in Mulder and Mortensen (eds.), *Among the Mormons,* 274-78.

[51] George Bourne, *Lorette: The History of Louise, Daughter of a Canadian Nun, Exhibiting the Interior of Female Convents* (New York, 1834), 176-77; Hogan, *Auricular Confession,* 271; Frances Stenhouse, *A Lady's Life among the Mormons: A Record of Personal Experiences as One of the Wives of a Mormon Elder* (New York, 1872), 77.

[52] *Anti-Masonic Review,* I (December, 1828), 24 ff.; *Cloven Foot,* 325-42, 357-58; Froiseth (ed.), *Women of Mormonism,* 317-18; Ward, *Female Life among the Mormons,* 428-29.

[53] Armstrong, *Masonry,* 22.

[54] *Free Masonry: A Poem,* p. iv.

[55] *Ibid.,* pp. iii, 51; Hopkins, *Renunciation of Free Masonry,* 5, 9-11; *Anti-Masonic Almanac,* 1830, pp. 28-29; Bernard, *Light on Masonry,* p. iii.

[56] Stenhouse, *Lady's Life among the Mormons,* 142-43.

[57] Hogan, *Auricular Confession,* 226-29, 233, 296-97.

David S. Reynolds

SOURCE: "Roman Catholic Fiction," in *Faith in Fiction: The Emergence of Religious Literature in America,* Harvard University Press, 1981, pp. 145-67.

[*In the essay below, Reynolds looks at Roman Catholic fiction and its character and themes, both before 1850, when it used theological and historical polemics to persuade, and after 1850, when it began to assimilate the prevailing anti-theological secularism.*]

Unlike Protestant novelists, who wished to find diverting, sentimental replacements for the rigorous theology of the Puritan past, Roman Catholics generally devoted their novels to attacking what they saw as Protestant divisiveness, theological evasion, and lack of logic. The free Biblical interpretation and privately formed faith that Protestant novels increasingly extolled were ultimate heresy for the Catholic writer, who tried to validate the authority of the historical True Church as a cure for contemporary Protestant corruption. While Protestant fiction was generally nontheoretical, much Catholic fiction before 1850 attempted to be intellectual and polemical.

This emphasis on reasoned debate was designed as both a foil to Protestant sentimentalism and a pointed reply to the growing number of Americans who dismissed Catholics as illiterate slum dwellers enslaved by the "Beast of Rome." Accordingly, most Catholic novels of the period include an account of a Protestant character who, after years of Catholic baiting and smug self-satisfaction, becomes miserably aware of Protestantism's shortcomings, often through the agency of a rational Catholic priest or lay person. And yet, despite this stress on reason and tradition, Catholic fiction made rhetorical use of sentimental devices which became progressively more prominent as time passed. Thus much of the interest of early Catholic fiction lies in the way its vaunted intellectualism was reinforced, with growing frequency, by secular props similar to those found in Protestant fiction of the time.

Protestantism, which had been called fragmented and confused by Catholics since the Reformation, was particularly vulnerable to Catholic criticism in nineteenth-century America. The right to private conscience and religious freedom guaranteed by the Constitution resulted in the proliferation of Protestant sects which were often doctrinally or politically antagonistic. In her preface to *Redwood* (1824) Catherine Sedgwick said that she wrote "at a period, and in a country of constant mutations, where old faiths are every year dissolving, and new ones every year forming."[1] As we have seen, the author of *The Soldier's Orphan* (1812) had claimed that every "free and accountable being" in America "has an equal right with his neighbour to form a creed for his own observance" (32): This democratic ethic placed renewed emphasis on private inquiry and toleration in religious matters, as external authority was seen as antithetical to individual freedom. Five new denominations of major importance would be founded by American Protestants in the nineteenth century; by 1960 the number of different Protestant sects would total more than two hundred. Thus, the century immediately following the Revolution saw a paradoxical combination of increasing theological similarities with growing sectarian schisms in American Protestantism.

The Catholic novelist capitalized on this post-Revolutionary religious ethic, converting into vices those values lauded by Protestants. The Catholic writer represented Protestant diversity as self-mocking fragmentation, private interpretation as the seedbed of religious chaos, toleration as theological relativism. Whereas Protestant authors, from writers of Oriental tales to Biblical novelists, attacked tyrannical authority on behalf of individual freedom, the Catholic novelist was quick to point out that without the guiding hand of authority, freedom can lapse into unregulated license, engendering mutually exclusive doctrines. The Catholic argument was an old one: there can be just one True Church derived from Christ, and the Catholic church is the only existing denomination that can justifiably lay claim to a link with early Christian times through a continuing tradition of ecclesiastical leaders, saints, and scholarly commentators. By definition, according to this view, Protestantism is merely an offshoot or modification of Catholicism, so that Protestant pretenses to originality are inaccurate. The corruptions Luther attributed to the Catholic church have been exceeded by those of Protestantism itself, which has created a battlefield of jarring sects each claiming to be the True Church. This familiar Catholic argument had special import in a period when the Unitarian controversy was raging, when the Plan of Union between Presbyterianism and Congregationalism was collapsing, when evangelical Calvinism was spawning many different sects.

In a sense, Protestant fiction of the period constituted a massive effort to fabricate a meeting place for schismatic religionists. Usually minimizing sectarian differences while endorsing universal religious principles, Protestant writers offered such commonly acceptable ideas as morality, goodness, and social activity to a religiously diversified nation. The Biblical novel provided, among other things, a surrogate connection to the early-Christian past that most American Protestants lacked; William Ware, for example, could imaginatively consummate his search for a Unitarian apostolic succession in his early essay by returning directly to Biblical times in his novels. To be sure, the doctrinal controversies of the period were reflected in the Protestant novel, as evidenced by such works as *Charles Observator, Justina, A New England Tale,* and *Jotham Anderson.* But most controversial Protestant novels were written before 1830, as writers of all sects tried to fabricate a unity in diversity in fiction that placed virtuous action at the center of faith.

The Catholic novel, which began to be written in America around 1830, tried to expose Protestant attempts at unity as fraudulent, ahistorical, and ephemeral. There is just one unity, the Catholic novelist stressed, the unity of the Church founded by Christ through the authority of Peter and maintained by the Holy Fathers for eighteen centuries. Protestants offer only pale copies of this grand unity and usually must resort to tricks or to false hope to do so.

The pre-1850 Catholic novelist faced a uniquely difficult task: to win the sympathy of predominantly Protestant readers who were apt to dislike not only Catholicism but authoritarian religion of any sort. To accomplish this task some writers stressed features of Catholicism that would be naturally attractive to Americans, such as the patriotism of Catholic soldiers during the Revolutionary War or the social work of groups such as the Sisters of Charity. More typically the Catholic novelist tried to defuse Protestant objections by portraying a vehement hater of Catholicism who comes to see the error of his prejudices. To oppose the common Protestant view of Catholicism as a sensuous religion of forms, the Catholic novelist deemphasized material emblems of faith. Indeed, the

extensive concrete descriptions of statues and icons in such Protestant novels as William Ware's *Probus* and Eliza B. Lee's *Parthenia* were generally avoided by the Catholic writers on behalf of more expository presentation of ideas.

Yet the Catholic novelist used common fictional devices to underscore rhetorically his religious message. For instance, a narrow and hateful Protestant preacher was often compared to a learned, urbane Catholic priest. Such a contrast cleverly overturned the normal conflict in Protestant novels—gloomy bigot versus tolerant protagonist—to make a case for Catholicism. Also, the Catholic writers of the period often invoked domestic sentiment and romantic love, which were standard features of Protestant fiction. Though the Catholic's final message was that the individual cannot create his own creed, all the authors borrowed the central Protestant premise of a restless individual protagonist seeking religious truth; exactly reversing the religious journey in Protestant novels, the Catholic writers showed a character emerging from the bigotry of Protestantism into the reasonableness and secure authoritarianism of the Catholic church. Some Catholic writers used the visionary mode to sanctify this journey. Combined with the increasing reliance on secular sentiment as time passed, these features of Catholic fiction suggest that in the process of appealing to a generally hostile audience, the Catholic novelist was forced to adopt several of the fictional techniques popularized by his Protestant opponents.

Catholic fiction in America before the Civil War was principally the product of the following novelists: Charles Constantine Pise, John Boyce, John T. Roddan, Hugh Quigley, Charles James Cannon, George Henry Miles, Jedediah Vincent Huntington, Anna Hanson Dorsey, Mrs. James Sadlier (formerly Mary Anne Madden), and Orestes Brownson.[2] Besides the fiction writen by these authors, there were individual efforts by other Catholics, including Mary Hughs's *The Two Schools* (1836), the anonymous *Father Oswald* (1843), and John D. Bryant's *Pauline Seward* (1847).

We find in this early Catholic fiction further evidence of the secularizing pattern apparent in much other religious fiction of the period. The earliest important novelists—Pise, Boyce, Roddan, and Quigley—were priests whose fiction passed from primarily intellectual defenses of doctrine to largely sentimental narratives illustrating practical Catholicism. In the 1840s these priest-novelists gave way to several Catholic lay persons—Cannon, Miles, Huntington, Dorsey, Sadlier—who increasingly deemphasized logic on behalf of pathos and adventure. Like many of the Protestant scribbling women of the 1840s and 1850s, these later Catholic writers were generally professional novelists trying to make a living through writing religious fiction: Cannon and Miles were determined to gain popularity, and

Dorsey and Sadlier each wrote more than thirty Catholic novels between 1845 and 1890. The best novelist of the group, Huntington, was also the most worldly; an avid reader of English and French romantic fiction, he was often praised and occasionally damned for the sensuous richness and realism of his descriptions. Much of the early Catholic fiction was reviewed by Orestes Brownson, who found several novels lacking in intellectual rigor but who nevertheless recognized the importance of fiction in promoting Catholicism. Brownson tried his hand at writing fiction, outdoing the reasoned argumentation of his Protestant *Charles Elwood* (1840) in his Catholic *The Two Brothers; or, Why Are You a Protestant?* (1847), after which he resorted to a more sensational approach in *The Spirit-Rapper* (1854). The general movement of popular Catholic writing was away from theology toward sentimental fiction. In the 1840s novels displaced doctrinal works as the most lucrative product of Catholic publishers, and in 1845 Edward Dunigan of New York inaugurated his Dunigan's Home Library Series of Religious and Moral Works for Popular Reading, which was composed largely of novels.

The Catholic novelist faced the delicate task of disproving Protestantism logically while appealing to the emotions in ways the American novel reader expected. More acutely than Protestant novelists, who were often willing to abandon dogma happily, Catholics felt the painful paradox of the question: How does one write an intellectual religious novel? The Catholic novelist wished to invoke the powerful scholarly tradition of his church and to contrast his own reason to the evasive tactics of his Protestant enemies. At the same time, he did not want to put his readers to sleep with dull polemics.

This tension was most explicitly expressed in Brownson's literary articles of the late 1840s. In an 1847 article on religious novels Brownson declared that the novel was "the most convenient literary form which can now be adopted."[3] The age demanded entertainment with its religion, and the novel was by far the most entertaining of popular genres. But Brownson was deeply disturbed by the failure of most religious novels, which he called "literary hybrids" combining "the sentimental story, and the grave religious discussion" (144). Brownson established the general rule that "they who are seriously disposed would prefer taking the theology by itself, and those who are not so disposed will skip it. The one class will regard the light and sentimental as an impertinence; and the other, the grave and religious as a *bore*" (144). Noting the prevalence of religious fiction in nineteenth-century America, Brownson declared that "we respect the rigidness of our Puritan ancestors more than we do the laxity of their descendants" (178). In an essay of 1848 entitled "Novel-Writing and Novel-Reading," denouncing J. D. Bryant's defense of religious novels as the proper

response to public demand, Brownson noted, "Study any age or nation, and you will find its peculiar heresy to have originated in the attempt to conform the church to its dominant ideas and sentiments, or to incorporate them into her teaching and practice" (223). Moreover, said Brownson, religious fiction is usually a literary monstrosity, since "the interest of a story is diverse from the interest excited by a logical discussion, and not compatible with it. The one demands action, movement, is impatient of delay, and hurries on to the end; the other demands quiet, repose, and suffers only the intellect to be active. It is impossible to combine them both in one and the same piece so as to produce unity of effect" (226). Religious novelists, Brownson went on, are wont to combine "profane love with an argument for religion," and "no two interests are more widely separated, or less capable of coalescing, than the interest of profane love and that of religion" (226). In the final analysis, religious novelists assume "that nature, as nature, nature without elevation or transformation by grace, may be pressed into the service of God" (230). In another essay of 1848, "Catholic Secular Literature," Brownson reiterated that religious novelists "secularize the spiritual, while we would spiritualize the secular" (299).

The fact that Brownson wrote four pieces of fiction in spite of his great reservations about religious novels points up the general problem of the Catholic novelist in nineteenth-century America. To overlook fiction altogether would be to risk losing the attention of an American public that was buying Protestant novels by the thousands. To write fiction was to risk debasing the sacrosanct tradition of Roman Catholic logic. If he tried too hard to be popular, the Catholic novelist might be dismissed as theologically flawed. If he tried to be intellectual, he might be called artistically inept. In a sense, the Catholic novelist, like the logical Calvinist of the period, was backed into a corner. He wanted to be entertaining but respectable, popular yet precise. He wanted to endorse divine grace and strong intellect through the avenues of nature and secular sentiment. The literary hybrids produced by Catholics between 1829 and 1855 reflect the plight of a logical religionist in a secular culture. By 1855 it had become apparent that the Catholic novelist had decided to conform to the culture he had been wooing for nearly three decades.

America's first important Catholic novelist, Charles Constantine Pise, wrote three novels that were pointedly reasoned and intellectual. Each of his novels is a doctrinal conversion drama mildly seasoned with domestic sentiment. The first, *Father Rowland* (1829), traces the conversion to Catholicism of Virginia Wolburn, a Baltimore Episcopalian who at first derides Catholics, through conversations with her parents, her sister Louisa, and particularly the refined Father Rowland. In *The Indian Cottage* (1830) the Unitarian

Elizabeth Preston adopts Catholicism after talking with Charles Clermont and his sisters. *Zenosius; or, The Pilgrim-Convert* (1845) allegorizes a young man's religious pilgrimage from a chaotic country, Sectarianism, to Rome.

Pise's basic story of a bigoted Protestant who comes to be convinced of Catholicism's reasonableness through careful deliberation epitomizes the most staid, conservative type of Catholic fiction. Strongest emotion in Pise's novels is directed to doctrinal matters, as when Father Rowland exclaims that American Protestantism is "the prolific parent of a thousand creeds, each contradicting each; all disagreeing; none admitting anything like a tribunal to decide their controversies; all appealing to the Bible, the Bible, the Bible!" Protestant Bible societies, Rowland continues, merely "scatter abroad the seeds of error: each individual interprets for himself, and forms a religion for himself," so that he can "make the scripture speak any language he pleases."[4] In each novel Pise depicts a learned authority, a priest or an educated lay person, who can explain the precepts and history of Catholicism to the searching Protestant. Pise avoids both lively adventure and romantic love in an effort to attain the quiet and repose that Brownson found essential to logical argument. Except for the allegorical Zenosius, Pise's characters are wealthy southern families who have leisure to discuss doctrinal niceties while enjoying peaceful Maryland sunsets.

But Pise, like most religious novelists, adopted fiction for rhetorical reasons, and secular sentiment often creeps into even his determinedly logical stories. Despite his pose of sobriety and equanimity, Pise discovers in fiction some anti-Protestant weapons which would be used by later Catholic novelists: appeals to American patriotism, contrasting personal descriptions of Protestants and Catholics, winning anecdotes, sorrowful deathbed scenes, and to a lesser extent, the visionary mode. By making the father of Virginia Wolburn a distinguished veteran of the Revolution, Pise plays on the democratic sympathies of Protestant readers. More significantly, by contrasting a handsome, forthright priest with an ugly, evasive Protestant minister, he plays on the average reader's sense of attraction and revulsion. While avoiding romantic love, Pise portrays the priest of his first novel as a pious young bachelor whose "unaffected gracefulness . . . could not but conciliate the prejudices of any company" (28). Rowland's history of the Catholic church is "interspersed with several amusing anecdotes," showing that the priest, "though grave, was facetious and lively, presenting a living picture of a truly pious man" (39). In contrast, his Episcopalian opponent, the Reverend Mr. Dorson, is "a tall, spare . . . person with a bald head, and a stern sanctimonious countenance" who makes certain "to allude in all his sermons to the *ignorance,* and *super-*stition, and *idolatry,* of the Catholic worship. Rome he styled Babylon. The Pope the beast. The Church the mother of corruption" (86). While Rowland desires honest discussion, Dorson tries "to evade it most dextrously," relying on vitriolic name calling (90). Louisa Wolburn is struck by the "difference between the calm, dispassionate reasoning of Mr. Rowland, and the vapid vituperation of Doctor Dorson" (98).

Pise repeats the contrast in *Indian Cottage:* the Catholic Charles Clermont is "elegant in his manners, and refined by the most polished education," while the Unitarian Alton is emotionally biased.[5] By embodying standard obloquies against Catholicism in disagreeable Protestant figures, Pise can overcome them through his appeals to the bourgeois values of his readers in his depictions of polished Catholic gentlemen.

Pise does not just use Protestant patriotism and anti-Catholic preconceptions to his own ends; he skillfully reverses common devices of Protestant fiction. This reversal is most apparent in the full title of his second novel, *The Indian Cottage: A Unitarian Story.* In 1830 the typical American reader might have picked up the book with expectations of another Unitarian Indian tale along the lines of Child's *Hobomok* or Sedgwick's *Hope Leslie.* The fact that the reader may have been disappointed to discover that "Indian Cottage" is simply the name of a Maryland mansion housing a Unitarian family that turns Catholic probably did not worry Pise; he at least caught the reader's eye and, perhaps, made him consider Catholicism. In his novels Pise often directs devices from Protestant fiction—deathbed sentiment, vernacular perspective, anecdotal persuasion, and even the visionary mode—to Catholic ends.

Pise masks his reversal of Protestant literary devices with conventional Catholic paeans to logic. His outlook is summed up by a priest in *Zenosius:* "Error should, certainly, be combated: but not with the arms of the flesh: not with impetuous abuse, not with passionate declamation against one another. If the Protestant believes one faith erroneous, let him confine himself to argument, to solid reasoning, to scriptural authority."[6] However, as we have seen, Pise, even while establishing himself as the most logical Catholic novelist America would produce, made subtle use of arms of the flesh in his novels. It was left to later Catholic writers to exaggerate the secular devices Pise had strategically covered with the guise of sober reason.

Mary Hughs's *The Two Schools* (1836) leaves behind Pise's doctrinal priorities and advances a creedless Catholicism of social action and feeling. The restrained domestic affection of Pise's Wolburn and Clermont families is replaced by Hughs's emotional portrait of the Monkton family, Anglicans who leave England for Baltimore, where they discover that a poor Catholic orphan, Mary McDonald, is in fact their long-lost daughter, Aline Monkton. The basic plot of Pise's novels—Protestant conversion to Catholicism—is echoed in Hughs's account of how the Anglican Augusta Monkton and her father adopt the Catholic faith as a result of their growing disaffection with Protestantism. But the reflective stasis of Pise's novels gives way in Hughs to dramatic movement as the Monktons wander from England to Baltimore and Wilmington in search of religious truth. Moreover, Pise's logical Catholic preceptors are replaced by secular exemplars: the Sisters of Charity, whose social work the Monktons come to admire, and the angelic Mary, who retains her peaceful faith in Catholicism despite poverty and solitude. Like a number of Calvinist and liberal novelists of the mid-1830s, Hughs finds in social activity and perseverance ideal alternatives to doctrinal religion.

Catholic fiction might have continued in Hugh's quietly noncontroversial vein had it not been for the increasingly rancorous anti-Catholicism that swept America between 1835 and 1850. The influx of Irish and European Catholics in the 1830s and 1840s caused great alarm in many Protestant circles and helped give rise to such nativist groups as the Know-Nothings. Several Protestant authors wrote vicious anti-Catholic novels that represented nunneries as whorehouses run by rum-drinking priests (see Chapter 7). Such Protestant criticism deserved stronger reply than staid, reasoned novels like Pise's or innocuous social-working dramas like Hughs's. At the same time, Catholics did not wish to lose their intellectual superiority by descending to the mudslinging tactics of their opponents. Therefore, they opted for fiction that combined solid Catholic argumentation with more sensational anti-Protestant devices. Catholic novelists after 1840 were more willing than Pise to take up arms of the flesh in the defense of their church.

As a result of the rising opposition to Catholicism in America, a new tone of defensive vindictiveness characterized several of the post-1840 works. *Father Oswald* (1843) was written, according to its preface, in reply to the anti-Catholic "Father Clement and many similar productions" since 1835. Presented as "an antidote to the baneful production of Father Clement," the book promises to answer all charges made in the anti-Catholic novel, "although they have been previously refuted a hundred times."[7] In his preface to *Harry Layden* (1842) Charles Cannon explains that the book "has been written—but with no controversial spirit—for the purpose of saying something in favour of that portion of the Christian family which every dabbler in literature feels himself at liberty to abuse."[8] Likewise, Hugh Quigley's *The Cross and the Shamrock* (1853) is prefaced by the assertion: "The corruption of the cheap trash literature, that is now ordinarily supplied for the amusement and instruction of the American people . . . calls for some antidote, some remedy."[9]

In keeping with such aims, post-1840 Catholic novelists gave new satiric point to their attacks on Protestantism. Unlike Pise, who had selected Episcopalian or Unitarian characters to outreason, the later writers often coupled their attacks on such mild characters with sharp caricature of more sensational Protestants—evangelical revivalists, Millerites, and so forth. In *Father Oswald* the dying William Smith is converted to Catholicism partly as result of the callous inattention of his Methodist pastor, Ebenezer, whose religion seems harsh and narrow. After Smith's death his antievangelical sentiments are repeated by a Catholic character who notes the "frightful spectacle" of "so many swarms of new sects, that rise up daily around us. In every village new meeting-houses are erected, and every illiterate fanatic quits the loom or the anvil, and, with all self-sufficiency, mounts to the pulpit to explain to the stupid crowd the deep mysteries of revelation." Such evangelism places the Bible in the hands of "every *unlearned* and *unstable* mechanic" who wishes to address "the gulled and gaping multitude."[10]

Charles Cannon similarly capitalizes on evangelical excesses. In *Harry Layden* he mocks the "great scandal" of Methodist camp meetings, where "the Christian heaven is described in the glowing colors of a Mahometan paradise; the praises of the 'Lamb' are sung with the frenzied ardor of Bacchanals; and even the Holy Name is mouthed with the most impious familiarity, to the horror of every right thinking man or woman present."[11] Cannon continues the attack in *Mora Carmody* (1844) and *Father Felix* (1845). Cannon's Mora is shocked by "the miserable jargon" of an itinerant who denounces the Pope as "the Son of Perdition, the Man of Sin, the Anti-Christ, foretold by the prophet."[12] In *Father Felix* a Millerite revival brings about the derangement of Julia Baldwin, whose former placidity is replaced by frenzied ravings which lead to her death.

Thus after 1840 Catholic novelists raised their voices in response to the clamorous vituperation that was coming from the Protestant press. The lascivious priest of the anti-Catholic novel was parodied by the ignorant, wild revivalist of the Catholic novel. But the Catholics did not wish to give themselves over to sheer emotionalism, for to do so would be to sacrifice their most dependable ally, logic. Thus, they presented their novels as reasoned refutations of unreasonable Protestant slander. Cannon, for example, denounced "those flagitious attacks upon the professors of the Catholic faith, with which the American press has lately teemed, that make up in abuse what they lack in argument."[13] Nearly every Catholic novel before 1850 contains a priest who defends such doctrines as transubstantiation, the Virgin Birth, and apostolic succession with cool wisdom. The priest normally stresses that Protestantism is hopelessly fragmented and that the final destination for the Protestant is either bewilderment or atheism.

And yet the Catholic novelist was fully aware that these were old arguments that might without sentimental refurbishment bore American readers. Accordingly, those secular arms of the flesh Pise had subtly used came to be utilized more explicitly and frequently by the post-1840 writers. Priests were not only learned but also well dressed and handsome, in contrast to their slovenly Protestant opponents. The domestic emotion Pise had tried to restrain became the key to conversion in several of the novels, and romantic love was a common theme. The Protestant couple of *Father Oswald,* for instance, separates when the wife adopts Catholicism and reunites when her husband follows her into the True Church. Cannon's orphaned Harry Layden wins love and wealth along with religion. The Protestant narrator of *Mora Carmody,* at first dismayed that Mora is a Catholic, is eventually won over as much by her winning demeanor as by her logic. In *Father Felix* Cannon connects Protestantism to seduction, madness, and murder while linking Catholicism to social advancement. A similarly sentimental scheme informs Bryant's *Pauline Seward* and nearly all the novels of Anna Dorsey. In many of the novels, deathbed scenes enforce the need for salvation in the Catholic Church. In short, the Catholic novelist after 1840 was using sentimental devices that had been standard features of Protestant fiction since the 1820s.

In addition, this later Catholic fiction, while always more doctrinal than its Protestant counterpart, relied increasingly on anecdotes and illustrations of religious truth. The priest figure was usually a good storyteller as well as a careful logician. *Father Felix* contains several interpolated religious legends, ranging from a story of medieval knighthood to a visionary tale, which dramatically accent the intellectual disquisitions of the main characters. In some novels an effort is made to reduce doctrinal references while extolling secular illustration. In the interest of "supplying the younger portion of the Catholic community with a source of mental recreation," Anna Dorsey emphasizes that she has merely "touched lightly on a few doctrinal points."[14] Indeed, her novels, which resemble those of the Calvinist Joseph Alden written during the same period, concentrate more on the tears of orphans than on the talk of priests. Likewise, in *Harry Layden,* Charles Cannon is willing to sidestep a key doctrinal discussion in the interest of getting on with the story:

> We are not writing a treatise on education, nor a volume of controversial divinity and will therefore, neither trace step by step, the progress of Harry in the path of learning, nor go over all the arguments made use of by Redmond in his conversations with Agneta, to prove that Catholicism—the religion of some of the wisest and best men the world has ever known—might have some claim to be considered Christianity. Nor will we describe the struggles of the ingenuous Agneta with herself, when obliged to abandon, one by one, the prejudices she had

cherished as truths, until she was forced to admit, that notwithstanding all she had heretofore heard and read, all that is essential to salvation may be found in the Church of Rome [35].

Evasion of doctrinal exposition had always been common in Protestant fiction in America; even relatively cerebral works such as *Jotham Anderson* and *A New England Tale* contain several passages that, like Cannon's, relegate vast intellectual inquiries to a vague sentence or two. But such circumvention was new to the Catholic novelist of the 1840s, who was now eager to avoid the appearance of writing a volume of controversial divinity.

After 1850 this movement to the sentimental and anecdotal was accelerated and was underscored by a minimizing of tedious argumentation that might alienate Protestant readers. Jedediah Vincent Huntington, an Anglican who was converted to Roman Catholicism in 1849, voiced the sentiments of many later novelists when in the mid-1850s he distinguished between "controversial" and "poetic" Catholic fiction. Echoing Brownson, Huntington wrote, "The modern controversial Catholic novel . . . is liable to the fatal objection of mixing things in themselves heterogeneous and incompatible." Dismissing the controversial novel as "essentially inartistic," Huntington declared that Catholic fiction should aim "to create the beautiful imitation of real human life, not to convince, not to refute even the most real and the most lamentable errors."[15] Huntington's interest in real human life was reflected in his five novels, which were more notable for their vivid realism and romantic adventure than for otherworldly contemplation or doctrinal subtlety. This secular emphasis sometimes angered Huntington's reviewers. In 1850 the *North American Review* found in his *Lady Alice* an "irreverent flippancy with which things sacred and things secular are constantly intermingled."[16] The *Review* lamented Huntington's "thoroughly licentious" and "voluptuous" accounts of concubinage, nude art models, and mixed public bathing, voicing its "solemn protest against the intrusion upon English literature, under the garb of religious purism, of the vilest forms and worst features of modern French fiction" (237).

In response to such criticism, Huntington tried to tame his impulse to graphic sensuous description, though it did surface in each of his four Catholic novels of the 1850s. For example, Huntington was condemned by several critics for allowing the heroine of *The Forest* (1852) to camp for a time with her lover in the North woods. Each of his Catholic novels made courtship prerequisite to conversion. *Rosemary* (1860), which dealt with such lively topics as clandestine marriages and reanimated corpses, was explained by the author as follows: "This is not a prayer-book, but a story written expressly to win the attention of those who will read nothing but stories, and sensational ones at that."[17] Mirroring this anecdotal propensity, Huntington's novels contain several storytelling characters and interpolated narratives. Alban of *Alban* (1853) and *The Forest* "can repeat whole novels from beginning to end."[18] In *The Forest* the Catholic heroine's long sentimental tale of the placidity of convent life effects the conversion of a Protestant girl, while Alban's intellectual cerebrations during a monastic retreat are dismissed with Huntington's statement that "it is not our intention to follow our hero through the course of this celebrated discipline" (277).

Other Catholic novelists after 1850 manifested this antitheological secularism in different ways. Such works as Anna Dorsey's *Woodreve Manor* (1852) and Charles Cannon's *Tighe Lyfford* (1859) have little Catholic content. Mrs. James Sadlier, adopting the favorite formula of Protestant domestic novelists, wrote numerous novels of displaced Irish orphans enduring Protestant obloquy and gaining money and marriage through firm adherence to simple Catholic principles. George Henry Miles's *Loretto* (1851) was "severely handled" by critics because it contained "no good solid arguments in it, extracted from standard theological works."[19] The heroine of Miles's *The Governess* (1851) brings about the conversion of a Protestant family not by argument but rather "by the force of example," giving rise to another evasion-of-exposition passage: "The winter passed in religious controversy, which we do not mean to repeat: there are so many better reasoners than Mary, that it is quite unnecessary to record her instructions."[20] Similarly, the Irish priest of Hugh Quigley's *The Cross and the Shamrock* (1853) shows "reluctance to enter into a theological discussion" with a Protestant character.[21] Quigley's sensational interests are reflected in this book, *The Cross and the Shamrock,* which associates camp meetings with sexual promiscuity and Protestantism in general with dissolution and suicide, as well as in his *Prophet of the Ruined Abbey* (1855) and *Profit and Loss* (1873), in which farcical anti-Protestant satire and stirring Irish legends predominate over logic.

This growing resistance to intellectual doctrine is most clearly illustrated in John Boyce's *Mary Lee* (1860). Boyce's special target is Orestes Brownson, who appears in the novel as Dr. Horseman-Henshaw, a recent convert to Catholicism whose ponderous logic contrasts with the simple emotional piety of the Irish heroine and a fun-loving priest. Like several other Catholic novelists of the day, Boyce had reason to be upset with Brownson. Although Brownson had lauded Boyce's *Shandy M'Guire* (1848), he had qualified his praise by stating, "We object to novels in general, because they are sentimental, and make the interest of their readers centre in a story of the rise, progress, and termination of the affection or passion of love."[22] Brownson had blasted Boyce's second book, *The Spaewife* (1853), calling it "too grave for fiction, and

too light for history.[23] Boyce responded with his caricature of Henshaw, who "as a polemic and logician . . . has very few equals" but who is coldly distant from practical, human Catholicism.[24] One of Boyce's Irish Catholics complains that Henshaw "wields theology like a sledge-hammer, and sends all Protestants to misery everlasting" (182). Another, noting that Henshaw "reviews every book he can lay his hands on—stories, novels, poetry, every thing," declares: "I think so little of his literary criticisms I don't care to read them" (165). In contrast to Henshaw, who believes that "intellectual men need intellectual treatment," Mary Lee wins over a Protestant girl "not by dosing her with dogmas, anathemas, and philosophy," but "by the mere example of her every-day life" (325, 324).

Thus post-1850 Catholic novelists, following a pattern similar to the one seen in the works of orthodox and liberal Protestant novelists, increasingly embraced quotidian example and noncontroversial piety, rejecting the more logically reasoned argumentation used by Pise and other priest-novelists before 1845.

In light of this movement toward the sentimental and anecdotal, it is not surprising that Orestes Brownson wrote several essays in 1847 and 1848 emphasizing the need for stricter logic in Roman Catholic fiction. The increasing use by Catholic novelists of the themes of love and adventure alarmed Brownson, who wished to reverse or at least retard the secularizing trend. But Brownson offered no real alternative to the writer of Catholic fiction. As we have seen, he could note that religious novelists "secularize the spiritual, while we would spiritualize the secular"; but how was such equivocal advice to be practically applied? He could declare that novelists "overlook the essential incongruity between nature and grace"; but how was intangible grace to be reproduced in fiction? He attacked J. D. Bryant's request for an adaptation to cultural tastes. Yet not only did he admit that the popular novel was "the most convenient form which can now be adopted," but he tempered his criticism of Anna Dorsey's *Conscience* (1856) by writing: "Let every man, every woman, old or young, that can write a passable book, write it. Even trash is better than nothing."[25] On the matter of religious fiction, Brownson was torn between the demands of culture and those of conscience, between popular appeal and doctrinal purity. Brownson's love affair with religious fiction was as painful as had been his infatuations with Presbyterianism, Unitarianism, socialism, and Transcendentalism—but it was much longer, as it began in the early 1840s and continued long after his conversion to Catholicism.

Both fascinated and repelled by religious fiction, Brownson made four efforts at writing fiction: *Charles Elwood* (1840), *The Two Brothers* (1847), "Uncle Jack and His Nephew" (1854), and *The Spirit-Rapper* (1854). In this fiction we see Brownson, first from a Protestant and then from a Catholic standpoint, struggling to locate a proper fictional voice. After mingling sentiment with argument in his first novel, he ascends to almost pure logic in his second and third tales, and then experiments with sensationalism in *The Spirit-Rapper*. The inconsistency in tone of these works suggests that even one of the most acute Roman Catholic thinkers in nineteenth-century America had extreme difficulty in discovering a fictional equipoise between religion and nature in the popular religious novel.

Many of Brownson's apprehensions are captured in his introductory apologia to *Charles Elwood:* "It may be objected that I have introduced too much fiction for a serious work, and too little, if I intended a regular-built novel."[26] His later novels and essays would constitute a prolonged attempt at deciding what was too much or too little fiction. In *Charles Elwood* Brownson essays a balanced combination of logic and emotion. He describes Elwood's painful passage from gloomy skepticism to piety as a result of his love for the dying Elizabeth Wyman and his intellectual dialogues with two progressive Protestants, Morton and Howard. Clearly Brownson in the novel is trying to expunge the frivolous in favor of the serious. He carefully records the cerebrations that lead Elwood from atheism to Protestantism. Basically, the argument is a fully developed version of the theme of most American Protestant novels of the period: that the religious sentiment beneath changeable creeds can be apprehended through free individual inquiry. Instead of resorting to indirect secular analogues like the Biblical novelist's Roman tyrant, Brownson directly attacks the "ecclesiastical tyranny" of Roman Catholicism and Calvinism, championing "individual reason" and every man's "right and power to form his own creed" (251).

And yet, despite this rational emphasis, Brownson does bend to the sentimental requirements of popular fiction. Branded a pariah by religionists, frustrated in love, finding no stoic or existential pleasure in life, Elwood before his conversion is a restless Wertherian seeker tailored to suit the romantic tastes of the reading public. He cries despondently over his disbelief and his lover's death and joyfully over his new-found faith. Even after his long talks with Morton and Howard, he is as much swayed by their benevolent example as by their logic. He can thus conclude: "As a general rule would you gain the reason you must win the heart. This is the secret of most conversions. There is no logic like love" (241).

In his effort to please both the sentimentalist and the logician Brownson pleased neither. *Charles Elwood* did not have popular success, and reviewers wrote contradictory evaluations of the book according to their doctrinal preferences. The *Christian Examiner* dubbed Brownson a "logic-grinder, without heart and

soul, or at best with nothing but a gizzard."[27] The conservative *Boston Quarterly Review,* arguing that Brownson resorted to "a subtler influence than logic" in the novel, said precisely the opposite:

> Abstract the personal interest taken in Charles himself, the aesthetic effect of his conversation with his betrothed, and of the moral beauty of Mr. Howard's life and generous friendship, and the life and force of the argument would be greatly impaired, and nearly all the efficacy of the work would be lost . . . Abstract the deep, earnest feeling, the passion even, that [Brownson] mingles with his arguments, to an extent perhaps little expected, and we apprehend his logic would be by no means remarkable.[28]

Thus, Brownson included in *Charles Elwood* both too little and too much fiction to satisfy anybody.

After he was converted to Catholicism in 1844, Brownson went through a period, roughly between 1847 and 1851, in which the logical side of *Charles Elwood* was exaggerated to fuel an antipathy to anything tinged with secular sentiment. The kind of intellectualism used by Elwood's teachers to support Protestantism was transformed in this later period to expository defenses of Catholicism and attacks on Protestantism in *Brownson's Quarterly Review.*

It was at this time that Brownson wrote the aridly logical *The Two Brothers; or, Why Are You a Protestant?* (1847). The novel consists of prolonged debates between John and James Milwood, brothers who were raised as Presbyterians and who have made adult choices, respectively, for Catholicism and Protestantism. In the face of his brother's spurious, emotional argumentation, John coolly performs dizzying intellectual feats to prove that Protestantism is a confused array of nonreligions which change God into a liar. Protestants, John says, are wont "to assume a bold and daring tone, to make broad and sweeping assertions, and to forego clear and exact statements, and close and rigid logic"; Catholics, in contrast, "speak to sober sense, to prudent judgement, and aim to convince the reason, instead of moving the sensibility and inflaming the passions."[29] John's logic is pointed in the opposite direction from that of the Protestant thinkers of *Charles Elwood.* The individual creation of religion recommended by Howard and Morton becomes, in the eyes of Brownson's Catholic spokesman, the cause of religious anarchy and relativism. In Protestantism, says John, "there is a multitude of sects, indeed, sometimes arranged under one common name, but without any common faith of principles, except that of hostility to the [Catholic] church" (268). Brownson keeps romantic love out of his novel; the two brothers are sexless mouthpieces for an inductive refutation of Protestantism. Even the conventional happy ending is eschewed, as James remains a hardened Catholic hater and John enters a monastery at the end.

While trying to offer a model of disinfected fiction to the Catholic novelists he was attacking in his essays of 1847-48, Brownson nevertheless does use a subtler influence than logic even in this highly intellectual novel. He has gotten rid of profane love here, but domestic and deathbed sentiment remains in the person of the brothers' mother, who, while dying, is tearfully converted to Catholicism. John is given the emotional advantage from the beginning by receiving his mother's blessing and by acting on her last request that he reconsider his childhood Presbyterianism. Brownson borrows from other Catholic novelists not only the deathbed scene but also the device of placing vehement anti-Catholicism in the mouth of a Protestant straw figure. James's first defense of Protestantism is a self-parodying torrent of vitriol: "I am a Protestant because the Romish Church is corrupt, the Mystery of Iniquity, the Man of Sin, Antichrist, the Whore of Babylon, drunk with the blood of the saints, a cage of unclean birds, cruel, oppressive, tyrannical, superstitious, idolatrous" (248). The reader is prepared by this outburst to agree with the later statement that Protestants are "far abler demogogues than logicians" (263). Furthermore, Brownson cleverly creates a devil in the ranks in his portrait of Wilson, a Presbyterian friend of James's who comes to criticize his own religion even more sharply than does John. "The time is not far distant," admits Wilson to James, "when you will have no Protestantism to defend, but each man will have a gospel of his own" (267). In sum, even while writing what is possibly the most studiously reasoned religious novel in American literature, Brownson makes rhetorical use of characterization and sentiment.

If *Charles Elwood* had been treated roughly by the public and by reviewers, *The Two Brothers* suffered an even worse fate: indifference. There is little evidence that the novel had a readership outside of regular subscribers to *Brownson's Quarterly Review,* in which it appeared serially. Brownson could intellectualize at length about what elements religious fiction should and should not contain, but he was finding the writing of such fiction difficult. The problem was really one of genre: to be theologically successful Brownson had to restrict himself to the essay; but to be popular he felt compelled to attempt fiction.

Criticized or ignored by reviewers and unsure of himself artistically, Brownson decided in *The Spirit-Rapper* (1854) to defy his critics by leaping over the boundary of genre altogether: "If the critics undertake to determine, by any recognized rules of art, to what class of literary productions the following unpretending work belongs, I think they will be sorely puzzled. I am sure I am puzzled myself to say what it is. It is not a novel; it is not a romance; it is not a biography

of a real individual; it is not a dissertation, an essay, or a regular treatise; and yet it perhaps has some elements of them all, thrown together in just such a way as best suited my convenience, or my purpose."[30] By now accustomed to both giving and receiving unfavorable reviews in his search for the ideal Catholic novel, Brownson invites his critics "to bestow upon the author as much of the castigation which, in his capacity of Reviewer, he has for many years been in the habit of bestowing on others, as they think proper" (1). The confident tone of the essays of 1847-48 has been replaced by a defensive, slightly cynical humor. The firm discrimination made in 1848 between the sentimental story and the grave religious discussion, between nature and grace, have given over to an ironic confession of literary puzzlement and possible failure. The issue is no longer a clear-cut conflict between too much and too little fiction; rather, it is a complex jugglery of genres and voices, none of which can be wholly accepted as the ideal ingredient of successful Catholic fiction.

As its preface indicates, *The Spirit-Rapper* is a potpourri of fiction, autobiography, history, satire, and theology. In several senses the book is notably different from Brownson's previous novels. Inductive logic has been replaced by flexible sentiment, a limited cast of characters by a multitude of religious voices, a nonadventurous plot by wide-ranging movement and even melodrama. Brownson's narrator, a liberal Protestant who is dabbling in mesmerism and spiritualism, meets the lovely Priscilla, a socialist despiser of despotic religions, who persuades him to join her World-Reform movement to overthrow the Catholic church. Along with Priscilla's husband, James, the two travel through Europe, where for six years they try to incite revolt against the Pope through a combined strategy of mind control and exhortation. Their attempts fail, as Pius IX causes a Catholic revival which crushes organized anti-Catholicism. Returning to America, the three reformers enter more troubled waters. The narrator becomes a gloomy atheist and is stabbed by James, who jealously suspects him of trying to steal his wife. The narrator becomes an invalid who is visited regularly by friends of various philosophical and religious outlooks. Meanwhile Priscilla, frustrated in love with the narrator, has been converted to Catholicism, which has been taught her by an erudite Franciscan monk whose brutal murder Priscilla later witnesses. The narrator follows a different road into the church. After trying to establish a rival religion to Christianity, a mixture of freethought and spiritualism, he at last espouses Catholicism because it is the only religion that distinguishes between "genuine and counterfeit spirit-manifestations" (191). Recognizing Satan, the narrator is forced to recognize Christ.

In this novel Brownson throws aside his earlier concern for strict logic and tightly regulated characterization and plot. He portrays many idiosyncratic characters who would have been banned from his previous fiction: Increase Mather Cotton, an Old Light Calvinist who mocks nineteenth-century liberalism's disbelief in devils; Edgerton and the American Orpheus, counterparts of Emerson and Alcott: Thomas Jefferson Andrew Jackson Hobbs, a populist demagogue; Rose Winter, a Jew who damns the New Testament; and various spiritualists, mesmerists, and radical reformers. Methodists are mocked as "so many bedlamites or howling dervishes" (11), and Joseph Smith is called "ignorant, illiterate, and weak" (99). In contrast to Brownson's novels and essays of the 1840s, this novel makes an allowance for profane love, borrowing from the popular sentimental novel the device of a love triangle that triggers a murder attempt. The narrator, despite his intelligence, is closer to the stormy, soul-searching protagonists of French romantic novels than to previous Brownson heroes such as John Milwood.

But the most thoroughly exploited area of sensationalism in the novel is spirit rapping and devil possession. Writing six years after the famous Fox rappings in New York, Brownson mentions not only the Fox sisters but also several other reports of spirit manifestations from modern and ancient historical records. Although Brownson's rather chaotic approach prevents him from fashioning a Catholic potboiler like William Peter Blatty's *The Exorcist,* Brownson anticipates Blatty's technique of positing an obverse spirituality through demon possession. One scene, in which Cotton orders a devil to leave a girl's body, presages the climactic moment of *The Exorcist.* Elsewhere, Brownson records instances of table lifting, violent body contortions, speaking in tongues, and Catholic exorcism. Brownson's goal is to destroy "the last infirmity of unbelief, the denial of the existence of the devil" (78). He cites Voltaire's exclamation, *"Sathan! c'est le Christianisme tout entier; PAS DE SATHAN, PAS DE SAUVEUR,"* explaining that "if there was no devil, the mission of Christ had no motive, no object, and Christianity is a fable" (93). Thus, the narrator's conversion comes only when he is convinced that Satan is a powerful being who is best explained and most successfully opposed by the Catholic church.

In *The Spirit-Rapper* Brownson has followed the pattern of those previous Catholic novelists whose foibles he pointed out in his essays of 1847-48. *The Spirit-Rapper* bears a relation to Brownson's earlier novels similar to that which the works of the other post-1840 writers bear to Pise's novels. Like Cannon and the author of *Father Oswald,* Brownson replaces logical refutation of reasonable Protestant denominations with caricature of more floridly emotional sects. He exceeds the other writers in his range of dramatic portrayals, as he describes excitingly radical movements which even the popularly oriented Cannon neglected. The vindictive post-1840 device of containing anti-

Catholicism through the depiction of misled Catholic baiters is expanded by Brownson to a complex plot involving Protestant reformers who scheme to subvert the Pope himself. The sentimentalism utilized by Huntington, Quigley, and Boyce is often invoked by Brownson, who heightens his religious dialogue with unrequited love, jealousy, revenge, and romantic ennui. All of these sensational tendencies are epitomized in Brownson's description of spirit manifestations. If *Charles Elwood* and *The Two Brothers* use a subtler influence than logic to endorse Catholicism, *The Spirit-Rapper,* like other Catholic novels after 1840, leaves behind cautious subtlety in favor of more explicitly combative and divertingly secular techniques.

The Spirit-Rapper is in part a sentimental dramatization of a central passage in Brownson's "Uncle Jack and His Nephew" (1854), a story that ran serially in the *Quarterly Review* during the months just prior to the publication of the novel. Among the arguments used by the Catholic uncle to his Protestant nephew is the following summation of Protestant history: "In religion Luther engendered Voltaire, in philosophy Descartes, in politics Jean Jacques Rousseau, in morals Helvetius. In religion you have ended in the rejection of the supernatural, in philosophy in doubt and nihilism, in politics in anarchy, in morals in the sanctification of lust."[31] This condemnation of Protestantism, stronger and more sweeping than any indictment in Brownson's fiction previous to "Uncle Jack," shows Brownson stating expositionally ideas that would be enacted sensationally in *The Spirit-Rapper.* The sanctification of lust here criticized becomes Priscilla's passion for the narrator during her Protestant period. Anarchy surfaces in the portrait of Protestant revolutionists, doubt and nihilism in the narrator's loss of faith before his conversion to Catholicism. Uncle Jack's strongest charge—the rejection of the supernatural— is answered by Brownson's graphic accounts of supernatural occurrences in the novel.

Having completed his secularizing cycle in *The Spirit-Rapper,* Brownson retreated in his later writings to the more conventional genres of unfictionalized autobiography, Catholic essays, and history. Apologetic from the beginning about his fiction, Brownson experimented with various balancings of logic and sentiment only to discover that the most convenient form was also the most artistically elusive.

Brownson stopped writing fiction in 1854, but he continued to review fiction regularly for the next two decades. His views of Henry Ward Beecher's *Norwood* and modern realist novels were predictable: he declared that such non-Catholic works remained in the realm of unsanctified nature and paganism. His attitudes towards what he came to call "Catholic secular literature" were more complex. He continued to treat the Catholic novel as a high ideal rarely realized in practice.

As late as the 1870s, shortly before his death, Brownson was still struggling to define Catholic fiction in a series of essays in his *Quarterly Review:* *"Mrs. Gerald's Niece"* (1870), "Religious Novels, and Woman versus Woman" (1873), "Catholic Popular Literature" (1872), and "Women's Novels" (1875). In these essays Brownson supported the broadening interest in fiction among Catholics while he lamented the failure of most religious novels. In "Religious Novels" he repeated his argument of 1848 that a mixture of love and doctrine creates "a literary monstrosity, which is equally indefensible under the relation of religion and that of art." "There are," he noted, " . . . very few of our authors of religious novels, even when they know their religion well enough to avoid all grave errors in the serious part of their productions, who have so thoroughly catholicized their whole nature, consecrated their imaginations, and conformed their tastes, mental habits and judgements, sentiments and affections, to the spirit of Catholicity, that when they write freely and spontaneously out from their own imaginations, they are sure to write nothing not fully in accordance with their religion."[32]

To be sure, the Catholic novel is, in Brownson's view, the best antidote to realism, that "most corrupting and infamous school of literature that has ever existed" (573). But in reality the antidote was becoming controlled by the poison, since post-1850 Catholic novelists were descending to realist secularism with disturbing frequency. In an effort to stem the secular tide Brownson reminded his readers: "The object of the Catholic novelist, or cultivator of light literature, is not or should not be to paint actual life, or life as we actually find it, but to idealize it, and raise it, as far as possible, to the Christian standard, not indeed by direct didactic discourses or sermonizing, which is out of place in a novel; but by the silent influence of the pictures presented, and the spirit that animates them" (572).

Instead of clarifying matters for the Catholic novelist, Brownson brought up an old paradox: there is no comfortable via media between direct didactic discourses and portraits of actual life for the Catholic author of popular fiction. Pise had tried to tip the fictional balance to the side of doctrine. Later novelists, such as Cannon, Dorsey, and the post-1850 authors, were more apt to find rhetorical reinforcements for doctrine in actual life.

Brownson himself had utilized first extreme logic and then extreme sensationalism before abandoning the writing of fiction for literary theorizing. By 1873 Brownson was sounding less like a prophetic elucidator of contemporary fictional tendencies than a reactionary purist in search of a genre that never did—and perhaps never could—exist.

Notes

[1] *Redwood,* p. xv.

[2] For a summary of the biographies of these writers, as well as descriptions of representative plots and typical critical reviews, see Willard Thorp, "Catholic Novelists in Defense of their Faith, 1829-1865," *Proceedings of the American Antiquarian Society,* 78 (April 1968), 25-117.

[3] *Works of . . . Brownson,* XIX, 149.

[4] *Father Rowland: A North American Tale* (Baltimore: Fielding Lucas, Jr., 1829), pp. 64, 65.

[5] *The Indian Cottage: A Unitarian Story* (Baltimore: Fielding Lucas, Jr.), p. 125.

[6] *Zenosius; or, The Pilgrim Convert* (New York: Dunigan, 1845), p. 80.

[7] *Father Oswald: A Genuine Catholic Story* (New York: Casserly and Sons, 1843), pp. vii, viii. *Father Clement* (1823), an anti-Catholic novel by the Scottish Grace Kennedy, had gained wide circulation in America in the 1820s and 1830s.

[8] *Harry Layden: A Tale* (New York: Boyle, 1842), pp. iii-iv.

[9] *The Cross and the Shamrock; or, How to Defend the Faith* (Boston: Patrick Donahoe, 1853), p. 6.

[10] *Father Oswald,* pp. 23-24.

[11] Cannon, *Harry Layden,* p. 46.

[12] *Mora Carmody; or, Woman's Influence* (New York: Dunigan, 1844), p. 23.

[13] *Father Felix* (New York: Dunigan, 1845), p. 50.

[14] Anna Dorsey, *The Sister of Charity* (New York: Dungian, 1846), p. 6.

[15] Quoted in James J. Walsh, "The Oxford Movement in America," *Records of the American Catholic Historical Society of Philadelphia,* XVI (Philadelphia, 1805), 436.

[16] *North American Review,* 70 (January 1850), 233.

[17] *Rosemary; or, Life and Death* (New York: Sadlier, 1860), p. 162.

[18] *The Forest* (New York: Redfield, 1852), p. 169.

[19] *Loretto; or, The Choice* (Baltimore: Hedian and O'Brien, 1851), p. iii.

[20] *The Governess; or, The Effects of Good Example* (Baltimore: Hedian and O'Brien, 1851), p. 251.

[21] *Cross and Shamrock,* p. 149.

[22] *Brownson's Quarterly Review,* 2nd Series, III (January 1849), 58.

[23] *Brownson's Quarterly Review,* 3rd Series, I (April 1853), 279.

[24] *Mary Lee; or, The Yankee in Ireland* (Baltimore: Kelly, Hedian, and Piet, 1860), p. 165.

[25] *Brownson's Quarterly Review,* New York Series, No. 2 (April 1856), 272.

[26] From *Charles Elwood; or, The Infidel Converted* (1840) in *Works of . . . Brownson,* IV, 178.

[27] *Christian Examiner and General Review,* 28 (May 1840), 180.

[28] "Charles Elwood Reviewed," *Boston Quarterly Review* (March 1842), in *Works of . . . Brownson,* VI, 318.

[29] *The Two Brothers; or, Why Are You a Protestant?* (1847), in *Works of . . . Brownson,* VI, 285.

[30] *The Spirit-Rapper: An Autobiography* (1854; rpt., Detroit: T. Nourse, 1884), p. 1.

[31] *Brownson's Quarterly Review,* 3rd Series, II (January 1854), 23.

[32] *Works of . . . Brownson,* XIX, 566.

Susan M. Griffin

SOURCE: "Awful Disclosures: Women's Evidence in the Escaped Nun's Tales," in *PMLA,* Vol. 111, No. 1, January, 1996, pp. 93-107.

[*Below, Griffin discusses the figure of the escapee in the anti-Catholic literature of the early nineteenth century. She relates questions of veracity concerning the escapees' claims to the larger question of the role of women in nineteenth-century American culture.*]

Between 1835 and 1860 Protestant Americans avidly read a series of reports by renegades from an ancient secret society: the church of Rome. Women's tales of escape from Catholicism were the most numerous and the most notorious of these reports; especially in the 1830s and 1850s, the runaway nun was a prominent figure in the American cultural and political imagination. As Richard Hofstader suggests, the renegade's role in establishing truth goes beyond the spy's: the renegade not only conveys but also *is* evidence. I argue that these female renegades reveal still more, for they disclose how questions of evidence were imbricated with the woman question in nineteenth-century American culture.

Anti-Catholicism was widespread during the antebellum period in which escaped nun's narratives proliferated. Fears that increasing immigration and a growing Roman Catholic population were threatening America's Protestant national identity fostered the formation of nativist groups in the 1830s and of the Know-Nothing Party in the 1850s. Protestant newspapers were, as Ray Allen Billington states, "with but few exceptions . . . given over" to anti-Catholic attacks, and bookstores devoted solely to anti-Catholic literature—primers, children's stories, travel books, novels, plays, verse, histories, gift books, almanacs, pamphlets, and sermons—flourished (*Protestant Crusade* 367, 345-51). In this atmosphere, narratives about runaways from Roman Catholic convents found a receptive audience. While some escaped nun's tales were published locally, others were issued by mainstream publishers like Van Nostrand and Dwight, D. Appleton, and Harper and Brothers. Maria Monk's *Awful Disclosures* (1836) was by all definitions a bestseller: 20,000 copies sold within a few weeks, 300,000 by 1860. Rebecca Theresa Reed's *Six Months in a Convent* (1835) sold 10,000 copies in the first week and an estimated 200,000 within a month. When Rosamond Culbertson's *Rosamond* (1836) was published in book form after its serial run, a second edition had to be issued within weeks. The publishers of Charles Frothingham's *Convent's Doom* (1854) claim to have sold 40,000 copies in ten days. Frothingham's *Six Hours in a Convent* (1854) went through eight editions in a year, and there were thirty-one editions of Isaac Kelso's *Danger in the Dark* (1854) within the same period.[1]

Without question, these narratives represent an attempt by American Protestantism to combat Roman Catholicism's influence. Yet this general anti-Catholic purpose does not fully account for the fascination with the figure of the escaped nun or for the intricate construction and corroboration of her testimony. At the historical moment when American women were shaping Protestantism in their own image,[2] these publications called the testimony of the religious woman into doubt. To her Protestant readers, the escaped nun simultaneously represented authenticity and unreliability: they knew what to expect from a woman who had been in a Catholic convent. While the escaped nun's story cannot claim the central place in nineteenth-century American culture that "woman's fiction" can (Baym), it nonetheless constitutes an alternative plot of some importance. For example, George Bourne's

Lorette (1833), the book that David S. Reynolds sees as the "prototype" of convent exposés (*Faith* 181), shares Frank Luther Mott's list of "Better Sellers" with Catherine Sedgwick's *Hope Leslie* and Susan Warner's *Queechy,* domestic novels that critics have recently made standard texts in studies of nineteenth-century American culture. The escaped nun echoes the emphasis mainstream writers of the period placed on women's spirituality. Yet her confirmation of this cultural dogma is narratologically structured to reveal an undercurrent of dissent. The multiple voices and forms and the visual, as well as verbal, rhetoric that the telling of the escaped nun's story entails work to destabilize feminine spiritual, religious, and moral authority, which the domestic novel instantiates.

The female renegade testifies to the awfulness of Romanism because who she is and what has happened to her tell her audience what Catholicism is. She is a victim of and a witness to popery's crimes. Yet perhaps, having chosen to enter the convent and take vows, she is also a perpetrator. The escaped nun attempts to bring the church of Rome to judgment, but her story and her self end up on trial. Thus, while Samuel B. Smith, the annotator of one escaped nun's narrative, claims that "with all this mass of positive, circumstantial, and presumptive evidence, there is not a jury in the world who would not pass the verdict, *guilty,* against the Reverend culprits, who, in this Narrative, are brought before the bar of public opinion," his own interventions in the narrative distinctly resemble advocacy for the defense (Culbertson 14). And the person he defends is the woman who reports the crime. As *Rosamond*'s publishers argue,

> Our criminal courts allow in evidence a witness to criminate associates in crime under open promise of pardon to himself. And why should we turn a deaf ear to the evidence of one, testifying without any conceivable motive but the good of others, under no influence but that of truth—under pressure of no circumstances but such as are calculated to give the greater weight to her evidence?

> (Culbertson 2)

The woman's circumstances, motives, criminality must all be addressed. Since she constitutes evidence, the renegade must be subjected to examination and interrogation. Reading her narrative means glossing her silences and elisions and testing her authenticity, as well as attending to her more deliberate disclosures.

The escaped nun's story is a familiar one in the annals of anti-Catholicism, not only because nineteenth-century American culture was saturated with anti-Catholic materials but also because the story draws on older traditions: the Gothic novel, American captivity narratives, and the literatures of British antipopery and French and Spanish anticlericalism.[3] The story typi-cally begins by describing how unsuspecting wealthy Protestant girls are enticed by beautiful music, lofty sentiments, charming rituals, and gorgeous decorations in Catholic convent schools. The girls are told that they can gain full access to the wonderful mysteries of convent life only by becoming nuns. This promise is borne out, since a young woman literally enters new areas of the convent once she takes vows. However, in the secret inner space of Catholicism, she finds not greater beauty and holiness but an ugly life of austerity and deprivation. The refined pursuits of the upper-class young lady are replaced with mindless, repetitive devotions and demeaning physical labor. Under the guise of penance, the new nun is regularly subjected to physical and mental tortures ranging from minor penalties (being forced to lick the shape of a cross on the ground is a favorite example) to more horrific punishments, like solitary confinement, starvation, and even murder. All communication with the outside world is cut off: letters are destroyed, visitors denied, false communications issued in the protagonist's name. Her privacy is systematically violated: her captors invade her room, eavesdrop on her conversations, spy on her actions, and assault her person. Inmates are forcibly imprisoned in the convent. Secrecy is vital because convents amass wealth (wrested from those who become nuns) and provide a training ground for spies and teachers of Catholic propaganda, activities essential to Rome's goal of conquering the United States. If nuns escape and tell their stories, Americans will abolish convents, and Rome's plot will fail.

Nuns must also be prevented from escaping because convents are essentially priests' brothels.[4] Priests can enter secretly, at any time of day or night, by means of concealed entrances and underground passages. The female inmates are either lascivious wantons or wretched victims of sexual and physical abuse. Those who refuse the priests' attentions are punished and, like the infants born as a result of priests' and nuns' illicit relations, eventually murdered. In the passages and rooms beneath the convent, dreadful penances are exacted, recalcitrant nuns imprisoned, and bodies disposed of. In several versions of the escaped nun's tale, the protagonist becomes the auditor or reader of other nuns' sad stories of entrapment and torture. The Gothic inheritance of the anti-Catholic novel is clearly at work in these multiple, framed narratives. As readers follow the heroine through the convent's maze of secret chambers and cells, they are in a narrative *mise en abyme,* enmeshed in the density, intricacy, and pervasiveness of popery's plots. For example, in *The Escaped Nun,* a compilation of nuns' stories, the author's personal history is interrupted for chapters at a time by the "History of the Orphan Nun of Capri" and the "Confessions of a Sister of Charity," both of which incorporate several individual narratives. These interruptions only add to the discontinuity and disorganization of the heroine's story, which bespeak the harried condition of Catholicism's victim, as well as her ingenuousness. The implication is that this is not a shameless woman's calculated bid for publicity and financial gain but the work of a retiring female, shattered by her immurement in the convent.

The best-known escaped nun's narratives were Reed's *Six Months in a Convent* and Monk's *Awful Disclosures,* both of which had hundreds of thousands of American readers.[5] The Charlestown burning in the first and the outrageous story in the second helped make these two versions of the escaped nun's tale notorious. The Ursuline convent on Mount Benedict in Charlestown, Massachusetts, housed a fashionable school for wealthy Protestant girls. Reed was an inmate of the convent and a teacher in the school for less than six months in 1831-32 before fleeing.[6] In 1834, Elizabeth Harrison also escaped, but she returned after a few days. Rumors in the *Mercantile Journal* and elsewhere implied that she had been taken back to the convent against her will. These events coincided with one of Lyman Beecher's visits to Boston, where he preached three provocative anti-Catholic sermons.[7] On the night of 11 August 1834, the convent was burned to the ground by a mob. The Catholic population and press blamed Reed for having inflamed local Protestants with misrepresentations of her convent experiences. Her supporters countered in 1835 by publishing her narrative "to vindicate her from unjust and unmanly aspersions which some friends of the Convent have indulged in toward her, and especially to advance the cause of truth" (Reed 13). The Catholic clergy, as well as the Protestant parents who had placed their daughters in the Ursuline school, responded to Reed's narrative by claiming the same objectives—vindicating beleaguered females and establishing truth (Moffatt).

Awful Disclosures, an international best-seller, told the horrific tale of Monk's experiences at and escape from the Hotel Dieu convent in Montreal. According to Billington (*Protestant Crusade*), the narrative was actually the work of two anti-Catholic ministers, J. J. Slocum and George Bourne, who insisted they had written at Monk's dictation. In addition to making "her" pronouncements in print, Monk appeared on public platforms, where she was joined by yet another escaped nun, Saint Francis Patrick, who claimed to have been Monk's fellow inmate at the Hotel Dieu. Monk was supported by the Protestant Reformation Society and the *American Protestant Vindicator* newspaper, at least until two inspections of the Hotel Dieu nunnery failed to substantiate any of her claims.

Reed's and Monk's first-person accounts of the horrors of convent life raised an immediate and sustained outcry. That the narratives' truth was contested underscores their political and cultural power: why else would high church officials like Bishop Fenwick of Boston have bothered to dispute their claims repeatedly? Public debate regarding the stories' veracity and the authors' identity and character took place not only in the religious press and in the pulpit but also within and by means of the genre of the escaped nun's narrative. *Six Months in a Convent and Awful Disclosures* spawned a group of answering fictions, some disputing, others supporting Reed's and Monk's claims. Examples include *Six Months in a House of Correction* (1835); Theodore Dwight's *Open Convents* (1836); Lucinda Martin Larned's *The American Nun* (1836); Mary Magdalen's *The Chronicles of Mount Benedict* (1837); Harry Hazel's *The Nun of St. Ursula* (1845); Thomas Ford Caldicott's *Hannah Corcoran* (1853); Frothingham's *Six Hours in a Convent* (1854), *The Convent's Doom* (1854), and *The Haunted Convent* (1854); and Lizzie St. John Eckel's *Maria Monk's Daughter* (1874).[8] Other fictions, not set at Mount Benedict or at the Hotel Dieu, engage Reed's and Monk's claims less directly but participate nonetheless in the cultural discourse on and of the escaped nun's tale and illustrate the ways in which this narrative traversed the culture. The 1833 *Lorette,* predating Reed's narrative by two years, was written by the same Bourne who aided Monk. Here I am concerned less with chronology than with the dialogue among the texts, including Culbertson's *Rosamond* (1836); Benjamin Barker's *Cecilia* (1845); Hyla's *The Convent and the Manse* (1853); Josephine Bunkley's *The Testimony of an Escaped Novice* (1855); *The Escaped Nun* (1855); Kelso's *Danger in the Dark* (1855); and William Earle Binder's *Madelon Hawley* (1857) and *Viola* (1858).

As a genre, the escaped nun's narrative includes some texts that purport to be factual accounts and others that declare their status as romance or fiction. (Of course, some "nonfictional" narratives—Monk's for example—have subsequently proved to be hoaxes. Nonetheless, *Awful Disclosures* continued to be reprinted, read, and cited as an authentic history at least through the end of the nineteenth century.) My analysis focuses on supposedly non-fictional narratives (Reed's *Six Months in a Convent,* Monk's *Awful Disclosures,* Dwight's *Open Convents,* Culbertson's *Rosamond,* Caldicott's *Hannah Corcoran, The Escaped Nun,* and Eckel's *Maria Monk's Daughter*) but also relies on contemporary parodies of the escaped nun's story (*Six Months in a House of Correction* and Mary Magdalen's *The Chronicles of Mount Benedict* [fig. 1]), which exaggerate its characteristics and techniques. However, these accounts cannot be considered in complete isolation from their more frankly fictionalized counterparts, with which they share characters, plot, and structure. As Reynolds points out, Reed's and Monk's narratives both follow and set fictional precedent (*Faith*). Indeed, Dwight cites Monk's novelistic style as "internal evidence" of her veracity: "the story, short as it is, for simplicity and pathos is not unworthy the genius and talents of a Scott" (116). The narratives' titles foreground their participation in an intertextual conversation about the escaped nun: for example, Reed's *Six Months in a Convent* is imitated by Frothingham's *Six Hours in a Convent* and parodied by *Six Months in a House of Correction*; Reed's and Monk's narratives are deliberately invoked in the titles of Mary Magdalen's *The Chronicles of Mount Benedict,* Hazel's *The Nun of St. Ursula, The Escaped Nun,* and Eckel's *Maria Monk's Daughter* and in the repeated use of the subtitle *A Tale of Charlestown in 1834.*

These texts anticipate challenges to the accuracy and authenticity of their evidence in similar ways. All the narratives, "fictional" and "nonfictional" alike, claim to be true. Further, in attempting to prove their own veracity, they rely on a common standard of evidence. For example, escaped nun's tales are regularly supplemented by documents authenticating their testimony and by corroborative footnotes, cross-references, and appendixes drawn from theological, historical, and even fictional works. While such documentation tends to be heavier in "nonfictional" narratives, it also plays a role in novels such as *Viola,* which includes footnotes citing Jesuit documents and anti-Catholic publications. Typically, the escaped nun's lived experience is said to guarantee the truth of her depiction of Romanism, but Frothingham offers his experience as the brother of a nun as proof of the veracity of his "Convent stories": "The single fact that a near relative of his was an inmate of the Convent at Charlestown, in 1834, is deemed sufficient to substantiate all statements presented the public as facts" (*Six Hours* 5). The title of Hazel's *The Nun of St. Ursula; or, The Burning of the Convent: A Romance of Mt. Benedict* may categorize the narrative as a romance, but it also ties the text to historical fact. Similarly, the illustrations depict both a fictional scene, "Cecile Taking the Veil" (3), and a verifiable public event, the "Destruction of the Charlestown Nunnery, August 24th, 1834" (65).

These generic crossings and confusions suggest that the escaped nun's narrative was positioned as a "romance of the real," a term coined by George Thompson in 1849 to differentiate his sensational novels of American urban life from conventional idealized romances. In doing so, Thompson assimilated his own fictional mode to contemporary investigative reports on slums, as Christopher Looby has shown. Both genres claim to uncover the fantastic truth, stranger than fiction, of crime and corruption in mid-nineteenth-century urban America. Looby's suggestion that the category of the exposé as "romance of the real" spanned nonfiction and romance in antebellum America[9] perhaps explains how escaped nun's narratives, from novels to newspaper reports, came to serve as evidentiary weapons in the fight against Rome.[10] While maintaining the distinction between narratives that

purport to be autobiographies and those that label themselves romances, I examine them together to underscore the ways in which reading an escaped nun's tale marshaled and confirmed recognized patterns of information for a Protestant audience. Tracing the profound intertextuality of the escaped nun's story suggests not only the cultural work that the narrative performed for its authors and audience but also the array of voices that cooperate and compete in the narrative's construction.

The escaped nun's narrative makes claims to truth based on first-person experience inaccessible to the general (Protestant) public. Even when the story is narrated in the third person, the point of view is that of the protagonist, whose scarred and debilitated body bears witness to her firsthand experience of the horrors of Catholicism. As Alexander Welsh demonstrates, in the late eighteenth and early nineteenth centuries, first-person testimony had been displaced by coherent narratives of circumstantial evidence "nearly everywhere: not only in literature but in criminal jurisprudence, natural science, natural religion, and history writing" (ix). Welsh describes how this shift in evidentiary standards affected the history of the novel:

> Before the nineteenth century, novels were typically surrounded by a false frame of pretended documentation . . . that purported to account for the real-life existence of the narrative they contained. But increasingly, through the conscious practice of Fielding and others, the claim to represent reality in novels was expressed by their internal connectedness of circumstances.
>
> (42)

The works that I am discussing are still engaged in the transition that Welsh explores, some retaining first-person testimony (e.g., Reed's *Six Months in a Convent,* Monk's *Awful Disclosures,* Culbertson's *Rosamond*), others switching to third person (e.g., Larned's *The American Nun,* Binder's *Viola*), still others combining both forms in framed narratives (e.g., Bourne's *Lorette,* Binder's *Madelon Hawley*).

How do these narratives prove that the proof they offer is valid? As the publishers of Reed's story neatly put it: "It is therefore simply a question of personal veracity, and of internal and external evidence of truth" (Reed 40). Both the authenticity of the speaker and the accuracy of her information must be externally verifiable and internally consistent. From the outset, these texts insistently present themselves as evidence: maps and floor plans, often printed as endpapers, introducing and framing the text, provide testable assertions about the secret spaces in convents. Cast as a kind of ethnography, marked by "thick description," the narratives are incredibly detailed, documenting the minutiae of convent life, explaining strange customs, translating foreign languages, delineating elaborate rituals. Scholarly apparatuses often lend legitimacy: footnotes, depositions, extracts from other texts, appendixes. In particular, narratives include page after page purportedly copied from works by Catholic clergymen. So marked is this tendency toward detailed, scholarly description that it becomes a principle source of humor in parodies of the escaped nun's narrative. For example, the narrator of *Six Months in a House of Correction* maintains that the tale's authenticity lies in its trivial details: "There is a minuteness of detail and a simple pathos in the narrative of Miss Dorah's adventures, which are in themselves unanswerable evidence of its truth" (64). This same work also parodies mercilessly the ethnographic stance attempted by most Protestant exposés of the secret practices of Catholics. The most innocuous remarks and events are solemnly pronounced "significant": the word *doctor* is footnoted ("the doctor is a person who tends upon the sick" [105]), and the phrase "No, not that" is said to "have a very deep meaning" (107).

Anti-Catholic texts claim to offer information impartially and to defer to their audience's judgment of the facts. Monk and Reed, for example, emphasize that all the documents from both sides have been included. Monk declares that she has "no intention of attempting to enforce the evidence presented in the testimonials," that she will "leave every reader to form his own conclusions independently and dispassionately" (253). The introduction to Caldicott's *Hannah Corcoran* states that the story is being presented to the public in order "to correct the many partial, inaccurate statements that have gone abroad, and to furnish the community with a narrative on which they may rely as being authentic" (iii).

Implicit in such professions of completeness is the juridical assumption that "[c]ircumstances do not lie."[11] Reed's publishers assume a stance at once dispassionate and prosecutorial in describing "the labor of seeing so many individuals, collecting such a mass of facts and testimony, and putting it together *correctly* . . . making this complete and unanswerable. We trust that, so far as the Narrative is concerned it will prove the 'End of Controversy'" (264). As Welsh suggests, such statements are designed to show that "the representation is conclusive: if it purports to review all the facts that is because, in the opinion of the person making the representation, the facts when considered rightly all point in one direction" (9). Circumstances do not lie only when they have been carefully and conclusively managed: a fact or circumstance means nothing in isolation. The renegade, reporter, autobiographer, detective, prosecutor, and novelist alike make meaning by ordering facts into a coherent, inclusive, believable account.

Evidence is managed in the escaped nun's tale not only by pedantic inclusiveness but also by the strategic omission of information. In introducing *Rosamond,* the ex-priest Samuel B. Smith expresses his regret that a series of letters written to Rosamond by the priest who imprisoned her have been lost or perhaps stolen: "these would have been an inestimable appendage to the work" (Culbertson 10). Smith calls on any reader who has come across these letters to turn them in so that they can be published. However, letters from another priest to his mistress furnish "further evidence of the truth and accuracy of the Narrative" (23). Yet even this evidence is incomplete, since some letters simply too foul to be published are omitted entirely; others are numbered and described but not reproduced (letter 7 "is of so indelicate a nature, that we have to suppress it" [28]); still others have their obscenity hidden "under the original cloak of Spanish." Nonetheless, since some readers would not have known Spanish, "we have translated what we dare to present in that language, into Latin" (23). Finally, although the handwriting is "almost illegible," two letters are given in holograph, printed so that a "blank in the fac-simile, marks the absence of what, in the original, would raise a blush on immodesty herself" (23; 11; fig. 2).

The cumulative effect of this editorial scrupulousness is to impress readers with the physical reality of the evidence and to convince them that real texts exist. Further, while rendering obscene material in Latin was by 1836 an editorial practice of long standing, here it is uniquely suited to Smith's anti-Catholicism. Smith sets up a continuum—horrible, fully accessible facts in English; worse, less accessible facts in Latin; still worse and even less accessible facts in Spanish; and inaccessible but by this point fully imaginable facts that are omitted—that invites reader participation in the pornographic construction of undeniable truth. So confident is Smith that his readership can supply images and narratives of priestly profligacy that he provides blank spaces for their inclusion. As Hofstader says, "Anti-Catholicism has always been the pornography of the Puritan" (21); Culbertson's audience knows Rosamond's story before reading it.

Reader participation is also critical to claims of probability, the evidentiary criterion addressed most directly in the escaped nun's tales.[12] The appendix to Reed's *Six Months in a Convent* explicitly takes up the "[p]rinciples on which the credibility of personal testimony depends," citing John Abercrombie's *Inquiries concerning the Intellectual Powers, and the Investigation of Truth:*

> In receiving facts upon testimony, we are much influenced by their accordance with facts with which we are already acquainted. This is what in common language we call their probability; and statements which are probable, that is, in accordance with

facts which we already know, are received upon a lower degree of evidence than those which are not in such accordance.

(146-47)

This standard of probability makes escaped nuns' accounts instantly verifiable because they employ narrative patterns and character types from Roman Catholicism's past. Ancient anecdotes are given life both by being inserted into nineteenth-century texts and by being enacted in the nineteenth-century world of the novel. Binder, the ex-priest who describes the imprisonment of Madelon Hawley, makes clear that hers is an old story: "thus was chronicled another of those crimes, which long since rendered the Romish Church notorious—which centuries ago, made black and fearful both the public and private history of her priesthood. Read there—if your eyes do not pale—the terrible catalogue of crimes" (*Madelon Hawley* 172-73). In Culbertson's *Rosamond*, Smith quotes descriptions by Bernard of Clairvaux, Agrippa von Nettesheim, Nicholas of Clémanges, and François Eudes de Mézeray of licentious popish clergymen's veiling women to prostitute them (58) and then shows Father Manuel doing precisely the same with Rosamond. If the narrative technique of multiplying nuns' life stories as the protagonist moves further into the convent shows the pervasiveness of Rome's evil influence, the inclusion of these historical precedents demonstrates its perdurability.

The weakness of an evidentiary standard that depends on the audience's reading history comes under parodic attack in *Six Months in a House of Correction* and *The Chronicles of Mount Benedict* (Mary Magdalen). In *The Chronicles of Mount Benedict,* the nun's tale is written to reveal not the horrors of Catholicism but the ludicrousness of Protestants' beliefs about Catholicism, beliefs founded on "the tales they read of popery as it was four hundred years ago" (xiii). The author's literalizing of anti-Catholicism's assumptions broadly undercuts the argument that medieval chronicles can illuminate the evils of nineteenth-century Catholicism. *The Chronicles of Mount Benedict,* which opens in fifteenth-century Germany, tells of the persecution of the beautiful virgin Maria Ursula by a hard-drinking, lust-mad priest, Father Pertinax, and his companions. All die, but the Pope decides to resurrect them so that Maria Ursula can establish an Ursuline convent in America: "Now, by mine infallibility . . . I have nothing to do but to fit them out with incorruptible and infallible bodies" (117). Thus equipped, Maria Ursula and Pertinax are sent "in some kind or other of a spiritual bark" (118), which arrives at Charlestown at 11:10:03.25, 21 July 1826, and they proceed to Mount Benedict. The outrageous transition from "popery as it was four hundred years ago" to Charlestown in 1826 parodies the anti-Catholic "knowledge" that nineteenth-century Protestant audiences

brought to their reading. The escaped nun's narrative enters an ongoing evidentiary debate that is incorporated within its covers through notes, appendixes, cross-references, and even title.

And yet what the audience already knows about the woman who bears witness to the awful truths of Catholicism is also what makes the evidentiary status of these narratives most problematic. To use the criteria outlined by Reed's publishers, the escaped nun's "personal veracity" is questionable because her tale exhibits "internal and external evidence of the truth" to its readership, which is already steeped in tales about the dishonesty of Catholics and women (40). Anti-Catholicism traditionally takes the honesty of Catholics as its target. The ex-priest William Hogan warns that Catholics are under specific dispensations regarding truth telling to non-Catholics: "*to keep no faith with heretics, but to destroy them, is one of the most solemn duties of a Catholic*" (*Synopsis* 100). Monk tells of the Catholic distinction between a "wicked" and a "religious" lie (71). Escaped nun's tales are laced with quotations from the works of the Church fathers that "prove" that Catholics are enjoined to use any means, however immoral, to advance papal power. And the dispensation of the confessional is taken to mean that Catholics can lie with impunity since they will shortly be forgiven for the sin.

If all Catholic speech is suspect, gender is an added complication in the accounts of escaped nuns. The uneasy status of women's evidence is tied to a variety of cultural and narratological assumptions about women and the public realm, about women's consistency, loyalty, and sincerity, and about the dangers of women's innocence and education. The most immediate problem the female renegade faces is that in telling her story publicly, she draws her modesty, respectability, and class standing into question. As Cathy N. Davidson notes, "Fame, for a woman, is by definition (gender definition), unfeminine, infamous" (127).[13] The publishers of *Six Months in a Convent* work hard to absolve Reed of all desire for publicity: "We wish it to be distinctly understood that the publication is not made at the instigation, or on the responsibility of the author. On the contrary, she has very reluctantly yielded to the force of circumstances and the dictates of duty" (13). Similarly, Caldicott makes sure to mention that his subject, Hannah Corcoran, "consents to give these facts publicity from no other motive than the hope that they may be made instrumental" (128). These women claim that they tell their stories of victimhood to prevent other young women from becoming victims; they sacrifice their own privacy and modesty to protect the privacy and modesty of others. Monk states repeatedly that she had no intention of publishing her story until she realized that it might provide a warning: "Although it was necessary to the cause of truth, that I should, in some degree, implicate myself, I have not hesitated to appear as a voluntary self-accuser before the world" (5). The implications of public speech by women explain why the prefatory and editorial defenses of escaped nuns' modesty are so insistent: though nunneries are false homes, perverse substitutes for the truly religious domestic realm of home and family, the escaped nun's narrative nonetheless describes a woman deliberately breaking free from a private, protected, spiritualized realm.

Even more compromising is the fact that this testimony is given by a woman whose honesty, that is to say, whose chastity, has already been compromised because she has been in a convent, one of the so-called priests' brothels. Disputes over the evidentiary status of the nun's story rapidly become disputes over the nun's sexual status. Norwood Damon, the author of *The Chronicles of Mount Benedict,* underscores the escaped nun's "fallen" status by using the pseudonym Mary Magdalen. The epigraph to *Awful Disclosures* illustrates how even what appears to be the most neutral and verifiable of facts—the floor plan of the convent—is, at the same time, a figure for the most epistemologically vexed object of interpretation—the sincerity of the teller. Invoking the whore of Babylon, the traditional Protestant metaphor for the Roman Catholic Church, Monk's epigraph figures the convent as the body of the scarlet woman: "Come out of her, my people, that ye be not partakers of her sin, and that ye receive not of her plagues."[14] If accurate, the floor plan that immediately prefaces this epigraph not only reveals the interior of the convent but also vouches for the escaped nun's authenticity as one who knows, who carries the truth of the convent out with her. With its false religious exterior and its hidden evil interior, the convent is implicitly contrasted with the sincere woman who has fled it. The woman's inside matches her outside, a metaphor that gains resonance from the nineteenth-century belief that underwrites the possibility of physical sincerity: when a woman blushes, pales, or faints, an "involuntary" feminine transparency allows her body to be read (Halttunen 58). Yet, the escaped nun's residency in the convent inevitably raises the possibility of her own duplicity. For the epigraph can be read as identifying both the inner convent and the woman who is its inmate as the whore of Babylon.

The Catholic establishment attacked the escaped nun in the press and in the pulpit. Having broken faith, the apostate is always already unreliable. As Reed's publishers quote the Boston newspaper the *Jesuit,* "Whenever a Catholic changes his religion, his motives and conduct are to be *invariably suspected,* and his *honesty* to be *never trusted*" (35). Larned's *The American Nun* addresses the more mixed Protestant response. The newly escaped Anna's plea for help is greeted with skepticism: "A runaway nun is not exactly such a companion as a clergyman of my age ought to be

seen with," demurs her rescuer. "A deep flush overspread the wan face of Anna, and for a time she remained silent; then said, 'It is true, I have no vouchers for the truth of my story'" (117). The apostate nun is a figure of shame. She has already proved herself unreliable by breaking her religious vows; now she divulges that which she has promised to keep secret.[15] The story that she tells only draws her integrity further into question. The Protestant clergyman who knows the awful "truth" about convents, who knows that the escaped nun's story of sexual persecution is "true," is also part of the audience that distrusts the honesty of any individual escaped nun.[16]

Many of the gaps in the escaped nun's narrative are strategic attempts to prove the female protagonist's innocence by demonstrating her lack of knowledge. The floor plan on which much of Monk's case rests designates not only the "[c]hamber where St. Frances was murdered" and the "[g]reat gloomy iron door" but also several spaces marked "unknown" and "secret apartments unknown." In recounting conversations with the Hotel Dieu gardener, the Sister of Charity in *The Escaped Nun* insists that she "did not know what to make of" his remarks and "had no idea of what he intended to hint at" yet makes clear to readers that the old man is raising poisonous herbs for the priests' murderous purposes (214-15). Like Henry James's Maisie, this innocent vessel carries awful truths to her audience. In *Rosamond,* the priest who has imprisoned the protagonist forces her to witness his rape of a fourteen-year-old girl. After a detailed discussion of the priest's plan and of the consequences, Rosamond states, "I could not support the horrible scene, but fainted" (Culbertson 105). Fainting at the crucial moment of sexual violation shields her from full knowledge of the crime. Since her own submission to the priest is never explicitly described, her unconsciousness here suggests sexual innocence—or at least a lack of consent.[17] Smith, the annotator of *Rosamond,* follows the description of the rape scene with a four-page footnote in which he analyzes the rhetorical effect of this lacuna in the text. He argues that if Rosamond had meant "to *appear* refined," she would have emphasized the fainting from the start (Culbertson 106). The order of the narration reveals Rosamond's artlessness and thus proves the sincerity of her account. Similarly, in several other versions of the escaped nun's story, the young woman is unconscious when her vows are "taken": while her Catholic oppressors view her silence as assent, her Protestant audience may have interpreted it as a form of resistance that preserved her honor and integrity.[18] Paradoxically, her refusal to speak as a nun indicates that—perhaps—she can be trusted to report honestly and sincerely as an authentic escaped nun.

These maneuverings between the reliable relation of facts and the insistent refusal to understand them present a novelistic pattern familiar at least since Richardson: the heroine's innocence is threatened for pages and pages of plot; if she is finally conquered, she dies, but if she escapes, she marries and lives happily ever after. Of the escaped nun's narratives I discuss, only *Awful Disclosures* breaks this narrative rule; Monk confesses that she is the living mother of a priest's child. But even in this case, the woman's life story becomes formulaic. Twentieth-century scholars inevitably "prove" Monk's dishonesty by describing how her life story ends: thirteen years after the publication of *Awful Disclosures,* Monk was arrested in "a house of ill fame" for robbing her male "companion of the moment," as Billington puts it (*Protestant Crusade* 108). Such a conclusion has been read as refuting the evidence she had presented over a decade earlier. By making the genre and plot of Monk's life readily recognizable (it is that kind of story; she is that kind of woman), her end determines her life.[19]

Monk's story concludes outside the confines of her book but within a familiar (didactic) pattern. This ending appears not only in twentieth-century histories of anti-Catholicism like Billington's but also in nineteenth-century accounts. Lizzie St. John Eckel, the author of *Maria Monk's Daughter: An Autobiography* (1874), describes Monk as a drunken, violent, abusive woman who dies, insane, in prison. In both her narrative and her notes, Monk's supposed daughter maintains that *Awful Disclosures*'s fabrications were framed to meet audience expectations: "in order the better to enlist their sympathies [Monk] would take care to shape her story so, as to suit the prejudices and partialities of those, whose protection she sought" (170-71). In this "true" account of her mother's storytelling, Eckel once again tells readers a tale they already know.

The outrageous Monk's ultimate confinement in the conventions of the fallen woman's story suggests that the escaped nun's tale can be read as another version of the seduction narrative, which attempts to define and control female sexuality. Indeed, Monk states, "Many an innocent girl may this year be exposed to the dangers of which I was ignorant. I am resolved, that so far as depends on me, not one more victim shall fall into the hands of those enemies in whose power I have so lately been" (4). While Monk stresses her role as victim of priestly debauchery, other antiCatholic writers focus more explicitly on female lasciviousness: "A destructive incredulity exists respecting the horrible impurity and deadly practice of Nuns, who are cloaked under various bewitching appellatives, and decorated in meretricious garbs expressly to ensnare and seduce our citizens," warns the author of *Female Convents* (De Potter ix). Somewhat more subtle are warnings about women's susceptibility to influence. Speaking of "the debauchery and wide spread iniquity" endemic to convents, Larned cautions, "[W]e are seldom aware how powerfully early impressions

affect the mind, and how much they influence the character in after life" (v).[20]

Yet the emphasis on questions of evidence, the attempts to bolster women's testimony with corroborative proofs from other (almost exclusively male) voices, and the ways strategies for validation undermine the women's reliability indicate that the escaped nun's tale is directed to other ends as well. In *Confidence Men and Painted Women* Karen Halttunen has shown how the weakening of family authority and of social deference that accompanied the shift from rural stability to urban mobility gave rise to cultural apprehensions about origins, authenticity, and sincerity. Those apprehensions were at work in Protestant suspicions about the secret society of Roman Catholics, as well as in uneasiness with the woman who was Catholicism's most notorious representative—the escaped nun. So, too, the rise of Jacksonian democracy, the birth of mass culture, and the increased immigration rate guaranteed an audience for these anti-Catholic tales (Archdeacon; Bennett; Billington, *Protestant Crusade;* Halttunen; Tyler). Indeed, Horace Mann's argument that only public education could undo the work of Catholic families and parish schools and remake delinquent youths into law-abiding American citizens might seem to suggest that fears about Irish and German immigration are the ultimate source of these stories, which center on attempts to escape from institutions of (mis)education.[21] Certainly most escaped nun's tales represent Catholic immigrants as contemptible (see, for example, Caldicott; Frothingham, *Convent's Doom* and *Six Hours;* Hazel).

This range of political and cultural forces, along with the widespread anti-Catholicism of the period, overdetermined the popularity of these narratives. But none of these factors explains why nunneries and nuns were the specific site of high cultural anxiety. The protagonists of these stories are not confidence men or painted women or truant Irish boys or even vulgar immigrant girls but young Protestant women. The evidentiary textures of these anti-Catholic texts may thus reveal a tension within Protestantism that is focused on the Protestant girl.[22] A number of nineteenth-century responses to these narratives support such a reading. Fanning the flames at Mount Benedict was a controversy among New England Protestants about religious choices: "all of the hatreds bred of the struggle then going on between liberal and fundamentalist religion in Massachusetts were centered on the Charlestown convent" (Billington, *Protestant Crusade* 69). By making the education of Protestant girls part of its mission, this Catholic institution provided upper-class Boston Unitarians with a means of circumventing the strict Congregationalism enforced in the public schools (69). One of a number of articles about Charlestown that appeared in the popular weekly the *Christian Watchman*[23] argues that to judge the events, readers must focus on the convent's essential character as "a school for the education of many Protestant females" ("Ursuline Convent"). In the letters appended to Moffatt's *An Answer to Six Months in a Convent,* fathers insist that they did not place their daughters in the Ursuline school to allow them religious choice. Repeatedly declaring, "I am not a Catholic," these men describe how they carefully chose the school and closely monitored their daughters' education.[24] A series of articles in the *Baltimore Literary and Religious Magazine* describing the escape of the nineteen-year-old Olevia Neal from a Carmelite convent stresses that "families not Catholic . . . have a direct personal interest in all the affairs of a body, one of whose chief objects is to proselyte protestant children" ("Review of the Correspondence" 485). Contrasting "the stout man" with "a weak girl," one article complains that there are no laws to protect "a poor female [who] may be morally influenced by friends, deluged by proselyting nuns, seduced by cunning priests, betrayed by the workings of her own fancy, misled by the irregular exercise of some of the best feelings of the heart" and calls on Protestant fathers to protect and, if need be, to rescue their daughters ("Review of the Case" 441). Insistently, the Protestant press evokes the image of a vulnerable daughter in need of strong paternal protection and control.

Anti-Catholic stories about escaped nuns express and contain a cultural anxiety about the new generation of daughters and their influence in the remaking of American religious practices. The tale that the runaway nun tells is a *spiritual* seduction story that attempts to define and control women's religion. During the period when escaped nun's tales proliferated, American Protestantism had moved from hierarchical, patriarchal Calvinism to an emphasis on the individual and the woman. In recent years, women's historians have charted the specific contours of this change (see, for example, Cott; Douglas; Ryan; Sklar), tracing its relation to domesticity and sentimental fiction and revealing its role in empowering American women at mid-century. The escaped nun's tale reflects a significant cultural response to the feminization of American religion. Rather than focus on the mother as "God in human form," as Jane Tompkins puts it (142), these narratives show the daughter at risk. What will happen if the American girl has religious choice? The escaped nun's story illustrates young women's incapacity to be trusted: her testimony is essential to unveiling the truth, but it also proves her vulnerability and fallibility. Indeed, the escaped nun makes a choice that proves her inability to choose. In the eyes of her Protestant audience, conversion to Catholicism means rejecting an independent, individual relationship to God. Entering the convent, a young woman abdicates her selfhood and cedes her autonomy to a corrupt and power-hungry priesthood.

These texts' visible demonstration that women cannot be trusted to speak alone further underscores such female incapacity. Independent testimony from women cannot stand on its own as proof; it must be framed and intercut with other forms of evidence. While corroboratory documents add weight to the escaped nun's testimony, their erudition also implies that a lack of education in theology, law, and history makes American women unfit for religious conversation and controversy; women are inevitably overcome by emotions, spiritually and sexually seduced. These daughters do not—perhaps cannot—know enough to defend themselves from papist priests. Insufficiently instructed at home, women end up in that false substitute for domesticity, the convent. The escaped nun's tale awfully discloses not only priests' plots and women's prisons but also the fundamental weakness of the female self on which the future of American Protestantism rests. The woman who gives evidence also serves as evidence—evidence that incriminates her self and her sex.

Notes

[1] Sales figures are from Billington, *Protestant Crusade,* and Mott. *Edition* is a vexed term in studies of nineteenth-century publishing; nonetheless, these multiple "editions" indicate substantial sales. Reynolds's *Beneath the American Renaissance* discusses canonical authors' reading and rewriting of popular anti-Catholic literature.

[2] On women's shaping influence on American Protestantism, see Cott; Douglas; Ryan; Sklar.

[3] For example, Arnheim's account of the English MP Charles Newdegate's campaign to open Roman Catholic convents to government inspection describes several notorious nineteenth-century escapes from English convents.

[4] On convents as priests' brothels, see, for example, Cross, as well as Hogan, "a former Roman Catholic priest," whose works were extremely popular (*Auricular Confession; Synopsis*).

[5] While several of the escaped nun's tales I discuss are set outside the continental United States (*Awful Disclosures,* as well as *Lorette* [Bourne] and *Cecilia* [Barker], in Canada; *Rosamond* [Culbertson] in Cuba), they nonetheless document anxiety about religion in America, as the permeability of United States borders in these texts makes clear. The religion of the Old World can indeed infiltrate New World countries. Because I want to focus on fears about religion in America, I do not discuss fictions written and published in America that describe convents and escapes set in England or continental Europe, for example, *Helen Mulgrave* (c. 1850) and *Sister Agnes* (1854).

[6] See Billington, *Protestant Crusade* (53-84), for a fuller account of these events.

[7] Beecher's most popular anti-Catholic sermon was published as *A Plea for the West* (1835). His son Edward Beecher, who was also involved in anti-Catholic activities, published *The Papal Conspiracy Exposed* in 1855. On his daughter Harriet Beecher Stowe's shifting attitudes towards Catholicism, see Hedrick.

[8] See Scank for a verse response to the Charlestown burning.

[9] Looby's suggestion is borne out in the antebellum exposé par excellence: the slave narrative. For example, Yellin describes Harriet Jacobs's use of fictional formulas in *Incidents in the Life of a Slave Girl,* and Stowe documents the factual basis of *Uncle Tom's Cabin* in prefatory remarks, in narrative intrusions, and in the subsequently published *Key to Uncle Tom's Cabin.* On the (white) generic forms imposed on African Americans' life stories, see Sekora.

[10] This is not a unique instance in nineteenth-century anti-Catholicism—in both the United States and Great Britain, fiction was regularly mined for the "facts" of Roman Catholic practice and doctrine. Novels like Eugène Sue's *The Wandering Jew* (*Le Juif errant;* 1844-45) were a major source of epigraphs, examples, notes, and appendixes for pamphlets, speeches, and essays.

[11] On the juridical history of this claim, see Welsh 1-42.

[12] On the importance of probability, see Welsh 69.

[13] On nineteenth-century American women and publicity, see Brodhead; Kelley.

[14] Billington reproduces this epigraph in the 1962 facsimile edition; the Arno reprint (Monk) omits the frontispiece.

[15] See Caldicott: "The only thing concerning which there can be any serious question in the minds of the candid will be the propriety, righteousness or lawfulness, of divulging that which Hannah promised to keep secret" (129).

[16] So strong is the identification of the escaped nun with the dishonest, unchaste woman that as late as the 1930s Billington dismissed first Monk and then Reed as a "chit of a girl" (*Awful Disclosures; Protestant Crusade* 71).

[17] See Yeazell on fainting in *Pamela* (85) and on the connections among women's chastity, modesty, and unconsciousness.

[18] See *The Nun of St. Ursula* (Hazel), as well as *The Escaped Nun,* whose protagonist describes herself as an "involuntary nun" (52).

[19] My point is not, of course, that Monk's story is true but that both nineteenth- and twentieth-century commentators consider her sexual status a relevant test of the story's truth.

[20] Both Davis and Bennett suggest that in describing sexual profligacy, these stories are expressing contemporary concern about declining moral standards, even as they provide a medium for fantasy. Bennett also links the sadism of these narratives to Protestant men's insecurity during this period.

[21] On the connection between the public school movement and anti-Catholicism, see Nasaw; Tyack and Hansot.

[22] Franchot's *Roads to Rome,* which appeared after I had completed work on this essay, also argues that "anti-Catholicism operated as an imaginative category of discourse through which antebellum American writers of popular and elite fictional and historical texts indirectly voiced the tensions and limitations of mainstream Protestant culture" (xvii). Specifically, Franchot maintains that convent narratives "voice the pressures of an emergent middle-class Protestant domesticity" (162). Franchot reads Monk's and Reed's narratives as "examples of a popular historiography" (135) and, in doing so, discusses the narratives' use of and status as evidence.

[23] I have not located circulation figures for 1835, but Kennedy lists the 1850 circulation as 10,200.

[24] Of the fourteen parents who write, only one is a woman.

Works Cited

Archdeacon, Thomas J. *Becoming American: An Ethnic History.* New York: Free, 1983.

Arnheim, Walter L. *Protestant versus Catholic in Mid-Victorian England: Mr. Newdegate and the Nuns.* Columbia: U of Missouri P, 1982.

Barker, Benjamin. *Cecilia; or, The White Nun of the Wilderness: A Romance of Love and Intrigue.* Boston: Gleason, 1845.

Baym, Nina. *Woman's Fiction: A Guide to Novels by and about Women in America, 1820-1870.* Ithaca: Cornell UP, 1978.

Beecher, Edward. *The Papal Conspiracy Exposed and Protestantism Defended in the Light of Reason, History, and Scripture.* 1855. New York: Arno, 1977.

Beecher, Lyman. *A Plea for the West.* 1835. New York: Arno, 1977.

Bennett, David H. *The Party of Fear: From Nativist Movements to the New Right in American History.* Chapel Hill: U of North Carolina P, 1988.

Billington, Ray Allen, introd. *Awful Disclosures of Maria Monk.* Hamden: Archon, 1962.

——. *The Protestant Crusade, 1800-1860: A Study of the Origins of American Nativism.* New York: Macmillan, 1938.

Binder, William Earle. *Madelon Hawley; or, The Jesuit and His Victim: A Revelation of Romanism.* New York: Dayton, 1857.

——. *Viola; or, The Triumphs of Love and Faith: A Tale of Plots and Counterplots.* New York: Evans, 1858.

Bourne, George. *Lorette: History of Louise: Daughter of a Canadian Nun, Exhibiting the Interior of Female Convents.* 1833. 2nd ed. New York: Small, 1834.

Brodhead, Richard. *Cultures of Letters: Scenes of Reading and Writing in Nineteenth-Century America.* Chicago: U of Chicago P, 1993.

Bunkley, Josephine M. *The Testimony of an Escaped Novice: From the Sisterhood of St. Joseph, Emmettsburg, Maryland, the Mother-House of the Sisters of Charity in the United States.* Philadelphia: Harper, 1855.

Caldicott, Thomas Ford. *Hannah Corcoran: An Authentic Narrative of Her Conversion from Romanism, Her Abduction from Charlestown, and the Treatment She Received during Her Absence.* Boston: Gould, 1853.

Cott, Nancy F. *The Bonds of Womanhood: "Woman's Sphere" in New England, 1780-1835.* New Haven: Yale UP, 1977.

Cross, Andrew B. *Priests' Prisons for Women; or, A Consideration of the Question, Whether Unmarried Foreign Priests Ought to Be Permitted to Erect Prisons. . . .* Baltimore: Sherwood, 1854.

Culbertson, Rosamond. *Rosamond; or, A Narrative of the Captivity and Sufferings of an American Female under the Popish Priests. . . .* Introd. and annotated by Samuel B. Smith. 2nd ed. New York: Leavitt, 1836.

Davidson, Cathy N. *Revolution and the Word: The Rise of the Novel in America.* New York: Oxford UP, 1986.

Davis, David Brion. "Some Themes of Counter-subversion: An Analysis of Anti-Masonic, Anti-Catholic, and Anti-Mormon Literature." *Mississippi Valley Historical Review* 47 (1960-61): 205-24.

[De Potter]. *Female Convents: Secrets of Nunneries Disclosed.* New York: Appleton, 1834.

Douglas, Ann. *The Feminization of American Culture.* New York: Knopf, 1977.

Dwight, Theodore. *Open Convents; or, Nunneries and Popish Seminaries Dangerous to the Morals, and Degrading to the Character of a Republican Community.* New York: Van Nostrand, 1836.

Eckel, L. St. John [Lizzie Harper]. *Maria Monk's Daughter: An Autobiography.* New York: United States, 1874.

The Escaped Nun; or, Disclosures of Convent Life. . . . New York: De Witt, 1855.

Franchot, Jenny. *Roads to Rome: The Antebellum Protestant Encounter with Catholicism.* Berkeley: U of California P, 1994.

Frothingham, Charles W. *The Convent's Doom: A Tale of Charlestown in 1834, also The Haunted Convent.* 5th ed. Boston: Graves, 1854.

——. *Six Hours in a Convent; or, The Stolen Nuns! A Tale of Charlestown in 1834.* 8th ed. Boston: Graves, 1855.

Halttunen, Karen. *Confidence Men and Painted Women: A Study of Middle-Class Culture in America, 1830-1870.* New Haven: Yale UP, 1982.

Hazel, Harry [Justin Jones]. *The Nun of St. Ursula; or, The Burning of the Convent: A Romance of Mt. Benedict.* Boston: Gleason, 1845.

Hedrick, Joan D. *Harriet Beecher Stowe: A Life.* New York: Oxford UP, 1994.

Helen Mulgrave; or, Jesuit Executorship: Being Passages in the Life of a Seceder from Romanism: An Autobiography. New York: De Witt, n.d.

Hofstader, Richard. *"The Paranoid Style in American Politics" and Other Essays.* 1965. Chicago: U of Chicago P, 1979.

Hogan, William. *Auricular Confession and Popish Nunneries.* 1845. 3rd ed. London: Hall, 1847.

——. *A Synopsis of Popery, As It Was and As It Is.* Boston: Saxton, 1845.

Hyla [Jane Dunbar Chaplin]. *The Convent and the Manse*. Boston: Jewett, 1853.

Kelley, Mary. *Private Woman, Public Stage: Literary Domesticity in Nineteenth-Century America*. New York: Oxford UP, 1984.

Kelso, Isaac. *Danger in the Dark: A Tale of Intrigue and Priestcraft*. 1854. 31st ed. Cincinnati: Queen City, 1855.

Kennedy, J. C. G. *Catalogue of the Newspapers and Periodicals Published in the United States*. New York: Livingston, 1852.

Larned, L[ucinda Martin]. *The American Nun; or, The Effects of Romance*. Boston: Otis, 1836.

Looby, Christopher. "George Thompson's 'Romance of the Real': Transgression and Taboo in American Sensation Fiction." *American Literature* 65 (1993): 651-72.

Mary Magdalen [Norwood Damon]. *The Chronicles of Mount Benedict: A Tale of the Ursuline Convent: The Quasi Production of Mary Magdalen*. Boston, 1837.

Moffatt, Mary Anne Ursula [Mary Edmund St. George]. *Answer to Six Months in a Convent, Exposing Its Falsehoods and Manifold Absurdities by the Lady Superior with Some Preliminary Remarks*. Boston: Eastburn, 1835.

Monk, Maria. *Awful Disclosures of the Hotel Dieu Nunnery of Montreal, Revised, with an Appendix*. 1836. New York: Arno, 1977.

Mott, Frank Luther. *Golden Multitudes: The Story of Best Sellers in the United States*. New York: Macmillan, 1947.

Nasaw, David. *Schooled to Order: A Social History of Public Schooling in the United States*. New York: Oxford UP, 1979.

Reed, Rebecca Theresa. *Six Months in a Convent; or, The Narrative of Rebecca Theresa Reed. . . .* 1835. New York: Arno, 1977.

"Review of the Case of Olevia Neal the Carmelite Nun, Commonly Called Sister Isabella." *Baltimore Literary and Religious Magazine* Oct. 1839: 433-46.

"Review of the Correspondence between the Archbishop and the Mayor of Baltimore." *Baltimore Literary and Religious Magazine* Nov. 1839: 481-96.

Reynolds, David S. *Beneath the American Renaissance: The Subversive Imagination in the Age of Emerson and Melville*. Cambridge: Harvard UP, 1988.

——. *Faith in Fiction: The Emergence of Religious Literature in America*. Cambridge: Harvard UP, 1981.

Ryan, Mary P. *Cradle of the Middle Class: The Family in Oneida County, New York, 1790-1865*. Cambridge: Cambridge UP, 1981.

Scank, Philemon [George Elder]. "The Ursuline Convent." *A Few Chapters to Brother Jonathan. . . .* Louisville, 1835. 7-34.

Sekora, John. "Black Message / White Envelope: Genre, Authenticity, and Authority in the Antebellum Slave Narrative." *Callaloo* 10 (1987): 482-515.

Sister Agnes; or, The Captive Nun: A Picture of Convent Life. New York: Riker, 1854.

Six Months in a House of Correction; or, The Narrative of Dorah Mahony. . . . Boston: Mussey, 1835.

Sklar, Kathryn Kish. *Catharine Beecher: A Study in American Domesticity*. New York: Norton, 1976.

Stowe, Harriet Beecher. *Uncle Tom's Cabin; or, Life among the Lowly*. Ed. Kathryn Kish Sklar. New York: Library of America, 1982.

——. *A Key to Uncle Tom's Cabin; Presenting the Original Facts and Documents upon Which the Story Is Founded: Together with Corroborative Statements Verifying the Truth of the Work*. Boston: Jewett, 1853.

Tompkins, Jane. *Sensational Designs: The Cultural Work of American Fiction, 1790-1860*. New York: Oxford UP, 1985.

Tyack, David, and Elizabeth Hansot. *Managers of Virtue: Public School Leadership in America, 1820-1980*. New York: Basic, 1982.

Tyler, Alice Felt. *Freedom's Ferment: Phases of American Social History from the Colonial Period to the Outbreak of the Civil War*. 1944. New York: Harper, 1962.

"The Ursuline Convent: No. 8." *Christian Watchman* 20 Mar. 1835:45.

Welsh, Alexander. *Strong Representations: Narrative and Circumstantial Evidence in England*. Baltimore: Johns Hopkins UP, 1992.

Yeazell, Ruth Bernard. *Fictions of Modesty: Women and Courtship in the English Novel*. Chicago: U of Chicago P, 1991.

Yellin, Jean Fagan, ed. *Incidents in the Life of a Slave Girl Written by Herself*. By Harriet Jacobs. Cambridge: Harvard UP, 1987.

CATHOLICISM IN LITERATURE

Jenny Franchot

SOURCE: "The Inquisitional Enclosures of Poe and Melville," in *Roads to Rome: The Antebellum Protestant Encounter with Catholicism*, University of California Press, 1994, pp. 162-81.

[*In this excerpt, Franchot examines Herman Melville's "Benito Cereno" and Edgar Allan Poe's "The Pit and the Pendulum" to demonstrate how elements of popular anti-Catholic tales of convent captivity became transformed in more literary tales of inquisitional and shipboard imprisonment.*]

The closely imagined relationship between popery and captivity initially established in the Indian captivity narrative developed, in nineteenth-century convent exposés, a crucial thematics of artifice. As we have seen in the narratives of Rebecca Reed and Maria Monk, convent terrors strategically deployed sham fears of Rome to voice the pressures of an emergent middle-class Protestant domesticity. As productions of a deviant female and popular voice, convent narratives imagined perverse domesticities in which an errant female voice, ambiguously positioned between working-class melodrama and middle-class sentiment, gained entry to Protestant parlors by cleansing itself of the impure attraction to Rome. The artifice at the heart of convent narratives—of persecuting figures dispatched from Rome—firmly situated the Protestant language of Romanism in the precariously privatized domain of family romance as well as the public terrain of political contestation. Rome was not only imaged polemically as the ethnic interloper in nativist conspiracy tracts but also figured sentimentally as a haunting memory, itself characterized by uncanny metaphor and fragmented, even implausible, narration, marks of fictional contrivance that point to submerged authenticities.

Antebellum Protestants experienced and contributed to this "dream logic" of Rome in varied ways.[1] But critical to our understanding of Romanism as a shaping force in the antebellum literary marketplace are the collective aspirations of this cultural logic that infiltrated from popular into elite fictions. In the "ascent" into higher canonical regions, this dream of Rome—nightmarish, comical, and baffling—found powerful vocalizations in writers of the American Renaissance, themselves imaginatively preoccupied with the terrors and representational challenges of alienation. In particular, Edgar Allan Poe's "Pit and the Pendulum," and Herman Melville's "Benito Cereno" translate the "womanly" dream logic of convent captivity into a "manly" logic of inquisitional or shipboard imprisonment.[2] Both texts displace overtly female preoccupations with the familial perversion of convents with images of the masculine psyche closed within Catholic powers or

ambiguously excluded by them. Voices of maidenhood and prostitution are supplanted by the voice of an ambiguously celibate masculinity whose largely unspoken patriarchal dominion in the familial enclosure of middle-class domesticity enables its exploration of extrafamilial spaces. Such expeditions finally deposit these celibate explorers in Romanized interiors that speak, not a dispossessed female language of hyperbolic conflict and sexualized violence, but an elite language of densely symbolic ambiguity. Thus Poe and Melville draw upon the language of Protestant captivity, Poe to dramatize the enigmatic pains of consciousness and Melville to construct the "knot" of slavery and racism embedded in the New England conscience.

Like convent captivity narratives, "The Pit and the Pendulum" and "Benito Cereno" picture the sufferings of an exaggeratedly privatized subjectivity, one rendered critically alone by virtue of its fascinated dread of Catholic power. If Puritan Indian captivity narratives figured the afflictions of papal bondage as genuine instances of the clash of imperial powers (both temporal and supernatural), these antebellum captivity narratives enjoy no such clarified relation between private and public. In these eminently self-conscious fictions, Roman Catholicism is no longer a rival imperial power but, to the contrary, a conspicuous anachronism, peripheral to the narratives' contemporary urgencies. Positioned off center, the Romanism of these captivity tales, particularly in its elusive religious malignity and the uncertainty of either capture or escape, distracts protagonists and readers alike from the true meanings of their victimization. Amasa Delano's "dreamy inquietude" aboard the *San Dominick* and Poe's narration of sickly fear inside the dungeon of the Spanish Inquisition are registered in the accents of a Protestant paranoia subjected to an ironic metanarrative gaze. If entrapment by Catholic powers exploits the nativist passions of Poe's and Melville's readers, Poe's narrator and Melville's Amasa Delano quickly transcend such crude simplicities of audience manipulation. Both tales consistently undermine the anti-Catholicism they invoke—not only to mock the nativist susceptibilities of the reading public but, in so doing, to question the very pretensions of narrative.

The unsettling combination of suffering and parody, of imprisonment as a sly, if not a playful, event, owes its peculiar tenor to the artificiality, even theatricality, of nativist captivity literature, with its characteristic blend of opportunism and genuine dread, of safe distance and dire involvement. The virtuosity of both narratives stems from their sustained and ambiguous mingling of sham and terror, their translation of nativism's exploitative melodramas into the aggressions of art. If the fraudulence of much nativist fiction reflected not only commercial opportunism but underlying doubts about the Catholic menace, Poe and Melville forged new authenticities, born of narrative elusiveness, from the inauthenticities of nativism.

In their religious manifestation, captivity narratives exerted a fascination born of the drama of suspended forgiveness. While the surface action of a narrative like Isaac Jogues's unfolded structures of merciful affliction, of the Lord forgiving and drawing his creature to him again, the interior drama threatened the reverse. Any number of seventeenth- and eighteenth-century narratives implicitly portrayed the suffering creature's forgiveness of God, the transition from anger to love, from insufferable fury to the prized condition of gratitude. As the popularity of the genre testifies, it was an absorbing dynamic, this adamant revision of resentment into bliss: With their developing capacity to reduce suffering, nineteenth-century Americans located in domesticity the pleasure of converting resentment and found it ever more difficult to perform an authentic submission. Increasingly, where suffering was concerned, the only bliss available was its cessation or, more realistically, its sentimental regulation.

Notwithstanding their release, such captives as Isaac Jogues or Mary Rowlandson sought to prolong their captivity, to dwell permanently inside the region of affliction. In the concluding lines to her captivity narrative, for example, Rowlandson jealously guards her battered consciousness from the soothing effects of the settlements and confesses to a new condition of sustained vigilance: "When others are sleeping, mine eyes are weeping!" Ironically, her greatest hope and necessity is to extend her captivity indefinitely, to maximize the moment of redemption by avoiding the closure of her experience. Thus she concludes in the atemporal, transcendental posture of the contemplative, bidding her readers, as Moses did the fleeing Israelites, to "stand still and see the salvation of the Lord."[3] In stark contrast to Rowlandson's newfound vigilance, Poe's narrator inches his way through an obsessively wakeful discourse in pursuit of the swoon, angling not for immortality but for oblivion. All he achieves is the horror of exposure, enduring the ceaseless recognition not of God but of his own consciousness: the eyes of punishment have replaced the gaze of faith: "Demon eyes, of a wild and ghastly vivacity, glared upon me in a thousand directions, where none had been visible before, and gleamed with the lurid lustre of a fire that I could not force my imagination to regard as unreal" (695).

> *I pondered upon all this frivolity until my teeth were on edge.*
>
> "The Pit and the Pendulum"

Having tripped and landed with his chin on the edge of the pit, the agonized hero of "The Pit and the Pendulum" congratulates himself for the second in a series of accidental deliverances. His lips suspended over the clammy vacancy of the pit, he enjoys to the full, like Maria Monk before him, the pleasures of the threshold; as another observer of popery's evil interiors, the narrator scrutinizes its gloomy recesses, eager simultaneously to pursue and escape its secrets. Grateful that live burial, the "most hideous of fates" (685), does not await him, he ventures into the perils of undifferentiated space, his curiosity enticed by the "blackness and vacancy" (685) through which he gropes. As prisoner of the Inquisition, Poe's narrator is lodged at the foundation of the edifice of Romanism—a visually duplicitous location where mechanical ingenuity endows his presumptively Napoleonic Age inquisitors with the technological powers of an industrializing America. The technical precision with which these inquisitors dominate the interior of the prison, invisibly engineering the movement of walls, floors, and swinging pendulum, registers envious antebellum suspicions of Rome's efficient technologies of the spirit. One contemporary observer of Catholicism commented on "the resources of that marvellous ecclesiastical system"—that is "so ingeniously contrived, so adroitly defended, so cunningly accommodated to human pride and weakness both."[4] Demoniac Catholic techniques to control both spirit and body marginalize Protestantism to an ever dwindling space of evasion. Progressively displaying its insidious creativity, the narrator's dungeon seemingly manipulates its own interior, from pit to pendulum to mechanized inferno, treating its victim to a series of spectacular disclosures whose unspeakability is cited in an ever more loquacious prose.

Unlike Maria Monk, who must be hit before she falls to the floor, Poe's narrator performs his own prostration, swooning before his own religious terrors. Enthralled by the pleasures of infantilization before the monkish power, this self-identified "recusant" (690) gazes up at the gleaming pendulum "as a child at some rare bauble" (691). Like other Protestant explorers of convents, catacombs, and confessionals, the narrator struggles for mastery by acting the detective, out to deduce not only the extent of Catholic iniquity but the intentions behind it. If Rebecca Reed and Maria Monk partially negotiate the challenges of this detective imperative by at least escaping, though in a state of continued bafflement, Poe's narrator frankly, luxuriously fails. His rationalist investigation cannot compete against the technical ingenuity of his captors, and in the face of their spectacular and disciplined violence he trails off into "vain, unconnected conjecture" (695). His attempts to decipher his plight are entirely secondary to the ardent predatory power of the wrathful church, which in pendulum form descends to the bound and childlike narrator, who can look *up*, but not *at* his persecutors.

The tale's pleasuring in the Inquisition recalls that of the New York showman who in 1842 exhibited a building of the Inquisition replete with common instruments of torture.[5] By the time of Poe's tale, the Inquisition and its ingenious tortures had become a form of popular entertainment. If the confessional offered the attractions of illicit intercourse, the Inquisition offered its own erotic intimacies. Bound in his oily bandage, Poe's narrator submits to the embrace of dungeon rats: "They pressed—they swarmed upon me in ever accumulating heaps. They writhed upon my throat; their cold lips sought my own" (694). The feminized posture of his plight disguises an aggressive, distinctly masculine desire to enter the persecutorial intimacies of Romanism. Juan Antonio Llorente's *History of the Inquisition of Spain* (London, 1826) describes how, on the opening of the Madrid Inquisition in 1820, a prisoner was discovered who was to die the following day by the pendulum method.[6] Whereas Llorente reports with objective restraint on the Inquisition as a thing of the past (albeit recent past), Poe invests his source material with the radical intimacy of his anonymous and confessional "I." This voice of suffering resurrects and appropriates the Inquisition as immediate antebellum context and symbol of its own indeterminate anguish.

The private taxonomy of captivity that forms the gruesome and comic focus of Poe's narrative neatly organizes the range of Protestant confinements in the ideological enclosure of Romanism; the spatial removes into Indian country of Puritan and Jesuit narrative become vertiginous descent into unconsciousness. Of the many horros that surround us, which is the worst? Poe, given to insistent scrutiny of the possible incarcerations available in this life, asks, in this tale above all, which captivity is the worst? Live entombment or the loathesome abyss?[7] The pit or the pendulum, the indifference of the void or the exquisite intimacy of the blade? Enamored of classification, the narrator must repeatedly submit to the Inquisition's sublime dismissal of his categories. The hero's hierarchy of punishments is subject to constant revision, as one torment leads into another, issuing finally into a competition of sufferings that renders distinction futile. "To the victims of its tyranny," explains this student of the Inquisition, "there was the choice of death with its direst physical agonies, or death with its most hideous moral horrors" (687). As his clinically precise discourse proceeds in its effort to survey the features of inquisitional captivity, the confinement becomes more boundless and uniform, the narrator's proliferating physiological detail finally pushing his captivity narrative to the edge of the ludicrous, where it is left to hover.

Thus the perceptual bondage suffered by Poe's bewildered "I" is both tortured and funny, a combination that forces the reader to dwell in a space as narrow as the narrator's—an uncomfortably shifting surrender to the tale's mimetic power where trust continually incites suspicion. Captivity as authorial joke is also

authorial menace. Objective tortures are endowed with a technological excess that incites reader engagement only to mock it, just as the original authenticities of the Protestant captivity tradition are rendered artificial to convey the emergent authenticities of a surrealist art in which the text's frank confession of its artifice testifies to its author's engagement with the finally unspecifiable urgencies of his idiosyncratic consciousness. Or in the authorial tones of Poe's captive to the Inquisition: "I saw the lips of the black-robed judges. They appeared to me white—whiter than the sheet upon which I trace these words—and thin even to grotesqueness" (681).

A virtuoso of studied authenticity, of a deflected sincerity like that of his artfully descending pendulum, Poe mimics the ambivalent blending of farce and dread that characterized conspiracy-minded nativists, for whom the foreign religion was sufficiently present yet unknown to make their accusations plausible. As the ultimate stylist of Protestant captivity, Poe uncovers the self-preoccupation at the heart of a tradition of practiced tremblings before the specter of the Inquisition.

As the primary vehicle of his religious burlesque, Poe's relentlessly physiological language supplants the "recusant" soul with a Protestant body as primary target of Catholic captivity, intrigue, and torture. While the narrator invokes the classical captivity narrative tradition by citing Scripture, confessing, like Hezekiah, to being "sick unto death" (Isaiah 38:1), his objective is hardly the education of the soul's ascetic powers by incarceration within the torments of the fallen world. His enclosed self immediately abandons the consolatory achronicity of biblical citation for a narrative of obsessive temporal precision, his rationalist language focusing on the flesh, a gaze that converts the pleasures of exegesis into those of "nausea" and "thrill." Intercessional wisdom fades into impotent spectral images as the "angel forms" of candle flames shift into "meaningless spectres" (682). This dissolution of scriptural context discloses a region of bodily obsession in which even the political menaces of Romanism, its proverbial systematized ingenuities, revert to a meaningless mechanization; thus the "inquisitorial voices seemed merged in one dreamy indeterminate hum" that simply suggests circularity, not revolt, the mere "idea of *revolution*—perhaps from its association in fancy with the burr of a mill-wheel" (681). In this sensationalized, and hence depoliticized, incarceration, religious captivity metaphorizes the impingements of consciousness, whose pressures urge one not toward God but toward the "sweet rest" (682) of the grave. Catholic persecutors become identified with the masochist energies of the modern subject—an "I" whose nationality, religion, and individual history are suppressed beneath a newly sensational language of disorientation and dispossession.

This deposit of the Inquisition at the heart of the narrator's dehistoricized subjectivity participates in the logic of convent captivity narrative, where maiden subjectivity can experience its purity only through identifying the mother superior as fallen mother. So Poe's narrative pictures the abjectly filial autobiographical subject as one pursuing contact with, and knowledge of, his inquisitional fathers. That he awakens already confined in a space that proceeds to dwindle makes of his every evasion an inevitable drawing closer. Poe's narrative, then, affords us a choreography of antebellum Protestant movement upon the shifting stage of Romanism. A benevolent version of this mobility appears in Hawthorne's admiring efforts to describe an Italian church: "Perhaps the best way to form some dim conception of it, is to imagine a little casket, all inlaid, in its inside, with precious stones, so that there shall not a hair's breadth be left un-precious-stoned; and then imagine this little bit of a casket increased to the magnitude of a great church, without losing anything of the intense glory that was compressed into its original small compass."[8] While Hawthorne can imaginatively shrink and then magnify the cathedral interior that so dazzled him, Poe's narrator is the hapless victim of such aesthetic play as his colorful dungeon looms large or shrinks at another's will.

Hope whispers falsely to the bound narrator, writhing before the pendulum's descent; so too his narrative, in its garrulous unspeakabilities, degrades the incarcerated logic at the heart of Jesuit or Puritan capture—a logic in which the bound body, imitating Christ's sacrificial immobility, gains access to a fluid, mobile subjectivity, one that not only can move into but also can move meanings. Here the body's fixity registers an exegetical fixity: the "heart's unnatural stillness" registers the "sudden motionlessness throughout all things" (683). Nor can the hero measure the site of his captivity, its beginnings and ends rendered identical by the "perfectly uniform" (685) wall. The hero's inability to decipher the meaning or measurements of a captivity transpiring within the "shadows of memory" (683) gains its cultural authenticity by reference to the "thousand vague rumors of the horrors of Toledo" (685)—imagined by antebellum Protestants as countless, incapable of final measurement.

Taunting the very religious fears he elicits, the narrator describes with studied artifice his fumbling along the slimy wall: "I followed it up; stepping with all the careful distrust with which certain antique narratives had inspired me" (685). Coyly alluding to the contemporary context of "no-popery" literature, Poe's captive urges his readers to understand his experience as authenticating their unease; glimpsing the pit, he assures us that the "death just avoided was of that very character which I had regarded as fabulous and frivolous in the tales respecting the Inquisition" (687). His horrors of consciousness are consistently subject to the satirical effect of this intertextuality. "Of the dungeons there had been strange things narrated—fables I had always deemed them—but yet strange, and too ghastly to repeat, save in a whisper" (685). With a teasing regularity that mimics the methodical enumeration of his sensations and gestures the narrator hints at the conventionality of his predicament, finally suggesting that his (and the reader's) real captivity is to no-popery literature. Thus his first trembling retreat from the pit's edge occurs within a sly reference to his past career as a reader of anti-Catholic fiction: "Neither could I forget what I had read of these pits—that the *sudden* extinction of life formed no part of their most horrible plan" (687).

Abruptly enabled by a "sulphurous lustre" (688) to see the true nature of his enclosure, the narrator confirms that the psychic void is reassuringly peopled with Catholic images, the walls everywhere "daubed in all the hideous and repulsive devices to which the charnel superstition of the monks has given rise" (689). These culturally self-reflexive motions of consciousness are doubly recontained by this invocation of monkish aesthetics, the skeletal forms displayed, as they were for American tourists in underground Rome, for his gruesome enjoyment. While the masochism of black vacancy yields to the sadism of monks who finally depict themselves as separate from the narrator so that the monologue of live entombment can at least become the dialogue of "inquisition," Poe's eccentric narrator is himself recontained as a character in no-popery literature. Like any reader of familiar texts, he appreciates his tormentor's deviation from the pit to the pendulum as an admirable instance of authorial ingenuity, aimed at preserving readerly interest: "The plunge into this pit I had avoided by the merest of accidents, and I knew that surprise, or entrapment into torment, formed an important portion of all the grotesquerie of these dungeon deaths. Having failed to fall, it was no part of the demon plan to hurl me into the abyss" (690). The captive's anticipatory knowledge of course is inverted by his narrative to cast him as a figure whose private reasonings are fully anticipated by his invisible persecutors. They have carefully kept his bound body from the descending path of the pendulum, their deep monkish intimacy with his most spontaneous unvoiced speculations rendering his every revelation already known, as happened to Rebecca Reed and Maria Monk before him. As past reader, current captive, and future author of anti-Catholic fictions, the narrator finds that his most frantic work is to disguise his entire knowledge of his inquisitors as their entire knowledge of him.

As one who knows all there is to know, he finally turns his rhetoric of teasing disclosure toward his readers, enticing and thwarting their engagement, refusing, unlike Maria Monk, to divulge what he sees in the pit's "inmost recesses" (696). Inquisitorial dalliance with his agonies models his own flirtation with the reader, enough so that the ingenuities of Catholic torture come to articulate how a burlesque of authorship simultaneously conveys the perils of its reading. Enticing the victim to cooperate in his own extinction, the inquisitors delight in surprise and protraction to enforce his acknowledgment of their punning, intertextual imaginations. As heretic pushed toward a mechanized auto-da-fé, in doubled bondage within a dungeon that itself flattens into a red hot lozenge, the narrator confesses to his captors' ingenious identification of deliverance and perdition. Springing away from the pendulum, he merely leaps toward their next narrative episode on the edge of the pit. "Free!—and in the grasp of the Inquisition!" (695) he cries as the walls begin to move. His best efforts to decipher and elude the "doom prepared . . . by monkish ingenuity in torture" (690) have failed, for the pendulum has sliced him free precisely that the walls might shove him into the pit.

In drawing the parallel between his narrator's frantic efforts to decipher the intentions of his inquisitional captors, his equally perplexed attempts to construct a sequential narrative from his memory fragments, and finally the reader's struggle to believe and disbelieve the manifest artifice of the narrative, "The Pit and the Pendulum" translates the legendary unspeakable filth within the recesses of Romanism—its impostures and secrecies—into the recalcitrant processes of a psychological realism struggling to represent a "memory which busies itself among forbidden things" (683). If captivity to Rome's agents in the New World formerly implicated Catholicism in the pleasures of regained spiritual vigilance and a revivified gratitude, it now belonged to the circuitous expeditions of the swoon into the unconscious and ambiguously beyond it. Captivity to Catholic mysteries has yielded to imprisonment in the menacing and maddeningly trivial confines of the writing psyche. The "seared and writhing body" (697) of Poe's narrator, a body whose "soul took a wild interest in trifles" (688), is the self-bound sequel to the heroic incandescence of Foxe's burning martyrs.

The Spaniard behind—his creature before: to rush from darkness to light was the involuntary choice.

"Benito Cereno"

In 1841, the nativist Joseph Berg uttered a revealing diatribe against the confessional:

We hear a great deal said about slavery in our day; and I abhor oppression in every shape; but I count the poor slave, who hoes his master's corn under the lash of a heartless overseer, a freeman, when compared with the man who breathes the atmosphere of liberty, and yet voluntarily fetters his

soul, and surrenders himself, bound hand and foot, to the sovereign will and pleasure of a popish priest.[9]

Berg was not alone is his astonishing opinion that the slave was better off than the Roman Catholic. His statement reveals a depressing capacity to rationalize chattel slavery as one (and not the worst) among a series of enslavements, a reasoning that suggests how images of bondage to papal captivity could minimize objections to race slavery. The priest is more fearsome than the slaveholder because Berg, racially and regionally, cannot identify with African Americans beyond the abolitionist stereotype of "the poor slave." The priest, unlike the planter, also enjoys the voluntary surrender of his victims. Berg's focus on this voluntarism at the heart of Catholic bondage reveals the uneasy masculinity of the Protestant temperament, which had long struggled with the theological imperative to enact a willing surrender to Christ.[10] If the seduction of females by priests registered the pressure of Protestant domesticity on the errant desires of women, the alleged psychological seduction of the male by priests violated cultural expectations of masculine autonomy—expectations that arose in order to legitimate the proliferating demands of the developing capitalist economy. Male victims of masculine power risked effeminization. As the fugitive slave Frederick Douglass well knew, the oratorical display of his own victimization at the hands of his former white masters encroached dangerously on the virility he also proudly claimed.[11]

Put simply, male victims always had to contend with the implication of complicity, a specter indeed more threatening than that faced by the slave, who, if "poor," at least did not volunteer for his or her fate. Perversely applying traditional Christian distinctions between spirit and flesh to condemn Romanism's spiritual tyranny or the bodily tyranny of slavery, northern nativists voiced their dread of such potentially all-male confessional intimacies. Like the fearsome image of miscegenation that haunted both pro- and antislavery white Americans, the threat of spiritual miscegenation as figured in anti-Catholic writing argued that mingling inevitably led to mixture—and in such mixtures all claims to purity were dangerously forsaken.

Melville's "Benito Cereno" (1855) probes these sexual, racial, and religious comminglings at work in the Protestant masculine imagination and brilliantly extends the logic of embattled purity to the challenges of narrative itself. Does purity afford one its vaunted insight into the workings of the contaminated enemy, casting light on its darkness? Or is purity a self-blinding force, repressing America's all too evident disturbances beneath a surface rhetoric of bemusement that genially minimizes what little remains to be seen? In the perceptions of Amasa Delano as he boards the *San*

Statue of the Roman Catholic saint Mary

Dominick, Melville images slavery in the New World as the secret text layered within the Protestant text of Rome. Delano's repeated deflection of a murderous racial reality into a fading world of ecclesiastical conflict was a familiar feature of nativist and abolitionist thought. "Benito Cereno" forcefully identifies the papal threat with the slaves and to that extent folds a southern voice of conspiratorial anxiety into Delano's northern ruminations that eventually lead him to conclude that Spaniard and African are piratically leagued against him. Delano was hardly unique in his misreading. Like Poe's "Pit and the Pendulum," Melville's Protestant captivity tale dramatizes the captive's plight as a protracted series of interpretive quandaries. But if Poe internalizes Catholicism to register the panic at the heart of his marginalized southern subjectivity, Melville insists on endowing it with the representational density and plausibility of conspiratorial narrative.

In 1853 the great diarist George Templeton Strong observed of a no-popery riot in New York: "If Roman Catholicism as transplanted here shall retain all its aggressive and exclusive features, in other words, its identity, I don't see but that a great religious war is a probable event in the history of the next hundred years; notwithstanding all our national indifference to religious forms."[12] Strong was right about the war but

wrong about the issue; his false prediction only too clearly recalls Amasa Delano's notorious naïveté aboard the *San Dominick*—a naïveté ideologically and aesthetically enabled by the suggestive convergence of black habit and black skin. Delano, the polite racist from Nantucket, is, we might argue, a representative northeasterner in his identification of slave ships and monasteries and a representative southerner in his perplexed musings on the black masks everywhere around him.[13]

When "Benito Cereno" was published in *Putnam's* in 1855, readers were well familiar with the ambiguous and ominous associations between Catholicism and slavery that Melville developed in his story, and with the narrative stance of confused and confusing perceptions of spiritual and bodily oppressions. In no-popery literature, the Catholic church itself moved treacherously across the boundary between profane and sacred—a division that powerfully informed domesticity's doctrine of "separate spheres," of prohibitions against interracial marriage, and of mounting northern hostilities to the South. Delano's voluntary captivity in what he initially views as a structure "like a white-washed monastery" (48), his alternately smug and frightened musings before its Old World secrets once aboard the *San Dominick* (nautical metonym of the Dominican-led Inquisition), reembody the hystericized interior of Poe's "Pit and the Pendulum" with the contemporary specifics of religious, racial, and regional conflict. If Poe's Seville dungeon is located at the geographic heart of the Spanish Inquisition, Melville's "Benito Cereno" sets that interior afloat; on the margins of European imperial power the self-described "little Jack of the Beach," Amasa Delano, meets up with the monasticized mysteries of the *San Dominick* "at the ends of the earth" (77). The *San Dominick*'s travels down the South American coast and its eventual forced passage back to Lima under the escort of the New England *Bachelor's Delight* free that Catholic interior from both its Old World touristic context and its domestic American context of Indian or convent captivity.

Only, like any traveler, Delano carries those domestic captivity narratives within him; he steps between the hatchet polishers "like one running the gauntlet" (59), compares a sailor peering at him to "an Indian [peering] from behind a hemlock" (74), a collapse of African and native American finally voiced by the narrator outside Delano's consciousness, when Africans are described fighting "Indian-like" as they "hurtled their hatchets" (101). Delano speaks as well a language of American travel abroad, transplanting the tourist rhetoric of European Catholicism onto the floating monastery. Like American tourists in Italy, baffled by their simultaneous exclusion from convents and confessionals and inclusion in the dazzling interiors of cathedrals and picture galleries, Delano is intrigued by the ship's visual self-presentation but mystified by the inhabitants. Indeed, just as the interest of antebellum tourist writings about Catholic Europe resides largely in the alternating collusion and confrontation between anti-Catholic ideology and the heterogeneous sights of Italy (in particular), so Melville fashions his narrative's intrigue from similar slippages among the conflicting forces of conventionalized anticipation, troubled perception, and disturbing memory. If those slippages occasionally enjoy the familiarity of the organic, his "old trepidations" recurring "like the ague" (78), they more frequently contradict one another forcefully enough to seem estranged, even uncanny. The circuitous inquiries and odd atmosphere of Delano's New World captivity, then, exhibit the suspended, rapt Protestant pace of exploration through convent, cathedral, and catacomb. As tourists pondered America in Rome (and convents back home), so Delano moves ideologically (and hence perceptually) through Europe to understand the Catholicism floating strangely before him. Whether readers shared in or disdained the nativist campaign against pope and immigrant, they would certainly recognize the narrative's peculiar tone of genial condescension flecked with abject dread, for it characterized discussions of the interlocking menaces of the 1850s: Romanism and slavery.

But if Delano, off the coast of Chile, must encounter the baffling metamorphoses of inquisitional power aboard the *San Dominick,* Melville carefully denies him the assurances of the Protestant captivity tradition. Its accoutrements are there and not there, vital yet absent, like the metaphors that enclose them. The ship appears "like" a monastery; its appearance "almost" leads Delano to imagine a "ship-load of monks" (48). That Delano first sees the Spanish slaver as crowded cloister registers the cultural error of nativism, in which racial blindness is enabled by religious illumination, a purifying light that mistakenly transforms slaves into monks. The ship, qua ship, enjoys a peculiarly intensified interiority by virtue of the sea's surrounding blankness; it is a particular kind of Catholic interior, for the malevolent fatherly power of Jesuit, of pope, and of the Dominican inquisitor in particular has been usurped—not conquered by Protestants but subversively appropriated by Africans. Many antebellum Protestants would agree with Delano's groping effort to situate Spaniards in the familiarites of Protestant English history by claiming that "the very word Spaniard has a curious, conspirator, Guy-Fawkish twang to it" (79). The blurred grammatical focus and casual tone of Delano's musings genially recognize the familiarity of the anti-Catholic code and the gentility of his partial refusal to believe in timeworn conspiracy. If to be a Spaniard still resonates with a "Guy-Fawkish twang," Delano subdues his conspiratorial gullibility, for he and his *Putnam's* readership know just what a "Guy-Fawkish twang" is—a threat rendered sufficiently

absurd by Protestant imperial power that it now sounds like a "twang."

While directing their suspicions toward immigrant Irish and (to a lesser extent) German Catholics, Protestant Americans accorded an aristocratic superiority to Spanish Catholicism. As home to the Jesuits and the Dominican Inquisition, Spanish Catholicism represented an ultimate (and in both senses of the word, a refined) fanaticism, one far superior in class terms to the impoverished and spiritually "docile," if politically threatening, Catholicism of the Irish. Indeed, the Catholic Cereno's symptoms are aristocratic ones, according to Delano's diagnosis: "Shut up in these oaken walls, chained to one dull round of command, whose unconditionality cloyed him, like some hypochondriac abbot he moved slowly about" (52). The Nantucket captain's sympathy with Cereno's burdens of command also suggests the shared commercial and class interests of northern "merchant princes" and southern "cotton kings"—alignments that only reluctantly succumbed to sectional animosity in the late 1850s. Indeed the "fraternal unreserve" (114) enjoyed between the two on the voyage back to Lima, while silent Babo lies imprisoned beneath, transiently recovers the solidarity of such alliances before the Negro's "shadow" (116) again interrupts the southerner's ability to communicate with his northern friend.

Melville's Catholic imagery invokes the Roman church's role in spurring the development of African slavery—a role that began, ironically, with the efforts of Las Casas to protect New World Indians from enslavement by suggesting the greater suitability of Africans.[14] Slavery in its later manifestation in Melville's narrative (set in 1799) is resolutely an affair of New Spain, not New England. Delano's suspicions of the apparently neurasthentic and morbidly reserved Cereno are traced to the pathology of Cereno's national type, his behavior "not unlike that which might be supposed to have been his imperial countryman's, Charles V., just previous to the anchoritish retirement of that monarch from the throne" (53). Delano's sentimental and sociable racism, which allows him to imaginatively berate Cereno as a bitter master and hence to locate him in English Protestant legends of Spanish cruelty in the New World, also allows him to chastise Cereno for his excessive familiarity with Africans. Reminding himself that "Spaniards in the main are as good folks as any in Duxbury, Massachusetts" (79), Delano minimizes national difference to ponder the internal mysteries of spirituality and temperament.

Thwarted by Don Benito's enigmatic reserve, Delano, in a series of unspoken ruminations, attempts to penetrate Don Benito's psychological interior. Indeed, until the long-delayed illumination of the racial meaning of the events surrounding him, Delano recurs to a religious, and at times medical, interpretation of the lassitude, disorder, and morbidity of life aboard the *San Dominick*. His Protestant exegesis of the "hypochondriac abbot" Don Benito, tended by Babo, his "friar" (57) on this "shipboard of monks," however, remains on the level of metaphor as Delano compares this baffling New World community to Old World Catholic morbidities. Anomalous and, as it turns out, finally unspeakable relations between Africans, English, and Spaniards in the New World gain a partial expressibility through their uncanny resemblance to the religious schism at the heart of Christianity. The cleansed and orderly procedures of Anglo-American subjectivity thus appraise with dismay the mingled items of Don Benito's cuddy, whose indiscriminate Catholic clutter contains both an actual and a metaphoric Catholicism. Delano notices a "thumbed missal" and a "meager crucifix" and then proceeds to metaphorize other items in the cuddy into his own ideological edifice of Romanism: thus the rigging lies "like a heap of poor friar's girdles"; the malacca cane settees are "uncomfortable to look at as inquisitors' racks" (82); and the barber chair "seemed some grotesque, middle-age engine of torment" and the sink "like a font" (83). This rush of remembered artifacts dismemebers Catholicism into an assemblage of books, clothing, and furniture that chaotically invokes the Franciscan order, the Inquistion, the sacrament of baptism, the Catholic liturgy. Delano's construction of this popish interior develops its grotesquerie from this jumbled collection of reminiscences and Roman artifacts. "This seems a sort of dormitory, sitting-room, sail-loft, chapel, armory, and private closet all together" (83), he remarks, troubled by the mixture of functions. As this paraphernalia prophesies the collapse of an antiquated Spanish imperial power before a modern Anglo-American one (whose interiors are well organized in their domestic rather than ecclesiastical piety), so the genre of Catholic captivity slips into Delano's subconscious, inhabiting the subordinated regions of fleeting intuition, suspended revelation, and haunting resemblance. Part of the tale's ideological subtlety is its simultaneous use of Delano's anti-Catholicism to voice his provincial views of New World politics and race and the rise and subsidence of the narrative's truth.[15]

In documenting the passage of a Protestant mind from naive confidence to vague suspicion, then to revelation and hard-hearted revenge, and finally to denial and forgetfulness, "Benito Cereno" forces apart and temporally orders the entangled skeins of ideology. Delano must forgo the religious for the racial narrative, must realize that the ship is no floating monastery of Old World tyrannies and impurities but a slave ship in which the Spaniard is not the powerful agent of Catholic imperial power but a feeble white man swooning before the ingenious tyrannies of the African.

In imagining the enslaved African as New World monk, Delano implicitly compares the masculine autonomy enjoyed on his ship, the *Bachelor's Delight,* to the suspicious collectivism of the slave ship's Catholic celibates. If New England bachelors advertise (without participating in) an unthreatening familial version of middle-class marriage, Catholic monks menace by their very numbers and anonymity. "Peering over the bulwarks were what really seemed, in the hazy distance, throngs of dark cowls; while, fitfully revealed through the open port-holes, other dark moving figures were dimly descried, as of Black Friars pacing the cloisters" (48). As an intermittently revelatory Catholic enclosure that entices Protestant exploration in order to punish it, the *Sun Dominick* enjoys the cover of Delano's religious blindness. Unable to see into monasticism, he is doubly distant from the truths of race slavery it disguises. Indeed, because his religious narrative imagines a superstitious, sickly Catholicism, Delano can exaggerate the difference between himself and Cereno; contemplating the Spaniard's seeming fear of the deceased, Delano muses, "How unlike are we made!" (61). The New England captain recurrently imagines Cereno's captivity in a morbid Catholicism that radically excludes the very idea of race slavery. Thus Cereno is strangely attended by Babo, who is "something like a begging friar of St. Francis" (57); Babo indeed is more a metaphor than a character, for his self is only partially revealed in the later trial depositions as the former "captain" of the slaves. That Delano understands Cereno as a religious rather than a political captive preserves both the racial hierarchy and Babo's unknowability. To recognize that Babo is a subversive African rather than a "deprecatory" (57) friar is to forgo the supremacies of Protestantism for the crisis of race war.

Ironically enough, the safety of this Protestant Gothic vision that enables Delano to imagine an impenetrable "subterranean vault" (96) rather than, as Cereno later describes it, a fully intentional inhabited community whose "every inch of ground [was] mined into honey-combs under you" (115) also provides him the hint. In his famous misreading of the shaving scene, Delano's focus on its inquisitional aspect truthfully communicates Babo's murderous power. The barber's seat does indeed work like "some grotesque, middle-age engine of torment"; musings on Babo's unwitting mimicry of the Inquisition do generate "the vagary, that in the black he saw a headsman, and in the white, a man at the block" (85). Babo's shaving of Don Benito, in its ceremonial, even ritual, precision, resonates with the legendary (and historical) calculations of a religiously motivated violence. At the same time, it possesses the vitality of historical anachronism; as countless Gothic narratives testify, psychic meaning accrues in proportion to a setting's historical displacement. Thus the Catholic imagery through which Delano haltingly approaches his enlightenment operates both sardonically and prophetically, simultaneously illuminating the limitations of his Massachusetts sensibility and pointing toward the presence of a novel malevolent power in the New World that jointly inhabits the story's exterior deceptions and its interior truth.

Like the blacks' staged reenactment of their former enslavement, Delano's interpretive recurrence to the enclosures of monastery and Inquisition (a recurrence in which the two are equated) appeals as well to anterior narratives of oppression. Each retrospection enables the other; Delano's monastic ruminations, in their focus on Cereno as the authoritarian "abbot" and Babo as faithful victim to the Spaniard's gloomy rule, make possible Babo's deception. Similarly, the slaves' staged reenactment of their former status—a collective theater that is always on the verge of disruption— fuels Delano's religious interpretation. The moments of near disruption—when Delano witnesses violence from black boy to white, when the knot is thrown to him, when he bids the "slaves" stand back—urge him to speculate on Cereno's improper use of authority as an instance of religious excess, one that resembles Charles V's "anchoritish retirement" from power. In constructing a New England subjectivity that persistently pathologizes the religious other in order to organize an otherwise baffling scenario, Melville satirizes its interpretive pretensions. Indeed, while Delano, precisely because he has categorized Cereno as the Catholic other, consigns himself to "again and again turning over in his mind the mysterious demeanor of Don Benito Cereno" (67), unable to decipher the catacomb environment, his own interior is seemingly transparent to the mutineers, who strike their hatchets "as in ominous comment on the white stranger's thoughts" (67).

Thus if Melville exploits antebellum preoccupations with the conventional monastic secrecies of Catholicism to introduce the radically unconventional duplicities of the African American, he endows the black man with monkish powers of collective organization and devious spiritual insight. Delano's uncertainties about his Catholic double—is he an invalid, an incompetent youth, an imposter?—finally urge him to embrace his own bewilderment as he concludes that "to the Spaniard's black-letter text, it was best, for awhile, to leave open margin" (65). The moment is an important one, for it signals the supersession of his conspiratorial religious vision, in which the sentimental vagaries of his anti-Catholicism falsely schematized black and white as

abbot and monk to obscure the murderous racial schism between them.

If neither Cereno nor Babo has access to Delano's Romanism, the narrative's concluding extracts from Cereno's deposition and the remarks upon that deposition invite the reader to marvel at Romanism's serendipitous contribution to Babo's conspiracy. Providing access to the interlocking processes of religious and racial conspiracy, Delano's language of mysterious interiors disguised by black cowls, black skins, and "black vapors" (69) is finally the language Melville uses to describe the elusive interior meanings of his fiction. If the deposition serves "as the key to fit into the lock of the complications which precede it, then, as a vault whose door has been flung back, the San Dominick's hull lies open to-day" (114). The force of this passage is not only to connect 1799 to the "today" of 1855 but also to register the ingenuity of authorial constructions over that of religious or racial conspiracy. The story finally wrenches Delano from his charitable musings on the twinned excesses of Catholics and slave-holders and violently repositions him within a vengeful vision of racial pollution. Delano's insidious transition is registered when "he smote Babo's hand down, but his own heart smote him harder. With infinite pity he withdrew his hold from Don Benito" (99). Delano's Gothic dread of Cereno is thus replaced by racial hatred, as the shadow of the Negro now covers that of the pope.

Cereno's leap toward Delano and the white man's conquest of the black rebel that ensues force the punitive logic of this polluted interiority onto the African. The blacks' bodies are open to white transgression while the sailors of the *Bachelor's Delight* are sealed off from penetration. The blacks' "red tongues lolled, wolf-like, from their black mouths. But the pale sailors' teeth were set" (102). Such racial thematics abruptly scissor Delano's musings and replace the recesses of papal iniquity with those of black bodies whose dark interiors are not uncanny so much as radically different—a difference that provokes the violent suppressions of the imperialist instead of the gingerly probings of the tourist.

Both the deposition extracts and the postdeposition narrative reintroduce the Catholicism that has been so abruptly jettisoned by the revelation of racial conspiracy. As a mark of the new sympathy between Spaniard and New Englander, Cereno, "courteous even to the point of religion" (115), acknowledges Delano's fraternal religious status; both men agree that they are protected by the "Prince of Heaven" (115); and Cereno even forgives Delano's misjudgment of the "recesses" (115) of his character. But this (racially homogeneous) ecumenical spirit, by which narrative sequence and white supremacy are restored, lapses again into the uncanny fragmented world of monasticism and narrative uncertainty. Prostrated and largely silenced by the "shadow" of "the negro" (116), Cereno retires once more, this time not to his cuddy but to a monastery, "where both physician and priest were his nurses, and a member of the order volunteered to be his one special guardian and consoler, by night and by day" (103). Thus the silenced, soon-to-be decapitated Babo is replaced by the monk Infelez; the illicit proximity practiced by the subversive African Babo, whose plotted narrative had forced whites to become his characters and no longer his author, reorganizes back into the European proximity of monk and spiritual patient. In larger narrative terms; Melville finally extracts the reader from the metaphoric to the deictic, from Delano's interior musings on the *San Dominick*'s resemblance to a monastery to an omniscient narrative that points, first, to the truths of slave conspiracy and, second, to those of monasticism. Cereno leaves Delano's "shipload of monks" for an omnisciently narrated pilgrimage to the monastery on Mount Agonia.

From these last exits of Babo and Benito Cereno, Delano is excluded. With his last words, which include his injunction to "forget it" (116), his world of New England Romanism vanishes from the text, replaced by the hidden monastic intimacies of Infelez and Cereno. That the text ejects Delano after he has urged us to forget what has happened does not signal the forgetting of the Protestant captivity tradition. On the contrary, the narrator supplants Delano and appropriates his mystified Romanizing gaze, enticed and thwarted by a foreign Catholic interiority. If the ship's hull has disclosed that antebellum America's secrets are those of race, not religion, those aboard retreat back into the mute Catholic interior. Babo's and Cereno's passage into voicelessness recontextualizes race within religion as the conspirator's decapitated head gazes toward (and into) St. Bartholomew's Church and toward (and onto) the monastery on Mount Agonia. In positioning these concluding narrative moments as all emanating from Babo's gaze, one directed on the Catholic "vaults" (117), Melville forcibly identifies his antebellum reader with Babo. We look at Babo's head, which, "fixed on a pole in the Plaza, met, unabashed, the gaze of the whites" (116), only to be suddenly looking with that head toward the church and monastery that enclose the vanishing Catholic slaveholders, Aranda and Cereno.

Babo's gaze recuperates and extends that of antebellum Protestantism, for it promises that one can gain access to the Catholic interior; not only does Babo stare into the vault that holds Aranda's bones, but his gaze, in following Cereno's funeral procession toward the monastery, is also there, narratively speaking, to greet him, for Babo's authorial inscription beneath Aranda's skeleton, "seguid vuestro jefe," is repeated in the narrator's final description of Cereno's end: "Benito Cereno, borne on the bier, did, indeed, follow his leader" (117). If Babo is victim finally to the allied Catholic and Protestant slaveholding powers of New Spain and New England, his displayed head, a "hive of subtlety" (116), suggests that he reclaims the cellular organization and ingenuities of the monastery for his own. Emerging as the conclusive monastic interior—collectively empowered and ingenious—that brain lodges itself in New Spain's literal Catholic edifices and in New England's metaphoric ones. As a final icon of religious difference, the monkish Babo subversively imitates New Spain to mock New England, master of both their guilty interiors.

Notes

[1] For an explication of such "dream logic" at work in dime-novel fiction, see Michael Denning, *Mechanic Accents*. The best scholarship on connections between "low," "middle," and "high" culture includes Lawrence W. Levine, *Highbrow, Lowbrow*. For a sustained treatment of these issues in the literary marketplace of the American Renaissance, see David Reynolds, *Beneath the American Renaissance*.

[2] Herman Melville, "Benito Cereno," in *The Piazza Tales and Other Prose Pieces, 1839-1860*. Parenthetical page references in the text are to this edition. Edgar Allan Poe, "The Pit and the Pendulum," in *Collected Works of Edgar Allan Poe*, vol. 2. Parenthetical page references in the text are to this edition.

[3] Mary Rowlandson, "The Sovereignty and Goodness of God," in Alden T. Vaughan and Edward W. Clark, *Puritans among the Indians*, 75.

[4] "The Artistic and Romantic View of the Church of the Middle Ages," *Christian Examiner* 45 (1849): 377.

[5] As reported by Ray Allen Billington, *The Protestant Crusade, 1800-1860*, 375 n.68.

[6] *The History of the Inquisition of Spain . . . of D. Juan Llorente*, preface.

[7] For a discussion of Poe's interest in premature burial and its impact on narration, see J. Gerald Kennedy, *Poe, Death, and the Life of Writing*, especially chap. 2. For an analysis of Poe's "supererogatory verbosity," see Louis A. Renza, "Poe's Secret Autobiography."

[8] Hawthorne, *The French and Italian Notebooks*, 48.

[9] Joseph F. Berg, *The Confessional; or, an Exposition of the Doctrine of Auricular Confession As Taught in the Standards of the Romish Church*, 75.

[10] The best account of these masculine struggles remains Philip Greven, *The Protestant Temperament.* For an account of the nativist Jane Swisshelm and her accusations of unbridled sexuality in the Church of Rome, see Peter F. Walker, *Moral Choices.* Swisshelm further observed: "To be a member of the Roman church was to be a friend of Southern interests." Walker links the abolitionist Moncure Conway's diatribes against Jesuitism to "pure naked rage, but it is a rage that has not been unequivocally focused on its real object" (73)—for Conway a "safe" attack. Swisshelm's attack on unions, slavery, and Catholicism is finally, according to Walker, a defense of the "individual workingman entrepreneur" (165) and the "competitive marketplace" (166)—a defense of sovereign selfhood against effeminizing tyrannies.

[11] See Michael Zuckerman, "Holy Wars, Civil Wars," for an account of the troubled acceptance of economic pressures on the part of Americans still believing in Christian norms of moderation, communality, and moral values. For an account of the volatile gender dynamics at work in Douglass's critique of slavery, see my "Punishment of Esther: Frederick Douglass and the Construction of the Feminine," in *Frederick Douglass: New Literary and Historical Essays,* ed. Eric Sundquist (New York: Cambridge University Press, 1991).

[12] *The Diary of George Templeton Strong,* 2:140.

[13] For one example of southern musings on the inner feelings behind the black "masks" of slaves, see Mary Chestnut's numerous entries in C. Vann Woodward, ed., *Mary Chestnut's Civil War Diary,* especially the "Witherspoon Murder Case," 209-19.

[14] Gloria Horsley-Meacham, "The Monastic Slaver," *New England Quarterly* 56 (1983): 261.

[15] Eric J. Sundquist, "Suspense and Tautology in 'Benito Cereno,'" *Glyph* 8 (1981): 109. See also Sundquist, "Benito Cereno and New World Slavery," in Sacvan Bercovitch, ed., *Reconstructing American Literary History,* 93-122. For a reading of the novella that stresses contemporary political ramifications, see Levine, *Conspiracy and Romance,* 165-233.

FURTHER READING

Criticism

Billington, Raymond A. "Tentative Bibliography of Anti-Catholic Propaganda in the United States." *The Catholic Historical Review* XVIII (April 1932-January 1933): 492.

   Attempts to list and classify all books, pamphlets, newspapers, and magazines published as anti-Catholic propaganda in the United States between 1800 and 1850.

——."The Literature of Anti-Catholicism." In The Protestant Crusade 1800-1860: A Study of the Origins of American Nativism, The Macmillan Company, 1938, pp. 345-79.

   Surveys the vast array of nativist anti-Catholic propaganda produced in the first half of the nineteenth century.

Dolan, Jay P. "Catholic Attitudes toward Protestants." In *Uncivil Religion: Interreligious Hostility in America,* edited by Robert N. Bellah and Frederick E. Greenspahn, pp. 72-86. New York: Crossroad Publishing Co., 1987.

   A discussion of the various ways in which Catholics regarded Protestants in the nineteenth century and how they responded to the latter's antagonism.

Elson, Ruth Miller. *Guardians of Tradition: American Schoolbooks of the Nineteenth Century.* Lincoln: University of Nebraska Press, 1964, 424 p.

   Discusses the contribution of school textbooks to the anti-Catholicism of the period.

Ewens, Mary. "Roles Seen in the Literature." In *The Role of the Nun in Nineteenth-Century America,* Arno Press, 1978, pp. 297-325.

   Examines the role of the nun in mid- to late-nineteenth century American fiction, showing how the popular portrayal and perception of the Roman Catholic nun shifted over time from one of intense negativity to one of ineffectual virtue.

Gorman, Robert. *Catholic Apologetical Literature in the United States (1784-1858). Studies in American Church History,* Vol. XXVIII. Washington, D.C.: The Catholic University of America, 1939, 192 p.

   Discusses the chief characteristics of Catholic apologetical literature between 1784 and 1858 and relates them to certain twentieth-century conditions.

Hofstadter, Richard. "The Paranoid Style in American Politics and Other Essays." In his *The Paranoid Style in American Politics and Other Essays.* pp. 3-40. New York: Alfred A. Knopf, 1966.

   Contains a useful discussion of the anti-Catholic movement in the 1820s and 1830s, its character, and some of the books that fostered it.

Miller, J. R. "Anti-Catholic Thought in Victorian Canada." *Canadian Historical Review* VI, no. 4 (1985): 474-94.

   Examines the social, political, and theological aspects of anti-Catholicism in Victorian Canada.

Thorp, Willard. "Catholic Novelists in Defense of Their Faith, 1829-1865." *Proceedings of the American Antiquarian Society* Vol. 78, pt 1 (1968): 25-117.

   A discussion of each of the Catholic apologetic novels with American themes published in the thirty-six years

between 1829 and 1865; included are several novels
with non-American themes, as well as a few from
Europe and Great Britain.

Hysteria in Nineteenth-Century Literature

INTRODUCTION

During the nineteenth century, the psychological disorder of hysteria became a major focus of cultural and medical study, and also increased in incidence both in Europe and the United States. Starting with Hippocrates's explanation of the disease as a wandering uterus, hysteria was considered a "female malady" and linked to the feminine, irrational, emotional, and sexually unrestrained. However, the social, economic, and political upheavals of the nineteenth century complicated conventional gender norms and brought discussion of hysteria out of a purely medical discourse and into a larger cultural one.

The evolution of hysteria from a medical curiosity to the focus of artistic and moral examination turned on an etiological shift—from looking for biological causes within female anatomy, to studying the emotional and social aspects of femininity. Hysteria seemed to simultaneously disrupt and reaffirm gender stereotypes, for it questioned the validity of the traditional dichotomies of passivity and activity, silence and speech, and weakness and strength. Among the varied and elusive symptoms of hysteria, aphonia—loss of speech—and blindness were prominent manifestations; the hysteric was deprived of the ability to directly articulate her experience, or to represent the world around her. The complex relation between the mute narrative that the hysteric enacted and the artistic imagination became a central issue for many writers. For them the illness and muteness of hysterics was not merely a void, but an insistent demand for attention and interpretation.

In examining the phenomenon of hysteria, nineteenth-century literary figures such as Gustave Flaubert, Honoré de Balzac, Henry James, George Eliot, Thomas Hardy, and William Wordsworth suggested a deeper relation between creativity and illness. These authors brought into question the identification of hysteria with female anatomy and gestured towards a more universal crisis of consciousness which erupts from the repression of desire. The linking of hysteria with reproductive disorders found its parallels in the connection between male hysteria, the disruption of the literary imagination, and the dramatic enactment of internal conflict. Through their use of hysterical characters, authors both alluded to and contributed to the cultural understanding of hysteria, focusing attention upon personal dynamics and articulation, and downplaying the role of physiological etiology.

Some novels, including Henry James's *The Bostonians* (1886) and Florence Nightingale's *Cassandra* (1852), associate hysteria either explicitly or implicitly with the new feminist movement of the nineteenth century. Works such as *The Diary of Alice James* (1894) portray the hysteric as a liminal figure, as one who is victimized by her illness but who also gains power from it. In contrast, Flaubert's *Madame Bovary* (1857) and Charlotte Brontë's *Jane Eyre* (1847) link hysteria to the repression of sexuality and thus reinscribe the identification of femininity in terms of reproduction and desire.

The literary appropriation of hysteria confronted gender stereotypes in a variety of ways. Some authors reinforced the association of women with maternal impulses (either repressed or fulfilled), while others responded to the cultural unrest of their time by questioning the validity of assumptions about gender traits. Hysteria became the disease of the imagination, the disease that silenced the voice but enacted the self-articulation of the feminine (and, more rarely, masculine) subject.

REPRESENTATIVE WORKS

Honoré de Balzac
Cousine Bette (novel) 1847

Charlotte Brontë
Jane Eyre (novel) 1847
Villette (novel) 1853

Samuel Taylor Coleridge
"Christabel" (poem) 1816

George Eliot
Daniel Deronda (novel) 1876

Gustave Flaubert
Madame Bovary (novel) 1857

Sigmund Freud
"Fragment of a Case of Hysteria" (case study) 1905

Charlotte Perkins Gilman
"The Yellow Wallpaper" (short story) 1892

Henrik Ibsen
Hedda Gabler (drama) 1890

Alice James
The Diary of Alice James (diary) 1894

Henry James
The Bostonians (novel) 1886
The Turn of the Screw (novella) 1897

Florence Nightingale
Cassandra (novel) 1852

George Sand
Lélia (novel) 1833

William Wordsworth
Lyrical Ballads (poetry) 1798

THE HISTORY OF HYSTERIA

Claire Kahane (essay date 1995)

SOURCE: "History/Hysteria: A Glance Backward," in
*Passions of the Voice: Hysteria, Narrative, and the
Figure of the Speaking Woman, 1850-1915,* The John
Hopkins University Press, 1995, pp. 1-13.

[*In the excerpt that follows, Kahane contends that the
second half of the nineteenth century was dominated
by cultural, political, and economic upheaval, accompanied by a conservative reaction to this upheaval;
this tension between radical change and static order,
Kahane maintains, is reflected in the structure of the
internal conflict expressed in hysteria.*]

> Wherever the hysteric goes, she brings war with
> her.

—Moustapha Safouan, "In Praise of Hysteria"

Change is the matter both of history and of narrative,
but as historians have remarked, England in the second
half of the nineteenth century seemed to experience its
mutability with extraordinary intensity. The sense of
cultural transformation that dominated both event and
discourse in the Victorian era has been repeatedly
chronicled; within one generation a technological revolution perhaps unparalleled until our own fin-de-siècle
computer age gave rise to material transformations that
radically altered the boundaries of the geosocial landscape. The rapid expansion of industrial capitalism and
its promotion of shifts of population, the emergence of
large urban centers with newly exploding populations
and new social classes, the invention of telegraph and
telephone, the expansion of railroads and steam power,
created a vertiginous sense of social and economic
acceleration to which Victorian discourse bore frequent
witness.[1]

Clearly such swift change breeds anxiety as well as
expectation, breeds a diffuse sense of being subject to
forces beyond one's comprehension or control, a sense
that went against the dominant Victorian ideal of progressive mastery and dominion in both politics and
culture. Thus, for example, Walter Bagehot in *Physics
and Politics* cannot quite remove the quasi-paranoid
intimations of invisible presences in his voice even as
he celebrates the new knowledge in physics: "One
peculiarity of this age is the sudden acquisition of much
physical knowledge. There is scarcely a department of
science which is the same, or at all the same, as it was
fifty years ago. A new world of inventions . . . has
grown up around us which we cannot help seeing, a
new world of ideas is in the air and affects us, though
we do not see it."[2] As Bagehot's text testifies, the very
word *new* emerges as a frequent incantation in the
discourse of the late nineteenth century—the New
Hedonism, the New Fiction, the New Realism, the New
Drama, the New Sciences, and, not least for my purposes, the New Woman—undermining the old certain-
ties that subtended the cultural order.[3]

What especially characterized this nervous age was that
a generalized anxiety about change became increasingly linked to a particular anxiety about the change in
and by women, a change that, as Peter Gay points out,
was brought about in great part by the very successes
of the bourgeois culture that was nervous.[4] If, for example, the speedy development of late-nineteenth-century capitalism called for a rapidly expanding work-
force; women in ever greater number participated in
that expansion. In the England of 1851 there had been
almost no women clerks; in 1861 there were 2,000;
and, by 1911, the number had mushroomed to 157,000.
Moreover, the growth of crowded urban centers, inevitably attended by poverty, unemployment, illness, and
crime, called for new social competencies and new
professional qualifications. Although women remained
a small minority in the professions—by 1897 there
were only 87 women doctors in all of England—middle-
class women took the lead as crusaders for social and
spiritual reform. Precisely in the name of those female
virtues conventionally attributed to them, women established reform societies, settlement houses, and educational alliances to address the needs of an expanding
new mass population. Even religion, the conventional
stronghold of patriarchal authority, was invaded by
these newly public women, who, newly inspired, used
the pulpit with millennial zeal to envision utopias in
which women prevailed as arbiters of morality and the
law. By the 1880s a new and increasingly vocal woman
had emerged in both England and America, confident
in her singularity, outspoken in the public arena, calling vociferously for suffrage and a legitimate voice in
the affairs of state.

Much like the response of many conservatives to the
second wave of feminism in the late 1960s, the social

critics of the time responded to the emergence of this New Woman by predicting the end of Western civilization. Ann Ardis points to an anonymously authored article in the *Westminster Review* that claimed that the New Woman was "intimately connected" with "the stirrings and rumblings now perceivable in the social and industrial world, the 'Bitter Cries' of the disinherited classes, the 'Social Wreckage' which is becoming able to make itself unpleasantly prominent, 'the Problems of Great Cities,' the spread of Socialism and Nihilism" (1990, 1). Certainly this link between rebellion in the working class and the increasingly militant calls for women's liberation was not without precedent. In mid-nineteenth-century America Harriet Beecher Stowe's *Uncle Tom's Cabin* drew an analogy between black slavery and the economically servile position of bourgeois white women; similarly, in England Charlotte Brontë's *Shirley,* specifically structured as a double narrative of political struggle and individual domestic conflict, depicted both working-class men and middle-class women as oppressed by a powerful male gentry indifferent to their claims, each barely containing a resentment that had no legitimate outlet. Increasingly, British discourse of the late nineteenth century identified women and labor—the title of Olive Schreiner's pioneering study—as the two great problems of modern social life. Both were represented as cauldrons of unrest, twins sources of a Pandora's box just waiting to be opened.

Thomas Laqueur has remarked of the French Revolution that "wherever boundaries were threatened arguments for fundamental sexual differences were shoved into the breach" (1986, 14); both England and America in the mid-nineteenth century seemed to require that supplementation. As Mary Poovey points out, a binary model of sexual difference had begun to dominate European culture by the late eighteenth century, but it reached its zenith in the mid-nineteenth century. Significantly, it took the body as the natural site of social as well as sexual difference, and as Poovey notes, that meant reproduction: "Emphasizing the incommensurability of male and female bodies entailed foregrounding the role of the reproductive system, effacing other kinds of differences" (1988, 6). By midcentury woman's maternal function was ubiquitously taken as the foundation both of her social identity and of her sexual desire. Late-eighteenth-century medical treatises, for example, had unselfconsciously described women as having large sexual appetites, but by the second half of the nineteenth century, most doctors deemed frigidity more natural for women, whose sensual pleasure was assimilated to their maternal function, appearing as tenderness rather than lust.

Of course, such a conflation of woman's desire with maternity was not new; woman's role as mother had long been propounded as a religious ideal. With the increasing valorization of the sciences in the bourgeois century (Gay 1984), however, medical discourse, as if appropriating the social authority previously deemed divine, defined and prescribed what was "natural" as a biocultural imperative. Between 1875 and 1900 a considerable number of physicians claimed that female emancipation would inevitably cause gynecological disease (Sensibar 1991).[5] Women were constantly warned by doctors about the horrendous physical consequences of the unnatural use of their minds: education would shrivel up women's reproductive organs; thinking robbed the ovaries of energy. Not surprisingly, hysteria, a pathology whose very name implicated women's reproductive system, was adduced as the inevitable consequence of this perverse intellectual and political transvestism.[6] As one American medical expert wrote,

> The nervous force, so necessary at puberty for the establishment of the menstrual function, is wasted on what may be compared as trifles to perfect health. . . . Bright eyes have been dulled by the brain-fag and sweet temper transformed into irritability, crossness and hysteria, while the womanhood of the land is deteriorating physically. (William Edgar Darnell, quoted in Smith-Rosenberg 1985, 259)

In the context of this pervasive medical legislation of woman's reproductive identity, the figure of the mother became not only an idealized trope of female nature and destiny but a site of psychic conflict as well.

It would be reductive to conclude that such arguments were universally accepted, however; certainly one can find dissenting opinions that encouraged the emancipatory project of young women, and even some conservative doctors relented in their pronouncements as more women entered institutions of higher education without ill effects.[7] Women doctors especially, although few in number, were among the most vocal in countering the assertions of male physicians; they blamed not education for women's illness but the class hypocrisy of a medical establishment that could argue simultaneously both for the working woman's greater powers of endurance and for the natural frailty of women. Nevertheless, blatant contradictions in the representations of women continued to circulate in Victorian discourse. Thus, for example, as Smith-Rosenberg remarks, at the same time that "the True Woman was emotional, dependent, and gentle—a born follower . . . the Ideal Mother, then and now, was expected to be strong, self-reliant, protective, an efficient caretaker in relation to children and home" (1985, 199).

Both meanings were fused into what has been called "the Cult of True Womanhood" (Welter 1966). Widely promulgated in mid-nineteenth-century fiction and poetry, this cult, with its doctrinaire insistence on separate spheres of action for men and women, had spawned perhaps the most tendentiously feminine-maternal figure, the "Angel in the House" who circulated in Coventry Patmore's popular tract-poem of that name (1854). Thirty years later Charles Darwin's *The Descent of Man* gave this essentialist separatist doctrine a scientific history by arguing that women had evolved differently from men, that their nurturant capacities naturally fitted them for home and hearth, while men had evolved aggressive abilities that suited them for competition in the public arena. Like Patmore's versified representation, Darwinian law represented woman as both nurturant and self-sacrificing, and thus the natural conservator of Victorian morality and civilization.

What seems obvious in retrospect is that the Victorian scripture on gender difference was being urgently disseminated at the very time that socioeconomic conditions, historical forces, and cultural representations were increasingly undermining it. Nina Auerbach's reading of the contradictory meanings of the Victorian woman, who was old maid, fallen woman, and angel in the house rolled into one, captures the complicated effects of the era's attempt to control the representation of women's nature. As Auerbach points out, "woman's very aura of exclusion gave her imaginative centrality in a culture increasingly alienated from itself. Powerful images of oppression became images of barely suppressed power, all the more grandly haunting because, unlike the hungry workers, woman ruled both the palace and the home while hovering simultaneously in the darkness without" (1982, 188). By the 1880s the Angel in the House was challenged by the appearance of "Novissima" (Ardis 1990, 1), the New Woman who rejected marriage and motherhood and provocatively contested the boundaries of those separate spheres.[8]

Yet clearly the very term *New Woman,* appearing ubiquitously in the popular press, had stirred up the demons of uncertainty not only about women's proper place, but about men's proper place as well. Elaine Showalter remarks that the New Woman "threatened to turn the world upside down and to be on top in a wild carnival of social and sexual misrule" (1990, 38).[9] Showalter's metaphor of sexual reversal, a common image for the cultural consequences of women's liberation in the popular iconography of the time, indicates the implicit challenge to heterosexual positioning that the New Woman conveyed, but nowhere more so than by mounting the platform and speaking, by putting herself actually on top. For it was particularly the feminist orators, who claimed an equal place in a *fraternal* order of culture, who took their political demands to the public platform, that most raised the hackles of the public about women's proper sexual place, if we can judge from the vehemence of popular critical reaction. From midcentury onward, antifeminist literature, cartoons, sermons, and caricatures increased in circulation. Typically, they took the form of questioning the gender identity of women who spoke in public; that is to say, they made the woman's public

voice the primary signifier of her problematic sexual being. American feminist conventions like those at Seneca Falls (1848) and Rochester (1852) had provoked fierce denunciations in the popular press, which represented the feminist orator as an unsexed woman. The *New York Herald* denounced feminist orators as "mannish women, like hens that crow" (September 12, 1852). Similarly, in England, *Punch* joined with the House of Commons to caricature women who took the podium as masculine harridans. "My hair is dark chestnut; my moustachios are rather lighter," *Punch* quipped, mimicking the voice of a female candidate for office (21 [1851], 157).[10] The mannish woman orator became an increasingly familiar figure in satiric novels; in *The Rebel of the Family,* the antifeminist writer Eliza Lynn Linton, who coined the phrase "shrieking sisterhood," referred to one "specimen of a female public orator" whose "case-hardened self sufficiency was as ugly as a physical deformity," and described another with suspiciously "close-cropped hair, a Tyrolese hat . . . a waistcoat and a short jacket" (quoted in Showalter 1990, 24).[11]

Paradoxically, feminist orators were portrayed not only as hermaphrodites but also as prostitutes, acting out a vulgar and suspect exhibitionism, which offended womanly proprieties. "There is something repugnant to the ordinary Englishman in the idea of a woman mounting the platform and facing the noisy, gaping, vulgar crowd of an election meeting," writes Mary Jeune in the 1890s ("English Women in Political Life," *North American Review* [1895]:453, quoted in Showalter 1990, 24). It is particularly ironic that not only does Jeune herself confound boundaries by speaking in the name of the English-*man,* but her "repugnance"—an affect associated with hysteria—itself suggests the hysterical ground of her response to the feminist orator. If these ubiquitous images of the woman orator pointed to the sexual anxieties of an aroused public, they also unveiled the cultural fantasy that provoked them: the freakish man-woman with a voice was the woman with a phallus, a vocal Medusa, to be suppressed for the sake of the social order, repressed for the sake of the psychological one.

It was no mere coincidence that at the same time that the woman orator became an increasingly audible and visible figure in the pulpit and on the podium, female hysteria, with its characteristic symptoms of aphonia and paralysis, swept across Europe and America in epidemic proportion.[12] Neil Hertz (1983) describes male hysteria in the eighteenth century as a response to the image of the anarchist woman of the French Revolution and its arousal of male castration anxiety. The nineteenth-century woman orator was also a kind of woman warrior, and it is not surprising that she provoked similar fears of being unmanned in her male audience. What is remarkable, however, is that this figure of the speaking woman also provoked women's anxiety—about the propriety of possessing the power of the voice, about having the phallus rather than being it, an anxiety whose effects are still evident in women's continued ambivalence about public speaking. To approach that ambivalence and its relation to hysteria, I want first to note that while feminist critics often conflate the feminist and the hysteric, seeing them as two sides of a singular political heroine—the revolutionary feminist-hysteric[13]—there is a significant distinction to be drawn between them as historical figures. The feminist and the hysteric presented mirror images of women's relation to the public voice: the feminist orator claimed an active subject position and the power of the voice; the hysteric passively acted out through her body what her voice could not speak.

If this mirror relation serves to describe an essential antithesis between the feminist and the hysteric, it also figures a psychic split *within* the hysteric, an internal division between active speaking subject and passive spoken object that inhibited if not totally suppressed her public voice.[14] Joan Rivière's well-known article "Womanliness as Masquerade" (1929; rpt. Burgin et al. 1986), although written in and about a later period, offers a useful point of entry into that division by its interrogation of a particular case of anxiety over the issue of public speaking. Rivière cites the case of a woman who seemed to have it all: a professional life that satisfied her ambitions, a family, a good sex life. As Rivière writes, "She had a high degree of adaptation to reality and managed to sustain good and appropriate relations with almost everyone with whom she came in contact" (36). There was a problem, however:

> She was an American woman engaged in work of a propagandist nature which consisted principally in speaking and writing. All her life a certain degree of anxiety, sometimes very severe, was experienced after every public performance, such as speaking to an audience. . . . She would be excited and apprehensive all night after, with misgivings whether she had done anything inappropriate, and obsessed by a need for reassurance. This need . . . led her compulsively on any such occasion to seek some attention or complimentary notice from a man or men at the close of the proceedings in which she had taken part or been the principal figure. (36)

Noting the "incongruity of this attitude with her highly impersonal and objective attitude during her intellectual performance" (36), Rivière locates its source in a doubled conflict familiar also to the etiology of hysteria: identification and rivalry with her mother (which implies desire for the father) and identification and rivalry with her father (which implies desire for the mother).

It is her rivalry with her father for the phallus, as Rivière describes it, which seems especially relevant for un-

derstanding why the feminist orator would provoke hysteria in women. For Rivière's patient public speaking "signified an exhibition of herself in possession of the father's penis, having castrated him" (39); her retreat to feminine behavior, her "womanliness as masquerade," was thus meant to ward off a feared punishment for appropriating the father's power.[15] The feminist orator could also be said to have stolen the father's phallus; but unlike the hysteric, she claimed her *right* to the phallus, her right to exceed the strictures of femininity, to compete with the father as an active, desiring subject. Circulating that claim in the expanding movement for women's suffrage, the feminist orator provoked a wishful identification among a good number of women auditors at the same time that she provoked an unconscious dread—an ambivalence that had mixed effects. While, as Judith Butler claims, the daughter's "rivalry with the father is not [necessarily] over the desire of the mother, but over the place of the father in public discourse as speaker" (1990, 51), it is virtually impossible to separate transgressive desire from rivalrous identification in this contestation with the father, which, at its worst, results in the kind of hysterical mutism that Henry James probes in *The Bostonians*. As with Rivière's early-twentieth-century patient, who was unable to either acknowledge the claim to the phallus and its oedipal ramifications or give it up, the hysterical woman of the nineteenth century kept silent her fantasmatic rivalry, and dissimulating by simulating femininity, spoke her divided desire in symptoms.

Hysteria has always been associated with femininity, from the Greek depiction of hysterics as lazy women with wandering wombs, through the demonically possessed women of the Middle Ages, to the nineteenth-century hysterics that fascinated Freud (Bernheimer 1990a). Moreover, as Ilza Veith (1965) points out in her extensive survey of the disease, historically "the symptoms were modified by the prevailing concept of the feminine ideal."[16] The relation between hysteria and the feminine ideal in the nineteenth century is further elucidated by Alan Krohn's (1978) observation that passivity has been a consistently central component of hysteria. The hysteric, Krohn argues in his cross-cultural study, uses the dominant myth of passivity in her or his culture to represent internal conflict. Since passivity, and particularly passive desire, came to define a normative and ideal femininity in the nineteenth century, the Victorian feminine ideal itself became a privileged site of hysterical ambivalence. Freud's opinion that what is repudiated in both sexes is femininity (1937, *SE* 23:250), specifically defined as passive desire, foreshadows the conclusions of these historical and cross-cultural studies. All suggest that both female and male hysterics were—are—involved in conflictual feminine identifications that they both desire and abhor.[17]

Even before the nineteenth century, femininity and passivity had been joined in the medical discourse on hysteria. "This disease attacks women more than men," wrote a Dr. Sydenham in the seventeenth century, "because they have a more delicate, less firm constitution, because they lead a softer life, and because they are accustomed to the luxuries and commodities of life and not to suffering" (quoted in Bernheimer 1990a, 12). Sydenham is credited with promoting the modern liberation of hysteria from its biological basis as a female disorder (Rousseau 1993, 144).[18] For Sydenham, hysteria was a common "affliction of the mind" induced by a passive lifestyle and thus a function of an increasingly affluent civilization. His female hysterics, all wealthy women, were especially suspect, however; leading "a softer life," they embodied more fully the social ills of the time. Sydenham's liberating definition of hysteria still cast the woman, "less firm" in constitution, as more "naturally" prone to hysteria.

Although men increasingly entered the ranks of hysterics throughout the eighteenth century, their susceptibility to hysteria was defined by their being "tender, nervous, brittle . . . either mentally or morally of feminine constitution" (Rousseau 1993, 170). Representations of male hysterics as "timid and fearful" or "coquettish and eccentric" (Showalter 1993, 289) reinforced the relation between hysteria and women, particularly women of a stereotypically fragile feminine constitution. Thus, although Enlightenment medicine continued to move away from the literalization of hysteria as a wandering womb to its being a more general signifier of a nervous disorder that afflicted both men and women, hysteria remained effectively tied to cultural definitions of a denigrated femininity. By the nineteenth century, hysteria had proliferated as a diagnosis. Covering a wide spectrum of physical disorders of uncertain origin, it remained doubly tainted both by its link to femininity and by a suspicion that it belonged to the realm of the imaginary.[19]

In the early nineteenth century the French physician Philippe Pinel, known as the "Liberator" for literally removing the chains from institutionalized patients, had proposed that some unacknowledged sexual transgression was part of the etiology of hysterical symptoms. Because hysteria resulted from deviant sexual conduct, Pinel recommended as a cure marriage and the family, a return to the sexual fix that was itself often an instigating factor in the etiology of the illness. If Pinel thus chained the hysteric to a suspect morality, he did make two significant contributions to the modern history of hysteria: (1) he empirically severed hysteria from biology, and therefore from an essential female nature, by demonstrating clinically that disorders associated with hysteria could not be traced to any organic changes in the brain or nervous system; (2) he used conversation to explore the source of his patients' disturbance, a method of treatment

that antedated the talking cure of psychoanalysis (Bernheimer 1990a, 5).

Perhaps more than any nineteenth-century figure before Freud, Jean Charcot contributed to a change in the perception of hysterics by extensively studying hysteria in men as well as women and delineating it as an actual pathology with precise laws.[20] Yet in spite of his categorization of hysteria as a non-gender-specific disorder, Charcot's most dramatic public representations of hysterics were of women. At his famous Leçons du Mardi, weekly lectures that took place in a hall beneath a picture of Pinel having the chains taken off the madmen in the Salpetrière, Charcot used hypnosis to produce, catalogue, and remove hysterical symptoms from women of different classes (Bernheimer 1990a, 6-7).

In composing the features of a mysterious behavior into a coherent, structured symptomatology, Charcot catalogued four phases in the hysterical attack that Freud records: (1) the epileptoid phase—convulsive attacks preceded by "aura sensations," especially the *globus hystericus* (spasms of the pharynx, "as though a lump were rising from the epigastrium to the throat"); (2) the *grands movements* phase—movements of wide compass, which Freud notes are elegantly performed; (3) the hallucinatory phase—the famous *attitudes passionelles,* "distinguished by attitudes and gestures which belong to scenes of passionate movement, which the patient hallucinates and often accompanies with the corresponding words"; during this attack consciousness is often lost; (4) the terminal delirium phase—the *grand attaque* (*SE* 1:42-43, 151). Although this description of the stages of intensification of a pathology has the structure of spectacle—indeed, Charcot made extensive use of photography in documenting and cataloguing hysterical symptoms[21]—its diachronic movement offers the rudiments of a sequenced story told through the hysterical body. That story moves from blocked orality to its liberation—from a lump coming up from within to an oral site of conflict at the throat, where it remains unexpressed; to the dissemination of that "lump" that blocks expression into a sexual scenario performed by body parts; and, finally, to orgiastic delirium. Charcot's ordering, which situates its initial conflict in the oral zone, would be elaborated by Freud, who gave the formal symptoms a particular content as the representation of an individual history, and joining temporality to meaning, foregrounded the importance of hysterical narration in finding a path to the cure.

In this regard, what proved most germane for the emergence of Freud's psychoanalysis was Charcot's demonstration through hypnosis that the hysteric's very consciousness was beyond her control, that she could speak and act from another place without being present as a subject of consciousness, that an erotic scenario unknown and unacknowledged was being articulated through her body and could be read. Writing of Charcot's patient and the *attitude passionelle,* Freud had remarked: "In many cases it is quite obvious that this phase comprises a memory from the patient's life. . . . Even when *attitudes passionelles* are lacking, hypnosis provides proof of psychical process such as is revealed in the phase *passionelle,* ie. a sexual scenario" (*SE* 1:151-52). Charcot's patients provided Freud with evidence of a disjunction among memory, sexuality, and consciousness, a disjunction in the very temporal reality of the subject that became the founding premise of his new science of the unconscious. Moreover, by reading the symptom as a linguistic representation of an unconscious conflict not available to the conscious subject, Freud challenged also the Enlightenment assumption of a unitary subject of language.

The move from Charcot to Freud, as Stephen Heath first remarked, is a move from the metaphorics of vision to voice, a move that subverted the distance between subject and object (1981, 202-4). If Charcot's careful visual charting had distanced and isolated the hysteric in the manner of objective science, Freud's method of listening to the speaking voice promoted proximity and the inevitable ambiguities associated with language. It also promoted a more permeable boundary between speaker and listener through the circulation of a disembodied voice. Indeed, the shift from vision to voice can also be seen as a shift in the aesthetics of narrative form, from a realism that makes extended use of objective description—those material details that so irritated Virginia Woolf in her critique of Arnold Bennett and John Galsworthy ("Modern Fiction" [1953])—to a modernism that insists on blurring the boundaries between the subject and object of representation through the permutations of an emphatically subjective narrative voice.[22] The case history, Freud's own new narrative genre, exemplifies the problematic consequences of this shift.[23]

Notes

[1] See Gay's extensive elaboration of the changes in Victorian life and their effects (1984).

[2] *Physics and Politics* (1872, 1; quoted in Gay 1984, 52-53).

[3] This characterization comes from Holbrook Jackson, *The Eighteen Nineties* (1913, 21-23; quoted in Gay 1984, 52).

[4] See Gay (1984), Showalter (1990), and Ardis (1990) for extended discussions of the cultural anxieties provoked by the New Woman in Victorian England. I take the statistics that follow from Gay's text. For an analogous discussion of the New Woman in the United States, see Smith-Rosenberg (1985, 245-96).

[5] Sensibar (1991) gives a good deal of useful historical information about hysteria and its medical context, claiming that it is essential to a reading of Henry James, *The Bostonians* (see my chap. 4). See also Showalter (1985); Sayers (1982).

[6] See Smith-Rosenberg's highly informed and informative chapter, "The Hysterical Woman," in *Disorderly Conduct* (1985) for an excellent overview of this issue. Gay also records striking examples of Harvard medical professor Edward Clarke's subjectively processed science, as, for example, the spurious case of Miss D., "who had entered Vassar at 14 healthy, began menstruation at 15, continued to study, recite, [and as a consequence] began to have fainting fits during exercises [and] graduated with impaired physique" (1984, 214-15).

[7] For refutations of such opinions as Darnell's and Clarke's, see Smith-Rosenberg's chapter "The New Woman as Androgyne" in *Disorderly Conduct* (1985).

[8] Ardis heroinizes the New Woman by pointing out that "the New Woman refused to be assimilated into the iconography of the Victorian 'Womanhood'" (1990, 2-3). See also Showalter (1990) on the sexual challenge of the New Woman.

[9] Showalter surveys the flourishing literature of female difference and emancipation in the final decades of the nineteenth century, including novels such as Gissing's *The Odd Women,* in which emancipation means the rejection of heterosexual marriage, and Walter Besant's *The Revolt of Men,* which represents a reversal of gender roles in a dystopian future.

[10] *History of Woman Suffrage,* ed. Elizabeth Cady Stanton, Susan B. Anthony, and Matilda Joslin Gage, vol. 1 (quoted in Gay 1984, 194).

[11] Interestingly, Henry James represents such a figure in the sexually ambiguous Dr. Prance in *The Bostonians,* but marks her as a sympathetic character by her taciturn alienation from feminist oratory.

[12] See Krohn (1978) for a discussion of the psychological features of this epidemic. Showalter (1985) provides a more extensive discussion of the meaning of hysteria for women in its nineteenth-century historical context.

[13] Hélène Cixous has been the most noteworthy feminist assuming this position; see her dialogue with Catherine Clément in *The Newly Born Woman* (1986).

[14] Oral fixations are also responsible for a cathexis of speaking, of the throat and the voice: some of Dora's and Anna O.'s symptoms suggest orality as the preferred mode of nonsatisfaction and anxiety (A. Anzieu 1990, 140-43).

[15] Heath (1986) has extrapolated from Rivière's case history a dynamic explanation of the problematics of femininity that also illuminates women's familiar ambivalence about public speaking.

[16] Veith describes the *Malleus Maleficarum* of 1494 as a document that "reveals beyond doubt that many, if not most, of the witches as well as a great number of their victims described therein were simply hysterics who had suffered from partial anesthesia, mutism, blindness, and convulsions, and above all, from a variety of sexual delusions" (1965, 61).

[17] For an elaboration of the ambivalence of male identity, see Silverman (1992). For a fuller discussion of the ways in which hysteria in both men and women is linked to the primary relation to an imaginary mother, and to oral conflicts, see David-Ménard (1989). A. Anzieu writes that hysteria involves "the erogenous diffusion of a mode of oral excitation to other parts of the body . . . namely a cathexis of the orifices of the body as erogenous place of passage. Persistence of the mouth-genital confusion is connected with this. . . . In men it reveals a fixation to early feminine identifications and difficulties whose form makes one inevitably think of hysteria" (1990, 121).

[18] Rousseau praises Sydenham for his "discovery" that hysteria imitates culture (1993, 102) and that the hysterical symptom was produced by stresses within the culture that it mimed. Rousseau presents a provocative historical reading of hysteria that explores the links between representation and pathology. See "A Strange Pathology" in Gilman et al. (1993).

[19] Smith-Rosenberg's discussion of the relation of hysteria to femaleness, while in many ways an excellent summary, oversimplifies its formulation in psychoanalysis: "It was defined as an entity that was peculiarly female and has almost always carried with it a pejorative implication" (1985, 197). Like Charcot before him, Freud took great pains to assert that hysteria was not limited to women, classing himself as a "petit hysteric." Moreover, Smith-Rosenberg's statement that "more recently, psychoanalysts such as Elizabeth Zetzel have refined this Freudian hypothesis, tracing the roots of hysteria to a woman's excessively ambivalent preoedipal relation with her mother and to the resulting complications of oedipal development and resolution" is misleading; the importance of the mother in hysterical etiologies was emphasized by Freud after the Dora case (see "Hysterical Phantasies and Their Relation to Bisexuality" (1908, *SE* 9) and developed more fully by subsequent psychoanalytic theorists.

[20] In his obituary notice of Charcot, Freud praised him for releasing the hysteric from the derogation to which she had been subject (*SE* 3:19).

[21] Charcot's famous photographs (published in three volumes, "Iconographie photographique de la salpetrière") captured women in various stages of the *attitude passionelle,* and portrayed types of erotic body language that continued to bind hysteria to the spectacle of a disturbing female sexual excess not unlike the image of the possessed woman of an earlier time.

[22] Woolf's essays on modernist writing, "Mr. Bennett and Mrs. Brown" and "Modern Fiction," can both be read as contrasting a visual mode of representation that focuses on perceived and bounded objects and a more subtle subjective representation of "the atoms as they fall upon the mind" (1953, 155).

[23] See Marcus (1990 [1974]) for a reading of Freud's case history as a great modernist novel.

Works Cited

Anzieu, Annie. 1990. "The Hysterical Envelope." In *Psychic Envelopes,* edited by Didier Anzieu. London: Karnac Books.

Ardis, Ann. 1990. *New Women, New Novels.* New Brunswick, N.J.: Rutgers University Press.

[Auerbach, Nina]. 1982. *Woman and the Demon: The Life of a Victorian Myth.* Cambridge: Harvard University Press.

Bernheimer, Charles. 1990a. Introduction to Part I. In *In Dora's Case: Freud-Hysteria-Feminism,* edited by Charles Bernheimer and Claire Kahane. 2d ed. New York: Columbia University Press.

[Brontë, Charlotte] 1974. *Shirley, a Tale.* Edited by Andrew and Judith Hook. Penguin English Library. Harmondsworth, England: Penguin Books.

Burgin, Victor, James Donald, and Cora Kaplan, eds. 1986. *Formations of Fantasy.* New York: Methuen.

Cixous, Hélène, and Catherine Clément. 1986. *The Newly Born Woman.* Translated by Betsy Wing. Minneapolis: University of Minnesota Press.

David-Ménard, Monique. 1989. *Hysteria from Freud to Lacan.* Ithaca: Cornell University Press.

Freud, Sigmund. 1959. *Standard Edition of the Complete Psychological Works.* Translated under the general editorship of James Strachey in collaboration with Anna Freud, assisted by Alix Strachey and Alan Tyson. 24 vols. London: The Hogarth Press and the Institute of Psychoanalysis.

Gay, Peter. 1984. *The Bourgeois Experience.* 2 vols. Vol. 1, *Education of the Senses.* Oxford: Oxford University Press.

Gilman, Sander L., et al., eds. 1993. *Hysteria beyond Freud.* Berkeley: University of California Press.

Heath, Stephen. 1981. *Questions of Cinema.* London: Macmillan.

Hertz, Neil. 1983. "Medusa's Head: Male Hysteria under Political Pressure." *Representations* 4 (Fall): 27-54.

[James, Henry]. 1976. *The Bostonians.* Edited by Alfred Habegger. Indianapolis: Bobbs-Merrill.

Krohn, Alan. 1978. *Hysteria: The Elusive Neurosis.* New York: International Universities Press.

Laqueur, Thomas. 1986. "Orgasm, Generation, and the Politics of Reproductive Biology." *Representations* 14 (Spring): 1-41.

Marcus, Steven. 1990. "Freud and Dora: Story, History, Case History." In *In Dora's Case: Freud-Hysteria-Feminism,* edited by Charles Bernheimer and Claire Kahane. 2d ed. New York: Columbia University Press.

Poovey, Mary. 1988. *Uneven Developments.* Chicago: University of Chicago Press.

Rivière, Joan. [1929] 1986. "Womanliness as Masquerade." In *Formations of Fantasy,* edited by Victor Burgin, James Donald, and Cora Kaplan. New York: Methuen.

Rousseau, George S. 1993. "A Strange Pathology." In *Hysteria beyond Freud,* edited by Sander L. Gilman et al. Berkeley: University of California Press.

Sayers, Janet. 1982. *Biological Politics: Feminist and Anti-Feminist Perspectives.* London: Tavistock; New York: Methuen.

Schreiner, Olive. 1976. *The Story of an African Farm.* New York: Schocken Books.

[Showalter, Elaine]. 1985. *The Female Malady: Women, Madness, and English Culture, 1830-1980.* New York: Pantheon.

———. 1990. *Sexual Anarchy.* New York: Viking.

———. 1993. "Hysteria, Feminism, and Gender." In *Hysteria beyond Freud.* Edited by Sandor Gilman et al. Berkeley: University of California Press.

Silverman, Kaja. 1992. *Male Subjectivity at the Margins.* New York: Routledge.

Smith-Rosenberg, Carroll. 1985. *Disorderly Conduct: Visions of Gender in Victorian America.* New York: Oxford University Press.

Veith, Ilza. 1965. *Hysteria: The History of a Disease.* Chicago: University of Chicago Press.

Welter, Barbara. 1966. "The Cult of True Womanhood: 1820-1860." *American Quarterly* 18 (Summer).

[Woolf, Virginia]. 1953. "Modern Fiction." In *The Common Reader.* First Series. Harvest Books. New York: Harcourt, Brace & World.

Evelyne Ender (essay date 1995)

SOURCE: "Nineteenth-Century Hysteria: The Medical Context," in *Sexing the Mind: Nineteenth-Century Fictions of Hysteria,* Cornell University Press, 1995, pp. 25-65.

[*In the following excerpt, Ender examines the ultimate convergence between differing explanations of hysteria—emotional/moral and physiological—and concludes that femininity is a predisposition for all of them.*]

> Hysteria! Why wouldn't this mystery become the matter and the substance of a literary work, this mystery that the Academy of medicine has not yet solved, and which is expressed in the case of women by the sensation of an ascending and asphyxiating lump (I am only talking about the main symptom) and which translates itself in the case of excitable men into powerlessness and a capacity for excesses of all kinds.
>
> —Baudelaire, *L'art romantique*

In May 1874 Gustave Flaubert wrote to his friend George Sand: "I am going to get rid of my congestion on the top of a mountain in Switzerland, following the advice of Doctor Hardy, who calls me 'a hysterical woman,' a profound statement, I find" (*Correspondance,* 467).[1] In the postscript of his next letter, signed "Cruchard," he added a tentative definition of his self-inflicted nickname: "More Cruchard than ever. I feel decrepit, flabby, worn out, sheik, deliquescent, in short, calm and moderate, which is the ultimate of decadence." In obedience to his doctor's prescription, he had just spent "twenty days on the Righi in order to breathe a little, to become sober, and to get rid of his neuropathy" (469). But Switzerland meant deep boredom: "Since you know Switzerland, no need to tell you more. And you would probably despise me too much if I told you that I am bored to death there" (475). A prolonged stay in a Magic Mountain village could indeed not have been the best remedy for this kind of hysterical behavior.

The letters of George Sand and Gustave Flaubert show that his hysteria took at times a more specific form, closer to the medical definitions. It is not only a disease of the imagination (such as his Emma Bovary experiences): the term describes as well his own ailing body. In a letter of 1867, Flaubert draws the list of his physical symptoms: "I feel palpitations in the heart for nothing—easy to understand, by the way, in an old hysteric like myself. For I maintain that men are hysterical just like women, and I am one of them. When I wrote *Salammbô* I had read 'the best authorities' on that subject and I have recognized all my symptoms: the *globus hystericus* and the harrowing pain at the back of the head. This is the outcome of our nice occupation: we torment ourselves body and soul" (*Corresponance,* 118). The fuller clinical picture would comprise as well certain hallucinations (described in a letter to Taine) and his seizures, which at the time were ascribed to his epilepsy, but might just as easily have been the paroxysmic expression of hysteria.

Flaubert's hysteria could be understood in its historical context as just another case in the epidemic of an illness so prevalent in his day that, according to Dr. Pierre Briquet (a contemporary of Flaubert), "one woman out of four as well as a sizable number of men seem to be affected by it."[2] It might also find a partial explanation in the writer's interest in medical textbooks. Flaubert, the son of a doctor, had read Bichat's *Anatomie générale* and his *Recherches physiologiques sur la vie et la mort,* Cabanis's *Rapport du physique et du moral,* Daremberg's *Histoire de la médecine* (and his *La médecine, histoires et doctrines*), and Garnier's *Traité des facultés de l'âme.* He also claimed to have studied "the best authors on hysteria," such as Jean-Louis Brachet (*Traité de l'hystérie*) and Pierre Briquet (*Traité clinique et thérapeutique de l'hystérie*). Given such abundant medical knowledge, one might risk the hypothesis that this case of hysteria may have been the outcome of readerly empathy—one which, under the writer's pen, produced descriptions and figurations that take on the appearance of the real, of a real case. Flaubert's hysteria thus belongs to literature, as an instance of the transformation of medical representations into literary production, as is attested by his letters to Sand on the subject.

The textbooks he had read drew on a variety of domains and discourses, and may well have encouraged the rich imaginative qualities that characterize his evocations of the illness. A nineteenth-century medical treatise typically would have combined, under the heading of hysteria, hard physical sciences (such as anatomy and physiology), clinical observations, speculations about the mind as well as philosophical and moral discussions, and mythical or literary examples. Matching the doctor's conception, the writer's hysteria expresses his aesthetic, moral, and psychological concerns. Flaubert's disquisitions on hysteria involve, moreover, a discussion of sexual difference, of that which at the time was called *le sexe*[3] For if, according to Naomi Schor, "their correspondence constitutes an exemplary attempt at carving out an intersubjective arena where sexual identity is shifting, mobile, severed from anatomy, unhampered by social norms" (*George Sand and Idealism,* 199), their exchanges on the theme of hysteria are the scene of an implicit, and sometimes explicit, questioning on the subject of the difference between the sexes. Thus Flaubert presents himself sometimes as *un vieil hystérique,* sometimes as *une femme hystérique,* and his insistence on being one or the other makes it clear that the subjective content of the illness must inevitably be gender-marked. In other words, the writer shows that although hysteria exists in both women (usually) and men (sometimes), its gender can never be a matter of indifference; hysteria seems, in effect, to have become the testing ground for sexual identities. The fullest enumeration of his symptoms opens the way for some thoughts on his powers of identification and on the sex changes they entail. While rereading *Consuelo* and *La comtesse de Rudolstadt* he felt "'amoureuse' de Liverani,"[4] and he concludes musingly that "this is because I have the two sexes maybe" (118).[5]

But this exchange of letters on hysteria takes a markedly more serious turn when George Sand, in her answer to Flaubert, expresses her ideas about sexual difference (*le sexe*). She responds to "Cruchard," in an unsigned letter:

> But what is it then to be hysterical? I have perhaps been that also. Maybe I am hysterical, but I don't know anything about it, since I never probed into this thing—I heard about it but did not study it. Is it not a kind of unease or anguish, caused by the desire of an impossible something or other? In that case, we are all affected by this strange illness, that is when we are endowed with some imagination; and why would such an illness have a sex?

> And there is more, for the people who are strong in anatomy: *there is only one sex.* A man and a woman. This is so much the same thing that it is hard to understand why societies have fed on a heap of subtle distinctions and reasonings on this subject. I have observed my son's childhood and development and the same in my daughter. My son was like myself, namely, much more of a woman than my daughter, who was a failed man. (*Correspondence,* 121)

What George Sand reveals here in substance is a conception of masculine and feminine as a difference within: the man and the woman, two declensions within the paradigm "one sex." While many of her contemporaries, such as the specialists in hysteria whose theories are discussed later in this chapter, were working hard at establishing a naturalized sexual identity, Sand expresses here her opposition to a model that ascribes a foundational value to the difference between the sexes. "There is only one sex" is underlined in Sand's text:

in its dismissal of a binary logic (one or the other sex), this statement would have had, in her day, the force of an oxymoron, and it is only within the modern notion of sexuality that it can really make sense. While acknowledging the existence of sexual difference, she highlights in her examples the versatility of its manifestations, which are detached from the anatomy, as if she had in mind some notions akin to our contemporary sexual positions, or to the French describing the assumption of sexual difference: "sexuation". She also acknowledges the effects of a belief in this difference—"the heap of subtle distinctions and reasonings"—and she concludes her discussion with an instance of what, to our modern critical gaze, might look like images of gendered subjectivities which would call for the words "feminine" and "masculine."

In her discussion of this passage, Naomi Schor argues that Sand's statement relies on a conventional model of androgyny; I suggest more optimistically that what the writer advances here, in a typically coy fashion, is the idea of gender.[6] Considering Sand's own disclaimer ("I don't know anything about this") it might of course be exaggerated to ascribe to her the elements of a theory of gender. After all, she developed her thoughts on the question almost casually, à propos of hysteria, and certainly made no claims for her scientific knowledge: since she had not studied the question, she could only speak from experience, as a mother. But if Sand is not a theoretician, let it be granted at least that here she writes about her awareness of gender.

In this conversation on hysteria she gets the better of Flaubert. Whereas he appears to flounder playfully in the murky limbo of his personal malaise, she provides a definition of the illness that approximates, in an uncanny fashion, what the philosopher Monique David-Ménard later writes on the question in 1986. Her notion that hysteria is the expression of a suffering bound up with the transgressions of the imagination or desire—hysteria as the pathological expression of the impossible—sketches the path to the philosopher's claim that hysteria is bound up with the failure of the symbolic, and is a construct of desire and thought around some impossible *jouissance*.[7] Whereas Flaubert's medical inclinations encourage him to play up the physical, bodily dimensions of the disease, Sand conceives of it as a phenomenon of the mind. When he insists on ascribing a sexual definition to the illness, she turns it into a universal human condition that touches those who have imagination.

My own inquiry into nineteenth-century medical texts on hysteria has led me to chart the rugged territory of a domain made up of science and imagination, where hysteria has become the figurehead for "the subtle distinctions and reasonings" that societies have fed upon the subject of sex. My inquiry traces as well the inscription of hysteria's symptoms and etiology on the

sexualized body, and from there into the mind, as part of a gendered identity. I thus show that, pace Sand, the disease has a sex, not given by nature of course, but produced by discursive formations infused with various mythologies concerning the female body and mind. But I might as well say at the outset that George Sand, and not Flaubert, has given the inspiration to this project: it was begun under the aegis of a feminist suspicion that an epidemic of hysteria of a kind that included no less than one woman out of four might teach more about the prejudice of male science than about hysteria or femininity, and would tell us more about minds than about bodies. The final section of this chapter thus shows how the "mental hysteria" (a term I owe to Jean-Jacques Virey) ascribed to nineteenth-century women is in effect the telltale sign of a regime of gender discrimination, where women function as the blank pages of men's texts, and where, moreover, sexual identity exists only as a parody or masquerade. While she plays, hysterically, at being a woman, he can reassure himself that he is a man.

Styles of the Flesh

Polymorphous, whimsical, elusive—this is how hysteria appears to the nineteenth-century doctor. Dr. Briquet, for instance, with his acknowledged taste for "the study of positivist science," began his detailed book on the subject by expressing strong reservations, for "hysteria is the very model of the unstable, the irregular, the fantastic, the unexpected . . . it is governed by no law, no rule . . . and no serious theory" (*Traité clinique et thérapeutique de l'hystérie*, iii), and yet he ended up publishing a treatise of more than seven hundred pages on the subject. The quest for the meaning of hysteria requires indeed the skills and dedication of a devoted reader: as a sign reinvented by every patient, it can only respond to the most persistent and detailed inquiry. To pierce its secrets would mean achieving distinction, and like so many of his colleagues Briquet seemed drawn by the very difficulty of the pursuit: the studies on hysteria seemed to proliferate in the nineteenth century at the same rate as the illness itself, like an epidemic.[8]

The first concern is to establish, with the help of anatomy or physiology, the organic origins of the illness. But because its manifestations are so various and complex, and the treatment so hazardous, a broader etiological approach is also necessary. Its enigmatic and sometimes spectacular aspects speak to the imagination and encourage an aesthetic approach, which is vividly present in descriptions that dwell at length on the bodily symptoms. But the body of the nineteenth-century hysteric is also the site of social and ethical regulations and of a power struggle whose violence is unmistakeable. "Nothing is more punitive than to give a disease a meaning—that meaning being invariably a moralistic one. Any important disease whose causality is murky, and for which treatment is ineffectual, tends to be awash in significance," writes Susan Sontag in her study of tuberculosis (58). The truth of her remark has found painful confirmation in our AIDS-haunted time. The texts on hysteria reveal a similar connivence between, on the one hand, the desire to know and understand the disease and, on the other, the urge to impose a whole array of moral norms. This preliminary inquiry into nineteenth-century medical representations of hysteria aims therefore at highlighting the complex mesh of discourses of knowledge, desire, and power that coalesce in the image of the hysteric. It focuses simultaneously on the emergence of a new topography of the disease, which reveals, in its remapping of the body-mind divide, an increasingly complex image of femininity.

The works of Voisin, Virey, Brachet, and Briquet, which span the years 1826 to 1859, all reject the older anatomical theories that tended to ascribe hysteria to the disorders of the uterus or to the whole genital system. For these doctors the origin of hysteria lies in some inherent predisposition: the hysteric is more easily affected by certain existential or social predicaments because endowed with a surplus of some quality such as passion (for Voisin), sensibility (Virey), nervous excitability (Brachet), or impressionability (Briquet). However, except for Voisin, these doctors persist in their conviction that the illness must be related to some anatomical or physiological dysfunctioning. The older model of the disease connected the symptoms to a specific part of the body marked by some excessive or pathological process. The new doctors too believe that hysteria originates in the body, but not in one part only; the totality of the female body, in its substance and its behavior, now participates in the illness.[9] Knife in hand, they therefore delve into its very fiber in order to detect the traces of an innate susceptibility to hysteria.

In *Traité de l'hystérie* Brachet, for example, celebrates with zest and in almost poetic terms the radical difference that characterizes the anatomized female body. The undisguised aim of this poetry of the shapes, tissues, organs, and physiological systems is to render legible, in the signs of nature, that is, in the organic body, an image of woman founded on the complex elaboration of a radical difference between the sexes. Extrapolating, systematizing, the doctor invents the features of a femininity that is no longer only ascribed to the reproductive sphere: women's bodies are inherently, in their smallest details, marked by significant distinctions.

Brachet's chapter titled "Etudes du physique et du moral de la femme" provides a good example. Having summarized most of the received opinions on the illness, the physician opposes to them his own scientific competence: long used to the amphitheater, he knows how to "perceive those nuances which distinguish women" (63). For indeed, "It is not only through the uterus that woman is what she is; she is such in her whole constitution. From head to foot, outside and inside, whatever part of the body you examine, you will find that she is everywhere the same. Everywhere will you find that her tissues and her organs differ from the same tissues and organs in a man" (63). But one need not be an anatomist, since the difference is perfectly clear on the surface:

> What a difference already in outward appearance, between this elegant and pretty figure and that tall and vigorously built body; between these graceful and round lines and those bones and muscles harshly revealed! What a difference between these soft and delicate features, and those protuberances, rough and vigorous, and those profound depressions. Doesn't her delicate and bright complexion distinguish her from man's complexion? Doesn't her hair always distinguish her from man's hair? Isn't her hair and the floss that shades some parts of her body much more delicate and softer? Don't we find significant differences between the sweet and sentimental expression of her physiognomy and the rude, martial, and sometimes harsh or majestic appearance of man? Every part of her body shows the same differences. Every part reflects the woman in her. Brow, nose, eyes, mouth, ears, chin, cheek, everything has its singularity, everything takes the imprint of her sex. (63-64)

Brachet approaches his anatomical inquiry into woman with the imagination of a poet; in his hand, the surgeon's knife that uncovers the organs, the tissues, the fibers, turns easily into the writer's pen. The descriptions of the female body are redolent with epithets evoking her delicacy, her softness, or refinement. Such "complicity between aesthetics and medicine" produces indeed what Judith Butler, in her study of gender, calls "styles of the flesh" (139).[10]

While they try to establish the characteristic features of the female body, the medical descriptions intersect with contemporary literary representations. Some pages of Brachet's treatise seem to have been lifted out of Balzac's *La peau de chagrin* or *Le lys dans la vallée*.[11] This is a common feature of our doctors' works. Not only does their language mime that of literary descriptions, but they often borrow, their prime clinical examples from fiction or mythology. These hysterical women go by the names Cleopatra, Lucretia, Phèdre, or Clarissa. Fictional creatures and cases drawn from the doctor's practice belong to one single descriptive project; they are part of a "generalized continuum which collectively produces the category 'woman'" (Solomon-Godeau, 236). That it should be possible to relate these texts on hysteria to Abigail Solomon-Godeau's study of erotic photography reveals to what extent Brachet and his colleagues drew on the conventions of nineteenth-century representation.[12] If woman as a unified concept exists, as she insistently does in these texts on hysteria, it is as a uniform, unified type. Thus Brachet can write: "Women seem to have been thrown into one common mould: among them one comes across a much more restricted variety of constitutions than among men. The exceptions are a mistake of nature" (64). Not surprisingly then, the doctor's search for the significant differences constitutive of "woman" both relies on and produces an amazing number of clichés. Scientific observation, from surface to depth into the inmost recesses of her anatomy, (re)produces the nineteenth-century topoi of what constitutes femininity. The treatise on hysteria looks increasingly like an *étude de moeurs,* a manual of hygiene or a treatise on morality. Science gives way to myth.

This close and spontaneous association of body and mind, a body that is intimately scanned by the anatomist's gaze and a mind scrutinized for its *affections morales,* is related to the emergence of a psychological discourse on the subject.[13] But more importantly, as Judith Butler suggests, this "psychological core" appears to be linked to the notions of "the ineffable interiority of [the subject's] sex and its true identity" (136). Given the systematic and repetitive nature of the doctors' descriptions, a brief overview will suffice. Voisin, who confines himself to a few general observations on anatomy, attributes to the female character the very same features of delicacy, softness, and grace that Brachet saw in the woman's body. Likewise Briquet, who tends to emphasize the moral aspect of the illness, resorts to a vocabulary that can be ascribed indifferently to external, physical traits and moral, psychological aspects. However, the descriptions of anatomy and physiology are increasingly related to an emerging psychological sphere, while the etiology of the disease is ascribed to some inner, mental causes. When Virey and Brachet insist on examining hysteria from a scientific perspective, they nevertheless end up reproducing, in the languages of anatomy and physiology, what are in fact its "moral" features. Whereas Voisin, who seems more interested in the "spiritual intimacy" of woman, speaks the language of sensibility and of Rousseau: "While my predecessors have been impressed by the striking qualities of woman, they have not given enough consideration to her sensibility, the natural violence of her feelings and of her inclinations, the predicaments of her social position . . . ; in one word, they have not read deeply enough into her heart; they have not unveiled its secrets, seen its agitations and torments, and, because of their ignorance of this *inner moral situation,* they have looked elsewhere for the causes of these nervous illnesses," (131, emphasis mine). Thirty years later, Pierre Briquet grapples with the etiology of hysteria by probing relentlessly into woman's "inner moral situation" and asking for the stories of her unhappiness. By 1859 the "female

malady" is indeed firmly anchored in the psychological sphere.[14]

Meanwhile, in the remaining observations on the physiology of woman, the drift toward speculation has become very apparent. Not that physiology produces knowledge about sexual difference; on the contrary, the fantasies born from a collective imagination of femininity sustain the errancies of the physiological inquiry. Brachet, for example, affirms, but cannot demonstrate, that the female nervous system is more impressionable so that the delicate nervous fiber of a woman "receives an influence that is quicker, more active and delicate, but also less strong and deep" (*Traité de l'hystérie,* 66). The idea is soon made into a principle so that he can adduce an impressive congeries of arguments: woman's impressionability is the source of her lymphatic temper, of a noticeable difference in her excretory functions, it makes her reach her full development earlier and have "rounder, softer and more delicate curves" (67). "Everybody knows," writes Brachet, "how easily the tears flow in a woman, how her perspiration and her cutaneous secretions come easily and abundantly, how quick her digestion is, because of the ready formation of gastric juice and of the more immediate secretion of her spleen. How finally the secreted urines seem to press and accumulate in her bladder to be evacuated more readily" (67). On the strength of such "observations," situated in a nebulous zone between physiology and the theory of emotions, Brachet comes to his decisive point: "you will see how both sensibility and mobility are different in the woman from what they are in the man. . . . Since we are so to speak immersed in an atmosphere of incitations of all kinds, the effect in woman is that her cerebral *appareil sensitif* is constantly active, that it continually receives strong impressions, that its life, in short, is only made of sensations, it is a real life of sensations" (68).[15] And he concludes, having asserted that this is why "painting and especially music have such a powerful sway over her," that "in man the intelligence comes first, and the impression second" (72), whereas "sensibility constitutes the whole of woman" (75).

"What is the state of a nervous system that is capable of such burning sensibility?" Virey asked in 1834 in the middle of his treatise, *De la femme sous ses rapports physiologique, moral et littéraire,* which deals abundantly with hysteria. This question still haunted Brachet in 1847; he tackled it at the end of his chapter "Etudes du physique et du moral de la femme." If one admits that women have a natural predisposition toward hysteria, he asks, why are they not all hysterical? Medical science is not yet able to answer such a question (which, he claims, is of "une haute physiologie pathologique") with a demonstration. But the conviction remains that, inscribed in the physiological processes, there must be a difference (*une modification*) that can account for this natural, almost spontaneous evolution from femininity into pathology. What such reasoning makes apparent, of course, is that while women are characterized by a modification, they can only figure as an exception or an accident in a system whose norm is the masculine. According to Brachet, "We shall then admit as a demonstrated fact that woman presents a special physiological modification of her nervous system, and especially of her cerebral nervous system; that she owes to this modification the differences that she presents in the exercise of this function, in her intelligence and in her character. We can then conclude that her greater predisposition toward hysteria is due to this modification, whereas hypochondria would typically be a man's lot" (*Traité de l'hystérie,* 96-97). In fact, the physiological cause of hysteria and of femininity (for so neat is their alignment that one can be substituted for the other) remains obscure and ungraspable. But against such uncertainties Brachet offers a single, resounding statement, "l'hystérie, c'est la femme," which succeeds in addressing the medical question (it is women—and not men usually—who are hysterical) as well as the sexual ideology (women are, by nature, hysterical). Mapped onto sexual difference, mental illnesses can be symmetrically divided: Brachet's treatise on hysteria finds its counterpart in his study on hypochondria, a masculine complaint.

In 1859 Briquet took up the same challenge and concluded with similarly ambiguous results, as a closer examination of his arguments shows. The following pronouncement relies on a problematic confusion between nature, represented by "l'encéphale de la femme," and culture, in the guise of a "destinée providentielle": "It is well established that there exists in the brain a portion that is destined to the affective passions; now, because of the social destination that has been assigned to her, in woman this portion is endowed with a quicker sensibility than that of man. From the liveliness of this sensibility derives a mode of reaction which is also particular to woman and which, whenever an impression on that portion of the brain has been either too strong or too painful, manifests itself in reactions which are also peculiar to her" (395). From the impersonal phrase "it is well established" (similar to Brachet's earlier formulation "everybody knows"), down to the slippery logical alignment, every rhetorical move of such a paragraph points to the confusions of the argument. In the guise of etiology, the science of hysteria can often do no better than confirm its own assumptions and prejudices.

Yet the seven hundred pages of Pierre Briquet's *Traité clinique et thérapeutique de l'hystérie* surely represent a monument of a positivist science. As a physician working in the Hôpital de la Charité, he and his assistants compiled statistics on 430 cases. He emphasizes in his treatise the etiology of the illness, which is skillfully organized along the main categories of *causes* *prédisposantes* and *causes déterminantes,* and, unlike his predecessors, Briquet kept his work free from literary contamination. He seemed to have read every traditional source on the subject, from Hippocrates to Galen, and was also well acquainted with the theories of his contemporaries. Confirmation for his hypotheses was sought among his partners, the urban family doctors: he was indeed determined to avoid the pitfalls of a traditional scholarly approach and to rely on observation and experience. But his magnum opus demonstrates little beyond the fact that the hysteric suffers from her propensity or her predisposition toward suffering. Since hysteria results from the coincidence between a developed sensibility and some particular circumstance or situation destined to affect it, and since women are by nature more sensitive (Briquet likes to use the word *impressionable*), then hysteria is necessarily connected to the female condition:

> In order to fulfill the great and noble mission devolved upon her, it was indispensable that [woman] be endowed with a great susceptibility to affective impressions [*impressions affectives*], that she be able somehow to feel everything in herself, and unfortunately, here as in everything else, the good can also produce evil, hysteria thus comes from this great susceptibility to affections. Let us imagine a man endowed with the faculty of being affected in the same way as a woman, he would become hysterical and consequently unfit for his predestined role, namely, that of protection and of strength. Hysteria in a man means the overthrow of the laws constitutive of our society. (101)

The opinion of our four doctors can be summarized as follows: Hysteria: *cause prédisposante* = femininity, *cause déterminante* = excess of emotion. "La femme est faite pour sentir et sentir c'est presque l'hystérie" (woman's destiny is to feel, but to feel is almost hysteria, 50), writes Briquet, and not surprisingly, he finds that one out of four women is affected by the disease. At this point, nineteenth-century hysteria looks very much like a parody of femininity. The cases of hysteria detected in men are very rare (one out of a hundred, Brachet claims [*Traité de l'hystérie,* 492]), and they are invariably ascribed to a process of feminization due to a faulty education or a defective constitution; it is such a short step from femininity to hysteria that in a man the illness can only be an aberration or else the sign of degeneracy. Thus Brachet writes: "This is why the man who is feminized by some constitutive predisposition, whether innate or acquired, by his education, by some prolonged or special illness, by a languid and overtly sentimental life, by excessive sensual pleasures, and so on, this is why, I say, this man who seems to have eyes, feet and hands only *ad honores* will be liable to experience hysteria" (98).[16] Indeed, the nineteenth-century study of hysteria participates in a conceptualization of a radical difference between the sexes, seemingly grounded in anatomical and physiological knowledge but in fact based on moral and cultural assumptions. This difference must be present from birth: Brachet denounces Rousseau's conviction that "in childhood there was no sex" (*Traité de l'hystérie,* 65). Although education or surroundings may exert some influence, the determining factor of hysteria consists in being female. When the whole of the woman's body bespeaks her propensity toward the illness, the discourse on hysteria all too easily enters into a circular logic, which plays off hysteria against femininity. Woman "is" her anatomy and her physiology, and beyond the aberrations, corruptions, and pathology that threaten her undoing, she remains herself, that is, as nature made her. "La femme reste femme" (76), writes Brachet, and "in spite of their efforts and their energetic style, one finds confirmation of the woman in Mme Rolland, Mme Deffant, in Mme Staël [*sic*], and even in this George Sand who appears to be ashamed of the sex that she should have honored" (73).

Such a belief defines the scope and the intent of the *médecine morale* that was professed by Voisin, Virey, Brachet, and Briquet: "true medicine in the case of women always consists in reinstating the order of nature" (*De la femme,* 74) writes Virey. Once he has described the illness and explored its causes, the doctor must find the necessary remedies to bring woman back to herself ("rendre la femme à elle-même"), to her own sphere and to her natural state or condition ("à son naturel"). Brachet presents in his concluding remarks what looks like a radical prophylactic: "one needs then, from very early on, to instruct the young girl to be what she is, and to be it fully: this is the only way to prepare for her a life of calm and to ensure that she will be happy" (*Traité de l'hystérie,"* 497).

"Does being female constitute a 'natural fact' or a cultural performance, or is 'naturalness' constituted through discursively constrained performative acts that produce the body through and within the categories of sex?" asks Judith Butler in the first pages of *Gender Trouble* (x). The preceding pages, with their emphasis on the systems of knowledge that defined or produced the nineteenth-century hysteric, appear to provide an indirect answer to this question. . . .

Notes

[1] The translations of the Flaubert-Sand letters are my own, but were emended whenever I felt Aimée Mackenzie or Francis Steegmuller provided better versions.

[2] The figure, taken from Briquet's extensive study, is cited in Pierre Larousse's *Grand dictionnaire universel du XIXème siècle.*

[3] *Le sexe* is what distinguishes men from women (from the Latin word *secare,* "to cut, to divide"). But this epistolary conversation between Flaubert and Sand shows that the older sense of the term, which emphasizes the mere fact of difference, was gradually giving way to the modern concept of sexuality. The *Grand Robert* proposes 1889 as the year *sexe* was first used to mean "l'ensemble des questions sexuelles (v. *sexualité, érotisme*)," while the more traditional *Littré* does not mention the newer sense of the word.

[4] The quotation marks emphasize the irregularity of the feminine grammatical gender as applied to the male subject. The translation of these nineteenth-century French authors reveals indeed the emergence of a notion of gender that is no longer merely grammatical; it testifies to a growing awareness of the complex cultural meanings associated with sexual difference. Gender is not merely a fact of language, but a question of subjective definition.

[5] In French, this passage reads, "j'ai les deux sexes." This formulation, in terms of "having a sex" rather than "being of one or the other sex," now seems awkward. The linguistic shift, however, registers a major change of sensibility, namely, the emergence of a gendered consciousness or being. Working on a parallel line of enquiry, Riley concludes her discussion of the place assigned to woman in the nineteenth-century elaboration of spirituality with the revealing statement: "As the neutral domains of the soul had contracted, so it had become possible to *be* a sex" (*"Am I That Name?"* 43).

[6] Naomi Schor describes this passage as "a curious combination of the radical and the conventional," but emphasizes in her interpretation what she deems the conventional aspects of Sand's conception, exemplified in her "sexism" and even "heterosexism" as well as in her single-sex model "of the order of the androgyne" (*George Sand and Idealism,* 196). My own *parti pris* goes the other way; however, in the last section of Chapter 5, I analyze Sand's intellectual timidity and her "hysterical" resistance to thinking.

[7] Monique David-Ménard defines this construct in "How the Mystery of Conversion is Constructed," pages 47-63 of *Hysteria from Freud to Lacan: Body and Language in Psychoanalysis.*

[8] This suggests, of course, that the illness results from a certain cultural and ideological configuration, which is what contemporary epidemiological approaches show as well: "The too frequent confusion . . . of typically socialized feminine behaviour with the diagnosis of hysteria must be kept in mind in any discussion of the epidemiology of the hysterical personality" (Mardi J. Horowitz, *Hysterical Personality,* 153).

[9] Hysteria enables us to document a historical process that has been described by the philosopher Denise Riley: "The whole meaning of 'woman' had been trans-

formed once the concept of the female person as thoroughly sexed through all her regions of being had become entrenched" (*"Am I That Name?"* 43).

[10] For a discussion of the complicity between aesthetics and medicine, see Barbara Johnson, "Is Female to Male as Ground Is to Figure?" as well as Michèle Le Doeuff, "Les chiasmes de Pierre Roussel." On the question of the stylization of the body, Butler writes: "if the body is not a 'being,' but a variable boundary, a surface whose permeability is politically regulated, a signifying practice within a cultural field of gender hierarchy and compulsory heterosexuality, then what language is left. . . . I suggest that gendered bodies are so many 'styles of the flesh.' These styles are never fully self-styled, for styles have a history, and those histories condition and limit the possibilities" (*Gender Trouble,* 139).

[11] This represents, as Anthony Mortimer has reminded me, a case of reciprocal influences, and the reverse applies as well: Balzac was fascinated by medicine and often used medical metaphors in his own fiction.

[12] See Abigail Solomon-Godeau's *Photography at the Dock: Essays on Photographic History, Institution, and Practices,* in particular, "Reconsidering Erotic Photography: Notes for a Project of Historical Salvage," which belongs to the section of the book titled "Photography and Sexual Difference."

[13] The term *moral* in the context of nineteenth-century psychiatry can be devoid of ethical connotations. It refers merely to "what belongs to the soul, in opposition to what belongs to the physical aspect" (*Littré*); it is synonymous with *mental, physique (Trésors de la langue francaise).* In the medical context, the term owes its popularity to Pierre Cabanis's study *Rapports du physique et du moral de l'homme* published in 1808. This *médecine morale* is discussed more fully, through a literary example, in Chapter 5.

[14] I borrowed this phrase from Elaine Showalter's groundbreaking study, *The Female Malady: Women, Madness, and English Culture, 1830-1980.*

[15] Or should one say "her life" rather than "its life"? The grammatical ambiguities of Brachet's prose make it impossible to distinguish if the phenomenon characterizes woman as a whole, or only a physiological process. The scientific description may be no more than a decoy destined to confirm the received opinion that "woman" equals "sensations."

[16] Brachet used the phrase "avoir l'hystérie," as one would say "avoir la gale" or "avoir la fièvre." This suggests that while women *are* hysterical, men catch hysteria like a foreign body or infection.

Works Cited

Baudelaire, Charles. *Curiosités esthétiques et L'art romantique.* Paris: Garnier, 1962.

Brachet, Jean-Louis. *Traité complet de l'hypochondrie.* Paris: Baillière, 1844.

———. *Traité de l'hystérie.* Paris: Baillière, 1847.

Briquet, Pierre. *Traité clinique et thérapeutique de l'hystérie.* Paris: Baillière, 1859.

Butler, Judith. *Gender Trouble: Feminism and the Subversion of Identity.* New York: Routledge, 1990.

David-Ménard, Monique. *Hysteria from Freud to Lacan: Body and Language in Psychoanalysis.* Trans. Catherine Porter. Ithaca: Cornell University Press, 1989.

Flaubert, Gustave. *The Letters of Gustave Flaubert, 1830-1857.* Ed. and trans. Francis Steegmuller. Cambridge: Harvard University Press, 1980.

———. *Madame Bovary.* Trans. Alan Russell. Harmondsworth: Penguin, 1987.

———. *Oeuvres.* Vol. I. Ed. A. Thibaudet and R. Dumesnil. Pléiade ed. Paris: Gallimard, 1966.

———. *Oeuvres complètes de Gustave Flaubert: Correspondance.* Paris: Connard, 1927.

Flaubert, Gustave, and George Sand. *Correspondance,* Ed. Alphonse Jacobs. Paris: Flammarion, 1981.

Horowitz, Mardi J. *Hysterical Personality.* New York: Jason Aronson, 1977.

Johnson, Barbara. "Is Female to Male as Ground Is to Figure?" In *Feminism and Psychoanalysis,* ed. Richard Feldstein and Judith Roof. Ithaca: Cornell University Press, 1989.

Larousse, Pierre, ed. *Grand dictionnaire universel du XIXème siècle.* Paris: Larousse, 1865-76.

Le Doeuff, Michèle. "Les chiasmes de Pierre Roussel (du savoir imaginaire à l'imaginaire savant)." In *L'imaginaire philosophique.* Paris: Payot, 1980.

Riley, Denise. *"Am I That Name?": Feminism and the Category of "Women" in History.* Minneapolis: University of Minnesota Press, 1988.

Sand, George. *Correspondance.* Vol. III. Ed. Georges Lubin. Paris: Garnier, 1967.

————. *Correspondance*. Vol. IV. Ed. Georges Lubin. Paris: Garnier, 1968.

————. *The George Sand-Gustave Flaubert Letters*. Trans. Aimée Mackenzie. Chicago: Academy Press, 1977. First ed. 1929.

[Schor, Naomi]. *George Sand and Idealism*. New York: Columbia University Press, 1993.

Showalter, Elaine. *The Female Malady: Women, Madness, and English Culture, 1830-1980*. New York: Pantheon, 1985.

Solomon-Godeau, Abigail. *Photography at the Dock: Essays on Photographic History, Institutions, and Practices*. Minneapolis: University of Minnesota Press, 1991.

Virey, Jean-Jacques. *De la femme sous ses rapports physiologique, moral et littéraire*. 3d ed. Brussels: Louis Hauman, 1834.

————. *Histoire naturelle du genre humain*. Paris: Crochard, 1824.

Voisin, François. *Des causes morales et physiques des maladies mentales et de quelques autres affections nerveuses telles que l'hystérie, la nymphomanie et le satyriasis*. Paris: Baillière, 1826.

THE GENDER OF HYSTERIA

Jan Goldstein (essay date 1991)

SOURCE: "The Uses of Male Hysteria: Medical and Literary Discourse in Nineteenth-Century France," in *Representations*, Vol. 34, Spring, 1991, pp. 134-65.

[*In the excerpt that follows, Goldstein argues that during the nineteenth century the phenomenon of male hysteria was developed through opposing interpretations: the medical community used it to reinscribe conventional gender definitions, while writers subverted such norms by associating hysteria with the desire for androgyny.*]

In the winter of 1867, Gustave Flaubert wrote to his good friend George Sand that he continued "to fiddle with" (*tripoter*) his current novel while living in complete solitude in the country. He passed entire weeks, he said, without exchanging a word with another human being and could perhaps best be compared to an anchorite whose "nights are black as ink" and who was "surrounded by a silence like that of the desert." In such an environment, he went on,

the sensibility becomes inordinately exalted. I experience flutterings of the heart for no reason at all—an understandable thing, moreover, in an old hysteric like me. For I maintain that men can be hysterics just like women, and that I am one. . . . I have recognized all my symptoms: the ball [rising in the throat], the [sensation of the] nail in the back of the skull.[1]

Some years later, in another letter to Sand, he mentioned with a hint of satisfaction that this self-diagnosis had been confirmed, if partially in jest, by a noted Paris medical authority. In making plans to vacation in the mountains of Switzerland, Flaubert was, he said, "obeying the advice of Dr. Hardy, who calls me 'an hysterical woman'—a phrase that I find profound."[2] So taken was Flaubert with this remark that he repeated it in another letter written the same day: "Dr. Hardy . . . calls me an hysterical old woman. 'Doctor,' I tell him, 'you are perfectly right.'"[3]

Flaubert's references to himself as hysterical, of which several more instances could be cited, raise the issue of the gender of hysteria in the nineteenth century. Clearly these references depend for their arresting force upon the audience's automatic association of hysteria with women, an association indelibly imprinted on the term by its ancient Greek etymology ("uterus") and its long, subsequent social development. But at the same time Flaubert's self-depictions violate and sever the association they assume. They suggest that if nineteenth-century hysteria was a conceptual space for the conventional, stereotypical definition of femininity, it was also, by that same token, potentially a conceptual space for the subversion of gender stereotypes. Through partaking of the pathological condition "hysteria," the man Flaubert might also lay claim to the attributes of femininity it had come to epitomize—here, nervous hypersensitivity, vulnerability, self-absorption—and hence implicitly achieve something of the status of androgyny. Applied by men to women, and most typically by male doctors to their female patients, the category "hysteria" was inevitably bound up in relations of power and generally served a stigmatizing, repressive function. But applied by a man to himself, that same category might disclose radical possibilities.

The purpose of this essay is to explore what might be called a contrapuntal tendency in the nineteenth-century French discourse about hysteria: the manner in which hysteria was used to destabilize the very gender definitions it had helped, and was still helping, to put into place. This contrapuntal tendency made itself heard only occasionally. It derived from the particular relationship between literary and medical discourse in nineteenth-century France, which ensured that hysteria would have a career in each discourse and, moreover, that these two careers would diverge. Hence, before proceeding further, we need to consider that literary-medical relationship and sketch it in broad outline.

We can approach it, or at least one side of it, by observing that Flaubert's flexible and creative manipulation of the category "hysteria" seems to have depended on his familiarity with technical discussions of the disease. When he announced to Sand that he was a male hysteric in 1867, he bolstered that assertion by citing the medical authorities: "When I was writing *Salammbô,* I read 'the best authors' on that subject, and I recognized all my symptoms."[4] In fact, Flaubert's researches into the medical literature on psychopathology long antedated the period at the end of the 1850s when he began *Salammbô.* His first "psycho-medical studies," as he called them, and which he described as having "so much beguiled" him, accompanied his work on *The Temptation of Saint Anthony* in the latter half of the 1840s; reminiscing on these studies, he could exclaim appreciatively, "There are treasures to be discovered in that material."[5]

We know very little about what, exactly, Flaubert read on hysteria at any point in his life, but that he had some direct exposure to the concept of male hysteria, and was aware of its controversial status in the medical community, seems probable. As part of his preparation for *Salammbô,* he consulted Dr. Hector Landouzy's *Traité complet de l'hystérie* (1846), a hefty tome that devotes a few pages to a skeptical and ultimately inconclusive review of the evidence for male hysteria offered by other physicians. Flaubert's careful, highly selective notes on Landouzy omit, however, any reference to this section of the text.[6] Flaubert was also in the habit of consulting the vast, multivolume medical dictionaries that the French produced during the nineteenth century to codify medical knowledge. Replying to Sainte-Beuve's review of *Salammbô,* for example, he protested that the ointment containing "bitches' milk" that the character Hanno rubs on his diseased skin was "not a 'joke,' but is *still* used as a remedy for leprosy; see the *Dictionnaire des sciences médicales,* article 'Leprosy.'"[7] Hence it is likely that Flaubert read the 1824 article on hysteria in the *Dictionnaire de médecine,* which argues strongly for the existence (though rarity) of hysteria in men.[8]

But whether or not he actually encountered the hypothesis of male hysteria in print, the catalogue of hysterical symptoms that he learned from other technical sources enabled him to interpret as hysterical the disturbing bodily phenomena he experienced firsthand. He practically acknowledged this as his modus operandi in a letter of 1859. "Every time you reflect on yourself, you find yourself sick; it is an axiom, be convinced of it! People beginning to study medicine discover every infirmity in themselves. . . . I have been through it and can say something about it."[9]

Flaubert's close relationship with medical knowledge was typical of that of many of his confreres. For reasons that have not yet been fully investigated, the men who became the canonical masters of the nineteenth-century French novel were all unusually well attuned to developments in medical science, especially those in the emergent specialty of psychiatry. Thus Stendhal could be found in the library of the Paris Faculty of Medicine in 1805 reading the recently published treatise on insanity by Dr. Philippe Pinel, the founding father of French psychiatry; he subsequently attempted to obtain the book for his personal collection.[10] Honoré de Balzac, who depicted himself as the taxonomist of the social world, read the medical literature voraciously, and his familiarity with the work of the Paris psychiatrist Etienne-Jean Georget, the chief popularizer of the new disease entity of monomania, led to a rather substantial population of monomaniacs among the characters of *La Comédie humaine.*[11] Flaubert's well-documented taste for medical literature seems to have stemmed from two biographical facts: he was the son of a provincial doctor, even growing up in a family apartment within the Rouen city hospital; and from early adulthood on, he was the intermittent victim of convulsive nervous seizures to which no clear diagnostic label could be affixed.[12] Emile Zola learned many of the principles of heredity he subsequently put to use in constructing the Rougon-Macquart series from a treatise by the psychiatrist Prosper Lucas.[13] Finally, Marcel Proust shared Flaubert's background as the son of a physician. In fact, the admissions registers of the Salpêtrière contain diagnoses of hystero-epilepsy signed by Dr. Adrien Proust, sometimes on the same page as similar diagnoses under the signature of Dr. Jean-Martin Charcot.[14]

Literary discourse and medical discourse intersected repeatedly in France during the nineteenth century, but it is striking that, at the points of intersection, the traffic went one way only. If nineteenth-century French novelists sought in medical texts superior insight into the human psyche, or scientific legitimation of their native intuitions, or a borrowed voice of authority with which to address the reading public, nineteenth-century French psychiatrists remained professionally uninterested in literary resources. One of the few psychiatric comments that I have found on the application of literary to psychiatric method condemns it outright, depicting the literary sensibility as a pitfall rather than a benefit to the psychiatric practitioner. In a discussion of styles of clinical observation in psychiatry, Dr. Jean-Pierre Falret noted at mid century that a highly distortive style resulted when the physician unwittingly imitated the novelist. Seeking to replace the chaos of nature with the order of art, such a physician ended up perceiving and representing each patient he encountered as a "character" in La Bruyère's sense, a person governed by a single passion or idea. He remained unaware of all the disconfirming clinical evidence screened out for the sake of his artistry. This observational style based on literary models, Falret concluded disparagingly, belonged to the "infancy" of the psychiatric specialty.[15]

In a formal treatise on hashish and insanity published in 1845, the psychiatrist Jacques-Joseph Moreau de Tours did, to be sure, quote a long account of the effects of smoking that drug written by Théophile Gautier (for whom Moreau had served as supplier). Moreau even initially expressed confidence about admitting the litterateur into the medical sanctum, noting that "hashish could find no more worthy an interpreter than the poetic imagination of Monsieur Gautier." But in his very next sentence, he seems to have been assailed by doubts—or by anticipated objections from his medical colleagues—about the propriety of using a literary source as scientific evidence. "Is there any need to add," he asked defensively, "that the brilliance of the style, and also perhaps a slight exaggeration in the language, should arouse no distrust about the truthfulness of this writer, who is, after all, only describing sensations already familiar to those who have some experience of hashish?"[16] In a very different context, the psychiatrist François Lélut revealed a quite similar belief in the incompatibility of literature and mental medicine. Bringing a collection of his own poetry before the public in 1840, he noted that its contents had been completed some twelve years before, when he was a young man in his mid twenties just embarking upon a psychiatric career. "What prevented me from publishing it then was the necessity I felt of making a profession of the science of man, a profession whose seriousness admits of no frivolous diversion."[17]

Toward the end of the century, as the psychiatric case study began to evolve into a long and complicated narrative form, a French psychiatrist might comment in passing that his account of a particular patient "savored of a novel."[18] But no self-congratulation should be inferred from such a remark, or from the comparable remark of Pierre Janet that a full description of his patients would more nearly approximate "a novel of manners and morals than it would a clinical observation."[19] Even Freud, who would later break from the strictly scientific mode of nineteenth-century medicine and tout the ability of psychoanalysis to synthesize science and poetic insight, experienced obvious discomfort with the *Studies on Hysteria* that he produced in the early 1890s. "Like other neuropathologists," he confessed in the middle of that work, "I was trained to employ local diagnoses and electro-prognosis, and it still strikes me as strange that the case studies I write should read like short stories and that, as one might say, they lack the serious stamp of science."[20]

For nineteenth-century psychiatrists, the "serious stamp of science" entailed avoidance not only of literary

modalities but also of subjective evidence. While empathy was a guiding principle of the pioneering psychiatric therapy called the moral treatment early in the century,[21] in matters of the classification and diagnosis of disease, objectivity and distance seem always to have been the unspoken rules. Even after the strict antinomies of mad and sane broke down in the latter part of the century, giving way to the intermediary zone of *demi-folie,* the psychiatrist was not supposed to recognize the "diseased" aspects of the patient in himself.[22] A psychiatric diagnosis was in the nineteenth century something that a doctor gave to the patient as an "other." Not until the advent of psychoanalysis would subjectivity be valorized as an appropriate instrument of medical-scientific investigation.

Thus nineteenth-century novelists such as Flaubert might be said to have had a larger repertory, a fuller range, than nineteenth-century psychiatrists. They absorbed and exploited medical knowledge, but even if they professed to emulate scientific objectivity— Flaubert's famous *impassibilité*—the free play of the imagination and the resources of subjective experience were still open to them. This difference between a capacious and a restricted discursive range is reflected in the difference between the literary and the medical handling of the hysteria concept, and especially the handling of the exceedingly "delicate point" of male hysteria.[23] Whereas the medical classification of disease was an effort to fix, delimit, and control disease cognitively, to establish the boundaries and norms that lent both precision and weight to the act of labeling some "other," the literary interest in disease included as one of its components a fascination with this "otherness," a tendency to recognize in it aspects of the self and to enlist it in the service of self-discovery. The first modality—objective and boundary constructing—produced the dominant themes in the nineteenth-century discourse on hysteria; the second modality— premised on the first, but subjective and boundary blurring—produced the occasional, subversive counterpoint to these same themes. In this essay, I take up each of these discourses in turn. I first explore the uses to which hysteria, and especially its male variety, was put by Flaubert and other nineteenth-century French writers, focusing on the way that diagnostic label could function as a metaphor for androgyny and hence as a challenge to prevailing gender norms. I then look at the far more circumscribed and culturally conservative role that male hysteria played within the psychiatric discourse of the same period.

The Hysteria of Literary Men

Let us turn first to Flaubert. His novels of the late 1850s and early 1860s, *Madame Bovary* and *Salammbô,* are in a sense suffused with hysteria, if one looks at the suggestive descriptions they contain and at the responses they elicited from contemporaries; yet the word *hysteria* never appears in them, nor in any of Flaubert's formal literary corpus until his last novel, *Bouvard and Pécuchet,* published in 1880.[24] Even without the cue of a precise label, nineteenth-century readers readily identified the *mal* of Emma Bovary. One critic summed her up as "that hysterical provincial, surfeited with pleasures [*jouissances*] and nonetheless always famished."[25] The 1857 review of the novel by Charles Baudelaire saw in Emma the image of the "hysterical poet" and asked rhetorically, "Why could hysteria, this physiological mystery, not serve as the central subject, the true foundation, of a literary work?"[26] Some two decades later an article in the *Revue des deux mondes* called Emma "the most animated, the most authentic of all the hysterics whose stories have been told by novelists" and praised Flaubert for describing her condition in a manner "so precise and seductive that one does not know whether to admire more the talents of the artist or the science of the observer."[27]

The case is similar though not as clear cut with *Salammbô,* Flaubert's exotic novel of ancient Carthage that dismayed so many of its critics. The only explicit disease in *Salammbô* is the gruesome dermatosis that eats away at the body of the magistrate Hanno and seems intended to symbolize the rot and moral decay of Carthaginian society as a whole. But many contemporary reviewers regarded the novel as dominated by pathology—it inaugurated, one said sardonically, "a new genre that I propose to call the *epileptic genre*"[28]— and they were quick to attribute mental pathology to both of the novel's main characters: Salammbô, a highborn virgin priestess of the cult of Tanit, the Carthaginian deity of love; and Mâtho, the Libyan mercenary "of colossal stature" who falls in love with her.

The consensus was that Mâtho was frankly insane, "seized by a kind of furious delirium at the sight and at the name of Salammbô,"[29] according to one critic, and gone "mad [*fou*] with wrath and pain" when Salammbô first disappears from view, according to another.[30] Salammbô, on the other hand, seemed to be suffering from a less flagrant pathology. The critics were struck by her dissociated states of consciousness and, extrapolating from the descriptions in Flaubert's text, they anticipated in uncanny fashion the central link between hysteria and hypnotic trance that Charcot would endeavor to establish two decades later. (Earlier in the nineteenth century, somnambulism enjoyed relatively minor status as a hysterical symptom.)[31] "One does not know if she is awake or if she sleeps, if she is conscious of her acts or if she is a prey to the hallucinations of the somnambulists," observed Saint-René Taillandier of Flaubert's heroine. Yet surely, he continued, she was a somnambulist, for how else could one make sense of the "bestial scene" in which she calmly wraps a python around her naked body?

Salammbô could be simultaneously "ecstatic" and "sensual" precisely because, in her peculiarly dissociated economy, "mind lacks consciousness of the incitements of the flesh."[32] While failing to provide such a subtle analysis of Salammbô's trancelike states, another critic explicitly linked them with hysteria. "Isolated in the midst of the crowd by her ecstasy," he wrote, Salammbô appeared in the opening scene of the novel like a "somnambulist pursuing I don't know what hysterical dream."[33]

Contemporaries may have read the figure of Salammbô, "Madame Bovary's oriental sister,"[34] somewhat less clearly as an hysteric than they had read her Rouennaise prototype. But Flaubert's letters together with the notes and rough drafts for his Carthaginian novel leave no doubt as to his intentions. "A propos of my *Salammbô,* I am busy with hysteria and insanity [*aliénation mentale*],"[35] he wrote to a friend, his pair of preoccupations corresponding well to the diagnoses that critics would later suggest for the characters of Salammbô and Mâtho respectively. To another friend he expressed, a few lines after discussing his progress on *Salammbô,* a wish to go to medical school "if I were ten years younger," or at least to have sufficient time to attend the "very curious little course" that the local asylum doctor was then giving for his close friends "on hysteria, nymphomania, and so on."[36] (Apparently Flaubert hoped to compensate for his nonattendance of this course by including Landouzy's *Traité complet de l'hystérie* in his broad, preparatory reading program for *Salammbô.*)[37] Two decades after the publication of the novel, he would even accept a depiction of it as being in some measure "about hysteria."[38] Against this background, it is hardly surprising to learn that, in one of his earliest sketches for his Carthaginian novel, Flaubert epitomized the virginal Salammbô as "intoxicated with the *mystico-hysterical* spirit" of the goddess of love and fertility.[39] Thus his characterization of Salammbô, like his characterization of Emma Bovary, joined hysteria together with two factors long believed to be predisposing causes of that disease: strong sexual impulses and exaggerated religious devotion.

Flaubert underscored the religious factor when he told Sainte-Beuve shortly after the publication of the novel that Salammbô was "a kind of Saint Theresa," a reference that plays on the long-standing medical identification of that Spanish Carmelite mystic as an hysteric.[40] And if we know from one letter of 1859 that Flaubert was thinking of hysteria as affiliated with nymphomania, we know from another of that same year that he was thinking about the psychopathogenic effects of religious devotion in women and the connection between intense female religiosity and erotic longings.

> It's a sad story that you tell me of that young girl, your relative, gone mad as a result of religious ideas, but it's a familiar one. You've got to have a robust temperament to ascend the summits of mysticism

without losing your head. And then, there is in all this (in women especially) questions of temperament that complicate the suffering. Don't you see that all of them are in love with Adonis? He is the eternal husband that they require. Ascetic or libidinous, they dream of love, the great love; and to cure them (at least temporarily), they need not an idea but a fact—a man, a child, a lover.[41]

The link between mysticism, repressed eroticism, and hysteria was apparently axiomatic in Flaubert's mind; it surfaced again when he wrote to Zola in 1874, praising the latter's new novel *La Conquête de Plassans*. In that novel, Zola's heroine Marthe discovers a deep religious sensibility in herself some months after her husband rents a room in their home to the town's new abbé. At about the same time that she begins to experience pious ecstasies, she develops a nervous malady. The two phenomena intensify in tandem, culminating in what Flaubert calls her "final avowal" of her carnal love for the priest living in her midst. Although Zola's novel leaves Marthe's sickness unnamed, Flaubert matter-of-factly identifies it in his letter as "her hysterical condition."[42]

This cursory consideration of the place of hysteria in Flaubert's prose indicates two aspects of his relationship to the disease category that are relevant to us here. First, hysteria was an implicit category in Flaubert's literary works but an explicit one for him when he wrote in the first person. While he seems to have deliberately avoided using the term in his novels, it appears at least a dozen times in his correspondence between 1852 and 1880[43]—a noteworthy tally given the fact that it was not until the early 1880s that, through the rise of Charcot and his school, hysteria gained widespread cultural currency and became "la question palpitante du jour" in France.[44] As we know from a letter to Sand, Flaubert took the nomenclature of the "psychological sciences" very seriously.[45] That he was more inclined to call hysteria by name in the relatively private sphere of letter writing than in the public one of novel writing was almost certainly an aesthetic strategy, part of Flaubert's project to create an impersonal, purely mimetic narrator reporting on the thingness of things without coloring them with his own affect, judgments, or particular funds of knowledge. But at the same time the selectivity of his usage may have reflected his perception of the category "hysteria" as existing in immediate relationship to himself.

Second, whatever medical sources he read, some of the views on hysteria that Flaubert absorbed in the 1850s and 1860s were not "contrapuntal" at all but were instead profoundly conventional. His facile comment that women who fell ill from mystical preoccupations were "all in love with Adonis" is a version of the old medical and popular representation of hysteria as "Venus attached to her prey."[46] It almost seems that in his *Dictionary of Received Ideas,* where he defined

"hysteria" as "confuse with nymphomania," Flaubert was satirizing not only the vulgar nineteenth-century understanding of the term but also his own earlier banality and *bêtise.* Nor was Flaubert above invoking hysteria explicitly and gratuitously in a way demeaning to women. Writing anxiously to a friend about the forthcoming trial of *Madame Bovary,* he suggested a strategy that might save him from "ruination": "What I need especially is men eminent by dint of their high office to vouch that I am not in the business of producing books for hysterical kitchen-maids."[47]

Yet if hysteria was for Flaubert on one level a tired cliché and a word that in its adjectival form always carried pejorative connotations and always modified women, on another level he found it an intensely interesting concept, one capable of expressive mutation. He seems to have linked it early on with his art and, in particular, with the often agonizing rhythm of his literary creativity. He first applied it to himself—something of a radical act, given the term's strong gender connotations—in 1852, in the context of a writing block of such massive proportions that he felt "mentally and physically annihilated, as after a great orgy" and had spent five hours lying on his divan in complete torpor, lacking both "the heart to make a gesture and the mind to have a thought." Whereas five days before, when his novel was "not moving," he had described himself as "having nerves set on edge like brass wires," he was now experiencing, he wrote, "hysterias of boredom"—a usage that finds support in the contemporary medical literature on hysterical symptoms.[48] And in his 1867 letter to Sand, at a time when he was not blocked in his creativity but was rather "sculpting my darling novel laboriously like a convict" in solitary confinement, he again linked hysteria to the stresses peculiar to literary labor: "All this results from our fine occupation."[49]

Perhaps, given the analogy and the pervasive unconscious association between literary creativity and female biological procreativity, the former was the logical area of discussion in which male appropriation of the hysteria concept could take place during the nineteenth century. From hysteria as a malfunction of the organs of female procreativity (the traditional Hippocratic formulation about the wandering womb still survived), there was only a short step to hysteria as a malfunction of the faculties of male artistic creativity. It is suggestive in this regard that, much like Flaubert, Stéphane Mallarmé applied hysteria to himself in his capacity as a writer, observing in a letter of 1869: "I have made a vow not to touch a pen from now [mid February] until Easter. . . . The simple act of writing installs hysteria in my head."[50] And it is significant that, when Flaubert ranged through Landouzy's encyclopedic treatise on hysteria, his note taking on the symptoms of that disease focused on the so-called ball. He jotted down information about the ball's ascendant trajectory from the lower abdomen to the thorax and its failure to return to its place of origin; about the sensations of "constriction" and "strangulation" in the throat that accompanied it; about the nonsensical "repetition[s] of a single word" and the indecipherable animal-like sounds—from "barks, howls, roars, yelps, down to the grunts of a pig"—that resulted from its obstructive presence.[51] Hysteria, it would seem, presented itself to Flaubert preeminently as an impairment in the capacity for linguistic expression. He was, furthermore, intrigued by those clinical descriptions in which the hysterical blockage appeared as literally displaced from the uterine region to the organs of speech or, figuratively, from the realm of biological procreativity to that of verbal production.

While Flaubert's connecting of hysteria to the labors of male writing can certainly be construed as an implicit assertion of androgyny—I take *androgyny* to mean here that condition under which the affective and behavioral characteristics of the sexes are not rigidly assigned[52]—it hardly makes a strong claim for his use of the hysteria concept as a mediator between dichotomous notions of gender. To bolster that strong claim, we must look at three bodies of evidence: Baudelaire's review of *Madame Bovary;* certain thematic patterns of that novel and of *Salammbô;* and finally, the Flaubert-Sand correspondence in which Flaubert's announcement of his male hysteria was embedded.

Flaubert regarded Baudelaire's review of *Madame Bovary* as the only fully satisfactory one the novel received, and it elicited his grateful encomium, "You have entered into the secrets of the book as though my brain were yours."[53] The review in fact turns on the issues of androgyny and hysteria, which are addressed in its final, climactic sections. Baudelaire characterizes *Madame Bovary* as a last-ditch effort to reinvigorate the moribund genre of the nineteenth-century novel, to shake up a complacent reading public by substituting icy detachment for engagement in the authorial voice and banality for deep significance in the subject matter. In carrying out this strategy, or artistic "wager," much depended upon the realization of the title character. Flaubert had to pour himself into Emma Bovary, or in Baudelaire's words,

> to divest himself of his actual sex and make himself into a woman. The result is miraculous, for despite his zeal at wearing masks he could not help but infuse some male blood into the veins of his creation. . . . Like a weapon-bearing Pallas issuing forth from the forehead of Zeus, *this bizarre androgyne* houses the seductiveness of a virile soul within a beautiful feminine body.

To prove his point, Baudelaire enumerates the "virile qualities" with which the author has "perhaps unconsciously" endowed Emma, and it is at the end of this enumeration that he introduces, or rather slips in, hysteria, relating that nervous disease to the subject of androgyny not so much by logical argument as by allusive juxtaposition. Emma's gender ambiguity emerges, he says, even during her adolescent convent days, when she exhibits both the "astonishing aptitude for life" that marks the "man of action" and the typically girlish tendency "to get intoxicated from" the lush trappings of Catholicism, "to gorge herself" on stained-glass windows and vespers music. But Emma offers an embellishment on this latter, passive, and characteristically feminine posture. She converts the true Christian God into "the God of her fantasy," one equipped "with spurs and mustaches"; and this eroticized transformation, entirely attributable to the condition of her "nerves," renders her the "hysterical poet."[54]

The meaning Baudelaire gives to *hysteria* here is itself ambiguous. The term seems to have two referents. First, there is the familiar equation of female mystical tendencies with hysteria and the contention that both serve as a screen for erotic longings—ideas to which Flaubert also gave credence, as we have already seen. But Baudelaire's *hysteria* seems to refer not merely to the supposedly feminine component of Emma's behavior in the convent but, more broadly, to her very coupling of male and female traits; it seems to be the expression of her "bizarre" androgyny. After all, what qualifies Emma as an hysteric in Baudelaire's view is the unorthodox metamorphosis of God that she enacts in fantasy; and Baudelaire had, earlier in the review, identified the faculty of "imagination" as "supreme," "tyrannical," and preeminently masculine.[55]

That Baudelaire intended to link hysteria with androgyny is borne out as well in the paragraph of the review devoted entirely to that nervous pathology. Here, consigning hysteria to the status of a "mystery" as yet unsolved by the Academy of Medicine,[56] he casually makes the controversial move of assuming its existence in both men and women. This move probably had autobiographical resonance: elsewhere in his writings, he, like Flaubert, depicted himself as an hysteric.[57] Developing the gender theme, Baudelaire ends his brief discussion of hysteria on a cryptic but highly evocative note. The principal symptom of the disease in women, the well-known "rising and strangulating ball," is, he tells us, "translated" in men into a symptomatology that combines various forms of "impotence" with a "proclivity to excess."

Read metaphorically, this clinical description could be taken to mean that hysteria represents in each sex an aspiration to androgyny—that is to say, a protest against conventional gender definitions and an (ultimately failed) attempt to transcend them. In women, according to Baudelaire's rendition, hysteria problematizes the organs of speech; the effort to escape the self-absorbed interiority of that pure bodily life to which society relegates women, to address the outside world in the "masculine" mode of language, is both highlighted and foiled. In men, hysteria problematizes the "masculine" mode of action through a vacillation between the desire to resign that mode utterly and embrace the "feminine" mode of impotent passivity and the compensatory desire to exaggerate action beyond measure.[58] The structure of Baudelaire's review at this juncture further indicates that he intended an integrative discussion of hysteria and androgyny, for immediately after the paragraph devoted to hysteria he returns quite explicitly to the androgyny motif. "*Intellectual women,*" he asserts, "owe [Flaubert] a debt of gratitude for having [in the character of Emma Bovary] elevated the female to a position of such efficacy, so far from the pure animal and so close to the ideal man, for having made her participate in that double nature of rational calculation and of dreaming that constitutes the perfect human being."[59]

Many twentieth-century commentators have elaborated upon the theme of androgyny in *Madame Bovary* first announced by Baudelaire, most notably Jean-Paul Sartre, who turned this aspect of Flaubert's novel into a fascinating, and vastly ambitious, research program:

> One problem then—without leaving the work itself; that is, the literary significations—is to ask ourselves why the author (that is, the pure synthetic activity which creates Madame Bovary) was able to metamorphose himself into a woman . . . what the artistic transformation of male into female means in the nineteenth century . . . and finally, just who Gustave Flaubert *must have been* in order to have within the field of his possibles the possibility of portraying himself as a woman. The reply is independent of all biography, since this problem could be posed in Kantian terms: "Under what conditions is the feminization of experience possible?"[60]

But these discussions by Sartre and others do not pick up Baudelaire's suggestion that Flaubert uses hysteria as the vehicle of androgyny, as the liminal ground where ordinary gender boundaries can be transgressed.

While *Salammbô* has elicited far less commentary—both in general, and as a novel about hysteria—it, too, is amenable to interpretation in terms of the conjoint theme of hysteria and androgyny. Certainly the novel plays on the binary opposition of male and female and on attempted mediations between the two.[61] This pattern is set forth in the opening scene when the rowdy, brawling, barbarian mercenaries—almost caricatures of masculinity—are suddenly interrupted by the ecstatic, virginal, lyre-playing Salammbô; she is accompanied by the "mediators," a corps of pallid, beardless, and hairless eunuch priests. Later in the novel, Flaubert explicitly underscores this mediation, noting of

Schahabarim, the eunuch priest who oversees Salammbô's religious training, "His condition established between them something like the equality of a common sex."[62]

That hysteria is another candidate for the mediating function in the novel can be inferred from a recent essay by Benjamin Bart that presents persuasive textual evidence for the proposition that Flaubert endowed Mâtho, the strapping Libyan mercenary, with the traits of an hysteric.[63] Building upon this suggestion, one can argue that both Mâtho and Salammbô are afflicted with hysteria: looking at the python, she experiences the hysterical ball ("another serpent slowly coming up in her throat to choke her"),[64] and confronted with her father's wrath, that same symptom condemns her to speechlessness ("She did not dare open her lips, yet she was choking with the need to voice her sorrow").[65] The common ground of hysteria thus mediates the polar opposition between these stereotypically male and female protagonists. Indeed, it helps to explain why the crucial scene in the tent, the supposed consummation of their passion, has been left so oddly ambiguous and unrealized. After all, Flaubert saw hysterical desire as essentially self-contradictory in its nature and hence not amenable to fulfillment. "In search of love and not of a lover," he laconically characterized Salammbô's "vague hysteria" in his notes for the novel.[66]

The early years of Flaubert's correspondence with George Sand provide another, more direct way to demonstrate the strength of the connection between androgyny and hysteria in Flaubert's mind. The friendship of these two writers, which effectively began in 1866 when he was forty-five and she sixty-two, has long puzzled critics, for the aesthetic philosophies of the two were (and would always remain) antithetical, and in his younger days Flaubert had even made contemptuous remarks about the flabby romanticism of Sand's novels and about the mindless "seamstresses" who read them.[67] A few months into the relationship, Flaubert was as puzzled by it as the critics later were. "Under what constellation were you born," he exclaimed to Sand, "that enabled you to unite in your person such diverse, numerous, and rare qualities! I don't know what kind of sentiment I bear for you, but I know that I feel a *specific* tenderness and one that I have never, up to this time, felt for anyone. . . . All the doors between the two of us are not yet open."[68]

What brought the two writers together for the first time was Flaubert's gratitude for the review of *Salammbô* that Sand published at the beginning of 1863—one of the few favorable assessments which that novel received. With her masculine pseudonym and intermittent assumption of a masculine demeanor, the bountifully maternal Sand was a kind of nineteenth-century French incarnation of androgyny. "That hermaphroditic writer," one critic had called her in the

George Sand (1804-1876).

1830s, reflecting the fact that she deliberately, and provocatively, insisted upon a male authorial identity despite the public's awareness of her actual gender. Another, pronouncing her "an enigmatic man and a phenomenal woman," speculated that Sand's power as a writer derived precisely from these "two opposing natures within a single being"—a being that would, he added, "honor whichever sex it deigned to choose."[69] Thus a shared fascination with gender definition, including a questioning of traditional gender boundaries, seems to have been an important, though tacit, factor underlying the soul union that Sand and Flaubert eventually forged. At least the letters leading up to and immediately following Flaubert's declaration of his hysterical pathology persistently reflect this theme.

At first, a spelling problem implicitly announces the theme. Flaubert addresses Sand as "cher maître," using the masculine form of the adjective—a mistake with respect to Sand's gender, though an accurate usage with respect to the masculine noun he has chosen for her ("master" instead of "mistress") in recognition of her senior status as a writer. The next time, he produces the spelling *chère maître* (the feminine form of the adjective), and twice after that, grown self-conscious

about the gender confusion that reflects itself in the orthography of this particular phrase as applied to Sand, he underlines the final *e* in *chère*.[70]

There is much play on the simulacrum of a cloistered life that Flaubert has arranged for himself, a motif that is important for us here for several reasons: because monks and nuns represent a particular variant on ordinary gender identity; because the enforced sexual abstinence and the religious exaltation of the formal cloistered life were routinely linked with female hysteria (Salammbô, as priestess of Tanit, falls into this category Carthaginian style); and because Flaubert would, in the critical 1867 letter, depict himself as an "anchorite." Thus, after her first visit to Flaubert at his home in Normandy, Sand writes, calling stark attention to her own female corporeality, "I was truly touched by the warm welcome I received in your monastic environment [*milieu de chanoine*], where a wandering animal of my species is an anomaly that could be found troublesome." A few weeks later, she calls Flaubert "my Benedictine, all alone in your ravishing monastery [*chartreuse*], working and never going out."[71] By return mail, Flaubert picks up the theme from another angle, informing her that he is reading through the ten volumes of her autobiography, and that "what struck me the most is the [section on] convent life. I have a lot of observations about all that to submit to you."[72] In *Histoire de ma vie,* Sand had described her early adolescent years in a Paris convent as a typical female experience ("More than one person of my sex will recognize [in this account] the sometimes good and sometimes bad effects of religious education"). She had passed through a series of stages: total rebellion against the institution; then an "ardent and agitated" mysticism; and finally, a "calm, firm, and lively devotion."[73] It seems likely that Flaubert was interested in her ability to move beyond the mystical stage, the one that he had portrayed as a kind of developmental impasse conducing to hysteria in both Emma Bovary and Salammbô. Indeed, as Flaubert could not have helped noticing, Sand mentions hysteria near the conclusion of her account of her convent days, explicitly distinguishing it from the "calm devotion" that she eventually achieved:

> Whoever has passed that way knows well that no terrestrial affection can give comparable intellectual satisfactions. This Jesus, as the mystics have interpreted and remade him for their purposes, is a friend, a brother, a father, whose constant presence, untiring solicitude, tenderness, and infinite patience can be compared to nothing in the realm of the real and the possible. I don't like the fact that nuns have made him their husband. *There is in that something that is bound to feed a hysterical mysticism, the most repugnant of the forms that mysticism can take.* This ideal love for Christ is without danger only during that period of life when the human passions are silent.[74]

To the motif of monastery and convent is joined the metaphor of literary creativity as biological procreativity that Sand contributes to the correspondence. She refers to a work in progress as "my fetus."[75] Regaled with details about the anguish that accompanies Flaubert's literary endeavors, she tells him that he has "the pains of childbirth" and that she empathizes with him as thoroughly as when "my daughter-in-law brings dear infants into the world," a process that causes Sand to become "more sick, and seriously so" than the woman actually in labor.[76] Another time, "astonished" by Flaubert's accounts of his difficulties as a writer, she does not use metaphors of female reproduction, but she counsels him to adopt a more passive, perhaps implicitly a more female, stance. "Ah well, when we are absolutely only instruments, it is still a pleasant condition and a sensation matched by no other to feel ourselves vibrate. Let the wind run up and down your strings a little, then. I think you make greater efforts than necessary, and that you ought more often to give free rein to the *other*."[77]

Even more striking are the two writers' explicit statements about a wish for, or about the actuality of, gender transformation. In the course of making plans to meet in Paris for the opening of a friend's play—a meeting that was, in effect, to be their first date—Sand writes, apparently alluding to her advanced age and the cessation of her menstrual cycle, "Since at present I am no longer a woman, if God were just I would become a man. I would have physical strength and would say to you, 'Let's go and take a trip to Carthage or some other place.' But, behold, one progresses toward a childhood which has neither sex nor energy."[78] Musing about his own aging process some four months later, Flaubert presents Sand's mirror image with respect to gender fantasies. "I believe that the heart does not grow old. There are even some people in whom it expands with age: I was more dried up and crabbed twenty years ago than I am today. I have been feminized [*je me suis féminisé*] and softened with wear and tear, as others become callous." The feminization Flaubert imputes to himself has thus been initially depicted in wholly positive terms: the feminine vulnerability he has acquired is equated with true vitality, with a capacity for openness and continued emotional growth. But Flaubert immediately renders his assessment of it ambiguous by injecting a negative note. "And that makes me indignant. I feel I'm becoming too soft. I am moved by nothing at all. Everything troubles and agitates me."[79]

Thus Flaubert begins by positing androgyny, that fluidity of gender definition which enables the integration of selected feminine traits into himself, as a desirable end. But he then partially retreats, fearfully enthralled, it would seem, by the low value placed on those traits by the culture at large, the general tendency to view female emotion as a sign of weakness, as intrinsically excessive and slightly ludicrous. At the time that he announced his identity as a male hysteric, then, Flaubert did so with an ambivalent commitment to the ideal of androgyny. Not surprisingly, he was much more able to appreciate the marks of Sand's androgynous condition than to affirm and cultivate that condition in himself. As he wrote in the very same letter in which he waffles on the value of his own feminization, "I, too, ask myself why I love you. Is it because you are a great Man, or because you are a charming being?"[80]

This affirmation of the androgynous ideal achieved by distancing that ideal from himself and displacing it onto a woman was not an entirely new emotional motif for Flaubert. Rather, it recalls a disappointed longing that had already colored his protracted sexual relationship with the writer Louise Colet. "I believed from the beginning that I would find in you less feminine personality, a more universal conception of life," he wrote to Colet with exasperation in 1846, going on to describe a personal ideal of "hermaphroditism" to which he imagined she could conform:

> I should like to make of you something entirely apart, neither [male] friend [*ami*] nor mistress. Both of those are too restrictive, too exclusive. One does not love one's friend enough, and one is too silly with one's mistress. It is the intermediate term I seek, the essence of those two sentiments combined. What I want, in short, is that, *like a new kind of hermaphrodite,* you give me all the joys of the flesh with your body, and all those of the soul with your mind.[81]

Flaubert feared that this concept was unclear, poorly articulated, even self-contradictory ("It's strange how bad my writing is in these letters to you. . . . Everything comes into collision, as if I wanted to say three words at once"),[82] but it persisted in his mind as an *idée fixe*. In the spring of 1854, a year before ending their liaison, he voiced it again to Colet in a more despairing tone. "I have always tried (but it seems to me that I failed) to make a sublime hermaphrodite of you."[83]

Sand's commitment to androgyny was, in her letters to Flaubert, much more inclusive and wholehearted than her correspondent's. It tended to take the form of so thoroughly undermining conventional distinctions between properly masculine and properly feminine traits that the category of gender nearly disappeared altogether.[84] Sand expressed this view quite succinctly in her reply to Flaubert's letter on his male hysteria. In the first place, she doubted that hysteria could be a gendered malady:

What does it mean to be hysterical? Perhaps I've also been so, perhaps I am now, but I know nothing about it, having never examined the matter thoroughly and having only heard about it secondhand without studying it. Isn't it a malaise, a great distress, caused by the desire for an impossible *something?* In that case, all of us who have imagination are afflicted with it, with that strange sickness. And why would such a malady have a sex?[85]

Thus, like Baudelaire in his review of *Madame Bovary,* Sand identified hysteria with the overreaching tendency of imagination; but since, unlike Baudelaire, she declined to identify imagination as a masculine faculty, hysteria became for her not a condition that mingled gender attributes but rather one simply without gender. In the next sentence of the same letter, she went on to question the validity of the very category of gender:

And then, for people knowledgeable in anatomy, *there is only one sex.* A man and a woman are so much the same thing that it is difficult to comprehend the heap of distinctions and subtle arguments about the subject that societies have fostered. I observed the infancy and the development of my son and daughter. My son was me, and consequently much more a woman than was my daughter, who was an unrealized man [*un homme pas réussi*].[86]

Medical Men Deploy Hysteria

This consideration of Flaubert and, to a lesser extent, Sand and Baudelaire, shows the use to which the hysteria concept could be put by French creative writers in the 1850s and 1860s. Construed metaphorically, it became the springboard for free-ranging and unorthodox ruminations about gender definition. Such ruminations were, in the case of Flaubert and almost certainly in the case of Baudelaire,[87] nourished by contact with the technical medical literature. But other factors must have nourished them as well. For example, if one accepts the claims of Freudian psychoanalysis, these writers may have been especially sensitive to the pervasive, unconscious fantasy of androgyny as expressed in the young child's belief in a phallic mother. Or, on the historical plane, they may have been influenced by the articulation of an androgynous ideal by such early nineteenth-century intellectual movements as Saint-Simonianism and Comtean positivism, which sought to achieve post-Revolutionary social stability by synthesizing the rational (and "male") element with the sentimental (and "female") one and which invented personifications of the desired synthesis.[88] At mid century Flaubert's close friend Maxime Du Camp even found this desirable androgynous synthesis embodied in the creative writer, a position consonant with that literary application of *hysteria* to the trials of male writing that we have noted. "The artist, and especially the poet," Du Camp asserted in a novel, "should be a sort of androgyne who combines in himself serenity and sensitivity, strength and tenderness"; he ought to be "a man in terms of intelligence, a woman in terms of heart." Interestingly enough, Du Camp attributed this opinion to his main character—a troubled young man, on the verge both of serious writing and of suicide, whom he described as a "hystero-melancholic."[89]

But what about nineteenth-century medical discourse itself? Although the medical community had furnished the discursive preconditions for the "discovery" of male hysteria and in fact engaged in intermittent debate about its existence throughout the nineteenth century, the medical supporters of that new category were not in a position to perceive or exploit its implications for the definition of gender. The field of vision of physicians and psychiatrists was effectively limited both by the discursive norms of medical science and by the nexus of power relations that enmeshed medical doctors as professional men who actively sought to increase the authority they commanded in society and whose expertise was, in turn, often sought after and applied by political agencies. These two factors combined to contain the cultural iconoclasm that might seem to have inhered in the male hysteria concept.

Throughout the nineteenth century, male hysteria entered medical discourse as the by-product of one or another more general scientific hypothesis. It was, consequently, regarded as far less interesting as a datum in itself than as evidence in support of that larger hypothesis. Thus the boldly inventive young Paris psychiatrist Georget propounded the existence of male hysteria in the 1820s in connection with his conviction, inspired by pioneering work in brain dissection, that all mental disease resulted from cerebral lesions. From this new theoretical perspective, hysteria became for Georget "an idiopathic affection of the brain . . . observable in both sexes." The long-standing belief that its locus was the female reproductive organs could, he said, be disproved both by documenting cases of hysteria in men and by showing that the uterus and ovaries simply lacked the neural "sympathies" necessary to spread a pathological condition throughout the organism as a whole.[90]

During the 1830s and 1840s, articles occasionally appeared in medical journals in Paris and the provinces painstakingly detailing the symptoms of a putative case of male hysteria and citing Georget as an authority on the theoretical possibility for such a clinical finding. But, as had been true for Georget himself, the subject really under discussion in such accounts was the bodily seat of hysteria.[91] The doctors failed to recognize—or, perhaps, automatically suppressed as irrelevant and inconvenient their unarticulated recognition—that their clinical findings might have implications for the definition of gender in the larger culture.

Some awareness of these general cultural issues was demonstrated by Dr. Pierre Briquet, whose monumental treatise on hysteria appeared in 1859. In affirming the existence (though extreme rarity) of hysteria in men and jettisoning the uterine theory of the disease, Briquet made clear that he hoped to contribute to the eradication of certain negative cultural stereotypes of women. Despite the connotations its name carried in the nonmedical world, hysteria was not, he said, a "shameful malady." It was not caused by unsatisfied sexual desires—a widespread belief that, according to Briquet, "tends to degrade women"—but rather by "the existence in women of the noblest and most admirable sentiments, ones which they alone are capable of feeling."[92] Denying hysteria all anatomical determinants, Briquet championed a psychophysiological theory of the disease that rooted it in the emotions mediated by the nervous system and that rendered it, if not exclusively female in its incidence, still an expression of characteristics that he regarded as feminine by nature.[93] "Woman has a noble mission of the greatest social importance—that of raising children, looking after the welfare of adults, and taking care of the elderly. To this end, she has been endowed with a special kind of sensibility, very different from that of men; and it is in this kind of sensibility that lies the source of hysteria."[94] The kind of sensibility to which Briquet was referring was in fact "an excess of sensibility," a disposition to feel intense and "incessant" emotion. Existing in women with "nothing to counterbalance it," it moved them to socially indispensable outpourings of tenderness and pity and also shaded by degrees into pathology.[95] Thus, with his particular slant on the social meaning of hysteria, Briquet valorized male hysteria as part of his project of desexualizing the disease while at the same time leaving it resoundingly gendered.

With the rise of Charcot and his Salpêtrière school in the 1870s and 1880s, everything about hysteria in France increased in scale[96]—the number of people diagnosed as afflicted with it, the popularization of knowledge about it, and, of particular interest here, the number of diagnosed male hysterics. A recent study has examined this last point in depth, ascertaining that some 20 to 25 percent of Charcot's published case studies of hysterics were in fact about men.[97] What are we to make of such avid interest in male hysteria on the part of Charcot and his disciples? Does it show that Charcot was free of the antifemale bias that had marked earlier medical research on hysteria, that his clinical gaze was, in this respect at least, a truly objective one? Might Charcot's erosion of the classically female nature of hysteria even mean that, like Flaubert, he entertained unconventional notions about gender definition?

Such a Charcot is not a very credible creature. For while Charcot's project entailed the affirmation of male hysteria, the doctor's real interest lay elsewhere. Much like Georget, he wanted to make a general theoretical point, one that happened to carry male hysteria along in its wake. In Charcot's case, that point concerned the universality of the clinical picture that hysteria presented and hence, ultimately, the legitimacy of hysteria as a diagnostic entity. Where his predecessors had found only a chaotic and chameleonlike bevy of symptoms, Charcot's much-hailed scientific achievement was to have found an orderly array; he had delineated four phases, or periods, of hysteria that, he asserted, "follow one another with the regularity of a mechanism." In other words, he had gained cognitive control over the disease (he still did not know how to cure it) by subsuming it under positive laws, and he made the supremely confident claim of the positivist: that the laws he had discovered and which governed hysteria were "valid for all countries, all times, all races" and "consequently universal."[98] Demonstrating the universality of hysteria thus became one of Charcot's continuing scientific preoccupations; and just as it led him to make retrospective diagnoses of that disease on the basis of the visual evidence contained in the paintings and woodcuts of past centuries, so it led him to emphasize the existence of hysteria in men.[99] The discussions of male hysteria in Charcot's lectures bear out this interpretation, for they are larded with explicit assertions about hysteria's "unity"—the single clinical picture that it presented in varied contexts.[100]

Other aspects of Charcot's work and public persona support this conclusion that his championing of male hysteria was not indicative of a revisionist attitude toward gender definition. For one thing, he appears to have barely tolerated the entrance of women into the medical profession. A late-nineteenth-century French feminist journal reproduced his remarks at the 1888 public dissertation defense of a young Polish woman aspiring to a degree from the Paris Faculty of Medicine. The first of the jurors to speak, Charcot unabashedly acknowledged that he had not read the thesis, a statistical study entitled "The Woman Doctor in the Nineteenth Century." But he nonetheless proceeded to develop a case against women doctors. "The special physiology of their sex," he said, including their monthly "indispositions," rendered them unsuitable to care for patients; but since French law had granted them the right to practice medicine, they should be confined to the humble position of country doctor rather than competing with men for lucrative and prestigious urban posts. Their career accomplishments must never be superior to those of their husband, for such a situation rendered a man "piteous alongside his wife." Charcot even invoked as relevant to the question at hand the natural "beauty of woman and the ugliness of the male sex." Women with careers, he noted, tended to "neglect their toilette," a dereliction of duty apparently countenanced by the Anglo-Saxons but unacceptable to the French as an "aesthetic people."[101]

Second, while Charcot's rendition of male hysteria was in many ways explicitly patterned on its female prototype, in certain details the disease also differed in its male and female victims—and the chief difference noted by Charcot paralleled and thus reaffirmed the most stereotypical notions of the difference between the sexes. Among the majority of female hysterics, "instability, mobility of symptoms" preponderated, and "the capricious course of the ailment is frequently interrupted by the most surprising strokes of theatricality." In the male, however, hysteria displayed none of this flightiness but presented an appropriately sober clinical picture "remarkable in the permanence and tenacity of the symptoms."[102]

Finally, looking at the social and ethnic backgrounds of the men whom Charcot judged to be hysterics, we find that male hysteria was a highly selective diagnosis. While female hysterics could be found in all social strata, male hysterics—at least those identified by Charcot—were, if French and Christian, almost invariably members of the working class or of the unemployed underworld. They might also be Jews or Arabs, in which case they could be either middle class or working class.[103] In other words, from the vantage point of the male, bourgeois, Christian doctor who made the diagnosis, the male hysteric remained the "other," as radically foreign and as extruded from the self as the female hysteric. Rather than introducing a fundamentally novel, nonstigmatizing element into the hysteria diagnosis, or seriously problematizing gender definition, or rendering the psychiatric doctor vulnerable to his own labels, Charcot's male hysteria was a variant on a familiar nineteenth-century rhetorical theme: it conflated forms of otherness, linking the characteristics of women with those of the lower classes or, alternatively, with those of the Orient.[104]

That Charcot's advocacy of male hysteria should respect rather than violate the status quo with respect to gender was in the first place dictated by the norms of medical scientific discourse, which sought to restrict the meanings of terms rather than to exploit their connotative or metaphorical possibilities. Charcot even paid obeisance to those norms when, in the course of affirming the positivity of hysteria as a diagnostic entity, he took the opportunity to denigrate the productions of literary men. Hysteria, he asserted, was "not one of those unknowns where one sees whatever one wishes." It was, in other words, "*not a novel:* hysteria has its laws."[105] But the fundamental conservatism of Charcot's male hysteria was also dictated by the complex of power relations in which his medical scientific discourse was involved.

As my earlier research has shown, Charcot's emphasis on hysteria was in part instrumental, serving to enhance the professional power of the psychiatric specialty and to facilitate psychiatry's collaboration with the anticlerical politics of the early Third Republic.[106] Most relevant here, a politics of gender went hand in hand with this professional expansion and republican entrenchment. It had long been axiomatic in French anticlerical thought that priests exercised their most tenacious control over the minds of women; hence the warning issued by the prominent republican politician Jules Ferry in 1870 that "women must belong to science, or else they will belong to the Church."[107] Now among the several ways to make women "belong to science" and, by extension, to the Republic, was to medicalize their bouts of indeterminate emotional distress, defining them as illnesses that required the consultation of a physician, rather than as moral failings or spiritual crises that required the guidance of a priest. From this perspective, disease categories such as hysteria or its cousin neurasthenia were permeated with political significance.

But the republican politics of gender extended further, furnishing a response not only to the traditional bonding of woman and priest but also to the new historical phenomenon of feminism. Although French feminism was a numerically unimpressive movement in the closing decades of the nineteenth century, Frenchmen typically perceived it as a serious threat to traditional gender relations and hence to that network of alliances between liberals and conservatives upon which the still fragile republican synthesis had been founded.[108] In face of such a threat, the utility of the hysteria diagnosis was unmistakable. For hysteria confirmed, in the supposedly neutral language of science, the weakness and vulnerability of women and thus their congenital lack of fitness for the traditionally male social roles that feminism sought to obtain for them. After all, French psychiatric doctors routinely described the victims of hysteria as deceitful, contrary, and capricious and sometimes even characterized the *normal* female character as "mildly hysterical."[109]

Given Charcot's thoroughgoing commitment to fin-de-siècle republican politics—a commitment that had redounded to his professional benefit, resulting in the creation of the first chair in nervous disease at the Paris Faculty of Medicine and the naming of Charcot as its first occupant—he could hardly have deployed his psychiatry to redefine gender. Or, more strongly put, discursive and political constraints combined to place gender redefinition outside Charcot's possibilities as a thinker, even when he was advancing as seemingly transgressive a category as male hysteria. If the dominant themes of the discourse on hysteria figured prominently in his repertory, their counterpoint eluded him.

A comparative remark is in order here. Wolf Lepenies recently suggested that the new discipline of sociology was in the nineteenth century caught between two rival epistemologies: the positivistic orientation that led it to imitate the natural sciences and the hermeneutical attitude that shifted it in the direction of literature.[110] The same cannot, however, be said of the new discipline of psychiatry, at least in France. There is nothing in the disciplinary experience of nineteenth-century French *médecine mentale* comparable to those "literary" moments that Lepenies has located for its sociological counterpart: Auguste Comte's love affair with Clotilde de Vaux, which led him to integrate emotion and poetry into his sociology, for example, or the utopian novel written by the fin-de-siècle sociologist Gabriel Trade. Firmly wedded to the scientific ethos of the Enlightenment, psychiatry remained insulated and aloof from the literary sensibility and counter-Enlightenment "culture of feeling" that periodically captivated sociology. As a result, the discourse of hysteria underwent quite separate developments in the literary and medical domains. Flaubert's male hysteric and Charcot's male hysteric were roughly contemporaneous constructions that bore the same name, but there was a radical disjunction between them.

The Parameters of Gender Redefinition Through Androgyny

Just how radical was the disjunction between literary and medical male hysteria, and how are we to construe its meaning? At the beginning of this essay, I called the nineteenth-century literary use of male hysteria a "subversive counterpoint" to its medical use in the same period. Now that I have presented my evidence, it is appropriate to step back and consider what the evidence really amounts to. Have I perhaps exaggerated my initial claim, been hornswoggled by a surface appearance of gender redefinition that masks a fundamental perpetuation of traditional stereotypes?

A case for the *lack* of subversiveness of male-hysteria-as-androgyny is in fact relatively easy to make. It rests upon the contention that, at least at the hands of Flaubert, the metaphorical identification of male hysteric and androgyne neither revalues the feminine nor alters the old hierarchy that subordinates the feminine to the masculine. After all, what Flaubert has done by declaring himself a male hysteric is to take upon himself a pathology, and a concept of the feminine as the pathological—fragile, hypersensitive, debarred from effective expression or action. In one of his letters to Sand, he did, to be sure, give a highly positive assessment of the female emotionality associated with hysteria, depicting it as inherently more vital than the phlegmatic rationalism that causes men to "dry up" as they advance in age. But, as we have seen, he turned against that idea almost as soon as he had given voice to it.

Hence (such an argument might continue), if Charcot used the hysteria concept, including its male variant, in the service of a kind of professional imperialism, expanding the patient population of the psychiatric

doctor to include the partly as well as the fully mad, Flaubert's use of that concept, though very different in substance, was equally imperialistic—and in its way as benighted as Charcot's with respect to gender issues. Flaubert enacted his imperialism in the personal as well as the professional realm. By defining himself as suffering from hysteria, he expanded the scope and aesthetic possibilities of his own personality, adding female modalities to his repertory without sacrificing male prerogatives. He thus exemplifies what Elaine Showalter has pejoratively called "critical cross-dressing," a form of self-representation as female by a literary man that shares the psychodynamics of literal male transvestism. In both its literary and its literal manifestations, according to Showalter, the assumption of a female persona functions psychologically not as a genuine tribute to the feminine but as a covert promotion of male power. The female impersonator takes great pride in the fact that he ultimately retains his masculinity and hence is able to shift back and forth between gender identities or to occupy both simultaneously, in the latter case incarnating a phallic woman. He regards himself as having the wherewithal to be, if he so chooses, a better woman than any biological female.[111]

Showalter's incisive critique of the strategy of critical cross-dressing doubles as a more general critique of the emancipatory potential of the androgyny concept. In this latter respect, her argument is part of a current in feminist thinking inaugurated in the mid 1970s in reaction against Carolyn Heilbrun's *Toward a Recognition of Androgyny*. Instead of seeing the ideal of androgyny as transcending dichotomous gender stereotypes and thus offering liberation to both women and men, feminist critics of androgyny have analyzed it as a deceptive and fundamentally male-centered ideal, either subsuming the feminine into the already dominant masculine (Showalter's point) or, in the form of the couple-as-androgyne, precluding the independent functioning of women in society.[112]

How then do these late-twentieth-century strictures against androgyny as an emancipatory ideal affect the thesis of this essay? They certainly call into question any implication that androgyny à la Flaubert can be held up today as an unassailable *normative* ideal for feminism. But they do not, I think, much affect the *historical* point that I have attempted to make: that in the nineteenth century and as a result of divergent epistemological norms, a single discursive object, male hysteria, underwent different developments in medical and literary discourse; that the medical usage conformed to the gender stereotypes enshrined in the nineteenth century's prevailing ideology of domesticity, while the literary usage challenged the dichotomous notion of gender. In the minds, conscious and unconscious, of the literary men who articulated it, male-hysteria-as-androgyny may not have been a completely laudable or revolutionary doctrine by some absolute, transhistorical standard. But in relative, historical terms—which is to say, within the bounds of its nineteenth-century context—it nonetheless retains its credentials as subversive. It opened up possibilities and alternatives otherwise hidden by the prevailing domestic doctrine that held that "nature" had made the sexes to fit a pattern of strict opposition, with rational, active men commanding the public life and passive but feelingful women consigned to a sheltered private sphere.

Notes

Earlier versions of this paper were presented at an interdisciplinary symposium on Representing Hysteria held at Trinity College, Hartford, Connecticut, in May 1988 and, later, at a meeting of the Workshop on the History of the Human Sciences at the University of Chicago. I am grateful to friends and colleagues for the helpful comments, criticisms, and suggestions they made on these and other occasions. In particular, I wish to thank Keith Baker, Janet Beizer, Priscilla Ferguson, Stephen Gabel, Robert Morrissey, Peter Novick, Lawrence Rothfield, Barbara Sicherman, George Stocking, and the editors of *Representations.*

[1] Gustave Flaubert to George Sand, 12-13 January 1867, in Flaubert and Sand, *Correspondance,* ed. Alphonse Jacobs (Paris, 1981), 117-18. The portion of the letter cited was omitted from the standard twentieth-century edition of Flaubert's *Correspondence,* that published by Editions Louis Conard, 13 vols. (Paris, 1926-64). Unless otherwise indicated, translations are my own.

[2] The reference is to Dr. Alfred Hardy, a highly respected Paris internist with a hospital appointment and a professorship at the Paris Faculty of Medicine. Like many experts in *pathologie interne* at this date, Hardy included mental and nervous pathology within his purview.

[3] Flaubert to Sand, 1 May 1874, *Correspondance,* 7:134; to Mme. Roger des Genettes of the same date, ibid., 137. By 1879, the doctor had changed but the diagnosis remained the same. As Flaubert wrote to his niece Caroline: "You know that I gorge myself on shrimp every day, being no longer able to eat meat. Fortin [Flaubert's local physician in Croisset] calls me more than ever 'a big hysterical girl'"; 25 April 1879, ibid., 8:261.

[4] Flaubert to Sand, 12-13 January 1867, Flaubert and Sand, *Correspondence,* 118.

[5] Flaubert to Mlle. Leroyer de Chantepie, 18 February 1859, *Correspondence,* 4:314. In the same letter, Flaubert declares, "The anatomy of the human heart has not yet been discerned. How, then, can you expect anyone to heal the heart? The unique glory of the nineteenth century will be to have begun these studies."

[6] The Bibliothèque nationale in Paris recently acquired a photocopy of Flaubert's undated "Notes de lecture pour *Salammbô*," a manuscript of sixty-three pages that includes two pages on Landouzy; see B.N. Manuscrits Don 37287, pp. 34-35. Hector Landouzy's discussion of "hystérie chez l'homme" occupies pp. 218-24 of his *Traité complet de l'hystérie* (Paris, 1846).

[7] Flaubert to Charles-Augustin Sainte-Beuve, December 1862, reprinted as an appendix in Sainte-Beuve, *Nouveaux Lundis,* 13 vols. (Paris, 1868-78), 4:437. The *Dictionnaire des sciences médicales* also appears in *Madame Bovary* and serves in that novel as the emblem of nineteenth-century medical knowledge; see the excellent analysis of this point by Lawrence Rothfield, "From Semiotic to Discursive Intertextuality: The Case of *Madame Bovary,*" *Novel* 19 (1985), esp. 59-60.

[8] See Etienne-Jean Georget, "Hystérie" (1824), *Dictionnaire de médecine,* 21, vols. (Paris, 1821-28), 11:532, 541. The comparable article in the *Dictionnaire des sciences médicales,* written by Jean-Baptiste Louyer-Villermay and published in 1818, acknowledged the occurrence of hysteria-like symptoms in men but insisted that they were distinguishable from true hysteria; 60 vols. (Paris, 1812-22), 23:229-30. Implicit in the author's discussion, however, is the fact that the existence of male hysteria was already a reputable hypothesis, if a controversial one, within the medical community.

[9] Flaubert to Mlle. Leroyer de Chantepie, 15 June 1859, *Correspondence,* 4:320.

[10] See Stendhal's journal of 1805, cited in Jules C. Alciatore, "Stendhal et Pinel," *Modern Philology* 45 (1947): 118; and a letter Stendhal received in 1806, cited in V. Del Litto, *La Vie intellectuelle de Stendhal* (Paris, 1959), 289, n. 76. For the full range of Stendhal's medical interests, see Jean Théodoridès, *Stendhal du côté de la science* (Aran, Switz., 1972), chap. 5.

[11] On Balzac's reading in technical medical sources, see, e.g., Madeleine Fargeaud, *Balzac et "La Recherche de l'absolu"* (Paris, 1968), 138-45. Monomania and monomaniacs make appearances in *Le Peau de chagrin, La Recherche de l'absolu, Eugénie Grandet, La Vieille Fille, Illusions perdues,* and *Pierrette;* on this point, see J.-L. Tritter, *Le Langage philosophique dans les oeuvres de Balzac* (Paris, 1976), 365.

[12] A biographical sketch of Flaubert stressing his connections with the world of medicine can be found in Roger L. Williams, *The Horror of Life* (Chicago, 1980), chap. 3.

[13] See. F. W. J. Hemmings, *Emile Zola,* 2nd ed. (Oxford, 1966), 56-59.

[14] See, for example, Archives de l'Assistance publique de Paris, Salpêtrière 6Q2-66, 5 March 1880 to 18 February 1881, nos. 37691 and 37717. Proust did not have a position at the Salpêtrière but in these and other instances functioned as the referring physician, arranging for the transfer of mentally ill patients from the Lariboisière Hospital.

[15] Jean-Pierre Falret, "Leçons faites à la Salpêtrière, 1850-51," reprinted in his *Des maladies mentales et des asiles d'aliénés* (Paris, 1864), 109-10, 139-40.

[16] Jacques-Joseph Moreau (de Tours), *Du hachisch et de l'aliénation mentale: Etudes psychologiques* (Paris, 1845), 20-21. Théophile Gautier's account, the feuilleton "Le Haschich," was originally published in *La Presse,* 10 July 1843, and subsequently reprinted in his *L'Orient,* 2 vols. (Paris, 1877), 2:47-56.

[17] Louis-François Lélut, *Poésies* (Paris, 1840), ix.

[18] The phrase comes from Philippe Tissié, *Les Aliénés voyageurs: Essai médico-psychologique* (Paris, 1887), 58, in the context of a particularly baroque tale of the exploits of one of the "traveling" lunatics referred to in the title.

[19] Pierre Janet, *Etat mental des hystériques,* 2 vols. (Paris, 1894), vol. 1, *Les Stigmates mentaux,* 224-25.

[20] Sigmund Freud and Josef Breuer, *Studies on Hysteria,* trans. James Strachey (New York, 1966), 201. The quotation comes from the "Discussion" of the case of Elisabeth von R., one of the cases written by Freud.

[21] See my discussion of the moral treatment in Jan Goldstein, *Console and Classify: The French Psychiatric Profession in the Nineteenth Century* (Cambridge, 1987), chap. 3.

[22] One exception is the early nineteenth-century psychiatrist Charles-Chrétien-Henri Marc, who acknowledged that he experienced, though only on a single occasion during his life, feelings that helped him to develop the concepts of instinctive impulsion and transitory madness. "I remember that, passing over the Pont-au-Change one day, and seeing sitting on the parapet a young stonemason who swung to and fro while eating his lunch, I was seized by the appalling desire to make him lose his balance and to hurl him into the river. This idea was only a flash; yet it inspired such horror in me that I rapidly crossed the street . . . thus promptly distancing myself from the object that had given rise to that hideous passing fancy"; quoted in René Semelaigne, *Les Pionniers de la psychiatrie fançaise avant et après Pinel,* 2 vols. (Paris, 1930-32), 1:122.

[23] The phrase is a doctor's: Landouzy, *Traité complet de l'hystérie,* 223, calls male hysteria "un des points les plus délicats de la science."

[24] This information was supplied by a computer scan of the ARTFL (American and French Research on the Treasury of the French Language) textual database at the University of Chicago. The database includes the Louis Conard edition (Paris, 1926-54) of Flaubert's *Oeuvres complètes.*

[25] Alcide Dusolier, "M. Gustave Flaubert," in *Nos gens de lettres: Leur caractère et leurs oeuvres* (Paris, 1864), 59. The essay, primarily a review of *Salammbô,* first appeared in the *Revue française* on 1 January 1863.

[26] Reprinted in Charles Baudelaire, *Oeuvres complètes,* 15 vols. (Paris, 1923-48), esp. 4:404.

[27] Charles Richet, "Les Démoniaques d'aujourd'hui," *Revue des deux mondes* 37 (1880): 340-72, esp. 348.

[28] Ed. Dargez, "La Quinzaine d'un liseur," *Le Figaro,* 4 December 1862, italics in the original. Dargez was not playing cruelly on Flaubert's own vulnerability to epileptoid seizures; this detail of Flaubert's biography was not made known to the public until Maxime Du Camp's revelations in the *Revue des deux mondes* in 1881; see Williams, *Horror of Life,* 124. Nor was Dargez's usage entirely idiosyncratic; by the 1880s *epileptic* had become a term associated with the artistic style of the performers at the café concert. See Rae Beth Gordon, "Le Caf'conc et l'hystérie," *Romantisme* 64 (1989): 53-66.

[29] Elme-Marie Caro, "Gustave Flaubert," in his *Poètes et romanciers* (Paris, 1888), 266. The article was originally published in *La France,* 9 December 1862.

[30] René-Gaspard-Ernest Saint-René Taillandier, "Le Réalisme épique dans le roman," *Revue des deux mondes,* 15 February 1863, 852.

[31] See Louyer-Villermé, "Hystérie," 242, which mentions it last in a paragraph devoted to "accidental symptoms"; and Pierre Briquet, *Traité clinique et thérapeutique de l'hystérie* (Paris, 1859), 412-14. On the other hand, neither Landouzy, *Traité complet de l'hystérie,* nor Jean-Louis Brachet, *Traité de l'hystérie* (Paris, 1847), include it in their chapters devoted to symptomatology.

[32] Saint-René Taillandier, "Réalisme épique," 854-55.

[33] B. Jouvin, "M. Gustave Flaubert: *Salammbô,*" *Le Figaro,* 28 December 1862.

[34] Caro, "Flaubert," 261.

[35] Flaubert to Mlle. Leroyer de Chantepie, 18 February 1859, *Correspondence,* 4:314.

[36] Flaubert to Ernest Feydeau, 29-30 November 1859, *Correspondence,* 4:349.

[37] Flaubert, "Notes de lecture pour *Salammbô*"; the reading program also included ancient and modern works on slavery, astronomy, political economy, and even serpents.

[38] See Flaubert to his niece Caroline, 18 April 1880, *Correspondence,* 9:23. Learning secondhand about Richet's "Les Démoniaques d'aujourd'hui" (see note 27 above), which a friend had accurately described to him both as being "about hysteria" and having "praised me as a physician," Flaubert here accepts the friend's misinformation that Richet had "cited *Salammbô* as proof." In fact, the article discusses hysteria in *Madame Bovary* and makes no mention of *Salammbô.*

[39] Quoted in Anne Green, *Flaubert and the Historical Novel: Salammbô Reassessed* (Cambridge, 1982), 36, my italics.

[40] Flaubert to Sainte-Beuve, December 1862, reprinted in Sainte-Beuve, *Nouveaux Lundis,* 4:437. The hysteria of Saint Theresa is mentioned in two medical sources with which Flaubert was almost certainly conversant: the article "Hystérie" in the *Dictionnaire des sciences médicales,* 23:235; and Briquet, *Traité clinique,* 409.

[41] Flaubert to Mlle. Leroyer de Chantepie, 18 February 1859, *Correspondence,* 4:313. The same letter, cited earlier, goes on to mention Flaubert's researches into hysteria in connection with *Salammbô.* Flaubert was very much a certain type of nineteenth-century Frenchman in the anticlericalism that marked his belief in the connection between piety and psychopathology. See his letter to Mlle. Leroyer de Chantepie, 15 June 1859: "In rereading your last two letters . . . I was sorry to see you so sad. Why do you persist in wanting to go to confession when the mere idea of it troubles you and the confessional itself occasions your relapses? Be, then, your own priest. . . . If I were your physician I would order an immediate visit to Paris, and if I were your spiritual director, I would forbid you access to the confessional" (4:320).

[42] Flaubert to Emile Zola, 3 June 1874, *Correspondence,* 7:143.

[43] My information is based on a computer search of the ARTFL database. I have added the critical letter to Sand of 1867 (not included in the Conard edition) to the tally.

[44] The phrase comes from Pierre Giffard, *Les Grands Bazars* (Paris, 1882), 157.

[45] See Flaubert to Sand, 29 September 1866, in Flaubert and Sand, *Correspondence,* 81: "The psychological sciences will stay where they lie—that is to say, in darkness and folly—insofar as they lack *a precise nomenclature* and the same expression can be employed to signify the most diverse ideas. When the categories are jumbled up, farewell moral philosophy!" (italics in the original).

[46] The quoted phrase comes from the physician Pierre Briquet, who explicitly represents it as a hoary stereotype in need of renovation; see his *Traité clinique,* vii.

[47] Flaubert to Emile Augier, 31 December 1856, *Correspondence,* suppl., vol. 1, pp. 213-14.

[48] Flaubert to Louise Colet, 8 April 1852, *Correspondence,* 2:386-87. For the nerve-brass wire analogy, see Flaubert to Colet, 3 April 1852, ibid., 2:383. The "lethargic" form of hysteria, as a variation on the standard form of the disease, is discussed in Brachet, *Traité de l'hystérie,* 285.

[49] Flaubert to Sand, 12-13 January 1867, Flaubert and Sand, *Correspondence,* 117-18.

[50] Stéphane Mallarmé to Henri Cazalis, 18 February 1869; in Mallarmé, *Correspondence, 1862-1871* (Paris, 1959), 301.

[51] Flaubert, "Notes de lecture pour *Salammbô*," 34.

[52] I am here following the definition of androgyny set forth by Carolyn G. Heilbrun, *Toward a Recognition of Androgyny* (1973; New York, 1982), esp. ix-x.

[53] See Francis Steegmuller, *Flaubert and Madame Bovary: A Double Portrait,* rev. ed. (Chicago, 1977), 339, 341.

[54] Charles Baudelaire, review of *Madame Bovary, Oeuvres complètes,* 4:400-404. I have combined elements of Paul de Man's translation of this essay in the Norton Critical Edition of *Madame Bovary* (New York, 1965; see esp. 339-41) with my own translation from the French.

[55] Ibid., 402. Imagination, says Baudelaire, is the masculine "substitute" for "what are called feelings" (*coeur*); the latter, entirely lacking a rational component, are "generally predominant in women, as they are in animals."

[56] His use of the Academy to stand for professional medicine suggests that he may have been reading the two treatises on hysteria that had received prizes from

that august institution and, hence, that he shared the taste for medical knowledge demonstrated by so many of his literary confreres. The relevant treatises, the most up-to-date books on the subject of hysteria before the appearance of Briquet's treatise in 1859, are Landouzy, *Traité complet de l'hystérie,* and Brachet, *Traité de l'hystérie;* both bear on their title pages the notation "Ouvrage couronné par l'Académic royale de médecine" (Recipient of an award from the Royal Academy of Medicine).

[57] See, e.g., *Fusées* 23: "J'ai cultivé mon hystérie avec jouissance et terreur" (I have cultivated my hysteria with pleasure and terror), an autobiographical note of 1862 in which hysteria is identified as a physical and psychological sensation of dizziness in face of an abyss (*gouffre*) and the latter is associated with such experiences as action, dreaming, memory, and desire; Charles Baudelaire, *Ecrits intimes,* ed. Jean-Paul Sartre (Paris, 1946), 32.

[58] That Baudelaire would later point to the hysterical potentiality of action in *Fusées* (see note above) squares with this characterization of male hysteria in his review of *Madame Bovary.*

[59] Baudelaire, review of *Madame Bovary,* 404-5, italics in the original.

[60] Jean-Paul Sartre, *Search for a Method,* trans. Hazel E. Barnes (New York, 1968), 140-41, italics in the original. Other commentators who have developed the androgyny theme are Dominick LaCapra, *Madame Bovary on Trial* (Ithaca, N.Y., 1982), 179-82; and Naomi Schor, "For a Restricted Thematics: Writing, Speech, and Difference in *Madame Bovary,*" in her *Breaking the Chain: Women, Theory, and French Realist Fiction* (New York, 1985), 3-28.

[61] Flaubert's own commentary on his novel stresses the super-masculinity of Mâtho and the super-femininity of Salammbô. In an early sketch for the novel, he succinctly described Mâtho as "the real man" (*le vrai homme*); see Green, *Flaubert and the Historical Novel,* 37. In a letter to a critic after the publication of the book, he depicted the deity Tanit, of whom Salammbô is a devotee, as "the goddess . . . of love, of the female, humid, fecund element"; see Flaubert to Guillaume Froehner, 21 January 1863, in *The Letters of Gustave Flaubert,* ed. and trans. Francis Steegmuller, 2 vols. (Cambridge, Mass., 1980-82), 2:55.

[62] Gustave Flaubert, *Salammbô,* trans. A.J. Krailsheimer (Harmondsworth, Eng., 1977), 169. I have altered the translation slightly.

[63] B. F. Bart, "Male Hysteria in *Salammbô,*" *Nineteenth-Century French Studies* 12 (1984): 313-21.

[64] Flaubert, *Salammbô,* 166.

[65] Ibid., 123.

[66] B.N. Manuscrits, Nouvelles acquisitions françaises 23662, p. 198. On the ambiguity and "undecidability" of the scene in the tent, see Bart, "Male Hysteria in *Salammbô,*" 317-19; and Naomi Schor, "*Salammbô* Unbound," in *Breaking the Chain,* esp. 118-19.

[67] The remarks, from Flaubert to Colet, 16 November 1852, and an 1843 draft of *The Sentimental Education,* respectively, are quoted by Alphonse Jacobs, Flaubert and Sand, *Correspondance,* 49-50. The letter to Colet is particularly vicious in its sexual characterization of Sand's prose: "In George Sand one perceives vaginal discharge [*fleurs blanches*]; it oozes, and the idea runs between the words as between thighs without muscles."

[68] Flaubert to Sand, 12-13 November 1866, ibid., 91-93.

[69] The quotations come from an unsigned review of *Heures du soir, livre des femmes*—an anthology of women's writing to which Sand contributed under a male signature!—in *Le Figaro,* 20 May 1833; and Jules Janin, "George Sand," in *Biographies des femmes auteurs contemporaines françaises* (Paris, 1836). Both are cited in Leyla Ezdinli, "George Sand's Literary Transvestism: Pre-texts and Contexts" (Ph.D. diss., Princeton University, 1988).

[70] For the four usages, see Flaubert to Sand, 12 February 1863, March-May 1866, 15 May 1866, and 8 September 1866, in Flaubert and Sand, *Correspondance,* 55, 60, 63, 74.

[71] Flaubert to Sand, 31 August 1866, 21 September 1866, in ibid., 72, 75.

[72] Flaubert to Sand, 22 September 1866, in ibid., 78.

[73] George Sand, *Histoire de ma vie,* in Sand, *Oeuvres autobiographiques,* ed. G. Lubin, 2 vols. (Paris, 1970), 1:869.

[74] Ibid., 964, my italics.

[75] Sand to Flaubert, 23 October 1866, in Flaubert and Sand, *Correspondance,* 86.

[76] Sand to Flaubert, 8 December 1866, in ibid., 108.

[77] Sand to Flaubert, 29 November 1866, in ibid., 102-3, italics in the original. Sand never mailed this letter, but instead sent another version of it, parallel in content, the next day.

[78] Sand to Flaubert, 1 October 1866, in ibid., 84.

[79] Flaubert to Sand, 23-24 January 1867, in ibid., 122.

[80] Ibid., capital letter in the original.

[81] Flaubert to Colet, 28 September 1846, *Correspondance,* 1:343, my italics. I have in most respects followed the excellent Steegmuller translation, *Letters,* 1:81-82.

[82] Ibid.

[83] Flaubert to Colet, 12-13 April 1854, in ibid., 4:58.

[84] For a typology of different varieties and subvarieties of the androgynous ideal, see Joyce Trebilcot, "Two Forms of Androgynism," in Mary Vetterling-Braggin, ed., *"Femininity," "Masculinity," and "Androgyny": A Modern Philosophical Discussion* (Totowa, N.J., 1982), 161-69, esp. 164.

[85] Sand to Flaubert, 15 January 1867, in Flaubert and Sand, *Correspondance,* 120. A survey of the ten published works of George Sand included in the ARTEL database revealed two references to the term *hysteria,* both in the context of female religious experience: the reference in the *Histoire de ma vie* of 1855 (see note 73 above) and a similar one some twenty years before in the novel *Lélia* (1833): "The naive poetry of primitive ages, the voluptuous canticles of Solomon . . . sometimes seemed to me more religious in their sublime nakedness than the mystical pantings and fanatical hysterias of Saint Theresa."

[86] Sand to Flaubert, 15 January 1867, in ibid., 120.

[87] *Fusées* 14, for example, indicates that Baudelaire had been reading the 1856 monograph of the psychiatrist Alexandre-Jacques-François Brierre de Boismont, *Du suicide et de la folie suicide.* See also my speculative gloss on his reference to the Academy of Medicine in his review of *Madame Bovary,* note 56 above.

[88] See, on this point, A. J. L. Busst, "The Image of the Androgyne in the Nineteenth Century," in Ian Fletcher, ed., *Romantic Mythologies* (New York, 1967), 1-95, esp. 3-4, and, on early nineteenth-century France, 12-39.

[89] Maxime Du Camp, *Mémoires d'un suicidé* (1853; new ed., Paris, 1876), 256. Du Camp's diagnosis of Jean-Marc, the *Suicidé* of the title, is found in the 1876 "Avertissement de cette nouvelle édition," vii, but it is entirely consistent with the description of Jean-Marc's malady in the original text. For the hysterical component, see, e.g., his dreaminess, mild catalepsy, sense of being inhabited by a demon, and tendency to ecstasy (46-47).

[90] See Georget's dictionary article "Hystérie," 541. On the scientific influences on Georget, see Goldstein, *Console and Classify,* 245-57.

[91] See, e.g., Dr. Mahot, "Observation chez l'homme des phénomènes dits hystériques," *Journal de la section de médecine de la Société académique de Nantes et du Département de la Loire-Inférieure* 15 (1839): 114-23, which cites Georget (115) but in the end comes out in favor of the uterine theory of hysteria, regarding the hysteria in a twenty-year-old mason as the result of a spinal lesion caused by a work accident and pointing out "the close sympathies by which the spine is linked to the uterus" (120); Dr. Mouchet, "Note sur un cas d'hystérie chez l'homme," *Gazette médicale de Paris,* 3rd ser., 3 (1848): 167-68, which concludes, "The careful observation of this patient seems to decide in favor of Georget, who placed the seat of hysteria in the brain"; and H. Desterne, hospital intern, "De l'hystérie chez l'homme," *Union médicale* 2 (28 September 1848): 455-57, which depicts its project as using clinical data to defend the thesis of Georget et al. against proponents of the "dogmatic" uterine hypothesis.

[92] Briquet, *Traité complet,* vii, 126.

[93] Ibid., 598-604.

[94] Ibid., 51.

[95] Ibid., 47, 48.

[96] These points are discussed in Jan Goldstein, "The Hysteria Diagnosis and the Politics of Anticlericalism in Late Nineteenth-Century France," *Journal of Modern History* 54 (1982): 209-39; an expanded version of that discussion appears in *Console and Classify,* chap. 9.

[97] Mark S. Micale, "Diagnostic Discriminations: Jean-Martin Charcot and the Nineteenth-Century Idea of Masculine Hysterical Neurosis" (Ph.D. diss., Yale University, 1987). Some of Charcot's published work on male hysteria was recently collected and reprinted; see Michèle Ouerd, ed., Jean-Martin Charcot, *Leçons sur l'hystérie virile* (Paris, 1984).

[98] Jean-Martin Charcot, "Leçon d'ouverture," *Progrès médical* 10 (1882): 336.

[99] The link between Charcot's claims of universality and his emphasis on male hysteria is made by Kenneth Levin, "Freud's Paper 'On Male Hysteria' and the Conflict Between Anatomical and Physiological Models," *Bulletin of the History of Medicine* 48 (1974): 377-97, esp. 381-82. I built upon Levin's argument, explicitly tying it to Charcot's commitment to positivism and to the political connotations of positivism, in "Hysteria Diagnosis," 234.

[100] See, e.g., Jean-Martin Charcot, *Leçons du mardi à la Salpêtrière,* 2 vols. (Paris, 1889), 2:36, 50.

[101] C. R. [Mme. C. Renooz], "Charcot dévoilé," *Revue scientifique des femmes* 1 (December 1888): 241-47,

esp. 241-45. The dissertation in question was written by Caroline Schulze. Charcot likewise used the occasion of the January 1889 defense of Blanche Edwards's dissertation, "De l'hémiplégie dans quelques affections nerveuses," to remark that female doctors should confine themselves to the treatment of women and children; see Mélanie Lipinska, *Histoire des femmes médecins depuis l'antiquité jusqu'à nos jours* (Paris, 1900), 426, n. 2.

[102] Jean-Martin Charcot, *Leçons sur les maladies du système nerveux faites à la Salpêtrière,* 3 vols. (Paris, 1875-83), 3:252-53. Charcot notes here that all female hysteria does not follow the "capricious" model. But he made his point about the basic difference between male and female hysterics repeatedly, observing more than a decade later, "I have already remarked many times that one should not expect to encounter in men that morbid *brio* so frequent in reality in women"; *Leçons du mardi,* 2:50.

[103] Michèle Ouerd, introduction to Charcot, *Leçons sur l'hystérie virile,* stresses the class background of Charcot's male hysterics; so does Micale, "Diagnostic Discriminations," which also discusses Charcot's Jewish and Arab cases. One late-nineteenth-century medical student researching male hysteria at the Necker Hospital found the disease most common among members of the liberal professions; see Auguste Klein, *De l'hystérie chez l'homme* (Paris, 1880), 14. But although Charcot cited Klein's work in support of the male hysteria diagnosis, Klein's specific sociological results did not, tellingly enough, affect the way Charcot represented the population of male hysterics.

[104] Michèle Ouerd makes the fascinating point that the wandering uterus motif of traditional hysteria was replicated by the unrooted, vagrant, and marginal social status of the male hysterics that predominated in Charcot's late case studies; see her introduction to Charcot, *Leçons sur l'hystérie virile,* 27-28. On the linkage of women and the lower classes in the context of a scientific and stigmatizing rhetoric in nineteenth-century France, see Susanna Barrows, *Distorting Mirrors: Visions of the Crowd in Late-Nineteenth-Century France* (New Haven, 1981), chap. 2; and Ruth Harris, "Murder Under Hypnosis in the Case of Gabrielle Bompard: Psychiatry in the Courtroom in Belle Epoque Paris," in W. F. Bynum, Roy Porter, and Michael Shepherd, eds., *The Anatomy of Madness: Essays in the History of Psychiatry,* 2 vols. (London, 1985), esp. 2:219-20. On the linkage of women and the Orient in nineteenth-century French discourse, see Edward W. Said, *Orientalism* (New York, 1979), 182, 186-88.

[105] Jean-Martin Charcot, "Contracture hystérique et aimants" (1878), in *Oeuvres complètes,* 9 vols. (Paris, 1888-94), 9:277, my italics.

[106] Goldstein, "Hysteria Diagnosis"; and Goldstein, *Console and Classify,* chap. 9.

[107] Quoted in Louis Legrand, *L'Influence du positivisme dans l'oeuvre scolaire de Jules Ferry* (Paris, 1961), 118.

[108] This argument is made by Debora L. Silverman, *Art Nouveau in Fin-de-Siècle France: Politics, Psychology, and Style* (Berkeley, 1989), chap. 4.

[109] See, e.g., Jules Falret, "Discussion de la folie raisonnante," *Annales médico-psychologiques,* 4th ser., 7 (1866): esp. 404-7; Charles Lasègue, "Les Hystér-iques, leur perversité, leurs mensonges," ibid., 6th ser., 6 (1881): 111-18; and, on the mild hysteria of normal women, Richet, "Les Démoniaques d'aujourd'hui," 346. Richet's point was cited in the work of Charcot's student Henri Huchard, "Caractère, moeurs, état mental des hystériques," *Archives de neurologie* 3 (1882): 206.

[110] Wolf Lepenies, *Between Literature and Science: The Rise of Sociology,* trans. R.J. Hollingdale (Cambridge, 1988), esp. introduction. Lepenies makes this case for France, England, and Germany.

[111] See Elaine Showalter, "Critical Cross-Dressing: Male Feminists and the Woman of the Year," *Raritan* 3 (Fall 1983): 130-49, esp. 138.

[112] An overview and bibliography of this debate can be found in William Veeder, *Mary Shelley and Frankenstein: The Fate of Androgyny* (Chicago, 1986), 234-35.

Colleen Hobbs (essay date 1993)

SOURCE: "Reading the Symptoms: An Exploration of Repression and Hysteria in Mary Shelley's *Frankenstein,*" in *Studies in the Novel,* Vol. XXV, No. 2, Summer, 1993, pp. 152-69.

[*In the excerpt that follows, Hobbs contends that Mary Shelley's Frankenstein is a character afflicted with a "female malady" brought on by his repression of stereotypically feminine traits.*]

Why isn't one a beastly girl and privileged to shriek?

Ford Madox Ford, *Parade's End,* 1925

Critics of Mary Shelley's *Frankenstein* have articulated a multiplicity of gendered characteristics in her protagonist, Victor Frankenstein. Those in the tradition of Ellen Moers interpret the novel as a birth myth, reading Victor as a life-giving mother.[1] These studies contrast with works focusing on the character's appropriation of the female realm, which find him to be a Promethean usurper "engaged upon a rape of nature."[2] And finally, Shelley's work has been mined for evidence that it blurs cultural definitions of gender by creating an androgynous figure.[3] Current critical debate has offered feminist readings of the implications for Shelley's ultra-feminine/hyper-masculine creation, but it has not examined the textual mechanism that Shelley herself uses to focus such an examination of gender socialization. I will suggest that Shelley provides us a locus for her critique of repressive artificial sexual roles in several symptoms and episodes of hysteria that she associates with Victor. In depicting Victor's response to the complications raised by his monster, Shelley attributes a classically female malady to a male character; simultaneously, she produces a site where orthodox gender stereotypes are revealed as inadequate, dangerous constructions. Beret Strong has argued that eighteenth-century hysteria theory combined corporeal symptoms associated with femininity with the masculine associations of reason: as a result, hysteria, in this period, "is located at the crossroads between masculine and feminine as they are culturally construed."[4] Shelley's character maps this intersection and the difficulties raised when the boundaries of gender are transgressed. A consideration of the complaint that Shelley calls "insanity, not of the understanding but of the heart," can sharpen our perception not only of her character's actions, but also of the author's commentary on the origins of depravity and monstrosity in Regency England.[5]

Eighteenth-century doctors increasingly defined hysteria as a "nervous disorder" associated with insanity; therefore, an examination of this social phenomenon must consider the terms in which hysteria and the "English Malady" are discussed during the reign of George III—Percy Shelley's "old, mad, blind, despised, and dying king."[6] In England as well as in France, Philippe Pinel's act of unchaining Paris' lunatics in 1793 symbolized the application of Reason to the problems of insanity: the mentally ill were no longer to be controlled through cruelty and force, but through a more humane system described as "moral management." Patients were seen as children to be controlled through discipline that emphasized "holding out encouragement and approbations to the deserving, [and] exerting the influence of the shame" upon the difficult.[7] Physicians attempted to correct disordered reasoning by controlling the minds of their patients, primarily by wearing down their opposition through rigorous treatments of solitary confinement, forced baths, and purges—laxatives, bleedings, emetics. John Ferriar, a physician in a Manchester asylum, offers insight into the issue of control between doctor and patient. He describes physicians' shift from physical to mental restraint of patients when he states that "though I would exclude everything painful and terrible, from a lunatic-house, yet the management of

hope and apprehension in the patient, forms the most useful part of discipline." His treatment of hysterics through "management of the mind" could be unrelenting.[8]

Hysteria's etymological and historical associations with the feminine are well known, and its manifestations in Victorian women have been the object of much study.[9] Hysteria in late eighteenth-century England has not received as much critical attention, but the ailment was so prevalent in 1784 that Thomas Syndenham routinely suspected it when diagnoses of female patients proved difficult.[10] Elaine Showalter's work has illustrated how Victorian doctors reduced the concepts of madness and hysteria to a specifically female complaint, yet the sensibilities of the early nineteenth century still could attribute hysteric symptoms to men. In 1823, a legal manual by a doctor and a lawyer illustrated "Feigned or Simulated Diseases" with the following account of hysteria:

> Dr. [William] Cullen is said to have been deceived by a man who, pretending to be affected with this disease [hysteria], was retained in the Edinburgh Infirmary as long as suited his convenience, and afterwards triumphantly acknowledged the deceit; affusion of cold water, low diet, and blisters, will generally furnish the means of detection.[11]

The authors' hostility toward the patient's deception and their willingness to punish it harshly become a commonplace in Victorian case studies; however, their casual inclusion of the example among a legal guide indicates that Shelley's depiction of a male hysteric would not have been without precedent.

Similarly, Ferriar can observe in 1799 that "men are frequently attacked by complaints which approach the hysterical type."[12] The doctor then makes a distinction that is particularly telling for readers of *Frankenstein*. He observes that insanity arises among men as a result of hard drinking, pride, disappointment, terror, and anxiety over business. Of these factors, only terror seems to address the concerns of Shelley's character. Ferriar's explanation of madness in women applies much more directly to Victor's situation: "From the peculiar situation of the other sex, their minds are sometimes deranged by the restraint or misdirection of passions, which were bestowed to constitute their happiness."[13] Although Shelley's text never uses the term "hysteria," her depiction of a character with an unspeakable secret suffers the same "restraint or misdirection of passions" that Ferriar specifically attributes to a female hysteric. Likewise, her character is shown to restrain his feelings for the best of motives—to "constitute the happiness" of his family and friends.

The medical profession's discussion of misdirected passions is further illustrated in the works of Rousseau, an author well known to both Shelley and her mother, Mary Wollstonecraft. The learned father of Rousseau's *Émile* espouses the Enlightenment models of education, order, and control through the training he gives his son. This narrator describes the feminine ideal of moderation through his heroine, Sophy, yet he grants the self-abnegating creature a measure of emotional excess on behalf of her loved ones. Rousseau's male character must endure this criticism from his father when courtship jeopardizes his emotional equilibrium:

> How pitiable you are going to be, thus subjected to your unruly passions! There will always be privations, losses, and alarms . . . How will you know how to sacrifice inclination to duty and to hold out against your heart in order to listen to your reason? . . . Inform me, then, at what crime a man stops when he has only the wishes of his heart for laws and knows how to resist nothing he desires?[14]

For Rousseau's narrator, passion is equated with anarchy and destitution, a message that never is painted so bleakly when applied to women. Sophy's emotional outbursts are discussed as threatening her character, but the very existence of civilization appears to depend on Émile's ability to resist the destructive force of his heart by applying the force of reason.[15]

Shelley's own family shows evidence of such instruction in this rational model of happiness through emotional restraint. Two-year-old William died in 1819—the third child lost to his parents in a little more than four years—and his passing left Mary Shelley inconsolable. When Percy asked his father-in-law to comfort the grieving mother, Godwin complied, but with a curious condolence. "You must . . . allow me the privilege of a father, and philosopher, in expostulating with you on this depression," he writes in a letter that offers more scolding than sympathy:

> I cannot but consider it as lowering your character in a memorable degree, and putting you quite among the commonality and mob of your sex, when I had thought I saw in you symptoms entitling you to be ranked among those noble spirits that do honour to our nature.[16]

Godwin argues here that his daughter is indulging in the weakness exhibited by the "mob of *your* sex" rather than exerting more of the control practiced by *"our"* noble spirits. His concern for strength of character assumes a connection between intense emotion and feminine inferiority that he contrasts with "noble" self-control. In addition, the contrast of "mob," "lowering," and "commonality" with "entitle[ment]," "rank," and "privilege" evokes a class ideology that again confirms masculine character and emotional restraint.

Shelley's fictional portrayal of grief in *Frankenstein* not only prefigures Godwin's response to an emotional crisis, but it replicates the sensibility of Reason and emotional restraint. Shelley creates the same terrible struggle for moderation between a learned father who shares Godwin's "philosophy" of logic and a passionate son struggling for self-control. In her representation, Alphonse lectures Victor on "the folly of giving way to immoderate grief" as the guilt-ridden protagonist mourns the deaths of William and Justine.[17] Shelley's character can avoid further censure only by adopting a strategy to avoid his father "until I had recovered myself so far as to be enabled to conceal those feelings that overpowered me" (pp. 91-92). She illustrates that the son has learned the father's lesson by having him uncritically repeat Alphonse's homily that "a human being in perfection ought always to preserve a calm and peaceful mind, and never to allow passion or transitory desire to disturb his tranquillity" (p. 51).

Given the coincidence between the scathing condolence Shelley received from her father and her fictional representations of grief, it is understandable that Anne Mellor would find Victor Frankenstein's statement of emotional control to be an "authorial credo and moral touchstone."[18] However, critics who credit the thoroughness of the character's emotional repression overlook the problems raised by Shelley's model of artificial tranquility. Shelley's novel complicates the question of emotional control by revealing its problematic implication with gender. According to Godwin's model, as we have seen, expression of grief characterizes only the common "mob" of women; therefore, the Promethean protagonist of *Frankenstein* resists "unmanly" emotions. As Marlon Ross's study illustrates, this Godwinian repression of the feminine reflects a specifically masculine ideology within Romantic poetics. Ross finds that in separating itself from the feminine influence of shared community values, Victor's project "looses his own unrestrained desire upon the world, a desire that is relentlessly aggressive, anarchic, and destructive."[19] While the monster illustrates the expression of Victor's unspeakable masculine desires, Shelley uses Victor's body to show the dangers of unspeakable feminine ones. She observes that because a social and psychological system categorizes strong emotion as feminine and common, the men who experience such emotion risk chaos: a redefinition of gender and class status. In examining Shelley's depiction of Victor's repression of the feminine, we must take into account the social and political consequences which occur when control gives way to an emotional transgression.

Shelley illustrates this redefinition most clearly in several episodes of hysteria that she associates with Victor—a character who may be less the phallic aggressor that some have described than a prototype for Freud's

Dora. By attributing hysteria to a male character, Shelley invites us to look for problems in the cultural orthodoxy of masculinity, especially as represented in Victor's project. The representation of a male hysteric in Shelley's text illustrates her belief that, despite a culture's artificial division of emotions by gender, the male body can, if need be, speak in a "feminine" voice.

As we have seen, the purveyors of "rational" medicine allowed men to experience hysteria for "manly" reasons: duplicity, drunkenness, and pride. Yet Victor Frankenstein, who attempts to heed Alphonse's maxims for moderation, transgresses the conventions of gender representation by being the wrong kind of hysteric. Not until his manly deathbed speech does Victor become the prideful, masculine hysteric of Ferriar's model. Instead, his behavior more closely replicates talkative, emotional, feminine hysteria. In his failure to uphold his father's standards for male reason and control, Victor articulates the schism between "masculine" and "feminine" behavior. In Shelley's narrative, the bourgeois Frankenstein family unit has maintained Alphonse's standards by insulating itself from the disruptive outside world. As Kate Ellis has argued, the members "wall in" domestic affection as they "[adjure] one another to repress their anger and grief for the sake of maintaining tranquility."[20] However, Ellis' model does not account for the manner in which the Frankenstein family has segregated masculine from feminine emotions. The iconic figure of Caroline Beaufort weeping on her father's coffin illustrates how gender intersects with demands for emotional control. Caroline is presented as a model of femininity, and her display is the only instance in the novel where grief is not only accepted, but valorized: the idealized image of Caroline "weeping bitterly" occurs early in Victor's autobiography and immediately defines the family pattern of female grief and its dependence upon male protection and control. Indeed, Alphonse finds a means of controlling even Caroline's moment of agony—the portrait he commissions captures her moment of despair in a manner that provides "an air of dignity and beauty, that hardly permitted the sentiment of pity" (p. 73). Her pain is now domesticated in a fashion that enhances the charm of her grieving demeanor, and the squalor and poverty of the "historical" situation are omitted to emphasize the scene's calm "dignity."[21] Alphonse's aesthetic revision of Caroline's history implies a patriarchal code—the father's ability to control the emotions of his entire family, sanitizing an occasion of despair for display over the family mantelpiece.

This depiction of Alphonse Frankenstein, like William Godwin's letter to Shelley, represents a code of emotional repression enforced by the male head of the household. Although her novel emphasizes Caroline's moment of grief, it is through Victor's self-conscious struggles that Shelley reveals the actual work of perpetuating a system designed to denigrate feminine outbursts in favor of masculine self-control. He is a model of Alphonse's ideas of "reason" and "moderation" when he chides Earnest for weeping at William's death, ordering him to "try to be more calm . . . you must assist me in acquiring sufficient calmness" (p. 74). However, Victor previously had admitted that "my tears flowed" as he looked on William's miniature before Earnest entered the room. In addition, he had shown no indication that Elizabeth, "for ever weeping," had acted inappropriately. His correction of Earnest's behavior further confirms the family's inability to cope with outward signs of male grief; the contradiction of this brotherly reprimand with Victor's own unseen tears alerts us to an interior struggle with his father's ideals of masculinity and reserve.

Emphasizing this code of restraint, Shelley shows Victor under the influence of other domestic models valorizing control. Caroline internalizes this repression to such an extent that she apologizes for not wanting to die. She reconsiders her wistful deathbed observance, "is it not hard to quit you all," and interprets her remark as an impropriety; she immediately qualifies her imagined transgression by saying that "these are not thoughts befitting me; I will endeavour to resign myself more cheerfully to death" (p. 38). Similarly, Alphonse refuses to display emotion after William's murder and, if allowed, would have changed the subject, "introduc[ing] some other topic than that of our disaster" (p. 75).

Shelley's treatment of the family psychodynamics makes it clear that, for the Frankensteins, grieving must be completed quickly and privately, and with the intervention of female nurturers who speed up the process. Alphonse's patriarchy, advancing a code of self-containment, charges these nurturers with responding to masculine demands for the kind of attention and comfort that will relieve them of emotional distress. Delegating these emotionally laden "feminine" tasks to women detaches men even more from this "unmanly" activity. For example, Elizabeth recognizes that her job following Caroline's death is to console the entire family. Victor recalls: "she felt that the most imperious duty, of rendering her uncle and cousins happy, had devolved upon her. She consoled me, amused her uncle, instructed my brothers . . . continually endeavouring to contribute to the happiness of others" (p. 39). Shelley's depiction of Elizabeth, as Ellis notes, spells out her "role in maintaining the atmosphere of continual sunshine in which Victor claims he spent *his* best years."[22] Although, as Shelley illustrates with Alphonse, men determine the rules of behavior, they give women the most visible role in the grieving process, and Alphonse deifies Caroline Beaufort as the perfect mourner. For men in such a world, Shelley's novel implies, repression is the only appropriate response to grief and, indeed, the only response accepted by Alphonse.

The Frankenstein men actively distance themselves from disturbing emotions, and their need for this insulating distance is apparent if we consider one particular consequence of unchecked feeling: sexual passion. Shelley indicates that, for the Frankenstein family, sexuality is the only subject more taboo than grief. In her novel of creation, the only scenes that obliquely indicate sexual desire are the monster's hovering over the sleeping Justine and his triumph over the prone body of Elizabeth. Shelley's narrative suggests the volatility of sexual passion and illustrates Alphonse's attempts to contain its power. For Victor's father, marriage is not a concession to love or physical attraction, but rather the culmination of a patriarchal ideal that will "[bestow] on the state sons."[23] Similarly, Shelley has Victor's quasi-incestuous relationship with Elizabeth emphasize compatibility, not the sexual chemistry. Elizabeth describes herself as "cousin and playmate"; Victor is her "constant friend and companion" (p. 185). Alphonse looks forward to their marriage as a time when "we shall all be united, and neither hopes or fears arise to disturb our domestic calm" (p. 150). Victor is decidedly guarded about marriage, and even in his most passionate declarations of love to Elizabeth, he can only consecrate to her his "endeavours for contentment" (p. 187). In Shelley's 1823 addition, she makes Victor reflect on his lack of feeling when, on his wedding day, he gazes at his bride and "instead of feeling the exultation of a—lover—a husband—a sudden gush of tears blinded my sight . . . Reason again awoke and [I shook] off all unmanly—or more properly *all natural thoughts of mischance*" (p. 190, emphasis mine). Shelley's text replicates Victor's turmoil on two levels. His fears of "mischance" are a conscious response to the monster's death threat, yet they apply to his unstated doubts about his cousinship with Elizabeth. The text emphasizes Victor's apprehension of this relationship by breaking the narrative as the character stumbles over the words "lover" and "husband."

Shelley emphasizes Victor's awareness, at this moment, of the contrast between lovers' passion and cousins' contentment, but she quells his contemplation through the quick return of "reason." In Victor's expression of discomfort, Shelley plants a telling comparison: his "unmanly thoughts"—in effect, a "feminine" admission of fear—are equated with what is properly "natural." She here reveals how Victor has consciously constructed the "manly" for himself, knowing that it involves "shaking off" his true feelings. The "manly," then, is Victor's denial of the disruptive and thus frightening possibility of physical passion, as well as the unseemly "feminine" admission of fear.

This urgency of self-control does not suggest that Victor is incapable of passion; Shelley instead shows that he is unwilling to bring it into the domestic realm. His passion is directed toward his work, which is safely outside the family circle. His descriptions of scientific discovery display a sexual tension that would have been inappropriate in Alphonse's home. Pursuing his studies, he is "exalted to a kind of transport"; he feels "delight and rapture" upon arriving at the "summit of my goals . . . [the] consummation of my toils" (p. 47). His rhetoric sounds like an address to a lover: he desires scientific discovery "with ardour," while his warmest feelings toward Elizabeth are decidedly less enthusiastic, no more than a platonic, "paradisiacal [dream] of love and joy" (p. 186). Shelley illustrates, then, that to maintain this code of masculinity, physical passion must be controlled to protect the interior, domestic world of serenity from the outside world of turbulent feeling.

Shelley's attention to repression in Victor's code of masculinity is significant because his version of the "manly" is maintained only by constant vigilance. Like William Godwin, Victor accepts an ideology of masculine control, feminine nurturing, and the sanctity of home at the expense of communication with family members. Yet after the creation of the monster and the crisis it precipitates, Victor no longer can meet these rigid demands. Victor has proven his feminine capacity for procreation and then denied that aspect of himself by abandoning his monster/child. The rejection of his disappointing but powerful offspring unleashes a truth about the denial of human feeling that sheer masculine repression can no longer control. Shelley makes its inadequacy clear in Victor's aborted attempt to share his emotional problems with Alphonse. Tortured by the guilt of irresponsibly engendering a life that has destroyed his family, Victor claims, as he has before, to have murdered William, Justine, and Henry. Although he would have "given the whole world to have confided the fatal secret," Victor always had refused to explain his self-accusations for fear of being labelled insane (p. 182). His father, who previously had ignored these outbursts, now responds in the manner Victor has predicted: "are you mad? My dear son, I entreat you never to make such an assertion again." Victor recalls that his statements

> convinced my father that my ideas were deranged, and he instantly changed the subject of our conversation, and to alter the course of my thoughts. He wished as much as possible to obliterate the memory of the scenes that had taken place in Ireland, and never alluded to them, or suffered me to speak of my misfortunes. (p. 183)

Alphonse shuts down Victor's every response to his crisis. He must not appear outwardly unhappy; he is accused of lunacy when he expresses his grief and guilt. Shelley takes away even his voice, since Victor is forbidden to broach the subject ever again. Shelley's articulation of this narrative raises a question: other than the rigorous self-control encouraged by

Alphonse—evident in the "utmost self-violence" Victor employs to quell the "imperious voice of wretchedness"—what opportunities for self-expression are available in such a controlled, "masculine" environment?

Shelley's answer to this question effectively subverts the patriarchal hierarchy epitomized by Alphonse. Victor revolts against his father's demands that he be the most "manly" of men by exhibiting the behavior of the most "womanly" women. She burdens her ultra-masculine character with a plethora of feelings and secrets that must be silenced, but she also provides him a method of revealing his emotions through an equally exaggerated inscription of femininity. Critics have explored hysteria's potential for protest and disruption and have examined how repressed hostility is transformed into physical symptoms like the fainting, trembling, and hallucinating that Victor exhibits.[24] These symptoms are evident in Shelley's character when, like the hysteric, he is unwilling to communicate a truth, either to himself or to those around him. Victor's behavior after creating the monster, for example, enacts a hysteric response both to the guilt of abandoning his creature and to his anxiety about hiding its existence from Clerval. "I dreaded to behold this monster," he says, "but I feared still more that Henry should see him" (p. 56). His fear of Henry's reaction demonstrates, as Ellis notes, "his inability to bring the Monster home" to the family that refuses to acknowledge the world's unpleasantness.[25] The tension between his need to deny his creature's existence and his wish to "bring home" the monster is resolved by a series of hysteric symptoms. After determining that his creature has fled, he clasps his hands, jumps over chairs, and indulges in "loud unrestrained, heartless laughter." He then hallucinates, seeing the monster "seize him," and falls down "in a fit" (p. 56).

The "feminine" component of such behavior, i.e. Victor's post-partum depression and agitation, is more evident if we compare it to that of the "lovely maniac" in Wollstonecraft's *Maria,* who sings ballads and utters "unconnected exclamations and questions . . . interrupted by fits of laughter."[26] Even the source of this character's madness has echoes of Victor's situation: "she had been married, against her inclination . . . [and] in consequence of his treatment, *or something which hung on her mind . . .* lost her senses" (emphasis mine). Showalter suggests that Wollstonecraft uses the asylum to illustrate confining masculine institutions that can drive women to insanity. Because women are traditionally associated with irrationality and the body—at the expense of the "noble spirits" of reason and mind that Godwin observed—"madness, even when experienced by men, is metaphorically and symbolically represented as feminine."[27] By attributing the most "feminine" of female traits to a male character, Shelley forces us to re-assess a character who, heretofore, seemed determined to impress us with his "manly"

control. Wollstonecraft uses hysteria to depict the oppression of women: Shelley employs the condition to uncover what is being repressed in and by Victor's code of masculinity. She calls into question her character's aggressive version of masculinity by shutting it down with an extreme inscription of the feminine that silences him when he wants to speak and paralyzes him when he most needs to act. Victor's hysteric symptoms illustrate that his body will address the message that his brain would deny: even rational "noble spirits" must attend to their emotions.

Through the depiction of such symptoms, Shelley can concisely communicate the numerous fears and anxieties that Victor is unable to articulate. In the novel's chronology, she shows Victor's first hysteric symptoms appearing as he constructs "a new species [that] would bless me as its creator" without reflecting on the ethical repercussions of his endeavor. Significantly, even at this stage, Shelley has his body signal that the project conflicts with his internal moral code. Victor outwardly asks himself no questions about the implications of his work. He sees it only as a scientific study that will "pour a torrent of light into our dark world" (p. 49). The act, as he sees it, is not an appropriation of the female act of birth and procreation, but an "[infusion of] spark" in the manner of the Old Testament God, or of Prometheus (p. 52). His body, however, sends a very resistant message that seems almost to replicate some of the conditions of pregnancy. He is "oppressed by a slow fever . . . [his] trembling hands almost refused to accomplish their task; I became as timid as a love-sick girl and alternate tremor and passionate ardour took the place of wholesome sensation and regulated ambition" (p. 51). For William Veeder, this passage offers evidence of effeminacy resulting from Victor's bifurcation of male from female. Shelley's message, however, does not so much polarize genders as it manifests a return of the repressed: Victor's body becomes the text of the feminine characteristics he has denied himself. The act of creation makes Victor physically feverish and ill; his hands, significantly, object to the task he sets before them. The timidity and tremors that Victor would attribute to nervousness are also signs of fear, but is he frightened by his grisly work, or by his unconscious anxiety about his appropriation of the female role? Victor refers to a tactic Alphonse has employed, hoping that "exercise and amusement would soon drive away such symptoms" (pp. 51-52), but since his afflictions are the result of mental, not just physical duress, they cannot be eradicated simply by amusement. Shelley reveals that the work Victor can describe as mere "regulated ambition" is loaded with ethical questions and, from the outset, his body reflects these inner doubts.[28]

Many of Victor's symptoms, then, are manifestations of his wish to conceal or deny his own creation, which is allied with disruptive emotions he must not bring home. These symptoms make literal his refusal to look upon his own work. His hysteric fit in Clerval's presence ends as Victor loses consciousness, an act that ensures he is "not the witness of [Henry's] grief; for I was lifeless."[29] The lengthy nervous fever following this fit allows him to avoid responsibility for his new creation. Even in his illness, however, he cannot entirely forget his accountability, since his guilty conscience imagines that "the form of the monster on whom I had bestowed existence was ever before my eyes" (p. 57).

Victor's symptoms also may be found in the "mist" that obscures his vision. It first occurs when he sees the creature on the glacier: "I was troubled: a mist came over my eyes, and I felt a faintness seize me . . . I trembled with rage and horror" (p. 94). Here, Shelley stages Victor's reaction to the monster—"mist," trembling, and faintness—as much more than a simple display of fear. Victor cannot admit to himself and cannot explain to others that he has neglected an obligation to a creature that endangers his family. He can do so only in Ireland, when informed of a murder. Although he is still unaware that Clerval is the victim, he begins to suspect the monster's involvement when told of the bruises on his neck: "I remembered the murder of my brother, and felt myself extremely agitated; my limbs trembled, and a mist came before my eyes" (p. 172). The repetition of these details indicates that Victor knows how this episode will end. He has refused to comply with the monster's demand for a companion, has destroyed the female creature as the monster watched, and has been threatened with retribution for failing to keep his promise. Shelley underscores Victor's capacity for repression by having him obliterate even this overwhelming evidence: the "mist" allows him to pretend, for a little longer, that he cannot see the tragedy for which he is responsible. When forced to view Clerval's body and to confront physical evidence of his action, he again loses consciousness and succumbs to a lengthy fever: "The human frame could no longer support the agonizing suffering that I endured, and I was carried out of the room in strong convulsions" (p. 174). Victor cannot bear the weight of his guilt, and so he again escapes into illness. But even his sickness bears out his inner feelings: his ailment is a fever, a symptom that indicates a burning admission of culpability.

If it is only through hysteria that Victor can voice the unspeakable, then his body speaks volumes on his wedding night. Here, Shelley brings to a climax the issues of hysteria and sexuality, just as the monster has promised all along. She has shown us Victor's perception that a union with his "more than sister" will prove problematic. Gilbert and Gubar see the relationship as one of "barely disguised incest."[30] and even Shelley's Alphonse wonders if Victor "regard[s] her as your sister, without any wish that she might become your wife" (p. 148). The narrative associates Victor's future bride with unnatural monstrosity in two forms. In an early dream after creating the monster, Victor's kiss (their *only* kiss) transforms Elizabeth into Victor's dead mother. He awakens from this vision of Elizabeth/Caroline to view the monster standing over his bed. This nightmare scene, George Levine notes, "conflates remarkably with the actual wedding night murder; in both, the Monster appears in the moonlight, looking in the first instance upon Victor's body, then upon Elizabeth's."[31] In addition to the doubling Levine observes, Shelley connects Elizabeth to the monster in another instance. On their honeymoon trip to Evian, the same trip where Victor stumbles over the term "lover," his vision becomes blurred while "gazing on the beloved face of Elizabeth" (p. 190). Just as a "mist" obscured Victor's view of the monster and the dead Clerval, so now "a sudden gush of tears blinded my sight and . . . I turned away to hide the involuntary emotion." Victor is concealing "unmanly" emotion, but he also is concealing the face of the woman whom he has married—the woman he associates with his uncontrollable creation and with an incestuous relation. Victor's last words to Elizabeth, then, are doubly loaded. When she asks "what is it you fear," his reply that "this night is dreadful, very dreadful," addresses both his stated apprehension about the monster and his unstated fear of consummating their marriage.

Shelley's exploration of her character's fears of sex and loss of control culminate in the scene of Elizabeth's murder. His reaction to Elizabeth's murder seems passive, or simply cowardly, only if insulated from questions about his ambivalence toward marriage, or more specifically, heterosexual passion. Victor's body shows, in effect, his fear that desire will kill the woman he has considered only in terms of her purity and innocence. When Victor hears his wife scream, "the whole truth rushed into my mind, my arms dropped, the motion of every muscle and fibre was suspended . . . this state lasted but for an instant; the scream was repeated, and I rushed into the room" (p. 193). Here, the character faints, just as he did when viewing Clerval's body. However, Shelley explicitly contrasts his former paralysis with the active role he takes after Elizabeth's death: "I *rushed* toward her, and embraced her *with ardour*" (emphasis mine). Significantly, Shelley crafts the novel's only erotic embrace to include a lifeless body, one that cannot arouse uncontrollable sexual passion and that will preserve the brother-sister relationship threatened by nuptial union. Her language suggests that Victor's paralysis in a situation demanding action is due to both the fear of defiling his bride's virginity and the fear of the unleashed powers of sexuality. Immediately after Victor hears screams, Shelley interrupts the narrative to have Victor recall Elizabeth as "the best hope, and the purest creature of the earth." Victor regains command of Elizabeth as a sexual being, emphatically closing down the possibility of passion and asserting her innocence to assure us that she *did* die before losing her virginity.

Here, then, we learn the knowledge that the Frankenstein family suppresses by focusing on compatibility and domestic tranquility, the knowledge that Victor's "workshop of filthy creation" tries to make obsolete. A scream from the room where Victor will consummate his marriage freezes him with fear because Victor's dread is not simply of the monster. His fear is of the terrifying sexual truth that, for a moment, he clearly sees: physical passion is unstable, disruptive, and irrational—the antithesis of the "tranquil" existence he has been trained to pursue. His fears, then, are not just of the explosive emotions Elizabeth and other women can unleash. He is, for a moment, aware of the duplicity involved in his own enactment of masculinity. If Victor's understanding of himself as a gendered being is determined on the basis of emotional control, then overpowering, hysterical symptoms reveal the frailty of his gendered construction. A man without rational self-control is what? A lunatic? A woman? According to Alphonse's code, he certainly cannot be a man. In this moment, when "the whole truth rushed into my mind," he unconsciously may wish for the monster's success in his murderous endeavour. The monster can remove both the doubts he feels about his sister/wife relationship with Elizabeth and terrifying possibilities opened by the sexual act. Shelley has emphasized her character's repeated refusal to examine these issues, and the fulfillment of the monster's promise will ensure the continued sublimation of passion in favor of detachment and Reason. On his wedding night, the moment that most acutely defines Victor as not-woman, Shelley's character refuses to fulfill the role of an aggressive, phallic male: "the motion of every muscle and fibre was suspended." Victor is implicated in Elizabeth's death not just, as Veeder argues, because he wishes to "transcend mortal unions" and achieve androgynous perfection. If Victor's body strives for a union, it is one that can call back the emotional range denied him by his culture's construction of masculinity. In this moment, his body resists its construction as a gendered self by refusing to rescue Elizabeth.[32]

Victor's hysteria results from his emotional constraints, in addition to the ethical questions raised by his creation of the monster. Not only must he restrain his grief for lost family members, but he also must cope with his feelings of guilt and responsibility for their deaths. Perhaps most difficult, though, is the repression of the self-doubt he feels about the moral questions the monster raises. His final speech, in which he reports that "I have been occupied in examining my past conduct; nor do I find it blameable," protests his innocence rather too much to indicate a guilt-free conscience. Victor has brought a creature into the world and abandoned it; a review of his actions, for all his rationalizing, seems to find him culpable. Shelley's

narrative unleashes a set of circumstances that her protagonist cannot control; his refusal to admit his own vulnerability ensures that the unexamined issues ultimately will consume him.

Shelley shows that Victor's failure is not so much that he made a monster, but that he failed to tell anyone about it. Because his scientific discoveries are covert and his personal fears are hidden, Victor faces his deepest fears in rational, manly privacy. Shelley indicates that the division of gender roles is dangerous not just because of its instability, but because it produces this isolation. When ideology circumscribes communication according to gender, too many important messages remain unsaid, messages that would articulate vital information concerning human pain and human need. In discussing Freud's hysteric patient Dora, Hélène Cixous describes the hysteric as resisting the family system by destroying its ability to function—a model that Shelley's systematic annihilation of the Frankensteins pushes to extreme limits. Cixous observes that the hysteric's resistance is driven by an unspoken need: "[t]he hysteric is not just someone who has had her words cut off, someone for whom the body speaks. It all starts with her anguish as it relates to desire and to the immensity of her desire."[33] To Freud's question "What do women want?" the hysteric would answer "everything": including, but not limited to, unconditional love, sexual gratification, and the support and empathy of family members. Like Freud, even William Godwin seems to divine that his daughter's despair articulates an unfulfilled desire. The letter of condolence concerning his grandchild's death, the letter in which he denies his daughter's right powerful, immoderate grief, continues by asking, "What do you want that you have not? You have the husband of your choice . . . You have all the goods of fortune, all the means of being useful to others, and shining in your proper sphere."[34] Godwin's harangue of his daughter's depression chides her for not properly appreciating the "goods of fortune" while, like Alphonse, he ignores her deeper, non-rational, emotional wants.

Shelley allows Elizabeth, the monster's final victim, to examine the human cost of remaining in one's "proper sphere." In her last moments, even Elizabeth seems to hear the hollowness in her instructions to "be calm, my dear Victor; I would sacrifice my life to your peace. We surely shall be happy: quiet in our native country, and not mingling in the world." Victor reports that Elizabeth weeps at her statement, "distrusting the very solace that she gave; but at the same time she smiled, that she might chase away the fiend that lurked in my heart" (p. 89). The fiend lurks in Elizabeth's heart as she altruistically attends to male discomfort, sacrificing her own desires in order to shore up men's emotional stability. It lurks in Victor's as he dutifully refuses to attend to the passionate, immoderate, "feminine" side of his nature. Mary Shelley's novel illustrates the manner in which a rational society has relegated even emotions to a Godwinian "proper sphere" in arbitrarily dividing them by gender; in the process, it has taken away the words of both men and women. The policy of reasoned control can be breached through the language of the body, but only imperfectly: this mute message carries force and integrity, but it ultimately depends on the sensitivity and skills of the interpreter, and, as we have seen, none of Shelley's characters can read Victor's somatic cries of distress. Shelley's characters must articulate their most essential needs with only the vocabulary of their bodies. In the silence that results, many monsters will be formed.

Notes

1 Readings in the tradition of Moers's "Female Gothic" in *Literary Women* (Garden City: Doubleday, 1976) explore the manner in which Shelley articulates particularly female questions through a male character. For example, Marc A. Rubenstein reads the novel as Shelley's attempt to define herself in relation to Mary Wollstonecraft (*"Frankenstein:* Search for the Mother," *Studies in Romanticism* 15 [1976]: 165-94). For Sandra Gilbert and Susan Gubar, the character is a fallen Eve, illustrating women's alienation in a patriarchal society (*The Madwoman in the Attic* [New Haven: Yale Univ. Press, 1979]). My interpretation is sharpened by a knowledge of this subtext of female birth, creation, and alienation.

2 Anne Mellor, *Mary Shelley, Her Life, Her Fiction, Her Monsters* (New York: Methuen, 1988), p. 86.

3 The most detailed discussion of this argument is William Veeder's *Mary Shelley and "Frankenstein," The Fate of Androgyny* (Chicago: Chicago Univ. Press, 1984). Veeder identifies moments in the text in which Victor is "effeminized" or in which he wills his "masculine self" into action, but, as Mellor's *Mary Shelley* observes, his categories of gender are essentialist: he never looks at these parts of the self as social constructions (p. 242). My use of the terms "masculine" and "feminine" in this discussion will refer to gendered, not biological, characteristics.

4 Beret E. Strong, "Foucault, Freud, and French Feminism: Theorizing Hysteria as Theorizing the Feminine," *Literature and Psychology* 35 (1989): 11.

5 Mary Shelley, *Frankenstein, or The Modern Prometheus,* ed. James Rieger (1974; rpt, Chicago: Chicago Univ. Press, 1982), p. 183. This passage is found in the addition to the Thomas copy, made in 1823.

6 Michel Foucault, *Madness and Civilization, A History of Insanity in the Age of Reason,* tr. Richard Howard (New York: Random House, Pantheon, 1965),

argues that hysteria's association with madness developed as physicians began to focus on the ailment's effects on the mind rather than the body: "as long as vapors were convulsions or strange sympathetic communications through the body, even when they led to fainting and loss of consciousness, they were not madness. But once the mind becomes blind through the very excess of sensibility—then madness appears" (p. 158).

7 *A Letter from J. Fothergill Relative to the Intended School at Ackworth* (1778), p. 17. Quoted in Anne Digby, *Madness, Morality and Medicine: A Study of the York Retreat, 1796-1914* (Cambridge: Cambridge Univ. Press, 1985), p. 60. Critics have refined Michel Foucault's argument in *Madness and Civilization* that Rationalism put "all forms of unreason . . . under lock and key." For example, Roy Porter's *Mind-Forg'd Manacles* discounts the notion that British lunatics were confined in great numbers and emphasizes the continuity between eighteenth-century medical practices and earlier methods of treatment (Cambridge: Harvard Univ. Press, 1987). In *Social Order/Mental Disorder* (London: Routledge, 1989), Andrew Scull argues that Foucault's model of repressive moral treatments diminishes the subtlety and pervasiveness that such a program might have exerted. For further discussion, see also Kathleen Jones, *Lunacy, Law, and Conscience, 1744-1845* (London: Routledge, 1955); William Parry-Jones, *The Trade in Lunacy,* (London: Routledge, 1972); and Robert Castel, *The Regulation of Madness,* trans. W.D. Halls, 1976 (Berkeley: Univ. of California Press, 1988).

8 John Ferriar, *Medical Histories and Reflections,* First American Edition (Philadelphia: Dobson, 1816), 2:188. This observation does not appear in Ferriar's original edition of 1799. A case study of an elderly man confined for lunacy illustrates Ferriar's methods. He reports that the patient is stubbornly "determined to retain his urine," apparently succeeding for three days. The patient's behavior speaks to the "reasonable" conditions that have deprived him of all other forms of autonomy: within the confines of an asylum, the sufferer can control only his body's wastes. Ferriar's treatment ignores the integrity of even his patient's body: he covertly adds an emetic to the elderly man's food, at which point the patient yields up both the contents of his stomach and his bladder (pp. 180-81).

9 Charles Bernheimer and Claire Kahane's collection *In Dora's Case: Freud—Hysteria—Feminism* (New York: Columbia Univ. Press, 1985) is representative of feminist criticism's exploration of hysteria and psychoanalysis, and Elaine Showalter's *The Female Malady* (New York: Pantheon, 1985) looks at nineteenth-century psychiatry's construction of madness as a female disorder.

10 Thomas Sydenham, *Médecine Practique* (Paris, 1784), pp. 400-404. Quoted in Foucault, pp. 149-50.

[11] J. A. Paris and J. S. M. Fonblanque, *Medical Jurisprudence* (London: Phillips and Yard, 1823), 2:362. This volume makes a clear distinction between insanity and hysteria, which is categorized with fictitious illnesses under the heading "Of Impositions." Their reference is to Cullen's piece in *Male's Elements of Jurical Medicine,* 2nd ed., p. 237.

[12] The case study of a hysterical seventeen-year-old boy is included in Ferriar's first edition of *Medical Histories and Reflections* and reprinted in his subsequent, expanded versions (1:57).

[13] Ferriar, p. 180.

[14] Jean-Jacques Rousseau, *Émile, or On Education,* trans. Allan Bloom (New York: Basic Books, 1979), p. 444. The Shelleys' reading diary records Shelley reading this text in 1815, and again in 1822. See *The Journals of Mary Shelley,* 2 vols., ed. Paula R. Feldman and Diana Scott-Kilvert (Oxford: Clarendon, 1987), 2:670.

[15] James O'Rourke traces Shelley's ambiguous response to Rousseau in "Nothing More Unnatural': Mary Shelley's Revision of Rousseau," *ELH* 56 (1989): 543-69. O'Rourke cites Shelley's article, "Rousseau," in *Lives of the Most Eminent Literary and Scientific Men of France* (London: Longman, 1839). In her review of his *Confessions,* Shelley berates Rousseau for leaving his five children in a foundling home and makes this observation of the author's model of human development: "nothing can be more unnatural than his natural man. The most characteristic part of man's nature is his affections" (p. 547).

[16] C. Kegan Paul, *William Godwin: His Friends and Contemporaries* (London: Henry S. King and Co., 1876), 2:269-70.

[17] Shelley, p. 86. After losing several children and her husband, Shelley must have found the phrase's Godwinian resonances too harsh. She canceled the passage in the 1823 Thomas copy, replacing it with a milder call for the moderation of grief: "he [Alphonse] called to his aid philosophy and reason, while he endeavoured to restore me to a calmer state of mind."

[18] Mellor, p. 122. Other critics have noted the character's denial of domesticity and the female. For Mary Poovey, *The Proper Lady and the Woman Writer* (Chicago: Chicago Univ. Press, 1983), this denial stems from Victor's aggressive, "egotistic" ambitions. Fred V. Randel reads Victor as a masculine character whose isolation from women leads to his ill-adjusted creation. See "*Frankenstein,* Feminism, and the Intertextuality of Mountains," *Studies in Romanticism* 24 (1985): 515-32.

[19] Marlon Ross, *The Contours of Masculine Desire* (Oxford: Oxford Univ. Press, 1989), p. 114. Ross notes Shelley's inscription of a "femininely influenced male" in the construction of Henry Clerval, a character that understands the necessity of domestic affection but is unable to bring his friend under the influence of the feminine. Shelley compares this character with Victor's fiancee, Ross observes, and she scripts his murder as retaliation for the monster's destroyed female mate. For further discussion of the masculine ideology of Romanticism, see *Romanticism and Feminism,* ed. Anne Mellor, (Bloomington: Indiana Univ. Press, 1988), and Mellor's "Why Women Didn't Like Romanticism," in *The Romantics and Us, Essays on Literature and Culture,* ed. G. Ruoff (New Brunswick: Rutgers Univ. Press, 1990).

[20] Kate Ellis, "Monsters in the Garden: Mary Shelley and the Bourgeois Family," in *The Endurance of "Frankenstein",* eds. George Levine and U. C. Knoepflmacher (Berkeley: Univ. of California Press, 1979), p. 138.

[21] William Veeder argues that Shelley constructs the passage as a tribute: "Mary then is careful to hang Caroline's portrait in the very place in Alphonse's home that the portrait of Mary Wollstonecraft hung in Godwin's—over the mantlepiece in the study" (p. 186).

[22] Ellis, p. 134.

[23] Shelley, p. 27. Compare to Rousseau's address from father to son in *Émile:* "In aspiring to the status of husband and a father, have you meditated enough upon its duties? When you become the head of a family you will become a member of your state, and do you know what it is to be a member of the state? Do you know what government, laws, and fatherland are? . . . Before taking a place in the civil order, learn to know it and to know what rank in it suits you" (p. 448).

[24] For example, Bernheimer's overview of Victorian hysteria finds that women "developed unconscious strategies whereby they disavowed the intense anger and aggressive impulses for which the culture gave them no outlet" (pp. 5-6). The danger in discussions of hysteric protest is the risk of valorizing women who often were incapacitated by the very protests they staged. Strong takes French feminists to task for this kind of glorification, finding that "though we can say that the hysteric speaks the truth of her difference by refusing the so-called 'health' of a sick system, refusal is not everything" (p. 24). Regardless of hysteria's effectiveness, it suggested a useful model of crossgendering for Shelley's project.

[25] Ellis, p. 140.

[26] Mary Wollstonecraft, *Maria, or The Wrongs of Woman* (New York: Norton, 1975), p. 37.

[27] Showalter, p. 4.

[28] Sara Coleridge notes this connection between mental and somatic symptoms in her 1834 essay "Nervousness," a work that draws on Bernard Mandeville's *A Treatise of the Hypochondriak and Hysterick Diseases* (1730). Coleridge reflects on her own "nervous derangement" of 1832, observing that it "manifests itself by so many different symptoms that the sufferers themselves are puzzled what to make of it, and others, looking at it from different points of view make wrong judgments on the case. *Those who perceive only how it affects the mind are apt to forget that it also weakens the body; those who perceive that it is a bodily disease wonder that it should produce any alteration in a well regulated mind*" (emphasis mine). In Bradford Mudge's *Sara Coleridge, A Victorian Daughter* (New Haven: Yale Univ. Press, 1989), p. 203.

[29] Shelley, p. 57. Robert Whytt's 1777 catalogue of hysteric symptoms in *Traité des Maladies Nerveuses* covers almost any conceivable ailment, including several found in Shelley's text: "an extraordinary sensation of cold and heat . . . syncopes and vaporous convulsions . . . palpitations of the heart; variations in the pulse; periodic headaches; vertigo and dizzy spells; diminution and failure of eyesight; depression, despair, melancholia or even madness; nightmares or incubi" (quoted in Foucault, p. 137).

[30] Gilbert and Gubar, p. 228.

[31] George Levine, "The Ambiguous Heritage of *Frankenstein,* in *The Endurance of "Frankenstein"*, p. 53.

[32] Veeder, p. 117. His examination of androgyny maintains that Elizabeth prevents Victor from achieving the solipsistic union he desires and that "only with her death, he unconsciously imagines, will free him to transcend mortal unions and reach immortality through Erotic self-union."

[33] Hélène Cixous and Catherine Clément, *The Newly Born Woman,* trans. Betsy Wing (1975; rpt. Minneapolis: Minnesota Univ. Press, 1986), pp. 154-55.

[34] Godwin, 2:269.

HYSTERIA AND WOMEN'S NARRATIVES

Mary Cappello (essay date 1988)

SOURCE: "Alice James: Neither Dead nor Recovered," in *American Imago*, Vol. 45, No. 2, Summer, 1988, pp. 127-62.

[*In the excerpt that follows, Cappello analyzes the relationship between femininity and self-articulation within the context of hysterical illness, using Alice James's* Diary *as an example.*]

I. Illness and Femininity; Hysteria and Writing

As I listen to the work of particular women who have achieved voice in twentieth century English-speaking culture, Plath, Sexton, and Woolf, for example, I am led to the question of whether a woman can do the new things with words that her self-expression calls for without getting ill or being perceived as ill; and, further, if she can make the necessary aesthetic gesture that compels her toward a new position in the community, in language, and stay alive. It is a general question for now, but it grows, for me, out of the particular phenomenon of hysteria as recorded in case studies and diaries of the nineteenth century.

Hysteria, the elusive playing out of often untranslatable signifiers on the female body, stands (or, more often, lies, writhing or numb) as a representation of what a woman could or couldn't, would or wouldn't, say. Hysteria is an outcome of the simultaneous compulsion toward and deflection of the position of object in a culture's definition of desire. Consequently, it gives birth to a "talking cure": a dialogue between circumvention and discovery; between the patient as analyst and the analyst as patient; between a new kind of patient and a revolutionary healer.

Since nineteenth century physicians named the womb as cause of all female ailments, it is not surprising that this nebulous "new" neuro-physio-psychological disorder would be called "hysteria." Nineteenth century doctors believed that "a woman's uterus and ovaries controlled her body and behavior from puberty through menopause" and that intellectual activity should not be undertaken by women as it would consume the vital energy needed to develop the reproductive organs.[1] It is a wonder that doctors, especially those who could say, "'it was as if the Almighty, in creating the female sex, had taken the uterus and built up a woman around it,'"[2] did not perform hysterec-tomies on hysterics. They did, however, "frequently recommend suffocating hysterical women until their fits stopped, beating them across the face and body with wet towels, ridiculing and exposing them in front of family and friends, showering them with icy water."[3] Such reactions wanted to close the curtain on the drama enacted by the hysterical woman. In Charcot's clinic, on the other hand, men "watched," and, more importantly, through Freud's revision and Anna O.'s initiation, doctors listened; hysteria invented the "talking cure," and with it the question of whether neurasthenia liberated or shackled women, freed or imprisoned them.

Hysterical women, especially invalid ones, escaped the roles foisted upon them by the culture insofar as they did not have to wife and mother, insofar as their bodies spoke an aggressive rebellion against descriptions of femininity. However, one might also say "this role inflicted great bodily (though non-organic) pain, provided no really new role or interest, and perpetuated—even increased—the patient's dependence on traditional role characteristics, especially that of passivity."[4] Did the hysterical woman possess the power to "explode linguistic conventions" and to "decompose the façade of orderly conduct" posed by the "reigning cultural order?"[5] Or, did the shifting and unpredictable, the fluid nature of hysterical symptoms not so much suggest a rupture of the reigning symbolic codes as it simply mirrored, in exaggerated ways, the paradoxes at the core of nineteenth century definitions of woman, "more spiritual than man, yet less intellectual, closer to the divine, yet prisoner of her most animal characteristics, more moral than man, yet less in control of her very morality"?[6] One might say that an unmarried woman's getting ill was not an extended statement against marriage, but a submission to the physician's warning that the "maiden lady" was more prone to disease than her "married sisters" and to a shorter life-span.[7] Or, the question could be posed as so many have raised it in relation to Dora—is the hysteric victim or heroine in the stories created about her and the stories she creates?[8]

Jean Strouse, in the introduction to her *Biography* of Alice James, tells us that "to make her into a heroine (or victim as heroine) now would be seriously to misconstrue her sufferings and her aims . . . Because she fought to define for herself what it meant to be Alice James, she gave posterity a way to think about who she was."[9] But I might just as easily say that the moment Alice James gets ill is the moment she stops trying to define herself, and perhaps this is because I want to reject the notion produced by nineteenth century culture, enacted by hysteria and represented and reproduced in some twentieth century American women's poetry that illness is a means of self-definition.

In a poem called, "The Addict," by Anne Sexton, the female voice engages the serious business of dying—a relation imagined with the mock indifference of an hysteric.[10] The addiction to sleeping pills, the illness, empowers her—she's "the queen of this condition." She practices dying as a response to the exercise of living; through sleep toward death she exorcises waking life. And, her inhabitance of a kind of sickbed is sexual, "a kind of marriage," and political, "a kind of war," "like any other sport / it's full of rules." It's reminiscent of the nurturative mother-child bond since the "pills are a mother, but better." It's finally a religious experience, ritualistic, sacrificial.

Approximately one hundred years earlier, Alice James exhibits a similar self-fashioning in what we know of

Henry James (1843-1916).

her life as an invalid hysteric and, more importantly for my purposes, what we can read in the *Diary* of her own making. If Anne Sexton had read Alice James, might she have been able to write a new female self into being? Or, is Sexton in fact taking up the reality generated by hysteria's texts as an *option?* Does Sexton write the poetry that Alice James could not produce? This essay will not answer the question of relations between centuries of women's writing, but it will watch the drama set in motion by Alice James and her illness. It will ask if Alice is actor or author in the staging of these inscriptions: her *Diary* and her hysteria. It will try to discover what Alice as hysteric could or could not write.

II. A History of Case Histories

There is Alice James and then there is her *Diary.* Both have been treated by literary history, a literary history written in part by her brothers, William and Henry, as well as by literary critics and biographers. Descriptions of Alice that have come down to us, with the exception of Jean Strouse's *Biography,* are perhaps less informed by the self constructed in her *Diary,* and more informed by inference from and reference to the male members of her family, especially her more famous older brothers. I want to begin by interplaying the ways in which Alice has been read and written with where we might let her take us now, especially if we decide to read the *Diary*.

One of the first important biographers to write Alice was F. O. Matthiessen who gave her a brief chapter in his book, *The James Family*. While the essay reads more like a necessary chapter in an otherwise significant and interesting work, its collage-like format serves as a representation of reader response. Matthiessen quotes Alice profusely, interspersing her words with an occasional comment of his own but without an attempt at dialogue or interpretation. Matthiessen's collection of fragments mimics the hysteric's disunion with herself; it resembles the loose associativeness of Alice's *Diary* entries, and, in doing so, suggests to me at least, that we need not read the *Diary*—here it is, after all, (and a shorter version, at that) in Matthiessen's book.

Matthiessen and other biographers usually begin their representation of Alice with a litany of diagnostic titles. Alice, Matthiessen tells us, is best understood as "rheumatic gout," "spinal neurosis," "cardiac complications," and "nervous hyperaesthesia."[11] He moves from here to the typical identification of the cause of these ailments, the aetiology of this Being, when he tells us that "her first breakdown as a girl would seem to have been brought on by the imponderable strain of being the youngest child and only girl in such an extraordinary family" (272); or, that more specifically, her illness arose from "the difficulty of being 'Nobody' among such notable brothers" (275). In fact, her best writing, Matthiessen announces, is that *called forth by the subjects* closest to her heart and consequently appears in her characterizations of William James and Henry James" (277, italics mine). Her best writing, he implies, is authored by her brothers.

Ruth Bernard Yeazell's sardonically titled *The Death and Letters of Alice James* suggests at first another reading that identifies with the hysteric, as the sarcasm of her title mimics the *belle indifference* that the patient takes toward her illness. She, too, represents Alice as "'heart attacks,'" "fainting spells," "aching head and stomach," and "paralyzed legs,"[12] but goes on to make us aware that, "The sickroom was of course a place Alice shared intermittently with most of the Jameses: neurasthenia, like intelligence, seems to have run in the family. Medical reports and advice fill their letters to one another: insomnia, digestive disorders, backaches, and headaches came and went among them in rapid succession" (3). And, Erik Erikson, in his *Identity, Youth and Crisis* will not report on Alice but on William James's "neurotic invalidism, his suicidal episodes and his father's anxiety attacks."[13] In other words, Yeazell and Erikson help us to see beyond explanations of Alice's "failure" that base their assumptions on something so simple as an inferiority complex. What may be noticed instead is not that she was the only sick one among the Jameses but that illness could be more readily taken up as a profession by her than by her brothers. Moreover, her struggle and consequent illness do emerge by virtue of her femininity but more specifically because she identifies with and takes cues from her father. This is implied but not explored when biographers like Matthiessen call her the "only girl." There were other women in the family, a mother and a live-in aunt. In fact, Alice's mother, Yeazell tells us, was "the single unequivocally healthy member of the family" (4, 22). Why, then, did Alice not identify with her mother, and what was her relation to the other female member of the family, Aunt Kate?

Millicent Bell writes that, "Amid the thrusting male egos of the household in which the mother was a domestic presence almost without color and outline, with no interest either in ideas or the world of outer enterprise, this brilliant spirited girl had no model of her own sex."[14] The dimension that Bell's description fails to elaborate is that of the father's role in making the mother vague. Henry James, Sr. imagined men and women absolutely—"Men alone were capable of sin—rage, lust, selfishness, doubt. Women knew nothing of temptation or skepticism."[15] A woman did not have the outline that activity in the world gives one; she existed, in Henry's view, as the receptacle of absolute purity into which a husband might retreat when his struggle with the ethical alternatives of experience overwhelmed him. Henry, Sr.'s position, it seems to me, rendered women at once innocuous and powerful, or necessarily innocuous because powerful. Henry, Sr. *needed* his wife, but he could only acknowledge his need by placing her in a subordinate realm—a behavior so common it has turned cliché.[16] But Henry, Sr. also insisted on being different from most men of his day through his rejection of "doing," or professional identification, and assertion of "being." The Jameses' father, in other words, desired vagueness and authority at once. Mary James, Alice's mother, may have sustained a relation with such a person without falling ill by continuing the bond between herself and her live-in sister, Kate. In Smith-Rosenberg's article on relations between women in the nineteenth century, women's life-long friendships with each other, impassioned letter-writing between even married women, and shared participation in important female rituals illuminate a "status and power" held by women separate from the heterosocial world in which they remained powerless.[17] The result for Alice, however, may have been that her mother's homosocial bonding, to borrow a term from Smith-Rosenberg, sealed her off from her daughter.

Alice indeed may have been more likely to identify with Aunt Kate if only to gain access to her mother.

When Strouse tells us that Kate was "prone to occasional 'nervous' troubles," that she was a better nurse than her sister, that she was politically opinionated (32), the possibility becomes even more viable: Alice too falls ill, she too devotes much of her *Diary* to voicing her own political concern. Aunt Kate's role would appear to be both attractive and repulsive to Alice. Strouse describes Kate's movement from being the James's family companion, to marrying, and divorcing mysteriously, only to return "home" (to the Jameses, of course) but this time with a "Mrs." forever attached to her name. Henry, Sr. described Kate as "'husband to Mary, a most considerate and devoted wife to me, and incomparable father and mother to our children'" (Strouse, 33). Alice, then, might fantasize a perfect Oedipal association with Aunt Kate's privileged position—a reading supported by a rivalry that develops between the aunt and niece when Kate will not easily give up her status. Yeazell's account of the receipt of Aunt Kate's "will that would effectively prevent her [Alice] . . . from subjecting the things to a will of her own" (39) is most telling in this regard; and, Alice's pitying response to Aunt Kate's death points to an underlying resentment of her while it clarifies the difficulty of ever identifying with her:

> Poor Aunt Kate's life on looking back to it with the new distinctness which the completion always gives, must seem to our point of view such a failure, a person so apparently meant for independence and a 'position' to have been so unable to have worked her way to them and instead voluntarily relegated herself to the contrary. But the truth was, as her long life showed, that she had but one *motif,* the intense longing to absorb herself in a few individuals, how she missed this and how much the individuals resisted her, was, thank Heaven, but faintly suspected by her. My failing her, after Mother's and Father's death, must have seemed to her a great and ungrateful betrayal; my inability to explain myself and hers to understand, in any way, the situation made it all the sadder and more ugly.[18]

Alice hides her own longing for identification by describing Aunt Kate as an unfulfilled role model. She also gives her a form that she never had while she was alive. Kate was, rather, a kind of floating signifier who could permeate any boundaries, take on various familial identities, but not have a unique one of her own. Marriage may have made Kate feel literally "out of place," the amorphous *place* she held in the James family; marriage may have demanded a too clear-cut role. All that Aunt Kate could offer Alice was an identity out of context.

Just as Aunt Kate's character finally becomes clearly delineated to Alice through her death, Alice becomes clear to herself in dying. Smith-Rosenberg speaks of childbirth as a rite of passage shared among women—"with a lengthy seclusion of the woman before and after delivery, severe restrictions on her activities, and finally a dramatic reemergence."[19] For Alice, the ritual was that of an illness, characterized by seclusion, supervised by a nurse and female companion, Katherine Loring; a ritual whose motive was death, followed by dramatic reemergence in the dissemination of her *Diary*.

But this state of affairs is provoked by other deaths and the dynamics induced by them. When Alice's mother dies, Alice seems to be given "new life,"[20] especially apparent in the subsequent nursing of Alice by her father. Hysteria, in fact, almost always draws as much attention to the illness of the father as it does the illness of the daughter. Hysteria is defined by this interconnection of ills as it so often comes after the nursing of a father, the death of a father, and a sick society's refusal to allow the daughter's identification with the father. In the case of Freud's Elisabeth von R., to cite one of many examples,

> it came about that she found herself drawn into especially intimate contact with her father, a vivacious man of the world, who used to say that this daughter of his took the place of a son and a friend with whom he could exchange thoughts. Although the girl's mind found intellectual stimulation from this relationship with her father, he did not fail to observe that her mental constitution was on that account departing from the ideal which people like to see realized in a girl . . . he often said she would find it hard to get a husband.[21]

Elisabeth's first symptoms appear while "playing the leading part" at her father's sickbed and take on full debilitating force after he dies. In becoming the patient after having acted as nurse, the hysteric, in a way, completes the identification with father. By perpetuating the position of patient, she keeps the father alive and so transforms guilt surrounding her father's death, from her failure as a nurse. But an illness like hysteria would not arise unless the identification with positions in the sick room were not already problematized. An hysteric's illness, in other words, grows already out of the initial problem she has, but does not acknowledge, with being in an undefined position of authority. It is a question of who is finally dominant, the patient or the nurse, especially when the patient is a father, and whether a woman can author as either one.

Leon Edel's language in the biographical introduction to the *Diary* speaks to the self-imposed containment of Alice's subjectivity when he writes, "she kept the record of her *sickroom world* in two *closely written* scribblers during the *final months* of her *abbreviated* life" (italics mine).[22] But Edel underestimates both cause and cure when he compares Alice James to Elizabeth Barrett Browning:

Elizabeth Barrett offers a record of an analogous kind of bedridden life and of her escape from it. But no Robert Browning came to carry Alice off to some Italy of her own. What we get instead, in the diary, is a sense of early frustration—that of a strong-limbed active girl who never found an opportunity to indulge in activity. In our time she would have played tennis, or gone water skiing or followed various forms of outdoor life. In earlier New England she wore long dresses, and sat decorously at dull teas—and had her periodic prostrations (8).

It does not take an acute intelligence to notice the shortcoming of Edel's response with its suggestion that all would have been different for Alice had she a man, a world elsewhere, and/or the wide world of sport. In Edel's reading, the "outdoors" has a static and universal meaning; he seems to say that if what were "out there" were different, Alice's response to life would be different, rather than locate the problem in how Alice read the outdoors or how she was taught to do so. Edel's comments fail to acknowledge the existence of a particular self acting and writing, feeling and thinking, in the setting of a complex and consequential social matrix. Otherwise, we might substitute Katherine Loring for Robert Browning and England for Italy and wonder why Alice was not happy. Such a reading wants to imagine how Alice might have been made comfortable when the issue is not why she was not "happy" but who she was able to be and what kind of self the culture, which includes her illness, enabled her to write. With this in mind, we can wonder how the *Diary* as a literary form might accomodate an hysterical personality; we can look at her relation to that form in particular and her attention to issues of form and formlessness in general.

Edel and Strouse seem compelled in their receipt and representations of Alice to offer detailed accounts of her death. So, too, Alice's brothers, especially William and Henry, write her into literary history through their letters, and most emphatically in those letters surrounding Alice's death and the unveiling of the previously unknown *Diary*.[23] William records a most peculiar reaction to news of Alice's cancer as he counsels her with the relief she will find once she is out of her body. In his letter to her, he writes: "'and when you're relieved from your post, just *that* bright note will remain behind [i.e., the more charming aspects of her personality] together with the inscrutable and mysterious character of the doom of nervous weakness which has chained you down for all these years'" (Matthiessen, 280). William, believer in free will, probably would not refer to his own "post," but here his sister has fulfilled a duty through illness, an illness which is alternately given responsibility for her oppression, an illness which will remain unknowable as long as femininity remains a secret. William goes on in the same letter to celebrate the imminent event of Alice's soul

leaving her body and can unabashedly say, "'You can't tell how I've pitied you.'" When Alice finally does die, William sends a telegram reflective of his *own* fantastical understanding of her position: "'I telegraphed you [Henry] this a.m. to make sure the death was not merely apparent . . . because her neurotic temperament and chronically reduced vitality are just the field for trance-tricks to play themselves upon'" (Yeazell, 45). Indeed, *William* typically created a "vague and extravagantly idealized image" of Alice in his correspondence to her.[24] Though Henry proved a more supportive presence to Alice throughout her life, he follows, to an extent, in William's vein by offering a fictionalized solution to her malaise afer she dies. After reading her *Diary,* he can say, "'However, what comes out in the book—as it came out to me in fact—is that she really was an Irishwoman . . . what a pity she wasn't born there—and had her health for it'" (Mattheissen, 285). The fact is that she was an American woman and did not have her health for it. But the reality of Alice James was clearly difficult for people close to home and helpless in her midst to acknowledge. When Katherine Loring makes copies of the *Diary* for Alice's brothers, Henry is astonished by its explicit gossip, and suggests that they edit the book for publication and burn their original copies.[25] Henry may have preferred that the book be fiction, though it is also imaginable that the brothers must have experienced guilt upon reading the *Diary,* its sick self-mocking voice struggling for authorship and companionship. Henry also thought that Alice might have produced something richer, say, if she were exposed to the world more; one wonders, then, how it could be possible, that from the locus of her sickroom, she exposed too much.

As the life and work of Alice James testifies, however, hysteria derives from and, in response, creates paradoxes. In fact, the elusiveness of hysteria, it would seem, caricatures its precipitating event: a distinct desire met with an indistinct position. To the extent that hysteria is a *dramatization* of inner conflict, it assumes a viewer; it is an illness which possibly generates itself for the edification of the viewer. In showing itself through the body, it insists on being read, but it simultaneously resists interpretation since a medical science grounded in somatic sources of illness must remain ignorant in its midst. Cast in other terms, the passive and active merge in hysteria as the hysteric opens herself to be read, i.e., through our watching she shall be acted upon, and resists being read, i.e., she demands a new way of reading. And, it is a reading that emphasizes form over content since hysteria foregrounds how the message is being said; a reading that, in blurring the distinction between reader and text, by constantly destabilizing the activity or passivity implicit in either, rejects a mode of perception based on dyadic opposition. Psychoanalysis, then, metaphorically responds by introducing a homeopathic rather than allopathic cure, by using some aspect of the illness to treat the illness, namely susceptibility to hypnosis; or, to give another example, by inducing the patient "to renounce an immediate and directly attainable yield of pleasure" even as this condition provoked the illness.[26]

Reading Alice James more specifically in the hysterical context she came to inhabit, we must wonder how identification with, and nursing of, the father played itself out in her case. As her father lay dying, Alice took the position of nurse, but, through what has been described as a gradual self-starvation, Henry, Sr. would not allow her help. Consequently, Alice retreated to her sick room, and predictably, Aunt Kate took over the role of nursing Henry. Alice's characterization of her symptoms in the *Diary* where she writes of how the "duties of doctor, nurse and strait-jacket" (149) were imposed upon her from within, speaks to the energized hyper-internalization of hysterical illness. As I shall show later, the hysteric is at a loss to find a correlative in the outside world to which her "self" might refer.

Alice's flight from the female role, so typical of the hysteric, her search for identity through the father, shows itself to the extent that she spiritualized her illness and associated it with affection and bonding. Alice's father, in Strouse's telling of the story, came to believe, after a childhood accident, that selfish pleasure incurred punishment and that "suffering brought love" (9). It is not surprising, then, that in one of her last *Diary* entries Alice asks if

> it is not wonderful that this *unholy granite substance in my breast* [her cancer] *should be the soil propitious for the perfect flowering of Katherine's unexampled genius for friendship and devotion.* The story of her watchfulness, patience and untiring resource cannot be told by my feeble pen, but all the pain and discomfort seem a slender price to pay for all the happiness and peace with which she fills my days (255; italics mine).

Henry, Sr's leg had to be amputated after suffering severe burns received while playing in his typically carefree way. The story of how Henry, Sr's formerly detached father came to love him after this episode, and Henry, Sr's subsequent incorporation of suffering into his world view and his conception of man's relation to the Divine, reads like a Puritanical conversion text. Later in life, he will deal with his own neuroses, the debilitating anxiety attacks for which he cannot find a cure, by spiritualizing them, by granting them the power and place of Swedenborgian vastations. When Alice falls ill, he will typically embrace her pain with religious fervor, described in a letter to his youngest son: "'Never have I had such deep tranquil joy in thinking of the Divine name revealed in Christ as in these profoundly trying experiences with Alice. I cer-

tainly never before saw such a believer in the truth of a better world as she is, when her suffering is most acute."[27]

If aspects of Alice's *Diary* certify the sickbed as a vehicle to eternity, thus linking father to daughter, her symptoms and subsequent curtailment of her creative expression grow up out of her father's denying her identification with him. When it seems clear that Alice and Katherine will be life-long companions, Henry, Jr. writes, "'There is about as much possibility of Alice's giving Katherine up as of giving her legs to be sawed off,'"[28] in other words, as much possibility as of her becoming father. The story, re-told by various critics, of Alice's conversation with her father concerning her own suicide, tells the most about Henry, Sr's denial of his daughter's will.[29] In short, he gives her permission but suggests that she do it "'in a perfectly gentle way in order not to distress her friends'" (Yeazell, 15). Yeazell reads the instance as a method of rendering the daughter powerless since Alice won't commit suicide once her father has given her the right to do so—then self-destruction would not work to break bonds.

As one who pays more particular attention to the *Diary* as a *literary text* than almost any other critic, Yeazell offers a careful reading of one of the most compelling passages in the *Diary,* Alice's self-description of hysteria, as an allegory of inner division.[30] Most notably, Yeazell emphasizes the splits implicit in the passage, between body and mind, as well as the particular detachment of the recording voice. I will take up the issue of *la belle indifference* implied by Alice's "quizzical self-mockery and her complete lack of self-pity, and the detachment with which she has schooled herself to observe her body as a bad experiment for which she is not responsible, and in which she refuses to let her mind become implicated" (Mattheissen, 272).[31] I will then assume a vantage point that considers the relations between an hysteric's self-fashioning and the aesthetic construction of a self, specifically, the difference between the making of oneself into a caricature and caricaturing an other through representation.

Doctors tell you, Alice James reflects, that you'll either get well or die; she remains "neither dead nor recovered,"[32] on a middle ground between exposure and closure, revealing and concealing. If Alice were to re-cover, perhaps she would gain new meaning; if dead, she might be revealed but self-lessly bare. Hysteria or invalidism as a means of signification is a way of telling the doctor or father, "your way of looking at my body can't cure me; in fact, your way makes me sick." One late nineteenth century neurologist calls hysteria a "disease in which it is unsafe to claim a conquest," while a pioneer gynecological specialist refers to the physician as "helpless" before the disease.[33] Indeed, the difficulty in treating hysteria arose partly from the fact that the physician had to rely so heavily on the *patient's* "word." But Alice James also wanted her peculiar disease, her state of mind/body, to be named by the presiding symbolic order, and this is why she rejoices when her doctor discovers her cancer.

Alice James lived a struggle between signifier and signified, a struggle between what she could signify and what she was meant to signify. Her retreat into illness posits her alternatives as the ability to signify to oneself but not to others or only to signify something by or because of others. In a letter to Fanny Morse, she says, "'You know ill or well one is never deprived of the power of standing for what one was *meant* to stand for and what more can life give us'" (Yeazell, 34). Perhaps this is what William meant by Alice's "post," but the *Diary* and Alice's illness tell us that Alice wanted to *turn herself* into meaning something. In a letter to William, she says, "I have always had a significance for myself' (Matthiessen, 282). After reading Alice's *Diary* and translating her illness, perhaps we can decide if she was at last only a "paralysed dictator,"[34] unwilling and compelled to be read according to the culture's precepts, unable to mean to others what she meant to herself.

III. Illness as Part of The Search for that Which is Greater Than Oneself: The Diary Proper

> Those great wars which the body wages with the mind a slave to it, in the solitude of the bedroom against the assault of fever or the oncome of melancholia, are neglected [by writers]. Nor is the reason far to seek. To look these things squarely in the face would need the courage of a lion-tamer; a robust philosophy; a reason rooted in the bowels of the earth. Short of these, this monster, the body, this miracle, its pain, will soon make us taper into mysticism, or rise with rapid beats of the wings, into the raptures of transcendentalism.

From "On Being Ill," Virginia Woolf

We can enter the *Diary* proper by considering two aspects of the original manuscript that practically stand for the dilemma played out in its pages: its size and the physical arrangement of its entries. Leon Edel, in describing the "bibliographical side of [his] task" in editing the manuscript (xi), refers us to the idiosyncracy of its being "contained in two ordinary English scribblers" (xi), or "two closely-written scribblers" (vii). In the context of this compact manuscript, moreover, Alice's habit was to use abbreviations, some of which Edel "spelled out as an aid to the reader" (x). The details of the *Diary*'s compression are not beside the point, I think; and, rather than, like Edel, conclude that Alice's utterance is "modest and personal" (22) if compared with her brother Henry's "soaring and beautiful works" (22), I would like to draw attention to the *Diary*'s self-consciously composed "smallness" as Alice's attempt to set limits on

what might otherwise emerge as a recoiling at the perceived "largeness," elasticity, or expansiveness of her body.

The materially shaped "Aloneness"[35] which the *Diary* is meant to dispel or transform is like the body which either needs to be dispensed with or re-made. Unable to achieve either the former (a death by separation) or the latter (a life by integration), Alice displaces her body onto the world outside of her sickroom as she attempts to give form to the overwhelming spirit of the outdoors. The world, as we shall see, is too much with rather than of her; it is the world beside herself The *Diary* then functions like Alice's illness by treating that world like an extra appendage that cannot be incorporated by Alice, that cannot make her whole, but which can serve as an instrument in the search for that which is greater than herself. The *Diary* is Alice's self-made companion through which she imagines the world as a companion, palpable and elusive as her caretakers, Katherine Loring and Nurse Bradford.

Like the series of companions that the *Diary* creates, the particular arrangement of entries in the *Diary* might suggest that there is no "development" in its pages. Instead we find a surrender to a reconciliation that Alice cannot achieve but which is forced on her by the breast cancer that she announces late in its pages. As Edel describes:

> The diarist began on page one, on the right-hand leaf at the front of each book, and continued on each successive right-hand leaf until the back of the book was reached. Then she turned it upside down; the blank pages were now on the right, and these were duly filled. Accordingly, when the diary is opened the text on the right-hand page is in the proper position, but that on the left is upside down (xi).

So long as a reader does not look at the two tracks suggested by this arrangement in relation to one another, they move forward and in sequence. If, however, they are considered in tandem, then the present appears to compete, through a backward and upside down movement, with the past. Alice used to be inspired by death, she tells us in one entry of the *Diary,* to the extent that death signified an end, a fulfillment. As death became more ungraspable to her, however, the "passion to achieve" passed over into an indifference and she began to approach both *life and death* with an even-hovering attention, and with a mere desire for sleep and silence. To Alice's mind, then, life is death turned on its head and written in reverse; or, "the shaping period is passed and one is fitted to every limitation through the long custom of surrender" (31). Alice's is an inactivity of body that cannot make its way (transcendentally) into metaphysics but only into decay. In the pages that follow, I will show how Alice's various positions—now spiritual, now artistic; now indifferent, now vain—continually prevent her from standing in the world even as they require the confines of her *Diary;* and, how hysterical self-caricaturing, by making living more difficult than writing, arrests the possibility of either.

To the end of her litany of Alice's medically named ills, Strouse adds the seemingly incongruous term, "spiritual crisis."[36] We can imagine Henry, Sr. describing Alice's condition in this way, since, as I have suggested earlier, he often thought of anxiety attacks and physical trauma as spiritual affairs. While for Henry, Sr., illness becomes a spiritual experience, for his daughter Alice, the failure to achieve the spiritual as defined by her father, the inability to make metaphor, makes her ill.

Like the weak-egoed sick person who tends, as Woolf suggests in my epigraph, to mystify and mysticize illness, Henry, Sr. and Alice used spirituality respectively as an end and a means of illness. We can recall, for example, Henry, Sr.'s propensity for conversion: he practiced conversion in courtship as he drew his fiancee, Mary, and her sister, Kate, away from Presbyterianism, and as he brought Mary to a civil ceremony in marriage;[37] his boyish plunges into pleasure "'had the effect often to convert God's chronic apathy or indifference into a sentiment of acute personal hostility'" (Strouse, 6); and, he encouraged his children, in Henry, Jr.'s words, to "'convert and convert' the raw data of experience into interesting forms of communication" (Strouse, xi). On the other hand, what will become in psychological terms, "conversion hysteria," has already begun for Alice as spiritual crisis. Alice converted not others, but herself, not her minimal experience but her inexpressible affects, into symptoms.

Alice's father's belief that "the condition of being was separate from and superior to any doing—in a word that identity was nothing but a state inwardly achieved" (Bell, 117) posed an extra-difficult if not impossible task for Alice. For Henry, Sr. this construction sprang from opposition to a "meaning" of maleness that said thou shalt act in the world, but Alice had no such definition of femaleness to respond to, no meaning against which such inwardness might rebel. Such transcendentalism as her father's requires, I think, a sense of self, an ego, to begin with. Inwardness placed alongside of inwardness, on the other hand, might induce invalidism, infantilism, silence, repose. While Henry's illness is imagined as the struggle between God and himself, Alice's becomes a more primary conflict of inner and outer. Henry, Sr. is already standing in the world when he images a mode of belief that Alice, out of the world, tries to mimic.

In the following entry, Alice, in trying to make good of her inexperience, reveals the extent to which desire has not been able to develop, the extent to which primary affects have not been met:

> I have seen so little that my memory is packed with little bits which have not been wiped out by great ones, so that it all seems like a reminiscence and as I go along the childish impressions of light and color come crawling back into my mind and with them the expectant, which then palpitated within me, lives for a ghostly moment (34).

Alice's wants are no more than a shadow in time here because a necessary "greatness" of perception, a looming and luminous thought has not emerged to make them real: in short, a certain outside world and concomittant expansiveness have not been taken in. But we cannot therefore stop at Strouse's assertion that Alice "was too much a part of the peculiar Jamesian universe to 'stand for' something larger than her own experience," or that Alice "made no claim to have carried on an exemplary struggle or to have achieved anything beyond the private measure of her own experience" (xiv-xv). Alice's illness and *Diary,* I think, read as a flight from her own experience, as a sign of the frustration of not being able to live *her own* experience, and as a search for something greater than herself—a belief which springs from the observation that things happen, things change, in spite of one's experience. Alice's record of "the success made up of all delicate shades and subtle tones, that *makes no sign,* but is known alone to the bosom that attains it" (87, italics mine) is not a record of private achievement but a justification for existence in a world where one is not able to achieve.

Thus Alice often shows herself giving into a larger than life authority, even as she wonders what she can 'stand for.' Sometimes that authority is nature, when, for example, Alice contemplates spring and decides it is the "most depressing moment of the year": "Spring not only depresses us physically, but in proportion to the revelation of natural beauty 'la souffrance innée . . . de n'être que nous, le désir vague d'en sortir et de nous mêler à l'être universel'—overwhelms us and fills us with despair" (95) (a translation of the French reads, "the suffering of being only ourselves, the vague desire to get out of it and to mingle with the universal being").

In another passage, that authority which draws attention to the ineffectualness of the self is history: "How wearing to the substance and exasperating to the nerves is the perpetual bewailing, wondering at and wishing to alter things happened, as if all personal concern didn't vanish as the 'happened' crystallizes into history" (231). But the conflict between having a self that can refer to something larger and outside it or not having a self at all is most interestingly pondered in the following passage which I quote at length:

> It's amusing to see how, even on my microscopic field, minute events are perpetually taking place illustrative of the broadest facts of human nature. Yesterday Nurse and I had a good laugh but I must allow that decidedly she 'had' me. I was thinking of something that interested me very much and my mind was suddenly flooded by one of those luminous waves that sweep out of consciousness all but the living sense and overpower one with joy in the rich, throbbing complexity of life, when suddenly I looked up at Nurse, who was dressing me, and saw her primitive, rudimentary expression (so common here) as of no inherited quarrel with her destiny of putting petticoats over my head; the poverty and deadness of it contrasted to the tide of speculation that was coursing thro' my brain made me exclaim, "Oh! Nurse, don't you wish you were inside of *me!*'—her look of dismay and vehement disclaimer—'Inside of you, Miss, when you have just had a sick head-ache for five days!'—gave a greater blow to my vanity, than that much battered article has ever received. The headache had gone off in the night and I had clean forgotten it—when the little wretch confronted me with it, at this sublime moment when I was feeling within me the potency of a Bismarck, and left me powerless before the immutable law that however great we may seem to our own consciousness no human being would exchange his for ours, and before the fact that *my* glorious role was to stand for *Sick headache* to mankind (48).

Alice seems to be saying that within her little life that contains a larger life, minute events occur which illustrate larger truths. So, too, the particular (the exchange between Alice and Nurse) that illustrates the general (the "immutable law") in this passage exemplifies the unlikelihood of particulars ever meeting generals or each other. It is as if Alice wants not only for her particular life to refer to the general, but she wants, as a consequence, individualities to merge. The impossibility of this leaves her with what she can stand for, necessitates her ill.

Alice's difficulties vis à vis the various figurations of authority in the *Diary* are perhaps better described as more complicated versions of Henry, Sr. and William's "inner struggle" as recapitulated by Erik Erikson. Theirs "concerned the identity of naked and stubborn selfhood so typical for extreme individualism, as against the surrender to some higher identity—be it outer and all-enveloping or inner and all-pervasive" (153). Alice's struggle seems to have occupied both realms as her individuality positioned itself in relation to an external father and internal God/father. She had as much difficulty with her desire to "knock off the head of the benignant pater" (149, the latinate form suggesting a God in father), as she did in wanting to "stay the will of God and add a second to the old man's hours" (125).

Finally, such tensions condition themselves in Alice's peculiar relation to the outdoors. Alice comes to see the outdoors as the place where the higher identity resides; the indoors as the place where the individual lives her life. If the indoors is the life, the outdoors is the after-life. People—brothers, aunts, fathers—then, no longer come between her and the higher identity, but are a means to it or messengers from it by way of letters or newspapers or visits (though these come rarely and mostly from Henry). If Alice is in the role of invalid, people can help her arrive at rather than obstruct her desire.

When Alice does go out, as we know from the *Diary*, she does so with an almost transcendental vigor that will render the exterior, interior or subjective. Nature becomes the great soothing good that waits beyond her sick room and that will take her into its arms when she dies.[38] Meanwhile, her visits to its sanctuary must be few; and, she will make herself a companion to herself by writing the *Diary:*

> I think that if I get into the habit of writing a bit about what happens, or rather what doesn't happen, I may lose a little of the sense of loneliness and desolation which abides with me. My circumstances allowing of nothing but the ejaculation of one-syllabled reflections, a written monologue by that most interesting being, *myself,* may have its yet to be discovered consolations. I shall at least have it all my own way and it may bring relief as an outlet to that geyser of emotions, sensations, speculations, and reflections which ferments perpetually within my poor old carcass for its sins; so here goes, my first Journal! (25)

Records of her journeys out repeat the consecrating effects of being in nature. Sometimes she "lay in the sun whilst they picked her flowerets, with a cuckoo in the distance, circling swallows overhead, broad sweeps of gentle wind slowly rustling thro' the trees near by" (27). Other times we find her, "lying in a meadow at Hawke's farm, absorbing like blotting-paper hay-ricks, hedges and trees" (33), letting nature write itself upon her so that "resignation in passivity" might have "spiritual significance" (56). The effort of reclining in nature is not only "divine" (35) but it "stirs unfathomable depths" (37), dulling her interest in receiving visitors. Visiting nature and writing the *Diary* get sexualized and become sublimations of relations that Alice cannot realize, in lines like the following: "If I were to make this a receptacle for feeble ejaculations over the scenery, what a terror it will be—I must however record the fact that today I entered into Paradise" (37).[39]

It is a wonder that Alice does not feel guiltily exposed in sharing these descriptions with us or that she does not feel that she is committing a desecration as she does when she reads a friend one of her father's letters and does not receive adequate response:

In a rash moment, panting to rise out of the trivial and draw a breath of *life,* I read one of Father's letters to a friend. It fell perfectly flat—Ah, what a wilted moment was that! I felt as if I had committed a desecration (84).

There is some suggestion of violation in the attempt to communicate what cannot be shared, with the implication that the relation to her father, or the unsharable content of her experience, preserves and is preserved by her illness. Yet, on some level, a reader cannot help feeling that the motive of the *Diary* is to share her secret relationships—to Nurse, Katherine, Henry, memories of her parents, herself, nature, her body, the body politic—all the activity of the indoors. To the extent that the *Diary* does both, reveal and conceal, it functions as a symptom. To the extent that Alice can never reconcile the indoors with the outdoors, she symptomatizes her communal and private selves.

Alice at once spiritualizes her position through the *Diary,* transcending the social, yet she presents herself as socially concerned. She undertakes the fabrication of a private world, a *Diary,* in which she voices concern for the other, the poor. But then she portrays herself as identifying with, even aspiring to the poor. "The Highest Divine order," she says, "is brought about by the humblest means" (223). And, she must sadly report that she is "hopelessly relegated among the smug and the comfortable" (55).

We must wonder, though, in light of her illness whether Alice did want "sympathy," or if, through her writing, reciprocity could be achieved. Perhaps what Alice wanted was the authority to make sympathetic connections, to decide where recognitions might occur. Virginia Woolf calls illness the "great confessional," where the main thing confessed is that we can do without sympathy:

> That illusion of a world so shaped that it echoes every groan, of human beings so tied together by common needs and fears that a twitch at one wrist jerks another, where however strange your experience other people have had it too, where however far you travel in your own mind someone has been there before you—is all an illusion. We do not know our own souls, let alone the souls of others. Human beings do not go hand in hand the whole stretch of the way. There is a virgin forest in each; a snowfield where even the print of birds' feet is unknown. Here we go alone, and like it better so. Always to have sympathy, always to be accompanied, always to be understood would be intolerable. But in health the genial pretence must be kept up and the effort renewed—to communicate, to civilize, to share, to cultivate the desert, educate the native, to work together by day and by night to sport (196).[40]

Illness, Woolf implies further, gives one a vantage point for feeling and reading the world that is separate, soli-tary, new, maybe even original. In illness, we feel words sensually, without the intrusion of reason (200); we read Shakespeare without the buzz of centuries of critics in our ears (201); we look up for the first time in years and perhaps notice the sky (196). One senses from the *Diary* that Alice James reads from a privileged position and, at least vicariously, notices the sky when she records in her commonplace book the following quotation from *War and Peace:*

> How was it I did not see that lofty sky before? And how happy I am to have found it at last. Yes! all is vanity, all is a cheat, except that infinite sky. There is nothing, nothing but that. But even that is not, there is nothing but peace and stillness. And thank God![41]

The passage looks back to a point Woolf goes on to make—that finally the sky is disinterested, indifferent, unsympathetic, and that illness is a solitary profession.

Often in the *Diary,* Alice James fashions herself a seer: she images the sick person as visionary or artist. "Heaven forbid that I should begin upon those that see not, it's too tragic" (33), she writes. He sensibility is often a painterly one as she notices the "infinite gradations of light and shade" (35) or when she impressionistically sees the peasant in the field as "'edgeless'" (34). She often finds herself before paintings in memory or in books (25, 30, 46, 28) and, at one point feels intense communion and insight before a Botticelli:

> Imagine the bliss of finding that I too was a 'sensitive,' and that I was not only 'mute before a Botticelli,' but that a Botticelli said an infinity of things to me—and this in a flash of mutual recognition, after the years of toil in trying to establish some sort of relation, either of speech or silence, with the Botticelli of Boston (47).

(She never records a similar experience with a book). On one trip into the countryside she says she

> behaved like a lunatic, à la Kingsley, over a farmhouse, a meadow, some trees and cawing rooks. Nurse says that there are some people downstairs who drive everywhere and admire nothing. How grateful I am that I actually do *see,* to my own consciousness, the quarter of an inch that my eyes fall upon; truly the subject is all that counts (31).

Here the ill one exerts uncorrupted vision; but, what can Alice finally create, what relationship can she have with what she sees? It is curious that she underscores subject in the above, for the hysteric, I think, is more object than anything else. The theater of hysteria's playing out demands, in fact, privileges, a viewer. The hysteric, unable to alter her self-perception or her perception of men, tries to change the way in which she is perceived.[42]

When the nurse asks Alice if she would like to be an artist, Alice imagines "the joy and despair of it! the joy of seeing with the trained eye and the despair of *doing* it" (31). In the rest of the passage, she writes tellingly, associatively, of the burden of some people's having many children, the feeling of her own exposure when someone comments on her charitableness, and the way in which her letters make her parents seem alive again—the despair and joy of it. Alice was best at what was perhaps a contradiction in terms—an internalized aesthetic. In a long French passage, she cheers the artist of the self and aggrandizes the peasant as she identifies, as a woman, with his oppression:

> Under this inspiration the humblest existences can become works of art far superior to the most beautiful symphonies and the most beautiful poems. Are not the works of art that one realizes in oneself the best? The others that are thrown outside on canvas or on paper are nothing but images, shadows. The work of life is a reality of the simple man; the poor peddlar from Faubourg St. Germain who makes of his life a poem of charity is worth more than a Homer (55).[43]

The psychology of hysteria's self-aesthetics is a complicated one and perhaps can be approached anew by a consideration of the oft-noted role of *caricature* in the hysteric's illness. Strouse quotes Nathan Hale's observation that

> hysteria sabotaged the 'civilized' norm of refinement in two ways, by 'fits,' outburst of emotion that directly violated it, or by incapacitating physical symptoms which because they made a woman helpless, caricatured the very delicacy and softness she and American men had been taught to reverence (106).

The specifics of those symptoms include speechlessness, loss of smell, taste or hearing, paralysis of the limbs and chronic fatigue. Thus, hysterics caricature their sensory deprivation and draw attention to the inadequate, undesirable definition of sensuality that characterized femininity. Hysteria draws attention to the literal monstrousness of women's being kept from speaking and moving in the world. An hysteric's acting is all histrionics:

> The most characteristic and dramatic symptom . . . was the hysterical 'fit.' Mimicking an epileptic seizure, these fits often occurred with shocking suddenness . . . It began with pain and tension, most frequently in the 'uterine area.' The sufferer alternately sobbed and laughed violently, complained of palpitations of the heart, clawed her throat as if strangling, and, at times, abruptly lost the power of hearing and speech. A death-like trance might follow,

lasting hours, even days. At other times violent convulsions—sometimes accompanied by hallucinations—seized her body.[44]

The hysterical fit makes the female body frighteningly present, a presence that demands self-punishment from the hysteric's (unspoken) point of view. I imagine the hysteric's psychic universe to consist of a profoundly, burdensomely present body detached from self, for it is an hysteric's body, not her self, that insists on its existence by getting ill. Such body consciousness or unconsciousness can be heard in images of the James family itself. Just as physicians "saw the body as a closed system possessing only a limited amount of vital force; energy expended in one area was necessarily removed from another,"[45] members of the James family subscribed to a 'bank-account' theory of family intelligence according to which Alice's intellectual achievement, for example, might deplete one of her brothers (Margolis, 565). Alice, then, was not so much a member of the James family as she was a member of a kind of James body. In one of her last *Diary* entries, she fears the "muscular demonstrations" that might occur at the moment of death: "for I occasionally have a quiver as of an expected dentistical wrench when I fancy the actual moment" (230). It is as if Alice fantasizes and fears death as a loosening of herself from the body that is the world, the mouth that is devouring her.

In such a pre-Oedipal sounding world, drawing a caricature as a mode of rebellion is impossible, but turning oneself into a caricature, hysteria seems to say, is not. There is a difference between creating a caricature, "the distorted reproduction of a recognizable likeness,"[46] and caricaturing through the body; between behavioral and illustrative or aesthetic caricaturing; between living an exaggeration and depicting one. There is a difference between setting up an image and deforming or destroying it, and merging with the image, embodying and enacting the image formerly represented in language.

"The serious artist according to academic tenets," writes Kris,

> creates beauty by liberating the perfect form that Nature sought to express in resistant matter. The caricaturist seeks for the perfect deformity, he shows how the soul of man would express itself in his body if only matter were sufficiently pliable to Nature's intentions (190).

An hysteric makes matter, that the caricaturist can only imagine, pliable, but at the cost of damaging herself. Hysteria also evokes the effigy as explored by Kris. The effigy is more primitive and magical than the caricature since the effigy is regarded "as identical with the person it represents" (183)—to destroy the effigy is to destroy the person—whereas the caricature wants to produce an effect on the spectator and does not seek to attack the person who is caricatured but to make use of his likeness.

The problem introduced by hysteria into these pictures is one in which a perception of oneself and oneself have become one and the same. In other words, what gets attacked in hysteria is a likeness and that likeness is the woman herself. There is no objective correlative for the self. If caricature is a "deliberate transformation of features in which the faults and weaknesses of the victim are exaggerated and brought to light" (189), hysteria exaggerates a quality of the self in order to bring to light the perception of the other. Cast in this framework, hysteria, it seems to me, exists somewhere between dreams and the comic. Hysteria, like dreams, is insular and governed by unconsciousness; unlike dreams, it is social. Kris speaks of the comic as an invitation to the other to "adopt a joint policy of aggression and regression" (180). No such joint policy seems the intention of hysteria-as-caricature; no one laughs at an hysterical fit. Yet its manifestation is aggressive and regressive. Perhaps we react as we might to a failed joke when the superego "objects to the manner of its disguise" (185); perhaps we disapprove of the speaker's implicit compulsion to confess (180). In any case, I think the question need be raised of how we react to what we see when we look at hysteria as well as how the nineteenth century viewer could respond.

Moreover, the question still remains of what the hysteric as caricaturist mocks: the self? the other? the other as it views the self? or the self as it enacts, expresses itself? And, what does an hysteric's *Diary* enable us to say? Are we appalled, sympathetic, analytical, indifferent? Do we laugh at Alice's wit, are we amused by her presentation of current events as riddles? Or is her sense of the comic in the *Diary* just as pallid as our response to her self-caricaturization?

An element that complements the peculiar place of the comic in hysteria is that of *la belle indifference.* After Freud's first interview with Elisabeth von R., he notices that she "seemed intelligent and mentally normal and bore her troubles, which interfered with her social life and pleasures, with a cheerful air—the *belle indifference* of a hysteric."[47] Alice James's mother, in reporting on Alice's fits, makes us aware of the indifferent attitude that accompanied them as she writes, "It is not in the least degree morbid in its character—her mind does not seem at all involved in it—she never dreads an attack and seems perfectly happy when they are over" (Strouse, 123). Or, we can go directly to the *Diary* to a passage of wry reflection on Alice's death:

> 'Tis a great waste that I didn't die whilst K. was here; she could have carried home the urn in her top berth and as she lay convulsed with seasickness it would have greatly assuaged her grief to have such a palpable assurance that that portion of me

hitherto so susceptible to the dread thing was reduced to ashes (88).

What purpose does this indifference serve and how is it beautiful? Here, it seems to be a way of enjoying without appearing to be gaining pleasure. In this passage, Alice is "playing" with Katherine, but because the topic surrounds her own death, we cannot believe she is having fun or at least we cannot participate in her joy. *La belle indifference* sets up separations— between the patient and her illness, as it obviates the guilt she might feel in embracing the ill; and between the viewer and any ordinary interpretations he might bring to the scene. It asserts an unconscious refusal, a will through unwillingness; it makes the illness seem to have a life of its own. Insofar as it "prefers not to," indifference is aggressive, but what makes it beautiful, benign, good—"belle," and who decides that it is so? Or, does the physician who gave it this description really not find it "belle" at all? Has the paradoxical nature of hysteria led the physician to ironize what he sees?

I cannot begin to answer these questions here, but I can take indifference toward the related issues of lying, self-exposition, and vanity, all of which show themselves in the *Diary,* all of which can impair just as they are necessarily called forth by the creation of art-ifice. There is a kind of hypocrisy implied in *la belle indifference,* in the insistent calmness of a nervous person, the carefreeness of a person in pain. But Alice James seems to believe that if we could laugh at ourselves more, we would be free of vanity (45). Self-distancing can be a virtue, but hysteria represents the objectification of the self taken to an extreme or gone awry. For Alice James, indifference does not engender self-revelation, i.e, it does not enable her to see herself more clearly, but, as a mode of covering over the self, enables it "to be." When Alice James quotes, "'Time does not work until we have ceased to watch him'" (45) she posits a belief in the stifling consequences of the gaze—as we watch things, we hold them, we render them static, she seems to say. Thus the hysteric, in pretending not to see her illness, lets it happen, enables herself to be *sick.* She is like the narrator in Poe's "Imp of the Perverse," who, driven to confess his crime knows that "to think" in his situation "was to be lost."[48]

Indifference, moreover, affords Alice profound freedom when she can use it to assert separation from moral codes—in the following passage, from the notion of a life after death:

> Vanity, however, maintains its undisputed sway, and I take satisfaction in feeling as much myself as ever, perhaps simply a more concentrated essence in this curtailment. If I could concern myself about the fate of my soul, it would give

doubtless a savor of uncertainty to the fleeting moments, but I never felt so absolutely uninterested in the poor, shabby, old thing. The fact is, I have been dead so long and it has been simply such a grim shoving of the hours behind me as I faced a ceaseless possible horror, since that hideous summer of '78, when I went down to the deep sea, its dark waters closed over me and I knew neither hope nor peace; that now it's only the shriveling of an empty pea pod that has to be completed (230).

Here, too, vanity is whimsically proposed as she simultaneously indicts herself for being vain, shows us the power it gives her, and makes us wonder to what extent vanity could be taken seriously by one so dead. Vanity, in Alice's words, is the "quality from which springs all the grotesque in life" (120); and the egotism of others makes her feel as if in the "presence of an unclothed being" (93). She, on the other hand, learned early to "clothe" herself "in neutral tints, walk by still waters, and possess her soul in silence" (95). The most unselfish, least vain and most truthful state is death, she implies, so that a person who commits suicide is "heroized" by her for being able to "suppress his vanity to the extent of confessing that the game is too hard" (52).

One of the difficulties Alice no doubt has with vanity is that vanity says I exist because I see myself, not because someone else sees me, not because I am perceived by another. Alice wants to make a scene but she does not want attention drawn to herself; she cannot take responsibility for the scene in the making: a not unlikely condition in a world where the male physician's gaze has determined what is ill and what will make one well, a not unlikely condition in a world where a woman's "secret internal organs" were said to "determine her behavior,"[49] where "all but gastronomic vice" was "denied" her "miserable sex" (212). Thus, Alice's hysteria elicits a kind of lying, and one which she unconsciously shows an awareness of when she begins a *Diary* entry on this uncanny note:

> Often in the stillness of the night the voice of a woman, hardly human in its sound, saying without pause, in a raucous monotone, 'you're a loi-er. You're a loi-er' mingled with the drunken notes of a man and with a feeble gin-suckled wail for chorus, reverberates within me (100).

Moreover, without the tools or the intent of a semiotician, Alice feels, I think, that communication necessarily entails lying. Love between men and women, she writes, "'involves a course of perpetual lying'" (86); and, in the same passage, she speaks the desire to strike a communion with the nurse but is continually frustrated by the nurse's "prevarication"—her training in placating the patient rather than under-

taking the serious inquiry into things that Alice wishes to experience with another.

In all this interplay between lying, exposure and vanity, however, what I cannot overlook is the virtual absence of these concerns *in relation to* the *Diary* that Alice is writing, the thing that she is creating. It is as if Alice were indifferent even to that. It is as if self-exposition, lying, and vanity are issues to be dealt with in living rather than writing for Alice. Writing a *Diary,* one senses, was not half as problematic or difficult for Alice as living in the world, and writing fiction, for example, might be harder than either.

The silent conversation between Alice's *Diary* and her illness made it possible for the *Diary* to accommodate an hysterical utterance; and, the continuous displacements of form and formlessness in the *Diary* prevent something like a personality from taking shape in its pages. Alice's comments on "form," which run throughout the *Diary,* present a boundary-less picture of where formlessness begins and form ends. Her relationship to form is ambiguous at best. We are told that Alice often ran words together so that "I am" would read "Iam" in her *Diary,* and that she made frequent use of abbreviations (Yeazell, 193-4), but she does this in a realm where free associativeness is the rule. Sometimes she merely accepts form—when she writes, "Just as the mind refuses to enjoy or to suffer save within limits, so does the heart refuse to love" (51)—but sometimes she desires it: "having been denied baptism by my parents, marriage by obtuse and imperceptive man, it seems too bad not to assist myself at this first and last ceremony" (216)—her death. Or, when writing serves as a harness for the divine, a limit on the infinite which might otherwise quite carry us away, she expresses that desire this way: "I think if I try a little and give it form its vague intensity will take limits to itself, and the 'divine anguish' of the myriad memories stirred grow less' (78). She is distressed by her "floating-particle sense" (51) and describes her attacks as dissolving experiences or "going to pie" (150), yet she wants limitlessness—"the delicious consciousness of wide spaces close at hand" (217)—and admires people whose characters are "stretchable" (56). Impulses that send Ishmael to sea, send Alice to bed. She wants her "bottled thunder" to burst forth as she writes, "How sick me gets of being 'good,' how much I should respect myself if I could burst out and make everyone wretched for 24 hours" (64).

From her retrospective description of America, one senses that she found it too difficult to stay inside there:

> What a longing to see a shaft of sunshine shimmering thro' the pines, breathe in the resinous air and throw my withered body down upon my mother earth, bury my face in the coarse grass,

worshipping all that the ugly, raw emptiness of the blessed land stands for—the embodiment of a Huge Chance for hemmed in Humanity! Its flexible conditions stretching and lending themselves to all sizes of man; pallid and naked of necessity; undraped by the illusions and mystery of a moss-grown, cobwebby past, but overflowing with a divine good-humor and benignancy—a helping hand for the faltering, an indulgent thought for the discredited, a heart of hope for every outcast of tradition! (119)

In England, on the other hand, "'form' is the god of gods" (217). Ironically, Alice retreats into form (the four walls of her sick room) so that she might approximate the formlessness (hysteria) of the after-life: "remaining here at loose ends seemed the only exit from chaos" (150). And, Alice, like her father, and like the God she imagines, is finally de-formed:[50]

> But of all the repulsions, the greatest is that of a religion subscribed to in conformity to an outward standard or respectability, not the spontaneous inspiration of the aspiring soul. A God with fixed and rigid outlines to be worshipped within a prescribed and strictly formal ritual, not a Deity that shapes himself from moment to moment to the need of the votary whose bosom glows with the living, ever clearer knowledge of divine things (196).

In Virginia Woolf's essay, "On Being Ill," Woolf fancies the sick person concocting romances about those who are absent. Alice James's *Diary* gives us no such stories, but over the years, it has been easier to make stories (biographies) about her than to submit her writing to serious inquiry. What *she* could tell us, after all, was hardly enough about *herself*.

Notes

[1] Carroll Smith-Rosenberg and Charles Rosenberg, "The Female Animal: Medical and Biological Views of Woman and Her Role in Nineteenth Century America," *Journal of American History*, (1973), 335.

[2] Quoted in Smith-Rosenberg and Rosenberg, 335.

[3] See Carroll Smith-Rosenberg, "The Hysterical Woman: Sex Roles and Role Conflict in Nineteenth Century America," *Social Research*, 39 (1972), 675.

[4] Smith-Rosenberg and Rosenberg, fn. 51, 355.

[5] Dianne Hunter, "Hysteria, Psychoanalysis and Feminism: The Case of Anna O.," *Feminist Studies*, 9 (1983), 466.

[6] Smith-Rosenberg and Rosenberg, 338.

[7] Smith-Rosenberg and Rosenberg, 336.

[8] I have Jane Gallop's essay specifically in mind here: "Keys to Dora," in Bernheimer and Kahane, eds., *In Dora's Case: Freud, Hysteria, Feminism* (Columbia University Press, 1985), 200-220.

[9] Jean Strouse, *Alice James* (Boston: Houghton Mifflin Company, 1980), xv.

[10] See Anne Sexton, *Complete Poems* (Boston: Houghton Mifflin Company, 1981), 165.

[11] F.O. Matthiessen, *The James Family* (New York: Alfred A. Knopf, 1947), 272.

[12] Ruth Bernard Yeazell, *The Death and Letters of Alice James* (Berkeley: University of California Press, 1981), 2.

[13] Erik H. Erikson, "William James, His Own Alienest" in *Identity, Youth and Crisis* (New York: W.W.Norton Co., 1968), 150-55.

[14] Millicent Bell, "Jamesian Being," *Virginia Quarterly Review*, 52 (1976), 124.

[15] Strouse, 13. Henry, Sr., according to Strouse, viewed women as "personifications of virtue, innocent purity, holy self-sacrifice," xiii. It might be interesting to explore Henry, Jr's novelistic preoccupation with "innocence" in the light of his father's views.

[16] During an anxiety attack, Henry, Sr. feels "the greatest desire to run incontinently to the foot of the stairs and shout for help to my wife'" and, as he finds no relief, he finally must communicate his "'doubt, anxiety and despair'" to his wife (Strouse, 14).

[17] Carroll Smith-Rosenberg, "The Female World of Love and Ritual: Relations Between Women in Nineteenth Century America," *Signs*, 1 (1975), 14.

[18] Quoted in Strouse, 286.

[19] Smith-Rosenberg, (1975), 23.

[20] See Yeazell, 22.

[21] Breuer and Freud, *Studies in Hysteria* in James Strachey, translator, *The Standard Edition of the Complete Psychological Works of Sigmund Freud* (London: The Hogarth Press, 1974), vol. 11, 140.

[22] Leon Edel, editor, *The Diary of Alice James* (New York: Penguin Books, 1964). preface, vii.

[23] Some critics also find Alice in Henry James's fiction—*Washington Square, The Bostonions,* and *The Wings of the Dove,* for example, but I will not take up that kind of reading here.

²⁴ For examples of this, see Yeazell, 8.

²⁵ It took many years for the *Diary* as a whole to arrive at publication. As late as 1934, it was published only as *part* of a volume which emphasized Wilky and Robertson, entitled *Alice James—Her Brothers, Her Journals*. Edel, viii.

²⁶ Sigmund Freud, "Some Character-Types Met With In Psychoanalytic Work" in *The Standard Edition of the Complete Psychological Works of Sigmund Freud,* vol. 14, 311.

²⁷ Edel, intro., 7. William James will also attack his bouts of depression and tendencies toward self-annihilation by taking a leap of "faith" into free will since he will "go a step further with his will, not only act with it, but believe as well; believe in his individual reality and creative power," (Erikson, 154), and by working to reconcile psycho-dynamics with religious experience. As Strouse describes, "William, meanwhile, was trying in the late 1800's to find a philosophy that would reconcile his own tormented nature with the laws of the universe" (126). Alice cannot make the move into health and writing, but death and writing.

²⁸ Edel, intro., 7.

²⁹ For one of several detailed descriptions of this exchange see Yeazell, 15.

³⁰ In a review article entitled, "The James Family," *American Quarterly,* Winter, 1982, 562-70, Anne T. Margolis accuses Yeazell of reductivism, but Margolis refuses to write of Alice on her own terms since her review of Strouse's and Yeazell's work includes and emphatically concludes with a review of volume III of Henry James' *Letters.* I quote, in part, the passage from Alice's *Diary* that receives a careful reading from Yeazell:

> As I used to sit immovable reading in the library with waves of violent inclination suddenly invading my muscles taking some one of their myriad forms such as throwing myself out of the window, or knocking off the head of the benignant pater as he sat with his silver locks, writing at his table, it used to seem to me that the only difference between me and the insane was that I had not only all the horrors and suffering of insanity but the duties of doctor, nurse, and strait-jacket imposed upon me, too. Conceive of never being without the sense that if you let yourself go for a moment your mechanism will fall into pie and that at some given moment you must abandon it all, let the dykes break and the flood sweep in, acknowledging yourself abjectly impotent before the immutable laws. When all one's moral and natural stock in trade is a temperament forbidding the abandonment of an inch or the relaxation of a muscle, 'tis a never-ending fight. When the fancy took me of a morning at school to

study my lessons by way of variety instead of shirking or wiggling thro' the most impossible sensations of upheaval, violent revolt in my head overtook me so that I had to "abandon" my brain, as it were. So it has always been, anything that sticks of itself is free to do so, but conscious and continuous cerebration is an impossible exercise and from just behind the eyes my head feels like a dense jungle into which no ray of light has ever penetrated. So, with the rest, you abandon the pit of your stomach, the palms of your hands, the soles of your feet, and refuse to keep them sane when you find in turn one moral impression after another producing despair in the one, terror in the other, anxiety in the third and so on until life becomes one long flight from remote suggestion and complicated eluding of the multi-fold traps set for your undoing (149).

³¹ Matthiessen also quotes a letter to William from Alice with the following added note from Katherine Loring: "'Alice discussed her demise with him as if she were talking about Queen Elizabeth'" (283).

³² *The Diary of Alice James,* 142: And these doctors tell you that you will die, or *recover!* But you *don't* recover. I have been at these alternations since I was nineteen and I am neither dead nor recovered—as I am now forty-two there has surely been time for either process.

³³ Carroll Smith-Rosenberg, (1972), 665, 676, fn.58.

³⁴ From a letter in Yeazell, 192.

³⁵ For examples of this, one might refer to the opening page of the *Diary* where Alice describes the motives of her embarkation, or to passages of reminiscence like the following (45):

> In those ghastly days, when I was by myself in the little house in Mt. Vernon Street, how I longed to flee in to the firemen next door and escape from the "Alone, Alone!" that echoed thro' the house, rustled down the stairs, whispered from the walls, and confronted me, like a material presence, as I sat waiting, counting the moments as they turned themselves from today into tomorrow . . .

³⁶ Strouse writes that Alice's condition was called at various points in her life, "neurasthenia, hysteria, rheumatic gout, suppressed gout, cardiac complication, spinal neurosis, nervous hyperesthesia and spiritual crisis" (ix).

³⁷ "In the comfortable parlor of Washington Square . . . [Mary and Kate] listened quietly to Henry James's denunciations of Presbyterian theology, and they soon withdrew from the Murry Street Church," Strouse, 5.

³⁸ Virginia Woolf, I think, provides us with a passage in *Orlando* which bears uncanny resemblance to Alice's state of mind, her perception of her position in the

world, but which reaches us through a comic remove and mastery in the self-conscious ironizing of Orlando. See *Orlando* (New York: Harcourt, Brace, and Jovanovich, 1950), 246-250. In fact, it seems to me that on more than one occasion, Woolf's characters read as parodic doubles of the portrait Alice paints of herself in her *Diary,* with the suggestion for further study of the difference between Woolf and Alice James's transformation of illness into word.

[39] As Freud has told us, "'Where hysteria is found there can no longer be any question of innocence of mind.'" Quoted in Sprengnether's essay, "Enforcing Oedipus: Freud and Dora," in *In Dora's Case,* 262.

[40] From Virginia Woolf, *Collected Essays* (New York: Harcourt, Brace, and World, 1967), vol. 14, 196.

[41] Quoted in Strouse, 269.

[42] The hysteric wants to be perceived differently by the father/doctor (with this in mind, we must consider what would constitute a cure) but the centrality of *being perceived* in the symptomatology as well as the *mirroring* or *mimicking* emergent in hysterical states implicates the mother as well.

[43] The passage reads in French:

> Sous cette inspiration les existences les plus humbles peuvent devenir des oeuvres d'art bien supérieures aux plus belles symphonies et aux plus beaux poèmes. Est-ce que les oeuvres d'art qu'on réalise en soi-même ne sont pas les meilleures? Les autres, qu'on jette en dehors sur la toile ou le papier, ne sont rien que des images, des ombres. L'oeuvre de la vie est une réalité d'homme simple, le pauvre revendeur du Faubourg St. Germain qui fait de sa vie un poème de charité, vaut mieux qu'Homère.

[44] Smith-Rosenberg, (1972), 661.

[45] Smith-Rosenberg and Rosenberg, 340.

[46] I will be referring to Ernst Kris's work on caricature and the comic in *Psychoanalytic Explorations in Art* (New York: Schocken Books, 1952), 84.

[47] Breuer and Freud, *Studies in Hysteria,* 135.

[48] From the *Selected Writings of Edgar Allan Poe,* Edward H. Davidson, ed. (Boston: Houghton Mifflin Company, 1956), 230:

> At first, I made an effort to shake off this nightmare of the soul. I walked vigorously—faster—still faster—at length I ran. I felt a maddening desire to shriek aloud. Every succeeding wave of thought overwhelmed me with new terror, for alas! I well, too well, understood that *to think* in my situation, was to be lost.

[49] Smith-Rosenberg and Rosenberg, 337. It is also important to note that Alice imagined her reader to be male: "I am as much amused, dear Inconnu (Please note the sex! pale shadow of Romance still-surviving even in the most rejected and despised by Man) . . ." (166)

[50] Other, more literal, aspects of form that might be contemplated include the French passages in the *Diary,* when they are Alice's or when they are borrowed; the dynamics of composing the *Diary,* i.e, Alice's habit of dictation through the Nurse or Katherine followed by revision; and Katherine's apparent need to give the *Diary* a closure by inscribing a paragraph of her own at the end, clearly addressed to a presumed reader.

Claire Kahane (essay date 1995)

SOURCE: "Invalids and Nurses: The Sisterhood of Rage," in *Passions of the Voice: Hysteria, Narrative, and the Figure of the Speaking Woman, 1850-1915,* The John Hopkins University Press, 1995, pp. 34-63.

[*In the excerpt that follows, Kahane examines several major works of literature to reveal the structure of hysteria as an aggressive act of self-expression.*]

> Hysteria is the daughter's disease.
>
> —Juliet Mitchell

> Daughter of the father? Or daughter of the mother?
>
> —Julia Kristeva

In reading Freud's case history of Dora for its illumination of hysterical narrative voice, I have explored Freud's desire more than Dora's, his symptomatic use of language more than hers. Yet, as Juliet Mitchell remarks, hysteria has been particularly the daughter's disease.[1] What does it mean to be a daughter in the narrative of psychoanalysis? Why is it so problematic? Freud's initial answer was that the daughter signifies the oedipal child who not only desires the father, but more specifically desires to be the object of the father's desire. It was a scene of passive submission to another's desire that Freud had first defined as the traumatic experience in the etiology of hysteria, and although he moved from the seduction theory, in which an early external trauma causes hysteria, to the theory of infantile fantasy, in which the subject's own transgressive desire is the origin of the symptom, even in fantasy the pleasure of being done to rather than doing, the proper feminine position, remained perilous for Freud as well as for his analysands. Desire in this form, as an eroticized submission as object, is the desire that Freud ultimately located in the death drive, in a primary masochism in which the subject seeks pleasure in a return to nonbeing, to nondifferentiation, to silence.

Masochism is thus a primary temptation in hysterical conflict, a seduction into objectification that erases the active subject of desire.

As the Dora case revealed, however, the hysterical daughter did not rest easy as a silent object. In conflict with that masochistic pleasure, she simultaneously struggled to assume the position of subject, to speak her desire. Since within the patriarchal ordering of subjectivity that dominated nineteenth-century discourse, to speak as an active subject was to occupy a masculine position, the voice of the female hysteric became a favored site of an ambivalence that troubled her speech. As we know, in the Dora case Freud analyzed this ambivalence as a matter of unconscious desire and identification: the hysteric was caught between an unacknowledged desire for the father—the core fantasy of the conventional female oedipal complex—and an acknowledged rivalrous identification with him that took a maternal figure as erotic object. Yet implicit in this formulation of sexual ambivalence is an aspect of hysteria that needs more attention: its spawning of rage. For at the heart of the daughter's oedipal oscillation was a more primal engagement with a maternal fantasm, an archaic figure of power and pleasure whose inevitable loss and social devaluation persisted as a burr in the daughter's psyche. Dora was a classic example of the daughter's ambivalent rejection of a devalued mother that inevitably provoked rage.

Although Freud's theorization of the function of rage remains slight and scattered among various texts,[2] he explicitly remarks upon the daughter's rage in his theorization of female psychosexual development, explaining her greater hostility toward the mother as deriving from her recognition of maternal lack ("Femininity," in *New Introductory Lectures,* 1933 [1932], *SE* 22:112-35). In Freud's narrative, the daughter, enraged at the mother for having deprived her of the valued phallus, repudiates her as a love object, a repudiation encouraged by patriarchal demands that she transfer her love to the father. More recent feminist reformulations expand this explanatory narrative to include the daughter's relation to the symbolic order and language. In Kristeva's account, in order to emerge as a subject of language, the daughter must disavow her primary identification with the maternal body and move toward an imaginary and symbolic identification with the father. This maternal disavowal generates a narcissistic crisis, resulting in a chronic melancholia and its concomitant, repressed rage.[3]

Luce Irigaray . . . describes a similar dilemma: "The girl's relationship with her mother is not lacking in ambivalence and becomes even more complicated when the little girl realizes that the phallic mother to whom—according to Freud—she addressed her love, is in fact castrated. This devaluation of the mother accompanies or follows on the devaluation of the little girl's own

Sigmund Freud (1856-1939).

sex organ" (1985a, 68). This oedipal turn from devalued mother to father initiates both a self-devaluation and a hysterical melancholia, a loss of the mother as loved and idealized object that is withdrawn from consciousness.[4] What is more, as Irigaray argues, girls lack access to "representations [that] will replace or assist this 'unconsciousness' in which is grounded the girl's conflictual relationship to her mother and to her sex organ. Which may result in their being 're-membered' in the form of 'somatic affections' that are characteristic of melancholia? And also, of course, of hysteria" (1985a, 68).[5] Since this maternal loss cannot be recuperated symbolically, the daughter must inscribe her desire through an alienating phallic signifier.

If Freud and French feminist psychoanalysts derive the daughter's rage from a recognition of maternal lack, Klein, a major theorist of infantile rage, locates its origin in a fantasy of maternal plenitude.[6] In Klein's view, this fantasy provokes oral-sadistic wishes to rob those parts of the mother where a fantasized fullness lies (her breasts, her body), to incorporate them in a totality that is the essence of primary narcissism. As Klein theorized, because such rage has as its aim the oral incorporation of the maternal body as well as its destruction, rage threatens to destroy the subject as well in a fusion that respects no boundaries. Thus, rage must be contained and loss gradually acknowledged as the subject moves through a primal mourning into what Klein called the depressive position.

Whatever their differences, these psychoanalytic theorists make a common point: the first lost object, which is also the first object of identification and the first object of rage, is the mother, the most ambivalently constructed other, who bears at the same time the traces of self. Certainly for an ambitious Victorian daughter, the stark disjunction between a paternal identification that validated her as speaking subject and a body that compelled her to identify with a devalued maternal object is repeatedly shown to provoke an unutterable rage. One thinks of Maggie destroying her doll in *The Mill on the Floss* in a paradigmatic repudiation of the maternal role that destroys the child-doll as well; or Dora, contemptuously negating her mother's importance in her story but in the process losing her own voice. Indeed, the daughter cannot negate the mother without also negating herself. Suspended at the oedipal moment in all its ambiguous and paralyzing potential, the daughter who succumbed to hysteria typically turned her rage against herself in a kind of masochistic biting of her own tongue instead of using it aggressively against the other and silently mimed in her body the script that had entrapped her.[7]

What would it mean for the invalidated daughter to have valid speech? to have a tongue? What would be said? and in what form? In asking these questions, women writers frequently transform the conventional figure of the patriarchal daughter into the rebellious sister in a discourse of equal rights—of liberty, equality, and fraternity—which values sorority as well. Yet although such writers as Charlotte Brontë and Olive Schreiner variously challenge fraternal privilege and paternal prohibitions in their fictions, their textual voices frequently betray their own bondage to those very prohibitions and the rage that is their affective complement. In what follows I want to look at the effects of rage on the narrative voices of three women whose writings represent three different genres: the *Diary* of Alice James; the polemical essay, *Cassandra,* of Florence Nightingale; and the novels *Shirley* and *Villette* of Charlotte Brontë. It is of perhaps more than passing interest that two of the three women were declared hysterics. James wrote her *Diary* during the final years of her life while sequestered in London with hysterical ailments until she succumbed with relief to a "real" one. Florence Nightingale, also housebound by hysterical debilities after her return from the Crimean War, began *Cassandra* as an autobiographical fiction meant to reveal the pathogenic nature of women's position in culture, but it became a long

and digressive essay that found no public audience during her own lifetime. In contrast, Charlotte Brontë became a professional writer, successfully able to represent as writing her ambivalent relation to cultural authority and narrative law. Yet the written discourse of all three can serve to illuminate the effects of rage on narrative voice.

Alice James had no public presence during her life, nor was she a writer by profession or self-proclamation. Unlike her famous brothers, who in spite of hysterical phenomena in their histories, inscribed themselves into public discourse, Alice James remained essentially the silent sister.[8] Hysterically invalided from the age of nineteen, she spent her life as the quintessential patient, her body the medium through which she covertly represented the problematics of her identity.[9] During the final years of her life, having followed Henry to London, housebound from ailments no doctor could diagnose as real, and cared for by her loyal friend and intimate companion, Katherine Loring, she took up the pen to record her life. Not surprisingly, her writing took the form of a diary, a private voice.

Yet clearly James intended her *Diary* to be read; Leon Edel notes that in 1894 she had four copies of the *Diary* printed, one for each of her brothers, and that she intended to publish the book if they approved ("Introduction" to *Diary,* 1964 [1982], vii). Moreover, in a number of comments she imagines herself exercising a public voice heard by others. In several entries she addresses an imaginary reader, who, significantly, was gendered male, an inflection especially striking since she dictated the better part of the *Diary* to Katherine Loring. But in this perversely gendered address, James' voice speaks the very contradiction of the hysteric: the imaginary ear of the listener/reader who confirms the speaking subject belongs to a man even when James is speaking literally to a woman. James herself comments on this incongruous imaginary male ear in her entry of January 1891, shortly before her death: "I am as much amused, dear Inconnu (please note the sex? pale shadow of Romance still surviving even in the most rejected and despised by Man) as you can be by these microscopic observations recorded of this mighty race" (166).

What strikes this reader is that the *Diary* seems unnecessarily narrow in the field of its attention: even in James' comments on reading—an area in which her observations could have transcended the confines of her domestic space—her thoughts are not allowed the expansion of significant reflection. Her remarks are crabbed or conversationally elliptical, her voice characterized more by biting commentary than by probing analysis or meditation.

Certainly although James writes in that most private of literary forms, the diary, the actual passages of introspection or self-reflection are few. When she does occasionally cast a cold eye on herself, what she reveals is a torturous self-division, as in this well-known passage in which she describes the aftereffects of her own first hysterical attack:

> As I lay prostrate after the storm with my mind luminous and active and susceptible of the clearest, strongest impressions, I saw so distinctly that it was a fight simply between my body and my will. . . . Owing to some physical weakness, . . . the moral power pauses . . . and refuses to maintain muscular sanity, worn out with the strain of its *constabulary* functions. As I used to sit immovable reading in the *library* with waves of violent inclination suddenly invading my muscles, taking some one of their myriad forms such as throwing myself out of the window, or knocking off the head of the benignant pater as he sat with his silver locks, writing at his table, it used to seem to me that the only difference between me and the insane was that I had not only all the horrors and suffering of insanity but the duties of doctor, nurse, and strait-jacket imposed upon me, too. Conceive of never being without the sense that if you let yourself go for a moment . . . you must abandon it all, let the dykes break and the flood sweep in, acknowledging yourself abjectly impotent before the immutable laws. When all one's moral and natural stock in trade is a temperament forbidding the abandonment of an inch or the relaxation of a muscle, 'tis a never-ending fight. (149)

The two forms of her violent inclination—self-destruction or the destruction of the father (and here a particularly archetypal father, the "benignant pater" writing)—and the totalistic either/or syntax speak a deeply regressive desire to break down the boundaries between self and other, here self and father, a desire to destroy the gendered polarities of the subject that confine her in the identity of the good daughter.

Appropriately, the setting of this melodrama is the father's library—the repository of patriarchy, where the daughter can read the script but not write it, a scene repeatedly invoked in late-nineteenth- and early-twentieth-century texts. Recall the provocative Maggie—a character James loved—reading her father's books, or Lucy Snowe in *Villette,* given instructional texts by M. Paul Emmanuel, or even Dora's dream of reading a big book. While Eliot's Maggie outdoes her brother in intellectual prowess, James' leading symptom is an intellectual inhibition. "Cerebration is an impossible exercise and from just behind the eyes my head feels like a dense jungle into which no ray of light has ever penetrated," she writes of her inability to study or think concentratedly without great anxiety (149). Given the phallic marking of intellectual activities—activities in which her particularly brilliant brothers excelled—it is not hard to loosen the knot of meanings in her inability to think, by which she avoids the domain of her brothers and performs a conventional femininity she also despised. "How sick one gets of being 'good,'" she writes. "How much I should respect myself if I could burst out and make every one wretched for 24 hours" (64). In a very real sense, Alice was "sick" of being "good."

This restriction of language and consciousness—a form of defense against knowing—was no doubt fostered by Alice's relation to William, who as Jean Strouse points out, played the flirtatious rake with his sister, his letters provocatively sprinkled with erotic double entendres (1980, 52-55). "If you had taken your pills last summer," William writes to her during one of her treatments for hysteria in New York, "you'd now be at home with my arm around you and the rich tones of my voice lingering in your ear" (110). Such amorous ambiguities between brother and sister were a staple of nineteenth-century discourse. If William's advantages provoked forbidden desire, his advantages encouraged envy and rage as well in his less fortunate sister, that is to say, encouraged her narcissistic identification with a male counterpart and its inherent aggressive rivalry. It was such an intermingling of desire and rage that George Eliot represented in the climactic brother-sister *liebestod* of Maggie and Tom, who are found reconciled to the extreme, drowned in an embrace in *The Mill on the Floss,* a novel especially dear to Alice James. One can even hear its final scene embedded in James' articulation of her own struggle to contain "the flood" within her, a trope of excess that took its toll on her body.

In this regard, it is especially striking that the most vigorous eruption of rage and energy in the chatty surface of James' prose is provoked by her reading of George Eliot's letters:

> Read the third volume of George Eliot's Letters and Journals at last. I'm glad I made myself do so for there is a faint spark of life and an occasional remotely humorous touch in the last half. But what a monument of ponderous dreariness the book! Not one outburst of joy, not one ray of humor, not one living breath in one of her letters or journals, the commonplace and platitude of these last, giving her impressions of the Continent, pictures and people, is simply incredible! Whether it is that her dank, moaning features haunt and pursue one through' the book, or not, but she makes upon me the impression, morally and physically, of mildew, or some morbid growth—a fungus of a pendulous shape, or as of something damp to the touch. I never had a stronger impression. Then to think of those books compact of wisdom, humor, and the richest humanity, and of her as the creator of the immortal *Maggie,* in short, what a horrible disillusion! Johnnie seems to have done his level best to wash out whatever little color the letters may have had by the unfortunate form in which he has seen fit to print them. (40-41)

The physical image by which she characterizes Eliot here is singularly repulsive and recalls the disgust at corporeality common to hysteria. What is it about Eliot that gives James the impression of a fungus, of something damp to the touch? If we follow the logic of the imagery, the morbid growth, the mildew, and fungus all share the quality of a repugnant and invasive parasitic dependence represented by tropes of abjection that are the antithesis of idealization. Certainly James' words, "I never had a stronger impression," suggest some very affective root has been tapped, and what follows next is its radical exposure: "On the subject of her marriage it is of course for an outsider criminal to say anything, but what a shock for her to say she felt as if her life were renewed and for her to express her sense of complacency in the vestry and church! What a betrayal of the much mentioned 'perfect love' of the past!" (41).

This sequence of associative enunciation, from Eliot as a damp fungus to her traitorous remarriage, suggests that her repulsion is associated with Eliot's indulgence of the body, imaged as a parasitic need for corporeal coupling at the expense of the ideal. Repeatedly James censures second marriages as an infidelity, a betrayal of an imagined "perfect love," and an unworthy craving for sensation.[10]

> January 23, 1891: How surprised and shocked I am to hear that Ellie Emmet, whose heart, I had been led to suppose, was seared by sorrow, is contemplating marriage again. . . . 'Twould seem to the inexperienced that one happy "go" at marriage would have given the full measure of connubial bliss, and all the chords of maternity have vibrated under the manipulation of six progeny, but man lives not to assimilate knowledge of the eternal essence of things, and only craves a renewal of sensation. (172)

As with her response to Eliot's remarriage, James here criticizes remarriage as a "renewal of sensation," censuring these women for taking pleasure in the body with which she was continually at war.[11]

The body as enemy is a pervasive trope of the *Diary*—and a trope that makes remarriage a virtually criminal act. Moreover, voicing the familiar dichotomy between European guilt and American innocence that informs her brother's fiction, James describes remarriage as an act that characterizes British women more than American, who sustain more loyally the Puritan ideal:

> The women seem to do here constantly what so rarely happens at home, marry again. 'Tis always a surprise, not that I have any foolish young inflexibility about it, for I am only too glad to see creatures grasp at anything, outside murder, theft or intoxication, from which they fancy they may extract happiness, but it reveals such a simple organization to be perpetually ready to renew experience in so confiding a manner. (102)

This sardonic juxtaposition of remarriage with murder, theft, and intoxication is followed by a startling synecdoche in which the moral integrity of the women who remarries is analogized to the female flesh having been torn, with its connotations of sexual violation:

> As they do it [remarry] within a year or two the moral flesh must be as healthy as that pink substance of which they are physically compact, the torn fibres healing themselves by first intention, evidently. The subjective experience being what survives from any relation, you would suppose that the wife part of you had been sufficiently developed in one experiment, at any rate that you would like to contemplate the situation a bit from the bereft point of view—but, no, they are ready to plunge *into love again* at a moment's notice—as if 'twere quantity, not quality, of emotion that counted. (103)

The trope of the daughter as a potentially torn fiber occurs again in her retelling of a familiar narrative paradigm: a daughter who dies from grief at her father's remarriage, "a little maid" who "passed with peaceful joy from amidst the vain shadows. Will there be no stirrings of remorse in her father's bosom for the brutalities which rent that delicate fibre?" (195-96). James' representation of the daughter as a delicate fiber torn by the father's brutalities recreates a perverse Gothic family romance in which the renewal of paternal desire results in the daughter's violation.

Given this representation of the inimical, vulnerable, or criminal body, it is intriguing to find that when James represents her parents' ideal marriage, she frames it by an association to her own body's vulnerability. Having just remarked on her "devilish headache," she first makes reference to the influenza epidemic and the danger of microbes invading her chamber. Immediately James' text converts the invasive material potential of actual microbes to "ghost microbes," a trope for old letters from her parents that have had a profound effect upon her, as she writes, "one of the most intense, exquisite and profoundly interesting experiences I ever had" (78). Although "ghost microbes" implies an infection by the past, the text quickly transforms this trope of the past as disease to the past as a fountain of perpetual nurturance:

> It seems now incredible to me that I should have drunk, as matter of course, at that ever springing fountain of responsive love and bathed all unconscious in that flood of human tenderness. The letters are made of the daily events of their pure simple lives, with souls unruffled by the ways of men, like special creatures, spiritualized and remote from coarser clay. Father ringing the changes upon Mother's perfections . . . and Mother's words breathing her extraordinary selfless devotion as if she simply embodied the unconscious essence of wife and motherhood. What a beautiful picture do they make for the thoughts of their children to dwell

upon! How the emotions of those two dreadful years, when I was wrenching myself away from them, surge thro' me. (79)

While her parents are represented as "remote from coarser clay," the physical underpinning of the image of her mother "breathing" selfless devotion is striking, especially if one recalls that the very dress of women in the mid-nineteenth century bound their respiration unnaturally. Certainly James seemed stifled in representing her mother, for aside from the above passage there is no anecdotal recall of her mother in the *Diary*. While her father and brothers are frequently remembered in writing, her mother remains an absence, the maternal voice and figure virtually effaced from representation. In its place are substitute women who, by virtue of their bodies, can in no way approach the disembodied ideal.

It is this very de-realization of the mother, her disembodiment and virtual absence from representation, which implicates her as a primary object of James' hysterical repression. Idealization as such eliminates the material presence of the mother; it obliterates the maternal body as well as the maternal voice. It is notable that her mother's voice is not embodied in dialogue, as is her father's and her brothers', and as are the voices of a host of minor characters. Indeed, in the *Diary*, her father's voice is all too present; in the above passage, James recollects her father's voice ringing the changes on a maternal perfection James could not dare dispute or equal.

One of the final entries is a more disquieting memory of her father's voice, this time ringing the changes on her own character in a manner that perhaps illuminates her earlier impulse to smash the paternal pate. Using a metaphor that discloses a nodal point of self-conflict, she recalls the disapproving "ring of Father's voice, as he anathematized some short-comings of mine in Newport one day: 'Oh, Alice, how hard you are!' and I can remember how penetrated I was, not for the first time, but often, with the truth of it, and saw the repulsion his nature with its ripe kernel of human benignancy felt—alas! through all these years, that hard core confronts me still" (192). Since this "hard core" signifies precisely those qualities that are her strengths, she is paradoxically confronted with an image of self that negates her; her very core identity becomes a wound induced by internalization of the condemnatory paternal voice. Close upon this recollection of paternal judgment is another memory that further elucidates her father's place in her internal script. Interestingly, it is a scene that reenacts Freud's theorization of the joke structure—a scene in which Alice listens passively, while two men, figures of patriarchal authority, tell a joke involving her. Emerson, her father's friend, asks another friend: "'And what sort of a girl is Alice?' . . . 'She has a highly moral nature.' . . . 'How in the world does her

father get on with her?'" (193). The punch line, so to speak, is the difference between her and her father, a moral difference in her favor. Yet she denies that difference by literally erasing herself as signifier in the next sentence: "But who shall relate that long alliance, made on one side of all tender affection, solicitous sympathy and paternal indulgence!"

Finally, then, it is a disturbing conflict about self-erasure in the name of the father—a self-erasure that also erases the mother—which inhibits self-representation in James' *Diary*. That erasure was extended to her body image, inducing a rage at the body that was paradoxically articulated through it.[12] At the same time, to undo that erasure, James makes herself a writing subject; but to avoid the implicit rivalry and aggressivity of that position—toward the father, toward her brothers—she writes a private text, a diary, and writes herself out of it as its primary subject. Only as the *Diary* closes on her last year, assuming what she called "a certain mortuary flavor," does she give voice to a greater self-reflexivity. "I would there were more bursts of enthusiasm, less of the carping tone through this, but I fear it comes by nature" (218). References to nature, to the body she could no longer ignore, increase, sharply etched by rage and self-loathing, while at the same time she continues to disclaim its significance:

> If the aim of life is the accretion of fat, the consumption of food unattended by digestive disorganization, and a succession of pleasurable sensations, there is no doubt that I am a failure, for as an animal form my insatiable vanity must allow that my existence doesn't justify itself, but every fibre protests against being taken simply as a sick carcass . . . for what power has dissolving flesh and aching bones to undermine a satisfaction made of imperishable things? (183)

Even as she approached the end and allowed herself to be the subject and object of her writing, she distanced her body by assuming the stance of pure percipient of its outline. "Of what matter can it be whether pain or pleasure has shaped and stamped the pulp within, as one is absorbed in the supreme interest of watching the outline and the tracery as the lines broaden for eternity" (232).

In spite of this self-representation as neutral observer, the lines that broadened were the lines she herself penned in the *Diary*, her textual voice giving her the only outline she still historically retains—as writer of the *Diary*. Not surprisingly, then, James continued to make manuscript corrections to the last, as if more than her life depended upon her words, so that, as Katherine Loring remarked, "although she was very weak and it tired her much to dictate, she could not get her head quiet until she had it written: then she was relieved" (232-33). While one must be very cautious about attributing psychological causality to physical events—cautious, that is to say, about privileging the imaginary as source of the real, especially given the very real suffering of Alice James—it remains an uncanny piece of James' history that she ultimately succumbed to breast cancer, a final physical symptom that exceeded the limits of the symbolic in its repudiation of the maternal signifier, and brought her a death she welcomed with relief.

If Alice James was the archetypal patient, Florence Nightingale has come to signify the archetypal nurse. Yet scratching the surface of this representation reveals a historical irony, since Nightingale, like James, lived the life of the patient, bedridden for most of her life. The figure of the nurse and its inversion, the patient, has dominated histories of hysterics—from Anna O.'s nursing of her father, which was followed by her own need to be nursed (now inscribed as a contemporary myth of the origins of psychoanalysis), to Freud's remembered relation to his nurse, constructed as an origin of his own hysterical proclivities.[13] That Nightingale chose nursing as her field—and battlefield—of action, concerned as it is with mastery of the passive and vulnerable body, but through the body of the other, is certainly not without relevance to the battles of her inner world. Yet, Nightingale thought of herself not as a practicing nurse, but as an administrator, as a fabricator of the nursing system, a role more symbolically coded as masculine. Nightingale's biographers indicate that she was disdainful of Victorian femininity and its domestic concerns and rejected being characterized as a nurse.[14] Nevertheless, in virtually creating the profession of the modern nurse and becoming that symbolic figure as well as a lifelong patient, Nightingale acted out in her own life a bifurcated identification with both a powerful maternal imago and its passive counterpart that was to plague both her writing voice and her body.

The youngest of two daughters, Nightingale grew up in a divided family constellation in which her father, who had rigorously educated her, was her intimate ally against the more conventional social demands of her mother and sister. This family friction took its toll: in her autobiographical writings she describes the dreamlike trances and religious hallucinations of her childhood, her sense that "she was a monster," and the voices she heard at traumatic moments in her adolescence calling her to a special destiny (Showalter 1977, 62). Defying her mother's strong censure for not marrying, Nightingale chose to commit herself instead to the vocation of nursing. Yet after her phenomenal success in the Crimean War, she returned to London with a host of symptoms—including heart palpitations and an extreme nausea when presented with food—and at the height of her reputation, she retired to her bed for almost half a century. That her illness was a

Florence Nightingale (1820-1910).

hysterical one is dramatically rendered by the fact that shortly after her mother's death, Nightingale, having been invalided for forty years, suddenly recovered, as if released from some magical entrapment.[15] Even invalided, however, she remained one of the most influential women in Europe, the founder of nursing as a respectable profession for middle-class women, and a prolific writer in the cause of health care reform.[16]

Although she was always writing—letters, reports, essays—writing is not what we associate with Nightingale. What she wanted to write—her own life story as admonitory narrative—she apparently could not. Among her papers is the fragmentary prose piece *Cassandra*, which began as an autobiographical novel but which she was unable to complete. Eventually, after many revisions, it metamorphosed into a long fractured essay, part of which has been published as a monograph by The Feminist Press. First written in 1852, before she took to her own bed, *Cassandra* was Nightingale's most persistent attempt to articulate her perception of the pathogenic conditions of women's lives. It is also a text that bears the classic marks of a hysterical discourse, riven by contradictory passions, digressive, fragmentary, inconsistent in its voice and subject position, a text that Lytton Strachey aptly characterized as a *cri de coeur* even though it had undergone repeated revisions (1918, 189).[17]

Nightingale's process of revising and rewriting from the early manuscript "novel" with its stilted artifice to the passionate cry of the essay instructively illuminates the nodal points of conflict that inhibited her ability to write a life-fiction.[18] In its first version *Cassandra* is framed as a third-person narrative but is "told" primarily in the firstperson voice of its tragic heroine Nofriani, a Venetian princes who, in a series of long dramatic dialogues with little action, complains of her situation as a woman to her brother Fariseo, whose function is to listen and confirm her concerns. Making use of what Marianne Hirsch calls "the man who would understand,"[19] a male double who is both self and other, this early version used the device of a social conversation between brother and sister to embed a critique of the social condition of women and its ill effects.

Yet in a gesture that seems to contradict her polemical intent, Nightingale places Nofriani in a conventionally romantic setting and makes her a romantic heroine who expresses from the outset a conventional melancholy and a desire for death:

> The night was mild & dark & cloudy. . . . All was still. "I alone am wandering in the bitterness of life without," she said. She went down where on the glassy dark pond the long shadows of the girdle of pines the tops of which seemed to touch heaven were lying. The swans were sleeping on their little island. Even the Muscovy ducks were not yet awake. But she had suffered so much that she had outlived even the desire to die. (Add.MS 45839, f.237; quoted in Snyder 1993, 26)

What is significantly different in this awkwardly artificial fiction is that it is a woman who articulates this conventional melancholy. As Juliana Schiesari argues, melancholy is a gendered affect, traditionally an affliction of great but tormented men. Certainly for the nineteenth century, the privileged melancholy subject was male, a Keats or a Byron but not a Dorothy Wordsworth, a Rochester but not a Jane Eyre. Moreover, melancholy was considered not merely an affect, but a form of male creativity; it was precisely the ability of the subject to speak his melancholy in language that gave it cultural value (Schiesari 1993, 1-7). In contrast, women were typically represented not as melancholic but as depressed, a difference signified by their absence of speech, by their withdrawal into silence. Nightingale's heroine, then, in being primarily a melancholy first-person voice, already transgresses the place of the woman in the nineteenth-century literature of melancholia. Nevertheless, her destiny is classically

feminine: after complaining of the social thwarting of women's desires, Nofriani dies, welcoming death in a gesture not unlike Alice James'. Significantly, it is the male voice of her brother that recounts her final words: "Free, free, oh! divine Freedom, art thou come at last? Welcome, beautiful Death!" (Add.MS 45839, f. 287; quoted in Snyder 1993, 26).

This conclusion, the declamation of a dying woman, was retained at the end of the final essay version as well, but in the essay the words are attributed to an anonymous dying woman by a voice external to the action. With the quotation marks of Nofriani's dialogue removed, the limited female voice and its melancholy romanticism are depersonalized and made into a general statement about women's unhappiness. Thus, Nightingale attempts to transform the romantic fantasy of a particular female subject into a generalized social criticism; failed novel is meant to be redeemed as political essay in great part through the transformation of the voice. To take another example, in the novel, Nofriani says that she is "too much ashamed of my dreams, which I thought were 'romantic' to tell them where I knew that they would be laughed at"; in the later essay version this embarrassment is made into a third-person description of a general condition: "thus women live—too much ashamed of their dreams, which they think 'romantic,' to tell them to be laughed at." Both cases, however, describe the inhibiting effects of shame—"too much ashamed of their dreams"—on women's narrative voice.

In this context the novel was obviously an inappropriate genre for Nightingale, for the novel requires a certain shamelessness, a scandalous exposure of dreams, a certain submission to fantasy, a letting go of the authorial first person. In her own attempted novel, that submission to fantasy had led Nightingale's heroine to a problematic flirtation with passivity and death. The essay, however, foregrounds authorial control and the authority of the first-person writing subject, and indeed, for that reason has been considered a male genre.[20] Paradoxically, the novel version of *Cassandra* insisted on the dominance of the first-person voice but at the same time too rigidly controlled it. Although the voice of the essay version is given more freedom, that, too, becomes problematic; the essay inconsistently shifts between third-person and first-person plural voices, digressing, obsessing, too often fracturing the focus of its argument. Significantly, in an intermediate stage, Nightingale excised the specifically feminine and thus culturally devalued narrative voice altogether; in this mediate version, the voice vacillates between a masculine first-person narrator, Fariseo, the brother who tells his sister's story, and an anonymous third-person narrator.

In the final essay, however, both Nofriani and Fariseo, brother and sister, are absorbed into another kind of splitting, an anonymous but gendered first-person plural and an authoritative third-person narrative voice, both of which eliminate the individual speaking subject and the potential shame at its revelations. The disembodied omniscient third-person voice can then speak with the authority of its transcendence, while the first-person plural "we" identifies with and explores the common concerns of women. Critiquing the detrimental effects of fantasy on women's psyches,[21] Nightingale uses the first-person plural to represent it as a dangerously seductive substitute for action: "We fast mentally, scourge ourselves morally, use the intellectual hair shirt, in order to subdue the perpetual daydreaming, which is so dangerous!" (1979, 27). Fantasy itself becomes the object to be repressed rather than available for fiction. Thus, through critique, Nightingale excises the exotic passages that had plagued the novel. The move from novel to essay thus shifts attention from inner desire to outer determinants in order to uncover and proclaim those social conditions that predispose women to invalidism and passivity, and to call for action.

Perhaps the most vivid of *Cassandra*'s warnings about the danger of the passive position is Nightingale's description of being "read aloud to," which she calls "the most miserable exercise of the human intellect": "It is like lying on one's back, with one's hands tied and having liquid poured down one's throat. Worse than that, because suffocation would immediately ensue and put a stop to this operation. But no suffocation would stop the other" (34). The violence of the metaphor in which listening to the voice of the other is the equivalent of being force-fed, a metaphor that would become a violent reality for militant suffragettes a generation later, and its oral site of conflict point again to a familiar hysterical fantasy of an intrusive and suffocating maternal body. (Nightingale actually suffered from a symptomatic and recurrent nausea, the most corporeal symptomatic rejection of maternal intrusion.)[22]

That the maternal voice is commonly experienced as an intrusive violation of boundaries (see chap. 2) lends a special resonance to Nightingale's representation of listening as an oral menace, as a violation of both her bodily limits and her psychological integrity.[23] Her response is to propose an antithetical image of desire: the daughter's passionate desire to talk. While mothers taught their daughters that women were not passionate, Nightingale writes, in fact, passion swells their imaginations. Given the straitjacket of femininity, romantic passion is displaced into a passion for sympathetic conversation, a passion for the voice. Thus, Nightingale represents the fantasy of a vocal interchange with an imaginary male double—recall Alice James' "Inconnu"—as the fulfillment of the daughter's desire:

That, with the phantom companion of their fancy, they talk (not love, they are too innocent, too pure, too full of genius and imagination for that, but) they talk, in fancy, of that which interests them most; they seek a companion for their every thought; the companion they find not in reality they seek in fancy, or if not that, if not absorbed in endless conversations, they see themselves engaged with him in stirring events. (26)

Romantic fiction, Nightingale suggests, appeals to women for the same reason: it encourages a fantasy of liberation through conversation with a sympathetic male other:

What are novels? What is the secret charm of every romance that ever was written? The first thing . . . is to place the persons together in circumstances which naturally call out the high feelings and thoughts of the character, which afford food for sympathy between them on these points—romantic events they are called. The second is that the heroine has generally no family ties (*almost invariably no mother*), or, if she has, these do not interfere with her entire independence. (28, italics mine)

Note the barely disguised wish to eliminate the mother, primary figure of interference with her independence, which appears in parentheses that restrain it. Simultaneously, the parentheses interrupt the linearity of the sentence by pointing to another track of association. Just as in this passage, the mother is displaced by the imaginary counterpart with whom the heroine can share "food for sympathy" rather than be force-fed, so in her own life Nightingale displaced her mother with actual counterparts, significant figures upon whom she depended for sympathy and whom she ruled as narcissistic extensions of her will and desire. When ultimately the exigencies of life caused an intimate to leave her, she responded to this separation with rage and symptoms.

In *Cassandra* Nightingale recognized that invalidism was a perverse form of aggressivity that both corrupts the individual life and impoverishes the symbolic order. In one of her formidable insights into the paralysis induced by a rage with no outlet she writes: "The great reformers of the world turn into the great misanthropists, if circumstances . . . do not permit them to act. *Christ, if he had been a woman, might have been nothing but a great complainer*" (53, italics mine). The paradox is rich: if Christ had been a woman, he would only have complained rather than acted. But also, if Christ had been a woman, his discourse would have been impotent; his audience would have heard and dismissed his message as only a complaint. Christ would have been Cassandra, the enraged prophet-daughter who speaks but is destined not to be heard, whose voice is stripped of any claim to authority. Like a number of women in conflict with patriarchal femininity, like Alice James hearing her father's voice, her brother's voice, writing to her male Inconnu, Nightingale here establishes the discursive potency of the male voice, and finds her imaginary counterpart, her ego ideal, in Christ—the prophet-*son*—who is empowered to speak as a woman never is.

In moving from fiction to essay, Nightingale was attempting to lend more urgency, immediacy, and authority to her voice. Just as the voice without quotation marks is more privileged in narrative as a source of authority, so the essay as a form is presumed to be more "true" than fiction. *Cassandra*'s fragmentation of the voice subverted the authority it attempted to claim: not surprisingly, it found no welcoming audience until recently. It is especially telling and historically prophetic, then, that Nightingale chose to name her writing voice and alter ego Cassandra, the mad prophet-daughter to whom no one listens. (Nightingale referred to herself as "poor Cassandra" in her letters and notes.) Ironically, Nightingale's own proper family name was itself a fiction, a name her father had appropriated in order to claim an inheritance. Was its allusion to the myth in which a woman's complaint is silenced by cutting out her tongue a constant reminder of her problematic place as speaking subject? Did Nightingale hear herself as Philomela as well as Cassandra? The excision of the woman's tongue is meant to destroy the female voice as logos, as meaning.[24] The voice of the woman in patriarchal discourse must remain the voice of the nightingale, a vocal image of pleasure rather than knowledge, sound without meaning, without pain. If the myth of the nightingale represents silence as the form of women's suffering at the hands of the patriarchal order, Nightingale's Cassandra managed to give suffering a voice and made pain a spur to social action: "Give us back our suffering, we cry to heaven in our hearts—suffering rather than indifferentism, for out of nothing comes nothing. But out of suffering may come the cure. Better have pain than paralysis!" (29). Although Nightingale herself refused the label *feminist, Cassandra* turned rage into outrage and thus turned the hysterical complaint to political account.

Charlotte Brontë can also be said to have turned the romantic complaint to political account by shifting from fiction to essay, but in Brontë's case, the political essay was typically embedded within the romantic fiction. Thus, for example, the narrator of *Jane Eyre,* in a sudden textual turn from narrative to argument, interpolates a passage on the need for action in women's lives:

> It is vain to say human beings ought to be dissatisfied with tranquility; they must have action; and they will make it if they cannot find it. . . . Women are supposed to be very calm generally; but women feel just as men feel; and it is narrow-minded in their more privileged fellow-creatures to

> say that they ought to confine themselves to making puddings and knitting stockings, to playing on the piano and embroidering bags. . . . It is thoughtless to condemn them, or laugh at them, if they seek to do more or learn more than custom has pronounced necessary for their sex.

> When thus alone I not unfrequently heard Grace Poole's laugh. (1960, 112-13)

Virginia Woolf cited this text as an example of a disturbance in the narrative voice caused by an uncontrolled eruption of Brontë's anger into her story (1957, 104). While a number of critics have censured Woolf for that critique and justified Brontë's digression on both political and narrative grounds,[25] clearly, there is an awkward break. In an interpolation that ruptures the narrative flow of the moment, Brontë's narrator temporarily leaves the story to make an eloquent and passionately felt first-person appeal for her right to the active subject position and then returns clumsily to her story. Significantly, it is an imaginary derisive *male* laugh that creates this division within her narrative voice, momentarily moving the voice away from the story and its mad-woman into a first-person complaint that exceeds the diegetic boundaries to implicate Brontë's authorial voice.

Similarly, in *Shirley,* in the midst of the narrator's description of the heroine's romantic disappointment, rage takes over the voice and diverts it, in a digression that, as in *Cassandra,* is spurred on by Brontë's outrage at the suppression of women's speech:

> A lover masculine so disappointed can speak and urge explanation; a lover feminine can say nothing: if she did, the result would be shame and anguish, inward remorse for self-treachery. Nature would brand such demonstration as a rebellion against her instincts, and would vindictively repay it afterwards by the thunderbolt of self-contempt smiting suddenly in secret. Take the matter as you find it; ask no questions; utter no remonstrances: it is your best wisdom. You expected bread, and you have got a stone; break your teeth on it, and don't shriek because the nerves are martyrized: do not doubt that your mental stomach—if you have such a thing—is strong as an ostrich's—the stone will digest. You held out your hand for an egg, and fate put into it a scorpion. Show no consternation: close your fingers firmly upon the fight; let it sting through your palm. Never mind: in time, after your hand and arm have swelled and quivered long with torture, the squeezed scorpion will die, and you will have learned the great lesson how to endure without a sob. (1974, 128)

The flood of affect that courses through this passage is more fervent than in Jane Eyre's speech. It recalls the more impassioned passages of Alice James' *Diary;* one hears the resentment at the freedom of the male voice to speak its desires, the shame of self-exposure that Nightingale articulated, features that identify this enraged third-person voice as a woman's. The metaphors of negative nurturance accuse the mother of deprivation; the lesson of martyrdom and silence accuses the patriarchal culture of oppression. If the voice vents its rage in an imperious staccato syntax, it also commands the female reader and the writer, both here temporarily merged into the second person, to endure without a sob.

Significantly, the admonition to endure without a sob, spoken in passionate irony by the narrative voice, is spoken in all seriousness by a maternal figure within the plot:

> "Rose, don't be too forward to talk," here interrupted Mrs. Yorke, in her usual kill-joy fashion; "nor Jessy either; it becomes all children, especially girls, to be silent in the presence of their elders."

> "Why have we tongues, then?" asked Jessy, pertly; while Rose only looked at her mother with an expression that seemed to say, she should take that maxim in, and think it over at her leisure. (172)

That maxim is precisely at the core of Brontë's fictional conflict, as she explores and tries to explode the patriarchal restrictions on the woman's tongue here transmitted by a "kill-joy" mother. Significantly, in *Shirley* both heroines fall ill precisely because they cannot "endure without a sob." Indeed, not only the heroines but also the hero succumbs to a mysterious illness, a ubiquitous trope in *Shirley* that is used to indicate not only the psychosomatic effects of repression on the characters, but a more extensive causal relation between repression and social disorder.

There are two plots in *Shirley:* a romance plot and a political plot. Both converge in making demands on a hero who becomes the antagonist of both. Caroline Helstone in the romance plot and the disaffected weavers in the political plot are shown to be subject to the callous indifference of the new phallic-capitalist hero Robert Moore and his cohort of fellow mercantilists. Caroline, rejected by Moore for materialist reasons—she is too poor to do him good in his obsession with rebuilding his family estate—and unable to articulate her anger, falls ill; the weavers, about to be supplanted by more efficient machines and refused recognition of their legitimate grievance, give voice to a resentment that turns into a violent action. Although Brontë's text recognizes the heroine's feelings of thwarted desire, her rage remains unacknowledged; repressed by both character and narrative voice, that rage is displaced into the political plot, where it is voiced by the disaffected workers. Only occasionally does rage break through directly in the narrative voice, as in the above passage, where it reveals a disruptive demand for women's speech.[26]

Shirley is Brontë's most explicitly feminist and political novel; it is also the most diffuse and disjointed one. Its narrative voice swings ambivalently between polarities we have discerned in Nightingale's text as well: between a conventional romanticism and its ironic subversion, between a pragmatic political discourse of equal rights and a more suspect appeal to the delights of mastery and submission, between a desire for dependence and a longing for autonomy. The plot is also riven by contradiction, veering between the sketchily conceived political plot of labor unrest and the romance plot that ambivalently heroizes the dominant master Moore. This division between the political and the romantic also suggests a conventionally gendered difference in narration, the former concerned with the public realm of rivalrous male power and the production of goods, the latter exploring the private province of women's desire. As other critics have also remarked, Brontë's uneven and fragmentary handling of the political plot makes it seem more an unsuccessful projection of the primary romance plot onto the historical stage than a developed political scenario in its own right.[27]

Within the romance plot, the narrative point of view is again split between the two heroines: Caroline Helstone, the virtuous and intelligent but docile and silent Victorian daughter, and her wealthy and feisty friend Shirley Keeldar, whose economic independence allows her a social freedom of speech unavailable to Caroline. Abandoned by her mother and reared by her misogynist uncle, Caroline has been trained to be silent, and thus suffers the familiar Brontëan torment of suppressed passion. In contrast, Shirley, who literally appropriates masculine authority by renaming herself Captain Keeldar, occupies a more privileged position, even demanding only half jokingly that she be addressed as a young lord. Under the protection of the masculine name and the social place it signifies, Shirley argues with the elders about female authority, brazenly defies her uncle in the matter of marriage, and imagines acting out a heroism beyond the confines of her estate.

If Brontë embodies a gendered active/passive dichotomy in the two heroines through their split relation to free speech, she again splits the conflict by representing that division within Shirley herself. Like the typical Brontë heroine, Shirley, confesses her taste for submission to a more powerful figure: "it is glorious to look up" (104). To satisfy that desire, Brontë introduces a late entry into the narrative, an almost literal deus ex machina, Louis Moore, Robert's long lost brother and Shirley's true but hitherto secret object of desire. A sensitive tutor rather than a ruthless businessman, Louis is brought in as a male supplement to relieve the rivalrous tension between the two women. Once Louis enters, each heroine has a proper mate; nothing of desire or rage remains. While he seems at first a more palatable hero, more vulnerable in his poverty, more sympathetic, indeed, more woman-like, very quickly, in spite of his poverty and lack of social power, Louis becomes a familiar Brontëan figure of male dominance, the Teacher to whom Shirley as student humbly bows, to whom she relinquishes the power of the voice.

Indeed, in the final chapters of *Shirley,* the narrative voice itself gets humble, shifting from Brontë's third-person voice to the first-person notebooks of Louis Moore, and thus yielding narrative authority to the male voice. It is as if the narrative voice, having repressed its desire to speak as a male subject with all the assumed mastery of that position, is finally gratified, revealing a major source of the text's symptomatic fragmentations. On the one hand, Brontë plays with and indulges in role reversals that unveil sexual difference as a kind of social masquerade, so that both male and female characters can be powerfully masculine or submissively feminine; on the other, she represents sexual desire as essentially dependent upon the heroine's submissive relation to a powerful male figure. Recurrently making her heroines bondswomen to romance, Brontë repeatedly undercuts her criticism of women's social oppression. Earlier in the novel, when Shirley, the figure who is invested with the power of the voice, uses it, it is Caroline, not her male auditors, who tells her: "Shirley, you chatter so, I can't fasten you: be still" (20). By the end of the novel, Brontë has not only inhibited Shirley's political speech, but has turned it into romantic chatter. If the novel begins with the question of the legitimacy of women's discursive authority, Brontë's implicit answer ultimately defeats the third-person female voice of *Shirley.*

Villette, Brontë's last novel, returns to these issues but avoids the pitfalls of *Shirley* by containing its conflict in the first-person female narrative voice of Lucy Snowe, a voice that emphatically does not chatter. Quite the contrary, Lucy withholds information, displaces her own desires onto other characters, even directly lies to both the reader and characters within the text, and generally evades her conventional narrative task of disclosure while seducing the reader into the interstices of allusion and innuendo. Lucy employs various strategies of dissemblance that bear an affinity to the strategies of the hysteric. She continually displaces herself as the subject of her story, switching narrative tracks a number of times to the stories of other characters—Paulina, Miss Marchmont, Ginevra—who are all represented as potential splits of the female subject of narrative action. Lucy hides her actions by narrative omissions of important details and her motivations by shifting at key moments of expected revelation to the more indirect modes of allegory and allusion, requiring the reader's interpretation to fill in the gaps. She promotes confusion by manipulating the ambiguities and duplicities of language itself, using terms that function like Freudian switchwords to suggest alternative paths of meaning.

Yet by these devices, Lucy also suggests the overdetermined nature of her desire and the difficulties of representing it through the conventions of Victorian narrative. Indeed, by alluding at various points to the problematics of women's writing and self-exposure, Lucy becomes a stand-in for the author behind the text, the narrative voice confusing the issues of authorship and inhibition confronting Brontë as a writer with the cultural limitations imposed on Lucy. Thus, both Brontë and Lucy hide in the shadows of a duplicitous discourse in order to exercise its power without revealing their own. At the same time, as in hysterical narrative, their very silences often result in a tortured syntax that itself divulges secrets they would withhold.[28] Within the context of my discussion, I want to focus on one untold secret: Lucy's passionate rage and its effects on her narrative voice.

Like *Shirley, Villette* is concerned with the silencing of the woman's voice; unlike *Jane Eyre,* it gives vent only indirectly to rage at being silenced, and then, lays blame on the woman's body. Take, for example, a key moment when Lucy wants to indulge her secret passion for Dr. John by an exchange of letters which, in displacing the corporeal presence of the voice, allows her to feel less inhibited in her expression. Brontë constructs Lucy's internal conflict as an allegorical dialogue with Reason, described as a cold and venomous stepmother: "Talk for you is good discipline," Reason tells her:

> "You converse imperfectly. While you speak there can be no oblivion of inferiority."

> "But," I again broke in, "where the bodily presence is weak and the speech contemptible, surely there cannot be error in making written language the medium of better utterance than faltering lips can achieve?" (1979, 306)

The passage introduces a difference between speech and writing that is essential to any interrogation of sexual difference, the difference the presence of the body makes in the articulation of the female subject. Although at this point in the novel, Lucy is refused the approval of Reason for desiring to disguise her weak "bodily presence" and its unwelcome revelations by writing rather than speaking, the question is not mute and recurs several times in the course of the novel. It is given another turn when Lucy undergoes an oral examination by "the professors" on the basis of their having seen an essay of hers. Confronted with their presence and their questions, she can only answer, "Je n'en sais rien" (493). As Brontë writes through Lucy, "Though answers to the questions surged up fast, my mind filling like a rising well, ideas were there, but not words. I either *could* not, or *would* not speak—I am not sure which: partly, I think my nerves had got wrong, and partly my humour was crossed" (493).

Recalling Alice James' intellectual constrictions, here Brontë's text makes clear the link between rage and the hysterical inhibition of the voice, especially as the passage continues:

> I wish I could have spoken with calm and dignity, or I wish my sense had sufficed to make me hold my tongue; that traitor tongue tripped, faltered. Beholding the judges cast . . . a hard look of triumph, and hearing the distressed tremor of my own voice, out I burst in a fit of choking tears. The emotion was far more of anger than grief; had I been a man and strong, I could have challenged that pair on the spot. (494)

In Brontë's text, the female voice is itself an ambivalent object, at once devalued as weak when tied to the limitations of its origin in the female body—the faltering lips—and made inarticulate by a rage that fractures language; but once projected into the disembodied voice of writing, and thus anonymous, that voice is empowered and empowering. Writing in this context becomes a phallic mask for the woman's voice; the disembodied voice of representation allows Brontë to lay claim to an equality that the female body as situated in a phallocentric order disallows. Without being physically subject to the gaze, one can "oubliez les professeurs" and speak through the disguise of language. That this remains a performance, however, with all the ambivalence implicit in speaking only through an other, remains a central insight of *Villette.*

Perhaps the most revealing passage that allows us to see the need for the mask as well as what it hides is Lucy's impassioned digression on the actress Vashti, in some sense that most potent but invisible presence in the novel. A foil to the fleshly Cleopatra, which the novel proffers as an image of the repulsive female body, Vashti is represented as transcending the limits of that body by the force of her articulated rage. Of course, as an actress, Vashti is performing a rage dissociated from her own existential being; indeed, the play she performs makes her passions the result of "evil forces" that inhabit her, "devils which cried sore and rent the tenement they haunted, but still refused to be exorcized" (339). Yet Brontë makes clear that the power of Vashti comes from her mastery of the passions she articulates rather than her being captured by them.

Indeed, while women's rage is conventionally allowed social expression by being contained as and in theatrical spectacle, in Brontë's representation of that spectacle, the actual body falls away, revealing the phenomenal power of rage to explode all limits. While we as readers are not given a direct description of Vashti's performance, we are given its reflection in Lucy's response, for once, without disguise. Lucy's articulated identification with Vashti allows her to break out of the mode of suppression and evasion that has charac-terized her own voice and actions. In a moment of extraordinary liberation and revelation, Lucy breaks open her carapace and with it the romance of Victorian fiction:

> I thought it was only a woman, though an unique woman, who moved in might and grace before this multitude. By-and-by I recognized my mistake. Behold! I found upon her something neither of woman nor of man: in each of her eyes sat a devil. These evil forces bore her through the tragedy, kept up her feeble strength—for she was but a frail creature; and as the action rose . . . how wildly they shook her with their passions of the pit! They wrote HELL on her straight, haughty brow. They turned her voice to the note of torment. They writhed her regal face to a demoniac mask. Hate and Murder and Madness incarnate she stood.
>
> It was a marvelous sight: a mighty revelation.
>
> It was a spectacle low, horrible, immoral. (339)

In Vashti as spectacle is exposed the rage that *Jane Eyre* keeps locked in the attic in the figure of Bertha. Moreover, unlike the masochistic hysteric, Vashti does not embrace her pain but attacks it; her rage is not turned inward but transgressively directed against the other. "To her, what hurts becomes immediately embodied; she looks on it as a thing that can be attacked, worried down, torn in shreds. . . . Before calamity she is a tigress; she rends her woes, shivers them in convulsed abhorrence. . . . Wicked perhaps she is, but also she is strong; and her strength has conquered Beauty, has overcome Grace, and bound both at her side, captives peerlessly fair, and docile as fair" (340). Paying tribute to a female figure freed by the license of poetic discourse from the corporeal limitations of both femininity and the body that represents it, *Villette* puts on stage a mighty paean to hatred, murder, and madness, whose meaning only Lucy consciously recognizes and approves, her own rhetoric liberated by this identification with rage. In contrast, Dr. John, the handsome hero of conventional romance and the keeper of the bourgeois flame, is made instinctively uncomfortable by Vashti. When Lucy asks his opinion, "He judged her as a woman, not an artist: it was a branding judgment" (342).

The appearance of Vashti in Lucy's narrative is a turning point in a novel that repeatedly turns from one narrative line to another. This turn, however, allows Lucy, and Brontë's narrative, to turn away from Dr. John, to bury his letter and the conventional romance plot it signifies. Thus, after Vashti's passions are released, a fire breaks out in the theater—one recalls Dora's dream-rescue by her father from her burning house—an event that brings back the Victorian angel in the house as the proper heroine of the Victorian domestic plot and compels Lucy to move into a new story. Thus, Lucy buries the letters of Dr. John. With that burial, M. Paul, until this point an emphatically little albeit comically ferocious figure, suddenly assumes the primary male place in a new plot of fraternal rather than romantic union. Or at least that is ostensibly what Lucy wants from him.

Yet if Brontë's narrative seemingly dispenses with romance, sexuality, and the problematic body, the turns are too quick and too many in this final section of the novel. Mme. Beck, Lucy's ambivalent model of female independence, whose faults have heretofore been indulged by Lucy, is abruptly and arbitrarily unmasked as a hateful rival, the bad mother as well as evil sister, Lucy's primary antagonist and the object of her rage. Dreamlike antagonists to Lucy's desire suddenly multiply: Mme. Walravens, Père Silas, and even the ghostly nun seem more dream visions than characters on the same plane as Lucy. The line between fantasy and reality becomes increasingly tenuous for the reader as Brontë through Lucy reaches for a new vision and a new destiny for the Victorian heroine.

The climax of this quest for a new vision is Lucy's fantasmatic midnight tour of the park, in which a drugged, cloaked, and seemingly disembodied Lucy floats around overhearing and overseeing the figures in her story. Interestingly, the only friendly figure in this dream space, the only one to recognize Lucy as Lucy in spite of her cloak, is the bookseller, who, telling her she "is not well placed" in her situation, secures Lucy a better place at the main event. Like a dream conversation, his diction resonates with alternative meanings that apply even more to Brontë as writer than to Lucy; neither can be "well placed" at the main event without the friendly bookseller, who disseminates the woman's voice as writing.

In Lucy's case, however, it is ultimately M. Paul who gives her a better place, by setting her up in her own school and thereby allowing her to live out her independence from the old school, Mme. Beck's school. Yet Brontë's old conflict still remains: if Paul is meant to be a brother spirit, another version of Hirsch's "the man who understands," he nevertheless also is the familiar dominant teacher-figure of Brontë's romances. This double view of the male hero, as fraternal and paternal, as equal and as superior, again returns us to Brontë's problematic configuration of desire as requiring two scenes: one of equality and one of dominance and submission. The narrative ultimately evades this dilemma by a sudden turn—Paul's ambiguous disappearance and presumed death, and Lucy's withdrawal from the social contest and the marriage plot which conventionally resolved it.

Although this ending, which allows Lucy to have her own place while not giving up the fantasy of romantic union in some beyond, is an advance over the contrived romantic ending of *Shirley,* it is not a resolution. Brontë permits Lucy her autonomy only by retaining the suspect trope of tragic thwarted passion, of an incomplete story, a story suspended rather than concluded. Indeed, if the final chapter is entitled "Finis," the narrative voice ironically refuses to put final closure to romantic desire. Instead, symptomatically marking this refusal by giving us a series of torturous sentence fragments that promote verbal ambiguity, by shifting back and forth from the past to a present tense that preserves a hovering stasis, the narrative voice projects a fissuring of meaning that resists closure or climax.[29] Moreover, the very page is fissured, as the syntax leaves large white spaces on the page that also presumably "let sunny imaginations hope" (596), spaces that also call the reader to imagine an unrepresented ending projected into the future. This is truly an hysterical strategy, for both reader and heroine remain locked in a state of ambivalent suspense, in that border territory that characterizes hysterical conflict: "Peace, be still! Oh! a thousand weepers, praying in agony on waiting shores, listened for that voice, but it was not uttered— not uttered till, when the hush came, some could not feel it: till, when the sun returned, his light was night to some!" (596).

Yet if *Villette* ends with fragments of a case of hysteria, it is also a powerful narrative exploration of various facets of hysterical subjectivity to the very end.[30] Indeed, *Villette* is Brontë's most complex and mature work precisely because rather than projecting the confusions of its utterance into a third-person voice, Brontë contains it within the voice of a discrete hysterical character, who reveals through the duplicities of her narration the problematics of the woman's speaking voice. This strategy makes *Villette* one of the great modern novels of the nineteenth century and precursor to such first-person modern tales of self-conscious self-revelation and repression as Ford Madox Ford's *The Good Soldier.* What becomes increasingly clear is that first-person narration is an effective way to contain and yet represent those splits in the voice of the subject that come to characterize modernist fiction, splits that are intricately bound up with gender ambivalence.

Notes

[1] Mitchell also constructs the daughter as a cultural position rather than an existential being (1984, 308-13).

[2] See *Beyond the Pleasure Principle* (1920, *SE* 18) and Lecture 33, "Femininity," in the *New Introductory Lectures on Psycho-Analysis* (1933 [1932], *SE* 22), respectively.

[3] See Kristeva's elaboration of these relations involving melancholy, masochism, and hatred in *Black Sun* (1989, 11-12). Freud argued that the loss of self-regard

typical in melancholia was a result of rage directed against the incorporated lost object, now part of the self. Freud discusses rage at the lost object in "Mourning and Melancholia" (1917 [1915], *SE* 14); also, in *The Ego and the Id,* 1923, *SE* 19: "In melancholia the object to which the super-ego's wrath applies has been taken into the ego by identification" (51).

[4] Freud's remarks on melancholia also support Irigaray's reading: "In melancholia," Freud had noted, "the object has not perhaps actually died, but has been lost . . . even if the patient cannot consciously perceive what [s]he lost" ("Mourning and Melancholia," 1917 [1915], *SE* 14:245). Freud's emphasis on *what* is lost turns the loss of the maternal object into a loss *in* the subject that cannot be represented.

[5] Montrelay also argues that the female subject is prevented by her position as object of desire from effectively distancing herself from the body without hysteria. "From now on, anxiety, tied to the presence of this body, can only be insistent, continuous. This body, so close, which she has to occupy, is an object in excess which must be 'lost,' that is to say, repressed, in order to be symbolized" (1978, 91-92). French feminist critics in particular have elaborated the ways in which the male child can position himself at a greater distance from the body, while the female is compelled by virtue of her identification with the mother, to be the body.

[6] See especially "Early Stages of the Oedipus Complex" (1928) and "Mourning and Its Relation to Manic-Depressive States" (1940), reprinted in *The Selected Melanie Klein* (1986).

[7] In describing the importance of oral fixations in hysteria, A. Anzieu notes that in the cases of both Dora and Anna O., conflict is situated in the throat and the voice (1990, 141). For a more extensive discussion of this same point, see David-Ménard (1989, 64-104). "Dora experiences everything by way of her mouth," David-Ménard writes. "Dora's mouth and throat are thus the theatre where she tries to articulate the way things are between the sexes" (90-91).

[8] It is well documented that both Henry and William suffered from physical ailments and effects no less mysterious and hysterical than Alice's. See especially Strouse (1980, 24-25, 110-11).

[9] Alice James had been diagnosed variously as hysterical, neurasthenic, melancholic—all related, and extremely common, disorders among women of her class and time. See Strouse (1980, 248) and Yeazell, "Introduction" (1981). In her *Diary* entry for February 21, 1890, she writes, "I had to peg away pretty hard between twelve and twenty-four 'killing myself' as someone calls it—absorbing in the bone that the better part is to clothe oneself in neutral tints, walk by still wa-

ters, and possess one's soul in silence" (1964, 95). It is fascinating to note that in the months after her mother's death, she was suddenly no invalid, but nursed her demanding and depressed father until he starved himself and died less than a year after his wife.

[10] Writing of a suffering English lady who was first married to a handsome cavalry officer by whom she had one daughter, and who after his death, married a stodgy curate by whom she had nine children, Alice James approvingly notes that the woman was berated by her daughter for her second marriage, and by her sister for having so many children and setting a bad example (October 12, 1890 [146-47]); see also the story of the daughter dying because of her father's remarriage, a story Henry James used as subject of "The Marriages" (April 22, 1891 [105]).

[11] In this way one can understand why her criticism of Eliot's remarriage is immediately followed by her unforgiving censure of Eliot's articulation of her pain:

> What an abject coward she seems to have been about physical pain, as if it weren't degrading enough to have headaches, without jotting them down in a row to stare at one for all time, thereby defeating the beneficient law which provides that physical pain is forgotten. If she related her diseases and her "depressions" and told for the good of others what armour she had forged against them, it would be conceivable, but they seem simply cherished as the vehicle for a moan. (40-42)

[12] Paradoxically, Alice James welcomed her illness as giving her substance; when she finally discovered that she had a tumor, she was elated to be able to name her problem as real: "Ever since I have been ill, I have longed and longed for some palpable disease, . . . but I was always driven back to stagger alone under the monstrous mass of subjective sensations which that sympathetic being 'the medical man' had no higher inspiration than to assure me I was personally responsible for" (207).

[13] See Swan (1974) for a full discussion of this complex maternal imaginary in Freud.

[14] For additional relevant biographical material on Florence Nightingale, see Stark's introduction to *Cassandra* (1979) and Woodham-Smith's biography (1951).

[15] In discussing motives for illness in the Dora case, Freud had pointed out that hysterical symptoms are typically "leveled at a particular person, and consequently vanish with that person's departure" (*SE* 7:61).

[16] See Stark's introduction to *Cassandra* (1979); Allen (1981); Showalter (1985); and Poovey (1988).

[17] Virginia Woolf similarly remarked that "Florence Nightingale shrieked aloud in her agony," and gave as footnote to this remark "See *Cassandra* by Florence Nightingale." See *A Room of One's Own.* (1957, 57).

[18] I first learned of the formless form of this document in conversation with Elaine Showalter. Subsequently, Katherine Snyder generously provided me with a copy of the original manuscript. I am greatly indebted to her transcription of Nightingale's first version of *Cassandra,* and her insightful and extensive discussion of manuscript changes in "From Novel to Essay: Gender and Revision in Florence Nightingale's *Cassandra*" (1993).

[19] See Hirsch's discussion of this imaginary relation in *The Mother-Daughter Plot* (1989, 57-60).

[20] Snyder (1993), in examining the social history behind the gendering of the essay as a masculine form, points out that nineteenth-century readers took the essay as a nonfictional and mimetic expression of the writer's actual self.

[21] Snyder notes such other alterations as Nightingale's excision of details that were autobiographical or too conventionally romantic, and her shortening of the heroine's fantasies (1993, 27-28).

[22] Significantly, it was Nightingale's father who actually read aloud to her, not her mother, though the conflict in its underlying oral structure remains tied to the maternal figure. Thus, her father takes his place with a number of maternal father figures who appear in hysterical histories. See my discussion of Olive Schreiner in chap. 5.

[23] As Silverman points out, "Since the voice is capable of being internalized at the same time as it is externalized it can spill over from subject to object and object to subject, violating bodily limits" (1988, 80).

[24] Psychoanalytically speaking, cutting out the tongue is a trope of castration, in particular, an excision of the power of speech. Its relation to the nightingale myth was reinforced for me recently when Professor Lia Lerner, of the Department of Spanish and Comparative Literature at Fordham University, called my attention to one of Boccaccio's stories in which a woman is holding a nightingale that suddenly is transformed into a penis. Making a similar point, Silverman writes that the "female voice provides the acoustic equivalent of an ejaculation" (1988, 68).

[25] See especially Showalter (1977, 285-90) and Gilbert and Gubar's chapter on Brontë (1979). For an admirable discussion of Woolf's fear of her own rage and its relation to her conviction that anger inevitably distorted art, see also Zwerdling (1986, 243-53).

[26] John Kucich (1987) reads Brontë's texts through their oppositional tensions between expression and repression. As Kucich astutely points out, in Brontë's texts "not only latent rage and subversive sexuality, but also the exploration of repression and desire itself . . . serve a libidinal structure in which both gestures are affirmed, and are to some degree reversible" (38). See also Auerbach (1973, 328-42) for a discussion of Brontë's divided voice as a psychic conflict that remains unresolved, and which Auerbach characterizes as abnormal.

[27] See, for example, Patrick Brantlinger on the confusion of the psychological with the social plot (1977, 124-27).

[28] There have been a good number of excellent extended and psychoanalytically informed readings of *Villette*. See especially Jacobus, "The Buried Letter" (1986).

[29] In a brilliant reading of *Villette's* lack of closure, Garrett Stewart notes that both the heroine's destiny and the death of M. Paul in a shipwreck are arrested. In the final passages, the present is read rather than the past and therefore the story is not past, not closed. As Stewart remarks, "The enunciation enjoins its own arrest" (unpublished manuscript). See also Garrett Stewart, "A Valediction For Bidding Mourning: Death and the Narratee in Brontë's *Villette,*" in *Death and Representation,* edited by Sarah Webster Goodwin and Elisabeth Bronfen (Baltimore: Johns Hopkins University Press, 1993), pp. 51-77.

[30] See Athena Vrettos (1990) for a comparison of Lucy's psychology and the neurotic symptoms of hysteria as discussed in nineteenth-century medical literature.

Works Cited

Allen, Donald R. 1981. "Florence Nightingale: Toward a Psychohistorical Interpretation." In *Florence Nightingale: Saint, Reformer, or Rebel?* edited by Raymond G. Herbert. Malabar, Fla.: Robert E. Krieger.

Anzieu, Annie. 1990. "The Hysterical Envelope." In *Psychic Envelopes,* edited by Didier Anzieu. London: Karnac Books.

Auerbach, Nina. 1973. "Charlotte Brontë: The Two Countries." *University of Toronto Quarterly* 42:328-42.

Brantlinger, Patrick. 1977. *The Spirit of Reform: British Literature and Politics, 1832-1867.* Cambridge: Harvard University Press.

Brontë, Charlotte. 1960. *Jane Eyre.* New York: New American Library.

————, 1974. *Shirley, a Tale*. Edited by Andrew and Judith Hook. Penguin English Library. Harmondsworth, England: Penguin Books.

————, 1979. *Villette*. Edited by Mark Lilly with an introduction by Tony Tanner. Penguin English Library: Harmondsworth, England: Penguin Books.

David-Ménard, Monique. 1989. *Hysteria from Freud to Lacan*. Ithaca: Cornell University Press.

Eliot, George [Mary Anne Evans]. 1966. *The Mill on the Floss*. Riverside Editions. Boston: Houghton Mifflin.

Freud, Sigmund. 1959. *Standard Edition of the Complete Psychological Works*. Translated under the general editorship of James Strachey in collaboration with Anna Freud, assisted by Alix Strachey and Alan Tyson. 24 vols. London: The Hogarth Press and the Institute of Psychoanalysis.

Gilbert, Sandra, and Susan Gubar. 1979. *The Madwoman in the Attic: The Woman Writer and the Nineteenth-Century Literary Imagination*. New Haven: Yale University Press.

Hirsch, Marianne. 1989. *The Mother-Daughter Plot: Narrative, Psychoanalysis, Feminism,* Bloomington: Indiana University Press.

Irigaray, Luce. 1985a. *Speculum of the Other Woman*. Translated by Gillian C. Gill. Ithaca: Cornell University Press.

Jacobus, Mary. 1986. "The Buried Letter." In *Reading Woman: Essays in Feminist Criticism*. New York: Columbia University Press.

James, Alice. 1964. *The Diary of Alice James*. Edited with an introduction by Leon Edel. New York: Dodd, Mead. Reprinted 1982: Penguin American Library. Harmondsworth, England: Penguin.

James, Henry. 1947. *The Notebooks of Henry James*. Edited by F. O. Matthiessen and Kenneth S. Murdock. New York: Oxford University Press.

Klein, Melanie. 1986. *The Selected Melanie Klein*. Edited by Juliet Mitchell. Harmondsworth, England: Penguin Books.

[Kristeva, Julia]. 1989. *Black Sun: Depression and Melancholia*. Translated by Leon S. Roudiez: New York: Columbia University Press.

Kucich, John. 1987. *Repression in Victorian Fiction: Charlotte Brontë, George Eliot and Charles Dickens*. Berkeley: University of California Press.

Mitchell, Juliet. 1984. *Women: The Longest Revolution*. New York: Pantheon.

Montrelay, Michele. 1978. "Inquiry into Femininity." *m/f* I:83-101.

Nightingale, Florence. 1979. *Cassandra*. New York: Feminist Press.

Poovey, Mary. 1988. *Uneven Developments*. Chicago: University of Chicago Press.

Schiesari, Juliana. 1993. *The Gendering of Melancholy*. Ithaca: Cornell University Press.

Schreiner, Olive. 1976. *The Story of an African Farm*. New York: Schocken Books.

Showalter, Elaine. 1977. *A Literature of Their Own: British Women Novelists from Brontë to Lessing*. Princeton: Princeton University Press.

————. 1985. *The Female Malady: Women, Madness, and English Culture, 1830-1980*. New York: Pantheon.

Silverman, Kaja. 1988. *The Acoustic Mirror*. Bloomington: Indiana University Press.

Snyder, Katherine. 1993. "From Novel to Essay: Gender and Revision in Florence Nightingale's *Cassandra*." In *The Politics of the Essay,* edited by Ruth-Ellen Boetcher Joeres and Elizabeth Mittman. Bloomington: Indiana University Press.

Stark, Myra. 1979. Introduction to *Cassandra,* by Florence Nightingale. New York: Feminist Press.

[Stewart, Carol]. 1993. "A Valediction For Bidding Mourning: Death and the Narratee in Brontë's *Villette*." In *Death and Representation,* edited by Sarah Webster Goodwin and Elisabeth Bronfen. Baltimore: Johns Hopkins University Press.

Strouse, Jean. 1980. *Alice James: A Biography*. New York: Houghton Mifflin.

Swan, Jim. 1974. "Mater and Nannie." *American Imago* 31(I): 1-64.

Vrettos, Athena. 1990. "From Neurosis to Narrative: The Private Life of the Nerves in *Villette* and *Daniel Deronda*." *Victorian Studies* 33(4):551-79.

[Woolf, Virginia]. 1957. *A Room of One's Own*. New York: Harcourt, Brace.

Yeazell, Ruth Bernard. 1981. Introduction to *The Death and Letters of Alice James*. Berkeley: University of California Press.

Zwerdling, Alex. 1986. *Virginia Woolf and the Real World*. Berkeley: University of California Press.

Evelyne Ender (essay date 1995)

SOURCE: "'Girls and Their Blind Visions': George Eliot, Hysteria, and History," in *Sexing the Mind: Nineteenth-Century Fictions of Hysteria*, Cornell University Press, 1995, pp. 229-72.

[*In the following excerpt, Ender contends that George Eliot's* Daniel Deronda *exemplifies the problematic manner in which hysteria—as an illness that simultaneously resists and demands interpretation—informs both the content and the structure of literary representation.*]

> What in the midst of that mighty drama are girls and their blind visions? They are the Yea or Nay of that good for which men are enduring and fighting. In these delicate vessels is borne onward through the ages the treasure of human affection.

—George Eliot, *Daniel Deronda*

The scandal and transgression associated with George Sand's name lie for the nineteenth century not so much in her works, where in spite of certain "confusions" morality is preserved, as in the apparent immorality of her existence. In her pretensions to virtue, Valentine outdoes her creator: Sand's realism endows her heroines with more conformism than the author herself ever achieved. Our archcritic, meanwhile, seems to pursue with a certain *frisson historique* the story of the woman whose "life . . . at its most active may fairly be described as an immunity from restrictive instincts more ably cultivated than any we know" ("George Sand," in *Literary Criticism*, 787). What ultimately draws Henry James's most passionate interests is the story of Sand's passions, because it speaks of the forbidden, of the extraordinary, and to borrow one of his images, of "soiled linen." The phase "soiled linen" belongs to his theory of representation which links Sand to Zola; it appears again as the critic greets the publication of her biography: "a tub of soiled linen which the muse of history, rolling her sleeves well up, has not even yet quite begun energetically and publicly to wash."[1] The figure shows James making the distinction between the clean and the dirty; what it does not reveal, however, is the fascination, the thrill—the frisson—that the spectacle of such corruption held for James. That fascination is expressed in a letter to Edith Wharton in which he remembers their joint visit to Nohant, Sand's home: "that wondrous day when we explored the very scene where they pigged so thrillingly together. What a crew, what *moeurs,* what habits, what conditions and relations every way—and what an altogether mighty and marvellous George, not diminished by all the

greasiness and smelliness in which she made herself (and so many other persons!) at home" (James and Wharton, 215). Or, differently, in the writerly glee with which the critic plays, in his 1897 essay, with sexual innuendo: "nothing is more striking than their convulsive effort either to reach up to it or to do without it. They would have given for it all else they possessed, but they only met in their struggle the inexorable *never*. They strain and pant and gasp, they beat the air in vain for the cup of cold water in their hell" (*Literary Criticism,* 745) or, later, not mincing his words: "so much publicity and palpability of 'heart,' so much experience reduced only to the terms of so many more or less greasy males" (773). Dirt, the impure, the immorality, all of this in the woman's quarters, when she should have been responsible for the rituals of purification. "Die quälende Reinmacherei der Mama"—these are Freud's words describing the mania for cleanliness that characterized Dora's mother (*SE* VII, 90). Indeed, in the shadow of Dora's involvement in the sexual traffic of fin-de-siècle Vienna, stands her mother, the instrument, martyr, and telling emblem of the nineteenth-century ideal of feminine purity.[2] Zola regularly fell in love with *blanchisseuses,* which, as James might have said, shows his fascination with dirty linen, or else his need for redemption.[3]

But enough of these scenarios of passion and perversion. This last incursion into Jamesian territory is intended above all to provide a context—the underside—for a discussion of a writer whom the nineteenth century would have singled out precisely for "her restrictive instincts" and dispassionate intellect. In *The Bostonians,* George Eliot makes an appearance as a deity presiding over woman's intellectual pursuits—a picture on the wall of the female academy gathered in Cape Cod. The dying Miss Birdseye, the skeptical "doctoress" Prance, Verena, and Olive (who like Eliot reads avidly the German philosophers) have taken up cloistered quarters to prepare Verena for her great public appearance at the Boston Music Hall. Olive has brought her lares: the complete works of George Eliot and—twice—the image of the Virgin: "Olive had taken her cottage furnished, but . . . the paucity of chairs was such that their little party used almost to sit down, to lie down in turn. On the other hand they had all George Eliot's writings, and two photographs of the Sistine Madonna" (344). Here James alludes teasingly to George Eliot's well-known admiration for Raphael's painting. These then are, in James's (satirical?) conception, the ornaments and effigies that adorn the altar of female knowledge. But there may be more truth than appears in this fictional play. While Olive's admiration for Eliot and the Virgin directs our gaze at Eliot's admiration for the Virgin, it also conjures up the image of Dora held in passionate absorption before the picture of the Madonna at the Dresden Museum, and even of Sand's Valentine praying to the Virgin in her private chapel. What emerges repeatedly from our nineteenth-century readings is a tableau—the woman gazing at the Virgin—which is like the matrix around which desire, knowledge, femininity, and moral purity find their articulation. And this tableau must be remembered as the emblem and memento of a scene of hysteria, whose actress is a woman.

Here then, briefly, is the account, according to George Eliot's biographers and critics, of another scene of hysteria.[4] In 1858, George Eliot spends six weeks in Dresden with her companion, George Henry Lewes. This is her second trip to Germany following what to her friends and acquaintances appeared to be a scandalous elopment: on the July 20, 1854, Mary Ann Evans had traveled to Weimar, semiclandestinely, with Lewes, a married man and father of a large family. During her second stay in Germany, she goes to the Dresden Museum almost daily, and on each visit pays homage to the Virgin, lingering for a long time in front of Raphael's Sistine Madonna. "Vor der Madonna verweilte sie zwei Stunden lang in still traümender Bewunderung," (she remained *two hours* in front the Sistine Madonna, rapt in silent admiration [*SE* VII, 96]), writes Freud about Dora's visit to the Dresden Museum; and his prose is infused here with phonemic patterns as if he had to convey his own writerly rapture in front of this tableau of femininity. For, it seems, while women admire the Virgin, men admire the picture of a woman "rapt in silent dreamy admiration" of the Virgin. Thus in the case of George Eliot and G. H. Lewes: "All other art seems only a preparation for the feeling of superiority of the madonna di San Sisto," she writes in a letter, and in her diary: "I sat down on the sofa opposite the picture for an instant, but a sort of awe, as if I were suddenly in the presence of some glorious being, made my heart swell too much for me to remain confortably, and we hurried out of the room." Meanwhile, in his own diary, Lewes writes about his own contemplations of the Virgin and mentions his hysteria (the result of identification maybe, for it seems to answer Eliot's own "swelling of the mother"): "I looked at the Raphael Madonna di San Sisto, till I felt quite hysterical."[5]

The veneration for the Virgin—which creates an unmistakable resemblance between the Jamesian and the Sandian heroines as well as between George Eliot and Dora—speaks of a desire for purity and of knowledge made of guilt. Always already fallen, the hysteric gazes passionately at the figure of a femininity that, in spite of its involvement in biological, bodily sexuality, has remained pure, serene, intact. For she has learned that while guilt should always be inscribed in the woman's body (unless her sex be hallowed by the marriage sacrament and destined to procreation), when it comes to her soul, redemption, as a return to an original purity, is impossible. This is the knowledge recounted in George Eliot's *Daniel Deronda,* in the story of Gwendolen Harleth: its theme, treated in the tragic

mode, is "the growth of [a woman's] conscience." Henry James's words concerning the heroine remind us aptly that her story might profitably be envisaged from the perspective of hysteria: "The universe forcing itself with a slow, inexorable pressure into a narrow, complacent, and yet after all extremely sensisitive mind, and making it ache with the pain of the process" ("*Daniel Deronda:* A Conversation," 990). Indeed, hysteria shows that (or explains why) against all intentions and desires, Eliot's narrative, whose originary impulse goes toward the representation of the "consciousness of a girl," ends up sacrificing the heroine to the rituals of conscience. "After all," writes Catherine Clément, "hysteria is the simplest of solutions, for to hold oneself in a state of permanent guilt is to constitute oneself as a subject" (*La jeune née,* 90). The following pages chart across Eliot's novel the path of an ethical and textual choice, that is, of a discourse, in which woman is shaped through a process of sublimation so as to embody, in her very hysteria, the harrowing pains of a conscience and beyond, a subjectivity whose characteristic mark is a state of expectancy and of suffering that is best described in the French expression *un être en souffrance.* From this perspective, Gwendolen's story becomes the nineteenth-century allegory of, and for all the waiting women, of all those whose story or history holds as yet only the promise of another beginning.

Woman as Spectacle

Daniel Deronda opens with an insistent peal of questions:

> Was she beautiful or not beautiful? and what was the secret of form or expression which gave the dynamic quality to her glance? Was the good or the evil genius dominant in those beams? Probably the evil; else why was the effect that of unrest rather than of undisturbed charm? Why was the wish to look again felt as coercion and not as a longing in which the whole being consents? (3)

Framed in the hero's mind, these questions set the tone for the aesthetic, epistemological, and moral examination of the heroine. George Sand's *Lélia* starts with a similar set of questions:

> "Who are you? and why is it that your love causes so much evil? There must be in you some terrible mystery unknown to men. Surely you are not a creature made of the same clay and inspired with the same life as we are! You are an angel or a demon, but you are not a human creature. Why hide from us your nature and your origin? Why live among us, if we are found lacking and we cannot understand you. If you come from God, speak, and we shall adore you. If you come from hell . . . You, from hell! You, so beautiful and so pure!. . . . And yet, Lélia, there is in you something infernal. Your

bitter smile belies the celestial promises of your glance." (3)

Indeed, whether as a conscious imitation or not, Eliot's novel begins where Sand began in 1832, with the question of woman. While it might have been interesting to pursue a comparison between the two texts to examine, for instance, how in both texts the conventions of narration break down under the pressures of such a question, my purpose here is more limited.[6] If I quote *Lélia,* it is in the interest of historical accuracy, to show how, with such a beginning, Eliot's novel seemingly abides by a traditional mode of representation: a woman is on display, her identity is put into question, and the gender of the viewer is predictable. In *Lélia* it is the poet Sténio who voices these questions. *Daniel Deronda* begins more subtly: the absence of quotation marks turns them into free indirect speech which typically enables the merging of the voice of narrator and protagonist. This ambiguity is resolved, however, at the beginning of the second paragraph, which begins, "She who raised these questions in Daniel Deronda's mind." The gaze is thus clearly identified as masculine, while the spectacle, inevitably, is that of woman.

The first paragraph sets the stage for a specularization of the heroine that constitutes a steady and easily identifiable strand in the whole novel. Gwendolen can be said to "exist" as surface projection of the images held in the gaze (and in the mind) of the men who shape her destiny: Deronda, Klesmer, Grandcourt, and a more undifferentiated group (made up of Mallinger, Gascoigne, and their likes). In this system of representation, the masculine gaze holds an overdetermined position: her image is sustained by those several men who observe and judge her, the unknown woman, the mystery. The novel produces, however, its hierarchy of gazes: while Deronda holds the highest position in this scale, the lowest level is occupied by those who, like Gascoigne, pronounce on "what maidens and wives are likely to know, do and suffer, having had a most imperfect observation of the particular maiden and wife in question" (*Daniel Deronda,* 704). Three types of gaze come into prominence, and they determine the heroine's *Bildung:* the hero's knowing and sympathetic gaze, Klesmer's aesthetic assessment (she is for him "a bit of *plastik*"), and Grandcourt's gaze of erotic possession and domination. Here *Bildung* means literally "shaping"; the multiple gaze bearing upon the woman seems to determine her outward shape. From a thematic perspective, the heroine's Bildungsroman, as her outward history, is clearly "male-authored": read for her actions, her acts, and for the way in which her body moves across time and space, Gwendolen is not more and not less than passive feminine matter moulded by the different perspectives of a masculine vision.

In this structure, Daniel holds a privileged position: "his grave and penetrating gaze" (302), "his activity of imagination on behalf of others" (162), and his general interest in female pathos ("those tragedies of the copse or hedgerow" [172]) designate him as an avatar of the perspicuous nineteenth-century moral doctor. The epigraph to the second chapter tellingly evokes the ghost of a Briquet who claimed he could, by the force of this gaze, tame or heal his hysterical patients. It announces too Freud's "keen, probing eyes" and his "piercing gaze" (Gay, 156-57, 613).

> This man contrives a secret 'twixt us two,
> That he may quell me with his meeting eyes
> Like one who quells a lioness at bay.
> (*Daniel Deronda,* 11)

The emphasis on a specular mode of knowing and of narrating the subject, so present in Eliot's novel, belongs to a pre-Freudian epistemology. Reading *Daniel Deronda* from the perspective of representation, it seems that the shift from gaze to voice, from the visual observation of the subject to the dialectic of narration and reconstruction that characterizes psychoanalysis is still to come. The notion that to see is to know, the idea that truth can be extracted from visible phenomena and that the gaze can be the finest instrument of intellectual mastery are some of the epistemological claims that this text tries to sustain.[7] Indeed, the femme fatale who figures at the center of *Daniel Deronda* ends up appearing to us modern readers as a forerunner of the heroines we are used to seeing in classical cinema. The fascination exerted by the feminine has had such a lasting hold on representation that, from *Lélia* to the modern actress, the woman as "icon: an image to be looked at by the spectator" (de Lauretis, 139) and as the object of endless interrogations, projections, and phantasies has undergone countless incarnations.[8]

The heroine inevitably occupies, to slip into Stanley Cavell's discourse about cinema, the focal point of the camera; she is that around which the spectacle turns.[9] Yet from the very beginning, Gwendolen's "iridescence" (36) challenges this structure: her aspect changes and, like a reflector, her image diffracts and refracts the look that tries to see her as one stable image. While she is endowed with an aura that draws the gaze to that which stands on the other side of the visible, the essential instability of her image signals that appearances might be deceptive. Her "iridescence" thus reinforces the suspicion that the first, strongly polarized questioning might have aroused: there may be more to this woman than meets the eye; vision, in the case of Gwendolen, cannot guarantee "epistemological certitude" (Doane, 107).

But the uncertainties that the representation of Gwendolen provokes do not merely derive from the changeable, unpredictable qualities of this "iridescent" object. As several critics have shown, *Daniel Deronda* reveals, when it comes to representing the heroine, a problem with the language of fiction which not even metaphor can solve.[10] If the specular image does not in fact give the "truth" about what is represented, the logical move would be to give representation an inward turn. One could indeed imagine that metaphors could be found that would render legible what the images hide or cannot say.[11] But at this point the narrator's critical stance, who speaks for "girls with their blind visions," and the general philosophical prejudice best known through Nietzsche's maxim that "woman closes her eyes to herself" seem to stand in the way of such a representation.[12] If girls are blind, and moreover only seem to know themselves as surfaces reflected in the gaze of the other, then to represent, even metaphorically, the substance that lies behind the surface becomes impossible. To enter the heroine's mind is, as the narrator claims repeatedly, to remain in the realm of appearances. Her mind is haunted by the ghostly and the phantasmal, and the questions raised at the beginning cannot be answered by another visual spectacle which would offer a truer vision of Gwendolen, one that would drive inward and provide a psychological anatomy of this particular woman. And yet, as Jacqueline Rose argues, "it is the dramatic staging, the spectacle itself to which the story seems ineluctably to return" (107). One could add that the spectacle threatens to engulf the process, if not the very possibility, of narration.

Indeed, the narrative voice ultimately fails to compensate for what the original investment in specular representation entailed, namely, a loss of inner vision or of psychological depths and shadings. There is then much that remains unsaid and unspoken, and also unknown, in this novel. But this is precisely where my interest begins, with the sense that the silences of Eliot's text are not empty, but rather that they demand to be read. The hold that the figure of Gwendolen has on the readers' imagination may well originate in our subliminal realization that there is much about her that calls for interpretation. This is where a new aspect of the fictions of hysteria comes to the fore.

Reversing the Gaze

From a narratological perspective, the several scenes of hysteria represented in the novel constitute spectacular instances of the predominance of representation over writing and voice, since they essentially rely on the violence and shock value of the image, as against the capacity of language to chart cohesive explanations or expressive descriptions of a subjectivity. Free indirect speech, for instance, is conspicuously absent in these scenes, while the words of direct speech (when they are not merely screams) are endowed with a phatic quality that places them almost beyond meaning: the narrator presents a description but seems to have lost all didactic or interpretative powers. The urge toward expression seems to override the ability to express. Like the reader, the narrative voice is faced with the notorious illegibility of hysteria, and this inevitably affects our reading: the sense-making process is brought to a halt by the sudden irruption of a spectacle. The scene of hysteria is a form of melodrama where the representation focuses on the body at the expense of the inner registrations of thought or consciousness expressed discursively. This scene opens up an abyss of incommensurability between the visible and the knowable, which in turn creates a desire to lift the veil, to go beyond the mere surface to probe into the depths. But it is a paradoxical figure, since it calls for a reading of depths and yet prohibits such reading because it is primarily spectacle and surface.

Working with representations of women in film, Mary Ann Doane argues that a discrepancy between the visible and the knowable is so often present in representations of women that it has created its own form of compensation: "the blindspot . . . is compensated for by an *over*-sight, a compulsion to see her, to imagine her, to make her revelatory of something," she writes (133). Neither an aesthetic concern nor a structure of desire can fully account for the fascination elicited by a *diva;* an epistemophilic drive is inevitably present as well, but only subliminally. But the hysteric is different since, in the spectacular and violent display of passions and pathos, she cries out to be heard, she demands to be understood and known. Hysteria always proclaims a secret and necessarily assumes a desire for knowledge. This is true as well, by implication, of a hysterical mode of representation. As we shall see, the hysterical heroine of Eliot's fiction addresses herself to the reader, and she says, just as Dora said to her analyst: "Read me." "Why was the wish to look again felt as coercion and not as a longing in which the whole being consents?" The coercive force of Gwendolen's image is thus the first sign of her unorthodox constitution, of her hysteria. This gaze (which is but a stronger form of the surreptitious or internalized glance that the hysteric always casts at the spectator for whom she performs) wants to obtain confirmation that she exists there, in the gaze of the other. In the dialectic of power and domination, the specular regime institutes the subsidiary position of a "returning" glance and thus instigates a reversal of power.

In fact, the "dynamic quality" of this glance troubled Eliot's readers from the very beginning. Her publisher, Blackwood, finds the term awkward and writes to the author, diplomatically: "I remember pausing at the use of the word dynamic in the very first sentence and I am not quite sure about it yet as it is a *dictionary* word to so many people" (*George Eliot Letters,* November 10, 1875, VI, 183). In the critical debate that James stages in "Daniel Deronda: A Conversation," Pulcheria believes the term reveals the author's pedantry and intellectualism. But maybe Eliot had settled for a word of the wrong register: in her days, "dynamic" belonged essentially to a scientific context and described, in physics, alchemy and homeopathic medicine, a force produced by an immaterial or spiritual influence. If, by definition or convention, woman is perceived above all as passive matter, one can see why, given the force of its original meaning, the term would have seemed out of place. But there may be more to this: a faint memory of a mythical figure, of Medusa's evil look, which blinds (de Lauretis, 110).

The word "dynamic," relayed by the notion of "coercion," is to be taken as the first symptom of a disturbance that promises an interesting reversal in the gendering that usually defines the spectacle of woman. If the structure of representation, as I have implied all along, assumes on the one side of the gender divide a desire to master, to know, to pierce surfaces in order to read depths (and this is precisely Deronda's original position) and places on the other, as the object of the unveiling, the woman as spectacle, then the fact that the woman looks back with a dynamic glance and somehow coerces the spectactor to look back at her will necessarily have an incidence on gender. Gwendolen's dynamic glance, the first sign of her hysteria, brings in its trail a radical questioning of the very foundations of the system of representation and sexual difference.

Gwendolen is entrusted with none of the gifts of vision, insight, or foresight that her "dynamic glance" could have entailed. This first glance, which the heroine returns to him, her spectator or reader, functions as a sign but does not correspond to a text. It belongs to a dynamics of power and desire, but does not elicit any knowledge. Indeed, from an epistemological point of view, it is a blank signifying nothing. But this precisely defines it as a symptom of hysteria, following the crucial distinction between signifiers and signs, which Monique David-Ménard highlights in Lacan's work. The symptoms of hysteria do not function as signifiers bound to other signifiers, but are signs "intended for someone" (194, n. 26). In other words, Gwendolen's "dynamic glance," as part of her hysteria, does not speak; it is merely an appeal to an other. As a particular aspect of Eliot's narratology, the scenes of hysteria must be perceived for what they are: failures in the process of signification; moments of textual absence or semantic void. They are "un-written" and offer no metaphors that could be read as vehicles of a latent content, they do not offer a set of signifiers which, once decoded, could lead us to a hidden or buried text. Hysteria, like its first annunciatory sign, the dynamic glance with which the novel opens, is the name given to a force that works insubstantially yet powerfully to attract us readers to confront under new terms, in a new guise, the object-subject of the spectacle, the uncharted space of what lies beyond the surface of woman's body.

However, the initial exchange of gazes does, in the course of the narrative, give way to a linguistic exchange, where the two protagonists, Gwendolen Harleth and Daniel Deronda, are involved in a reciprocation of affect and knowledge that seems to foreshadow an analytical scene. As has often been noted, the confessional mode of their conversations, where the heroine represents to the hero her beliefs, her emotions; and her fears, and, moreover, her increasing depen'ence on such moments create a transferential stage similar to that of the Freudian talking cure. The hero's openly declared inability to respond to the intensity of Gwendolen's demand hints at a demise of the analytical mind in front of a woman's desire that takes us all the way to the story of Freud and Dora. Such is, it seems, the benumbing effect of their *hysterica passio* that these hysterical women leave their analysts-counselors with no words to answer: it took Freud four years to overcome the silence that followed Dora's parting words, and Deronda is left speechless in his last encounter with Gwendolen: "[he] could not speak again" (750).

In fact, the dialogue between Gwendolen and Deronda drifts repeatedly into the unspeakable. "There was a long silence between them" (747), "she could not finish" (750): the last scene between them, with its exemplary dramaturgy, is punctuated by similar comments, while the dialogue is regularly supplanted by visual registration or the description of gestures and bodily attitude. "Her withered look of grief" (750); "He met his upward look of sorrow with something like a return of consciousness after fainting" (749); "Gwendolen had sat like a statue with her wrists lying over each other and her eyes fixed—the intensity of her mental action arresting all other excitation" (748): these examples, selected at random from the description of the protagonists' last encounter, show well enough the convergence of bodily representation with mental phenomena. The silence which inhabits them cannot rest as mere void or absence but, on the contrary, puts a further demand on the reader to respond to what remains unspeakable or unanswered in this novel's "struggle of language and consciousness" (Hertz, "Some Words," 283). It has other consequences as well, where a discussion of representation not only raises narratological, literary questions, but also philosophical issues. These can be foregrounded in a critical moment of a scene of hysteria.

> Suddenly loosing Deronda's hand, she started up, stretching her arms to their full length upward, and said with a sort of moan—

> "I have been a cruel woman! What can *I* do but cry for help? *I* am sinking. Die—die—you are forsaken—

go down, go down into darkness. Forsaken—no pity—*I* shall be forsaken."

> She sank in her chair again and broke into sobs. Even Deronda had no place in her consciousness at that moment. He was completely unmanned. (646)[13]

This passage is excerpted from the scene of confession that follows Grandcourt's death, where the reader has been asked to "imagine the conflict of feeling that kept [Deronda] silent," as the hero only reluctantly hears a confession that is part of "an exaggerating medium of excitement and horror" and "a state of delirium" (642). It shows the heroine in the thralls of a mental pain and anguish that can only be expressed, it seems, in these theatrical gestures and failed utterances suggestive of hysteria. The sobs that end this outburst foreshadow Gwendolen's "hysterical crying" at the very end of her confession (653).

This moment in Eliot's text is a particularly interesting instance of the failed conversations and the kinds of impasses of knowledge that hysteria can provoke. The confession does not in fact bring relief, nor does it, if we conceive of it as a case of transference, succeed either in achieving the undoing of symptoms or in bringing about knowledge "through the active mediation of signifying language" (Felman, *Lacan,* 56). The divide that opens between the protagonists evokes then almost too literally "the radical castration of the mastery of consciousness": "Deronda had no place in her consciousness. . . . He was completely unmanned."[14]

The implications of such statements can best be understood by comparing the text with one Eliot certainly knew well, since she translated it, and which might have been the model for such a scene:

> In another I first have the consciousness of humanity; through him I first learn, I first feel, that I am a man: in my love for him it is first clear to me that he belongs to me and I to him, that we two cannot be without each other, that only community constitutes humanity. But morally, also, there is a qualitative, critical distinction between the *I* and *thou.* My fellow-man is my objective conscience.[15]

This quotation from Feuerbach's *Essence of Christianity* is echoed, for instance, in the narrator's comment about the insistent demand Gwendolen puts on Deronda's sympathy and understanding: "Those who trust us educate us" (401). The relation between the protagonists, between the suffering woman and her confessor, represents indeed an education into sympathy and otherness. Gwendolen is for Deronda, who in that scene is unmistakably the center of consciousness, the indispensable "other" who determines his humanity. It is possible then that the intense and extreme nature of such an exchange does not merely derive

from the author's desire to represent some extreme affective states, but that it signals as well the philosophical stakes that are put into play here. Given the nature of the wager that lies in such an encounter between an *I* and a *Thou*—the very definition of what makes a man, *ein Mensch*—the conversation would naturally have to reach the intensity of melodrama.[16]

As we begin to match the philosopher's text against Eliot's fiction, however, their overall similarity dissolves under the pressure of their differences. "In another I first have the consciousness of humanity," writes the philosopher. With respect to Daniel, it might be accurate to say that he finds in the other, namely, Gwendolen, "the consciousness of humanity." But the hero is so ostensibly denied a place in Gwendolen's consciousness ("Even Deronda had no place in her consciousness at that moment") that the philosopher's statement, which is predicated upon reciprocity, no longer applies: she cannot find in him the same "consciousness of humanity." The theory does not work equally well for the hysteric and the analyst-confessor, for the woman and the man: we must then assume that in Gwendolen's case, consciousness cannot be produced in the intersubjective scenario, but elsewhere and differently. The reciprocity in Eliot's text is merely the physical and affective experience of holding hands, sharing tears, exchanging kisses: but these bodily gestures evocative of shared emotion or sympathy are too obviously at a great remove from Feuerbach's definition of consciousness or conscience. Eliot writes, "Sobs rose, and great tears fell fast. Deronda would not let her hands go—held them still with one of his, and himself pressed her handkerchief against her eyes. . . . She bent foward to kiss his cheek, and he kissed hers. Then they looked at each other for an instant with clasped hands, and he turned away" (749-50). Pathos can blur the boundaries between subjects (whose sobs? whose tears? are they only Gwendolen's?), but consciousness, even though defined by Feuerbach as a sense of belonging, is predicated upon a notion of identity that maintains the separation and difference between the self and the other. This is not to say that Eliot's text wants to hold up this moment of shared sentiment as a new model for (inter)subjectivity, but rather that she, so to speak, stops short in the middle of the impulse that Feuerbach's text could have given her. Body language is not even a substitute for consciousness or conscience; it expresses their demise. Moreover, a true exchange of the kind that Feuerbach imagines is impossible—what can she know of "humanity" in the throes of such hysteria?

Because it fails to imagine or believe in the possibility of such a community of consciousness or cannot conceive of a consciousness constructed communally in shared, reciprocal understanding or love, Eliot's text seems to hint at the failure or at least at the limitations of a theory of sympathy. While her version of a conversation takes this unexpected negative turn, it suggests that some forms of human interaction cannot so easily be resolved into cognitive or moral solutions. This is where the humanist conception promoted by Feuerbach begins to founder. Read in light of the fictional passage, the philosophical text emerges as an insistently universalizing statement. This appears especially in the original German text, where the word *Mensch* (expressing a non-gender-marked humanity) gives to Feuerbach's statement on reciprocity and intersubjectivity its full force. This confident universalism cannot be retreived in the English translation "man" or, in Eliot's formulation, "fellow-man." Thus the writer's skepticism comes back like a ghost to haunt Feuerbach's theory, and it raises the question of gender: Which of the sexes figures behind the statement "I first learn, I first feel that I am a man"? Eliot's representation of a conversation is bound to raise such questions as Who learns what from whom? Who, of man or woman, is the subject who learns, and which object or instrument?

This pedagogical point is in fact raised earlier in the novel and resolved in an unambiguous fashion—he learns from her: "Young reverence for one who is also young is the most coercive of all. . . . But the coercion is often stronger on the one who takes the reverence. Those who trust us educate us. And perhaps in that ideal consecration of Gwendolen's, some education was being prepared for Deronda" (401). That she should teach him the moral imperative—that the moral sphere of man should be produced by some feminine influence—should not surprise us: the alliance of femininity with some higher moral sphere is a staple of the Victorian idealization of woman, even though we might be left wondering at the meaning of "ideal consecration." Is she going to be his muse? a vestal virgin? Or more like a victim sacrificed on the altar of good moral knowledge? It is true that this passage, unlike the earlier scene, allows us to imagine conversations that do not fail, where conscience now finds a place and maybe even consciousness—although this might mean putting too much weight on the word "education." However, this still leaves burning the issue of gender, and nothing suggests that a man and a woman can exchange positions—that she, for instance, could be the subject of such an apprenticeship.

This incursion into Feuerbach's text has made it possible to identify what is the irrevocably gendered nature of a scene of consciousness predicated upon the needs and urgencies that impel her to go to him as to a fellow soul. It also puts a different, more skeptical light on Deronda's natural sympathy, this spontaneous impulse that leads him to encounter the other in the guise of girls and their tragedies. George Eliot's novel acts as a reminder that such a humanist dialectic more likely than not will stop in the first stage, and it will go only one way, from the man to the woman; it can even be sustained between a man and two different feminine others, as shown in the hero's double allegiance to Mirah and to Gwendolen. It fails to work in the other direction. To then narrow the divide between theory and fiction would be to gloss over what is, after all, the most startling aspect of Eliot's reworking of Feuerbach: that it shows the impossiblity of sustaining the model of a general humanism when it is applied to the "consciousness of a girl." Centered around a woman, the scene of consciousness as it had been sketched or dreamt by the philosopher collapses, and with it the other who, rendered unable to take his "place" and his share in it, is now "unmanned."

The philosophical implications of the closing word of this scene—"unmanned"—may well be the most troubling and difficult to grasp. Within a psychological frame, the term can be accounted for easily enough as a figure, while it could hold pride of place in a feminist reading intent on deciphering in the novel the signs of a power struggle.[17] But what is the meaning of this "unmanning" in light of the previous discussion? What is it indeed to be thrown from the happy, innocent state of being a man "before gender" (like the subject of "I first learn, I first feel that I am a man") into history that is now gendered and to find oneself "unmanned"? Within such a narrative, the scene's last word could be read as a statement bearing on the consequences of such a conversation or even as a warning. It would say that in that space of intersubjective relations, the masculinist stance must be returned to the neuter; losing the mark of virility, one is neither more nor less than a man (*Mensch*) before men (humanity). A Deronda unmanned would then no longer know or speak as a man (*Mann*) but would, albeit through some painful loss, rejoin the common fold of humanity.

Or are we to envisage a more radical process: a neutralization of the man in Deronda, as a "destruction of the peculiar properties of" and a "counteracting of the effect of"? Another interpretation indeed suggests that the hero's demise implied by this last word is the irresistible effect of Gwendolen's own power. The conversation ends, it will be remembered, with the assertion of her consciousness and the simultaneous exclusion of his: "he had no place in her consciousness." This statement could have far-reaching consequences. If the fictional scenario were to prevail (and not the philosopher's plot), we would see the end of reciprocity of consciousness that Feuerbach imagined. The other vanishes into thin air: what remains, alone, is one sovereign narcissistic subject, who seems immune from lack.[18]

Meanwhile, the negation of *him* induced in the process of constructing *her* consciousness cannot be canceled out and is surely not a matter of indifference: inscribed in the term "unmanned," there is a loss that speaks of a difference, an antagonism, and an inevitable suffering that the philosopher had perhaps never envisaged, but which the novelist recounts in the story of Gwendolen's hysteria. It may be then that Deronda's "unmanning" constitutes the farthest-reaching effect of Gwendolen's dynamic, hysterical glance and of the coercion that it exerts: held frozen within the masculine gaze for her femininity, she can only, like Medusa, evoke the presence of his own lack—and then "neutering" would be the better word. Eliot's fictional response to Feuerbach in the form of a scene of consciousness that is now irremediably gendered opens wide, wider than ever anticipated, the divide between the sexes. The image of an easy, tension-free scene of exchange and dialogue vanishes; in its place is violence, pain, and the irretrievable gap that separates him from her, like the end of all conversation.

Consciousness Is Not an Agent but a Symptom

As a fiction of sexual identity, George Eliot's *Daniel Deronda* tells then the story of the differences between a man, Daniel Deronda, and a woman, Gwendolen Harleth.[19] On Daniel's side of the divide is a gradual involvement in the history of humanity and the eventual discovery of a vocation. On Gwendolen's is a coming into consciousness as conscience and a progressive freezing into an immobility suggestive of a state of expectancy and suffering. The extent of the heroine's estrangement can be measured in two comments ascribed to the narrator which appear in the scene that represents the last conversation between the two protagonists:

> The world seemed to be getting larger round poor Gwendolen, and she more solitary and helpless in the midst. The thought that he might come back after going to the East, sank before the bewildering vision of these wide-stretching purposes in which she felt herself reduced to a mere speck. (747)

> That was the sort of crisis which was at this moment beginning in Gwendolen's small life: she was for the first time feeling the pressure of a vast mysterious movement, for the first time being dislodged from her supremacy in her own world, and getting a sense that her horizon was but the the dipping onward of an existence with which her own was revolving. (748)

At the close of the novel, the heroine is granted an insight into her condition, which, although minimal (no more than a "bewildering vision" and "a sense that"), might yet stand for a newly achieved consciousness. These two passages can be understood to represent the inaugural moment of the heroine's growth into awareness of her place in the vaster scheme of things. They sketch a move from a self-centered to a relational positioning in the world; breaking out of the narcissistic circle, she now places herself in a wider plot, which in the second description resembles the

grand design of history—"the dipping onward of an existence with which her own was revolving." The move is from outside to inside, from a solitary, useless, single life to the collective communal project.

The end may thus have brought about the heroine's redemption; this new awareness could then be read as the clearest sign of her "recoverable nature" and thus answer Deronda's fond wish that after the crisis of her husband's drowning, the heroine may yet be saved. It may be that this ending answers as well a more general wish, of the kind expressed in *Lélia,* for instance, where the heroine prays on two important occasions to be released from the exile that has been inflicted on her, as a woman petrified in her solipsistic suffering.[20] We may have to accept that to conclude Gwendolen's story in this fashion is to give her the most moral as well as the most positive of ends: endowed with a place in history, she is saved—for history at least. We might also consider that Gwendolen's last outburst of hysteria, which follows this conversation, differs from all the others in that it precedes some final remission, as the emphasis on "living" suggests: "'I am going to live,' said Gwendolen, bursting out hysterically, . . . she fell continually into fits of shrieking, but cried in the midst of them to her mother, 'Don't be afraid. I shall live. I mean to live'" (751).

Yet one might be inclined to exclaim, echoing the narrator, "poor Gwendolen," for the knowledge comes very late, and not as a gradual enlightment under the power of reason, but as yet another violent crisis of *hysterical passio*—as a drama of affect combined with pathos, which leaves her "look[ing] very ill" (750). "Poor Gwendolen" too because she has clearly not retrieved the intellectual ascendancy that, earlier on, she had held over Deronda, and which left him helpless and unmanned, with no influence over her consciousness. (But then, had we not been told all along in the novel that it is morally objectionable to "make another's loss one's gain"?) Moreover, one might be inclined to respond to this conclusion with the words of Simone de Beauvoir (from *Pour une morale de l'ambiguïté*) and endorse her rebellious stance: "to live is merely not to die, and then human existence is no different from some absurd vegetating state" (quoted in Kruks, 14).

Readerly sympathy will not take us far, however; it is from a logical, narratological point of view that the ending must be examined. This view makes us envisage what constitutes the central paradox of Eliot's novel, a paradox, moreover, that explains the presence of hysteria as the figure that, textually and philosophically, can best represent such a contradiction.

> There comes a terrible moment to many souls when the great movements of the world, the larger destinies of mankind, which have lain aloof in the

newspapers and other neglected reading, enter like an earthquake into their own lives—when the slow urgency of growing generations turns into the tread of an invading army or the dire clash of civil war, and grey fathers know nothing to seek for but the corpses of their blooming sons, and girls forget all vanity to make lint and bandages which may serve for the shattered limbs of their betrothed husbands. (747-48)

This is how the narrator of Eliot's novel, shifting his/her stance, reconsiders the heroine's predicament: having been "reduced to a mere speck," she figures in the next sentence among those "many souls" now unquestionably aligned within the more orthodox plot of a male-centered history. As "generations" are turned into armies, "grey fathers" look for their sons, and "girls" attend to their husbands, the heroine finds her (proper) place in the common fold of humanity, in a situation where her sex can no longer grant her a special claim on our pity.

This is not the narrator's first excursus into history, however. Earlier in the novel and in conjunction with the memorable discussion of girls as "delicate vessels," the narrator had raised similarly the specter of a war in which women mourn for husbands and sons, and men endure the loss of bread, "a time when the soul of man was waking to pulses which had for centuries been beating in him unheard" (109). "The soul of man," *die menschliche Seele*—Eliot's language when she writes about history inevitably harks back to the ungendered world of a Feuerbach. Yet this happens precisely when the novel raises twice, in the most explicit fashion, the question of woman's place in the vast scheme of the history of humanity. The historical theme is framed by two questions, the first concerning *a* girl, the second girls as a species:

Could there be a slenderer, more insignificant thread in human history than this consciousness of a girl, busy with her small inferences of the way in which she could make her life pleasant?—in a time, too. . . .

What in the midst of that mighty drama are girls and their blind visions? They are the Yea or Nay of that good for which men are enduring and fighting. In these delicate vessels is borne onward through the ages the treasure of human affections. (109)

In this novel the other sex is indeed the object of a relentless examination, which begins, on the first page, with Deronda's questions and is also, as we saw, promoted by the "visual structure" of the representation itself. But here the question mark that first surrounds the "striking girl" (8) has been displaced onto a different, more philosophical level: it is, this time, not the nature of the object that mat-

ters, but, at a further remove, the nature of our investment in the object. Why do we care? the narrator seems to say, and the first question is answered implicitly in differential terms: because girls are different they cannot be effortlessly subsumed under the wider, more familiar category of history. The question What are girls? arises then as a difference or supplement that cannot be comprehended under the wider rubric of those "larger destinies of mankind": her story is whatever that history cannot comprehend.

Here the ending ("the bewildering visions of these wide-stretching purposes in which she felt herself reduced to a mere speck") strikes me as providing a puzzling answer to such a questioning: "a mere speck" can hardly meet the demands of "what are girls and their blind visions?" granted even that "a mere speck" might stand closer to Gwendolen's voice than to the narrator's. Common sense suggests that if it had been a mere speck, the "consciousness of that girl" would not have borne 750-odd pages of narration, even shared with the hero. Yet she is described as little more than a speck, a dot that trails into near silence. Indeed, even the ending does not help: when Gwendolen's full measure is taken, we see the startlingly narrow scope of her fulfillment, especially when compared with the heroic promises held by his "wide-stretching purposes." What remains is the thinnest of threads, slender to the point of unnarratable tenuousness, and the question is not answered: what about the girls and their blind visions?

Nor is the question answered in the preceding narration, for it is only at the end of the novel that the notion of consciousness becomes meaningful, when the final crisis brings about the inaugural moment which hints at a "reformed" heroine. Before that the term is insubstantial, a mere cipher that surrounds the inner side, the unrepresentable inward drama. "Pale as one of the sheeted dead . . . a wild amazed consciousness in her eyes, as if she had waked up in a world where some judgment was impending" (638)—when the context reveals such vivid and extreme figures of emotion, the word "consciousness" looks almost like a misnomer, and the more so when "judgment" is experienced in the guise of a moral sanction given by an entity that is so clearly a stranger to the self. How indeed can you identify a consciousness when what is presented is the mere bodily registration of emotion? Thus, although the psychological discourse of the novel seems to rely at regular intervals on the word "consciousness" as a way of designating the heroine's autonomous, individual inner sphere, it is only in the final crisis that we can decipher its fuller meaning and begin to trace its history. But this deferral leaves the question mostly unanswered: the novel has yet to produce the story of Gwendolen's newly acquired consciousness.

The final stage of Gwendolen's story shapes the "consciousness of a girl" within the confines of a mighty closet drama and in the form of negation. In the last scene of the novel, the heroine is the living refutation of the metaphor which, in the earlier stages, appeared to account for her significance: it seems impossible to imagine Gwendolen as a "delicate vessel" bearing "the treasure of human affection." Whatever the level at which we read her, more literally as a "vessel-womb" or as a token within the more complex system of a relational and transferential staging, Gwendolen reveals the demise of the meanings that the narrator earlier located in the history of girls and their blind visions. As the scales fall from her eyes, she can only look at the world through the tears of her ultimate chastisement and renunciation. "To be one of the best women, who make others glad that they were born" is indeed a strange reformulation of the earlier proposition, one that entails such a reduction that it contains none of the forward-looking, creative, perhaps procreative possibilities of her former incarnation as a vessel of human affection. Furthermore, when compared with the earlier passage, this scene offers no resting place to that treasure of affection put into circulation. "The burthen of that difficult rectitude towards him was a weight her frame tottered under" (750): the transfer of conscience from him to her amounts to a moral imperative, an imperative that threatens to crush her. Indeed, after Daniel's departure, the heroine breaks down, or rather breaks into hysteria: such is the expenditure of grief and need in this final, cathartic crisis that it leaves her with no more than a thread of history ahead of her: "I shall live. I shall be better" (750). In its depiction of woman's fate, *Daniel Deronda* works toward entropy. After this last hysterical outburst, the consciousness of the girl, born from her ashes, appears to begin in a new cycle, yet to be written. To be merely living is not much of a story and is surely, in terms of human history, the most minimal of beginnings.

Perhaps the solution to the quandary that Eliot's novel sets up—how can that "mere speck," a girl with her blind visions matter to the world—simply cannot be found at the level of a narrative resolution, and perhaps the secret of Gwendolen's history lies, in fact, in the figuration. "In these delicate vessels is borne onward through the ages the treasure of human affection" appears indeed to provide the most immediate response to the general interrogation: "what in the midst of that mighty drama are girls and their blind visions?" "A vessel," the writer answers, which like a womb is the instrument of generation. The attention paid to such a slender thread would then find its justification because the thread is woven into the great chain of being in which the subject's erotic fate is inscribed. It appears that, conventionally enough, the author holds that "in the case of woman" it is love that matters above all, and the novel could do no more than rehearse the topos of woman's definition and circumscription within

the sphere of affect. That woman possesses emotions, feelings, and passions suffices to guarantee that she is a subject: a consciousness would then be the mere recording of those affective impressions related to her inscription within the erotic plot.

Nevertheless, it seems hardly defensible to argue that a woman's consciousness can be defined, solely and completely, within this generational plot. This again would make of "consciousness" a misnomer, for the very definition of the term holds that consciousness is necessarily manifested as judgment and consequently thinking and that it cannot be reduced merely to affect, or to erotic and sexual components.[21] In fact even a cursory glance at *Daniel Deronda* shows the narrator enquiring relentlessly about Gwendolen's ideas and testing her on her ability of make adequate judgments. In order to stand by the notion that a girl's consciousness can be measured merely in affective terms, the author would have had to remain blind to her own performance.

In this instance it might be helpful to bear in mind Freud's analogous pronouncement about woman's desire being primarily erotic and man's turning on ambition: an examination of his case histories shows that a persistent questioning of woman's knowledge and judgment runs counter to the theoretical emphasis on erotic wishes. Eliot's novel shows the same thing—that it might be easier to discourse on woman's emotional life than on her intelligence. Fortunately, however, *Daniel Deronda* easily convinces us that, as James remarked in one of his letters on George Eliot, "We know all about the female heart; but apparently there is a female brain too!" (*Selected Letters,* 104). Unquestionably, the consciousness at stake here stretches beyond its definition as affect.

It may be then that I have interpreted the figure too literally and that it deserves to be read within a wider symbolic economy. Couldn't we say that the "consciousness of a girl" matters because of the particular dynamic or economy that it enables or triggers? The statement indeed implies that consciousness "means" because it carries, conveys, transports that which as a "treasure" constitutes a precious value in a system of exchanges. Since I have already (in my earlier discussion of James's appropriation of Eliot's formulation) tackled the question of woman as a metaphor for the subject in nineteenth-century writing, I focus here, more narrowly and in light of Eliot's project, on the nature of this symbolic exchange whereby the "consciousness of a girl" becomes the bearer of affective investments.

Critics have often enough used the psychoanalytical model to explain the relation between the hero and the heroine in *Daniel Deronda,*[22] but a phenomenon of transference is involved as well on a different level, providing another answer to the question of the investment carried by the "consciousness of a girl." The analytical frame is not only pertinent for the conversations between Deronda and Gwendolen; it can be shifted to encompass the relation between the reader and the subject of the text as a relation that owes its existence, if we pursue the narrator's claim, to our affective investment in the figure. Our willingness as readers to follow the "insignificant thread" is determined by an interest that indeed mere curiosity or desire for knowledge could not solely warrant. It relies on a closer "implication' in the symptom observed" (Felman, *Lacan,* 23) and is inseparable from an intersubjective context created by our affective involvement in the heroine's drama. Our interest in "girls and their blind visions" is thus always, just like Deronda's, "personal" and yet "ex-centric" to our conscious readerly self (Felman, 123), and hence simultaneously impersonal. "Girls and their blind visions" are thus the instrument in a general "human" (and the term is of course predictable within Eliot's humanism) dialectical process of discovery. Their otherness, termed as insignificance and blindness, works incrementally on a more general, universal history. "*The* treasure of human affection" is, as my emphasis on the definite article suggests, a formulation that is so general as to be beyond attribution either to those men "enduring and fighting" evoked in the previous statement or to some specific interest in the object (such as Deronda's, for instance). In short, the investment in girls and their blind visions is collective and marks a universal dependence on the human affection that is rehearsed between us and them on the transferential stage of our reading.

This alone can explain why the "consciousness of a girl" remains a concept endowed with meaning and value in Eliot's novel, even when it eludes both the representation and the knowledge that come with narration. This is how the most tenuous and smallest inferences that sketch out her life still belong to the web of a history that knows many seemingly mightier dramas. It is precisely because it is so thin or broken that the discourse of the hysterical heroine comes to mean so much; we are drawn by the unrepresentable. Hysteria as the stage of woman's disposession and as a symptom of consciousness acts here as a vivid reminder of the secret territory that remains to be seen, known, and understood, a territory that escapes the ready perceptions of representation. Hysteria signifies the demise of the heroine's consciousness yet invites us visibly and insistently to read this absence. Read in light of the narrator's comments on "girls and their blind visions," the heroine's hysteria is less a figure of madness or suffering than the sign of a crisis of consciousness which repeats itself until the "terrible moment" of revelation endows the heroine with its substitue—a conscience. Thus I devote the last part of this chapter to a critical exploration of the most spectacular of the scenes of hysteria in *Daniel Deronda:* Gwendolen's wedding night. This is my answer to the

invitation to read hysteria. By shifting my perspective from the philosophical content of representation to the performative dimensions of Eliot's writing, I show how hysteria, when it is understood as a textual phenomenon and literary representation, can teach us to read more attentively the text of woman's history and consciousness which Eliot has woven into her novel.

Reading Hysteria

Three scenes of hysteria hold a conspicuous place in *Daniel Deronda:* the first occurs when Gwendolen, playing Hermione in a game of charades, freezes in terror as a sliding panel reveals "the picture of the dead face and the fleeing figure" (91). Later in the novel, the heroine is faced with the same figure, but this time it takes the identifiable form of her drowned husband's face: her anguished memory leads her to rehearse compulsively in her mind a scene (as a memory or phantasy?) that shows "his face above the water," "the dead face—dead, dead," and herself "leaping from [her] crime" (648). Here again, but this time with Daniel in attendance and in the role of confessor and analyst, the heroine, who is held in the throes of some unspeakable, unutterable memory or desire, breaks into "hysterical crying" (653). In Eliot's text, the notion of hysteria, always conveyed in its milder adjectival form ("hysterical") or as a description of a behavior ("hysterics"), is usually associated with the heroine's "discourse of imaginative fears" (394) as what best represents to a late nineteenth-century reader the heroine's unexpected, theatrical behavior as well as mental suffering accompanied by a state of dissociation. In such scenes too, "words [are] no better than chips" (558), and failing to relate discursively the adventures that befall Gwendolen's consciousness, the narrative progression seemingly comes to a halt. The discursive flow is arrested in scenes or tableaux that rely on the reader's visualization of the heroine's condition as a bodily performance. The evocation of gestures, shrieks, and sobs replaces the dialogue or interior monologue, while the description, with its particular rhythms, intensities and figures, alludes to some unutterable or irrepresentable inner drama.

Hysteria could profitably be studied as part of the elaborate moral and psychological discourse of Eliot's novel, but emphasis on its literary aspects shows that it holds much more in store than the mere registration of the subject's positioning within such a frame.[23] As an element in the particular narratology and dramaturgy of subjectivity, it deserves to be scanned for its critical and literary significations. My theme in this last part then is hysteria as *une chose littéraire* (borrowing Shoshana Felman's term), namely, as an aspect of what literature is and what literature only, among other competing discourses such as philosophy, psychology, or history, can perform. The scene under scrutiny is that of Gwendolen's wedding night, in the closing pages of chapter 31 of *Daniel Deronda,* and it provides us with the first elements of a rhetoric and poetics of hysteria organized around the following notions: the letter, dissociation, the signifier, displacement, condensation, and the phantasmatic.

The letter. The scene of hysteria begins—the term must not be understood in its temporal sense, but as origin and causation—with a double injunction to read, which is presented at its center: "It was legible as print and thrust its words upon her" (330). The heroine's receipt of the letter triggers the crisis of hysteria, while "legible as print," the letter of the text, which is addressed to us its readers, implicitly enjoins us with a similar burden of interpretation. But before addressing the question of the statement's figural meaning, I must unravel its elements from the perspective of narrative. Putting their imprint on the heroine's mind ("those written words kept repeating themselves in her"), the words of the letter constitute the *cause provocante* of the illness: they are the text of her hysteria and what determines its performance. The analyst might say that it is because these words, although "legible as print," exceed the mind's ability to interpret them, or because they touch consciousness at a point of lack or failure of symbolization, that they give way to symptoms (David-Ménard, 66). Let it be stated, on the other hand, that the text expresses no such thing, yet it matches the letter, without any transition or mediation, with the representation of a hysterical body. The content of this message keeps recurring under various forms, while the later insistent reappearance in chapter 35 of the very words of the letter is proof that they literally cannot be absorbed by the mind: "The words of that letter kept repeating themselves, and hung on her consciousness with the weight of a prophetic doom" (395). If words are what keeps the heroine in the sphere of visions, of dread, and of the phantasmal, then it can only be true that the letter represents the crux of the heroine's failed consciousness and the secret of her illness. But this letter belongs, at the same time, to the text of which we are the readers. Jerry Aline Flieger tells us that "according to Freud's own view of it as 'compromise formation' or symptom of desire, the literary text may be considered to be a 'letter in circulation,' which is at once metaphoric in nature—as symptom of the repressed tragic conflict between law and desire—and metonymic in function, driven by a never-assuaged *désir* addressed, like the purloined letter, to the other it both reaches and misses" (205). Although it bears on the literary text in general, this statement offers a vivid reminder that the hysteric's letter (as what consitutes her hysteria) is always susceptible to enfold us in its secret. Within the fiction, it is to the heroine that the words appear "legible as print," but print they are for us especially, the readers of Eliot's fiction. The letter is not only the site of the unresolved conflict embodied in Gwendolen Harleth; it is also an injunction to us, readers of the novel, to engage, as if

by some compensatory logic, with its demand to be interpreted. "Read me" says the letter of Eliot's text thrust upon us, and where Gwendolen in her hysteria fails, we readers are called on to witness the scene of her trauma and to respond to its provocation of violence and mystery, for such a theater of sensation,[24] with its "spasm of terror," "its tremors of lips and hands," its "hysterical violence," could hardly leave us indifferent.

However, in this instance and unlike what we saw in the Jamesian scenario, the scene is presented in such a way as to prevent our total involvement or identification. A very noticeable, because unique, shift of person that occurs in the middle of the narration positions us, irrevocably, as the readers/viewers of the scene: "But coming near herself you might have seen the tremor in her lips and hands." As it breaks away from the impersonal narrative voice focusing on its object (framing the hysteric in a tableau), the narration resorts to apostrophe and conjures up an "I-you" structure: taking on a voice, the narrator summons the absent reader to be a witness. But beyond its emotive function (as increasing the pathos of the scene), this rhetorical move functions in a deictic fashion, as the marker of the reader's position. Indeed, as he examines the role of person in writing, Roland Barthes speaks of a "mixed system of person and non person," characteristic of discourse, and aligns the pronouns "you" and "I" on the side of the personal, as entailing the speaker's participation in the statement (*Rustle of Language,* 16). He remarks further that "this double system . . . produces an ambiguous consciousness which manages to keep the personal quality of what is stated, yet periodically breaking off the reader's participation in the statement." One could argue, conversely, that a shift of person as emphatic as this apostrophe calling on our participation in the scene of hysteria creates a consciousness in the reader, and this without the usual ambiguity. The reader is separated from the hysteric's nonconsciousness and is yet held in its thrall, and it is then to him that the burden of consciousness falls, unambiguously, and this in the act of reading her hysteria.

Dissociation. The letter, I have argued, is only the *cause provocante* of Gwendolen's hysteria; it is the factor that brings about the crisis, but this is not where the illness truly begins. It is indeed in the use of the reflexive person or pronoun that the first signs of hysterical dissociation can be detected: "Gwendolen . . . threw herself into a chair by the glowing hearth, and saw herself repeated in glass panels with all her faint-green satin surroundings" (329). This formulation, which distinguishes carefully between the agent and the subject of the action, is symptomatic of the increasing dissociation which the heroine is made to experience in her growing hysteria. Earlier, as if in anticipation of the later drama, we see that Gwendolen moves toward her wedding night with a sense of "an insistent penetration of suppressed experience." The heroine's state of mind is represented as an invasive process, and seems to respond to the sway of some inner psychical division. This dissociation is rendered more perceptible in the metaphor that envisages that same mental space in the guise of a theater, the subject having become the bemused, distant witness of her own existence: "Was not all her hurrying life of the last three months a show in which her consciousness was a wondering spectator?" Gwendolen's "seeing herself" is indeed part of a general emphasis on reflexive constructions such as "felt herself," "threw herself," "saw herself." The specular division created in the process is relayed, meanwhile, by another analogous dissociation which relies on the autonomous life or, rather, activity that is given to bodily parts in descriptions of her sensations: "her heart gave a leap," "a new spasm of terror made her lean forward." The choice of language evokes in both these cases, and through a cumulative process, the yawning gap that figures in the place of a unified, masterful consciousness. It should not surprise us then that the onset of hysterical crisis is registered by a combination of the two forms of dissociation, an "act of seeing" conflated with a bodily response: "the sight of him brought a new nervous shock, and Gwendolen screamed again and again with hysterical violence" (331).

The fate of Gwendolen's consciousness in the scene of hysteria can thus be traced in the following fashion: overwhelmed by the perception and its affect, the subject has lost her reflexive faculty, and responds to the trauma with a body in motion, a body as emotion that erupts into screaming and shrieking. The dispersal, splitting, fading of the subject which was initiated even before the fatal letter "thrust its fatal print upon her" assumes the climactic form of a hysterical fit. The only unified knowledge that the heroine holds is that of "feeling ill." Meanwhile, as the specular, reflexive ability is taken away from the hysteric, consciousness becomes also the reader's share: "She could not see the reflections of herself then, they were like so many women petrified white." Who indeed is made to see here, if not the reader, through the agency of the narrator? And what is to be seen? The text answers first with a metaphor, but then, reinstating the stance of the distant, analytical observer, gives up the pretense of mapping out the heroine's inner progress. The scene of hysteria is described from outside, and eventually through her husband's bewildered, critical gaze, but it is no longer enacted in the rhetorical and metaphorical figurations of the writing. The text or letter of Gwendolen's hysteria and of her missing consciousness must then be read in the interval that separates the first specular moment, ascribed to the heroine ("she saw herself"), from its demise and the substitution of the reader ("she could not see the reflections . . . coming near herself"). If here, as so often in nineteenth-century texts, vision is made to stand for knowledge, we can conclude that Gwendolen's entry into the hys-

terical scenario is matched by the decline of her consciousness.

The literary scene of hysteria is meanwhile inevitably predicated upon a redoubling of vision. The stance of the "wondering spectator," which is initially ascribed to the heroine watching her own self in performance, also defines the reader's position. This structural overlay, where the gaze within the scene is matched by another gaze that is to be located outside of the framed tableau (where, in other words, the action is so insistently drawn back to the "ostensive presentation" or revelation of an "arrested scene") presents, as Alexander Gelley has shown, the "structure of phantasy (or phantasm) as a scene of desire."[25] Expressed intradiegetically as well as extradiegetically, the desire to hold her in focus must necessarily be ascribed to the agent or entity that endorses the act of representation, which expresses in the writing its investment in the contents of the scene. Since the scene mainly shows but does not narrate, it might be tempting to view it from a distance, like a spectacle, and to seize on its obvious melodramatic features and to interpret it sequentially, as a causal interlinking of behavior and action. But the rhetoric of Eliot's writing forbids such an easy move and sustains other exigencies. "Coming near," as we are invited to do by the narrator, we soon find that the scene of hysteria must be read along an axis that is not merely temporal, chronological, sequential, but requires us rather to decipher positionalities of desire within a field of representation that is envisaged in its specular, metaphorical, or figurative aspects.

The signifier. As a first instance of this demand for an enhanced form of readerly implication, I examine here a grammatical irregularity in a discussion that should mark a noticeable shift of attention from the discourse of representation to the performance of writing.[26] What on the surface may be taken as a slip of the author's pen is examined as a symptom. Thus we find in Eliot's text on hysteria an unusual, ungrammatical occurrence of a reflexive pronoun: "But coming near herself you might have seen the tremor in her lips and hands" (331). What are we to make of this foreign body in the sentence, "herself," whose effect can surely not be reduced to mere redundancy? It might be accounted for easily enough as part of the general emphasis on reflexive constructions: "herself" repeats the pronoun of the previous sentence ("she could not see the reflections of herself then") and also harks back to the moment preceding the crisis, which relies heavily, as we have seen, on such dissociations ("she felt herself being led," "she threw herself"). But "herself" carries as well, like a ghostly presence, the reflexive "yourself." The implied presence, like a modulation or echo of this "yourself" that the grammatical slippage makes possible, reinforces the apostrophe: our identification with the hysteric might then be stronger than acknowledged.[27]

Furthermore, putting the emphasis on "self" this time, we would be able to foreground the covert expression of a "self" or subject that lies behind the hysteric's ostentatious performance. The grammatical error and ambiguity of the reflexive "herself" reveal then the multiplicity of subjective positions involved in the scene of hysteria. Overdetermination, that is, a plurality of meanings but also a plurality of determinations, is the rule as we read the signifier as a symptoms. The slip of a pen can also be taken as a reminder of the several desires that converge around the scene of hysteria: the referent of the symptomatic word could be, as I have shown, the hysteric involved in her own subjective drama or the spectator who participates in it in the intersubjective mode of transference. In addition it might also involve the subject involved in the writing: "coming near myself."

Moving away from representation to envisage the transitive meanings of "to write," one is inevitably confronted with such ghostly referents and above all with the figure of the writer. Roland Barthes discusses precisely this literary phenomenon, using the example of the middle voice of the verb "to sacrifice": "in the case of the active voice, the action is performed outside the subject, for although the priest makes the sacrifice, he is not affected by it; in the case of the middle voice, on the contrary, by acting, the subject affects himself, he always remains inside the action, even if that action involves an object" (*Rustle of Language,* 18). His illustration of what writing means, in the guise of a linguistic analysis of the verb "to sacrifice," turns out to be particularly appropriate for this examination of the scene of hysteria: for the victim of "textual" hysteria, just like the victim of sacrifice, invokes a multiple cast of characters and is always apt to provoke their affective involvement. Indeed, Eliot's slip of the pen shows that the difference between the narrator's voice and the author's presence, just like that between the priest who officiates as a sacrificer and the person who makes a sacrifice for himself or herself, might be much smaller than suspected. Under "herself" speaks the "I" that had effaced itself from the representation but returns in the symptoms of the writing. The agrammaticality produced in the writing speaks of affect and desire, when the representation tended on the contrary, as we saw, to contain and to frame affects and desire within the scene of hysteria while establishing, on the outside, the stance of a viewer-analyst.[28] An examination of the signifier in the scene of hysteria is bound to evoke an autobiographical subtext, not as the representation of the author, but rather, to borrow one of Louis Marin's propositions on autobiography, because "the autobiographical text in the place of the subject will be haunted [*travaillé*] by an originary, inaudible voice, which it echoes in its signifiers" (43).

Displacement. The symptom represents one element in a general configuration, and it remains essential not to lose sight of the general form taken by the illness. This leads us inevitably to ask, in the most blatant fashion, about the outcome of the wedding night. How do the expected erotics of the scene give way to hysteria? While the substitution of hysteria for the *nuit de noces* has become by now a familiar situation, we are not dispensed from attending to the particular form it takes in Eliot's novel. Ellen Moers describes, in vivid terms, what she thinks happened during the wedding night: "There is of course nothing that could remotely be called pornographic in George Eliot's treatment of Gwendolen's deflowering by her husband Grandcourt; the matter is not even mentioned, directly. But indirectly, by means of the jewel-case, George Eliot conveys all that need be told about Gwendolen's hysterical, virginal frigidity: about Grandcourt's sadistic tastes; and about, in addition, mercenary marriages, wedding night customs, and sexual hypocrisy in the Victorian age" (253). Another enthusiastic and sensitive reader of Eliot, George Steiner, has praised eloquently this author's uncanny ability to represent, in her use of figurative language, the intimate, private scene of erotic life. Steiner wrote the following comment about *Middlemarch,* but the same would surely hold true for the later novel: "George Eliot's perceptions of sexual feeling, the closeness of observation she brings to bear on erotic sensibility and conflict, yield nothing to that of the moderns. In most instances what passes for characteristic post-Freudian insight is, by comparison, shallow. But these perceptions and the free play of imaginative recognition are immensely in advance of, immensely more explicit than, the vocabulary available to a serious novelist of the 1870s" (105). James too, it will be remembered, singled out Eliot among all other nineteenth-century British writers for her ability to convey erotic meanings. Indeed there seems to be general agreement among her readers that George Eliot is able to convey in her figurative language the sense of the sexual, eroticized body. This scene is no exception.

In this instance, however, the thread of the erotic is very tenuous. Apart from a first kiss on the lips and Grandcourt's pressing Gwendolen's hands to his lips somewhat later in the bedroom, no gesture of love is represented. There may be, on the other hand, more than a hint of eroticism in a decor that is warm, glowing, conducive to "creeping luxurious languor," and is framed with a reference to its ceilings, which show a Spring shedding flowers and Zephyrs blowing trumpets (329). There are then enough indications to suggest that the heroine is entering a bower of love. One might even decipher in the move from antechamber (*Vorhof*) to boudoir a progress within a geography of sex not unlike that which Freud examined at length in Dora's second dream. The sexual symbolism of the adder, of the box, of the jewel is unmistakable, whereas the words "penetration" and "thrust," used at the beginning of the scene to describe the heroine's mental experience, appear in this light as strange equivocations. While undeniably present, the erotic or sexual body is, however, the object of considerable displacements.

But the most visible phenomenon of such a scene is a lack of symbolization of the sexual body and the substitution of hysterical symptoms. The heroine's "pleasure-body" is conspicuously missing, while the affective, expressive charge is displaced on her hysteria. That Gwendolen's erotic body should not exist here, but that meanwhile another body should be drawn—with its tremors, pallors, shrieks, and fits—shows indeed how close the representation comes to the clinical definition of hysteria as "a deficiency in the subject's symbolization of the body" (David-Ménard, 44). In its failure to convey the "perceptual reality" of a pleasure-body, the text reveals the symptoms of hysteria as they are defined by Monique David-Ménard: "It is now clear where this reversal leads: from the omnipresence of the hysterics' body to the eyes of a fascinated observer, the study of sensorimotor functions permeated by language leads us to say that that ostentation is only the obtrusive side of the hysteric's absence with respect to her own body, for want of symbolization. The hysteric has no body, for something in the history of her body could not be formulated, except in symptoms" (66).

David-Ménard's study begins with an investigation into the meaning of Dora's disgust, in the wake of Freud's observation that "I should without question consider a person hysterical in whom an occasion for sexual excitement elicited feelings that were preponderantly or exclusively unpleasurable" (*SE* II, 28). "I hate the touch of woollen cloth touching me" (103), Gwendolen exclaims when asked why she does not dance the waltz. The disgust Eliot attributes to her heroine ("she objected with a sort of physical repulsion to being directly made love to" [63]) may be part of a pattern of hysteria. One is then increasingly tempted to ascribe to Eliot the unerring eye of an analyst and the uncanny foresight into psychological processes that have only been understood in our century. What is one to make then of such an anachronism?

It is precisely because the scene of hysteria presented in *Daniel Deronda* in 1876 comes before Freud, and before the kind of theoretical insight found in case histories such as that of Dora (1905) or Wolf Man (1909), that a psychoanalytical interpretation can work so well. François Roustang in *Un destin si funeste* speaks tellingly of the cultural, temporal gap that constitutes the necessary condition for rendering analysis operational. Analysis can only work, he claims, if "the theory stands ahead of the cultural situation of the symptom by one step"—*en avance d'un temps* (91). In other words, the analytical stance depends on invention: it is predicated upon the fact that there is, in its

object, something yet to be known.[29] George Eliot's novel benefits from being read psychoanalytically precisely because it exhibits in its textual "symptoms" a *méconnaissance* analogous to the "ignorance" displayed by the hysterical patient who provoked Roustang's commentary. Our stakes differ, however, in that unlike the analyst who strives for a cure, I rely on a psychoanalytical reading for what it shows in terms of a history of a woman's consciousness. In the fragmentary elements that emerge from a psychoanalytical reading lies the unspoken, unrepresented side of the history of the gendered subject that gets written in Eliot's fiction.

Condensation. The scene of hysteria in *Daniel Deronda* turns upon the letter sent by Lydia Glasher: while it can be read within the narrative sequence as what provokes the crisis, it also constitutes the focal point of the heroine's "discourse of imaginative fears." What it performs, as a curse, is made possible by what it carries as a signifier; this is why we must proceed to unravel the figures and stories that it condenses.

The language speaks here of a desire for knowledge. The overall narrative takes on the appearance, as Peter Brooks has remarked, of "a plot of female curiosity" (*Body Work,* 252). The sequence is revealing: Gwendolen receives a packet, sealed by a paper, which shows a letter that covers a box in which are to be found the jewels: "She knew the handwriting of the address, it was as if an adder had lain on them." A later repetition of the same motive, in the guise of a memory, foregrounds what the narrative sequence, conceived as a progressive unveiling, has rendered visible, namely, the imbrication of the letter with the jewels: "they had horrible words clinging and crawling about them as from some bad dream, whose images lingered on her perturbed sense" (397). "The perturbed sense," of which Gwendolen's hysteria is the sign, lies then at the convergence of a handwriting (Lydia Glasher's), the jewels (Grandcourt's inheritance through his mother), and those words that kill (the letter on the jewels).

One can detect in the succession of unveiling, unwrapping, and uncovering, just as in Dora's second dream, the representation of an epistemophilic drive. A similar "symbolic geography of sex" makes of the jewel case (*Schmuckkästchen*) the equivalent of the female body, while the unmistakeably phallic symbol of the adder evokes a male body. This complex figure, which in the letter and the box holds emblematically both a female and a male body, looks like the very site of an engendering. And it is this figure which triggers, repeatedly, the hysteria: "It seemed at first as if Gwendolen's eyes were spellbound in reading the horrible words of the letter over and over again as a doom of penance; but suddenly a new spasm of terror. . . ." The adderlike words draw repeatedly Gwendolen's inner and outer gaze, bringing in their trail the whole sequence of bodily symptoms as well as the mental dissociation-dissolution characteristic of hysteria. Indeed, whereas in the first stage the figure holds the heroine in the thralls of a visual fascination, it reverbates in a second stage, described in chapter 35, in the inner space of her mind. The letter, the text insistently proclaims, is what is given to the heroine by way of a consciousness: it "hangs on her consciousness," "gnawing trouble in her consciousness," "the words of that letter kept repeating themselves, and hung on her consciousness with the weight of a prophetic doom" (395).

Between the first trauma and its repetition as memory, the "hysterical violence" has become "violent hysterics." The change in the wording is revealing enough: it registers the fact that the violence has been internalized as symptomatic behavior. The effect of the letter reverberates far beyond the initial shock, as a reminiscence: "the words had nestled their venomous life within her, and stirred continually the vision of the scene at the Whispering Stone." The letter then works proleptically as well as retroactively, taking the heroine back to another moment of terror: "Gwendolen, watching Mrs. Glasher's face while she spoke, felt a sort of terror: it was as if some ghastly vision had come to her in a dream and said, 'I am a woman's life'" (137). What looms behind Gwendolen's hysteria is the image of the rival woman, who, like Medea to Creusa, curses the other woman's marriage with her poisoned gift.[30] This image, moreover, offers Gwendolen a counterpart to the dead face of her husband, condenses in it like a vision, a knowledge that is unmistakeably gender inflected. It seems indeed that the letter of Eliot's text is ultimately about a history peculiar to women and about some hard-earned visionary knowledge.

The phantasmatic. "She could not see the reflections of herself then: they were like so many women petrified white, but coming near herself you might have seen the tremor in her lips and hands" (331). This is hysteria seen from outside, framed by the spectator's gaze. But the simile reveals, simultaneously, an attempt to show from inside, but through the power of an analogy, the loss of identity and the paralysis that affects the heroine: "so many women petrified white." The self-seeking gaze is met, it seems, with a phenomenon of petrification, or, to return to the body, it is supplanted by the movement or position of frozen terror. "I feel petrified" this hysteric says, implicitly. Hysteria here again works by condensation: Gwensdolen's stance is another reminder of the encounter with the other woman at Whispering Stone and more pointedly of the later "Medusa-apparition in Hyde Park" of the same Lydia Glasher. Eliot's text of hysteria overlaps in an uncanny fashion with Freud's presentation of the mythical encounter with Medusa: "The hair

upon Medusa's head is frequently represented in works of art in the form of snakes, and these once again are derived from the castration complex. . . . The sight of Medusa's head makes the spectator stiff with terror, turns him into stone. . . . The symbol of horror is worn upon her dress by the virgin goddess Athene. And rightly so, for thus she becomes a woman who is unapproachable and repels all sexual desires—since she displays the terrifying genitals of the Mother" (*SE* XVIII, 273). Because it evokes the castration complex—fear of the loss or absence that marks the woman's genitals for the viewer—the image of Medusa strikes the spectator with terror and turns him (or her?) to stone. Would a Freudian interpretation of the myth allow for such a substitution of pronouns? Freud's insistence on Medusa's apotropaic function suggests a negative answer. Eliot's text, however, displays an array of female images that strike another woman with terror and violence: the Furies at the end of this passage, the specular demultiplication of those "women petrified white," the allusion to Medea and Creusa, and finally the encounter between the two rival women under the auspices of Medusa. The text's obsession with the myth of Medusa confirms what is so conspicuously enacted in Gwendolen's hysterical symptoms: that hysteria is the sign of the hysteric's inability to assume her own body. These encounters with Medusa represent another, this time wholly negative, version of the scene of transmission between women. Faced with this specular other who resembles herself, a woman, the heroine cannot bear what she sees, and "closing her eyes to herself," she flees into the terrors of hysteria.

In Eliot's text, the scene of hysteria is not bisexual (unlike what we saw in *Valentine*), but it does resemble Dora's story in the interpretation of Lacan and David-Ménard: it shows the impossibility of sustaining one's gender in the grammar of the sexes and represents "a passionate denial of sexual difference that seeks to attribute to the other a kind of responsibility for having spoiled sexuality" (David-Ménard, 102). The scene of female rivalry that looms behind the scene of hysteria suggests that, as David-Ménard writes about Dora, "the other woman fascinates through the power to swallow up the patient's entire existence, a power attributed to her, when she 'steals' from the patient the heterosexual object of her desire" (100). The hysteria represented in Eliot's text begins then with the story of a woman who attempts to steal back a husband whom the other wants. Glasher steals Grandcourt on the wedding night: "the man you have married has a withered heart. His best young love was mine; you could not take that from me when you took the rest. It is dead; but I am the grave. . . ." (330). And in this it seems, Eliot may not only uncannily have anticipated Dora's hysteria but may also have invented her own. It might be that in writing about her heroine's hysteria she shows her glimpses of her unconscious. Barthes's comments on modern writing seem, in this instance, truer than ever: "Thus, in the middle voice of *to write,* the distance between *scriptor* and language diminishes asymptomatically. . . . In the modern verb of middle voice *to write,* the subject is constituted as immediately contemporary with the writing, being effected and affected by it" (*Rustle of Language,* 19). Neil Hertz has written suggestively on the personal allegory that lies behind Eliot's writing:

> To seek an author's personal allegory behind the realistic surface she has woven is often as unrewarding as it is methodologically dubious, but in the case of George Eliot's works, because they are explicitly about the imagining of others—about the status of the image of one person in the imagining mind of another—the play between the imaginer and the imagined, between author and character, and the possibility of a narcissistic confusion developing between the one and the other has already been thematized and made available for interpretations. (*End of the Line,* 82)

The sheer dramatic intensity, the theatricalization of the representation, as well as the writing's overbearing and repetitive investment in figures suggest indeed that the scene of hysteria fulfills in Eliot's novel the role of a phantasmatic, in the sense given to the term by Kaja Silverman.[31] Thus, in my literary interpretation of hysteria, I have not only encountered the "author inside the text" (in the guise of a narrator or as a kind of stage director of a hysterical scenario, with the heroine as leading actress), but I have also found myself reading what Silverman calls the "text 'inside' the author—for the scenario for passion, or, to be more precise, the 'scene' of authorial desire" (*Acoustic Mirror,* 216).

In the heroine's hysterical screaming and in the tremor of her lips and hands, the representation meets with the writing, and the difference between what writes and what gets written vanishes. A moment like this enables us to touch, at some tangential point, the unsayable and unrepresentable that haunts the imagination of the woman holding the pen. In the case of George Eliot, just as was true of George Sand, the "phantasmata" speak of gender. The figures of Gwendolen's hysteria, meanwhile, designate the proximity between the writer and her creation, and they mark the convergence between art and life, between the performance of writing and the enactment of some deeply subjective event or experience. When Gwendolen reads death in the letter addressed to her by Lydia Glasher, when she flees in terror from an impending guilt, the heroine's screaming cannot be separated from the writer's. Hysteria then, sprung from this discrepancy where the will to express meets the impossibility of representing, evokes in the negative mode a desire for consciousness.

But this implies that we resist the lure of the representation that would suggest that the meaning of hysteria lies solely in its pathos and that the heroine's story signifies only in terms of its affective contents. Because Eliot's hysterical writing in *Daniel Deronda* presses upon us the obligation to read its figurations and because, moreover, in this instance "the process of reading is assimilated very tightly to the silent movement of thought within us" (Beer, 214), we can identify this desire for consciousness. As the written and writing figure of knowledge and desire caught between recognition and terror, the scene of hysteria bespeaks a desire that is neither fiction nor reality, but that like any true fantasy might come much closer to identifying a subject than any stories or histories that can be told. If Eliot faces in this novel the impossibility of retracing the "consciousness of a girl," it may be because, coming close to such a theme, she encounters too much forgetting, too much blindness. We have to remember, however, that hysteria is nothing but a sign, an invitation to read, that it does not reveal a code that would enable us to lift the secret; it just spins its own stories. Pulling off the veil, as my psychoanalytical reading has attempted to do, amounts to revealing the undivulged secret and the silence that ultimately lie behind writing.

The Inward Turn

"In the case of Gwendolen Harleth. Eliot seems to equate the necessity of narrative, of biographical meaning, with the woman's life, with the sphere of inwardness—affirming in this manner a fundamental tradition of the novel," Peter Brooks writes suggestively in *Body Work* (255). The concept of inwardness can indeed justify Eliot's interest in representing consciousness in her novel; it explains, moreover, the inward turn that history takes when woman is its subject. It also throws a different perspective on the closure applied to Gwendolen's story: if her life relies on "being" (when his consists in "doing"), then the heroine, in her frozen, but knowing predicament, singled out by her peers "to be one of the best of women, who make others glad that they were born," reaches her apotheosis precisely there, in that absolute inwardness of nonaction that defines her new beginning. Moreover, the old saying remains true *pati natae:* in the feminine mode, to be is to suffer, and to know, for a woman, is to suffer the pains and pangs of a private history written in the body before it emerges, if it ever does, into consciousness.

Read for this "introversion" and as a forerunner of the stream-of-consciousness novel, the story of Gwendolen can be strung consistently and right to its end on the line drawn by this inward progress toward the more exquisite pains or intensities of a fuller consciousness, one that knows how to subsume emotions and affections under the higher categories of morality. Or more appropriately, because of the weight given to the mortifications that come with a moral imperative, her story can be summarized as the denial of consciousness, and the upholding of conscience in its stead. "Her remorse was the precious sign of a recoverable nature," comments the analytical and critical voice belonging to Deronda or to the narrator, after one of Gwendolen's hysterical breakdowns. In this way the tale of her woes never trails far from a story of hysteria, at least as our nineteenth-century doctors identified it. Just as in Sand's *Valentine,* hysteria speaks in Eliot's text of an ethical and aesthetic choice that imposes on woman the pains and pangs of conscience, and models her on a pattern of sublime, ineffable spiritual pain. "Hysteria"—the words of Clément are worth repeating—"is the simplest of solutions: to hold oneself in a state of permanent guilt is to constitute oneself as a subject" (*La jeune née,* 90).

But, as we saw, hysteria is not only a theme in Eliot's novel; it is also a form of representation. The narrative process, which takes the heroine through the different stages of her *Bildung,* is repeatedly halted by a form of "freeze-framing" which, as a scene or tableau, is insistently visual and yet invites us repeatedly to read beyond the visible. Beyond the spectacle of woman's assumption of a conscience that the novel represents, one is faced then in the scenes of hysteria with a language that seems to work "at the point of fragility of the symbolic" (David-Ménard, 188). As my first, resistant interpretation of the novel's terms and of its ending have suggested, Eliot's project of representing the "consciousness of a girl" is riddled with difficulties and contradictions. A closer examination of the writing that characterizes the scene of hysteria has shown that the sense of such scenes threatens to collapse altogether under the weight of the unknown and the unrepresentable which stand in the place of her consciousness.

The symptoms of such a negation can be seen at a narratological level, as the narration can be shown to shuttle back and forth, repeatedly, between narrative and scene or, to shift registers, between discourse and performance. As a literary phenomenon, hysterical representation mimes in its accents and displacements a signification that cannot be articulated discursively. Indeed, as Lacan has shown, it eludes discourse defined as what is *réfléchi, articulable, accessible* (as thought, expression, and communication) and it exists only as image or hallucination (*Ethique,* 60). The effects of hysteria are not merely linguistic; they also affect our understanding of representation. They are a reminder of a pervasive and insistent negation or repression that, in the nineteenth century, came to bear upon the consciousness ascribed to woman. They show that the inward turn the novel has given to history ultimately leads, like Woolf's fishing line, to some inexpressible, unrepresentable bedrock. Hysteria is here again the equivalent of a veil, which separates this time representation from the unrepresentable.

Gwendolen's consciousness, her inwardness, cannot be staged fully as representation and narrative but is mapped around moments of textual intensity which appear to be the figured enactment, in the timeless (because activated in every reading), nonnarratable space of writing, of an unconscious. In her attempt to write the fiction of her heroine's consciousness, Eliot gives her novel a form more radical than has generally been appreciated: she endows her character with a depth of unspokenness and with the kinds of displacements and metaphors that do not really represent a consciousness but rather end up delineating the latter around the borders of a textual unconscious. Indeed, if, as has often been suggested, "George Eliot had anticipated Freud in her presentation of the urgencies of transferential need" (Hertz, "Some Words," 291), not enough has been said about the "struggle of language and consciousness' waged in this text, where Eliot anticipates both modernism, as a style, and psychoanalysis, as a new understanding of subjectivity.

If the project of narrating the consciousness of a girl is halted repeatedly by the fact that no more can be shown or said than this freezing into a screaming, sobbing, or shrieking stance, then these moments of hysterical crisis are for us readers of the "consciousness of a girl" the precious signs of a negativity that cries out to be heard. The hysteria represented and enacted in Eliot's text is then the nodal point of a critical interpretation which analyzes the meaning and assesses the implications of the blindness of vision that affects the heroine. From this perspective, the textualized symptoms of hysteria, which must be understood as failures in symbolization or ungraspable metaphors, constitute nevertheless the realities of the female subject that figures at the center of Eliot's novel; her consciousness can then be mapped out against the backdrop of her hysteria. But it might be more appropriate to reverse the relation between ground and figure, and to say that her hysteria, which is turned toward an unconscious and the play of signifiers, traces the contours of a consciousness, as a secret history of knowledge and desire. "The universe forcing itself with a slow, inexorable pressure into a narrow, complacent, and yet after all extremely sensitive mind, and making it ache with the process—that is Gwendolen's story," Henry James writes ("*Daniel Deronda:* A Conversation," 990). Gwendolen's *pathologein,* her hysteria, deserves more than just a sympathetic or mournful glance ("another one of those suffering women!"); it needs to be interpreted on its own terms, as a figure that defines the "interiority" of woman's history as imagined by Eliot.

The insistence on bodily phenomena that characterizes the scenes of hysteria in *Daniel Deronda* must be understood as the representation by default, as the underside of a gender-marked consciousness. At the same time, I am well aware that hysteria also has a history, in our modern critical times, as "a privileged dramatization of female sexuality" (Irigaray, 70) and that, moreover, its reliance on the body as a site of signification might single it out as ideal terrain for the decipherment of the semiotic, in the sense given to this term by Julia Kristeva. I have chosen, however, to interrogate Gwendolen's hysteria from the perspective of language and consciousness, and I have put the emphasis on the linguistic predicament, the failure of symbolization that defines hysteria *in* literature, but also *as* literature. "Words were no better than chips," the narrator exclaims, when commenting on the failure of language between Grandcourt and Gwendolen ("her passion had no weapons" [558]). I find myself inclined to trust the theoretical insight of the teller of the tale. Reading hysteria against the body, I propose that hysteria is then the symptom of language's inability to answer the writer's need to express some particularly feminine history. That history, while marked significantly by failure in the symbolization of desire and the prohibition of jouissance,[32] cannot be reduced to either pure affect or body language. It accounts for a form of *Aufmerksamkeit,* for a perception and an awareness that are, however, marked by a denial. Working within a model of negation makes it impossible to decipher in the hysteric's body a femininity brought back to its bodily and behavioral components. I have chosen, on the contrary, responding to the philosopher's invitation, to read "the history of the subject's desire, in so far that this history is inscribed on his or her body" (David-Ménard, 59). It can still be said that Eliot's attempts to revise history to include the private dramas and ecstasies of "girls and their blind visions" have taken a peculiar and paradoxical form. But it may be that writers feel more acutely and are able to register more accurately the failures in knowledge because they experience them first hand, confronted as they are with the errancies and lacks that define the languages of the "unsayable" and the unpresentable. It seems crucial to me to grant them this particular insight and to read them by taking the risk of that ambivalent knowledge.

This attempt to reflect on consciousness and gender through the figurations of hysteria constitutes then a variation or modulation of similar projects—by Foucault, Derrida, Felman, and Cavell—which associate the cogito with a scene or play of madness. Because it belongs so typically to the feminine gender, because it became, in the nineteenth century above all, the madness that is peculiar to women, and because it is so charged semiotically, hysteria has enabled me to reflect upon a gender-marked consciousness. It could be argued then that it is precisely there, in the *méconnaissance* of desire and *jouissance,* that a feminine consciousness or history necessarily begins and, simultaneously, threatens to founder in Eliot's project. In that sense Gwendolen's hysteria is about the engulfment of knowledge in the repetitive play of a desire that does not know itself. The particular but exemplary predicament embodied in Gwendolen's hysteria is that of a feminine blindness of vision. In her book *Acoustic Mirror,* Kaja Silverman argues forcefully that there can be no subject without the specular and insists on defining woman's subjectivity in its psychic dimensions: "as a projection inward from the surface of the (constructed) body" (147). It also seems to me that much is to be gained (from a feminist perspective but also for a better understanding of Eliot's writing) if we, as readers, attempt to follow the path of this inward turn. The female subject that is held in focus in the scene of hysteria tells stories of a kind that must indeed take their meaningful place in our modern Western history.

Notes

[1] James, "George Sand," in *Literary Criticism,* 741; the letter is quoted by Leon Edel, *The Life of Henry James* II, 313-34.

[2] In the words of Freud: "I never made her mother's acquaintance. From the accounts given me by the girl and her father, I was led to imagine her as an uncultivated woman and above all as a foolish one, who had concentrated all her interests upon domestic affairs. . . . She presented the picture, in fact, of what might be called the 'housewife's psychosis'" ([Freud, Sigmund, *Standard Edition of the Complete Psychological Works* (1959) Hereafter *SE*.] VII, 20).

[3] The detour through the German text shows more palpably what is at stake in such figurations, namely an attempt to project onto woman the burden of reinstating a pristine purity (of the kind invoked in the concept of pudicity [*pudicité*]). It is not merely a question of cleaning, but of purifying and making white, as is conveyed so well by the French term for laundresses: *blanchisseuses.*

[4] See in particular Mary Jacobus, "*Dora and the Pregnant Madonna,*" in *Reading Woman: Essays in Feminist Criticism.* The rapprochement she establishes between Eliot and Dora greatly helped my own understanding of these instances of hysterical admiration.

[5] Eliot's remarks are quoted from *George Eliot Letters* II, 471-72 and from J. W. Cross, *George Eliot's Life* II, 58. Lewes's words are quoted in a note by Gordon Haight (*Letters* II, 472n). These passages are discussed by Jacobus, *Reading Woman.*

[6] "I would suggest that a good many late nineteenth-century texts can profitably be called premodernist and hysterical, that as symptomatic narratives, they articulate the problematics of sexual difference, a difference challenged in great part by nineteenth-century feminism," Kahane writes suggestively ("Hysteria, Feminism, and the Case of *The Bostonians,*" 286). Indeed

we should not be surprised that the narrative conventions break down under the pressure of a questioning, which, as I tried to show in Chapter 4, challenges the conventional epistemological frames. But *Lélia* more than *Daniel Deronda* generally subverts the generic conventions of the novel.

[7] The limits of this epistemology of the visible are shown in the episode of Grandcourt's death, where the meaning of Gwendolen's action (who throws the rope a little too late to save her husband) cannot be subsumed under its outward appearance. Thus Deronda's unresolved, unanswerable question: "And it has all remained in your imagination. It has gone on only in your thought. To the last the evil temptation has been resisted?" (*Daniel Deronda*, 644). The narrator probes this question as s/he discusses the heroine's desire (648-49).

[8] For a particularly enlightening discussion of this topic, see Doane, "Veiling over Desire."

[9] See Stanley Cavell's discussion of the genre, which he calls, in "Naughty Orators: Negation of Voice in *Gaslight*," the "melodrama of the unknown woman" (340).

[10] Richard Freadman in particular emphasizes George Eliot's "interest in the powers and limitations of language" and the "semiotic concern" perceptible in her novel (*Eliot, James and the Fictional Self*, 63-64). See also William Myers, *The Teaching of George Eliot*, 224-25; and Elizabeth Ermath, *George Eliot*, 129-30.

[11] Here we might be faced with a case of anasemia—an irreducible difference of nature between what the figure might say and what it is destined to describe. On this question see Derrida's "Me-Psychoanalysis."

[12] The phrase is quoted by Doane, "Veiling over Desire," 123. See also the last section of Chapter I where I raise the question of woman's blindness to herself.

[13] With such dramatic emphases and "mimetic" punctuation, Eliot's style seems here to emulate a theatrical or melodramatic mode. Similar instances occur in *Deronda* on pages 642 and 717.

[14] This phrase appears in Felman's definition of the unconscious: "The unconscious, therefore, is the radical castration of the mastery of consciousness, which turns out to be forever incomplete, illusory, and self-deceptive" (*Jacques Lacan and the Adventure of Insight: Psychoanalysis in Contemporary Culture*, 57). It could be argued that it is the return of the repressed which renders the conversation impossible.

[15] I owe this suggestive passage to Richard Freadman's invaluable study *Eliot, James and the Fictional Self: A Study in Character and Narration*, 64. Singling out two strands of philosophical sources that to him "appear especially germane to such a novel as *Deronda*," he quotes as one of them this passage from Feuerbach's *The Essence of Christianity* in Eliot's own translation (158).

"An dem Anderen habe ich erst das Bewusstsein der Menschheit; durch ihn erst erfahre, fühle ich, dass ich *Mensch* bin; in der Liebe zu ihm wird mir erst klar, dass er zu mir und ich zu ihm gehöre, dass wir beide nicht ohne einander sein können, dass nur die Gemeinsamkeit die Menschheit ausmacht. Aber ebenso findet auch moralisch ein *qualitativer* ein *kritischer* Unterschied zwischen dem Ich und Du statt. Der Andere ist mein *gegenständliches* Gewissen" (Ludwig Feuer-bach, *Das Wesen des Christenthums*, 191). Notice the shift of vocabulary: *Bewusstsein* (consciousness), once infused with a moral dimension, becomes indeed *Gewissen* (conscience).

[16] As Peter Brooks (to whom I am greatly indebted for this discussion of hysterical representation) has shown in *Melodramatic Imagination:* "The site of [the] drama, the ontology of the true subject, is not easily established: the narrative must push toward it, the pressure of the prose must uncover it. We might say that the center of interest and the scene of the underlying drama reside within what we could call the 'moral occult,' the domain of operative spiritual values which is both indicated within and masked by the surface of reality" (5).

[17] It is between the mother and son, Daniel and Alcharisi, that the struggle for power is explicitly wagered.

[18] "In other words, does he admit that woman is the only one to know the secret, to know the final answer to the riddle [*énigme*], that she most assuredly does not want to give it away (since she is, or believes herself to be, self-sufficient) and has no need of any complicity? Such is the path opened up by 'On Narcissism,' a painful path for the man who complains of woman's inaccessiblity, of her coldness, and of her 'enigmatic,' undecipherable nature," writes Kofman with regards to Freud ("Narcissistic Woman," 223-24). Kofman's words greatly illuminate George Eliot's novel if we accept that, as the "new Oedipus," Freud offers the paradigm of the masculine position or attitude. It is against this irreducible self-sufficient otherness of the feminine, embodied in Gwendolen, that Eliot's narrative seems to struggle; the ultimate sacrifice of such a "beautiful" heroine testifies to Eliot's deep revulsion against "feminine" narcissism.

[19] The phrase in the heading is a misappropriation of G. H. Lewes's definition: "Consciousness is not an agent but a symptom,' mind constitutes 'the activities of the whole organism in correspondence with a physi-

cal and social medium'" (quoted in Freadman, *Eliot, James and the Fictional Self,* 65). I have given Lewes's words a more literal meaning than they obviously held for him.

20 Gwendolen is not the first literary heroine to express the burden of woman's isolation from history. The following excerpt from Lélia's complaint evokes the same predicament: "Pourquoi m'avez-vous fait naître femme, si vous vouliez un peu plus tard me changer en pierre et me laisser inutile en dehors de la vie commune?" (Why have you made me a woman, if soon after you would change me into stone and make of me a useless being cut off from communal life? [99]).

21 As Jean Hyppolite has shown in his commentary on Freud's *Verneinung,* even within a model of subjectivity such as the one developed by Freud, which gives crucial importance to "human affections," consciousness is necessarily made of those other faculties, judgment and thinking. See "A Spoken Commentary on Freud's *Verneinung*".

22 "It is a commonplace that George Eliot had anticipated Freud—in her presentation of the urgencies of transferential need as they shape Gwendolen's painful talks with Daniel, and, more compellingly still, in her exploration of repression and of the terrors associated with the return of repressed images and feelings," writes Neil Hertz in "Some Words in George Eliot: Nullify, Neutral, Numb, Number," 291.

23 "The moral examination of female psychology—in which we classically locate the depth of George Eliot's fully human perception—is therefore doubly contaminated. By the sexual fantasy which supports it as well as by all the questions of social inequality and misery which this attention directed at the woman serves to displace," writes Jacqueline Rose in "George Eliot and the Spectacle of Woman," (*Sexuality in the Field of Vision,* 113). Built on similar premises, our approaches diverge since Rose endorses a marxistfeminist approach whereas my own theme—the burden gender places on bourgeois Western women (and, by implication, on men)—leads me to focus singlemindedly on the philosophical and historical implications of such a phenomenon, but without taking into account social and economic determinations.

24 On the question of reading the "sensation novel," see D. A. Miller's brilliant analysis, focusing on the readers' "hystericized bodies," in the introduction to "*Cage aux folles:* Sensation and Gender in Wilkie Collins's *The Woman in White,*" 187-88.

25 "In episodes of this type the effect is that of an arrested scene, nearly a tableau, since what they consist of is nothing but the ostensive presentation of a figure or setting. The action of such scenes is not an action within the scene but the presenting or disclosing of the scene," writes Alexander Gelley in his analysis of the scene in Hawthorne's short story "Wakefield" (*Narrative Crossings: Theory and Pragmatics of Prose Fiction,* 159). The scene of hysteria in *Daniel Deronda* seems a particularly apt illustration of what his theory of the scene highlights, namely, a shift in representation from the outer to the inner stage.

26 Marc Redfield first drew my attention, a long time ago, to this unusual grammatical feature.

27 These are the kinds of "transegmental drifts" that Stewart analyzes in *Reading Voices.* "[In his discussion of *Finnegan's Wake*] Derrida comes as close as anywhere in his work to acknowledging the pressure, however phantasmal, of pronunciation upon script," Stewart writes (245). I argue, similarly, that Eliot's grammatical slip reveals "the pressure, however, phantasmal" of voice upon writing.

28 For the relation between linguistic forms and affect, see Gilles Deleuze's ground-breaking study "The Schizophrenic and Language: Surface and Depth in Lewis Carroll and Antonin Artaud." Given the unusual rhythms, intensities, and displacements of Eliot's writing of hysteria, it could be said that her text produces as well "passion-words" and "action-words" (291) and reveals a tension (and not a radical break) between "language-affect" and "the organization of language" (287).

On the difference between writing and representation, see Roland Barthes, *Le plaisir du texte,* 88-90:

> This is representation, really: when nothing gets out, springs out of the frame: of the painting, the book, the screen.

29 Or put differently: "The effect of the theory corresponded to what it invented in relation to the cultural coordinates of the interlocutor (or analysand)" (Roustang, *Un destin si funeste,* 91).

30 See my discussion in Chapter 4 in the section titled "Between Women."

31 In her theorization of the "female authorial voice," Silverman suggests there are at least two "points of entry that help to organize the authorial corpus": nodal points (made of the repetition of sound, image, scene), and "a sound, image, scene, or sequence which is marked through some kind of formal excess" (*Acoustic Mirror,* 218).

32 This is how hysteria is defined by David-Ménard, in the wake of Lacan, in *Hysteria from Freud to Lacan,* 44.

Works Cited

Barthes, Roland. *Le plaisir du texte,* Paris: Seuil, 1973.

—————. *The Rustle of Language.* Trans. Richard Howard. Berkeley: University of California Press, 1989.

Beauvoir, Simone de. *Le deuxième sexe.* Paris: Gallimard, 1976.

Brooks, Peter. *Body Work: Objects of Desire in Modern Narrative.* Cambridge: Harvard University Press, 1993.

—————. *The Melodramatic Imagination: Balzac, Henry James and the Mode of Excess.* New York: Columbia University Press, 1985.

Cavell, Stanley. "Naughty Orators: Negation of Voice in *Gaslight.*" In *Languages of the Unsayable: The Play of Negativity in Literature and Literary Theory,* ed. Sanford Budick and Wolfgang Iser. New York: Columbia University Press, 1989.

Clément, Catherine, and Hélène Cixous. *La jeune née.* Paris: Union Générale d'Éditions, 1975.

Cross, John W. *George Eliot's Life as Related in Her Letters and Journal,* ed. by her husband. 3 vols. London: Blackwood, 1885.

David-Ménard, Monique. *Hysteria from Freud to Lacan: Body and Language in Psychoanalysis.* Trans. Catherine Porter. Ithaca: Cornell University Press, 1989.

de Lauretis, Teresa. *Alice Doesn't: Feminism, Semiotics, Cinema.* Bloomington: Indiana University Press, 1984.

Deleuze, Gilles. "The Schizophrenic and Languages: Surface and Depth in Lewis Carroll and Antonin Artaud." In *Textual Strategies,* ed. Josué Harari. Ithaca: Cornell University Press, 1979.

[Derrida, Jacques]. "Me-Psychoanalysis: An Introduction to the Translation of 'The Shell and the Kernel' by Nicolas Abraham." *Diacritics* 9 (1979).

Doane, Mary Ann. "Veiling over Desire: Close-ups of the Woman." In *Feminism and Psychoanalysis,* ed. Richard Feldstein and Judith Roof. Ithaca: Cornell University Press, 1989.

Edel, Leon. *The Life of Henry James.* 2 vols. Harmondsworth: Penguin, 1977.

Eliot, George. *Daniel Deronda.* Ed. Graham H. Handley. Oxford: Clarendon Press, 1984.

—————. *The George Eliot Letters.* Ed. Gordon S. Haight. 9 vols. New Haven: Yale University Press, 1954-1978.

Ermarth, Elizabeth Deeds. *George Eliot.* Princeton: Princeton University Press, 1985.

Felman, Shoshana. *Jacques Lacan and the Adventure of Insight: Psychoanalysis in Contemporary Culture.* Cambridge: Harvard University Press, 1987.

Feuerbach, Ludwig. *The Essence of Christianity.* Trans. George Eliot. 2d ed. London: Trübner, 1881.

Flieger, Jerry Aline. "Entertaining the Ménage à Trois: Psychoanalysis, Feminism, and Literature." In *Feminism and Psychoanalysis,* ed. Richard Feldstein and Judith Root. Ithaca: Cornell University Press, 1989.

[Foucault, Michel]. *La volonté de savoir: Histoire de la sexualité I.* Paris: Gallimard, 1976.

Freadman, Richard. *Eliot, James and the Fictional Self: A Study in Character and Narration.* London: Macmillan, 1986.

[Freud, Sigmund]. *The Standard Edition of the Complete Psychological Works of Sigmund Freud.* Trans. under the direction of James Strachey. 24 vols. London: Hogarth Press, 1959-72. Cited throughout as *SE.*

Gay, Peter. *Freud: A Life for Our Time.* New York: Doubleday, 1989.

Gelley, Alexander. *Narrative Crossings: Theory and Pragmatics of Prose Fiction.* Baltimore: Johns Hopkins University Press, 1987.

Haight, Gordon. *George Eliot, a Biography.* Oxford: Oxford University Press, 1968.

Hertz, Neil. "Dora's Secrets, Freud's Techniques." In *In Dora's Case: Freud, Hysteria, Feminism,* ed. Charles Bernheimer and Claire Kahane. New York: Columbia University Press, 1985.

—————. *The End of the Line.* New York: Oxford University Press, 1985.

—————. "Some Words in George Eliot: Nullify, Neutral, Numb, Number." In *Languages of the Unsayable,* ed. Sanford Budick and Wolfgang Iser. New York: Columbia University Press, 1989.

Hyppolite, Jean. "A Spoken Commentary on Freud's *Verneinung.*" In *The Seminar of Jacques Lacan, Book I,* trans. John Forrester. New York: Norton, 1988.

[Jacobus, Mary]. *Reading Woman: Essays in Feminist Criticism*. London: Methuen, 1986.

[James, Henry]. *The Bostonians*. Oxford: Oxford University Press, 1984.

———. *The Complete Notebooks of Henry James*. Ed. Leon Edel and Lyall H. Powers. Oxford: Oxford University Press, 1987.

———. *"Daniel Deronda: A Conversation."* In *Essays on Literature, American Writers, English Writers*. Ed. Leon Edel. New York: Library of America, 1984.

———. *Letters*. Vol. IV (1895-1916). Ed. Leon Edel. Cambridge: Harvard University Press, 1984.

———. *Literary Criticism: French Writers, Other European Writers, the Prefaces to the New York Edition*. Ed. Leon Edel. Cambridge: Library of America, 1984.

———. *Selected Letters*. Ed. Leon Edel. Cambridge: Harvard University Press, 1987.

James, Henry, and Edith Wharton. *Letters, 1900-1915*. Ed. Lyall L. Powers. New York: Charles Scribner's Sons, 1990.

Kahane, Claire. "Hysteria, Feminism, and the Case of *The Bostonians*." In *Feminism and Psychoanalysis,* ed. Richard Feldstein and Judith Roof. Ithaca: Cornell University Press, 1989.

[Kofman, Sarah]. "The Narcissistic Woman: Freud and Girard." In *French Feminist Thought: A Reader,* ed. Toril Moi. London: Blackwell, 1987.

Lacan, Jacques. "Intervention on Transference." In *In Dora's Case: Freud, Hysteria, Feminism,* ed. Charles Bernheimer and Claire Kahane. New York: Columbia University Press, 1985.

Miller, D. A. *"Cage aux Folles:* Sensation and Gender in Wilkie Collins's *The Woman in White*." In *Speaking of Gender,* ed. Elaine Showalter. New York: Routledge, 1989.

Moers, Ellen. *Literary Women*. London: Woman's Press, 1986.

Myers, William. *The Teaching of George Eliot*. Leicester: Leicester University Press, 1984.

Rose, Jacqueline. *Sexuality and the Field of Vision*. London: Verso, 1986.

Roustang, François. *Un destin si funeste*. Paris: Minuit, 1976.

[Sand, George]. *Lélia*. Ed. Pierre Reboul. Paris: Garnier, 1960.

———. *Lélia*. Trans. Maria Espinosa. Bloomington: Indiana University Press, 1978.

———. *Valentine*. Geneva: Slatkine Reprints, 1980. Reprint of the Editions de Paris, 1863-1926.

———. *Valentine*. Trans. George Burnham Ives. Chicago: Academy Press, 1978.

Silverman, Kaja. *The Acoustic Mirror: The Female Voice in Psychoanalysis and Cinema*. Indianapolis: Indiana University Press, 1988.

Steiner, George. "Eros and Idiom." *On Difficulty and Other Essays*. Oxford: Oxford University Press, 1978.

Stewart, Garrett. *Reading Voices: Literature and the Phonotext*. Berkeley: University of California Press, 1990.

HYSTERIA IN NINETEENTH-CENTURY POETRY

Karen Swann (essay date 1984)

SOURCE: "'Christabel': The Wandering Mother and the Enigma of Form," in *Studies in Romantcism*, Vol. 23, No. 4, Winter, 1984, pp. 533-53.

[*In the following excerpt, Swann asserts that in "Christabel" Coleridge explores the complex and multifaceted relations between hysteria—as a socially disruptive moment—and the Law—as masculine, rational control through social conventionality.*]

The first questions Christabel asks Geraldine refer to identity and origins: "who art thou?" and "how camest thou here?" Geraldine's response is oblique; in effect she replies, "I am like you, and my story is like your own":

> My sire is of a noble line,
> And my name is Geraldine:
> Five warriors seized me yestermorn,
> Me, even me, a maid forlorn: . . .
>
> They spurred amain, their steeds were white:
> And once we crossed the shade of night.
> As sure as Heaven shall rescue me,
> I have no thought what men they be;
> Nor do I know how long it is
> (For I have lain entranced I wis)
> Since one, the tallest of the five,

Took me from the palfrey's back,
A weary woman, scarce alive. . . .

Whither they went I cannot tell—
I thought I heard, some minutes past,
Sounds as of a castle bell.
Stretch forth thy hand (thus ended she),
And help a wretched maid to flee.

(ll. 79-104)[1]

Geraldine's tale echoes and anticipates Christabel's. Christabel is also first introduced as the daughter of a "noble" father; she, too, experiences things she "cannot tell," calls on Heaven to rescue her, crosses threshholds and falls into trances. But in contrast to the story "Christabel," often criticized for its ambiguities, Geraldine's tale presents sexual and moral categories as unambiguous and distinct: villainous male force appropriates and silences an innocent female victim. This difference effects a corresponding clarification of genre. Geraldine translates "Christabel" into the familiar terms of the tale of terror.

Geraldine's translation would appear to establish the identity of the woman. Ultimately, however, her story complicates the issue of feminine identity by suggesting its entanglement, at the origin, with genre. How one takes Geraldine depends on one's sense of the "line" of representations she comes from. For Christabel, but also, for any absorbed reader of circulating library romances, Geraldine's story of abduction works as a seduction—Christabel recognizes Geraldine as a certain type of heroine and embraces her.[2] More guarded readers appropriate Geraldine as confidently as Christabel does, but they see her quite differently. Charles Tomlinson, for example, reads "Christabel" as "a tale of terror," but in contrast to Geraldine's own story casts her in the role of villain, while for Patricia Adair, Geraldine is betrayed by her very conventionality: she tells her story in "rather unconvincing and second-rate verse which was, no doubt, deliberately meant to sound false."[3] Geraldine is "false" because she comes from an ignoble line of Gothic temptresses, or, in the case of other critics, because she can be traced back to the ignoble Duessa and to a host of other predatory figures. Tellingly these sophisticated readers, who employ literary history to read Geraldine as a figure of untruth, are the worst ruffians—they either refuse to hear the woman's story of her own abduction, or assume that her protests are really a come-on.

Geraldine may be Christabel's ghost or projection as many critics have suggested, but only if we acknowledge that Christabel produces herself as a received representation—a feminine character who in turn raises the ghosts of different subtexts, each dictating a reading of her as victim or seductress, good or evil, genuine or affected. I will be arguing in this essay that "Christabel" both dramatizes and provokes hysteria. The poem explores the possessing force of certain bodies—Geraldine's, of course, but also bodies of literary convention, which I am calling "genres." Particularly in Coleridge's day, debates on literary decorum allowed the gendering of structure in a way that seemed to assuage anxiety about the subject's relation to cultural forms. Questions involving the subject's autonomy could be framed as an opposition between authentic, contained "manly" speech and "feminine" bodies—the utterly conventional yet licentiously imaginative female characters, readers, and genres of the circulating libraries. In "Christabel," Coleridge both capitalizes on and exposes culture's tactical gendering of formal questions. The poem invites us to link the displacing movement of cultural forms through subjects to the "feminine" malady of hysteria and the "feminine" genres of the circulating library; at the same time, it mockingly and dreamily informs us that hysteria is the condition of all subjects in discourse, and that the attribution of this condition to feminine bodies is a conventional, hysterical response.

I

If Coleridge were thinking of dramatizing hysteria in a poem, he might have turned to Burton's account of "Maids', Nuns', and Widows' Melancholy" in *The Anatomy of Melancholy,* a book he knew well. According to Burton, hysterics "think themselves bewitched":

> Some think they see visions, confer with spirits and devils, they shall surely be damned, are afraid of some treachery, imminent danger, and the like, they will not speak, make answer to any question, but are almost distracted, mad, or stupid for the time, and by fits. . . . [4]

The malady befalls barren or celibate women; among these, Catholic noblewomen who are forced to remain idle are particularly susceptible. Most of the symptoms Burton catalogues are touched on in the passage quoted above. Hysterics have visions and are afraid "by fits"—the "fits of the mother" or womb ("the heart itself beats, is sore grieved, and faints . . . like fits of the mother" [p. 415]). The symptom which most interests Burton, though, is the inability of hysterics to communicate their troubles: they "cannot tell" what ails them. This fact becomes a refrain of his own exposition: "and yet will not, cannot again tell how, where, or what offends them"; "many of them cannot tell how to express themselves in words, or how it holds them, what ails them; you cannot understand them, or well tell what to make of their sayings" (p. 416).

They "cannot tell," and *you* cannot "well tell" what to make of them: the phenomenon of their blocked or incomprehensible speech seems to produce similar ef-

Samuel Taylor Coleridge (1772-1834).

fects in the writer. And indeed, Burton's impetous and fitful prose in many respects resembles the discourse of the hysteric, into whose point of view he regularly tumbles ("Some *think* they see visions," but "they *shall* surely be damned" [my italics]). Far from resisting this identification, Burton makes narrative capital from the slippage, as here, when he allows himself to become "carried away" by sympathy for the Christabel-like afflicted:

> I do not so much pity them that may otherwise be eased, but those alone that out of a strong temperament, innate constitution, are violently carried away with this torrent of inward humours, and though very modest of themselves, sober, religious, virtuous, and well given (as many so distressed maids are), yet cannot make resistance. . . .

and then, as if shaking off a "fit," comically pauses to reflect on his own indecorous "torrents":

> But where am I? Into what subject have I rushed? What have I to do with nuns, maids, virgins, widows? I am a bachelor myself, and lead a monastic life in a college: *nae ego sane ineptus qui haec dixerim,* I confess 'tis an indecorum, and as Pallas, a virgin, blushed when Jupiter by chance spake of love matters in her presence, and turned away her face, *me reprimam;* though my subject necessarily require it, I will say no more. (p. 417)

Protesting all the while his ignorance of women, the "old bachelor" coyly figures himself as a virgin whose body betrays her when desire takes her unawares. He also takes the part of the apparently more knowing and self-controlled Jupiter, but only to suggest that the latter's fatherly indifference is an act. For whether he is an artful or artless seducer, Jupiter himself appears only to rush into speech "by chance"—the "chance," we suspect, of finding himself in such close proximity to his virginal daughter. The woman whose desire is written on her body is like the man who makes love the "matter" of his discourse: both attempt to disguise desire, and become the more seductive when desire is revealed in the context of their attempts to suppress it.

The story of Pallas and Jupiter is placed at a strategic point in Burton's chapter. It punctuates his resolve to check the torrents of his narrative, a resolve immediately and engagingly broken when, more "by chance" than design, he finds he has to say something more ("And yet I must and will say something more"). This time he is prompted by his commiseration with all distressed women to launch an attack on "them that are in fault,"

> . . . those tyrannizing pseudo-politicians, superstitious orders, rash vows, hard-hearted parents, guardians, unnatural friends, allies (call them how you will), those careless and stupid overseers . . .

those fathers and parental substitutes (particularly the Church), who "suppress the vigour of youth" and ensure the orderly descent of their estates through the enforced celibacy of their daughters (p. 418). An "old bachelor" who leads a monastic life in a college; whose own discourse, like the discourse of the hysteric, seems to be the product of a strained compromise between lawless impulses and the claims of order; who might himself be said to be possessed by spirits and the dead language in which they wrote, ends his discussion of "maids', nuns', and widows' melancholy" by championing those who "cannot tell" against the ungenerous legislators of the world.

There are suggestive correspondences between Burton's chapter on hysteria and "Christabel." Christabel is a virtuous Catholic gentlewoman whose lover is away, possibly at the behest of her father, out of whose castle she "steals" at the beginning of the poem. Whether or not he is responsible for blighting love affairs,[5] Sir Leoline has affinities with both of Burton's father-figures: like the "pseudopoliticians" he is intimately linked with repressive law; like Jupiter, his relation to his daughter is somewhat suspect. Moreover, the poem's descriptions of Christabel's experiences—first with the possibly supernatural Geraldine and later, with a traumatic memory or scene which comes over her by fits and bars her from telling—and its insistent references to a "mother" who at one point threatens to block

Geraldine's speech ("Off, wandering mother!" [l. 205]), follow Burton's account of the characteristic symptoms of hysteria. But Coleridge may have appreciated most the comic slippages in Burton's narrative between the slightly hysterical scholar whose business it is to "tell" and the women who are the matter of his discourse. When he came to write "Christabel," Coleridge told the story through narrators who are as enigmatic as the women they tell about—we cannot "well tell" if they are one voice or two. More than any detail of the plot, the participation of these narrators in the "feminine" exchanges they describe, and the poem's playful suggestion that hysteria cannot be restricted to *feminine* bodies, marks the kinship of "Christabel" and Burton's text.

II

Who is Geraldine and where does she come from? Possibly, from Christabel. In the opening of the poem Christabel has gone into the woods to pray for her absent lover after having had uneasy dreams "all yesternight"—"Dreams, that made her moan and leap, / As on her bed she lay in sleep," we are told in the 1816 version of the poem. In the woods *two* ladies perform the actions of moaning and leaping which, yesternight, *one* lady had performed alone:

> The lady leaps up suddenly,
> The lovely lady, Christabel!
> It moaned as near, as near can be,
> But what it is she cannot tell—
> On the other side it seems to be,
> Of the huge, broad-breasted, old oak tree.
>
> (1816: ll. 37-42)

For a moment we, too, are in the woods, particularly if, like the poem's "first" readers, we already know something of the plot. Does "the lady" refer to Christabel or Geraldine? Is her leaping up the cause or effect of fright? The next lines supply answers to these questions, and as the scene proceeds "it" resolves into the distinct, articulate character Geraldine. For a moment's space, however, we entertain the notion that an uneasy lady leaped up suddenly and terrified herself.

Burton says of hysterics, "some think they see visions, confer with spirits and devils, they shall surely be damned." Geraldine is such a "vision." She appears in response to what Burton implies and psychoanalysis declares are the wishes of hysterics—to get around patriarchal law, which legislates desire. In the beginning of the poem Christabel "cannot tell" what ails her, but critics have theorized from her sighs that she is suffering from romance, from frustrated love for the "lover that's far away," for the Baron, or even, for the mother.[6] Geraldine, who appears as if in answer to Christabel's prayer, "steals" with her back into the castle, sleeps with her "as a mother with her child," and then meets the Baron's embrace, allows the performance of these wishes. Moreover, like an hysterical symptom, which figures both desire and its repression, Geraldine also fulfills the last clause of Burton's formula: although much is ambiguous *before* she appears, it is not until she appears that Christabel feels "damned," and that we are invited to moralize ambiguity as duplicity, the cause of "sorrow and shame" (ll. 270, 296, 674).

As well as answering *Christabel's* desires, however, Geraldine answers the indeterminacy of the narrative and the reader's expectancy. The wood outside the Baron's castle is not the "natural" world, as is often declared,[7] but a world stocked with cultural artifacts. Before Geraldine ever appears it is haunted by the ghosts of old stories: familiar settings and props function as portents, both for the superstitious and the well-read. The wood and the midnight hour are the "moment's space" where innocence is traditionally put to the test, or when spirits walk abroad; other details—the cock's crow at midnight, the mastiff's unrest, the contracted moon—we know to be art's way of signifying nature's response to human disorder. These so-called "Gothic trappings" ensnare us because they mean nothing ("Tu-whit, tu-whoo") and too much: like the sighs we seize on as evidence of Christabel's inner life, they gesture to an enigma, something as yet hidden from view. Geraldine makes "answer meet" to these suspensions of the narrative, not by providing closure, but by representing indeterminacy:

> There she sees a damsel bright,
> Drest in a silken robe of white,
> That shadowy in the moonlight shone:
> The neck that made that white robe wan,
> Her stately neck, and arms were bare;
> Her blue-veined feet unsandal'd were,
> And wildly glittered here and there
> The gems entangled in her hair.
>
> (ll. 58-65)

Precipitating out of the Gothic atmosphere, Geraldine promises to contain in herself an entrapping play of surfaces and shadows; with her appearance suspense resolves into a familiar sign of ambiguity.

Geraldine is a fantasy, produced by the psychic operations of condensation and displacement. On the one hand, her function is to objectify: she intervenes in moments of interpretive crisis as a legible representation—a "vision," a story, and a plot. At the same time, though, she, the story she tells, and the plot she seems to set in motion are all displacing performances of ambiguities she might at first promise to "answer" more decisively. After she pops up, two women dramatize the implied doubleness of the daughter who "stole" along the forest keeping her thoughts to herself (l. 31).

Very little else changes. Prompted by an uneasy dream one women "stole" out of her father's castle; two women return to it "as if in stealth" (l. 120), and by the end of Part I Christabel has simply resumed "fearfully dreaming," at least according to the narrator (l. 294). The spell that becomes "lord of her utterance" (l. 268) that night does not more than render explicit the inhibition of her "telling" already operative in the opening scene of the poem, where her silence was obscurely connected to the brooding, dreaming "lord" of the castle, the father who loved the daughter "so well." By the end of the poem we have simply returned to where we began: Christabel is "inly praying" once again, this time at the "old" Baron's feet, and once again Geraldine is on "the other side" (l. 614).

While it proposes an answer to the question "who art thou?" this reading only makes Christabel's second question to Geraldine more problematic: Geraldine is a fantasy, but she does not seem to "come from" any locatable place. The many source studies of the poem have shown that her origins are as much in literature as in Christabel: she first appears to the latter as a highly aestheticized object, and first speaks, many readers think to her discredit, in a highly encoded discourse. A material, communally available representation, she could have been dreamed up by any of the characters to whom she appears in the course of the poem—by the uneasy dreamer Christabel, but also by the Baron, into whose castle she steals while he is asleep, and, Christabel suggests, dreaming uneasily (l. 165), or by Bracy, whose dream of her seems to "live upon [his] eye" the next day (l. 559). She could even be part of *our* dream. For in "Christabel" as in all of his poems of the supernatural, Coleridge plots to turn us into dreamers—to "procure" our "willing suspension of disbelief," our happy relinquishment of the reality principle. In "Christabel" as in dreams there is no version of the negative: questions raise possibilities that are neither confirmed nor wholly dismissed ("Is it the wind . . . ? / There is not wind enough . . ." [ll. 44-45]). Tags drift from one "lady" to another, suggesting the affinity of apparent adversaries; signs are familiar yet unreadable, laden with associations which neither exclude each other nor resolve into univocality.

Geraldine intervenes into these several dreamlike states as a figure of the imaginary itself—a figure whose legibility derives from its status within the symbolic order. She obeys the laws which structure all psychic phenomena, including dreams, jokes, and hysteria, the malady which allowed Freud to "discover" these very laws. The latter, however, do not explain why *particular* representations become collectively privileged. Why, at moments when they brush with the (il-)logic of the unconscious, do subjects automatically, even hysterically, produce certain *gendered* sights and stories?—produce the image of a radically divided woman, or of two women in each other's arms; and produce

the story of a woman who seduces, and/or is seduced, abducted, and silenced by a father, a seducer, and/or a ruffian? This story, including all the ambiguities that make it hard to "tell," is of course the story of hysteria as told by Burton, and later, painstakingly reconstructed by Freud from its plural, displacing performances on the bodies of women. Even the common reader would know it, however, for it describes all the permutations of the romance plot—a form largely, but not exclusively, associated with a body of popular, "feminine" literature.

If a body like Geraldine's pops up from behind a tree when all the witnesses are in the woods, it is no accident: everyone thinks feminine forms appropriately represent the dangers and attractions of fantasy life. Coleridge, who dramatized the highly overdetermined romance/hysteria plot in "Christabel" and happily flaunted feminine bodies when it suited him, was no exception. But I want to argue, first by looking at his generic play, and then by examining his treatment of the family romance, that in "Christabel" he was also mockingly obtruding, a conspiracy to view, allowing us to see "feminine" genre and gender alike as cultural fantasy.

III

"Christabel's" narrators are themselves hysterics. The poem's interlocutor and respondent mime the entanglement of Geraldine and Christabel—I call them "they," but it is not clear if we hear two voices or one. Like the women they describe, they are overmastered by "visions." Repeatedly, they abandon an authoritative point of view to fall into the story's present; or they engage in transferential exchanges with the characters whose plot they are narrating. In the opening scene, for example, one of them plunges into the tale to plead to and for Christabel: "Hush, beating heart of Christabel! / Jesu, Maria, shield her well!" As if she hears, a stanza later Christabel cries out, "Mary mother, save me now!" (ll. 53-54, 69). Further on, the sequence is reversed when the speaker seems to take up Christabel's speech. She has just assured Geraldine that Sir Leoline will "guide and guard [her] safe and free" (l. 110); although the narrators generally are not as trusting as Christabel, one seems inspired by her confidence to echo her, twice: "So free from danger, free from fear / They crossed the court: right glad they were" (ll. 135-36, 143-44).

These narrators create the conditions and logic of dream: like them, and because of them, the reader is impotent to decide the poem's ambiguities from a position outside its fictions. Furthermore, the poem's "fictions" seem to be about little else than these formal slippages. The repressed of "Christabel's" dreamwork is almost too visible to be seen—not a particular psychic content but literary conventions themselves, like those which demand that narrators speak from privileged points of view, and important for this argument, bodies of conventions or "genres." "Christabel" obtrudes genre to our notice. The Gothic atmosphere of the first stanza, with its enumerations of ominously coincident bird and clock noises, goes slightly bad in the second—partly because of the very presence of the shocking "mastiff bitch," but also because both mastiff and narrator become heady with coincidence: making answer to the clock, "Four for the quarters, and twelve for the hour . . . Sixteen short howls, not over loud," she becomes an obvious piece of Gothic machinery (ll. 10-13). A similar generic disturbance occurs between Part I, told more or less in the "tale of terror" convention, and its conclusion, which recapitulates the story in a new convention, that of sentimental fiction. Suddenly Christabel "means" "a bourgeois lady of delicate, even saccharine, sensibility": "Her face, oh call it fair not pale, / And both blue eyes more bright than clear, / Each about to have a tear" (ll. 289-91). As suddenly, the narrators are exposed in a desperate act of wielding genre, using convention to force legibility on a sight that won't be explained.

Once we become aware of these instabilities, no stretch of the poem is exempt. In life women might faint, dogs might moan, and fires might flare up without anyone remarking it; if these coincide in story, they mean something. When they coincide in the overloaded, tonally unsettling Part I of "Christabel" they simultaneously draw attention to themselves as elements of a code. Although we may think of genres as vessels which successive authors infuse with original content, "Christabel's" "originality" is to expose them as the means by which significance is produced and contained.

This analysis raises the issue of the generic status of "Christabel." What is its literary genre? But also, what genre of psychic phenomenon does the poem aspire to—is it like a dream, as we first proposed, or like a joke? The latter question may not immediately seem important, since jokes and dreams have so much in common: like hysteria, they work by condensation and displacement to bring the repressed to light.[8] But for the poem's first readers, at least, it clearly mattered which was which. The reviewers of 1816 fiercely protested the poem's "licentious" mixing of joke and dream, categories of psychic phenomena which they translated into literary categories: was "Christabel" a bit of "doggrel," a wild, weird tale of terror, or a fantastic combination of the two? (Modern readers, less tuned to genre play, have decided the question by not hearing the jokes.)[9] Coleridge's contemporaries recognized that jokes and dreams demand different attitudes: if one responds to "Christabel" as though it were just a wild weird tale, and it turns out to be a joke, then the joke is on oneself. "Christabel" frightened its reviewers, not because it was such a successful tale of terror, but because they couldn't decide what sort of tale it was.

"Christabel" made its first readers hysterical because it is not one genre or another but a joke on our desire to decide genre. As such, it turned a "merely" formal question into a matter of one upsmanship. Most of the critics responded by redirecting the joke, giving the impression that it was on the poem and the author. Coleridge, they claimed, mixed the genres of joke and dream, not as a joke, but in a dream. What is telling is their almost universal decision to recast these issues of literary and formal mastery into the more obviously charged and manageable terms of sexual difference. According to them, the poem was, after all, just one of those tales of terror which ladies like to read ("For what woman of fashion would not purchase a book recommended by Lord Byron?" asks the *AntiJacobin*[10]); the author, variously described as an "enchanted virgin," an "old nurse," a "dreamer"—by implication, a hysteric—simply could not control the discourses that spoke through him like so many "lords" of his utterance.[11]

Gendering the formal question, the reviewers reenact the scene of Geraldine's first appearance: then, too, a variety of characters responded to indeterminacy by producing a feminine body at once utterly conventional and too full of significance. In critical discourse as in fantasy life, it seems, feminine forms—the derogated genres of the circulating library, the feminized body of the author, or the body of Geraldine—represent the enigma of form itself. Female bodies "naturally" seem to figure an ungraspable truth: that form, habitually viewed as the arbitrary, contingent vessel of more enduring meanings, is yet the source and determinant of all meanings, whether the subject's or the world's.

Displacing what is problematic about form onto the feminine gender ultimately serves the hypothetical authenticity and integrity of masculine gender and "manly" language. Look, for example, at the opening lines of the passage Hazlitt selects as the only "genuine burst of humanity" "worthy of the author" in the whole poem—the only place where "no dream oppresses him, no spell binds him"[12].

> Alas! they had been friends in youth;
> But whispering tongues can poison truth;
> And constancy lives in realms above;
> And life is thorny; and youth is vain;
> And to be wroth with one we love
> Doth work like madness in the brain.
> And thus it chanced, as I divine,
> With Roland and Sir Leoline.
>
> (ll. 408-15)

Hazlitt was not alone in his approbation: many reviewers of the poem quoted this passage with approval, and Coleridge himself called them "the best & sweetest Lines [he] ever wrote."[13] They are indeed outstanding—the only moment, in this tale about mysterious exchanges among women, when an already-past, already-interpreted, fully-breached male friendship is encountered. For those of us who don't equate "manliness" with universality and authenticity, this unremarked confluence of masculine subject-matter and "genuine" discourse is of course suspicious: it's not *simply* purity of style that made this passage the standard against which all other Christabellian discourse could be measured and found "licentious," "indecorous," "affected"—in short, effeminate.

But here, we are anticipated by the passage itself, which exposes "manliness" as a gendered convention. When the narrator begins this impassioned flight, we assume he speaks from privileged knowledge: why else such drama? Several lines later, though, he betrays that this is all something he has "divined," something that may have chanced. "Chancing" on a situation that really spoke to him—a ruined manly friendship—the narrator has constructed a "divination" based on what he knows—about constancy (it isn't to be found on earth), life (it's thorny), and youth (it's vain). Although he is more caught up in his speech than she, his voice is as "hollow" as Geraldine's. His flight or "genuine burst of humanity" is a fit of the mother, and a mocking treatment of manly discourse on the part of Coleridge, whose later accession to the going opinion was either a private joke or a guilty, revisionary reading of his licentious youth. If this tonal instability was lost on "Christabel's" reviewers, it can only be because, like the narrator himself, they were reading hysterically: a "vision" of autonomous male identities caused them automatically to produce a set of received ideas about manly discourse.

"Christabel" exposes the conventionality of manly authenticity and the giddiness of manly decorum; in the same move, it suggests that attributing hysteria to feminine forms is a hysterical response to a more general condition. In the poem as elsewhere, "the feminine" is the locus of erotic and generic license: this can have the exciting charge of perversity or madness, or can seem absolutely conventional, affected. "Christabel" contrives to have these alternatives redound on the reader, who continually feels mad or just stupid, unable to "tell" how to characterize the verse at any given point. Here is Christabel "imprisoned" in the arms of Geraldine:

> With open eyes (ah woe is me!)
> Asleep, and dreaming fearfully,
> Fearfully dreaming, yet, I wis,
> Dreaming that alone, which is—
> O sorrow and shame! Can this be she,
> The lady, who knelt at the old oak tree?
> And lo! the worker of these harms,
> That holds the maiden in her arms,
> Seems to slumber still and mild,
> As a mother with her child.

>   (ll. 292-301)

Geraldine's arms, the scene of the close embrace, and the conclusion as a whole, which recasts part I as a sentimental narrative—all in some sense work to imprison the significances of the text. Yet the scenario only imperfectly traps, and closes not at all, the questions which circulated through part I. Identity is still a matter of debate, and still hangs on a suggestively ambiguous "she" ("Can this be she?"). Even the women's gender identities and roles are undecidable, their single embrace "read" by multiple, superimposed relationships. Geraldine, a "lady" like Christabel, is also sleeping with Christabel; a "worker of harms," a ruffian-like assaultor of unspecified gender, she is also like a "mild," protective mother. If in keeping with the sentimentality of this section of the poem, the mother/child analogy is introduced to clean up the post-coital embrace of the women, it redounds to suggest the eroticism of maternal attention. These ghostly stories, all already raised in the text of Part I, work to create the compellingly charged erotic ambivalence of "Christabel"—ambivalence about becoming absorbed into a body which may be "the same" as one's own, or may belong to an adversary, a "worker of harms," and which is associated with, or represented by, the maternal body.

Christabel's situation, including, perhaps her feminine situation, is contagious. The narrator, who seems overmastered by the very spell he is describing, can only direct us to a "sight" ("And lo!"), the significance of which he "cannot tell." His speech breaks down before the woman who is "dreaming fearfully, / Fearfully dreaming," before the form that may conceal "that alone, which is."

The narrator circles round but cannot tell the enigma of form, of the body or sign that is at once meaningless and too full of significance. His own discourse repeats the paradox of the "sight," and becomes a locus of the reader's interpretive breakdown. His lament strikes us as coming from "genuine" distress at the remembrance of Christabel's horrible predicament. But particularly in context, the lines—

> With open eyes (ah woe is me!)
> Asleep and dreaming fearfully,
> Fearfully dreaming, yet, I wis,
> Dreaming that alone which is—

raise the ghost of a sentimental style that as a matter of course suppresses all distressing sights and implications, while coyly directing the reader to what's not being said. To decide the narrator's credibility—is he bewildered or merely "affected," effeminate; could he even be camping it up?—it is necessary to bring genre to bear, to decide whether Gothic or sentimental romance is a determining convention. This is simultaneously to recognize that the voice we have been hearing cannot be authentic—if mad, it speaks in the tale of terror's legislated mad discourse; that genres are constructs which produce meaning for the subject; and that genres, like fantasy, reproduce the indeterminacies they at first appear to limit or control. Our relation to Christabel's narrators is like theirs to Christabel: the enigmatic form of their discourse turns us into hysterical readers, subject to the possessing, conventional bodies that that discourse raises in us.

IV

"Christabel's" romance plot suggests that our culture's hysterical relation to feminine forms—or its hysterical feminization of form—has its origins in the family romance. The poem invites us to distinguish between paternal and feminine orders of experience. The father's sphere is the Law—a legislative, symbolic order structured according to a divisive logic:

> Each matin bell, the Baron saith,
> Knells us back to a world of death.
> These words Sir Leoline first said,
> When he rose and found his lady dead:
> These words Sir Leoline will say
> Many a morn to his dying day!
>
> And hence the custom and law began
> That still at dawn the sacristan,
> Who duly pulls the heavy bell,
> Five and forty beads must tell
> Between each stroke—a warning knell,
> Which not a soul can choose but hear
> From Bratha Head to Wyndermere.

> (ll. 332-44)

The Baron's response to a traumatic event is to commemorate it. Every day, punctually, he relives the loss of "his lady," spacing and controlling the recurrences of his sorrow. By institutionalizing the observance, he turns a private grief into a public ceremony. The compulsive becomes the compulsory: the sacristan "duly" pulls his bell, and "not a soul can choose but hear."

Separation is something of a habit with the Baron. Three other times during the poem he attempts to stabilize his relation to a disturbing person or event by opening out a "space between" (l. 349). In the past, the narrator "divine[s]," Sir Leoline had been "wroth" with Lord Roland (ll. 412-13). Wrath and the threat of madness precipitate a separation which leaves each scarred (ll. 421-22). The speaker "ween[s]" these scars will never go away and seems to guess right, since the Baron's memory of that friendship revives when Geraldine appears on the scene and tells her story:

> Sir Leoline, a moment's space,
> Stood gazing on the damsel's face:

> And the youthful Lord of Tryermaine
> Came back upon his heart again.

> (ll. 427-30)

For a second time the Baron experiences maddening confusion, here obscurely related to the striking together of "youthful lord" and "damsel," known and new, past and present, revived love and recognized loss. Once again he becomes wrathful ("His noble heart swelled high with rage" [l. 432]), and introduces a "law" of deathly separation: he will "dislodge" the "reptile souls" of Geraldine's abductors "from the bodies and forms of men" [ll. 442-43]. Finally, for a third time the Baron meets "[swelling] rage and pain" (l. 638) and "confusion" (l. 639) with division: in the last stanza of the poem, "turning from his own sweet maid," he leads Geraldine off (l. 653).

The Baron's customs and laws divide and oppose potential "sames" or potentially intermingling parts of "the same." In contrast, femininity bewilders the narrator because one can never tell if identities and differences are constant, "the same": "Can this be she, / The lady, who knelt at the old oak tree?" (ll. 296-97); "And Christabel awoke and spied / The same who lay down by her side— / Oh rather say, the same . . ." (ll. 370-71). Tales, glances, and verbal tags circulate between Christabel and Geraldine throughout the poem: each is a "lady," each makes "answer meet" to the other. These exchanges could be said to obey the law of "the mother." Her function has puzzled some critics, who have found it hard to reconcile her angelic guardianship of Christabel with her likeness to Geraldine.[14] Coleridge, however, intended "Christabel's" mother to be a punning, rather than a stable, character. Referring simultaneously to the malady of hysteria, the womb whose vaporish fantasies were thought to block the hysteric's speech, and the female parent, "the mother" is an exemplarily vagrant sign, whose shifts of meaning obey the very "laws" which determine the characteristic displacements of hysteria.

The mother escapes the Baron's divisive categories. Neither opposites nor "the same," Geraldine and Christabel are identically self-divided, each subject to a "sight" or "weight" whose history and effects she "cannot tell." The Baron might attempt to redress such duplicity by dislodging offending "souls" from the "bodies and forms" they occupy. The "mother," however, is neither spirit nor body. Dying the hour Christabel was born, she inhabits her daughter as an already-dislodged form, or in psychoanalytic terms, as an alien internal entity or fantasy.[15] At times Christabel feels this "weight" as the fully external, "weary weight" of Geraldine (l. 131), at times as an inner "vision" which "falls" on her. Where the Baron imagines parenthood bestowing on him all the privileges of ownership ("*his own* sweet maid"), possession by the "mother" breaks down privilege, including that of an original, controlling term. The "weight" or "sight" is both within and without, both the fantasy that cannot be told and the representation that makes it legible.

The Baron also remembers the mother by a weary weight, but he gets someone else to heft it: every morning his sacristan "duly pulls the heavy bell" which "not a soul can choose but hear." Obviously the organizations we have been calling the father's and the mother's exist in some relation to one another. A feminist reading of this relation might charge the Law with producing hysterics, women who "cannot tell" what ails them because the Law legislates against every voice but its own. The *Baron* stifles the daughter by his oppressive, deathly presence: stealing back into his castle with Geraldine, Christabel passes his room "as still as death / With stifled breath" (l. 171). "The mother"—the malady of hysteria—symptomatically represents the daughter's internalization of patriarchal law. This reading is supported by Burton, who laid the daughter's troubles on the pseudopoliticians, and by Geraldine, who identifies the curse that prevents Christabel from "telling" as masculine prohibition: the sign which seals them both up is a "lord" of utterance and an "overmastering" spell.

A plot as popular as this one, however, is probably overdetermined. "Christabel" invites at least two other readings of the relation between hysteria and the law. First, that hysteria produces the Law: repeatedly, the Baron opens out a space between himself and perceived threats in order to "shield" himself from overmastering confusion or madness. Second, that the Law is just one form of hysteria. According to the narrator, the Baron's cutting efforts leave him internally scarred. The space between is also a mark within, from which no "shield" can protect him. Like the hysteric he is always vulnerable to a recurrence of "swelling" confusion, a revival of the already-internalized mark, to which he responds with another legislative cut. The Law resembles hysteria in its defenses and effects: it attempts to decide irresolution by producing something "on the other side," and its cuts leave the legislator subject to recurrences.[16]

"Christabel" invites us to decide there is only one significant "sight"—Geraldine's bosom; and to infer that it is women who can have no discourse within the law. But at the same time it allows us to see hysteria as the coincidence of superimposed fields: as a metaphysical condition of the speaking subject, as a malady historically affecting women who suffer under patriarchal law, and as a fantasy of patriarchal culture—a representation which figures the subject's alienation from the symbolic order on the bodies of women. Christabel and Geraldine, who enter the Baron's castle while he sleeps, enact their 'own' fantasy and his dream.

To account for the power of this dream, we might try tracing it back to the origin. At the moment the Baron is about to cast off his only child, a protesting narrator invokes the mother:

> Why is thy cheek so wan and wild,
> Sir Leoline? Thy only child
> Lies at thy feet, thy joy, thy pride,
> So fair, so innocent, so mild;
> The same, for whom thy lady died!
> O by the pangs of her dear mother
> Think thou no evil of thy child!
> For her, and thee, and for no other,
> She prayed the moment ere she died:
> Prayed that the babe for whom she died,
> Might prove her dear lord's joy and pride!
>   That prayer her deadly pangs beguiled,
>   Sir Leoline!
>   And wouldst thou wrong thy only child,
>   Her child and thine?
>
> (ll. 621-35)

These lines refer us back to the opening of part II, where custom and law were instituted in response to a "lady's" death. This "lady" was also a mother, the narrator reminds us here; her death was simultaneous with a birth, her "pangs"—at once labor and death pangs—were beguiled by prayers, her suffering mingled with joy.

The Baron's law is an interpretive moment: he decides to read the occasion as a death only. His action anticipates his later disavowal of Christabel, which occurs almost as if in response to the narrator's reminder that she is "[thy lady's] child and thine"; and it resonates with Geraldine's response when, diverted from her plot for a moment as love for Christabel and longing for the mother rise up in her, she collects herself by flinging off the latter ("Off, wandering mother!" [l. 205]). In each case, a feminine body comes to represent a threat to the wishfully autonomous self. "Christabel," with its punning allusions to "the mother," invites us to speculate that the "law" of gender, which legislates the systematic exclusion of feminine forms, is connected to the experience of maternal attention. In this view, representations of feminine bodies as sites of non-self-identity all take revenge on the maternal body, which, in its historical role as the first "worker of harms," is the agent through which identity is constituted on a split. The mother "wounds" with her love, constituting the subject as originally, irreducibly divided, marked by the meanings and desires of the Other.

This reading, however, may play into the hands of the patriarchs. Historically, they have used maternity to ground a question of origins; they have used gender to naturalize what is in fact a function of genre—of constructs which are only meaningful within an already-originated cultural order. To suggest that misogyny can be traced to experience of the mother, to attribute it to blind revenge for the subject's condition, is to give it a sort of tragic weight. It's also to forget the tone of "Christabel." The urbane ironist and even the apparently less controlled patriarch of that poem suggest that the projects of culture are at once more political and more finessed than what we've just described. The Baron's exclusion and readmission of women amounts to a kind of play. He guards his fantasied autonomy by opening out spaces between—between bodies, genders, generations. He lives in a deathly, "dreary" world, until his "dream" of radically split women reanimates it with desire. With the appearance of Geraldine, the threat of abduction—a threat for every subject in discourse—can be rewritten, flirted with, in dreams of seduction which repeat, at a safe distance, the "confusions" of first love. That night, a fantasized feminine body—single yet double, like the mother's when pregnant with child, or the hysteric's when inhabited by the vaporish conceptions of an origin which is never *her* origin—performs exchanges with another body like her own. These women figure but only imperfectly contain impropriety, allowing its threats and attractions to return to the Baron's world as a taint. Geraldine moves from Christabel's bed to his arms, supplanting the daughter who had supplanted the mother; for a moment, she produces in him the illusion that one can "forget . . . age" (l. 431) and all that has intervened, and recapture the fantasied past, when exchanges traversed the laws of self-identity and even the laws of gender.

V

Coleridge, who capitalizes on the potential of feminine bodies to eroticize masculine discourse, is himself a pseudopolitician; at the same time, like the hysteric he seems to counter the Law. Drawing together matters of form and desire, his discussion of meter in the Preface to "Christabel" nicely illustrates this double relation to the symbolic order. On the one hand, the principle the author lays down is strikingly consonant with the Baron's tolling "custom and law":

> I have only to add that the metre of Christabel is not, properly speaking, irregular, though it may seem so from its being founded on a new principle: namely, that of counting in each line the accents, not the syllables. Though the latter may vary from seven to twelve, yet in each line the accents will be found to be only four. Nevertheless, this occasional variation in number of syllables is not introduced wantonly, or for the mere ends of convenience, but in correspondence with some transition in the nature of the imagery or passion.

"Christabel's" metrics are figured in the poem as the ringing of the Baron's clock and matin bell. Coleridge's "principle," however, is designed to accommodate, not just the Baron, who would institute unvarying repetition, but also the movement of desire, "transition[s] in the nature of the imagery or passion."

Coleridge's meter, or more broadly, his joking treatment of gender and genre, can thus be seen as a compromise between the Law's reificatory strategies and the potentially wanton, disruptive liveliness of passion—a compromise which ultimately benefits the ironist who acquiesces to the laws he also exposes as interested. Yet Coleridge's play, which mocks the law of gender/genre by too faithfully reinscribing its conventions, also opens up the possibility of a more radical collapse between the positions of patriarch, hysteric, and ironist: it exposes the wantonness of the Law, and allows one to discover the laws of desire; it suggests that the Law itself may be inseparable from the operations of desire. When Bracy the Bard hears the Baron's deathly matin bell, he declares, "So let it knell!"—

> There is no lack of such, I ween,
> As well fill up the space between.
> In Langdale Pike and Witch's Lair,
> And Dungeon-ghyll so foully rent,
> With ropes of rock and bells of air
> Three sinful sextons' ghosts are pent,
> Who all give back, one after t'other,
> The death-note to their living brother;
> And oft too, by the knell offended,
> Just as their one! two! three! is ended,
> The devil mocks the doleful tale
> With a merry peal from Borodale.
>
> (ll. 348-59)

Bracy's accession echoes Christabel's words at the end of Part 1, when she announces her obedience to Geraldine's request: "So let it be!" (l. 235). Bracy is in league with the hysteric, and Coleridge with them all—and all submit to the Law. When Christabel steals into her father's house with Geraldine, we "cannot tell" if her silence is the absolute solicitude of a dutiful daughter or a sign of subversive intent: does hysteria come from too much or too little respect for the father? In a sense it doesn't matter, since the effects are the same for the Baron and us: her very unreadability draws out and mocks his and our possessing desire to decide meaning. Her strategy resembles Bracy's—apparently without doing anything himself, he simply "lets" the law mock its own voice. It echoes through hollow, rent spaces, which in dutifully returning its knell, elude its efforts to control the significance of an event. "Telling" notes become the occasion of ghostly echoes, which in turn generate Bracy's lively ghost stories; finally, as if by way of commentary, the "devil" makes merry mockery of the whole phenomenon. The passage describes in little the narrative tactics of "Christabel." By too-dutiful accession to the laws of gender and genre, "Christabel" exposes their strategies to view, letting the Law subvert itself.

Notes

[1] Quotations from "Christabel" and its preface are taken from *Coleridge's Poetical Works,* ed. Ernest Hartley Coleridge (1912; rpt. Oxford: Oxford U. Press, 1969).

[2] See Susan Luther, "'Christabel' as Dream Reverie," *Romantic Reassessments* 61, ed. Dr. James Hogg (Salzburg: Institut fur Englische Sprache und Literatur, Univ. Salzburg A5020, 1976), for the argument that Christabel is a reader of romances.

[3] "'Christabel'" (1955), rpt. in *The Ancient Mariner and Other Poems: A Casebook,* eds. Alun R. Jones and William Tydemann (London and Basingstoke: Macmillan, 1973), p. 235; *The Waking Dream: A Study of Coleridge's Poetry* (London: Edward Arnold, 1967), p. 146.

[4] *The Anatomy of Melancholy,* ed. Holbrook Jackson (New York: Random House-Vintage Books, 1977), p. 416. Future references to this edition appear in the text.

[5] In "Sir Cauline," the ballad from which Coleridge took the name Christabel, this is the case; that Christabel's lover is dismissed by her father.

[6] See for example Roy Basler, *Sex, Symbolism, and Psychology in Literature* (New Brunswick: Rutgers U. Press, 1948), p. 41; Gerald Enscoe, *Eros and the Romantics* (The Hague and Paris: Mouton, 1967), pp. 44-45; Jonas Spatz, "The Mystery of Eros: Sexual Initiation in Coleridge's 'Christabel,'" *PMLA* 90 (1975), 112-13; Barbara A. Schapiro, *The Romantic Mother: Narcissistic Patterns in Romantic Poetry* (Baltimore and London: Johns Hopkins U. Press, 1983), 61-85.

[7] See for example Enscoe, p. 43; John Beer, *Coleridge's Poetic Intelligence* (London and Basingstoke: Macmillan, 1977), p. 187; and H. W. Piper, "The Disunity of *Christabel* and the Fall of Nature," *Essays in Criticism* 28 (1978), 216-27.

[8] Or so Freud claims in *Jokes and their Relation to the Unconscious,* chapter VI ("Jokes, Dreams, and the Unconscious"), trans. James Strachey (New York: Norton, 1963), pp. 159-80.

[9] For examples of the reviews, see *The Romantic Reviewed,* ed. Donald H. Reiman (New York and London: Garland, 1977), II, 666, 239. Modern critics sometimes notice tonal or generic instability as "falls" into Gothic trickery, into caricature of the Gothic, or into sentimentality; see for example Max Schulz, *The Poetic Voices of Coleridge* (Detroit: Wayne State U. Press, 1963), pp. 66-71; and Paul Edwards and MacDonald Emslie, "'Thoughts all so unlike each other': The Paradoxical in *Christabel,*" *English Studies* 52 (1971), 328.

The latter suggest these discrepancies are intended to shock.

[10] *Romantics Reviewed* I, 23.

[11] *Romantics Reviewed* I, 373; II, 866; II, 531. I discuss these reviews more fully in my essay "Literary Gentlemen and Lovely Ladies: The Debate on the Character of 'Christabel,'" forthcoming in *ELH.*

[12] *Romantics Reviewed* II, 531.

[13] *Collected Letters of Samuel Taylor Coleridge,* ed. Earl Leslie Griggs (Oxford: Clarendon Press, 1956-71), III, 435.

[14] See for example Abe Delson, "The Function of Geraldine in *Christabel:* A Critical Perspective and Interpretation," *English Studies* 61 (1980), 130-41; and Enscoe, p. 46.

[15] My understanding of fantasy here follows that of Jean Laplanche and J.-B Pontalis in their "Fantasy and the Origins of Sexuality," *International Journal of Psycho-Analysis* 49 (1968), 1-18.

[16] My argument here is indebted to Richard Rand's discussion of the ubiquitous "mark" in "Geraldine," *Glyph* 3 (1978), 74-97.

Alan J. Bewell (essay date 1986)

SOURCE: "A 'Word Scarce Said': Hysteria and Witchcraft in Wordsworth's 'Experimental' Poetry of 1797-1798," in *ELH,* Vol. 53, No. 2, Summer, 1986, pp. 357-90.

[*In the excerpt that follows, Bewell discusses Wordsworth's use of the hysteric and her roots in the figure of the witch to examine the connection between language and the creative imagination.*]

> Old Susan, she who dwells alone,
> Is sick, and makes a piteous moan,
> As if her very life would fail.
>
> There's not a house within a mile,
> No hand to help them in distress;
> Old Susan lies a-bed in pain,
> And sorely puzzled are the twain,
> For what she ails they cannot guess.[1]

Susan Gale's strange disease and unusual cure have received little critical attention from readers of "The Idiot Boy"—so little, in fact, that no one has felt it worth clarifying what her illness actually is. The doctor never arrives to give a diagnosis, so descriptions of her sickness, from Southey's term "indisposed" to John

Danby's "imaginary illness" and "psychological bed-riddenness," have been decidedly vague.[2] For most readers, her illness is psychosomatic, of relative unimportance, except as a comic device that occasions Johnny's mock epic quest. Like Betty Foy's terrors, Susan's disease would seem but another instance of the work of "Female Wit," creating "mighty Contests" from "trivial Things" (*Rape of the Lock*). Nevertheless, in the 1800 preface to *Lyrical Ballads,* speaking of both "The Idiot Boy" and "The Mad Mother," Wordsworth places the female imagination at the center of these poems when he states that they trace "the maternal passion through many of its more subtle windings" (*PW* 2:388n).

It is not by chance that Susan, like many of the other women that will interest Wordsworth during this time, is described as "she who dwells alone" (19). In Wordsworth's reference to "maternal passion" (which is, as he later notes, either "connubial or parental")[3] and its "subtle windings," one can discern the figural survival of the traditional medical discourse on hysteria. For centuries, in highly metaphoric descriptions of female physiology, medicine had explained the disease in terms of "unnatural states" of the womb—the hungry up-and-down wanderings and complicated windings of the uterus, or the poisonous and corrupt "vapors" rising from a diseased womb.[4] Hysteria (or the Mother, the Incubus, spleen, vapors) was usually accompanied by a sensation of "suffocation," pressure felt on the chest or a choking feeling in the throat. But it was known also for its mimetic powers, its protean mimicry of other diseases. "The shapes of *Proteus,* or the colours of the *chameleon,* are not more numerous and inconstant, than the variations of the hypochondriac and hysteric disease," writes the Edinburgh doctor Robert Whytt.[5] Significantly, the imagination was rarely absent from these discussions. As Edward Jorden, who reintroduced the ancient notion of hysteria as a sex-linked disease, writes: "we doe observe that most commonly besides the indisposition of the bodie: there is also some melancholike or capricious conceit . . . which being . . . removed the disease is easily overcome."[6] As neurology supplanted humoral psychology in the seventeenth century, the uterus came less frequently to be mentioned in connection with hysteria, but the imagination retained (in fact, gained in) its importance. Now physicians began citing the strange and powerful effects of a combination of passions and strong imagination upon the body and weak nerves, a condition to which women were particularly prone. "Women are more subject than Men to Diseases arising from the Passions of the Mind," writes the Italian physician Georgi Baglivi, "and more violently affected with them, by Reason of the Timorousness and Weakness of their Sex." Treatment consists, therefore, in seeking to reduce "the disorderly Motions of the Imagination [the "subtle windings" of the "maternal passion"] to their Primitive Regularity."[7]

This link between hysteria and the imagination, as well as its fashionable popularity among the wealthy, led to its being a frequent object of satire throughout the eighteenth century. "Vapourish people are perpetual subjects for diseases to work upon," remarks Robert Lovelace in *Clarissa.* "*Name* but the malady, and it is *theirs* in a moment." Susan's psychosomatic illness is not removed, therefore, from a context of satire. Her most notable and strangest antecedents appear in Pope's catalogue "Of Bodies chang'd to various Forms" by the "*Hysteric* or *Poetic* Fit":

> Here living *Teapots* stand, one Arm held out,
> One bent; the Handle this, and that the Spout:
> A Pipkin there like *Homer's Tripod* walks;
> Here sighs a Jar, and there a Goose-pye talks;
> Men prove with Child, as pow'rful Fancy works,
> And Maids turn'd Bottels, call aloud for Corks.
>
> (*The Rape of the Lock* 4.48, 60, 49-54)

In a society that accorded the female imagination extraordinary powers, it is not surprising that Pope would focus upon its modes and workings, deified by Belinda, to criticize the misuse of the imagination he saw pervading Augustan England. Yet if hysteria was a popular object of satire, among doctors and philosophers, who saw in "the strange and wonderful phenomena of hysteria"[8] a profound and disturbing proof of the body's compliance with the promptings, demands, and intentions of the imagination, the disease remained a subject of considerable interest. Hysteria had become an exemplary *disease of the imagination*. Through the observation of women afflicted by it, the amazing powers of the imagination and bodily imitation were made visible to the eye, not as abstract principles, but as forces, "monstrous and terrible to beholde,"[9] seen palpably operating on women's bodies, behavior, and speech.

Though eighteenth-century medicine was primarily mechanistic in orientation, its increasing interest in psychopathology brought aspects of it into close proximity with poetics. As L. J. Rather has observed, physicians commonly ascribed (partly because of inadequate physiological knowledge) "as much or more in the way of bodily change to the emotions or 'power of the imagination' than would all but the most convinced proponents of the psychological causation of disease today."[10] In describing the various "diseases of the imagination," their force and effects, their causes and cures, medicine developed a complex and extensive discourse on the imagination, and on suggestion, association, sympathy, and imitation. "It appears almost incredible," Peter Shaw writes in *The Reflector* (1750), "what great Effects the Imagination has upon Patients."[11] Medical discourse was rich in spectacular accounts of individuals possessed by their imaginations, and these cases gave to its discussions of the imaginations, a strangeness, vivacity, and concreteness that exercised a profound, if rarely acknowledged, influence on philosophy and literature. Where the modern doctor sees a tubercular condition, the eighteenth-century doctor saw the wasting power of melancholy and nostalgia.[12] In the obsessive ravings of madmen, the fits of epileptics, the convulsions of religious enthusiasts, the rage of the hydrophobic, but most of all in the strange bodily afflictions occasioned by melancholy, spleen, or hysteria, physicians set aside physical causes and diagnosed the sublime and threatening presence of a diseased imagination.

It is this horizon of inquiry, I believe, rather than a misogynistic desire to satirize spinsters, that underlies Susan Gale's appearance in "The Idiot Boy." The medical and philosophical discourse that made hysterical women victims of the workings of a powerful imagination also made them a key for unlocking the mysteries of "a mind beset / With images, and haunted by itself" (1805 *Prelude* 6.179-80). Just as Freud, a century later, turned to "hysterical women" as a scientific point of departure for psychoanalysis, Wordsworth also found in these women a medium of speculative argument, a means for observing and forcefully delineating, as he notes in connection with *Lyrical Ballads,* the manner in which "language and the human mind act and react on each other" (*PW* 2:385). In seeking a language to describe and understand his own imagination, Wordsworth turned to a certain kind of discourse—to medicine—and to a certain figure that inhabited it, the "hysterical woman."

It should be equally stressed, however, that even though medical discourse, as I intend to show, fostered and authorized to a large degree his decision to use descriptions of these women as a vehicle of aesthetic inquiry, Wordsworth appears to have been equally intent on comically deflating its importance in the poem. The episode can thus be seen as paradigmatic of the ambiguous way in which Wordsworth's "experimental" poems are linked to contemporary medicine, for it simultaneously draws upon and conceals the modes of inquiry and concerns that initially sponsored it. Simultaneously engaged in taking up and displacing their philosophical preconditions and theoretical purposes, they have the uncanny status of being demonstrations in what remains an implied, absent, or submerged framework of speculation.

The paradox of Wordsworthian observation is that his eye is attracted to specific kinds of marginal individuals for reasons that his poetry will not admit. In examining his representation of hysterical women, then, we are in the difficult position of needing to read his poetry against the grain, asking questions and reconstructing operant discourses that the poems were written to counteract or make irrelevant. Yet by recovering this language, we will be able to recognize the revaluation of, and strategical distancing from, these women and the medical discourse that first represented them.

I

Wordsworth was writing at a time when a knowledge of medicine was understood as a prerequisite for empirical speculation. G. S. Rousseau points out that Locke's *Essay,* by combining ethics and physiology, placed medical theory at the center of philosophical debate until the end of the eighteenth century.[13] In fact, as Hans-Jürgen Schings has shown, the "philosophical doctor" became, during this period, a popular literary type.[14] Given the importance of the natural sciences and medicine within philosophy, it is not surprising that Coleridge and Wordsworth decided in 1798 to visit Germany, where Coleridge met Johann Friedrich Blumenbach, the famous anthropologist and comparative anatomist, and Wordsworth sought to furnish himself "with a tolerable stock of information in natural science" (*EY,* 213). Nor is it surprising that in late February or early March, 1798, the poet, seeking material for *The Recluse,* his "philosophic poem" on "nature, man, and society," would have turned to Erasmus Darwin's *Zoönomia.* At the very beginning of the period in which *Peter Bell* and *Lyrical Ballads* were conceived and written, Wordsworth urges the printer Joseph Cottle to send him this encyclopedic medical treatise *"by the first carrier"* (*EY,* 199; author's emphasis). Though approximately two weeks later, Dorothy writes that these volumes have answered Wordsworth's purpose in writing for them, it was not until May 9th that they were returned (*EY,* 214-15, 218).

Zoönomia was of major importance to the experimentalism of *Lyrical Ballads.* As James Averill has argued, the poet drew from *Zoönomia* the associationist theory of perception that earlier critics, such as Arthur Beatty, attributed to David Hartley.[15] More significantly, however, he found within its pages a demonstration of the speculative uses of the "case history." Arranged under classificatory headings, often amounting to little more than an anecdote, a few words, or a short paragraph, the case histories that form so large a part of *Zoönomia* are more than just examples or illustrations. They play an integral role in Darwin's speculations on human nature, and represent, as legal cases do in law, a basic figural medium of empirical argumentation, the place where philosophical hypotheses were tested on the bodies and minds of the observed. In the "case history" Wordsworth found a mode of writing that could be adapted to poetic as well as philosophical argument, one well suited for the observation, dramatic display, and interpretation of the workings of the imagination. Yet, it should be recognized, he was also aware of its shortcomings. In connection with George Crabbe's poetry, Wordsworth writes that "the Muses

William Wordsworth (1770-1850).

And Susan now begins to fear
Of sad mischances not a few,
That Johnny may perhaps be drowned;
Or lost, perhaps, and never found;
Which they must both for ever rue.

(177-81)

"Present fears are less than horrible imaginings" (*Macbeth* 1.3.136), and Susan, in ignorance of what is happening to Johnny, imagines the direst of situations:

Long time lay Susan lost in thought;
And many dreadful fears beset her,
Both for her Messenger and Nurse;
And, as her mind grew worse and worse,
Her body—it grew better.

She turned, she tossed herself in bed,
On all sides doubts and terrors met her;
Point after point did she discuss;
And, while her mind was fighting thus,
Her body still grew better.

"Alas! what is become of them?
These fears can never be endured;
I'll to the wood."—The word scarce said,
Did Susan rise up from her bed,
As if by magic cured.

(412-26)

have just about as much to do [with 'mere matters of fact'] as they have with a Collection of medical reports, or of Law cases" (*MY* 1:268). Though the medical and philosophical case history provided Wordsworth with a vocabulary for taking up poetic, moral, and philosophical concerns, it was a discursive form that could not enter poetry directly, without substantial revaluation.

The very fact that no critic has felt called upon to ask what illness Susan Gale suffers from is a gauge to Wordsworth's success in transforming the case history. Just as his representation of Johnny in the poem redefines popular and medical conceptions of idiocy, Wordsworth replaces the objectivity and detachment claimed by the case history with the observations of a comic narrator, and asks the reader to laugh, yet sympathize fully, with Susan's dilemma. Her sickness is at once a neighborhood calling card and a symptom of a lonely spinster's need for love (both sexual and social). Simultaneously, her therapy reflects the concerns that made the observation of hysterical or melancholic women a staging ground for a broader inquiry into the powers of imagination and poetic language. It begins early in the poem, shortly after Betty leaves in search of her son:

Within this imaginative psychotherapy, mental terror is substituted for bodily pains: the "dreadful fears" and "doubts and terrors" conjured by Susan's imagination replace the pains of hysteria.[16] The logic of this transference, central to Wordsworthian poetics, is partly explained by Edmund Burke, who argues that pain and fear have a common physiological basis and "act upon the same parts of the body, and in the same manner, though somewhat differing in degree. . . . The only difference between pain and terror, is, that things which cause pain operate on the mind, by the intervention of the body; whereas things which cause terror generally affect the bodily organs by the operation of the mind suggesting the danger."[17] Yet in Susan's case this metaphoric displacement is not based, as Burke argues, on a physiological mechanism, but instead on the fact that pain and terror represent alternate modes of imaginative activity. Therapy consists in a rechanneling of the imagination so that instead of speaking unconsciously, in bodily symptoms and physical pain, the imagination finds expression in images and symbols. The poet's task, akin to the psychoanalyst's, is that of alleviating physical suffering by providing the imagination with language. Not surprisingly, it finds its conclusion in a "word scarce said," whereupon Susan rises "As if by magic cured."

The narrator's declaration that this cure works like "magic" requires that another facet of the history of hysteria be addressed: its intimate connection with witchcraft. Though Betty Foy and Susan Gale never *say* what they believe to be the cause of this lonely woman's illness, instead remaining "sorely puzzled" (25) by her pains, we need not doubt that they are convinced she is bewitched. In a world still enchanted by "goblins," "ghosts," and "wandering gypsy-folk" (226-30) who threaten to steal straying children, the lack of a natural explanation or remedy for a disease has the status of a diagnosis of its supernatural causes. Because these women "cannot guess" the natural causes of Susan's illness, they cannot conceive of a natural remedy. Susan's piteous "There's nothing that can ease my pain" (198) thus stands as an oblique assertion of witchcraft. Wordsworth's interest in such a case is in keeping with both the experimentalism of the poem and its parody and revaluation of the "supernatural ballad," popularized during the 1790s by William Taylor's translations of Gottfried Bürger's "Lenore" and "Des Pfarrers Tochter von Taubenhain." The villagers' reluctance to verbalize their suspicions does not indicate an absence of witchcraft, but instead reflects the deep-felt anxiety about the performative powers of words that is characteristic of societies in which magic is practiced. When words can wound and cure and are no sooner said than they become realities, speech is not used lightly and some things are best left unsaid. Betty can sit for hours in a "sad *quandary,*" because "there's *nobody to say* / If she must go, or she must stay!" (168-70; my emphasis). But "at the first word that Susan said" (184), her mind is made up and she is off in search for her son, partly to prevent Susan from finishing her sentence "'God forbid it should be true!'" (183). In like manner, Susan can deliberate "Point after point," attempting to rationalize the doubts and terrors meeting her "On all sides," but it is not until she declares, "'I'll to the wood,'" that she is able to "rise up from her bed, / As if by magic cured." Betty and Susan consider her cure a miracle, cause for as "merry meeting / As ever was in Christendom" (430-31). However, readers are also provided with the alternative, hinted at by a "somewhat grim" (259) country doctor's presence, of viewing the case in naturalistic terms as a demonstration of the psychology of magic.

Historically, hysteria played a major role in the demystification of witchcraft. In fact, one of the first major advances of modern psychiatry came through its transformation of the witch and her victim into melancholy or hysterical women. By so doing, instances of witchcraft became the proper concern of physicians, rather than judges or theologians, and the witch entered into "case histories" as part of the empirical discourse on the imagination. Significantly, Edward Jorden reintroduced the concept of hysteria after attending the 1602 trial of Elizabeth Jackson for having bewitched Mary Glover. *A briefe discourse on the Suffocation of the mother,* written to counter the influence of King James's *Daemonologie,* aimed to show that cases of demonic possession were really attributable to the "varietie" and "strangenesse" of the symptoms of hysteria.[18] The work was indebted to Reginald Scot's *The Discoverie of Witchcraft,* which argued that the belief in witchcraft ultimately has its source in the strong and confused imaginations of melancholy women, often brought on by menopause. "This strong imagination, with this strange event," John Cotta argues in 1612, "have intangled many a poore spinster in a thicker string then her cunning could untwist, to save the cracking of her neck."[19] In his *The Displaying of Supposed Witchcraft* (1677), John Webster complains of the superstitious beliefs of the villagers in Northern England, thus providing a context for our understanding of "The Idiot Boy": "In all its parts in the North of *England,* where Ignorance, Popery, and superstition doth much abound, the common people, if they chance to have any sort of the Epilepsie, Palsie, Convulsions or the like, do presently perswade themselves that they are bewitched, fore-spoken, blasted, fairy-taken, or haunted with some evil spirit, and the like." Where Betty and Susan see witchcraft, Webster sees a "depraved and prepossessed imagination."[20]

This association (even interchangeability) between witchcraft and hysteria, one that foregrounds the powers of a strong imagination, is of central importance to Wordsworth's 1797-1798 representation of witches in "The Three Graves," "The Mad Mother," "Goody Blake and Harry Gill," and "The Thorn." In these poems isolated or abandoned women come to serve as the empirical medium for recovering origins, subjects of a study of the original workings of the imagination and its power to produce such weird forms of delirium and bodily symptoms that they might appear to be "under the dominion of spells."[21]

II

Though the sphere of supernatural agency was certainly diminished by the transformation of the witch into a hysterical woman, the realm of the imaginary was greatly expanded. No longer primarily an object of theological speculation or superstition, the witch could become part of empirical inquiries into the powers of the imagination. It is in this ambiguous form, as a figure inhabiting a liminal zone between supernaturalism and medical discourse, that the witch enters Wordsworth's poetry. In the fragmentary "Three Graves," which Wordsworth began in 1797 and Coleridge later took up in 1798, the manner in which psychopathology and poetics converged on the witch/hysteric is clear.

In his note to the poem Coleridge indicates the critical interest in the connections between psychopathology and witchcraft that gave rise to it. Based on an actual incident, "positive facts, and of no very distant date," the poem would have provided "a striking proof of the possible effect on the imagination, from an idea violently and suddenly impressed on it." It would have followed, he declares, "the progress and symptoms of the morbid action on the fancy" in three women, each recognizably prone to hysteria—a lonely widow "bordering on her fortieth year"[22]; her daughter Mary, a "barren wife"; and Ellen, a "maid forlorn."[23] Even Edward, who is the object of their rivalry, falls victim to hysteria. His surprise upon hearing the widow's proposal of marriage, Coleridge tells us, combined with "the effect of horror he felt, acting as it were hysterically on his nervous system," makes him fling "her from him and burst into a fit of laughter." Wordsworth writes that the rejected widow, furious, frustrated, and embarrassed, falls to her knees and, resorting to witchcraft, curses both her daughter and future son-in-law, angrily taunting them:

> "I am a woman weak and old,
>   Why turn a thought on me?
>
> What can an aged mother do,
>   And what have ye to dread?
> A curse is wind, it hath no shape
> To haunt your marriage-bed."
>
> (WW, 196-201)

As in the case of Susan, Wordsworth uses such situations to foreground the performative powers of language. "A curse is wind"; a word is as transitory as breath; it has "no shape," no substance. Yet the mother knows that her words can invoke spirits, the earthly "Spirits of the Mind" (*Peter Bell*) and imagination.

There is no reason to doubt Coleridge's claim for the poem's factuality. As Pierre Bayle observes, cases where newlyweds came to believe that their marriage-bed was bewitched were quite common at this time:

> I could not restrain myself from making you recall something which is without doubt very common in your Province, and which visibly demonstrates what the imagination can accomplish. Several men are unable to consummate their marriage, and believe that this impotence is the effect of a spell. From then on, the newlyweds regard each other with an evil eye, and their discord descends sometimes into a most horrible enmity: the sight of one makes the other shiver. What I tell you here are not old wive's tales, but certain and incontestable facts which only too often come into the sight and ken of all the neighbours in the provinces, where much faith is put in the traditions of witchcraft.[24]

Bayle demystifies witchcraft, telling us that these superstitions supply us with a visible demonstration of "what the imagination can accomplish." "An imagination that is alarmed by the fear of a witch's spell," he writes, "can overthrow the animal economy and produce those extravagant symptoms that exasperate the most expert medical doctors."[25] Initially functioning as explanations and excuses for "impotence," these beliefs lead inevitably to suspicion, "discord," and, finally, "most horrible enmity" between the newlyweds; the imagination invests the "evil eye" with real power and "the sight of one makes the other shiver."

It appears that "The Three Graves" would have recounted a similar train of events, as understood by a superstitious, seventy-year old sexton, in which the young couple's belief in the marriage-bed curse prevents them from having sexual relations (she remains a "barren wife") and progressively leads to mutual enmity. Upon first hearing the curse, writes Wordsworth, Mary believes that "the bed beneath her stirred" (WW, 157). And Coleridge, aware (perhaps from his reading in Bayle) that "the common opinion is that witches visit this evil service upon newlyweds by pronouncing certain words during the nuptial benediction,"[26] describes how she imagines her mother cursing her "when the Vicar join'd their hands":

> Her limbs did creep and freeze:
> And when they prayed, she thought she saw
> Her mother on her knees.
>
> (240-43)

When Mary leaves the church, just as her feet touch the "mossy track" (a symbol that will reappear in "The Thorn"), she falls victim to hysteria, the Suffocation of the mother:

> The shade o'er-flushed her limbs with heat—
>   Then came a chill like death:
> And when the merry bells rang out,
>   *They seemed to stop her breath.*
>
> (251-55, my emphasis)

Though the subsequent "progress . . . of the morbid action" on Mary's imagination remains incomplete, Ellen's case, also fragmentary, is similar and provides more clues concerning the direction the poem would have taken.

It is of the essence of the mother's curse, itself expressive of a love born from her having "fed upon the sight" of the young lovers' "'course of wooing'" (WW, 56, 52), that the young couple should also find itself repeating the original love triangle.[27] Ellen, "at whose house / Young Edward woo'd his wife" (316-17), falls mimetically in love with Edward and, after also being cursed by the mother, becomes a rival lover. "They clung round him [Edward] with their arms," Coleridge writes, "Both Ellen and his wife" (379-80), the latter now reduced to a common noun. And when Edward cries,

> Ellen did not weep at all,
> But closelier did she cling,

And turned her face and looked as if
She saw some frightful thing.

(385-88)

We later discover that this "frightful thing" that Ellen imagines clinging "on his breast" is Mary, who, in her imagination, has become a diabolical double of the mother:

And with a kind of shriek she cried.
"Oh Christ! you're like your mother!"

(446-47)

This doubling is essential to the working out of Edward's curse, for symbolically Edward *does* marry "the mother," as is clear in his reference to Mary in his nightmare—"A mother too!" (522). The progress of Ellen's hysteria is fragmentary: the curse appears to have produced a "sore grief . . . haunting in her brain" (428-29), she grows "thin" (430), and suffers from "convulsion" (437). However, in an isolated fragment, written by Wordsworth, we are given at once an extraordinary representation of madness and Wordsworth's most explicit representation of a case of bodily possession. Ellen's body becomes the stage for melancholy's appearance as nightmarish spectacle:

And she was pinched and pricked with pins,
And twitched with cord and wire;
And starting from her seat would cry,
"It is a stool of fire."
And she would bare her maiden breast,
And if you looked would shew
The milk which clinging imps of hell
And sucking daemons drew.

(WW, 205-13)

Ellen's morbid extravagance, her belief that she is being "pinched and pricked with pins" and her display of milk flowing from her "maiden breast," evokes the histrionics of the witch-trials, where legal and medical cases converged as women's bodies took central stage as evidence in judicial proceedings. As if her breasts were "witches teats," those insensible protruberances where the witch fed her familiars, discovered by pricking the body "with pins," Ellen displays what she takes to be the *indicia* of possession. It is easy, perhaps, to dismiss the possibility that Ellen is diabolically possessed, but the possibility that her breasts actually do give milk nevertheless poses a problem. If there is, indeed, lactation, it is either a symptom of her desire to be a mother, and thus an illustration of the powerful workings of the imagination, or possibly, since we lack the intervening narrative, an indication that she has indeed become one, her madness arising, perhaps, because she has been abandoned by her lover (Edward?) or has lost her child. Though either interpretation is possible, the ambiguity is not without significance, for we will see this problematic interpretive framework repeated in "The Mad Mother" and "The Thorn."

III

Though Wordsworth's reasons for abandoning "The Three Graves" early in 1798 (when Coleridge began composition of the poem) are not clear, his later criticism that it was "too shocking and painful, and not sufficiently sweetened by any healing views" (*PW* 1:374), suggests that he was dissatisfied with the way that it addressed the relationship of medicine and poetry, in its representation of individuals possessed by their imaginations. Significantly, at the same time, he began composition of three other witchcraft poems— "Goody Blake and Harry Gill," "The Mad Mother," and "The Thorn." It appears likely that each represents an attempt to solve the problem posed by the failure of the earlier poem—that of rejecting the detached language of the case history without relinquishing the ability to take up the speculative questions, relating to the imagination, that had found their locus in descriptions of witch/hysterics. Wordsworth's answer, especially in the later witchcraft poems, is to deny the dispassionate neutrality of the observer, by showing that such "cases" tell as much about the anxieties and emotions of those who narrate them as they do about their subjects.

"Goody Blake and Harry Gill," a "True Story" (as the subtitle indicates) of a farmer in Warwickshire falling victim to witchcraft, is one of the first of the poems written for *Lyrical Ballads*. Drawn almost verbatim from the copy of *Zoönomia* that Wordsworth borrowed from Cottle in early March, from the section dealing with *mania mutabilis*, it is the least successful of these poems in distancing itself from medical discourse, for its proximity to the medical case history is apparent. It should be recognized that a case history is not a simple narrative or description, but has, because of its inclusion of an explicit hermeneutical aspect, a twofold structure: the systematic elaboration of categories, the theoretical headings, the generalized descriptions of diseases, and the speculative introductions and conclusions to the case histories that make up *Zoönomia* are not extrinsic or separate from them, but instead are the interpretive framework within which each case is to be read. In many of the experimental poems one sees a severance of these two parts and an excision of the theoretical framework; their philosophical purposes are intentionally left undefined, giving them the character of illustrations to unknown or absent texts. Perhaps recognizing the difficult demands thereby placed upon his readers to supply their necessary reflective context, in the 1800 preface to *Lyrical Ballads* Wordsworth supplied short statements of their speculative concerns. In connection with "Goody Blake and Harry Gill," he writes that he "wished to draw attention to the truth that the power of the human imagination is sufficient to produce such changes even in our physical nature as might almost appear miraculous. The truth is an important one; the fact (for it is a *fact*) is a valuable illustration of it" (*PW* 2:401n). Though the poem retains the objective narrational mode of the case history, it uses psychopathology as a key to demonstrate the power of the imagination to shape and organize even bodily processes: it examines the psychical construction of a witch—the process whereby old women are made into witches by the imaginations of their accusers—and the fearsome power, especially the power of language, arising from this fiction.

Harry, a "lusty drover" (17), has long suspected that the old weaver Goody Blake has been pilfering kindling from his hedge over the course of the winter. He decides, therefore, to catch her in the act. On a particularly cold night, after lying in wait for her behind a barley rick, he hears her busily filling her apron with twigs and, almost like a predatory animal, "springs" on her and "fiercely" (91) grabs and shakes her, crying" 'I've caught you then at last!'" (92). There is little attempt to suppress the implied sexual aggression; Harry, like Peter Bell, takes pleasure in unrestrained violence and uncontested possession. The old cottager, overcome by the ferocity of the attack, falls on her knees (like the mother in "The Three Graves"), and, as a last resort, "her withered arm uprearing" (97), prays that if Harry cannot sympathize with the coldness felt by others, he should feel it physically:

> "God! who art never out of hearing,
> O may he never more be warm!"
> The cold, cold moon above her head,
> Thus on her knees did Goody pray.
>
> (99-102)

Goody Blake may indeed believe her words summon up divine powers (even the victims of social ostracism make whatever use they can of a stereotype). But it is clear that they function without "the intervention of supernatural agency" (*PW* 2:331), beneath a bare and vacant heaven, its only inhabitant the "cold, cold moon." They depend instead upon the imagination of her *human* auditor. Harry "heard what she had said / And icy cold he turned away" (103-4).

Harry falls victim to a self-made fiction. "Old and poor" (21), "housed alone" (36), living outside the village "on a hill's northern side" (30), a nocturnal creature whose crimes, even though petty, take place at night, Goody Blake easily fits the traditional stereotype of the witch. Darwin even says she looks "like a witch in a play," and Southey, in his review of *Lyrical Ballads,* thought that the poem was likely to "promote the popular superstition of witchcraft."[28] All that is needed, therefore, is for her "prayer" to follow the conventional pattern of admonitory magic for Harry to be convinced that it is his luck to have stumbled onto a witch and to be filled with icy horror. The resulting bizarre illness confirms his belief:

> 'Twas all in vain, a useless matter,
> And blankets were about him pinned;
> Yet still his jaws and teeth they clatter,
> Like a loose casement in the wind.
> And Harry's flesh it fell away;
> And all who see him say, 'tis plain,
> That, live as long as live he may,
> He never will be warm again.
>
> (113-20)

Harry's disease manifests a double relation. It is an *accusation,* and thus a projection of his own coldheartedness upon the old woman. Yet it is also a form of *punishment,* and thus reflects, at the level of his body, the inceptive stages of *conscience* and *guilt,* the sense that he has violated the primitive law of charity. As historians of witchcraft like Alan Macfarlane and Keith Thomas have suggested, witchcraft accusations reflected social ambivalence toward Christian charity. Joseph Addison makes a similar point: "When an old Woman begins to doat, and grow chargeable to a Parish, she is generally turned into a Witch, and fills the whole Country with extravagant Fancies, imaginary Distempers, and terrifying Dreams. In the mean time, the poor Wretch that is the innocent Occasion of so many Evils begins to be frighted at her self, and sometimes confesses secret Commerces and Familiarities that her Imagination forms in a delirius old Age. This frequently cuts off Charity from the greatest Objects of Compassion, and inspires People with a Malevolence towards those poor decrepid Parts of our Species, in whom Human Nature is defaced by Infirmity and Dotage."[29] Like Peter Bell's sympathy, guilt and charity seem to come from the outside, but are, in fact, products of the mind's terrified recoil from the sublime threat of its own projections and conjurations.

IV

"The Mad Mother," one of the most powerful and least understood poems of *Lyrical Ballads,* places extraordinary demands upon the reader, for in this poem Wordsworth not only displaces the interpretive framework of the "case history"—by using a deserted woman, insane through melancholy and loss, as a vehicle for examining the relationship between the imagination and passion—but also disrupts radically its narrative structure. The case history form hardly extends beyond the first stanza, which provides relevant biographical information:

> Her eyes are wild, her head is bare,
> The sun has burnt her coal-black hair;
> Her eyebrows have a rusty stain,
> And she came far from over the main.

She has a baby on her arm,
Or else she were alone:
And underneath the hay-stack warm,
And on the greenwood stone,
She talked and sung the woods among,
And it was in the English tongue.

(1-10)

At this point, instead of using the neutral, objective tone of reportage preferred by physicians, Wordsworth shifts to dramatic monologue and depicts the woman's madness from within—the woman's case history as *she* sees and understands it, a history not yet fully disentangled from delirium.[30] The resulting poem, as it moves ambiguously among the tense and conflicting emotions of love, anger, and fear, constitutes an extraordinary psychological portrait of the melancholy of the "witch."

The woman's monologue (dialogue?) is spoken in a rare moment of lucidity brought about by the child's suckling at her breast. As James H. Averill has noted, Wordsworth drew the idea of the child's power to alleviate insanity from *Zoönomia*, in which Darwin writes:

> Where the cause is of a temporary nature, as in puerperal insanity, there is reason to hope, that the disease will cease, when the bruises, or other painful sensations attending this state, are removed. In these cases the child should be brought frequently to the mother, and applied to her breast, if she will suffer it, and this *whether she at first attends to it or not: as by a few trials it frequently excites the storgé, or maternal affection, and removes the insanity, as I have witnessed.*"[31]

The possibility that an insane woman might not be conscious of the suckling child during the period when it is drawing her out of her delirium provides Wordsworth with the premise for an extraordinary excursion into madness. He focuses upon that moment when the child's face, transformed by the supernatural phantasms of the woman's mind, gives way to naturalized perception and to the woman's ecstatic joy in recognizing her child. Like someone just awakened from a dream, the woman remembers that moment when the face of the child suddenly appeared, displacing the fiendish faces of the creatures of her insanity:

> "A fire was once within my brain;
> And in my head a dull, dull pain;
> And fiendish faces, one, two, three,
> Hung at my breast, and pulled at me;
> But then there came a sight of joy;
> It came at once to do me good;
> I waked, and saw my little boy,
> My little boy of flesh and blood;
> Oh joy for me that sight to see!
> For he was here, and only he."

(21-30)

"My little boy, / My little boy," she exclaims, happy in seeing "that sight of joy," *her* child "of flesh and blood" suckling at her breast. But her joy in seeing "he . . . here, and only he" is also one in having escaped a supernatural nightmare, in which she was possessed, like Ellen of "The Three Graves," by the "fiendish faces" of incubi "hanging" and "pulling" at her breast. Significantly, in both her mad and lucid moments, it is her suckling child that she sees, yet in her madness its face goes unrecognized and is instead transformed into the horrific faces of diabolic imps.

Wordsworth is not depicting a case of possession, but instead a disease, the Incubus, or Nightmare, as it was often called. "Sleepers," Burton writes in the *Anatomy of Melancholy,* "by reason of humours, concours of vapours troubling the phantasy, imagine many times absurd & prodigious things, & in such as are troubled with Incubus, or witch-ridden (as we call it); if they lie on their backs, they suppose an old woman rides, & sits hard upon them, that they are almost stifled for want of breath, when there is nothing offends but a concours of bad humours, which trouble the phantasy."[32] Like Fuseli's reclining woman in *The Nightmare,* a popular painting that Wordsworth is likely to have known (if not through an engraving, through one of the many political parodies done of it during the 1780s and 1790s, for instance, those by T. Rowlandson, Robert Newton, and Temple Webb), the woman, "almost stifled for want of breath," has fallen victim to her "phantasy," and in her delirium (perhaps because of the weight of the child) has imagined that she was being ridden by the devil's incubi.[33] When the child's suckling and caresses have freed her from the Incubus, loosening "something at my chest," she is able to breathe once more:

> "Oh! press me with thy little hand;
> It loosens something at my chest;
> About that tight and deadly band
> I feel thy little fingers prest.
> The breeze I see is in the tree:
> It comes to cool my babe and me.

(35-40)

The child's love "cools" her "blood" and "brain" (32) (the breast/fire antithesis at work in the fragment on Ellen's hysteria) and makes possible her perception of "The breeze . . . in the tree" that "comes to cool my babe and me."

The willingness of witches to confess, Reginald Scot argued, is not evidence of guilt, but a sign of their melancholy imaginations: "the force which melancholie hath, and the effects that it worketh in the bodie of a man, or rather of a woman, are almost incredible. For as some of these melancholike persons imagine, they are witches and by witchcraft can worke woonders, and doo what they list: so doo other, troubled with this disease, imagine manie strange, incredible, and impossible things."[34] The mother's melancholy leads to a similar inability to distinguish what is real from what is unreal in her past, whether the "fiendish faces" of her delirium are *memories* (and she, a witch) or only *imaginings*. Given her tangled confusion about what constitutes her past, the existence of a child leads to a distressing problem. Who is its father? And how is she to establish its paternity? Seeking evidence of his parentage, whether her son is the offspring of a natural or infernal father, the woman anxiously scrutinizes his face, hoping to discover the image of the father. As she becomes progressively more sane, the child's face becomes increasingly human. She begins to sort out her past. "'I am thy father's wedded wife'" (72), she joyously affirms, as she remembers the "poor man" (78) who deserted her, their marriage, and "*his* sweet boy" (75, my emphasis), the issue of their union. However, just at the moment when she begins to hope to "live in honesty" (74) and to "pray / For him that's gone and far away" (79-80), the child finishes suckling, and the mother begins to relapse into madness:

> "My little babe! thy lips are still,
> And thou hast almost sucked thy fill.
> —Where art thou gone, my own dear child?"
>
> (83-85)

In that terrible pause, after the end-stopped declaration of the child's having finished nursing, and before the mother's pathetic call for her lost child, her son's origins have once more fallen into doubt, as he increasingly takes on the devilish face of the incubus:

> "What wicked looks are those I see?
> Alas! alas! that look so wild,
> *It never, never came from me:*
> If thou art mad, my pretty lad,
> Then I must be for ever sad."
>
> (86-90, my emphasis)

"When a woman yields to an incubus," writes Norman Cohn, "she imperils her eternal salvation."[35] To be "for ever sad," forever melancholy, is to be forever a witch, unable to pray, in league with the devil, embraced not by a wedding band, but by the "tight and deadly band" of the Incubus.

Since the child's "face," like the face of the child reflected in the water of the pond in "The Thorn," is a projection, its two faces—as child or imp—suggest that the mother is attempting to deal with an unconscious emotional ambivalence, certainly directed toward the Janus-like father, attempting to comprehend her contradictory feelings of love, anger, and resentment toward the husband who abandoned her.[36] Her language consequently has a contradictory aspect, as each image is structured by displacement and overdetermination. Her breast is the confused seat of her love for both the child and its "father" (he who "cares not for my breast" [61]). This confusion between maternal and sexual love, in which each is displaced upon the other, also extends into her delirium where it engenders, in the supernatural register, the child's and father's demonic counterparts. The child, who is the symbolic locus of these ambivalences, and like a projective screen, "Doth gather passion from his mother's eye" (1805 *Prelude* 2.243), is not removed from them. One of the more poignant tensions in the poem, resulting from this ambivalence, is her fear that if, indeed, she is a witch, then she is also probably capable of infanticide. As Scot observes, it was generally believed that witches usually killed "infants of their own kind," often using them to make "witches salve," "the ointments, whereby they ride in the aire" and escape harm.[37] The mother's attempts to comfort her child—"lovely baby, do not fear! / I pray thee have no fear of me. . . . I cannot work thee any woe" (15-16, 20)—express her own anxiety. And the protection she offers also is not without its dark ironies:

> "And do not dread the waves below,
> When o'er the sea-rock's edge we go;
> The high crag cannot work me harm,
> Nor leaping torrents when they howl;
> The babe I carry on my arm
> He saves for me my precious soul."
>
> (43-48)

The child is all that stands between the mother and damnation, and she would save it; but to do so, to prevent the "sea-rock's edge," the "high crag," and "leaping torrents" from doing herself or her baby harm, she would need the powers that only witchcraft and the witch's ointment can give.

The concluding stanza of the poem intensifies the poignancy of a mother's agonizing desire to hold onto her son, her sanity, and her "precious soul." Her solution is to seek escape in the woods:

> "Oh! smile on me, my little lamb!
> For I thy own dear mother am:
> My love for thee has well been tried:
> I've sought thy father far and wide.
> I know the poisons of the shade;
> I know the earth-nuts fit for food:
> Then, pretty dear, be not afraid:
> We'll find thy father in the wood.
> Now laugh and be gay, to the woods away!
> And there, my babe, we'll live for aye."
>
> (91-98)

For a single woman with child, as the sad case of Martha Ray makes plain, the forest is a refuge from villagers' "taunts" (71) and, as "tried" suggests, possible prosecution. The progress of the witch/hysteric is one of increasing movement away from society. Yet because "the wood" is also where witches held their sabbats, murdered their bastard children, and engaged in orgies with the devil, it is a refuge that is likely to increase their suspicion, as well as her confusion. She would live on "earth-nuts," yet she also knows "the poisons of the shade"—one of the arts of witchcraft. The final lines of the poem, in which laughter and gaiety are closer to hysteria than joy, fully dramatize the confusion and anguish of this melancholy woman, hoping to find "thy father in the wood."

V

Some called it madness; such indeed it was,

. . . . .

If prophesy be madness; if things viewed
By poets of old time, and higher up
By the first men, earth's first inhabitants,
May in these tutored days no more be seen
With undisordered sight.

(1805 *Prelude* 3.147-55)

For Wordsworth, abnormal psychology was not without its "prophetic" side. If "things viewed / By poets of old time" and "By the first men, earth's first inhabitants" cannot be seen "With undisordered sight," then in the "disorder" of the witch/hysteric, older than Christianity, one might still observe the original powers of primitive imagination and trace the origin and progress of those institutions based upon it. The madness that placed these women at the geographical margins of society, in proximity with nature, also placed them at its historical edges. As Coleridge's note to "The Three Graves" indicates, the poem was not primarily concerned with the psychopathology of witchcraft, but was conceived as a *domestic anthropology,* which would show that the powers of the primitive imagination are not restricted to the magic of "savage or barbarous tribes," but can be found at work in everyday life:

> I had been reading Bryan Edwards's account of the effects of the *Oby* witchcraft on the Negroes in the West Indies, and Hearne's deeply interesting anecdotes of similar workings on the imagination of the Copper Indians (those of my readers who have it in their power will be well repaid for the trouble of referring to those works for the passages alluded to); and I conceived the design of shewing that instances of this kind are not peculiar to savage or barbarous tribes, and of illustrating the mode in which the mind is affected in these cases.[38]

In "The Thorn" anthropological inquiry and "prophesy" are affiliated in a similar fashion, as the "madness" of Martha Ray provides an empirical vehicle for an extraordinary experimental account of the genesis of language, poetry, and myth.

As a synthesis of the dramatic perspectives of both the witch and her accuser, the poem represents Wordsworth's culminating and most complex representation of the witch/hysteric. Surprisingly, even though its adjacency to the case histories of *Zoönomia* is less apparent than in any of the other poems, it is also the poem in which the conflict between medical and traditional interpretations of witchcraft is most clearly drawn.[39] Distancing, however, is achieved in another way, by Wordsworth's setting the described action in the remote past: the poem is meant to be read as a *literary ballad* (probably modeled, as de Selincourt points out, upon a ballad from David Herd's *Ancient and Modern Scottish Songs*), *written during the latter half of the seventeenth century,* when witchcraft beliefs existed alongside the newly emerging methods and procedures of the New Science. For twenty years, Martha Ray, a woman loved, then jilted by Stephen Hill, has haunted a lonely spot high in the mountains outside the village. Nobody actually knows why:

> "Now wherefore, thus, by day and night,
> In rain, in tempest, and in snow,
> Thus to the dreary mountain-top
> Does this poor Woman go?
>
> . . . . .
>
> I cannot tell; I wish I could;
> For the true reason no one knows.

(78-81, 89-90)

But everyone in the village has an opinion. Some hold that this "poor Woman," whose situation is even more extreme than that of the "Mad Mother," is suffering from hysteria or melancholy, "A fire . . . kindled in her breast" (120) by her abandonment:

> "Her state to any eye was plain;
> She was with child, and she was mad;
> Yet often was she sober sad
> From her exceeding pain."

(127-30)

And, increasing her misery and madness, she has lost her child (by miscarriage or stillbirth). Others in the village interpret her case differently and suspect her of being both an infanticide and a witch. "[S]ome," who "remember well" (152), say she "Would up the mountain often climb" (154) "full six months" (122) after she went mad, approximately when the child was due. "If a child to her was born" no one knows, or "if 'twas born alive or dead" cannot "*with proof* be said" (148-51, my emphasis). But all that winter when, late at night, the wind "blew from the mountain-peak" frequented by Martha Ray, these villagers, when they stood in the "churchyard path," heard the wild cries of what seemed a meeting of the "living" and the "dead":

"For many a time and oft were heard
Cries coming from the mountain head:
Some plainly living voices were;
And others, I've heard many swear,
Were voices of the dead."

(159-63)

These may have been Martha Ray's cries, distorted by the wind; but since their source was "the mountain head," the usual site for nocturnal sabbats, it is not surprising that some would conclude that she had entered into a compact with the devil and murdered her child at the sabbat.

It is significant that though these villagers *suspect* Martha Ray, they never legally accuse her. As Alan Macfarlane has noted, witchcraft accusations were rarely spontaneous, spur-of-the-moment charges made by individuals, but instead reflected a *community consensus,* reached over a long period of time:

> Witchcraft suspicions tended to move in an ever-widening ripple through the village, the final accusation being based on a general consensus of opinion which rested on the mutual exchange of fears through gossip. . . . Counter-action against witches was a village affair in its later stages. Not merely the concern of an individual, it mobilized a number of emotional forces in the parish. . . . When enough proof was accumulated, and the village was united, the prosecution would occur.[40]

With a subtle understanding of the social dynamics of witchcraft accusations, Wordsworth depicts the atmosphere of suspicion and doubt, the constant rumor, gossip, and debate that preceded, often by many years, the reaching of a consensus and the initiation of legal action against a witch. In this instance, general agreement has not been reached.

The superstitious members of the village believe that enough evidence can be found to justify legal action and have made "an oath that she / Should be to public justice brought" (221-22). "I've heard," says the old mariner, "the moss is spotted red / With drops of that poor infant's blood" (210-11), but he finds it difficult to accept that Martha Ray is an infanticide. The villagers also believe they know where the child was buried, knowledge gained by resorting to a form of "crystal-gazing," one of the more popular forms of "white magic" used by cunning folk to recover treasure and stolen goods or to reveal the future. In mirror-magic the client or, more commonly, a *scryor* (usually a young boy), by looking into a reflecting surface, such as a mirror, beryl, swordblade, or basin of water, would conjure a figure (devil or angel) who would assist him, often in the search for buried treasure. As Reginald Scot observes, this figure often took the "faire forme of a boy twelve yeares of age," who then would be

asked "if there be anie treasure hidden in such a place N. & wherein it lieth, and how manie foot from this peece of earth, east, west, north, or south."[41] In "The Thorn," the villagers also conjure a child, but Wordsworth, no more a believer in mirror-magic than Scot was, makes it clear that what is reflected by the surface has been projected upon it by the seeker's imagination:

> "Some say, if to the pond you go,
> And fix on it a steady view,
> The shadow of a babe you trace,
> A baby and a baby's face,
> And that it looks at you;
> Whene'er you look on it, 'tis plain
> The baby looks at you again."

(214-20)

Assured of the location of the child's grave, the villagers set out to recover "the little infant's bones" (223), the "treasure" buried beneath the hill of moss. And these would have been enough to justify an accusation, for as Jean Bodin argued:

> If anie womans child chance to die at hir hand, so as no bodie knoweth how; it may not be thought or presumed that the mother killed it, except she be supposed a witch: and in that case it is otherwise, for she must upon that presumption be executed; except she can proove the negative or contrarie.

> Item, if the child of a woman that is suspected to be a witch, be lacking or gone from hir; it is to be presumed, that she hath sacrificed it to the divell: except she can proove the negative or contrarie."[42]

Proof of infanticide was tantamount to proof of witchcraft, especially when combined with a history of suspected witchcraft, the responsibility resting with the accused to "proove the negative or contrarie." But, as in "Goody Blake and Harry Gill," Wordsworth seeks to show that primitive superstition enforces its own kind of charity. When the villagers began digging for "proof" (151), "instantly the hill of moss / Before their eyes began to stir!" (225-26). Fearful of what this sight might portend, they decided to let matters stand. Though Martha Ray has escaped legal prosecution, there is nothing optimistic about the conclusion of the poem. Like many of the women who eventually came to be convicted of witchcraft, she still remains within the pale of suspicion, ostracized from the community and a continual object of fear, hostility, gossip, and debate.

This conflict and uncertainty are clearly manifested in the mind and language of the narrator of "The Thorn," whose "superstitious imagination" is, as Stephen Parrish has cogently argued, "the subject of the poem." Geoffrey Hartman sees in this "slow and teasing narrative" the exposure of "a mind shying from, yet drawn to, a compulsive center of interest."[43] This center is his earliest memory, a primal scene of terror that happened *before he had a language to describe it*. While climbing among the hills, when the old sailor first came to this seaside village and had not yet "heard of Martha's name" (173), he was caught in a terrible storm:

> "'Twas mist and rain, and storm and rain:
> No screen, no fence could I discover;
> And then the wind! in sooth, it was
> A wind full ten times over.
> I looked around, I thought I saw
> A jutting crag,—and off I ran,
> Head-foremost, through the driving rain,
> The shelter of the crag to gain;
> And, as I am a man,
> Instead of jutting crag, I found
> A Woman seated on the ground."
>
> "I did not speak—I saw her face;
> Her face!—it was enough for me;
> I turned about and heard her cry,
> 'Oh misery! oh misery!'"
>
> (177-91)

Seeking a rock, he came upon what seemed an isolated woman, her body so close to the earth that she had almost become part of it, suffering, like mad Lear, the brunt of the storm. Terror preceded language: "I did not speak—I saw her face; / Her face!—it was enough for me." Only after he "turned about," away from this primal image, did he find words to begin to convey its effect upon him, the words initially given to him by this woman, upon which his own narrative will subsequently be built, "Oh misery! oh misery!"

In his anxious effort to explain its effect upon him, the old sailor vacillates between two systems of explanation, from the "hinterland of broad folk attitudes,"[44] the superstitions that give rise to storytelling, to an almost compulsive emphasis upon ethnographic description and scientific measurement, the experimentalism of the New Science. Arising after he had "turned about," these explanatory systems have the status of screen memories. Not only do they stand in for this original event, but they have become so linked to it that the sailor, despite his sense of the insufficiency of his language, is unable to separate what he originally saw from its subsequent reconstruction in memory.

"Sea-faring folk," Herder observes, "still remain particularly attached to superstition and the marvellous. Since they have to attend to wind and weather, to small signs and portents, since their fate depends on phenomena of the upper atmosphere, they have good reason to heed such signs, to look on them with a kind of reverent wonder and to develop as it were a science of portents."[45] To a superstitious sailor—a perfect subject for a study, as Wordsworth writes in his note to "The Thorn," "of the general laws by which superstition acts upon the mind" (*PW* 2:512)—the connection between the storm, the pond, and a woman, seated on the ground, repeating the words "Oh misery! oh misery" almost as if they were part of a spell, would have been obvious. For centuries, *tempesterii,* claiming the power to raise winds and storms, had haunted seaports and had cajoled money out of sailors hoping for safe voyages.[46] Among the superstitious, Reginald Scot declares, "a clap of thunder, or a gale of wind is no sooner heard, but either they run to ring bels, or crie out to burne witches. . . ."[47] Storms could be raised in a number of ways. However, as Norman Cohn observes, the technique often "consisted of beating, stirring or splashing water. A pond was ideal for the purpose, but if none was available it was enough to make a small hole in the ground, fill it with water or even with one's own urine, and stir this with one's finger."[48] Having come upon what seemed a lonely woman beside a pond in such a storm ("A wind full ten times over"), engaged in the incantatory repetition of words, the sailor is not without fears that he, like Harry Gill, has stumbled upon a witch.

Except for his repeated mention of her "scarlet cloak," the old mariner does not describe Martha Ray, so it is not certain whether her physical appearance corresponds to the stereotype of the witch. In fact, Wordsworth's major criticism of Sir George Beaumont's painting of "The Thorn" was that "the female figure . . . [is] too old and decrepit for one likely to frequent an eminence on such a call" (*PW* 2:512n). Yet it is significant, in ways that support Stephen Parrish's contention that the sailor did not actually see Martha Ray, only "a gnarled old tree hung with moss," that even if she does not resemble a witch, the thorn *does*.[49] "Toothless" (*PW* 2:240n), "old and grey," with "knotted joints," this "wretched thing forlorn" (adjectives also used in connection with Martha Ray) "looks so old / In truth, you'd find it hard to say / How it could ever have been young." Like the woman, the thorn struggles against "a *melancholy* crop" (my emphasis) that is "bent / With plain and manifest intent" on burying it forever. In Wordsworth's well-known description of the origin of ancient myths, in book 4 of *The Excursion,* he suggests that they originate from the imagination's being "lord / Of observations natural" (4.707-8). In "more distant ages of the world," Wordsworth writes, "Withered boughs grotesque, / Stripped of their leaves and twigs by hoary age" became "lurking Satyrs, a wild brood / Of gamesome Deities" (4.847, 879-86). "The Thorn" shows how the mythology of witchcraft—perhaps born from a person's "observing, on the ridge of Quantock Hill, on a stormy day, a thorn which . . . had often [been] passed in calm and bright weather" (*PW* 2:510) without being noticed—subsequently comes to be applied to individuals.

Whether the image of Martha Ray compulsively repeating her few words "Oh misery! oh misery! / Oh woe is me! oh misery!" (65-66) was a fiction engendered by the winds or by the sailor's memory, it provided Wordsworth with a staging ground for an inquiry into the origin of human language and myth. It is not a coincidence that the poem's parallelisms, especially Martha Ray's expression of her suffering, are modeled, as Wordsworth indicates in his note to the poem, upon Hebrew poetry, upon "innumerable passages from the Bible, and from the impassioned poetry of every nation" (*PW* 2:513). Lowth's treatment of the Bible as "the primeval and genuine poetry," or Herder's claim that it represented the "most ancient records of the human mind and heart . . . the simplest forms, by which the human soul expressed its thoughts," made the Bible the obvious model for an experimental ballad aimed at dramatizing the primitive origins of poetry and passion.[50] Yet Wordsworth's anthropological speculation goes even further. With few words at her disposal, and these primarily interjections, Martha Ray clings to the words that approximate her pain best. Strikingly, this clinging to a word not only produces repetition (and thus poetry), but also a *new* phrase, "Oh woe is me!" as an assonantal variation of "Oh misery!" This movement, at once linguistic and cognitive, from interjection to statement, passionate expression to rudimentary reflection, represents an epitome of eighteenth-century accounts of the origin and progress of human language.

As a crucial figure in Wordsworth's mythology of origins, the lonely witch/hysteric provided him with the figural and empirical means for imagining the genesis of language and culture. Hers was a savage imagination, inhabiting the borderland of nature and society and moving between the supernatural and domesticated spheres of the imagination, and she came to occupy a primal space in Wordsworth's imagination, "as holy and enchanted / As e'er beneath a waning moon was haunted / By woman wailing for her demon-lover."

VI

Since eighteenth-century medicine and philosophy had already made mad women the subjects of observation in a discourse on the imagination, it was not by accident that Wordsworth, beginning work on the philosophical poem *The Recluse*, would have hoped to find in the tragic story of Margaret's abandonment and madness a suitable site for elaborating the "Colours & forms of a strange discipline"—a theory of the therapeutic powers of poetic language.[51] Yet because, for Wordsworth, to represent the witch/hysteric was not to describe her melancholy with clinical detachment, but instead *to confront* and possibly to fall victim to a being largely of one's own creation, his representations posit a different, more emotionally charged, stance toward her than the evaluative stance of medicine. "'I never heard, of such as dare" the old sailor of "The Thorn" tells us, "Approach the spot when she is there'"

(98-99). As the embodiment of primal imagination, the "disorder" that his poetry draws upon yet seeks to counteract and domesticate, as the bestower of both trauma and language, the witch/hysteric remains an ambivalent figure to Wordsworth, as threatening and as fascinating to him as his imagination. The distancing strategies of the witchcraft poems should not be viewed, therefore, only in terms of his revaluation of medical and philosophical discourse—they also reflect the contradictory, sublimational processes that lie at the basis of his poetry.

The later poetry displays an increasing effacement of the witch/hysteric. In the 1799 *Prelude,* in the poet's description of a "naked pool," a beacon on a "lonely eminence," and a "woman," her psychological state (like Susan *gale*'s) expressed metonymically by "garments vexed and tossed / By the strong wind," one can recognize a reworking of the anxieties of "The Thorn." Medical, philosophical, and anthropological speculation still converge upon this woman, and the deficiencies of language are again foregrounded—the need for "Colours and words that are unknown to man / To paint the visionary dreariness" (1.321-27) of the scene. Nevertheless, the woman's madness is represented at a greater distance, and the speculative focus of the passage has shifted to the self. In *Resolution and Independence,* one finds a starker, more patriarchal conception of poetic origins, and a more general effacement of the female imagination, as Wordsworth rewrites the supernatural origins of poetry in more masculine terms. Yet the preoccupation with melancholy and magic, and the presence, after a terrible tempest, of a stonelike leech-gatherer, stirring and "conning" the muddy waters of a pond "As if he had been reading in a book," wearing "a Cloak, the same as women wear" (*PW* 2.238n), his body, through sickness or pain, 'bent to a hoop,' still betray, though in a far more concealed fashion, the poem's debt to the experimental concerns of the *Lyrical Ballads*.[52] In "The Solitary Reaper," the concerns that first drew Wordsworth's eye toward lonely women speaking are still present, yet the poem aims at subsuming the woman's status as imaginative threat in order to celebrate her civilizing powers. "Single," "solitary," "alone" in the field, hers is "a melancholy strain," of "natural sorrow, loss, or pain," or of "old, unhappy, far-off things," a primordial song whose power over the listener is prelinguistic, for it is sung in a language unknown to the listener. "O'er the sickle bending," she emblematizes the conjunction of death and poetry, but now her song speaks the fertility of the female voice and womb, "for the Vale profound / Is overflowing with the sound." Like language, which was born "Among Arabian sands," her song moves northward, breaking "the silence of the seas / Among the farthest Hebrides" and connecting the ancient past with the present.[53] The lonely witch has been displaced by the solitary agricultural laborer; her unfulfilled desire now takes the form of a love song and a harvest requiem.

Notes

[1] Unless otherwise indicated, citations to Wordsworth's poetry are from *The Poetical Works of William Wordsworth,* ed. E. de Selincourt, 2nd ed. (Oxford: Clarendon Press, 1952), abbreviated as *PW.* Citations to *The Prelude* are from *The Prelude 1799, 1805, 1850,* ed. Jonathan Wordsworth, M. H. Abrams, and Stephen Gill (New York and London: Norton, 1979).

[2] *Critical Review,* 2nd series, 24 (Oct. 1798): 198, in *The Romantics Reviewed: Contemporary Reviews of British Romantic Writers,* ed. Donald H. Reiman, 3 pts. (New York and London: Garland, 1972), A, 1:307; *The Simple Wordsworth* (New York: Barnes and Noble, 1961), 52-54.

[3] *The Letters of William and Dorothy Wordsworth: The Middle Years, 1806-1811,* ed. Ernest de Selincourt, 2nd ed. (Oxford: Clarendon Press, 1969), 1:336, subsequently abbreviated as *MY.* Citations to *The Letters of William and Dorothy Wordsworth: The Early Years, 1787-1805,* ed. Ernest de Selincourt, 2nd ed. (Oxford: Clarendon Press, 1967) are abbreviated as *EY.*

[4] William Harvey, *On Parturation,* in *The Works of William Harvey, M.D.,* trans. Robert Willis (London: Sydenham Society, 1847), 543.

[5] Robert Whytt, *Observations on the Nature, Causes, and Cure of those Disorders which have been commonly called Nervous, Hypochondriac, or Hysteric: to which are prefixed some Remarks on the Sympathy of the Nerves,* 2nd ed. (Edinburgh: T. Becket, 1765), 96. See also, for example, Edward Jorden, *A Disease Called the Suffocation of the Mother* (1603: reprint, New York: Da Capo Press, 1971), 1; and Thomas Sydenham, "Epistolary Dissertation," in *The Works of Thomas Sydenham, M.D.,* trans. Dr. Greenhill (London: Sydenham Society, 1848), 2:85.

[6] *The Suffocation of the Mother,* 26.

[7] *The Practice of Physic, reduc'd to the ancient Way of Observations, containing a just Parallel between the Wisdom of the Ancients and the Hypothesis's of Modern Physicians* (London: Andrew Bell, 1704), 179, 185.

[8] Sigmund Freud, "Fragment of an Analysis of a Case of Hysteria," in the *Standard Edition of the Complete Psychological Works of Sigmund Freud,* trans, and ed. James Strachey (London: Hogarth Press, 1964), 7:24.

[9] *Suffocation of the Mother,* 2.

[10] *Mind and Body in Eighteenth Century Medicine: A Study Based on Jerome Gaub's De regimine mentis* (Berkeley and Los Angeles: Univ. of California Press, 1965), 17.

[11] *The Reflector: representing human affairs, as they are; and may be improved* (London: T. Longman, 1750), 228.

[12] For discussions of the contemporary understanding of psychosomatic illnesses, see Jean Starobinski, "The Idea of Nostalgia," *Diogenes* 54 (1966): 81-103; and G. S. Rousseau, "Nymphomania, Bienville and the rise of erotic sensibility," in *Sexuality in eighteenth-century Britain,* ed. Paul-Gabriel Boucé (Totowa, N.J.: Barnes and Noble, 1982): 95-119.

[13] "Nerves, Spirits, and Fibres: Towards Defining the Origins of Sensibility," in *Studies in the Eighteenth Century III,* ed. R. F. Brissendon and J. C. Eade (Toronto, Ont. and Buffalo, N.Y.: Univ. of Toronto Press, 1976), 151.

[14] *Melancholie und Aufklärung: Melancholiker und ihre Kritiker in Erfahrungssee-lenkunde und Literatur des 18 Jahrhunderts* (Stuttgart: Metzler, 1977), 16-40.

[15] See "Wordsworth and 'Natural Science': The Poetry of 1798," *Journal of English and German Philology* 77 (1978): 232-46 and *Wordsworth and the Poetry of Human Suffering* (Ithaca: Cornell Univ. Press, 1980), 152-66.

[16] The efficacy of this therapy may reflect conventional notions, discussed by Michel Foucault, of the connection between idleness and disease, an idea exemplified by the American physician Benjamin Rush's explanation of the positive effect of the American Revolution upon hysterics: "Many persons of infirm and delicate habits, were restored to perfect health, by the change of place or occupation, to which the war exposed them. This was the case in a more especial manner with hysterical women, who were much interested in the successful issue of the contest. . . . It may perhaps help to extend our ideas of the influence of the passions upon diseases, to add, that when either love, jealousy, grief, or even devotion, wholly engross the female mind, they seldom fail, in like manner, to cure or to suspend hysterical complaints" ("An Account of the Influence . . . of the American Revolution upon the Human Body," in *Medical Inquiries and Observations,* 3rd ed. [Philadelphia: Hopkins and Earle, 1809], 1:238).

[17] *A Philosophical Enquiry into the Origin of our Ideas of the Sublime and Beautiful,* ed. James T. Boulton (London: Routledge and Kegan Paul, 1958), 131-32.

[18] *The Suffocation of the Mother,* 1. Wordsworth's abortive political satire "Imitation of Juvenal" ridicules the *Daemonologie* and suggests that James whetted "his kingly faculties to chase / Legions of devils through a key-hole's space" (ll. 113-14).

[19] *A short discoverie of the unobserved dangers of severall sorts of ignorant and unconsiderate practisers of physicke in England* (London: Jones and Boyle, 1612), 54.

[20] *The Displaying of Supposed Witchcraft* (London: J. M., 1677), 323-24.

[21] William Harvey, *On Parturation,* 543.

[22] *The Complete Poetical Works of Samuel Taylor Coleridge,* ed. Ernest Hartley Coleridge, 2 vols. (Oxford: Clarendon Press, 1912), 1:268-69.

[23] *William Wordsworth: The Poems,* ed. John O. Hayden, 2 vols. (New Haven: Yale Univ. Press, 1981), 1:245. Because no complete text is available, lines cited from those parts assigned to Wordsworth will be prefaced by his initials.

[24] *Réponse aux Questions d'un Provincial,* in *Oeuvres Diverses de M. Pierre Bayle,* 4 vols. (La Haye: P. Husson, 1725-31), 3:561, my translation.

[25] *Réponse* 3:559.

[26] *Réponse* 3:561.

[27] Coleridge further developed this complex conjunction of magic, possession, sexuality, and mimetic transference in the love triangle of *Christabel,* begun in 1797. Karen Swann, in "'Christabel': The Wandering Mother and the Enigma of Form" *Studies in Romanticism* 23 (1984): 533-53, has analyzed suggestively the role that hysteria plays in Coleridge's poetry.

[28] Erasmus Darwin, *Zoönomia: or, The Laws of Life,* 2 vols. (London: J. Johnson, 1794-96), 2:359; *Critical Review,* 200.

[29] *Spectator* no. 117, in *Selected Essays from "The Tatler," "The Spectator," and "The Guardian,"* ed. Daniel McDonald (Indianapolis and New York: Bobbs-Merrill, 1973), 298. See also, Alan Macfarlane, *Witchcraft in Tudor and Stuart England: A Regional and Comparative Study* (New York: Harper and Row, 1970); and Keith Thomas, *Religion and the Decline of Magic* (New York: Charles Scribners, 1971).

[30] Robert Langbaum downplays the importance of language in "The Mad Mother" and, therefore, does not feel that the poem is really a dramatic monologue (*The Poetry of Experience: The Dramatic Monologue in Modern Literary Tradition* [New York: Random House, 1957], 71-72).

[31] *Poetry of Human Suffering,* 156; *Zoönomia* 2:360, my emphasis.

[32] *The Anatomy of Melancholy,* ed. Floyd Dell and Paul Jordan-Smith (New York: Tudor Publishing, 1927), 220.

[33] Reginald Scot recounts a priest's story of his nightly meetings with a succubus: "There commeth unto mee, almost everie night, a certeine woman, unknowne unto me, and lieth so heavie upon my brest, that I cannot fetch my breath, neither have anie power to crie, neither doo my hands serve me to shoove hir awaie, nor my feete to go from hir." Scot reassured the priest that he was not possessed, but "vexed with a disease called *Incubus,* or the mare; and the residue was phantasie and vaine imagination" (*The Discoverie of Witchcraft,* intro, Montague Summers [London: J. Rodker, 1930], 4.9:47-48). The Incubus is a "bodilie disease . . . although it extend unto the trouble of the mind: which of some is called The mare, oppressing manie in their sleep so sore, as they are not able to call for helpe, or stir themselves under the burthen of that heavie humor, which is ingendred of a thicke vapor proceeding from the cruditie and rawnesse in the stomach: which ascending up into the head oppresseth the braine, in so much as manie are much infeebled therebie, as being nightlie haunted therewith" (4.11:49).

[34] *The Discoverie of Witchcraft* 3.9:30.

[35] *Europe's Inner Demons: An Enquiry Inspired by the Great Witch-Hunt* (New York: Basic Books, 1975), 236.

[36] The problem posed by the child's bearing the face of the father is a central point of ambivalence in "Lady Anne Bothwell's Lament," a ballad from Percy's *Reliques of Ancient English Poetry* that Wordsworth drew upon in composing the poem. There, the woman, seduced and abandoned, claims that she still loves the boy's father, yet fears that he might grow up to be like him:

> But smile not, as thy father did,
> To cozen maids: nay God forbid!
> Bot yett I feire, thou wilt gae neire
> Thy fatheris hart, and face to beire.

The way in which the figure of the deserted woman images the mother "as hostile and treacherous, in the form of a denying and rejecting Nature, and also as a suffering victim" (125) is profitably examined in psychoanalytic terms by Barbara A. Schapiro in *The Romantic Mother: Narcissistic Patterns in Romantic Poetry* (Baltimore and London: The Johns Hopkins Univ. Press, 1983).

[37] *The Discovery of Witchcraft* 1.4:5, 3.1:23.

[38] *Complete Poetical Works* 1:269.

[39] James H. Averill has argued that Wordsworth's "remarkably dubious" (*Poetry of Human Suffering,* 167) allusion to James Hackman's murder of Martha Ray, Basil Montagu's grandmother, on April 7, 1779 was influenced by Darwin's mention of the case in *Zoönomia,* as an illustration of an extreme stage of *erotomania,* a "furious or melancholy insanity" (2:365). The close connection between sexuality and hysteria, love and madness, in this case would have been of special interest to Wordsworth. By naming his witch "Martha Ray," he reaffirms that the witch is not the *cause,* but the *victim,* of the aggressive imaginings of her accusers. Ironically, Martha Ray was shot as she left a performance of *Love in a Village.*

[40] *Witchcraft in Tudor and Stuart England,* 110-12.

[41] *The Discoverie of Witchcraft* 15.16:245-46.

[42] Cited in Scot, *The Discoverie of Witchcraft* 2.5:14.

[43] *The Art of the "Lyrical Ballads"* (Cambridge: Harvard Univ. Press, 1973), 100, 99; *Wordsworth's Poetry 1787-1814* (1964; reprint, New Haven and London: Yale Univ. Press, 1971), 147-48. For a subtle interpretation of "The Thorn" as "mental theater," in which the speaker displays the "dramatic incapacity of experience to explain passion" (282), of language to encompass "the open site of desire" (283), see Jerome Christensen, "Wordsworth's Misery, Coleridge's Woe: Reading 'The Thorn,'" *Papers on Language and Literature* 16 (1980): 268-86.

[44] Danby, *The Simple Wordsworth* (New York: Barnes and Noble, 1961), 60.

[45] "Journal of My Voyage in the Year 1769," trans. F. M. Barnard, in *J. G. Herder on Social and Political Culture* (Cambridge: Cambridge Univ. Press, 1969), 71.

[46] Wordsworth's decision to depict the mind of a superstitious seventeenth-century mariner suggests that "The Thorn" is a pastiche of the *Rime of the Ancient Mariner* aimed at revaluing Coleridge's theory of the supernatural. It is likely that the same passage from Captain George Shelvocke's *A Voyage Round the World by the Way of the Great South Sea* (London: J. Senex, 1726) that Wordsworth recalled in suggesting that Coleridge have the mariner kill an albatross equally informs his depiction of the old sailor's encounter with a "weather-witch." Having described the terrible weather south of the Straits of le Mair, Shelvocke writes that his crew saw no living thing save "a disconsolate black *Albitross,* who accompanied us for several days, hovering about us as if he had lost himself, till *Hatley,* (my second Captain) observing, in one of his melancholy fits, that this bird was always hovering near us, imagin'd, from his colour, that it might be some ill omen. That which, I suppose, induced him the more to encourage his superstition, was the continued series of contrary tempestuous winds, which had oppress'd us ever since we had got into this sea. But be that as it would, he, after some fruitless attempts, at length, shot the *Albitross,* not doubting (perhaps) that we should have a fair wind after it" (72-73). As in "The Thorn," conceived as Words-worth tells us, when he observed, "on the ridge of Quantock Hill, on a stormy day, a thorn," and set out to make it "permanently an impressive object as the storm . . . made it to my eyes" (*PW* 2:511), a melancholy sailor's superstitious identification of a natural creature, emerging from the mists, with the cause of tempests invests it with supernatural powers. Coleridge's sophisticated understanding of the supernatural has recently been the subject of three very fine studies: E. S. Shaffer, *"Kubla Khan" and The Fall of Jerusalem: The Mythological School in Biblical Criticism and Secular Literature 1770-1880* (Cambridge: Cambridge Univ. Press, 1975); Jerome McGann, "The Meaning of the Ancient Mariner," *Critical Inquiry* 8 (1981): 35-67; and Leslie Brisman, "Coleridge and the Supernatural," *Studies in Romanticism* 21 (1982): 123-59. No comparable work has yet been done, however, on Wordsworth's rich debts to eighteenth-century biblical theory.

[47] *The Discoverie of Witchcraft* 1.1:1.

[48] *Europe's Inner Demons,* 153.

[49] *The Art of the Lyrical Ballads,* 101.

[50] *Lectures on the Sacred Poetry of the Hebrews,* trans. G. Gregory, 3rd ed. (London: Thomas Tegg & Son, 1835), 1:50; *The Spirit of Hebrew Poetry,* trans. James Marsh (Burlington: Edward Smith, 1833), 21, 45.

[51] Wordsworth, "The Ruined Cottage," in *"The Ruined Cottage" and "The Pedlar,"* ed. James Butler (Ithaca: Cornell Univ. Press, 1979), 257.

[52] Prospero, in *The Tempest,* describes the "foul witch Sycorax" as being "with age and envy . . . grown into a hoop" (1.2.258-59). K. M. Briggs observes that "this was often popularly taken as a sign of witchcraft" (*Pale Hecate's Team: An Examination of the Beliefs on Witchcraft and Magic among Shakespeare's Contemporaries and His Immediate Successors* [New York: Humanities Press, 1962], 83).

[53] The south-to-north "progress of poetry" (as well as its east-to-west movement) is suggestively discussed by Geoffrey Hartman, in "Blake and the Progress of Poesy," in *Beyond Formalism: Literary Essays 1958-70* (New Haven: Yale Univ. Press, 1970), 193-205.

FURTHER READING

Auerbach, Nina. "Magi and Maidens: The Romance of the Victorian Freud." *Critical Inquiry* 8, No. 2 (Winter 1981): 281-300.

Discusses the role of mythology in the discourse on hysteria and considers the claim that such mythologies can be utilized to affirm female authority.

Brady, Kristin. "Textual Hysteria: Hardy's Narrator on Women." In *The Sense of Sex: Feminist Perspectives on Hardy*, edited by Margaret R. Higonnet, pp. 87-106. Chicago: University of Illinois Press, 1993.

Examines the evolution of Hardy's rendering of female characters in the context of Victorian tensions about femininity and sexuality.

Cummings, Katherine. *Telling Tales: The Hysteric's Seduction in Fiction and Theory*. Stanford: Stanford University Press, 1991, 298 p.

Discusses the appropriation of the figure of the hysteric as the object of seduction in Freudian theory and canonical literature.

Diamond, Elin. "Realism and Hysteria: Towards a Feminist Mimesis." *Discourse* 13, No. 1 (Fall-Winter 1990-91): 59-92.

Contends that realism, as a mimetic and mythologizing form of representation, has typically hysterical characteristics.

Fontana, Ernest. "Virginal Hysteria in Tennyson's *The Hesperides*." *Concerning Poetry* 8, No. 2 (Fall 1975): 17-20.

Interprets Tennyson's *The Hesperides* as a psychological study of emotion and sensuality, rather than as a parable about abstract artistic imagination.

Herndl, Diane Price. "The Writing Cure: Charlotte Perkins Gilman, Anna O., and 'Hysterical' Writing." *National Women's Studies Association Journal* 1, No. 1 (Autumn 1988): 52-74.

Analyzes the complex interaction between hysteria and speech in women's writing of the late nineteenth century and discusses their utilization of the "male" structure of language.

Johnston, Ruth D. "*The Professor*: Charlotte Brontë's Hysterical Text, or Realistic Narrative and the Ideology of the Subject from a Feminist Perspective." In *Dickens Studies Annual: Essays on Victorian Fiction* 18, edited by Michael Tinko, Fred Kaplan, and Edward Guiliano, pp. 353-80. New York: AMS Press, 1989.

Examines the possibility of constructing a feminine subjectivity and identity in representation, particularly in "hysterical texts."

Kahane, Claire. "Hysteria, Feminism, and the Case of *The Bostonians*." In *Feminism and Psychoanalysis*, edited by Richard Feldstein and Judith Roof, pp. 280-97. Ithaca: Cornell University Press, 1989.

Contends that two major historical developments in the second half of the nineteenth century—the study of hysteria and the feminist movement—disrupt conventional accounts of women's silence in ways that are only superficially opposed.

Matlock, Jann. *Scenes of Seduction: Prostitution, Hysteria, and Reading Difference in Nineteenth-Century France*. New York: Columbia University Press, 1994, 422 p.

Examines the representation of hysteria and the phenomenon of "reading the female body" that links the discourse on prostitution, as portrayed in nineteenth-century French literature.

Matus, Jill L. "Saint Teresa, Hypatia, and *Middlemarch*." *Journal of the History of Sexuality* 1, No. 2 (October 1990): 215-40.

Analyzes the depiction of Saint Teresa in George Eliot's *Middlemarch* in order to illuminate the relation between sexual repression, transcendence, and hysteria.

Mitchell, Juliet. "From King Lear to Anna O. and Beyond: Some Speculative Theses on Hysteria and the Traditionless Self." *The Yale Journal of Criticism* 5, No. 2 (Spring 1992): 91-107.

Discusses the significance of death in the interpretations and symbolism of hysteria.

Renner, Stanley. "'Red hair, very red, close-curling': Sexual Hysteria, Physiognomical Bogeyman, and the 'Ghosts' in *The Turn of the Screw*." In *The Turn of the Screw*, by Henry James, edited by Peter G. Beidler, pp. 223-41. New York: St. Martin's Press, 1995.

Argues that *The Turn of the Screw* represents a dramatization of hysteria arising from the repression of sexual desire.

Rothfield, Lawrence. "From Semiotic to Discursive Intertextuality: The Case of *Madame Bovary*." *Novel: A Forum on Fiction* 19, No. 1 (Fall 1985): 57-81.

Traces the characterization of Emma Bovary through a focus on hysteria and medicine.

The Irish Famine as Represented in Nineteenth-Century Literature

INTRODUCTION

By 1845, Ireland had become familiar with the unreliability of their staple crop—they had suffered through intermittent potato crop failures throughout the previous one hundred or so years, and the hunger that resulted from the failures of 1800, 1817, and 1822 had even been widespread enough to have been described as "famine." So when the crop of 1845—which by early indications promised to be bountiful—began to fail due to an inexplicable rot that destroyed the potatoes even before they had been dug up, many believed that the abundance of the crop would compensate for these losses. By winter, however, the rot had even blackened and spoiled the tubers that had been stored in pits. Reports of potato crop failures in the United States and, later, Europe, had made their way to England and Ireland, but in general the British government ignored the ramifications of the possibility that the disease would make its way to Ireland. Meanwhile, the Irish farmer made extra efforts to ensure that the crop of 1846-47 would be better. In fact, this season became known as "Black '47," the year in which the potato disease destroyed crops throughout the countryside; the year that marked the beginning of the "Great Famine"; and the first of several years in which record numbers of people died from starvation, malnutrition, dysentery, cholera, and typhoid fever. The Famine claimed countless numbers of victims (estimates range into the millions) throughout the late 1840s. Many of those who managed to stay alive fled to other countries, often to the United States. A cure for the potato blight (the disease was actually a fungus which was eventually identified as *Phythophthora infestans*) was not developed until 1882.

Critics note that the literature of this time period is scarred with incomplete, disjointed images—such as the "skeletal spectre" of death—which recur throughout the poetry and prose. Many Famine writers begin to describe a scene of a starving child, or a cabin whose emaciated inhabitants lie dead in the corner, only to abruptly depart from the image, refusing to detail it further. Often the same writers note their uncertainty regarding their ability, or even their right, to describe with words the horror of the Famine. This uncertainty, and these fragmented images, are the thread which binds together the vast array of Famine literature.

The political history of the Famine years is touched upon to varying degrees in the novels, poetry, and narratives of the time period. This history is not just that of Ireland, but that of England as well, for Ireland's history is inextricably tangled with England's. In 1801, the Act of Union between England and Ireland had made the two countries one, merging their economies and political structures; and historians, among others interested in the affairs of England and Ireland, have debated the role of British politics in the Famine. Some pose the question of whether the disaster could have been averted altogether, or, at the very least, if the suffering could have been assuaged to a greater degree than it was in reality. Others defend Britain's policies. Even some of the literature of the time period, especially Anthony Trollope's *Castle Richmond* (1860), while sympathizing with the victims of the Famine, seems to argue that the Famine was a "blessing in disguise" for the Irish, brought about by either God or nature, in that it created the suffering necessary for the emergence of a more equitable social order. From this standpoint—that the Famine was required either by nature or by God—Britain's policy of limited intervention is justified. Many contemporary and modern observers, however, revolted by the concept of the Famine as a blessing of any kind, agree that the British government did too little, too late, for the nation it occupied.

For a variety of reasons, the social, political, and economic structure of pre-Famine Ireland, which had been occupied for decades by the English, left Irish peasants in a position of absolute dependence upon the land, and on the potato in particular, for their existence. Irish farmers were tenants, most often renting land from absentee English or Irish landlords. The Irish paid a high price for the land—many times much higher than its actual value—but they had little choice, for without land, the Irish farmer had no means of supporting his family. As the population as well as unemployment increased, the rented land was subdivided until several families settled on a patch that could only grow enough potatoes to support one family. When the disease struck potato crops in 1845, and as crop failures continued throughout the next several years, the effect on a people completely reliant on one crop was utter devastation.

At the time of the Famine, England was experiencing its own economic crisis, and the concerns of Ireland were often viewed as trivial in light of this. Reports of widespread famine in Ireland were accused of being exaggerated. A few government officials advocated public relief efforts in Ireland, and finally, in 1847, some government aid was provided in the form of public works projects, soup kitchens, and workhouses. Critics of Britain's aid, contemporary and modern, argue that none of these efforts addressed the agricultural issues that formed the heart of the Famine problem. Britain's relief efforts, or lack thereof, also became a rallying point for the Irish nationalist movement during these years, and the literature of the time period, particularly poetry, which details the suffering of Famine victims was praised and published by Irish nationalist papers, including *The Nation* and *The United Irishman*. These publications, however, were often either ignored or derided in England.

Novels written during this time period were authored by upper-class men and women, rather than by the peasantry decimated by famine, and often came down rather softly on the British handling of the Famine, even as they offered harsh and painful images of Famine victims. The most frequently noted problem of most Famine novels—cited by contemporary and modern critics alike—is the apparent conflict between the story itself and famine analysis. Often the Famine backdrop is a marginal, and even obtrusive, part of the novels. This problem is shared by two of the most well-known nineteenth-century Famine novels: Trollope's *Castle Richmond* and William Carleton's *The Black Prophet* (1847). Modern analysis of Trollope's work, however, has attempted to prove that the Famine is neither incidental to *Castle Richmond* nor a separate story that should have been handled as such, as previously argued in the May, 1860, edition of the *Saturday Review*. Rather, critic Hugh Hennedy argues that Trollope parallels the plight of the Fitzgerald family with the plight of Ireland itself: as the Fitzgerald family emerges strengthened after its dealings with an unscrupulous member of the middle class, so does the whole of Ireland emerge "almost with triumph" from the Famine, as "the idle, genteel class has been cut up root and branch" and the "poor cotter . . . has risen from his bed of suffering a better man." Similarly, Christopher Morash demonstrates that the seemingly incidental depiction of the Famine in the novels of the time actually serves a purpose. Morash contends that *Castle Richmond* and two other novels (Margaret Brew's *The Chronicles of Castle Cloyne; or, Pictures of the Munster People* [1885] and Annie Keary's *Castle Daly: The Story of an Irish Home Thirty Years Ago* [1875]) view the Famine as "a Malthusian 'check' upon extravagance, moderating the two extremes of society, making them both more like the middle class." While the advent of this new social order is prescribed by the conventions of the novel, Morash maintains, the authors convey details about Famine suffering as a reminder that establishing an empowered middle class comes at a heavy cost.

Like these novels' apparently incidental depictions of the Famine, which arguably convey a larger meaning,

Famine poetry contains fragmented, unfinished images which seem to stop short of portraying the fully horrific nature of the Famine. Modern critics, such as Morash, maintain that the disjointed and incomplete nature of these images stems from the hesitancy of Famine poets to describe the indescribable. Such images include that of death as a "skeletal spectre" (due to the emaciated appearance of the living and the dead) and that of the "green-mouthed corpse" (referring to individuals who tried to eat grass to ease their hunger but died nonetheless, often with masticated grass still in their mouths). The reuse of these images in later Famine writings, Morash explains, contributed to the formation of collective, constructive memories among the Irish as a people, and that such memories are displayed in twentieth-century art and literature, including the 1990 film *The Field*. In a separate essay, Morash also discusses the role of Famine poetry, particularly that of the millenarianism movement and poets such as James Clarence Mangan, in supporting the Irish nationalist movement. Critic Margaret Kelleher agrees with the significance Morash attributes to Famine poetry when, in her discussion of the poetry most often published in widely available Irish periodicals, she states that such works "played an important role in nationalist famine historiography." Kelleher lists the themes of eviction, starvation, and emigration as highly prevalent in Famine poetry. Nationalists sought to use the poetic depiction of these themes, the results of the Famine, to incite rebellion against England.

In addition to poetry and novels, eye-witness accounts were transcribed during the Famine. Such narratives, some twentieth-century critics argue, have long been overlooked by historians. Kelleher asserts that this dismissal is perhaps due to the fear by some historians that the material is too subjective or overly emotional. She maintains that a significant amount of research on the nature and influence of such accounts has yet to be undertaken and offers her own examination of the first-hand experiences of one American woman—Asenath Nicholson—during the Famine years. K. D. M. Snell agrees that the eye-witness narratives are sources too often discounted by historians. Snell describes one such account, that of the Scottish-born Alexander Somerville, who traveled throughout Ireland during 1847 and recorded all aspects of rural life, including the human effects of the Famine, and issues such as tenant rights, the dependance of the Irish peasant on the land, and the Poor-Law system. Just as such accounts are so frequently overlooked by modern scholars, contemporary readers often considered the reports exaggerated in order to muster sympathy for the Irish among the British, or to urge the revolt of the Irish against the British. In fact, in 1845, an editorial in the *Achill Herald* summarized the work of Nicholson: "It appears to us that the principal object of this woman's mission is to create a spirit of discontent among the lower orders and to dispose them to regard their superiors as so many unfeeling oppressors. . . ."

The Irish Famine has been compared to the Holocaust in dimension, despite other obvious differences. It is not surprising, therefore, that the literature of the time period has been undergoing such a thorough re-examination by twentieth-century readers and critics. Modern reviewers of Famine literature, poetry, and narratives are perhaps as much moved to horror and its accompanying sympathy by the stark depictions of the Famine—sometimes edged with agony and despair, sometimes softened but rarely eased by memory—as they are by an effort to learn about and from the historical event itself.

REPRESENTATIVE WORKS

Margaret Brew
The Chronicles of Castle Cloyne; or, Pictures of the Munster People (novel) 1885

William Carleton
The Black Prophet (novel) 1847

Aubrey De Vere
"The Desolation of the West" (poem) 1869
"Ode: After One of the Famine Years" (poem) 1869

Samuel Ferguson
"Dublin: A Poem in Imitation of the Third Satire of Juvenal" (satire) 1849
"Inheritor and Economist: A Poem" (satire) 1849

John De Jean Frazer
"The Harvest Pledge" (poem) 1848
"The Artisan's Apology for Emigrating" (poem) 1849

Mary Anne Hoare
Shamrock Leaves (tales and sketches) 1851

Annie Keary
Castle Daly: The Story of an Irish Home Thirty Years Ago (novel) 1875

John Keegan
"To the Cholera" (poem) 1848

James Clarence Mangan
"The Warning Voice" (poem) 1846
"A Vision: A.D. 1848" (poem) 1848
"The Famine" (poem) 1849
"The Funerals" (poem) 1849

Thomas D'Arcy McGee
"Life and Land" (also published as "The Famine in the Land" (poem) 1847
"The Living and the Dead" (poem) 1847

Mary Anne Sadlier
New Lights (novel) 1853

James Tighe
"The Boreen Side" (poem) 1849

Anthony Trollope
Castle Richmond (novel) 1860

Elizabeth Hely Walshe
Golden Hills (novel) 1865

Jane Wilde ('Speranza')
"The Famine Year" (poem) 1847

Richard D'Alton Williams
"Lord of Hosts" (poem) 1848
"Lament for Clarence Mangan" (poem) 1849

OVERVIEWS

Margaret Kelleher (essay date 1995)

SOURCE: "Irish Famine in Literature," in *The Great Irish Famine*, edited by Cathal Póirtéir, Mercier Press, 1995, pp. 232-47.

[*In the following excerpt, Kelleher surveys Famine novels and poetry, maintaining that one of the primary issues concerning nineteenth-century Famine literature is the fulfillment of "its role in preserving and shaping the memory of famine for succeeding generations."*]

In William Carleton's famine novel, *The Black Prophet,* the narrator hesitates before the task of describing a famine victim with the exclamation, 'But how shall we describe it?'[1] Such a question recurs throughout Irish famine literature: can the experience of famine be expressed; is language adequate to a description of famine's horrors? Fears as to language's adequacy in face of overwhelming events also appear in other literary contexts, most famously in writings concerning the Holocaust by George Steiner and others. Steiner's work expresses a further anxiety as to whether such representations should even be attempted: 'The world of Auschwitz lies outside speech as it lies outside reason. To speak of the *unspeakable* is to risk the survivance of language as creator and bearer of humane, rational truth'.[2]

Analogies between famine and the Holocaust, while suggestive, are limited; but significant comments on the role of literature have emerged in response to Steiner's challenge. Critics such as Laurence Langer and Paul Ricoeur emphasise literature's distinctive power to 'make present' the historical experience, thus '*mak-*

ing such reality "possible" for the imagination'[3] in what Ricoeur has called the 'quasi-intuitiveness of fiction'.[4] In Irish famine literature, questions about language's competence give way to a detailed attempt at representation. Nineteenth and twentieth-century literary works thus reveal both the difficulties encountered and the strategies necessary in making the events of famine imaginatively accessible for their readers.

Carleton's novel *The Black Prophet* is one of the earliest and most famous of Irish famine novels. First published in *The Dublin University Magazine* in 1846 in eight parts, and set 'some twenty and odd years ago', its story employs details from the famines of 1817 and 1822. The first instalments, beginning in May 1846 after the partial failure of the potato crop, had themselves a prophetic quality in their anticipation of a further recurrence of famine; by December when the final chapters were published, the contemporary significance of this 'Tale of Irish famine' had become acutely clear: 'The sufferings of that year of famine we have endeavoured to bring before those who may have the power in their hands of assuaging the similar horrors which have revisited our country in this.' Carleton's novel has an explicit interventionist role, seeking, as he explained in the preface to the single-volume edition of February 1847, 'to awaken those who legislate for us into something like a humane perception of a calamity that has been almost perennial in this country' and to stir readers' 'sympathy' into 'benevolence'. In addition, Carleton's preface characterises the very purchase of the novel by the reader—inevitably a member of 'the higher and wealthier classes'—as equivalent to a charitable act, this some 150 years before the 'pioneering' Band-aid appeal!

William Carleton (1794-1869).

The Black Prophet exemplifies many of the difficulties faced by novels in representing the event of famine, its causation, progress and effects. Famine constitutes only one of its plots, along with a conventional love story and murder mystery. References to famine include a number of strong indictments of the legislature for its history of 'illiberal legislation and unjustifiable neglect', and its failure to provide a 'better and more comfortable provision of food for the indigent and the poor'. This neglect, Carleton argues, has allowed 'provision-dealers of all kinds, mealmongers, forestallers, butchers, bakers and huxters' to 'combine together and sustain such a general monopoly of food, as is at variance with the spirit of all law and humanity' constituting 'a kind of artificial famine in the country'. These comments contrast sharply with definitions of government responsibility held by many of Carleton's contemporaries, while his identification of an 'artificial famine', created by monopoly rather than food shortage, anticipates recent work on the significance of food distribution and entitlements. The progressive nature of this analysis initially carries over into a sympathetic depiction of famine victims, people 'impelled by hunger

and general misery'. Carleton's representation of famine crowds, however, becomes increasingly ambivalent, as evidenced in a profusion of oxymorons and other dualisms: 'dull but frantic tumult', 'wolfish and frightful gluttony on the part of the starving people', who possess an 'expression which seemed partly the wild excitement of temporary frenzy, and partly the dull, hopeless apathy of fatuity'. This ambivalence seems to originate in the author's fear of the activity and potential violence of those who are starving. In these passages, the starving poor appear less as victims of a neglectful legislature and more as creatures dangerously misguided, now 'victims of a quick and powerful contagion which spread the insane spirit of violence' rather than victims of disease and starvation. Carleton's characterisation of famine victims thus works against some of the implications of his political analyses. In addition, the differing, even competing, requirements, of story and famine analysis become clear as the novel ends: one family, the chief characters in the story, has its land and fortune restored as the story draws neatly to a close; the fortunes of the other 'starving people' are ignored.

The difficulties in combining famine material with conventional fictional plots can also be seen in Anthony Trollope's novel, *Castle Richmond*.[5] Trollope had lived in Ireland from 1841 to 1850, and intermittently in the 1850s. Written in 1859, on the eve of Trollope's final departure from Ireland, *Castle Richmond* is set in the south of Ireland, in counties Cork and Kerry, and covers what the author calls the 'Famine year' of 1846-7. The majority of the novel consists of a sentimental love story, with familiar nineteenth-century ingredients of illegitimacy and blackmail; the curious presence of famine material in the background led an early reviewer to declare that 'the milk and the water really should be in separate pails'.[6] One of the functions of *Castle Richmond*'s famine references is to assert the heroic status and attractiveness of Herbert, the chief character, in the face of the reader's quite likely view to the contrary; Herbert's work in famine relief seems, at least partly, intended to counteract the threat of the reader's growing dislike. Trollope's more detailed treatment of famine occurs through a series of encounters between upper class characters and the starving poor. These episodes allow the author to discourse on political economy and the dangers of 'promiscuous charity', especially in light of the apathy of the poor, and are intended to illustrate the operations of a power which was to Trollope 'prompt, wise and beneficent'. The characterisation of famine victims in *Castle Richmond* employs gender terms which recur throughout famine representations: male characters, though apathetic and idle, are situated on relief works, while females seek charity or remain within the domestic scene. In addition, female victims receive a physical scrutiny and inspection unparalleled in male representations. In contrast to Trollope's intention, the manner of his depiction of famine victims, the anxiety released by the encounter between the upper class and the starving, threatens to uncover very different power-relations.

While Carleton and Trollope's works constitute the two most famous nineteenth-century Famine novels, many other fictional treatments exist, a majority of which were written by women.

In 1851, Mary Anne Hoare published *Shamrock Leaves,* a collection of tales and sketches gathered 'from the famine-stricken fields of my native country', in which she argues that the horrors of Ugolino's dungeon, as depicted by Dante, 'fade into nothingness before the everyday tragedies of our Irish cabins'.[7] Controversial famine issues make an early appearance in famine fiction: Mary Anne Sadlier's *New Lights* (1853) strongly condemns the evils of prosleytism in the context of famine while Elizabeth Hely Walshe's *Golden Hills* (1865) depicts agrarian outrages and attempted assassinations by 'a lawless Riband tribunal.'[8] Other novels link the 1840s Famine to the events of 1848, as in Annie Keary's *Castle Daly: the Story of an Irish Home Thirty Years Ago*.[9] Annie Keary was the English daughter of an Irish-born clergyman; her novel, deemed by John O'Leary, Rosa Mulholland and others to be the best Irish novel of its time, was based on memories of conversations with her father and a total of two weeks spent in Ireland!

Other famine stories, such as 'The Hungry Death' by Rosa Mulholland and *Rose O'Connor* by Emily Fox, concern famines or periods of distress later than the 1840s.[10] Late nineteenth-century novels such as Margaret Brew's *The Chronicles of Castle Cloyne*[11] and Louisa Field's *Denis*[12] directly engage with contested issues in famine historiography such as the role of the landowning class, Brew emphasising that for the landed proprietors, 'with very few exceptions, the ruin, if it had come more slowly, did not come the less surely or pitilessly'. Given the extent of fictional writing about famine, it is not surprising that, in 1875, a writer in *The Saturday Review* noted that Irish events in the 1840s, including the Famine, compared to the French Revolution in providing writers with 'an inexhaustible mine of stirring incident', 'a mass of kaleidoscopic material that may be thrown together a thousand times'.[13]

A central question with regard to nineteenth-century famine literature is its role in preserving and shaping the memory of famine for succeeding generations. The majority of famine fiction was published either in London or jointly in Dublin and London, though a few novels were published in North America. This suggests that these narratives possessed a particularly significant function in terms of a British audience, a view supported by reviews of and prefaces to the novels. Famine stories were sometimes welcomed as explanations of the 'abiding Irish difficulty' for those 'perplexed by the contradictory versions of the present state of Ireland'; other reviewers were less sympathetic, seeing them as proof of the intractability of the Irish.[14] In the preface to her novel *Denis,* Louisa Field strongly emphasised the contemporary role of a famine story in throwing 'some light on circumstances and characteristics too often unknown and ignored, which yet are vital factors in that vast and ever-recurring problem, the Irish Question'.

The difficulties of representing famine included, for many writers, fears of being charged with exaggeration; frequently the defence employed involves an interesting configuration of issues of 'imaginative truth' and 'historical fact'. As early as 1847 Carleton argues that events in the 'present time' prove 'how far the strongest imagery of fiction is frequently transcended by the terrible realities of Truth'. Thus, as Mary Anne Hoare notes, the 'inventions of fiction' are rivalled, even surpassed, by 'matters of fact'. Similarly in 1865, Elizabeth Walshe defends her novel against charges of being overdrawn or exaggerated by bidding her readers to study the historical record: 'Let the files of contemporary journals, or the reports made to parliament be examined, and it will be found that the reality was far more terrible than anything which has been told in the "Golden Hills".' Ironically some years earlier, in 1850, in a letter to *The Examiner*, Anthony Trollope had refuted angrily the veracity of such reports in contemporary journals, declaring their accounts to be 'horrid novels'.[15] Nineteenth-century famine writings produce striking inversions of literary fiction and historical fact—where imaginative fictions are deemed more credible than 'the terrible realities of Truth'.

Nineteenth-century literature also includes a substantial amount of famine poetry, much of which was published contemporaneously with the 1840s Famine in periodicals such as *The Dublin University Magazine, The Nation,* and the short-lived journals *The Cork Magazine* (1847-8), *The Irishman* (1849-50) and *The United Irishman* (February-May 1848). As Chris Morash, editor of *The Hungry Voice,* an anthology of Irish famine poetry, notes: 'these contributors were by and large professionals from the middle class'—lawyers, doctors as well as journalists.[16] Nineteenth-century famine poetry varies from the fiery, apocalyptic visions of James Clarence Mangan, Jane Wilde and Richard D'Alton Williams, with their images of 'Revolution's red abyss' and the avenging 'Angel of the Trumpet', to more individualised, lyrical ballads such as Rosa Muholland's Wordsworthian 'A Lay of the Irish Famine' (1900). Poems such as 'The Famine Year' by Jane Wilde ('Speranza'), first published in *The Nation* on 23 January 1847 and later frequently anthologised, played an important role in nationalist famine historiography:

> Weary men, what reap ye?—Golden corn for
>   the stranger.
> What sow ye?—Human corses that wait for
>   the avenger.
> Fainting forms, hunger-stricken, what see you
>   in the offing?
> Stately ships to bear our food away, amid the
>   stranger's scoffing.

In many poetic treatments, famine is retold as part of the story of eviction, starvation and emigration, as in the famous 'Lament of the Irish Emigrant' ('I'm sitting on the stile, Mary') by Helena Dufferin (1807-1867), or Jane Wilde's 'The Exodus' (1864):

> 'A million a decade!' Count ten by ten,
>   Column and line of the record fair;
> Each unit stands for ten thousand men,
>   Staring with blank, dead eyeballs there;
>   Strewn like blasted trees on the sod,
>   Men that were made in the image of
>   God . . .

> 'A million a decade!' What does it mean?
>   A Nation dying of inner decay—
> A churchyard silence where life has been—
>   The base of the pyramid crumbling away—
>   A drift of men gone over the sea,
>   A drift of the dead where men should be.

Motifs which recur in famine poetry include images of an infant at the 'clay-cold breast' of its mother (Matthew MaGrath's 'One of Many', 1849) or the mother's lament, often delivered at the grave of her child. 'The Dying Mother's Lament' by John Keegan (1809-1849) constitutes one of the most frequently-anthologised famine poems, appearing in Daniel Connolly's American-published *The Household Library of Ireland's Poets* with Wilde's 'The Voice of the Poor', Dufferin's 'The Irish Emigrant's Lament' and 'The Black Forty-six' by Alfred Perceval Graves.[17] The popular *Gill's Irish Reciter,* first published in 1907 and selling four thousand copies within little more than six months of publication, also reproduced Keegan's lament.[18] Frequently, within depictions of famine mothers, analogies are drawn with Mary, the mother of Christ, as in Keegan's lament, while other poems present horrific images of mothers, closer to Medea than the Madonna, as in the anonymous 'Thanatos, 1849':

> The mother-love was warm and true; the Want
>   was long withstood—
> Strength failed at last; she gorged the flesh—
>   the offspring of her blood.

As may be seen throughout famine representations, female images are chosen to represent famine's worst consequences, in characterisations ranging from heroic self-sacrifice to 'monstrous' perversions of 'Nature'.

One of the most striking of famine poets is James Clarence Mangan (1803-1849), of whom Richard D'Alton Williams, in his 'Lament for Clarence Mangan' (1849), wrote:

> Thou wert a voice of God on earth—of those
>   prophetic souls
> Who hear the fearful thunder in the Future's
>   womb that rolls.

Mangan's work had indeed a prophetic quality; his 'Warning Voice' published in *The Nation,* 21 February 1846, prophesied that 'A day is at hand / Of trial and trouble / And woe in the land!'

The chronology of famine was to prove tragically linked with Mangan's own life; his poem 'The Famine' appeared in *The Irishman* on 9 June 1849, eleven days before his death of malnutrition, during a cholera epidemic in Dublin.[19] This interweaving of Mangan's personal fate and that of the land in general becomes explicit in his poem 'Siberia' (1846) with its portrait of a landscape of 'blight and death':

> And the exile there
>   Is one with those;
> They are part, and he is part,
> For the sands are in his heart,
>   And the killing snows.

Similarly, Mangan's poem 'The Funerals' (1849) creates a terrifying vision of 'endless Funerals' sweeping onward, over an 'Earth' which has become 'one groanful grave', a vision both surreal and mercilessly real, of overwhelming power:

> It was as though my Life were gone
>   With what I saw!
> Here were the FUNERALS of my thoughts as
>   well!
> The Dead and I at last were One!
> An ecstasy of chilling awe
>   Mastered my spirit as a spell.

Mangan's work contains powerful tensions between his determination to represent the contemporary horrors and his fear of language's inadequacy; thus in 'A Voice of Encouragement—A New Year's Lay', published in *The Nation* on 1 January 1848, the poet exhorts himself to

> Follow your destiny up! Work! Write! Preach
>   to arouse and
> Warn, and watch, and encourage! Dangers, no
>   doubt, surround you—
> But for Ten threatening you now, you will
>   soon be appalled by a Thousand
> If you forsake the course to which Virtue and
>   Honour have bound you!

Yet his poems also record Mangan's fear that the experience cannot be conveyed:

> But oh! No horror overdarks
> The stanzas of my gloomsome verse
>   Like that which then weighed down my
>   soul!
>
> ('The Funerals')

The 'Voice of Encouragement' concludes with the 'mission unspoken', recognising that the 'Impending Era' will enter 'the secret heart', silently:

> Cloaked in the Hall, the Envoy stands, his
>   mission unspoken,
> While the pale, banquetless guests await in
>   trembling to hear it.

In 1910, in the preface to her novel, *The Hunger,* Mildred Darby ('Andrew Merry') noted that 'Few people of the present generation know more of the appalling catastrophe than its broad outlines, gathered from some attenuated volume of Irish History';[20] fictions such as Darby's were to play an important part in constructing and preserving a famine memory. Twentieth-century literary representations were to encounter further difficulties since famine was now a historical event no longer verifiable by personal testimony and also a central and increasingly controversial event in the national chronology. As Paul Ricoeur has noted, 'As soon as a story is well known—and such is the case with most traditional and popular narratives as well as with the national chronicles of the founding events of a given community—retelling takes the place of telling.'[21] The 'Great Famine' has received a number of twentieth-century retellings, in fiction, poetry and drama, each situating it within the 'national chronicle' but in very different ways.

Liam O'Flaherty's novel, *Famine* is the most famous of Irish Famine stories; translated into French, Spanish, Portuguese, Dutch and German, it remains in print.[22] In one of the earliest reviews of the novel, Seán O'Faoláin declared: 'It is tremendous. It is biblical. It is the best Irish historical novel to date.'[23] First published in 1937, *Famine* emerged while the new state was still in the process of self-definition and as a particular version of the 'national chronicle', the Irish Constitution, was being written. The novel's powerful immediacy, from its detailed opening chapters to the quiet tragedy of Brian Kilmartin's death makes it, for this reader, the most successful Famine narrative; as the *Irish Book Lover* reviewer in 1937 noted: 'there are moments in it that have the heroic quality of sudden piercing lines in an old saga.'[24] Much of the novel's historical detail comes from Canon John O'Rourke's *The History of the Great Irish Famine of 1847 with Notices of Earlier Irish Famines,* first published in 1874; in terms of causation, O'Flaherty shares O'Rourke's interpretation that the famine demonstrated England's ability and unwillingness to 'save the lives of five million of her own subjects'.[25] The novel displays some difficulty in combining historical explanation with individualised characterisation; some of the historical comment is introduced quite awkwardly while the centre of investigation increasingly moves to the dilemmas and horrors experienced by female victims such as abandonment of children, prostitution and infanticide; thus a domestic sphere deflects political and socio-economic analysis.

Both the challenges faced by famine representations and O'Flaherty's particular successes may be seen in his memorable final chapter which tells of the death of Brian Kilmartin in quiet yet piercing detail:

> He clutched the handle of the spade, leaned forward, threatened the frosty earth with the point, and raised his foot. There was a deep, gurgling sound in his

throat and he fell forward headlong. The spade skidded away over the frost and rolled into a hollow. The old man lay still with his arms stretched out.

In stark contrast to other characterisations of famine victims, O'Flaherty presents a victim who has a name, a voice, a family, a past, an individual identity. As a confrontation between the individual and inexorable circumstance, Brian's death is tragic; this tragedy, however, occurs as a force associated more with Nature and the inevitable than the politics of starvation. The novel's political comment is to be found instead in the context of its other ending, Mary and Martin's departure for America. In an image repeated throughout nationalist historiography, sacks of grain are taken abroad for transport to England as ships are loaded with people bound for America. The reference to emigrants' 'cries of future vengeance' invokes events in Irish history from the story's end in 1847 to the time of its publication in 1937 and underlines O'Flaherty's own myth-making activity. The 1840s Famine proved part of the charter-myth of Irish-America, a community which was and continues to be a significant part of O'Flaherty's audience. *Famine*'s first reviewers recognised its mythic aspect, suggesting that O'Flaherty had 'in some sort fulfilled a destiny by writing this book', as well as its function as history: 'it is not only a story but a history told in terms of men and women'.[26] . . .

Notes

[1] William Carleton, *The Black Prophet* [1847], Shannon: Irish University Press, 1972, p. 344.

[2] George Steiner, *Literature and Silence: Essays 1958-1966* [1966], new edition: London and Boston: Faber and Faber, 1985, p. 146.

[3] Laurence Langer, *The Holocaust and the Literary Imagination*, New Haven: Yale, 1975, p. 8.

[4] Paul Ricoeur, *Time and Narrative*, Vol. 3. Translated by Kathleen McLaughlin and David Pellauer, London and Chicago: Chicago University Press, 1988, p. 188.

[5] Anthony Trollope, *Castle Richmond* [1860], Oxford: University Press, 1989.

[6] *The Saturday Review*, 19 May 1860, pp. 643-4.

[7] Mary Anne Hoare, *Shamrock Leaves*, Dublin: McGlashan; London: Partridge & Oakey, 1851, p. 206.

[8] Mary Anne Sadlier, *New Lights*, New York: Sadlier, 1853; Elizabeth Hely Walshe, *Golden Hills*, London: Religious Tract Society, 1865, p. 6.

[9] Annie Keary, *Castle Daly: The Story of an Irish Home Thirty Years Ago*, London: Macmillan, 1875; reprinted New York: Garland, 1879.

[10] Emily Fox ('Toler King'), *Rose O'Connor*, Chicago: Sumner, 1880. Rosa Mulholland, 'The Hungry Death' in W. B. Yeats (ed.) *Representative Irish Tales*, New York and London: Putnam, 1891; reprinted with a foreword by Mary Helen Thuente, Gerrards Cross: Colin Smythe, 1979.

[11] Margaret Brew, *The Chronicles of Castle Cloyne*, London: Chapman and Hall, 1884; 1885 edition reprinted New York: Garland, 1979.

[12] Louisa Field, *Denis*, London: Macmillan, 1896.

[13] *The Saturday Review*, 40 (1875) pp. 470-1.

[14] *cf.* review of *Castle Daly* in *The Graphic* (21 August 1875) and Stanley Lane-Poole 'Annie Keary' in *Macmillan's Magazine* 42 (1880), p. 263.

[15] *The Examiner*, 6 April 1850, p. 217.

[16] Chris Morash, *The Hungry Voice: Poetry of the Irish Famine*, Dublin: Irish Academic Press, 1989. The nineteenth-century poems referred to in this text are available in this anthology.

[17] Daniel Connolly, *The Household Library of Ireland's Poets*, New York; privately published, 1887.

[18] *Gill's Irish Reciter*, edited by J. J. O'Kelly, Dublin: Gill, 1907.

[19] Mangan's death has been attributed both to cholera and to starvation; in *Nationalism and Minor Literature: James Clarence Mangan and the Emergence of Irish Cultural Nationalism* (California: University of Press, 1987), David Lloyd notes that Mangan's death took place in the cholera sheds of the Meath Hospital but was diagnosed as due to starvation.

[20] Mildred Darby ('Andrew Merry'), *The Hunger: Being Realities of the Famine Years in Ireland, 1845 to 1848*, London: Melrose, 1910, p. 1.

[21] Paul Ricoeur, 'Narrative Time', *Critical Inquiry* (1980), p. 179.

[22] Liam O'Flaherty, *Famine* [1937], Dublin: Wolfhound, 1979.

[23] Seán O'Faolain, review of *Famine*, *Ireland Today* II. 2 (February 1937), pp. 81-2

[24] M. L., review of *Famine*, *Irish Book Lover* 25 (January-February 1937), pp. 22-3.

[25] John O'Rourke, *The History of the Great Irish Famine of 1847 with Notices of Earlier Irish Famines*, 1874. Abridged edition, London: Veritas, 1989, p. 98.

[26] M. L., review of *Famine, Irish Book Lover* 25 (January-February 1937), pp. 22-3.

. . . . .

An excerpt from *The Black Prophet* (1847) by William Carleton:

". . . Isn't the Almighty, in his wrath, this moment proclaimin' it through the heavens and the airth? Look about you, and say what is it you see that doesn't foretell famine—famine—famine! Doesn't the dark wet day an' the rain, rain, rain, foretell it? Doesn't the rottin' crops, the unhealthy air, an' the green damp foretell it? Doesn't the sky without a sun, the heavy clouds, an' the angry fire of the West foretell it? Isn't the airth a page of prophecy, an' the sky a page of prophecy, where every man may read of famine, pestilence, an' death? The airth is softened for the grave, an' in the black clouds of heaven you may see the death-hearses movin' slowly along—funeral afther funeral—funeral afther funeral—an' nothing to folly them but lamentation an' woe, by the widow an' orphan—the fatherless, the motherless, an' the childless—woe an' lamentation—lamentation an' woe."

William Carleton, in The Black Prophet, *1847, reprinted by Woodstock Books, 1996.*

Chris Morash (essay date 1996)

SOURCE: "Literature, Memory, Atrocity," in *"Fearful Realities": New Perspectives on the Famine*, edited by Chris Morash and Richard Hayes, Irish Academic Press, 1996, pp. 110-18.

[*In the essay that follows, Morash explores the manner by which Famine literature constructed collective memories of the Famine, maintaining that literature contemporary with the Famine contains "iconic fragments," images that are disjointed and incomplete due to the writers' belief in the inadequacy of language to convey the true horror of the Famine. Morash goes on to argue that these images have been liberally borrowed from by later Famine writers.*]

[*Scene: Pub interior*]

Bull McCabe: Who would insult me by bidding for my field here in Carraigthomond?

Mick Flanagan: There might be outsiders, Bull.

Bull: Outsiders? Outsiders? Are these the same 'outsiders' who took the corn from our mouths when the potatoes went rotten in the ditches?

Flanagan: Ah, now Bull . . .

Bull: Are these the same 'outsiders' who took the meat from the tables when we lay in the ditches with the grass juice running green from our mouths?

Flanagan: Take it easy . . .

Bull: Are these the same 'outsiders' who drove us to the coffin ships and scattered us to the four corners of the earth? Are these the same 'outsiders' who watched whilst our valley went silent except for the sound of the last starving child?

Flanagan: The English are gone, Bull.

Bull: Gone. Because I drove 'em out. Me. And my kind. Gone. But not forgotten, Flanagan. No 'outsider' will bid for my field.[1]

This scene from Jim Sheridan's 1990 film, *The Field,* is among the more recent (and, given the film's success, among the most widely distributed) representations of the Great Irish Famine of the 1840s. However, like many such representations, it can only invoke the Famine because of an almost invisible form of anachronism which becomes apparent when we focus on the language used by Richard Harris's character, the Bull McCabe: 'took the corn from *our* mouths'; '*we* lay in the ditches with the grass juice running green from *our* mouths'; 'drove *us* to the coffin ships and scattered *us* to the four corners of the earth'. When McCabe speaks of the Famine, it is as if it were something that had happened to him, something he remembered. And yet, as the pub owner, Mick Flanagan, reminds us, 'the English are gone'—that is to say, at the very least, the film is set after 1922; indeed, the car and clothes owned by Tom Berenger's character, 'the Yank', suggest that it may be set more than a decade later.[2] This means that in order to have an actual memory of the Famine, the Bull McCabe would have to be at least in his nineties—which he obviously is not unless he is an exceptionally spry ninety.

How do we explain this apparent anachronism? Has Sheridan slipped up in his chronology? Or is it naive to expect such verisimilitude in a film which tries so earnestly in its final moments to mythologise the past? Neither answer is fully satisfactory. Instead, we must think of 'memory' as it is used in this scene as the middle term in an equation connecting literature and atrocity.

Literature

When I first saw this scene in *The Field,* I was reminded of a passage dealing with the Famine in Canon Sheehan's 1905 novel, *Glenanaar:*

It is an appalling picture, that which springs up to memory. Gaunt spectres move here and there, looking at one another out of hollow eyes of despair and gloom.[3]

Although Sheehan claims that this image of the Famine 'springs to memory', 'memory' is here playing the same trick that we saw in *The Field*. Neither Canon Sheehan, nor the narrator-priest who is his fictional replacement, could, in fact, 'remember' the Famine. Sheehan was not born until 1852, when the Famine was, for all intents and purposes, over. So, as in the case of Bull McCabe, we have to ask: what is he 'remembering'?

We can begin to find an answer to this question by looking at the rest of the passage:

> It is an appalling picture, that which springs up to memory. Gaunt spectres move here and there, looking at one another out of hollow eyes of despair and gloom. Ghosts walk the land. Great giant figures, reduced to skeletons by hunger, shake in their clothes, which hang loose around their attenuated frames . . . Here and there by the wayside a corpse stares at the passers-by, as it lies against the hedge where it had sought shelter. The pallor of its face is darkened by lines of green around the mouth, the dry juice of grass and nettles.[4]

All of the images which appear in this passage can be found in earlier attempts to write the Famine. This suggests that what Sheehan is actually 'remembering' are other Famine texts. Indeed, in many cases, his memory extends to the vocabulary of those earlier texts, particularly in his use of the word 'spectre'. For instance, if we turn back to the Famine literature of the late 1840s, we will find poems such as 'The Spectre':

> Far west a grim shadow was seen, as 'tis said,
> Like a spectre from Famine and Pestilence
>   bred:
> His gaunt giant-form, with pale Poverty wed . . .[5]

Employing a variation on this motif, the *Mayo Constitution* reported in 1848 that 'the streets of every town in the county are overrun by stalking skeletons'.[6] Moreover, this image of the Famine as a 'stalking skeleton' or 'spectre' was still in use as Sheehan was writing in 1905. For instance, a Catholic Truth Society pamphlet from the turn of the century, entitled *The Famine Years,* contains the following passage:

> The dread *spectre* of famine had already set foot on the shores of Ireland, and was making ready to *stalk* through the fruitful land, from north to south, from east to west [emphasis added].[7]

Later in the same Catholic Truth Society pamphlet, we find the image of the corpse with a green mouth, mentioned by both Sheehan and the Bull McCabe:

> In Mayo a man, who had been observed searching for shell-fish on the seashore, was afterwards found dead, after vainly endeavouring to satisfy the cravings of devouring hunger with grass and turf.[8]

Once again, this image has a genealogy as an image of the Famine going back to the 1840s, and can be found in Famine-era texts such as 'The Boreen Side', by James Tighe, which first appeared in 1849:

> A stripling, the last of his race, lies dead
> In a nook by the Boreen side;
> The rivulet runs by his board and his bed,
> Where he ate the green cresses and died.[9]

In tracing the use of these images as representations of the Famine of the 1840s, I am not disputing that they correspond to a concrete reality, albeit an absent one. Their appearance in numerous newspaper reports, travellers' journals, and government documents of the period suggests that such horrific images were originally intended to be mimetic representations of things that actually existed. For instance, in a newspaper account of an inquest held in 1848, we find the image of the corpse with the green mouth:

> A poor man, whose name we could not learn . . . lay down on the roadside, where shortly after he was found dead, his face turned to the earth, and a portion of the grass and turf on which he lay masticated in his mouth.[10]

What interests me about such representations is not whether or not they were once empirically true; we can never fully answer that question. Instead, I want to focus on the way in which they were transformed in the process of textual transmission, which happens in and through language.

We must begin by recognising that even before the Famine was acknowledged as a complete event, it was in the process of being textually encoded in a limited number of clearly defined images. Indeed, for an event which we customarily think of as being vast, the archive of images in which it is represented is relatively small and circumscribed. As the nineteenth century progressed, these images became more and more rigidly defined, taking on the characteristics of Lyotard's 'rigid designators'. By the 1870s the Famine had become an increasingly potent element in the propaganda war which accompanied the struggle for land ownership, and as a consequence Famine images such as the 'stalking spectre' and the green-mouthed corpse were repeated in magazines like the *Irish Monthly Magazine* until they had the boldly defined outlines of religious icons. By the turn of the century, such images were so widely known that they could be said to constitute a form of collectively maintained 'memory'.

Memory

When I call these images from the archive of Famine literature 'memories', I am not thinking of memory here as passive recollection; instead, I am thinking of what memory theorists call 'constructive memory', which integrates past, present and future in such as way as to create the impression of a 'unified personal history'.[11] When constructive memories are shared by a group of people—as indeed they must be if they originate in a printed text—they create the impression of a unified collective history, in which the memories of the individual and memories shared by the literate members of society as a whole are the same. If we think of textually generated memories in this manner, it becomes apparent that they have an ideological function—indeed, they are almost pure ideology, insofar as they create an illusion of complete identity between the individual and society.

In order to understand the ideological function of these textually generated memories, it is necessary to understand something of their form. Like the Bull McCabe's account of the Famine, or the passage from Canon Sheehan's *Glenanaar*, most representations of the Famine tend to be made up of static, iconic tableaux, each existing in a single timeless moment. Even attempts at longer Famine narratives, stretching from William Carleton's 1847 novel, *The Black Prophet*, to John Banville's 1973 novel, *Birchwood*, incorporate these iconic representations of the Famine, but rarely use them as causal elements in the plot. In *The Black Prophet*, for instance, when the conventional blackmail story which gives the novel its form has been resolved, the Famine disappears. In the case of *Birchwood*, with its postmodern refiguration of cause and effect in narrative structure, the Famine is brought in as yet one more element in a shifting collage of public and family history. In these two very different Famine novels, and in others written in the decades which separate them, we find that there is no single metanarrative of the Famine in literature. Instead, we find that the Famine as a textual event is composed of a group of images whose meaning does not derive from their strategic location within a narrative, but rather from the strangeness and horror of the images themselves, as dislocated, isolated emblems of suffering.

The disconnected form of these images means that they are available for appropriation by other narratives, other forms of discourse. Reading through the literature of the Famine, one finds that such appropriation is rife. For instance, in John Mitchel's *Last Conquest of Ireland (Perhaps)* of 1864 there is an often quoted passage describing the condition of the countryside after the failure of the potato crop. It appears, however, in the midst of his account of the nationalist attempt to win an election in Galway in 1847:

In the depth of winter we travelled to Galway, through the very centre of that fertile island, and saw sights that will never wholly leave the eyes that beheld them:—cowering wretches, almost naked in the savage weather, prowling in turnip-fields, and endeavouring to grub up roots which had been left, but running to hide as the mail-coach rolled by; . . . groups and families, sitting or wandering on the high-road, with failing steps and dim, patient eyes, gazing hopelessly into infinite darkness; before them, around them, above them, nothing but darkness and despair.[12]

With the Miltonic echoes of the final phrases, this is a powerful representation of human suffering; however, it appears in Mitchel's narrative only as an aside in a chapter that is primarily concerned with the campaign for the Galway election. Mitchel later makes a half-hearted attempt to suggest that in such extreme conditions, he was 'justified in urging so desperate a measure' as revolution.[13] The passage, however, is not fully integrated in the text, and it is the failure of the nationalists to win the Galway election rather than the suffering of the 'cowering wretches' which becomes the rationale for taking up arms.

Moreover, this passage in *The Last Conquest* shares with a number of other Famine texts a detached perspective, as the narrator views the starving peasantry through the windows of a moving coach. For instance, there is an often reprinted account of the Famine by Father Theobald Matthew in which he describes travelling from Dublin to Cork by coach, and seeing 'the wretched people seated on the fences of their decaying gardens, wringing their hands and wailing bitterly the destruction that had left them foodless'.[14] Later, in a 1937 Famine novel by Louis J. Walsh, entitled *The Next Time*, the hero, travelling by coach from Dublin to his home in Gortnanaan, sees 'cowering wretches, almost naked in the savage weather, endeavouring to grub up roots that had been left behind in the ground'[15] in a passage which, like many others in the novel, shamelessly echoes Mitchel's *Last Conquest*.

Hence, the fragmentary way in which the Famine is represented makes it liable to appropriation by larger narratives, such as those of Mitchel, Fr Matthew, and Louis J. Walsh. Having no narrative of their own, put possessing a hard-edged clarity that has been refined through decades of repetition, these Famine icons are transmitted to us like something flashing by the windows of a moving coach—unforgettable glimpses of a narrative whose full development is always just beyond our line of vision.

Atrocity

We can begin to understand the resistance of these Famine icons to longer, sequential narratives by turning to two Famine texts. The first, a poem called 'The

A poor Irish family in front of their sod house, 1849.

Three Angels', was written in 1848 by a working class nationalist, John De Jean Frazer:

> Some gathered their kith to a fugitive band
> And sought the stars of a happier land;—
> Themselves and their kindred, thro' sheer despair,
> Some slew, in belief that *to slay* was *to spare!*—
> A cannibal fierceness but ill-suppressed
> In many—made some—we must veil the rest![16]

Frazer's poem can be read in the context of a passage from William Carleton's 1851 novel, *The Squanders of Castle Squander,* in which he describes a cemetery being desecrated by wild dogs:

> Round about the awful cemetery, were numbers of gaunt and starving dogs, whose skeleton bodies and fearful howlings indicated the ravenous fury with which they awaited an opportunity to drag the unfortunate dead from their shallow graves and glut themselves upon their bodies. Here and there an arm; in another place a head (half-eaten by some famished mongrel, who had been frightened from his prey), or a leg, dragged partially from the earth, and half-mangled, might be seen; altogether, presenting such a combination of horrible imagery as can scarcely be conceived by our readers.[17]

These images of cannibalism and desecration of the dead constitute another of the memories which make up the archive of Famine literature. In the texts of both Frazer and Carleton, however, there is an inability to complete the image. 'We must veil the rest', writes Frazer; 'such horrible imagery', writes Carleton, 'can scarcely be conceived by our readers'. Commenting on representations of the Irish Famine, Steven Marcus notes: 'The constant refrain of those who observed the famine is, "It cannot be described". "The scenes which presented themselves were such as no tongue or pen can convey the slightest idea of". "It is impossible to go through the detail". "Believe me, my dear Sir, the reality in most cases far exceeded description. Indeed none can conceive what it was but those who were in it." ' As Marcus points out, these are very modern voices, telling us that 'however mad, wild, or grotesque art may seem to be, it can never touch or approach the madness of reality'.[18] They also help to explain why the literature of the Famine contains so many iconic fragments. The unwillingness of these commentators to describe the scenes of Famine suffering is more than simply mid-Victorian prudishness or a conventional nod in the direction of an unspeakable sublime. After all, it was in the interest of Irish nationalist writers and those campaigning for greater government intervention to emphasise the suffering caused by the Famine; and yet a militant nationalist such as John De Jean Frazer is as inclined to 'veil the rest' as his imperialist, free market counterparts. Instead, we must consider structural incompletion as a feature of the representation of atrocity.

'Atrocity' is a word to be used with the greatest of care in relation to the Famine, for it suggests elements of intentionality which simplify matters to an unacceptable degree. Nonetheless, Lawrence Langer's 1975 study, *The Holocaust and the Literary Imagination,* provides a useful definition of the term when considering the writing of the Famine when he writes of a similar inability to construct sequential narratives among writers dealing with the Holocaust. 'The kind of atrocity at issue here', he writes, 'assaulted the very coherence of time and led to the breakdown of "chronology" as a meaningful conception'.[19] When we are talking about atrocity—at least in Langer's sense—we are talking about suffering that is disproportionate to its causes: hugely, grossly disproportionate. Because atrocity upsets our sense of cause and effect, it hampers our ability to construct sequential narratives which follow the conventions of mimetic literary representation. It may well be as a consequence of this breakdown of literary convention that the literature of the Famine is constructed as an archive of free-floating signs, capable of incorporation in any number of sequential semiotic systems, including the constructive personal memory which seeks to unite past, present and future in the creation of an individual identity.

In an early essay, 'A Kind of Survivor', George Steiner attests to the ability of such textually generated shards of memory to become a part of an individual's sense of identity. Steiner begins the essay by describing himself as a 'kind of survivor' of the Holocaust:

> Not literally. Due to my father's foresight . . . I came to America in January 1940, during the phoney war. We left France, where I was born and brought up, in safety. So I happened not to be there when the names were called out . . . But in another sense I am a survivor, and not intact . . . If that which haunts me and controls my habits of feeling strikes many of those I should be intimate and working with in my present world as remotely sinister and artificial, it is because the black mystery of what happened in Europe is to me indivisible from my own identity.[20]

The literature of the Famine provokes something of the same response; when we read a Famine text, we too feel that we are 'a kind of survivor'. It may be that when we encounter these shattered fragments of the past, we wish to complete them; and the only way in which we can do so is by internalising them, making them part of the narrative of our own memories.

When we do embrace these icons as part of our own past, however, we must undertake a project which Steiner's recent literary criticism has resisted with a stridency which makes his work look increasingly archaic; we must constantly remind ourselves that we are participating in ideology. In accepting these shared memories, we are enlisting ourselves as part of a group—a nation, a tribe, a race. In keeping these memories alive, we may be doing no more than bearing witness, trying to make whole that which the form of these images tells us can never be made whole. But such a longing for wholeness is not without its dangers; and it is here that the final mention of the Famine in *The Field* can act as a warning. As the Bull McCabe beats the 'outsider' to death by slamming his head repeatedly against a rock, he bellows to his son:

> See this fella here? See this Yank? His family lived around here, but when the going got tough they ran away to America. They ran away from the Famine— while we stayed. Do you understand? We stayed! We stayed!! We stayed!!!![21]

This should serve to remind us that while memories created by literature and born of atrocity may often seem like a testimony of human decency, they nonetheless have the potential to perpetuate the atrocity which they memorialise by providing the justification for a future which is envisaged in terms of the iconic, clearly-defined narrative structure which the past so often lacks.

Notes

[1] Jim Sheridan (dir.), *The Field* (Granada Films, 1990).

[2] Sheridan deliberately strips *The Field* of the references to television and aeroplanes which occur in the John B. Keane play on which the film is based, thereby locating it earlier than the 1965 setting of the play.

[3] Patrick Sheehan, *Glenanaar* (London, 1905; Rpt. Dublin, 1989), pp. 198-9.

[4] Ibid., pp. 198-9.

[5] H. D., 'The Spectre: Stanzas With Illustrations' in Chris Morash (ed.), *The Hungry Voice: The Poetry of the Irish Famine* (Dublin, 1989), p. 261.

[6] 'Death by Starvation' in *United Irishman* i, 5 (11 March 1848), p. 46.

[7] Joseph Guinan, *The Famine Years* (Dublin, 1908), p. 15.

[8] Ibid., p. 15.

[9] James Tighe, 'The Boreen Side', in Morash, *The Hungry Voice*, p. 73.

[10] 'Inquests' in *United Irishman* i, 14 (13 May 1848), p. 211.

[11] Gillian Cohen, *Memory in the Real World* (East Sussex, 1989), p. 219. See also Maurice Halbwachs, *The Collective Memory* (New York, 1980).

[12] John Mitchel, *The Last Conquest of Ireland (Perhaps)* (Glasgow, n.d [1861]), p. 147.

[13] Ibid., p. 150.

[14] Theobald Matthew in John O'Rourke, *History of the Great Irish Famine* (Dublin, 1875), p. 149.

[15] L. J. Walsh, *The Next Time: A Story of 'Forty Eight* (Dublin, 1919), p. 155.

[16] John 'de Jean' Frazer, in Morash, *The Hungry Voice*, p. 187.

[17] William Carleton, *The Squanders of Castle Squander* (2 vols., London, 1852), ii, p. 138.

[18] Steven Marcus, 'Hunger and Ideology' in *Representations: Essays on Literature and Society* (New York, 1990), pp. 10-11.

[19] L. L. Langer, *The Holocaust and the Literary Imagination* (London, 1975), p. 251.

[20] George Steiner, 'A Kind of Survivor', in *Language and Silence: Essays 1958-1966* (London, 1985), p. 164.

[21] Sheridan, *The Field*.

HISTORICAL BACKGROUND

A. M. Sullivan (essay date 1877)

SOURCE: "The Black Forty-Seven," in *New Ireland*, Sampson Low, Marston, Searle, and Rivington, 1877, pp. 121-43.

> . . . The whole of [Ireland's] structure, the minute subdivisions, the closely-packed population existing at the lowest level, the high rents, the frantic competition for land, had been produced by the potato. The conditions of life in Ireland and the existence of the Irish people depended on the potato entirely and exclusively. . . .
>
> . . . . .
>
> [If] the potato did fail, neither meal nor anything else could replace it. There could be no question of resorting to an equally cheap food, no such food existed, nor could potato cultivation be replaced, except after a long period, by the cultivation of any other food. 'What hope is there for a nation that lives on potatoes!' wrote an English official. . . .
>
> *Cecil Woodham-Smith, in* The Great Hunger: Ireland, 1845-1849, *Harper and Row, 1962.*

[The following essay is taken from Sullivan's New Ireland, *which was published just thirty years after the Famine of 1847. In the essay Sullivan attempts not a "formal history" of the Famine, but a history based on his own "personal observation," describing the political, social, and economic forces that contributed to the great tragedy.]*

There is probably no subject on which such painful misunderstanding and bitter recrimination have prevailed between the peoples of England and Ireland as the Irish famine. The enmities and antagonisms arising out of other historical events were at all events comprehensible. The havoc and devastation which ensued upon the Royalist-Cromwellian war of 1641-1650, the confiscations and proscriptions which followed the Stuart struggle in 1690, the insurrection of 1798, and the overthrow of the Irish constitution in 1800, were causes of ire, on the one side or the other, as to the reality of which there was at least no controversy. But it was not so in this case. The English people, remembering only the sympathy and compassion which they felt, the splendid contributions which they freely bestowed in that sad time, are shocked and angered beyond endurance when they hear Irishmen refer to the famine as a "slaughter." In Ireland, on the other hand, the burning memory of horrors which more prompt and competent action on the part of the ruling authorities might have considerably averted, seems to overwhelm all other recollection, and the noble generosity of the English people appears to be forgotten in a frenzy of reproach against the English Government of that day.

I know not whether the time has even yet arrived when that theme can be fairly treated, and when a calm and just apportionment of blame and merit may be attempted. To-day, full thirty years after the event, I tremble to contemplate it.

In 1841 the population of Ireland was 8,175,124 souls. By 1845 it had probably reached to nearly nine million. The increase had been fairly continuous for at least a century, and had become rapid between 1820 and 1840. To any one looking beneath the surface the condition of the country was painfully precarious. Nine millions of a population living at best in a light-hearted and hopeful hand-to-mouth contentment, totally dependent on the hazards of one crop, destitute of manufacturing industries, and utterly without reserve or resource to fall back upon in time of reverse; what did all this mean but a state of things critical and alarming in the extreme? Yet no one seemed conscious of danger. The potato crop had been abundant for four or five years, and respite from dearth and distress was comparative happiness and prosperity. Moreover, the temperance movement had come to make the "good times" still better. Everything looked bright. No one concerned himself to discover how slender and treacherous was the foundation for this general hopefulness and confidence.

Yet signs of the coming storm had been given. Partial famine caused by failing harvests had indeed been intermittent in Ireland, and quite recently warnings that ought not to have been mistaken or neglected had given notice that the esculent which formed the sole dependence of the peasant millions was subject to some mysterious blight. In 1844 it was stricken in America, but in Ireland the yield was healthy and plentiful as ever. The harvest of 1845 promised to be the richest gathered for many years. Suddenly, in one short month, in one week it might be said, the withering breath of a simoom seemed to sweep the land, blasting all in its path. I myself saw whole tracts of potato growth changed *in one night* from smiling luxuriance to a shrivelled and blackened waste. A shout of alarm arose. But the buoyant nature of the Celtic peasant did not yet give way. The crop was so profuse that it was expected the healthy portion would reach an average result. Winter revealed the alarming fact that the tubers had rotted in pit and store-house. Nevertheless the farmers, like hapless men who double their stakes to recover losses, made only the more strenuous exertions to till a larger breadth in 1846. Although already feeling the pinch of sore distress, if not actual famine, they worked as if for dear life; they begged and borrowed on any terms the means whereby to crop the land once more. The pawn-offices were choked with the humble finery that had shone at the village dance or christening feast; the banks and local moneylenders were besieged with appeals for credit. Meals were stinted, backs were bared. Anything, anything to tide over the interval to the harvest of "Forty-six."

O God, it is a dreadful thought that all this effort was but more surely leading them to ruin! It was this harvest of Forty-six that sealed their doom. Not partially but completely, utterly, hopelessly it perished. As in the previous year, all promised brightly up to the close of July. Then, suddenly, in a night, whole areas were blighted; and this time, alas! no portion of the crop escaped. A cry of agony and despair went up all over the land. The last desperate stake for life had been played, and all was lost.

The doomed people realised but too well what was before them. Last year's premonitory sufferings had exhausted them; and now?—they must die!

My native district figures largely in the gloomy record of that dreadful time. I saw the horrible phantasmagoria—would God it were but that!—pass before my eyes. Blank stolid dismay, a sort of stupor, fell upon the people, contrasting remarkably with the fierce energy put forth a year before. It was no uncommon sight to see the cottier and his little family seated on the garden fence gazing all day long in moody silence at the blighted plot that had been their last hope. Nothing could arouse them. You spoke; they answered not. You tried to cheer them; they shook their heads. I never saw so sudden and so terrible a transformation.

When first in the autumn of 1845 the partial blight appeared, wise voices were raised in warning to the Government that a frightful catastrophe was at hand; yet even then began that fatal circumlocution and inaptness which it maddens one to think of. It would be utter injustice to deny that the Government made exertions which judged by ordinary emergencies would be prompt and considerable. But judged by the awful magnitude of the evil then at hand or actually befallen, they were fatally tardy and inadequate. When at length the executive did hurry, the blunders of precipitancy outdid the disasters of excessive deliberation.

In truth the Irish famine was one of those stupendous calamities which the rules and formulæ of ordinary constitutional administration were unable to cope with, and which could be efficiently encountered only by the concentration of plenary powers and resources in some competent "despotism" located in the scene of disaster. It was easy to foresee the result of an attempt to deal "at long range" with such an evil—to manage it from Downing Street, London, according to orthodox routine. Again and again the Government were warned, not by heedless orators or popular leaders, but by men of the highest position and soundest repute in Ireland, that even with the very best intentions on their part, mistake and failure must abound in any attempt to grapple with the famine by the ordinary machinery of Government. Many efforts, bold and able efforts, were made by the Government and by Parliament eighteen months subsequently—I refer especially to the measures taken in the session of 1847. But, unfortunately, everything seemed to come too late. Delay made all the difference. In October 1845 the Irish Mansion House Relief Committee implored the Government to call Parliament together and throw open the ports. The Government refused. Again and again the terrible urgency of the case, the magnitude of the disaster at hand, was pressed on the executive. It was the obstinate refusal of Lord John Russell to listen to these remonstrances and entreaties, and the sad verification subsequently of these apprehensions, that implanted in the Irish mind the bitter memories which still occasionally find vent in passionate accusation of "England."

Not but the Government had many and weighty arguments in behalf of the course they took. Firstly, they feared exaggeration, and waited for official investigation and report. [The truth is, the fight over the Corn Law question in England at the time was peculiarly unfortunate for Ireland; because the protectionist press and politicians felt it a duty strenuously to deny there was any danger of famine, lest such a circumstance should be made a pretext for Free Trade. Thus the Duke of Richmond, on the 9th of December 1845, speaking at the Agricultural Protection Society, said: "With respect to the cry of 'Famine,' he believed that it was perfectly illusory, and no man of respectability could have put it in good faith if he had been acquainted with the facts within the knowledge of their society."

At Warwick, on the 31st of December, Mr. Newdegate carried a resolution testifying against "the fallacy and mischief of the reports of a deficient harvest," and affirming that "there was no reasonable ground for apprehending a scarcity of food."

Like declarations abounded in England up to a late period of the famine, and, no doubt, considerably retarded the prompt action of the Government.] Even when official testimony was forthcoming, the Cabinet in London erred, as the Irish peasantry did, in trusting somewhat that the harvest of 1846 would change gloom to joy. When the worst came in 1846-47, much precious time was lost through misunderstanding and recrimination between the Irish landlords and the executive; charges of neglect of duties on one hand, and of incapacity on the other, passing freely to and fro. No doubt the Government feared waste, prodigality, and abuse if it placed absolute power and unlimited supplies in the hands of an Irish board; and one must allow that, to a commercial-minded people, the violations of the doctrines of political economy involved in every suggestion and demand shouted across the Channel from Ireland were very alarming. Yet in the end it was found—all too late, unfortunately—that those doctrines were inapplicable in such a case. They had to be flung aside in 1847. Had they been discarded a year or two sooner a million of lives might have been saved.

The situation bristled with difficulties. "Do not demoralise the people by pauper doles, but give them employment," said one counsellor. "Beware how you interfere with the labour market," answered another. "It is no use voting millions to be paid away on relief works while you allow the price of food to be run up four hundred per cent.; set up Government depôts for sale of food at reasonable price," cried many wise and far-seeing men. "Utterly opposed to the teachings of Adam Smith," responded Lord John Russell.

At first the establishment of public soupkitchens under local relief committees, subsidised by Government, was relied upon to arrest the famine. I doubt if the world ever saw so huge a demoralisation, so great a degradation, visited upon a once high-spirited and sensitive people. All over the country large iron boilers were set up in which what was called "soup" was concocted; later on Indian-meal stirabout was boiled. Around these boilers on the roadside there daily moaned and shrieked and fought and scuffled crowds of gaunt, cadaverous creatures that once had been men and women made in the image of God. The feeding of dogs in a kennel was far more decent and orderly. I once thought—ay, and often bitterly said, in public and in private—that never, never would our people recover the shameful humiliation of that brutal public soupboiler scheme. I frequently stood and watched the scene till tears blinded me and I almost chocked with grief and passion. It was heart-breaking, almost maddening, to see; but help for it there was none.

The Irish poor-law system early broke down under the strain which the famine imposed. Until 1846 the workhouses were shunned and detested by the Irish poor. Relief of destitution had always been regarded by the Irish as a sort of religious duty or fraternal succour. Poverty was a misfortune, not a crime. When, however, relief was offered, on the penal condition of an imprisonment that sundered the family tie, and which, by destroying home, howsoever humble, shut out all hope of future recovery, it was indignantly spurned. Scores of times I have seen some poor widow before the workhouse board clasp her little children tightly to her heart and sob aloud, "No, no, your honour. If they are to be parted from me I'll not come in. I'll beg the wide world with them."

But soon beneath the devouring pangs of starvation even this holy affection had to give way, and the famishing people poured into the workhouses, which soon choked with the dying and the dead. Such privations had been endured in every case before this hated ordeal was faced, that the people entered the Bastille merely to die. The parting scenes of husband and wife, father and mother and children, at the board-room door would melt a heart of stone. Too well they felt it was to be an eternal severance, and that this loving embrace was to be their last on earth. The warders tore them asunder—the husband from the wife, the mother from the child—for "discipline" required that it should be so. But, with the famine fever in every ward, and the air around them laden with disease and death, they knew their fate, and parted like victims at the foot of the guillotine.

It was not long until the workhouses overflowed and could admit no more. Rapidly as the death-rate made vacancies, the pressure of applicants overpowered all resources. Worse still, bankruptcy came on many a union. In some the poor-rate rose to twenty-two shillings on the pound, and very nearly the entire rural population of several were needing relief. In a few cases, I am sorry to say, the horrible idea seemed to seize the landowners on the boards that all rates would be ineffectual, and that, as their imposition would result only in ruining "property," it was as well to "let things take their course." Happily an act of Parliament was passed in 1846 which gave the poor-law commissioners in Dublin power to deal with cases of delay or refusal to make adequate provision for maintenance of the workhouse. All such boards were abolished by sealed order, and paid vice-guardians were appointed in their place. To these, as well as to elected boards willing to face their duty, the commissioners were empowered to advance, by way of loan, secured on the lands within the union, funds sufficient to carry on the poor-law system. Had it not been for this arrangement, the workhouses would have closed altogether in many parts of the country.

The conduct of the Irish landlords throughout the famine period has been variously described, and has been, I believe, generally condemned. I consider the censure visited on them too sweeping. I hold it to be in some respects cruelly unjust. On many of them no blame too heavy could possibly fall. A large number were permanent absentees; their ranks were swelled by several who early fled the post of duty at home—cowardly and selfish deserters of a brave and faithful people. Of those who remained, some may have grown callous; it is impossible to contest authentic instances of brutal heartlessness here and there. But granting all that has to be entered on the dark debtor side, the overwhelming balance is the other way. The bulk of the resident Irish landlords manfully did their best in that dread hour. [No adequate tribute has ever been paid to the memory of those Irish landlords—and they were men of every party and creed—who perished martyrs to duty in that awful time; who did not fly the plague-reeking workhouse or fever-tainted court. Their names would make a goodly roll of honour. The people of Bantry still mourn for Mr. Richard White of Inchiclogh, cousin of Lord Bantry, who early fell in this way. Mr. Martin, M.P.—"Dick Martin," Prince of Connemara—caught fever while acting as a magistrate, and was swept away. One of the most touching stories I ever heard was that told me by an eye-witness of how Mr. Nolan of Ballinderry (father of Captain J. P. Nolan, M.P.), braving the deadly typhus in Tuam workhouse, was struck down, amidst the grief of a people who mourn him to this day.] If they did too little compared with what the landlord class in England would have done in similar case, it was because little was in their power. The famine found most of the resident landed gentry of Ireland on the brink of ruin. They were heritors of estates heavily overweighted with the debts of a bygone generation. Broad lands and lordly mansions were held by them on settlements and conditions that allowed small scope for the exercise of individual liberality. To these landowners the failure of one year's rental receipts meant mortgage foreclosure and hopeless ruin. Yet cases might be named by the score in which such men scorned to avert by pressure on their suffering tenantry the fate they saw impending over them. They "went down with the ship."

In the autumn of 1846 relief works were set on foot, the Government having received parliamentary authority to grant baronial loans for such undertakings. There might have been found many ways of applying these funds in reproductive employment, but the modes decided on were draining and road-making. Of course it was not possible to provide very rapidly the engineering staff requisite for surveying and laying out so many thousands of new roads all over the country; but eventually the scheme was somehow hurried into operation. The result was in every sense deplorable failure. The wretched people were by this time too wasted and emaciated to work. The endeavour to do so under an inclement winter sky only hastened death. They tottered at daybreak to the roll-call; vainly tried to wheel the barrow or ply the pick, but fainted away on the "cutting," or lay down on the wayside to rise no more. As for the "roads" on which so much money was wasted, and on which so many lives were sacrificed, hardly any of them were finished. Miles of grass-grown earthworks throughout the country now mark their course and commemorate for posterity one of the gigantic blunders of the famine time.

The first remarkable sign of the havoc which death was making was the decline and disappearance of funerals. Amongst the Irish people a funeral was always a great display, and participation in the procession was for all neighbours and friends a sacred duty. A "poor" funeral—that is, one thinly attended—was considered disrespectful to the deceased and reproachful to the living. The humblest peasant was borne to the grave by a parochial *cortége*. But one could observe in the summer of '46 that, as funerals became more frequent, there was a rapid decline in the number of attendants, until at length persons were stopped on the road and requested to assist in conveying the coffin a little way further. Soon, alas! neither coffin nor shroud could be supplied. Daily in the street and on the footway some poor creature lay down as if to sleep, and presently was stiff and stark. In our district it was a common occurrence to find on opening the front door in early morning, leaning against it, the corpse of some victim who in the night time had "rested" in its shelter. We raised a public subscription, and employed two men with horse and cart to go around each day and gather up the dead. One by one they were taken to a great pit at Ardnabrahair Abbey, and dropped through the hinged bottom of a "trap-coffin" into a common grave below. In the remoter rural districts even this rude sepulture was impossible. In the field and by the ditch side the victims lay as they fell, till some charitable hand was found to cover them with the adjacent soil.

It was the fever which supervened on the famine that wrought the greatest slaughter and spread the greatest terror. For this destroyer when it came spared no class, rich or poor. As long as it was "the hunger" alone that raged, it was no deadly peril to visit the sufferers; but not so now. To come within the reach of this contagion was certain death. Whole families perished unvisited and unassisted. By levelling above their corpses the sheeling in which they died, the neighbours gave them a grave. [I myself assisted in such a task under heartrending circumstances in June 1847.]

No pen can trace nor tongue relate the countless deeds of heroism and self-sacrifice which this dreadful visitation called forth on the part, preeminently, of two classes in the community—the Catholic clergy and the dispensary doctors of Ireland. I have named the Catholic clergy, not that those of the Protestant denominations did not furnish many instances of devotion fully as striking, but because on the former obviously fell the brunt of the trial. [The Protestant curate of my native parish in 1847 was the Rev. Alexander Ben Hallowell, subsequently rector of Clonakilty, and now I believe residing somewhere in Lancashire. There were comparatively few of his own flock in a way to suffer from the famine; but he dared death daily in his desperate efforts to save the perishing creatures around him. A poor hunchback named Richard O'Brien lay dying of the plague in a deserted hovel at a place called "the Custom Gap." Mr. Hallowell, passing by, heard the moans and went in. A shocking sight met his view. On some rotten straw in a dark corner lay poor "Dick" naked, except for a few rags across his body. Mr. Hallowell rushed to the door and saw a young friend on the road: "Run, run with this shilling and buy me some wine," he cried. Then he re-entered the hovel, stripped off his own clothes, and with his own hands put upon the plague-stricken hunchback the flannel vest and drawers and the shirt of which he had just divested himself. I know this to be true. *I* was the "young friend" who went for and brought the wine.] For them there was no flinching. A call to administer the last rites of religion to the inmate of a plague-ward or fever-shed *must* be, and is, obeyed by the Catholic priest, though death to himself be the well-known

consequence. The fatality amongst the two classes I have mentioned, clergymen and doctors, was lamentable. Christian heroes, martyrs for humanity, their names are blazoned on no courtly roll; yet shall they shine upon an eternal page, brighter than the stars!

But even this dark cloud of the Irish famine had its silver lining. If it is painful to recall the disastrous errors of irresolution and panic, one can linger gratefully over memories of Samaritan philanthropy, of efficacious generosity, of tenderest sympathy. The people of England behaved nobly; and assuredly not less munificent were the citizens of the great American Republic, which had already become the home of thousands of the Irish race. From every considerable town in England there poured subscriptions, amounting in the aggregate to hundreds of thousands of pounds. From America came a truly touching demonstration of national sympathy. Some citizens of the States contributed two shiploads of breadstuffs, and the American Government decided to furnish the ships which should bring the offering to the Irish shore. Accordingly two war-vessels, the *Macedonian* and the *Jamestown* frigates, having had their armaments removed, their "gun-decks" displaced and cargo bulk-heads put up, were filled to the gunwale with best American flour and biscuits, and despatched on their errand of mercy. It happened that just previously the British naval authorities had rather strictly refused the loan of a ship for a like purpose, as being quite opposed to all departmental regulations (which, to be sure, it was), and a good deal of angry feeling was called forth by the refusal. Yet had it a requiting contrast in the despatch from England, by voluntary associations there, of several deputations or embassies of succour, charged to visit personally the districts in Ireland most severely afflicted, and to distribute with their own hands the benefactions they brought.

Foremost in this blessed work were the Society of Friends, the English members of that body co-operating with its central committee in Dublin. Amongst the most active and fearless of their representatives was a young Yorkshire Quaker, whose name, I doubt not, is still warmly remembered by Connemara peasants. He drove from village to village, he walked bog and moor, rowed the lake and climbed the mountain, fought death, as it were, hand to hand, in brave resolution to save the people. His correspondence from the scene of his labours would constitute in itself a graphic memorial of the Irish famine. That young "Yorkshire Quaker" of 1847 was destined a quarter of a century later to be known to the empire as a minister of the Crown—the Right Hon. W. E. Forster, M.P.

In truth, until the appearance a few years since of the Rev. Mr. O'Rorke's excellent volume, the *History of the Irish Famine,* the only competent record of the events of that time was the *Report of the Society of*

Friends' Irish Relief Committee. It is a remarkable fact that the traveller who now visits the west and south of Ireland, and seeks to gather from the people reminiscences of the famine time, will find praise and blame a good deal mingled as to nearly every other relief agency of the period; but naught save grateful recollection of the unostentatious, kindly, prompt, generous, and efficacious action of the Friends' committee. Fondly as the Catholic Irish revere the memory of their own priests who suffered with and died for them in that fearful time, they give a place in their prayers to the "good Quakers, God bless them," Jonathan Pim, Richard Allen, Richard Webb, and William Edward Forster.

The Irish famine of 1847 had results, social and political, that constitute it one of the most important events in Irish history for more than two hundred years. It is impossible for any one who knew the country previous to that period, and who has thoughtfully studied it since, to avoid the conclusion that so much has been destroyed, or so greatly changed, that the Ireland of old times will be seen no more.

The losses will, I would fain hope, be in a great degree repaired; the gains entirely retained. Yet much that was precious was engulfed, I fear, beyond recovery. "Here are twenty miles of country, sir," said a dispensary doctor to me, "and before the famine there was not a padlock from end to end of it." Under the pressure of hunger, ravenous creatures prowled around barn and storehouse, stealing corn, potatoes, cabbage, turnips—anything, in a word, that might be eaten. Later on the fields had to be watched, gun in hand, or the seed was rooted up and devoured raw. This state of things struck a fatal blow at some of the most beautiful traits of Irish rural life. It destroyed the simple confidence that bolted no door; it banished for ever a custom which throughout the island was of almost universal obligation—the housing for the night, with cheerful welcome, of any poor wayfarer who claimed hospitality. Fear of "the fever," even where no apprehension of robbery was entertained, closed every door, and the custom, once killed off, has not revived. A thousand kindly usages and neighbourly courtesies were swept away. When *sauve qui peut* had resounded throughout a country for three years of alarm and disaster, human nature becomes contracted in its sympathies, and "every one for himself" becomes a maxim of life and conduct long after. The open-handed, openhearted ways of the rural population have been visibly affected by the "Forty-seven" ordeal. Their ancient sports and pastimes everywhere disappeared, and in many parts of Ireland have never returned. The outdoor games, the hurling-match, and the village dance are seen no more.

With the greater seriousness of character which the famine period has imprinted on the Irish people, some notable changes for the better must be recognised. Providence, forethought, economy are studied and valued as they never were before. There is more method, strictness, and punctuality in business transactions. There is a graver sense of responsibility on all hands. For the first time the future seems to be earnestly thought of, and its possible vicissitudes kept in view. More steadiness of purpose, more firmness and determination of character, mark the Irish peasantry of the new era. God has willed that in the midst of such awful sufferings some share of blessings should fall on the sorely shattered nation.

A. Nicholson describes a starving man:

[R]eader, if you have never seen a starving human being, *may you never!* In my childhood I had been frightened with the stories of ghosts, and had seen actual skeletons; but imagination had come short of the sight of this man. And here, to those who have never watched the progress of protracted hunger, it might be proper to say, that persons will live for months, and pass through different stages, and life will struggle on to maintain her lawful hold, if occasional scanty supplies are given, till the walking skeleton is reduced to a state of inanity—he sees you not, he heeds you not, neither does he beg. The first stage is somewhat clamorous—will not easily be put off; the next is patient, passive stupidity; and the last is idiocy. In the second stage they will stand at a window for hours, without asking charity, giving a vacant stare, and not until peremptorily driven away will they move. In the last state, the head bends forward, and they walk with long strides, and pass you unheedingly. The man before mentioned was emaciated to the last degree; he was tall, his eyes prominent, his skin shriveled, his manner cringing and childlike; and the impression *then* and *there* made never *has* nor never *can* be effaced; it was the *first*, and the beginning of these dreadful days yet in reserve. . . .

A. Nicholson, in Annals of the Famine in Ireland, in 1847, 1848, and 1849, *E. French, 1851.*

Cormac Ó Gráda (essay date 1989)

SOURCE: "The Great Hunger 1845-1850," in *The Great Irish Famine*, Macmillan Education Ltd., 1989, pp. 39-64.

[*In this excerpt from his book-length study of Ireland's pre-Famine population and economy, the Famine itself, and the years following the Famine, Ó Gráda outlines in brief the history of the Famine, from 1845 through 1850, including the political, economic, and human dimensions of the Famine as well as the subsequent relief efforts made by the British government.*]

The arrival of *Phythophthora infestans* or potato blight in Ireland was first noted in the press on 6 September 1845. The 'New Disease' had already struck in the US in the summer of 1843. According to a contemporary account from there, 'potatoes [were] subject to dry rot, attacking some in the hill, and some in the heap, and fatal to the whole wherever it makes its appearance, causing them to rot and emit a very offensive stench'.[27] The blight then crossed the ocean by a mysterious route, reaching Ireland via Continental Europe and England. The news that Ireland had been hit caused the London *Gardener's Chronicle* to stop press, but local reports from Ireland were initially reassuring. Reaction in financial and commodity markets was minimal. Indeed the movement of potato prices on the Dublin market in the autumn of 1845 reflects this. Lumpers, which fetched 16d. to 20d. per hundredweight (or 50 kilos) in the second week of September, could still be bought for less than 18d. until near the end of November. (Then, it is true, prices rose beyond 2 shillings, and had passed 3 shillings by April 1846.) In political circles, however, the gravity of the situation soon became a 'party' issue: 'to profess belief in . . . the existence of a formidable potato blight, was as sure a method of being branded a radical, as to propose to destroy the Church.'[28] Constabulary crop returns soon put an end to the confusion; they suggested that less than half the crop had been lost, though the poor, who tended to plant their potatoes late, were worst hit.

The disease was, of course, a mystery. Most botanists agreed with Professor Lindley, eminent editor of the *Gardener's Chronicle,* who blamed the still, damp weather for the excess moisture that caused the tubers to rot. A fungal specialist, Rev. M.J. Berkeley, correctly diagnosed the mould on the plants as a 'vampire' fungus that fed on healthy potatoes, but the fungal hypothesis was scoffed at by most experts. Lindley dominated the official committee of inquiry ordered by Peel, now Prime Minister, and so the disease was diagnosed as a kind of wet rot. The committee's report suggested storage in well-ventilated pits as the best remedy: corollary remedies included dousing in quicklime, exposure to air, kiln drying, and a cover of ashes.[29] The blight excited enormous interest in the gardening and scientific press for a time, but Bourke [1964] suggests that 'few authentic clues' stand out amid the welter of hunches and assertions. Not that a different diagnosis would have eliminated the problem: an antidote for potato blight (copper sulphate solution) was not discovered until 1882. (Ironically the salutory effect of copper had been noted in Swansea in 1846, but quickly forgotten.) Acceptance of Berkeley's diagnosis would have dictated felling diseased tubers, thereby delaying the blight's progress. But that would not have mattered much. More important, the blight which, as noted above, had severely damaged the US potato crop in 1843, did so again in the US in 1844 and 1845 [Bourke, "The Scientific Investigation of the Potato

Blight in 1845-6," in *Irish Historical Studies,* 13, 1962]. Had the fungal diagnosis been more widely accepted, might this tendency for the disease to recur have reduced the widespread complacency about the prospects of the 1846 Irish potato harvest?

Sir Robert Peel, long familiar with Irish problems—he had been Irish Secretary in 1822 and Home Secretary subsequently—acted quickly [O'Rourke, *History of the Great Irish Famine of 1847,* 1902, *122-30*]. Against Treasury advice, he engaged the merchant house of Baring Brothers in November 1845 to purchase £100,000 worth of maize and meal—enough to feed 1 million people for over a month—in America. A buffer stock was built without fuss or publicity. In the event, it was hardly needed. Though history books often date the Famine from the first onslaught of the blight, few people perished in the 1845-6 season. This remarkable achievement was partly due to the efficacy of relief, but partly too to the country's ability to handle such a shortfall, provided the next year's crop was not long delayed.

(i) Chronology

The renewed and more complete failure of the potato in 1846 heralded the true beginning of the Great Famine. Another failure had not been anticipated, for despite the previous year's poor harvest, the potato acreage was close to an all-time high in 1846. In the early summer the potato plots bloomed 'like flower gardens', but any hopes that the blight might prove a one-year wonder soon vanished. The tell-tale discoloured leaves and stalks and the stench were everywhere, and another police report based on returns from all over the country put the average yield at less than half a ton per acre (compared to the usual six to seven tons). The prices of potatoes of all varieties rocketed. Cups, which had been worth less than 2 shillings per hundredweight (or 50 kilos) on the Dublin market in October 1845 were selling for over 7 shillings a year later, while the price of the lowly Lumper had jumped from about 16d. to 6 shillings.[30] The average agricultural wage per day was now less than the cost of a poor man's food, making no allowance for those dependent on him. Famine loomed. The new minority Whig administration of Lord John Russell faced urgent pleas for public works and controls on the grain trade. But having berated the Tories for over-reacting in 1845-6, Russell's policy was one of wait-and-see.

The numbers starving to death began to mount alarmingly in the autumn of 1846, and reports of some particularly gruesome cases soon began to appear in the press. Some of these are described at length by Woodham-Smith [*The Great Hunger: Ireland, 1845-49,* 1962] and Kee [*Ireland: A History,* 1981], but in the retreat from 'emotiveness' mentioned earlier, other accounts shun them.[31] Yet reports such as the follow-

Famine victims receive clothing and other assistance in Kilrush, Ireland, 1849.

ing pair from south-west Cork, usually considered the worst-hit area in the early stages of the Famine, are at the heart of the famine story. They make it 'a palpable thing', adding context to the matchstick scavengers portrayed in the *Illustrated London News* in 1847 and 1848, and widely reproduced since [Edwards and Williams, *The Great Famine: Studies in Irish History,* 1956; Irish University Press, 'Famine Series', 1968; Woodham-Smith, 1962]:[32]

> The famine grew more horrible towards the end of December 1846, many were buried with neither inquest nor coffin. An inquest was held by Dr. Sweetman on three bodies. The first was that of the father of two very young children whose mother had already died of starvation. His death became known only when the two children toddled into the village of Schull. They were crying of hunger and complaining that their father would not speak to them for four days; they told how he was 'as cold as a flag'. The other bodies on which an inquest was held were those of a mother and child who had both died of starvation. The remains had been gnawed by rats.

Other accounts, like this horrific report from Caheragh in the Cork *Southern Reporter,* were widely publicized:

'The following is a statement of what I *saw* yesterday evening on the lands of Toureen. In a cabbage garden I saw (as I was informed) the bodies of Kate Barry and her two children very lightly covered with earth, the hands and legs of her large body entirely exposed, the flesh completely eaten off by the dogs, the skin and hair of the head lying within a couple of yards of the skull, which, when I first threw my eyes on it, I thought to be part of a horse's tail. Within about thirty yards of the above-mentioned garden, at the opposite side of the road, are two most wretched-looking old houses, with two dead bodies in each, Norry Regan, Tom Barry, Nelly Barry (a little girl), and Charles McCarthy (a little boy), all dead about a fortnight, and not yet interred; Tim Donovan, Darrig, on the same farm, died on Saturday, his wife and sister the only people I saw about the cabin, said they had no means to bury him. You will think this very horrifying; but were you to witness the state of the dead and dying here at Toureen, it would be too much for flesh and blood to behold. May the Lord avert, by his gracious interposition, the merited tokens of his displeasure.'

I need make no comment on this, but ask, *are we living in a portion of the United Kingdom?* (emphasis in the original)

Soon notices of 'deaths by starvation' lost their news-worthiness. The contemporary shock value of testimony such as that just quoted is difficult to evaluate. A generation ago the right-wing historian Max Hartwell ventured that people like himself 'well disciplined by familiarity with concentration camps' are left 'comparatively unmoved' by the scandal of child labour during the Industrial Revolution.[33] The assessment of 'emotive' accounts of Famine starvation in Irish historiography is similar: contemporary policy-makers, inured to—and constrained by—mass misery, took them in their stride, and no more should be expected of them. Later generations, then, should not set anachronistically high standards for the politicians and bureaucrats of the 1840s. But this perspective ignores the fact that in Ireland most decent people were shocked [compare also Woods, "American Travellers in Ireland Before and During the Great Famine: A Case of Culture-Shock," in Wolfgang Zach and Heinz Kosok (eds), *Literary Interrelations,* 1987], and clamoured for government to act. Even that most doctrinaire of policy-makers, Treasury Under Secretary Charles Trevelyan, was jolted by reports such as those just quoted for a time, and the immediate policy response was influenced by the publicity given to mass mortality.

The poor reacted vigorously at first to the crisis. Food rioting was widespread, and secret agrarian societies (locally organized but generically known as Ribbonmen) stepped up their activities [Donnelly, *The Land and People of Nineteenth-century Cork,* 1973, *187-91*].[34] Still, the full story of this popular resistance and its repression, which holds great potential for comparative insight on issues such as the moral economy and farmer-labourer conflict, remains to be told. Meanwhile the crime statistics help highlight the extent of the upsurge. They show, for example, that the number of persons committed for trial rose from an average of less than 20,000 in 1842-6 to 31,209 in 1847, 38,522 in 1848, and 41,989 in 1849.[35] Cross-tabulations by type of crime show that the surge was more the product of desperation than of malice: the number of commitals for non-violent offences against property trebled, while that for offences against the person (homicide, wounding, and sexual offences) hardly rose at all. The dramatic rise in the proportion of illiterates among those charged during the Famine (from 30 to over 40 per cent) also supports this interpretation. Striking too is the persistence of high crime rates until 1849, after which the crime rate dropped off sharply.

The mounting death toll prompted a series of policy initiatives. The then-traditional policy of providing work for the poor on public schemes through a Board of Works had been reintroduced by Peel in March 1846. This continued but with more central supervision, with Russell's Labour Rate Act. The cost of acceptable schemes was to fall 'entirely on persons possessed of property in the distressed districts'. Nevertheless, a flood of applications ensued, and for a time the Board was handling about 1,000 letters a day. The official in charge, Colonel Harry Jones, described the Board of Works in the following months as 'a great bazaar' [quoted in Griffiths, 1970]. Whitehall insisted on projects combining a high social and low private value. There was a cry in Ireland for 'reproductive' works, meaning land reclamation, drainage projects, and estate improvement generally. It was held that these would directly raise farm output, but the official preference for schemes such as road works and quays won out. The skill intensity of the projects selected was necessarily low: 'the work was chosen for the people, not the people for the work'. By October 1846 hundreds of projects were already employing over 100,000 people; 20,000 of the workers lived in a single county—Clare—while the whole province of Ulster accounted for only 1,200.

The schemes were proposed by local 'presentment sessions', bodies composed of local taxpayers with ultimate responsibility for repaying the cost. A sense of desperation, coupled perhaps with the conviction that government in the end would not exact repayment in full, bred fiscal irresponsibility. There was never the slightest hope that local taxpayers could repay the cost of all the schemes proposed, or even those sanctioned by the Board of Works. By the end of 1846 the Board was already exasperated, but the number of relief works under its aegis continued to mount, and by the following spring they had cost nearly £5 million. At the peak in March 1847 a vast army of almost three-quarters of a million was employed, at less than a subsistence wage, on works which made little sense in terms either of economy or their goal of staving off famine. Partly because they were failing in their main task, partly because it was feared that they would 'crowd out' farm work, they were quickly disbanded in the spring of 1847. This policy reversal left its mark on the rural landscape; it left farmers cut off from their fields by unfinished roads, cottages isolated on cuttings, 'constant and unsightly monument(s) of a disastrous period'. Such eyesores would have been a small price to pay for staving off starvation, but the Board's low-wage policy ruled that out. In a pointed 'final report' on its relief role, the Board expressed the hope that 'labour will not in future be lowered to the purpose of relief, nor relief deprived of its character of benevolence' [Irish University Press, 'Famine series', 1968, *vol. 8, 383*].

The provision of 'soup' or gruel—in effect 'any food cooked in a boiler, and distributed in a liquid state' [O'Rourke, 1902, *427*]—under the Destitute Poor (Ireland) Act, which came into operation in March 1847, seemed a step in the right direction. It attempted to tackle the problem of subsistence directly, and was less likely than the public works to 'crowd out' other employment. The cost was supposed to come from rates and charity, supplemented *pro rata* by government aid. During the summer of 1847 millions of meals were provided by local relief committees: in July the number fed reached 3 million daily. In some places more meals were provided daily than there were people. The distribution of soup was an impressive feat, and historians rate the scheme a success. The soup kitchens have not been subjected to close analytical scrutiny, however. True, mortality fell off during the summer of 1847 but this was, in part at least, a seasonal phenomenon. Whether soup alone would have prevented the mass mortality of the following winter is a moot point, because the last of the government soup kitchens were wound up, amid protest, at the end of September 1847. In practice the food value of the often watery soup was low, and the people were routinely humiliated by being made to queue for hours. Yet this was arguably 'by far the most effective of all the methods adopted by government' [Donnelly, 1988].

The Irish Poor Law Extension Act of June 1847 switched the main burden of relief to the Irish Poor Law system. The switch was prompted by a fall in food prices and an anticipated seasonal rise in the demand for labour. The workhouses, it was believed, could now cope with the numbers requiring relief. However, the workhouse system had been devised for the quite different purpose of coping with non-crisis poverty. It could not handle the larger responsibility, and during 1848 one-quarter of all Boards of Guardians, mainly those located in the poorest areas, were dissolved by the Commissioners in Dublin. Cross-subsidization *within* Ireland through the highly unpopular 'rate-in-aid' shifted some of the burden to more prosperous unions [Woodham-Smith, 1962, *378-9*]. Clearly the workhouses themselves, though they had greatly expanded their capacity, could not house all the poor. Outdoor relief was widely relied on: in July 1849 the workhouses still housed over 200,000 people, but another 800,000 were on outdoor relief. The principle of 'less eligibility' was pressed home by the infamous Gregory Clause, which barred tenants who held more than one-quarter of an acre of land from relief. But the decision, taken in the summer of 1847, to throw the burden of relief on the Irish Poor Law and the Irish taxpayer was the most cynical move of all. It amounted to a declaration that, as far as Whitehall was concerned, the Famine was over. This callous act, born of ideology and frustration, prolonged the crisis. In the west roadside deaths were still commonplace in the winter of 1848-9 [Ó Gráda, *Ireland Before and After the Famine: Explorations in Economic History 1800-1930*, 1988, 86-8; Woodham-Smith, 1962, *406-7*].

Unfortunately for Ireland, the height of the Famine period—late 1846 and early 1847—was one of financial crisis in Britain. The 'railway mania' which began in 1845 had run its course, and bad harvests in both Ireland and Britain in 1846 led to a huge trade deficit and consequent drain of bullion on the Bank of England. The ensuing sharp rise in the cost of credit embarrassed many companies. The value of cotton output fell by a quarter. The financial crisis of 1847 thus had 'real' origins, though it was exacerbated (so most economists argue) by the restrictiveness of the Bank Act of 1844. The crisis was relatively short-lived, but it was one of the nineteenth century's worst, and from Ireland's point of view the timing was inauspicious. With the plight of the Bank of England to worry them, it is easier to see how Ireland's problems took a back seat in the minds of Russell and Wood.

The history of the Famine has always been handled without due attention to its short-term impact on the Irish economy. The crisis left no sector unscathed. Censal occupational data show that while agriculture was worst hit, other sectors, dependent either directly or indirectly on purchases from farmers and labourers, suffered severely too. . . . The dramatic and sustained falling off in monetary circulation can be explained neither by the crisis of 1847 (which it outlasted) nor legislative reform. Its connection with the Famine is underlined by the dramatic drop in the circulation of low-denomination banknotes, used in transactions such as wage payments and the business dealings of the poor. The amount of silver species held by the banks . . . also fell markedly.[36] 1846 was a boom year for business and banks, but 1847 presented difficulties as the price of corn plummeted, and rents were not paid.[37] These years saw too the creation of Ireland's rail system. Between 1845 and 1853 track mileage grew from 70 to 700 miles, and in 1846-8 railway construction projects employed on average about 40,000 men. The benefits of railway investment for the Irish economy proved more lasting than those of the roads and bridges built by a far larger army of emaciated workers on public relief. But while the long-run consequences of the network were very important, this railway boom could do little to alleviate the Famine.[38]

The trend of weekly deaths in the poorhouses is a fallible but still useful indication of the spread of the deaths over time. The numbers highlight the seasonality of deaths and—more importantly—the long-drawn-out character of the crisis [Mokyr and Ó Gráda, "New Developments in Irish Population History, 1700-1845," *Economic History Review,* 47 1984, *84-6*]. Now famine deaths, it is true, usually outlast the literal shortage of food, but in Ireland what shocks is the *size* of the excess mortality in 1848-50. The continuing winter mortality peaks point like accusing fingers pointed at the official determination to declare the crisis over in the summer of 1847. The precise number who died will never be known, though guesses abound [Boyle and Ó Gráda, "Fertility Trends, Excess Mortality, and the Great Irish Famine, *Demography,* 23 1986; Cousens, "The Regional Variation in Emigration from Ireland Between 1821 and 1841," *Proceedings of the Royal*

Irish Academy, 63, 1963; Mokyr, "The Deadly Fungus," *Research in Population Economics,* 2, 1980b]. Some recent revisionist accounts have reduced the figure to 0.5 million, but Woodham-Smith has proposed 1.5 million [1962, *411*] and the *New Encyclopedia Britannica* puts deaths as high as 2-3 million.[39] Civil registration data on mortality are lacking, but by extrapolating the censal population estimates of 1841 to 1851, and allowing for non-crisis mortality and migration, an estimate of famine mortality is generated as a residual. In practice, incomplete Famine emigration data present a problem. No proper count was kept of the *flow* to Britain: only data on the number of Irish living in Britain in 1851 are available. Nor do passenger list tabulations, the best source on the numbers who boarded ships to move further afield, capture everybody either. In calculating excess mortality it is thus easy for the historian to consign to a premature grave some who escaped abroad unnoticed. For what they are worth, two recent estimates confirm the traditional guess of an excess mortality of 1 million, or one-in-nine of the whole population [Mokyr, 1980b; Boyle and Ó Gráda, 1986). Both ignore the difficulties of disentangling cholera deaths from the total, and base their assumptions about 'normal' mortality on imperfect censal data. Mokyr [1980b] reminds us that the Famine also reduced the birth rate below the 'normal' level, and argues the case for including such averted births as famine victims. He puts their number at about 0.4 million.[40]

If scientific diagnosis of the potato blight was crude, medical science was ineffective in preventing the ensuing deaths. Ireland had a large number of hospitals (about 40 regular and 60 fever hospitals) and over 600 dispensaries. These hospitals and dispensaries, largely the relics of earlier crises, survived on a combination of public funds and local enterprise. Worthy institutions, they were often poorly managed, and their spread was inverse to need. Medical practitioners grumbled about their rewards for famine duties. The work was dangerous, however: 36 of the 473 men appointed as medical officers by the Board of Health died of the occupational hazard of famine fever. But medical men had no remedies for fever or dysentery beyond what commonsense dictated. The treatment meted out in fever hospitals in the 1840s—deemed 'lazarettos for the reception of the sick' by Dublin's leading physician, Dominick Corrigan—was still fumigation with sulphuric acid and 'nitre', and the baking of victims' clothes.[41]

Those who died better-publicized deaths during the first famine winter in places such as Skibbereen perished of starvation, and of dysentery induced by infected and unwholesome foods. But 'no famine, no fever', and later deaths were disproportionately due to fever. Relapsing sickness, a less virulent form of fever endemic in Ireland, was accompanied by (and sometimes confused with) the more murderous typhus.

Typhus was more likely to attack all socioeconomic groups, and once the rich contracted it, they were more likely to succumb than the poor. The cholera epidemic of 1849 was undoubtedly intensified by the Famine. Cholera's first visitation in 1832-3 had killed 25,000. The higher toll in 1849-50—the 1851 census put the total at 36,000—may be attributed in large part to the effects of the Famine, for a double reason: casualties were more frequent where the Famine was gravest and, besides, well-fed people can usually withstand or recover from cholera infection.

Who perished? The Famine presumably forced many families, like the occupants of an overloaded lifeboat, to make life-and-death choices: an equal sharing of the burden of hunger might have doomed all. Were the young sacrificed so that others might live? The admittedly curious tale of an infant 'at the mother's breast [who] had to be removed' so that its teenage brother 'might receive sustenance from his mother to enable him to remain at work' highlights the issue [O'Rourke, 1902, *274*]. A recent study of the Famine's incidence by age and sex shows that crisis mortality was almost a straightforward multiple of ordinary mortality. Children under 10 years and old people over 60 were overrepresented among the famine dead; they accounted for less than one-third of the population but three-fifths of the deaths. Thus in a sense the very old and young were 'sacrificed'. But such proportions held in normal times also [Boyle and Ó Gráda, 1986]. In this the Great Famine resembled the Bengali famine of 1940-3. The pattern is by no means inevitable, however [Watkins and Menken, "Famines in Historical Perspective," *Population and Development Review,* II 1985, *654-6*]; Irish famine mortality was the product of a particular combination of the 'lifeboat ethics' described above, dysentery which tended to target the young, and typhus which was more inclined to attack the elderly.

(ii) Ideology and Relief

The history of the Irish Famine is also British political history. By mid-October 1845 the potato failure had convinced Peel that only 'the removal of all impediments to the import of all kinds of human food' would remove the threat of famine, and this dramatic reversal of a key Tory policy—the Corn Laws—led to his political downfall eight months later [Gash, *Sir Robert Peel,* 1972, *538*]. Other leading politicians of the day, from Whig (or Liberal Party) leader Lord John Russell to Tory protectionist Lord George Bentinck, were less inclined to bend their previous views. The range of attitudes in high places towards public help for the Irish is curious. In terms of today's political alignments, the Tories of the time would be considered 'liberal'. Peel's determined action in 1845-6 has often been contrasted with the harsh policies of Russell and Wood at the height of the Famine,[42] while Bentinck was a vocal supporter of more spending in Ireland, in particular on railways. Against this, Whig spokesmen such as Whately and Senior believed that preventing mass mortality was simply impossible. Even attempting to do so was wrong, since it would bankrupt Irish landlords, and the ensuing demoralization would destroy 'industry' and 'self-dependence' and ultimately put a stop to economic activity. The Whigs, too, were consistent in their faith in the market, and their text might have been Adam Smith's dictum that 'the free exercise (of trade) is not only the best palliative of the inconveniences of a dearth, but the best preventative of that calamity'.[43]

The contrast oversimplifies, for Peel as long ago as 1822 had articulated those same fears of generous relief now so emphasized by the Whigs. But he had felt and insisted too that 'the exigency of the present case precludes any consideration of ultimate results'.[44] Nor were political groupings in the 1840s as ideologically monolithic as today. Clarendon, the Whig Lord Lieutenant, was much more eager for aid than his colleagues in Whitehall. The split in the Tory ranks on the Corn Laws spilled over into Irish policy, and after his defeat in July 1846 Peel tended to support the Whig ministry against Bentinck from the backbenches. Again, some of the Whig reluctance to spend may be traced to their wish to embarrass Irish landlords, in the main supporters of the Tories. But once more the distinction is hardly clearcut, since several leading Irish landlords were influential Whigs. Yet the ideological tensions that divided Whig and Tory on the Poor Law and factory legislation are also reflected in Famine relief policy. In line with their more *noblesse oblige* attitude toward social welfare legislation, the Tories at least paid lip service to more food aid, a less restrictive use of the Poor Law, more public spending on the infrastructure, and subsidies to improving landlords.

Leading Whigs and Radicals, by contrast, insisted on the evils of public charity and the 'inevitability' of the outcome. They were strongly supported in this by the *Edinburgh Review* and the fledgling *Economist*. Avoiding deaths was not the prime Whig preoccupation: relief would shift the distribution of food 'from the more meritorious to the less', because 'if left to the natural law of distribution, those who deserved more would obtain it'.[45] Thus in the Commons Russell refused to commit himself to saving lives as the prime objective, and some Whig ideologues such as Nassau Senior and *The Economist*'s Thomas Wilson ('it is no man's business to provide for another') countenanced large-scale mortality with equanimity. In India as in Ireland, Whig logic highlighted the abuses of intervention, and made light of the cost in human lives [Ambirajan, *Classical Political Economy and British Policy in India,* 1978, *ch. 3*]. It is easy to see why populist and socialist critics saw this as Malthusian murder by the invisible hand [see Gibbon, 1975]. Ironically historians have been dismissive of the likes of Bentinck and William

Smith O'Brien, who showed far more humanity than either, say, Lord Brougham or John Roebuck, MP for Bath, remembered today as enlightened men. But historical wrath has been reserved for permanent Treasury Under-Secretary Charles Trevelyan, the able but arrogant mandarin responsible for day-to-day policy decisions during the Famine. Trevelyan, very much the villain in Woodham-Smith's plot [1962], has an able defender in Austin Bourke, who contrasts Trevelyan's more dogmatic pronouncements under Russell with a more flexible stance earlier under Peel.[46] With Russell in command, claims Bourke, Trevelyan's humanitarian instincts could find no voice. An analysis of Trevelyan's private papers, however, lends little support to this view. It shows that the Under-Secretary, a deeply religious man, fully believed throughout that the Famine had been ordained by God to teach the Irish a lesson, and therefore should not be too much interfered with [Hart, "Sir Charles Trevelyan at the Treasury," *English Historical Review,* LXXV, 1960]. In India, Trevelyan's thinking on Ireland was invoked by bureaucrats in the 1850s to justify keeping interference to a minimum [Ambirajan, 1978, *79*].

The Whig belief in the power of free markets to direct food where most needed dictated a policy of *laissez-faire* in so far as supply was concerned. Demand would be met by the purchasing power of money wages earned on the public works. Tying relief to work would minimize sponging, and limiting works to infrastructural projects would leave private investment unaffected. In theory the policy thus aimed at distortion-free relief. In practice, however, relief measures taken during the worst of the crisis were reluctant and wrong-headed. As noted earlier, policy relied on competitive market forces to keep prices down. High prices would increase supply either through imports or reduced exports of grain. In economic jargon this amounts to no more than the hope that the market provides a Pareto-optimal outcome . . . even in famine conditions. Whether the market was powerful enough to control speculation and hoarding is difficult to say. Folklore and literary fiction stress the huge profits made by village merchant-cum-usurers, but the man in the street typically cannot distinguish between hoarding and supply-and-demand fundamentals as the cause of high prices. While some traders in remote areas no doubt prospered— even government acknowledged as much—there is no theoretical presumption that monopoly power rises in times of crisis. Hard evidence is lacking. The gombeen-man or 'meal-monger', vilified in folk memory but without whom matters might have been worse still, certainly charged more during the Famine than before. But was this monopoly extortion, or a reaction to higher default rates? The unlovable gombeenmen have left few traces for the historian to assess. The evidence from the country's biggest potato market, that of Dublin, is at least consistent with no hoarding, because hoarding would have led to high prices after harvest-time, but a smaller rise in price thereafter as traders rid themselves of their hoards before they rotted in the late spring or early summer. This implies a seasonal price pattern not observed in the data [Ó Gráda, 1988, *ch. 3*]. Thus it would seem that deaths were not due to the failure of the market to work. The question warrants full investigation, especially since research elsewhere points to speculative bubbles and market failure during famines.[47]

The massive mortality has understandably prompted the verdict that 'relief operations . . . made no impression on starvation' [Gibbon, 1975, *132*]. None of the policies pursued was beyond criticism. The public works were a tremendous achievement in *bureaucratic* terms, and made sense to the extent that most of the money went to labourers. About 90 per cent of the outlays went on wages, and the necessarily large bureaucracy took only 7 per cent. Nor is the inevitable petty cheating and malingering, sensationalized by critics at the time [e.g. Senior, 1968], the issue. There were more serious problems. First, as already noted, the outcome too often was 'work which will answer no other purpose than that of obstructing the public conveyances' [Woodham-Smith, 1962, *180*]. From October 1846 landlords were allowed to sponsor works that would improve their properties, provided they accepted responsibility for all the charges incurred. The conditions were too onerous, and this measure achieved little. The maximum number employed on estate improvement never reached more than a tiny fraction of those on the roads. Second, payment by results on the public works benefited those with some capital and those still healthy, and widened the gap between these and the most needy over time. By the end of 1846 the Board was already declaring that the problem had become 'one of food, not labour' [Irish University Press, 'Famine Series', 1968, *VIII, 383*], but the claim is imprecise. What was lacking was the *purchasing power* to command subsistence at prevailing prices. On average, the Board paid its workers about 12d. *per diem,* enough for a family to subsist on in normal times, but now literally a starvation wage [Irish University Press, 'Famine Series', 1968, *VI, 190-1; VII, 537*]. Third, money spent on the works did not always necessarily reflect famine conditions, because the local organization necessary to request schemes seems to have been lacking in some of the worst blackspots. The cost of the projects constructed by starving workers was high, of course. In south-west Cork in 1845 the regular presentment sessions were allowing 12 shillings per perch for roads; by the end of the following year, the cost was over £2, stark evidence both of enforcement problems and the declining strength of workers.[48]

Another key element of policy, local responsibility, told most against those areas least equipped to fend for themselves. Thus though thousands were starving in west Cork in December 1846, even there the *'main point'* was to get local subscriptions, since 'there must be somebody . . . capable of some contribution'. Matching grants represented a peculiarly regressive form of governmental assistance [Irish University Press, 'Famine Series', 1962, *5, 849*].

The public works may have provided the framework, but they failed to provide the funds for preventing starvation. Mass emigration, properly subsidized and regulated, would also have reduced mortality. Instead, the government relied largely on unaided individual effort. To a widely-supported scheme of assisted emigration to Canada proposed in the spring of 1847, Russell's riposte was dismissive [O'Rourke, 1902, *493-6*]. Of course, the crisis produced a massive exodus regardless: between 1845 and 1855 about 1.5 million left for good, double the numbers that would have left otherwise. Emigration in 1845 was unaffected by the blight. Next year's blight did not strike until the usual passage season was almost over, yet over 100,000 left for North America, the highest in any year until then. But 1847 produced an exodus of one-quarter of a million, and an average outflow of 200,000 or more was recorded for the next five years. Then the numbers fell and were down to about 70,000 by 1855. Most of this migration was unaided by other than family members, often through emigrant remittances. Recent calculations imply that no more than 3 or 4 per cent had their passages paid by landlord or government, though others were subsidized by charity and rent rebates [Fitzpatrick, *Irish Emigration 1801-1921,* 1984; Edwards and Williams, 1956, *ch. 6*]. Most of the migrants ended up in the United States.

Not surprisingly, the Famine migration differed from earlier movements in several respects [Fitzpatrick; Miller, *Emigrants and Exiles,* 1985; MacDonagh in Edwards and Williams, 1956]. First the poor were better represented, though the very poorest were more likely to succumb to the Famine at home than to emigrate. Second, it was more likely to consist of family groupings than either earlier or later movements. Third, the regional composition of the Famine exodus was different too. As noted earlier, migration before 1845 tended to be from the richer provinces of Leinster and Ulster, but the Famine gave the spur to mass migration from the poorer west and south-west, establishing a trend that has lasted till this day. Fourth, the migration of 1847 exacted a higher toll in lives *en route* than earlier crossings. In theory the emigrant was protected from corrupt agents and shipowners by the Passenger Acts, but the machinery and personnel in place for enforcing existing controls were completely inadequate. The screening of passengers already stricken with fever was inadequate, and overcrowding and the lack of proper food and medical care led to more. Mortality on the Atlantic passage in 1847, particularly on the Canadian route, was high [Mokyr, *Why Ireland Starved: A Quan-*

titative and Analytical History of the Irish Economy, 1800-1845, 1983, 267-8; MacDonagh in Edwards and Williams, 1956; McDonagh, A Pattern of Government Growth, 1961]. The emigration commissioners charged with protecting passengers from abuse reacted timorously, 'oppressed by a sense of general Treasury disapproval'. Legislation could not have eliminated all abuses without placing the traffic as a whole at risk. Some emigrants were bound to perish: the supply of proper ships and medical inspectors was too inelastic in the short run to cope. Yet here too dogmatism cost lives, before the existing legislation was tightened up and acted upon. The outcome was a retreat from laissez-faire and free contract [McDonagh, 1961].[49]

The sums spent on relief by government are on record. In 1850 the Treasury put its outlay since 1845 at just over £8 million. The remission of public works loans and the soup kitchens accounted for less than half of this; the rest was in the form of loans which had not been repaid by 1850. These were consolidated then, and written off in 1853. Ireland spent more than this on famine relief. The poor rates produced over £7 million, while landlords spent an unknown amount privately, and borrowed over a million [Donnelly, 1989]. Historians disagree about the significance of the sums spent by government. The tone of Edwards and Williams [1956, vii-xvi] is distinctly apologetic; awestruck by the '[impressive] extent of the actual outlay', they urge that to expect more is anachronistic. However, they chose to ignore those contemporary critics who repeatedly protested at the stinginess of aid. Complaints that 'England could find a hundred millions of money to spend in fighting the Grand Turk', 20 millions to compensate West Indian slave-owners for freeing their slaves, or a similar sum for 'the luxury of shooting King Theodore', while funds could not be found to save Irish lives, were commonplace [O'Rourke, 1902, 162; Ó Gráda, 1988, ch. 3]. A curious feature of the literature is that non-Irish Famine specialists are less inhibited than Irish historians in their critiques of policy. Thus Mokyr [1983, 291-2] and Donnelly [1988] stress the limitations of relief policy. And, relative to output or total government spending, spending on Irish famine relief indeed seems small. Spread out over the period of the Famine, outlays were about 0.3 per cent of GNP or 2-3 per cent of public expenditure. Total gross public liabilities were less after the Famine than before it. Such arithmetic exaggerates the impact of relief, since much of the generosity was ex post. Had this been fully grasped before, spending might have been geared more towards helping the most needy. Like the British standard-of-living debate, positions on the Great Famine tend to reflect political biases. Thus it is hardly surprising, however depressing, to find the eminent historian John Clapham claiming 'that the indiscriminate provision of relief . . . was still further directing the Irish from the steady industry and increased self-help which alone, in

the end, could save them', or Ireland's leading Marxist thinker insisting instead that 'England made the Famine by a rigid application of the economic principles that lie at the base of capitalist society'.[50]

Private generosity helped, but was unequal to the problem [Woodham-Smith, 1962, 382-3]. The generosity of some groups, including the much-publicized efforts of the Society of Friends, was matched by those who raised funds, largely under Catholic auspices, in America and Australia. Emigrant remittances flowed in too [Miller, 1985]. Nearer home, however, private charity was in short supply during the Great Famine. English charity had been crucial in 1822 and 1831. What changed in the interim? Several possible reasons have been outlined by Tim O'Neill. The passing of the Irish Poor Law in 1838 may have crowded out some private charity, and the feeling in middle-class Britain that Irish property was reneging on its responsibilities was encouraged by ministers and the press. But exaggerated perceptions of Irish criminality, anti-Catholic bigotry, and British disillusionment with agitator-parliamentarian Daniel O'Connell and his campaign for the Repeal of the Union, all played a role [see Senior, Essays, Conversations and Journals Relating to Ireland, 1868].[51] Finally, 'donor fatigue' is indicated by the ebbing of private charity in 1848 and later. . . .

Notes

. . . . .

[27] Quoted in N.E. Stevens, 'The Dark Ages in Plant Pathology in America', Journal of the Washington Academy of Sciences, 23 (15 September 1933), 441.

[28] (Isaac Butt), 'The Famine in the Land', Dublin University Magazine, vol. 29 (1847), 502.

[29] P. Hickey, 'A Study of Four Peninsular Parishes in West Cork 1796-1855' (Ph.D. thesis, National University of Ireland, 1980), pp. 303-11.

[30] This did not result in higher potato consumption. The Famine thus produced no evidence for potatoes being a 'Giffen' . . . good [see Dwyer and Lindsay, 1984].

[31] Daly's otherwise excellent survey [Daly, 1986] omits such accounts entirely. In this, it reflects the dispassionate, sanitized approach to the Great Famine now dominant in Irish historical scholarship.

[32] Hickey, op. cit., p. 361.

[33] R.M. Hartwell, 'Interpretations of the Industrial Revolution', Journal of Economic History, XIX (1959), 229-49.

[34] Charles Townshend, *Political Violence in Ireland: Government and Resistance since 1848* (Oxford, 1983), pp. 18-21. See too Jonathan Pim, 'Address Delivered at the Opening of the Session of the Society', *Journal of the Dublin Statistical Society,* I (1855-6), 18-19, 30-1.

[35] Data on the number of crimes reported tell a similar story, though they peak earlier. Crimes outside the Dublin metropolitan area rose from 8,088 in 1845 to 12,380 in 1846, and peaked at 20,986 in 1847. They exceeded 14,000 in both 1848 and 1849, and then dropped off sharply. Cf. State Papers Office Dublin, Returns of Outrages 1846-55.

[36] See 'The Agricultural and Commercial Condition of Ireland: The Bank Returns', *Dublin University Magazine,* 34 (1849), 372-80. These numbers are a better measure of the Famine's impact than the trend in bank deposits, which fell in 1847 but rose thereafter. Cf. Philip Ollerenshaw, *Banking in Nineteenth-Century Ireland: The Belfast Banks, 1825-1914* (Manchester, 1987), pp. 70-2.

[37] F.G. Hall, *The Bank of Ireland 1783-1946* (Dublin, 1947), pp. 216-24.

[38] Joseph Lee, 'An Economic History of Early Irish Railways' (unpublished M.A. thesis, National University of Ireland, 1965), pp. 140-2, 170-2.

[39] Compare Mary Daly, *The Economic History of Ireland since 1800* (Dublin, 1980), pp. 20-1: T. Garvin, *The Evolution of Irish Nationalist Politics* (Dublin, 1981), p. 54; *Encyclopedia Britannica* (15 edn, New York, 1974), p. 674.

[40] However, as Kennedy [1983, *210*] points out, Mokyr overlooks the 'reincarnation' of some of these as the children of emigrants.

[41] See Peter Froggatt, 'The Response of the Medical Profession to the Great Famine', in [Crawford, 1987].

[42] Compare the contrast in India a few decades later between two successive Governors General, one throwing 'all his resources into saving lives', the other 'trusting to the workings of the market to perform the same job'. S. Ambirajan, 'Malthusian Theory and Indian Famine Policy in the Nineteenth Century', *Population Studies,* 30 (1976), 6.

[43] A. Smith, *An Inquiry into the Nature and Causes of the Wealth of Nations* (Oxford, 1976), p. 532. Compare P. Samuelson, *Economics,* 7th edn (New York, 1967), p. 45 (quoted in Ambirajan, p. 63n).

[44] O'Neill, 'The Famine of 1822', ch.3, p.51.

[45] *The Economist,* 30 January 1847.

[46] Austin Bourke, 'Apologia for a Dead Civil Servant', *Irish Times,* 5-6 July 1977.

[47] See e.g. Salim Rashid, 'The Policy of Laissez-Faire During Scarcities', *Economic Journal,* 90 (1980), and Martin Ravallion, *Markets and Famines* (Oxford, 1987).

[48] Hickey, *op. cit.,* p. 356.

[49] See too Philip Taylor, *The Distant Magnet: European Migration to the U.S.A.* (London, 1972), pp. 107-16.

[50] J.H. Clapham, 'A Source for the Historian', in *The Economist 1843-1943: A Centenary Volume* (Oxford, 1943), p. 39; James Connolly, quoted in [Gibbon, 1975].

[51] T. O'Neill, 'The State, Poverty and Distress', pp. 304-6.

. . . . .

Works Cited

E. M. Crawford (ed.), *Famine: The Irish Experience 900-1900: Subsistence Crises and Famine in Ireland* (Edinburgh, 1989). Proceedings of a conference on Irish famines held in Belfast, April 1987.

M. Daly, *The Great Famine in Ireland* (Dublin, 1986).

G.P. Dwyer Jr. and C.M. Lindsay, 'Robert Giffen and the Irish Potato', *American Economic Review,* 74 (1984), 188-92.

P. Gibbon, 'Colonialism and the Great Starvation in Ireland 1845-9' *Race and Class,* 17 (1975).

L. Kennedy, 'Studies in Irish Econometric History', *Irish Historical Studies,* XXIII (1983).

FAMINE NOVELS

Hugh L. Hennedy (essay date 1972)

SOURCE: "Love and Famine, Family and Country in Trollope's *Castle Richmond*," in *Éire-Ireland*, Vol. 7, No. 4, Winter, 1972, pp. 48-66.

[*In the following essay, Hennedy examines the relationship in Anthony Trollope's* Castle Richmond *(1860) between the love story and the Famine backdrop. The critic argues, contrary to earlier scholarship, that Trollope established a thematic and situational parallelism in the novel between family and country, but concedes that both examples of such parallelism suffer to a degree from disproportion.*]

Although *Castle Richmond* (1860), Anthony Trollope's ninth novel, "was at once translated into five different languages—Dutch, Danish, French, German, and Russian . . ." and "No other Trollope novel was so honored,"[1] it has not turned out to be one of Trollope's more popular novels. It has not, for instance, been reprinted in the Oxford World's Classics series, the edition that contains more of Trollope's novels than any other modern edition.[2] And one critic in the twentieth century has even gone so far as to damn *Castle Richmond* as one of Trollope's absolute failures, as one of the six Trollope novels "that may be eternally and remorselessly forgotten as though they had never been born."[3]

When, however, he came to write his autobiography some fifteen years after the publication of *Castle Richmond,* Trollope had by no means forgotten the novel. Declaring that he had "not looked at *Castle Richmond* since it was published," he nevertheless asserted that he remembered "all the incidents." But as vividly as *Castle Richmond* may have continued to live in his mind, he was well aware that it had not gone over well with his public, had not been "A success,—even though the plot is a fairly good plot, and is much more of a plot than I have generally been able to find."[4]

The novel's failure to find favor with the public Trollope attributed to two causes, one extrinsic—his English readers' dislike of Irish stories—and one intrinsic—weak characterization. Not all of his critics have agreed with Trollope that the characterization in *Castle Richmond* is weak,[5] but whatever the cause or causes, the fact is clear that *Castle Richmond* has not been a popular novel, neither in Trollope's day nor in ours.

As might be expected, the novel's lack of popular success has been reflected in and paralleled by a relative lack of critical interest, which lack is something of a blessing if one assumes, as I do, that *Castle Richmond,* though it may not be one of Trollope's best novels, is deserving not of oblivion but of serious reading and critical attention today. The lack is something of a blessing because in the little criticism that there is, one can see so clearly what the central critical problem is. That problem was first stated in an unsigned notice published in the *Saturday Review* in May, 1860, the year of the novel's first publication. After suggesting that "It is impossible not to feel that . . . [the Irish famine] was the part of it about which Mr. Trollope really cared, but that, as he had to get a novel out of it, he was in duty bound to mix up a hash of Desmonds and Fitzgeralds with the Indian meal on which his mind was fixed as he wrote," the reviewer (changing his metaphor somewhat) concludes by stating that the story of the famine and the love story, "the milk and the water[,] really should be in separate pails."[6]

An excerpt from an article in *The Dublin Evening Post,* September 9, 1845:

In the part of *The Evening Post* dedicated to the interests of the farming world, we have made rather an ample report of a matter of great importance indeed, namely, the failure of the potato crop—very extensively in the United States, to a great extent in Flanders and France, and to an appreciable amount in England. We have heard something of the kind in our own country—especially along the coast—but we believe that no apprehension whatever is entertained even of a partial failure of the potato crop in Ireland. . . .

But, the general failures of which we read, are producing serious apprehensions. Yet, surely the United States have little real cause to fear. If the potato were entirely extirpated, the people would enjoy an ample sufficiency of food. It is in the densely packed communities of Europe that the failure would be alarming, and in no country more, or so much, than in our own.

But, happily, there is no ground for any apprehensions of the kind in Ireland. There may have been partial failures in some localities; but, we believe that there was never a more abundant potato crop in Ireland than there is at present.

An anonymous writer, in The Dublin Evening Post, *September 9, 1845, reprinted in* The Irish Famine, *by Noel Kissane, National Library of Ireland, 1995.*

Later critics have put it in other ways,[7] but most of the critics who have chosen to say something about *Castle Richmond* have repeated, though they may not have known they were doing so, the *Saturday Review*'s objection: the famine setting, as effective as it may be in itself, is obtrusive, it has little or nothing to do with the bulk of the novel, the love story. The central critical question about *Castle Richmond,* then, has remained, from Trollope's day to ours, this: How, if at all, is the famine related to the love plot?[8]

In May, 1860, the same month that the question was first asked, a good beginning of an answer was made in an unsigned review in the *Spectator.* The reviewer did not try to argue that there are serious causal connections between the famine and the love story, but he did praise Trollope's handling of the relationship between the two:

Mr. Trollope's new novel has its scene in the south of Ireland, in the year of the Famine; but none of its main issues are evolved out of that great calamity. Their connexion with it is casual, and just close enough to furnish in a suitable manner the secondary machinery and incidents of the story, to supply occasion for some of the comings and goings, the occupations and the talk of the dramatis personae, and to give to the story of the principal personages such a background of local and historical reality as serves to heighten its scenic illusion, and does not injuriously distract attention from the leading theme. The author's management of this portion of his materials is exceedingly judicious.[9]

If the connections are not causal but casual, they do serve the purposes of realism and help to make the romantic elements of the novel more believable. If we are given a convincing setting, one that we can respond to because we know it really existed and the author really knew it, should this setting not help us respond well to the main action that takes place within this setting?

There is much to be said for such a line of reasoning, but it must also be said that it allows one of the main issues—whether or not the setting is so vivid or compelling as to "distract attention from the leading theme"—to be begged. Furthermore, one should probably not be quite so ready to concede that there are no causal ties between the famine setting and the love story.[10] Trollope, in any event, explicitly relates the famine to his hero's[11] fortunes as lover and heir in at least two instances, and these should be looked at before conclusions about causal connections are accepted.

In the first instance, Herbert Fitzgerald, seeking shelter from a rain squall, has just encountered in a roadside cabin stripped bare of furniture and utensils a starving mother and her two children, one dead and the other dying. After spreading his silk handkerchief over the naked corpse of the child and then giving the mother some money and a promise to send help to her, Herbert leaves the cabin: "Herbert, as he remounted his horse and rode quietly on, forgot for a while both himself and Clara Desmond. Whatever might be the extent of his own calamity, how could he think himself unhappy after what he had seen? How could he repine at ought that the world had done for him, having now witnessed to how low a state of misery a fellow human being might be brought? Could he, after that, dare to consider himself unfortunate?" (pp. 580-581)

Herbert does not soon forget his experience in the cabin, but since it does not alter his future course of action—he would have gone on loving Clara and intending to marry her whether or not he had stopped in the cabin—that experience cannot be said to affect the action of the novel causally. Still, it puts the love story, for Herbert and for us, in a certain perspective; it reminds him and us of the general misery within which particular misery, or happiness, in this novel, occurs. Doing that, it blunts, though it does not destroy, our concern for Herbert and his problems. In this way, the famine becomes frame as well as background for the love story. In this way, to change the metaphor, a damper is, by anticipation, put upon the happy—happy for Herbert if not for many of the other characters—conclusion of the love story.

In the concluding chapter of the novel, the emphasis is not, of course, placed upon the unhappiness of Herbert Fitzgerald, for, having come into his inheritance and knowing that soon he will be enfolded by the arms of his bride, Herbert is not unhappy. Still, he has not forgotten his experience in the cabin, and "Of all those who did true good conscientious work at this time, none exceeded in energy our friend Herbert Fitzgerald. . . . It seemed to him as though some thank-offering were due from him for all the good things that Providence had showered upon him, and the best thank-offering that he could give was a devoted attention to the interest of the poor around him." (p. 753)

Here, one can see, causality is at work, for at the end of the novel, Herbert, a central character of the love story, is moved by his knowledge of the reality and extent of the misery around him to act in a certain way. If this causality does not have much to do with the working-out of the plot, it is, nevertheless, causality.

But it is neither Herbert's happiness nor his awareness of the plight of the starving which impresses one most at the end of the novel. It is, rather, a general mood of sadness and misery which is most impressive. For if when the novel ends Herbert and Clare share a modest, modified-by-awareness happiness, Clara's mother, Lady Desmond, finding her title little compensation for her poverty and loneliness, is decidedly unhappy. And she is not the only unhappy character at the end. Herbert's mother, Lady Fitzgerald, is unhappy, and so are Owen Fitzgerald, Clara's first suitor, and Patrick Desmond, Clara's brother. Though their reasons for unhappiness differ, these four major characters are alike inasmuch as each suffers. And it is the suffering of these characters, rather than the joys of the newly-weds, which stands out at the end of the novel. Given the famine setting, it is not appropriate that the final note of this novel is sad, that the final tone is one of quiet anguish?

The setting of *Castle Richmond*, then, by influencing some of the actions of the hero and by contributing an air of realism and a mood of sadness to a story which, on the whole, is far from happy, makes a real and valid contribution to the overall effect. Is this enough, however? Is this all that Trollope means when in his last chapter he says that if he believed in using sub-titles, he "might have called this 'A Tale of the Famine Year in Ireland' "? (p. 751) Is this enough to demonstrate that the setting does not unduly take interest away from the love story? If this is all, one might very well say, this is not enough. The rest of this article will attempt to show that this, indeed, is not all, that the famine setting is related to the love story of *Castle Richmond* in important ways not yet touched upon.

When Robert M. Polhemus observes that in *Castle Richmond* "The most interesting characters are starved for love, and Ireland, where the novel is set during the ghastly famine of 1846-1848, is starved for food,"[12] he touches upon a possible way in which setting and story are related—they are related, Polhemus assumes, by means of parallelism. Although some critics have argued that Trollope was in the habit of using parallel structure and parallel characterization,[13] only John E. Dustin, so far as I know, has explicitly said that *Castle Richmond* employs parallelism. But after saying that "Trollope eventually developed his skill in observing analogies, comparisons, and special relationships into a highly refined technique of parallel characterization and parallel plotting," Dustin goes on to say that "the technique . . . offers facile opportunities for padding," and *Castle Richmond* is one of the novels where the technique is in fact used for purposes of padding.[14] Insofar as Polhemus and Dustin note that Trollope uses forms of parallelism in *Castle Richmond,* they are right; Polhemus, however, is wrong in referring to a potential parallel as if it were an actual one, and Dustin is wrong in suggesting that parallelism is used in *Castle Richmond* for purposes of padding.

Although Trollope did not choose to develop a parallel between the Irish people, starving for food, and the major characters of the novel, starving for love, he did choose to establish and develop many parallels, parallels between places, for instance (Castle Richmond and Desmond Court), and parallels between characters (Herbert and Owen Fitzgerald, Mr. Townsend and Father Bernard, Sir Thomas and his son, Herbert, and Matthew Mollett and his son, Aby). But there are so many of these parallels—more examples of the types already mentioned but more types too—that it would not be expedient to try to name or consider them all. The key parallel in the novel, however, can and will be named and its use considered at some length.

The key parallel in *Castle Richmond* is quite a bit like one of the parallels employed by Shakespeare in *Richard II,* where (especially in V.ii.) the coming discord in the state is foreshadowed and projected by the discord in the family of the Duke of York. Trollope does not emphasize discord precisely but he does work with the family-state parallel, does present the plights of the Fitzgerald family at Castle Richmond and of the Irish nation everywhere as being similar, if not essentially identical.

Just after recording the death of Sir Thomas Fitzgerald, Herbert's father, Trollope explicitly links together the Fitzgeralds of Castle Richmond and the poor of the nation dying from the famine: "At any rate, there was the famine, undoubted now by any one; and death, who in visiting Castle Richmond may be said to have knocked at the towers of a king, was busy enough also among the cabins of the poor." (p. 531) But it is not just death that, in Trollope's view, links together family and country; in this novel, before death comes suffering, and Trollope sees the family and the country as suffering in much the same way, as being afflicted in similar fashions.

The suffering at Castle Richmond, suffering at first largely borne by Sir Thomas, is to a great extent caused by doubt about the validity of the marriage between Sir Thomas and Lady Fitzgerald. Trying to protect his wife's good name and his son's inheritance, Sir Thomas for some time pays blackmail to Matthew Mollett, the man who claims to be Lady Fitzgerald's first and, in the eyes of the law, only husband. Sir Thomas's anguish about the state of his marriage is aggravated by the hold that Mollett has on him and by his worries about the way the blackmail money is draining his estate. Those worries, Trollope makes clear, are well founded, for, as Mr. Prendergast, the family friend and legal advisor from London, knows, "such leeches as Mr. Mollett never leave the skin as long as there is a drop of blood left within the veins." (p. 365)

The economic distresses of the Irish nation before the coming of the famine were not, in Trollope's view, caused by a dubious marriage, a marriage between the Irish and the English, say (though if he cared to, no doubt, he could have developed this analogy), nor, directly, at least, by absentee landlords, but by the misuse of the profit-rent system by ill-educated, unprincipled, rapacious members, both Protestant and Roman Catholic, of the middle classes: "Young men were brought up to do nothing. Property was regarded as having no duties attached to it. Men became rapacious, and determined to extract the uttermost farthing out of the land within their power, let the consequences to the people on that land be what they might. . . . The scourge of Ireland was the existence of a class who looked to be gentlemen living on their property, but who should have earned their bread by the work of their brain, or, failing that, by the sweat of their brow." (p. 103) Trollope does not explicitly call these profit-renters, these middlemen, leeches or blackmailers, but it is clear that he saw them as in the process of bleeding the country dry, just as the Molletts were bleeding the family at Castle Richmond dry.

That neither the Molletts nor the profit-renters succeed in sucking all the life out of their victims is the result of outside intervention. Mr. Prendergast, when bidden, comes to the aid of the Fitzgerald family, and God, apparently unbidden, comes to the aid of Ireland.[15] Neither brings immediate or easy comfort, for Mr. Prendergast insists that the truth about Lady Fitzgerald's marital status be made generally known, and God visits the potato blight and consequent famine upon

Ireland. But as severe and painful as these methods are,[16] the finally important thing about them is that they work. Making public the doubtful status of Lady Fitzgerald's marriage immediately puts to an end any further possibilities of blackmail and ultimately leads to the discovery of the truth that the marriage is valid and Herbert is the rightful heir to Castle Richmond. Similarly, the famine turns out to be a manifestation not of God's wrath but of his mercy,[17] for

> It is with thorough rejoicing, almost with triumph, that I declare that the idle, genteel class has been cut up root and branch, has been driven forth out of its holding into the wide world, and has been punished with the penalty of extermination. The poor cotter suffered sorely under the famine, and under the pestilence which followed the famine; but he, as a class, has risen from his bed of suffering a better man. He is thriving as a labourer either in his own country or in some newer—for him better— land to which he has emigrated. He, even in Ireland, can now get eight and nine shillings a-week easier and with more constancy than he could get four some fifteen years since. But the other man is gone, and his place is left happily vacant. (p. 105)

One may very well have doubts about the appropriateness of seeing, in whatever perspective, such a terrible event as the famine as an act of mercy, just as one may wonder about the validity of Trollope's sanguine view of the Irish economy in 1860, but the point is that *Castle Richmond* portrays both the Fitzgerald family and the Irish nation as being better off as the result of the brushing off from them of leech-like middlemen. The point is that in *Castle Richmond* Trollope establishes and develops a central parallel between family and country, that the problems of the Fitzgerald family are presented as being remarkably similar to those of the Irish nation.

Shakespeare, it has been noted, does something similar in *Richard II,* but there is at least one significant difference: in the English history play, the smaller unit, the family, is used to throw light on the central subject, the state; in the Irish novel, the smaller unit, the family, is, at least ostensibly, the central subject, and the state, apparently, is being used to illuminate it. If indeed one sees the Irish nation in *Castle Richmond* as being used to throw light on the Fitzgerald family, one may very well feel a lack of proportion in the novel, for the potato famine is surely too big and grave a subject to be used simply for familial purposes. If, on the other hand, one supposes that the real subject of the novel is the state of the nation during the potato famine, then one seems still to be faced with disproportion, for most of the novel is directly concerned with the problems of the Fitzgeralds, so that portraying the Irish nation largely by means of the Fitzgeralds would appear to be a remarkably indirect way of proceeding.

One could reply to the first argument of disproportion that Trollope, instead of simply repeating Shakespeare's practice, is doing something original, and to the second that, as a matter of fact, that is the way art does most of the time proceed, that is, by means of indirection, but although there would be much truth in both replies, they would not be fully satisfactory, for disproportion, if it really exists, cannot simply be explained away. Still, without trying to explain away the problem of possible disproportion, one may try to approach the problem from somewhat different angles.

One approach is by way of emotional intensity. The moments in the novel that must stand out most clearly in the memories of most of its readers are those when familial and national concerns, love story and famine, are most clearly present together—moments such as the one already referred to when Herbert enters the cabin of the starving woman, or those earlier moments when the miserable Herbert, walking through the rain and mud to Desmond Court to break the news of the doubtful validity of his claim to be the heir of Castle Richmond, passes through the gauntlet of miserable Irishmen working on the road near Gortnaclough and then wanders into that wretched village, only to leave it again soon afterwards (Chapter XXV).[18] In such moments in the novel, the effect is not so much one of misery doubled as of misery squared—squared but at the same time controlled by perspective. Someone might, of course, object that the power of such moments is itself good evidence of disproportion, for the most powerful moments in this kind of novel should be those which are directly and exclusively the province of the love story. Such an objection, however, assumes that Trollope intended *Castle Richmond* to be a conventional love story, and the generally sad ending—sad despite the union of Herbert and Clara—is by itself fairly conclusive evidence that *Castle Richmond* was not intended to be a conventional love story. The way Trollope relates the famine and the love story, then, may disappoint the expectations of some novel readers but the emotional effects that he does achieve, being more than adequate to make up for disappointed expectations, are by no means evidence of disproportion. They are, rather, evidence of control.

Another approach to the problem of possible disproportion is by way of theme. When Mr. Prendergast tells Mrs. Jones, who thinks she can help her mistress by keeping the truth concealed, that " 'Truth is always the best, you know' " (p. 363), he not only states with great explicitness one of the morals of *Castle Richmond* and one of the principles which Trollope affirms over and over in his novels, but he also sounds the central theme of the novel, the theme first sounded on the novel's first page and last sounded on its last. The theme is that of truth.[19]

Trollope begins *Castle Richmond* by saying that although he is aware "That there is a strong feeling against things Irish," this novel is set in Ireland, for "if I ought to know anything about any place, I ought to know something about Ireland" (p. 1) and "I am now leaving the Green Isle and my old friends, and would fain say a word of them as I do so. If I do not say that word now it will never be said." (p. 3) In other words, he writes now about Ireland, despite the prejudices against the subject, because now he can tell the truth about it. Later, when the prejudices against the subject may be less strong, he will be less able to speak the truth about it.

Castle Richmond ends when Patrick Desmond tells Owen Fitzgerald, with whom he is traveling, that he has to leave him for a while.

> "They want me to be home," he had said one morning to his friend.
>
> "Ah, yes; I suppose so."
>
> "Do you know why?" They had never spoken a word about Clara since they had left England together, and the earl now dreaded to mention her name.
>
> "Know why!" replied Owen; "of course I do. It is to give away your sister. Go home, Desmond, my boy; when you have returned we will talk about her. I shall bear it better when I know that she is his wife." (pp. 756-757)

Patrick does not have to tell Owen the whole bitter truth; he knows it already.

If *Castle Richmond* is concerned with truth in the beginning and at the end, in between the concern with truth is also very much in evidence. The story, for instance, is filled with reports and tidings. There are reports of the goings on at Owen Fitzgerald's place, reports, that is, of "the Hap House Orgies"; reports of the impending marriage of Owen to Lady Desmond; reports from France of the death of Mr. Talbot (Matthew Mollett), the husband of Mary Wainwright (Lady Fitzgerald). And there are the tidings of Owen's apparent inheritance brought to Hap House, separately, by Aby Mollett and Mr. Prendergast; the tidings of Herbert's apparent loss of inheritance brought to Desmond Court by Herbert himself; the tidings that come to Owen "that Clara was still within his reach if only he were master of Castle Richmond" (p. 633); the new tidings about Matthew Mollett's marital status sent, by letter, to Mr. Prendergast by Aby Mollett. These and other reports and tidings, permeating the novel as they do, make the reader, who is often more critical than the recipients of the reports and tidings, wonder about their truth, for if it seems pretty clear that they are not completely true, it also seems clear that they are not completely false.

The novel's concern with truth is also projected through the prejudices of some of the characters, especially their religious prejudices. Mr. Townsend, the rector of Drumbarrow, is prejudiced against Catholics: "few men carried their Protestant fervour further than he did. A cross was to him what a red cloth is supposed to be to a bull; and so averse was he to the intercession of saints, that he always regarded as a wolf in sheep's clothing a certain English clergyman who had written to him a letter dated from the feast of St. Michael and All Angels." (p. 157) But if Mr. Townsend's prejudices are strong, those of his wife (and of her friend, Aunt Letty Fitzgerald) who, believing "that there was some college or club of papists at Oxford, emissaries of the Pope or of the Jesuits," is convinced that "if there were left any real Protestant truth in the Church of England, that Church should look to feed her lambs by the hands of shepherds chosen from . . . [Trinity College, Dublin], and from that seminary only," (p. 164) are even stronger. Given this attitude in the Townsend household, it is no wonder that at the beginning of the novel Mr. Townsend and the Rev. Bernard M'Carthy, the parish priest of Drumbarrow, hate each other. They are hardly acquainted, of course, but Father Bernard "was as firmly convinced of the inward, heart-destroying iniquity of the parson as the parson was of that of the priest. And so these two men had learned to hate each other. And yet neither of them were bad men." (p. 160) As the novel progresses and Mr. Townsend and Father Bernard are brought together by their work on the famine relief committee, they get to know each other, and each gradually discovers that his counterpart, far from being a man of iniquity, is a decent, hard-working Christian. The prejudices of some of his characters offer Trollope opportunities for comic relief in a novel which deals for the most part with pretty solemn material, and Trollope seizes his opportunities and gets his laughs at the expense of the Townsends, Aunt Letty, and Father Bernard, but all the time he is working with the theme of truth, all the time showing how difficult it often is for people to see the truth.

But if the novel is much concerned with the difficulty of finding out the truth, it is also much concerned with the difficulty of speaking out the truth when one knows it or thinks he knows it. That, after all, is a good part of Sir Thomas's problem: he thinks he knows the truth about his marital status but he cannot bring himself to make what he thinks he knows public. It is not until the arrival of Mr. Prendergast that Sir Thomas can bring himself to face the reality of the situation: "It certainly was necessary that the whole truth in this matter should be made known and declared openly. This fair inheritance must go to the right owner and not to the wrong. . . . Justice in this case was clear, and the truth must be declared. But then they must take good care to find out absolutely what the truth was." (p. 334)[20]

But if Sir Thomas is the character in the novel who is most spectacularly placed in the painful position of having to speak out the truth, he is by no means the only one so placed.[21] Clara, for instance, is urged a number of times by Owen Fitzgerald to speak out. The first time, "She did not tell him in words that so it had been; but she looked into his face with a glance of doubt and pain that answered his question as plainly as any words could have done." (p. 38) The second time, "some sound did fall from her lips. But yet it was so soft, so gentle, so slight, that it could hardly be said to reach even a lover's ear. Fitzgerald, however, made the most of it. Whether it were Yes, or whether it were No, he took it as being favourable, and Lady Clara Desmond gave him no sign to show that he was mistaken." (pp. 41-42) The third and climactic time, she still does not speak loudly. When Owen asks her, " 'Whom is it then you love?' " she replies, " 'Herbert Fitzgerald'. . . . The words hardly formed themselves into a whisper, but nevertheless they were audible enough to him." (p. 664)

It can hardly be said that Clara speaks up in any of these instances, but what she really thinks and feels is made known each time. Clara's mother, the countess, is much more skillful than her artless daughter in concealing her thoughts and feelings, for she has had plenty of practice. Trollope explains that she had not "been accustomed to speak out her thoughts. But she had ever been accustomed to conceal them." (p. 490) Still, even she finally speaks out, and when she does, she speaks up clearly enough: " 'And as we must part I will tell you all. Owen Fitzgerald, I have loved you with all my heart,—with all the love that a woman has to give. I have loved you, and have never loved any other.' " (p. 745) This declaration makes for a big and painful scene. It is the last big scene of the novel and it is painful for Owen and the reader as well as for the countess.

Painful as it is, however, Trollope no doubt approves of this speaking out just as he approves of the making public the doubtful status of the Fitzgerald marriage. He states his position several times through Mr. Prendergast, as when that friend of the family tells Mrs. Jones, without metaphor, that " 'Truth is always the best, you know' " (p. 363) and when he lectures Herbert, with the aid of metaphor, that " 'in such matters we can only sail safely by the truth. There is no other compass worth a man's while to look at!' " (p. 386) And he also states his position in his own voice: "We have all heard of demonstrative people. A demonstrative person, I take it, is he who is desirous of speaking out what is in his heart. For myself I am inclined to think that such speaking out has its good ends. . . . What is in a man, let it come out and be known to

those around him; if it be bad it will find correction; if it be good it will spread and be beneficent." (pp. 559-560) Many people today who may never have heard of Anthony Trollope would find this statement of position familiar and congenial, at least up until the point where correction makes its appearance.

But Trollope does not rely on statement alone to make his position clear, for the tale, as Lawrence would say, also makes the point that speaking out is good. After all, it is only after the doubts about the Fitzgerald marriage are made known to Mr. Prendergast and the public that any kind of search for the truth is begun. And that search, though difficult, finally proves successful, so that the reader comes to see that at the heart of the plot finding the truth and telling the truth become practically one and the same action. As the inheritance plot and the love plot turn out to be two strands of the same plot, so two major thematic strands become one.

And if the tale manifests Trollope's attitude toward finding and speaking out the truth, what he does with his setting repeats, parallels, the action of the tale. For as painful as facing up to the truth may be for the Fitzgerald family and as terrible as the famine is for the Irish nation, they are preferable to being endlessly blackmailed by the Molletts or continually blighted by bad economic practices. So if the family because it brings what it knows of the truth to light finally comes into secure possession of its rightful estate, the nation, in Trollope's view, is better off after the famine than before, because now such weaknesses of the economic system as the abuse of profit-rent and the over-reliance on the potato, having been exposed, are (supposedly) eliminated.

Though the subject of Trollope's handling of the theme of truth in *Castle Richmond* has been by no means exhausted—the very important condition of being true, for instance, has not even been touched on, let alone related to the acts of seeking the truth and speaking it out—it is not necessary to continue indefinitely the exposition of Trollope's handling of the theme, for the present concern is not the theme itself but the way the theme throws light on Trollope's employment of parallelism in the novel. That some kind of thematic parallelism exists has been demonstrated: the ultimate beneficence of painful truth for the family is paralleled by the usefulness of the truths about the nation's economy driven home by the terrible, providential famine. The question is, Are the proportions right? One further consideration of Trollope's handling of the theme of truth in the novel should lead to an answer.

Unlike, say, *The Small House at Allington, Castle Richmond* is not a Trollope novel notable for its imagery. It does employ a certain amount of animal imagery, however, and its use of one animal, the fox, is to the point now. When a fox first appears in the novel, it is a real fox, the fox hunted down on Owen Fitzgerald's grounds and finally killed near the door of Hap House. The fox meets its fate in the same thicket into which Aby Mollett on the same day had been pitched by Owen. In case the reader might miss the connection, Trollope takes pains to underline it: "The poor fox, with his last gasp of strength, had betaken himself to the thicket before the door, and there the hounds had killed him, at the very spot on which Aby Mollett had fallen." (p. 430) The fox, then, is used to establish a parallel with Aby. As the fox suffers at the hands of the hunters, Aby has suffered at Owen's hands. But beyond this meaning there seems to be foreshadowing: as the elusive fox was eventually cornered and trapped, so finally will the blackmailing Molletts be exposed.

The hint of foreshadowing is confirmed when later on in the novel the reader reaches the chapters (XXXIX and XL) entitled "Fox-Hunting in Spinney Lane" and "The Fox in His Earth." In these chapters, something interesting happens to the fox image-parallel. For if the first human fox in the novel is Aby, in these chapters both Molletts are treated as foxes, neither of whom Mr. Prendergast would have hesitated to deliver up "to be devoured by the dogs of the law; but he did not the less love them tenderly while they were yet running." (p. 673) But after a while, it becomes apparent that the fox that Mr. Prendergast is interested in is the father, Matthew Mollett, the "fox he knew to be lying in ambush upstairs. It was of course possible that old Mollett should slip away out of the back door and over a wall. If foxes did not do those sort of things they would not be worth half the attention that is paid to them. But Mr. Prendergast was well on the scent; all that a sportsman wants is good scent." (p. 682) So the fox image, begun as a parallel, develops into a regular conceit, and the imagistic light used first to illuminate Aby, the son, shifts onto Matthew, the father.

And the shifting does not stop at this point, for before the novel is over, the fox image has come very close to becoming a symbol for the truth itself. In the last chapter, the reader is told that the marriage between Clara and Herbert "did not take place till full six months after the period to which our story has brought us." (p. 753) During this time, "Mr. Die and Mr. Prendergast were certainly going about, still drawing all coverts far and near, lest their fox might not have been fairly run to his last earth." (p. 754) By this point in the story, the Molletts have been rendered ineffective. Neither of them is any longer a threat. The elusive fox which has run through so much of the novel turns out finally to be neither an animal nor a person but the truth about the marriage and the inheritance, that truth which at times has seemed so clear and at other times so doubtful. Is it not appropriate that a novel much concerned with the problems of finding and revealing the truth

Anthony Trollope (1815-1882).

should employ as a key image a fox, a fox which changes its meaning as it moves through the novel?

The last question, sounding as rhetorical as it does, appears to need no answer, yet it leads to what may be a serious weakness of *Castle Richmond*. Yes, the shifting fox image, though at times Trollope's handling of it may seem a bit too precious for some readers, is an appropriate image for a novel much concerned with the difficulty of apprehending the truth. The trouble is that all of *Castle Richmond* does not convey this difficulty, for if Trollope's portrayal of the novel's setting does succeed in conveying much of the pain and misery caused by the truth-revealing famine, it does not communicate enough sense of mystery. Why this calamity: That is a difficult question, one not to be answered with an easy answer. Trollope's answer— the famine is a providential act operating for the eventual economic benefit of Ireland—may not be precisely an easy answer, but it is an answer that he has ready at the very beginning of his novel. It may very well be an answer that he has had to struggle to reach, but he does not convey much sense of that struggle to the reader. And because the reader does not experience the difficulty of discovering the truth about the nation, as he does experience the difficulty of discovering the truth about the family, he may come away from *Castle Richmond* with some well-grounded feeling of disproportion.

One might argue that one of the pleasures in reading Trollope comes from the feeling of being in the company of a man who most emphatically knows what he is talking about, and as a matter of fact there is considerable assurance in the handling of the love story as well as in the treatment of the famine. "Truth is always the best" is, after all, not a principle that Trollope discovers during the course of *Castle Richmond*. It is, rather, like his understanding of the meaning of the famine, something that he brings with him at the start of the novel.

The argument is sound as far as it goes but it does not get as far as the question of the sense of difficulty in discovering truth. Because he does begin with certain principles, Trollope can with confidence give himself up to the imagining of how various kinds of people might act and react as the facts of a situation seem to change and then change again. Though solidly based on principle, the experience for the reader is one of considerable uncertainty.[22] But it is that uncertainty which is lacking in the reader's experience of the famine.

Castle Richmond, then, whether considered from the point of view of situational or thematic parallelism, suffers from a certain amount of disproportion. But it is also a work with considerably more coherence than up to now it has generally been credited with, for if the family-country parallel may be a bit out of proportion here and there, it does exist, and by means of it Trollope makes all kinds and numbers of connections within his novel. And by bringing the characters of his love story into contact with the starving Irish peasantry, he achieves a number of affecting, memorable fictional moments. Far from being an absolute failure, *Castle Richmond*, for people interested in the novel and/or Ireland, has much to give.

Notes

1 Bradford A. Booth, *Anthony Trollope: Aspects of His Life and Art* (Bloomington: Indiana Univ. Press, 1958), p. 243.

2 About thirty of Trollope's forty-seven novels have been made available to modern readers in the World's Classics edition.

3 Hugh Walpole, *Anthony Trollope* (New York: Macmillan, 1928), p. 122. The other five condemned to oblivion by Walpole are *Marion Fay, The Struggles of Brown, Jones, and Robinson, The Bertrams, Lady Anna*, and *An Old Man's Love*. When Walpole suggests that *Castle Richmond* contains "some mildly pleasant Irish

backgrounds," one concludes that he has taken his own advice and already forgotten the novel, for the Irish background, being one of suffering and starvation, is anything but pleasant. Such a critical practice can hardly be recommended, though one may admire the manly consistency involved in it.

4 *An Autobiography*, ed. Frederick Page (London: Oxford Univ. Press, 1950), p. 156.

5 For instance, in *Anthony Trollope: His Public Services, Private Friends, and Literary Originals* (London and New York: Lane; Toronto: Bell & Cockburn, 1913), pp. 130-131. T. H. S. Escott, Trollope's first biographer, has high praise for the characterizations of both Lady Desmond and Clara, her daughter, two of the characters that Trollope in the *Autobiography* (p. 157) singles out for dispraise.

6 Donald Smalley, ed., *Trollope: The Critical Heritage* (London: Routledge & Kegan Paul; New York: Barnes & Noble, 1969), pp. 113-114.

7 For instance—Wilson Barr Gragg ("Anthony Trollope: 'An Advanced Conservative-Liberal' " [Evanston: Northwestern Univ. Diss., 1948], p. 242): "the plight of the Irish during the Potato Famine is related in frequent expository passages with sympathy and detail, but these are digressions from a plot which could as well have been laid in England"; John Hagan ("The Major Novels of Anthony Trollope: An Interpretation and Critique" [Chicago: Univ. of Chicago Diss., 1957], p. 230): "the grim subject of the Famine is powerfully dealt with, but it can easily be skipped (existing as independently of the love story with which it alternates as the separate layers of a cake)"; Christiaan C. Koets (*Female Characters in the Work of Anthony Trollope* [Gouda: Van Tilburg, 1933], pp. 8-9): "it is rather difficult to trace any organic connection between the plot of the novel and the description of the famine"; Michael Sadleir (*Trollope: A Commentary*, rev. American ed. [New York: Farrar, Straus, 1947], p. 387): *Castle Richmond* is "a document, not a work of art"; John H. Wildman (*Anthony Trollope's England* [Providence: Brown Univ. Press, 1940], p. 34): "*Castle Richmond* (1860), his third novel on Ireland, is another curiously poor novel; and probably, from the point of view of form, it is his worst; or rather, the worst of the novels he wrote with an intimate knowledge of his subject."

8 There are other questions, of course, but they are either not so central or not so accessible to literary criticism. Trollope himself has raised the question of characterization, but effectiveness of characterization hardly seems to be a question that can be argued, though the functions of characters can be discussed and demonstrated. The quality of the novel, as the discussion up to this point has indicated, is debatable, but a de-

cision about quality depends partly upon the question of the effectiveness of characterization and partly upon the question of coherence, which, for this reason among others, claims priority. A very important question raised by a novel which, like this one, has a definite historical setting is, How valid is the novel's rendering and interpretation of history? But this question is probably more properly addressed to the historian than to the literary critic. It is too bad that Cecil Woodham-Smith does not concern herself with this question in *The Great Hunger: Ireland* 1845-9 (London: Hamish Hamilton, 1962).

[9] Smalley, p. 115.

[10] It is possible to speak of the love story as the only plot of *Castle Richmond* because although the novel at first appears to be working with two separate plots—the love plot and the blackmail or inheritance plot—it becomes apparent after a while that the blackmail plot affects the love plot so closely that for all intents and purposes the two merge. So far as I know, no one has ever objected to the relationship in the novel of the love and blackmail elements, whether they be regarded as being carried by two plots or one. For the sake of convenience, then, but with considerable objective justification, I shall continue to refer to both the love and blackmail-inheritance elements of the novel under the rubrics, "love story" or "love plot."

When Trollope praises the plot *Castle Richmond* in the *Autobiography,* he is no doubt thinking of the way the love and blackmail-inheritance elements of the novel merge. He may also be thinking of the almost Racinian effect he achieves through his plot reversals, each of which forces the main characters to re-evaluate their positions and courses of action. At the beginning of the novel, Herbert Fitzgerald seems to be the heir of Castle Richmond. At the end, he is certainly so. But in between the beginning and the end, the inheritance seems to slip from his hands into those of his cousin, Owen Fitzgerald. Lady Desmond, basing herself on what she believes to be the true state of the inheritance, takes at least four different positions in regard to the disposal of her daughter Clara's hand in marriage. The other characters change their positions too, but less often, which is part of the point. Given this kind of plot, it is highly appropriate that in the final big scene of the novel, Lady Desmond, Phaedra-like, declares her love for the younger and pained Owen Fitzgerald.

[11] Strictly speaking, the novel has no hero. Trollope puts it this way: "It is impossible that these volumes should be graced by any hero, for the story does not admit of one. But if there were to be a hero, Herbert Fitzgerald would be the man" (*Castle Richmond* [London and New York: Land, 1906], p. 70. This is the edition I use throughout this article.) For the sake of convenience, Herbert shall occasionally be referred to as the novel's hero.

[12] *The Changing World of Anthony Trollope* (Berkeley and Los Angeles: Univ. of California Press, 1968), p. 63.

[13] Most notably Maude Houston ("Structure and Plot in *The Warden,*" UTSE, 34 [1955], 107-113), Arthur Mizener ("Anthony Trollope: The Palliser Novels," in *From Jane Austen to Joseph Conrad: Essays Collected in Memory of James T. Hillhouse,* ed. Robert C. Rathburn and Martin Steinmann, Jr. [Minneapolis: Univ. of Minnesota Press, 1958]), and Jerome Thale ("The Problem of Structure in Trollope," NCF, 15 [1960-61], 147-157).

[14] "Anthony Trollope: A Study in Recurrence" (Urbana: Univ. of Illinois Diss., 1958), pp. 50, 63-64.

[15] Although Mr. Prendergast's role in the love-inheritance story is usually presented as paralleling the role of God in the famine background, at one point at least God, who in his mercy brought the famine to Ireland, is seen as having in his mercy brought sorrow to Castle Richmond, for Herbert prays "that they all in that family might be enabled to bear the heavy sorrows which God in his mercy and wisdom had now thought fit to lay upon them." (pp. 393-394) In this perspective, Mr. Prendergast loses some dignity, though his role remains providential.

[16] Trollope makes his attitude toward pain fairly clear when he says, "It is the flinching from pain which makes pain so painful." (p. 153)

[17] Trollope makes no bones about declaring that he believes in God's mercy but not his wrath: "But though I do not believe in exhibitions of God's anger, I do believe in exhibitions of his mercy. When men by their folly and by the shortness of their vision have brought upon themselves penalties which seem to be overwhelming, to which no end can be seen, which would be overwhelming were no aid coming to us but our own, then God raises his hand, not in anger, but in mercy, and by his wisdom does for us that for which our own wisdom has been insufficient." (p. 102)

[18] These two trips constitute one of the many particular parallels in the novel. On both occasions, the unhappy Herbert, on his way from Castle Richmond to Desmond Court, is caught in the rain. But there are some differences, some slight, perhaps, and some important. Herbert, for instance, walks the first time and rides the second. The first time, Herbert is so wrapped up in his own misery that he hardly notices the misery of the Irish working men, but when he emerges from the cabin during the second trip, he has been much moved by

the misery within and is thus enabled to see his own misery in a truer light.

[19] For a discussion of how Trollope handles the theme of truth in a slightly earlier novel, *Doctor Thorne* (1858), where it is important though not central, see Chapter IV of my *Unity in Barsetshire* (The Hague: Mouton, 1971).

[20] One of the ironies of the novel resides in the fact that Mr. Prendergast, who sees so clearly what must be done, almost fails to discover the truth about the Fitzgerald marriage. Rather late in the game and almost by accident, he begins to investigate the possibility that leads to the discovery that Mollett was already married when he met and wooed Mary Wainwright.

[21] Here we get back to some of the particular parallels of the novel.

[22] But not an uncertainty to be compared with that generated by one of Trollope's favorite authors, Cervantes, in *Don Quixote*. Part of the difference probably lies in the fact that in the Spanish work the basic principles themselves—the falsity of books of chivalry, say—shift and are subject to change and re-evaluation.

Max Hastings (essay date 1994)

SOURCE: An introduction to *Castle Richmond*, by Anthony Trollope, edited by David Skilton, The Trollope Society, 1994, pp. vii-xvi.

[*In this excerpt from Hastings' introduction to Anthony Trollope's* Castle Richmond *(1860), the critic argues that a primary reason for the novel's commercial failure was the fact that Victorians preferred not to read about such an unpleasant chapter from recent history, and later readers, Hastings contends, have looked disfavorably upon both the "detachment with which Trollope wrote of the famine and its consequences" and Trollope's apparent view that the Famine was a "blessing in disguise."*]

. . . [T]he most persistent and damaging criticism of *Castle Richmond* since its publication is directed against Trollope's attempt to marry his romance to a backdrop of one of the greatest tragedies of the nineteenth century, the Irish potato famine. 'Those who saw its course, and watched its victims', he wrote sombrely, 'will not readily forget what they saw.'

Indeed they did not. In 1845, the Irish population of 8.25 million amounted to half that of Britain. Yet six years later the Irish total had fallen to 6.5 million. Death and emigration had disposed of the balance in a

---

> **An excerpt from Anthony Trollope's novel** *Castle Richmond* **(1860):**
>
> They who were in the south of Ireland during the winter of 1846-47 will not readily forget the agony of that period. For many, many years preceding and up to that time, the increasing swarms of the country had been fed upon the potato, and upon the potato only; and now all at once the potato failed them, and the greater part of eight million human beings were left without food.
>
> The destruction of the potato was the work of God; and it was natural to attribute the sufferings which at once overwhelmed the unfortunate country to God's anger—to his wrath for the misdeeds of which that country had been guilty. For myself, I do not believe in such exhibitions of God's anger. When wars come, and pestilence, and famine; when the people of a land are worse than decimated, and the living hardly able to bury the dead, I cannot coincide with those who would deprecate God's wrath by prayers. I do not believe that our God stalks darkly along the clouds, laying thousands low with the arrows of death, and those thousands the most ignorant, because men who are not ignorant have displeased Him. Nor, if in his wisdom He did do so, can I think that men's prayers would hinder that which his wisdom had seen to be good and right.
>
> But though I do not believe in exhibitions of God's anger, I do believe in exhibitions of his mercy. When men by their folly and by the shortness of their vision have brought upon themselves penalties which seem to be overwhelming, to which no end can be seen, which would be overwhelming were no aid coming to us but our own, then God raises his hand not in anger but in mercy, and by his wisdom does for us that for which our own wisdom has been insufficient.
>
> *Anthony Trollope, in* Castle Richmond, *1860, edited by David Skilton, reprinted by The Trollope Society, 1994.*

---

terrible natural catastrophe. The verdict of historians is almost unanimous, that the Government at Westminster acted wholly inadequately to assuage the disaster that followed the failure of successive potato harvests, which should have provided the sole means of sustenance for most of the Irish rural population.

Lord John Russell himself, as Prime Minister in January 1847, said that the famine was 'such as has not been known in modern times; indeed I should say it is like a famine of the thirteenth century acting upon a population of the nineteenth'. Yet it was Lord John who, despite this knowledge, exposed the destitute millions of Ireland to the mercy of wholly inadequate local Poor Rates, and refused assistance when the second total failure of the potato took place in 1848. The Government's pledge to feed starving children was broken. Cecil Woodham-Smith has written: 'Since Britain was passing through a financial crisis, the justification of the Government's action was expediency, but it is difficult to reconcile expediency with duty and moral principles.'

Mrs Woodham-Smith's verdict on the British response to the Irish famine is devastating. She acknowledges that, in the first period from 1845 to 1847, substantial and speedy aid was sent, to the considerable value of £8 million. Yet, in the second period, pitifully little was done. 'Neither during the famine nor for decades afterwards', writes Mrs Woodham-Smith, 'were any measures of reconstruction or agricultural improvement attempted, and this neglect condemned Ireland to decline.' When the second potato harvest failed in 1848, Lord John Russell threw up his hands in disgust. 'In 1847', he said, 'eight millions were advanced to enable the Irish to supply the loss of the potato crops and to cast about them for some less precarious food . . . The result is that they have placed more dependence on the potato than ever and have again been deceived. How can such a people be assisted?' This was the background against which must be viewed the benign view of official policy expressed by Trollope in *Castle Richmond*.

The Victorians, in some respects the most sentimental of people, yet in others notably ruthless, did not want their leisure reading interwoven with a fragment of recent history they preferred to forget. This was a major contributory factor to the commercial failure of *Castle Richmond*. But later readers, also, have been dismayed by the detachment with which Trollope wrote of the famine and its consequences. A notably damaging passage is often quoted by critics:

> Such having been the state of the country, such its wretchedness, a merciful God sent the remedy which might avail to arrest it; and we—we deprecated his wrath. But all this will soon be known and acknowledged; acknowledged as it is acknowledged that new cities rise up in splendour from the ashes into which old cities have been consumed by fire. If this beneficent agency did not from time to time disencumber our crowded places, we should ever be living in narrow alleys with stinking gutters, and supply of water at the minimum.

Trollope sought to argue, therefore, that the famine was a blessing in disguise—God's way of redressing the natural balance in hopelessly overcrowded rural areas of Ireland, where few peasant landholdings exceeded half an acre, bounded by mud walls. We all recognise that death was much closer to every citizen of the British Isles in the nineteenth century than it is to ourselves in the twentieth. But Trollope's verdict seems indeed harsh measure, the ultimate expression of Victorian faith in the policy of *laissez-faire*.

Having read Woodham-Smith or the words of Russell, it is not easy to indulge Trollope's defence of government policy in responding to the famine, which he acclaims as 'prompt, wise, and beneficent; and I have to say also that the efforts of those who managed the poor were, as a rule, unremitting, honest, impartial, and successful'.

Yet, paradoxically, the author was by no means blind to suffering, or to Irish sentiment. Trollope understood and explained to the readers of *Castle Richmond* why the Irish poor were, in the eyes of the Ascendancy, so unappreciative of the relief they were offered—the Indian corn and the directions to the nearest workhouse:

> To call them ungrateful would imply too deep a reproach, for their convictions were that they were being ill used by the upper classes. When they received bad meal which they could not cook, and even in their extreme hunger could hardly eat half-cooked; when they were desired to leave their cabins and gardens, and flock into the wretched barracks which were prepared for them; when they saw their children wasting away under a suddenly altered system of diet, it would have been unreasonable to expect that they should have been grateful. Grateful for what?

Some of the vignettes of the famine in *Castle Richmond* offer powerful testimony to its horrors: Herbert Fitzgerald taking shelter from a rainstorm in the cabin of a peasant woman with her dead and dying children; the meetings of local dignitaries, to debate measures to alleviate suffering—'and now the famine was in full swing; and strange to say, men had ceased to be uncomfortable about it—such men, anyway, as Mr Somers and Mr Townsend'; Herbert Fitzgerald's meeting with a starving family at the gates of Desmond Court; the great heap of wheelbarrows by the roadside, relic of the ill-fated government programme of public works to justify paying a wage to the starving.

Yet Trollope failed convincingly to bring together his romance and the dreadful experience of the population beyond the gates of the great houses. Although the Castle Richmond family went out among the villages to do their best to bring relief, the chief impression of the famine's impact upon the Fitzgeralds and Desmonds is of inconvenience and dismay, at the margins of the narrative. In reality, among most of the landed classes it was probably just so. But some readers are left with a sense of unease and even repugnance.

The best explanation of Trollope's attitude is that, while he was a great writer, he was also a civil servant. All his instincts directed him towards respect for the authorities and for the difficulties of government. Some of the passages from *Castle Richmond* quoted above should acquit him of the charge of complacency levelled by critics against his view of the famine. He records with terrible vividness the sufferings of the Irish poor. But it is impossible to defend his verdict, that when the famine was over, the past could be set aside, as Ireland advanced once again into the sunshine.

Most historians share the view that the famine permanently altered the course of Irish history, and set nationalists upon a path from which they would never turn back, their passions inflamed by the conviction that the experience of the famine demonstrated that Englishmen could not be entrusted with the humane stewardship of Irish affairs. This is a judgement from which many modern Englishmen and women would find it difficult to dissent. . . .

Chris Morash (essay date 1995)

SOURCE: "Malthus and Famine Novel," in *Writing The Irish Famine*, Oxford at the Clarendon Press, 1995, pp. 30-51.

[*In the following essay, Morash analyzes three Famine novels in relation to the Malthusian principles of population—that an "unchecked" population will increase at a much higher rate than will the subsistence level, unless the population is "checked" by some type of disaster, such as famine, war, or disease. Morash argues that the Malthusian principles are present in the novels, suggesting that the Famine—the "check"—is the fault of the "extravagance" of both the aristocracy (for its lavish monetary expenditures) and the peasantry (for the size of their families). Morash maintains, however, that the social order which is created out of the chaos of the Famine—with the new prominence of the middle class—is dictated by the conventions of the novel, and that the authors' depictions of Famine victims serve as a reminder to readers of the cost of establishing a new social order.*]

Malthusian Narratives

Malthus's principle of population, Darwin's theory of evolution, and the nineteenth-century novel are all narratives which share what Gillian Beer has identified as a 'preoccupation with time and with change'. Defining the situation more precisely, George Levine argues in *Darwin and the Novelists* that 'science enters most Victorian fiction not so much in the shape of ideas, as, quite literally, in the shape of its shape, its form, as well as in the patterns it exploits and develops, the relationships it allows'.[1] These formal permissions, rather than any simple idea of the 'influence', constitute the active relationship between Malthusian and Darwinian discourses, and the novel. When reading William Steuart Trench's *Ierne* in the context of his efforts to depopulate Kenmare, for instance, we

glimpse the structural analogies between Malthusian theories of population control and conventional elements of fictional narrative such as marriage (selective breeding), postponed marriage (preventive population control), the failed love affair (preclusion from breeding), exile (positive population control), and inheritance (heredity),[2] Far from being distracting pieces of narrative machinery which obscure the 'real' representation of the Famine, the conventional elements of Victorian fiction give the Famine form and hence meaning, constructing ethical subjects in the midst of atrocity. And always, even when he is not mentioned by name, Malthus stands behind this process, ghost-writing the shape of narrative.

While it might be argued that the linear form of the realist novel has a tendency to write all history as progress, three novels in particular inscribe the Famine in narratives of social improvement: Anthony Trollope's *Castle Richmond* of 1860; Annie Keary's *Castle Daly: The Story of An Irish Home Thirty Years Ago* of 1875; and Margaret Brew's *The Chronicles of Castle Cloyne: Or, Pictures of the Munster People*, published in 1885. These novels share more than the similarity of their titles with Maria Edgeworth's *Castle Rackrent* of 1800; they also share in the construction of a narrative of the transition from an aristocratic to a bourgeois society which Edgeworth intimates, but leaves enigmatically unresolved.[3] With the last of the Rackrents dead, and with Jason the land agent poised to take over the estate in the novel's final pages, her narrator, Thady M'Quirk, relates that 'others say Jason won't have the lands at any rate—many wishes it so—for my part, I'm tired of wishing for any thing in this world, after all I've seen in it—but I'll say nothing.'[4] If, as Kenneth Burke argues, 'critical and imaginative works are answers to questions posed by the situations in which they arose',[5] *Castle Richmond, Castle Daly,* and *Castle Cloyne* can be read as attempts to respond to Edgeworth's unanswered question: what happens when Jason moves into the castle?

If Edgeworth was worried in 1800 that the landowning aristocracy to which she belonged must either reform or perish, the effect of the Famine on land prices a half-century later was to make these fears all the more real, in effect transforming the Famine into an emblem of social change. 'English capitalists', writes Elizabeth Smith in her 1848 diary, 'are waiting till the glut in the market still further reduces the value of the land. It can now be had for fifteen or sixteen years' purchase; they expect it to fall to twelve. This will annihilate our present aristocracy.'[6] What would have made this prospect all the more threatening to Smith is the ease with which the 'annihilation' of the aristocracy could be accommodated to a Malthusian narrative of progress. In his 1847 account of his travels in the west of Ireland, the Quaker William Bennett makes this point with blunt directness:

Here is society dislocated at *both ends*. . . . The natural influences and expenditure of property in creating artificial wants and means of livelihood, withdrawn from their own sources, and the people thrown back upon the veriest thriftlessness and least remove above the lowest animal conditions of life! Under such a state of things,—not the accident of to-day, but the steady and regular growth of years and a system,—a population is nurtured, treading constantly on the borders of starvation; checked only by a crisis like the present, to which it inevitably leads, and almost verifying the worst Malthusian doctrines.[7]

In pointing to the dislocation of 'both ends' of society—the large landowner at the upper end, and the peasant at the lower—Bennett presents what is to be one of the recurrent structural features of the Malthusian interpretation of the Famine. The Famine is read as being attributable to the extravagance of two classes: the aristocracy and the peasantry. The aristocracy are seen as being extravagant in their monetary expenditure and their mode of living; the peasantry, in the size of their families. In both instances, the Famine acts as a Malthusian 'check' upon extravagance, moderating the two extremes of society, making them both more like the middle class. It is this Malthusian metanarrative of class change, with its Darwinian overtones, which we see acted out in the novels of Annie Keary, Margaret Brew, and Anthony Trollope in the decades after the Famine.

Castles Under Siege

Of the three 'castle' novels, Annie Keary's *Castle Daly* takes up the challenge of *Castle Rackrent* most directly—indeed, the novel even includes a cameo appearance by Edgeworth's narrator, Thady M'Quirk. In *Castle Daly* an English brother and sister, John and Bride Thornley, emigrate to Ireland to manage their aristocratic cousin's property, the eponymous Castle Daly. During the Famine, the kindly, responsible Thornleys loan the feckless Dalys more and more money, eventually becoming full owners of Castle Daly, which they transform into an efficient and profitable operation. Such social change, the novel suggests, is inevitable—as Bride Thornley makes clear:

> The sort of interdependence and mutual affection and interest between rich and poor you look back upon is a remnant of the old clan feeling, and has, no doubt, a great deal of beauty and poetry about it. I can understand the revolt you feel against it being merged into the hard individualism of the stage of society that has to follow. It looks ugly in the first stern form of struggle it has to take, but it must come and work out into its own good.[8]

The Darwinian class 'struggle' which Keary establishes between the Irish 'old clan feeling' and the English

bourgeois individualism 'that *has to* follow' also has a colonial dimension. 'To us,' Macaulay had written in 1835, 'we will own, nothing is so interesting and delightful as to contemplate the steps by which . . . the England of the crusaders, monks, schoolmen, astrologers, serfs, outlaws, became the England which we know and love, the classic ground of liberty.'[9] English history, in its dominant formulation, was a progress from feudalism to bourgeois 'liberty' in a historiographic metanarrative which was given the sanction of science by Darwinian evolution. Ireland, with its perceived lack of a middle class, can thus be written as one of the last bastions of 'old clan feeling', an archaic form of English culture, the chimpanzee to England's *homo sapiens*.

Castle Daly is an attempt to reconcile, in the aesthetic realm of the novel, the 'ugliness' of the English 'stern individualism' which '*has to* follow' with the Irish 'beauty and poetry' of a social order which the text simultaneously laments and refutes. The heroine of the novel, Ellen Daly, is the daughter of an English mother and a well-meaning but reckless Irish landlord straight out of the pages of *Castle Rackrent*. Her mother died while Ellen was a child, leaving her 'long enough with my [peasant] foster-mother to remember the cabin life perfectly',[10] and thereby providing her with the credentials to be a 'wild Irish girl' in the mould of Lady Morgan's eponymous heroine. Her brother, Pelham Daly, by contrast, was raised as the English gentleman suggested by his name—an intertextual borrowing from Bulwer-Lytton's 1828 novel, *Pelham: or the adventures of a gentleman*. Over the course of the novel, these two characters marry their temperamental and national opposites—in Ellen's case, the calm, rational Englishman, John Thornley; in Pelham's case, an impetuous English girl named Lesbia Maynard. And, as in Trench's *Ierne*, there is a male 'Celtic' character, Ellen's brother Conor Daly, a follower of Young Ireland, who does not fit into the structure of pairings and is exiled at the novel's end. Those who are able to achieve balance, the novel's structure suggests, are able to progress through marriage into the next generation; those who seek revolution are denied the opportunity to partake of evolutionary change.

As these almost allegorical characters negotiate allegiances, they debate the Famine in ways which create discursive frames for their positions. John Thornley, for instance, a land agent and an occasional contributor to the *Edinburgh Review,* articulates the Malthusian perspective of the English and Irish ruling classes when he declares that 'there will come some good out of the present misery, you may be sure. It is good for the country that the surplus population is driven away, even by stress of famine, to seek more prosperous homes elsewhere, leaving the land to be made the best of.' Ellen's brother, Conor, responds to this with the orthodox Young Ireland rejection of the need for emigration:

> Everywhere roofless villages and deserted homes, and only here and there a few companionless people who have lost all instinct of nationality, guarding riches that are not their own. *That* would be your good; but that is just the fate we Young Irelanders are resolved to make one stand against before it is quite too late—one struggle to keep Ireland and her people together.[11]

Ellen stands between these two positions, accepting the logic of Thornley's arguments, but susceptible to the emotional appeal of her brother's position. However, by equating these interpretative positions metaphorically with fictional characters, *Castle Daly* allows the logic of novelistic convention to determine the shape of social debate. In the end, Ellen comes to accept Thornley's position not because his arguments have been more persuasive than those of her brother, but because the conventions of romantic fiction lead the reader to expect that the heroine's primary allegiance will shift from her brother to her lover. It is at such moments that the logic of fictional narrative imposes itself on the shape of history.

The same writing of social change in terms of the conventions of fiction takes place in Trollope's *Castle Richmond,* where the plot revolves around two men competing for the love of the same woman. Trollope expands the architectural metaphor upon which the 'castle' novel depends as a genre by associating each of his three main characters with an architectural style. The aristocratic heroine and object of pursuit, Clara Desmond, lives in Desmond Court, which, Trollope tells us: 'is a huge place—huge, ungainly, and uselessly extensive; built at a time when, at any rate in Ireland, men considered neither beauty, aptitude, nor economy'. 'Nothing', in the narrator's judgement, 'can well be more desolate.' Clara's earliest suitor is Owen Fitzgerald, a young bachelor who has come into possession of Hap House, 'such a pleasant, comfortable residence, too large no doubt for such a property, as is so often the case in Ireland'. However, the 'pleasantness' of Hap House is suspect, for it is not based on social responsibility. 'A house,' we are told, 'if it be not pleasant by domestic pleasant things, must be made pleasant by pleasure. And a bachelor's pleasures in his own house are always dangerous.' Finally, there is Herbert Fitzgerald, who cuts a less dashing figure than his cousin Owen. Herbert lives with his parents and sisters in the eponymous Castle Richmond, a building which lacks 'any of those interesting picturesque faults' which Trollope considers to be associated with 'Irish castles': 'Castle Richmond had no appearance of having been thrown out of its own windows. It was a good, substantial, modern family residence, built not more than thirty years since.'

With this simple architectural motif, Trollope establishes three alternate versions of a ruling class: the extravagant *ancien régime* (Desmond Court) and the equally extravagant *nouveau* aristocratic (Hap House)—both instances of 'property . . . regarded as having no duties attached to it'[12]—and the 'substantial, modern' middle class (Castle Richmond). As was the case in *Castle Daly,* however, the social order which emerges victorious from the disorganization of the Famine is determined not purely by any yardstick of justice or ability, but by the dictates of fictional convention. Herbert Fitzgerald, the responsible young bourgeois landowner, marries Clara Desmond and thereby reconciles her to the values of the middle class at the end of the novel because he is the hero of the novel and she is the heroine. 'What is important in narrative', Joep Leerssen reminds us, 'is not how characters are, but how their behavior relates to the audience's expectations concerning them.'[13] We all know from the outset that Clara cannot possibly marry Owen of Hap House, because Owen is a rake. And yet, when Owen goes into exile and Clara's stubbornly aristocratic mother, Lady Desmond, locks herself up in the 'gloomy prison' of Desmond Court, the outcome of the romantic plot becomes a symbolic enactment of what Trollope claims to have been a general rout of the aristocracy in the wake of the Famine. 'It is with thorough rejoicing,' he writes in his authorial persona, 'almost with triumph, that I declare that the idle, genteel class has been cut up root and branch, has been driven forth out of its holding into the wide world, and has been punished with the penalty of extermination.'[14] Defining himself as an 'advanced Conservative-Liberal' in his 1883 *Autobiography,* Trollope makes clear the narrative of historical progress which forms the ideological framework for this rejoicing. 'The advanced Conservative-Liberal', writes Trollope, sees history as 'a series of steps towards that human millennium of which he dreams. He is even willing to help the many to ascend the ladder a little, though he knows, as they come up towards him, he must go down to meet them.'[15]

There is a similar form of 'advanced Conservative-Liberal' politics in Margaret Brew's 1885 novel, *The Chronicles of Castle Cloyne,* although its relation to narrative convention is slightly different. Where Trollope in *Castle Richmond* and Keary in *Castle Daly* wrote only of the descent of the aristocracy to the level of the bourgeoisie, Brew splits her narrative into two parts, one dealing with the rise of a peasant, the other dealing with the fall of an aristocrat:

> There are two different stories running side by side through the book, each having but slight connection with the other. This was to show how universal was the action of the Famine, and how impartial in its effects. Peer and peasant, landlord and tenant, the home of the great, the cabin of the lowly, all were alike brought under its terrible influence, and all alike were compelled to bend beneath the storm.

Some had vitality enough to survive it, and lift their heads once more above the water, but more—and these last were the great majority—went down beneath the waves of utter and hopeless ruin, never to rise again.[16]

One narrative in *Castle Cloyne* follows Oonagh Mac-Dermott, a peasant woman, as she grows to adulthood during the Famine; the other narrative follows the heir to the estate on which Oonagh lives, Hyacinth Dillon, during the same period. Apart from their mutual friendship with the local priest, however, neither character comes into contact with the other during the course of the novel. Instead, the relationship between the two narratives is structural; both narratives, plotting the fall and rise of their respective characters, are Comic.

Like so much of our critical vocabulary for discussing these structural patterns, the word 'Comic' has so many different meanings that at times it almost appears to be meaningless. Here we can take it to refer to those U-shaped narratives, like Shakespeare's *A Midsummer Night's Dream,* where an initial period of social control collapses into a dark night of chaos, which in turn is succeeded by a new, more stable, social order, usually signalled by a marriage. The novel, as the form in which 'the anomalous individual learns to be reconciled with society and its project',[17] is ideally suited to tell these Comic tales of social integration.

In *Castle Cloyne,* Oonagh's story begins in an Edenic pre-Famine world, which is thrown into turmoil by the failure of the potato crop. One by one, Oonagh's friends and family succumb to starvation and disease, and Oonagh finds herself driven out of her smallholding, forced to become a travelling pedlar. After much hardship, however, she finds that her new life provides her with greater wealth than she had known as part of a cottier family:

> In a little time she [Oonagh] found, to her great surprise, that she had some small surplus at the end of every quarter. It might be sometimes a few pence only, and sometimes a few shillings. These were carefully put by until they mounted up to a couple of pounds. . . . She had put it together by hard work, and much self-sacrifice, and the thought that she had it, and could draw upon it in case of sickness, or any future emergency, made her heart feel very light and happy.[18]

Eventually, Oonagh's 'couple of pounds' becomes enough to enable her to buy a shop, marking her move out of the peasantry into the lower middle class. This change in the character's social status corresponds to a formal change in the text. In the early sections of the novel, Brew provides her readers with the 'pictures of the Munster people' promised in the book's subtitle.

These anecdotes of peasant life owe much, as the title suggests, to early collections such as Gerald Griffin's *Tales of the Munster Festivals* and Carleton's *Traits and Stories of the Irish Peasantry*. However, as the peasant characters who feature in the anecdotes are decimated by hunger and disease, the peasant genre of the anecdote itself disappears, and Oonagh's narrative of absorption into the middle class takes the form of the progressive linearity of the novel.

The sections of *Castle Cloyne* dealing with Hyacinth, the aristocrat and landowner, map a trajectory of social change which mirrors the story of Oonagh's fall and rise from the opposite end of the social spectrum. In the early part of the novel, Hyacinth and his father are Rackrentian figures, squandering borrowed money on election campaigns, dodging bailiffs, and providing lavish entertainments for ungrateful retainers. However, with the onset of the Famine, the Dillons are forced to sell Castle Cloyne to a 'London hotel-keeper' at 'an enormous sacrifice, not much more than seven years' purchase . . . owing to the dreadful state of the country, and the tightness of the money markets'.[19] And yet, in spite of her sympathetic portrayal of these aristocratic characters, Brew adds her voice to the chorus singing the praises of modernity as the old estates are broken up:

> There were not wanting those who sorrowed for the old gentry, and thought that the world must surely be coming to an end, when they were so utterly rooted out of the land in which they had been established for centuries; others stoutly maintained that the system which had tolerated them so long, was as unwholesome as it was obsolete, and that the new blood and fresh energy that had replaced them all over the country, would vastly serve to advance its real interests, and develop its numerous and latent resources.

As the phrase 'new blood' with its unspoken debt to Darwinian evolutionary theory suggests, there is a measure of equivocation in *Castle Cloyne*'s use of the Comic metanarrative to write the story of the Irish aristocracy. The peasant character, Oonagh, survives by evolving—penny by penny and shilling by shilling—to fit the changing economic order of Ireland in the 1840s. By contrast, the aristocratic Hyacinth finds himself shipped off to the Californian gold rush of 1849, where he simply digs up enough gold to buy back Castle Cloyne. Although by the novel's end he too has joined the ranks of a cautious, mercantile middle class—his wedding is described as 'the quietest of all quiet weddings, though a very happy one'[20]—his survival as a character stretches the capabilities of fictional convention into the realm of the *deus ex machina*. In terms of the novel's enplotment, it is fortuitous rather than necessary, suggesting that Hyacinth's story could just as easily be written as Tragedy.

That Ghastly, Livid Face

On the level of narrative structure, the Famine operates as an agent of Darwinian social change in all three of these novels. In this regard, Brew, Keary, and Trollope are, in their various ways, part of the same discursive formation as the texts of Senior, Trench, Trevelyan, and others. At the same time, however, the form of the novel disrupts certain aspects of this formation. As a genre, the novel is concerned primarily with the integration of the individual into the social order; this means that while the realistic novel may discuss social classes, it is necessarily concerned with the construction of individual characters. Malthusian and Darwinian metanarratives of progress may have made it possible to accept the 'extermination' of entire classes or categories of beings; it is impossible, however, to imagine Trollope treating the death of an individual character with the same 'thorough rejoicing' and 'triumph' with which he celebrates the 'penalty of extermination' inflicted upon an entire class.

It is thus to the suffering individual that we must turn if we are to see the narrative of progress disrupted. In particular, as the suffering caused by Famine is engraved upon the body, the writing of the body of the Famine victim reminds us of the Famine dead on whose absence the new order of history as progress is founded. In Margaret Brew's *Castle Cloyne,* for instance, the story of Oonagh's triumphant progress into the mercantile economy is troubled by a passage in which she discovers the corpse of Pleasant John, the thriftless peasant whom she loved, but never married:

> There was no kind hand near him at the last to close his eyes, for they were wide open, and their fixed and glassy stare was perfectly horrible to look on. The worn face was half covered by a stubbly black beard of a fortnight's growth, and was like nothing earthly but a yellow parchment mask, wrinkled, haggard, and careworn. The throat and chest, laid bare by having the quilt drawn down, were so thin that the bones were in a manner held together only by the skin, and could literally be counted.[21]

There is a detail lavished on the body in this passage which recalls us to the singularity of each human body: the 'glassy stare' of the eyes; the 'stubbly black beard'; throat, chest, bones, skin. The narrative of *Castle Cloyne* may be structured in such a way that it is desirable that the peasants and aristocrats of an 'unwholesome' and 'obsolete' system of landholding should be exterminated so that they can be replaced by 'new blood'. It may also speak of a peasantry capable of 'suffering with sublime endurance, and dying with patient resignation'[22] due to the strength of their religious convictions. Yet neither of these metanarratives can adequately accommodate the 'yellow parchment mask' of the dead man's face. We find a similar moment in Thackeray's *Irish Sketch Book* of 1842, when he acknowledges the effect of individual faces on his appreciation of the Irish landscape. 'The traveller is haunted by the face of popular starvation,' writes Thackeray; 'that ghastly livid face interposing itself between you and it [the landscape].'[23]

Similarly, in Annie Keary's *Castle Daly,* John Thornley is shown throughout the novel speaking 'eagerly of it [the Famine] for the sake of searching out analogies to its woes in the past periods of history; fitting cause and effect, and probable remote consequences, with a satisfaction in the completeness of the chain of reasoning'. However, his ability to contain the Famine in discourse is disrupted when he encounters the body— and, more precisely, the face—of a starving woman. 'A figure was half-seated on the ground with its back to the wall,' the passage begins. 'A child's form lay motionless across its knees, the head rested on a stone in the wall, and there was light enough through a crevice above to show . . . the death-pale, hollow face, with dropped jaw, and half-closed eyes that looked so strangely without seeing.'[24] Prior to this encounter with a suffering individual, Thornley had accepted, on principle, that 'the want of due appreciation of the subtler emotions and spiritual sources of individual and national life was a fatal hindrance to penetrating the truth of things'. After looking on the face of death his theoretical acceptance of the need for 'subtler emotions and spiritual sources' is transformed into what can only be described as a form of religious revival. Leaving the cabin, he and Ellen Daly flee from the 'death-pale, hollow face' of starvation, and stumble into a Roman Catholic church service taking place in a nearby village:

> At another time John might have listened critically— questioning the wisdom or utility of such an exercise [as the sermon] under such circumstances; but now kneeling on the mud floor among that sea of pale faces that were gradually losing their ghastliness under the illumination of hope in the Unseen, thus set forth before eyes that in every other quarter beheld only despair, he could not question.[25]

The 'death-pale face' of the starving is transformed by the presence of religious ritual into the 'sea of pale faces that were gradually losing their ghastliness under the illumination of hope in the Unseen'. In rewriting the face of the starving woman in this way, *Castle Daly* attempts to accommodate the singularity of the face by submerging it in a 'sea of pale faces' whose suffering is given meaning by religious ritual. Here the novel finds itself confronting two incompatible regimes of truth: Thornley's rational world of 'fitting cause to effect', and the 'illumination of hope in the Unseen', to which Ellen is sympathetic. The novel attempts to accommodate these two contradictory orders of perception by mobilizing the reader's expectations of romantic fiction as Ellen holds out her hand to Thornley at the end of the sermon, paving the way for the novel's conventional resolution in the marriage of the 'wild Irish girl' and the rational Englishman. And yet, the disruptive force of the 'death-pale' face of the starving woman resists this narrativization, and continues to trouble the novel's final moments as Ellen looks out over a landscape haunted by absence. John, she muses, 'is so convinced that the character of this part of the country needs must be changed, and that to discourage the emigration, induce people to settle here in their former numbers, would only lead to another famine, that he cannot mourn as I do over the deserted villages and the silent hill-sides.'[26]

Suffering Subjects

Herbert Fitzgerald, the prudent bourgeois hero who triumphs in Trollope's *Castle Richmond,* had, we are told, 'learned deep lessons of political economy'. And so when, riding through the Cork countryside to meet Clara Desmond, he meets a woman with five starving children who beg him for money, he refuses. To give 'promiscuous charity', his theoretical lessons had taught him, was to waste valuable resources. However, when the woman threatens to go to Herbert's rival, Owen Fitzgerald, for assistance, saying 'Mr. Owen won't be afther sending me to the Kanturk union', Herbert offers her money in some confusion:

> Herbert Fitzgerald, from the first moment of his interrogating the woman, had of course known that he would give her somewhat. In spite of all his political economy, there were but few days in which he did not empty his pocket of his loose silver, with these culpable deviations from his theoretical philosophy. But yet he felt that it was his duty to insist on his rules, as far as his heart would allow him to do so.[27]

It might be argued that Herbert's 'culpable deviations from his theoretical philosophy' are part of the 'anti-systematic, anti-doctrinal, antipreceptual'[28] ethics which Ruth apRoberts has identified throughout Trollope's work. However, in this particular passage in *Castle Richmond,* the narrative context of these 'deviations' suggests something else. Rather than resolving the contradiction between individual need and economic theory, Herbert's response to starvation in this passage is based on his desire to impress Clara Desmond. If he does not help the starving woman, his rival will. As in *Castle Daly* and *Castle Cloyne,* issues of economic theory and individual suffering are here resolved through the conventions of the fictional romantic narrative. However, unlike Keary and Brew, Trollope seems determined to push the issue further; and so in *Castle Richmond* there are two more confrontations with the individual face of Famine.

In both of these encounters, Herbert is on a journey from Castle Richmond to Desmond Court: in the first, his mission is to inform Clara Desmond that he will no longer be able to marry her because he has been disinherited; in the second, he is going to tell her that he is bound for London to win back his place in society by studying law. On the first journey, he passes through a group of starving men employed on a government works project but turns a deaf ear to their petitions as he struggles 'through the slush and across the chasm, regardless of it all'. 'Nothing', comments Trollope, 'is so powerful in making a man selfish as misfortune.' Upon his arrival at Desmond Court, 'wet through and covered with mud',[29] Herbert is rejected by Clara's mother because he has been dispossessed. Herbert's first confrontation with suffering is thus associated with defeat in his personal affairs, even though there is no causal connection between the two.

In his second encounter with a Famine victim, the difference in Herbert's response indicates the degree to which he has become reconciled to the contradictory values of bourgeois society. Travelling through a wasteland of abandoned cottages to announce to Clara his intention to work for a living, he stops to shelter from the rain in a small cabin:

> Squatting in the middle of the cabin, seated on her legs crossed under her, with nothing between her and the wet earth, there crouched a woman with a child in her arms. . . . She had on her some rag of clothing which barely sufficed to cover her nakedness, and the baby which she held in her arms was covered in some sort . . . her rough short hair hung down upon her back, clotted with dirt, and the head and face of the child which she held was covered with dirt and sores. On no more wretched object, in its desolate solitude, did the eye of man ever fall.

As his eyes adjust to the darkness Herbert comes to realize that the baby is dead; he first experiences disgust, and then pity:

> So he took from his pocket his silk handkerchief, and, returning to the corner of the cabin, spread it as a covering over the corpse. At first he did not like to touch the small naked dwindled remains of humanity from which life had fled; but gradually he overcame his disgust, and kneeling down, he straightened the limbs and closed the eyes, and folded the handkerchief round the slender body.

In this simple act of compassion the transformation of Herbert into a responsible subject is completed. 'He forgot for a while both himself and Clara Desmond . . . how could he repine at aught that the world had done for him, having now witnessed to how low a state of misery a fellow human being might be brought?'[30] The body of the Famine victim forces on Herbert a recognition of the reality of another's existence as analogous to his own existence. This ethical response, however, is formulated in a context of paradox. Herbert's attempt to understand the dying woman's suffering in terms of his own suffering brings an awareness of the disproportion between his suffering and hers—an awareness forced on the reader by the detail of the 'silk handkerchief' which contrasts so abruptly with the image of the famished infant. 'Could he,' the novel asks us, 'after that, dare to consider himself unfortunate?' The anonymous woman holding the body of her dead child both demands and denies the possibility of empathy. And it is this tension which generates the desire for an ethics of empathy, even if that project must be founded on its own failure.

Civilization's Hungry Double

When Trollope tells his readers in the opening pages of *Castle Richmond* that 'neither Sir Thomas [Herbert's father], nor Sir Thomas's house [Castle Richmond] had about them any of those interesting picturesque faults which are so generally attributed to Irish landlords and Irish castles', he is signalling to his readers that he is making a departure from the conventions of representations of Ireland in fiction. 'As regards its appearance,' Trollope writes, 'Castle Richmond might have been in Hampshire or Essex; and as regards his property, Sir Thomas Fitzgerald might have been a Leicestershire baronet.'[31] Indeed, there are no Ribbonmen, Whiteboys, or Young Irelanders in the novel; there are no recipes for whiskey punch,[32] no Thadyesque faithful retainers, no grasping estate agents; nor is Cork city written in terms which greatly differ from a large market town in Trollope's Barsetshire. This is more than simply a case of a writer being unable to create characters outside of his own social sphere. Trollope announces in his opening pages that, in writing of Ireland, he is writing of Ireland as a part of Great Britain; and, as such, his text is meant to apply to all inhabitants of Great Britain: 'No one will think that Hampshire is better for such a purpose than Cumberland, or Essex than Leicestershire. What abstract objection can there then be to the county Cork?' On one hand, this refusal to grant Ireland a unique identity is a form of literary unionism; but there is more to it than that.

Trollope realizes that his readers will make a distinction between Hampshire and Cork, regardless of the Act of Union. 'I fear that Irish character is in these days considered almost as unattractive as historical incident,' he writes; 'but nevertheless I will make the attempt.'[33] The comparison here between 'Irish character' and 'historical incident' is telling in the light of Georg Lukács's observations on the change in the use of history in the novel after the revolutions of 1848. Prior to 1848, argues Lukács, pointing to the novels of Walter Scott, 'the people play the chief role actively and passively, in action and suffering'; after 1848 'characters cease to be really historical; the historical events become external and exotic, a merely decorative backdrop'. Lukács attributes this 'crisis of bourgeois realism' to the changed perception of the idea of progress after 1848:

> The most notable writers and thinkers of the period before 1848 made their most important step forward by giving an historical formulation to the idea of progress. . . . However, the events of the class struggle presented to the ideologists of the bourgeoisie so threatening a prospect for the future of their society and class, that the disinterested courage with which the contradictions of progress had been disclosed and declared was bound to disappear [in the period after 1848].[34]

For Trollope, as for Annie Keary and Margaret Brew, the representation of Irish poverty served the same function as the sort of pre-1848 historical analysis Lukács is describing here, exposing a set of 'contradictions of progress' made all the more complex by the colonial relations between England and Ireland. By the time Keary's *Castle Daly* was published in 1875, Gladstone's first Land Act had been in effect for five years, and by the time Brew's *Castle Cloyne* appeared in 1885, the Ashbourne Act was before Parliament and the Land League agitation of the early 1880s had given a new urgency to the whole question of land ownership. As these novelists were writing, land was changing possession, moving from a hereditary aristocracy to the middle classes. In the writing of this class change as social progress, the Famine acts as an emblematic moment of abrupt transition.

The Famine, claimed William Steuart Trench in his 1868 *Realities of Irish Life,* 'removed the needy country gentlemen, and forced them to sell their estates into the hands of capitalists'[35]—which was indeed the case. However, as recent statistical analyses of property sales in the wake of the Famine demonstrate, more often than not Irish estates were broken up and bought by Irish buyers. 'Out of 7,489 buyers up to the end of August 1857,' writes James Donnelly of the Encumbered Estates Court, 'just 309, or 4 per cent, were of English, Scottish, or foreign background; all the rest were Irish.'[36] It is in this that we can identify one of the unpleasant 'contradictions of progress' forced on English and unionist commentators by the changes in land ownership which followed the Famine. When Trench goes on to announce that the Famine 'brought over hundreds of Scotchmen and Englishmen, who have farmed on an extended and more scientific system than had before then been the practice in Ireland',[37] there is an element of wishful thinking in the assertion. In 1848 it may have been possible for John Hamilton, for instance, writing in a pamphlet predicated on the ubiquitous disease metaphor—*Ireland's Recovery and Ire-*

land's Health—to claim that 'the introduction of enterprising purchasers and improvers of land, from England and Scotland' would be 'one of the surest tokens of Ireland's health', making Ireland feel 'herself *a part of the empire,* and not merely a conquered province'.[38] By the time Trench and Keary are writing twenty years later, it would have become clear that this was not going to happen. The old estates may have been broken up; but the vast majority of their purchasers had come from within Ireland, as Margaret Brew's 1885 novel recognizes.

Consequently, we can understand attempts to write narratives in the 1860s and 1870s in which the Famine paves the way for 'hundreds of Scotchmen and Englishmen' as what Fredric Jameson calls 'ideological acts in their own right' which have 'the function of inventing imaginary or formal "solutions" to unresolvable social contradictions'.[39] Such solutions however, go beyond a simple regret that an opportunity for a free-market recolonization of Ireland had been missed. In *Castle Daly,* and in a more complex way in *Castle Richmond* with its ambivalently Irish/English characters, there is an attempt to construct a narrative of history in which the social progress of Ireland and the social progress of England are more than just compatible. In *Castle Richmond,* the social situations of England and Ireland become identical.

This strategy, however, opens up a series of frightening vistas. If an equivalence is established between Cork and Cumberland, Ireland becomes England's double, and the narrative of history which constructs Irish culture as an immature version of English culture becomes reversible. Once Ireland and England are written as mirror images of each other, as they are in *Castle Richmond,* it becomes equally possible that Ireland presents not an image of England's past, but an image of England's future—a future of crumbling traditions and swarming poverty in which England is unrecognizable to itself.

Writing Ireland as England's horrid twin extends back to the period before the Famine. On the eve of the Famine in 1844, for instance, Trollope's friend and contemporary William Thackeray wrote: 'Poverty and misery have, it seems their sublime, and that sublime is to be found in Ireland.'[40] In the same mode, Thomas Carlyle, during his Irish journey of 1849, wrote that 'Ireland really *is* my problem; the breaking point of the huge suppuration which all British and European society now is. Set down in Ireland, one might at least feel, "Here is Thy problem: In God's name, what wilt Thou do with it?" '[41] Later in the century, Henry Fawcett, MP and Cambridge Professor of Political Economy, was to make a more Malthusian use of Famine Ireland as a warning to England. In an 1871 lecture on English poverty, he told his audience:

It cannot be right or wise that, following the example of Ireland, we should observe the growth of poverty, we should know that an increasing population is each year pressing more severely upon our sources of employment, and upon our supplies of food, and yet anticipate with complacency the advent of the day when the people will be compelled by dire necessity to emigrate in masses or to seek refuge in some other drastic remedy.[42]

The 'drastic remedy' could equally be famine or revolution; the vagueness of the formulation allows both possibilities to occupy the same discursive space. *Castle Richmond, Castle Daly,* and *Castle Cloyne* attempt to use the narrative form of the novel to separate the threats of mass poverty and violent social reorganization, integrating the Famine into the narrative of evolutionary, progressive change. However, the very necessity for carrying out this process suggests the unspoken alternative: Famine Ireland is not just the site of a terrifying Otherness; it is a possible future for England. Once it comes to be read as such, an ethics of empathy—an ability to see the Self in the Other—becomes a matter of survival for the ruling classes.

'I do not believe', writes Trollope in his authorial persona, 'that our God stalks darkly along the clouds, laying thousands low with the arrows of death, and those thousands the most ignorant, because men who are not ignorant have displeased Him.' God strikes not in anger, Trollope claims, but in mercy. 'There comes upon us some strange disease, and we bid Him to stay his hand. But the disease, when it has passed by, has taught us lessons of cleanliness, which no master less stern would have made acceptable.' As the metaphor of the disease and the cure makes clear, the invocation of an active God is as much a figure of speech here as it is a theological position; what is really at stake is the ability of those who survive to learn from crisis. Hence, not only does the Famine stand as a 'lesson' to Ireland, Trollope's fictional representation of a young landowner learning empathy is also meant to be taken as a 'lesson' by his readers. 'Many a young English country gentleman', Trollope points out, 'might take a lesson from Sir Herbert Fitzgerald in the duties peculiar to his position.'[43] Here we have an instance of what David Lloyd identifies as 'the end of the novel's "narrative of representation" ', which is 'the production of ethical subjects, and not merely their figuration'.[44] The 'lesson' which Trollope wants to inculcate in his readers depends upon the severity of the Famine. For Trollope, the Irish Famine was not different in kind to the suffering endured by the English poor in 'Hampshire or Essex'; it was, however, different in scale, and that changed everything. When Herbert Fitzgerald is forced to confront the face of the starving woman, he confronts the contingency of his own existence, on both a personal and a social level, and the manner in which he does so is one which would not be forced upon him in a society in which poverty existed at a constant level. Similarly, there is a conventional blackmail plot in *Castle Richmond,* which seems unrelated to the Famine background, but which acts in a manner analogous to the Famine in so far as it forces Herbert to face the contingent nature of his inheritance.[45]

In forcing this recognition on his characters, we might think that Trollope in *Castle Richmond* is rectifying the lack of engagement with the contradictions of progress which Lukács detects in the novel after 1848. However, while the passages dealing with the victims of the Famine do provide a shock of ethical awareness, the final lines of the novel pronounce the triumph of progress in terms which erase the suffering on which such an awareness depends:

> If one did in truth write a tale of the famine, after that it would behove the author to write a tale of the pestilence; and then another, a tale of the exodus. These three wonderful events, following each other, were the blessings coming from Omniscience and Omnipotence by which the black clouds were driven away from the Irish firmament. If one, through it all, could have dared to hope, and have had from the first that wisdom which has learned to acknowledge that His mercy endureth for ever! And then the same author going on with his series would give in his last set,—Ireland in her prosperity.[46]

Read in the context of his public support for the measures of Charles Trevelyan and the Whig government during the Famine,[47] Trollope's almost ecstatic vision of 'Omniscience and Omnipotence' driving the 'black clouds' away 'from the Irish firmament' can be placed beside Trevelyan's claim that 'supreme wisdom has educed permanent good out of transient evil'.[48] In both of these narratives, as in the novels of Annie Keary and Margaret Brew, progress is reified as a reconciling supernatural force which not only justifies starvation, but requires it. In the narrative of progress, the Famine becomes civilization's hungry double.

Notes

[1] G. Beer, *Darwin's Plots* (London, 1983), 7; G. Levine, *Darwin and the Novelists* (London, 1988), 13.

[2] J. R. Reed, *Victorian Conventions* (Athens, Ohio, 1975), 105, 216-49, 268. Reed's study constitutes a dictionary of narrative convention in the Victorian novel.

[3] It is tempting to trace this historical narrative through the genre of the 'castle novel', beginning with the celebration of aristocracy in Walpole's *Castle of Otranto* of 1765, through the unresolved transition between aristocracy and bourgeoisie in *Castle Rackrent,* to the Famine 'castle novels' which consolidate the social change.

[4] M. Edgeworth, *Castle Rackrent* ([1800]; Oxford, 1980), 96.

[5] K. Burke, *The Philosophy of Literary Form* ([1941]; Berkeley, Calif., 1973), 1.

[6] E. Smith *The Irish Journals of Elizabeth Smith* (Oxford, 1980), 205.

[7] W. Bennett, *Narrative of a Recent Journey of Six Weeks in Ireland* (Dublin, 1847), 24.

[8] A. Keary, *Castle Daly* ([1875]; New York, 1979), ii. 200.

[9] T. B. Macaulay, 'Sir James Mackintosh', in *Critical and Historical Essays Contributed to the Edinburgh Review* (London, 1903), ii. 73.

[10] Keary, *Castle Daly,* ii. 123.

[11] Keary, *Castle Daly,* 123.

[12] A. Trollope, *Castle Richmond* ([1860]; New York, 1984), 3, 6, 59.

[13] J. Th. Leerssen, 'Mimesis and Stereotype', *Yearbook of European Studies* IV (1991), 169.

[14] Trollope, *Castle Richmond,* 59, 439.

[15] A. Trollope, *An Autobiography* ([1883]; London, 1947), 245.

[16] Margaret Brew, *The Chronicles of Castle Cloyne* ([1885]; New York, 1979), i, p. viii.

[17] D. Lloyd, 'Violence and the Constitution of the Novel', in *Anomalous States* (Dublin, 1993), 134.

[18] Brew, *Castle Cloyne,* ii. 327-8.

[19] Ibid. ii. 284; ii. 179. Donnelly records sales as low as five years' purchase in the early years of the Encumbered Estates Courts, although by the mid-1850s prices had recovered to the levels of the late 1830s. J. S. Donnelly, Jr., 'Landlords and Tenants', in W. E. Vaughan (ed.), *A New History of Ireland* (Oxford, 1989), v. 347.

[20] Brew, *Castle Cloyne,* ii. 170; ii. 277.

[21] Brew, *Castle Cloyne,* ii. 286.

[22] Ibid. 163.

[23] W. M. Thackeray, *Irish Sketch Book* ([1842]; Dublin, 1990), 83.

[24] Keary, *Castle Daly,* ii. 248-9; iii. 35-6.

[25] Keary, *Castle Daly,* ii. 249; iii. 47-8.

[26] Ibid. iii. 349.

[27] Trollope, *Castle Richmond,* 169-71.

[28] R. apRoberts, *Trollope* (London, 1971), 123.

[29] Trollope, *Castle Richmond,* 257, 261.

[30] Ibid. 331, 335.

[31] Ibid. 2-3.

[32] Both Sir Patrick and Sir Condy Rackrent in *Castle Rackrent* die while drinking whiskey punch: Edgeworth, *Castle Rackrent,* 38 and 91. See also the sections devoted to whiskey punch parties in William Carleton, *The Squanders of Castle Squander* (London, 1852), i. 58-61, 132-4; and Gerald Griffin, *The Collegians* (London, 1829), ii. 35-59.

[33] Trollope, *Castle Richmond,* 2.

[34] G. Lukács, *The Historical Novel* ([1937]; Harmondsworth, 1969), 205-6, 276.

[35] W. S. Trench, *Realities of Irish Life* (London, 1868), 105.

[36] Donnelly, 'Landlords and Tenants', 348. It has also been argued that many existing landlords consolidated their positions in the first half of the 1850s. See W. E. Vaughan, *Landlords and Tenants in Mid-Victorian Ireland* (Oxford, 1994), 16-18.

[37] Trench, *Realities of Irish Life,* 105.

[38] J. Hamilton, *Ireland's Recovery and Ireland's Health* (Dublin, 1848), 45.

[39] F. Jameson, *The Political Unconscious* (London, 1981), 79.

[40] W. M. Thackeray, *Contributions to the Morning Chronicle* (Urbana, Ill., 1955), 1.

[41] T. Carlyle, *Reminiscences of My Irish Journey in 1849* (London, 1882), 1.

[42] H. Fawcett, *Pauperism* (London, 1871), 106-7.

[43] Trollope, *Castle Richmond,* 58-9; 438.

[44] Lloyd, 'Violence and the Constitution of the Novel', 134.

[45] Stephen Wall notes that 'inheritance and guilt' form a recurring motif in Trollope's work, playing a central structural role in *Orley Farm, Lady Anna, Ralph the Heir,* and *Mr Scarborough's Family.* S. Wall, *Trollope and Character* (Boston and London, 1988), 287. For a further discussion of the function of the blackmail plot in *Castle Richmond,* see H. Hennedy, 'Love and Famine, Family and Country in Trollope's *Castle Richmond',* *Eire/Ireland* VII: 4 (Winter 1972), 48-66.

[46] Trollope, *Castle Richmond,* 438.

[47] Trollope, *Autobiography,* 69.

[48] C. Trevelyan, *The Irish Crisis* ([1848]; London, 1880), 1.

Works Cited

apRoberts, R., *Trollope: Artist and Moralist* (London, 1971).

Beer, G., *Darwin's Plots: Evolutionary Narrative in Darwin, George Eliot and Nineteenth Century Fiction* (London, 1983).

Bennett, W., *Narrative of a Recent Journey of Six Weeks in Ireland* (Dublin, 1847).

Brew, M., *The Chronicles of Castle Cloyne: Or, Pictures of the Munster People* ([1885]; New York, 1979).

Burke, K., *The Philosophy of Literary Form: Studies in Symbolic Action* ([1941]; Berkeley, Calif., 1973).

[Carleton, W.,] *The Squanders of Castle Squander* (2 vols.; London, 1852).

Carlyle, T., *Reminiscences of My Irish Journey in 1849* (London, 1882).

Edgeworth, M., *Castle Rackrent,* ed. G. Watson ([1800]; Oxford, 1980).

Fawcett, H., *Pauperism: Its Causes and Remedies* (London, 1871).

Griffin, G., *The Collegians* (3 vols.; London, 1829).

Hamilton, J., *Ireland's Recovery and Ireland's Health* (Dublin, 1848).

Hennedy, H., 'Love and Famine, Family and Country in Trollope's *Castle Richmond',* *Eire/Ireland* VII: 4 (Winter 1972), 48-66.

Jameson, F., *The Political Unconscious: Narrative as Socially Symbolic Act* (London, 1981).

Keary, A., *Castle Daly: The Story of An Irish Home Thirty Years Ago* ([1875]; 3 vols.; New York, 1979).

Leerssen, J. Th., 'Mimesis and Stereotype', *Yearbook of European Studies* IV (1991), 165-75.

Lloyd, D., *Anomalous States: Irish Writing and the Post-Colonial Moment* (Dublin, 1993).

Lukács, G., *The Historical Novel,* trans. H. and S. Mitchell ([1937]; Harmondsworth, 1969).

Macaulay, T. B., *Critical and Historical Essays Contributed to the Edinburgh Review,* ed. F. C. Montague (3 vols.; London, 1903).

Reed, J. R., *Victorian Conventions* (Athens, Ohio, 1975).

Smith, E., *The Irish Journals of Elizabeth Smith: 1840-1850,* ed. D. Thompson and M. McGusty (Oxford, 1980).

[W. M. Thackeray], *Irish Sketch Book: 1842* ([1842]; Dublin, 1990).

———. *William Makepeace Thackeray: Contributions to the Morning Chronicle,* ed. N. G. Ray (Urbana, Ill., 1955).

[Trench, W. S.], *Realities of Irish Life* (London, 1868).

Trevelyan, C., *The Irish Crisis: Being a Narrative of the Measures for the Relief of the Distress Caused by the Great Irish Famine of 1846-7* ([1848]; London, 1880).

Trollope, A., *An Autobiography,* ed. B. A. Booth ([1883]; London, 1947).

———. *Castle Richmond* ([1860]; New York, 1984).

Wall, S., *Trollope and Character* (Boston and London, 1988).

FAMINE POETRY

Chris Morash (essay date 1989)

SOURCE: An introduction to *The Hungry Voice: The Poetry of the Irish Famine*, edited by Chris Morash, Irish Academic Press, 1989, pp. 15-39.

[*In the following survey of Famine poetry, Morash claims that the Famine "left the poets of the 1840s abandoned by tradition," citing the difficulties the poets experienced trying to respond to the enormous tragedy and the fact that the subject matter resisted the Victorian poetic tendency to marry form with meaning.*]

It is not the literal past, the 'facts' of history'
   that shape us,
but images of the past embodied in language.'
   Brian Friel, *Translations*

If you were to hike across Achill Island in County Mayo, you would find a village of roofless cottages in the island's centre, the empty shells of an entire community, piled stone upon stone. Their counterparts can be found singly and in clusters throughout every county in Ireland. There, on that silent hillside, it takes little effort of the imagination to see the peasant farmer of the first half of the last century carrying each one of those stones from his tiny, irregular field, lifting it and fitting it into place in the wall, stone upon stone. The mind's eye sees his young wife, holding the first of many children, tending to the pig, or digging at the small patch of ground that was to become the potato garden. However, the imagination begins to strain when it tries to imagine three million such farmers, each carefully piling stone upon stone. And it balks entirely when asked to imagine all three million either dead or packed into the holds of emigrant ships.

And yet, that is what happened. Early in the autumn of 1845, a fungus, now known to have been *phythopthera infestans,* drifted invisibly across the Irish Sea. The weather had been warm and damp—conditions which favoured the blight—and by October the potatoes were in varying states of rot throughout the entire country. That winter, stories of food shortages began to filter in to the cities, and by the summer of 1846 streams of emaciated refugees were beginning to flee from a countryside that had become a nightmare to crowd the poorhouses, public works schemes, soup kitchens and docksides. In the wake of this destitution, the diseases always endemic within the population erupted, primarily typhus and dysentry; these in turn were followed by the cholera epidemic which swept Europe in 1849. In April of that year, a visitor to Limerick would report being shown 'one mass grave, in a field on the outside of the city, near the poor house, into which nearly two thousand bodies had been gathered in less than a month.'[1] The Census of 1851 shows an estimated 'excess mortality' for the period of over a million persons; a further two million are estimated to have fled the country. But those are only estimates; we will probably never know for sure how many anonymous thousands died alone in their remote stone cottages, or how many perished between the decks of the coffin ships.

This holocaust took place at a time of great turmoil throughout Europe. In Portugal and Poland there was civil war. In Italy, Guiseppe Mazzini was bringing together the disaffected and the ambitious under the banner of Young Europe. In England, the Chartist movement looked as if it might ignite a popular revolution. These stirrings of discontent came to a boil in

The Irish village of Movern is deserted due to the great famine of the 1840s.

1848 when in February the poor of Paris took to the barricades; by May, Marx and Engels had published the Communist Manifesto, and by the year's end there had been serious uprisings in Berlin, Milan, Warsaw, Prague and Austria. 'In the past year thrones have been overturned, principalities shaken, and powers humbled', commented the *Dublin University Magazine* in January, 1849. 'From its centre to its extremities, Europe has been convulsed.'[2] One cartoon of the period in *Punch* shows a horse-drawn carriage, labelled 'The New Continental Coach', whipping along at breakneck speed, scattering monarchs in its path. In the background stands 'The British Lion Inn,' a bastion of stability; however, barely discernible in the dust behind the Inn the simianized figure of Paddy waves his shillelagh, cheering the coach on its way. Ireland in 1848 seemed ready to plunge into the European revolutionary maelstrom, possibly carrying England with her. And it could be argued that a revolution occurred, although it was not the one planned by those who were forging pikes and digging up their old muskets; that revolution fizzled out with a skirmish in a cabbage patch in County Tipperary. The real revolution lasted much longer, and had a much more profound influence on the future nation.

The social changes that took place in Ireland during the Famine were little different in kind from the types of change that had been in progress since at least the beginning of the nineteenth century. The fall in agricultural prices after the Napoleonic Wars, and the

decreased profitability of tillage exports as compared to livestock exports all meant that, for a significant segment of the rural labouring population, hunger was common during that part of the year prior to the harvest, after the previous year's supplies had been exhausted. In 1800, 1817 and 1822 this hunger was so widespread as to have been designated as 'famine'. However, hardship was not the exclusive preserve of the small farmer; the large landowner, whose sole wealth was in his property, was finding it increasingly difficult to generate a profit from his impoverished tenantry. As the century progressed, the position of the landed gentry was further undermined by the granting of Catholic Emancipation in 1829 and the repeal of the Corn Laws in 1845; but it was the Famine of 1845-49 that gave the final push to the teetering edifice of many a country manor, just as it tumbled so many of the single-roomed cottages of the poor. As early as 1800, in Maria Edgeworth's novel, *Castle Rackrent,* we have an account of the old neo-feudal system of land-holding beginning to break down as more and more landlords became bankrupt and a predominantly Catholic middle class, made up of merchants, lawyers and larger farmers moved in to buy up portions of the old estates. As the self-made land speculator, Jason M'Quirk, asks in *Castle Rackrent,* 'When there's no cash, what can a gentleman do but go to the land?'[3] And it was from this chaos of evictions, bankruptcy, emigration and legislative change that we can trace the development of the middle class revolution that was to consolidate itself with the granting of the Land Acts in the latter half of the century. One novelist of the Famine, Elizabeth Hely Walshe, saw the situation like this:

> In 1850 the horizon was clearing. The lessening agricultural population had more elbow room . . . overgrown estates, encumbered with heavy charges, were broken into a variety of smaller properties, freed from burden, passing from the effete hands of the old possessors into the vigorous hands of men from the middle class.[4]

For the poet living in an age when social change is occurring on an epic scale, the nature of that change will influence the type of aesthetic decisions the poet must make. Famine, perhaps more than any other agent of change, forces the poet to make difficult choices; for while the sight of so many of his fellow creatures driven to the limits of existence cries out for some sort of response, famine does not sit comfortably in any of the established poetic idioms of the English tradition. Had the Great Famine taken place a half century earlier, it could have found expression in a native Gaelic tradition that embraced a long history of famine, exile and destitution. But by the 1840s, all of the great Irish language poets of the eighteenth century were gone, and the Gaelic revival that was to come at the end of the nineteenth century was still fifty years away. Although with some poets, notably Mangan, we see the first attempts to adapt Irish models to the English language, on the whole the only available poetic models came from a country in which famine was a foreign concept. Had the same number of people died in battle as died from hunger and disease, there would have been a tradition on which to draw going right back to 'The Battle of Maldon' (c. 1000)—the same tradition out of which Tennyson was able to create 'The Charge of the Light Brigade' (1854) only a few weeks after the event itself. Famine, however, left the poets of the 1840s abandoned by tradition. Many of the poets in this anthology [*The Hungry Voice: The Poetry of the Irish Famine*] turned to the all-embracing lyric, choosing to focus on an emotional expression of their own reactions to individual instances of suffering. Of those who tried to take a wider view, there was a contrary tendency to sidestep the physical realities of starvation by placing the Famine in a religious or mythological context.

In this respect, Sir Samuel Ferguson's two long satires of 1849, 'Inheritor and Economist', and 'Dublin', are virtually unique among the poems of the era in their attempts to comprehend the state of Famine Ireland in a verse form that takes account of the wider network of social and economic relationships in which any individual is necessarily enmeshed. When the potato blight first hit Ireland in the autumn of 1845, Ferguson, a successful lawyer and antiquarian, was on the Continent, researching manuscript sources of early Irish history. His verse translations of these ancient Gaelic

epics in the years after the Famine were to earn him the respect of Yeats and to secure for him a place in the history of Irish literature. However, when he returned to Ireland in 1846 to find the country in a state of crisis, he not only laid aside the legendary material on which he had been working he also began to modify his political views. As a younger man, he had been a strong supporter of the union with England and had published anti-nationalist poetry, such as 'An Irish Garland', which appeared in *Blackwood's Magazine* in 1833. In the wake of the potato failure, Ferguson felt so perturbed at the sufferings of the peasantry, and the financial ruin of the gentry, that he felt himself uncharacteristically drawn to the politics of repeal. He even went so far as to address a meeting of the Protestant Repeal Association in May of 1848, at the height of the insurrectionary excitement, and later went on to make a successful defence of the poet Richard D'Alton Williams against a charge of treason felony.

However, the militant nationalism espoused by Williams and the Young Irelanders was not Ferguson's nationalism, and the difference registers itself in their respective verse forms. Williams favours short lines, strong rhymes, martial rhythms, and direct, imperative statements that aim to link the listener with the speaking voice of the poem:

> Come! hand in hand, at Heaven's command,
> Whose voice through the people rolls,
> Let us bravely stand, for our lives and land,
> And prove that men have souls!
> ('Hand in Hand', lines 9-12)

Although the internal rhymes might be taken to indicate an early Gaelic model, the exclamatory tone suggests that the strongest influence is probably an imitator of Shelley in an ecstatic moment. Ferguson, on the other hand, looks back beyond Romanticism; his two satires turn to the poets of Augustan England for their models, with their characteristic long lines, rhymed couplets, and cool, sardonic perspective. Indeed, 'Dublin,' which Ferguson tells us is 'In Imitation of the Third Satire of Juvenal,' owes more to Samuel Johnson's version of the Third Satire, his 'London' of 1738, than it does to Juvenal's original. This Augustan verse form, the urbane vehicle of oratorical wit, was the very antithesis of the overt emotionalism of Young Ireland, and, as such, was the perfect idiom for the nationalism to which Ferguson was attracted during the years of the Famine. The heroes of Ferguson's nationalist tradition, as he lists them in 'Dublin', are neither Wolfe Tone nor Robert Emmet; they are the august eighteenth century statesmen of the Parliament of 1782—Grattan, Bushe and Plunket. And it is not on the historic fields of Tara and Clontarf, newly reconsecrated by O'Connell's 'monster meetings', that he finds the ruins of squandered nobility. For Ferguson, the monument to the Ireland that had been lost is the

Parliament Building on College Green, forced into ignomious service as a bank:

> Here, where old Freedom used to wait
> Her darling Grattan at the gate,
> Now little clerks in hall and colonnade
> Tot the poor items of provincial trade;
> So changed, alas!—since, sped by cruel fates,
> Our three-per-cents expelled our three estates.
> ('Inheritor and Economist,' lines 23-26; 33-34)

As Ferguson was writing his satires in the spring of 1849, the dust was still settling from the previous year—a year which not only had seen the dramatic spectacle of widespread revolution but also had witnessed a much more low key event in the publication of J.S. Mill's *Principles of Political Economy*. While most of his contemporaries were luridly imagining—either in fear or in anticipation—an Ireland overrun by bands of rebels, Ferguson was able to perceive that the slow, unheroic implementation of the theory of free market 'political economy' was the agent of change that formed the more potent threat to the Ireland to which he wanted to belong. And just as the 'little clerks', whom Yeats was later to describe 'fumbling in a greasy till,'[5] oust the noble Grattan from the Parliament Buildings in 'Dublin,' so too does the 'Economist' in 'Inheritor and Economist' drive the landed 'Inheritor' and his family from their ancestral acres. In both poems, Ferguson is turning back to the eighteenth century, to the age from which he had taken his verse forms, to find the two figures who represented the last hope of a real possibility of leadership for the Protestant Ascendancy—the parliamentary nationalist, and the eighteenth century landed nobleman—both of whom had been made anachronistic not by any pike-wielding revolutionary, but by the utilitarian determination of a mercantile class to create a cash-based economy:

> So shall we speedily the land behold
> Once more exchangeable for British gold;
> And in its Castle-Rack-Rent mansions see
> A bran-new Cheesemonger propriet'ry,
> Able in all things, save alone thy grace,
> Gentility, to fill a gentry's place.
> ('Inheritor and Economist', lines 505-510)

Ferguson was not to go as far as Yeats in embracing the revolutionary tradition as a means of ennobling the 'bran-new Cheesemonger propriet'ry', (although his 'Lament for Thomas Davis' takes him several steps in that direction); nonetheless, in 'Inheritor and Economist', he is battling, Cuchulain-like, the first waves of Yeats' 'filthy modern tide'.[6] The ultimate futility of any challenge to such a complex and widely-based social change registers in the internal stresses and strains in Ferguson's verse. Both 'Dublin' and 'Inheritor and Economist' use the freedom of the couplet to allow the ramifications of political and economic theories to develop from a perspective which, if somewhat jaundiced, is nonetheless emotionally detached. However, towards the end of 'Dublin', the speaking voice of the poem changes as Ferguson introduces a section that is stylistically inconsistent in its emotional immediacy and yet is justified by the latent bitterness of the rest of the poem:

> Here men of feeling, ere they grow old,
> Die of the very horrors they behold.
> 'Tis hard to sleep when one has just stood by
> And seen a strong man of sheer hunger die;
> 'Tis hard to draw an easy, healthful breath,
> In fields that sicken with the air of death.
> ('Dublin', lines 177-182)

A similar breakdown in the satiric distance maintained throughout the poem takes places at the end of 'Inheritor and Economist.' Even more than 'Dublin', this poem constitutes a sustained analysis of the economic factors at work in Ireland during the Famine years, doggedly outlining the day-to-day realities of managing an estate. However, in its final lines, the poem transforms itself into an apostrophe to the poet's 'poor native land':

> Thy day prefixed in God's eternal doom,
> May long be longed for; but the day will
>   come
> When heaven shall also give its sign to thee,
> Thy Diocletians fallen, thy people free.
> ('Inheritor & Economist', lines 549-552)

Faced with an unrecoverable past, and the unpalatable present that the harsh light of satire has shown him, Ferguson takes a third option; he chooses to place the fate of Ireland in the context of a divinely ordered history. Ireland must wait for the 'sign' before coming into her kingdom.

Ferguson was too deeply rooted in Enlightenment ideals of rationality to promote such doctrines at any length. His slip into the language of prophecy is no more than an illuminating aberration. For many of his contemporaries, however, the images of the prophetic books of the Bible provided a central means of comprehending the accelerated change brought on by the Famine. In the light of the research that has been done on millenarianism since the publication of Norman Cohn's *Pursuit of the Millennium* in 1957, this should hardly seem surprising. In his pioneering study, Cohn found that poverty, even the direst poverty, is not in itself sufficient to trigger millenarian hopes, for the impoverished society very often generates a passive stability of the sort J.M. Synge was to idealize in his portrayal of the remnant of the pre-Famine peasantry on the Aran Islands. Millenarianism is much more likely to arise when the impoverished society comes into close contact with a more affluent society, creating a disparity between expectations and their possibilities for fulfilment. 'The torture of Tantalus' is how William Drennan Jr describes the aggravated colonial situation of Famine Ireland in his poem '1848'. When the political apparatus for change seems to be out of control, one of the few historical paradigms to offer the possibility of a return to an ordered society is that which promises complete this-worldly salvation brought about by an other-worldly agency—the millenarian paradigm.

If Famine Ireland was ripe for a millenarian prophet, no one was better suited to fill that role than James Clarence Mangan. More than any other single poet, Mangan established the millenarian idiom of Famine poetry with 'The Warning Voice', 'The Peal of Another Trumpet' and 'A Vision: 1848'. Born in penury, and struggling all of his life with drug addiction, Mangan was to carry the mantle of poet-prophet from his verse into his public persona, transforming himself into an urban version of the prophecy man desribed by Carleton in *The Black Prophet*. One contemporary describes Mangan thus:

> When he emerged into daylight, he was dressed in a blue cloak, mid-summer or midwinter, and a hat of fantastic shape, under which golden hair, as fine and silky as a woman's, hung in unkempt tangles, and deep blue eyes lighted a face as colourless as parchment. He looked like the spectre of some German romance rather than a living creature.[7]

Whether he believed, or believed intermittently, in the power of Mangan the prophet, it was a posture that provided Mangan the poet with the metaphor for which he had been searching throughout his career in his exploration of sublime terror in the face of death, and what might lie beyond death. Although his early work is an idiosyncratic mixture of giddy parodies, acrostics, Wertherian melancholia, 'translations' from imaginary Persian poets, as well as successful translations from the Irish, the backbone of this eclectic collection is comprised of a group of deeply personal poems of spiritual desolation. As early as 1833, the imagery of his Famine poetry is presaged in such pieces as 'Life is the Desert and the Solitude', 'Disaster', and 'A Broken-Hearted Lay':

> Weep for one blank, one desert epoch in
> The history of the heart; it is the time
> When all which dazzled us no more can win.[8]

In the years leading up to the Famine, Mangan began to explore the potential of the role of prophet in the desert; in 'The Coming Event', written on the very eve of the Famine in 1844, he makes the link between the imminence of his own approaching death and the imminence of the Last Judgement:

> Shadows of changes are seen in advance,
>   Whose epochs are nearing;
> And days are at hand when the Best will
>   require
>   All means of salvation,
> And the souls of men shall be tried in the fire
>   Of the Final Probation.

By the end of the poem, however, the world historical nature of the 'Coming Event' has shrunken to the dimensions of a skull, as a single man confronts his end alone:

> Spend all, sinew, soul, in your zeal to atone
>   For the past and its errors;
> So best shall ye bear to encounter alone
>   THE EVENT and its terrors.[9]

As the world around Mangan came increasingly to resemble the desert of his nightmares in the final years of his life, the themes which had long haunted his work, themes of isolation, spiritual exile, and metaphysical terror, found their objective correlatives in the state of Famine Ireland. It was as if the spiritual malaise of one man had been realized in the landscape of a nation. As he saw the horsemen of war, famine and pestilence ride roughshod over Ireland, the millenarian dimension of Mangan's confrontation with death became inflamed and its images more sharply defined. He found omens and portents in public events, and these in turn, by their life-threatening nature, both intensified his spiritual anxiety and expanded the metaphorical possibilities for its expression. By the time he came to write 'A Vision' in 1848, Mangan was finding places for specific political developments of the recent past in the jigsaw puzzle of Biblical prophecy, identifying the young men of the nationalist movement with the divinely chosen elite to whom he increasingly addressed himself:

> Youths! Compatriots! Friends! Men for the
>   time that is nearing!
> Spirits appointed by Heaven to front the storm
>   and the trouble!
>   ('A Voice of Encouragement', lines 1-2)

However, as in most millenarian visions of salvation drawn from the Judeo-Christian tradition, Mangan's young heroes are not to come into their kingdom unscathed. If one is to usher in an apocalypse, the reasons for doing so can not be more or less correct; they must be absolutely correct. The enemy must be absolutely evil, and the chosen absolutely good. In the Old Testament and Book of Revelations, the chosen remnant achieve this purity by suffering conquest, exile, famine and pestilence. As those very tribulations were visited upon Ireland in the 1840s, it became possible for a poet like Mangan to interpret the suffering they caused as being directed toward a similar purpose:

The ANOINTED must fall—
The Weak Ones must yield
Up in silence their breath
　Ere the Last Scene of all,
For that scene must behold
But stern spirits
　When the Lord takes the field.
Therefore Famine first came
And then Pestilence came.
　　　　　　('A Vision,' lines 64-72)

Later, we will see how Aubrey De Vere developed the theme of the sanctity of suffering in a more orthodox religious context. Mangan, however, lacked the stabilizing influence of orthodoxy, and as a consequence his prophecy poems of the Famine veer wildly between poles of wild elation and profound despair. The years of crisis and sorrow constitute a test; to succeed is to win the favour of God; to fail is damnation. Hence, he is able to exult in 'When Hearts Were Trumps':

Love will yet abolish Pain,
　As by necromancy;
And, friends, trust me; your—(not *my*)—
　Offspring will have wondered
Much at myriad changes—by
　ANNO NINETEEN-HUNDRED!
　　　　　('When Hearts were Trumps', lines 41-48)

Yet, in another poem, 'The Groans of Despair', he writes:

The wrath of God, the avenging sword
　Of Heav'n burns in my breast alway
With ever freshly torturing flame!
　And desolateness and terror
　　Have made me their dark mate—
The ghastly brood of sin and error
Repented all—TOO LATE![10]

What began as a structure to impart meaning to physical suffering becomes itself the source of a deeper spiritual suffering under the burdensome sense of sin and isolation which permeates Mangan's world. His best work is to be found in the handful of poems written during the Famine years in which he is able to go beyond the sources of his almost unbearable anxiety to a direct apprehension of that anxiety itself. In the realm of 'pain acute, yet dead' of 'Siberia', for instance, Mangan is able to unite the existential horror he had long felt at the knowledge of his own impending death with the bleak, death-strewn landscape of Famine Ireland in a single, forceful image of desolation in which neither the public nor the private is foregrounded. He was to write increasingly in this mode right up until the end. Although not up to the standard of 'Siberia', the same painful awareness of death haunts the final poem he was to publish, 'The Famine', which appeared eleven days before cholera

and malnutrition finally brought about his death on June 20, 1849:

Despair? Yes! For a blight fell on the land—
　The soil, heaven-blasted, yielded food no
　　more—
The Irish serf became a Being banned—
　Life-exiled as none ever was before.
The old man died beside his hovel's hearth,
The young man stretched himself along the
　earth,
　　And perished, stricken to the core!
　　　　　　　('The Famine,' lines 22-28)

While Mangan presents us with the unique case of a poet whose private obsessions found a form in millenarian interpretations of the world around him, he was not alone in his use of the images and paradigms of prophecy during the Famine years. Thomas D'Arcy McGee, Richard D'Alton Williams, Speranza, John De Jean Frazer, and other less prolific nationalist poets, as well as the Orange poet Robert Young, were all to attempt the role of prophet in the years leading up to 1848. But can this flood of chiliastic verse, particularly among nationalists, be taken as evidence of a full-fledged millenarian movement in Ireland during the 1840s? Comparative studies have shown that 'millenarianism is born out of great distress coupled with political helplessness.'[11] In order to begin to determine the millenarian status of Famine Ireland, it is necessary to ask who was in great distress, and who was feeling the burden of political helplessness. With a few notable exceptions, the main poetic activity of those years took place in the periodicals, the most important of which was *The Nation,* and its successors, the *United Irishman,* and *The Irishman.* A closer look at these newspapers reveals that their contributors were by and large professionals from the middle class: Thomas Davis, John Mitchel, and John O'Hagan were lawyers. Kevin Izod O'Doherty, and Richard D'Alton Williams were doctors. Indeed, it was said at the time that if you were ill you had a better chance of finding a doctor in D'Olier street (where *The Nation* had its offices) than you did in Jervis street (site of one of the main Dublin hospitals). There were, of course, exceptions. Mangan was never far from abject poverty. John Keegan, educated at a hedge school, was buried in a pauper's plot when he died in 1849. But, on the whole, the men and women who were writing prophecies of the coming millennium were members of a class who, were it not for Ireland's colonial status, would have been in positions of political power. While this urban, Dublin-based middle class were agitating for reform, the real impact of the Famine was being felt by an entirely different class of rural peasantry, who were, for the most part, politically passive during the Famine years. It is difficult to measure political involvement in what was a limited democracy; however, one indicator suggests the political apathy that covered the countryside. Daniel

O'Connell had funded both the earlier Catholic Emancipation movement and his later Repeal Association by means of a weekly 'rent,' donated primarily by small farmers throughout the countryside. For years this 'rent' had brought the Association a substantial weekly sum. But as the Famine progressed, the amounts dwindled, until, on the week of June 6, 1848—at the very height of the insurrectionary fever, if one reads *The Irishman* or the *Irish Felon*—the 'rent' collected from the entire country amounted to a mere £12. The following week the Repeal Association was disbanded.

It is because of this disjunction between the class who were suffering the greatest oppression, and the class who were using the imagery of Biblical salvation to articulate their struggle to free themselves from a situation of political helplessness that Irish millenarianism takes its peculiar form. There is an air of unreality about the whole enterprise, beginning with the notion of using English language newspapers to preach rebellion to a largely Irish speaking peasantry, most of whom would have had no money to buy newspapers and considered themselves lucky if they had enough to buy their food and pay their rent. The western peasantry, desperately trying to survive, were oblivious to the affluent young Dublin poets like Richard D'Alton Williams who were fascinated by the idea of an apocalypse that would right every wrong:

> Ere we burst the chains that gore us,
> Ere the tide of battle rolls,
> May thine angels camp around us,
> Nerve our hearts and cleanse our souls!
>   ('Lord of Hosts', lines 21-24)

The same newspaper that carried Williams' strident cries for the tide of battle to roll forth and rejuvenate the soil with the blood of young heroes was also publishing a series of lengthy pieces of undergraduate humour that Williams was writing, entitled 'The Adventures of a Medical Student'. While it may not seem remarkable that Williams should have exhibited this form of cultural schizophrenia, it does seem striking in retrospect that neither he nor his editors should have found it disturbing or even incongruous that a university prankster should have been praying for Armageddon. Like many of his contemporaries in the nationalist press, Williams was promoting a millenarian fantasy that had little correspondence to the reality of the world around him. Nonetheless, *The Nation* poets repeatedly used the chiaroscuro opposition of absolute good and absolute evil to rehearse the tale of the perfidious Saxon and the sorrowing Gael; and they dropped delicious hints as to the nature of the golden age that was to follow the cleansing blood bath. For Thomas D'Arcy McGee in particular, the New Jerusalem was to be a world peopled by refugees from the poems of Thomas Moore—harp-plucking bards, stout-hearted warriors, and holy monks living in round towers. This dream perspective permeates even to the level of details such as the weapons that the peasantry are urged to take up: spears, swords and staffs predominate—hardly very effective tactical weaponry in 1848. Indeed, the unreality of the whole neo-mediaeval vision of bardic Ireland became glaringly apparent in August of 1848 when William Smith O'Brien attempted to conduct a rebellion with due respect for the laws of property and chivalry, and promptly earned himself a passage to Australia at Her Majesty's expense, after a farcical, but gentlemanly, skirmish.

The difficulty of the nationalist position registers itself in this tension between the rhetorical ideal and the reality of conditions in Famine Ireland. A comparison between the newspapers that supported the Union with Britain, and those which were in favour of Repeal, shows a marked tendency among the latter to emphasize the more graphic physical details of death by starvation. John Mitchel's *United Irishman*, for instance, was filled week after week with headlines such as 'Horse Eaten By Human Beings', and 'The Shroudless and Coffinless Dead', which shared the page with Mitchel's own militant harangues.[12] Some of the most successful poems of the period are the sentimental pieces from occasional contributors that focus on a single graphic image of suffering. James Tighe's 'The Boreen Side', for instance, appeared in the radical *Irishman:*

> A stripling, the last of his race, lies dead
> In a nook by the Boreen side;
> The rivulet runs by his board and bed,
> Where he ate the green cresses and died.
>   ('The Boreen Side', lines 1-4)

Yet, the very degradation that was generating so much sympathy for the nationalist cause, even among such unlikely people as Samuel Ferguson, was the very thing that was withering the strong arms of the Celtic warriors, belying the shining utopia of the nationalist rhetoric. As reports of the numbers who had died began to reveal the horrific extent of the disaster, it became increasingly difficult to reconcile rhetoric and reality—a difficulty which takes an explicit form in the rejection of statistical truth in Speranza's 'The Exodus':

> 'A million a decade!' calmly and cold
> The units are read by our statesmen sage;
> Little they think of a Nation old,
> Fading away from History's page.
>   ('The Exodus', lines 1-4)

Because the nationalist use of millenarianism entailed this uneasy rejection of the world of statesmen and statistics, and yet tried to operate at the same time as political allegory, it occupies a poetic space supported by neither public nor personal truth. Whereas Mangan believed that if the 'Coming Event' did not take a collective, earthly form, it was sure to take a personal, spiritual form, there is no evidence of this personal conviction in a poet like Williams. Consequently, whereas millenarian imagery provided Mangan with an accurate metaphor for the awesome reality of personal judgement, for many of his co-contributors to the nationalist press such imagery was an evasion of the reality of political impotence.

And yet, in spite of their weaknesses and blind spots—or perhaps because of them—the verses published by these young nationalists have been among the most popular and influential works of Famine poetry. If anything, this body of poetry gained in effectiveness as the ever increasing assimilation of the peasantry into the rural middle classes eased the disjunction between image and audience that had existed when the poems were first published. As the descendants of the Famine generation were becoming a part of the struggle for land and power, they were also becoming a part of the book-buying public. Between the founding of the Tenant League in 1850, and the final Land Act of 1923, the poetry of *The Nation* was republished in an avalanche of anthologies and garlands; indeed, it was often claimed that the best selling Irish book of the entire nineteenth century was *The Spirit of the Nation* anthology. The influence of individual pieces extended even further. Williams' 'Lord of Hosts' can be found sharing the page with popular music hall numbers and 'minstrel' songs in the weekly *Harding's Dublin Songster* in the first decades of this century. Speranza's 'Famine Year' made its way into the school textbooks in 1929, when it was included in *Ballads of Irish History for Schools,* where it would have left several generations of Irish school children with a millenarian interpretation of the Famine:

> We are wretches, famished, scorned, human
>   tools to build your pride,
> But God will yet take vengeance for the souls
>   for whom Christ died.
> Now is your hour of pleasure—bask ye in the
>   world's caress;
> But our whitening bones against ye will rise
>   as witnesses,
> From the cabins and ditches, in their charred
>   uncoffin'd masses,
> For the Angel of the Trumpet will know them
>   as he passes.
> A ghastly spectral army, before the great God
>   we'll stand,
> And arraign ye as our murderers, the spoilers
>   of our land.
>   ('The Famine Year', lines 41-8)

The very exuberance of the vision of the brave new Ireland that was the key to the popularity of this body of verse held within itself the seeds of a corresponding despondency. As might have been expected, the inability of a nation devastated by famine to become the New Jerusalem led many of those who had preached that dream most fervently—including McGee and Williams—to emigrate after the collapse of the rising in 1848. Others, like Speranza and John O'Hagan, settled back into that world of statisticians and statesmen which their poetry had previously rejected. It was not only the social structure of Ireland that was undergoing a massive change during the Famine years. These young men and women themselves—most of whom were in their early twenties—underwent personal change at the same accelerated pace as the world around them, as they were forced to abandon the adolescent idealism of romantic nationalism and accept the disillusioning realities of their situation in a famished colony. At the age of twenty-four, Martin MacDermott wrote:

> I have seen death strike so fast
>   That the churchyards could not hold—
> Though torn into one yawning grave—
> The remnants of the young, the brave,
>   The bright-eyed and the bold.
> I must be very, very old—
>   A very Old, Old Man.
>   ('A Very Old, Old Man', lines 54-60)

This tone of exhaustion is echoed throughout much of the later Famine poetry from *The Nation*. John De Jean Frazer, for instance, was a young carpenter who in 1848 was writing some of the most overtly militant verse of the period. His 'Harvest Pledge' appeared in *The Nation* in July, embellished with all of the neo-mediaevalisms of the genre:

> So the serfs, in the face of the Lord of the
>   Manor,
> Set a spear for a shaft and sheaf for a banner;
> And said: 'If *we* choose, from the sward to
>   the sky,
> From centre to shore, thou shouldst yield—or
>   die!'
>   ('The Harvest Pledge', lines 31-34)

However, by the following year his ringing confidence had fled. Although he still reiterated his constant theme of a workman's right to a decent living, it had become a plea rather than a demand in 'The Artisan's Apology for Emigrating' of 1849:

> Day and night we are wrapped in a desperate
>   strife,
> Not for national glory, but personal life;
> And our hair raineth sweat, like the clouds on
>   the soil;
> Yet the ass, with his thistle, has more for his
>   toil!

Or, lacking employment, our energies rust;
Our ambitions decay into ashes and dust.
　　　　('The Artisan's Apology For Emigrating',
　　　　　　　　　　　　　　　　　　lines 39-44)

Like the English Romantic poets of a generation before him, faced with the degeneration of the ideals of the French Revolution, or like many of the poets to have emerged out of Northern Ireland after the collapse of the Civil Rights movement, Frazer seems to have been attempting to find a more personal poetry, a poetry 'not for national glory, but personal life'. However, unlike most of his co-contributors to the nationalist press, Frazer was a working man whose 'desperate strife' to support himself and his family in the shattered economy of Famine Ireland made it impossible for him to disentangle the personal from the political. He stopped writing poetry after the death of his son during the cholera epidemic of 1849. In 1851, some of his more affluent associates from *The Nation* attempted to help him out financially by publishing a collected edition of his poems; it did little good. The following year he died in poverty.

Where Frazer's precarious social position made the personal political, Aubrey De Vere, ensconced in his Curragh Chase estate, was able to confine his public work during the Famine to his efforts on behalf of his tenantry, and to his prose writings, chief among which is his *English Misrule and Irish Misdeeds* of 1848. His Famine poetry, however, is delimited to a personal exploration of spirituality. Indeed, the Famine seems to have generated much of its compelling literary interest for De Vere precisely because the suffering he saw about him brought him into an active dialogue with his faith, heightening an already intense religious awareness that owed much to his friendship with Newman and his interest in the Oxford Movement. In his 'Ode: After One of the Famine Years', he writes:

A cry from famished vales I hear,
　That cry which others hear not.
Sad eyes, as of a moontide ghost,
　Whose grief, not grace, first won me,
'Mid regal pomps ye haunt me most:—
　There most your power is on me.
　　　　('Ode: After One of the Famine Years',
　　　　　　　　　　　　　　　　　　lines 27-32)

There is a stately, almost languid elegance to the world of 'moontide ghosts' of De Vere's Famine poetry. His is an empty landscape of:

Far-circling wastes. Far-bending skies,
Clouds as at Nature's obsequies
　Slow trailing scarf and pall.
　　　　('The Desolation of the West',
　　　　　　　　　　　　　　　　　　lines 7-9)

The peace that De Vere finds in this 'realm untenanted' ('The Desolation of the West', line 6) begs comparison with the Famine landscape of Mangan. Whereas Mangan's world is one where 'Nought is felt but dullest pain / Pain acute, yet dead' ('Siberia', lines 14-15), De Vere is able to move beyond the pain to a beatific vision. The chief difference between the two lies in their respective temporal perspectives. Mangan's best Famine poetry, such as 'Siberia', speaks with a Beckettian voice from the interminable, tormented 'now' of the last seconds of doubt before death. De Vere, on the other hand, is usually writing in the past tense:

And in my spirit grew and gathered
Knowledge that Ireland's worst was
　weathered,
　Her last dread penance paid;
Conviction that for earthly scath
In world-wide victories of her Faith
　Atonement should be made.
　　　　('The Desolation of the West', lines 49-54)

De Vere's Famine poetry takes an essentially preterist stance; the apocalypse has taken place, and it is now time to look to the New Jerusalem. He is able to work from this position because unlike Mangan he never shows any doubt of his own salvation, and unlike the young political millenarians of *The Nation,* he does not think of the golden age to be ushered in by the suffering of the Famine in political terms. De Vere's interpretation of the Famine was rather 'Conviction that for earthly scath / In worldwide victories of her Faith / Atonement should be made.' Consequently, he is able to proclaim at the end of 'The Desolation of the West':

A Land become a Monument!
Man works: but God's concealed intent
　Converts his worst to best.
The first of altars was a tomb—
Ireland! thy grave-stones shall become
　God's altar in the west!
　　　　('The Desolation of the West', lines 73-78)

When a poet uses such a vast frame of reference, there is always the danger that the central problem of suffering will be dwarfed, and ultimately dehumanized. Although De Vere occasionally does allow the interpretation to overwhelm the event, his poetry is never less than a serious attempt to assail the problem of suffering. In his 'Ode', for instance, he voices a doubt as to the very legitimacy of writing poetry about the Famine:

I come, and bring not song; for why
　Should grief from fancy borrow?
Why should a lute prolong a sigh,

Sophisticating sorrow?
          ('Ode: After One of the Famine Years',
                   lines 73-76)

De Vere's question foreshadows T.W. Adorno's assertion that to write poetry after Auschwitz would be barbaric. There is a fundamental ethical question at stake here: is it morally correct to allow art to impose its order on an experience whose essentially horrific nature lies in its very chaos? Is it right to 'sophisticate sorrow?' Writing from a Christian perspective, De Vere's position seems to be that not only is it right, but it is necessary to understand the Famine as a part of the unfolding of God's design for humanity extending back through centuries of suffering:

  Sleep well, unsung by idle rhymes,
    Ye sufferers late and lowly;
  Ye saints and seers of earlier times,
    Sleep well in cloisters holy!
          ('Ode: After One of the Famine Years',
                   lines 105-108)

When De Vere equates the Famine dead with the 'saints and seers of earlier times', he is creating a context in which the deaths of the anonymous thousands who died of starvation and disease have a meaning. His Christian strategy parallels that of the nationalist writers who attempted to include the Famine dead among the pantheon of martyrs who had died for Irish freedom. However, what struck so many observers of the period was the banality conferred on suffering by the sheer scale of the Famine. A manufacturer from Manchester, Spencer T. Hall, arriving in Limerick in 1847, shared the surprise of many who were shocked at the almost complete absence of burial rites in a society so famous for its wakes. 'It happened', he records in his journal, 'that a man died of hunger and lay for the greater part of a week in a cow cabin, without any one making the slightest preparation for burying him!'[13] As we find in so many accounts of the Famine, it is not the fact of death itself which so affronts the observer, but the ignoble means of death, and the facelessness of the victims after death. Although it would be unwise to equate the Irish Famine and the Holocaust too rigorously (for there are major causal and motivational differences), it is worth remembering that the bureaucratic nature of evil during the Third Reich remains one of the most problematic features of the Nazi era. Similarly, when writing of the Famine, contemporary authors repeatedly refer to the Kafkaesque nature of the world around them. In 'Inheritor and Economist', for instance, Ferguson describes the proliferation of bureaucrats in an Irish Poor Law Union thus:

  Make haste, appoint one Chief Commissioner
  To supervise all Beggarland's concerns,
  Fifty inspectors, chiefs, and subalterns;

Fifty collectors, with good sureties,
To gather in the dues: then add to these
Five hundred guardians, vice and volunteer—
Five hundred clerks at fifty pounds a-year;
Five hundred masters, and five hundred
  dames,
Five hundred Health-Board doctors of all
  names;
Five hundred builders from the Board of
  Works,
Five hundred Chaplains, and five hundred
  clerks.
       ('Inheritor and Economist', lines 220-230)

At the opposite end of the political spectrum, John Mitchel can be found grappling with the same invasion of civil servants in his *Last Conquest of Ireland (Perhaps)*:

If one should narrate how the cause of his country was stricken down in open battle, and blasted to pieces with shot and shell, there might be a certain mournful pride in dwelling upon the gallant resistance . . . but to describe how the spirit of a country has been broken and subdued by beggarly famine;—how her national aspirations have been not choked in her own blood, nobly shed on the field, but strangled by red tape;—how her life and soul have been ameliorated and civilized out of her;—how she died of political economy, and was buried under tons of official stationary;—this is a dreary task, which I wish some one else had undertaken.[14]

Such honesty about the problem of finding a response is rare; the Famine cried out to be falsified, for the random and widespread devastation caused by the intangible agents of fungus and bureaucracy did not lend itself to models of heroic martyrdom, either religious or political, that were capable of giving a meaning to death in other circumstances.

The questions this posed for the poet of the 1840s go straight to the heart of pre-modernist aesthetics. Victorian poetry and the various traditions to which it was heir had meaning; it had form, and was about the imposition of form and meaning on those aspects of experience, whether love or nature, that threatened to escape the snares of meaning. A poet such as Aubrey De Vere simply did not have at his disposal forms that allowed for formlessness, nor structures that admitted the existence of meaninglessness. In such a context, Mangan's verse appears more modern (and hence is attracting more recent critical attention than De Vere's), because his personal idiosyncrasies led him to break forms and admit the possibility of meaninglessness in the interstices of his own radical metaphysical doubt; De Vere, by comparison, with his formal and theological confidence, today sounds distinctly dated. Much of the poetry in this anthology [*The Hungry Voice:*

Poetry of the Irish Famine] shows the strain of having been created within a conventional framework that did not pertain to the situation to which it strove to respond. The millenarian imagery examined at length above is but one example of the latent apprehension of meaninglessness generating a search for alternative conventions. Instead of turning to the obvious Biblical text with which to encompass the problem of suffering, the Book of Job, or even instead of turning to the passages dealing with suffering in the Gospels, the majority of the Famine poets who attempted to work within a Biblical framework drew on what is probably the most imagerially chaotic book in the Bible, the Book of Revelations, as the only Biblical text capable of providing images as extreme and as disorienting as the world around them had suddenly become:

> The wondrous things foretold by JOHN were
>   realized at last,
> And APOLLYON came on earth, to blacken and
>   to blast.
>
> ('Thanatos, 1849', lines 9-10)

But let us return to Adorno's challenge, adapted to the present circumstances.

No poetry after the Famine?

The answer of the combined voices of the poets in [*The Hungry Voice*] would seem to say that poetry is not only a possibility in such conditions, it is a necessity; for it is that which cannot be articulated which must be articulated. History provides us with facts, and continues to do so with increasing sophistication; but literature provides us with the response to those facts—or, if not the response, at least the possibility of a response. It still remains impossible to fully comprehend what it meant for those three million small farmers to stand outside their stone cottages and watch their sole source of food decay into black putrification. In *Language and Silence*, George Steiner writes: 'The world of Auschwitz lies outside speech as it lies outside reason.'[15] The same could be said of the world of the Famine. But the attempt to contain that world within language, even if doomed to failure, had to be attempted, just as we must try to understand the images that those attempts have bequeathed to us. So while we can recognize the basic inadequacy of all paradigms of comprehension—whether rational, romantic, political, religious, or millenarian—and the continued inadequacy of all subsequent paradigms, including this one, we must also recognize that their failure does not entail their dismissal. Even if each individual paradigm can be said to have failed, the plurality of views presented in [*The Hungry Voice*] constitutes a multifaceted text with more extensive claims to adequacy than any single one of its constituent parts; indeed, it could even be said to have greater claims to adequacy than a single long unified text, such as a novel. However, this

does not mean that we should ignore the uniqueness of each one of the poems that follows: they are not merely a variety of strategies of evasion. Each of the poems in [*The Hungry Voice*] is an attempt at understanding that in itself constitutes a simple, Sisyphusian form of heroism that is at the basis any movement towards an adequate response to atrocity.

Notes

[1] Spencer T. Hall, *Life and Death in Ireland* (Manchester, J.T. Parkes, 1850), p. 38.

[2] Kappa, 'France: A Retrospect of the Year 1848,' *Dublin University Magazine,* Vol. 33, No. 193 (January 1849), p. 134.

[3] Maria Edgeworth, *Castle Rackrent.* Vol. I of *Tales and Miscellaneous Pieces* (London: Thomas Davison, 1825), p. 70.

[4] Elizabeth Hely Walshe, *Golden Hills* (London: The Religious Tract Society, 1865), p. 266.

[5] W.B. Yeats, 'September, 1913,' in *Collected Poems* (London: Macmillan, 1985), p.120.

[6] Y. B. Yeats, 'The Statues,' in *Collected Poems,* p. 376.

[7] Sir Charles Gavan Duffy, 'Personal Memories of James C. Mangan,' *Dublin Review,* Vol. 142, No. 285 (April, 1908), p. 278.

[8] James Clarence Mangan, 'A Broken Hearted Lay,' *Poems of James Clarence Mangan,* ed. D. J. O'Donoghue (Dublin: M.H. Gill, 1922), p. 124.

[9] James Clarence Mangan, 'The Coming Event,' *Poems,* p. 143.

[10] James Clarence Mangan, 'The Groans of Despair,' *Poems,* p. 125.

[11] Yonina Talmon, 'Millenarian Movements,' *Archives euroéennes de sociologie,* Vol. 7, No. 2 (1966), p. 185.

[12] *The United Irishman,* Vol. 1, No. 2 (Feb. 19, 1848), p. 23.

[13] Hall, *Life and Death in Ireland,* p. 20.

[14] John Mitchel, *The Last Conquest of Ireland (Perhaps)* (London: Burns, Oates & Washbourne, 1861), pp. 138-9.

[15] George Steiner, *Language and Silence* (London: Faber & Faber, 1985), p. 146.

FAMINE LETTERS
AND EYE-WITNESS ACCOUNTS

K. D. M. Snell (essay date 1994)

SOURCE: "Alexander Somerville and the Irish Famine," in *Letters from Ireland during the Famine of 1847*, by Alexander Somerville, edited by K. D. M. Snell, Irish Academic Press, 1994, pp. 7-24.

[*The following is an introduction to Scottish writer Alexander Somerville's* Letters from Ireland (*the letters were originally published at the time of their composition [1847] in newspaper reports in the* Manchester Examiner, *and later as part of Somerville's* The Whistler at the Plough [1852]). *Snell offers a brief biography of Somerville—explaining the writer's sympathy with Ireland and the Famine victims—then makes use of quotations from Somerville's writings to depict the candid and often poetic nature of his account of the Famine and of Ireland's political and economic situation.*]

At an early point in his investigation of Ireland during the great famine, Alexander Somerville found himself one morning in Clonmel, on the 29th January, 1847. He had decided to accompany a convoy about to set off towards Waterford, to distribute Indian corn to the starving population. It was half past five and still dark, the morning was stormy, rain poured from a blackened and sullen sky, and there was a strong but increasingly saturated military escort gathering to accompany the laden carts.

Somerville waited. And as he surveyed the drenched scene, he commented on how few travellers stirred anywhere without fortifying themselves with weapons. Apparently the state of the country was such that pay clerks at public works were often attacked and robbed; land stewards and agents also never felt themselves to be safe. Such people, like commercial travellers, merchants, property owners and many others, went everywhere heavily armed. Somerville described how men came into hotels, and in taking off their coats, relieved themselves of a heavy burden of guns and pistols, which they carried or secreted in various parts of their clothing. He said that he had himself been warned that if he was to travel through the Irish country he had better arm himself in a similar fashion. Accordingly, he wrote, 'as arming seemed the order of the day, I armed myself . . . I took one of my carpet bags and emptied everything of luggage kind out; took it to a baker's shop and purchased several shillings' worth of loaves of bread, and to a general dealer's shop, and purchased a piece of cheese. I put them in the bag, put the bag on the car by my side, ready, if any hungry Tipperarian or dweller on the Waterford mountains should present a blunderbuss at me, to put my hand into the

bag, pull out, present, and throw to him a bullet of bread; not fearing but that this style of defence would be more effective than a defence by powder and lead.'[1] This passage reveals much about Somerville, about his abhorrence of repression and of his deeply sympathetic attitude towards the starving people of Ireland during the famine.

Alexander Somerville, known as 'The Whistler at the Plough', had himself been born into deep poverty in 1811, the eleventh child of a family living in a one-roomed, tiled hovel in Oldhamstocks, East Lothian. The hovel was windowless, except for a single pane of glass, owned and treasured by his farm labouring father, who moved it with him every time he changed his residence. His father had been born in Nether-aichlin-Sky, Perthshire, and his mother came from Ayton in Berwickshire. Both his parents were from very poor Scottish labouring families. Alexander himself had worked in his youth as a farm helper, plough-boy, sawyer, limekiln labourer, stone breaker, sheep shearer, itinerant harvester, drainer, quarryman, and dock labourer. This was not a promising start in life for a man of letters—a man whose voluminous writings included this forceful and very humane account of Ireland during the famine, first published as newspaper reports in the *Manchester Examiner,* and subsequently as part of his *The Whistler at the Plough* in 1852.[2] It is now reprinted under the title Somerville himself gave it.

One can best understand the sympathetic position he took during the Irish famine by appreciating the poverty he experienced as a farm worker, and the injustice he suffered at the hands of the British army. Much is known about him, for he was the author of a very readable nineteenth-century working-class autobiography, *The Autobiography of a Working Man* (1848).[3] In this he describes his childhood. 'I came into the family at a time when I could have been very well spared', he wrote, referring to the famine prices of 1811-13 and the poverty in which he grew up. His mother worked in the fields. His schooling had to be delayed because his parents could not find adequate clothing for him, other than the rags he normally wore. He was accordingly mistreated by the other children at school on account of his raggedness. His fondness for history— he was to write a history of the British Legion and the 1835-7 war in Spain, and a history of free trade and the Anti-Corn Law League[4]—began when he befriended an old blind shepherd, who held imaginary conversations with Elizabethan courtiers. At an young age he began his miscellany of employments in agriculture and other labouring work. The early pages of his *Autobiography* tell much about working conditions in his region of Scotland at the time. On harvest migration for example, such a prevalent feature of nineteenth-century Irish life, he wrote that 'To us who went from Lothian to the Merse, the higher wages was always the ruling cause of our migration, and no amount of work . . . deterred us.'[5] But it was a difficult time, with many men facing unemployment, and there was much political agitation to improve miserable living standards. Somerville seems to have joined in some of the activity in Edinburgh in support of political reform. After failing to find employment as a librarian (he was considered socially too inferior for such a job), and being unsuccessful in trying to attract subscriptions for a newspaper, Somerville himself enlisted in the Scots Greys.

In doing this, he set in train the tragic and brutal course of events which made him celebrated among the public, and which had a major influence on his later development and attitudes. The harrowing story is told in considerable detail in his *Autobiography*. He first served in Brighton, and was then marched to Birmingham, through the rural areas affected by the 'Captain Swing' unrest of 1830-1. Birmingham on the eve of the Reform Act was regarded as a danger to the political establishment, a hotbed of radical reformist ideas, one of the main venues for Reform riots. The Scots Greys were ordered to sharpen their swords to prepare to deal with crowd trouble. It was only a decade or so since the Peterloo Massacre of innocent civilians.

It was then that Somerville wrote a letter to the editor of the *Weekly Dispatch*. He said that while the Scots Greys could be relied upon to put down disorderly conduct, they should never be ordered to lift up arms against the liberties of the country and peaceful demonstrations of the people. The inexperienced officer in charge, Major Wyndham, saw fit to take this as a libel on the regiment. Accordingly, Somerville was then charged at an informal and very hastily convened 'court martial' with a trumped up offence, and was sentenced to a military flogging of two hundred lashes. He refused to grovel before Major Wyndham in the anticipated manner, refused to accept rum from the other soldiers before the flogging, and bore the flogging in silence in front of the regiment on parade. The relentlessly detailed pages telling of it in his *Autobiography* provide a harrowing and enduring castigation on the British army at this time. 'I put my tongue between my teeth, held it there, and bit it almost in two pieces. What with the blood from my tongue, and my lips, which I had also bitten, and the blood from my lungs, or some other internal part ruptured by the writhing agony, I was almost choked, and became black in the face . . . Only fifty had been inflicted, and the time since they began was like a long period of life: I felt as if I had lived all the time of my real life in pain and torture, and that the time when existence had pleasure in it was a dream, long, long gone by.'[6] Finally, after a hundred lashes, he was taken down in case he died— and in the hospital afterwards said, 'This shall be heard of, yet; I shall make it as public over England as newspapers can make it.'[7]

His case became front-page news, discussed in Parliament, referred to the King. The incident was officially investigated, and the regiment's officers were execrated in public by indignant crowds. There were large popular demonstrations against flogging in the army. The English rural labouring poor were as sympathetic to his case as were workers in the towns. Major Wyndham received an official reprimand. Somerville became a hero of the reform movement, used for political ends, in many cases against his inclinations. A public subscription was started for him. He met and was befriended by William Cobbett, a man who also had considerable experience of the army, who had made his voice heard against military flogging, and who had written at length on conditions in Ireland, often in a similar tone to that later adopted by Somerville.[8] Cobbett offered him advice on a career as a writer. Somerville was able in August 1832 to purchase his release from the army, and he returned to Scotland, where he went back to work as a wood sawyer in Edinburgh. His efforts to start a paper and then a shop were unsuccessful. So he joined the so-called 'British Legion', serving with it for two years in Spain, involved in the very grim warfare of 1835-7 on behalf of Queen Isabella against her uncle, Don Carlos. He received special commendations and was promoted to lieutenant, before being invalided out in 1837 with a bullet in his arm which he carried with him to the grave.

His politics were not of the more radical kind, and he became increasingly 'conservative' during his life— although his conservatism was of an idiosyncratic, humane and economically liberal kind, informed also by his Scottish covenanting background. In the 1830s he supported the transported Tolpuddle Martyrs, but berated trade-union leaders for seizing on the Martyrs' cause in an opportunistic way, which was not primarily concerned with the plight of the persecuted Dorset labourers. He condemned anti-combination laws, but criticised restrictions on entry practised by trade unions via apprenticeship, and the unions' secrecy. In 1837 he published his *Narrative of the British Legion in Spain,* an account of his military experience of the Spanish Civil War of 1835-7.

This was followed by his *Warnings to the People on Street Warfare,* attacking the 'instructions' issued by the revolutionary Colonel Francis Maceroni to the people on street warfare. Somerville argued for the futility of using violence in England to achieve political ends.[9] He had returned in the autumn of 1837 with first-hand experience of the brutal savagery of war in Spain; and he was soon introduced to two members of a Chartist 'Secret Committee of War', as an experienced soldier 'who could give a practical opinion of the feasibility of their intended insurrection'. Somerville, a huge and powerfully built man himself told the secret committee that he had seen, besides the horrors of bloodshed and death in battle, 'fertile fields trodden under the hoofs and wheels of the artillery . . . vines cut down . . . the houses of rich and poor . . . of political and non-political inhabitants, battered to atoms.'[10] In particular, he attacked what he called the 'absurd . . . dangerous, warlike notions' of the Chartist Peter McDouall, pointing out that, unlike continental soldiers, British troops were unlikely to go over to the side of crowds, and that the army was a formidable force for civilians to confront.[11]

He wrote to similar effect, in his *Public and Personal Affairs,* of how 'the agitation in the manufacturing districts is high enough for immediate action, and from a too well grounded discontent—but that agitation is not yet national, nor from the mingled indifference and opposition of the middle classes will it soon become general—therefore an armed movement must be defeated.'[12] There were some who tried to persuade him to join the 'Welsh insurrection of 1839'—the Newport Rising—but he refused to become involved.[13] He also wrote critically of the Chartist Land Plan in the *Manchester Examiner,* as he does on occasion in the *Letters from Ireland,* basing his view on an assessment of the questionable viability of extremely small-scale peasant holdings, as found in many parts of northern and western pre-famine Ireland.[14] Indeed, his criticism was such that two historians have since referred to him as 'the vitriolic anti-Land Plan propagandist.'[15]

It is for the part Somerville played in the troubles of these years that he has been remembered, mainly by historians of Chartism. Yet it is probable that his best literary work was his subsequent rural commentaries on Ireland, Scotland and England: devoting himself largely to social and economic topics and their political ramifications, writing for the *Morning Chronicle* and the *Manchester Examiner,* with a particular sympathy for the work of the Anti-Corn Law League. *The Whistler at the Plough,* his *Letters from Ireland during the Famine of 1847,* and his *Free Trade and the League* were written around this time, when his public influence was undoubtedly at its height.

A meeting with Richard Cobden, following letters Somerville had published in the *Morning Chronicle* in 1842 on the Corn Laws, began his career as a rural writer. He was supported by the Anti-Corn Law League to report on rural conditions. Known to the League's organisers as a rather difficult fellow they called 'Reuben'—whose occasional drinking bouts they tolerated because of his excellent and authoritative prose—he published his writings under the authorship of 'One who has Whistled at the Plough'. Somerville's views on English and Irish rural society were widely discussed at the time, for he was a persuasive, intelligent and often moving writer. He tells us that 'I resolved to write . . . in a manner . . . which eschewed the didactic and the still less welcome array of dry figures, which in newspapers had hitherto made agricultural politics an unin-

teresting subject, and to take up a style of narrative and description.'[16] After an earlier tour of Ireland in 1843—and extracts from his letters written during that tour are published here, as he included them—Somerville visited Ireland again for a second and more extended time. His purpose now was to report on conditions in 1847, the worst year of the tragic potato famine. The result was a remarkable and well-informed account of the structure and problems of rural life during that famine, an account that has altogether been missed by historians.

'Famine, fever, and the worst ills of the worst times of poor Ireland, were then at their crisis', he wrote in his *Autobiography.*[17] Very small subdivided holdings in many regions, and a rural population that had been growing rapidly since the 1770s, had become inextricably reliant upon the potato. Famine was nothing new to Ireland—there had been such catastrophes before, for example in 1740-1, 1745-6, 1755, 1766, 1783, and 1816-19. However, the significance and scale of the famine in the 1840s, and its chronic associated illnesses (typhus, dysentery, cholera, scurvy, and what contemporaries called 'relapsing sickness'), were unprecedented, and were to have enormous social, economic and political repercussions. The potato crop had been initially hit by a ruinous fungal infection, *phythophthora infestans,* in 1845, which had spread after previously appearing in America in 1843. Because of the prevailing damp conditions in Ireland the blight persisted and intensified in 1846, 1847 and 1848, in very many areas turning the staple crop into a stinking putrid mess: described by one official as like 'acres blackened as if steeped in tar'.[18] There was no remedy for such blight until the later nineteenth-century use of copper sulphate solution. Munster and Connaught were especially devastated, but almost all regions were affected, with the least impact in the north-east. Until shortly before Somerville's visit, the government's handling of the crisis had been relatively generous. From the summer of 1847 it was notable that a far more neglectful response set in, which Somerville himself was not in a position to predict or assess.[19] Some of his comments on public generosity from across the water perhaps need to be read with this in mind. The government's reaction, the political disputes over economic policy, the inadequacy of the public works laid on to provide employment, the operation of the recently established Irish poor law, the efficacy of the soup kitchens and food supplies—these have all been vigorously debated ever since, as they were by Somerville.[20]

Somerville recalled how he 'was sent from England by the proprietors of the *Manchester Examiner,* to travel through Ireland, to examine into its actual condition, without regard to political or religious parties, and to report to that paper what I saw. This task I fulfilled.'[21] In doing so, he himself succumbed to one of the virulent fevers that accompanied the famine: 'Upon my first arrival in Dublin from England, I was taken suddenly and seriously ill while visiting some of the deplorable abodes of poverty and disease in that city. When I recovered sufficiently to be able to write, I reflected on the chances of recurring illness and death, while travelling in the fevered, famine-stricken, crime-committing districts of the south and west of Ireland; and that if I did not write this chapter [of my *Autobiography*] then, I might pass from the world without its facts being known.'[22]

Unlike so many others, he survived. But the fear and melancholy of death, at this time in Ireland, were pervasive. They seep insidiously and sadly through his writing, enveloping the reader and entreating the need for further understanding. They are the omnipresent background to his accounts of fever, the food depots and public works, the activities of the military, the life-destroying evictions and 'clearances', or the agitations of the Irish poor. Because of the famine, perhaps a million people died.[23] In all, probably over a third the Irish population either died or were forced (often in horrendous circumstances) to emigrate.[24] The famine initiated a long-lasting decline in population, and major changes in agricultural life. Its political consequences for Ireland were far-reaching. And its memory pulses through modern efforts to alleviate such conditions elsewhere. Somerville wrote of 'all the ghastly faces, hollow and shrunken, which I have seen, with death looking out of the eyes . . . the masses of population amongst whom I have travelled through Tipperary and part of this county [Limerick], sinking from health to sickness, from life to death—not yet dead, but more terrible to look upon and think upon than if they were dead . . . glaring horribly upon the passer by.'[25] In Roscommon, 'the people are literally crawling to their graves, their eyes starting in their heads with stomach torture.'[26] 'No newspaper account of the distress is exaggerated. The people are famishing. It will be my business to give such details as I meet with as soon as I can.'[27] Somerville, a hardened soldier and a mercenary familiar with the ferocity of the Spanish Civil War, could now write that 'Never, in the known history of mankind, was there a country and its people so dislocated as Ireland is now; so inextricably revelled, and its people in such imminent hazard of perishing utterly.'[28]

Somerville's purpose in England had been to investigate the possibility and results of Corn Law repeal. By 1847 this cause was won. In Ireland his priority was to convince a sceptical British public, and their politicians, that a disaster was occurring of enormous and unrecognised proportions. He wanted also to comprehend how conditions had deteriorated to such a point. He was a man capable of compelling rhetorical effect in his writing, but his discussion here was level-headed, accusatory and indignant, but still analytical, always urgent. If Somerville can be said to lay blame anywhere for what he saw, and for the causes of the famine, it was at the doors of the larger Irish landlords, regardless of their faith or politics. However, he went beyond superficial allocation of blame—outlining the structural problems of the Irish agrarian economy, dealing with the problems of entailed estates, tenant right, inadequate leases and the disincentives for tenants to improve land, the Irish poor-law question, dependency upon land, the considerable extent of subletting, and the conacre and rundale systems. He made detailed comparisons between the respective circumstances of Irish and English agriculture, and also discussed the reasons for the lack of Irish industrial development compared to England.

It is surprising that historians have hitherto missed his work. In Britain at any rate, this may owe something to the fact that Somerville's views were so sympathetic to the Irish peasant farmers, and highly critical of what he recognised as the incompetence, greed or wastefulness of an all too often parasitic landlord class. Certainly, Somerville had a political stance and his own economic views to communicate, like all other commentators. The passages in [*Letters from Ireland*] where he outlines his own version of political economy are not always compelling, though they bear witness to the extent to which even his assertive and independent mind was constrained by certain intellectual axioms of his time. However, it is worth noting his dismissal of the population theory of Malthus, even in Ireland during the famine, and indeed some more recent historians have cast doubt on whether the famine was predominantly a case of Malthusian over-population.[29] Among many contemporaries, Malthusian argument coupled with free-market dogma and anti-Irish prejudice were used to justify limited intervention during the famine. This was not a stance Somerville shared, although he was worried that traders might avoid supplying the worst hit areas of Ireland if they suspected that government intervention and supply would lower prices. Somerville took pains to declare his politics and economic views throughout. It is clear that he saw the causes of the famine as lying in avoidable institutional, legal and structural flaws rather than in the 'natural' (i.e. inevitable) causes which were emphasised by many in 'responsible' positions as an excuse for inaction. Somerville's journalistic skill, his literary and descriptive imagination, and his sympathy for the Irish people produced a deeply humane account of the hardships suffered, their structural causes, and the inadequate attempts to relieve them.

Somerville's own background was Scottish Calvinist. He spoke 'broad Scotch'. However, that did not stand in the way of his defence of Irish Catholicism. Nor did it stop him condemning some Protestant landlord abuses in the strongest terms.[30] He wrote that 'The reverence with which these poor flesh-worn peasants speak of sacred things is very remarkable';[31] but one finds in him no condescension or anti-Irish sentiment. He criticised the view that 'the Catholic religion . . . disqualified the Irish for industrial enterprise', stressing the obvious exceptions to this in Europe.[32] He strongly condemned penal laws prejudicial to Catholics, and the eviction of Catholic tenants in favour of Protestants. With regard to large Protestant landlords, Somerville was particularly outspoken. The small tenantry, he wrote, 'have no security of tenure, and sad experience tells them that to enrich the soil is to invite an ejectment. Many of them . . . have leases, but even a lease in Ireland is no security. A landlord has only to make a profession of a wish to exchange a Catholic tenantry for Protestants, and, under cover of such a pretence, he may commit . . . the most damnable and detestable robberies.'[33] Further, he commented in scathing terms on that kind of Protestant landlord who 'looks to improved agriculture as a means of church proselytism. He mingles the produce of the farm-yard and the Thirty-nine Articles together, the stall feeding of cattle and attendance at the Protestant church, the instructions on thorough drainage and the instructions in the church catechism. A new dwelling-house, or barn, or stable, or road is equivalent on his estate to a new religion. The use of a bull of improved breed is associated with a renunciation of the bulls of Rome. No man on earth save an Irish landlord could be found to mingle such things together.'[34]

A large number of the worst Irish landlords, Somerville believed, had 'brought Ireland to a condition unparalleled in the history of nations.'[35] As a class, he thought that they stood 'at the very bottom of the scale of honest and honourable men.'[36] Indeed, 'the Irish landlord is only a rent-eater, and his agent a rent-extractor, neither of them adding to the resources of the farm—not even by making roads or erecting buildings.'[37] There was almost a complete lack of trust between landlord and tenant, which explained an absence of agricultural improvement, and much of the unrest and behaviour of the Irish rural poor.[38] The Irish themselves, he insisted, were not 'a naturally turbulent and assassin race'; they should be treated with fairness and trusted, in a way that was certainly not prevailing landlord practice. The tenants were very suspicious of agricultural innovation, because 'they have invariably seen, that such doctrines, and specimens, and injunctions to improve, were only preparatory to their being sacrificed and their land seized. And in a country almost devoid of trade and manufactures, to be turned out of a holding of land is a calamity on a family like a death stroke.'[39] Land—the control over it, and the desire for it—was the key to almost everything in rural Ireland.

He was even harsher on Irish landlords than he had been on their counterparts in England in *The Whistler at the Plough,* a book which itself mounts a considerable attack on English landed power. He appreciated the difficulties faced by some landlords, and the scale of their indebtedness, but his sympathy did not extend far. Land, he insisted, must be made saleable; the law of entail had to be reformed. This was essential if new owners, with capital to invest, were to be attracted. Furthermore, tenants were being politically regulated and intimidated in a wholly unjustifiable manner, and leases were manipulated to such ends, with tenants removed for political reasons.[40] Agricultural improvement was constantly hindered by landlords' policies of exacting exorbitant rents. 'Idle, dissolute, and improvident proprietary classes exact, and compulsorily exact, from the cultivators all their capital, the improving cultivator only being a mark for the landlord's cupidity.'[41] The Repealer gentry were little better than their English and Protestant counterparts in such regards.[42]

Neither were larger landlords helping much towards the relief of the starving poor. 'In no place can I see, or ascertain by inquiry, that the nobility or landowning gentry are contributing [to relief committees], save in the most paltry sums; most of them give nothing at all. A landlord who has nominally an income of £20,000 per annum . . . puts his name down, in the county of Cork, for £5. Another in Tipperary county, who either is rich or lives as if he were rich, puts his name down for £4'[43] Nor did they accept attempts to make them personally responsible for maintaining the poor of their parishes or unions, as was being advocated by some reformers of the poor law. Somerville believed that this would be equitable—'so that owners of property may be taxed for the poor according to their merits in giving employment to the poor', an interesting view on the obligations of property.[44] However, he added, this would be resisted 'to the uttermost.'[45] Very many landlords, like Lord Lucan, were refusing to pay poor rates, and by so doing were 'dooming their . . . people to desolation and death.'[46]

In addition, some were arranging for large sums to be spent on building workhouses on their estates, gaining by selling land to the poor-law commissioners for the buildings (even though these were often remotely sited away from the population). Such landlords planned to have the property on their estates. They would then refuse to pay poor rates, thus guaranteeing the failure of the poor law, and so forcing poor-law authorities to leave the buildings unused. In due course they would adopt these buildings for their own use. Somerville also complained of the way in which many landlords were manipulating the cess (a local rate for the constabulary, roads, compensation against 'outrages' and so on), and extracting tolls and customs. The proceeds of these were being used to adorn their houses, build private extensions, bridges and the like for their own private advantage, rather than for the good of the community and the alleviation of suffering.[47] Similar corruption prevailed in connection with railway construction.[48]

Irish crofters during the great famine.

The evictions and settlement clearances at this time have been much discussed. Somerville provides further documentation. Not only did landlords 'prevent, whenever they can, the erection of new houses';[49] but they were clearing their land of inhabitants to take advantage of the current public 'provision' for those people.[50] The poor law, the soup kitchens and the armed police all facilitated such activities. While in England, rural depopulation was said to be due to the attraction of urban industrial employment, in Ireland such employment was unavailable, and 'clearances' were forced, coercive and intolerable. Somerville complained of how the present time was an opportunistic one for evictions: 'We have England paying out of English taxes all those armed men, and providing them with bullets, bayonets, swords, guns, and gunpowder, to unhouse and turn to the frosts of February those tenants and their families.'[51] He told of how over all the south and west of Ireland the wrecks of dwellings were visible, the roofs torn off, and the walls demolished, testimony to evictions and to measures taken to prevent tenants returning to the homes they had built. In Ballinamuck, the scene of the 1978 French-English conflict, the entire village had been de-populated and destroyed by Lord Lorton, a 'mischievous bigot'. 'Ballinamuck was destroyed because a jury would not decide that one of its inhabitants was guilty'[52]—guilty, that is, of the murder of a northerner whom Lord Lorton had brought in to replace an ejected Catholic tenant. Somerville complains bitterly that English tax payers were having to pay for such repression, with starvation and death as its result.

Catholic tenants had almost no legal recourse. This was too expensive, and landlords' exorbitant fees had to be paid by the tenant. Where damages were awarded against landlords, they were absurdly low, unlike their incidence on tenants. The law overtly favoured landlords. Tenants were impoverished by legal actions; even when they were in the right, they could be ruined because of legal delays. Measures were taken to force tenants into arrears, causing their eviction.[53] One landlord had even purchased from the creditor a debt incurred by one of his tenants, so that he could then evict the tenant. Where leases existed, they were often held by landlords, rather than legally surrendered to tenants. In such cases, political subjugation was the aim.[54] Lord Devon's Commission of 1844 had complained that tenants often had difficulty in enforcing the production of leases.[55] Somerville endorsed this, and felt that the leases themselves sometimes 'read like a sarcastic chapter from *Punch* . . . The law-jargon of [the leases of Lord Clancarty or Lord Palmerston, in Galway, Sligo or Roscommon] is hopelessly unintelligible.'[56] A fault of Irish agriculture thus reproduced one often found in England, and constraining and absurd clauses in leases further obstructed agricultural improvement.

Somerville repeatedly dwelt on Ireland's potential for economic and industrial growth. Its lead, copper and iron-ore resources were extensive; its natural harbours, navigable rivers and geographical situation were enviable; its potential agricultural wealth self-evident, even if currently extorted in poverty-inducing rent. There were no insurmountable cultural barriers to industrial wealth, although some to whom Somerville talked felt it a 'crime' to have capital to carry on a business. He comments at one point on attitudes antagonistic to profit, and a reluctance to trade unless under compulsion.[57] He also felt that the Irish were badly served by traditional leaders, 'territorial legislators' like Smith O'Brien, by the pro-repeal gentry, by 'the ancient race of landlords', who all too often knew little of their country, and shared the faults of outside Protestant and non-resident landlords.[58] Beyond all the necessary agricultural reforms, Somerville urged the need for industrial developments, for without them population would be surplus to land, agriculture would lack markets, and a more complex monied economy would not evolve. Many of the stumbling blocks in Irish rural society existed also in England, but England was safeguarded from their ill-consequences by its industrial and urban home markets. 'It is in the natural order of things for agriculture to be profitless without a manufacturing and trading population to purchase and consume the agricultural produce', he wrote, without analysing further the effects on Ireland of the industrial revolution in England, or discussing the constraints on Irish industrial growth imposed by England in the past.[59] For as long as Ireland remained a purely agricultural nation, controlled by near-feudal landlords, it would be liable to famine.

One of the most telling features of Somerville's literary style is his eye for detail—for rents, wages, rates, regional types of farming, the way people armed and conducted themselves, or how the famine had affected particular individuals. Much of his prose comprises close description of the agriculture of different parts of Ireland, and his assessment of its unrealised potential. His versatility also impresses the reader, for example the way in which poetic description of landscape is juxtaposed against harsh realism to considerable effect. He uses a variety of literary devices to persuade his readers, all of which convey his empathy.[60] He had

an excellent eye for symbolic example. Throughout, he was imaginative and open-minded about the possibilities of alternative agricultural systems, as found elsewhere. For the historian his use of verbatim oral evidence is especially valuable, a technique not found among many other writers on the famine. Somerville is careful to allow farmers and the poor to speak for themselves. One will not find in his writing the tendency to impose certain stereotyped views onto the people discussed—unlike many others, he was certainly no prejudiced armchair commentator, reluctant to move into the crowd or across muddy fields. He took considerable pains to report circumstances as he saw them on the ground.

In short, it is time now to rediscover his work on Ireland and to absorb it into modern analysis of the tragic event it documents. Had Somerville written to support the political establishment, ignored conditions he witnessed, or pretended (like many others) that they were 'natural', inescapable or just another case of 'Irish exaggeration', his future in England would have been more secure. However, as proved when he was in the army, such a course was never his inclination. As the only (and very brief) biographical account of his life put it: 'Sympathetic and sensitive to a degree, he might have fared better in this world had he been less so.'[61] He was outspoken to an extent that many found embarrassing, and this had already cost him a British military flogging. His concern for the Irish rural poor and their plight overrode any temptation to political ingratiation. He was often criticized for the social views he stated, and he gained little economic security because of them.

After his work on Ireland he continued to write for many years, but largely in another country. He emigrated to Canada in 1859. Sadly, his wife died just eleven months after his arrival there, although they left a number of children who settled in America and Canada. Despite many literary initiatives,[62] his own fortunes did not improve. Late in life he listed his writings, including his account of Ireland, and remarked that 'it will be seen that many of the subjects are, unfortunately, such as an author may become poor upon, rather than popular and well remunerated.'[63] His earlier sympathetic attitude towards the Irish in the 1840s seems to have taken some knocks following the Fenian attack on Upper Canada in May, 1866, under General John O'Neill, with the seizure of Fort Erie, and the attacks on St. Armand and Frelighsburg.[64] On these occasions he defended the Upper Canadians, on the grounds that their livelihoods and new homes were being threatened, and that they were not themselves involved in the controversy in Britain over Ireland.[65]

Somerville died in 1885, aged seventy-four, in poverty in a squalid boarding house in Toronto. For some years he had been sleeping throughout the year in a woodshed outside, with the snow in winter seeping through the window—much as it had done, no doubt, around his father's moveable pane of glass, in the cottages of his childhood in the Lothians. And it is certain that, all those years later, he had not forgotten the deplorable scenes he had witnessed during the famine: men like 'the phantom farmer, Thomas Killaheel', who had followed him at one point, while on the hillside two 'spectre children' had stood leaning on their long and narrow spades, 'spades made for spectres to dig with.' Thomas Killaheel 'said nothing, but looked—oh! such looks, and thin jaws! . . . The lean man looked as if his spirit, starved in his own thin flesh, would leave him and take up its abode with me. I even felt it going through me as if looking into the innermost pores of my body for food to eat and for seed oats. It moved through the veins with the blood, and finding no seed oats there, nor food, searched through every pocket to the bottom, and returned again and searched the flesh and blood to the very heart; the poor man all the while gazing at me as if to see what the lean spirit might find; and it searched the more keenly that he spoke not a word.'[66] Thomas Killaheel may have spoken not a word, but Alexander Somerville wrote for him. [*Letters from Ireland*] is Somerville's eye-witness account of that worst tragedy of Irish history, 'the great hunger'.

Notes

[1] *Letters from Ireland during the Famine of 1847*, p. 449 (hereafter *Letters*). On people arming themselves, see C. Woodham-Smith, *The Great Hunger: Ireland, 1845-9* (1962), pp. 150-1.

[2] The original pp. 433-624 of *The Whistler at the Plough* (Manchester, 1852) are reprinted here, using the title *Letters from Ireland During the Famine of 1847* which Somerville gave them. His 'Extracts from Irish *Letters*', on the state of Ireland in 1843, are included at the end, just as he published them. There is a further discussion of Irish rural conditions in 1843 in *The Whistler at the Plough* (1852 ed.), pp. 185-192, entitled 'Journey from Navan to Trim. Visit to the birthplace of the Duke of Wellington in 1843'. This has been reprinted here as an Appendix. The English and Scottish part of *The Whistler at the Plough* has been reprinted as a separate book, under that title, by Merlin Press, 1989, edited by K.D.M. Snell.

[3] Alexander Somerville, *The Autobiography of a Working Man* (1848, 1951 ed.). This autobiography provided the basis for the summary of the life of 'a peasant, bred and nurtured under the most disadvantageous circumstances' in Scotland, in R.M. Garnier, *Annals of the British Peasantry* (1895), pp. 321-8.

[4] A. Somerville, *History of the British Legion and War in Spain* (1839); and his *Free Trade and the League:*

a Biographical History (1852), the latter originally published with *The Whistler at the Plough*.

[5] *Autobiography*, p. 107.

[6] *Autobiography*, p. 189.

[7] *Autobiography*, p. 190

[8] See D. Knight (ed), *Cobbett in Ireland; a Warning to England* (1984).

[9] *Narrative of the British Legion in Spain* (1837); *Warnings to the People on Street Warfare. A Series of Weekly Letters* (1839). Francis Maceroni's instructions were issued in his *Defensive Instructions for the People in Street Warfare* (1832, 1834). Somerville also wrote *Public and Personal Affairs. Being an Enquiry into the Physical Strength of the People, in which the Value of their Pikes and Rifles is compared with that of the Grape Shot . . . of the Woolwich Artillery* (1839). For brief discussions of Somerville's role in the controversy over Chartist physical force tactics, see W.T. Ward, *Chartism* (1973), p. 262; F.C. Mather (ed), *Chartism and Society: an Anthology of Documents* (1980), pp. 37, 139, 246; M. Hovell, *The Chartist Movement* (Manchester, 1918, 1970 ed.); H. Weisser, *British Working-Class Movements and Europe, 1815-48* (Manchester, 1975), p. 100; A. Plummer, *Bronterre: A Political Biography of Bronterre O'Brien, 1804-1864* (1971), pp. 107-9, 137; and see Somerville's *Autobiography*.

[10] Plummer, *Bronterre*, pp. 107-8.

[11] Weisser, *British Working-Class Movements and Europe*, p. 100. On McDouall, see for example J. Epstein, *The Lion of Freedom; Feargus O'Connor and the Chartist Movement, 1832-1842* (1982), eg. pp. 197, 221, 271-2, 295-7.

[12] Plummer, *Bronterre*, p. 109.

[13] Plummer, *Bronterre*, p. 137.

[14] See for example, L.H. Lees, *Exiles of Erin* (Manchester, 1979), p. 25.

[15] J. Epstein & D. Thompson (eds), *The Chartist Experience: Studies in Working-Class Radicalism and Culture, 1830-60* (1982), p. 302. See also A.R. Schoyen, *The Chartist Challenge; a Portrait of George Julian Harney* (1958), p. 174; Ward, *Chartism*, pp. 192, 199; A. Somerville, *Cobdenic Policy the Internal Enemy of England* (1854), ch. 5; and his *The Land Plan of Feargus O'Connor* (Manchester, 1847).

[16] *The Whistler at the Plough*, p. 4.

[17] *Autobiography*, p. 256.

[18] Woodham-Smith, *The Great Hunger*, p. 362.

[19] See e.g. ibid., pp. 408-9.

[20] For further discussion of the famine and its historiography, see the select bibliography provided here.

[21] *Autobiography*, p. 256. For discussion of other visitors' accounts of Ireland during the famine, see C. Woods, 'American travellers in Ireland before and during the Great Famine: a case of culture shock', in W. Zach & H. Kosok (eds), *Literary Interrelations: Ireland, England and the World*, Vol. 3. *National Images and Stereotypes* (Tubingen, 1987), pp. 77-84.

[22] *Autobiography*, p. 256. For discussion of the famine fevers, see Woodham-Smith, *The Great Hunger*, pp. 188-204.

[23] See C. O'Grada, *The Great Irish Famine* (1989), pp. 48-9.

[24] See Woodham-Smith, *The Great Hunger*, pp. 206-69.

[25] *Letters*, p. 56.

[26] *Letters*, p. 77.

[27] *Letters*, pp. 28. Other contemporaries condemned the view that the severity of famine was being exaggerated. See Woodham-Smith, *The Great Hunger*, pp. 157-69.

[28] *Letters*, p. 31.

[29] See in particular J. Mokyr, *Why Ireland Starved: A Quantitative and Analytical History of the Irish Economy, 1800-1850* (1983, 1985 ed.).

[30] E.g., *Letters*, p. 103.

[31] *Letters*, p. 149.

[32] *Letters*, p. 177.

[33] *The Whistler at the Plough*, p. 187. Reprinted as an appendix in *Letters*.

[34] *Letters*, p. 77.

[35] *Letters*, p. 206.

[36] *Letters*, p. 118.

[37] *Letters*, p. 78.

[38] For further analysis of the classes of rural Ireland at this time, see e.g. S. Clark, 'The importance of agrarian classes: agrarian class structure and collective action in nineteenth-century Ireland', in P.J. Drudy (ed), *Ireland: Land, Politics and People* (Cambridge, 1982), pp. 11-36.

[39] *The Whistler at the Plough*, pp. 187-8. For one of many similar assessments, see A. Bisset, *Notes on the Anti-Corn Law Struggle* (1884), pp. 194-6, who complains of 'the disgrace of the frightful robbery committed on those poor Irish labourer-tenants', who after often considerably improving their properties 'had the alternative given them of either having their rents at once raised to the full value of the improvements or of being turned adrift to wander about as vagabonds on the face of the earth, and carry with them to America an exile's sorrows and an outlaw's hate—for though it may be shown to be in accordance with the *form of law*, it was a robbery of the most cruel nature—a robbery that took advantage of the best qualities of the victims to make those very qualities the instruments of their destruction . . . The inhabitants of Ireland have taken up a deep and murderous hatred towards the inhabitants of Great Britain'.

[40] *Letters*, pp. 89 ff, 116, 121-2.

[41] *Letters*, p. 98.

[42] *Letters*, p. 97.

[43] *Letters*, pp. 56-7.

[44] *Letters*, p. 82.

[45] *Letters*, p. 67.

[46] *Letters*, p. 87.

[47] *Letters*, pp. 115-19.

[48] *Letters*, pp. 58 ff.

[49] *Letters*, p. 136.

[50] *Letters*, p. 82.

[51] *Letters*, p. 76.

[52] *Letters*, pp. 93-4.

[53] *Letters*, p. 188.

[54] *Letters*, pp. 121-2.

[55] *Letters*, p. 122.

[56] *Letters*, p. 155.

[57] *Letters*, pp. 67-8.

[58] *Letters,* pp. 145-7.

[59] *Letters,* p. 98.

[60] Richard Cobden wrote in another context of Somerville's style that 'The difficulty with Somerville [is] to condense sufficiently his narrative—this would not be easy even with one who had a style less flowing and imaginative than he.' See J. Morley, *The Life of Richard Carlile* (1881), vol. 2, pp. 54-5.

[61] W.M. Sandison, 'Alexander Somerville', *Border Magazine,* XVIII, no. 207 (March, 1913), separately printed as a supplement, to which reference is made here, p. 6.

[62] See the Bibliography of his writings in my edition of his *The Whistler at the Plough* (1989 edn), for further information on his considerable literary output. He also founded and for a while edited the *Canadian Illustrated News,* was editor of the *Church Herald,* and wrote on behalf of the Immigration Department of the Ontario Government, again much concerned with Irish affairs.

[63] W.M. Sandison, *Alexander Somerville, "The Whistler at the Plough"* (1913, reprinted from the *Border Magazine,* March, 1913), p. 8.

[64] The Fenian Brotherhood had been organised in Dublin in 1858, and in New York in 1859—they planned to establish a republic in Canada.

[65] He wrote a *Narrative of the Fenian Invasion of Canada* (Hamilton, Canada, 1866).

[66] *Letters,* p. 153.

Margaret Kelleher (essay date 1996)

SOURCE: "The Female Gaze: Asenath Nicholson's Famine Narrative," in *"Fearful Realities": New Perspectives on the Famine,* edited by Chris Morash and Richard Hayes, Irish Academic Press, 1996, pp. 119-30.

[*In the following essay, Kelleher re-examines the eye-witness account of the Famine by Asenath Nicholson, an American teacher who traveled to Ireland during the Famine in order to "personally investigate the condition of the poor" and to distribute Bibles. Kelleher analyzes Nicholson's writings from a feminine viewpoint, as defined by modern feminist film theory, and demonstrates the differences between Nicholson's accounts and contemporary male observations of the Famine and its victims.*]

Asenath Nicholson's record of 'The Famine of 1847, '48 and '49', first published in 1850 as the third part

---

> **An excerpt from Gerald Keegan's diary, dated May 27th, 1847, in which he describes the sufferings and indignities he and his fellow emigrants endured while escaping the Famine:**
>
> . . . I have told, in my own simple way, the story of how the poor and the dispossessed and the patriots are being treated in my country. I have tried to give a word picture of the intensity of their sufferings and, above all, of the indignities which have been heaped upon them. My only regret is the limitations that words have, in any attempt to use them to express the unfathomable depths of misery to which countless thousands have been reduced by famine and pestilence and persecution. If our trials stemmed from natural causes, from all those contingencies and disasters that are legally classified as acts of God, they would in many ways be more bearable. But the famine was an artificial one and pestilence followed naturally in its wake. After being deprived of food and the basic right to possess land freely in our own country, we were subjected to ruthless persecution by hordes of ruffians who were hired to molest us in every possible way. The final blow for all of the dispossessed was to be driven from our land and transported, in the holds of the most dilapidated vessels in the world, to a foreign land. Far from exaggerating anything in this story, I have merely touched the surface of the massive tragedy. If this is the end of my story I sincerely hope that it contains enough of the truth to let the world know how sorely we have been tried by the tribulations we have endured.
>
> *Gerald Keegan, in* Famine Diary: Journey to a New World, *edited by James J. Mangan, Wolfhound Press, 1991.*

---

of her study of Irish history entitled *Lights and Shades of Ireland,* is one of a large number of eye-witness accounts from the period. These descriptive and individualised narratives by contemporary observers such as Nicholas Cummins, William Bennett, William Forster and Sydney Osborne constitute a significant but frequently neglected historical source. The omission or scant reference to these writings in Famine historiography suggests a fear, on the part of some historians, of their emotive potential along with a suspicion that they do not constitute a sufficiently objective source. In those histories where eye-witness accounts are mentioned, they frequently serve as a type of shorthand for famine's effects, given in isolation from other aspects of the Famine study and without any detailed analysis of their original context, audience or reception. Substantial work is yet to be done on the nature and influence of observers' accounts, in relation both to the original context in which they appeared and the occasions in which they have been reproduced, albeit infrequent. The texts of these accounts themselves deserve a close examination, moving beyond questions of putative accuracy to the type of detail chosen for representation, the existence of recurring motifs, the role of the observer and the creation of a famine spectacle. Drawing from cinematic theories of 'gaze' and 'spectacle', this article presents a re-reading or re-visioning of Asenath Nicholson's famine account; revision, in the words of Adrienne Rich, being 'the act of looking back, of seeing with fresh eyes, of entering an old text from a new critical direction.'[1]

Contemporary film criticism, in particular the work of feminist film theorists, provides a richly suggestive perspective from which to view the writings of Nicholson and others. In a pioneering article, entitled 'Visual Pleasure and Narrative Cinema' and published in 1975, Laura Mulvey argued that mainstream cinema invites the spectator to identify with a male gaze which objectifies the female; woman is thus the object of the gaze, 'to-be-looked-at-ness'.[2] Mulvey's identification of 'woman as image, man as bearer of the look' is exemplified throughout representations of famine, in which individual victims are characterised most frequently as female, by predominantly male observers. Developing Mulvey's work, some film critics have investigated the nature of a female gaze and the positioning of a female spectator: what happens when a woman looks?[3] In exploring these questions, feminist film theory faces many of the problems and dangers encountered by feminist literary studies: defining the realm of the female may involve positing a female specificity, woman as nature, as mother, which reproduces and reinforces the old dualisms of culture and nature. Female perspectives also risk becoming an unchallengeable 'authentic' expression. With reference to this particular study of Nicholson's famine text, the danger is of positing a 'pure female gaze'.

The writings of Judith Mayne and Christine Gledhill, two more recent theorists, resonate in interesting ways with Nicholson's narrative. In arguing that film theory's over-concentration on the psycho-linguistic has neglected social, economic and political practices, Gledhill's work parallels the move by other feminist writers from the 'textual' to the 'social' subject.[4] Her work is of particular interest in studying famine texts, both in its emphasis on the importance of social and economic formations and in its identification of 'textual negotiation'. Gledhill defines the dynamics of a text and of its reception as processes of 'negotiation' in which 'meaning arises out of a struggle or negotiation between competing frames of reference, motivation and experience'; the critic is thus one who analyses 'the conditions and possibilities of reading', who 'opens up the negotiations of the text in order to animate the contradictions in play.'[5]

Drawing from analysis of the novel, Judith Mayne similarly defines narrative as a 'form of negotiation', in this case between the private and the public spheres, with female writing in novels and in cinema involving an 'intensification' of such negotiations.[6] As a summary of women's relationship to the cinema, Mayne has formulated the expressive phrase, 'the woman at the keyhole':

> On one side of the corridor is a woman who peeks, on the other, the woman who is, as it were, on display . . . The history of women's relationship to the cinema, from this side of the keyhole, has been a series of tentative peeks; that threshold . . . crossed with difficulty.[7]

The key-hole and threshold mark the boundary between public and private spheres, between outside and inside; rooms and homes being viewed traditionally as women's space. Drawing on the work of women filmmakers, Mayne contemplates what happens 'if women cast a cinematic gaze inside rooms': the construction of narrative space from a female perspective.[8] Nicholson's famine writing, read in light of these studies, demonstrates the operations of a female gaze, its specific negotiations and thresholds 'crossed with difficulty'.

Asenath Hatch Nicholson was born in Vermont in the late eighteenth century, where she worked as a teacher, before moving to New York in the 1830s. A strict teetotaller and vegetarian, and follower of Sylvester Graham, a Presbyterian minister, she opened the Graham Temperance Boarding-house in New York, later described as 'the resort of hundreds of choice spirits from all parts of the country, including most of the names of those who were engaged in measures of social reform.'[9] Nicholson first arrived in Ireland in June 1844; her book, *Ireland's Welcome to the Stranger; or, Excursions through Ireland in 1844, and 1845, for the purpose of personally investigating the condition of the poor,* first published in 1847, records her travels around Ireland, staying in lodging-houses and in cabins, including the homes of servant-girls whom Nicholson had employed in New York.[10] As well as 'personally investigating the condition of the poor' Nicholson sought to distribute and read the Bible among the Irish, having obtained a stock of Bibles, some in English and some in Irish, from the Hibernian Bible Society. Nicholson's independence of spirit and her ability to disturb and perplex her contemporaries are clear from the memorable editorial published in the *Achill Herald* of June 1845:

> She lodges with the peasantry, and alleges that her object is to become acquainted with Irish character. This stranger is evidently a person of some talent, and although the singular course which she pursues is utterly at variance with the modesty and retiredness to which the Bible gives a prominent place in its delineation of a virtuous female, she professes to have no ordinary regard for that Holy Book . . . It appears to us that the principal object

of this woman's mission is to create a spirit of discontent among the lower orders and to dispose them to regard their superiors as so many unfeeling oppressors . . . There is nothing either in her conduct or conversation to justify the supposition of insanity, and we strongly suspect that she is the emissary of some democratic or revolutionary society.[11]

Nicholson's particular denominational affiliation remains unclear; Alfred Sheppard, author of the preface to the 1926 reprint of *Ireland's Welcome,* notes that nowhere does Nicholson give a clue to her own denomination, 'if indeed it had any other member than herself'.[12] Similarly, in *Lights and Shades of Ireland,* Nicholson gives a detailed account of the various denominations existing in Ireland such as Presbyterians, the Society of Friends, Methodists and others, and describes herself as 'a listener who belongs to no one of them'.[13]

Returning to Ireland in late 1846, Nicholson spent the next two years travelling around famine-stricken areas: based in Dublin for six months, she moved in July 1847 to the north of Ireland, visiting Belfast, Donegal, Derry, Arranmore; the autumn of 1847 and winter 1847-8 she spent in the west, including Tuam, Ballina, Achill Island; in summer and autumn 1848 she visited Munster, before leaving Ireland in late 1848 or early 1849. Nicholson's account of what she had seen, entitled *The Famine of 1847, '48 and '49,* was first published in London in 1850, along with her accounts of early Irish history and of 'saints, kings, and poets, of the early ages'. In April 1851, the famine account was published in New York as a separate volume; a 'tale of woe' which, according to its editor 'J.L.', 'should be read by the whole American people; it will have a salutary effect upon their minds, to appreciate more fully the depth of oppression and wretchedness from which the Irish poor escape in coming to this land of plenty.'[14]

Both Nicholson's commentaries and the author herself emphasise the breadth and depth of her investigation, entering people's homes, in city and countryside: 'walking and riding, with money and without, in castle and cabin, in bog and in glen, by land and by water, in church and in chapel, with rector, curate and priest.'[15] In the preface to *Lights and Shades* the author warns the reader of the horrors, the 'fearful realities' which she has witnessed, and stresses the uniqueness of her perspective:

The reader of these pages should be told that, if strange things are recorded, it was because strange things were seen; and if strange things were seen which no other writer has written, it was because no other writer has visited the same places, under the same circumstances. No other writer ever explored mountain and glen for four years, with the same object in view; . . . And now, while looking

at them calmly at a distance, they appear, even to myself, more like a dream than reality, because they appear out of *common course,* and out of the order of even nature itself. But they *are* realities, and many of them fearful ones—*realities* which none but eye-witnesses can understand, and none but those who passed through them can *feel.*

The distinctive nature of her position is attributed both to her identity as woman: 'My task was a different one—operating individually. I took my own time and way—as woman is wont to do, when at her own option'[16], and as 'foreigner':

I was attached to England as the race from which I descended, and pitied Ireland for her sufferings, rather than I admired her for any virtues which she might possess; consequently my mind was so balanced between the two, that on which side the scale might have preponderated, the danger of blind partiality would not have been so great.[17]

Later Nicholson identifies a bias to which she, as female outsider, is distinctively vulnerable: 'the danger of that excessive pity or blind fondness, which a kind mother feels for a deformed or half-idiot child, which all the world, if not the *father* himself, sets aside as a thing of nought.'[18]

Nicholson's famine narrative includes a number of striking individualised accounts, offered almost reluctantly and quite apologetically, as 'specimens, not wishing to be tedious with such narrations, only to show the character of the famine, and its effects in general on the sufferers, with whom I was conversant.'[19] Two of the most memorable descriptions of famine victims occur quite early in the narrative, while Nicholson is still in Dublin, and provide interesting examples of Nicholson's singular 'negotiations', with regard to her own position and her encounters with others.

Nicholson's first sight of 'a starving person' occurs in Kingstown/Dun Laoghaire:

A servant in the house where I was stopping, at Kingstown, said that the milk woman wished me to see a man near by, that was in a state of actual starvation; and he was going out to attempt to work on the Queen's highway; a little labour was beginning outside the house, and fifteen-pence-a-day stimulated this poor man, who had seven to support, his rent to pay, and fuel to buy.[20]

The description of her encounter with the starving man is prefaced by an apostrophe to the reader:

and reader, if you never have seen a starving being, *may you never!* In my childhood I had been frighted with the stories of ghosts, and had seen actual skeletons; but imagination had come short of the sight of this man . . . [he] was emaciated to the last degree; he was tall, his eyes prominent, his skin shrivelled, his manner cringing and childlike; and the impression *then* and *there* made never *has* nor ever *can* be effaced.[21]

Nicholson's observations contain motifs common to other eye-witness accounts: the physical description of the man, the sense of a reality exceeding the possibilities of imagination. Much less frequent is her explicit inclusion of political and economic analysis, in this case a ringing condemnation of official methods of payment: 'Workmen are not paid at night on the public works, they must wait a week; and if they commence labour in a state of hunger, they often die before the week expires.' In contrast to many other eye-witness accounts in which encountering and distributing famine relief requires male authorization and mediation, frequently from local ministers, priests or doctors, Nicholson's distribution of food occurs during the family's absence, with help provided by the servant. References to entrances and gates, which carry crucial material consequences, permeate Nicholson's narrative: the labourers are 'called in' to the kitchen for food while others are fed at the door; the eventual locking of the gate, the barring of access, painfully signifies the exhaustion of supplies; while an unexpected donation from New York allows the unlocking of the gate, once the 'man of the house' has left for his business in Dublin.

Soon after this episode, Nicholson details another encounter, on this occasion with a widow who she meets 'creeping upon the street, one cold night', carrying 'a few boxes of matches, to see if she could sell them, for she told me she could not yet bring herself to beg; she could work, and was willing to, could she get knitting or sewing.'[22] The woman is reluctant to give Nicholson the number of her home; having given an indirect promise to call some future day and meaning to take the woman 'by surprise', Nicholson recounts that 'at ten the next morning my way was made into that fearful street, and still more fearful alley, which led to the cheerless abode I entered.' Her journey through the city's 'retired streets and dark alleys' involves 'finding my way through darkness and filth' until 'a sight opened upon me, which, speaking moderately was startling.' The description of this sight, as Nicholson's gaze travels around the room, from the dark corner at her right to the other side of the empty grate, includes features common to other famine accounts: the empty fire, the woman without a dress, pawned to pay rent, the man without a coat 'likewise pawned', and Nicholson's initial muteness at the sight. Less frequent is the breaking of the pause by the widow

Nicholson had encountered earlier; very rarely in such accounts do the suffering victims speak. In this case, a conversation takes place, one of the women is named, and, even rarer, the encounter emerges as the first of many such visits: 'daily did I go and cook their food, or see it cooked.'[23]

Nicholson's repeated crossing of the threshold of this 'forbidding', 'uncomfortable' and 'wretched' abode occurs in marked contrast to many other eye-witness accounts in which the beholder remains standing at the threshold or outside. The following extract from the Earl of Dufferin's account of his one-day visit to Skibbereen in 1847 is typical in its positioning of the male spectator:

> Conversing on these subjects, we reached a most miserable portion of the town; the houses were mere hovels, dark and dismal in the inside, damp and filthy to the most offensive degree. So universal and virulent was the fever, that we were forced to choose among several houses to discover one or more which it would be safe to enter. At length, Mr Townsend singled out one. We stood on the threshold and looked in; the darkness of the interior was such, that we were scarcely able to distinguish objects; the walls were bare, the floor of mud, and not a vestige of furniture.[24]

The perspectives offered by Dufferin and other contemporary observers further exemplify Laura Mulvey's comments on the gendered split between spectacle and narrative: women, or famine victims, represent 'icon' or 'spectacle' while the male protagonist 'articulates the look and creates the action.'[25] In Nicholson's narrative, however, both the female protagonist/narrator and the women she observes possess an active role. Most rarely, Nicholson's entrance into the people's home and her giving of food are reciprocated: 'Often late in the evening would I hear a soft footstep on the stairs, followed by a gentle tap, and the unassuming Mary would enter with her bountiful supply of fire kindling.'[26] In addition, as part of a continued emphasis throughout her narrative on women's desire and duty to work, Mary and her friend are presented as 'good expert knitters and good sempstresses' who repair Nicholson's clothing.

The account of the 1840s famine provided in *Lights and Shades of Ireland* is also distinguished by its interweaving of detailed analysis of famine's causation with representation of famine's effects. Nicholson engages directly and vehemently with contemporary views such as the attribution of famine to God's providence: 'God is slandered, where it is called an unavoidably dispensation of His wise providence, to which we should all humbly bow, as a chastisement which could not be avoided'.[27] Her comments on the availability of food provide an early treatment of what has become one of the most controversial issues in famine history: the question of the existence of 'sufficient' food in Ireland; while they also anticipate late twentieth-century debates as to the relation between famine and entitlement to food:

> and never was a famine on earth, in *any* part, when there was not an abundance in *some* part, to make up all the deficiency; . . . Yes, unhesitatingly may it be said, that there was not a week during that famine, but there was sufficient food for the wants of that week, and *more* than sufficient.[28]

Nicholson also castigates the government systems charged with transportation and distribution of grain, her strong individual grievance being the wasting of grain on the making of alcohol, while she deems many government officials or 'hirelings' guilty of crimes ranging from unnecessary delay in distribution of relief to direct embezzlement of government funds. Arguing that if the 'immediate breaking forth' of famine 'could not have been foreseen or prevented, its sad effects might have been met without the loss of life,' she concludes, in a bitter satire of political economy, that 'the principle of throwing away life today, lest means to protect it to-morrow might be lessened, was fully and practically carried on and carried out.'[29]

On a number of occasions in her narrative, Nicholson draws analogies between the position of American slaves and the Irish lower-classes: 'never had I seen slaves so degraded . . . These poor creatures are in as virtual bondage to their landlords and superiors as is possible for mind and body to be.'[30] In a passage strikingly prophetic of studies on the origins and ambivalences of colonial discourse,[31] she declares that existing laws

> possess the unvarying principle of fixing deeply and firmly in the heart of the oppressor a hatred towards the very being that he has unjustly coerced, and the very degradation to which he has reduced him becomes the very cause of his aversion towards him.[32]

Along with her detailing of encounters with individual famine victims and her forceful political analysis of 'oppression', Nicholson stresses that her 'greatest object in writing this sketch of the famine' was to show its effects on all classes, rather than to detail scenes of death by starvation.'[33] Yet the distinctive quality both of Nicholson and of her writings arises from her extensive visits among the lower classes of Irish society. This 'looking into' the lives of the poor, ironically, at first facilitated Nicholson's entrance into upper-class society:

> The people of Dublin, among the comfortable classes, whatever hospitality they might manifest towards guests and visitors, had never troubled themselves by looking into the real *home* wants of the suffering poor. Enough they thought that societies of all kinds abounded, and a poor-house besides, were claims upon their purses to a full equivalent for all their consciences required, and to visit them was quite *un-lady-like*, if not dangerous. To many of those I had access as a matter of curiosity, to hear from me the tales of starvation, which they were now to have dealt out unsparingly; and so kind were the most of them that the interview generally ended by an invitation to eat, which was never refused when needed, and the meal thus saved was always given to the hungry.[34]

Nicholson's account affords to the 'comfortable classes' a certain voyeuristic pleasure, 'the impression of looking in on a private world unaware of the spectator's own existence',[35] a curiosity, even voyeurism, shared by future audiences.

These visits, however, were to render the American 'foreigner' increasingly suspicious to her contemporaries. Nicholson herself mimics the voices of her critics, such as the 'nominal professor': ' "We do not understand your object, and do you go into the miserable cabins among the lower order." '[36] Although, in the early part of her famine narrative, Nicholson comments that the events of 1846 onwards allowed easier and more frequent access for outsiders, 'Poverty was divested of every mask; and from the mud cabin to the estated gentleman's abode, all strangers who wished, without the usual circuitous ceremony, could gain access,'[37] the later chapters suggest that her visits into Irish homes, particularly the homes of the poor, were made increasingly difficult by famine. *Ireland's Welcome to the Stranger,* Nicholson's earlier work, includes many accounts of staying overnight in cabins, with detailed descriptions of cabin interiors and bedding arrangements; significantly fewer of these are to be found in her famine work. On a number of occasions, Nicholson admits her reluctance to enter cabins: of her visit to Arranmore, Co. Donegal, she writes: 'We went from cabin to cabin till I begged the curate to show me no more.'[38] On these occasions, Nicholson's famine discourse displays a marked struggle between competing judgements, sometimes bordering on animalistic terms and struggling to retain a humanised discourse:

> they stood up before us in a speechless, vacant, staring, stupid, yet most eloquent posture, mutely *graphically* saying, 'Here we are, your bone and your flesh, made in God's image like you. *Look at us!* What brought us here?' . . . when we entered they saluted us by crawling on all fours towards us, and trying to give some token of welcome.[39]

In some of the most moving scenes in Nicholson's 'sketch' of famine, those seeking relief press against windows and doors, the threshold between the woman observer and famine victims now increasingly difficult to cross. In the home of the Hewitson family in Derry, 'the lower window-frame in the kitchen was of board instead of glass, this all having been broken by the pressure of faces continually there';[40] at Newport,

> the door and window of the kind Mrs Arthur wore a spectacle of distress indescribable; naked, cold and dying, standing like petrified statues at the window, or imploring, for God's sake, a little food, till I almost wished that I might flee into the wilderness, far, far from the abode of any living creature.[41]

Soon afterwards, Nicholson is at dinner with a company of ministers during which she criticises their luxurious fare, in particular their taking of alcohol, citing the suffering of the people; the Marriage of Cana is cited in reply,

> when in an hour after dinner the tea was served, as is the custom in Ireland, one of the daughters of the family passing a window, looked down upon the pavement and saw a corpse with a blanket spread over it, lying upon the walk beneath the window. It was a mother and infant, dead, and a daughter of 16 had brought and laid her there, hoping to induce the people to put her in a coffin; and as if she had been listening to the conversation at the dinner of the want of coffins, she had placed her mother under the very window and eye, where those wine-bibing ministers might apply the lesson. All was hushed, the blinds were down, and a few sixpences were quite unostentatiously sent out to the poor girl, as a beginning, to procure a coffin. The lesson ended here.[42]

The episode is an interesting one for a number of reasons; clearly displayed, along with Nicholson's strong objections to alcohol, are her alienation from most of the company inside, her imaginative sympathy with the girl outside which extends to some knowledge of the girl's age and purpose, and her recognition of the desperate efforts of the poor to ensure a proper burial for their dead.

By early 1847, during her travels in Connaught, the overwhelming nature of what Nicholson has witnessed becomes clear:

> A cabin was seen closed one day a little out of the town, when a man had the curiosity to open it, and in a dark corner he found a family of the father, mother, and two children, lying in close compact. The father was considerably decomposed; the mother, it appeared, had died last, and probably fastened the door, which was always the custom when all hope was extinguished, to get into the darkest corner and die, where passersby could not see them. Such *family* scenes were quite common, and the cabin was generally pulled down upon them for a grave. The man called, begging me to look in. *I did not,* and *could not* endure, as the famine progressed, such sights, as well as at the first, they were too *real,* and these realities became a dread. In all my former walks over the island, by day or night, no shrinking or fear of danger ever retarded in the least my progress; but now, the horror of meeting living walking ghosts, or stumbling upon the dead in my path at night, inclined me to keep within when necessity did not call.[43]

In what are now familiar terms in Nicholson's writing, the horror of the family's death is expressed in terms of 'inside' and 'outside', of uncrossed thresholds: the mother fastens the door so that others may not enter, Nicholson is, by now, unable to even 'look in' and, in stark contrast to her earlier 'excursions', increasingly stays 'within'.

In August 1848 in a letter published in the *Cork Examiner,* William O'Connor wrote, with regard to Asenath Nicholson:

> It is a singular spectacle to witness—a lady gently nurtured and brought up, giving up, for a time, home and country and kindred—visiting a land stricken with famine—traversing on foot that land from boundary to boundary, making her way over solitary mountains and treading through remote glens, where scarcely the steps of civilisation have reached, sharing the scanty potato of the poor but hospitable people, and lying down after a day of toil, in the miserable but secure cabin of a Kerry or Connaught peasant.[44]

Nicholson's writings present, in many ways, a 'singular spectacle', both in the details of famine conditions and in the character of their observer. Her account illustrates the negotiations which she attempted, both personally—across geographical and class divisions, and in the narration of famine—between analysis of famine's effects and causation; it remains a significant testimony to the 'fearful realities' of the 1840s famine.

Notes

[1] Adrienne Rich, 'When We Dead Awaken: Writing as Re-Vision' in *On Lies, Secrets and Silence* (New York, 1979), p. 35.

[2] Laura Mulvey, 'Visual Pleasure and Narrative Cinema' in *Screen* xiv, 3 (1975), pp. 6-18.

[3] See Linda Williams, 'When the Woman Looks' in M.A. Doane, P. Mellencamp and L. Williams (eds),

Re-Vision: Essays in Feminist Film Criticism (Maryland/Los Angeles, 1984); Lorraine Gamman and Margaret Marshment, *The Female Gaze* (London, 1988) and E.A. Kaplan, *Women and Film: Both Sides of the Camera* (London, 1983).

[4] Christine Gledhill, 'Recent Developments in Feminist Film Criticism' in *Quarterly Review of Film Studies* iii, 4 (1978), republished in Doane et al., *Re-Vision*, pp. 18-48; idem, 'Pleasurable Negotiations' in E.D. Pribram (ed.), *Female Spectators* (London, 1988), pp. 64-89.

[5] Gledhill, 'Pleasurable Negotiations', pp. 68, 74-5.

[6] Judith Mayne, 'The Woman at the Keyhole: Women's Cinema and Feminist Criticism' in *New German Critique* xxiii (1981), republished in Doane et al., *Re-Vision*, pp. 49-66.

[7] Ibid., pp. 54-5.

[8] Ibid., p. 55.

[9] J.L., 'Introduction' in Asenath Nicholson, *Annals of the Famine in Ireland, in 1847, 1848, and 1849* (New York, 1851).

[10] Asenath Nicholson, *Ireland's Welcome to the Stranger; or, Excursions through Ireland in 1844, and 1845, for the Purpose of Personally Investigating the Condition of the Poor* (London, 1847).

[11] *Achill Missionary Herald and Western Witness*, 25 June 1845, p. 65.

[12] A.T. Sheppard, 'Introduction' in Asenath Nicholson, *The Bible in Ireland* (abridged version of *Ireland's Welcome;* London, 1926).

[13] Asenath Nicholson, *Lights and Shades of Ireland* (London, 1850) p. 419.

[14] J. L., 'Introduction' in Asenath Nicholson, *Annals of the Famine in Ireland, in 1847, 1848, and 1849* (New York, 1851).

[15] Nicholson, *Lights and Shades of Ireland*, p. 438.

[16] Ibid., p. 229.

[17] Ibid., pp. 8-9.

[18] Ibid., p. 10.

[19] Ibid., p. 233.

[20] Ibid., p. 224. This episode and other extracts from Nicholson's famine narrative have been anthologised in Seamus Deane (ed.), *The Field Day Anthology of Irish Writing,* (3 vols., Derry, 1991), ii, pp. 133-45.

[21] Nicholson, *Lights and Shades of Ireland,* pp. 224-5.

[22] Ibid., p. 230.

[23] Ibid., pp. 231-2.

[24] Earl of Dufferin and Hon. G.F. Boyle, *Narrative of a Journey from Oxford to Skibbereen during the Year of the Irish Famine* (Oxford, 1847), pp. 12-13.

[25] Mulvey, 'Visual Pleasure', pp. 12-13.

[26] Nicholson, *Lights and Shades of Ireland,* p. 232.

[27] Ibid., p. 237.

[28] Ibid., pp. 237-9.

[29] Ibid., p. 239.

[30] Ibid., p. 301.

[31] See, for example, Homi Bhabha, 'The Other Question: The Stereotype and Colonial Discourse' in *Screen* xxiv, 6 (1983), pp. 18-36.

[32] Nicholson, *Lights and Shades of Ireland,* p. 408.

[33] Ibid., p. 25.

[34] Ibid., p. 234.

[35] Williams, 'When the Woman Looks', p. 83.

[36] Nicholson, *Lights and Shades of Ireland,* p. 429.

[37] Ibid., p. 246.

[38] Ibid., p. 271.

[39] Ibid.

[40] Ibid., p. 256.

[41] Ibid., p. 284.

[42] Ibid., p. 294.

[43] Ibid., p. 330.

[44] William O'Connor, letter to *Cork Examiner,* 31 August 1848, quoted in Nicholson, *Lights and Shades,* p. 385.

An excerpt from a traditional tale about the mysterious appearance of food, recorded by a resident of county Cork:

I often heard of Mrs. Ned Fitzgerald, Mountinfant, two miles north of our village. . . . This good woman never refused to give her skim milk to the poor and often her husband used to blame her for giving away the milk and letting the calves go hungry.

It was told how one day he was ploughing near the house and he saw so many poor people leaving the house with 'gallons' of milk on their heads that he got vexed and made for the house to scold his wife for giving away so much milk. He said to her: 'You are giving away all my milk and starving my calves and not caring a bit what price they'd be making'. She said the calves had grass and water and wouldn't starve, and that she couldn't refuse poor neighbours a drop of milk for starving children. 'There's milk going all day', he said, 'and come now and show me what you have for the calves in the evening'. He ran out to the dairy himself and she thought: 'Tis unknown what he'll do when he finds all the pans empty'. But when he went into the place, lo and behold, all the pans were full of milk as if she had given nothing away; full of milk and cream they were, though he had seen milk being taken away all day. He got an awful surprise and went away back to his plough; and 'twas said he never again interfered with his good wife about what milk she'd give away to the poor; and his calves grew and thrived and he never had better calves than he had that very year when his wife had all the milk given away to the children of her poor neighbours.

An anonymous storyteller, reprinted in The Great Famine: Studies in Irish History, 1845-52, *edited by R. Dudley Edwards and T. Desmond Williams, Russell and Russell, 1976.*

FURTHER READING

Brown, Malcolm. "Black '47." In *The Politics of Irish Literature: From Thomas Davis to W. B. Yeats*, pp. 85-102. Seattle: University of Washington Press, 1972.

> Discusses the political events in Ireland, especially the activities of the Irish nationalist movement, during the worst year of the Famine, 1847.

Kissane, Noel. *The Irish Famine: A Documentary History.* Dublin: National Library of Ireland, 1995, 184 p.

> Chronicles the history of the Famine through the extracts, accounts, and reports of the "traveller, parliamentarian, civil servant, botanist, professional reporter, or bystander."

McHugh, Roger J. "The Famine in Irish Oral Tradition." In *The Great Famine: Studies in Irish History, 1845-52.* Eds. R. Dudley Edwards and T. Desmond Williams, pp. 391-436. New York: Russell and Russell, 1956.

> With the aid of the Irish Folklore Commission, surveys the Irish oral treatment of the Famine, covering such topics as the blight itself, the food available during the Famine, the public relief efforts, disease, death, and the effects of the Famine on the Irish countryside.

Woodham-Smith, Cecil. *The Great Hunger: Ireland, 1845-1849.* New York: Harper and Row, 1962, 510 p.

> This much-cited reference offers a comprehensive treatment of the history of the Famine, and includes analyses of the human, political, and economic conditions of Ireland prior to and during the Famine, as well as discussion of the impact of British policies on Ireland during these years.

Nineteenth-Century Native American Autobiography

INTRODUCTION

Native American autobiographies of the nineteenth century have a peculiar difficulty: both the authenticity of Native American authorship and the applicability of the term "autobiography" are questioned by scholars. Situated during the transition from oral to written literature, most of these works were edited and/or translated by members of white society, and therefore are commonly identified as "collaborative" projects. The earliest narratives were written by Native Americans converted to Christianity, and simultaneously romanticized "primitive" existence and vilified so-called "heathen" beliefs. Throughout the nineteenth century—particularly with the rise of forced assimilation, the establishment of reservations, and the end of military resistance—narratives become increasingly secular and concerned with the political situation of Native Americans. In addition, toward the turn of the century, in response to a growing concern over the fading of traditional culture, ethnographic studies focused upon representative lives, whereas earlier interest had centered on such figures as ministers, warriors, and leaders.

Although some autobiographies reflect conciliatory responses to the dominance of Western culture and some are profoundly informed by sentimentality and the stereotype of the "noble savage," others, such as Sarah Winnemucca Hopkins's *Life Among the Paiutes* (1883), question the social and cultural disruption of the nineteenth century. Native American authors were acculturated to Western society to varying degrees and represent, in Arnold Krupat's words, a textual "frontier" by which traditional modes of self-expression, such as the pictographs of the Plains Indians (as Hertha Wong argues), were gradually displaced by the specifically Euro-American genre of autobiography. Accordingly, some autobiographies, including Simon Pokagon's *Life of O-Gi-Maw-Kwe-Mit-I-Gwa-Ki: Queen of the Woods* (1899), incorporate mythical elements with more realistic experiences. Recent scholars contend, citing such elements, that these autobiographies are not merely "transparent," but rather reflect a self-consciously literary style. The popular interest in these narratives increased toward the end of the nineteenth century, despite mixed critical reviews. More recent scholars have studied the conception of the "self" expressed in these works, as well as how the autobiographies reflect the series of political, cultural, and literary transitions that occurred as con-tact between the Native American and Euro-American cultures continued to increase.

REPRESENTATIVE WORKS

William Apes (or Apess)
A Son of the Forest: The Experience of William Apes, a Native of the Forest (autobiography) 1829

Hendrick Aupaumut
A Narrative of an Embassy to the Western Indians, from the Original Manuscript of Hendrick Aupaumut, with Prefatory Remarks by Dr. B. H. Coates (autobiography) 1827

Black Elk
Black Elk Speaks (autobiography) 1932

Black Hawk
Life of Ma-ka-tai-me-she-kia-kiak, or Black Hawk (autobiography) 1833

Andrew J. Blackbird
Ottawa and Chippewa Indians (memoirs) 1887

Sam Blowsnake [Big Winnebago and Crashing Thunder]
The Autobiography of a Winnebago Indian (autobiography) 1920
Crashing Thunder (autobiography) 1926

Chainbreaker [Governor Blacksnake]
*Chainbreaker: The Revolutionary War Memoirs of Governor Blacksnake (autobiography) 1989

George Copway
The Life, History, and Travels of Kah-ge-ga-gah-bowh (George Copway [also published as *Recollections of a Forest Life*] (autobiography) 1847

Charles A. Eastman
Indian Boyhood (autobiography) 1902
From the Deep Woods to Civilization: Chapters in the Autobiography of an Indian (autobiography) 1916

Sarah Winnemucca Hopkins
Life Among the Paiutes: Their Wrongs and Claims (autobiography) 1883

Peter Jacobs
  Journal of the Reverend Peter Jacobs (autobiography) 1857

Peter Jones
  The Life and Journals of Kah-ke-we-quo-na-by (autobiography) 1860

Maungwudaus [George Henry]
  An Account of the Chippewa Indians, Who Have Been Traveling Among the Whites (autobiography) 1848

Simon Pokagon
  O-Gi-Maw-Kwe-Mit-I-Gwa-Ki: Queen of the Woods (autobiography) 1899

Two Leggings
  **Two Leggings: The Making of a Crow Warrior* (autobiography) 1967

Chainbreaker was told to Benjamin Williams sometime between 1833 and 1843.

**Two Leggings* was composed from 1919-23.

OVERVIEW

Arnold Krupat (essay date 1992)

SOURCE: An introduction to *Native American Autobiography*, edited by Arnold Krupat, The University of Wisconsin Press, 1994, pp. 3-17.

[*In the following excerpt from his introduction to his anthology, Krupat reviews the historical trends and the major issues involved in Native American autobiography.*]

The genre of writing referred to in the West as *autobiography* had no close parallel in the traditional cultures of the indigenous inhabitants of the Americas, misnamed "Indians." Like people the world over, the tribes recorded various kinds of personal experience, but the western notion of representing the whole of any one person's life—from childhood through adolescence to adulthood and old age—was, in the most literal way, foreign to the cultures of the present-day United States. The high regard in which the modern West holds egocentric, autonomous individualism—the "auto" part of "autobiography"—found almost no parallel whatever in the communally oriented cultures of Native America.

Just as the "auto" part of "autobiography" was alien to Native understanding, so, too, was the "graph" part, for alphabetic writing was not present among the cultures of Native America. Tribal people were oral people who represented personal experience performatively and dramatically to an audience. Personal exploits might be presented pictographically (i.e., in tipi decorations or other types of drawing), but never in alphabetic writing. When, after considerable contact with the Euramerican invader-settlers, some Native people did attempt to offer extensive life histories, these made their way into writing in two distinct but related forms. One of these I refer to as "autobiographies by Indians," and the other as "Indian autobiographies."

Autobiographies by Indians are individually composed texts, and, like western autobiographies, they are indeed written by those whose lives they chronicle. For the Native American to become author of such a text requires that he—and later also she—must have become "educated" and "civilized" and, in the vast majority of cases, also Christianized. Indian autobiographies, as I have detailed the matter elsewhere, are not actually self-written, but are, rather, texts marked by the principle of original, bicultural composite composition. That is to say, these texts are the end-products of a rather complex process involving a three-part collaboration between a white editor-amanuensis who edits, polishes, revises, or otherwise fixes the "form" of the text in writing, a Native "subject" whose orally presented life story serves as the "content" of the autobiographical narrative, and, in almost all cases, a mixedblood interpreter/translator whose exact contribution to the autobiographical project remains one of the least understood aspects of Indian autobiography. Historically, Indian autobiographies have been produced under the sign of history and (social) science, while, with certain exceptions, autobiographies by Indians have been produced under the sign of religion, nonscientific cultural commentary, and art.

Both Indian autobiographies and autobiographies by Indians may be seen as the textual equivalent of the "frontier," as the discursive ground on which two extremely different cultures met and interacted. In this regard, Native American autobiography may usefully be studied for what it tells us about Native culture, Euramerican culture, the view each had of the other, and the shifting relations, i.e., the discursive/textual relations but also material relations of power, between them. In the multicultural age we all inhabit, self-life-writing by Indians—Native American autobiography—is important not only for its intrinsic interest, but also because it can provide a different, alternate, or, indeed, radically *other* perspective on the meaning of the terms ("self-life-writing") one cannot help but use in referring to it.

For example, Native American conceptions of the self tend toward integrative rather than oppositional relations with others. Whereas the modern West has tended to define personal identity as involving the successful mediation of an opposition between the individual and society, Native Americans have instead tended to define themselves as persons by successfully integrating themselves into the relevant social groupings—kin, clan, band, etc.—of their respective societies. On the Plains, to be sure, glory and honor were intensely sought by male warriors who wanted, individually, to be "great men," but even on the Plains, any personal greatness was important primarily for the good of "the people." These conceptions of the self may be viewed as "synecdochic," i.e., based on part-to-whole relations, rather than "metonymic," i.e., as in the part-to-part relations that most frequently dominate Euramerican autobiography.

In the same way that Native American autobiography can put the western concept of the self in perspective by making us see that what we have taken as only natural is, instead, a matter of cultural convention, so, too, can it offer a critical perspective on the western conception of the importance of writing. This is a subject that has occupied the attention of a great many theorists of late, perhaps because we are currently in a stage of transition to what Walter Ong has called a "secondary orality," a condition in which print media and writing certainly exist but do not occupy the social-functional position they held before the computer revolution.

Let me turn here to a brief historical sketch of Native American autobiography.

The earliest Native American autobiography I know is an autobiography by an Indian, by the Reverend Samson Occom, a Mohegan, who produced a short narrative of his life in 1768. In 1791, Hendrik Aupaumut, referred to as a "Mahican," included a good deal of what might be taken as autobiographical material in his *Journal of a Mission to the Western Tribes of Indians*. Neither of these texts was published in its author's lifetime, Occom's reposing for many years in the Dartmouth College Library before finally appearing in 1982, Aupaumut's seeing print—somewhat obscurely—in 1827. This latter date is perhaps not strictly an accident, for it was in the second quarter of the nineteenth century that American interest in the first-person life history (only recently, in 1808, named autobiography by the British poet Robert Southey) began to grow. Just two years after Aupaumut's work, the Reverend William Apess, a Pequot and a Methodist minister, published the first extended autobiography by an Indian to attract a relatively wide readership. Apess's *A Son of the Forest: The Experience of William Apess a Native of the Forest, Written by Himself,* appeared in 1829, and went through several editions in its author's lifetime. It is the christianized Indian's relation to Euramerican religion that thematically dominates the early period of autobiographies by Indians.

Only a few years after Apess's autobiography was published, there appeared in the West (Cincinnati) the first of those compositely produced texts I call Indian autobiographies. This was the *Life of Ma-Ka-tai-she-me-kia-kiak, or Black Hawk,* the autobiography not of a Christian Indian but, rather, of a resisting Indian who came to public attention as a result of his military opposition to the encroachment of whites onto Indian lands. After being defeated in the Black Hawk War of 1832, the last Indian war to be fought (for the most part) east of the Mississippi, Black Hawk endured imprisonment and a public tour of the East before being allowed to return home. Once back on his ancestral lands on the Rock River in Illinois, he narrated the story of his life. Black Hawk was a traditionally-raised Sac and Fox person who did not speak English and did not write any language—nor is it clear, in the distinction proposed by Watson and Watson-Franke, whether his autobiography was "elicited or prompted by another person" or whether it was, instead, "self-initiated."[1] Indeed, this distinction itself, while logically tenable, is empirically almost impossible to apply. Black Hawk's editor, the young journalist J.B. Patterson, claimed that Black Hawk himself initiated the autobiographical project, but we also know that Black Hawk was much solicited by various Euramericans for the story of his life, and he may have been urged in this direction by Native people, too. In any case, even if the Native subject of an Indian autobiography was pressed to the task by a journalist, historian, or anthropologist, we now understand that only those Native persons who found such a task consistent with their own needs and desires eventually complied. This would be the case as well for autobiographies by Indians, for even these ostensibly "self-initiated" texts were not "initiated" in a vacuum, but in a cultural and historical context which "prompted" some Indians who could write about themselves to do so while others simply did not.

Although I believe that we can rarely know with any assurance the full motivation behind a given Indian autobiography, we can in many cases know something about what may be called its mode of production. Here, again, Black Hawk's autobiography is exemplary, for the text is one that comes into being through the collaborative labor of Black Hawk, who is its subject and the person to whom the "I" of the text refers; of Antoine LeClair, a mixedblood person who served as official government interpreter to the Sac and Fox Indians, and who transcribed and translated the old war chief's words into written English; and of J. B. Patterson, who ultimately "edits"—inscribes and fixes in writing—the text we read as "Black Hawk's autobiography." What kind of transcription LeClair must have made, in that age before the tape recorder, we do not know, nor do we know what kind of English LeClair would have written by way of translation, inasmuch as no notes or transcripts seem to have survived.

It is reasonable to imagine, however, that LeClair presented Patterson with a text in what has since been called "Red English," the English that Native people with little or no formal schooling speak and sometimes write. In the absence of a text from LeClair, it may be useful to cite an autobiographical text roughly contemporary with his—one which, like Black Hawk's story, is more a military memoir (in this case, of the American Revolution and the War of 1812) than a personal narrative. I quote here a brief passage from the autobiography of Chainbreaker, also known to the whites as Governor Blacksnake. Somewhere between the years 1833 and 1843, when he was ninety or a hundred years old, Chainbreaker told his story to Benjamin Williams, who was nearly fifty years his junior and, like Chainbreaker, a Seneca. Williams' manuscript was not taken up by an editor until very recently (1989), when Thomas Abler prepared it for print. Abler's editing, however, is very different from that of J. B. Patterson, in that he has not transformed Williams' text into standard English, as Patterson almost surely did for LeClair's text. In the quotation below, the square brackets are Abler's additions:

> The year [1799] Certifies that from a personal Acquanted called good lake—that year he was Sick Confined on his bed he was not able to Rise from the bed and it hapen one morning He was called to Rise and go to Door. He Did So—Saw three [or four?—both have been written] person Standing by the Door And Take hands with him all—and comminced That he felt Vend [faint] and fall down on the ground By theirs feets and lost his Senses. . . . [2]

What I would have the reader consider is that there are, broadly speaking, two ways to read this sort of text. One way is to take it as a rather pathetic approximation of the conventional standard of educated authors. The other is to take it not so much as *failed* English but as an invention, a hybrid or creolized language *based on* English. Standard English provides a vocabulary and a set of grammatical rules, which, on the one hand, may have been imperfectly mastered but which, on the other, may simply have been adapted, creatively manipulated for the purposes at hand, and, of course, manipulated in relation to the writer's prior familiarity with another language (Seneca).

I do not for a moment suggest that Benjamin Williams was consciously engaged in inventive experimentation, nor does it seem likely to me that, if we did have a manuscript from Antoine LeClair, we would necessarily find it a shining example of the creative transformation of English. I do, however, suggest that the reader worry less about the formal "errors" of this English and try to imagine more the Indian linguistic modes that it may convey. Like Black Hawk's autobiography, many of the Indian autobiographies we read in "good" English have some intermediate version—intermediate between *speech* in a Native language and *writing* in standard English—that exists, or once existed, in some variant of this written "Red English," or "Reservation English."

One version or another of the triangulated textual generation of Black Hawk's autobiography—Indian sub-ject, mixedblood interpreter/translator, Euramerican editor/amanuensis—became standard for the texts I call Indian autobiographies; and it is important to keep in mind the very particular mode of production of these texts, because it bears, among other things, upon the virtually irresistible question of whether or to what degree Indian autobiographies give us the "real" or "authentic" Indian.

To open this question is potentially to lead the reader into a patch of theoretical thorns. One line of thought urges that we give up entirely the desire for "reference," the desire to encounter the "real" Black Hawk and other persons we know to have existed outside of and beyond the words of their autobiographical texts, but whom we can only know through the words of those and other texts. Another, oppositional, line of thought insists upon the referentiality of the autobiographical text, admitting that, while the language of the text inevitably mediates our encounter with the real, historical subject of the autobiography, still, the abiding appeal of autobiography is exactly the sense we have of an encounter with lives other than and apart from our own. If the former view insists that any feel for the real is only a produced effect of language, the latter tends to insist upon the autobiographical "pact" between writer and reader involving a conventionally-prescribed commitment to tell the "truth," albeit in words. I incline to the latter view while taking very seriously the warnings of the former as to the inevitable disparities between—in the terms of Michel Foucault—the order of words and the order of things.

As I have noted above, the Indian autobiography in its first manifestations appears as a historical document of the nineteenth century, as whites urge Indians who had resisted the "advance" of "civilization" to tell their story and explain their resistance. Interest in the resisting Indian, the world-historical chief or warrior, would persist well into the twentieth century, no longer as a "dominant" societal concern, in Raymond Williams' sense, but as a "residual" one. From early in the twentieth century, Native persons were approached for their life stories not because they had uniquely distinguished themselves in war or diplomacy or any other public or historical activity, but because they were considered "representative" of their culture, persons who might be attended to precisely because they were *not* extraordinary, because they were *not* among those great men whose biographies, as Thomas Carlyle had put it, comprised what we call history. Rather, as Paul Radin said of the informant he named "Crashing Thunder," the appropriate subject of the anthropological life history would more nearly be "a representative middle-aged individual of moderate ability," one who could "describe his life in relation to the social group in which he had grown up."[3]

In an approximately parallel fashion, autobiographies by Indians in the late nineteenth and early twentieth century may be said to shift their emphasis from a relation to Euramerican religion to a relation to Euramerican culture and society, as in the texts of Charles Alexander Eastman, Gertrude Bonnin, and Luther Standing Bear, among others. These Native writers spoke for the ongoing value of traditional tribal ways, while generally accepting many of the values of the dominant "civilization."

It is clearly social science, in the form of an anthropological interest in the professionally and academically defined categories of culture and culture-and-personality that dominates the production of Indian autobiographies from about 1913 (the date of Paul Radin's first Winnebago autobiography) into at least the early 1940s, when Franz Boas, the dominant figure in American anthropology for half a century, called life histories of use only for illustrating the "perversion of truth by the play of memory with the past."[4] Parallel to the work of the professional anthropologists in this period, however, are the efforts of "amateurs"—journalists, westerners, and devotees of things Indian—in obtaining the life stories of warriors like Wooden Leg, who participated in the Custer fight (1876), Yellow Wolf, who was part of the "flight" of the Nez Perces (1877), and Plenty-Coups, chief of the Crow, among other aged Natives who saw and made "history."

Although non-Natives continue to this day to produce Indian autobiographies in collaboration with Native people, the most noted Native American autobiographies of late have been autobiographies by Indians, the self-written texts of Native people who first came to public notice as artists, as writers of poetry and fiction. I am thinking foremost of N. Scott Momaday, whose 1969 Pulitzer Prize for the novel *House Made of Dawn* ushered in the contemporary "Native American Renaissance" in written literature. Momaday's two autobiographies, *The Way to Rainy Mountain* (1969), in which oral and tribal histories are combined with the author's personal history, and *The Names* (1976), in which reflections on this personal history are combined with passages of modernist prose-poetry and family photographs, are widely known and have been widely influential. They have, for example, influenced Leslie Marmon Silko, whose novel *Ceremony* (1977) first brought her to the attention of the dominant culture, and whose loosely autobiographical text, *Storyteller* (1981), includes not only photographs of the author and her family, but short stories and poems as well. At least one anthology of autobiographical statements by Native-American writers currently exists, and there are several collections of interviews with Native American artists which provide a good deal of autobiographical reflection. Most recently, the mixed-blood Chippewa novelist and poet Gerald Vizenor has produced a substantial body of autobiographical writing. . . .

With respect to the material I have selected and my arrangement of the volume [*Native American Autobiography: An Anthology*] as a whole, let me say the following. With the exception of Part One, I have generally followed a chronological order from the eighteenth century to the present. In parts Two and Three, which present Native American autobiographies of the eighteenth and nineteenth centuries, I have taken Native "response" to the white invaders—i.e., the decisions to become Christian or resisting Indians—as a useful ordering principle. My decision here may be criticized for ethnocentrism, since, even though the response is *Indian,* it is the Euramerican invaders who are represented as acting, with Native peoples re-acting. The only answer to such a charge is that history did, in fact, happen this way. From perhaps the sixteenth century in the Southwest, and from early in the seventeenth century on the East Coast, in the Mid-Atlantic and the Southeast, Native Americans had to factor into their lives the presence and pressures of an increasingly numerous, highly aggressive group of new arrivals. This is not to say that Native people stopped doing most of what they had always done, or that they adopted a new center to their lives. It is to say that for many of the Native persons who came to the autobiographical project, their lives could not be recounted independently of some relation-reaction to the encroaching whites. (The exceptions to this generalization have their life stories grouped in Part One, "Traditional Lives," about which I shall have more to say below.) In the excerpts both from the converts' and the combatants' life histories, I have tried to present, in whatever measure possible, some sense of both the ongoing, uninterrupted quality of these lives and the temporally specific, new, and unprecedented reactiveness of these lives.

For all that I have taken acceptance or rejection of Christianity and Euramerican "civilization" as providing useful distinctions among eighteenth- and nineteenth-century Native American autobiographies, it is hardly the case that these categories account for all the Indian lives written during this period. Paul Cuffe's brief autobiography (1839), for example, tells the story of a part-black, part-Indian seaman who shows no particular interest in Christianity, and active resistance to white dominance in Cuffe's New York of the 1830s was altogether a thing of the past. Something similar would be true for the Seneca Chainbreaker, also known as Governor Blacksnake, whom I have mentioned above: his life could not, no more than Paul Cuffe's, easily be thematized in terms of a resistance to or acceptance of Christianity and "civilization." We could also say much the same sort of thing of Okah Tubbee, part black and part Choctaw, whose extraordinary story of his life in Mississippi was published in 1848.

With regard to those many Native American autobiographers for whom my Christian/resisting distinction accounts relatively well, it should not be thought that either acceptance or resistance can directly be translated into some version of treason or heroism. While an older climate of opinion would have approved the converts and scorned or pitied the traditionalists, it is more likely, these days, that the reader's sympathies will lie with the resisters rather than with the Christian Indians. Such good/bad or hero/traitor judgments will do no service to the particular persons and texts involved, regardless of the criteria for "goodness," "heroism," or their presumed antitheses.

William Apess, for example, while a passionate convert to Methodism, was equally passionate as an activist for Native American rights, and in his denunciation of racism in all its forms. Along with his autobiographical texts, he published a "Eulogy on King Philip," which named this warrior chief of the Pequots the greatest man that America ever produced. In a later day, Charles Alexander Eastman, a university and medical school graduate and youthful practicioner ministering to the Lakota at Wounded Knee, for all his movement "from the deep woods to civilization," fought tirelessly for the recognition of the worth of traditional Native American values. His autobiographies are structured in a manner easily recognizable to Euramericans as rags-to-riches success stories of the type frequently associated with the name of Horatio Alger, but they are equally structured (if perhaps more loosely and less recognizably) according to a fairly widespread Native use of what Robin McGrath, in her comments on Inuit Eskimo autobiography, refers to as "a sort of male Cinderella."[6] This figure is represented by "the orphan boy Kaujjarkuk" among the Inuit and by other traditionally known protagonists among other Native peoples. Eastman's "baby name" in Lakota (Sioux) was Hakada, "the pitiful last [of five children]." From the victory at lacrosse that won him the name of Ohiyesa, "the winner," to his success as a kind of young warrior in the white man's world, Eastman's narrative of his rise to prominence has traditional Native as well as Euramerican models.

This may also be the place to say that the reader should not assume that persons named "Wooden Leg" or "Black Elk" are somehow "more Indian" or "authentic" than persons named "William Apess," "Charles Alexander Eastman," or "Maria Chona." Eastman, as I have just noted, was also known as "Ohiyesa," although he did not publish under that name—as Zitkala Sa was also Gertrude Bonnin, or, indeed, the great Sequoyah, inventor of the Cherokee syllabary, was also George Guess, and as the Paiute Wovoka, initiator of the Ghost Dance religion, was also Jack Wilson. We need to recall that the Spanish in the Southwest tended to bestow names familiar to them, names, for example, like Maria Chona, rather than—as the English did at least sometimes—to translate names from the Indian, e.g., "Chainbreaker" or "Black Hawk."

Once the West was "won," and the "frontier" closed, Indian acceptance or rejection of "civilization" was no longer an issue of historical concern for Americans; rather, the only issue seemed to be whether the Indian would "vanish" or survive. For the American Indian to survive, it was assumed that he or she would have to become the Indian-American, and, like other hyphenate Americans (Italian-American, Chinese-American, etc.), be melted into general Christian, bourgeois, capitalist citizenship. Government policy toward Native people in this period was founded on the Dawes or General Allotment Act of 1887, which sought to destroy tribal culture by an attack on the tribally (e.g., communally, "communistically") held landbase. The project was, in many ways, a continuation of the effort, in a phrase of Captain Richard Pratt, founder of the Carlisle Indian school, to "Kill the Indian and Save the Man." The autobiographical texts in Part Four of the anthology, "The Closed Frontier," provide personal responses to this exceedingly difficult—some have called it "transitional"—time for Native American people.

One response to the generally accepted notion that the Indian as Indian could not survive was what came to be called "salvage anthropology," a determined effort on the part of professional anthropologists to document the record of cultures presumably slated for oblivion. This led to those Indian autobiographies I have grouped under the heading for Part Five [of *Native American Autobiography*], "The Anthropologists' Indians." Here, again, it needs to be said that such a phrase is not meant to imply in any way that the Native people who complied with the anthropologists' request to "tell the story of their life" somehow betrayed themselves or their culture, yielding themselves up to alien purposes. To the contrary, the more these matters have been studied of late, the more it has become apparent that the Native subjects of the anthropologists' life histories had their own purposes for engaging in the autobiographical project; they "used" the anthropologists to the same or even greater extent than the anthropologists "used" them.

While the professional anthropologists were interested in Indians as the embodiment of a particular culture, there remained, as I have said, a number of amateurs who were still interested in those surviving Native people who had, indeed, made "history." Their labors resulted in the composite composition of such Indian autobiographies as those of Yellow Wolf, Wooden Leg, and Geronimo, among many others. Although the "resisting Indians" had resisted somewhere between 1832 and 1890, many accounts of their resistance did not appear until the 1930s, a period marked by intense concern to overturn the materially and culturally destructive Dawes Act. The Merriam Report of 1928 severely criticized federal Indian policy, and, upon Franklin Roosevelt's election to the presidency, major changes were instituted. Roosevelt's appointment of John Collier, a strong and knowledgeable admirer of Native American cultures, led to the passage in 1934 of the Wheeler-Howard Act, (also called the Indian Reorganization Act), which gave Native Americans an opportunity to decide for themselves how they would live. Their decision, unfortunately, had to be made known to the federal government by parliamentary means that were untraditional, and, indeed, to many Native people repugnant; nonetheless, for all its defects, Wheeler-Howard was a clear admission on the part of the federal government of the worth and potential viability of Native cultures. . . .

Notes

[1] Lawrence Watson and Maria Barbara Watson-Franke, *Interpreting Life Histories* (New Brunswick, NJ: Rutgers Univ. Press, 1985), p. 2.

[2] *Chainbreaker: The Revolutionary War Memoirs of Governor Blacksnake,* as told to Benjamin Williams (Lincoln: Univ. of Nebraska Press, 1989), p. 210.

[3] *The Autobiography of a Winnebago Indian* (New York: Dover, 1963), p. 2.

[4] Franz Boas, "Recent Anthropology II," *Science* 98 (1943): 335. . . .

[6] Robin McGrath, "Oral Influences in Contemporary Inuit Literature," in *The Native in Literature: Canadian and Comparative Perspectives,* ed. Thomas King, Cheryl Calver, and Helen Hoy (Oakville, Ontario: ECW Press, 1987), p. 161.

PROBLEMS OF AUTHORSHIP

Donald Jackson (essay date 1955)

SOURCE: An introduction to *Black Hawk*, edited by Donald Jackson, University of Illinois Press, 1964, pp. 1-40.

[*In the following excerpt, originally written in 1955, Jackson examines the complex issue of the authenticity of Black Hawk's memoirs.*]

Since the first appearance of the autobiography [*Life of Ma-ka-tai-me-she-kia-kiak, or Black Hawk*] in 1833, its accuracy, authenticity, and style have been both praised and damned. The fault that critics find with it is usually expressed in one or more of these comments: Black Hawk didn't dictate it; the facts are garbled; no Indian would talk that way; no Indian would ever think of dictating his life story; LeClaire, the interpreter, was an unreliable halfbreed.

The conflicting judgments can be shown best by quotation. The *North American Review,* January, 1835, ran a review of the book which contained this passage on pp. 69-70:

> It is almost the only one we have ever read, in which we feel perfect confidence, that the author sincerely believes that every thing he has set down is the truth, the whole truth, and nothing but the truth. That it is the *bona fide* work of Black Hawk, we have the respectable testimony of Antoine Le Clair, the government interpreter for the Sacs and Foxes, and what (as we have not the honor of being acquainted with that gentleman,) we deem more conclusive, the intrinsic evidence of the work itself. We will venture to affirm, and (having long dwelt among the aborigines, we conceive ourself entitled to do so,) that no one but a Sac Indian could have written or dictated such a composition. No white man, however great his ability may be, could have executed a work so thoroughly and truly Indian. Many of the facts therein contained are, moreover, known to us to be true, and of many others we have the testimony of the oral tradition of the country. We think, therefore, we may say that the authenticity of the work is unquestionable. . . . The only drawback upon our credence is the intermixture of courtly phrases, and the figures of speech, which our novelists are so fond of putting into the mouths of Indians. These are, doubtless, to be attributed to the bad taste of Black Hawk's amanuensis.

A contrary opinion appeared in 1854 when ex-Governor Thomas Ford published his *History of Illinois*. In a note on p. 110, referring to the autobiography, he said:

> This work has misled many. Black Hawk knew but little, if anything, about it. In point of fact, it was got up from the statements of Mr. Antoine Le Clere and Col. Davenport, and was written by a printer, and was never intended for anything but a catchpenny publication. Mr. Le Clere was a half-breed Indian interpreter. . . .

More recent critics have included the government attorneys participating in hearings before the Indian Claims Commission in Washington, August, 1953. They argued that the Sauk and Fox, seeking payment for lands taken from them in 1804, were basing some of their testimony upon statements in the Black Hawk autobiography—a book which history had already discredited.[43]

Skepticism such as this is understandable when one considers the complicated way in which the book was created. According to its proprietors it was dictated by Black Hawk, translated into English by the interpreter, and put into manuscript form by its editor. The difficulties of thus getting the revelations of an Indian into print, with faithfulness to fact and style, are apparent.

Antoine LeClaire said that Black Hawk approached him in August, 1833, with the desire to tell his life story. It is quite likely that he was given the idea while touring in the East. If Black Hawk were to make such a tour today, dozens of well-wishers would hasten to tell him, "You ought to write all this down and send it in." Undoubtedly he heard the same advice in 1833. And Colonel Thomas McKenney, interviewing him in Philadelphia, may also have suggested it to him. Although LeClaire spoke English (with a French accent) he was not a trained writer, and so he turned to John B. Patterson, a young newspaper editor, for help in getting the narrative into manuscript form. Both men swore that the final manuscript was a true account of what Black Hawk told them.

Doubters persisted. When Thomas Ford published his deprecating statement many years later, Patterson was publisher of an Illinois newspaper, the *Oquawka Spectator*. A short time after the Ford history appeared, Patterson attacked it in the pages of the *Spectator*. He called the autobiography a literal translation of Black Hawk's own statements and said he wondered if Ford had ever seen a copy of the book.[44]

Since there are no known documents by which the authenticity of the work can be established, except the signed statements of LeClaire and Patterson, much depends upon an evaluation of those men.

Ford's statement that LeClaire was a halfbreed is true; but the implication that he was therefore untrustworthy or incompetent is belied by LeClaire's record. He was born in 1797, the son of a French-Canadian father and a Potawatomi mother. Under the sponsorship of William Clark he learned English and, allegedly, more than a dozen Indian languages, and in 1818 he was employed at Fort Armstrong as an interpreter. He served in this capacity for many years, became well known to every Indian in the area, and signed his name as interpreter to eleven treaties. In the vital treaty of September, 1832, at the close of the Black Hawk War, the Indians insisted that LeClaire be given two sections of land as a reward for faithful service. To this request General Scott replied, "It is with much pleasure that we agree to the reservation for the benefit of your faithful Interpreter. We believe that he has been faithful to both sides, to the Americans as well as to the Sac and Fox nation."[45]

LeClaire prospered with his land and with his trading business; at one time in later life he was worth half a million dollars. He was one of the founders of Davenport, Iowa, and his portrait appeared on the first five-dollar bill, authorized in 1858, for issuance by the Iowa State Bank.[46]

Patterson, born in 1806, had come to the frontier from Virginia in 1832 to visit relatives. When the war with Black Hawk began, and the publisher of the Galena newspaper, the *Galenian,* went off to join the troops, Patterson took charge. He was sworn into service as a militiaman but not as a combatant; he was detailed as regimental printer to Colonel James Strode's regiment. After the war he traded with the Indians, opened a retail store in Oquawka (south of Rock Island in Henderson County), and finally began his own newspaper in 1848. With his son, E. N. H. Patterson, he published the *Spectator* for more than forty years.[47]

In phrasing Black Hawk's story, young Patterson no doubt felt that he was conforming to the best traditions of frontier journalism. Simplicity of style had not yet become a desirable attribute in the newspaper world; a noble Indian deserved noble prose. As a result we find Black Hawk talking of "the vicissitudes of war," and using such poetic words as "whilst," "thither," and "o'er." Patterson emphasized awkwardly humorous passages with exclamation marks. He retained certain Indian terms for a picturesque touch, and so we find Black Hawk referring to President Jackson's "wigwam," and calling newspaper editors "village criers."

To evaluate the autobiography properly we must take care to distinguish between *accuracy* and *authenticity*. The accuracy we may test by checking with contemporary documents; the authenticity—the genuineness of the book as an utterance of Black Hawk—is harder to determine.

There are inaccuracies throughout the book, but they are not basic. If Black Hawk dictated the story, the errors may be attributed to his understandable bias, his failing memory, and the involved procedure by which his words reached the printed page. Under these circumstances it is surprising that the book is so accurate.

But now we must ponder the matter of authenticity. Both LeClaire and Patterson declared, in the 1833 edition, that the book was a true record. Patterson reaffirmed this in his blast at Ford and again in the appendix to his 1882 edition. When he reissued the book in 1882, nearly fifty years after its original publication, Patterson wrote on p. 178: "After we had finished his autobiography the interpreter read it over to him carefully, and explained it thoroughly, so that he might make any needed corrections, by adding to, or taking from the narrations; but he did not desire to change it in any material manner."

Judge James Hall, writing in *History of the Indian Tribes* a few years after the autobiography appeared, said he knew that Black Hawk had acknowledged it as authentic. Hall was a reputable writer who had met and talked with Black Hawk, was acquainted with LeClaire and probably Patterson, and had no reason to misrepresent the situation.

If we wish to doubt the validity of the work, there is a document which could provide a foundation for our suspicions. The files of the Illinois State Historical Library contain a report by Major John Dement, written after the war, giving his own account of the battle at Kellogg's Grove. On the last page is a note by Dement, dated December 16, 1833, saying, "The account here with forwarded is a copy on [of] an account furnished the publisher of Black Hawk's Biography." This tells us little, for if Patterson had wished to concoct an account of the war he could have turned to the files of his own *Galenian,* where most of the action was reported in detail. There is nothing in Black Hawk's account to show that it is based on Dement's.

The text of Black Hawk's story as it appears in the following pages is a literal reprint of the 1833 edition. If we had only this edition and its subsequent reissues to consider, and if we could develop nothing more questionable than Major Dement's note, we could feel rather safe about the authenticity of the autobiography. But we must also deal with the 1882 edition.

When Patterson, as an old man, published his revised edition of the book, he made substantial changes in the wording of many passages and he introduced new material—attributing it to Black Hawk. The differing language of the two editions shows that Patterson succeeded in making Black Hawk sound even less aboriginal in 1882 then he had in 1833. Here are some typical changes:

1833 edition	1882 edition
. . . by the annihilation, if possible, of all their race.	. . . by the utter annihilation, if possible, of the last remnant of their tribe.
He gave us a variety of presents, and plenty of provisions.	He gave us a great variety of presents, and an abundance of provisions.
I paid several visits to Fort Armstrong during the summer, and was always well treated.	I paid several visits to Fort Armstrong, at Rock Island, during the summer, and was always well received by the gentlemanly officers stationed there, who were distinguished for their bravery, and they never trampled upon an enemy's rights.

These are unimportant changes from the standpoint of accuracy, though the last one casts doubt upon Patterson's claim that the book is a "literal translation" of Black Hawk's words. They are not nearly as significant as the completely new portions that Patterson added. The new material includes (1) a tale about Elijah Kilbourn, allegedly captured by Black Hawk and forced to live with the Sauk for three years, then recaptured during the Black Hawk War; (2) a paragraph about Black Hawk's "watch tower" on the Mississippi; (3) a legend about a pair of Indian lovers buried beneath a rock slide; (4) a passage about the persons who accompanied Black Hawk on his trip to the East, containing errors of fact; (5) a verbatim account of a speech made in honor of Black Hawk by John A. Graham, in New York.

In weaving this new material into the text, Patterson made no attempt to indicate that it was new or that it was never related by Black Hawk. When referring to the Kilbourn affair in his commentary on the war, p. 158, he said, "Mr. K. is the man Black Hawk *makes mention of* in his narrative as having been taken captive during our last war with Great Britain, and by him adopted into the Sac tribe; and again taken prisoner by three of his braves at the battle of Sycamore creek." [Italics added.]

If Patterson altered Black Hawk's story in the 1882 edition, must we assume that he did so forty-nine years earlier in the 1833 edition? Not necessarily. The Patterson of 1882, to whom the Black Hawk period was a fading memory, certainly must have viewed the book differently than he had as a young printer working closely with LeClaire and Black Hawk. He was probably more concerned in 1882 with telling a story than with preserving a document of American history; and his two associates were not there to confirm or deny. If we are to evaluate Black Hawk's story properly, we must disregard the 1882 edition and stick with the 1833 edition, which, despite the intrusive hands of interpreter and editor, is basically a tale told by an Indian from an Indian point of view.

Like much Americana, it is a tragic tale, for tragedy and inequity are certain in the re-peopling of a continent. Black Hawk's seventy-year lifetime was one of struggle and change—from his early battles with the Osage to his last miserable flight before an American army. He saw Spanish rule give way to American rule, and the westward press of settlers that resulted. He saw America and Great Britain involved in a disgraceful war, and he fought on the British side until he grew tired of it. When he drew his mark on the white man's treaty papers, it was always with the fear that the covenants would not hold.

Black Hawk was never a great Indian statesman like Tecumseh or a persuasive orator like Keokuk. He was not a hereditary chief or a medicine man. He was only a stubborn warrior brooding upon the certainty that his people must fight to survive.

The Indians used to say that a white settlement was like a spot of raccoon grease on a new blanket. When you first saw the tiny stain you did not realize how wide and how fast it would spread. Black Hawk's story is the narrative of a man who saw the vast stain of American settlement widening across the Midwest, darkening all the lands of his ancestors. Keokuk was a smooth talker and a politician who planned to co-exist with the Americans; Black Hawk was a bull-headed fighter who chose a bitter last stand against extinction. And both men went down, for their day in history had passed.

Abbreviations

IHI—Illinois State Historical Library Black. Hawk War collection of about 1,100 documents, augmented by 900 or more in photostat and microfilm from the National Archives.

ICC—Indian Claims Commission. Testimony, Sac and Fox Tribe of Oklahoma, *et al.,* v. United States, Docket 83, 1953. Mimeographed copy in the Illinois State Historical Library.

NA—National Archives. Material found in the following files:

AGO—Adjutant General's Office

OIA—Office of Indian Affairs

SW—Office of the Secretary of War

Works cited

Black Hawk. *Life of Ma-ka-tai-me-she-kia-kiak or Black Hawk.* Cincinnati, 1833. Reissued in Boston, 1834 (two editions); London, 1836; Cooperstown, 1842; Leeuwarden, Netherlands (trans.), 1847; Chicago, 1916; Iowa City, 1932.

———. *Autobiography of Ma-ka-tai-me-she-kia-kiak, or Black Hawk.* Oquawka, Ill., 1882. Reissued in Rock Island, Ill., 1912.

Ford, Thomas. *A History of Illinois.* Chicago, 1854.

"Life of Black Hawk," a review in *North American Review,* 40 (1835) 68-87.

"Life of Ma-ka-tai-me-she-kia-kiak, or Black Hawk," a review in *American Quarterly Review,* 35 (1834) 426-48.

McKenney, Thomas L., and James Hall. *History of the Indian Tribes of North America.* 3 vols. Philadelphia, 1836-44. The edition cited was edited by Frederick Webb Hodge, 3 vols., published in Edinburgh, 1933-34.

Snyder, Charles. "Antoine LeClaire, the First Proprietor of Davenport," *Annals of Iowa,* 3rd ser., 23 (1941-42) 79-117.

Notes

[43] Mimeographed testimony, Sac and Fox Indian Tribes of Oklahoma vs. U. S., Docket 83, 1953, before the Indian Claims Commission. Copy in the Illinois State Historical Library. Cited hereafter as ICC.

[44] Issue of Jan. 23, 1855.

[45] Minutes of the first conference held between U. S. representatives and the Indians at Rock Island, Sept. 19, 1832. Records of the U. S. Senate, 22nd Cong., NA. Seen in ICC as Petitioners' Exhibit 254.

[46] LeClaire was a tremendous man, reportedly weighing 385 pounds in 1844, but his size did not seem to hinder his movement about the country on horseback or in carriages. Most of the biographical data about him in the above paragraphs is from Synder, 79-117.

[47] See an account of Patterson's life in *History of Mercer and Henderson Counties* (Chicago, 1882, p. 922).

Arnold Krupat (essay date 1985)

SOURCE: "Indian Autobiography: Origins, Type, and Function," in *For Those Who Come After: A Study of Native American Autobiography,* The University of California Press, 1985, pp. 28-53.

[*In the following essay, Krupat defines Native American autobiography as "original bicultural composite composition"—texts written during the transition from oral to written literature, and produced through the collaboration of members of two distinct cultures—in order to distinguish these works from traditional Western autobiography.*]

The group of texts I propose to call Indian autobiographies and to treat as a literary genre has been almost entirely ignored by students of American literature—who have, otherwise, been quite interested in the autobiography as literature. This may be because, as already noted, these particular autobiographies were explicitly presented by the whites who wrote them down and published them as historical or ethnographic documents. Perhaps, too, their neglect results from the fact that Indian autobiographies were indeed written by whites, not by the Indians of whose lives they speak; thus, no Indian autobiography, strictly considered, conforms to the definition of autobiography "we all know," as James Cox states it, "a narrative of a person's life written by himself."[1]

"View of Black Hawk Pointe," a lithograph by J. E. Dillingham.

"Autobiography" as a particular form of self-written life is a European invention of comparatively recent date. Southey is credited with coining the word in English in 1809, and the earliest American book title I have discovered to use it is from 1832. Great labor has recently been expended in the effort to define "autobiography" as a genre. For our purposes, we may note only that the autobiographical project, as we usually understand it, is marked by egocentric individualism, historicism, and writing. These are all present in European and Euramerican culture after the revolutionary last quarter of the eighteenth century. But none has ever characterized the native cultures of the present-day United States.

Although the Indians' sense of personal freedom, worth, and responsibility became legendary, the "autonomy of the [male] individual" was always subordinated to communal and collective requirements.[2] That egocentric individualism associated with the names of Byron or Rousseau, the cultivation of originality and differentness, was never legitimated by native cultures, to which celebration of the hero-as-solitary would have been incomprehensible.

Neither is the post-Napoleonic sense of progressive, linear history at all like the historical sense found among

Indian cultures. (A strict account would require noting many variations.) The Sioux have a well-known proverb to the effect that "A people without history is like wind on the buffalo grass." But the understanding of "history" at issue here, if European analogues may be invoked, is more nearly Hellenic than Hebraic. Or, somewhat more precisely, history is not evolutionary, teleological, or progressive. Means for preserving tribal memory were developed in all "culture areas," but these did not privilege the dimensions of causality and uniqueness which mark the modern forms of Euramerican historicism.

Further, while no culture is possible without writing in some very broad sense, no Indian culture developed the phonetic alphabet which Lewis Henry Morgan isolated as the distinctive feature of "civilized" culture. Patterns worked in wampum belts, tattoos, pictographs painted on animal skins or in sand may all be considered forms of "writing." But the black-on-white which distinguishes scription from diction for the Euramerican, the letter and the book, were not found among native cultures in the precontact period. Even later—after John Eliot had transcribed the Bible into a Massachusetts dialect of the Algonquian language in the seventeenth century; after Sequoyah, in the early nineteenth century, had devised a Cherokee syllabary; or the Dakota language, by the late nineteenth century, had become available for inscription—the presence of the grapheme still signified for the Indian the cultural other, the track of the Indo-European snake in the American garden.

Strictly speaking, therefore, Indian autobiography is a contradiction in terms. Indian autobiographies are collaborative efforts, jointly produced by some white who translates, transcribes, compiles, edits, interprets, polishes, and ultimately determines the form of the text in writing, and by an Indian who is its subject and whose life becomes the content of the "autobiography" whose title may bear his name.

I may now state the principle constituting the Indian autobiography as a genre as the principle of *original bicultural composite composition*. I mean thus to distinguish Indian autobiographies from autobiographies by "civilized" or christianized Indians whose texts originate with them and contain, inevitably, a bicultural element, yet are not compositely produced. I mean, as well, to distinguish Indian autobiographies from traditional Native American literature in textual form in which, although there is bicultural composite composition, there is no question of personal origination. Unlike traditional Native literature, the Indian autobiography has no prior model in the collective practice of tribal cultures.

Although there will always be debatable cases (e.g., I would class the many "as-told-to" autobiographies of Indians which have appeared in the twentieth century among autobiographies-by-Indians rather than Indian autobiographies because their subjects' competence in written English allows them to take responsibility for the form of the work to a degree impossible for most Native American subjects of Indian autobiography: but this is, to be sure, a judgment of degree, not kind), it should be possible to demonstrate this particular mode of production for any text claimed for the genre. In this respect, I follow a structural or "syntactic" definition of genre, as in the following formulation of Tzvetan Todorov: "When we examine works of literature from the perspective of genre, we engage in a very particular enterprise: we discover a principle operative in a number of texts, rather than what is specific about each of them."[3] But this turns us back to the issue with which we began: to what extent is it responsible to treat works presented as contributions to history and ethnography as works of literature?

It is surely true that all texts, social-scientific as well as literary, share a narrative dimension, and that no text can evade the orders of language to achieve an innocent or neutral representation of "the order of things." Yet social-scientific and literary texts each have a different epistemological status, the one being bound by the real, the other free of it, at least to the extent it may willfully transform or distort the real. This difference informs the different natures of the scientific and the literary reading as well. The scientific reading is impelled by the desire to foreground the real, to pass as rapidly as possible beyond the orders of the signifier to an engagement with the real-as-signified. (This last, to be sure, is a problematic category: the real need not be taken as transcendental ground but as the ultimate horizon of the text, as history in a specifically Marxian sense, or as the world beyond the text.) The justification for a scientific reading—the condition for cognitive responsibility—typically refers to authorial intention as this is conveyed not so much (or only) through the biography of the author as through his or her text's relation to those discursive rules which define scientific texts.

The decision to read texts discursively marked as scientific in a literary way may also be responsible, however. In such a case we must require the instantiation of sufficient reasons to override the authorial/discursive markings. I would justify a literary reading for Indian autobiographies by reference to the principle of original bicultural composite composition, which constitutes them as a genre of writing. Their particular mode of production means that in Indian autobiographies there is, in Jakobsonian terms, an actual doubling of the sender and of the cultural code which complicates the signifier in precisely historical and demonstrable ways. A literary reading, as I have said, foregrounds not the real-signified but the signifier and the formal signifying practices of the text. Because these practices are determined not only by language but by history, in particular the relations between the general mode of production and the literary mode of production, it should be clear that the scientific and the literary reading differ in no way absolutely but only in their emphases. Given the presence of two persons, two cultures, two modes of production, as well as two languages at work in the formation of the Indian autobiography, it seems reasonable to examine the signifier and the text's signifying practices in some detail, regardless of whether—and how—one may seek passage to the world beyond the text.

The principle of original bicultural composite composition, which provides the key to the Indian autobiography's discursive type, provides as well the key to its discursive function, its purposive dimension as an act of power and will. For to see the Indian autobiography as a ground on which two cultures meet is to see it as the textual equivalent of the frontier. Here, the frontier does not only mean the furthest line of points to which "civilization" has extended itself; rather, to adopt the systemic view of the contemporary ethnohistorian, the frontier also signifies "the reciprocal relationship between two cultures in contact."[4] But, however much it may have been "reciprocal," the "relationship" between Native Americans and Euramericans was never—with the exception, perhaps, of moments during the eighteenth century—one between equals. For the whites, the advance of the frontier always meant domination and appropriation, and the movement westward was achieved not only with the power of the sword but of the pen as well. To win the continent required not only troops and technology but a discourse of what Foucault would call *assujettissement,* of—in Edward Said's description—"the subjugation of individuals in societies" (or of whole societies) "to some suprapersonal discipline or authority."[5]

During the nineteenth century, part of that discipline was the idea of progressive history as a "scientific" determinism or "law" which authorized the doctrine of cultural evolution, the belief that "civilization" must everywhere replace "savagery." This was the official sanction for the removal of the eastern tribes west of the Mississippi in the 1830s as it was the unofficial sanction for the enormous body of writing about Indians that appeared in these same years. Along with novels, poems, plays, and "histories" of Indians, the decade of Indian Removal saw the production of a new form of writing "by" as well as about Indians, the Indian autobiography. Following native defeat in the Black Hawk War, J. B. Patterson, in 1833, published the first Indian autobiography, the *Life of Ma-Ka-tai-me-she-kia-kiak or Black Hawk.* As Black Hawk had submitted to Euramerican military and political forms, so he now submitted to Euramerican discursive form. But the form of writing offered to this Indian who could not write was not the eighteenth-century "life-and-times" biography; instead, it was the newer form of personal history, the autobiography. Produced as an acknowledgement of Indian defeat, in the ideological service of progressive expansionism, the book made by Patterson and Black Hawk, by admitting an Indian to the ranks of the self-represented, also questioned progressivist expansionism. For the production of an Indian's own statement of his inevitable disappearance required that the Indian be represented as speaking in his own voice. Unlike Indian biographies, Indian autobiographies require contact with living Indians, for it is the central convention of autobiography that the subject speaks for himself. And it is in its presentation of an Indian voice not as vanished and silent, but as still living and able to be heard that the oppositional potential of Indian autobiography resides.

During the first stages of the "invasion of America," the East itself was West, and the towns of the "frontier" were named "Plimoth," Jamestown, and Boston.[6] Contact between the Euramerican invader-settlers and Native Americans led to conflict; the most common "reciprocal relationships" were conquest and captivity, and it should come as no surprise that the first two indigenous forms of history-writing developed in the New World were the Indian War Narrative and the Indian Captivity Narrative.

Recognizing the insatiable colonial appetite for land, Indians—for the most part—chose the "wrong" side in the American Revolution and suffered the consequences of British defeat. By the end of the eighteenth century, the American invasion had pushed forward into the Ohio valley and Daniel Boone's "dark and bloody ground" of "Kentucke" where the by-now traditional frontier relations of battle and bondage were reestablished. Indians fought Americans once more in 1812 and once more lost. After the Treaty of Ghent in 1815, the natives could no longer hope for European support to check the further advance of the new American nation. Jackson's election to the presidency, signaling the rise of the West, signaled also the fall of the red man, for Indian Removal now became a national, not merely a local, priority.

"Indian-haters" avid to appropriate native holdings, and "Indian-lovers" avid to protect the "noble" Red Man from white drink, disease, and depredation joined in supporting the Indian Removal Bill which, after fierce debate in Congress, was passed into law on 28 May 1830. The opposition included Davey Crockett, a western rival of Jackson, and John Quincy Adams, quintessential easterner. For the decade of the 1830s, response to the plight of the Indian was of paramount importance to American thought about history and science.

The forcible removal of the eastern tribes into the "Great American Desert" west of the Mississippi was generally viewed—sadly or gladly—as the inevitable consequence of the advance of civilization. Not white cupidity, but the "scientific law" of cultural evolution, popularly equated with the "doctrine of progress," determined the disappearance of the natives, giving an odor of sanctity to the most violent acts of exploitation and providing the ideological authorization for the wholesale destruction of Native cultures.

Or, rather, for the accession of "nature" to "culture." For, as Roy Harvey Pearce showed some time ago, in nineteenth-century American discourse, Indian "savages" had no "culture." The "customs" of "savagery" could not be dignified as a different form of culture from Euramerican "civilization," nor even a different stage of culture; rather, they were to be seen as the antithesis of culture, its zero degree.[7] In the seventies and eighties after Morgan had defined "savagery" as an evolutionary stage prior to "barbarism" (the category into which most American Indians actually fell), which was itself but a stage prior to "civilization," Friends of the Indian succeeded in their fight to declare the Indian indeed civilizable. But for the 1830s and 1840s, the "savage" remained the one who could never be civilized. As the "Jew" is to the anti-Semite, in Sartre's analysis, or the Oriental to the European in Edward Said's analysis, so was the "savage" to the "civilized" American of the nineteenth century the term for radical alterity, a condition of being which no act could contradict.

Because the Indian "savage" could not himself be "civilized," "civilization" could not help but supplant him. The "aborigines," "Persons of little worth found cumbering the soil," in Ambrose Bierce's unsentimental definition, "soon cease to cumber; they fertilize."[8] As American troops removed Indians to the West in the 1830s, a very considerable interest in this material for fertilizer developed, and a great deal of writing about the "vanishing American" began to appear. New Captivity Narratives, authentic and apocryphal, were rushed to press while older Captivities, along with Indian War Narratives, were reprinted. Cooper's fiction reached the height of its popularity in this period, and gave voice to the typical eastern sadness at the passing of a primitive but noble race. Not sadness but satisfaction was the attitude more usual to the westerner (or southerner), and expressed in the Indian fiction of Robert Bird and William Gilmore Simms, novelists whose knowledge of Indians, unlike Cooper's, was derived not only from the library but from contact as well.

Painters as well as writers became Indian "historians," setting themselves the task of representing Indian life before it was gone forever. George Catlin, still the best known of the Indian-painters, left Pennsylvania for the West in 1830, the year of the Removal Act; his task, he wrote, was to rescue "from oblivion the looks and customs of the vanishing races of native man in America."[9] In every case, as A. D. Coleman has only recently written of the photographer Edward Curtis, a later "historian" of the still-vanishing Indian, all those who took the Indian as their subject sought "to document all aspects of a marvelous culture which was being inexorably destroyed, in such a way as to retain the spirit of the culture and keep it alive."[10] Only the spirit of Indian culture might be kept alive; no intervention in history was believed possible to save it materially from inexorable destruction. And even that spirit would have to be kept alive by those allied to its destroyers: for only they possessed the means of documentation and representation. The Indian himself did not paint things as they "really were"; the Indian could not write. His part was to pose—and disappear.

The West saw the destruction of the Indians not only as inevitable but also as just; but the East, which did not doubt the inevitability of it all, nonetheless questioned its justice. Considering the deeds of their own forebears, ministers in Boston protested Jackson's Indian policy, concerned that the "mistakes of the Puritan founders," their "historical blunders," not be repeated on the "frontier."[11] Urging that we learn from

the past, these easterners provided a powerful impetus for the writing of Puritan history. But there was other writing to be undertaken as well, "an act of mere justice to the fame and the memories of many wise, brilliant, brave and generous men—patriots, orators, warriors and statesmen,—who ruled over barbarian communities, and were indeed themselves barbarians," as B. B. Thatcher explained in the preface to his *Indian Biography* which, along with Samuel G. Drake's *Indian Biography,* was published in Boston in 1832. "We owe, and our Fathers owed, too much to the Indians . . . to deny them the poor restitution of historical justice at least," Thatcher continued, adding darkly, "however the issue may have been or may be with themselves."[12]

The form Thatcher and Drake chose for restitution was the "life-and-times" form of eighteenth-century biography. Their Indians are represented as eminent men in the neoclassic mold but they are not yet conceived of as heroes. Biography writing in the West, on the contrary, was very much engaged with the heroic and produced not only lives of that nearly legendary, Indian-like white hero, Daniel Boone, but, in time, the lives of Indians as well.

In view of Richard Slotkin's influential work on the Boone material which privileges the explanatory categories of myth and archetype, it seems important to point out that the search for an American hero was rooted not only in some universal human longing, but in some very specific nineteenth-century ideas about history, science, and law.[13] Interest in the *heldensleben* in mid-nineteenth-century America was spurred by a concern to discover an individual author of events and to locate historical beginnings—rather than absolute origins, in Said's useful distinction—in personal action. We need only think of Carlyle, the contemporary of these American hero-seekers, to recall how great an explanatory force the belief in "great men" once had. Carlyle's dictum that history is "the essence of innumerable biographies"—an opinion shared on these shores by Emerson and Thoreau—is the essence of the nineteenth-century romantic reaction against neoclassic Universal History which, as Louis Mink has written, simply "never made room for . . . the uniqueness, vividness, and intrinsic value of individuals."[14] What is curious to note is that the reaction against Universal History, as Mink further remarks, does not prevent its simultaneous survival in the guise of the doctrine of progress. In this context, autobiography, the self-written narrative of the "hero's" life, will become available both to support this "suprapersonal discipline" yet also potentially to oppose it.

For the decade of Indian Removal was also the decade when a conjunction of historicism and egocentric individualism first brought autobiography as a term and a type of writing to America. In Boston, in the same year Thatcher and Drake issued their Indian biographies, the seventeenth-century "personal narrative" of Thomas Sheperd was published as an "autobiography"; *The Autobiography of Thomas Sheperd, the Celebrated Minister of Cambridge, New England* is the first American book I have found to use the term *autobiography* in its title. The following year, Asa Greene became the first American to apply the term to a "narrative of [his] life written by himself," when he published, in New York, *A Yankee Among the Nullifiers, an Auto-Biography,* under the pseudonym Elnathan Elmwood.

Although Elnathan Elmwood has lapsed into obscurity, we still think of autobiography as a Yankee affair. Those we usually place in the great tradition of personal narrative or autobiography in America—Jonathan Edwards in the colonial period, Benjamin Franklin in the Revolutionary period, Henry Thoreau in the period preceding the Civil War—are all easterners. So, too, are Henry Adams, the next major figure in this tradition, and, to step into the twentieth century, Gertrude Stein as well. From the first days of settlement until the end of the nineteenth century, the American self tended to locate its peculiar national distinctiveness in relation to a perceived opposition between the European, the "man of culture," and the Indian, the "child of nature." And, for the writers I have named, the European polarity was decisive. The works of eastern autobiography from Edwards through Stein are old-world-oriented and self-consciously literary. (Edwards, Franklin, and Thoreau, however, wrote extensively about Indians.) These autobiographers were conscious of themselves as writers when it was writing that precisely distinguished the European "man of culture" from "nature's child," the Indian—who did not write. The classic eastern autobiographies include scenes of writing (and reading) as important to self-definition. Only with Thoreau, formed in the Jacksonian era of the rise of the West and intense concern with Indians, did the "natural" polarity enter into the autobiographical project. Thoreau's movement from the study to the woods and back was an exemplary journey as fact and as metaphor for Americans of the 1830s and 1840s. (It is interesting, too, to note that pencil-making and surveying were Thoreau's only ordinary sources of income after he stopped keeping school.)

But there is another tradition of autobiography in America for which the Indian polarity was definitive. In this tradition, we have the autobiographies of Daniel Boone, Davey Crockett, Kit Carson, Jim Beckwourth, and Sam Houston. Unlike Yankee autobiography, the western tradition is restless, mobile and, reflecting the split between "high" and "low" culture already hardening in the age of Jackson, explicitly anti-literary. The subjects of western autobiography are all "world-historical" chiefs whose public reputations, like that of Andrew Jackson himself, were first established by Indian-fighting. Yet these men, in comparison to the European or the American easterner, seemed themselves to be "Indians," men of action not letters, hunters and warriors, not preachers of farmers, neither book-keepers nor book-writers. Nearly or wholly illiterate, they rejected the fall into writing and civilization, and balked at cultivating either the field or the page. Defined by Indian War and voluntary or involuntary Indian Captivity, these western autobiographers did not settle down long enough to establish their texts in writing, which, as an act, they largely scorned. Invoking the "natural," oral tradition of the Indian, telling *coup* stories or tall tales, the western autobiographer lived his life apart from writing, going so far as to entrust its actual inscription to another.

Although the "real" Daniel Boone at least once carried a copy of *Gulliver* with him, as the story of the naming of Lulbegrud Creek attests, he was not, himself, interested in writing. If he kept notes for a story of his life, as he was urged, they have not survived. Fairly consistent in signing correspondence "your omble Sarvent," Boone, it would seem, attempted to pass "naturally" from diction to scription.[15] His was exactly the orthographical and grammatological theory Colonel David Crockett espoused in the preface to his autobiography: "I despise this way of spelling contrary to nature. And as for grammar, it's pretty much a thing of nothing at last, after all the fuss that's made about it."[16]

But even Crockett had to acknowledge, as Boone before him had done in collaborating with John Filson, that the book of a man's life cannot be made strictly according to "nature." In Louis Renza's phrase, "Autobiography . . . transforms empirical facts into *arti*-facts."[17] Thus the western autobiographer encountered a problem different from any faced by his eastern counterpart. For, when the eastern autobiographer looked to Europe for a model of the self, he also found a formal model for his book. But, if the western autobiographer, looking to the Indian, found a valuable experiential model, he found no textual model whatever. The solution to this problem turned out to be submission to varying degrees of collaborative composition, where the empirical, natural, and historical "facts" of a man's life were the contribution of the nominal subject of the autobiographical book, while its artifactuality, its grammar, and writing were the contribution of one accredited as the culture-bearer: the journalist-editor or, in Crockett's scornful term, the "critic . . . a sort of vermin," who was, finally, the book's author in the strictly etymological sense (*augere*) of one who augments as well as originates.[18]

Boone's "autobiography," the first of this western line, was written by John Filson, a Pennsylvania schoolmaster saturated in eighteenth-century biographical conventions. Crockett insisted of his "autobiography" that "the whole book is my own, and every sentiment and sentence in it." Yet he "would not be such a fool, or knave either, as to deny that I have had it hastily run over by a friend or so, and that some little alterations have been made in the spelling and grammar." Perhaps the book "is the worse of even that"; still, there is no avoiding "a little correcting of the spelling and the grammar to make them fit for use."[19] To make the book of Kit Carson's life "fit for use" took very nearly an absolute division of compositional labor, for Carson could neither read nor write. Approaching the Indian in incomprehensibility, Carson spoke a language "markedly" different, according to M. M. Quaife, "from ordinary literary English," and expressed his "sentiments" in a "patois" common to mountain men.[20] Sam Houston's autobiography required the mediation of C. E. Lester. When James Beckwourth, born of mixed black and white parentage, who rose to the status of War Chief of the Crow, returned to Euramerican ways and to autobiography, he required the aid of T. D. Bonner to write the book of his life.[21] Thus eastern Indian biography with its orientation to "historical justice" through the textual representation of individual Indian lives provided the motive force for Indian autobiography, while western autobiography with its discovery of composite authorship provided the solution to its formal problem.

After passage of the Indian Removal Act, William Hagan wrote:

> Most of the tribes were prevailed upon to remove by the routine methods of persuasion or bribery or threats, or some combination of these. The three exceptions were a band of confederated Sacs and Foxes, the Creeks, and the Seminoles. Back in 1804 the Sacs and Foxes had signed a treaty under suspicious circumstances at the request of Governor Harrison. It provided for a cession of their lands east of the Mississippi, but did not require removal until the line of settlement reached them. Most of the tribesmen were ignorant of the situation until in the late 1820's peremptory demands were made on them to move. Then a faction led by old war chief Black Hawk, who had opposed the Americans in the War of 1812 and had subsequently plagued government agents by his conservative policies, denied the validity of the 1804 treaty.[22]

Eventually, in April of 1832, the Black Hawk War broke out, a fifteen-week affair in which large numbers of Illinois militia (among them the young Abraham Lincoln), together with detachments of federal troops, decimated and demoralized Black Hawk's band sufficiently to induce the chief's surrender. Following months of imprisonment at Jefferson Barracks (where Catlin among others came to preserve him on canvas), Black Hawk was brought before his contemporary, the Great War Chief of the whites, "Old Hickory," Andrew Jackson. After their meeting, apparently unaware of the partial coincidence of their routes, the two warriors set out on a tour of the East where both Black Hawk and the president received, to borrow Davey Crockett's phrase, "much custom." Black Hawk was briefly detained at Fortress Monroe and then returned to his people on the Rock River. It was at this time, according to Antoine LeClair, the government interpreter for the Sacs and Foxes, that Black Hawk approached him and did "express a great desire to have a History of his Life written and published."[23]

Although he was highly regarded by both Indians and whites as an interpreter, and reputedly competent in some dozen Native languages, LeClair did not speak English as his own first language. For this (or some other) reason, he engaged the assistance of young J. B. Patterson, editor of the Galena, Illinois, *Galenian*. And it was Patterson, in the role of Black Hawk's editor and amenuensis, who actually wrote the history of Black Hawk's life.

According to LeClair and Patterson, Black Hawk dictated to LeClair who translated his words into English; these were then edited into final form by Patterson. In his 1882 reissue of the *Life*, Patterson wrote, "After we had finished his [Black Hawk's] autobiography the interpreter read it over to him carefully, and explained it thoroughly, so that he might make any needed corrections, by adding to, or taking from the narrations; he did not desire to change it in any material manner."[24] This was a recollection a full half century after the fact, however; but it is all we know of how the manuscript was actually produced. For, as Donald Jackson, Black Hawk's most recent editor, attests, "there are no known documents by which the authenticity of the work can be established."[25]

In a prefatory "Advertisement" from the "Editor," Patterson writes, "It is presumed no apology will be required for presenting to the public, the life of a Hero who has lately taken such high rank among the distinguished individuals of America." The first part of this is entirely conventional and parallels Thatcher's opening statement: "The Author does not propose an elaborate explanation or an apology of any kind, for the benefit of the following work."[26] But the proposal of Black Hawk's as a "Hero's" life goes beyond Thatcher whose Indians, "remarkable characters"—as his title page puts it—though they may have been, are not yet "heroes." Moreover, although they are "individuals who have been distinguished among the North American natives," this is not necessarily to give them "high rank among the distinguished individuals of America" as a whole. Patterson goes beyond Thatcher not only in permitting Black Hawk the context of heroism and national distinction but also in relinquishing his claim to the full authority of the "Author" for the more limited power of editorship. Thus on the title page of each Indian autobiography there appears that fraternal couple so frequently invoked by the American imagination, the White Man and the Indian—Natty Bumppo and Chingachgook, Ishmael and Queequeg, the Lone Ranger and Tonto—but with a difference. For the claim of Indian autobiography is that the white man is silent while the Indian, no longer a mute or monosyllabic figure, speaks for himself.

Patterson's relation to Black Hawk replicates Filson's relation to Boone, and it is indicative of the West's "literary reconciliation to identification with the Indian" that there is extended the graphological supplement, the distinctive property of "civilization," not only to the Indian-like white frontiersman but to Indian "nature" itself.[27] In this way, Black Hawk, no less than the great Boone himself, may speak his life in writing.

The formal similarity of western autobiography and Indian autobiography may be extended to a functional similarity as well—but only to a point. Both, that is, function to affirm the central authority of American progressivist ideology, offering testimony to the inevitable replacement of "savagery" by "civilization." Filson's Boone concludes his "autobiography," saying:

> . . . I now live in peace and safety, enjoying the sweets of liberty, and the bounties of Providence, with my once fellow-sufferers, in this delightful country, which I have seen purchased with a vast expence of blood and treasure, delighting in the prospect of its being, in a short time, one of the most opulent and powerful states on the continent of North-America; which with the love and gratitude of my country-men, I esteem a sufficient reward for all my toil and dangers.[28]

Boone's life and his book are evidence that the long knife and long rifle are adequate to the work of "civilization," driving the "savage" out and transforming the "wilderness" into "one of the most opulent and powerful states on the continent of North-America." Black Hawk concludes his "autobiography" with the assurance that "the white man will always be welcome in our village or camps, as a brother . . . and may the watch-word between Americans and Sacs and Foxes, ever be—'*Friendship*'!" (Jackson, *Black Hawk,* pp. 153-154). But these are not the words of a man basking in success and looking forward to glory; rather, as Black Hawk has announced in the dedication of his book to Brigadier General H. Atkinson, his "conqueror," they are the words of one who is "now an obscure member of a nation, that formerly honored and respected [his] opinions . . . [and one who hopes] you may never experience the humility that the power of the American government has reduced me to." Admitting "the power of the American government," Indian autobiography takes its place beside western autobiography in a discourse of *assujettissement,* the ideological authorization for displacement of the Native.

Whereas victory is the enabling condition of western autobiography, defeat is the enabling condition of Indian autobiography. The narrative of the life of the western hero follows the "emplotment" of American history as the nineteenth century conceived it, and is figured as "comedy," the just progression to a "happy ending" in which the red-skinned "blocking characters" are overcome. "The society emerging at the conclusion of comedy," as Northrop Frye has written, "represents . . . a kind of moral norm, or pragmatically free society."[29] And so it is in *The Autobiography of Daniel Boone.* Its structure is not only determined by the "facts" of Boone's life, nor even strictly—in Hayden White's terms—by the pregeneric figural preferences of John Filson, but, as well, by the authority and discipline of discourse. The narrative of the life of the Indian "hero" replicates the general ideology of the period formally by structuring that life as a story of decline and fall, or—apparently—as tragedy. (This gives us the curious paradox of *heldensleben* as prisoner-of-war narrative.) For it is only when the Indian subject of an autobiography acknowledges his defeat, when he becomes what Patterson calls a "State-prisoner," that he can appear as a "hero." Even as a "State-prisoner," Patterson writes in his "Advertisement," "in every situation [Black Hawk] is still the Chief of his Band [he has however been superseded by Keokuk], asserting their rights with dignity, fairness, and courage." Perhaps; yet it is only as a "State-prisoner" that he can assert anything at all, or be "allowed to make known to the world the injuries his people have received from the whites." Native American decline is the necessary condition for the comic ascent of Euramerican civilization, and it is by means of this particular structure—the apparent tragedy as actual comedy—that the silent, absent editor speaks his acceptance of progressivist ideology, confirming the inevitability of Indian defeat in the manner of western autobiography.

But Patterson's *Black Hawk* also strongly questions the justice of Indian defeat in the manner of eastern Indian biography. According to Patterson, Black Hawk "thinks justice is not done to himself or nation" in hitherto-published accounts of the War (although Black Hawk could not actually have read them), and part of the motive force behind the Black Hawk-(LeClair)-Patterson collaboration is the performance of an act of textual "justice." Patterson includes many instances of the "injuries" done to Black Hawk and his people, and, speaking in his own voice, he explicitly criticizes the Treaty of 1804. Patterson also draws back from full responsibility for anything in the book that may seem to the "whites" too strong in criticism of their behavior. The concluding paragraph of his "Advertisement" announces that "The Editor has written this work according to the dictation of Black Hawk, through the United States Interpreter, at the Sac and Fox Agency of Rock Island. He does not, therefore, consider himself responsible for any of the facts or views, contained in it."

Rather than weakening the oppositional force of the book, Patterson's disclaimer is, instead, the announcement of its formal expression. For the *Life* of Black Hawk is not a biography but an autobiography; if Patterson is not "responsible" for what Black Hawk says, then Black Hawk himself must be responsible. Here is the unprecedented instance of an Indian speaking for himself.

Unlike the eastern Indian-biographer, Patterson did not make his book from the safe distance of Boston or New York, nor was his subject the "life-and-times" of some bygone noble barbarian. Patterson came from Illinois, and he wrote from Rock Island only a year after the Black Hawk War. In just five more years, even a western Indian-biographer could echo Thatcher and the ministers of Boston on the Indians; in a biography of Black Hawk published in Cincinnati in 1838, Benjamin Drake wrote, "Have we not more frequently met [the Indians] in bad faith than in a Christian spirit?" And Drake accepted full responsibility for his book's purpose "to awaken the public mind to a sense of the wrongs inflicted on the Indians."[30]

I would not minimize the efforts of Samuel Drake, B. B. Thatcher, or Benjamin Drake to do "justice" to the Indian in writing. Yet unlike Patterson, these men adopted the biographical not the autobiographical form which, whatever its author's intentions, cannot help but function in support of the belief that the "savage" has no intelligible voice of his own, that the "civilized" man of letters must speak for him if he is to be heard at all. The Indian biographer, master of books and writing, required no contact with his subject; he had no need to enter into a reciprocal relationship with him. According to Samuel Drake, his *Indian Biography* takes "much of" its material "from manuscripts never before published"; its title page is adorned with a verse from Byron and, interestingly, a verse of Isaiah from what Drake calls the "Indian Bible," no native product but the white man's gift to the red.[31] Appropriately, Drake's book is published by Josiah Drake at the Antiquarian Bookstore, first established in 1830, the year of the Indian Removal Bill. Thatcher, too, is almost entirely indebted to the "archive" for his work, like Drake exploiting the resources of the Antiquarian Bookstore as well as materials from the Harvard Library and other collections.

Turning to books, not to Indians, Drake and Thatcher retained their "exteriority" and kept the full *authority* of the author not as augmentor but as originator. Although the Indian biographer approached the *impensé,* the epistemic unthinkable of the period, when he suggested that Indians "must . . . vanish" only if the constant "wrongs inflicted" on them forced them to vanish, he never went so far as to grant the Indian the right to speak for himself. Whatever injustices and injuries he protested, he was not yet able to protest in the actual form of his work what Gilles DeLeuze has called the indignity of speaking for others. With all his sympathy for the Indian, the Indian biographer still defined him as he would be defined by Robert Frost's murderous Miller, in "The Vanishing Red," as ". . . one who had no right to be heard from."

But it is the central convention of autobiography that its subject speaks for himself. Black Hawk may speak in Patterson's presence, but "The Editor," as we have noted, ". . . does not . . . consider himself responsible . . ." for what is said; in his choice of the autobiographical form, Patterson speaks against progressivist ideology. As discursive equivalent of the frontier, the textual ground on which two cultures meet, the Indian autobiography requires contact between its subject-author and its editor-author. If the relationship is unequal, it is nonetheless genuinely reciprocal. Only by submitting to the Euramerican form of autobiography could Black Hawk speak to the whites at all; only by accepting the graphematic supplement of the editor and the fall into writing and culture could Black Hawk achieve the book of his life, whose final form was not his to determine. Yet an Indian autobiography could be achieved by no white alone. Only by acknowledging reciprocity, abandoning the authority of the author for the more limited authority of editorship, and entering into "contact" with Black Hawk, could Patterson produce the book of an Indian life, a book in which a still-living and formerly unheard voice emerged to speak for itself. This Indian voice—translated, transcribed, edited, polished, interpreted though it was—had never before sounded, not in western autobiography (hostile to it though indebted to it), nor in eastern Indian biography (sympathetic to it but formally indifferent to it).

Patterson's *Life of Black Hawk* was sufficiently popular to justify four more editions the following year in the East and, after many years, an edition published in St. Louis in 1882.[32] For this, the last edition published in Patterson's lifetime, the "editor and sole proprietor" of the *Life,* as he then called himself, provided some revisions of the text, adding material, expanding certain descriptions, and generally elaborating the diction. For these changes, Patterson was alone responsible, Black Hawk having died in 1838. The 1882 edition also received a new title, for the *Life* now became *The Autobiography of Ma-Ka-Tai-Me-She-Kia-Kiak.* Subsequent editions have tended to use the 1882 title, though reprinting the 1833 text as closer to Black Hawk's "own words." Despite this continued interest in Patterson's work, the remaining years of the nineteenth century present no other fully developed instance of Indian autobiography.

Notes

[1] James M. Cox, "Autobiography and America," in *Aspects of Narrative: Selected Papers from the English Institute,* ed. J. Hillis Miller (New York, 1971), p. 145.

[2] George and Louise Spindler, "American Indian Personality Types and Their Sociocultural Roots," quoted by Harold E. Driver, *Indians of North America,* 2d ed., rev. (Chicago, 1975), p. 434.

[3] Tzvetan Todorov, *The Fantastic: A Structural Approach to a Literary Genre,* trans. Richard Howard (Ithaca, N.Y., 1975), p. 3.

[4] James Axtell, "The Ethnohistory of Early America: A Review Essay," *The William and Mary Quarterly* 35 (Jan. 1978):116.

[5] Edward Said, "The Problem of Textuality: Two Exemplary Positions," *Critical Inquiry* 4 (1978):675, and 709n.

[6] See Francis Jennings, *The Invasion of America: Indians, Colonialism, and the Cant of Conquest* (New York, 1976).

[7] See Roy Harvey Pearce, *Savagism and Civilization* (Baltimore, 1967), originally published in 1953 as *The Savages of America: A Study of the Indian and the Idea of Civilization,* chap. 4, "The Zero of Human Society: The Idea of the Savage."

[8] Ambrose Bierce, *The Devil's Dictionary* (New York, 1958), p. 7. Bierce wrote his definitions between 1881 and 1906.

[9] Quoted by Marjorie Halpin in her introduction to Catlin's *Letters and Notes on the Manners, Customs, and Conditions of North American Indians* (New York, 1973), I:ix. Catlin's work was first published in London in 1841.

[10] A. D. Coleman in an introduction to Edward S. Curtis, *Portraits from North American Indian Life* (n.p., 1972), p. v. Curtis's work was originally published in a limited edition of five hundred sets (priced at $3,000 each) in 1907-1908.

[11] William Fenton in his introduction to B. B. Thatcher's *Indian Biography* (Glorieta, N.M., 1973), unpaged. This is a reprint of the New York edition of 1832; an edition appeared in Boston in the same year.

[12] Thatcher, *Indian Biography,* unpaged. Further quotations from Thatcher are taken from this preface.

[13] See Richard Slotkin, *Regeneration Through Violence: The Mythology of the American Frontier, 1600-1860* (Middletown, Conn., 1974), especially chaps. 9 and 10.

[14] Louis O. Mink, "Narrative Form as a Cognitive Instrument," in *The Writing of History: Literary Form and Historical Understanding,* eds. R. H. Canary and Henry Kozicki (Madison, 1978), p. 138.

[15] Quoted in John Bakeless, *Daniel Boone: Master of the Wilderness* (New York, 1939), passim.

[16] David Crockett, in the preface to his *A Narrative of the Life of David Crockett of the State of Tennessee, Written by Himself,* ed. Joseph J. Arpad (New Haven, 1972), p. 47. Crockett's *Narrative* was originally published in Philadelphia in 1834.

[17] Louis P. Renza, "The Veto of the Imagination: A Theory of Autobiography," *New Literary History* 9 (1977):2. Renza's sentence concludes, autobiography "is definable as a form of 'prose fiction.'"

[18] Ibid.

[19] Crockett, *A Narrative,* pp. 47-48.

[20] In his introduction to *Kit Carson's Autobiography,* edited by Quaife (Chicago, 1935; rpt. Lincoln, Nebr., n.d.), pp. xvii-xxviii. The *Autobiography* was originally published in late 1858 or early 1859 in New York.

[21] See the *Life of Sam Houston of Texas* (New York, 1855), unsigned, by Charles Edward Lester, under Houston's supervision; also the *Life of General Sam Houston: A Short Autobiography* (Austin, Tex., 1964), originally published in 1855; and T. D. Bonner, *The Life and Adventures of James P. Beckwourth* (New York, 1969), originally published in New York in 1856.

[22] William T. Hagan, *American Indians,* rev. ed. (Chicago, 1979), p. 72.

[23] Translator's preface to *Black Hawk: An Autobiography,* ed. Donald Jackson (Urbana, 1964), unpaged. The full title of the original 1833 edition published at Cincinnati is the *Life of Ma-Ka-Tai-Me-She-Kia-Kiak or Black Hawk, embracing the Tradition of his Nation—Indian Wars in which he has been engaged—Cause of joining the British in their late War with America, and its History—Description of the Rock-River Village—Manners and Customs—Encroachments by the Whites, Contrary to Treaty—Removal from his Village in 1831. With an Account of the Cause and General History of the Late War, his Surrender and Confinement at Jefferson Barracks, and Travels through the United States. Dictated by Himself.* All quotations are from Jackson's edition in which the translator's preface, Black Hawk's dedication, and the editor's "Advertise-

ment" are unpaged. Page references will be given in the text.

[24] Quoted by Donald Jackson in his introduction to *Black Hawk: An Autobiography*, p. 28.

[25] Ibid., p. 26.

[26] Thatcher, preface to *Indian Biography*, unpaged.

[27] Slotkin, *Regeneration Through Violence*, p. 426.

[28] John Filson, *The Discovery, Settlement and Present State of Kentucke*, which includes as an appendix "The Adventures of Col. Daniel Boon, one of the first settlers, containing a 'Narrative of the Wars of Kentucke'" (Gloucester, Mass., 1975), pp. 81-82. Filson's book was originally published in Wilmington, Delaware, in 1784.

[29] *Emplotment* is Hayden White's term for the large structures Frye would probably call "myths," as they appear in the narratives of "history." See Hayden White, *Metahistory: The Historical Imagination in Nineteenth-Century Europe* (Baltimore, 1973), and "The Historical Text as Literary Artifact," in *The Writing of History*, eds. Canary and Kozicki. The quotations from Frye are from the *Anatomy of Criticism* (New York, 1965), pp. 169ff.

[30] Benjamin F. Drake, *The Life and Adventures of Black Hawk* (Cincinnati, 1838), pp. 20-21.

[31] From the title page of the first edition, Boston, 1832.

[32] Two editions in Boston in 1834; one in Philadelphia in 1834, together with an account of "a Lady who was taken prisoner by the Indians"; and one in New York in 1834. Other editions: London, 1836; Cooperstown, 1842; Boston, 1845; Leeuwarden, Netherlands, 1847—this is listed in Sabin, *Bibliotheca Americana: Dictionary of Books Relating to America from its Discovery to the Present Time* (New York, 1868; rpt. New York, n.d.) under LeClair's pseudonym, "R. Postumus"; Cincinnati, 1858; St. Louis, 1882; Chicago, 1916; and Iowa City, 1932.

THE EVOLUTION OF NATIVE AMERICAN AUTOBIOGRAPHY

A. LaVonne Brown Ruoff (essay date 1990)

SOURCE: "Three Nineteenth-Century American Indian Autobiographers," in *Redefining American Literary History*, edited by A. LaVonne Brown Ruoff and Jerry W. Ward, Jr., The Modern Language Association of America, 1990, pp. 251-69.

[*In the essay that follows, Ruoff contends that Native American autobiographies became more intensely focused on Native American-white political relations, and more self-reflectively literary, over the course of the nineteenth century.*]

Since the early nineteenth century, American Indians have written personal narratives and autobiographies more consistently than any other form of prose.[1] The structure of these personal narratives reflects a diverse range of influences, from Western European forms of spiritual autobiography and slave narratives to the oral traditions of Native America. The full-length confessions or autobiographies of Western European literature are not part of Indian oral tradition. As Barre Toelken points out, in many tribes "one is not to speak of himself in any full way until after he has become someone—such as having had many children or an illustrious life."[2] Nevertheless, as H. David Brumble III makes clear in *American Indian Autobiography*, there were at least six forms of American Indian preliterate autobiographical narratives: coup tales, which described feats of bravery; less formal and usually more detailed stories of warfare and hunting; self-examinations, such as confessions required for participation in rituals or accounts of misfortunes and illnesses; self-vindications; educational narratives; and tales of the acquisition of powers (22-23). Although some Indian authors of personal narratives consciously adopted literary forms popular among white readers, they often blended these with tribal narrative in which personal history was expressed within the contexts of the myths, stories, and histories of their tribes or bands, clans, and families. These narratives also incorporated forceful commentary on whites' treatment of Indians.

This essay will trace the evolution of American Indian written autobiographies in the nineteenth century through the personal narratives of three authors, from the East, Midwest, and West: William Apes (Pequot), George Copway (Ojibwa), and Sarah Winnemucca (Paiute).[3] It will also examine the relation of these works to the history and literature of the age and the influence of such forms as spiritual confessions, missionary reminiscences, and slave narratives; it will discuss, as well, the influence of American Indian oral traditions.

When Indian authors first began to write personal narratives, the word *autobiography* was not in general use. Coined by Robert Southey in 1809, the term did not appear in the titles of books published in the United States until the 1830s. During the first half of the century, American Indian authors were more influenced in their choice of autobiographical form by spiritual confessions, which describe the subject's private or inner life, than by memoirs, which chronicle the subject's public career. As Christian converts, the earliest Indian autobiographers consciously modeled their works on religious narratives, especially on spiritual confessions and missionary reminiscences. Perhaps less consciously, some Indian authors, or their editors or publishers, also incorporated aspects of the slave narratives, which themselves were influenced by religious narratives.

The spiritual confessions were logical models both for religious and ideological reasons. They linked Indian autobiographers to Protestant literary traditions and identified the authors as civilized Christians whose experiences were as legitimate subjects of written analysis as were those of other Christians. As G. A. Starr points out, writing any kind of autobiography assumes both one's own importance and the appropriateness of writing about one's experiences. Implicit in these assumptions is the Protestant principle that only an individual's exertions can influence his or her soul. Consequently each person must examine carefully the events in the development of the soul. Also implicit is the belief that because spiritual life varies little from person to person, individuals can measure their spiritual state by that of others. The double value of spiritual autobiographies was that at the same time that they chronicled the author's spiritual development, they enabled readers to repeat the process by identifying with the writer's spiritual pilgrimages (Starr 5, 14, 19, 27). Although early Indian autobiographers used the structural pattern of the spiritual confession, later writers combined this form with descriptions of their missionary activities as they spread the word of God and of their own salvation.

The task of achieving credibility for their personal narratives was as formidable to American Indians as it was to former slaves. On the one hand, the narrators had to convince their readers that they were members of the human race whose experiences were legitimate subjects of autobiography and whose accounts of these experiences were accurate. On the other hand, they had the moral obligation to portray the harsh injustices they and their fellows suffered at the hands of Christian whites. While chronicling their struggles either to achieve or maintain a sense of individual identity, these narrators had to avoid antagonizing their white audiences. They also had the dual task of describing experiences common to slaves or Indians and those unique to themselves. However, these narrators were not typical of the groups they characterized because they could read and write. In addition, fugitive slaves who wrote were different from other slaves by having escaped bondage, and Christian Indians differed from others by having rejected native for white religion (Butterfield 15-18; F. S. Foster 67-70).

When the first personal narratives by American Indians were published in the late 1820s, the tide of popular taste and of Indian-white relations ensured a ready audience for Indian authors. During this decade, increased literacy and cheaper methods of book production resulted in an expanded market for all kinds of books. Religious, slave, and captivity narratives as well as works about the West were popular during the 1820s and 1830s. The image of the Indians in captivity narratives as unfeeling savages competed with their representation as the "noble-but-doomed redmen" in Cooper's *Leather-Stocking Tales*, widely read during this period (Pearce, "Red Gifts" 196-236; Berkhofer 86-95). The success of these narratives and the public's continuing interest in Indians stimulated the Indians to publish their own autobiographies.

Indian-white relations also influenced the content and popularity of Indian autobiographies. The death knell of Indian hopes for retaining tribal lands east of the Mississippi was sounded in 1830 with the passage of the Indian Removal Act, which authorized the federal government to resettle Indians from these areas to Indian Territory, now Oklahoma, and other locations deemed suitable. As Indian presence became less threatening, whites increasingly wanted to read about vanished red men or assimilated Indian converts to Christianity.

II

The first published, full-life history written by an Indian is William Apes's *Son of the Forest: The Experience of William Apes, a Native of the Forest* (1829).[4] Published in the midst of the controversy over removal, Apes's autobiography, which appeared in a revised and expanded edition in 1831, is a testimony both to the essential humanity of Indian people and to their potential for adapting to white concepts of civilization.[5] *A Son of the Forest* follows the basic structure of the spiritual confession. Because Apes (b. 1798) was not raised in a traditional Indian culture, he does not include the description of tribal life and history that characterizes the autobiographies of Copway and Winnemucca. Physically abused by his alcoholic grandparents, four-year-old Apes was taken from them, nursed for a year by a white couple, and then bound out at age five to a series of white families. He ran off at age fourteen to join the army during the War of 1812. Later he became a Methodist minister.

Like the slave narrators, Apes recognizes the necessity of establishing the authenticity of his autobiography.[6] Early in the second edition, Apes assures his readers that he has told the truth because he must answer to God for every word written. He also authenticates his background by describing his ancestry. Apes's mother was a full-blood Pequot, although his father was half white. His paternal grandmother was a full-blood member of the Pequot tribe. In both editions of *A Son of the Forest*, Apes states that she was descended from King Philip (Wampanoag).[7]

Apes's account of his experiences is especially interesting because he was raised among Indians only until he was four years old. Apes's parents separated when he was around three, leaving their children in the care of the maternal grandparents. Apes movingly describes how his intoxicated grandmother beat him unmercifully with a club, breaking his arm in three places. Lest his audience attribute such abuse to cruelty inherent in the Indian character, Apes emphasizes that only when drunk did his maternal grandparents abuse the children. He also stresses that his paternal grandparents were gentle Christians. Blaming whites, rather than his maternal grandparents, for the abuse, Apes uses the episode to introduce one of the dominant themes of nineteenth-century autobiographies—the destructive impact of white-introduced alcohol on Indian life:

> [Whites] introduced among my countrymen, that bane of comfort and happiness, ardent spirits— seduced them into a love of it, and when under its unhappy influence, wronged them out of their lawful possessions—that land, where reposed the ashes of their sires; and not only so, but they committed violence of the most revolting kind upon the persons of the female portion of the tribe, who previous to the introduction among them of the arts, and vices, and debaucheries of the whites, were as unoffending and happy as they roamed over their goodly possessions, as any people on whom the sun of heaven ever shown. (14)

Like the authors of spiritual confessions and slave narratives, Apes gives little information about his personal life, devoting his autobiography primarily to his journey toward salvation.[8] Apes couples the description of his spiritual journey with that of his progress toward racial and individual identity, another characteristic of slave narratives. The book follows the structure of contemporary religious confessions in which the narrator moves through specific stages: growing awareness of God's power, conversion, questioning of faith, fall from grace, and recovery. Like many writers about religious conversion, Apes was converted after a vivid dream revealed to him the horrors of hell. In 1813, fifteen-year-old Apes converted to Christianity and became a Methodist. What determined Apes's conversion was a sermon on Christ's death as the atonement for the world's sins: "I felt convinced that Christ died for all mankind—that age, sect, colour, country, or situation made no difference. I felt an assurance that I was included in the plan of redemption with all my brethren" (41).

A Son of the Forest bears a strong relationship to slave narratives in its emphasis on white injustice. Apes introduces this theme at the beginning of the second edition when he describes how whites stole the land and ravished the daughters of the Pequots, who welcomed whites to their land "in that spirit of kindness, so peculiar to the redmen of the woods" (8). He objects to the word "Indian," which whites frequently used as an epithet, and substitutes "natives" as a more appropriate term. As an Indian raised among whites, Apes experienced the terror that stereotypical stories about savage Indians aroused in children. Such stories made Apes so afraid of his fellow natives that threats to send the young boy to live with Indians effectively controlled his behavior. Especially dramatic is his account of how, while gathering berries in the woods, Apes was frightened by some white females with dark complexions: "I broke from the party with my utmost speed, and I could not master courage enough to look behind until I had reached home. By this time my imagination had pictured out a tale of blood, and as soon as I regained breath sufficient to answer the questions which my master asked, I informed him that we had met a body of the natives in the woods . . ." (22).

Only later did Apes realize that although whites filled him with stories of Indian cruelty, they never told him how cruelly whites had treated Indians. As a bound servant who could be sold at the whim of his masters until age twenty-one, Apes endured experiences similar to those of the slave narrators. He protests the unfeeling manner in which these sales occurred: "If my consent had been solicited as a matter of form, I should not have felt so bad. But to be sold to, and treated unkindly, by those who had got our father's lands for nothing, was too much to bear" (35).

In *A Son of the Forest,* Apes uses a simple, straightforward style to chronicle the events in his life. His own particular style is evident both in his use of "now" as a transition between parts of an episode or between his narration and commentary and in his choice of a first-person narrative voice. Although he does not embellish his autobiography with re-creations of scenes enlivened with direct quotations or detailed descriptions, Apes focuses occasionally on experiences that reveal his state of mind.

Apes departs from this plain style in his account of his conversion, in which he uses the rhapsodic language conventional in spiritual autobiographies to describe his emotional responses. While working in a garden, Apes found that his "heart melted into tenderness—my soul was filled with love—love to God, and love to all mankind. Oh how my poor heart swelled with joy" (45). Apes then saw God in everything. He was so filled with love for people that he would have "pressed them to my bosom, as they were more precious to me than gold" (45). Both in these passages and in his commentaries on white injustice to Indians, Apes adopts the oratorical style that characterizes so much of his later writing.

In his brief autobiography in *The Experiences of Five Christian Indians of the Pequod Tribe* (1833; revised and republished in 1837 as *Experience of Five Christian Indians, of the Pequod Tribe*), Apes is far more critical of whites than he was in *A Son of the Forest.*

Later Indian authors also expressed more disillusionment with whites in their second autobiographies than they did in their first. Twenty of the forty-seven pages of the 1833 edition of *The Experiences of Five Christian Indians* are devoted to Apes's autobiography, which emphasizes his religious progress. Apes also speaks out against whites' unjust treatment of him as a child and adolescent. Describing his conflicts with one master over his desire to attend religious meetings after his conversion, Apes comments:

> How hard it is to be robbed of all our earthly rights and deprived of the means of grace, merely because the skin is of a different color; such has been the case with us poor colored people. I would ask the white man, if he thinks that he can be justified in making just such a being as I am, or any other person in the world unhappy; and although the white man finds so much fault because God had made us thus, yet if I have any vanity about it, I choose to remain as I am, and praise my Maker while I live, that Indians he has made. (17; 1833)

Apes's last two books grew out of his commitment to the fight for Indian rights. He describes the Mashpee struggle to retain self-government in *Indian Nullification of the Unconstitutional Laws of Massachusetts, Relative to the Marshpee Tribe* (1835), one of the most powerful pieces of Indian protest literature of the first half of the nineteenth century.[9] His efforts helped the Mashpees regain their rights, one of the few such Indian victories in the 1830s. Apes's final work is the eloquent *Eulogy on King Philip* (1836), originally delivered as a series of lectures at the Odeon in Boston. Apes disappeared from public view after this work has published, and the details of his later life are unknown.

III

The publication of Apes's autobiographies did not immediately inspire other Indian authors to publish theirs. Not until 1847 was another full autobiography published by an Indian writer. Educated Indians had little leisure to write personal narratives, because they devoted their energies to helping their people retain tribal lands, obtain just compensation for land cessions, or gain civil rights. No sooner was removal implemented than whites violated it by migrating westward into Indian territories. What began as a stream of settlers in the 1830s became a flood by the 1850s.

During removal, white authors lamented the passing of the "noble savage" doomed to extinction by the necessity of "Manifest Destiny." Cooper's *Leather-Stocking Tales* vividly portray this stereotype, as do the narratives about famous Indians and their tribes. In 1833, the narrated Indian autobiography, a major literary form in the late nineteenth and twentieth centuries, was introduced, with the publication of *Life of Ma-ka-tai-me-she-kia-kiak, or Black Hawk.* Narrated by Black Hawk (Sauk) to translator Antoine Le Claire and revised for publication by John B. Patterson, this popular book went through five editions by 1847. Biographical dictionaries of famous Indians were also published during this period (Berkhofer 88-89; Pearce, "The Zero of Human Society" 118; Krupat, *For Those* 34-35, 45-47).

Paralleling the interest in the "noble-but-doomed" Indian were scientific studies of the Indian published in the late 1830s (Bieder 309-12). One of the most influential was Henry Rowe Schoolcraft's *Algic Researches,* a study of Ojibwa and Ottawa cultures. Longfellow's popular *Song of Hiawatha,* published after the enthusiasm for the noble savage had waned, strongly reflects Schoolcraft's influence.

The success of books about Indians in the 1830s created a literary climate favorable to the appearance of the Ojibwa writer George Copway (1818-69). To an American public imbued with the belief that the noble red man must assimilate or perish, this Ojibwa convert to Methodism from the woodlands of midwestern Canada seemed to represent what the Indian must become in order to survive—the embodiment of both the noble virtues from the savage past and the Western European culture from the civilized present. The public eagerly embraced Copway, who cast himself in this image in his *The Life, History, and Travels of Kah-ge-ga-gah-bowh (George Copway)* (1847). Enthusiasm for this autobiography was so great that it was reprinted in six editions in one year. A slightly revised edition, to which Copway added speeches and published letters, appeared in 1850 under two different titles: *The Life, Letters and Speeches of Kah-ge-ga-gah-bowh: Or, G. Copway* (New York) and *Recollections of a Forest Life: Or, The Life and Travels of Kah-ge-ga-gah-bowh* (London).[10]

Copway was born near the mouth of the Trent River, in Upper Canada, and was raised as a traditional Ojibwa until 1827, when his parents converted to Christianity. Following the death of his mother in 1830, Copway became a convert and later occasionally attended the Methodist Mission School at Rice Lake, Ontario. During 1834-36, he helped Methodist missionaries spread the gospel among the Lake Superior Ojibwa. In 1838, he entered Ebenezer Manual Labor School at Jacksonville, Illinois, where he received his only formal education. After he left school, Copway traveled in the East before returning to Rice Lake, where he met and married Elizabeth Howell, a white woman. Until 1842, the Copways served as missionaries to the Indian tribes of Wisconsin and Minnesota. Accepted as a preacher by the Wesleyan Methodist Canadian Conference, Copway also was briefly a missionary in Upper Canada. The high point of his career in Canada was his election, in 1845, as vice president of the Grand Council of Methodist Ojibwas of Upper Canada. Later that year, both the Saugeen and Rice Lake bands accused him of embezzlement. After being imprisoned briefly in the summer of 1846, Copway was expelled from the Canadian Conference and went to the United States. Befriended by American Methodists, Copway launched a new career as a lecturer and writer on Indian affairs.

Copway's *Life, Letters and Speeches* incorporates traditions from earlier written personal histories and from American Indian oral narratives. It reflects the influence of the slave narratives in its emphasis on documentation. Like the slave narrators and like Apes, Copway felt he must prove that he was an educated man capable of writing an autobiography. In a prefatory "Word to the Reader," Copway acknowledges that he has had only three years of school and has spoken English only a few years.[11] However, he assures his readers that although a friend corrected all serious grammatical errors, Copway himself both planned and wrote the volume.[12] To substantiate his literacy and status in the world, he buttresses his volume with literary quotations and documentation, particularly in the second edition, to which he added speeches and published letters.

The structure of Copway's autobiography is far more complex than that of Apes's. The first part is an ethnographic account of Ojibwa culture, in which Copway balances general descriptions with specific examples from personal experience. The second part is devoted to the conversions of his band, family, and himself; the third, to his role as mediator between Indians and whites; and the fourth, to a history of Ojibwa-white relations in the recent past. Copway's blending of myth, history, and recent events, and his combining of tribal ethnohistory and personal experience create a structure of personal narrative that later American Indian autobiographers followed. This mixed form, which differs from the more linear, personal confession or life history found in non-Indian autobiographies, was congenial to Indian narrators accustomed to viewing their lives within the history of their tribe or band, clan, and family. Julie Cruikshank makes clear the distinction between Indian and non-Indian concepts of autobiography in the introduction to *Life Lived like a Story*. As Cruikshank compiled the personal narratives of three Yukon women, she found that they responded to her questions about secular events by telling traditional stories. Each explained that "these narratives were important to record *as part of* her life story." According to Cruikshank, the women's accounts included not only reminiscences of the kind we associate with autobiography but also detailed narratives on mythological themes. Cruikshank also notes that these women embedded songs in their chronicles, which they framed with genealogies and with long lists of personal and place names that appear to have both metaphoric and mnemonic value: the women "talk about their lives

using an oral tradition grounded in local idiom and a mutually shared body of knowledge" (ms. 2-5). Copway's autobiography reflects this perspective—of narrating one's life within a tribal context—as do numerous other American Indian oral and written personal histories. Copway, like the Yukon women Cruikshank interviewed, incorporates myths, stories, and songs into his personal narrative. In *The Traditional History and Characteristic Sketches of the Ojibway Nation,* Copway emphasized the importance of storytelling to him and his people:

> There is not a lake or mountain that has not connected with it some story of delight or wonder, and nearly every beast and bird is the subject of the story-teller, being said to have transformed itself at some prior time into some mysterious formation—of men going to live in the stars, and of imaginary beings in the air, whose rushing passage roars in the distant whirlwinds. (95-96)

By beginning his narrative with the description of his life as an Ojibwa, Copway demonstrates his strong identification with his tribal culture. In its nostalgia for the tribal past, Copway's autobiography bears a stronger relationship to the narratives published by African slaves in the late eighteenth century than to those by African American slaves in the nineteenth. For example, *The Interesting Narrative of the Life of Olaudah Equiano, or Gustavus Vassa, the African* (1789) begins with accounts of the geography and culture of his native land, Benin (now part of Nigeria), his family, and childhood (F. S. Foster 47). Like the Africans captured on their native continent and transported to North America, Copway and many of the nineteenth-century Native American writers who followed him retained vivid memories of the free tribal life. Copway and other Christian Indian writers, like the African slave writers, undertook the dual task of demonstrating to their audiences both the virtues of traditional tribal life and the capacity of their race to adapt to white civilization after conversion and education in Western European traditions (F. S. Foster 11-13, 44-47). Copway's goal is not to give an exhaustive account of his life and thoughts but rather to present himself as a typical Indian who, after conversion, exemplifies the ability of his tribe to become worthy members of mainstream society. Reticence to discuss one's personal life is characteristic of spiritual confessions and slave narratives as well as many American Indian personal histories.

In the ethnographic sections on Ojibwa life, Copway adopts an overwhelmingly romantic and nostalgic tone. He unabashedly appeals to American affection for the stereotype of the Indian as a child of nature at the same time that he uses himself as an example of the Indian's adaptability to white civilization: "I loved the woods, and the chase. I had the nature for it, and gloried in nothing else. The mind for letters was in me, *but was asleep* until the dawn of Christianity arose, and awoke the slumbers of my soul into energy and action" (11). The ethnographic sections are designed to persuade his audience of the value of tribal culture and of the essential humanity of Indian people, goals adopted by later Indian autobiographers as well. For example, he stresses that the Ojibwa moral code, which embodies universal human values, links Indian and white cultures. Quoting maxims that emphasize kindness, generosity, and respect for parents, the aged, and the indigent, the author concludes that adherence to these precepts brought Indians peace and happiness until they were weaned away by the white man's whiskey. His descriptions of visions also suggest a common ground between Indian and white cultures. Visions and dreams played an important role in the Christian conversion literature of the period and were the subject of Indian oral autobiographies. Throughout this work, Copway stresses that the differences between whites and Indians consist of language and custom rather than humanity.

Copway uses his own experiences to personalize his generalizations about tribal worldviews and customs. Particularly effective are the sketches of his life with his parents. In one of the most moving episodes, the family almost starves after being imprisoned in their birchbark wigwam for eleven days by heavy snow, with only boiled birch-bark, beaver skins, and old moccasins for food. By the tenth day, most of the family was too weak to walk: "Oh how distressing to see the starving Indians lying about the wigwam with hungry and eager looks; the children would cry for something to eat. My poor mother would heave *bitter sighs of despair,* the tears falling from her cheeks profusely as she kissed us. Wood, though plenty, could not be obtained, on account of the feebleness of our limbs" (35). The family was saved when a vision led Copway's father to beaver swimming under the ice of a nearby river. The poignancy of such hardships tempers the idyllic scenes of Indian life amid the gentle beauty of nature.

Just as his boyhood experiences illuminate Ojibwa life in general, Copway's descriptions of their conversion and of his own exemplify the power of Christianity to uplift Indians from the darkness of tribal religions and the degradation inflicted on them by whites luring Indians into alcoholism. The account of his spiritual awakening follows the literary conventions of confessions. While attending a church service to hear a powerful preacher, Copway tried to pray but could not. Suddenly, he saw a torch: "The small brilliant light came near to me, and fell upon my head, and then ran all over and through me. . . . I arose; and O! how happy I was! I felt light as a feather. I clapped my hands, and exclaimed in English, *"Glory to Jesus"* (62).

Although Copway expresses the feelings of unworthiness traditional to confessional literature, he casts these in distinctly racial terms. Like Apes, Copway felt God was *"too great* to listen to the words of a poor Indian boy" (62). The appeal of Christianity is the same as it was for Apes—equality with whites. As Copway reminds his audience, "the Great Spirit is no respecter of persons; He had made of one blood all the nations of the earth; He loves all his children alike; and his highest attributes are *love, mercy, and justice.* If this be so—and who dare doubt it?—will He not stretch out his hand and help them, and avenge their wrongs?" (157).

The sections of the book that deal with the author's missionary work replace the conventional fall from grace and subsequent recapture of faith found in confessional narratives. Leaving the safety of his home, Copway journeys into the wilds, where his spiritual and physical courage is tested. His harrowing adventures among the Great Lakes Ojibwas appealed to his audience's taste for the sensational and are comparable to those in the Indian captivity, slave, and missionary narratives of the period.

Indian-white relations are a focus of the autobiography, especially white treatment of Indians in the wilderness and the author's impressions of white civilization during his travels; specific recommendations are made for improved relations. Copway strongly criticizes whites for introducing alcohol, which undermined Ojibwa values and family life, and for failing to send missionaries to the Indians. Christianity and education, Copway argues, are what Indians needed to achieve advancement in religion, literature, the arts and sciences.

The work incorporates a variety of styles. In the narrative portions, Copway adopts a plain, journalistic style, while in his discussions of government policy, he employs an oratorical one. In the philosophical sections, Copway unfortunately uses a rhapsodic tone that undercuts the realism of the autobiography, although it undoubtedly appealed to the taste of the average reader. The influence of Byron's *Childe Harold's Pilgrimage* is evident both in Copway's comment that he views his life "like the mariner on the wide ocean, without a compass, in the dark night, as he watches the heavens for the north star" and in subsequent stanzas, which have a distinctly Byronic flavor (13).

After the publication of *The Life, History and Travels,* Copway lectured in the East, South, and Midwest on his plan for a separate Indian state, advocated in his pamphlet *Organization of a New Indian Territory, East of the Missouri River.* The lectures in the East enabled Copway to meet the well-known scholars Henry Rowe Schoolcraft and Francis Parkman, as well as Longfellow, Irving, and Cooper, who provided moral and financial encouragement for his later publishing projects.

Copway's second book, *The Traditional History and Characteristic Sketches of the Ojibway Nation,* was the first published book-length history of that tribe written by an Indian; it later appeared under the title *Indian Life and Indian History.* In it, Copway is far more critical of whites than he was in his autobiography. The author reached the zenith of his career in the years 1850-51, when he represented the Christian Indians at the World Peace Congress held in Germany. Copway visited Britain and the Continent before attending the congress, where he created a stir by delivering a lengthy antiwar speech while garbed in his Ojibwa finery. Returning from Europe in December 1850, Copway hurriedly stitched together *Running Sketches of Men and Places, in England, France, Germany, Belgium, and Scotland.*[13] Unfortunately, this travel book, one of the first by an Indian, is padded with newspaper accounts of his triumphal lecture tours in Britain and descriptions taken from other travel books. Between July and October 1851, he established the short-lived journal *Copway's American Indian.*[14] The year 1851 marked the end of his successful career as a writer and of his close relations with eastern intellectuals, now impatient with his too frequent appeals for money.

Little is known of Copway's later life. He recruited Canadian Indians to serve in the American Civil War and surfaced again in 1867, when, in the *Detroit Free Press,* he advertised himself as a healer. The following year, after apparently abandoning his wife and daughter, Copway arrived alone at Lac-des-deux-Montagnes, a large Algonquian and Iroquois mission about thirty miles northwest of Montreal. Describing himself as a pagan, Copway announced his intention to convert to Catholicism. On 17 January 1869, he was baptized Joseph-Antoine. Several days later he died on the evening of his first communion.

IV

Few Indians published during the three decades following the publication of Copway's works. From the 1850s to the 1890s, most of the works by Indian authors were histories of woodland tribes from the East and Midwest.[15] The history of literature written by American Indians parallels the history of white migration across the country. After pressure from white settlement forced Indians onto reservations and pressure from the federal government forced Indian children to be sent to white-run schools, Indians from the Plains and Far West educated in these schools began, at the turn of the century, to publish their autobiographies.

Hostile government policies and public attitudes created a climate generally unfavorable to the development of Indian literature. White audiences were far more interested in the accounts of explorers, settlers, and gold miners than in those of Indians who suffered as a result of the western conquest.

The stereotypes of the "noble savage" and "red devil" persisted, however. Authors like Bret Harte and Mark Twain adopted popular prejudices against the Indian, vividly illustrated in the latter's description of the Gosiute in *Roughing It.* The public's earlier interest in the "noble-but-doomed redman" from the East and Midwest was replaced by its antagonism to the fighting tribes of the West. Among the few authors adopting a romantic treatment of the Indian was Joaquin Miller, who revived the "noble savage" in his *Life among the Modocs.* Helen Hunt Jackson in *A Century of Dishonor* (1881) gave a realistic assessment of Indians and of the injustice of American policies toward them (Berkhofer 104-06).

The decline of the public's fascination with the Indian as a subject for serious literature paralleled the erosion of its fascination with the ex-slave. After abolition, slavery was a subject to be forgotten and the existence of racial prejudice one to be ignored (Cooley 8; Hart 113-14; F. S. Foster 60). While public interest was beginning to wane in the late 1850s, however, slave narrators were altering their life histories in ways later reflected in those by American Indians. Increasingly conscious of their own sense of individual and racial identity, slave narrators resisted the demands of white abolitionists that they simply retell their stories according to accepted formulas. Abandoning the Christian structure and tone of earlier nineteenth-century narratives, they focused less narrowly on the flight from slavery and forthrightly criticized the prejudice they encountered in the North.[16]

One of the few Indian autobiographies published during the last half of the nineteenth century was Sarah Winnemucca's *Life among the Piutes.* The fiery Winnemucca (Thocmetony; Paiute; 1844-91) was the first Indian woman writer of personal and tribal history. Like the slave narrators of the second half of the century, Winnemucca abandons the strongly Christian flavor of earlier personal narratives; unlike Apes and Copway, she does not pattern her narrative after spiritual confessions and missionary reminiscences. Her emphasis on personal experience as part of the ethnohistory of her tribe owes more to tribal narrative traditions than to religious ones. Further, her life history is considerably more militant than theirs.

Winnemucca's *Life among the Piutes* also differs from typical women's autobiographies. In *A Poetics of Women's Autobiography,* Sidonie Smith comments that women autobiographers deal with two stories. On the one hand, the woman autobiographer "engages in the fiction of selfhood that constitutes the discourse of man and that conveys by the way a vision of the fabricating power of male subjectivity." On the other hand, because the story of man is not exactly her story, woman's "relationship to the empowering figure of male selfhood is inevitably problematic." Matters are further complicated by the fact that she must also "engage the fictions of selfhood that constitute the idea of woman and that specify the parameters of female subjectivity, including woman's problematic relationship to language, desire, power, and meaning." This leads Smith to conclude that because the ideology of gender makes woman's life history a nonstory, the ideal woman is "self-effacing rather than self-promoting" and her "natural" story shapes itself "not around the public, heroic life but around the fluid, circumstantial, contingent responsiveness to others that, according to patriarchal ideology, characterizes the life of women but not autobiography" (50).

Smith notes that when the autobiographer is a woman of color or of the working class, she faces even more complex imbroglios of male-female figures:

> Here identities of race and class, sometimes even of nationality, intersect and confound those of gender. As a result, she is doubly or triply the subject of other people's representations, turned again and again in stories that reflect and promote certain forms of selfhood identified with class, race, and nationality as well as with sex. In every case, moreover, she remains marginalized in that she finds herself resident on the margins of discourse, always removed from the center of power within the culture she inhabits. (51)[17]

Although marginalized within the dominant society because of her racial heritage, Winnemucca played a central role in her tribe. Born near the sink of the Humboldt River in Nevada, she was the granddaughter of Truckee, who, Winnemucca claimed, was chief of all the Paiutes, and the daughter of Old Winnemucca, who succeeded his father as chief. Because she and her family followed Truckee's policy of peaceful coexistence with whites, Winnemucca spent much of her life as a liaison between Paiutes and whites.[18] As such she became a courageous and eloquent spokeswoman for her people, pleading the Paiute cause before government officials and the general public. Far from being marginalized, Winnemucca's role as advocate made her the mightiest word warrior of her tribe. In "Indian Women's Personal Narrative," Kathleen Mullen Sands concludes that Winnemucca portrays herself in opposing roles in her autobiography: male and female, private and public: "She not only presents herself as a warrior for Indian justice, but she also develops a portrait of a child terrified by white power who, toward the end of her narrative, has become a dedicated teacher of Indian pupils—a version of motherhood" (ms. 19). In *American Indian Autobiography,* Brumble perceptively argues that *Life among the Piutes* is a kind of coup tale in which Winnemucca records her deeds in order to establish how she ought to be regarded, as have such Indian men as Two Leggings and White Bull (65-66).

Life among the Piutes covers the period from Winnemucca's birth to 1883, four decades that roughly encompass the first contacts between whites and Paiutes, through their many conflicts with whites, resettlements, and negotiations to receive justice from the federal government. After the discovery of gold in California, in 1849, pressures increased on the tribe as hordes of emigrants passed through Paiute territory on their way to the California goldfields, Idaho ore deposits, or Oregon timber. Winnemucca's disillusionment with federal Indian policy and with its agents aroused her to take the Paiute cause to the public. Encouraged by the success of her first lecture in San Francisco in 1879, she toured the East, delivering more than three hundred speeches. In Boston, she was befriended by Elizabeth Palmer Peabody, well known for her support of kindergarten education, and by her sister Mary Tyler Mann, widow of Horace. Through their intercession, Winnemucca was invited to speak in the homes of such distinguished Bostonians as Ralph Waldo Emerson, John Greenleaf Whittier, and Senator Henry L. Dawes. Enthusiastic response to her lectures and support from Mary Mann led Winnemucca to write *Life among the Piutes,* a blend of autobiography, ethnography, and history of Paiute-white relations between 1844 and 1883. Both in her lectures and in her book, Winnemucca staunchly supported the General Allotment Act, sponsored by Senator Dawes, under which Indians would be allotted tribal lands in severalty.[19]

In the book, Winnemucca combines the authenticating devices and narrative techniques of earlier Indian autobiographies with dramatic re-creations of episodes from her own and her family's personal experiences, a combination that makes the book one of the most colorful personal and tribal histories of the nineteenth century. Like Apes and Copway, Winnemucca is careful to validate her narrative. Her editor, Mary Mann, emphatically states in the "Editor's Preface" that her own "editing has consisted in copying the original manuscript in correct orthography and punctuation, with occasional emendations by the author" (ii). Winnemucca appends many documents attesting to her high moral character and to her services as an interpreter and intermediary for the government. In fact, such documents were necessary not only to establish her credibility as someone capable of writing a true account of her own life and history of her tribe but also to defend herself against scurrilous attacks on her virtue and honesty. For example, *The Council Fire and Arbitrator,* a monthly journal supposedly devoted to "civilization" and the "rights of American Indians," publicized accusations that Major William V. Rinehart, an agent whom Winnemucca harshly criticized, had sent to prejudice officials against her on her first trip to Washington: "She is notorious for her untruthfulness as to be wholly unreliable. She is known . . . to have been a common camp follower, consorting with common soldiers" (qtd. in Canfield 204). To combat such libels, Winnemucca published tributes from Brevet Major General Oliver Howard and other high-ranking officers with whom she served. Although such authenticating devices are common in slave narratives, Brumble also links her use of them to the oral traditions of self-vindication in American Indian personal narratives (*Autobiography* 69).

Unlike Apes and Copway, Winnemucca does not make the spiritual journey a central element in her narrative. She also departs from their example by being much more critical of white hypocrisy; her critical tone parallels that of post-Civil War slave narrators. In fact, her central theme is Indian-white relations, a secondary theme in the narratives by Apes and Copway. The emphasis is clear in the organization of the narrative. Part 1 consists of a single chapter on the background of her family and on the impact of white migration on Paiute life after 1844. Part 2, also composed of only one chapter, describes the domestic and social moralities of the Paiutes and provides ethnographic information about the tribe. The six chapters of part 3 are devoted to the conflicts between the Paiutes and whites from 1860 to 1883, as the Indians struggled to retain their native land, were moved from one reservation to another, and attempted to gain allotments on the Malheur agency in Oregon.

Life among the Piutes is more personalized than the autobiographies of Apes and Copway, a trend in slave narratives after the 1850s as well. The work contains a detailed account of Winnemucca's childhood, stressing, in particular, her strong attachment to her grandfather, Truckee, and her intense fear of white men, who reminded her of owls. Although she provides little information about herself as an adolescent and adult, Winnemucca reveals far more of her adult personality than Apes and Copway. The sensitive side of her nature is illustrated in her anguish when she must tell the Paiutes that they will be forced to move in midwinter to the Yakima agency—despite government assurances at the end of the Bannock War that the tribe would not be relocated. Her anguish is deepened by her realization that the Paiutes will say that she lied. Wishing that this were her last day in "this cruel world," Winnemucca questions the motives of a president who would force the weakened Paiutes to travel through freezing cold and deep snows to Yakima: "Oh what can the President be thinking about? Oh, tell me, what is he? Is he man or beast? Yes, he must be a beast; if he has no feeling for my people, surely he ought to have some for the soldiers" (204, 205).

The personal characteristics Winnemucca most consistently demonstrates are courage and stamina, particularly in her account of her role in the Bannock War. Her exploits rival those of the western adventure tales and recall the harrowing experiences of the heroines of captivity and slave narratives. Between 13 and 15 June 1878, Winnemucca rode 223 miles, on horseback and by wagon, between the Indian and army lines, in danger both from the warring Bannocks and from whites eager to kill her for helping the Paiutes.

Winnemucca is acutely conscious that the role she played in Paiute-white relations was unusual for a woman. In addition to the dangers encountered by any emissary passing between enemy lines, Winnemucca and her sister Mattie, who often accompanied her, faced the threat of rape. Warned by her cousin that whites had been lassoing Paiute women and doing "fearful" things to them, Winnemucca asserted: "If such an outrageous thing is to happen to me, it will not be done by one man or two, while there are two women with knives, for I know what an Indian can do. She can never be outraged by one man; but she may by two" (228). That Winnemucca was prepared to defend herself is illustrated by the incident in which she and her sister were forced by circumstances to share one room overnight with eight cowboys. Touched by one of them during the night, Winnemucca jumped up, punched the offender in the face, and warned: "Go away, or I will cut you to pieces, you mean man!" The startled culprit fled before she could carry out her threat (231).

Winnemucca's narrow escapes titillated the reading public's taste for both the imminence of sexuality and the triumph of virtue. The literary descendants of Pamela were expected to die rather than face dishonor, a fate they usually managed to escape. Sexual violence was a staple of both captivity and slave narratives. The women in captivity narratives trusted to their God to deliver them from the danger of rape or servitude as the captive wives of "heathen savages." If such narratives convinced whites of the innate cruelty of nonwhites, the slave narratives reminded whites of their own brutality. The degradation of slave women at the hands of masters provided the writers of slave narratives with the opportunity to demonstrate how the slave system destroyed the morality of blacks and whites.[20] Unlike the heroines of sentimental literature or of captivity and slave narratives, Winnemucca is not a victim but rather an independent woman determined to fight off her attackers. Her strength of character, as well as a fast horse and sharp knife, enable her to achieve victories denied to her literary sisters. They also distinguish her life history from the less dramatic accounts by other women autobiographers.

The description of the impact of white migration into Paiute territory provides a dramatic backdrop for Winnemucca's discussions of tribal beliefs and customs, which reflect the oral tradition of linking personal narrative to a family, clan, and tribal context. Her detailed accounts of the roles played by girls and women represent a subject receiving little emphasis in nineteenth-century autobiographies and ethnographies. Her description of the Paiute councils is an eloquent reminder that Indian women in traditional cultures had political power that was denied to white women in the "civilized" society: "The women know as much as the men do and their advice is often asked. We have a republic as well as you. The council-tent is our Congress, and anybody can speak who has anything to say, women and all. . . . If women would go into your Congress, I think justice would soon be done to the Indians" (53). Like Copway, Winnemucca stresses the importance of dreams in tribal culture. She vividly illustrates the Paiutes' belief in the truth of dreams when she describes how her father gathered his people to tell them that his vision foretold their destruction by whites. The incident also demonstrates the tribe's process of making decisions by consensus, when its members agree to follow his advice to retreat to the mountains.

In the longest section of *Life among the Piutes,* chronicling the tribe's relations with whites in the 1860s and 1870s, Indian agents got rich, Winnemucca charges, by starting their own stores and then bringing in cattlemen to pay them a dollar a head to graze their cattle on reservation land. Winnemucca bitterly attacks Major Rinehart, the agent at the Malheur reservation, and the Rev. James H. Wilbur, agent of the Yakima reservation in Washington, to which the Paiutes were sent.

Stylistically, *Life among the Piutes* is the most interesting of the three autobiographies, primarily because its author effectively dramatizes key episodes. Carolyn S. Fowler suggests that Winnemucca's re-creation of dialogue derives from the quotative style of Northern Paiute narratives (40). Dramatizing scenes and reproducing dialogue enable Winnemucca to strengthen her attacks against her adversaries by including the testimony of witnesses. The technique emphasizes, as well, the influence of the performance aspects of storytelling in native oral traditions. Examples of her narrative skill occur in the scene in which her grandfather calls his people together to retell the Paiute origin myth (6-7) and in her dramatization of Truckee's death, in 1859, in which she weaves together the threads of autobiography, ethnography, and Indian-white relations that dominate the book. Truckee's final speeches express his love for his family, his wish that his granddaughters be sent to a convent school, and his concern for good relations between Paiutes and whites. The author eloquently describes her grief at his passing: "I could not speak. I felt the world growing cold; everything seemed dark. The great light had gone out. I had father, mother, brothers, and sisters; it seemed I would rather lose all of them than my poor grandpa" (69). Her grief was shared by the Paiutes, who gathered from near and far for his deathwatch and funeral.

Like Apes and Copway, Winnemucca uses oratorical power to great effect in arousing the sympathy of her audience. One of the best examples of this style is her final exhortation:

> For shame! for shame! You dare to cry out Liberty, when you hold us in places against our will, driving us from place to place as if we were beasts. Ah, there is one thing you cannot say of the Indian. You call him savage, and everything that is bad, but one; but, thanks be to God, I am so proud to say that my people have never outraged your women, or have even insulted them by looks or words. . . . Oh, my dear readers, talk for us, and if the white people will treat us like human beings, we will behave like a people; but if we are treated by white savages as if we are savages, we are relentless and desperate; yet no more so than any other badly treated people. Oh, dear friends, I am pleading for God and for humanity. (243-44)

Life among the Piutes is the only book Winnemucca ever published. In 1882, the year before her book appeared, she published an article on Paiute ethnography, "The Pah-Utes," in *The Californian.* Despite her acute observations of Paiute life, her skillful storytelling, and her often eloquent style, Winnemucca did not continue her career as a writer. In 1884, she returned to her brother Naches's farm near Lovelock, Nevada, to establish a school for Paiute children. Ill health, despondence over marital difficulties, and lack of money forced her to abandon the school in 1887. Four years later she died.

V

Over the course of the nineteenth century, both the form and content of American Indian autobiographies changed substantially, reflecting the authors' increasing emphasis on personal accounts of tribal cultures and Indian-white relations, as well as shifts in popular taste. Although Apes's *Son of the Forest* follows the traditions of the spiritual confession, Copway combines this form with the missionary reminiscence and with tribal ethnohistory in his *Life, History, and Travels of Kah-ge-ga-gah-bowh.* The circumstances of Apes's upbringing and the acculturation of the Pequots precluded a detailed discussion of Pequot society. From the publication of Copway's and Winnemucca's autobiographies to the present, Indian authors have made tribal culture and history important parts of their life stories, reflecting their continuing perception of themselves as part of a tribal community, even after conversion and entry into a predominantly Western society. Stress, too, is placed on the art of storytelling. The plain chronicling of events that characterizes much of Apes's book gives way to the dramatization of scenes in Winnemucca's narrative. The result is greater realism and immediacy. Furthermore, Indian authors' movement away from the restrictive religious narrative and toward evocation of personal experiences parallels a similar trend among African American authors. It reflects the influence of the performances of oral narratives that Copway and Winnemucca observed during childhood.

Childhood memories play a significant part in the personal narratives of American Indians. Apes focuses on his spiritual experiences as a boy in order to illustrate his early religious devotion, a theme common to spiritual confessions, and to demonstrate the destruction of Indian family life resulting from the whites' introduction of alcohol and the indenturing of Indian children to whites. Copway devotes even more attention to his childhood than Apes does, in order to illustrate both the mutual bonds of affection that held Indian families together and the methods used to educate Ojibwa children in tribal customs and worldviews. Neither Apes, Copway, nor Winnemucca, however, examines the psychological influences of childhood on adult personality, as do early nineteenth-century European autobiographers.

Both Apes and Copway depict themselves as Christian Indians; Copway also presents himself as an Indian man of letters. Their common goal is to represent themselves as examples of what Indians can become if whites give them the opportunity to be converted and to be educated in white culture. The life histories of Indians, as well as of former slaves, were vehicles for demonstrating the potential of their races to become part of "civilized" society. The autobiographies were intended to educate white audiences about the injustice of their race to nonwhites. Like many of the slave narrators, Apes, Copway, and Winnemucca were eloquent orators in the cause of their people before they became authors. Although the theme of white injustice to Indians runs through the personal narratives of Apes and Copway, it is dominant in that of Winnemucca and in slave narratives as well.

The increasingly strong criticism of white injustice reflects the desperate plight of Indians by the end of the century and also parallels the growing militancy in the slave narratives published after the mid-1850s. By educating white audiences about the value of Indian culture and by advocating an Indian state west of the Missouri River, Copway hoped to ensure a tranquil life for Woodland Indians. By the time that white migration reached the Paiutes of the Far West, however, no such hope remained. Writers like Copway and Winnemucca put their faith in a policy of individual land allotments. All three authors appealed to their Christian audience's humanity. Winnemucca, however, realized that recitations of the value of tribal culture were not enough; she attacked those individuals responsible for the treatment of her people. In their oratorical styles, Apes and Copway undoubtedly reflected the influence of the evangelical tradition, although Native Americans have a heritage of oratory in rituals, council meetings, announcements of victory, formal petitions, addresses of welcome, and expressions of personal feeling. Growing up as they did in tribal societies, Copway and Winnemucca certainly drew on their mastery of traditional oratory. Whatever their approach to writing autobiography, all three authors

recognized the importance of the English language in their resistance to white encroachment. For them, the written word became a new weapon in the Indian's battle for survival.

Notes

[1] Research for this essay was done under a grant from the Research Division, NEH.

[2] "Cultural Bilingualism and Composition" 29-30. Toelken emphasizes that Indian students at the University of Oregon who held such an attitude toward the self would simply not write autobiographical theme assignments. Because narrated autobiographies are oral literature, they are not included in this study. Brumble provides a general study of the subject. For bibliographic information about American Indian autobiographies, see his *Annotated Bibliography of American Indian and Eskimo Autobiographies* and "The Autobiographies," supplement to the former appended to *American Indian Autobiography*.

[3] For general information on the Pequot and Ojibwa tribes, see Trigger. For material on the northern Paiutes, see Steward and Wheeler-Voegelin.

[4] The first written autobiographical narrative to be published is Hendrick Aupaumut's (Mohegan) *Narrative of an Embassy to the Western Indians* (1827). However, it is a journal rather than a full-life narrative. In 1791 Aupaumut recorded his experiences as he traveled for eleven months among the Miamis, Senecas, Ottawas, Shawnees, Onondagas, Wyandots, and others. See Brumble, "Autobiographies" in *American Indian Autobiography* 214-15.

[5] Unless otherwise indicated, all quotations are from the 1831 edition. For an account of Apes's career, see McQuaid.

[6] For a discussion of the methods slaves used to authenticate their autobiographies, see Stepto, *From behind the Veil* (ch. 1). F. S. Foster notes that antebellum slave narratives usually begin with what is known about the former slave's birth and childhood (55).

[7] Chief sachem of the Wampanoag Indians and son of Massasoit (d. 1662), Metacomet (c. 1639-76) was given the name King Philip by the English. Because Philip was a Wampanoag, Apes's paternal grandmother would have to be part Wampanoag if she were a blood relative to Philip. However, the relationship could have existed through adoption or membership in the same clan. The Pequots may have originally traced descent through the female line (Salwen 167). Both the Pequots and Wampanoags suffered grave losses because of the Puritans' conquest of their lands during the Pequot War (1637) and King Philip's War (1672-76). Jennings

refers to these as the First and Second Puritan Conquests. A strong supporter of the English until pushed beyond endurance, Philip united many New England tribes against the whites. However, the Pequots, who shared with the Wampanoags a long enmity against their neighbors the Narragansetts, sided with the English. For a brief account of these conflicts, see Washburn, "Seventeenth-Century Indian Wars." For fuller accounts see Jennings; D. E. Leach.

[8] Pascal comments that the autobiographer relates experiences rather than facts—that is, the interaction of a person and events (16). According to Starr, spiritual autobiographies placed little emphasis on the actual recording of experience. Undertaken as religious exercises, these works used facts purely as grounds for reflection (27). Shea notes that in the spiritual autobiographies of early America, the autobiographical act is reduced to testifying that one has conformed to certain patterns of feeling and behavior (91). F. S. Foster indicates that slave narratives did not include positive information unless it could directly be used to contrast with a negative experience or to document slave customs: "Courtships and marriages, for example, occur between the lines or are briefly and impersonally mentioned" (112).

[9] Although Joseph Sabin notes that "the real author of this work is said to be William J. Snelling," I find no evidence to support this claim (1: 229).

[10] All citations are to the 1850 edition. For biographical information, see D. B. Smith, "Kahgegagahbowh" and "Life of George Copway." See also Knobel.

[11] D. B. Smith indicates that Copway's accounts of his formal education vary. In his *Life* Copway indicates that James Evans instructed him in the alphabet (1830) and that between 1832 and 1834 he attended school at Rice Lake as "often as possible." He declares (in his *History*) that "twenty months passed in a school in Illinois has been the sum-total of my schooling. . . ." In *Running Sketches,* Copway contradicts both versions by claiming that he "was just learning" his English alphabet in 1839 (personal correspondence).

[12] Elizabeth Howell Copway is probably the "friend" who helped her husband prepare his autobiography. Copway was traveling much of the time that it was being prepared. Her letters indicate that she wrote well and she probably suggested the literary quotations Copway included in his works (Smith, "The Life of George Copway" 13-14, 17).

[13] Only one year later, William Wells Brown published the first travel book by an African-American writer, *Three Years in Europe* (Andrews, "1850s" 45 and n.).

[14] Three years earlier, in 1848, Maungwudaus (Ojibwa) had published a brief work entitled *An Account of the Chippewa Indians.* Knobel argues that Copway's autobiography, plan for a separate Indian territory, history of the Ojibwas, and newspaper were his responses to the efforts of the Lake Superior Ojibwa to resist removal. In 1847, Commissioner of Indian Affairs William Medill attempted to secure removal of the Ojibwa to central Minnesota from lands ceded them in 1842. Strongly opposed to this proposal, the Lake Superior bands sent a delegation to Washington in 1849 to persuade the president and Congress to allow them to retain land in Wisconsin and Upper Michigan. In 1850, however, President Zachary Taylor authorized immediate and complete removal of the Ojibwas from the lands ceded in 1842 (174-82).

[15] See, for example, Jones [Kahkewaquonaby] (Ojibwa), *Life* and *History,* both published by Jones's wife after his death; Clarke (Wyandot), *Origin;* Elias Johnson (Tuscarora), *Legends;* Warren, *History;* and Blackbird [Mackawdebenessy] (Ottawa) *History.*

[16] This change is exemplified in two of Frederick Douglass's autobiographies. Although, in his *Narrative,* Douglass examines his life as a slave and gives little information about his life as a freeman, he is optimistic about the future. In *My Bondage* Douglass reassesses his life from twenty-one years of slavery through seventeen years of freedom. Clearly restive under abolitionist demands that he simply tell his story, Douglass was no longer content merely to narrate wrongs; he now wanted to denounce them (Andrews, "1850s" 43, 55-60; Butterfield, ch. 4).

[17] S. Smith gives an excellent summary of the theoretical approaches to autobiography in her chapter "Autobiography Criticism and the Problematics of Gender" (*Poetics* 3-43). See also Jelinek, "Introduction: Women's Autobiography and the Male Tradition" in *Women's Autobiography* (1-20). As Sands points out, in "Indian Women's Personal Narrative," books on women's autobiography have not dealt with American Indian life histories. One of the few books to treat this topic is Bataille and Sands.

[18] For a full-length biography, see Canfield. Additional biographical information is contained in articles by Brimlow; C. Fowler; P. Stewart.

[19] The General Allotment Act of 1887 was designed to end the reservation system. Under the act, supported by both reformers and opportunists, Indians who took their land in severalty became citizens of the United States and were subject to all its obligations. Although the act was passed to enable Indians to become prosperous landowners, the measure instead ushered in an era in which Indians lost their land by fraud and force. By 1934, sixty percent of the land owned by Indians in 1887 had passed from their control. See Washburn, *The Indian in America* 242-43. For an Indian view of

the impact of allotment, see D'Arcy McNickle (Cree-Salish), *Native American Tribalism* 80-85, 91-92, an excellent source for the history of Indian-white relations in the twentieth century.

[20] F. S. Foster 132, 58. Harriet A. Brent Jacobs (Linda Brent) treats the theme of sexual harassment in *Incidents in the Life of a Slave Girl* (1861). Elizabeth Keckley's *Behind the Scenes* (1868) treats this theme briefly.

In *American Indian Autobiography*, Brumble concludes that *Life among the Piutes* was probably not influenced by written captivity or slave narratives. Brumble, whose comments are based on a draft of my essay, asserts that "we should not simply *assume* the degree of literacy and breadth of reading which Ruoff's argument would require of Winnemucca" (61, 63, 69). He believes that the elements of sexual violence and daring adventures in Winnemucca's autobiography that I point out as present in captivity and slave narratives "tell us more about Winnemucca's audience than about what might have influenced Winnemucca in writing her autobiography" (61).

Brumble misinterprets the thrust of my argument, which is that Winnemucca's and Copway's autobiographies in particular reflect a complex blend of influences: Native American oral traditions and popular literary forms. This does not suggest that Apes, Copway, or Winnemucca, all of whom had very little education, read widely in the genres whose forms and themes may be reflected in their work. We simply do not know what or how much they read. Such parallels may well reflect other kinds of influences. All three were skilled and experienced platform speakers who developed dramatic presentations of their life histories to convince their audiences of the virtues and values of their native cultures and to horrify their listeners with vivid descriptions of the suffering that whites inflicted on American Indians. To gain the attention of their audiences, they structured their narratives to reflect not only native oral traditions but also the forms and themes to which their readers would respond. The presence of aspects of popular literature in their autobiographies may reflect the narrators' responses to their non-Indian audiences, spouses, friends, and editors. Consequently, these parallels may well mirror the taste of the age rather than the literary background of the narrators.

Works Cited

Autobiography

Cruikshank, Julie, Angela Sidney, Kitty Smith, and Annie Ned. *Life Lived like a Story: Life Stories of Three Yukon Elders*. American Indian Lives. Lincoln: U of Nebraska P, 1991.

Primary Works

Apes, William (Pequot). *Eulogy on King Philip, as Pronounced at the Odeon, in Federal Street, Boston, by the Rev. William Apes, an Indian*. Boston: Author, 1836. Nonfiction prose.

————. *The Experiences of Five Christian Indians of the Pequod Tribe*. Boston: Dow, 1833. Rev. and repub. as *Experience of Five Christian Indians, of the Pequod Tribe*. Boston: Printed for the Publisher, 1837. Nonfiction.

————. *Indian Nullification of the Unconstitutional Laws of Massachusetts, Relative to the Marshpee Tribe: Or, The Pretended Riot Explained*. 1835. Foreword Jack Campisi. Stanfordville: Coleman, 1979. Nonfiction.

————. *A Son of the Forest: The Experience of William Apes, a Native of the Forest, Comprising a Notice of the Pequod Tribe of Indians*. New York: Author, 1829. Repub. as *A Son of the Forest. The Experience of William Apes, a Native of the Forest*. 2nd ed. rev. and cor. New York: Author, 1831. Autobiography.

Aupaumut, Hendrick (Mohegan). *A Narrative of an Embassy to the Western Indians, from the Original Manuscript of Hendrick Aupaumut, with Prefatory Remarks by Dr. B. H. Coates. Pennsylvania Historical Soc. Memoirs* 2.1 (1827): 61-131. Autobiography.

Black Hawk (Sauk). Antoine Le Claire and John B. Patterson. *Black Hawk, an Autobiography*. Orig. pub. as *Life of Ma-ka-tai-me-she-kia-kiha, or Black Hawk*. 1833. Ed. with new introd. Donald Jackson. Urbana: U of Illinois P, 1955. Autobiography.

Clarke, Peter Dooyentate (Wyandot). *Origin and Traditional History of the Wyandotts, and Sketches of Other Indian Tribes of North America: True Traditional Stories of Tecumseh and His League, in the Years 1811 and 1812*. Toronto: Hunter, 1870.

Copway, George (Ojibwa). *The Life, History, and Travels of Kah-ge-ga-gah-bowh (George Copway . . .)*. Albany: Weed, 1847. Rev. ed. *The Life, Letters and Speeches of Kah-ge-ga-gah-bowh: Or, G. Copway. . . .* New York: Benedict, 1850.

————. *Organization of a New Indian Territory, East of the Missouri River. Arguments and Reasons Submitted to the Honorable Members of the Senate and House of Representatives to the 31st Congress of the United States; by the Indian Chief Kah-ge-ga-gah-bouh [sic], or Geo. Copway*. New York: Benedict, 1850. Nonfiction.

————. *Running Sketches of Men and Places, in England, France, Germany, Belgium, and Scotland*. New York: Riker, 1851. Nonfiction prose.

————. *The Traditional History and Characteristic Sketches of the Ojibway Nation*. London: Gilpin, 1850. Repub. as *Indian Life and Indian History, by an Indian Author, Embracing the Traditions of the North American Indian Tribes Regarding Themselves, Particularly of That Most Important of All the Tribes, the Ojibways*. 1858. New York: AMS, 1977.

Johnson, Emily Pauline (Mohawk). *Canadian Born*. Toronto: Morang, 1903. Poetry.

————. *Flint and Feather*. Toronto: Musson, 1912. Markam: PaperJacks, 1973. Poetry.

————. *The Moccasin Maker*. 1913. Ed., annot., and introd. A. LaVonne Brown Ruoff. Tucson: U of Arizona P, 1987. Fiction and nonfiction.

————. *The Shagganappi*. Introd. Ernest Thompson Seton. Vancouver: Briggs, 1913. Short fiction.

————. *The White Wampum*. London: Bodley Head, 1895. Poetry.

Jones, Peter [Kahkewaquonaby] (Ojibwa). *History of the Ojebway Indians: With Especial Reference to Their Conversion to Christianity*. 1861. Freeport: Books for Libraries, 1970. Nonfiction.

————. *Life and Journals of Kah-ke-wa-quo-na-by (Rev. Peter Jones), Wesleyan Missionary*. Pub. under the direction of the Missionary Comm., Canada Conference. Toronto: Green, 1860. Nonfiction.

Maungwudaus [George Henry] (Chippewa). *An Account of the Chippewa Indians, Who Have Been Travelling among the Whites, in the United States, England, Ireland, Scotland, France and Belgium*. Boston: Author, 1848. Autobiography.

Winnemucca, Sarah [Hopkins] (Thocmetony; Paiute). *Life among the Piutes: Their Wrongs and Claims*. Ed. Mrs. Horace Mann. 1883. Bishop: Chalfant, 1969. Autobiography.

Secondary Works

Andrews, William L. "The 1850s: The First Afro-American Literary Renaissance." *Literary Romanticism in America*. Ed. Andrews. Baton Rouge: Louisiana State UP, 1981. 38-60.

Bataille, Gretchen M., and Kathleen Mullen Sands. *American Indian Women: Telling Their Lives*. Lincoln: U of Nebraska P, 1984.

Berkhofer, Robert F., Jr. *The White Man's Indian: Images of the American Indian from Columbus to the Present*. 1978. New York: Vintage, 1979.

Brimlow, George F. "The Life of Sarah Winnemucca: The Formative Years." *Oregon Historical Quarterly* 58 (1952): 103-34.

Brumble, H. David, III. *American Indian Autobiography*. Berkeley: U of California P, 1988.

Butterfield, Stephen. *Black Autobiography in America*. Amherst: U of Massachusetts P, 1974.

Canfield, Gae Whitney. *Sarah Winnemucca of the Northern Paiutes*. Norman: U of Oklahoma P, 1983.

Cooley, Thomas. *Educated Lives: The Rise of Modern Autobiography in America*. Columbus: Ohio State UP, 1976.

Foster, Frances Smith. *Witnessing Slavery: The Development of the Antebellum Slave Narratives*. Contributions in Afro-American and African Studies 46. Westport: Greenwood, 1979.

Hart, James. *The Popular Book: A History of America's Literary Taste*. New York: Oxford UP, 1950.

Jackson, Helen Hunt. *A Century of Dishonor: The Early Crusade for Indian Reform*. 1886. St. Clair Shores: Scholarly, 1973.

Jelinek, Estelle, ed. *Women's Autobiography: Essays in Criticism*. Bloomington: Indiana UP, 1980.

Jennings, Francis. *The Invasion of America: Indians, Colonialism, and the Cant of Conquest*. 1975. New York: Norton, 1976.

Knobel, Dale T. "Know-Nothings and Indians: Strange Bedfellows?" *Western Historical Quarterly* 15 (1984): 175-98.

Krupat, Arnold. *For Those Who Come After: A Study of Native American Autobiography*. Los Angeles: U of California P, 1985.

Leach, Douglas Edward. *Flintlock and Tomahawk: New England in King Philip's War*. 1958. New York: Norton, 1966.

Longfellow, Henry Wadsworth. *The Song of Hiawatha*. 1855. Facs. ed. New York: Crown, 1969.

McNickle, D'Arcy. *Native American Tribalism: Indian Survivals and Renewals*. New York: Oxford UP, 1973.

McQuaid, Kim. "William Apes, Pequot, an Indian Reformer in the Jackson Era." *New England Quarterly* 50 (1977): 605-25.

Pascal, Roy. *Design and Truth in Autobiography*. Cambridge: Harvard UP, 1960.

Pearce, Roy Harvey. "Red Gifts and White: The Image in Fiction." Pearce, *Savagism, Savages of America,* 196-236.

———. *Savagism and Civilization: A Study of the Indian and the American Mind.* 1953. Rpt. as *The Savages of America: A Study of the Indian and the Idea of Civilization.* Baltimore: Johns Hopkins UP, 1965. Rpt. under original title. Introd. Arnold Krupat. Afterword Pearce. Berkeley: U of California P, 1988.

Sabin, Joseph. *A Dictionary of Books Relating to America, from Its Discovery to the Present Time.* New York: Sabin, 1868.

Salwen, Bert. "Indians of Southern New England and Long Island." Trigger, *Northeast* 160-76.

Sands, Kathleen Mullen. "Indian Women's Personal Narrative: Voices Past and Present." *American Women's Autobiography.* Ed. Margot Culley. Madison: U of Wisconsin P, forthcoming.

Schoolcraft, Henry Rowe. *Algic Researches, Comprising Inquiries Respecting the Mental Characteristics of the North American Indian.* 2 vols. New York: Harper, 1839.

Shea, Daniel B., Jr. *Spiritual Autobiography in Early America.* Princeton: Princeton UP, 1968.

Smith, Donald B. "Kahgegagahbowh." *Dictionary of Canadian Biography.* Ed. George W. Brown et al. 1961-70 ed. 9: 419-21.

———. "The Life of George Copway or Kah-ge-ga-gah-bowh (1818-1869) and a Review of His Writings." *Journal of Canadian Studies* 23.3 (1988): 5-38.

Smith, Sidonie. *A Poetics of Women's Autobiography: Marginality and the Fictions of Self-Representation.* Bloomington: Indiana UP, 1987.

Starr, G. A. *Defoe and Spiritual Autobiography.* Princeton: Princeton UP, 1965.

Stepto, Robert B. *From behind the Veil: A Study of Afro-American Narratives.* Urbana: U of Illinois P, 1979.

Steward, Julian H., and Erminie Wheeler-Voegelin. *The Northern Paiute Indians.* Vol. 3 of *The Paiute Indians.* New York: Garland, 1974.

Toelken, J. Barre. "Cultural Bilingualism and Composition: Native American Education at the University of Oregon." *English for American Indians* (1971): 19-32.

Trigger, Bruce, ed. *Northeast.* Vol. 15 of *Handbook of the North American Indians.* Ed. William C. Sturtevant. Washington: Smithsonian, 1978.

Twain, Mark. *Roughing It.* 1872. Vol. 2 of *The Works of Mark Twain.* Ed. Franklin Rogers and Paul Baender. Berkeley: U of California P, 1972.

Washburn, Wilcomb E. *The Indian in America.* New York: Harper, 1975.

Winnemucca, Sarah [Hopkins]. "The Pah-Utes." *The Californian* 6 (1882): 252-56.

Arnold Krupat (essay date 1991)

SOURCE: "Native American Autobiography and the Synecdochic Self," *American Autobiography: Retrospect and Prospect,* edited by Paul John Eakin, The University of Wisconsin Press, 1991, pp. 171-94.

[*In the following excerpt, Krupat investigates how the concept of the "self" operates in Native American autobiographies. The critic analyzes William Apes' writings in particular in order to support his contention that the "Native American self" can be described as an "I-am-We experience . . . where such a phrase indicates that I understand myself as a self only in relation to the coherent and bounded whole of which I am a part."*]

Although studies of Native American autobiography have become more numerous of late, no one of them has yet taken as a central focus the matter that has perhaps more than any other occupied students of Western autobiography: the nature of the self presented in these texts. This is not to indicate an error or omission; on the contrary, inasmuch as the centrality of the self in Western autobiography finds no close parallel in Native American autobiography, any immediate orientation toward the self would inevitably have seemed ethnocentric, or at the least premature. But to say that the typical Western understanding of the self is neither prioritized nor valorized in Native American autobiography is not to say that all modes of subjectivity are, therefore, absent or unimportant in these texts. Whether or not Paul Heelas is correct in his sweeping suggestion that "the autonomous self is universal" (48), it is very likely the case that some sense of self—perhaps Amelie Rorty's "reflective, conscious subject of experience, a subject that is not identical with any set of its experiences, memories or traits, but is that which *has* all of them" (11)—is indeed to be found universally, and therefore also present among Native American people.

The problem is that every term in Rorty's (or any other) description is culturally inflected, determined in its meaning by the specific codes according to which we differentially "have," as historically and geographically situated men and women, our similar "experiences" as human beings.[1] What, after all, does it mean for the

Koya to be "reflective," for the Yaqui to be "conscious," for the Talensi to be a "subject," for the Ilongot to "remember"? Humans are or do all of these things, and we are or do them in the same ways—differently. Considerations of this sort have animated work in the ethnography of the self, from its rudimentary and initially "anti-psychological"[2] beginnings in the form of "culture and personality" studies from about 1910 on, to its current existence in the form of a decidedly "psychological anthropology." Yet for all of this work, we are still far from any conceptual and terminological consensus about how to speak of the *self*, the *individual*, or the *ego*, the *I*, or *me*, the *modal personality*, the *model of identity*—or, indeed, the *subject*,—where each of these terms signals not only a personal preference, a research interest or emphasis, but also, as Paul Smith has recently shown, a disciplinary affiliation (*subjects* coming more or less from philosophy, *selves* from the humanities, *egos* and *modal personalities* from the social sciences, etc.).[3] Even to the extent that we do know how these terms apply to the West, we know less well how they apply (or don't apply) to the rest, whose thought on such matters is reduced (or elevated) to the level of "indigenous psychologies."[4]

Studies of this sort are barely a century old, so that it would be premature to abandon, as a certain postmodernist strain of thought would urge, further efforts in the direction of some greater accuracy of description and explanation. Yet it is necessary to acknowledge here a practical rather than a theoretical problem certain to beset advances along these lines, one akin to a problem that Freud posited for the general prospects of psychoanalysis.[5] I refer to the fact that while it is a fairly simple matter to convince people that their eating or greeting habits are cultural rather than natural, it is considerably more difficult to convince them that the ways in which they think and deeply feel about themselves are also more nearly culturally than biologically determined. And modern, Western concepts of the self are so thoroughly committed to notions of interiority and individualism that even anthropologically sophisticated Westerners tend to construct their accounts of the varieties of selfhood as evolutionary narratives, telling stories of a progression from the social and public orientation of ancient or "primitive" self-conception (the self as social "person") to the modern, Western, "civilized," egocentric/individualist sense of self.[6]

This tendency may be responsible for the comic plot of Marcel Mauss's 1938 essay, most recently translated as "A Category of the Human Mind: The Notion of Person; the Notion of Self." This classic piece tells a story which has as its happy ending the emergence of the *moi*, the Western postromantic self as veritably "sacred," a construction that surpasses the *personnage* models of the Native Americans, Mauss's chief illustrative example, and the *personnalité* models of ancient and/or non-Western peoples generally. For Mauss, Native American self-consciousness was minimal, or, better, defined by the etymology of the word *person* (*personne, personnage*), from Latin *persona, per sonare,* as this referred to the mask through which the actor spoke his role in public. Not an individual with rights and responsibilities before the law (this must await the Roman addition of the right to a personal *praenomen,* or "forename," and the Christian invention of "the moral person"), the Indian was rather the representative of his ancestor or his clan, an actor who merely performed his appointed character. He (*she* was rarely at issue) knew nothing of that consciousness which is self-consciousness as "an act of the 'self'," which, from Fichte on, saw "the revolution in mentalities . . . accomplished" (Mauss, 22). The modern *moi,* I will suggest, may be seen at its apogee in such texts as Gerard Manley Hopkins's "As king-fishers catch fire, dragonflies draw flame," where the inward self appears both as actor "in God's eye," and unique romantic consciousness. For Hopkins,

> Each mortal thing does one thing and the
> same:
> Deals out that being indoors each one dwells;
> Selves—goes itself; *myself* it speaks and
> spells,
> Crying *What I do is me: for that I came* (51).

But this lovely indoor self, in Mauss's tale, unfortunately was never present to the poor outdoor Indian.

In his ultimate celebration of the inward self, Mauss, as a number of commentators have noted, seems to renege on his initial promise to "leave aside everything which relates to the 'self' (*moi*), the conscious personality as such," and to focus instead on the "social history" (3) of the person, the category of prime concern to Mauss's uncle and *maître,* Emile Durkheim, as it was to the major but—at least in literary circles—somewhat obscure figure, George Herbert Mead. Mead's "social theory of the self," as Stephen Lukes has remarked, sought "to explain how it can be, in all societies and cultures, that [in Mead's words, now]

> all selves are constituted by or in terms of the social
> process, and are individual reflections of it [yet]
> every individual self has its own peculiar individuality,
> its own unique pattern (Lukes, 287).

In this regard, any attempt to privilege the sacred inviolability of the self by setting it in opposition to society or culture, standard Western bourgeois practice at least since Fichte, involves a significant loss of understanding. To avoid just such a loss, indeed, to achieve some gain in understanding, we get, in the forties and fifties, a redescription of the Native American sense of self by such writers as Dorothy Lee and George Devereux, among others, in ways that seek not to make it seem "primitive" and retrograde, but progressively wiser than the West in its comprehension of the dynamics of self and society: here is comedy once again, only with a different protagonist.[7] It was Devereux's opinion that for the Native Americans, "maximum individuation and maximum socialization go hand in hand" ("From Anxiety to Method," 291), while Lee concluded that Lakota cultures demonstrate "autonomy and community in transaction" ("Autonomy," 41). Of the Wintu self, Lee noted (her generalizations supported by impressionistically selective citations from Wintu grammar and diction), that it is

> not clearly opposed to the other, neither is it clearly identical with or incorporated in the other. On most occasions it participates to some extent in the other, and is of equal status to the other . . . ("Conception of the Self," 137).

Wintu know "society" more easily than the "self," the reverse of our Western knowledge, but most of all, Wintu seem to have found a way to reconcile what often appears to Euro-Americans as an opposition between self and society.[8]

In any event, insofar as we would attempt to generalize about the Native American self from the available studies, that self would seem to be less attracted to introspection, integration, expansion, or fulfilment than the Western self appears to be. It would seem relatively uninterested in such things as the "I-am-Me" experience,[9] and a sense of uniqueness or individuality. More positively, one might perhaps instantiate an I-am-We experience as descriptive of the Native sense of self, where such a phrase indicates that I understand myself as a self only in relation to the coherent and bounded whole of which I am a part (e.g., the preceding quotation from Lee above). Here, Jane Fajans's distinction between the "*person* as a bounded entity invested with specific patterns of social behavior, normative powers, and restraints, and the *individual* as an entity with interiorized conscience, feelings, goals, motivations, and aspirations" (370; my emphasis) is useful. Native Americans (along with most of the world's people, it would seem) tend to construct themselves not as individuals but as persons, who, because of their sensitivity to social "restraints," may well feel more nearly "under control," in Andrew Lock's term, rather than "in control" (28ff), the sense of self more typical of Western "individuals" oriented toward interiority. It needs to be said that this subjective sense of the matter does not mean that Native American "persons" are, in point of objective fact, more "controlled" than Euro-American "individuals," nor that their sense of operative "restraints" corresponds closely to what the Western bourgeois individual would understand by such terms. . . .

Native American autobiography, a post-contact phenomenon, as I have detailed the matter elsewhere,[20]

exists in two forms, the Indian autobiography and the autobiography by an Indian. The first of these is constituted as a genre of writing by its original, bicultural, composite composition, the product of a collaboration between the Native American subject of the autobiography, who provides its "content," and its Euro-American editor, who ultimately provides its "form" by fixing the text in writing. Autobiographies by Indians, however, are indeed self-written lives; there is no compositeness to their composition, although inasmuch as their subject, in order to *write* a life, must have become "civilized" (in many cases Christianized as well), there remains the element of biculturalism. In both sorts of texts, let me claim, we find a privileging of the synecdochic relation of part-to-whole over the metonymic relation of part-to-part.[21]

At this point, the reader may well expect some illustrative demonstration of a synecdochic nature to make its entrance, a detailed reading of a single text being offered as representative of a larger body of autobiographical work; nor will I fail to conform to such expectation. I have chosen to consider an autobiography by an Indian rather than an Indian autobiography for two reasons. First, every aspect of the Indian autobiography, including the particular sense of self conveyed, is at least theoretically ascribable to its non-Native editor as much as to its Native subject. This fact raises questions it would be too cumbersome to deal with just here. More importantly, to work with the autobiographies of traditional, tribal persons—and Indian autobiographies are almost exclusively focused on this sort of person—and then to show that they are indeed traditionally tribal, relationally synecdochic, courts even a greater circularity than such exercises must inevitably involve. As noted, Indians who write their own life stories must first have learned to write and, at least to that extent, been influenced by the dominant Euro-American culture. To see whether their autobiographical presentations of self, therefore, have also been influenced by the dominant culture—whether they have, in my terms, tended to move from synecdochic to metonymic senses of the self—seems the more interesting tack to take. I proceed now to consider the autobiographical work of the Reverend William Apes (1798-1837).

One of the very first autobiographies by an Indian is *A Son of the Forest* (1829) by the mixed-blood Pequot and Methodist preacher, the Reverend William Apes.[22] This text was followed in 1833 by Apes's the *Experiences of Five Christian Indians of the Pequod Tribe*, the first chapter of which, the "Experience of the Missionary," offers a second brief autobiography by Apes ("the Missionary"). This makes no reference to *A Son of the Forest* but instead promises a further autobiographical volume, "a book of 300 pages, 18mo. in size; and there, the reader will find particulars respecting my life" (4). Apes was never to write such a book, although his further publications—*Indian Nullification of the Unconstitutional Laws of Massachusetts, Relative to the Marshpee Tribe* (1835), in part an account of political work on behalf of the Mashpees which landed him in prison, and *Eulogy on King Philip* (1836), a fierce attack on the Puritan origins of American racism—are both intensely personal. All of his texts, I would suggest, may fruitfully be read as pieces of an extended autobiography.

By 1798, the year of William Apes's birth, Pequot cultural integrity was at a low point. This is to say that aboriginal lands had been usurped or heavily encroached upon by whites, so that traditional ecological economies and cultural practices were severely disrupted where they were not entirely destroyed. Disease, alcoholism, and Christianity served as further agents undermining tribal coherence and cultural competence, with predictable effects on Native self-conception—although Apes came to view Christianity as part of the solution, rather than part of the problem. Apes did not live long with his parents, who tended to move about considerably. Placed with his grandparents, Apes was so cruelly treated—at the age of four, his arm was broken in three places (*Son of the Forest*, 12) as the result of a drunken beating administered by his grandmother—that he eventually was sent to live "among good Christian people" (13). Their goodness did not prevent them from "selling" (31) him to a judge who worked him and "sold" (35) him to someone else. I will not detail Apes's life-adventures further[23]; suffice it to say that he eventually became a convert to evangelical Methodism, attaining to the position of licensed Methodist "exhorter," (111) although the license to preach which he desired was still, at the conclusion of *A Son of the Forest*, withheld from him.

At this point in his life, Apes seems to see himself as something like Mauss's Christian "'moral person',," virtually "a metaphysical entity" (19). Although Mauss reads the Christian stage of Western self-conception as a step on the way toward (these are, of course, my terms, not those of Mauss) metonymic construals of self, it needs to be said that this is by no means the only reading possible. Christian tradition gives us abundant instances of solitary individuals seeking relation foremost with God (e.g., the early desert fathers, medieval mystics, Louis Dumont's "outworldly" Christian individuals), but it also gives us abundant images of individuals defined foremost by a sense of commonality and community (Dumont's post-Calvinist "inwardly" Christians). For every "I" focused exclusively on "Thou"; for everyone trying to love her particularized neighbor, there are also those who are committed to doing unto *all* others as they would be done to themselves; those committed to what William Bradford called "the church or commonwealth" (39), made up of persons who believe that (I return to Dumont) "we should embody that other world in our determined action upon this one" (116).

It is this latter sense of Christian self-definition that is important to Apes, nor does he fail to grasp its political implications. Towards the close of *A Son of the Forest,* Apes writes

> I feel a great deal happier in the *new* [Methodist Society] than I did in the *old* [Methodist Episcopal] church—the government of the first is founded on *republican,* while that of the latter is founded on *monarchial* principles . . . (115).

And Apes "rejoice[s] sincerely in the spread of the principles of civil and religious liberty—may they ever be found 'hand in hand' . . ." (115). He believes that

> If these blessed principles prevail . . . the image of God in his members will be a sufficient passport to all Christian privileges; and all the followers of the most high will unite together in singing the song of praise, *Glory to God in the highest, &c.* (115).

In this way Apes seeks to replace the lost paradise of the Pequot—what he called in the first paragraph of his autobiography, "the goodly heritage occupied by this once peaceable and happy tribe" (7)—with the paradise regained in Christ. The tribe to which he would now belong, defining himself by his membership, is that of "the followers of the most high." Obviously enough, "*all* the followers of the most high" (my emphasis) must include Indians—at least those Native "members" of the saved in whom "the image of God" is to "be a sufficient passport to all Christian privileges." "Look brethren," Apes exhorts in his penultimate paragraph,

> at the natives of the forest—they come, notwithstanding you call them *"savage,"* from the "east and from the west, the north and the south," and will occupy [because the last shall be first?] seats in the kingdom of heaven before you (116).

Yet for all that Christian Indians will share equally with Christian whites a heavenly heritage in the future, those same Indians, now, in the present, are abused and discriminated against by whites. Nor is it Indians only, as Apes came increasingly to understand, but blacks and all people of color[24] who suffer from American racial prejudice. Here, the incompatibility of Christianity and racism emerges as a major theme of William Apes's subsequent writing (as it would, of course, become a theme of Frederick Douglass and the abolitionists). I shall try to say in a moment how this bears on the question of his synecdochic self-definition.

Consider, in these regards, Apes's second brief autobiography, "The Experience of the Missionary." Addressed to the "youth," "those poor children of the forest, who have had taken from them their once delightful plains, and homes of their peaceable habitations . . ." (*Experience of Five Indians,* 3), Apes's account of his life here places a particular emphasis on those aspects of his suffering that occurred because of race prejudice. In a text of only seventeen pages, Apes's increased awareness of the problem of color in America is indicated by such phrases and sentences as "Had my skin been white . . ." (8); "Now, if my face had been white . . ." (9), "I would ask the white man, if he thinks that he can be justified in making just such a being as I am . . . unhappy . . . because God has made us thus . . ." (17); "I was already a hissing-stock and a by-word in the world, merely because I was a child of the forest . . ." (19); and so on.

In these regards, consider also that the cover of the first edition of *The Experience,* gives its full title as *The Experiences of Five Christian Indians: or The Indian's Looking Glass for the White Man.* But *The Indian's Looking Glass . . .* is not merely an alternate title for the collection of autobiographies, but the title of a pamphlet or sermon that appears after the fifth "Experience," at the end of the book. This is a brilliant and violent attack on racism. I will quote its first sentences; they indicate, I believe, a new strength and stylistic assurance.[25] Apes begins,

> Having a desire to place a few things before my fellow creatures who are travelling with me to the grave, and to that God who is the maker and preserver both of the white man and the Indian, whose abilities are the same, and who are to be judged by one God, who will show no favor to outward appearances, but will judge righteousness. Now I ask if degradation has not been heaped long enough upon the Indians (53)?

The *or* in the compound title—*or,* that is, instead of *and*—on the cover would seem to urge that the whole of Apes's book be taken as providing a "looking glass" for the white man. And what that looking glass reflects above all are the "national crimes" (56) of white Americans. Here is the extraordinary passage in which this phrase occurs; I believe it is worth quoting at length:

> Assemble all nations together in your imagination, and then let the whites be seated amongst them, and then let us look for the whites, and I doubt not it would be hard finding them; for to the rest of the nations, they are still but a handful. Now suppose these skins were put together, and each skin had its national crimes written upon it[26]—which skin do you think would have the greatest? I will ask one question more. Can you charge the Indians with robbing a nation almost of their whole Continent, and murdering their women and children, and then depriving the remainder of their lawful rights, that nature and God require them to have? And to cap the climax, rob another nation to till their grounds, and welter out their days under the lash with hunger

and fatigue under the scorching rays of a burning sun? I should look at all the skins, and I know that when I cast my eye upon that white skin, and if I saw those crimes written upon it, I should enter my protest against it immediately, and cleave to that which is more honorable. And I can tell you that I am satisfied with the manner of my creation, fully— whether others are or not (56).

Apes's next work (the *Indian Nullification*) continues his concern with racism, announcing it explicitly as central to his life. Writing in the third person, Apes announces in his Introduction that the author

> wishes to say in the first place, that the causes of the prevalent prejudice against his race have been his study from his childhood upwards. That their colour should be a reason to treat one portion of the human race with insult and abuse has always seemed to him strange; believing that God has given to all men an equal right to possess and occupy the earth, and to enjoy the fruits thereof, without any such distinction (10).

Apes now sees himself quite self-consciously as the prophet of color-blind Christianity, and this bears upon the question of self-definition inasmuch as it would seem he can be fully himself only as an Indian member of the tribe of the nonracist saved. It is the part-to-whole relation in which the self as such is validated only in its social-collective (Christian) personhood that is important to Apes. But let us come finally to William Apes's last known text, the *Eulogy on King Philip.*

Apes's turn to King Philip is rather a return, for the initial sentence of his first work, *A Son of the Forest,* had described its author as "a native of the American soil, and a descendant of one of the principal chiefs of the Pequod tribe, so well known in that part of American history called King Philip's Wars" (7). It was Philip's defeat in war which initiated the Pequots' loss "of the[ir] goodly heritage," and so it may come as no surprise to discover that a vindication of Philip, the narrative reconstitution of his "defeat" as a victory, now becomes for Apes the necessary condition for any recuperation of that "goodly heritage." The *Eulogy* proclaims Philip "the greatest man that was ever in America" (55-56), providing a revisionist history of the Pilgrim invasion: "the seed of iniquity and prejudice was sown in that day" (21), when the Pilgrims invaded these shores, Apes writes. Speaking to the descendants of the Pilgrims and Puritans in Boston, Apes would yet say,

> Let the children of the pilgrims blush, while the son of the forest drops a tear, and groans over the fate of his murdered and departed fathers. He would say to the sons of the pilgrims, (as Job said about his birth day,) let the day be dark, the 22d of December,

1622; let it be forgotten in your celebration, in your speeches, and by the burying of the Rock that your fathers first put their foot upon. For be it remembered, although the gospel is said to be glad tidings to all people, yet we poor Indians never have found those who brought it as messengers of mercy, but contrawise. We say therefore, let every man of color wrap himself in mourning, for the 22d of December and the 4th of July are days of mourning and not of joy (20).

And so, Apes continues, "while you ask yourselves, what do they, the Indians, want? you have only to look at the unjust laws made for them, and say they want what I want," which is that "all men must operate under one general law" (59). That law is to be, as Apes had earlier written, both "civil and religious," (*Son of the Forest,* 115), for it is the implication of Christianity as Apes understands it that the "image of God in his members," be the "sufficient passport to all Christian privileges" (*Son of the Forest,* 115), not only in Heaven but here on earth as well—and, as he says, "first, in New England" (*Eulogy,* 59).

Curiously—amazingly?—Apes's *Eulogy* was sufficiently popular to warrant a second edition in 1837, after which year, as I have noted, no more is known of the Reverend William Apes. So far as his writings may be taken as formally and informally autobiographical, it seems reasonable to suggest that they show him as engaged in a very particular form of synecdochic self-definition. Recalling from the first a lost tribal identity and a "goodly heritage" in which all share together, he attempts with increasing self-consciousness to reconstitute and redefine his "tribe" and its "heritage" in Christian terms as a means of constituting and defining himself—this latter process, in typical Native American fashion, hardly self-conscious at all. The tribe to which Apes will ultimately belong must finally be made up not so much of Pequots or Puritans, not even only of Christians, "but [of] men" (*Eulogy,* 59). In the end, Apes is simply an Indian member of the color-blind saved, one of those nonracist Christians who, like most Indians traditionally, are usually more interested in their integration within a principled community rather than in their unique or "sacred" individuality.

Apes's synecdochic presentation of self finds parallels in a great many autobiographies by Indians. I would instance first Sarah Winnemucca Hopkins's *Life Among the Paiutes: Their Wrongs and Claims* (1883), whose very title proclaims her individual life as comprehensible foremost in relation to the collective experience of her tribe. Then there is Charles Alexander Eastman's *From the Deep Woods to Civilization: Chapters in the Autobiography of an Indian* (1916) with its conclusion, "I am an Indian. . . . I am an American" (195). Approaching the present, there is Leslie Marmon Silko's *Storyteller* (1981) which, as I have described it else-

where,[27] conceives of individual identity only in functional relation to the tribe. Silko, as a contemporary Laguna "storyteller," takes her place in a line of "storytellers as far back as memory goes" ("Dedication," n.p.); she is what she does to sustain her community. Finally, we may look to the ongoing autobiographical projects of the Minnesota Chippewa novelist and critic, Gerald Vizenor, who, in his recent "Crows Written on the Poplars: Autocritical Autobiographies," invokes the "mixedblood," the trickster, and the author as categories in relation to which he may define himself. Inasmuch as "mixedbloods loosen the seams in the shrouds of identity" (101), they have a ready relation to tricksters—those jokers, shape-changers, and limit-challengers—and to writers of fiction, poetry, or criticism who are all, if true to their vocation, focused on the powers of the imagination. And Vizenor will define himself as one of the mixed-bloods, tricksters, and writers—for all that these each take self-definition as a loose and impermanent thing.

For all of this, I would not want to be understood as claiming that all autobiographies by Indians must necessarily be unimpressed by varieties of individualism, nor that all autobiographies by Native people must take synecdoche as their defining figure. The autobiographies by the much-acclaimed N. Scott Momaday, a Kiowa, seem to me as metonymic in their orientation as those by Rousseau and Thoreau, for example.[28] In the same way, Western autobiography is hardly constrained to metonymic strategies. Some autobiographical writing by Western women and certain forms of Christian autobiography, as I have noted above, are quite likely to adopt synecdochic types of self-identification, as are the autobiographies of writers whose deep commitment to political egalitarianism works to structure their self-conception in a part-to-whole manner: I think here, for example of Prince Peter Kropotkin, Emma Goldman, and, more recently, Assata Shakur.[29] For all that, so far as one may generalize, it nonetheless seems true that Native American autobiography is marked by the figure of synecdoche in its presentation of the self.

Notes

[1] If not another "problem," another consideration is that while *some* sense of self may be universal, that sense of self, whatever it may be, does not receive cultural validation. As we shall see, not selfhood, hallmark of "individualist" society, so much as personhood, hallmark of the "holist" society (Dumont, *passim*), is what is found among most of the world's people.

[2] Clyde Kluckhohn, quoted by A. I. Hallowell ("The Self," 387n). I would not be quite so certain as Marsella, DeVos, and Hsu, writing at the meridian of Reaganism, that "The Self has returned!" (n.p.), nor so unequivocally cheered if that were indeed the case. Neverthe-

less, it does seem to be true that psychological anthropology, for better or worse, is currently on an upswing and that its focus of study is whatever name we choose to give to the unitary male's or female's own sense of him- or herself as a unit entity. Almost by definition, a strictly conceived *psychological* anthropology tends to privilege the individual perception of self, projecting a Western bourgeois bias. For a tough, ideologically-inflected account of the early culture and personality movement, see Harris. Although culture-and-personality studies may be dated from as early as 1910, their influence, through Benedict, Mead, and others (cf. n. 7, below) is more nearly a matter of the thirties. Hsu is particularly hostile to *personality* as the reference term for this type of study, which may account for the title of his co-edited text, *Culture and Self.* Thomas Williams lists over a hundred and twenty references that permit the interested reader to trace the historical trajectory from culture and personality to psychological anthropology in his "The Development of Psychological Anthropology," the introduction to a collection of essays on the subject. For the "continuities" between the two orientations, see also the study by Philip K. Bock. Victor Barnouw's textbook, in its fourth edition as of 1985, still adheres to the older nomenclature for its title. The introduction by John Kirkpatrick and Geoffrey M. White to their *Person, Self, and Experience: Exploring Pacific Ethnopsychologies* offers a particularly sophisticated and thoughtful account of these matters. The journal, *Ethos,* published by the American Society for Psychological Anthropology was founded in 1973.

3 See Smith, *Discerning the Subject.*

4 See, for example, Heelas and Lock, eds., *Indigenous Psychologies.*

5 Sigmund Freud, "One of the Difficulties of Psychoanalysis."

6 Paul Heelas, who develops practical applications of Andrew Lock's distinction between concepts of the self as "in control" or "under control," according to what he calls "idealist" or *"passiones"* models (39ff), quotes Edward Tylor, Lucien Levy-Bruhl, and C. Hallpike in ways that would seem to indicate their attachment to a Western view for all their (rudimentary, in Tylor's case) commitment to versions of cultural relativism.

7 But there is a complicated history here, which, although it is beyond the scope of this paper, is very well worth detailing. The background involves Ruth Benedict's prescriptive "descriptions" in *Patterns of Culture* of Native American personality clusters; Margaret Mead's Pacific excursus in *Coming of Age in Samoa;* and Erik Erikson's intervention culminating in detailed accounts in *Childhood in Society* of correla-

tions (Erikson being quite careful to deny any claim to statements of a directly causal nature) between Yurok and Sioux childrearing practices and adult character structures. The work of Anthony Wallace with the Tuscarora and A. I. Hallowell with the Ojibwa also deserves mention, as does that of George Spindler and the "rorschachists." George Devereux's important invention, as it were, of ethnopsychoanalysis, commences with the practical demonstration of his *Reality and Dream: the Psychoanalysis of a Plains Indian,* and achieves full theoretical statement in *From Anxiety to Method.* Current work along a variety of these lines, as I have noted above, is abundant. Still, the conclusions of Richard Shweder's recent three-part essay, "Rethinking Culture and Personality Theory," is that "Most of the postulates of the culture and personality school . . . worked out in the 1940s and 1950s . . . do not weather well under empirical and conceptual scrutiny" (I:255-6). Shweder's own positions are "worked out" in his "Does the concept of the person vary cross-culturally?" (co-authored with Edmund J. Bourne).

8 To the extent this is true, it might then be said that some Native American cultures seem to have reconciled the apparently antithetical implications of the English words *subject* and *individual,* for all that these are often used as synonyms. As Raymond Williams has usefully pointed out, the etymology of the first, from the Latin *sub-* and *jactum* (p.p.), to be thrown under or beneath, persists in the senses of being subject to, the subject of, subjected, and so forth (e.g., Lock's self "under control"). The etymology of *individual,* however, continues to carry with it the original sense of "indivisible," as if one were fully present to oneself and uniquely empowered as causal agent (e.g., Lock's self "in control"). This sense of the individual, espoused ahistorically by a certain vulgar humanism in the fifties, called forth an equivalently vulgar antihumanism in the sixties and after (as, e.g., in much of Foucault), with no place whatever for the active force of human agency. For a fine account of these matters, see Kate Soper's *Humanism and Anti-Humanism.*

9 For the "I-am-me" experience, see Eakin (217-9). . . .

20 See my *For Those Who Come After.*

21 Gerard Genette quotes an early text of Mauss, the 1902 *Esquisse d'une theorie de la magie [Sketch of a Theory of Magic]* to the effect that "The simplest form [of association by contiguity] is the identification of the part with the whole" (108). Thus Mauss's early sense of the simple or primitive nature of synecdoche would seem to accord with his late sense of the simple or primitive nature of *personnage* concepts of self.

22 Apes was preceded as an autobiographer by the Reverend Samson Occom, a Mohegan, who wrote a brief account of his life in 1762, and by Hendrick

Aupaumut, generally referred to as a Mahican, who produced a text in 1792 that at least contained a good deal of autobiographical material. The *Memoir of Catherine Brown, a Christian Indian of the Cherokee Nation,* as edited by the missionary Rufus Anderson, appeared in the same year, 1829, as Apes's text. The very brief life history of Paul Cuffe, like Apes, a Pequot, appeared in 1839. By that time the first Indian autobiography, J. B. Patterson's *Life of Black Hawk* (1833) had been published. For further references, see the indispensable annotated bibliography by David Brumble *(An Annotated Bibliography)* and its "Supplement," as well as Brumble's recent full-length study, *American Indian Autobiography.* My own book *(For Those Who Come After),* as well as the introduction to Swann and Krupat, may also prove helpful.

23 A further account of Apes's life and work, most particularly in relation to the Bakhtinian concern with the plural elements of "individual" speech appears in my "Monologue and Dialogue in Native American Autobiography."

24 This includes the Jews, who, as Apes writes in *The Indian's Looking Glass,* "are a colored people, especially those living in the East, where Christ was born . . ." (60)!

25 The grammar, to be sure, is questionable, the two sentences properly constituting but a single sentence. But it should be remembered that Apes's written style is very much the transcription of an oral manner. Whatever he may or may not have known and remembered of aboriginal orality, his commitment to a Christian tradition of "exhorting" and "preaching" provides a continuity with Native modes of communication. It is fitting, therefore, that his final work is "only" the text of what was orally "pronounced at the Odeon."

26 I find it difficult not to think of Kafka's "In the Penal Colony," just here. Apes's image of corporeal criminal inscription resonates with a good deal of contemporary theoretical work.

27 See my "Monologue and Dialogue."

28 See Momaday, *The Way to Rainy Mountain* and *The Names,* and my discussion in the study cited in note 27.

29 See Kropotkin, *Memoirs of a Revolutionist;* Goldman, *Living My Life,* and Shakur, *Assata.* Shakur's use of lowercase *i* within sentences (she capitalizes *I* at the beginning of sentences, where all letters equivalently get to appear in uppercase) seems a gesture in the interest of bringing the individual ego back to proper scale as simply an existant among others.

Works Cited

Apes, William. *A Son of the Forest: The Experience of William Apes, a Native of the Forest.* New York: Published by the Author, 1829.

———. *The Experience of Five Christian Indians of the Pequod Tribe; or the Indian's Looking-Glass for the White Man.* Boston: James B. Dow, 1833.

———. *Indian Nullification of the Unconstitutional Laws of Massachusetts, Relative to the Marshpee Tribe: or, The Pretended Riot Explained.* Boston: Jonathan Howe, 1835.

———. *Eulogy on King Philip, as Pronounced at the Odeon in Federal Street, Boston, by the Rev. William Apes, an Indian, January 8, 1836.* [Boston: 1836]. Reprint. Brookfield, MA: Lincoln A. Dexter, 1985.

Aupaumut, Hendrick. *A Narrative of an Embassy to the Western Indians, from the Original Manuscript of Hendrick Aupaumut, with Prefatory Remarks by Dr. B. H. Coates.* [1791]. *Pennsylvania Historical Society Memoirs* 2, pt. I (1827): 61-131.

Barnouw, Victor. *Culture and Personality.* Homewood, IL: Dorsey, 1985.

Benedict, Ruth. *Patterns of Culture.* [1934]. New York: Mentor, 1946.

Black Elk. *Black Elk Speaks.* [1932]. Ed. John G. Neihardt. Lincoln: University of Nebraska Press, 1979.

Black Hawk. *Black Hawk: An Autobiography.* [1833]. Ed. Donald Jackson. Champaign-Urbana: University of Illinois Press, 1964.

Bock, Philip K. *Continuities in Psychological Anthropology.* San Francisco: W. H. Freeman, 1980.

Brown, Catherine. *Memoirs of Catherine Brown a Christian Indian of the Cherokee Nation.* Ed. Rufus B. Anderson. Philadelphia: American Sunday School Union, 1824.

Brumble, David. *An Annotated Bibliography of American Indian and Eskimo Autobiographies.* Lincoln: University of Nebraska Press, 1981.

———. "A Supplement to *An Annotated Bibliography of American Indian and Eskimo Autobiographies.*" *Western American Literature* 17 (1982): 242-60.

———. *American Indian Autobiography.* Berkeley: University of California Press, 1988.

Cuffe, Paul. *Narrative of the Life and Adventures of Paul Cuffe, Pequot Indian: During Thirty Years at Sea, and in Travelling in Foreign Lands*. Vernon [?]: Horace N. Bill, 1839.

Devereux, George. *From Anxiety to Method in the Behavioral Sciences*. The Hague: Mouton, 1967.

———. *Reality and Dream: Psychotherapy of a Plains Indian*. [1951]. Garden City, NY: Anchor, 1969.

Dumont, Louis. "A Modified View of Our Origins: The Christian Beginnings of Modern Individualism." In Carrithers, Collins, and Lukes, eds., *Category*, 93-122.

Eakin, Paul John. *Fictions in Autobiography*. Princeton: Princeton University Press, 1985.

Eastman, Charles Alexander. *From the Deep Woods to Civilization: Chapters in the Autobiography of an Indian*. [1916]. Lincoln: University of Nebraska Press, 1977.

Erikson, Eric. *Childhood and Society*. [1950]. New York: W. W. Norton, 1963.

Fajans, Jane. "The Person in Social Context: The Social Character of Baining 'Psychology'." In White and Kirkpatrick, eds. *Person, Self, and Experience*, 367-400.

Freud, Sigmund. "One of the Difficulties of Psychoanalysis." In *Collected Papers of Sigmund Freud*. Vol. 4. Trans. Joan Riviere. London: Hogarth, 1925, 347-56.

Genette, Gerard. *Figures of Literary Discourse*, Tr. Alan Sheridan, New York: Columbia University Press, 1982.

Goldman, Emma. *Living My Life*. 2 vols. [1931]. New York: Dover, 1970.

Hallowell, A.I. "The Self and Its Behavioral Environment." In *Culture and Experience*. Philadelphia: University of Pennsylvania Press, 1955, 75-111.

Harris, Marvin. *The Rise of Anthropological Theory*. New York: Crowell, 1968.

Heelas, Paul. "The Model Applied: Anthropology and Indigenous Psychologies." In Heelas and Lock, eds., *Indigenous Psychologies*, 39-64.

Heelas, Paul, and Andrew Lock, eds. *Indigenous Psychologies: The Anthropology of the Self*. London: Academic, 1981.

Hopkins, Gerard Manley. A Selection of His Poems and Prose. Ed. W. H. Gardner, Baltimore: Penguin, 1953.

Hopkins, Sarah Winnemucca. *Life Among the Piutes: Their Wrongs and Claims*. [1883]. Ed. Mrs. Horace Mann. Bishop, CA: Chalfant Press, 1969.

Kropotkin, Peter. *Memoirs of a Revolutionist*. [1899]. Gloucester, MA: Peter Smith, 1967.

Krupat, Arnold. *For Those Who Come After: a Study of Native American Autobiography*. Berkeley and Los Angeles: University of California Press, 1985.

———. "Monologue and Dialogue in Native American Autobiography." In *The Voice in the Margin: Native American Literature and the Canon*. Berkeley: University of California Press, 1989.

Lee, Dorothy. "The Conception of the Self Among the Wintu Indians." *Freedom and Culture*. Englewood Cliffs, NJ: Prentice-Hall, 1959, 131-140.

———. "Autonomy and Community." In *Valuing the Self: What We Can Learn from Other Cultures*. Prospect Heights, IL: Waveland, 1986, 28-41.

Lock, Andrew. "Universals in Human Conception." In Heelas and Lock, eds., *Indigenous Psychologies*, 19-38.

Lukes, Steven. "Conclusion." In Carrithers, Collins, and Lukes, eds., *Category*, 282-301.

Marcella, Anthony J.; George DeVos; and Francis L. K. Hsu, eds. *Culture and Self: Asian and Western Perspectives*. New York: Tavistock, 1985.

Mauss, Marcel. "A Category of the Human Mind: The Notion of Person; the Notion of Self." [1938]. Trans. W. D. Halls. In Carrithers, Collins, and Lukes, eds., *Category*, 1-25.

Mead, Margaret. *Coming of Age in Samoa*. [1928]. New York: Mentor, 1953.

Momaday, N. Scott. *The Way to Rainy Mountain*. [1969]. New York: Ballantine, 1973.

———. *The Names*. New York: Harper & Row, 1976.

O'Brien, Lynne Woods. *Plains Indian Autobiographies*. Boise, ID: Boise State College Press, 1973.

Occom, Samson. "A Short Narrative of My Life." In *The Elders Wrote: An Autobiography of Early Prose by North American Indians, 1768-1931*. [1762]. Ed. Bernd Peyer. Berlin: Dietrich Reimer Verlag, 1982, 12-18.

Rorty, Amelie O. *The Identities of Persons*. Berkeley and Los Angeles: University of California Press, 1976.

Shakur, Assata. *Assata*. Westport, CT: Lawrence Hill, 1987.

Shweder, Richard A. "Rethinking Culture and Personality Theory." Part I. "A Critical Examination of Two Classical Postulates." *Ethos*. 7(1979): 255-78.

———. "Rethinking Culture and Personality Theory." Part II. "A Critical Examination of Two More Classical Postulates." *Ethos*. 7 (1979): 279-311.

———. "Rethinking Culture and Personality Theory." Part III. "From Genesis and Typology to Hermeneutics and Dynamics." *Ethos*. 8(1980): 60-94.

Shweder, Richard A., and Edmund J. Bourne. "Does the Concept of the Person Vary Cross-Culturally?" In *Culture Theory: Essays on Mind, Self, and Emotion.* Ed. Richard A. Shweder and Robert LeVine. Cambridge: Cambridge University Press, 1984, 158-99.

Silko, Leslie Marmon. *Storyteller*. New York: Seaver Books, 1981.

Smith, M. Brewster. "The Metaphorical Basis of Selfhood." In Marsella, DeVos, and Hsu, eds., *Culture and Self,* 56-88.

Smith, Paul. *Discerning the Subject*. Minneapolis: University of Minnesota Press, 1988.

Soper, Kate. *Humanism and Anti-Humanism*. London: Hutchinson, 1986.

Spindler, George D., and Louise S. Spindler. "American Indian Personality Types and Their Sociocultural Roots." *Annals of the American Academy of Political and Social Science*. 311(1957): 147-57.

Stein, Gertrude. *Everybody's Autobiography*. New York: Random House, 1937.

Swann, Brian, and Arnold Krupat, eds. *I Tell You Now: Autobiographical Essays by Native American Writers.* Lincoln: University of Nebraska Press, 1987.

Vizenor, Gerald. "Crows Written on the Poplars: Autocritical Autobiographies." In Swann and Krupat, eds., *I Tell You Now,* 99-109.

Wallace, Anthony. "The Modal Personality Structure of the Tuscarora Indians as Revealed by the Rorschach Test." *Bureau of American Ethnology Bulletin No. 150.* Washington, DC: Smithsonian Institution, 1952.

White, Geoffrey M., and John Kirkpatrick, *Person, Self, and Experience: Exploring Pacific Ethnopsychologies.* Berkeley and Los Angeles: University of California Press, 1985.

Williams, Raymond. *Keywords*. New York: Oxford University Press, 1976.

Williams, Thomas R., ed. *Psychological Anthropology.* The Hague: Mouton, 1975.

POLITICAL ISSUES

Bernd C. Peyer

SOURCE: "Autobiographical Works by Native Americans," in *Ameriksastudien/American Studies (Amst),* J. B. Metzlersche Verlagsbuchhandlung Stuttgart, Vol. 26, No. 3/4, 1981, pp. 386-402.

[*In the excerpt that follows, Peyer provides a historical account of Native American autobiography, with primary consideration of its political implications.*]

> To the white man many things done by the Indian are inexplicable, though he continues to write much of the visible and exterior life with explanations that are more often than not erroneous. The inner life of the Indian is, of course, a closed book to the white man.
>
> Luther Standing Bear[1]

The autobiography has long been a popular source of inside information for those interested in cultures other than their own. In the case of Native American cultures, the term has been used predominantly for those accounts recorded and written down by an intermediary, an editor, and, to a lesser extent, those works published in a cooperative effort between the editor and the subject, with the former doing the actual writing. That is to say, the bulk of the material known and categorized as Native American autobiography is made up of works either "edited by" or "as told to" non-Native Americans. Certainly this is due in part to historical circumstances, as there was apparently no elaborate system of writing in North America prior to contact and most Native Americans did not speak a European language for some time, let alone write in one. Yet, contrary to what might be expected, there are a good number of works published by Native Americans that go back at least as far as the 18th century and these include several autobiographies.[2] The fact that this material has been available but ignored until recently, seems to imply a matter of choice on the part of publishers and readers as well as being due to language barriers. Whatever the reasons may be, paternalism, preference for accounts by less acculturated individuals, or simply because Whites have easier access to publishing facilities, they are sure to be quite complex and not of primary concern in this article. Nor is it my intent to analyse Native American autobiographies in terms of "authenticity", as it has already been done elsewhere.[3] Besides, to speak of "authenticity" is, in this writer's opinion, dangerously close to the very dubious practice of defining "real Indians." More important is the awareness of the possibility of outside manipulation in the individual Native American's choice to communicate in the form of autobiographical literature.

Most standard dictionaries define autobiography as the art or practice of writing down one's own life narrative. Although this is an overly simplified definition, it still clearly emphasizes the act of writing itself as an integral aspect of this genre. Communication between cultures becomes meaningful when there are individuals who can share a language, and the literature written by Native Americans in English represents an effort to communicate in the foreign language of a conquering society that is either unwilling or unable to learn theirs. This process becomes more complicated, however, when the motivation and the presentation are carried out by someone other than the subject. The anthropologist as editor, for instance, might well have a specific interest long before conducting the actual interview with the subject. As social scientists are primarily concerned with ethnic groups, they may pay closer attention to that which identifies the individual as a member of such a group, or the "ethnic identity." What happens in this case to the motivation or language of the individual whose life is to be narrated? The editor is not only in the position to filter out what he considers to be important, but also to manipulate the style and content of the subject's account. The editor's influence would be considerably less in a direct and untranslated recording, but this is seldom the case with published autobiographies. Thus it can happen that the subject, rather than having the freedom to express himself in a language formed by his own style and content, becomes a symbol for what others think a Native American should be.[4] To quote George Devereux: "If one is nothing but a Spartan, a capitalist, a proletarian, or a Buddhist, one is next door to being nothing and therefore even to not being at all."[5]

This problem is evident, for instance, with John Neihardt's *Black Elk Speaks,* one of the most popular autobiographies. The subject, Black Elk, apparently motivated by the fear that his knowledge might be lost to his people after his death, narrates his life in the Lakota language to another member of his community, who in turn translates what he has heard and understood into a foreign language. The actual writing is finally performed by John Neihardt, who is not only a member of a different culture with little knowledge of the Lakota language, but also a fairly established poet with his own literary style. Thus, even if the events in Black Elk's life have been recorded faithfully, they are recreated in a language which, according to the author's introduction in a 1972 reprint, can only reflect "the mood and manner of the old man's narrative."

The considerations presented above are not so much a comment on the value of recorded autobiographies, many of which, including *Black Elk Speaks,* are excellently written source books that even meet the general approval of Native American scholars. Instead, they stress the importance of those autobiographies written by Native Americans themselves in the English language, if only for the reason that they have received relatively little attention. I am aware, of course, that this type of autobiography is also subject to manipulation. A few of the writers, such as Copway, Winnemucca, Eastman, and Standing Bear, have apparently received some superficial help with their orthography and all of the writers were at the mercy of a publisher's demands. Nevertheless, one may assume that these writers were fairly fluent in the English language and that their autobiographies, as compared to the recorded type, represent a maximum of involvement by the subject at a given time and a minimum in the manipulation of his literary product. Furthermore, they are entirely free of difficulties caused by translations. The fact that knowledge of the English language implies a certain degree of acculturation on the part of the writers should not be reason enough to doubt the "authenticity" of their works. On the contrary, it would seem to make them of special interest. If one considers that what is understood to be meaningful for Native Americans has almost entirely been formulated by Whites, then the use of the English language as a vehicle for communication in any literary form is of such political import that the serious scholar would be ill advised to ignore it. It is the main purpose of this article, therefore, to acquaint the reader briefly with autobiographies written by Native Americans, presenting these in a historically relevant chronological order with some statements on the individual writer's attitudes towards his culture and that of the conquering society.

Although there are numerous documented letters written early in the 17th century by pupils of missionaries like John Eliot, Native American literature in English probably begins with the writings of Samson Occom in the latter part of the 18th century.[6] Occom was a converted Mohegan who achieved some renown during his time in the colonies and England, both as orator and writer. Together with his teacher Eleazor Wheelock, he originated the plan to unite all Christian Indians into one tribe and was instrumental in the founding of Brother-town, one of the so called "Praying Indian" towns. His major works are *A Sermon at the Execution of Moses Paul,* which went through at least 19 editions after its initial publication in 1772—Occom also published this sermon in the form of a long poem that same year—and *A Choice Collection of Hymns and Spiritual Songs,* published in 1774 and containing several of his own compositions. Occom may also be the first Native American to undertake the task of writing an autobiography. He began working on it September 17, 1768, motivated by some of the slander

Black Elk being protected by the sacred bow.

that had been written about him. In his own words: "finding many gross mistakes in their Account, I thought it my Duty to give a Short, Plain, and Honest Account of my Self, that these, who may hereafter see it may know the truth Concerning me." Unfortunately, Occom never completed his autobiography, but the twelve page manuscript is still available with the Wheelock Papers at Dartmouth University. In it he very briefly sketches his conversion at the age of sixteen, his education under Wheelock and the Indian Charity School, and his subsequent work as a teacher and missionary among some of the Eastern tribes. The short autobiographical account ends with a bitter complaint against the policy of the Church to pay White missionaries much more than their Native American counterparts. No further mention is made of the "gross mistakes" in other accounts about him, by which he was probably referring to the various rumors of his being an alcoholic. Also contained among the Wheelock Papers and the Collections of the Connecticut Historical Society are several letters and diaries by Occom and his Mohegan pupil Joseph Johnson, who was con-

sidered to be a most promising scholar before his unexpected death in ca. 1776.[7]

Another autobiographical account written in the 18th century, actually a first person travelogue, is Hendrick Aupaumut's *A Narrative of an Embassy to the Western Indians,* but it was not published until 1827. The Mohegan Aupaumut enlisted in the Revolutionary War as a scout and was given the title Captain Hendrick. Later he served the newly formed republic on several occasions as an emissary to various tribes. His last voyage is recorded in the publication mentioned above, which is written in an interesting grammatical form, probably shaped by his own language, and contains many renditions in English of speeches made by Native American leaders with whom he had to confer, as well as his answers to them. Although Aupaumut gives a lengthy and detailed account of his travels to and conferences with tribal delegations, he says virtually nothing about himself, either past or present. His narrative was intended as a documentary of his activities as an emissary, rather than self-expression.

In the 19th century the number of publications by Native Americans increases unproportionately. The autobiographies that appeared during the first two-thirds of this century were predominantly authored by converted Native Americans, most of them active Methodists. The Church at that time had sole control over the education of Native Americans and was undoubtedly the only institution with a vested interest in such publications. This interest, of course, brought forth a specific type of autobiographical work in which the life narratives of the individual authors exemplify Christian ideals and focus upon their conversion. Conversion invariably meant the rejection of a previous way of life and the acceptance of the "superiority" of the dominant culture. Nevertheless, they still reflect the political views of a certain faction of assimilated Native Americans who, relative to their position in historical time, managed to express some criticism of the new culture they had adopted. The language in these Christian oriented autobiographies is borrowed directly from the Bible.

The earliest, and most self-expressive, autobiography of this period was published in 1828 by the Pequot William Apes. Perhaps more so than most other Native American autobiographies, *A Son of the Forest* is a reflective documentation of a marginal existence between two incompatible cultures. Apes was abandoned by his half-blood father and full-blood mother at the age of three and taken in by his alcoholic maternal grandparents. After he was almost beaten to death by his grandmother, one of his uncles gave him up for adoption to a poor White family. Apes'autobiography is a long narrative describing his early life as an indentured servant, his escape after having been bought and sold by various families, his adventures as a soldier in the War of 1812, and finally the events that led up to his conversion by the Protestant Methodists who also ordained him. Apes later published enough works to earn himself the title of "the writing Indian." The core of his autobiography is the moment of conversion and the resistance to various temptations, especially alcohol, much of which is also described in another publication of his entitled *The Experiences of Five Christian Indians of the Pequot Tribe* (1833). Basically, it was fear of death and hell—both concepts having been used to intimidate him by his foster parents—that led to a series of revelations or visions resembling seizures that left him disabled for days, which he then interpreted as God's command for his conversion. Interestingly enough, he was forcefully detained in his religious fervor by his foster parents, who apparently could not accept the idea of a Native American becoming a preacher. In later life he was actually censured several times for preaching without a license, which he finally obtained from the Methodists, at that time a marginal and controversial sect. Although his activities as a preacher undoubtedly gave him a degree of social mobility otherwise hardly attainable in his

position, there is no reason to question his faith in Christianity, which he ultimately accepted as a solution to all differences between Native Americans and Whites. At the same time he is openly critical in all of his writings of White racist attitudes, the exploitation of Native American land base, and the highly profitable traffic with alcohol. His demands for better education and equal opportunity are not far removed from those made by many contemporary Native American progressives. This critical stance, however, developed at a later stage in his life. In his autobiography he mentions that he once thought it disgraceful to be called an Indian. He heard so many gruesome stories about his own people that he ran away in fright when he met agroup of sunburned White women in the woods whom he had mistaken for Indians.

The autobiographies appearing after Apes' were George Copway's *The Life, History, and Travels, of Kah-ge-ga-gah-bowh*, published in 1847 and later reprinted in England (1851) under the title *Recollections of a Forest Life*, Peter Jacobs' *Journal of the Reverend Peter Jacobs*, published in 1857, and Peter Jones' *The Life and Journals of Kah-ke-wa-quo-na-by*, published in 1860. In contrast to Apes, all three authors were brought up traditionally and in the security of a stable family relationship. However, their acceptance of newly imposed values on the one hand, and their rejection of traditional life on the other, are much more pronounced in their writings than in those of their forerunner.

Copway was probably the most popular writer of this period. Several of his works were also published in England. Copway was a full-blood Ojibway whose father held a key position within the tribe and, like his contemporaries Jacobs and Jones who were also Ojibway, he spent his entire childhood in the traditional way, neither learning English nor converting to Christianity until his early teens. The first half of his autobiography is a rather euphoric description of his youth in terms that fit well into the "noble savage" concept which was then steadily gaining in popularity. As the title to the English edition already insinuates, there are long statements eulogizing the freedom and purity of an existence with nature. It is possible that either he or the helpful "firend" mentioned in the introduction were well aware of how far a positive description of traditional life could go in such a publication. At any rate, he closes the chapters on his youth with an unmistakeable rejection of the Native American spiritual world. "In the days of our ignorance we used to dance around a fire. I shudder when I think of those days of our darkness. I thought the Spirit would be kind to me if I danced before the old men; and day after day, or night after night, I have been employed with others in this way. I thank God that those days will never return."[8] This contradictive relationship to his own culture is typical for most of the early Native American authors, a situation that has often received the label of "bi-culturalism." But it is also questionable whether Copway and other authors were entirely free to express all of their thoughts on the matter. After his involuntary break with the Canadian Methodists he went to live in the U. S., where he established himself as a writer, orator and self-appointed spokesman for Native American rights. His main political goal, for which he travelled several times around the country as a lobbyist, was to convince the government to grant Native Americans part of what was then called the Northwest Territory, which he ultimately hoped to see integrated into the Union as a separate Native American state.[9]

Another autobiographical work by George Copway was published in 1851 under the title *Running Sketches of Men and Places*. This is a unique narrative of his extensive travels throughout the British Isles and continental Europe and his experiences as a Native American delegate to the Third General Peace Congress held in Frankfurt, Germany, on August 22 through 24, 1850. A similar but much shorter publication appeared a few years earlier, in 1848, titled *An Account of the Chippewa Indians*. This was written by Maungwudaus, an Ojibway leader who taught himself how to speak and write the English language well enough to become a principal interpreter for the British government in Canada. In 1843 he embarked upon a tour of England and continental Europe along with an Ottawa and Ojibwa dance troupe which was eventually sponsored by George Catlin. His account is a highly interesting document as it contains the candid views of a 19th century Native American—in this case not a preacher—on the "strange" habits and customs of the Europeans.

The two titles published by Jacobs and Jones are actually journals of their missionary activities with minute day to day accounts of religious services, sermons, meetings, and travels to and from tribal communities. Both, however, begin with a chapter giving a brief life narrative of the author by the author, which concentrates on the experience of conversion. Jacobs was converted by the Methodists some five days after Jones, whom he mentions in his narrative. His is the most abrupt break with traditional life, about which he writes: "I, as well as the people of my tribe, was very cruel and wicked, because there was no fear of God in our heart, and no fear of punishment; but every man settles his own affairs by the force of his tomahawk; that is to say, by burying his tomahawk in the people's heads, and that ends all disputes. The Indians made their women do all the work, and the men did little or nothing in heathen life."[10] Jacobs was ordained in England in 1842 and subsequrntly served as a missionary to tribes in the Hudson's Bay Territory.

Peter Jones was a mixed-blood of Welch descent but his early education was left up to his full-blood mother, who brought him up within the Native American community. At the age of nine he was adopted by an Ojibway named Captain Jim who then sent him to a mission school five years later. Jones was not converted until 1823, when he was 21 years old. In his narrative he mentions that he was long torn between Christianity and the spiritual way of his people, mainly because of the contradictions he had observed between the Whites' behavior and their religion. His final moment of conversion came during a campmeeting held by a group of Wesleyans, after a four-day-and-night marathon session of songs and prayers in which he accepted "God, the Father, Son, and Holy Ghost, and gladly renounced the world, the flesh, and the devil." Although as fervent a Christian as Jacobs, his views on traditional life were not nearly as negative. In another one of his publications he goes so far as to conclude that Native Americans were much better off before the arrival of Europeans and their alcohol.[11] The bulk of his literary work, however, is in the translation of Biblical texts into the Ojibway language.

Another autobiography published early in the 19th century which, like Copway's and Maungwudaus' travelogs, doesn't fit into the pattern of the Christian autobiographies, is Paul Cuffe's *Narrative of the Life and Adventures of Paul Cuffe, a Pequot Indian,* appearing in 1839.[12] This is a short but moving account of some thirty years spent at sea, full of adventurous escapades that approach the level of a good "yarn." Cuffe makes absolutely no mention of his life prior to becoming a sailor; in fact, the only reason to consider this work as a Native American autobiography is in the title itself. This is apparently the son of Paul Cuffe, a mixed-blood of African and Native American descent who married a Wampanoag woman and later became known for his efforts to resettle freed U.S. Blacks in Africa.

The last quarter of the 19th century saw several major changes that had a direct effect upon the content and style of Native American literature. First of all, as part of the policy of forced assimilation which was to culminate into the Dawes Act of 1887, responsibility over the education of Native Americans was shifted away from the missions to federally financed boarding schools. This enabled some Native Americans to obtain an education which was not dominated by any religious denomination and, as a consequence, the literature published during and after this period is no longer the work of preachers. At the same time, the end of all militarily potential resistance by 1890, at the latest, and the consequent establishment of reservations, gave rise to a renewed interest in Native American cultures, if only because it was assumed that they would soon vanish for ever. This period is dominated by people like Franz Boas, William Powell, and James Mooney, who brought in what has been called "the golden age" of anthropology. Together with the rise of numerous organizations of "friends", this created a greater market for Native American literature with an emphasis on traditional life. Thus, the works written by Native Americans during this period include much more ethnohistorical detail and, as the situation on the reservations quickly became unbearable, turn more and more critical of the conquering society. Finally, the steady growth of the publishing industry opened up new possibilities for the authors, who had hitherto been limited to small private or Church owned enterprises.

Of the many works written by Native American during the latter part of the 19th century, at least three were autobiographical: Sarah Hopkins Winnemucca's *Life Among the Paiutes* (1883), Andrew J. Blackbird's *Ottawa and Chippewa Indians* (1887), and Simon Pokagon's *O-Gi-Maw-Kwe-Mit-I-Gwa-Ki: Queen of the Woods* (1899).

Sarah Winnemucca is probably the first major female Native American writer. Although a somewhat controversial figure for her cooperation with the U.S. Army in affairs concerning the Paiutes of Nevada, she was very active as a writer and did a great deal to publicize the corruption and criminal behaviour of the Indian agents in the area. She also made one the first attempts—after the so called Five Civilized Tribes—at self-determination in education by founding a small school for Native Americans, which she managed to keep going for some years despite the almost total lack of funding. Her autobiography covers the period between 1844 and 1883, and is one of the most effective documentations of the tragic fate of the tribes in Nevada and California. One reason for its popularity at the time is the fact that it is written in a narrative style that reads almost like a novel. The incredible deprivations and the cruelties inflicted upon her people are rendered without any apparent bitterness or sensationalism. Individual settlers and especially Indian agents are made responsible for the situation, rather than White society in general. Her cooperation with the Army is, according to her autobiography, a desperate effort to prevent further depradations by civilians who were otherwise free to practice genocide at will. Her publications—two in all—and her various lecturing tours were an important part of her individual effort to focus public attention on the problems facing her people.

Blackbird's book is an historical account of the Ottawa and the Ojibway, interspersed with his own personal experiences. At the urge of his father, apparently an assimilationist leader of a Native American community at L'Arbre Croche in present day Michigan, Blackbird first attended a missionary school for a few years and later enrolled at the Yipsilanti State Normal School for two years, until he was forced to withdraw due to the lack of funds. Blackbird's life ambition had been to obtain a higher education, but it was effectively thwarted by a hostile Indian agent who continually refused him access to funds set aside for the educa-

tion of the Ojibway under the Treaty of Detroit in 1855. Much like Apes, Blackbird was forced into a marginal position, making a meager living as a blacksmith, shopkeeper, postmaster, and U.S. interpreter. His disappointment with White society comes through in all of his literary work, in which the right of Native Americans to a proper education, to equal opportunity in the professions, and to full citizenship are championed.[13]

The third writer mentioned was once considered to be "the best educated and most distinguished full-blooded Indian in America."[14] Simon Pokagon was brought up by an assimilationist father who had apparently sold some of the Potawatomie lands that now make up the city of Chicago. After having learned English at the age of twelve from some missionaries, he went on to attend several schools and colleges over a period of about eight years. He was also in favor of an effective assimilation of Native Americans into the conquering society, but strove in numerous published articles and monographs to correct misconceptions and stereotypes concerning his people's history. Although *Queen of the Woods* was published as an autobiography, it is in fact one of the first works of fiction by a Native American. Basically it is autobiographical, telling the story of Simon Pokagon's own marriage during a summer hunting trip, with practically all of the personal details corresponding to actual experience. However, he combines several elements that seem to come out of Native American oral tradition—his wife is transformed into a quasi-mythical figure with supernatural powers over all animals—in order to make a literary statement against alcohol abuse. In the end, his wife and two children die melodramatically as a direct or indirect result of alcoholism. Pokagon may be the first author to strive for a literary style in an autobiography, bringing into it elements of fantasy that foreshadow some of the contemporary works in this genre to be mentioned later.

At the turn of the century, literary production shifts almost entirely to the Plains tribes. This is due probably to the special attention given to these tribes by Whites after the so called Indian Wars during the latter part of the 19th century, a popularity which is still evident today. At the same time, members of the only recently subdued Plains tribes infused both Native American politics and literature with an obstinate pride in tradition and a determined critical stance against the conquering society. In 1911, a major national organization was founded, the Society of American Indians, which included many of the important writers as active members. The literary works by some of these author-politicians carried over into the 30's, thus wielding some influence—and vice versa—on the policies of John Collier and other reformers of the "Indian New Deal" era. These authors also enjoyed much more public attention than any of their predecessors. Their works include the following autobiographies: *The Middle Five,* published by Francis LaFlesche in 1900, *Indian Boyhood* and *From the Deep Woods to Civilization,* published by Charles Eastman in 1902 and 1916, *American Indian Stories,* published by Gertrude Bonnin in 1921, *My People the Sioux* and *Land of the Spotted Eagle,* published by Luther Standing Bear in 1928 and 1933, and *Flaming Arrow's People,* published by James Paytiamo in 1932. . . .

Notes

[1] Luther, Standing Bear, *Land of the Spotted Eagle* (Lincoln: Bison Books, 1978), repr. of the 1933 ed., p. xv.

[2] See Bernd C., Peyer, "A Bibliography of Native American Prose Prior to the 20th Century," *Wassajal The Indian Historian,* 13, III, (Sept., 1980), 23-25.

[3] William Bloodworth, "Varieties of American Indian Autobiography," *Melus,* 5, (1978), 67-81.

[4] For a brief essay on the difficulties imposed on Native American writers and artists due to stereotyping see Richard Aitson, "Some Observations on Contemporary Native American Literature," *Four Winds,* (Summer, 1980), 28-31, 80.

[5] George Devereux, "Ethnic Identity: Its Logical Foundations and its Dysfunctions," in George De Vos and Lola Romanucci-Ross, (eds.), *Ethnic Identity* (Palo Alto, Ca.: Mayfield Publ. Co., 1975), p. 68.

[6] Walter T. Meserve, "English Works of Seventeenth-Century Indians," *American Quarterly,* 8, III, (1956), 264-277.

[7] William DeLoss Love, *Samson Occom and the Christian Indians of New England* (Boston: Pilgrim Press, 1899).

[8] George Copway, *The Life, History, and Travels of Kah-ge-ga-gah-bowh* (Albany, N.Y.: Weed & Parsons, 1847), p. 26

[9] George Copway, *Organization of a new Indian Territory:* (New York: S.W. Benedict, 1850).

[10] Peter Jacobs, *Journal of the Reverend Peter Jacobs* (Toronto: Anson Green, 1857), p. 3

[11] Peter Jones, *History of the Ojebway Indians* (London: A. W. Bennett, 1861), pp. 25-30.

[12] See H. N. Sherwood, "Paul Cuffe," *The Journal of Negro History,* 8, (1923), 153-232.

[13] See also Andrew J. Blackbird, *The Indian Problem, From the Indian's Standpoint* (Philadelphia: National Indian Association, 1900).

[14] Cecilia B. Buechner, "The Pokagons," *Indiana Historical Society Publications,* 10, V, (1933), 318-328. . . .

Gae Whitney Canfield (essay date 1983)

SOURCE: "A Trip to the East," in *Sarah Winnemucca of the Northern Paiutes,* University of Oklahoma Press, 1983, pp. 200-13.

[*In the following excerpt Canfield recounts the circumstances that led to the writing of Sarah Hopkins Winnemucca's autobiography, and the political views Winnemucca expressed in her numerous lectures.*]

Two influential Boston sisters were to be Sarah's mainstays for several years to come. First was Elizabeth Palmer Peabody, who, from the time when she first met Sarah and heard her impassioned plea for the Paiutes and other American Indians, continued faithfully to support her cause.

Outwardly Elizabeth was a chunky spinster, always dressed in the same black silk, but she had created an illustrious aura about herself from her associations with the Concord Transcendentalists, whose books she published. Her own learned lectures and writings on world history, plus her dynamic enthusiasm and support for the establishment of German kindergartens in the United States, added to her stature.

Elizabeth's sister, Mary Mann, was the widow of Horace Mann. Though not so dynamic as her impulsive, talkative sister, she was accomplished as a writer and was instrumental in organizing and supporting Elizabeth's many ventures into humanitarian causes. A third sister, Sophia Peabody, had married Nathanial Hawthorne, but she was deceased before Sarah and Lewis reached Boston in the spring of 1883.

When Sarah arrived in Boston, Elizabeth was seventy-nine years old and had suffered a slight stroke but she soon began working assiduously for the cause of the "Princess" Sarah Winnemucca. She proposed that Sarah give a series of lectures, so that subscribers would learn the history and culture of the Paiutes as well as their present circumstances. When Sarah found that she could cover only a few points in each lecture, she became determined to write about her people at length.[1] Elizabeth was willing to see that the book was published. It would be a means of introducing Sarah and her cause and also would bring in revenue.

Thus Sarah gained innumerable speaking engagements up and down the East Coast before large church gatherings and Indian Association groups. She brought a new awareness to her audiences of the plight of the American Indian: their lack of land, sustenance, citizenship, and the rights that go with citizenship. She

Winnemucca (The Giver), 1880.

reminded her audiences that the Indians had no representation in the United States government.

Sarah lectured in New York, Connecticut, Rhode Island, Maryland, Massachusetts, and Pennsylvania within the first few months of her stay in the East. She enjoyed creating a dramatic impression, dressed in fringed buckskin and beads, with armlets and bracelets adorning her arms and wrists. She even included the affectation of a gold crown on her head and a wampum bag of velvet, decorated with an embroidered cupid, hanging from her waist.[2]

The first lecture in Boston, where she spoke on the shortcomings of Father Wilbur, offended an influential Methodist woman, who had expected Sarah to tone down her criticisms in return for support and hospitality. Sarah did not bow to such pressure. As a result opposition started against her, including the Women's Association of the Methodist church.[3]

Sarah, however, was moving in select circles, thanks to Elizabeth Peabody and Mary Mann. John Greenleaf Whittier, Ralph Waldo Emerson, and Justice Oliver Wendell Holmes were made aware of her cause through

Elizabeth, who knew everybody of consequence in New England. She was a guest of Mrs. Ole Bull, the wife of the famous musician, and spoke to the students of Vassar College by invitation of their president.[4]

One early lecture in Boston was intended for women only. Sarah spoke of the domestic education given by Paiute grandmothers to the youth of both sexes concerning their relations with each other before and after marriage. It was "a lecture which never failed to excite the moral enthusiasm of every woman that heard it," according to Elizabeth.[5] The elderly woman was convinced by Sarah that the Paiutes' education of their young was based on "natural religion and family moralities."[6]

As well as lecturing, Sarah found time to write *Life Among the Piutes: Their Wrongs and Claims,* the story of her own life arranged in eight chapters. In the book she made the Paiute woman's position in councils and family life sound somewhat liberated: "The women know as much as the men do, and their advice is often asked. We have a republic as well as you. The counciltent is our Congress, and anybody can speak who has anything to say, women and all." She described how women were quite willing to go into battle alongside their husbands, if need be.[7]

Mary offered to edit Sarah's manuscript and found it difficult work. She wrote a friend:

> I wish you could see her manuscript as a matter of curiosity. I don't think the English language ever got such a treatment before. I have to recur to her sometimes to know what a word is, as spelling is an unknown quantity to her, as you mathematicians would express it. She often takes syllables off of words & adds them or rather prefixes them to other words, but the story is heart-breaking, and told with a simplicity & eloquence that cannot be described, for it is not high-faluting eloquence, tho' sometimes it lapses into verse (and quite poetical verse too). I was always considered fanatical about Indians, but I have a wholly new conception of them now, and we civilized people may well stand abashed before their purity of life & their truthfulness.[8]

Doubtless, Sarah's purpose in writing and lecturing at this hard pace was partly to provide much-needed financial support for her and Lewis. Mary Mann understood, however, that her principal motive was "to influence the public mind by the details of the Indian wrongs she can give so as to induce Congress to give them their farms in severalty and give them rights to defend them in the courts." There was also an effort underway to form an association to aid Sarah's educational plans.[9]

Sarah trod on dangerous ground in most of her speeches. She said: "I have asked the agents why they did these wrong things. They have told me it is necessary for them to do so in order to get money enough to send to the great white Father at Washington to keep their position. I assure you that there is an Indian ring; that it is a corrupt ring, and that it has its head and shoulders in the treasury at Washington."[10]

The Council Fire and Arbitrator, a monthly journal purportedly devoted to the "civilization" and rights of American Indians, called Sarah "an Amazonian champion of the Army [who] was being used as a tool of the army officers to create public sentiment in favor of the transfer of the Indian Bureau to the War Department." *The Council Fire* publicized the Indian Bureau files on Sarah and the affidavits that Rinehart had sent to prejudice officials against her on her first trip to Washington: "She is so notorious for her untruthfulness as to be wholly unreliable. She is known . . . to have been a common camp follower, consorting with common soldiers. It is a great outrage on the respectable people of Boston for General Howard or any other officer of the army to foist such a woman of any race upon them."[11]

In Nevada the *Winnemucca Silver State,* which was not always kind to Sarah, came to her defense this time:

> Now, because she states, before an audience in Boston, what the whites in Nevada and on the frontier generally know to be facts, the "Council Fire," the Washington organ of the Indian Bureau, roundly abuses her. . . . Without attempting to refute or dispute her assertions, which it undoubtedly knows would be futile, it endeavors to break their force by attacking her character. It adopts the tactics of the ring organs generally, and instead of showing wherein she has misrepresented the Indian agents, it contents itself with slandering her, ignoring the fact that it is the Indian Bureau System not Sarah Winnemucca's character, that the people are interested in and that is under discussion."[12]

Elizabeth Peabody and Mary Mann decided that they should add an appendix to Sarah's book with letters of recommendation and affirmation in defense of her character. M. S. Bonnifield, the Winnemucca attorney, who had transmitted the *Council Fire* article to the editor of the *Silver State,* wrote the following: "I take pleasure in saying that I have known you personally and by reputation ever since 1869. Your conduct has always been exemplary, so far as I know. I have never heard your veracity or chastity questioned in this community." It must have been a moment of regret for Sarah and her defenders when a letter was received from General Howard with the request that it not be published. Howard had led many battles for the Union during the Civil War, losing his right arm at Fair Oaks, Virginia, in 1862. He had ridden unarmed into an Apache stronghold in 1872 to treat with Cochise. Devoted to the betterment of the Negro, he was named head of the Freedman's Bureau after the Civil War and was president of Howard University between 1869 and 1873. Now his courage left him. His reason was:

> My feeling towards Mrs. Hopkins is like yours, but for reasons which are imperative with me, I cannot publish a letter in defence of her character. I will say to you that when with me, or near me, her behavior was above reproach. I think her ardent love for her people, and her profound sympathy for them, has led her into several errors with regard to them, and her desires, in this respect, are positively against my own views or recommendations [referring to the removal of Leggin's band from Yakima], but this, in no way, affects the question of Sarah's moral character. . . . Should I write I would lay myself open to be assailed by the same bad man, who is thoroughly wicked, and unscrupulous. . . . You may show this to any of your friends, but do not publish it.[13]

Upon reading this letter Elizabeth Peabody wrote in the margin in her distinctive handwriting the name unstated by Howard, "Agent Rhinehart."

If a general of the army was wary of Rinehart's wrath, one can understand Sarah's predicament. An earlier letter of General Howard's was, however, printed in the appendix of *Life Among the Piutes,* along with many statements of high regard by army officers who had worked with Sarah during the Bannock War. The commander of the Military Division of the Pacific at the Presidio in San Francisco, Major General Irvin McDowell, pointedly made it his last act before his retirement on October 15, 1882, to offer a military escort to Leggins's band back to their home near Camp McDermit.[14] McDowell's offer was duly rejected, however, by Commissioner H. Price of the Office of Indian Affairs.[15]

The policy, instituted by President Grant in 1870, to use Christian agents, rather than military men, on Indian reservations had been termed "the Quaker policy." When Sarah spoke before the Universal Peace Union, the *Council Fire* criticized that organization for placing her on their agenda. In September, 1883, the Peace Union's president, Alfred H. Love, wrote a letter to the *Council Fire* in response:

> Sarah Winnemucca came thoroughly endorsed by prominent Boston friends of peace. She was as free as anyone else to express her views. We were gainers by hearing her. She modestly waited to be heard, and when she spoke, affirmed our resolutions.

> We think her reference to the army meant she preferred it to the loose, uncontrolled, and unscrupulous spectators and adventurers and recreant agents. . . .

> I wish the Quaker policy could be better understood. It comprehends more than opposition to military

surveillance. It accepts the good wherever found. . . . In reference to this person, once the Indian girl of the West, even if the statements you make be true, would it not be kind to keep them from the public. Suppose she had been attracted by the soldiers with their gay trappings, and perhaps their promises of favors; they are called Christians, she is styled savage. What wonder if she went astray? Of whom should we expect the most? Who were more to blame?

I would like to see those who dare make the personal affidavits you quote. Rather should we applaud this woman for now coming forth in all of womanly dignity and earnestness and upholding justice, virtue, and peace. The true Quaker policy is to encourage the good everywhere and in every thing.

Sarah wrote: "Everyone knows what a woman must suffer who undertakes to act against bad men. My reputation has been assailed, and it is done so cunningly that I cannot prove it to be unjust. I can only protest that it is unjust, and say that wherever I have been known, I have been believed and trusted.[16]

Every effort was made by Sarah and her Boston friends to get the autobiography printed, bound, and out to the public before the next session of Congress, when the legislators expected to consider legislation for the benefit of the Indians. Subscriptions were gotten up to help defray expenses, and the price of the book was expected to be one dollar per copy. John Greenleaf Whittier subscribed for ten dollars' worth, and Mrs. Ralph Waldo Emerson for the same amount. Elizabeth found five persons who underwrote the expenses of publication for a total of $600. Thus, when Sarah sold her 600 copies, the money that she received was free and clear and helped pay her expenses.[17]

Mary and Elizabeth had always lived frugally, and now they were in modest rented rooms at 54 Bowdoin Street in Boston. Elizabeth had earned her own living since age sixteen, and Mary, the widow of an honest politician and liberal educator, had never experienced a surplus of funds. Yet they willingly gave their limited resources to this new cause. In her typical lengthy sentences and almost undecipherable slanting scrawl, Elizabeth also wrote letters to friends and congressmen regarding her good friend Mrs. Hopkins. The following appeal to Congressman Newton Booth was typical:

I have been all my life a student of Indian history and character, a great uncle of mine who was a Revolutionary officer having married an Indian princess [who] brot up her family so nobly and wisely as to have been a lesson to her civilized relations by marriage, a family that yield now some of the most respected citizens of Michigan. . . . I hope you will think it worthwhile to look into her

book the first book of Indian literature—I will send you the appendix to it which contains her credentials. . . . The degree of ignorant nonsense that prevails is comparable to what was upon the negro question *fifty years ago* and will seem as amazing fifty years hence as that does now. I shall send you her book when it comes out.[18]

In this time of absorbing productivity for Sarah, who often bedded and boarded with Elizabeth and Mary, where was Lewis Hopkins, her husband? He traveled with Sarah often, sometimes introducing his wife to her audiences, and helped with the autobiography by visiting the Boston Athenaeum and other institutions for background material.[19]

A typical scenario for one of Sarah's lectures occurred in Philadelphia in Christ Episcopal Church. At least an hour before the time appointed for the lecture, masses of people began to crowd into the church's front entrance. They continued to file in until the entire building, including the galleries, aisles, and chancel steps, was completely packed.

After the singing of a hymn the rector introduced Lewis Hopkins as the husband of "Princess Winnemucca." Lewis gave a brief sketch of his wife's history and stated the purpose of Sarah's visit to the East.[20] Sarah then flashed him an appreciative smile and told her story in such a way that the audience was overcome with emotion. For almost an hour she spoke very effectively. Afterwards people crowded around, wanting to touch the hand of this resplendent Indian woman wearing a gold crown and intricately beaded buckskin dress. Sarah's dark eyes glowed with enjoyment at the attention. Elizabeth Peabody, who often sat on the rostrum with her protégé, commented that, although she had heard Sarah lecture fifty times, each speech was different, because she never spoke from notes, but from her heart.[21]

After her lectures Sarah would obligingly sign copies of *Life Among the Piutes* for those of her followers who wished to purchase the handsome volume. The book contained 268 pages, including the 20-page appendix. The title was stamped in gold on the spine of the green or red cloth cover (the color was different in various printings). In her editor's preface Mary Mann had written: "At this moment, when the United States seem waking up to their duty to the original possessors of our immense territory, it is of the first importance to hear what only an Indian and an Indian woman can tell. To tell it was her own deep impulse, and the dying charge given her by her father, the truly parental chief of his beloved tribe."

Senator Henry L. Dawes invited Sarah and Elizabeth to his home and arranged for Sarah to lecture there one evening. Aware that the senator could make some of her ideas into law, Sarah spoke with special animation, and Dawes was greatly moved by her speech. He took her into his study and had a long talk with her—promising he would bring her before the Indian committee of which he was chairman. He encouraged her to continue speaking, because it was desirable that she "stir hearts," as she had done that day, to press congress to consideration of the Indian question.[22]

Sarah lectured in Providence, Rhode Island; Hartford, Connecticut; New York City, Newburgh, and Poughkeepsie, New York; Dorset, Vermont; Boston, Salem, Cambridge, Germantown, and Pittsfield, Massachusetts; and Philadelphia. She circulated a petition, which was signed by almost five thousand people, asking that the Indians be given lands in severalty and rights of citizenship.[23] Plans were afoot for three representatives to present the legislation in the House. Thus the "princess" was happy, feeling that her efforts for the cause of her people might yet be successful. She bought a fine overcoat for Natchez, who, when he received it found it much too large and generously gave it to his half brother Lee, who was especially tall and broad-shouldered.[24]

Through the Christmas season Mary Mann stayed at home collecting and mending serviceable clothes to send to the Paiutes in Nevada. Though she could not afford Christmas cards for her friends, she sent a large barrel of used goods to the Paiutes. She hoped it was not as cold in Nevada as it was in Boston, where she sat frozen by the fireside.[25] Elizabeth was expected home for the holidays. Sarah and Lewis were to move to Baltimore, where a series of lectures was planned.[26]

When the bells rang in the New Year of 1884, Sarah may have kissed Lewis without hesitation, but she may also have ignored a growing discontent in the relationship. Hopkins had helped her in Washington, visiting the Library of Congress for material for her book. He had sat on the lecture platforms, and with his gentle manners he had charmed those with whom he came in contact. At the same time the joint bank account of the Hopkinses was a temptation to Lewis's gambling propensities. He and Sarah had agreed in principle that most of the money that they collected for the cause should be reserved for a school that Sarah intended to start for Paiute children in Nevada,[27] though, of course, the expenses of traveling and accommodations had to be met before banking the remainder. Six months after they had arrived in the East the *Council Fire* had accused Hopkins of squandering funds given to Sarah for the benefit of her people in "low gambling dens in Boston." The article said, "When Sarah complained of this to her husband his reply was, 'You need not say anything; if I should tell your Boston friends what I know about you, you would not hold your head so high.'"[28]

According to Elizabeth, Sarah spoke in Baltimore sixty-six times in a variety of places, including churches of various denominations and the Young Men's Christian Association. The Methodist Episcopal Church seemed to enjoy a special claim on her presence.[29] Admission was charged, from ten to twenty-five cents, and copies of *Life Among the Piutes* were sold after the lectures. The Hopkinses were dependent on Sarah for their income,[30] and her competition in Baltimore was of the highest quality, including the Shakespearian actor Edwin Booth and Henry Ward Beecher, who was heralded as the "World's greatest orator." The autobiography, personally autographed by Sarah, was also made available through the mails for one dollar. If a purchaser so wished, he could receive an autographed picture of the "princess" for another fifty cents.[31] Lewis acted as her agent, responding personally to such requests. . . .

Notes

[1] Hopkins, *Life Among the Piutes,* editor's preface. Also, Elizabeth P. Peabody, *The Piutes: Second Report,* p. 7.

[2] *Boston Evening Transcript,* May 3, 1883, p. 2, col. 6.

[3] Elizabeth P. Peabody, *Sarah Winnemucca's Practical Solution of the Indian Problem,* p. 24.

[4] Peabody, *The Piutes: Second Report,* p. 7.

[5] Ibid., p. 5.

[6] Peabody, *Sarah Winnemucca's Practical Solution,* pp. 8-9.

[7] Hopkins, *Life Among the Piutes,* p. 53.

[8] Mary Mann to Miss Eleanor Lewis, April 25, 1883, Olive Kettering Library, Antioch College, Yellow Springs, Ohio.

[9] Ibid.

[10] *Boston Evening Transcript,* May 3, 1883, p. 2, col. 6. Thomas Tibbles, a white writer married to a Ponca Indian woman (Susette La Flesche), had recently written of the "Hidden Power" by which Indians were kept as the helpless wards of the agents, their self-respect lost while the contractors on the reservation became affluent.

[11] *Council Fire and Arbitrator* 6 (May, 1883): 69.

[12] *Silver State,* June 19, 1883.

[13] General O. O. Howard to Mrs. Mary Mann, September 13, 1883, Olive Kettering Library, Antioch College.

[14] Hopkins, *Life Among the Piutes,* pp. 250-51.

[15] Ibid., pp. 256-57.

[16] Ibid, p. 258.

[17] Elizabeth P. Peabody to the Honorable J. B. Long, January 11, 1884, Massachusetts Historical Society, Boston.

[18] Elizabeth P. Peabody to Congressman Newton Booth [1883], Olive Kettering Library, Antioch College.

[19] Hopkins, *Life Among the Piutes,* p. 76.

[20] *Silver State,* November 7, 1883.

[21] Elizabeth P. Peabody to the Honorable J. B. Long, March [27?], 1884, Massachusetts Historical Society.

[22] Elizabeth P. Peabody to Edwin Munroe Bacon [1883], Olive Kettering Library, Antioch College.

[23] Mary Mann to Miss Eleanor Lewis, December 24, 1883, Olive Kettering Library, Antioch College.

[24] *Silver State,* December 13, 1883.

[25] Mary Mann to Miss Eleanor Lewis, December 24, 1883.

[26] *Silver State,* December 5, 1883.

[27] Peabody, *The Piutes: Second Report,* p. 8.

[28] *Council Fire and Arbitrator* 6 (May, 1883): 135.

[29] Advertisements for Sarah's lectures appeared in the *Baltimore Sun* under "Special Notices" during the winter of 1884.

[30] Peabody, *The Piutes: Second Report,* p. 7.

[31] Lewis H. Hopkins to a subscriber for Sarah's book, May 10, 1884, Museum and Library of Maryland History, Maryland Historical Society, Baltimore. . . .

Works Cited

Books and Articles

Council Fire 6 (May, 1883):69.

Council Fire 6 (September, 1883):134.

Hopkins, Sarah Winnemucca. *Life Among the Piutes: Their Wrongs and Claims.* Edited by Mrs. Horace Mann. Boston and New York: privately printed, 1883. Reprint. Bishop, Calif.: Chalfant Press, 1969.

Peabody, Elizabeth P. *The Piutes: Second Report of the Model School of Sarah Winnemucca.* Cambridge, Mass.: John Wilcox and Son, 1887.

———. *Sarah Winnemucca's Practical Solution of the Indian Problem.* Cambridge, Mass.: John Wilcox and Son, 1886.

Tharp, Louise Hall. *The Peabody Sisters of Salem.* Boston: Little, Brown and Co., 1950.

Periodicals

Baltimore Sun

Boston Evening Transcript

Daily Silver State (Winnemucca, Nev.)

Silver State (Winnemucca, Nev.)

Manuscript Materials

Mann, Mary. Personal correspondence. Olive Kettering Library, Antioch College, Yellow Springs, Ohio.

Peabody, Elizabeth Palmer. Personal correspondence. Olive Kettering Library, Antioch College, Yellow Springs, Ohio; and Massachusetts Historical Society, Boston, Massachusetts.

An excerpt from Sara Winnemucca Hopkins' *Life among the Piutes* (1883):

Oh, what a fright we all got one morning to hear some white people were coming. Every one ran as best they could. My poor mother was left with my little sister and me. Oh, I never can forget it. My poor mother was carrying my little sister on her back, and trying to make me run; but I was so frightened I could not move my feet, and while my poor mother was trying to get me along my aunt overtook us, and she said to my mother: "Let us bury our girls, or we shall all be killed and eaten up." So they went to work and buried us, and told us if we heard any noise not to cry out, for if we did they would surely kill us and eat us. So our mothers buried me and my cousin, planted sage bushes over our faces to keep the sun from burning them, and there we were left all day.

Oh, can any one imagine my feelings *buried alive,* thinking every minute that I was to be unburied and eaten up by the people that my grandfather loved so much? With my heart throbbing, and not daring to breathe, we lay there all day. It seemed that the night would never come. Thanks be to God! the night came at last. Oh, how I cried and said: "Oh, father, have you forgotten me? Are you never coming for me?" I cried so I thought my very heartstrings would break.

Sara Winnemucca Hopkins, in Life among the Piutes: Their Wrongs and Claims, *edited by Mrs. Horace Mann, G.P. Putnam's Sons, 1883.*

GENDER AND AUTOBIOGRAPHY

Gretchen M. Bataille and Kathleen Mullen Sands (essay date 1984)

SOURCE: "The Ethnographic Perspective: Early Recorders," in *American Indian Women: Telling Their Lives*, University of Nebraska Press, 1984, pp. 27-46.

[*In the following essay, Bataille and Sands discuss the movement toward the ethnographic study of Native American life, which included a new focus on the female experience.*]

> To fail to understand another person's life story is, in general, to reject one's own humanity. Whether recorded in the extremity of personal or cultural annihilation, or in the midst of joy and productivity, the anthropological life history offers a positive moral opportunity to pass on stories that might otherwise never be told. For those who are bearers of a tradition, the opportunity to tell their story can be a gift; reassurance that they are indeed still alive, that their voices will be heard, and that their cultures can survive. It is a gift of equal importance for those generations to come who will take up that tradition and shape it to their own needs as the future unfolds.
>
> L. L. Langness and Gelya Frank, *Lives: An Anthropological Approach to Biography*

In *Lives: An Anthropological Approach to Biography*, L. L. Langness and Gelya Frank discuss the life-history method in anthropology that emerged primarily out of research on American Indians.[1] It is this pioneering effort of recording life stories that is examined in this chapter, particularly as these works have illustrated women's views of their lives and cultures. Although the early ethnographic autobiographies do not approach the literary quality of those life stories that came later, they did serve as models for subsequent works and suggested that the lives of Indian women deserved examination within the context of tribe and culture.

At the end of the nineteenth century and early in the twentieth century a rising interest in native customs and an increasing desire "to salvage the remains of a culture" prompted anthropologists and ethnologists to begin recording life stories. The purpose was not to focus on an individual life, but rather to use a single life to illuminate a culture. The women whose lives were recorded during that period were the mothers and wives of the tribe, revealing the day-to-day events of their lives. Their stories differ from the stories of their male contemporaries in that they do not tell of war but

rather of the gathering of herbs. They focus on preparing buffalo rather than hunting it, and they tell of raising children rather than of racing horses. These differences reflect the division of roles in the cultures. More than anything else, these stories reflect the relationships of women and men within a tribe.

As these life stories moved from the traditional oral mode to the recorded written form, much of the element of storytelling was inevitably lost. When the stories were written down, facial expressions, hand movements, and pauses were lost on the printed page. Editors decided what elements were significant to a woman's life or, more often, significant to field research on a given tribe. Indian women recognized that the essence of their lives could not always be communicated in a "foreign" language and that events which they thought significant might be considered naive or unimportant by their white interviewers. Taboos were broken: to tell the story of the family, women were often forced to speak the names of the dead.

Ethnographers had a distinct purpose for wanting to hear the stories; they were after linguistic or anthropological data to round out field reports. The material chosen for inclusion by these editors represented what they thought was significant. Many of the earliest collectors perceived themselves as necessary to salvage what would soon be lost: "It is evident that aboriginal manners and customs are rapidly disappearing, but notwithstanding that disappearance much remains unknown, and there has come a more urgent necessity to preserve for posterity by adequate record the many survivals before they disappear forever."[2]

The attitude of the "white man's burden" predominated in the earliest recorded autobiographies. Early ethnologists regarded the life stories as only a small part of the total field report on a given group, however. Often these narratives were published as miscellaneous additions to a tribal study. Franz Boas described autobiographies as being "of limited value, and useful chiefly for the study of the perversion of truth by memory."[3] In an article on the use of autobiographical evidence Alfred Kroeber explains that "among nonliterate tribal folk some normal elderly persons are likely to feel their life not as something interesting in its individuation and distinctiveness, but as an exemplification of a socialization. Such a person is conscious of himself first of all as a preserver and transmitter of his culture."[4]

Paul Radin had expressed similar sentiments earlier: "A native informant is, at best, interested merely in satisfying the demands of the investigator." One of the drawbacks to acquiring accurate and complete information, Radin believed, was that most investigators do not spend enough time with the tribes or individuals. Even when recorders were conscientious, Radin postulated, the final result was completely tinged with the investigator's emotional tone and "quite unsafe to follow." Despite the drawbacks, autobiography has been viewed throughout the century as a useful tool for anthropological research: "Such personal reminiscences and impressions, inadequate as they are, are likely to throw more light on the workings of the mind and emotions of primitive man than any amount of speculation from a sophisticated ethnologist or ethnological theorist."[5] It is these various assumptions that are reflected in some of the earliest autobiographies, particularly those discussed in this chapter.

One of the earliest recorders of information about North American Indian tribes was Truman Michelson. Among his published studies of tribes in the Midwest are recordings of ceremonies, descriptions of the contents of sacred bundles, accounts of funerals, and brief autobiographies. Through three narratives of American Indian women, Truman Michelson provides a generalized view of the lives of Indian women in traditional societies during a period of transition. "The Autobiography of a Fox Indian Woman," obtained in 1918, tells the story of a Mesquakie (Fox) woman who had been born in the late 1800s and who had had several children and three husbands. "Narrative of an Arapaho Woman" was obtained in 1932 from an informant born in 1855 and thus much older than the Fox woman—seventy-seven years old—when she told her story. The exact age of the Cheyenne woman in "The Narrative of a Southern Cheyenne Woman" is not indicated. The story was obtained in 1931, however, and the informant says that her mother is eighty years old, thus the narrator had also experienced the changes wrought upon American Indian tribes at the turn of the century.[6]

Much of Michelson's work was published in the volumes of the Bureau of American Ethnology, and in each case he prefaces his reports with the required introduction. This introductory material is useful, for it makes clear that Michelson relied heavily on tribal members to help him secure informants, dictate, and translate the information. In his work with the Mesquakies (Foxes) of Iowa, several tribal names appear repeatedly. It is also obvious that Michelson trusted those who were recording for him, and that he perceived his job to be the final ordering and structuring of both the original and the translation. It is useful to the linguistic scholar that Michelson frequently published both the native and English texts, making comparisons possible. The emphasis on linguistics suggests, however, that Michelson may have been less interested in the particular content and cultural information contained in the personal narratives and more interested in the linguistic patterns and variations in usage. He does not place emphasis on the informants as individual human beings; they are subjects expected to provide information, usually in a relatively short time. They are rarely named—often at their own request, because

they were divulging information about the tribe or ceremonies which should have remained secret.

Despite some of these flaws, Michelson's accounts provide three early autobiographies in which American Indian women recorded their own impressions of their lives without editorial pressures: "No attempt was made to influence the informant in any way; so that the contents are the things which seem of importance to herself."[7] Michelson did serve as editor, however, and writes in the introduction to "The Autobiography of a Fox Woman," "It may be noted that at times the original autobiography was too naive and frank for European taste, and so a few sentences have been deleted."[8]

The three narratives tell of common experiences. All three women recall learning their roles from their mothers or other female relatives. Their stories dwell on their marriages, their children, and the roles other family members played in arranging marriages and caring for the children. All three emphasize the nature of proper behavior: they were concerned about what others might think of them should they talk to boys, remain out after dark, fail to protect their virtue, or become the object of community gossip. They had learned their lessons well and strove to be model women in their communities. Even after her marriage, the Southern Cheyenne woman was concerned about what others might think of her: "After I was married I thought I would have more freedom in going about with my girlfriends, but my mother watched me more closely. . . . This was done to prevent any gossip from my husband's people."[9]

None of the three narratives was recorded as literary autobiography. They appear as incidental records that were part of collections of ethnographic data on particular tribes. The exclusion of significant information, such as ages of the informants, and the emphasis on linguistic notes suggest that the collection of life stories was not the primary objective of Michelson's work. Michelson's admission that portions of the Fox autobiography which he felt were "too naive and frank for European taste" were omitted suggests further that the study had strictly defined parameters. Despite his interest in all facets of Fox life, Michelson recognized that explicit accounts of menstruation and childbirth would have to be omitted. His interest in the individual lives of these women was secondary to his interest in the languages, the tribes, and the general cultures, so he could justify omission of detailed information given by the informant.

Michelson's earliest recorded autobiography and longest narrative was obtained from a Fox (Mesquakie) woman in Tama, Iowa. The Fox woman was born many years after the Mesquakie Indians had returned to their "home" along the Iowa River. Her autobiography makes no reference to the politics involved in that move, nor does it deal with factionalism or clan differences within the tribe, yet the period at the turn of the century was a difficult time internally for the Mesquakies. There was controversy over the position of chief and continuing strife between the conservatives and progressives. The federal government had opened an Indian boarding school in 1898, but the Mesquakies refused to send their children, and the school was forced to close by 1911. In 1913 the Mesquakies performed the first public powwow, inviting the people of Tama to observe. Mesquakie history shows that the first two decades of the twentieth century were years of change for the people and a time of increasing contact with the government and their white neighbors.[10] Yet none of this is reflected in the collected life story.

The Fox woman's autobiography is the story of one woman growing up in this culture which, despite the intrusions of the outside, yet today maintains many of the traditions of the past. Her life story focuses on her tribal education and integration into the ways of her people, what she was expected to know in order to take her place within that society. She tells of "growing up"—making dolls, planting, weaving belts, and learning the many necessary tasks which would be hers as a woman. Her concern is personal—her education, marriage, and children. She is seen as a somewhat isolated figure; the important relationships are with family members, and there are only vague allusions to friends and others in the community. Tribal connections seem important only for ceremonial needs, like adoptions, giveaways, and funerals. Her strength is derived from the extended family, first her mother and uncles, later her own children. Much of the material in the Fox woman's narrative appears in a slightly different form in the information dictated to Michelson by Harry Lincoln, which appeared as "How Meskwaki Children Should Be Brought Up" in *American Indian Life,*[11] which suggests that the narrative presents fairly typical behavior.

The events leading up to the time of recording help explain both the history of the Mesquakies and why some tribal members were eager to cooperate with Michelson in recording their customs. In 1840 Governor Robert Lucas of the Iowa Territory reported, "The Sac and Fox Indians . . . are fast progressing toward extermination."[12] Over fifty years later, E. Sidney Hartland, in the preface to Mary Alicia Owen's book *Folklore of the Musquakie Indians of North America,* wrote, "They have been beaten; and they are now a dying people. Their blood may be mingled with that of their conquerors and thus their life may in some measure be perpetuated. But their ancient beliefs and institutions are passing away forever."[13] Most observers had written the Mesquakies off by 1900, but these predictions did not come true. The Mesquakie Indians today live on the Mesquaki Settlement near Tama, Iowa. The story of their removal to Kansas in 1846 as a result of the Treaty of 1842 and their subsequent return in 1856 to purchase land is unique in American Indian history. The Mesquakies today are still traditional people who have maintained their tribal ways and preserved their stories.

Despite the constancy in Mesquakie behavior, much of what has been written by outsiders has been inaccurate. Michelson, relying on some of the earlier published reports on the Mesquakies, perpetuated the inaccurate tribal designation. The name *Fox (Renard)* was given to a group of people encountered by French trader-explorers early in the nineteenth century and designated clan identity of that group rather than tribal affiliation. The name, once assigned, remained, although the designation the people have for themselves is *Mesquakie,* "The Red Earth People." Michelson knew this and referred to it in published reports, but he chose the government's label to designate the tribe for this autobiography. In Parson's *American Indian Life,* however, he used the tribal name Mesquakie (Meskwaki).

Michelson was not the first to do field research on the Mesquakies. One of the earliest writers to discuss Mesquakie customs was Mary Alicia Owen. Her limited vision is obvious in several areas, and her accounts of Mesquakie life are contradicted in the Fox woman's autobiography and by Michelson in other publications. In discussing clan affiliation, Owen states that women belong to their father's totem, but that if the father dies or the parents are divorced the woman goes to her mother's totem. She states further that a woman belongs to her husband's totem when she marries.[14] This is clearly not the case. The Mesquakies are patrilineal, and children always belong to their father's clan even though they may at times participate in the activities of other clans.[15] The Fox woman made no reference to her clan membership, perhaps because she took it for granted.

The Fox woman discusses mourning in her account, and her experiences are quite different from the customs Owen describes. Owen recounts the "cries and shrieks" of women in mourning; but Mesquakie women act more in the manner described in the Fox woman's narrative: "I undid my hair and loosened it. For several nights I could not sleep as I was sorrowful. . . . I wore black clothing. . . . I was fasting. . . . Soon I would walk far off to cry, it was far off so that it would not be known."[16]

The description of the Fox woman's behavior after the death of her second husband appears consistent with Mesquakie practice then and now. Even today public emotions are deemed a "show" and only a pretense of grieving. William Jones, an anthropologist of Fox descent, confirmed that stoic behavior was expected, pointing out that a widow was mocked and insulted if she wept for her husband.[17] After her husband's death, the Fox woman did not show her emotions openly, she participated in the traditional giveaway, and she mourned appropriately for four years. She was now a true Mesquakie woman; she had fulfilled the necessary roles expected of her, and she was sad but satisfied.

Although it is unlikely that this one woman's life is representative of all Mesquakie women, her narrative does provide an insider's perspective on the role of women within the tribe. It is possible to evaluate the narrative in several ways: comparison with available information on the Mesquakies, comparison with the perceptions of Mesquakie women today, and the study of the autobiography as literary document. In particular, how does this early ethnographic autobiography fit into the loose genre of autobiographies of American Indian women?

Michelson's means of obtaining the narrative deserves examination. The number of people through whom this story was told almost guaranteed that there would be some errors in translation that might mislead a reader. The story, told in Mesquakie to Harry Lincoln, corrected by his wife, Dalottiwa, translated by Horace Poweshiek, and finally edited and published by Truman Michelson, had been dictated only once. Two years passed between the first dictation and the final translation. Harry Lincoln was half Mesquakie and half Winnebago; his wife was Mesquakie, as is Horace Poweshiek, who is now probably the oldest Mesquakie living on the Settlement near Tama, Iowa.

Poweshiek served as a translater for many of Michelson's publications and years later emerged in Mesquakie history as one of the men appointed to draft a constitution in accordance with the Indian Reorganization Act of 1934. He was at that time a member of the Young Bear faction and a progressive. This group was pro-white and ultimately was successful in getting the new constitution approved by the tribe.[18] Because Michelson does not deal with the politics on the Settlement, we do not know if the Fox woman represented the conservative or progressive faction, nor do we know how politics may have influenced the translations. (This is not a minor point; factionalism continues to be a divisive factor on the Mesquakie Settlement.)

There are some statements in the narrative that require clarification and explanation. Because of the brevity of the narrative there often are events that are not explained. For example, the Fox woman is warned against sleeping over at the wickiups of her friends. Although this appears to be a practice that in itself is inoccuous, it is, in fact, a part of the discipline a young girl must learn lest she get into the habit of sleeping in different places. A contemporary Mesquakie woman stated the reason very succinctly: girls who don't learn this early will end up "sleeping around" when they become women.[19] During a discussion of proper behavior for young girls, Adeline Wanatee, today a Mesquakie grandmother, revealed that girls are told they should not watch dogs copulate; her own mother had taught her that.[20]

Michelson's translation dealing with menstruation says that "The state of being a young woman is evil."[21] Yet the Mesquakie word *myanetwima* means more literally *bad*, or, in this context, *unclean*. This Mesquakie attitude is a part of a lifeway that recognizes opposites as well as the reconciliation of those opposites. Although a woman during her period was isolated—another way of teaching discipline—that time was also positive in that it marked the beginning of womanhood and promised the potential of motherhood. Rather than the manitous or gods "hating" the event, they took pity on her, or felt sorry for her, knowing the loneliness of isolation and the fear associated with the first experience of womanhood. The matter-of-fact attitude of the mother contrasts with the honest fear expressed by the narrator when she first menstruates. The practice of isolation was necessary to keep the power contained. Adeline Wanatee interprets the experience simply: "Men have visions, women have children."[22] The power associated with the two acts is comparable and explains why isolation is a factor in vision seeking as well as in response to bodily changes associated with menstruation and childbirth. Michelson's translation then imposes a negative value on this event which was not, and is not, present in Mesquakie society.[23]

The Fox woman makes many references to her mother's control over her. It was her mother, not a male relative, who made the decision about whom the woman would marry. Later the narrator indicates that immorality regarding men would bring shame to her brothers or uncles, so it is clear she also considers the effects her actions might have on her male relatives. It was only after her mother's death that the Fox woman believed she was free to marry the man she had always loved, for only then was she released from the traditional obligations.

The use of terms such as *mother* and *grandmother* does not conform to non-Indian labels for relatives. The label *grandmother* was assigned to several women; in fact, almost any older woman or medicine woman is likely to be referred to as *grandmother*. The label connotes wisdom and evokes respect. One cannot be a medicine woman until after menopause, suggesting further the respect and responsibility of age. Maternal involvement in the life of a daughter is confirmed by present-day Mesquakie society. Mrs. Wanatee said that her own mother was influential in her decision not to be sterilized after she had had three children; she had five more children, the last when she was fifty-three years old.[24]

The Fox woman revealed the importance of children in her life. When her first baby died, she feared her own complicity because of the unloving relationship she had with her husband. Her mother had warned her of the evils of anger:

"Finally you will make your son angry if you are always having trouble with each other. Babies die when they become angry," I was told.

Soon, when our little boy nearly knew how to talk, he became ill. I felt very sorrowful. Later on, indeed, he died. It is surely very hard to have death (in the family). One cannot help feeling badly. "That is why I told you about it when you were both unfortunately frightening him," I was told. . . . I felt worse after he was buried.[25]

Never happy with this first husband, the Fox woman shows great strength and independence by leaving him and marrying her first love, a man whose attitude was completely different from that of the first husband. She loves her second husband and he is good to her, but he dies, leaving her childless. After a proper mourning period, she allows a suitor to court her and decides to marry again. She states, however, that the only reason for her remarriage was to have children: "If I had had a child I should have never married again."[26] Childbirth and children were necessary to carry out her role as a Mesquakie woman. Although the narrator recognized the pain associated with childbirth, she was also aware of the important responsibility women have in continuing the tribe.

For we women have a hard time at childbirth. We suffer. Some are killed by the babies. But we are not afraid of it, as we have been made to be that way. That is probably the reason why we are not afraid of it. Oh, if we were all afraid of it, when we all became old, that is as far as we could go. We should not be able to branch out (to a new generation).[27]

Given the circumscribed purposes Michelson had for obtaining the Fox woman's life story, evaluation of the document as autobiography raises several issues. Certainly the narrative is valuable as ethnography, as a reflection of the day-to-day responsibilities of Mesquakie women, and as a record of the moral and domestic education of a young Indian girl. The Fox woman clearly is the central character, yet we know little of her psychological motivation or her real reactions to the many events of her life. We know her only through what she is willing to tell us through translators, some of whom were male, and through what intermediaries ultimately decided was worth preserving.

The setting, the Mesquakie Settlement outside of Tama, is not significant in the telling of the story. The location is not mentioned either in the introduction or in the body of the narrative. Presumably, those anthropologists who followed Michelson's fieldwork were aware that the Mesquakies lived in Iowa. Certainly the narrator perceived no need to describe either the landscape or her immediate physical environment.

If the story had been told when the Fox woman was older we might have expected to see a turning point in her life or a climactic moment. As it is, she has experienced a great deal—three marriages, the death of children and a loved spouse, and the birth of more children—yet she has many more years to live. Ironically, she does indeed perceive her life to have reached a climax of sorts. She has borne children and now feels her role has been played out: "After we had many children then my husband died. 'Well, I shall never marry again,' I thought, 'for now these children of mine will help me (get a living),' I thought."[28]

The narrative tells of her preparation for her role as a Fox woman, and having learned and having fulfilled that role, she can begin to prepare for that time when, past her child-bearing years, she will act in the role of teacher for younger girls, perhaps even become a medicine woman herself.

Michelson collected two additional accounts from Indian women, but both are fragmentary in comparison with the Fox woman's story. The two narratives obtained in the 1930s are brief and incomplete, resulting in interesting but stylistically flat accounts. A. L. Kroeber cites Michelson's "The Narrative of a Southern Cheyenne Woman" and "Narrative of an Arapaho Woman" as examples in which the narrator supresses individuality and personal feeling in order to express the accepted social standards of the group.[29] These two reports disclose family relationships, courtship and marriage, and some ritual, and both the informants and the editor make it clear that there are omissions.

In the summer of 1931 Mack Haag, working for Michelson, obtained the record of a Southern Cheyenne woman in Calumet, Oklahoma, which was published by Michelson. It is a brief story, one that hardly does justice to the life of its teller. The Cheyenne woman tells of childhood play, of her arranged marriage, eight children, and the death of her husband; she ends with a brief account of the Sacrifice Offering Ceremony, in which she participated to fulfill her dead husband's pledge.

The narrator tells of her instruction in the practical ways of the tribe: "My mother taught me everything connected with the tipi."[30] Her mother taught her in other "ways" as well, particularly the "way" of the oral tradition. She mentions incidents that she does not remember happening but which were passed on orally by her mother and have thus become a part of her personal history. She tells also of learning social norms:

"My aunt told me not to play with young men."[31] The emphasis on morality among Cheyenne women had been confirmed earlier by George Bird Grinnell: "The women of the Cheyennes are famous among all western tribes for their chastity."[32]

She understood well her role within the family and the culture and acknowledged her position: "My parents were very proud of me. In fact they treated me as if I were a male member of the family." Her awareness of male and female roles appears frequently in the narrative. The limitations of gender are apparent in her statement about the Tipi Decorators, the woman's society to which she belonged. In speaking of the Tipi Decorators, the Southern Cheyenne woman says, "I was very carefully instructed never to disclose the ceremony in the presence of males. So I shall be obliged to discontinue the subject." Ceremonial information is generally missing from this and from the other narratives obtained by Michelson, perhaps because the narratives were brief, or because Michelson recorded ceremonial practices elsewhere. The Cheyenne woman refers to old women and "sacred ritualistic ceremonies" without explanation. She does give descriptive details of the preparation for the Sacrifice Offering and includes information about the altar, but the narrative ends abruptly with the conclusion of her description of the ceremony.[33] As readers we do not know if she ended the recording session feeling she had already shared too much, or if the recorder, perhaps anxious only for the ethnographic detail about the Sacrifice Offering, ended the session when he had obtained his information. In any case, the narrative is brief and appears unfinished. It is a sketch rather than a developed literary document.

In 1932 Jesse Rowlodge obtained a narrative from a seventy-seven-year-old Arapaho woman near Geary, Oklahoma, and it was published by Michelson as "Narrative of an Arapaho Woman." This is a short account, in part because the narrator indicates she had only a few days to provide Rowlodge with information. As had the Cheyenne informant, this narrator stressed the teachings from her mother and paternal aunts. Respect, however, was reserved for male relatives; she does not mention private experiences "out of respect to my brothers and male cousins."[34]

Michelson's comment in the Introduction prefaces the narrative ambiguously:

> Most early writers on the Arapaho have a poor opinion of Arapaho in contrast with Cheyenne women. Were this expressed only by sensational and unreliable "authorities," I should pay no attention to it; but as sober and reliable a writer as Clark confirms this; he also condemns some other tribes and praises the Sioux and Cheyenne for the morality of their women. As far as the Arapaho are concerned, I am inclined to believe that their unfavorable reputation is due to the fact that some institutional practices recorded by other writers and myself were observed and supposed to be of every day occurrence, whereas they are strictly circumscribed and do not justify the opinions expressed.[35]

Grinnell had written earlier about the "notorious looseness of [Arapaho] women" in his work on the Cheyenne.[36] This woman does not fit the negative stereotype to which Michelson alludes, however; instead, she stresses the instruction she received, mentions that Arapaho mothers watched their daughters strictly at all times, and observes the commitment to tribal custom in respecting her brother's wishes concerning her marriage. Although she describes her pleasure at having a certain degree of freedom during her marriage, her behavior is not described as immoral or loose.

The narrator states that she left her third husband when he chose to take another wife, describes each of her four marriages, and explains why she sacrificed a finger to elicit good health for her sister. In all of the telling she is direct and explicit.

The conclusion of the narrative, however, resonates with wistfulness for the "old days," making clear again that this is a life story of a woman who has experienced profound changes in her life:

> There were no briar weeds, or stickers, or burrs; so the children as well as their parents were nearly always barefooted. All that one could see on the prairies was grass, buffalo grass and blue stem. When camps were pitched we would make our beds on the ground with grass for under cushions. The air was always fresh. We wore no head-shade; in fact we didn't mind the weather in those days.[37]

The literary value of these personal narratives recorded by Michelson lies in their representation of a particular mode of autobiography. The women whose lives are documented presumably did not initiate the activity. They were willing and perhaps paid volunteers for ethnographic fieldwork on their tribes. Kroeber reports that the Arapaho and Cheyenne narratives were recorded by younger native tribesmen, probably kinsmen, so we do not know what cultural restrictions may have been operative.[38] There is no indication that the women had an opportunity to read or correct the final versions; they may not have seen them or known the use which was made of them. The narratives were parts of much longer commissioned reports and as such were for an audience of professionals in the discipline rather than for the public at large.

It is obvious that there was no attempt to produce literary documents, even though the Fox woman's account comes close to being readable as a sustained narrative. Despite the initial purposes, these narratives are valuable today as records of these women's lives and how they perceived them. It is clear that they viewed their roles as women as tribally defined, almost rigid. Their stories are not told to glorify themselves, examine tribal politics, criticize white society, or emulate non-Indian autobiography. Instead, they forthrightly tell of the events of their lives. Although Michelson's consistent intent was to record ethnographic documents, the individuality of the narrators persists. It appears impossible to depersonalize an individual life or to reduce the drama of real life to anthropological data.

Close examination of these recorded autobiographies invites us to focus on the relationship between the narrator and recorder; however, Michelson's distance from his informants allows only speculation about what kind of interaction he had with the women whose lives he chronicled. Like several early ethnographic autobiographies, Michelson's accounts do not provide many insights into the intimate lives of these women.

Clearly, the beginning of the twentieth century was a period of experimentation in the recording of life stories. While some, such as Michelson, focused on accounts that revealed general lifeways and linguistic analyses, other recorders, such as Gilbert L. Wilson, Frank Linderman, and Ruth Bunzel, spent more time getting to know their informants as individual members of their tribes. They also provided much ethnographic information, particularly Wilson in his study of Hidatsa agriculture and Bunzel in her study of Zuni linguistics, but their sensitivity to their narrators provided for more interesting autobiographical accounts.

In 1906 Gilbert L. Wilson and his brother Frederick went to Fort Berthold Reservation and established a friendship with the Hidatsa Indians who were living there. Wilson, an ordained Presbyterian minister, spent a considerable amount of time with the Hidatsas, first doing ethnological fieldwork for the American Museum of Natural History and later as a doctoral candidate at the University of Minnesota. He sought out a "representative agriculturalist" and in 1912 recorded the story of Buffalo Bird Woman (also known as Waheeneewea, Maxi'diwiac, and Mahidiwia); in 1913 he recorded the life story of her son Edward Goodbird (Tsaka'Kasakic). The result of Wilson's thesis work on Hidatsa agriculture, *Agriculture of the Hidatsa Indians: An Indian Interpretation,* was published in 1917.[39] Wilson established a solid relationship with Goodbird, his translator; and Buffalo Bird Woman, Goodbird's mother, became Wilson's adopted mother and his principal informant. Her accounts of corn planting were "taken down almost literally as translated by Goodbird."[40] Wilson was determined to let Buffalo Bird Woman's words remain the focus of his research:

The writer claims no credit beyond arranging the material and putting the interpreter's Indian-English translations into proper idiom. Bits of Indian philosophy and shrewd or humorous observations found in the narrative are not the writer's, but the informant's, and are as they fell from her lips. The writer has sincerely endeavored to add to the narrative essentially nothing of his own. . . . It is an Indian woman's interpretation of economics; the thought she gave to her fields; the philosophy of her labors.[41]

Buffalo Bird Woman's account is appropriately literary, for she begins with the Hidatsa creation myth, telling the story of the tribe's ascent up a vine from the bottom of Devil's Lake. Only half of the tribe climbed to the surface, leaving the rest still drumming beneath the water. Practically every chapter includes storytelling, accounts of social relationships, and details of her own experiences. She gives a careful account of her female lineage, including biological as well as social mothers and grandmothers, before she begins to tell of planting the gardens. Although Wilson was writing ethnography, he recognized that corn and tobacco planting among the Hidatsas could not be separated from myth and ritual.

In 1921 Wilson published the autobiography *Waheenee: An Indian Girl's Story, Told by Herself,* a book suitable for children as well as for an adult audience, incorporating much of the information he had included in his scholarly account with the addition of details about Buffalo Bird Woman's life. The book was originally intended for children, thus it focuses on the child's life, giving only brief mention of her arranged marriage to Magpie and her later marriage to Son-of-a-star, a Mandan. At the conclusion, the narrator jumps ahead from the birth of Goodbird to fifty years later when she is telling her story as an eighty-three-year-old woman. Wilson writes, "The aim has been not to give a biography of Waheenee, but a series of stories illustrating the philosophy, the Indian-thinking of her life."[42] It is clear that Wilson recognized that this was not a chronological autobiography, but rather a philosophical account written to provide young readers with an understanding of this Hidatsa woman who had experienced the forced move in 1885 from the Knife River Villages, where she had been born about 1839, to Fort Berthold Reservation and who, as an old woman, recognized how much life had changed for her people and her family. Wilson's relationship with Buffalo Bird Woman and Goodbird is close, and he is sensitive to the different perspectives of the mother and her son. Goodbird, a Christian, did not identify with his mother's views of the past, believing instead that life would be better with the new ways: "We Hidatsas know that our Indian ways will soon perish; but we feel no anger. The government has given us a good reservation, and we think the new way better for our children."[43]

The different perspectives of mother and son reflect the intrusions of missionaries, the government, and anthropologists upon Hidatsa culture. Goodbird had been sent to a mission school, and he became pastor of the Congregational Chapel at Independence. He spoke Hidatsa, Mandan, Dakota, and English and dictated his autobiography to Wilson in English. Buffalo Bird Woman, however, spoke no English, and her communication with Wilson was through her son. Wilson analyzes Buffalo Bird Woman's philosophy: "She is a conservative and sighs for the good old times, yet is aware that the younger generation of Indians must adopt civilized ways." Despite some ethnocentrism in Wilson's analysis, it is clear he was sympathetic to his narrator: "May the Indian woman's story of her toil be a plea for our better appreciation of her race."[44]

Another ethnographer who published a life story of an Indian woman was Frank Linderman. He was intimately involved with his seventy-four-year-old informant, and the life story of Pretty-shield reflects, both in content and in style, their close relationship. *Pretty-shield: Medicine Woman of the Crows* was first published (as *Red Mother*) in 1932. This account was translated from Crow to English, and Linderman is present throughout the text providing explanatory comments that another anthropologist might have relegated to notes or an appendix. We learn as part of the running commentary that Pretty-shield received four dollars for her recording session, that she shared women's jokes with her interpreter Goes-together that she would not share with Linderman, and that she irreverently spoke the names of the dead to tell a more complete story. Pretty-shield is aware of the changes that have been wrought on her life, and she shares her frustrations: "I am trying to live a life I do not understand. . . . Ours was a different world before the buffalo went away, and I belong to that other world."[45] Linderman does little restructuring of the text, allowing Pretty-shield's childhood stories to be included at the place she remembered them rather than at the chronological moment. The story is a wistful one, a story of remembering and of questioning: "How could we live in the old way when everything was gone?"[46]

In 1926 Ruth Bunzel from the Department of Anthropology at Columbia University was studying the Zuni language, and she was fortunate in having as her interpreter Flora Zuni, a thirty-six-year-old woman who spoke both English and Zuni. During her second summer with the Zuni people, Bunzel recorded the brief autobiography of Lina Zuni, Flora's seventy-year-old mother. Flora Zuni was both translator and interpreter for her mother, resulting in the unique circumstance of having a completely female "team" telling, translating, and recording a woman's life story. In the Foreword to *Zuni Texts* Bunzel credits Flora Zuni for her careful interpretation and corrections of the text. Although Bunzel's concern was with language, she apparently believed the record of Lina Zuni's life, most often described as one of poverty, was significant. She includes Lina Zuni's oft-repeated phrase "We were very poor" and retains the original sentence structure; for example, "Very terrible were the words of the old people."[47] Lina Zuni recounts "how I came to be alive, how I grew up like a poor person." In her brief account she tells of rituals and prayers, and of old animosities between the Zunis and the Navajos. She ends with her uncle's advice: "Do not think of where you have come from, but rather look forward to where you are to go."[48] By means of this brief life story Bunzel adds a human quality to the study of Zuni linguistics and in the process provides yet another glimpse into the lives of American Indian women.

All of the autobiographies discussed in this chapter were recorded as ethnographic documents, and they share some characteristics. The women told their stories through interpreters to recorders who were more interested in language and culture than in autobiography. Despite the original purposes for the publications, however, the recorders often became involved in the lives of their informants; some, such as Wilson, became adopted relatives. Those recorders who knew their subjects well were able to communicate the lives with sensitivity and insight, providing the reader with a more full account of an individual life. Upon careful examination, it is clear that these early ethnographers provided the basic patterns for life stories that were to follow.

Notes

[1] L. L. Langness and Gelya Frank, *Lives: An Anthropological Approach to Biography* (Novato, CA: Chandler and Sharp, 1981).

[2] J. Walter Fewkes, *Fortieth Annual Report of the Bureau of American Ethnology* (1925), p. 1.

[3] Boas, as quoted in A. L. Kroeber, *The Nature of Culture* (Chicago: University of Chicago Press, 1952), p. 320.

[4] Ibid., p. 324.

[5] Paul Radin, *The Autobiography of a Winnebago Indian* (New York: Dover, 1963), pp. 1-2.

[6] Michelson, "The Narrative of a Southern Cheyenne Woman," [(*Smithsonian Miscellaneous Collections* 87, 1932)] 1-13; idem, "The Autobiography of a Fox Indian Woman," [(*Bureau of American Ethnology Fortieth Annual Report*, 1925)] pp. 291-349; idem, "Narrative of an Arapaho Woman," [(*American Anthropologist* 35, Oct.-Dec. 1933)] pp. 595-610.

[7] Idem, "The Autobiography of a Fox Indian Woman," p. 295.

[8] Ibid., p. 298.

[9] Idem, "The Narrative of a Southern Cheyenne Woman," p. 17.

[10] Richard Frank Brown, "A Social History of the Mesquakie Indians, 1800-1963" (Master's Thesis, Iowa State University, 1964), pp. 68-72.

[11] Elsie Clews Parsons, American Indian Life (New York: Viking Press, 1922), pp. 81-86.

[12] William T. Hagen, *The Sac and Fox Indians* (Norman: University of Oklahoma Press, 1958), p. 205.

[13] Mary Alicia Owen, *Folklore of the Musquakie Indians of North America* (London: David Nutt, 1904), p. vi.

[14] Ibid., p. 39.

[15] Michelson, "The Autobiography of a Fox Woman," p. 341.

[16] Ibid., pp. 329-31.

[17] William Jones, *Ethnography of the Fox Indians,* Smithsonian Institution, BAE Bulletin 125 (Washington, D.C.: U.S. Government Printing Office, 1939), p. 69.

[18] Brown, "A Social History," p. 80.

[19] Interview with Priscilla Wanatee, Mesquakie Settlement, Tama, Iowa, February 28, 1980.

[20] Interview with Adeline Wanatee, Mesquakie Settlement, Tama, Iowa, February 28, 1980. Adeline Wanatee, a Mesquakie woman, was eight years old when Harry Lincoln recorded the life of a Fox woman later published by Truman Michelson. Mrs. Wanatee answered questions about the manuscript and provided invaluable assistance with the Mesquakie language. Her daughter-in-law, Priscilla Wanatee, offered comments on the expected behavior patterns of young Mesquakie women today that mirror those recorded in the past.

[21] Michelson, "The Autobiography of a Fox Indian Woman," p. 303.

[22] Interview with Adeline Wanatee, Mesquakie Settlement, Tama, Iowa, February 28, 1980.

[23] For a discussion of the derivation of the use of *unclean* to describe women during their menstrual periods, see Ruth M. Underhill, *Red Man's Religion: Beliefs and Practices of the Indians North of Mexico* (Chicago: University of Chicago Press, 1965), pp. 51-61.

[24] Interview with Adeline Wanatee, Mesquakie Settlement, Tama, Iowa, February 28, 1980.

[25] Michelson, "The Autobiography of a Fox Indian Woman," p. 321.

[26] Ibid., p. 335.

[27] Ibid., 317.

[28] Ibid., p. 337.

[29] Kroeber, *The Nature of Culture,* p. 324.

[30] Michelson, "The Narrative of a Southern Cheyenne Woman," p. 2.

[31] Ibid, p. 3.

[32] George Bird Grinnell, *The Cheyenne Indians: Their History and Ways of Life* (New Haven: Yale University Press, 1923), p. 156.

[33] Michelson, "The Narrative of a Southern Cheyenne Woman," pp. 2, 9.

[34] Michelson, "Narrative of an Arapaho Woman," p. 609.

[35] Ibid., p. 596.

[36] Grinnell, *Cheyenne Indians,* p. 156.

[37] "Narrative of an Arapaho Woman," p. 610.

[38] Kroeber, *The Nature of Culture,* p. 325.

[39] Gilbert Livingstone Wilson, *Agriculture of the Hidatsa Indians: An Indian Interpretation* (Minneapolis: University of Minnesota Studies in the Social Sciences No. 9, 1917); idem, *Goodbird the Indian: His Story Told by Himself to Gilbert L. Wilson* (New York: Fleming H. Revell Co., 1914).

[40] Wilson, *Agriculture of the Hidatsa,* p. 3.

[41] Ibid., p. 5.

[42] Wilson, *Waheenee,* p. 189.

[43] Wilson, *Goodbird the Indian,* p. 79.

[44] Wilson, *Agriculture of the Hidatsa,* pp. 4-5.

[45] Linderman, *Pretty-shield,* pp. 24, 70.

[46] Ibid., p. 250.

[47] Ruth L. Bunzel, *Zuni Texts* (New York: G. E. Stechert and Co., 1933), p. 81.

[48] Ibid., p. 96.

Kathleen Mullen Sands (essay date 1992)

SOURCE: "Indian Women's Personal Narrative: Voices Past and Present," in *American Women's Autobiography: Fea(s)ts of Memory*, edited by Margo Culley, The University of Wisconsin Press, 1992, pp. 268-94.

[*In the excerpt below, Sands argues for the importance of Native American women's narratives of the nineteenth and twentieth centuries, focusing in particular on Sarah Winnemucca Hopkins'* Life among the Piutes *(1883).*]

American Indian women are essential to America's record of historical development. Where would America be without Pocahontas' timely rescue of John Smith? What would have become of the Lewis and Clark expedition without the loyal guidance of Sacagawea? Yet from the beginning of colonization, Native American women have been accorded recognition only as symbols of a primitive nobility which contributed to the progress of the American enterprise. And even that symbology is ambivalent; the reverse of the Indian "princess" is the "squaw," an object of sexual abuse and debasement. Thus the powerful image of the "princess" is neutralized by the powerless image of the native woman as "object of scornful convenience" (Green 713).

In the American mind, the Indian woman in relation to Indian men is insignificant—a breeder of "papooses," gatherer of berries and roots, and curer of buffalo hides. Reduced to menial tasks, she remains humble and mute. In relationship to colonizing males she is either primitive sexual object or dusky virgin "royalty"—an abstraction to be manipulated for political or physical motives—easily abandoned because she has no distinct personal identity. Her existence, as portrayed consistently through American history and popular culture, is defined exclusively in relationship to her usefulness to males. As Cherokee critic Rayna Green comments:

> It is time that the Princess herself is rescued and the squaw relieved of her obligatory service. The Native American woman, like all women, needs definition that stands apart from that of males, red or white. Certainly, the Native woman needs to be defined as Indian, in Indian terms. (714)

The princess/squaw stereotypes, however comforting they may be to the American sensibility, allow the American Indian woman not only to be marginalized by race and sex, but, perhaps more than any other minority group in America, to be perversely distorted.[1] By examining the lives of real Indian women, historical and contemporary, some appreciation for the substance and range of American Indian women's lives may be achieved, and the absurdly elevating and demeaning images traditionally attached to them may begin to lose their power.

American Indian women have had force and voice within their own tribes. Traditionally Indian women have been repositories of knowledge to be passed down from generation to generation, and they have also been the keepers of spiritual ideals and tribal values. As one contemporary Navajo woman points out, in the American stereotype "the Indian woman is totally a cardboard figure, a shadow of the man. In reality the women are the lifeline of their people" (Bataille 5). Frequently they have been powerful forces in the leadership of their tribes in roles as curers, warriors, and as respected counselors. As Sioux spokesman Vine Deloria, Sr., points out, "men did not hold office without the approval of the mature women of the tribe, and if they did not fulfill their responsibilities adequately, they were not likely to be given roles of power again" (Bataille and Sands 18). One Indian woman sums up this balance of roles by saying:

> There was a very fine line, a fine bond between a man and a woman and their responsibility as members of a tribe. . . . every single tribe believed that both sides had to equally join together in balance or there would be no life. You have to have a man and a woman and with that there is unity and balance and harmony in the world. (Bataille 6)

Native American women, then, have traditionally been and still are central to tribal well-being. At the center of kinship systems in matrilineal societies, tribal women may control substantial amounts of property. Tribal societies consider menstruating women extremely powerful, and mature women are held in high esteem for their wisdom and knowledge. It is no wonder, then, that many Indian women reject the notion of women's liberation, finding within their own societies suitable outlets for their needs and ambitions without rupturing the fabric of their traditional communities. However, it must be recognized that power does not constitute dominance within Indian tribes, and tribal roles and behavior for both men and women are carefully defined and regulated by such means as ceremonial obligations and community gossip; so while Native American women have been misperceived by Euro-Americans and do, in fact, have considerable influence within their tribes, limitations, rooted firmly in tradition, do govern their behavior.

Though the impact of Indian women on mainstream culture has been largely a product of misinformation, stereotyping, and political convenience, Indian women have, over the past century and a half, been frequent and eloquent spokespersons for their tribes and activists for Indian causes.[2] Many tribal women have also chosen to tell or write their life stories for a nontribal readership, giving voice to a wide range of personal intentions and experiences. However, despite the substantial canon of American Indian women's autobiographical publications (Bataille and Sands; Brumble, *Annotated Bibliography*), little attention has been given to these works even by scholars in the field of autobiography and American Indian literatures.[3] In many cases, this is because the works are hard to find, often obscured by misclassification in libraries (anything Indian must be anthropology) or not kept in print by publishers or marketed widely. And, of course, like all women's literature, these texts suffer from marginalization, but to a much higher degree, particularly when they challenge the princess/squaw image of Indian women held so dearly by American culture. As Sidonie Smith points out:

> if the autobiographer is a woman of color or a working class woman, she faces even more complex imbroglios of male-female figures: Here ideologies of race and class, sometimes even of nationality, intersect and confound those of gender. As a result, she is doubly or triply the subject of other people's representation, turned again and again in stories that reflect and promote certain forms of selfhood identified with class, race, and nationality as well as sex. In every case, moreover, she remains marginalized in that she finds herself resident on the margins of discourse, always removed from the center of power within the culture she inhabits. (51)

Indian women autobiographers participate in two cultures, tribal and Euro-American, yet reception and recognition of personal narratives by Indian women are rare indeed, because the marginality of Indian women's autobiographies also is complicated by factors unique to their tribal source.

Autobiography is not an indigenous form of literature for American Indian peoples. The traditional literature of tribal peoples is oral in nature and communal in source—myths, tales, songs, and chants performed in ceremonial context or told for the purpose of instructing and entertaining the community. Only since the nineteenth century have Indian people used written forms to record their histories and produce literary works, and until this century only a minority of Indians wrote English, making their production of text very minimal until relatively recently. Furthermore, tribal societies do not value individualism or self-assertion in the Euro-American sense highly, so to relate one's life story is to put oneself forward in a way that may elicit criticism from one's own community. Added to this is the fact that cross-cultural writing requires complex processes to make what is "foreign" accessible to the mainstream of American culture.

To most Americans, Indian culture remains exotic and unknown; moreover, representing Native American experience is further complicated by the fact that Indian culture is not homogeneous but made up of several hundred separate cultures with separate languages and literatures, so cultural and linguistic translations are necessary for a wide readership. And, as in mainstream and other American minority cultures, the female autobiographical tradition is separate from the male tradition. Autobiographies of Indian men tend to focus on public lives; their subjects are figures of historical importance—chiefs, warriors, medicine men—while the autobiographies of Indian women tend to focus on private lives, examining personal relationships and individual growth and concentrating on everyday events and activities.[4]

Finally, the process of Indian personal narrative is often collaborative—a tribal person narrating to a nontribal collector/editor. The intervention of a mediator between the narrator and the reader complicates the issues of voice and reliability enormously since the published narrative is actually a bicultural composition (Krupat, "Indian Autobiography"). Speaking of cross-cultural writing, anthropologist James Clifford states, "Literary processes—metaphor, figuration, narrative—affect the ways cultural phenomena are registered, from the first jotted 'observations,' to the completed book, to the ways these configurations 'make sense' in determined acts of reading" (Clifford and Marcus 4). Even if the intention of Indian personal narrative is not literary, the writing of lives employs culturally defined cognitive processes and narrative techniques that affect cultural representation; the text is both a cultural and a personal interpretation in which the narrator "in a sense, makes or remakes" (Personal Narrative Group 101) her life and its cultural context through language. Moreover, bicultural narrative doesn't simply double the problem of reliability, it multiplies the complexity of interpretation. The relationship between truth and illusion, story and reality is one not only of intimate codependence but of multiple codependences affected by colonialism.

In many cases, tribal people have been interviewed about their lives by historians or anthropologists seeking ethnographic data. Yet even in anthropological writing, as Clifford Geertz points out, truths are only partial—ethnographic fictions (15)—constructs of language and memory that bring to the reader ways of imagining lives and cultures.[5] In every collaborative narrative, the power relationship is unequal and the intended audience is outside the tribal group, so dominant culture forms and interpretations overpower the indigenous narrative style. In some cases ethnographic intent leads to short, episodic narratives collected to illustrate anthropological categories; in others a full life history is presented but with little attention to aesthetic techniques or style, particularly not Native style. Thus the term autobiography, which is always difficult to define, becomes particularly problematical in reference to American Indian personal narrative since autobiography generally presumes literary intention and form. "Personal narrative" or "life history" (Frank, 72) describes many of these texts more accurately though some Indian narratives are, despite their ethnographic genesis, of recognized literary merit and fit commonly held notions of autobiography (Neihardt; Underhill), and others have been written consciously as literary works.[6] Whether literary or ethnographic, the cross-cultural discourse required to represent the life and culture of a tribal person to a nontribal reader is complex and adds to the already problematical nature of autobiographical process.

And to further complicate the study of Indian personal narrative, three separate traditions of autobiography coexist: composite, written, and multiform. The bicultural composite often described by the terms "as-told-to" or "life history" is characterized by oral narration by the subject, and recording, structuring, and editing by a nontribal person to form an extensive record of the subject's life.[7] This form should not, however, be seen as an early stage in the development of Indian autobiography since it is still being produced today and has coexisted with the written tradition over the past century and a half. The written text, often affected by extensive editing by a nontribal person, may too share, in varying degrees, the bicultural method of composition.[8] The multiform text, a recent innovation by contemporary Indian creative writers, mixes oral tradition, personal narrative, fiction, and poetry into works which might best be described as cultural memoirs composed and controlled by tribal authors.[9]

Autobiographical works by American Indians, because of the variety of forms of discourse used in their production, defy genre categorization and are best examined as processes of personal narration.[10]

Though the three processes referred to are not gender specific, gender must be considered in examining autobiographical works by American Indians, because it not only establishes the public/private contrast in these texts but has impact on the issues of reader reception and critical assessment. Because warriors and medicine men, like Geronimo or Black Elk, have historical recognition apart from their narratives, their autobiographical texts receive far greater critical attention than those written by Indian women who have no public reputation. Hence, female narratives are, as in mainstream literature, marginalized because their content does not seem significant. Indian women, not generally actors in the public arena, create narratives, it is assumed, essentially repetitious of one another, focusing on childhood, puberty, marriage and childbearing, and old age. Readers expect little variety or significance. Even for the purposes of ethnography, women's lives often claim attention only in terms of their generative and male-supporting roles, so in some cases

little beyond data supporting representative social roles has been gathered and published. If it has traditionally been a negative characteristic for tribal people to put themselves forward, the woman who narrates her individual experience, particularly if she presents herself as other than representative of tribal norms, calls particularly negative attention to herself. She places herself in double jeopardy, criticized within her tribe and unlikely to find validation for her experience or narration in the world of her nontribal audience either, because it generally upholds male dominated criteria for autobiographical writing and clings to the princess/squaw image tenaciously. As Sidonie Smith says:

> Since the ideology of gender makes of woman's life script a nonstory, a silent space, a gap in patriarchal culture, the ideal woman is self-effacing rather than self-promoting, and her "natural" story shapes itself not around public, heroic life but around the fluid, circumstantial, contingent responsiveness to others, that according to patriarchal ideology, characterizes the life of woman but not autobiography. (50)

The American Indian woman who, either through a nontribal collector/editor, or by her own pen, ventures to call attention to her life, whether as representative or, more dangerously yet, as unique risks censure at home, tepid reception in the dominant culture, and indifference from scholars even in the field of Indian studies.

It is a wonder, given this personal and literary peril, that any Indian women have chosen to share their life stories. Some have, in fact, remained anonymous informants for anthropologists, but most of the over one hundred and thirty autobiographical texts by Indian women[11] carry the narrators' names, and many are powerful and eloquent statements of personal and cultural survival.

Written Autobiography

One of the earliest written autobiographies by an American Indian is Sarah Winnemucca Hopkins' *Life among the Piutes: Their Wrongs and Claims,* published in 1883. As the title suggests, this autobiography is not only a personal narrative, but also a cultural history of the Northern Paiute tribe from early contact with whites to the 1880s, and a plea for an end to unjust treatment of her people.

Thocmentony (translated Shell Flower), as she was named when she was born, probably in 1844, in the vicinity of Humboldt Lake in present-day northern Nevada, was the granddaughter of Truckee "who had been a guide to early emigrants crossing the Great Basin" and leader of the Numa, as the Northern Paiutes called themselves (Canfield 4). She was the daughter of Winnemucca, an important antelope shaman who became the leader and spokesman for his tribe upon Truckee's death. Sarah Winnemucca was born into an important family at a time of rapid and bewildering change for her people.

Her first encounter with whites was filled with terror. Stories of cannibalism in the doomed Donner party had filtered into the tribe and become the basis of stories of fierce whites who would eat Numas (Hopkins 11), so Thocmentony did not believe her grandfather's story about the tradition of the white men as prophesied benevolent lost brothers of the Numa (Canfield 6). Frightened by the approach of a party of whites, Thocmentony's mother buried Thocmentony and her cousin to the neck and hid them under sagebrush, leaving them there all day until she could safely return to uncover them. The trauma of this event stayed with the child, making her fearful and timid, especially after one of her uncles was killed by a party of whites (Hopkins 20). She was especially terrified when her grandfather insisted that his daughter and granddaughter and other kinsmen accompany him to California. During the journey, gifts of sugar from white settlers and the kind nursing of a white woman when Thocmentony became ill with poison oak finally dissolved her fear of "the owls," as the Numa called white people because of their bearded faces and light eyes (Hopkins 11-32). In fact, she was so thoroughly taken with her nurse she claims in her autobiography that this incident made her "come to love the white people" (Hopkins 33). By 1858, in fact, Sarah and her sister were living with a white family and learning English rapidly (Hopkins 58). The timid little girl who had been mute, too afraid even to speak her native language around whites, was finding her voice and would soon become an interpreter for negotiations between the army and her people though she was only an adolescent. Her skill as a translator and her position as a member of the most prominent family in the tribe brought her to the very center of her tribe's negotiations with Indian agents and army officers and rapidly led to her role as spokeswoman for her people to white society in western towns and cities and eventually as a lecturer and lobbyist for Indian causes in the eastern United States.

Sarah Winnemucca, as she became known to whites, wrote her autobiography to reach a wider audience than her lectures could in order to convince the white world that her people were not bloodthirsty savages but decent people willing to coexist peacefully with the growing white population in their traditional homeland (now western Nevada, southeastern Oregon, and northeastern California), if only the injustices and corruption of Indian policy could be redressed.

In Elizabeth Palmer Peabody and Mary Mann, the widow of Horace Mann, Sarah Winnemucca found loyal support; Peabody found her lecturing engagements and

Mann volunteered to edit Sarah's book, which she quickly found to be quite a task. Writing about the narrative of this self-educated Indian woman, Mann says:

> I wish you could see her manuscript as a matter of curiosity. I don't think the English language ever got such treatment before. I have to recur to her sometimes to know what a word is, as spelling is an unknown quantity to her. . . . She often takes syllables off of words & adds them or rather prefixes them to other words, but the story is heart-breaking, and told with simplicity & eloquence that cannot be described, for it is not high-faluting eloquence, tho' sometimes it lapses into verse (and quite poetical verse too). I was always considered fanatical about Indians, but I have a wholly new conception of them now, and we civilized people may well stand abashed before their purity of life & their truthfulness. (Canfield 201)

Mann's enthusiasm for the project did not fade despite Sarah's unorthodox writing; in fact, she aided in defraying publication costs by getting subscriptions to underwrite printing. Mann's comments on the project are particularly useful because they verify that Sarah Winnemucca composed her autobiography with relatively little help from Mann, who writes in the preface, "My editing has consisted in copying the original manuscript in correct orthography and punctuation, with occasional emendations by the author, of a book which is an heroic act on the part of the writer" (Hopkins 3).

Sarah Winnemucca's personal narrative fits poorly into the genre of women's autobiography as reminiscence; rather, because of the very public nature of her life, it corresponds more accurately to the memoir style of male autobiography. That her mentors were active in the transcendentalist movement and that she had become quite sophisticated in eastern society suggest that she may well have been deliberately modeling Victorian male autobiographies, though that must remain purely speculation, since no records exist of literary influences on her text. The political nature of her authorial intent must also be taken into account, and so must the nature of her life experience. A pivotal figure in the relations of her tribe with the military and bureaucratic agencies of the United States government,[12] she acted as a scout for the U.S. Army under General Howard's command in the Bannock War (Canfield 141). In the appendix to her autobiography, a letter written in 1878, by R. F. Bernard, a cavalry captain, verifies her role:

> This is to certify that Sara Winnemucca has rendered most valuable services during the operations of this year against the hostile Bannock and Piute Indians. About the commencement of hostilities, she went for me from my camp to that of the hostiles, distant about a hundred miles, and returned bringing

exceedingly valuable information concerning their number, location, intentions, etc., and she also succeeded in getting her father, the Piute chief Winnemucca, with many of his band, to leave the enemy and go to Camp McDermit, Nevada, where they remained during the summer campaign. (Hopkins 259)

Sarah's version of these events is considerably more dramatic:

> This was the hardest work I ever did for the government in all my life—the whole round trip, from 10 o'clock June 13 up to June 15, arriving back at 5:30 P.M., having been in the saddle night and day; distance, about two hundred and twenty-three miles. Yes, I went for the government when the officers could not get an Indian man or a white man to go for love or money. I, only an Indian woman, went and saved my father and his people. (Hopkins 164)

Her vision of herself as a warrior woman dominates this summary and interpretation of her actions. She presents herself as a hero, brave beyond either Indian or white males, yet speaks of herself as "only" an Indian woman, a dramatic contrast that indicates her awareness of her readership who certainly would not expect such bravery of a "squaw."

Winnemucca does not, however, reject the Euro-American stereotype of "princess"; she allows herself to be billed as "Princess Sarah Winnemucca of the Piutes" for her lectures (Canfield 200), perhaps in this case deliberately using the stereotype of exotic royalty to work for her cause.

Sarah Winnemucca is a very self-conscious narrator. At work here are "strategies by which the author seeks to explain or justify her current sense of herself, a need which might be especially strong in a woman who feels herself moving into uncharted waters . . ." (Chevigny 83). She writes her narrative directly to her audience, frequently addressing them in the second person and using genteel language as when she describes the traditional flower festival among her people:

> Oh, with what eagerness we girls used to watch every spring for the time when we could meet with our hearts' delight, the young men, whom in civilized life you call beaux. We would all go in company to see if the flowers we were named for were yet in bloom, for almost all the girls are named for flowers. (Hopkins 46)

Note the term "civilized." It is hard to believe that she sees white society as more civilized than her own; she frequently chastises whites for their perfidy in dealing with Indians and portrays her people as trustworthy,

gentle, clean, hospitable, and above all, moral—far superior to the corrupt agents who steal their food rations and keep the income from tribal farming for their own enrichment. It is clear who she thinks is really civilized, but she knows how to play her audience and uses her "only an Indian woman" pose to gain sympathy for her cause, just as she uses the image of the exotic "princess" to fill a lecture hall.

Winnemucca takes considerable pains to give details of traditional life, especially the training of young men and women for adult roles as spouses and parents. In her chapter entitled "Domestic and Social Moralities" she also makes it clear that women have power within her tribe. She writes:

> The women know as much as the men do, and their advice is often asked. We have a republic as well as you. The council-tent is our Congress, and anybody can speak who has anything to say, women and all. (Hopkins 53)

She continues, giving an account of a woman who takes her fallen uncle's place in battle. Winnemucca, herself, of course, remains the ultimate warrior of her tribe, risking her life to rescue her people and also fighting for her people in the council tents, lecture halls, and even the halls of Congress and of the White House itself, yet maintaining the demeanor of a humble Indian woman when it suits her need for audience reception. Adroit at two techniques, she uses a conventional autobiographical form for her time, and she manipulates her status as an Indian woman in her own favor. She has it both ways—male and female, private and public. Not only does she present herself as a warrior for Indian justice, but she also develops a portrait of a child terrified by white power who, toward the end of her narrative, has become a dedicated teacher of Indian pupils—a version of motherhood.

The fact that she is a woman is a great asset for her in reaching her audience. Male Indian warriors may threaten; look at Geronimo, Sitting Bull, etc., but a woman as warrior, in alliance with the U.S. Army and her own people, is safe—a powerful yet acceptable image, not so very different from Pocahontas after all, especially considering she has a white man for a husband. She ironically fits all the conventions already well established in the American mind and thus gains reader acceptance despite her strident accusations of injustice toward her people. Winnemucca does call very public attention to herself, not so much by writing her autobiography as by appearing as the "princess" in full buckskin dress before audiences on both Pacific and Atlantic coasts, speaking out to whites on behalf of Indians, pointing out the misuse of Indian women by white men, accusing whites of lying to Indians. She also calls attention to herself in her own tribe. As interpreter between tribe and whites, she is particularly vulnerable to criticism if things do not go as promised, if blankets and food are not delivered as scheduled, or land settlements she negotiated in Washington are not implemented. She is an easy scapegoat among her people, and as a highly unconventional representative of Indian women in white society, is also open to scrutiny and occasional barbs, particularly about her liaisons with white men, including two marriages. The first marriage to a drunken gambler who wasted her meager resources was disastrous, and the second, to Louis Hopkins, was stormy and unconventional. In part, the autobiography defends her against gossip about her private life and criticism of her public life; it is a rationale—but clearly not an apology—for the unusual thrust of her life in a period of Victorian sensibilities in white society and confusing social change in tribal society. Sarah Winnemucca's autobiography explains her public life and makes a case for her integrity as a Northern Paiute woman working for understanding and cooperation between tribal people and the dominant society.

The reliability of the Winnemucca text, as with all autobiographical texts, is suspect particularly because she uses her life story to promote the cause of her own personal integrity and the broader cause of tribal justice—she has axes to grind. It is also suspect at another level. Included in the text, in fact dominant in it, lengthy speeches and dialogues highly unlikely to have been remembered and written verbatim are presented in the conventional forms of quoted monologue and dialogue, and thus purport to be accurate. These techniques suggest a considerable use of poetic license, recollections edited with political as well as artistic intent in mind, other voices played through the voice of the narrator, noticeably in the narrator's narrative style. The text is not a polyphony; only the single voice of Winnemucca actually narrates dramatic events and characters. She creates speeches by her grandfather to move a white audience to admire him and the nature of tribal culture. Sarah's dialogues with military officers, white settlers, her family, and others enhance her own stature and her case for justice toward the Paiutes. In the name of justice, she sees manipulation of the past as fair. Her "fictions," as Geertz would put it, however suspect, make the autobiography far livelier than it would be without such dramatic devices.

Sarah Winnemucca places herself at the center of every event and action in the autobiography, from her description of her terror at the first contact with whites, where, actually, she is only a bit player, to her daring rescue of her father and his band, where she is indeed center stage, to her negotiations with congressmen and cabinet members. It is Winnemucca's verve, her certainty of the epic nature of her life, her absolute dedication, despite enormous personal sacrifice, and her genteelly Victorian use of language that work in concert to move the reader and convince the audience of the justice of Indian rights even a century after its first publication. . . .

Notes

[1] Rosaldo and Lamphere clarify this problem: "Because men everywhere tend to have more prestige than women, and because men are usually associated with social roles of dominance and authority, most previous descriptions of social processes have treated women as being theoretically uninteresting. Women who exercise power are seen as deviants, manipulators, or, at best, exceptions. And women's goals and ideologies are assumed to be coordinate with those of men" (9).

[2] Notable examples are Zitkala-Sa (Gertrude Bonnin), a Sioux woman who wrote three autobiographical essays published in *Atlantic Monthly* in 1900; Ada Deer, a contemporary Menominee woman active in the restoration of her tribe's rights and author of an autobiography, *Speaking Out;* Susette La Flesche, activist for her Omaha tribe and the Ponca tribe in the 1870s and subject of the biography *Bright Eyes* by Dorothy Clark Wilson.

[3] American Indian autobiography scholars Lynne Woods O'Brien, William F. Smith, Jr., Arnold Krupat do not include analysis of Indian women's autobiographies in their critical studies; nor do autobiography scholars Estelle C. Jelinek, Domna C. Stanton, Sidonie Smith, or the Personal Narratives Group. Work since the mid-1980s shows some increase in attention to Native American women narrators. H. David Brumble addresses women's narratives in the first two chapters of his book *American Indian Autobiography,* and Hertha Wong briefly mentions Plains quilts and Navajo weaving as forms of women's autobiography. Helen Carr offers a substantial analysis of two Native women's narratives, *Autobiography of a Fox Woman* and *Autobiography of a Papago Woman,* which reveals the colonial ethnocentricity of the collectors of these texts. Kathleen M. Sands applies new ethnographic theory to a Papago autobiography. Arnold Krupat, in "The Dialogic of Silko's Storyteller," provides a reading of Silko's multigenre collection as autobiography, emphasizing the polyvocal character of the volume and the self-reflexive nature of the discourse as it incorporates traditional stories, voices from the community, and recollection. This essay is useful to compare with my designation of this volume as a multiform autobiography later in this essay. A. LaVonne Ruoff gives a detailed analysis of the Winnemucca narrative useful for comparison with the analysis of the same text given in this essay. Clearly, a great deal more critical work will be required in order to develop critical theory and methodology appropriate for Native American women's autobiographies.

[4] See Bataille and Sands, especially chap. 1, for a discussion of the form and content of Indian women's personal narrative.

[5] In *The Interpretation of Cultures* Clifford Geertz uses the term "fictions" to describe anthropological writing "in the sense that they are 'something made,' 'something fashioned' . . . not that they are false . . ." (15). James Clifford, in his essay "On Ethnographic Allegory," makes a strong case for the term allegory to describe anthropological field reporting, on the basis that representations of other cultures are convincing or rich to the degree allegories "stand behind the controlled fictions of difference and similitude that we call ethnographic accounts" (101). For an analysis of a Native American woman's autobiography grounded in current ethnography theory, see Sands. Collection and critical analysis of any form of Native text, of course, is an act of colonization and often reveals as much about the non-Native culture as it does about the Native text and culture, since colonization is a matter as much of language as of action, and, as Clifford suggests, may be defined as the continuous replacement of an indigenous allegory by a colonial one. Exposure of the colonial allegory, as it is imbedded in collected versions of Native texts and the critical discourse about them, is being facilitated by the current crisis in ethnography though it is unlikely that any theory or methodology will eradicate ethnocentricity; this crisis will, one hopes, sensitize scholars and generate more incorporation of Native metacommentary in the field of Native American studies. Autobiographies by indigenous women, despite the imposition upon them of Euro-American forms and interpretation, are, as the Personal Narrative Group points out, "particularly effective sources of counterhegemonic insight because they expose the viewpoint embedded in dominant ideology as particularist rather than universal, and because they reveal the reality of a life that defies or contradicts the rules" (7), and question the cultural norms of the dominant society.

[6] See Kiowa poet and Pulitzer Prize-winning novelist N. Scott Momaday's *The Names: A Memoir* for an example.

[7] Quoting Langness, *The Life History in Anthropological Science*, Susan N. G. Geiger says: "Although the demarcations between types of oral data are not always clear, a life history is generally distinguishable from other kinds of oral documentation as 'an extensive record of a person's life told to and recorded by another, who then edits and writes the life as though it were autobiography'" (336).

[8] For an example of the editorial control of a written autobiography, see the analysis of Anna Moore Shaw's *A Pima Past* in Bataille and Sands 89-99.

[9] See N. Scott Momaday's *The Way to Rainy Mountain;* also Leslie Marmon Silko's *Storyteller,* which is discussed later in this essay.

[10] For a more complete discussion of sources of and influences on American Indian autobiography, see Bataille and Sands 3-20.

[11] H. David Brumble's *Annotated Bibliography of American Indian and Eskimo Autobiographies* and "A Supplement to An Annotated Bibliography of American Indian and Eskimo Autobiographies" include 133 American Indian women and 444 American Indian men.

[12] Several biographers call Sarah Winnemucca Hopkins a chief; one, by Dorothy Nafus Morrison, is titled *Chief Sarah: Sarah Winnemucca's Fight for Indian Rights*. As a spokesperson, negotiator, and warrior, she does, in fact, fill the role of a chief though she never bore the title; however in one speech, her father said, "Now hereafter we will look on her as our chieftain, for none of us are worthy of being chief but her" (193), or at least in her autobiography she reports that that is what he said. . . .

Works Cited

Bataille, Gretchen. "An Interview with Geraldine Keams." *Explorations in Ethnic Studies,* 10/1 (1987), 1-7.

———, and Kathleen M. Sands. *American Indian Women Telling Their Lives*. Lincoln: University of Nebraska Press, 1984.

Brumble, H. David. *American Indian Autobiography*. Los Angeles: University of California Press, 1988.

———. *An Annotated Bibliography of American Indian and Eskimo Autobiographies*. Lincoln: University of Nebraska Press, 1981.

———. "A Supplement to An Annotated Bibliography of American Indian and Eskimo Autobiographies." *Western American Literature,* 17 (November 1982), 243-60.

Canfield, Gae Whitney. *Sarah Winnemucca of the Northern Paiutes*. Norman, University of Oklahoma Press, 1931.

Carr, Helen. "In Other Words: Native American Women's Autobiography." In *Life/Lines,* ed. Bella Brodzki and Celeste Schenck. Ithaca: Cornell University Press, 1988.

Chevigny, Bell Gale. "Daughters Writing: Toward a Theory of Women's Biography." *Feminist Studies,* 9/1 (1983), 79-102.

Clifford, James. "On Ethnographic Allegory." In *Writing Cultures: The Poetics and Politics of Ethnography,* ed. Clifford and George E. Marcus. Berkeley: University of California Press, 1986.

Frank, Geyla. "Finding the Common Denominator: A Phenomenological Critique of Life History Method." *Ethos,* 7/1 (1981), 68-93.

Geertz, Clifford. *The Interpretation of Cultures.* New York: Basic Books, 1973.

Geiger, Susan N. G. "Women's Life Histories: Method and Content." *Signs,* 11/1 (1986), 344-51.

Green, Rayna. "The Pocahontas Perplex: The Image of Indian Women in American Culture." *Massachusetts Review,* 16/4 (1976), 698-714.

Hopkins, Sarah Winnemucca. *Life among the Piutes: Their Wrongs and Claims.* Boston: Printed for the Author, 1883. Photographically reproduced by Chalfant Press, Bishop, CA, 1969.

Jelinek, Estelle C. *The Tradition of Women's Autobiography: From Antiquity to the Present.* Boston: Twayne Publishers, 1986.

———. *Women's Autobiography: Essays in Criticism.* Bloomington: Indiana University Press, 1980.

Koehler, Lyle. "Native Women of the Americas: A Bibliography." *Frontiers,* 6 (Autumn 1982), 73-93.

Krupat, Arnold. "The Dialogic of Silko's Storyteller." In *Narrative Chance: Post-modern Discourse on Native American Indian Literatures,* ed. Gerald Vizenor. Albuquerque: University of New Mexico Press, 1989.

———. *For Those Who Come After: A Study of Native American Autobiography.* Berkeley: University of California Press, 1985.

———. "The Indian Autobiography: Origins, Type, and Functions." *American Literature,* 53 (March 1981), 22-42.

Langness, L. L. *The Life History in Anthropological Science.* Boston: Holt, Rinehart and Winston, 1965.

Momaday, N. Scott. *The Names, A Memoir.* New York: Harper Colophon Books, 1976.

———. *The Way to Rainy Mountain.* Albuquerque: University of New Mexico Press, 1969.

Morrison, Dorothy Nafus. *Chief Sarah: Sarah Winnemucca's Fight for Indian Rights.* New York: Atheneum, 1980.

Neihardt, John G. *Black Elk Speaks: Being the Life Story of a Holy Man of the Oglala Sioux.* Lincoln: University of Nebraska Press, 1961.

O'Brien, Lynne Woods. *Plains Indian Autobiographies.* Idaho: Boise College, 1973.

Personal Narratives Group. *Interpreting Women's Lives: Feminist Theory and Personal Narratives.* Bloomington: Indiana University Press, 1989.

Rosaldo, Michelle Zimbalist, and Louise Lamphere, eds. *Women, Culture, and Society.* Stanford: Stanford University Press, 1974.

Ruoff, A. LaVonne. "Nineteenth-Century American Indian Autobiographers: William Apes, George Copway, and Sarah Winnemucca." In *The New American Literary History,* ed. Jerry Ward. New York: MLA, 1991.

Sands, Kathleen M. "Ethnography, Autobiography, and Fiction: Narrative Strategies in Cultural Analysis." In *Native American Literatures,* ed. Laura Coltelli. Pisa, Italy: Servizio Editoriale Universitario, 1989.

Silko, Leslie Marmon. *Storyteller,* New York: Seaver Books, 1981.

Smith, Sidonie. *A Poetics of Women's Autobiography: Marginality and the Fictions of Self-Representation.* Bloomington: Indiana University Press, 1987.

Smith, William F., Jr. "American Indian Autobiographies." *American Indian Quarterly,* 2 (Autumn 1975), 237-45.

Stanton, Domna C., ed. *The Female Autograph.* New York: New York Literary Forum, 1984.

Swan, Brian, and Arnold Krupat. *I Tell You Now: Autobiographical Essays by Native American Writers.* Lincoln: University of Nebraska Press, 1987.

Underhill, Ruth M. *Papago Woman.* New York: Holt Rinehart, and Winston, 1979.

Wong, Hertha. "Pre-literate Native American Autobiography: Forms of Personal Narrative." *Melus,* 14/1 (Spring 1987), 17-32. . . .

Timothy Sweet (essay date 1993)

SOURCE: "Masculinity and Self-Performance in the Life of Black Hawk," in *American Literature,* Vol. 65, No. 3, September, 1993, pp. 475-99.

[*In the essay that follows, Sweet discusses the role of Native American masculine identity in the autobiography of Black Hawk, a Sauk warrior who was defeated by the U. S. army in 1832.*]

> Traditional tribal lifestyles are more often gynocratic than not, and they are never patriarchal.—Paula Gunn Allen, *The Sacred Hoop*

It is not customary for us to say much about our women, as they generally perform their part cheerfully, and never interfere with business belonging to the men!—Black Hawk, *Life of Black Hawk*

In *The Sacred Hoop,* Paula Gunn Allen articulates the need to recover the original feminine traditions of American tribal peoples as part of a general critique of white Western patriarchy. Traditional tribal lifestyles, according to Allen, underwent an incomplete but significant transformation from gynocratic to patriarchal modes as a result of contact with Europeans who enforced their own values, especially Christian misogyny, in their dealings with Native Americans. Whether or not "the physical and cultural genocide of American Indian tribes is and was mostly about patriarchal fear of gynocracy," it is certainly true that the European conquest of the Americas brought about significant alterations in the gender structures of Native American cultures, as it did in every other facet of tribal life.[1] Yet if femininity was altered, so was masculinity. Thus Allen's project of "recovering the feminine," articulated in the subtitle of her important study, must be complemented by an endeavor to recover the masculine in order to attain a full understanding of gender in American tribal societies. The feminine roles that Allen valorizes did not exist in isolation but rather in mutually enabling relations with various masculine roles such as shaman, healer, hunter, politician, and defender of the tribe, all of which were altered in some way by the European conquest.[2]

A good place to begin investigating these concerns is the autobiographical *Life of Black Hawk.*[3] Here we read the personal narrative of a Sauk war chief, a man who in 1832 led a small band in the only violent resistance to Indian Removal in the old Northwest. Threatened by soldiers who were coming to force his people from the village of Saukenuk on the Rock River in Illinois, which had been ceded by a suspect treaty in 1804 (discussed below), Black Hawk moved his band of men, women, and children to the north, attempting to rendezvous with the Winnebago and Potawatomi in Wisconsin, and, as he thought, British forces in Canada. He then intended to return and retake Saukenuk. But he had been deceived by a Sauk chief, Neapope ("Broth"), and a crossblood Sauk-Winnebago, Wabokieshiek ("White Cloud" or "Prophet"), about the possibility of an alliance with the British.[4] After the discovery of this deception, the war took the form of a strategic retreat to the west, with Black Hawk attempting to protect his band from massacre by the Illinois Mounted Volunteers on the one hand and attack by the Sioux on the other. The majority of the Sauk and Fox did not participate in the war; they had been persuaded by Black Hawk's political rival Keokuk to remove west of the Mississippi as the treaty specified. The war marked a turning point in Sauk political and cultural history. Through subsequent negotiations they lost all of the

land west of the Mississippi that had been granted to them (in perpetuity, of course) by the treaty of 1804. Once a powerful force in the Mississippi Valley, by 1845 they were confined to a tiny reservation in Kansas, ironically at the headwaters of a river named for their traditional enemies, the Osage.[5]

While other traditionally masculine tribal roles, such as hunter, were also altered by white conquest, the significance of the *Life of Black Hawk* consists in its representation of the collision between the specific Sauk tradition for the masculine gendering of the self as a warrior and the U.S. government policy, also enacted by "warriors," that sought to eliminate the Native American warrior tradition in order to control and ultimately eradicate tribal cultural wholes. This government policy is exemplified in the treaty of 1804, which Black Hawk regarded as invalid since he did not think the signers represented the Sauk interest. The primary intent of the treaty was, of course, the acquisition of Sauk and Fox land (bounded by the Mississippi and Illinois Rivers) and the removal of the tribes west of the Mississippi. But it held other, deeper cultural implications as well, in specifying that the tribes could no longer be responsible for their own defense. The treaty stipulated that the tribes must place themselves "under the protection of the United States, and of no other power whatsoever," that they must not take "private revenge or retaliation" for violations of the treaty but instead appeal to a judicial process administered by the United States government, and that they must "put an end to the bloody war which has heretofore raged between their tribes and those of the Great and Little Osages."[6] Strict adherence to these conditions would alter the gender economy of the tribe by minimizing the importance of warriors. The defeat of the Sauk in the Black Hawk war confirmed this alteration, ensuring that warriors no longer had a legitimate cultural role to play. In the face of white military and political efforts to emasculate the tribal warrior, the *Life of Black Hawk* emerges as an attempt to preserve his traditions.

Black Hawk's story was translated into English and published in late 1833, the year after the war. The actual oral narratives of the war that Black Hawk told to his Sauk contemporaries are unavailable. But we can assume that the conventions governing such narratives would have shaped his telling of the story to a white audience. Given both the social relations surrounding the traditions of Sauk men's personal narratives and the circumstances determining the production of the *Life of Black Hawk,* Black Hawk appears to us primarily as a defender of the tribe, a warrior, and not as a hunter or a seeker of visions or other possible subject-positions. In the partiality of that representation vis-à-vis whatever his "whole" sense of self might have been, we will find a fundamental connection between personal narrative and the construction of masculinity in Sauk society. This connection is put into question by the context of Black Hawk's defeat and the telling of his story to the victors, but it is nevertheless available to a careful reader of the *Life*.

The *Life of Black Hawk* is told by an unassimilated Sauk. The telling is mediated by two men. Antoine LeClair, a crossblood (French-Canadian and Potawatomi) who was fluent in several tribal languages as well as French and English and had been employed by the U.S. government since 1818 as an interpreter, reported that in August of 1833 Black Hawk approached him at the Rock Island Indian Agency and "express[ed] a great desire to have a History of his Life written and published" (*L*, 35). LeClair enlisted the editorial assistance of John Patterson, a newspaper editor. Patterson provided no account of the nature and extent of his editing, and it is not clear whether he ever spoke to Black Hawk in person. All manuscripts and correspondence surrounding the collaboration have been lost.[7] However, prefaces to the *Life* by both LeClair and Patterson attest to the text's fidelity to Black Hawk's actual words.

It was not unusual in the nineteenth century for tribal leaders to want representations of themselves produced for white audiences. While "as told to" personal narratives were rare—for reasons related to logistics and the literary marketplace—painted portraits were common. The usual itinerary of a tribal delegation to Washington included sitting for portraits, which were then displayed in the Indian Gallery at the War Department. The men were usually gratified that their images were thus preserved and publicized; some demanded copies to take home with them. One writer describing the Winnebago delegation in 1850 remarked that "nothing pleased them so much as to tell them that their likenesses were in the War Department, and that their fame was spread through the world."[8] While Black Hawk's desire for fame is evident, his motivations go beyond this and he takes a more active role in self-representation than merely sitting for a portrait (although, as I will discuss below, he did this as well).

The immediate audience for Black Hawk's narrative is the United States government as represented in the person of the interpreter LeClair and the physical space of the Rock Island Agency—a situation in some ways analogous to delegation portraiture. However, according to LeClair's preface, Black Hawk envisioned a wider audience, desiring "(as he said), 'that the people of the United States, (among whom he had been travelling, and by whom he had been treated with great respect, friendship, and hospitality,) might know the *causes* that had impelled him to act as he had done, and the *principles* by which he was governed'" (*L*, 35). Supposing the accuracy of LeClair's story and translation here, we can see that Black Hawk believed

in both the possibility of cross-cultural communication and the interest of white readers in his story. That is, Black Hawk demonstrated his awareness that the *Life* would be what Arnold Krupat calls a "bicultural composite composition."[9]

The most theoretically sophisticated treatment of "bicultural composition" is given in Krupat's *The Voice in the Margin: Native American Literature and the Canon,* which provides a useful framework for understanding the relation between the textual structures and social contexts of Native American literature by analyzing textual production in terms of Mikhail Bakhtin's *The Dialogic Imagination*.[10] Krupat, who has provided the only substantial readings to date of the *Life of Black Hawk,* identifies a tension in the text between genuine cross-cultural dialogue, evidenced by its autobiographical form (the fact that Black Hawk speaks for himself rather than being represented as the subject of a historical narrative), and white monologue, evidenced by Patterson's editorial procedure. In following the chronological imperative of European autobiography, Patterson made Black Hawk's words conform to the dominant discourse for dealing with Indians—"savagism"—which "claimed as a necessity of nature the accession of Indian savagery to white civilization."[11] This discourse, Krupat argues, produced a generic narrative structure of "decline and fall in the comic mode."[12] That is, the overall Jacksonian-progressivist ideological narrative of westward expansion determined the textualization in English of any story of Indian-white interaction, no matter who narrated it originally, as a comedy in which "the red-skinned 'blocking characters' are overcome" to produce the "happy ending" of white settlement.[13] Alternatively, such a narrative could be read as a tragedy of a noble people doomed by the "flaw" of Indianness without distorting the Jacksonian-progressive master narrative. The difference between these modes lies in nineteenth-century white attitudes toward the master narrative—Western Indian-hating or Eastern philanthropy.[14] We will need to read from neither of these positions if we hope to recover tribal tradition from a text that seems, in its overall narrative structure, to be so completely co-opted.

Bakhtin's later work on "speech genres" provides an additional analytical frame for investigating the questions of gender that I raised at the beginning of this essay. Speech genres are "relatively stable types of utterance" ranging in verbal complexity from primary genres, such as the conventional "short rejoinders of daily dialogue" or "the brief standard military command," through secondary genres such as "the diverse forms of scientific statement and all literary genres."[15] Secondary genres are composed of strings of primary genres which are "absorb[ed] and digest[ed]" in various conventional ways.[16] The concept of speech genre can be used to theorize both H. David Brumble's empirical catalogue of preliterate autobiographical traditions—coup tales, informal autobiographical tales, self-examinations, self-vindications, educational narratives, and stories of the acquisition of powers—and the English textualization of these traditions.[17] If we understand the *Life of Black Hawk* as merely an assemblage of utterances in various complex speech genres translated by LeClair and organized by Patterson, we can watch the teleological narrative dissolve into more localized sets of verbal conventions, some of which function to construct and maintain gender roles in Sauk culture.

Before investigating gender roles, however, we must understand the cross-cultural speech genre of ethnography which is essential to an identification of Black Hawk's subject position in the text.[18] The *Life* contains a good deal of ethnographic material, which is placed between Black Hawk's criticism of the dubious treaty of 1804 (the conditions of which compel Black Hawk to go to war) and the account of the war itself; this placement is probably due to Patterson's desire to heighten the dramatic impact of the narrative through a contrast of genres. Regardless of its placement, it is interesting in itself as an example of the cross-cultural dialogization of speech genres. The ethnographic description is oriented toward whites (since Black Hawk would not need to explain these things to his own people), and yet it depends on a "native informant." Further embedded within the ethnographic description are various traditional tribal genres; for example, Black Hawk's account of the ceremony celebrating the new corn leads him into telling a story that might be told at this ceremony: "When the corn is fit to use, another great ceremony takes place, with feasting, and returning thanks to the Great Spirit for giving us corn. I will here relate the manner in which corn first came. According to tradition, handed down to our people, a beautiful woman was seen to descend from the clouds . . ." (*L*, 93). When the story of the woman who brings beans, corn, and tobacco is told within the context of ethnography, it becomes dialogized toward its white audience. As such, the story becomes alienated from its original, tribal orientation; for although LeClair and Patterson textualize it in a way that registers Black Hawk's consciousness of the continuity of oral transmission, the story's traditional social context has been radically altered by virtue not only of its appearing in print for white readers, but, even prior to this, by Black Hawk's telling it to the government employee LeClair rather than to the Sauk.

Black Hawk himself is aware of the cross-cultural situation of this particular telling of the story of Corn Woman. He concludes by acknowledging the dialogic frame without vitiating the legitimacy of the place of the story within the Sauk worldview, which is attempting to come to terms with the presence of whites in America: "The two first [corn and beans] have, ever since, been cultivated by our people, as our principal provisions—and the last used for smoking. The white people have since found out the latter, and seem to

relish it as much as we do" (*L*, 94). The story's contextualization transforms it into ethnographic information, while demonstrating how one speech genre (ethnography) can operate on another (sacred story) to produce a cross-cultural text that does not destroy the legitimacy of the original, monologic story. Enabling the dissemination of the story by telling it within this context, Black Hawk builds a cultural bridge to the whites based on a common appreciation for tobacco. White readers are of course free to make their own assessment of the story as "myth"—and in so doing would be operating on it with their own speech genres (for example, theological or scientific discourses)— but nothing in the text itself especially encourages them to do so. Black Hawk thus represents himself as one firmly grounded in tribal tradition, implicitly emphasizing not his uniqueness or individuality (conventions of modern, white autobiography), but his cultural sameness with other Sauks and his qualification to explain Sauk ways to the whites.

Black Hawk's sense of his cultural sameness with other Sauks is fundamentally important, for his credibility and honor with respect to the main events of the *Life*— his self-identification as warrior and his conduct in the war—depend on his ability to represent himself as following the way of the Sauk, always in comparison with his political rival Keokuk, who is from Black Hawk's perspective too much under the influence of whites. Black Hawk attempts to discredit Keokuk, who agreed to abide by the treaty of 1804, by suggesting that he does not possess the qualities of a warrior. Thus Keokuk, as he comes to be represented in the *Life of Black Hawk,* would not have been entitled to tell the kind of personal narrative that Black Hawk tells. Yet the U.S. government chose to regard Keokuk as "chief" of the Sauks, and he became powerful and influential among his own people even before Black Hawk's defeat in 1832.[19]

Black Hawk's sense of social position is heavily invested in his self-representation as a Sauk who makes no gestures toward assimilation. In this way he is unlike "civilized Indians" such as Samson Occom and William Apes, who in their autobiographies voice the dominant white discourses of salvationism and progressivism in attempting to produce narratives of assimilation. Black Hawk does not write in his own "voice" but has his words transcribed and translated for him, a situation that embroiled contemporary readers in questions of the text's "authenticity"[20] but that interestingly preserves the integrity of Black Hawk's status as an unassimilated Sauk. Patterson makes a point of including on facing pages both a phonetic transcription and a translation (the English version is labeled a "Dedication") of Black Hawk's opening address to the victorious General Atkinson. This address calls on Atkinson to "vouch for the facts contained in my narrative, so far as they came under your observation" (*L*, 37). The facing-page layout would have been far too cumbersome to carry through the entire book, but its use here indicates a desire to represent the voice of the text as Black Hawk's own. Thus, despite the Jacksonian-progressivist context, a Native American (in this instance, Sauk) worldview is acknowledged through language, as it is not when Native Americans such as Occom and Apes write in English in the eighteenth and nineteenth centuries. Unlike John Neihardt's treatment of Black Elk's voice in *Black Elk Speaks,* there is no reason to believe Patterson edited out any evidence of assimilation to white culture.[21] For example, the accounts of trading with whites and descriptions of the impact of that trade (such as the increasing use of alcohol) are integrated without comment into the section of the text describing "our customs, and the manner we live" (*L,* 87). Indeed, in 1833 the newspaperman Patterson would have had every political incentive to preserve or even to fabricate such evidence, which would demonstrate an Indian's acknowledgment of the superiority of white ways. Black Hawk is instead seen to acknowledge only the superiority of white military force, and on his own terms—the terms of a Sauk warrior. As he states at the beginning of his address to Atkinson, "The changes of fortune, and vicissitudes of war, made you my conqueror" (*L,* 37).

In attempting to imagine what the terms of the Sauk warrior might be, we must bear in mind recent caveats about the difficulties of regarding any printed text as an "Indian autobiography" while hoping that the project of coming to some understanding of the warrior Black Hawk and his world is not impossible. An analysis of two categories of speech genre is relevant to developing such an understanding: first, the textual presentations directed toward a white audience, which belong to the "ethnographic" genre described above; second, the oral presentations by means of which Black Hawk's Sauk identity is established and maintained in his own society. Of course, the latter are necessarily mediated for us by the former. To put it another way, Black Hawk's Sauk identity must be seen to influence the textualized, translated (self-)presentation of "Black Hawk" in an important way—if not in terms of overall narrative structure, then in terms of topics or speech genres.

Black Hawk's self-representation as a warrior evokes two traditional, preliterate speech genres: the coup tale and the self-vindication narrative. Brumble characterizes the entire *Life of Black Hawk* as a self-vindication narrative and argues that in telling such a story Black Hawk was "acting in a perfectly traditional manner."[22] Equally important, however, is the coup tale—or, more precisely, the warrior's self-defining performance. Chronologically, the first life event of Black Hawk's narrative occurs at age fifteen (in contrast to Western autobiography, in which childhood is often assumed to be significant in the formation of character). Along

with his father, he joins a war party against the Osages and kills his first enemy:

> Standing by my father's side, I saw him kill his antagonist, and tear the scalp from his head. Fired with valor and ambition, I rushed furiously upon another, smote him to the earth with my tomahawk— run [*sic*] my lance through his body—took off his scalp, and returned in triumph to my father! He said nothing, but looked pleased. This was the first man I killed! . . . Our party then returned to our village, and danced over the scalps we had taken. This was the first time that I was permitted to join in a scalp-dance. (*L,* 47)

The killing itself is important in two ways: of course it contributes to the Sauk victory in this battle, but it also enables Black Hawk to establish a new position in the community. He is formally acknowledged as a warrior for the first time by means of his participation in the scalp dance. Whites might miss the full significance of this narrative for Black Hawk's self-presentation if not for the apparently ethnographic orientation of the last sentence.[23]

This first act of self-performance authorizes Black Hawk to consolidate his new identity in further action (he reports, for example, that a subsequent successful raid "gained for me great applause" [*L,* 47]). Yet further ceremonies are at least equally important in the construction and maintenance of identity. One such ceremony, the "national dance," is described in some detail in a later ethnographic passage which clearly shows the fundamental link between warrior identity and self-performance in Sauk culture:

> The large square in the village is swept and prepared for the purpose. The chiefs and old warriors, take seats on mats which have been spread at the upper end of the square—the drummers and singers come next, and the braves and women form the sides, leaving a large space in the middle. The drums beat, and the singers commence. A warrior enters the square, keeping time with the music. He shows the manner he started on a war party—how he approached the enemy—he strikes, and describes the way he killed him. All join in applause. He then leaves the square, and another enters and takes his place. Such of our young men as have not been out in war parties, and killed an enemy, stand back ashamed—not being able to enter the square. I remember that I was ashamed to look where our young women stood, before I could take my stand in the square as a warrior.
>
> What pleasure it is to an old warrior, to see his son come forward and relate his exploits—it makes him feel young again, and induces him to enter the square, and "fight his battles o'er again." (*L,* 91-92)

With this information, the reader is in a position to understand the importance of self-performative activity in the establishment and maintenance of a particular configuration of masculine identity in Sauk culture: the moment of (communally validated) self-definition as a warrior is simultaneously the moment of (again, communally validated) self-definition as *self-definer*.[24] The warrior is necessarily an autobiographer. This moment is repeated periodically throughout the warrior's life. There would, of course, be other contexts in which masculinity is defined in other terms, such as the ceremony following a young man's first successful hunt, but these would not necessarily admit repeated performative validation.[25]

An important component of this performance is the possibility of meeting the gaze of those whom the tribe acknowledges as sexually available women. Males who cannot participate in this dance are defined only negatively, as not warriors and not fully masculine in this context; they are "ashamed to look where our young women stood." About Black Hawk's life before his first kill the text is utterly silent, mirroring the nonidentity of these unfortunate youths. This silence indicates that the self-presentation of the warrior configuration of masculinity is linked with the very possibility of self-presentation itself. The sexual competition implied in Black Hawk's account of the national dance suggests that the moment of self-definition contains an element of sexual self-objectification. This moment, in which the warrior becomes both masculine subject and sexual object, suggests that gender is constructed according to a paradigm more complex than that of traditional Western patriarchy, in which "woman" is marked (only) as object and "man" (only) as subject: for the Sauk man, both subject and object positions are occupied at once. Additionally, it is not merely the moment of self-objectification before the female gaze that is significant, but the other warriors' observation of this moment as well. The entire community is fully involved.

The sexual politics surrounding the perception of men by women, however, remain unexamined in the context of Black Hawk's situation as narrator of the *Life*. The printed narrative emerges as a textual trace of Black Hawk's attempt to recover the original oral-performative definition of identity not primarily in relation to Sauk women but rather in relation to white soldiers and Sauk warriors, now that the war and Keokuk's accession to power seem to put his masculinity into question. At this point the originary relation between masculinity and formal self-presentation in Sauk culture, like the story of Corn Woman, is mediated by the ethnographic frame of the text. This mediation, the crossing of cultural boundaries, holds potential consequences for the gendering of the subject that Black Hawk attempts to overcome. He is describing the "national dance" for white readers, placing it within the context of events that take place after the corn is planted and within the larger context of his general description of Sauk life. Thus, while we can

recognize how Black Hawk, like most Sauk men, established and maintained a gendered identity by means of personal narrative embodied in a ceremonial performance of his warrior role, we must also recognize the possibility that this gendered identity is alienated from him by the nonceremonial context of the interviews with the translator LeClair and by the medium of print technology. Without full communal authorization, accounts of wartime exploits may be mere idle boasts.

Black Hawk is no doubt aware of the difference in the production of identity between participating in a tribal ceremony and describing this participation to an agent of the U.S. government. Yet he knows that to present his already actualized, gendered self to whites who do not share this ceremonial context he must go through the discourse of ethnography and the medium of print, so that whites "might know the *causes* that had impelled him to act as he had done, and the *principles* by which he was governed" (*L,* 35). The "causes" of the war were the 1804 treaty of cession and Keokuk's inability or unwillingness to renegotiate; the "principles" were those of the Sauk warrior who, since he did not personally recognize the treaty, felt compelled to prevent the expropriation of the lands of the people for whom he took responsibility. In this narrative he attempts a cross-cultural authorization of his status as warrior, which embroils him in political controversy with Keokuk, whom he knows the whites regard as the "chief" of the Sauks and Foxes.

Black Hawk's descriptions of Keokuk typically mark the latter as a nonwarrior and, more generally, as one who violates Sauk tradition at crucial moments—in contrast to Black Hawk himself, who always demonstrates his centeredness within the traditional tribal worldview. Here, for example, is his assessment of the political situation on the eve of the war:

> We were a divided people, forming two parties. Ke-o-kuck being at the head of one, willing to barter our rights merely for the good opinion of the whites; and cowardly enough to desert our village to them. I was at the head of the other party, and was determined to hold on to my village, although I had been *ordered* to leave it. But, I considered, as myself and band had no agency in selling our country . . . that we could not be *forced* away. I refused, therefore, to quit my village. It was here, that I was born—and here lie the bones of many friends and relations. For this spot I felt a sacred reverence, and never could consent to leave it, without being forced therefrom. (*L,* 107)

Black Hawk argues that "my reason tells me that *land cannot be sold*. . . . Nothing can be sold, but such things as can be carried away" (*L,* 101). Keokuk had, in Black Hawk's view, both affirmed the white idea of land ownership and denigrated the warrior tradition in his negotiations with the whites:

Ke-o-kuck came to the village; but his object was to persuade others to follow him to the Ioway [i.e., to the Iowa River where a new village site had been specified by the U.S. government]. He had accomplished nothing towards making arrangements for us to remain, or to exchange other lands for our village. There was no more friendship existing between us. I looked upon him as a coward, and no brave, to abandon his village to be occupied by strangers. (*L,* 101)

As Black Hawk clarifies the political situation, he impugns Keokuk's masculinity and thus questions his qualifications to assume such a position of leadership.

Keokuk had not always held precisely this view of the treaty, but Black Hawk had long suspected his political qualifications. Black Hawk had returned from the War of 1812 (in which he had fought on the side of the British) to find that Keokuk had been named "war-chief of the braves then in the village" (*L,* 72). Black Hawk's report of how this had happened in his absence is tinged with irony. U.S. soldiers had been spotted in the vicinity and a council had been called, which decided that the people ought to leave the village temporarily: "Ke-o-kuck, during the sitting of the council, had been standing at the door of the lodge, (*not being allowed to enter, having never killed an enemy,*) where he remained until old Wa-co-me came out. He then told him that he had heard what they had decided upon, and was anxious to be permitted to go in and speak, before the council adjourned!" (*L,* 72, emphasis added). Keokuk persuaded the council to appoint him war-chief, possibly (although Black Hawk does not say so) because there were few experienced warriors currently in the village, most having been for some time at the war.[26] Again, inflecting the entire political-historical discourse is the sense of Keokuk's not having achieved a tribally confirmed status as warrior. This war party might provide Keokuk with the opportunity to achieve this status, as Black Hawk had long since done, through ceremonial self-performance. Black Hawk's historical account continues: "He marshalled his braves—sent out spies—and advanced with a party himself. . . . They returned without seeing an enemy. The Americans did not come to our village. All were well satisfied with the appointment of Ke-o-kuck. He used every precaution that our people should not be surprised. This is the manner in which, and the cause of, his receiving the appointment. I was satisfied, and then started to visit my wife and children" (*L,* 73). Although Black Hawk himself professes to be "satisfied," he does not say whether it is with the fact that no enemies attacked the village, with Keokuk's appointment in general, or with the fact that Keokuk got no opportunity to prove himself a warrior (thus confirming Black Hawk's view of him as "no brave"). The reminder that Keokuk was not yet formally recognized as a warrior indicates Black Hawk's suspicion and makes it seem as if Keokuk was merely lucky that no enemies were near. The odd conclusion of the story—the reiteration of the topic—marks it as somehow questionable, as if the insistence that this is the complete explanation covers some incompleteness; perhaps it is meant to cast suspicion on Keokuk's credentials. By the time of the war twenty years later it is still not clear whether Keokuk has ever engaged an enemy in battle. All subsequent mentions of him in the *Life of Black Hawk* characterize him, with historical accuracy, as a protreaty spokesman, while none refer to any exploits in battle.[27]

Keokuk's position gained him favorable portrayal by whites, which contrasts interestingly with Black Hawk's view of him and with the whites' view of Black Hawk. For George Catlin, it is Keokuk, not Black Hawk, who represents the epitome of Sauk manhood at this historical moment—the pacified and potentially civilizable warrior. One of Catlin's portraits, made during a visit to "Kee-o-kuk's village of Sacs and Foxes" on the Des Moines River in 1835, shows Keokuk holding a tomahawk in the right hand and a feathered staff in the left. . . .[28] Catlin insists on the authenticity of this representation. Keokuk, he writes, "is the present chief of the tribe, a dignified and proud man, with a good share of talent, and vanity enough to force into action all the wit and judgement he possesses, in order to command the attention and respect of the world. . . . In this portrait I have represented him in the costume, precisely, in which he was dressed when he stood for it, with his shield on his arm, and his staff (insignia of office) in his left hand."[29] Linked with this portrait is a verbal image of Keokuk as the supposed true defender of the tribe—but one who uses means approved by the whites: "There is no Indian chief on the frontier better known at this time, or more highly appreciated for his eloquence, as a public speaker, than Kee-o-kuk; as he has repeatedly visited Washington and others of our Atlantic towns, and made his speeches before thousands, when he has been contending for his people's rights, in their stipulations with the United States Government, for the sale of their lands."[30] The tomahawk had appeared in the portrait by both Keokuk's own choice and Catlin's approval.[31] Catlin's verbal description omits any mention of this sign of warrior status, implying new limits on Sauk masculinity in the postsubjugation period: only the role of politician, a role easily managed by the U.S. government and military, is relevant. However, the tomahawk is clearly depicted, suggesting the form that Keokuk's masculinity could take under freer circumstances.

In contrast, Catlin emasculates the public image of Black Hawk both verbally and visually. Black Hawk sat for Catlin in late 1832 or early 1833, while he was imprisoned at Jefferson Barracks south of St. Louis.[32] The conventional bust-length portrait made at this time would be unremarkable but for the tail feathers of a black hawk held in the right hand. . . .[33] Where Keokuk's tomahawk could be taken to mark him as a potential warrior, Black Hawk's pose seems feminine, as if he were an elegant lady holding a fan. Thus Catlin takes the man's very name and uses it as a device to re-gender his identity for a white audience. Catlin's verbal description of Black Hawk, included in his account of his visit to "Kee-o-kuk's village" in 1835, does not emphasize the feminine connotations of the 1832-33 portrait. Nevertheless, the description serves to cast doubt on Black Hawk's credentials as a warrior:

> [Black Hawk] was defeated by General Atkinson, and held a prisoner of war, and sent through Washington and other Eastern cities, with a number of others, *to be gazed at.*

> This man, whose name has carried a sort of terror through the country where it has been sounded, has been distinguished as a speaker or counsellor rather than as a warrior; and I believe it has been pretty generally admitted, that "Nah-pope" and the "Prophet" were, in fact, the instigators of the war; and either of them with much higher claims for the name of warrior than Black Hawk ever had.[34]

Catlin's assault on Black Hawk's masculine identity is threefold. If he was a warrior, then he was defeated and exhibited as a prisoner of war. But in fact he was not really a warrior and did not instigate the war. Moreover, as a statesman he was not nearly so impressive, by comparison, as Keokuk. Where Catlin describes Keokuk's presence among the whites in terms of action, speaking for his people's rights, he describes Black Hawk as passive, occupying the conventionally feminine position (in Western tradition) of the object of a "gaze"—a position emphasized by the particular pose of the portrait. However, it is doubtful that Sauks, unfamiliar with the conventions of the nineteenth-century drawing room, would have read the same feminine connotations into Black Hawk's pose, because to them the feathers would signify the man's name and thus connote all the deeds performed under that name. Their reading of the portrait would depend on their opinion of the man, an opinion that would be formed communally, in the contexts of warfare and ceremony.

Catlin's second portrait of Keokuk . . . more strongly represents him as a warrior than does the first, and thus provides an emphatic contrast to Catlin's femi-nized representation of Black Hawk. Although this pose can be said to represent a tribal warrior, Catlin's mod-els are European baroque monuments of military offic-ers reining in powerful, spirited horses, on their way to performing heroic, liberating deeds. It is, perhaps, the archetypal image of the warrior in white Western cul-ture. However, Catlin's verbal description also estab-lishes Keokuk's legitimacy as a warrior in Sauk terms by remarking that "his scalps were attached to the bridle-bits."[35] At the same time, Catlin reminds us that

the status of warrior among the Sauk is now merely ornamental. He says that it is Keokuk's "vanity" in his "fine appearance on horseback" (rather than any fame that Keokuk has gained as a warrior) that convinced him to paint this second portrait. Catlin's remark that "the horse that he rode was the best animal on the frontier; a fine blooded horse, for which he gave the price of 300 dollars, a thing that he was quite able to, who had the distribution of 50,000 dollars annuities, annually, amongst his people" reminds us that the enabling condition of Keokuk's particular pose on this magnificent horse is U.S. government patronage and administrative control.[36]

Black Hawk describes a similar pose, connoting the heroic warrior but without the subtext of white con-trol, at a key moment of the war: "I was mounted on a fine horse, and was pleased to see my warriors so brave. I addressed them in a loud voice, telling them to stand their ground, and never yield it to the enemy" (*L,* 134). But, as always, his band is woefully outnum-bered. Black Hawk admits that he is simply directing a strategic retreat, defending women and children from potential massacre with a loss of six men. As he often does, he here hopes that an understanding of the war-rior code will vindicate his actions: "I would not have fought there, but to gain time for my women and chil-dren to cross to an island. A warrior will duly appre-ciate the embarrassments I labored under—and what-ever may be the sentiments of the *white people,* in relation to this battle, my nation, though fallen, will award to me the reputation of a great brave, in con-ducting it" (*L,* 135). This is one of the clearest in-stances of the "self-vindication" speech genre, encap-sulating what Brumble argues is the intention of the entire narrative. In this passage Black Hawk is more concerned with his status among the Sauks than among the whites, but the reference to a generic "warrior" does not exclude whites—not, at least, the whites who matter to him, the soldiers such as General Atkinson who would be in the best position to understand him.

Applying the warrior code as a single standard that he believes ought to be universal, Black Hawk is highly critical of instances in which Indians or whites do not behave in a manner he considers honorable.[37] Through-out the text we see Black Hawk appealing to the idea that the values of the warrior ought to transcend cul-tural differences. Being told of West Point, "the place where the Americans dance their national dance," Black Hawk infers a commonality with the self-performance of warriors in the Sauk "national dance"; West Point, in his interpretation, is "where the old warriors recount to their young men, what they have done, to stimulate them to go and do likewise. This surprised me, as I did not think the whites understood our way of making braves" (*L,* 92). Black Hawk's conflation of West Point with the "nation" may be every U.S. Army officer's fantasy, but it is a drastic misunderstanding of the narrow way in which a white soldier's identity is established in a "nation" that is basically non-communal. Yet it is in this context that we must interpret Black Hawk's argument that white "war chiefs"—rather than the usual notoriously corrupt and avaricious merchants—ought to serve as Indian agents (*L,* 151). Such an idea may strike us as naive, but it demonstrates a non-Western conception of politics that is at the core of Black Hawk's understanding of himself and his place in Sauk society. The Sauks never waged war with the intention of violently imposing their own social, economic, and political structures on another people—in contrast to the whites, who in the nineteenth century engaged in warfare primarily as a means of imperial conquest (and arguably still do).

Contemporary whites formed a better opinion of Keokuk, the politician who conformed to U.S. policies and avoided war, than of Black Hawk, the warrior who followed the Sauk way and felt honor bound to fight. Catlin also implies that many Sauks thought quite highly of Keokuk in the years following the war. At this time, of course, the ability to collect government money—at which Keokuk excelled—was of paramount importance, while traditional Sauk conceptions of warfare were impossible to implement in any serious way. Catlin describes an incident in the late 1830s that illustrates these issues. He reports that Keokuk and several other Sauk and Fox men had an opportunity to view the portrait of Keokuk on horseback when they attended one of Catlin's lectures on "Customs of the Indians" during a visit to New York City: "During the Lecture, I placed a series of portraits on my easel before the audience . . . and at last I placed this portrait of Kee-o-kuk before them, when they all sprung up and hailed it with a piercing yell. After the noise had subsided, Kee-o-kuk arose, and addressed the audience in these words:—'My friends, I hope you will pardon my men for making so much noise, as they were very much excited by seeing me on my favorite war-horse, which they all recognized in a moment.'"[38] Here we see a staging of communal validation apparently similar to that reported by Black Hawk, in which members of the tribe formally acknowledge the status of a warrior. The situation differs, however: the event to which the men respond is not a living ceremony, but a static image. The effect may be similar, but it is Catlin's performance, rather than Keokuk's, to which the men respond: they see in the image of the mounted warrior a potential for the defense of the tribe that, in not having been tested as Black Hawk's had been, retains its ideological power.

This episode confirms the white intervention into the gendering of the Sauk male enacted by the war. Black Hawk, potentially emasculated by his defeat, must employ traditional speech genres—now necessarily mediated by nontraditional ones—in order to reaffirm his identity. Keokuk, in contrast, has gained his el-

evated position by virtue of his role as subaltern for the U.S. government. The Sauk men who saw Catlin's painting in New York were not Black Hawk's partisans, of course, but followers of Keokuk. Even so, it is not clear that they cheered for the specific image of Keokuk as warrior; as Keokuk himself reports it, they cheered not simply for him but for his horse (which was, ironically, paid for by the government that oppressed them). They may, more generally, have been cheering for any white acknowledgment of the Sauk warrior tradition which could no longer occupy an integral place in their society.

Arnold Krupat points out that Black Hawk's defeat (and the Jacksonian master narrative of Native American defeat more generally) was the "enabling condition" of the production of the *Life of Black Hawk.*[39] But it is highly unlikely that Black Hawk himself came to think in Jacksonian-progressivist terms. There is nothing in Black Hawk's opening address to General Atkinson that can be interpreted as an admission of the justness of Indian Removal, while there is a great deal in the narrative, such as Black Hawk's views on land tenancy and treaties, which is openly critical of U.S. policies (and we will never know if he said more). The narrative does end with Black Hawk's proclamation of friendship for his former enemies: "from my heart I assure them, that the white man will always be welcome in our village or camps, as a brother. The tomahawk is buried forever! We will forget what has past—and may the watchword between the Americans and Sacs and Foxes, ever be—'*Friendship!*'" (*L,* 153-54). We must recall that it is the editor Patterson, and not Black Hawk, who places these words at the end of the narrative, thus implying that they bear a teleological significance. Having been defeated in war with no practical hope of revenge, having spent some time in an Army prison camp, and now like the rest of his tribe dependent on government annuities for his livelihood, Black Hawk has something to gain—or at least nothing to lose—by professing "friendship" somewhere in the course of his narrative. In any case, Black Hawk hopes that the "friendship" will be structured in terms of the mutual respect of one warrior for another. That is, even in his overt concession of defeat (burying the tomahawk—which leaves open the possibility that it can be dug up again) he never fully surrenders his warrior identity. While a prisoner in the East after his defeat, he witnesses a militia exercise in Baltimore, his account of which is placed near the conclusion of the text: "The chiefs and men were well dressed, and exhibited quite a warlike appearance. I think our system of military parade far better than that of the whites—but, as I am now done going to war, I will not describe it, or say any thing more about war, or the preparations necessary for it'" (*L,* 147). The *occupatio* here reiterates the warrior theme of the entire text and reminds us that the terms of the "friendship" as Black Hawk conceives it depend on the mutual respect of warriors.

Ironically, Black Hawk's identity is preserved not despite but because of textual mediation. Traditional conditions for the preservation of that identity no longer exist in Sauk culture, having been vitiated by the defeat and containment of the tribe, which eliminated the warrior's cultural position. In response to this drastic re-ordering of Sauk society, Black Hawk enjoins his white readers to validate his identity. The methods of cross-cultural textual production—the transcription, translation, and editing of Black Hawk's narrating voice—embroil us in questions about the text's "authenticity"; yet a preoccupation with "authenticity" may mislead us. The necessary interventions between voice and text, explicitly indicated for us by the phonetic transcription and accompanying English translation of the opening address to General Atkinson, identify Black Hawk as a tribal warrior who is not assimilated to the Jacksonian master narrative but who nevertheless hopes for some translatability of the warrior code in order to promote an understanding and dissemination of the terms of his identity.

Notes

1 Paula Gunn Allen, *The Sacred Hoop: Recovering the Feminine in American Indian Traditions* (Boston: Beacon, 1986), 3.

2 This is not to say that there was an absolute binary division between "masculine" and "feminine" as single paradigms for identity; not every man or woman played every culturally available role. For example, among the Ojibwa, warriors were usually not simultaneously civil leaders; see Basil Johnston, *Ojibway Heritage* (New York: Columbia Univ. Press, 1976), 67-69. The role of the *berdache,* still evidently an integral part of Sauk and Fox culture when George Catlin visited them in 1835, indicates some fluidity in the relation of sex to gender. Catlin's account reveals the whites' desire to eliminate an indeterminacy that they found unsettling: the *berdache* is "a man dressed in woman's clothes, as he is known to be all his life, and for extraordinary privileges which he is known to possess, he is driven to the most servile and degrading duties. . . . [He] is looked upon as *medicine* and sacred, and a feast is given to him annually. . . . This is one of the most unaccountable and disgusting customs that I have ever met with in the Indian country . . . and for further account of it I am constrained to refer the reader to the country where it is practised, and where I should wish that it might be extinguished before it be more fully recorded" (George Catlin, *North American Indians,* 2 vols. [1841; rpt., Edinburgh: John Grant, 1926], 2:243-44). Allen argues that homosexual practices and identities generally were socially valorized in a great number of tribes prior to white contact but later became increasingly subject to white repression, which tribal peoples themselves internalized (197-200).

3 *Life of Ma-ka-tai-me-she-kia-kiak, or Black Hawk . . . Dictated by Himself* (Cincinnati, 1833), in *Black Hawk: An Autobiography,* ed. Donald Jackson (Urbana: Univ. of Illinois Press, 1964), 33-154. All quotations from this work will be documented parenthetically in the text using the abbreviation *L.*

4 A remark on names is in order here. It seems to be conventional to use the English translation "Black Hawk," but to use phonetic spellings of other Sauk names rather than translations, especially in the case of Keokuk ("Watchful Fox"). I continue this practice to avoid confusion. As will become apparent, there are variant spellings of "Keokuk"; I have chosen the simplest.

5 For a more detailed history, see William T. Hagan, *The Sac and Fox Indians* (Norman: Univ. of Oklahoma Press, 1958).

6 Jackson, 157, 158, 159-60. Jackson provides the entire text of the treaty.

7 Jackson, 26.

8 Herman J. Viola, *The Indian Legacy of Charles Bird King* (Washington: Smithsonian Institution, 1976), 65.

9 Arnold Krupat, *For Those Who Come After: A Study of Native American Autobiography* (Berkeley: Univ. of California Press, 1985), 31. This idea is central to all treatments of the genre. See H. David Brumble III, *American Indian Autobiography* (Berkeley: Univ. of California Press, 1988); Hertha D. Wong, "Pre-literate Native American Autobiography: Forms of Personal Narrative," *MELUS* 14 (1987): 17-32.

10 Arnold Krupat, *The Voice in the Margin: Native American Literature and the Canon* (Berkeley: Univ. of California Press, 1989), 135-43. See also Hertha D. Wong, "Pictographs as Autobiography: Plains Indian Sketchbooks of the Late Nineteenth and Early Twentieth Centuries," *American Literary History* 1 (1987): 296.

11 Krupat, *Voice,* 149, 150.

12 Krupat, *For Those,* 116.

13 Krupat, *For Those,* 48.

14 An elegiac mode—evident, for example, in *The Last of the Mohicans*—also seems prevalent. Since the inevitability of death is an important elegiac topos, the application of this topos to the supposed death of an entire culture, allegorized in a single Indian character, would also be consistent with the Jacksonian master narrative.

[15] M. M. Bakhtin, "The Problem of Speech Genres," in *Speech Genres and Other Late Essays,* ed. Caryl Emerson and Michael Holquist (Austin: Univ. of Texas Press, 1986), 60-61.

[16] Bakhtin, 62. Although Bakhtin (who was surprisingly uninterested in traditional oral cultures) discusses only written complex or secondary speech genres, it is clear that oral genres such as oratory, legend, historical narrative, and the like are built of combinations of primary genres in much the same way as their written counterparts. The concept of "*speech* genre" need not be taken to imply the logocentric privileging of speech as somehow prior to writing, given Derrida's argument that oral speech acts are already culturally encoded—already "written"—and thus their position with respect to the individual subject is as mediated as acts of writing are; see Jacques Derrida, "Signature Event Context," in *Margins of Philosophy* (Chicago: Univ. of Chicago Press, 1982), 307-30. Bakhtin's and Derrida's positions are similar in this respect, since Bakhtin stresses the conventional nature of speech genres. However, since I am not performing a merely linguistic analysis, it is finally only complex speech genres, especially various forms of narrative, that will interest me here.

[17] See Brumble, 21-47.

[18] I am using the term "ethnography" loosely here to refer to material that we would now recognize as bearing ethnographic significance, regardless of the original process of collecting and presenting the information. Krupat points out that Patterson would have considered himself a historian rather than an ethnographer and speculates that "the cultural material . . . probably was Black Hawk's voluntary contribution" (*Voice,* 153).

[19] Black Hawk was never a civil chief, as distinct from a war chief, nor was Keokuk a civil chief until the U.S. government made him one. Keokuk had been a client of Indian Agent William Clark since 1820. Clark's generous patronage contributed to the growth of Keokuk's influence (and the consequent waning of Black Hawk's) among many of the Sauk, whose traditional economic base was by this time seriously eroded; see Hagan, 89.

[20] On the question of authenticity, see Jackson, 24-30. Some contemporaries thought it a hoax; others believed it was genuine. Hagan, Jackson, Brumble, and Krupat do not doubt that the story originated with Black Hawk, although only Krupat ponders the theoretical implications of terms such as "authenticity" and "origin."

[21] See Thomas Couser, "Black Elk Speaks with Forked Tongue," in *Studies in Autobiography,* ed. James Olney (New York: Oxford Univ. Press, 1982), 73-88. Couser argues that in editing out evidence of Black Elk's assimilation—e.g., his conversion to Catholicism and role

on the reservation as catechist—Neihardt was "trying to make [the story] more Indian" but as a consequence "made it less autobiographical" (88).

[22] Brumble, 39.

[23] While the specification of what is "permitted" would go without saying among the adults of the Sauk community who witnessed Black Hawk's first participation in the scalp dance, it is possible that this apparently ethnographic sentence has its origin in precontact tribal speech genres as well. Such an explanation might be offered to a member of another tribe who was unfamiliar with Sauk ways (another sort of ethnographic function) or to young members of the tribe who were being formally or informally instructed about appropriate behavior.

[24] Wong points out the importance of communally oriented "dramatic" forms of "self-expression" among plains tribes as well (29).

[25] Johnston describes the first hunt ceremony among the Ojibwa, a neighboring people of the same Algonquin language and culture group as the Sauk, although he does not specify a self-presentational aspect of the ceremony that would parallel the Sauk national dance (142). Unlike the first hunt ceremony, which is enacted only once, the Sauk scalp dance and national dance offer the opportunity to renew and reaffirm identity.

[26] There is no way to confirm this story. Hagan's only source for his account (57) appears to be Black Hawk's narrative.

[27] Hagan, whose only source for tribal origin is the *Life of Black Hawk,* does not record any instance of Keokuk's fighting against the whites. It seems likely that he fought against other tribes—an important issue in view of his position in Sauk politics.

[28] Catlin, 169.

[29] Catlin, 238.

[30] Ibid.

[31] According to Catlin, Keokuk "brought in all his costly wardrobe, that I might select for his portrait such as suited me best; but at once named (of his own accord) the one that was purely Indian. . . . In it I painted him at full length" (170). It is likely that Keokuk frequently presented this self-image to white painters. A portrait by Charles Bird King painted in Washington in 1829 shows a similar pose and props, except that the shield is missing and Keokuk wears only a loincloth; this painting is reproduced in Andrew J. Cosentino, *The Paintings of Charles Bird King* (Washington: Smithsonian Institution, 1977), 171. A portrait by J. O. Lewis painted at the Prairie du Chien Indian Agency in 1825 shows

at the Prairie du Chien Indian Agency in 1825 shows Keokuk holding a similar feathered staff in his right hand (in this case the staff is tipped with a spear point) but no tomahawk (reproduced in Hagan, 50).

[32] Jackson, 8.

[33] Jackson identifies Black Hawk's namesake as a "sparrow hawk" (2).

[34] Catlin, 239, emphasis added.

[35] Catlin, 240.

[36] Catlin, 240-41.

[37] For example, both the whites and the Sioux come in for criticism by this standard when Black Hawk reports surrendering only to find that "a large body of Sioux had pursued, and killed, a number of our women and children who had got safely across the Mississippi. The whites ought not to have permitted such conduct—none but *cowards* would ever have been guilty of such cruelty—which has always been practiced on our nation by the Sioux" (*L*, 140).

[38] Catlin, 241.

[39] Krupat, *For Those*, 48.

An excerpt from Black Hawk's *Life of Ma-ka-tai-me-she-kia-kiak, or Black Hawk* (1833):

I will here relate the manner in which corn first came. According to tradition, handed down to our people, a beautiful woman was seen to descend from the clouds, and alight upon the earth, by two of our ancestors, who had killed a deer, and were sitting by a fire, roasting a part of it to eat. They were astonished at seeing her, and concluded that she must be hungry, and had smelt the meat—and immediately went to her, taking with them a piece of the roasted venison. They presented it to her, and she eat—and told them to return to the spot where she was sitting, at the end of one year, and they would find a reward for their kindness and generosity. She then ascended to the clouds, and disappeared. The two men returned to their village, and explained to the nation what they had seen, done, and heard—but were laughed at by their people. When the period arrived, for them to visit this consecrated ground, where they were to find a reward for their attention to the beautiful woman of the clouds, they went with a large party, and found, where her right hand had rested on the ground, *corn* growing—and where the left hand had rested, *beans*—and immediately where she had been seated, *tobacco.*

Black Hawk, in Life of Ma-ka-tai-me-she-kia-kiak, or Black Hawk, *1833, reprinted in* Native American Autobiography, *edited by Arnold Krupat, University of Wisconsin Press, 1994.*

Brigitte Georgi-Findlay (essay date 1993)

SOURCE: "The Frontiers of Native American Women's Writing: Sarah Winnemucca's Life among the Piutes," in *New Voices in Native American Literary Criticism*, edited by Arnold Krupat, Smithsonian Institution Press, 1993, pp. 222-52.

[*In the essay that follows, Georgi-Findlay examines the American frontier experience from the perspective of a Native American woman—Sarah Winnemucca Hopkins—using her* Life among the Piutes *to discuss the role of gender in such areas as assimilation, Native American/white relations, literary style, and sexual and political power.*]

The study of the history, literature, and popular mythology of American westward expansion and the frontier West has, during the past decades, undergone some crucial reconsideration, if not revision, through the inclusion of two new angles of vision: the focus on the tribal people dispossessed by the westward movement and, more recently, on the largely ignored and for a long time invisible participation of women in this move west. These two relatively new fields of study, it would appear, do not have much in common with each other—except, of course, for their combined efforts to rewrite previously excluded groups of people as presences and agents into American history and literature. Thus it should not come as a surprise that both areas have kept rather aloof from each other and have only recently approached each other in studies focusing on Native American women. Both areas of study, however, may be made profitable for each other also in the reconsideration of the frontier experience in American literature and culture, from which both Native American and female voices have long been absent. Focusing on one of the first autobiographical narratives written by a Native American woman, Sarah Winnemucca Hopkins's *Life among the Piutes: Their wrongs and claims* (1883),[1] I aim at such a reconsideration of the frontier experience from the female and the Native American point of view, by drawing on some of the critical questions raised by both fields of study.

Historical research on the American frontier has tended to view westward expansion as a predominantly male activity, and studies dealing with the "popular mythology of the frontier"[2] have defined it as a cultural idea almost exclusively linked to and shaped by male concerns, although admittedly assigning women an important symbolic presence.[3] Both have for a long time based their evidence on texts written by white men. However, recent historical research, mostly undertaken by women, has established women's presence on the various western frontiers on the basis of their published and private writings in the form of travel narratives, memoirs, diaries, and letters.[4] In their writings, these westering women have recorded their encounters with native women—sometimes expressing unconcealed racism and ethnocentrism, sometimes full of fear and distrust, and sometimes with a refreshing openness and willingness to understand the "other," as represented by tribal cultures and people, in a way that leaves us wondering about the impact of these encounters on tribal women, both on a cultural as well as an interpersonal level. One of the main problems in the study of the female experience of the frontier is, of course, the problem of written evidence. Researchers have so far mostly focused on the experience of Euroamerican middle-class women for the obvious reason that these more or less educated women furnished the largest part of the written material on the female frontier. During the 1980s, however, large retrieval efforts have resulted in the recovery and establishment of an ever increasing store of women's texts on the frontiers, which has also multiplied the complexity of perspectives.[5] Aware of the immense variety of women's experience, researchers increasingly emphasize the need to consider the impact of many cultures when studying women and call for a "new multicultural framework."[6] Of course, the admittedly problematic text status and limited amount of the material which is available to study the experiences especially of Native American women, consisting to a large degree of originally oral narratives and raising serious questions of authorship, have prevented researchers so far from taking a closer look at native women's texts. However, studies on Native American autobiographies on the one hand, and of women's autobiographies on the other hand, have already developed methodological approaches to the interpretation of these difficult texts.[7] As a matter of fact, it is remarkable that the studies of both Native American and women's autobiographies deal with similar difficulties and often come up with similar conclusions. Here I only want to point to the questions of authorship and voice, the role of the "framing" of texts through prefaces, appendixes, and generic conventions, to the special circumstances of text production, distribution, and reception, as well as to the issues of power and authority surrounding editor-narrator relations. Both areas of study often come to the conclusion that the characteristics identified as generic to the American autobiography are largely based on the study of texts by male white Americans; both often contend that the concept of self-projected in the "master texts" of the American autobiography informs neither—or only marginally—the autobiographical narratives of tribal people nor those of women.[8]

While researchers on the female frontier have recently called for a multicultural framework in the study of women's experiences of the western frontiers, Native American studies, both anthropological and literary, have begun to focus on Native American women and to put emphasis on the construction and role of gender in North American tribal cultures.[9] Although the studies of Native American literature have come to acknowledge the prominence of contemporary native women writers and the important thematic and formal role of gender in contemporary Native American literary works,[10] they have not considered well enough the role of gender in earlier Native American literature. These literary expressions of Native Americans in the eighteenth and nineteenth centuries have been interpreted mainly in the context of political Indian-white relations, of acculturation and assimilation, an approach which is of course fully legitimized by the circumstances surrounding and motivating the production of these early texts.[11] I would argue, however, that we have not considered well enough the role of gender in the history of Indian-white relations, of cultural contact, colonization, and assimilation—especially in the interpretation of the texts written, authored or coauthored, or narrated by Native American women. Shouldn't we wonder whether the experience and process of assimilation is different for native women than for native men?[12] How did cultural contact, colonization, and change affect tribal women? How did it affect their views of themselves as tribal persons and as women, and how did they express these views in their autobiographical narratives?[13] And how did these women place themselves within the changing world of the western frontiers? These, I would suggest, are the questions that may add new angles of vision to the study of early native women's texts.

One of the first autobiographical texts written by a Native American woman, Sarah Winnemucca Hopkins's *Life among the Piutes,* seems to me to be a case in point, since it demonstrates the need for an interpretation that is sensitive to the complex role of gender and gender relations in the narrator's appeal for the vindication of her people's rights. In the following I want to suggest that this text may be read in more than one context. It may be read, of course, as a Native American autobiographical narrative that incorporates a political message. Yet, I would argue, it is not only a political statement on Indian-white power relations toward the end of the nineteenth century, but is itself shaped by the realities of sexual politics in Indian-white relations. At the same time, it may be read as an example of women's writing on the western frontier, a reading which is suggested by the fact that the text is anthologized in collections of western women's writing.[14] Sarah Winnemucca was born, as she states in her autobiographical narrative, "somewhere near 1844" near the sink of the Humboldt River in what is now western Nevada. She came from a Northern Paiute[15] family that from the time of first contact with whites had advocated peaceful coexistence. Her maternal grandfather Truckee, who she claimed was the chief of all the Paiutes, welcomed early explorers and settlers and served as a guide to various emigrant parties traveling to California. He had fought in California with John C. Frémont in his Mexican campaigns and befriended white families and individuals throughout northern

"Ma-Ka-Tai-Me-She-Kia-Kiah. Black Hawk, A Saukie Brave."

egon, after they had been crowded onto the Yakima Reservation in Washington. The government, however, provided neither supplies nor transportation for the tribe's return. Disillusioned with federal Indian policy and its agents, Sarah started taking the Paiute cause to the public. Encouraged by the success of her first lecture in San Francisco in 1879, she went east on a lecture tour. Giving nearly three hundred talks between April 1883 and August 1884, from Boston and New York to Baltimore and Washington, she exposed inequities in federal Indian policy and the corruption of federal Indian agents and called for the restoration of lands in severalty to the Paiutes. In Boston she met Elizabeth Palmer Peabody, the promoter of kindergarten education and publisher of the works of the transcendentalists, and her sister Mary Mann, who took up the Paiutes' cause.[18] Under their direction, she also spoke in the homes of Ralph Waldo Emerson, John Greenleaf Whittier, and those of congressmen, among them Senator Henry Dawes.[19] Evidently encouraged by the two women, Sarah Winnemucca, now Mrs. Hopkins, wrote her autobiographical book *Life among the Piutes,* which was edited by Mary Mann and published in 1883 by Elizabeth Palmer Peabody. This book, which contains the text of a petition requesting the grant of lands in severalty to the Paiutes at Malheur Reservation, is together with her lectures generally claimed to have lent support to the passage of the General Allotment Act, also known as the Dawes Act, in 1887.[20]

Nevada and California. Sarah's father, Old Winnemucca, succeeded Truckee as chief.[16]

By the time she reached adulthood, Sarah Winnemucca was in the public eye as an "Indian Princess"[17] and a spokeswoman of the Paiute tribe. At the age of twenty, she appeared on stage with her family, acting in Indian *tableaux vivants* and interpreting for her father in his attempts to mediate between the Paiutes and the citizens of Virginia City. At twenty-four she was a figure of some prominence and influence, serving as a liaison between the Paiutes and the whites in her people's native Nevada and in Oregon, where they were assigned to the Malheur Reservation, soon living lives of poverty dependent on the whims of an Indian agent. During the Bannock War of 1878 she acted in the controversial role of the army's emissary to recalcitrant bands of Paiutes and Bannocks, bringing them onto the reservations. Already in 1870, a letter she had written on the plight of the Paiutes was published by *Harper's Weekly,* attracting the attention of eastern Indian reformers particularly after its republication in the appendix of Helen Hunt Jackson's *A Century of Dishonor* (1881). After the Bannock War, Sarah accompanied her father and her brother Natchez to Washington to talk to President Hayes and to obtain from secretary of the interior Carl Schurz permission for the Paiutes to return to the Malheur Reservation in Or-

Consequently, Bernd C. Peyer has read Sarah Winnemucca's autobiography, together with other autobiographical texts of the period, as a political text in the context of Indian-white political relations in the last quarter of the nineteenth century. In his reading, these texts reflect changes of the time both in federal Indian policy and in the public interest in Indian affairs. Thus the lessened focus on the religious conversion experience, which had been so prominent in earlier autobiographical works, is explained by the secularization of Indian education, which no longer aims predominantly at the education and training of preachers. At the same time, the end of any major Native American military resistance by 1890 at the latest and the confinement of tribes on reservations gave rise to a scholarly and humanist interest in the history and fate of Native Americans, which, together with the founding of numerous organizations of "friends," created a greater market for Native American literature with an emphasis on traditional life. Thus, Peyer argues, the works written by Native Americans during this period, among them that of Sarah Winnemucca, include much more ethnohistorical detail and, as the situation on the reservations quickly became unbearable, turn more and more critical of the conquering society.[21]

In a similar fashion, A. LaVonne Brown Ruoff notes that Winnemucca's text, unlike the earlier autobiographies of William Apes and George Copway, is not influenced by religious autobiographies, and that its central theme is not the conversion experience, but Indian-white relations.[22] Contradicting Bernd Peyer, however, she contends that hostile government policies and public attitudes created a climate generally unfavorable to the development of Native American literature during this period. White audiences, she argues, were far more interested in reading the accounts of the explorers, settlers, and gold miners who conquered the West than they were in reading of Native American suffering brought about by this conquest.[23] This would suggest that Native American literature of the time had, so to speak, to compete with western literature. Yet, although Ruoff discovers allusions to dime-novel westerns in Winnemucca's text, she does not elaborate further on this interesting intertextual aspect and on the whole seems to privilege a reading of the autobiography as a political statement supporting the General Allotment Act. In another publication Ruoff argues that *Life among the Piutes* should be understood in the light of contemporary literary trends and types, such as the captivity narratives and the slave narratives. She points to a number of features that the text has in common with such narratives, such as some sexual violence and lots of daring adventures.[24] In reaction to this argument, H. David Brumble regards it as unlikely that Winnemucca herself was familiar with such literature. He asks that we "not simply *assume* the degree of literacy and the breadth of reading which Ruoff's argument would require of Winnemucca"[25] and argues that Winnemucca's autobiography was not influenced by written captivity or slave narratives, but seems instead to owe a good deal to preliterate autobiographical traditions. He proposes to look at Winnemucca instead as a well-experienced *speaker* who adapted Paiute oral conventions to the uses of the pen and to the entertainment and persuasion of white audiences. By the time she came to write her narrative down, he argues, Winnemucca would have delivered it, in parts, on many occasions, and she would have had a lively sense of how white audiences had responded to the various versions of particular episodes. Thus we need not assume that Winnemucca was at all aware of literary models, but we have to take into account that she had learned a great deal about her white audience.[26]

My reading of *Life among the Piutes* sustains Peyer's and Ruoff's interpretations of the autobiography as a text of some political impact in the area of Indian policy, although I cannot fully follow the connections Peyer draws between changes in federal Indian policy and the impact of these changes on the content and style of Native American literature in the last quarter of the nineteenth century. As the title suggests, the work may be identified as both autobiographical and ethnographic. In it Winnemucca tells the story of Indian dispossession and legal incapacitation, exemplified in the case of her tribe, the Northern Paiutes. Its publication may

be seen as a sign of increasing humanitarian concern among eastern reformers for the plight of Native Americans, and also of changes in the federal Indian policy leading to the Dawes Act of 1887. Moreover, H. David Brumble's reading of the text as following a preliterate autobiographical tradition seems to be a convincing explanation for the striking differences distinguishing it from both the earlier and later Native American autobiographies of William Apes (1829), George Copway (1847), Charles Eastman (1902, 1916), and Joseph Griffis (1915). These differences consist, for instance, in the absence of turning points or conversion experiences as well as in Winnemucca's reference to her actions as solely motivated by the service to her people. As Brumble suggests, she seems mainly concerned with setting down her deeds, assuming, with other male Native autobiographers, that she may rise in the regard of her tribe by the telling of these deeds, thus implicitly assuming an audience with Paiute habits of mind, not Christian.[27] From this vantage point, he comes to the conclusion that "for all her acquaintance with the Transcendentalists, for all her Indian activism, Winnemucca retained an essentially tribal sense of self,"[28] an interpretation that justly contradicts Bataille's and Sands's claim that Winnemucca's autobiography is "heavily biased by her acculturated and Christianized point of view."[29] Although it supports his interpretation in many of its main arguments, my reading of the text will try to expand its focus by pointing to another one of its dimensions which has so far not been considered. Concurring with Brumble's thesis that Winnemucca was less aware of literary models than of the potential response of her white— and potentially tribal—audience to her speeches, I want to suggest that Winnemucca's identity as a woman and the way her womanhood is, so to speak, "incorporated" into her text, form an important part of Winnemucca's dialogue with her public that should not be underestimated. I would even go so far as to suggest that the very fact that Winnemucca was a woman was crucial in the public reception of her person, her lectures, and her book by a contemporary audience.[30] A reading of the text from this perspective, however, will necessarily lead to a modification of Brumble's suggestion that Sarah Winnemucca retained an essentially tribal self throughout her autobiographical narrative.

When I reread Winnemucca's *Life among the Piutes* in terms of what it might reveal about being a Native American woman in the transitional culture of the frontier West, I was appalled at the sense of personal pain, yet also of personal pride, pervading the text; but I was also surprised at the way this woman had written herself, or possibly, had been written into the text. What difference did it make, I wondered, that the author of this bitter attack on the reservation system was a woman, and a Native American woman at that? Hers is a distressing story that aims at her audience's emotional commitment and concern. That the author is a woman seems to be part of this effect; that the editor is a woman is evidence of the fact, of which a contemporary public doubtless had been aware, that toward the end of the nineteenth century women played an important part in the reform movements of the time, and particularly in the Indian reform movement, where women's organizations in fact had initially formulated policies that were later endorsed by other groups and adopted by the government.[31]

Although most critics note Sarah Winnemucca's exceptional position as the female public voice of her tribe, none of them has considered the implications of this exceptionalism in the text itself. In his preface to the 1969 reprint of the text, M. R. Harrington remarks that "not often has an Indian woman been allowed to become so vocal and to bring the history of her people before the public." Ruoff as well notes this exceptionalism and points to Winnemucca's emphasis on the roles played by women in achieving peace for her people, yet does not go beyond relating the narrative of Winnemucca's daring exploits to the western dime novels featuring adventurous heroines.[32] Peyer points to Winnemucca's position as the first major female Native American writer, and Fowler argues that the events of Winnemucca's life suggest clearly some of the motives that led her to speak for Indian rights at a time when a Native American *woman* would hardly be respected for doing so.[33] Only Brumble registers Winnemucca's own explanation of the position of women in the tribe and draws the conclusion that "Winnemucca wants to be remembered in this way, as a woman who was brave as any man, as a woman who did great things."[34] I would go even farther and argue that the female presence of Sarah Winnemucca in her text extends this traditional tribal role by incorporating references to concepts of Victorian womanhood, and is thus in fact much more ambiguous than Brumble suggests.[35]

The reports on Sarah Winnemucca's public appearances support the idea that she was aware of the effect she had on her public in the romantic role of the "Indian Princess," a role certainly not entirely of her own making.[36] In a similar fashion, she seems to capitalize on this romantic public image in her lectures and her autobiographical narrative for the purpose of winning her audience's sympathy for her tribe. However, in *Life among the Piutes* this self-stylization as an Indian princess takes on exactly the paradoxical quality of the image of the Indian woman in American culture, which Rayna Green had stressed: Sarah faces what Green describes as the basic crux of the Native American woman, the impossibility "to be seen as real . . . As some abstract, noble Princess tied to 'America' and to sacrificial zeal, she has power as a symbol. As the Squaw, a depersonalized object of scornful convenience, she is powerless."[37] Linked to the main narrative dealing with the story of her tribe, we discover a

subtext of personal defense, which has led Brumble to read the text as "an extended self-vindication, as an attempt to defend her own reputation and that of her family and her tribe," relating it to a preliterate, tribal conception of autobiography "as a way to answer slander," and arguing that "Indians of many tribes were answering their accusers with autobiographical narratives long before the Paiutes came into contact with the white man."[38] As a matter of fact, Winnemucca's own person is at times so overwhelmingly present in the narrative of her tribe's plight that we might be tempted to read the text as an enterprise of self-aggrandizement in the tradition of the male American autobiography—an enterprise that, to my knowledge, no American woman had undertaken so far. It also seems to be no coincidence that, as Catherine S. Fowler has pointed out, Winnemucca emerges in the works of cultural anthropologists as a controversial figure, a woman with two faces.[39] Considering the fact that she is writing against the silencing of Native American tribal voices in the context of a paternalistic federal Indian policy, her focus on her own person may of course be seen as a strategy of authentication, of claiming authority and representativity as a spokeswoman of her tribe. And yet what distinguishes Sarah's strategy of claiming authority from other native authors' strategies, say, for instance, from that of Charles Eastman, is not only the absence of the discourse of conversion, but also the awareness, ever present in her text, that this claim of authority is in a problematic way tied to issues of gender. I would argue therefore that the subtext of personal defense implies that Winnemucca had to defend herself against attacks particularly aimed at her as a woman. This becomes especially clear when we consider the framework of the book, which is provided not only by a foreword of the editor, but also by an appendix—a well-known and important textual device in the publication of Native American autobiographies as well as of slave narratives—that includes affidavits testifying to the respectable and reliable character of Sarah Winnemucca Hopkins, and thus implying, although rather subtly and unobtrusively, that her respectability must somehow have been questioned. Read against this framework, the issues of sexuality and morality written into the text take on a new meaning: what is negotiated in her presentation of Indian-white relations is not only the issue of the dispossession of tribal land, an issue a white audience dedicated to the rhetoric of national westward expansion would not have espoused without restrictions, but also the outrageous issues of sexual violence and miscegenation revealed in the violation of native women's bodies by white men.

The personal attacks against Sarah Winnemucca, as they are indirectly referred to in the affidavits in the book's appendix, seem even tame compared to the press reports and letters written about Sarah and sent to officials in Washington: Sarah is described as nothing less than a prostitute, an easy woman, a common camp follower.[40] Now we begin to identify the voices Sarah must implicitly have been writing against: those who disclaim her authority as a political spokeswoman by disclaiming her respectability as a woman, by exposing the woman who speaks and acts in public as a "public woman,"[41] by putting the Native American "princess" in her negative stereotypical place as savage woman, as "squaw," a promiscuous consort lacking "civilized" womanly virtue and restraint. As a matter of fact, even today's critics feel compelled to apologize for Sarah Winnemucca's supposedly unwomanly habits.[42] If we take further into consideration that Sarah reportedly had to defend herself against other Native women's insults as well as that her book was written during a lecture tour in the East, encouraged by, edited, and promoted by women active in or affiliated with various reform movements known for their concern for morality, domesticity, and the integrity of the family, we may assume the high importance this issue of respectability—and, implicitly, of sexuality, seduction, and slandered virtue—must have had in the production, promotion, and reception of the text.[43]

Life among the Piutes is apparently the result of a collaboration, or rather, of a dialogue of voices, female and male, eastern and western, Indian and white. Yet it is not the collaboration of a tribal person with one of the increasing numbers of anthropologists, as will be the case with many of the Native American autobiographies produced in the first decades of the twentieth century, which were informed by the scientific concerns of the young discipline of cultural anthropology.[44] It is a collaboration between women of two cultures. Arnold Krupat has suggested that "to see the Indian autobiography as a ground on which two cultures meet is to see it as the textual equivalent of the frontier."[45] In this sense, Winnemucca's *Life* could be read as a textual equivalent of a woman's frontier which is defined by the boundaries and reciprocal relationships between her native culture on the one hand and both eastern and western cultures on the other hand.

In her preface, Mary Mann describes the book as "an heroic act on the part of the writer," and as "the first outbreak of the American Indian in human literature, [which] has a single aim—to *tell the truth* as it lies in the heart and mind of a true patriot, and one whose knowledge of the two races gives her an opportunity of comparing them justly." She describes the motivation of Sarah Winnemucca, who is, in view of the attacks upon her respectability, significantly referred to as Mrs. Hopkins, to write the book: "Finding that in extemporaneous speech she could only speak at one time of a few points, she determined to write out the most important part of what she wished to say." She draws attention to the importance of the book at a particular historical instance: "At this moment, when the United States seems waking up to their duty to the original possessors of our immense territory, it is of the first importance to hear what only an Indian *and an Indian woman* [my emphasis] can tell." Why should it be of the first importance, at that particular historical moment, to hear what only an Indian woman can tell? Because, I would suggest, Indian reform is regarded, at this historical moment, as a domain which is of particular concern to women. The book is thus placed in a feminine discourse which assumes moral responsibility in the realm of political reform.

Mary Mann further informs her readers that the writing of the book was Sarah's "own deep impulse, and the dying charge given her by her father, the truly parental chief of his beloved tribe." Sarah Winnemucca herself will, in her narrative, legitimize her own role as spokeswoman with her family position as granddaughter of Truckee, whom she introduces as chief of the entire Paiute nation[46] and as daughter of Winnemucca, whom she describes as the legitimate successor of Truckee. Thus she suggests that her authority is based on kinship and relation: she is spokeswoman first by way of relation, and only secondarily by way of education. The idea is also underlined by her devaluation of her educational training. In this she distinguishes herself from other authors of Native American autobiographies who present themselves as educated Christians.

Mary Mann describes her own editing as "copying the original manuscript in correct orthography and punctuation, with occasional emendation by the author." The final version of the text is credited as Sarah's own: "In fighting with her literary deficiencies she loses some of the fervid eloquence which her extraordinary command of the English language enables her to utter, but I am confident that no one would desire that her own original words should be altered." To a friend, however, Mary Mann had confided that she had found the work of editing the manuscript rather difficult, which suggests not only that she may have interfered in the original text more than she cared to admit in her preface, but also that she may have realized the oral dimension of Sarah's written text:

> I wish you could see her manuscript as a matter of curiosity. I don't think the English language ever got such a treatment before. I have to recur to her sometimes to know what a word is, as spelling is an unknown quantity to her, as you mathematicians would express it. She often takes syllables off of words & adds them or rather prefixes them to other words, but the story is heart-breaking, and told with a simplicity & eloquence that cannot be described, for it is not high-faluting eloquence, tho' sometimes it lapses into verse (and quite poetical verse too). I was always considered fanatical about Indians, but I have a wholly new conception of them now, and we civilized people may well stand abashed before their purity of life & their truthfulness.[47]

Sarah Winnemucca's *Life among the Piutes* is arranged in eight chapters, following in general a linear chronology of events from her childhood to the present in 1882-83. As a child she witnesses the first encounters between Paiutes and white people in the 1840s and 1850s and the impact of the westward movement on the overland trails on tribal life. Retrospectively, she describes the first coming of white people as the central event of her childhood, the event that marks the beginning of the story of her life, and that—as in many other Native autobiographical narratives—is seen prophesied in visions and dreams.[48] Thus she puts herself in the position of both tribal historian and autobiographical narrator. From the beginning of her text, she uses direct speech and dialogue as narrative devices, which give the text an extraordinary vividness and preserve a sense of the oral quality of her narration; at the same time they add a dramatic element to her story, especially in the rendering of speeches. The purpose of this first chapter is clearly to establish the peaceful intent of the Paiutes in their relations with whites, revising the idea of hostile savages promoted by bloodcurdling tales of emigrant trains attacked by Paiute bands in the years of increasing emigration to California. As a matter of fact, the coming of the emigrant trains every summer lends a structure and repetitive rhythmic pattern to the narrative, which reproduces the movement of white people closing in upon the migratory Paiutes from all sides. The Paiutes' frontier, the encounter with a foreign people on the territory they call their homeland, of course does not resemble the Turnerian concept of *the* American frontier. Although the Paiutes are reaching out to welcome the strangers, they are encircled and finally expelled from their homeland.

When she was a very small child, Sarah tells her readers, a party of white people was seen traveling eastward from California. They were people who kept at a distance (5). During the following years these emigrants came closer with every annual emigration. More emigrants came, and one summer—which must have been 1846, two years after Sarah's birth—her grandfather goes to California with a party of Paiutes to help Frémont against the Mexicans. Very late that same fall, Sarah reports, the emigrants kept coming and were forced to live among the Paiutes during the winter. The following spring, there were "fearful news coming from different tribes, that the people whom they called their white brothers were killing everybody that came their way, and all the Indian tribes had gone into the mountains to save their lives" (11). Then Winnemucca describes the psychological effect of these news on her tribe by dwelling on the special sense of fear and horror this brought to the lives of women and children. Women covered long distances when gathering food, and the dramatic episode Sarah tells of her mother burying her in order to hide her from white people serves to demonstrate this sense of fear and horror shared by women and children. In an inversion of the pattern of the Indian captivity narrative, she casts white people in the role of savages and cannibals, and dwells on the emotional effect of this incident on herself:

> Oh, can any one imagine my feelings *buried alive,* thinking every minute that I was to be unburied and eaten up by the people that my grandfather loved so much? . . . Oh, can any one in this world ever imagine what were my feelings when I was dug up by my poor mother and father? (12)

The idea that white people were cannibals, that "we shall all be killed and eaten up" (11) seems to have haunted especially the women after talk had come up that a party of emigrants "ate each other up in the mountains last winter"—a possible reference to the Donner party, thus locating the incidents in the year 1846.

Drawing a connection between past and present, Winnemucca now uses sentimental language to narrate the story of her life in terms of a tragic plot:

> I was once buried alive; but my second burial shall be for ever, where no father or mother will come and dig me up. It shall not be with throbbing heart that I shall listen for coming footsteps. I shall be in the sweet rest of peace—I, the chieftain's weary daughter. (12)

This use of the stylized phrase of the "chieftain's weary daughter" is the only instance in which Sarah Winnemucca draws openly on the romantic figure of the Indian princess. It has to be noted that in other instances she uses her claim of being the chief's daughter not in order to possibly attain an exotic effect, but in order to establish her authority to speak up and act for her people.

When Sarah was about ten years old, her grandfather "prevailed with his people to go with him to California" (21). As his daughter, Sarah's mother accompanies him with her children, and they spend part of a year near San Jose. The trip to California marks Sarah's first direct contact with white emigrants and their way of life; at the same time her own presence in the narrative becomes stronger. Increasingly interlaced in the story of Indian-white relations, dominated by her grandfather's policy of peaceful coexistence, is the story of Sarah's own extreme reaction to his efforts: she pictures herself as a unique child who was crying more, was afraid more than any of the other children (28), a child who kept her distance from her grandfather, whom she held responsible for having exposed the family to the white "owls," and thus acts badly and rebellious. She pictures herself frantic with fear whenever confronted with white people, dancing round "like the wild one, which I was" (25).

Thus we see Sarah first as a child who is extremely violent in her instinctual resistance to contact with white people, and it is significant that this resistance, which she obviously shares with her mother, is only slowly overcome by white women's acts of kindness in order to be reinstated by acts of violence committed by white men. The first white person Sarah encounters is indeed a woman who gives the children sugar (23). And when little Sarah lies sick with the unforeseen effects of having eaten too much cake, she remembers, "some one came that had a voice like an angel." This was "the good white woman" who had come every day to see her, had made her well, and had given her her own dead child's clothes (31-33). Soon, however, the theme of sexual violence is introduced. The band leaves Stockton for the San Joaquin River, where the Paiute men work as vaqueros for a rancher. Here she reports, still from the perspective of the child, of the first incident of sexual violence by hinting that white men had attempted to rape her sister (37). This first part of the narrative establishes her as a child who feels instinctively threatened by white men taking the role of "hostiles" or savages uprooting Paiute family life. It establishes her as a special child, the daughter and granddaughter of chiefs, who perceives herself first in relation to her family, then in relation to her tribe, which is the subject of her second chapter. That this second chapter is titled "Domestic and Social Moralities" and not, as might have been expected, "Domestic . . . Manners," seems to underline the general intent of demonstrating the moral integrity of traditional Paiute upbringing and training: "Our children are very carefully taught to be good" (45). It is a chapter in which Sarah assumes the position of tribal ethnographer, at the same time inscribing herself, as female member of the community, into the description of the Paiute Flower Festival, a female puberty ceremony. It is also a chapter that discusses the issue of gender relations before and after white contact. Here it is significant that Sarah Winnemucca repeatedly emphasizes the controlled and morally pure quality of gender relations in a tribal context: "Our young women are not allowed to talk to any young man that is not their cousin, except at the festive dances" (45). Her description of the Flower Festival gives a sense of the possibilities for self-admiration and self-esteem available to Paiute girls, imagining, dancing, and singing themselves as flowers in bloom, admired by the young men who sing and dance with them. This moral integrity of gender relations and of women's self-esteem, Sarah argues, suffered a deterioration after Indian-white contact: "My people have been so unhappy . . . The mothers are afraid to have more children, for fear they shall have daughters, who are not safe even in their mother's presence" (48). Indian-white relations, she suggests, had a different dimension for native women than for native men. Her description of traditional marriage customs then emphasizes the women's freedom in choosing a husband, the husband's duty to assume all his wife's household work during a certain period before the birth of the first child, and the extent of power wives have over their husbands. When Sarah Winnemucca points to the possible superiority of Indian education over white child training, this is supported by the editor who in a footnote recommends the principles of Indian training as being "worthy the imitation of the whites" (51).[49] Sarah Winnemucca's account of the principles of Indian training leads her to emphasize the role of women in tribal politics, stating that "if the women are interested they can share in the talks" of the tribal council:

> The women know as much as the men do, and their advice is often asked. We have a republic as well as you. The council-tent is our Congress, and anybody can speak who has anything to say, women and all. They are always interested in what their husbands are doing and thinking about. And they take some part even in the wars. (53)

At the same time she comments on the gendered power relations in white America: "If women could go into your Congress I think justice would soon be done to the Indians" (53). If we read this text in the context of white women's demands for political participation and the growing presence of women in public affairs, a context possibly mediated by Sarah's interaction with her editor as well as with other white women, this chapter may be seen to serve as another legitimation of Sarah's own role as public woman and tribal spokeswoman, and of the roles of woman scout and woman warrior she will subsequently assume further in her account. Thus, in the second chapter, she establishes her role as tribal spokeswoman by pointing to the role of women in the political affairs of the tribe and, in contrast to white "domestic feminism," emphasizing the absence of a separation of female and male spheres in tribal culture. At the beginning of the third chapter, she announces: "I will now stop writing about myself and family and tribe customs, and tell about the wars, and the causes of the wars. I will jump over six years" (58). She locates the events within her own history, remembering that she and her sister "were living at this time in Genoa with Major Ormsby's family, who took us as playmates for their little girl. While with them we learned the English language very fast, for they were very kind to us. This was in the year 1858, I think" (58). When, in 1873, Sarah Winnemucca was interviewed by a reporter of the *Nevada State Journal,* she revealed that she was adopted by a Mrs. Roach, worked for several white families, and that she and her sister, while they lived in Major Ormsby's household, worked at household chores and helped serve passengers.[50] In her autobiography, however, she leaves out this part of her circumstances which reveals the common practice of frontier families to adopt Paiute children, who were expected to earn their keep, and mentions the educational effect of this practice. Yet this first experience in education is not centered on by Sarah

Winnemucca as a crucial formative event. As a matter of fact, her allusions to her education are always cursory, never at the narrative center. Her emphasis is on the repetitive acts of violence marking the beginning of strained Indian-white relations in Nevada. Even the racist attitudes that terminated her attendance of a San Jose convent school remain uncommented. She simply states that they "were only there a little while, say three weeks, when complaints were made to the sisters by wealthy parents about Indians being in school with their children" (70).

Shortly after the children had to leave school, the "war of 1860" broke out, as she reports, with the kidnapping and rape of two twelve-year-old Paiute girls by white men (70-71). After a war of three months, a treaty was made, giving the Pyramid Lake Reservation to the Paiutes (73). Reservation life begins, which for the people will mean dispossession, increasing encroachment upon their land by cattle ranchers, dependence on Indian agents, hunger, starvation, and powerlessness. The description of this process of dispossession will now be at the center of Sarah's narrative, which exposes the lawless practices of Indian agents, criticizes the reservation system sharply, and argues that Indian affairs should be assigned to the military.

Again the facts of her personal life are only cursorily mentioned. The following passage is typical of the way in which Sarah Winnemucca writes her own story, as a secondary but striking presence into her narrative:

> I will tell you the doings of the agents in that agency. The first six who came I did not know. In 1866, after my poor mother and sister Mary died, I came down from Virginia City to live with my brother Natchez, while there were some white men living on the agency. (79)

Telling the story of her people's plight, she only hints at the personal tragedies in her life, leaving the reader wondering about the causes of her separations from her people, about her work and her life. Canfield reveals in her biography that Sarah Winnemucca must have come into the public eye as an "Indian princess" at about that time.[51] Yet Sarah does not tell of this; neither does she tell of her father's loss of authority and trust with the white settlers at about 1866. Is her move to live with her brother, one wonders, a forced or voluntary removal from the white society of Virginia City?[52]

As soon as Sarah is on the reservation, she seems to be in a prominent position as interpreter and peacemaker, serving as go-between in the dealings of the Paiutes with their Indian agents. We see her as the one who, with her brother, warns the agent of plans to kill him (79-80), we see her jumping "on a horse, bareback" (80) to go and meet her brother at a time of danger,

and we see her receiving a letter by an officer, addressed to her, and asking her and her brother for a meeting with the soldiers (82). It becomes clear that this prominent position is not only related to her family's position in the tribe, but also to her ability to speak English, to read and write, although she discounts the latter abilities (82-83). She begins to talk for her people with the soldiers. Yet it is significant that in this role she pictures herself as reluctant and needy of protection, "because I was afraid of the soldiers" (84). We see Sarah crying all the while when she is asked by the soldiers to help them bring her father's band onto the army post (85). Her brother, upon leaving his sister to the care of the Colonel, asks "that no soldiers talk to her" (100). When talking to some other Indians, he expresses his fears that the soldiers "might abuse her" (101-102). When her brother is gone, she goes to the commanding officer and tells him: "Colonel, I am here all alone with so many men, I am afraid. I want your protection. I want you to protect me against your soldiers, and I want you to protect my people also" (103). That she deemed it necessary to stress her respectable womanhood repeatedly in these allusions to her endangered virtue demonstrates the force of the voices she is speaking up against. It also demonstrates that her narrative is located, either by herself or by her editor, within a feminine discourse of respectable womanhood, with a stress on morality as a key term. This is further underlined by the fact that the book was published under Winnemucca's married name. This denial of erotic relations between the "Indian Princess" and the soldiers, and the attempt to de-eroticize her own presence as an Indian woman among white men form important strategies of the book; these go, however, curiously unnoticed in some of today's historical literature, which seems to thrive on this eroticism.[53] Of course, Sarah Winnemucca's favorable view of the army is shaped by practical, although controversial, considerations based on the Paiutes' experience:

> Can you wonder, dear readers, that I like to have my people taken care of by the army? It is said that I am working in the interest of the army, and as if they wanted all this care. It is not so; but they know more about the Indians than any citizens do, and are always friendly. (93)

Yet these considerations are everywhere linked to the theme of sexual violence. Apparently in order to demonstrate the need for the army's protection against white settlers, she adds an episode that emphasizes the unprotected situation of native women in the area. Sarah Winnemucca may be influential as a political spokeswoman, yet she is constantly molested as a woman—except when she is among the soldiers:

> The last time sister and I were on a visit to our people at our old home, just before I was married,

we stopped with a white lady named Nichols, at Wadsworth, Nevada. . . . Some one tried to break through our bedroom door. . . . This is the kind of people, dear reader, that the government sends to teach us at Pyramid Lake Reservation. (94)

After we have seen her as peacemaker and interpreter trying to dissuade her people from going to war, there is a break of about six years in her narrative again. Chapter VI begins with a reference to the year 1875: "In 1875 I was in Camp Harney, Oregon, to see my father. It was in May" (105). Invited to act as interpreter for her people at the Malheur Reservation in Oregon, she accepts the offer, "for I had no other way of making a living for myself" (105). She pictures the people as living happily and prospering under agent Parrish, with his brother's wife, the "white lily," as a kind school teacher, loved by everyone, and assisted by Sarah. Yet again a time full of hope for a better and possibly self-determined future comes to an end when the civilian agent, in the course of the implementation of Grant's Indian policy, is supplanted by a religious man. Under the new agent Rinehart[54] the Paiutes are again dependent and starving. As the voice of her people, Sarah becomes the target of the agent's anger. Caught up in the conflict between the Department of the Interior and the War Department for control of Indian affairs, she is inevitably discharged from her position and expelled from the reservation. Moreover, agent Rinehart will try to destroy her credibility by denouncing her as a harlot and camp follower, when she reports him to Washington.

Of course, Sarah Winnemucca's main purpose is to tell about her people and not about herself. Yet at chronological breaks like these, one becomes aware of the sometimes dangerously voyeuristic nature of the interpretation of any life story—with the lure of exoticism added in the case of a Native American woman's life story. Why else should we be so curious about these years missing in her story? Canfield reveals what seems to be left out here, and what a contemporary audience potentially was, at least in part, aware of: a letter by Sarah Winnemucca criticizing the reservation system, passed on to the Indian Commissioner Parker; an article on her in the May 7, 1870, issue of *Harper's Weekly;* a Boise, Idaho, editor's unfavorable reaction to Sarah's publicity, picturing her as an unwashed, unattractive savage; an August 1870 interview in the San Francisco *Alta California;* an 1871 elopement with and marriage to a Lieutenant Bartlett, a marriage that was unacceptable to her father and brother, who did not want to see her any more; a letter to General Ord, again critical of the reservation system, with repercussions both in Nevada and Washington; after the breakup of her marriage, work as a hospital matron at Camp McDermitt; after an argument with the commanding officer a move to Winnemucca and work as a glovemaker, milliner, and interpreter. During that time

she repeatedly makes the local news: she is reported to have fought with another Paiute woman who slandered her virtue and she is said to be living with an Indian named Jones.[55] Subsequently she is reported to live in Winnemucca, where within a few weeks the *Winnemucca Silver State* commented on her activities. She had gotten into another fight with another Indian woman, and was soon thereafter accused of cutting a man with a knife. Sarah had felt that her dignity was threatened because a man had touched her without permission. The "Piute Princess," as the newspapers called her, was put in the county jail overnight. In November 1876 Sarah got married, apparently for the third time. Her husband was Joseph Satwaller.[56]

What personal tragedies are hidden behind the lines of her autobiographical narrative? As a woman of two worlds, Sarah Winnemucca must have provoked criticism from both sides, walking a tightrope between two cultures. She must have found herself in the position of an outsider, not living on the reservation, but in various frontier towns, trying to make a living, and at the same time trying to speak up for her starving people in interviews, and to get her family's love back. Yet it is significant that she chooses not to talk about her life in Virginia City and the other frontier towns, and instead talks about her deeds in the service of her people. While her life as a woman in frontier towns is the focus of press reports, and may well have contributed to her popularity built on the image of the Indian princess, she herself is concerned with placing her life both within the context of the story of her tribe, and, possibly with a view to a female audience, within the context of feminine respectability.

When she takes up the narration again, after her dismissal from her interpreter's position, it is three years later. In the winter of 1878, we find her "living at the head of John Day's river with a lady by the name of Courley" (137). Having apparently had no news from Malheur for quite some time, she is asked for her help by her people: new trouble is ahead on the Bannock reservation after two white men were killed and a Bannock girl was raped; Bannocks keep trying to get the Paiutes to go to war with them against the whites. Yet Sarah repeatedly declines, since she feels powerless on account of "being a woman" (139). At last she agrees to go to Washington for them, an enterprise that will have to be postponed after the outbreak of the Bannock war. She asks to be of service to the army and acts as scout in the military campaign against the Bannocks, a service that will provoke criticism from her own people. The account of her participation in this campaign, however, is one of the most vivid parts of her book, where she now pictures herself as a female daredevil, courageous and unafraid, undertaking what neither Paiute nor white men would undertake "for love or money," leading scouting parties of fearful men (151, 155) and rescuing her people held prisoners at the camp of the "hostile" Bannocks. At the same time she takes care to emphasize that despite all this she has not lost her genteel standards of womanhood. We see her riding in the sidesaddle, wearing a riding dress (152). On the way to the camp of the "hostiles," as she terms the Bannocks, she is in the position of leader, giving orders, encouraging fearful men, guiding them over difficult terrain only she is familiar with. The only impression of the country we get is that it is rocky, full of steep mountains, and without water (155, 158).[57] Even during her daring exploits, she remains a lady; her brother tells her to "take off your hat and your dress and unbraid your hair" (158), thus again revealing her genteel appearance to her readers. Yet the heroic nature of her action is immediately revised as the act of a daughter, when she quotes her father welcoming her with the words: "Oh, my dear little girl, and what is it? Have you come to save me yet? My little child is in great danger" (159). After the rescue of her father's band from captivity, Sarah and her sister-in-law Mattie undertake the dangerous enterprise of bringing a message back to the troops: "Away we started over the hills and valleys. We had to go about seventy-five miles through the country. No water" (164). Thereafter, the two women start for Camp Lyon, and Sarah declares that she "was as mad as could be because I wanted to go right after the hostile Bannocks" (165). It is clear that the role in which she casts herself here is the role of a warrior. When she is asked by General Howard to go with a dispatch to Camp Harney, she refuses an escort: "No, Mattie and I will go alone, for no white man can keep up with us. We can go alone quicker than with soldiers" (167). Yet one of the soldiers insists, "as there were bad white men who might harm us" (167). When a battle ensues between soldiers and "hostiles," she "did not feel any fear. I asked the general to let me go to the front line where the soldiers were fighting" (176). She draws attention to the heroism of this army, applying a cultural key term usually including Native Americans: "Dear reader, if you could only know the difficulties of this wilderness you could then appreciate their loyal service" (176). Subsequently, she casts herself in the role of the Indian fighter: "we struck the Indian rear guard. . . . We went in hot pursuit of the Indians" (178-80).

When she returns to her band's camp, she is welcomed by her family as a woman warrior, putting the Paiute men to shame. It is important how she relates this story of her elevation to the status of a warrior: it is contained in the speeches of her father and brother. Her brother scolds his young men: "I am afraid, my young men, you are not doing your duty; for I have here in my camp a warrior who has just arrived" (189). Old Winnemucca speaks in the same way to his people:

> Oh! for shame! for shame to you, young men, who ought to have come with this news to me! I am

much pained because my dear daughter has come with the fearful things which have happened in the war. Oh, yes! my child's name is so far beyond yours; none of you can ever come up to hers. Her name is everywhere and every one praises her. Oh! how thankful I felt that it is my own child who has saved so many lives, not only mine, but a great many, both whites and her own, people. Now hereafter we will look on her as our chieftain, for none of us are worthy of being chief but her, and all I can say to you is to send her to the wars and you stay and do women's work, and talk as women do. (193)

Thus Sarah Winnemucca has legitimized her role and established her authority as spokeswoman on multiple levels: by way of family and kinship, by pointing to the role of women in the political affairs of the tribe, and by becoming a tribal warrior hero, elevated by her chieftain father to the status of female chieftain. I agree with H. David Brumble that it sounds rather like the assertion of her deeds in the traditional manner of a coup tale[58] than like an apology when Sarah sums up her work for the army:

> This was the hardest work I ever did for the government in all my life. . . . Yes, I went for the government when the officers could not get an Indian man or a white man to go for love or money. I, only an Indian woman, went and saved my father and his people. (164)

Yet while Sarah Winnemucca may present her acts in terms of a Paiute role model, her voice still remains that of an individual woman under attack from two sides. Moreover, as she now reveals, the fact that she had never spoken with her own voice, but always in the words of others, becomes the more problematic with the breakdown of tribal authority structures. Probably Sarah would not have helped gathering together the Paiutes if she had known what was ahead of them. Soon she receives order that they were to be taken to the Yakima Reservation in the middle of winter, and it becomes increasingly difficult for Sarah to act as the voice of the people and of the soldiers at the same time: she is held responsible for the army's and government's promises conveyed by her to her people. The increasing difficulty of speaking in the words of others is revealed in a dialogue between her and Mattie. Mattie replies to Sarah's fear that her people will think her to have worked against them: "Well, sister, we cannot help it if the white people won't keep their word. We can't help it. We have to work for them and if they get our people not to love us, by telling what is not true to them, what can we do? It is they, not us" (204). It is the beginning of a tragedy, of the Paiute trail of tears to the Yakima reservation in the winter of 1878-79 where they will go hungry again as they had done before. It is also the beginning of a personal tragedy: her people do not believe her any more and refuse to speak to her (208). The public lecture platform becomes her new domain of activity. She reports that she went away in November 1879 to Vancouver, Washington Territory, to see General Howard, going on to San Francisco to lecture: "Well, while I was lecturing in San Francisco, a great deal was said about it through the Western country. The papers said I was coming East to lecture" (207). When she was getting ready, a telegram arrived from Washington, asking her, her father and brother, and another chief to see the president (207). Her editor notes,

> Mrs. Hopkins has not told in the text of the very great impression made by her lectures in San Francisco, showing up the iniquity of the agent Reinhard. It was, doubtless, the rumor of the excitement she caused which led to her being sent for to Washington. Reinhard could not contradict her there, where he and she were so well known, and therefore he probably wrote to Washington and told some story for himself. (217)

Thus, although Sarah herself understates the political effect of her lectures, her editor elevates her to a central position as political spokeswoman of the tribe in Washington. And in fact, Canfield's research suggests that Sarah's popularity may well have had a political impact. Yet it also suggests that any public comment on Sarah, whether positive or negative, was tied to conceptions of her womanhood, either as the good, motherly "Indian Princess" or the bad, lewd "Indian Squaw." On her arrival in San Francisco, Sarah Winnemucca found herself something of a celebrity, who had been in the public eye during the Bannock War. The newspapers headlined her as "The Princess Sarah," or wrote of her as "Nature's child."[59] The *San Francisco Chronicle* reported:

> Sarah has undergone hardships and dared dangers that few men would be willing to face, but she has not lost her womanly qualities, and succeeded during her visit in coaxing into her lap two little timid "palefaced" children usually shy of strangers, who soon lost their fear of her dark skin, won by her warm and genial ways.

In the same paper, however, she was also described as having had "an extensive and diversified matrimonial experience, the number of her white husbands being variously estimated at from three to seven." Sarah subsequently gave an interview in which she refuted that report, mentioning her marriage to Bartlett and subsequent divorce and a second marriage to an Indian, who grossly mistreated her.[60] That her popularity had political repercussions is demonstrated in the letters agent Rinehart sent to the Indian Department, in which he called Sarah a "low, unprincipled Indian woman of questionable virtue and veracity as well, who was formerly Interpreter at the Agency and who

was discharged for untruthfulness, gambling and other bad conduct."[61] That her lectures did have a political effect is also suggested in her description of the Paiutes' visit to Washington in January 1880. There she is asked by Secretary Schurz not to lecture (221) and the whole group is kept from reporters and other interested parties (219). At the White House, however, "[a] great many ladies were there to see us" (222), among them apparently Elizabeth Palmer Peabody,[62] while President Hayes only grants them a handshake.

The group's mission is met with only a limited success. Although Secretary Schurz has granted the Paiutes to live on the Malheur Reservation, the government provides neither supplies nor transportation for the tribe's return. Before she knows this, however, Sarah goes on another mission with another Paiute woman, trying to get her people to go to the agency. Again she emphasizes the boldness of the undertaking for two unaccompanied women, when she quotes her cousin Joe Winnemucca welcoming her with the words: "That can't be, you two women, all alone" (227). He accompanies the women to the next place, warning them:

> He said there were very bad men there. Sometimes they would throw a rope over our women, and do fearful things to them. "Oh, my poor cousins," he said, "my heart aches for you, for I am afraid they will do something fearful to you. They do not care for anything. They do most terrible outrageous things to our women." (228)

Sarah herself is rather explicit about the subject of rape here, yet she speaks not as a helpless, fearful frontier woman but as a Native American woman who can defend herself to a certain extent: "If such an outrageous thing is to happen to me, it will not be done by one man or two, while there are two women with knives, for I know what an Indian woman can do. She can never be outraged by one man: but she may by two" (228). And, she adds:

> It is something an Indian woman dare not say till she has been overcome by one man, for there is no man living that can do anything to a woman if she does not wish him to. My dear reader, I have not lived in this world for over thirty or forty years for nothing, and I know what I am talking about. (228)

When they leave the house the next morning, their host's Spanish boarders are after them "like wild men" (229). However, they manage to reach the next house safely. In a breathless manner she dwells on the dangers the road poses to Native American women, dangers which are linked to the absence of white women: "No white women on all the places where we stopped,—all men,—yet we were treated kindly by all of them, so far" (230-231). When they spend the night at a place where cowboys stay over night, she is molested, yet manages to give the man "a blow right in the face" (231). When they arrive at Camp Harney, there "were only three ladies at the post. The captain's wife and the other officers' wives were kind to me while I stayed there" (232). In this context it should be noted that her remarks on and descriptions of white women always serve rather strategic functions in her narrative. There are good women like the emigrant woman who nursed her back to health when she was a child, or like the "white lily," whom she assisted as teacher of the Paiute children. There are also army officers' wives who represent genteel womanhood and protection against potential molestations, and who supply Sarah with dresses (169). Yet she also presents another kind of womanhood, such as the woman who wants to see Sarah hang, for reasons we are not informed about: "Dear reader, this is the kind of white women that are in the West. They are always ready to condemn me" (168). In another passage, she describes an Indian agent's wife: "She had a Bible with her. Ah! ah! What do you think the Bible was? Why it was a pack of cards. She would sit every day and play cards with men, and every evening, too. She was an Indian agent's wife" (223). On the whole, she seems to present western women with an eye to an eastern female audience and their assumed standards of morality.

The last part of the book is dominated by a note of personal defense against attacks from two sides. Back at the Yakima reservation, some of her people accuse her of having sold them to the soldiers, yet she is defended by the women: "We knew she would not do such a thing" (235). She herself tells her people:

> You can say what you like about me. You have a right to say I have sold you. It looks so. I have told you many things which are not my own words, but the words of the agents and the soldiers. I know I have told you more lies than I have hair on my head. I tell you, my dear children, I have never told you my own words; they were the words of the white people, not mine. (236)

At the end of her narrative, Sarah Winnemucca is a woman in between, attacked from all sides—a woman desperately alone, yet trying to assume a collective voice. As if she had given up her own voice as speaker, and deferred the talking to her readers, she now appeals to them in the name of all tribes:

> Hear our pitiful cry to you, sweep away the agency system; give us homes to live in, for God's sake and for humanity's sake. I left my poor people in despair, I knew I had so many against me . . . I see that all who say they are working for Indians are against me. (243)

And she goes on to appeal not only to her readers' national values, but also to their sense of morality.

Again she speaks as part of a group, of Indians confronting whites:

> For shame! for shame! You dare to cry out Liberty, when you hold us in places against our will, driving us from place to place as if we were beasts. Ah, there is one thing you cannot say of the Indian. You call him savage, and everything that is bad but one; but, thanks be to God, I am so proud to say that my people have never outraged your women, or have even insulted them by looks or words. Can you say the same of the negroes or the whites? They do commit some most horrible outrages on your women, but you do not drive them round like dogs. Oh, my dear readers, talk for us, and if the white people will treat us like human beings, we will behave like a people; but if we are treated by white savages as if we are savages, we are relentless and desperate; yet not more so than any other badly treated people. Oh, dear friends, I am pleading for God and for humanity. (244)

And thus ends her autobiographical narrative: "Finding it impossible to do any thing for my people I did not return to Yakima, but after I left Vancouver Barracks I went to my sister in Montana. After my marriage to Mr. Hopkins I visited my people once more at Pyramid Lake Reservation, and they urged me again to come to the East and talk for them, and so I have come" (246).

Appended to the main text is a note by the editor asking readers to sign the petition made by Sarah Winnemucca to the next Congress, asking to restore Malheur Reservation in severalty to the Paiutes, and to let the portion of Paiutes removed to Yakima return to Malheur. The language of the petition reveals its link to a female rhetoric of domesticity:

> And especially do we petition for the return of that portion of the tribe arbitrarily removed from the Malheur Reservation . . . in which removal families were ruthlessly separated, and have never ceased to pine for husbands, wives, and children, which restoration was pledged to them by the Secretary of the Interior in 1880, but has not been fulfilled. (247)

Mary Mann finally draws attention to the last three pages of the appendix, which

> will show that the friends of the agents she criticizes are active to discredit her; but it has been ascertained that every definite charge made to the Indian office has no better endorsement than the name of Reinhard, who is characterized, to my personal knowledge, by some of the army officers who have known of his proceedings, as "a thoroughly wicked and unscrupulous man." (248)[63]

The appendix is not only commented on by the editor, but also held together by Sarah's voice who finally places her text within the context of a campaign aimed at discrediting her as a spokes*woman:*

> I know now, from the highest authority, that the government was deceived by the agent, Renehart, who said the Indians would not stay at the Malheur Reservation. After being driven away by starvation, after having had every promise broken, falsehoods were told about them and *there was no one to take their part but a woman. Every one knows what a woman must suffer who undertakes to act against bad men. My reputation has been assailed, and it is done so cunningly that I cannot prove it to be unjust. I can only protest that it is unjust, and say that wherever I have been known, I have been believed and trusted.* . . . Those who have maligned me have not known me. It is true that my people sometimes distrust me, but that is because words have been put into my mouth which have turned out to be nothing but idle wind. Promises have been made to me in high places that have not been kept, and I have had to suffer for this in the loss of my people's confidence. (258)

Sarah Winnemucca Hopkins's *Life among the Piutes* has answered many of my initial questions about the role of gender in Indian-white relations and about the way cultural contact affected Native American women's lives. Indian-white relations, as they emerge in Sarah's narrative, are highly charged with the issues of sexual violence and sexual stereotyping. Sarah herself uses her text to fight against stereotypical images of Native American women, and although she draws on the image of the Indian princess, it mainly serves as a legitimizing strategy to underline her authority as spokeswoman. Her narrative represents the attempt of a Native American woman to become real as a woman beyond stereotypes. It also counters the image of Sarah as the "fallen woman" by depicting her relationship with her sister-in-law and other women, and by presenting her, also through the voice of her editor, as part of a female community. Acculturation, however, is a double-edged sword in Sarah's narrative, as ambiguous as the image of Sarah's personality which emerges in this text. As the product of an encounter between female voices, East and West, white and Indian, the narrative presents a rather complex concept of the woman and tribal person. By referring to the role of women in the political affairs of the Paiute band, and by emphasizing the absence of the separation of female and male spheres in the tribe, Sarah Winnemucca draws authority for her public role as spokeswoman from both this position of women within the tribe and from her kinship position as daughter and granddaughter of chiefs. Placing her life story within the context of the story of her tribe, she takes on the various roles of peacemaker, interpreter, helper of both whites and Paiutes, as scout, chieftain, and woman warrior, thus legitimizing her public role with role models which are apparently in accord with Paiute

concepts of womanhood. Her acts of heroism and self-reliance thus have their roots in her conception of her Native American womanhood.

On the other hand, Sarah Winnemucca draws upon images of genteel Victorian womanhood by presenting herself, within the context of feminine respectability, as a lady in appearance and manners, distancing herself from the image of the erotic or even lewd Native American "squaw." Yet whenever she emphasizes her own morality and modesty, she explains their rationale by pointing to her Paiute upbringing, and it is the voice of the editor that relates principles of Paiute womanhood to those of white respectable womanhood. When Sarah Winnemucca is seen crying, she cries over the plight of her people, which of course may have a special effect on her audience since it shows her as a sensitive woman. However, references to other aspects of "true womanhood," such as piety, submissiveness, and domesticity, are significantly lacking. Sarah Winnemucca does not present herself as a religious woman. Neither does she claim for herself a "civilizing" influence on her people. References to these aspects of ideal white womanhood are, however, contained in her remarks on white women which underline her own arguments by valuing genteel army wives and kind pioneer women over rough frontier women and immoral Indian agents' wives. Although Sarah hints at her domestic work for white women in Nevada and Oregon, there are no references to herself as a domestic woman. The idea, or rather the ideology, of "domestic feminism" so often elaborated on in the literature on white nineteenth-century women is only appealed to in references to her people's search for a permanent home where families can be reunited. She herself presents herself rather as a working woman who, although proud of her achievements, describes them as acts of necessity and duty.

Sarah Winnemucca's narrative exemplifies the necessity for a multicultural framework in the study of women's experience, which so far has focused predominantly on white middle-class women—a framework that should also allow for an analysis that takes class into account. What is presented in Sarah Winnemucca's *Life among the Piutes,* is the image of a complex personality who draws her strength from a cultural encounter whose negative impact, in the form of the white control of Native American lives, is at the center of her story. How far Sarah had control over her own narrative in the encounter with her editor and publisher, still remains to be debated. Nevertheless, although the nature of these women's collaboration still needs to be investigated more thoroughly, I would venture the thesis that this text is very much Sarah's own in the sense that she can present the complexity of her situation, both as a mouthpiece of many voices, and as a woman who is forced to find her own voice in order to defend her personal dignity. Sarah Winnemucca emerges, on the one hand, as an individual who has to defend her reputation as a modest and respectable Native American woman against both white and Indian voices, a woman who stands alone under attacks from various sides. On the other hand, she transgresses the boundaries imposed on white respectable womanhood. We see her as a tribal person committed to her people through bonds of love and kinship, drawing strength for her heroic deeds from an allegedly tribal, or rather Indian, role model of the woman warrior. It is her gender which, in the eyes of both her supporters and her attackers, singles her out. She has spoken out both as a daughter and a Paiute spokesperson, never claiming a voice of her own. But she was most vulnerable and alone when she had to find her own voice as a woman between two worlds.

Notes

1 Hopkins (1969).

2 The term has been used by Slotkin (1973).

3 Slotkin (1973) shows how women have been used as the motive behind male manipulation and destruction of both the natural world and the indigenous inhabitants of the frontier. Women are symbolically present in the popular mythology of the frontier as civilizing maternal forces from whom men flee into the wilderness or as legitimation for the conquest of Indian land.

4 See Jeffrey (1979); Faragher (1979); Schlissel (1982); Myres (1982); Riley (1988). The only major work dealing with the imaginative constructs women have projected onto the western frontiers in their literary writings is Kolodny (1984). A textual study of women's private writings has been undertaken by Hampsten (1982). Articles of an interdisciplinary sort on western women have been collected in Armitage and Jameson (1987) and Norwood and Monk (1987).

5 See Riley (1985:83-84).

6 See Jensen and Miller (1980:185). See also DuBois and Ruiz (1990). Riley (1984:xvi) has examined the relationship between white women and Native Americans, taking as her basis the diaries and letters of westering women. Yet she puts no special focus on the relations between white and Native American women. The perspective of her study is "that of white history rather than white-Indian or Indian history." Myres (1982) has included Native American women's perspectives, based on a reading of oral and written sources. The articles included in Myres (1982) and Norwood and Monk (1987) demonstrate this growing concern for a multicultural framework in the study of western women.

7 On Native American autobiography see Krupat (1985); Brumble (1988); Sands (1982:55-65); Theisz (1981:65-

80). On women's autobiography and personal narratives, see Personal Narratives Group (1989); Hoffmann and Culley (1985); Brodzki and Schenck (1988); Buss (1989:1-17).

8 Krupat (1985:31) has argued that the principle constituting the Native American autobiography as a genre is the principle of "original bicultural composite composition." Krupat (1989:133-134, 141, 149) refines this definition by describing the model of the Native American autobiography as a dialogic model of the self. In their introduction, Brodzki and Schenck (1988:2) state that "the implicit attitude toward the masculine representative self . . . is reflective . . . of a generic exclusivity in the critical treatment of autobiography, rendering this model inadequate for a theory of women's autobiography." They regard "self-definition in relation to significant others" (Brodzki and Schenck 1988:8) as the most pervasive characteristic of the female autobiography.

9 See Albers and Medicine (1983); Green (1983); Powers (1986); Liberty (1982:10-19); Mathes (1980:20-25). See also Williams (1986).

10 See the literary criticism on Silko's novel *Ceremony,* for example, Herzog (1985:25-36); Rubenstein (1987); Allen (1986:118-126).

11 See Peyer (1981:1-12; 386-402).

12 This issue is discussed in Armitage and Jameson (1987:51ff). Various papers in this collection, particularly those by Kirk and Smith, explore whether gender has an impact on intercultural relationships, and whether women and men view people of different cultures differently.

13 The value of an interpretation of Native American women's life stories for an understanding of the complexities of cultural contact and change is increasingly acknowledged. One of the first works analyzing these life stories was Bataille and Sands (1984). Carr's (1988:131-153) excellent essay on native women's life stories of the twentieth century, which has profited from recent research in both feminist and poststructuralist theory, demonstrates the fruitfulness of an approach that is sensitive to the textuality and the special "framing" of these texts.

14 See Fischer (1977); Luchetti (1982); Moynihan, Armitage, and Dichamp (1990).

15 In the historical and anthropological literature, there are many variations for the spelling of *Paiute.* I have used the popular blanket term *Paiute* throughout the text, except in direct quotations.

16 See Hopkins (1969:5), chaps. 1-4; Fowler (1978:33-42); Ruoff (1982:151-152).

[17] The term *Indian Princess* occurs very often in the literature on Sarah Winnemucca. Gehm (1975) uses the term rather uncritically, without being aware of the ideological implications of this stereotype. Green (1975:698-714) has explored how the paradoxical but positive image of the Indian Princess, "exotic and sexual, yet maternal and contradictorily virginal" (Green 1975:709-710), is paired with the negative image of the Indian Squaw in the national imagination. Both the native woman's "nobility as a Princess and her savagery as a Squaw are defined in terms of her relationships with male figures" (Green 1975:703), either as exotic helper and guide, whose "sexuality can be hinted at but never realized" (Green 1975:711) or as real woman and sexual partner, in which case the positive image is converted into a negative one.

[18] Peabody's letters of the years 1883-1887 show how Sarah and the Paiute case figure prominently in the old lady's correspondence before her death in 1894. See Ronda (1984:esp. 397-398, 414-415, 439-440, 442-443).

[19] For these biographical details, see Canfield (1983).

[20] See Fowler (1978:38); Brumble (1988:61); Ruoff (1982:151).

[21] See Peyer (1981:6, 392).

[22] See Ruoff (1987:1041).

[23] See Ruoff (1987:1040).

[24] See Ruoff (1990). I am relying here on Brumble's interpretation of Ruoff's article, since I have not yet been able to locate the publication.

[25] See Brumble (1988:63).

[26] See Brumble (1988:69-71).

[27] See Brumble (1988:65-66).

[28] See Brumble (1988:71).

[29] See Bataille and Sands (1984:21).

[30] This argument is partially supported by Canfield's biography of Sarah Winnemucca, which is an invaluable source on the reception of her lectures, since it collects evidence from both the eastern and the western contemporary press. Although she is concerned mainly with the accurate historical compilation of the "facts" of a life gathered from various sources, and does not consider the textual implications of her sources, Canfield (1983) provides a fascinating reconstruction of the life of Sarah Winnemucca.

[31] See Mathes (1990:15-16, esp. 14).

[32] See Ruoff (1987:1041).

[33] See Peyer (1981:392); Fowler (1978:33).

[34] See Brumble (1988:65).

[35] Much of the scholarship on nineteenth-century women's history is based on the assumption that women's lives, particularly among the emerging bourgeoisie in the first half of the nineteenth century, were lived in a separate domestic "sphere," on which basis they were able to claim a kind of social power distinct from that of men. Reified in prescriptive literature, realized in daily life, and ritualized in female collectivities, this "woman's sphere" came to be seen as the foundation of women's culture and community within the Victorian middle class. See Hewitt (1990:1-14). Welter (1966:151-174) has first identified the construction of a new ideology of gender that defined the "true woman" as pious, pure, domestic, and submissive. Other formative works on Victorian womanhood are Cott (1977); Smith-Rosenberg (1975:1-29).

[36] Note the way Sarah appears as the "Indian Princess" in De Quille (1947:11-12, 201-202).

[37] See Green (1975:713).

[38] See Brumble (1988:68, 69).

[39] See Fowler (1978:33): "Robert Heizer (1960:3) suggests that her 'selfless motives and tremendous energies and high purpose make her a person to admire in the history of our far West.' Omer Stewart (1939:129) on the other hand, described her as 'ambitious, educated, . . . trying to attain self-aggrandizement by exalting her father.'"

[40] See Canfield (1983:172ff) where she quotes affidavits to Washington, signed by nine gentlemen of Canyon City: "That this woman has been several times married, but that by reason of her adulterous and drunken habits, neither squawmen nor Indians would long live with her, that in addition to her character of Harlot and drunkard, she merits and possesses that of a notorious liar and malicious schemer [*sic*]."

[41] Ryan (1990:48-94) discusses this double bind of women who began to claim the public, political arena for themselves in Victorian America.

[42] See Fowler (1978:37): "In all fairness to her detractors, Sarah was short tempered, particularly in the context of offenses to her people, and she was known to take a drink and to scream and swear on occasion. She also had three husbands, two of them White men."

[43] Note especially the titles of Peabody's and Mann's publications that emphasize the "moral" as a key term,

although it might have had a different significance for nineteenth-century readers than for a twentieth-century audience. See Peabody and Mann (1870); Peabody (1874).

[44] See Krupat (1985:33).

[45] See Krupat (1985:33).

[46] See Hopkins (1969:5); further references to the autobiography will appear in the text.

[47] Quoted in Canfield (1983:203).

[48] See the autobiography of Black Hawk (1964); see also *Co-ge-we-a, the Half-Blood* (Mourning Dove 1927).

[49] Here Mann admires the Native American emphasis on teaching "a great deal about nature; how to observe the habits of plants and animals," criticizes Indian-white relations, and charges her own country, by quoting from Helen Hunt Jackson's *A Century of Dishonor,* with Christian bigotry: "Thus Christendom missed the moral reformation it might have had, if they had become acquainted with the noble Five Nations, and others whom they have exterminated" (Mann 1870:52).

[50] See Canfield (1983:11).

[51] See Canfield (1983:36-42).

[52] Brimlow (1952:118), attempts to fill this gap: "Intermittently, Sarah had been doing housework for white families in Virginia City. She observed the frothy night life and participated in sociable dances, but she spent some of the hard-earned money on books to piece out her education." In a footnote he adds, with an obvious allusion to De Quille's romanticization of Sarah Winnemucca: "Written and oral evidence, for the most part, refutes stress misplaced on Sarah's frailty of character in this period. Obviously miscalculated is making Sarah a Gold Canyon frontier dance-hall girl in the early 1850s, as related in print from time to time. She had not attained teen age until about 1857."

[53] See Brimlow (1952:121), who describes events later in Sarah's life:

> Coincidentally with the winding up of Crook's campaign, Sarah and Natchez accompanied Company M, First United States Calvalry, from western Nevada to Fort McDermitt. On the slow journey by horseback, she warded off flirtations by emboldened troopers. She was not unattractive. A tri-cornered scarlet shawl kept alkali dust out of her glossy black hair. Her well-spaced black eyes often blinked mirthfully and her deep-red lips puckered teasingly. At the left side of a two-inch beaded belt, cleating a ruffled pink waist and a dark green overskirt, swung a sheathed knife. High-laced shoes peeked from underneath fringes of petticoats.

[54] Both Canfield (1983) and Gehm (1975), in their biographies of Sarah Winnemucca, spell the agent's name as Rinehart, while in *Life among the Piutes* it appears as Reinhard or even Renehart.

[55] See Canfield (1983:60-82).

[56] See Canfield (1983:92).

[57] This absence of explicit landscape description in Native American women's (and men's) texts is emphasized by Brumble (1988:198). He argues against Bataille's and Sands's (1984:3) assertion that one of the "basic characteristics" oral Indian literature "shares" with American Indian women's autobiography is the "concern with landscape." In an interesting article on Hispanic women artists of the Southwest, Stoller (1987:125-145) argues that Hispanic women artists, like Indian artists, have felt little need to represent their physical environment in other than abstract forms.

[58] See Brumble (1988:66).

[59] See Canfield (1983:164).

[60] See Canfield (1983:163).

[61] Quoted by Canfield (1983:163).

[62] That Peabody was present at this occasion is suggested by Gehm (1975:20-21).

[63] Peabody (1874:415) emphasized the same in a letter she wrote to the editor of the *Boston Daily Advertiser* in 1883: "Now I want to tell you how she has been misrepresented in some quarters—& how every thing has been thoroughly investigated & every thing is perfectly right about her. She has shared our bed & board for months this last summer and fall. I want the Daily Advertiser to recognize her & her cause—& think you will agree." One can imagine how important the support of this woman must have been for Sarah Winnemucca Hopkins at this difficult time in her life.

Works Cited

Albers, Patricia, and Beatrice Medicine. 1983. *The Hidden Half: Studies of Plains Indian Women.* Washington, D.C.: University Press of America.

Allen, Paula Gunn, ed. 1982. *Studies in American Indian Literature.* New York: Modern Language Association.

———. 1986. *The Sacred Hoop: Recovering the Feminine in American Indian Traditions.* Boston: Beacon Press.

Armitage, Susan, and Elizabeth Jameson, eds. 1989. *The Women's West*. Norman and London: University of Oklahoma Press.

Bataille, Gretchen, and Kathleen Sands. 1984. *American Indian Women: Telling Their Lives*. Lincoln and London: University of Nebraska Press.

Black Hawk. 1964. *Black Hawk: An Autobiography*. Edited by Donald Jackson. Urbana: University of Illinois Press.

Brimlow, George F. 1952. "The Life of Sarah Winnemucca: The Formative Years." *Oregon Historical Quarterly,* June 2:103-134.

Brodzki, Bella, and Celeste Schenck, eds. 1988. *Life/Lines: Theorizing Women's Autobiography*. Ithaca and London: Cornell University Press.

Brumble, H. David. 1988. *American Indian Autobiography*. Berkeley: University of California Press.

Buss, Helen M. 1989. "'The Dear Domestic Circle': Frameworks of the Literary Study of Women's Personal Narratives in Archival Collections." *Studies in Canadian Fiction* 1-17.

Canfield, Gae Whitney. 1983. *Sarah Winnemucca of the Northern Paiutes*. Norman: University of Oklahoma Press.

Carr, Helen. 1988. "In Other Words: Native American Women's Autobiography." In *Life/Lines,* edited by Bella Brodzki and Celeste Schenck, 131-153. Ithaca and London: Cornell University Press.

Cott, Nancy. *The Bonds of Womanhood: 'Women's Sphere' in New England, 1780-1835*. New Haven: Yale University Press.

De Quille, Dan (William Wright). 1947 [1876]. *The Big Bonanza*. New York: Knopf.

DuBois, Carol, and Vicki L. Ruiz, eds. 1990. *Unequal Sisters: A Multicultural Reader in U.S. Women's History*. New York and London: Routledge.

Faragher, John Mack. 1979. *Women and Men on the Overland Trail*. New Haven and London: Yale University Press.

Fischer, Christiane, ed. 1977. *Let Them Speak for Themselves: Women in the American West*. Hamden, Conn.: Shoestring Press.

Fowler, Catherine S. 1978. "Sarah Winnemucca, Northern Paiute, 1844-1891." In *American Indian Intellectuals,* edited by Margot Liberty, 33-42. St. Paul: West Publishing.

Gehm, Katherine. 1975. *Sarah Winnemucca: Most Extraordinary Woman of the Paiute Nation*. Phoenix: O'Sullivan.

Green, Rayna. 1975. "The Pocahontas Perplex: The Image of Indian Women in American Culture." *The Massachusetts Review,* Autumn 16:698-714.

———. 1980. "Native American Women." *Signs,* Winter 6:248-267.

———. 1983. *Native American Women: A Contextual Bibliography*. Bloomington: Indiana University Press.

Hampsten, Elizabeth. 1982. *Read This Only to Yourself: The Private Writings of Midwestern Women, 1880-1910*. Bloomington: Indiana University Press.

Herzog, Kristin. 1985. "Feeling Man and Thinking Woman: Gender in Silko's *Ceremony*." *MELUS,* Spring 12:1:25-36.

Hewitt, Nancy A. 1990. "Beyond the Search for Sisterhood: American Women's History in the 1980s." In *Unequal Sisters,* edited by Carol DuBois and Vicki L. Ruiz, 1-14. New York and London: Routledge.

Hoffmann, Leonore, and Margo Culley, eds. 1985. *Women's Personal Narratives: Essays in Criticism and Pedagogy*. New York: Modern Language Association.

Hopkins, Sarah Winnemucca. 1969 [1883]. *Life among the Piutes: Their Wrongs and Claims*. Edited by Mrs. Horace Mann. Bishop, Calif.: Sierra Media.

Jeffrey, Julie Roy. 1979. *Frontier Women: The Trans-Mississippi West 1840-1880*. New York: Hill and Wang.

Jensen, Joan, and Darlis A. Miller. 1980. "The Gentle Tamers Revisited: New Approaches to the History of Women in the American West." *Pacific Historical Review* 49:2:173-212.

Kolodny, Annette. 1984. *The Land Before Her: Fantasy and Experience of the American Frontiers, 1630-1860*. Chapel Hill and London: University of North Carolina Press.

Krupat, Arnold. 1985. *For Those Who Come After: A Study of Native American Autobiography*. Berkeley: University of California Press.

———. 1989. *The Voice in the Margin: Native American Literature and the Canon*. Berkeley: University of California Press.

Liberty, Margot. 1982. "Hell Came with Horses: Plains Indian Women in the Equestrian Era." *Montana, The Magazine of Western History,* Summer 32:10-19.

Luchetti, Cathy, in collaboration with Carol Olwell. 1982. *Women of the West.* St. George, Ut.: Antelope Island Press.

Mann, Mary Tyler, and Elizabeth Palmer Peabody. 1870. *Moral Culture of Infancy and Kindergarten Guide.* New York: Schenterhorn.

Mathes, Valerie Sherer. 1980. "American Indian Women and the Catholic Church." *North Dakota History,* Fall 20-25.

———. 1990. *Helen Hunt Jackson and Her Indian Reform Legacy.* Austin: University of Texas Press.

Mourning Dove (Hum-ishu-ma). 1929. *Co-ge-we-a, The Half-Blood: A Depiction of the Great Montana Cattle Range,* as told to Sho-pow-tan. Boston: Four Seas.

Moynihan, Ruth B., Susan Armitage, and Christiane Fischer Dichamp, eds. 1990. *So Much to Be Done: Women Settlers on the Mining and Ranching Frontier.* Lincoln and London: University of Nebraska Press.

Myres, Sandra L. 1982. *Westering Women and the Frontier Experience, 1800-1915.* Albuquerque: University of New Mexico Press.

Norwood, Vera, and Janice Monk, eds. 1987. *The Desert Is No Lady: Southwestern Landscapes in Women's Writing and Art.* New Haven and London: Yale University Press.

Peabody, Elizabeth Palmer. 1874. *Record of Mr. Alcott's School, Exemplifying the Principles and Methods of Moral Culture.* 3d ed. Boston: Roberts Brothers.

Personal Narratives Group, ed. 1989. *Interpreting Women's Lives: Feminist Theory and Personal Narratives.* Bloomington: Indiana University Press.

Peyer, Bernd C. 1981. "Autobiographical Works Written by Native Americans." *Amerikastudien/American Studies* 26:3/4:386-402.

———. 1981. "The Importance of Native American Authors." *American Indian Culture and Research Journal* 5:3:1-12.

Powers, Marla. 1986. *Oglala Women: Myth, Ritual, and Reality.* Chicago: University of Chicago Press.

Riley, Glenda. 1984. *Women and Indians on the Frontier, 1825-1915.* Albuquerque: University of New Mexico Press.

———. 1985. "Women on the Great Plains: Recent Developments in Research." *Great Plains Quarterly* 5:2:81-92.

———. 1988. *The Female Frontier: A Comparative View of Women on the Prairie and Plains.* Lawrence: University Press of Kansas.

Ronda, Bruce A., ed. 1984. *Letters of Elizabeth Palmer Peabody: American Renaissance Woman.* Middletown, Conn.: Wesleyan University Press.

Rubenstein, Roberta. 1987. *Boundaries of the Self: Gender, Culture, Fiction.* Urbana and Chicago: University of Illinois Press.

Ruoff, A. LaVonne Brown. 1982. "Old Traditions and New Forms." In *Studies in American Indian Literature,* edited by Paula Gunn Allen, 147-168. New York: Modern Language Association.

———. 1987. "Western American Indian Writers, 1854-1960." In *A Literary History of the American West,* edited by The Western Literature Association, 1038-1057. Fort Worth: Texas Christian University Press.

———. 1990. "Nineteenth-Century American Indian Autobiographers: William Apes, George Copway, and Sarah Winnemucca." In *Redefining American Literary History,* edited by A. LaVonne Ruoff and Jerry Ward. New York: Modern Language Association.

Ryan, Mary. 1990. *Women in Public: Between Banners and Ballots, 1825-1880.* Baltimore: Johns Hopkins Press.

Sands, Kathleen Mullen. 1982. "American Indian Autobiography," in *Studies in American Indian Literature,* edited by Paula Gunn Allen, 55-65. New York: Modern Language Association.

Schlissel, Lillian. 1982. *Women's Diaries of the Westward Journey.* New York: Schocken Books.

Schlissel, Lillian, Vicki L. Ruiz, and Janice Monk, eds. 1988. *Western Women: Their Land, Their Lives.* Albuquerque: University of New Mexico Press.

Slotkin, Richard. 1973. *Regeneration through Violence: The Mythology of the American Frontier, 1600-1860.* Middletown, Conn.: Wesleyan University Press.

Smith-Rosenberg, Carroll. 1975. "The Female World of Love and Ritual: Relations between Women in Nineteenth-Century America." *Signs,* Autumn 1:1-29.

Stoller, Marianne L. 1987. "Peregrinas with Many Visions: Hispanic Women Artists of New Mexico, Southern Colorado, and Texas." In *The Desert Is No Lady,* edited by Vera Norwood and Janice Monk, 125-145. New Haven and London: Yale University Press.

Theisz, R. D. 1981. "The Critical Collaboration: Introductions as a Gateway to the Study of Native American Bi-Autobiography." *American Culture and Research Journal* 5:1:65-80.

Williams, Walter L. 1986. *The Spirit and the Flesh: Sexual Diversity in American Indian Culture*. Boston: Beacon Press.

AUTOBIOGRAPHICAL WORKS DURING THE TURN OF THE CENTURY

H. David Brumble III (essay date 1985)

SOURCE: "Albert Hensley's Two Autobiographies," in *American Quarterly*, Johns Hopkins University Press, Vol. 37, No. 5, Winter, 1985, pp. 702-18.

[*In the essay that follows, Brumble disputes the common conception of Native American autobiographies as "transparent" rather than consciously literary, and claims that works such as those by Albert Hensley, a, member of the Winnebago tribe, reflect a deliberate narrative coherence.*]

Peyote, The Divine Cactus, The Vision Sender, Came to the Wisconsin Winnebago in the last decade of the nineteenth century, years that were especially difficult for that Indian tribe. Most Americans were still convinced that America was the great melting pot, and so believed as well that it was the manifest duty of Indians to melt as soon as possible. The official expression of this sentiment was the Dawes Act of 1887, which aimed to break up the tribes and tribal predilections by dividing up the reservations into individual allotments for individual Indians. Like the Indians of many other tribes, the Winnebagos were divided in their response to these pressures to abandon the old ways, to melt—to become "civilized." Some remained adamant in their belief that their Winnebago traditions ought to be maintained, that their children ought still to be initiated into the old ceremonies, and that they ought still to fast for visions. Sam Blowsnake, for example, tells us in his autobiography, *Crashing Thunder,*[1] that his father encouraged him in these years not only to seek a vision, but to go on the warpath as well. And so he and some other Winnebago young men went to a neighboring village and killed an unfortunate Potawatomi, who was laboring there as a blacksmith. But times had changed. These young men could not tell of their deeds about the campfire—not for fear of avenging Potawatomis, not even for fear of the cavalry, but for fear of the *police*. Eventually Blowsnake and his fellow warriors would be brought to trial for murder.

Other Winnebagos were convinced that it was not only expedient but right to melt into the larger American society. Still others managed to live in both worlds, to

respect the old ways and yet to farm their land, as the Bureau of Indian Affairs encouraged them to do—a first step on the road to civilization. An alarming number of Winnebagos were choosing alcohol.

Then came peyote. Ancient of use in Mexico, but new to the northern plains, peyote made sharper the divisions, more bitter the conflicts among the Winnebago. The traditionalists were appalled by this new religion with its antitribal, pan-Indian tendencies, its elaborate Indian-Christian rituals, and its scorn for the old ways. But for the converts, these were exciting times. They felt that they were surely seeing dream eagles larger and more colorful than any Winnebago had ever been able to call forth by mere fasting. The promise of their religion and their church was as yet undiminished. And, undoubtedly, the antipathy of the traditional Winnebago helped to unify the Peyotists and to make clear the difference between the two groups.

One of the most important figures among the Winnebago Peyotists during these years was Albert Hensley. He is best known for having introduced the Bible and other Christian elements into the Winnebago peyote ritual.[2] Interestingly enough, Hensley left not one but two autobiographies. Both narratives are engaging for what they tell us about Winnebago history and Peyote Cult history; both are also useful to set beside the remarkable number of autobiographical narratives by other Winnebago Peyotists.[3] But Hensley's two narratives are especially important in that they typify two distinct stages in the history of American Indian autobiography.

Nearly everyone who writes about American Indian autobiography mentions at some point that autobiography was not a genre indigenous to Indian cultures.[4] Hensley's two autobiographies, however, show how deeply and how early—in terms of the Indians' adoption of Anglo-American ways—autobiographical forms entered into Indian cultures. Not only could Hensley make use of autobiography for his own rhetorical and hortatory purposes, as we shall see; he could even choose between two quite separate autobiographical traditions. These two forms, furthermore, were available to him and to other Winnebagos as a part of their oral culture! Taken together, then, these two narratives make our understanding of Hensley—and of the history of American Indian autobiography—more problematic.

The first narrative was elicited by anthropologist Paul Radin in 1908, who then published it in his chapter on the Peyote Cult in *The Winnebago Tribe.*[5] The second was written by Hensley himself in 1916, in a letter to Miss Millie V. Gaither, the superintendent of the Carlisle (Pennsylvania) Indian school which Hensley had attended and where his daughters were then boarding.[6] One of Gaither's letters explains how Hensley came to write his autobiography:

Last September Albert Hensley and Levi StCyr of Thurston, Nebraska, both former students of Carlisle, placed their little girls in this school. They took the children home for the holidays and brought them back after Christmas. Mr. Hensley brought his sister's two little girls with his children[7] on their return, and while in Sioux City had all their photographs taken with himself.

He is such a splendid man. I wrote asking him if I might send the photograph to the "Arrow." In his reply, he wrote a story of his life. I enclose it thinking you might get extracts from it for the "Arrow." Am sorry not to have a picture of Mr. StCyr and his children also.

Yours very truly,
Millie V. Gaither
Superintendent

Both narratives are printed below. Except for some regularization of Hensley's punctuation in the 1916 narrative, nothing has been altered.

1908

I am 37 years old. It was 37 years ago that my mother gave birth to me in an old-fashioned reed lodge. When I was a year old she died and my grandmother took care of me. I had come into the world a healthy child, but bad luck was apparently to pursue me, for when I was 7 years old my grandmother died. Then my father took care of me. At that time he began to be a bad man; he was a drunkard and a horse thief. He would frequently get into trouble and run away, always taking me along with him, however. On one occasion we fled to Wisconsin, and there we stayed two years. We got along pretty well, and there my father married again. By his second wife he had three children.

After a while he got into trouble again, and misfortune followed misfortune. People were killing each other, and I was left alone. If at any time of my life I was in trouble it was then. I was never happy. Once I did not have anything to eat for four days. We had fled to the wilderness, and it was raining continually. The country was flooded with high water, and we sat on top of a tree. It was impossible to sleep, for if we went to sleep we would fall off into the water, which was very deep. The shore was quite far away. As we were prominent people, we soon heard that my father had been freed. We were very happy, and went back to our people.

At that time a young man named Young-Bear was starting for Nebraska, and he said that he would take me along. I was very happy. So in that manner I was brought into this country. Here I have had only happy days. When my father got married everyone disliked me. When I worked I was working for my father, and all the money I earned I had to give to him.

After a while I went to school, and although I liked it I ran away and then went to school at Carlisle. I wanted to lead a good life. At school I knew that they would take care of me and love me. I was very shy and lacked a strong character at that time. If a person told me to do anything I would always obey immediately. Everybody loved me. I stayed there six months. I was also taught Christianity there. When I came back to my country the Episcopalian people told me that they wanted me to be diligent in religious matters and never to forsake the religion of the Son of God. I also desired to do that. I entered the church that we had in our country and I stayed with them six years.

At that time the Winnebago with whom I associated were heavy drinkers, and after a while they induced me to drink also. I became as wicked as they. I learned how to gamble and I worked for the devil all that time. I even taught the Winnebago how to be bad.

After a while they began eating peyote, and as I was in the habit of doing everything I saw, I thought I would do it, too. I asked them whether I could join, and they permitted me. At that time I had a position at the county commissioner's office. I ate the peyote and liked it very much. Then the authorities tried to stop the Indians from eating peyote, and I was supposed to see that the law was enforced. I continued eating peyote and enjoying it. All the evil that was in me I forgot. From that time to the present my actions have been quite different from what they used to be. I am only working for what is good; not that I mean to say that I am good.

After that I married and now I have three children, and it would not have been right for me to continue in my wickedness. I resolved that thereafter I would behave as a grown-up man ought to behave. I resolved never to be idle again and to work so that I could supply my wife and children with food and necessities, that I would be ready to help them whenever they were in need. Here in my own country would I remain till I died. This (peyote) religion was good. All the evil is gone and hereafter I will choose my path carefully.

. . . . .

1916

Thurston, Nebr.
Febr. 22nd, 1916

Miss M. V. Gaither
Springfield, S.D.

Dear Miss Gaither:

I received your letter and I was very glad to hear from you and the girls. We are all well here at home.

I have no objection if you wanted to put our picture in the "Arrow," and I will give you the brief history of my miserable life.

My mother died while I was yet a baby, so my grandmother (my father's mother) raise me on gravy, and she also died when I was five years old. Then I was kicked here and there in different families, and when I was seven years old my father took me and made me work for him, what little I could do, til I was Sixteen. The Alloting Agent, Miss Alice Fletcher[8] came, year 1887, and she saw me twice, and both time she said to me, I ought to be in school. We talked through an interpreter, and I told her, I have tried to go to school. Even at Agency School, my father would not let me, and I told her, if she can obtain permission from my father, I would go any where to school, but she fail, and I supposed she was very sorry for me, and next time I saw her, she asked me if I was still in notion to go to school, and I told her I was, and [she] asked me if I would run away from my father, if she get me the ticket to Carlisle. Pa? And I told her I would, so she arrange certain night and certain place to meet, so we carried out, and I was taken to Bancroft, Nebr., Thirty-two miles from the Winnebago Ag'cy.

I started to ran away from my father, Dec. 18th, 1888, and I got to Carlisle on Dec. 22nd, 1888, and in April 24th, 1889, I went out in the country,[9] Rushville, Bucks Co., Pa., and I happened to struck a very mean man to work for, but I stayed there for two seasons getting only ten dollars a month, but I worked just as hard as though I was getting $40.00 a month.[10]

And went back to Carlisle Sept. 12th, 1980. And I was out again April 14th, 1892, at Bryn Mawr, Montgomery Co., Pa. At last I worked for very kind man, and he gave me $35.00 a month,[11] and I only worked there for five month and went back to Carlisle Sept. 12th, 1892, and I stayed til I was send back to Nebraska to die. They thought I was consumped. I left Carlisle June 15th, 1895. I never graduate, although I was in the senior class for three month. And I learn to be steam-plumber, including carpentering and blacksmithing. When I came back to Winnebago Agency, I was well in side of two month, and I was offered the position of chief of police, and beside I was promise a better place later on and gladly accepted it. And about two months late[r] I was promoted to the Agency blacksmith, and three years late[r] I was promoted again as an Agency Interpreter, and again eighteen month later I was given a better place. I worked with John K. Rankin, an Allotting Agent.

I worked with him three years, and then I was elected as a county commissioner in our county (Thurston Co., Nebr.), and I serve one term and refuse the

Second Term, and in mean time I got married to Martha Henry. She never have any schooling, because her parents were oppose of schooling. There were five girls and two boys that they never went to a day to school, but she was a good worker.

And then we move on farm of one hundred and Sixty acres, near Thurston, Nebr.

We now got five healthy children and we are always happy and made good living on farm and independent. I will now conclude with best wishes to your future welfare.

I am your friend,
Albert Hensley

The first thing to notice about these narratives is that they do not simply string together episodes; each is *connected,* unified by a single idea of the self. This sharply distinguishes Hensley's little autobiographies from many other early Indian autobiographical narratives. Nonliterate Indians were quite capable of telling stories about their deeds without learning anything about "autobiography" from Anglos—and many such stories have been published. Fine Day (Cree, born circa 1853), for example, has some splendid stories to tell about his battles and his curings.[12] Gregorio (Navajo, born circa 1902) tells about his work as a hand trembler, and about his marriage and his sheepherding.[13] Wolf Chief (Hidatsa, born 1849) tells about his battles with the Crows and about his Sun Dances, and he narrates a blood-curdling story about his eagle trapping.[14] Maxidiwiac speaks movingly of her work as a farmer, of her relation to her work and her plants.[15] But we do not find these Indians telling stories in such a way as to suggest exactly how they came to be just the men or women they were. These Indians tell of deeds done, of hardships endured, of marvels witnessed, of crops harvested, of buffalos killed, and of ceremonies accomplished. They do not relate their tales each to each; their tales are not designed to work together to convey a unified idea of the narrator as an *individual,* separate, distinct, and different from what he or she might have been.

Where the Indian's sense of identity is still largely tribal, there is no autobiography as Rousseau, Henry Adams, and many other modern autobiographers have led us to expect.[16] Rousseau, for example, tells us early in the *Confessions* that he was born in weakly condition, and that his mother died delivering him. We are to infer that suffering was his lot from the very beginning. Patterns emerge; the form takes shape. Henry Adams became the man he was, he tells us, because in him the eighteenth century and the machine age found their intersection:

He and his eighteenth-century, troglodytic Boston were suddenly cut apart—separated forever—in act if not in sentiment, by the opening of the Boston and Albany Railroad; the appearance of the first Cunard steamers in the bay; and the telegraphic messages which carried from Baltimore to Washington the news that Henry Clay and James K. Polk were nominated for the Presidency. This was May, 1844; he was six years old; his new world was ready for use and only fragments of the old met his eyes.[17]

Rousseau is confident that his life might have been otherwise had his mother lived: confident that with different beginnings and different turnings along the way, he might have been a different man. Adams is keenly aware, too, that he would have been a very different man had he been born fifty years earlier. He is the man his education has made him. Adams and Rousseau are typical of modern autobiographers, then, in that they are aware of themselves as individuals, and conscious of the fact that other conditions and experiences might have led to different selves.[18]

On the other hand, an Indian living in the old way had little sense of an individual self apart from the tribe or clan, little sense that he might have been a different self had he been born in a different lodge, or had he, say, spent more time learning about plants and less time hunting. Karl Weintraub, in his history of Western autobiography, tries to account for the same habit of mind among the ancients:

> Ask a Homeric hero who he is, and most likely he will answer: I am Telemachus, the son of Odysseus, the son of Laertes, the son of Autolykus. . . . Individuals were embedded in the social mass of given blood relations. In fundamental ways, often so hard for us who live in a highly differentiated society of individualists and individualities to understand, these early lives are enmeshed in and derive their meaning from basic social and kinship relations.

The hero may stand out, "but only as the representative of his society's values."[19] No other definition of the self is a possibility to be considered. Homer's heroes, for example, may sometimes wonder if the rewards of the soldier's life are worth the expense of blood and fear; they may wonder if they ought to leave the war to return home to hearths and wives—but it would no more occur to them to do what Adams does, to account for just how it was that they came by their particular constellation of values and desires, than it would occur to them to wonder just how it was that their horses were horses and not sheep. And so we find among the ancient Greeks and Romans—and among the traditional Indians—only the accounts of deeds done, the collections of episodes of autobiography. Where no other way of life is imagined as a possibility, it makes no sense to discuss how one's experiences have led exactly to *this* life, *this* self, and

no other. (Where there seem to be exceptions among the Indians, one should beware the hand of the Anglo editor.)

Hensley, with his incomplete Carlisle education, was much more nearly "civilized" than was Fine Day or Wolf Chief, or the Sioux Black Elk who speaks to us from the pages of John Neihardt's *Black Elk Speaks*. On the other hand, Hensley is a good deal less educated, and good deal farther from "civilization" than were other contemporary Indians who wrote their own autobiographies. Although Hensley was twenty-one when he left Carlisle, the school provided no more than what was essentially a grammar-school education along with some training for the trades. Considering the short distance Hensley had traveled along the narrow road between the two cultures, he was able to tell his life story in a remarkably consistent way—indeed, in *two* remarkably consistent ways. The conception of self differs in the two narratives, but each narrative is unified by a consistent conception of the self.

In the 1916 narrative, Hensley is inviting Gaither to understand his life in much the same way Charles Alexander Eastman asks his readers to understand his life in *From the Deep Woods to Civilization,*[20] which was, incidentally, published in the same year. Both Eastman and Hensley see themselves as having progressed, as having climbed the ladder of civilization. Eastman, who climbed several rungs higher than Hensley, would certainly have realized that, in going from the "Deep Woods" of the Santee Sioux to graduation from the Boston University Medical School, he was a living embodiment of Social Darwinist theories of racial-cultural progression. Hensley would not have read Darwin or Spencer—but he had drunk deep of the closely related assumptions that had guided his teachers at the Carlisle Indian School.

Captain Richard Pratt, "the Father of Indian Education," founded Carlisle in 1879. The school was to be the working out of his faith that Indians were equal in potential to whites, but that this potential could only be realized if the Indian purged himself of all within him that was tribal, if he evolved, then, from a lower level of human development to a higher. "Kill the Indian, save the man" was Pratt's motto. And if a man were to be saved, he had to be educated to work in the American way. The Indian must be made ready to progress, to "melt"—the metaphor was current—into American society. Self-help was what was needed; self-help, education and hard work could turn Indians into Americans.[21]

This attitude is inherent in the 1916 narrative. Hensley, by dint of hard work and education, has left behind the squalor of his Indian childhood. His own children are not being raised "on gravy." He has even managed to achieve what the Bureau of Indian Affairs hoped its Indians would accomplish as their first step in their progress, their evolution, toward civilization: he has become a successful farmer. This idea of steady progress through self-help and education unifies the 1916 narrative; this is the idea which here gives unity to Hensley's conception of himself.

There are Indian autobiographies, contemporaneous with Hensley's, that share these assumptions, and others which are unified by this same conception of individual and racial progress. The subtitle, for example, of Joseph Griffis' 1915 autobiography, *Tahan,* is "Out of Savagery into Civilization." In his preface Griffis wrote that he saw himself as having progressed from being a leader of savages to being "the friend of the scientist and the literary critic."[22] Thomas Wildcat Alford is another case in point. In his autobiography, *Civilization* (1936) he sometimes yearns for primitive innocence—but he never really doubts that he was driven by an "inner voice" to seek in modern America a "better way of living than [his] people knew."[23] Hensley is like these Indians in that he is asking us to see him as an individual example of racial progress.

Let us now turn to Hensley's earlier autobiography. Radin worked intensively among the Winnebago in the years between the years 1908 and 1913, the period that the Winnebagos were split down the middle in their attitudes toward the old ways. For the Peyotists the old ways were the ways of darkness; peyote was the light. With the Christianizing of the Peyote Cult among the Winnebago, for which Hensley was largely responsible, the old ways were made to seem even worse. With their Bible and their belief in Christ, the newly baptized Peyotists could now regard the traditionalists as pagans. They could regard their long-haired brothers as the Israelites regarded the Philistines. The Medicine Dance was an abomination and the medicine bundles were pagan fetishes with power only to mislead their followers.

It is not surprising, then, that Radin found his most willing informants among the Peyotists. Having grown up in the old ways, they could tell Radin what he wanted to know about those traditions; being converts to the Peyote Cult, and so convinced of the evil of the old ways, they were not at all hesitant to speak to Radin concerning matters which traditional Winnebagos still regarded as taboo. Hensley was one of the first Winnebagos to serve Radin as an informant; Radin asked him for the story of his life during his first year of fieldwork among the Winnebagos.

The first questions that must be raised by the 1908 narrative concern the language, which differs markedly in sentence structure and "correctness" from that of the 1916 narrative. It is possible that Radin collected the narrative in English—Hensley did serve for a time as Agency interpreter—and then edited it toward standard English. It is even possible that Hensley

wrote the narrative in Winnebago. As Radin explained in his preface to *The Winnebago Tribe:*

> Owing to the fact that the Winnebago have for some time been accustomed to the use of a syllabic alphabet borrowed from the Sauk and the Fox, it was a comparatively easy task to induce them to write down their mythology, and at times, their ceremonies. . . . [24]

Somewhere, Radin's memory is playing him false. He later stated that ninety percent of his texts in the syllabary were written by one man, Sam Blowsnake.[25] (Blowsnake wrote his autobiography, for example, in the syllabary.) Given the mass of material which Radin collected from so many different Winnebago informants, it is unlikely that Hensley's little autobiography is one of the few syllabary texts not written by Blowsnake.

It is much more likely that the narrative, as we have it, is a translation of Hensley's Winnebago. In his preface to *The Winnebago Tribe* Radin wrote that he tried "whenever it was possible . . . to obtain information in Winnebago." Probably, Radin took down Hensley's oral narrative in phonetic script. Then Radin's Winnebago assistant, Oliver Lamere, probably provided a translation. Radin, finally, would have checked Lamere's translation (Radin's Winnebago was, evidently, quite respectable) and polished the English. We know enough about Radin's work as an editor of such texts[26] to know that he was quite capable of working some changes upon the original, but that these changes would likely not be such as to affect the shape or intent of Hensley's narrative.

The way in which this autobiography is unified, then, is almost certainly Hensley's own device. Here too, Hensley conveys a unified conception of himself. Now, however, the unifying principle is not the school and self-help, but rather peyote and the religion of Christian renewal. In fact, the narrative is structured like so many other Christian conversion stories. Early in his life, Hensley was under the influence of wicked people—his father was "a drunkard and a horse thief." And so Hensley himself was weak and inclined to sin: "Although I liked it," he says of his first school, "I ran away." He was "shy and lacked strong character." As weak as he was, though, he "wanted to lead a good life." He was taught Christianity at Carlisle, but weakling that he was, *Winnebago* that he was, sinner that he was, he sank deeper and deeper until he "even taught the Winnebago how to be bad." Then the peyote eaters entered into his life, and so he is able to say, in the present tense now, "I am only working for what is good"; although with Christian-Peyotist humility he is quick to add, "not that I mean to say that I am good."

In the 1908 narrative, then, it is not Carlisle that made Hensley the man he is; indeed, according to this conversion narrative, it was while he was at Carlisle that he was weak and easily led. In the 1916 narrative, it was during the time at Carlisle that he was willing to work hard, even though he was not well paid. According to the later narrative, Carlisle prepared him to make his way in the modern world—and so after Carlisle his life was a steady progress from reservation, to Carlisle, to chief of police, to Agency blacksmith, to Agency interpreter, to assistant to the alloting agent, to county commissioner.

Although Hensley was still an active Peyotist in 1916, there is no mention of sinful ways or even of peyote in the 1916 narrative. On the other hand, in the 1908 narrative Hensley is intending to demonstrate the efficacy of the Christian-Peyote way, and so peyote must be seen to work a transformation, a reformation. Therefore Hensley tells of his sins. And if his sins are to be emphasized, his schooling must minimized. In the 1908 narrative he gives himself just six months at Carlisle! Clearly, Hensley must regard both peyote and Carlisle as transformative—and so in each narrative the one must be minimized in order to allow the other full credit for his conversion.

How can we account for the differences? In the first place, Hensley clearly had a sense of two very different audiences. He wrote his 1916 autobiography for a school superintendent—his daughters' school superintendent, a person not likely to approve of peyote. In 1908, on the other hand, he was speaking with Radin, who was asking him questions not about Carlisle, but about Winnebago ways and about the Peyote Cult. And Radin, as part of his field methodology, was asking questions in such a way as to make his Peyotist informants feel religiously obligated to respond. For example, Jaspar Blowsnake, another important figure in the Winnebago Peyote Cult, wove Radin into "the whole fabric of his life," making Radin "the pre-ordained one who had sensed what was the proper time to come among the Winnebago."[27] Radin elicited information from Sam Blowsnake which it was taboo for traditional Winnebagos to reveal by urging him to tell about the old ways so that future generations would not be misled.[28]

But it is not enough to point to two different audiences, because the differences in the two narratives have to do with more than merely selecting incidents which would please a certain audience. Hensley was actually working self-consciously in two distinct autobiographical traditions: the Peyote Conversion Narrative and the Carlisle Success Story.

The autobiography of Sam Blowsnake provides an excellent example of the Peyote Conversion Narrative. After telling us about his life of sin and seeking, Blowsnake says, finally:

> Before I thought that I knew something but really I knew nothing. It is only now that I have true knowledge. In my former life I was like one deaf and blind. My heart ached when I thought of what I had done. Never again will I do it. This medicine alone is holy, has made me good and rid me of evil.[29]

Hensley, of course, would not have read Blowsnake's autobiography. But *with* Blowsnake he did hear many, many Peyote Conversion/Confession Narratives during peyote meetings. As another Winnebago Peyotist, Oliver Lamere, described these meetings. "If a person eats peyote and does not repent openly, he has a guilty conscience, which leaves him as soom as the repentance has been made." Indeed, "After the peyote had begun to have an appreciable effect . . . the ceremony consists exclusively of a repetition of the ritualistic unit and confessions."[30] The confessional autobiography which Hensley narrated for Radin must, then, be very like similar narratives that he had delivered during peyote meetings, very like the many other confessional narratives he heard there.

Hensley probably had not heard quite so many Carlisle Success Stories, but he must have heard some since they were an important part of the recruiting effort of Carlisle and the other boarding schools—the "away schools," as some Indians poignantly called them. It is easy to imagine the sorts of stories that would be necessary to persuade anxious parents to send their children to such a faraway place as Carlisle. Luther Standing Bear's autobiography, *My People the Sioux,* has a chapter devoted to "Recruiting for Carlisle," detailing the efforts on the Rosebud reservation:

> About this time (1882) Captain Pratt thought that it would be a good idea to send some of the more advanced Indian boys back to the reservation, in order to show the Indians there that they were really learning the white man's ways. By doing this, he hoped to induce more of the Indian children to come to the school.

Back on the Rosebud reservation, young Standing Bear was soon allowed to "work in the blacksmith shop, making stovepipes and elbows, as a demonstration of [his] education acquired in the school." He continues, "We were all very sincere in our desire to show what we learned, in order to interest more of the children to go back to Carlisle School."

But so many of the Rosebud's children had died at schools far from home, and the people of the Rosebud had experienced so little which would incline them to trust white people and their institutions, that parents were fearful of sending their children away.

> To settle the matter it was decided to hold a big council. I was designated to speak. I felt very

important, as many of the leading chiefs were to be present. . . . I told them all about the training we received in the East. . . . And after I had finished talking, my father rose and told of his visit to Carlisle. . . . and what an improvement the children had shown in learning and acquiring the ways of the white people. . . . He then said: ". . . I know this learning of the white man's way is good for my children."[31]

Standing Bear and the other children from Carlisle stopped at other reservations as well. They returned to Carlisle with fifty-two new children for the school. Hensley, who began at Carlisle in 1888, can hardly have missed hearing such speeches.

This analysis, however, still leaves may questions unanswered. The suggestion that Hensley composed his two autobiographies according to two different autobiographical traditions does not explain, for example, why the 1916 narrative is so much more tightly unified than the earlier one. It is difficult to find a single detail in the letter to Gaither which does not work to convey Hensley's conception of himself as a Carlisle Success Story. Even the propriety of the heading, the salutation, and the conventionality of the closing suggests Hensley's mastery of the norms that Pratt had sought to impart to his charges at Carlisle.

In the 1908 narrative, on the other hand, while we recognize the unifying idea, we see as well that there are a number of details which do not seem to fit. In the fourth sentence Hensley says "bad luck was apparently to pursue me." We are prepared, then, for a story about a figure beset by "misfortune after misfortune"—but the story turns out to be about sin and redemption and reformation. Hensley tells us that his father was "a bad man . . . a drunkard and a horse thief," and then suddenly he says, "we were prominent people." The whole episode of the flood is very strange, disoriented. We understand Hensley to mean himself and his father when he says "we sat on top of a tree," but then *they* heard that his father was *freed*. Then Young Bear takes Hensley to Nebraska, where he had "only happy days," and there he became "wicked." He was a peyote eater, and he was responsible for rooting out peyote.

These discontinuities are partly, perhaps largely, a result of the circumstances of the narration. This autobiography was almost certainly delivered orally. In talking with one another we typically leave unspoken much that would have to be made explicit were we to tell our story in writing. And since Hensley's narrative was almost certainly not taken down in shorthand, it could not have been delivered continuously. There would have been pauses, questions, backtracking, starting again. It would have been difficult for even Anthony Trollope to maintain a narrative thread under such conditions.

Still, it is tempting to see in this disjointed telling of a life a disjointed life. Where Hensley tried to force the odds and ends of his life into the unifying mold of the Peyote Conversion Story, we may see a consciousness struggling to conform itself to a new ideal. Hensley was at first a dirt-poor Winnebago, then a Carlisle school boy, then an Episcopalian, and finally a Peyotist. He was also (although he does not mention this in either autobiography) for a time a member of the Society of American Indians, an important, early pan-Indian movement. He attended the first conference of the Society in 1911 and several other conferences as well. Curiously then, Hensley was, during the same years, a Peyotist and a member of an organization whose members were divided in their attitudes toward peyote, but who finally voted, in 1916, to support the Gandy Bill to outlaw peyote.[32]

Hensley remembers his father as "prominent" and as "bad." At one moment he seems to be speaking out of his remembered Winnebago sense of his father. The next moment he seems to be speaking out of his Peyotist/Christian/Carlisle/pan-Indian sense of his father. According to this uneasy constellation of values, his father would be "bad" simply because he was a long-hair, a Winnebago. Hensley's determination to distance himself from such a tribal conception of himself is perhaps most strikingly evident in his attempts (with John Rave) to affiliate their peyote church with a local Prostestant church (whose clergyman rebuffed them).[33]

Again, the conception of himself which Hensley wishes to convey in the 1908 narrative is very like Sam Blowsnake's conception of *him*self as we find it in *Crashing Thunder*. Both Hensley and Blowsnake are convinced that their conversion to peyote has opened a huge gulf between their Peyotist present and their wicked, wandering, Winnebago tribal past. But both autobiographies in fact seem to *us* clearly to have been composed by men with their feet planted in at least two cultures. The watery peyote infusion with which these men were baptized may have washed away their sins; their tribal past seems to have been more nearly indelible.

The 1916 autobiography was written, not oral. Perhaps the leisure for reflection and revision which writing allows is largley responsible for the more controlled idea of himself which this autobiography conveys. But the passage of eight years' time has allowed Hensley to settle into his new way(s) of life. In the 1916 autobiography it appears that Hensley has managed to conform his conception of himself to a nontribal ideal. If the 1908 autobiography seems to us to be richer, more alive, we may be sensing some of what Hensley struggled to give up over the long course of his "melting."

Two autobiographies, two conceptions of self, each tailored for a particular audience and occasion—all this Hensley manages within the spacious boundaries of the Winnebago oral traditions of these years. In order to tell the first life story and write the second, then, Hensley need not have read a single autobiography. Hensley's narratives, then, offer a nice indication of just how early (in terms of the movement from traditional ways to modern American ways) Indians could make use of autobiography for their own purposes. Yet these two narratives bear upon other issues as well. They may serve as a gentle warning to those who persist in regarding Indian literature—and particularly Indian autobiographies—as transparent. It has long been a cliche of literary analysis of Euro-American texts that circumstances of composition are important considerations. But this still seems to be at issue for some who study American Indian literature. Some, like William F. Smith,[34] write as though the editors of Indian autobiographies played no role at all. Smith compares the structure of S.M. Barrett's *Geronimo*[35] and Kinney Griffith's *The First Hundred Years of Nino Cochise*[36] for example, without even mentioning that both are as-told-to autobiographies. In spite of what he might have learned from Sally McClusky[37] about Neihardt's contributions to *Black Elk Speaks,* Smith still writes as though the "structure" of the book were all Black Elk's own. And Jeffrey Hanson, in his introduction to the very welcome reprint of *Waheenee: An Indian Girl's Story, told by Herself to Gilbert L. Wilson,*[38] has not a word to say about the composition of the book, and so does nothing to correct the erroneous impression left by the subtitle.

Vina Deloria's response to the recent *Black Elk Speaks* scholarship is that it does not matter "if we are talking with Black Elk or John Neihardt." It is easy to understand Deloria's concern; he is speaking as a believer, as one for whom Black Elk's words "now bid fair to become the canon or at least the theological core of a North American Indian theological canon."[39] To detail Neihardt's contribution to *Black Elk Speaks* might seem to diminish what is Indian in the book. It is more difficult to understand why a non-Indian scholar like Karl Kroeber should put himself on record as agreeing with Deloria that distinctions between Neihardt and Black Elk do not matter.[40]

In fact, recent scholarship is making it very clear indeed that such distinctions do matter: Arnold Krupat on *Geronimo*, Gretchen Bataille and Kay Sands on *Papago Women*, Krupat and Brumble on *Crashing Thunder,* Michael Castro and Clyde Holler on *Black Elk Speaks,* and especially Raymond de Mallie's meticulous edition of, and commentary upon, the Neihardt-Black Elk manuscripts.[41] It is becoming increasing evident that may of the Indian autobiographies can best be understood as *bi*-cultural narratives, as texts wherein the assumptions of Indian autobiographer *and* Anglo editor are at work. Far from being diminished by such considerations, the Indian autobiographers are emerging as more complex, more human, and even larger than their editors' conception.

The two Hensley autobiographies will help to make the same point, that American Indian autobiographies can not be counted upon to be transparent, that to study an Indian's autobiography is not the same as studying his life. Hensley shows us that an Indian who has begun to conceive of an individual—as opposed to a tribal—self at all may be quite capable of conceiving of more than one self, and of suiting the autobiographical self and so the whole pattern of his life to a particular audience and occasion. Hensley has left a record of just two of the ways in which he imagined himself; but he must have imagined himself in other ways as well. And we must guess that this man had a lively, perhaps a painful, awareness of yet other selves that might have been.

Notes

[1] Paul Radin, ed., *Crashing Thunder,* Native American Autobiography Series, Vol. 1 (1926: Lincoln: Univ. of Nebraska Press, 1983).

[2] See Weston La Barre, *The Peyote Cult* (New York: Schocken, 1971), 73-74. La Barre's is still the best history of the Peyote Cult. See also Hazel W. Hertzberg, *The Search for an American Indian Identity: Modern Pan-Indian Movements* (Syracuse: Syracuse Univ. Press, 1981), 274. See also fellow-peyotist Oliver Lamere's remembrances of Hensley in Paul Radin, *The Winnebago Tribe* (1923; rpt. Lincoln: Univ. of Nebraska Press, 1970), 347.

[3] Sam Blowsnake's autobiography was edited by Paul Radin, *The Autobiography of a Winnebago Indian* (1920; rpt. New York: Dover, 1963). (Radin later expanded this narrative by adding material elicited from Blowsnake at other times, resulting in *Crashing Thunder.*) For Jasper Blowsnake's autobiography, see Radin, "Personal Reminiscences of a Winnebago Indian," *Journal of American Folklore,* 26 (1913), 293-318. For Mountain Wolf Woman's autobiography, see Nancy O. Lurie, *Mountain Wolf Woman, Sister of Crashing Thunder: The Autobiography of a Winnebago Indian* (Ann Arbor: Univ. of Michigan Press, 1961). For John Rave's autobiography, see Radin, *The Winnebago Tribe,* 341-46.

[4] See, e.g., Arnold Krupat, "The Indian Autobiography: Origins, Type, and Function," in Brian Swann, ed., *Smoothing the Ground: Essays on Native American Oral Literature* (Berkeley: Univ. of California Press, 1983), 261; H. David Brumble III, *An Annotated Bibliography of American Indian and Eskimo Autobiographies* (Lincoln: Univ. of Nebraska Press, 1981), 1-2; Lynne Woods O'Brien, *Plains Indian Autobiography* (Boise, Idaho: Boise State College Western Writers Series, 1973), 5; Clyde Kluckhorn, "The Personal Document in Anthropological Science," in Louis Gottschalk, et al., *The Use of Personal Docu-*

ments in History, Anthropology and Sociology, Social Science Research Bulletin, no. 53, 77-123.

[5] Radin, *The Winnebago Tribe,* 349-50; this is reprinted below with the kind permission of the Univ. of Nebraska Press.

[6] I would like to thank Mr. Robert Kvasnicka, of the General Services Administration, National Archives and Records Service, in Washington, D.C., for locating these Hensley documents and making them available to me. The originals may be consulted in the National Archives, as Records of the Bureau of Indian Affairs, RG 75, Carlisle Indian School Records, 2144. I am indepted to Hertzberg, *American Indian Indentity,* 340, for bringing the Hensley letter to my attention.

[7] Hensley's daughter's names were Agnes and Esther Hensley; the nieces were Alice and Margaret Irwin (Carlisle Indian School Records, 2144).

[8] Fletcher was also an anthropologist.

[9] This is a reference to the Carlisle Outing System. Captain Richard Pratt, the founder of Carlisle, had as his goal the quick assimilation of his Indian charges into American society. Individual students, then, were sent to live with approved families in nearby communities, where they worked and attended school. They were visited periodically by the Carlisle Outing Agent. See Hertzberg, *American Indian Identity,* 16.

[10] Hensley worked for E.V. Barr of Gladwyne, Montgomery Co., Pa., from April to September, 1891 (Carlisle Indian School Records, 2144).

[11] Hensley worked for A. Kruesen of Newton, Montgomery Co., Pa., from March to September 1894 (ibid.).

[12] For autobiographical narratives by Fine Day, see David G. Mandelbaum, *The Plains Cree, Anthropological Papers of the American Museum of Natural History,* 37 (1940), especially 198, 224-26, 253, 256, 278, 301-06, 313-16. See also Adolph Hungry Wolf, *My Cree People* (Invermere, B.C.: Good Medicine Books, 1973). This book is a collection of Fine Day's stories, culled from Mandelbaum's field notes, some of which appeared in *The Plains Cree,* See Brumble, *Annotated Bibliography,* no. 175.

[13] See *Gregorio, the Hand-Trembler, Papers of the Peabody Museum of American Archeology and Ethnology,* 40, no. 1 (1949).

[14] For autobiographical narratives by Wolf Chief, see Robert H. Lowie, "Sun Dance of the Shoshoni, Ute, and Hidatsa," *Anthropological Papers of the American Museum of Natural History,* 16, pt. 5 (1919), 421-27; Gilbert L. Wilson, *Hidatsa Horse and Dog Culture,* *Anthropological Papers of the American Museum of Natural History,* 15, no. 2 (1924), 125-311; idem, *Hidatsa Eagle Trapping, Anthropological Papers of the American Museum of Natural History,* 30, no. 4 (1928), 99-245, passim.

[15] Gilbert L. Wilson, *Agriculture of the Hidatsa Culture: An Indian Interpretation, University of Minnesota Studies in the Social Sciences,* no. 9 (1917).

[16] My sense of the characteristics of modern autobiography is largely derived from Karl Weintraub, *The Value of the Individual: Self and Circumstance in Autobiography* (Chicago: Univ. of Chicago Press, 1978).

[17] Adams, *The Education of Henry Adams* (1918; rpt. Boston: Houghton Mifflin, 1961), 3.

[18] See Weintraub, *The Value of the Individual,* passim.

[19] Ibid., 2-4. For one of many anthropologists who make essentially the same point, see Kluckhohn, "The Personal Document," 119. Carter Revard, "History, Myth, and Identity among Osages and Other Peoples," *Denver Quarterly,* 14 (1980), 84-87, makes this distinction, too, in the course of his insightful comparison of Geronimo's autobiography (*Geronimo's Story of His Life,* ed. S.M. Barrett [New York: Duffield, 1906]) and the autobiography of a younger "civilized" Apache, Jason Betzinez (*I fought with Geronimo,* ed. W.S. Nye [Harrisburg, Pa.: Stackpole, 1969]).

[20] Eastman, *From the Deep Woods to Civilization* (1916; rpt. Lincoln: Univ. of Nebraska Press, 1977). This book takes up where Eastman's *Indian Boyhood* (1902; rpt. Boston: Little, Brown, 1922) leaves off. In the second book Eastman is less critical of the reservation Indians and more skeptical of "civilization"—Eastman had been the first doctor in attendance upon those who survived the massacre at Wounded Knee—but it may generally be said that he sees the Indians' problems with whites as springing from the faults of individuals rather than from "civilization" as a whole.

[21] Hertzberg, *American Indian Identity,* 15-19, provides a good introduction to the history and principles of Carlisle.

[22] Griffis, *Tahan* (New York: George H. Doran, 1915). A new edition of this book is being prepared, with a new introduction by Joseph K. Griffis, Jr., for early publication in the Native American Autobiography Series (Lincoln: Univ. of Nebraska Press).

[23] Thomas Wildcat Alford, *Civilization,* ed. Forence Drake (Norman: Univ. of Oklahoma Press, 1936), 77.

[24] Radin, *The Winnebago Tribe,* xv.

25 Radin, *The Culture of the Winnebagos: As Described by Themselves, Indiana University Publications in Anthropology and Linguistics,* Memoir no. 2 (1949), 4.

26 See Arnold Krupat's Introduction and Appendix to the edition of *Crashing Thunder* cited above.

27 As found in Radin, *Crashing Thunder,* x.

28 Radin, *The Autobiography of a Winnebago Indian,* 67.

29 Radin, *Crashing Thunder,* 184. See Brumble, "Sam Blowsnake's Confessions: *Crashing Thunder* and the History of American Indian Autobiography," *Canadian Review of American Studies,* 16 (1985), 271-82.

30 As found in Radin, *The Winnebago Tribe,* 341.

31 Luther Standing Bear, *My People the Sioux* (1928; rpt. Lincoln: Univ. of Nebraska Press, 1975), 161-163.

32 See Hertzberg, *American Indian Identity,* 83, 124-125, 247-48.

33 Ibid., 248.

34 "American Indian Autobiographies," *American Indian Quarterly,* 2 (1975), 237-45.

35 Barrett, *Geronimo* (New York: Duffield and Co., 1906).

36 Griffith, *The First Hundred Years of Nino Cochise* (London: Abelard-Schuman, 1971).

37 "*Black Elk Speaks,* and So Does John Neihardt," *Western American Literature,* 6 (1972), 231-42.

38 Hanson,*Waheenee: An Indian Girl's Story, Told by Herself to Gilbert L. Wilson* (Lincoln: Univ. Of Nebraska Press, 1981).

39 Deloria, in his Introduction to the 1979 edition of *Black Elk Speaks* (Univ. of Nebraska Press, 1979), xiv.

40 Karl Kroeber, "Reasoning Together," in Swann, *Smoothing the Ground,* 348.

41 Arnold Krupat, *For Those Whom Come After: A Study of Native American Autobiography* (Berkeley: Univ. of California Press, 1985): Gretchen Bataille and Kathleen Sands, *American Indian Women: Telling Their Lives* (Lincoln: Univ. of Nebraska Press, 1984), 47-48; Ruth Underhill, *Papago Woman* (New York: Holt, 1979); Krupat, Introduction and Appendix to *Crashing Thunder,* Brumble, "Sam Blowsnake's Confessions": Michael Castro, *Intrepreting the Indian: Twentieth-Century Posts and the Native American* (Albuquerque: Univ. of New Mexico Press, 1983); Clyde Holler, "Lakota Religion and Tragedy; The Theology of *Black Elk Speaks,*" *Journal of the American Academy of Religion,* 52 (1984), 19-45; Raymond De Mallie, *The Sixth Grandfather* (Lincoln: Univ. of Nebraska Press, 1984).

H. David Brumble III (essay date 1988)

SOURCE: "The Preliterate Traditions at Work: White Bull, Two Leggings, and Sarah Winnemucca," in *American Indian Autobiography,* University of California Press, 1988, pp. 48-71.

[*In the following excerpt Brumble considers two contrasting Native American autobiographies—Two Leggings: The Making of a Crow Warrior and Sarah Winnemucca Hopkins' Life among the Piutes—and examines the contexts in which each were composed, edited, and published.*]

Two Leggings

Two Leggings, a River Crow Indian, was born about 1847. He was a warrior, as tender of his reputation as Achilles, as eager as Ajax for honor and booty. Like White Bull, he delighted in war, the hunt, and the stealing of horses. In 1888, just two years before Wounded Knee, he led what was almost certainly the last Crow war party. He was a seeker after visions, and to this end he danced in the Sun Dance lodge, leaning back against the pull of the thongs slowly tearing through the flesh on his chest. To this end he fasted in prairie-dog villages and on mountain tops. And to this end he cut off the tip of a finger with a stone knife. And he cut into his arm the shapes of horses' hooves—the horses he hoped to steal from the Sioux and the Piegan. Not least remarkably, this man has left us an autobiography.

In 1918 William Wildschut, a Dutch-born businessman and amateur ethnologist, moved to Billings, Montana. Wildschut met Two Leggings in the summer of 1919, and soon they were embarked upon the autobiographical project that continued until Two Leggings's death in 1923 ([Peter Nabokov's introduction to *Two Leggings: The Making of a Crow Warrior,* 1967], xiii). Wildschut, then, was one of a number of Indian enthusiasts early in this century who collected memories in order to preserve something of "authentic" Indian life before it vanished utterly from the face of the West. The engine of nostalgia worked always in such books. . . . But in Wildschut these motivations were muted by the demands of science for objectivity, for Wildschut was a scientist, albeit an amateur. (His work was sufficiently careful that the Museum of the American Indian has seen fit to publish two collections of his notes, *Crow Indian Beadwork* [1959] and *Crow Indian Medicine Bundles* [1960].) And the scientists, too, were collecting autobiographical narratives. Franz Boas had taught a generation of anthropologists that collection was more important than theorizing, that the theorizing could wait until the data were in, and the data were fast vanishing along with the "authentic" Indians. He had taught them, too, as one of the corollaries of his cultural relativism, that it was important to discover the Indians' *own* sense of their culture. As Paul Radin wrote in his introduction to Sam Blowsnake's *Autobiography of a Winnebago Indian,* it was necessary to get "the facts in an emotional setting"; autobiography, Radin argued, allows this (2).

Autobiography, then, would not only allow us to recognize the Indians' own view, it would humanize the anthropological facts that were the Boasians' stock in trade.[9] It must have been balm to the soul of such an amateur as Wildschut to read Boas urging that collection of data was more important than the elaboration of theory. And as an amateur, he must have appreciated the concern which was then being expressed that the cold, hard ethnographic facts be humanized. So Wildschut was one of the earliest collectors of ethnographic autobiography. He was transcribing Two Leggings's remembrances before the appearance in 1919 of Goddard's and Wallis's accounts of the Plains Sun Dance, both of which made use of brief personal narratives for illustrative purposes. And Wildschut was well under way before Radin's publication in 1920 of Blowsnake's *Autobiography of a Winnebago Indian,* the book that is generally credited with having ignited the interest in autobiography for ethnographic purposes.

Wildschut edited all that he collected into 480 pages of florid prose. But, alas, he found no publisher. *Two Leggings* languished on the shelf for some forty years, until 1962, when Peter Nabokov engaged himself to reedit the manuscript. To read Nabokov's statement of his method and its rationale—and the before-and-after passages he provides to illustrate his method (213-217)—is to be convinced that he has worked a small miracle with his rewriting, making believable sentences out of Wildschut's fantasy of Indian drawing-room prose. But still, all of this places us at four removes from Two Leggings. Two Leggings spoke through an interpreter; the interpreter's words were transcribed; Wildschut reordered the transcription and embellished the prose; Nabokov rewrote Wildschut. After all this tampering, we certainly cannot hope to identify any of the characteristic features of Crow narrative style. As Nabokov wrote, Wildschut "could not have been aware of the close attention Crows paid to antithesis, parallelism, repetition, hyperbole, soliloquy, rhetorical queries, and symbolic expressions" (213), and so virtually all such sentence-level stylistic features are lost to us. But much as Two Leggings's words have been reworked, we may still recognize in the autobiography the lineaments of some preliterate autobiographical traditions.

Consider, for example, Two Leggings's motivation for collaborating with Wildschut. A hawk, it seems, appeared to Two Leggings in a vision. The hawk was The Bird Above All The Mountains, and it told Two Leggings that he would be known by "people all over the earth" (63). Two Leggings told Wildschut,

> I . . . think he was telling me that one day a white man would be sent to write my life in a book so that people all over the earth would read my story. You are the one to tell about my life and it will soon travel all over the earth. (205-206)

His motivations seem to have been exactly like White Bull's in writing his *Personal Narrative* and in his work with Vestal on his biography. "When our book is published," White Bull said to Vestal, "my name will be remembered and my story read so long as men can read it" (Vestal, 1984 [1934]:255-256). Two Leggings understood his own autobiographical labors in just this way. One of his visions had foretold that his glory would be known all over the world—and, lo, here was Wildschut to take it all down, to make a book of his deeds. Two Leggings must have imagined the book that was to be as the most wondrously extended set of coup tales the Crows had ever known.

Two Leggings, like White Bull, would tell his coup tales in order to establish and confirm who he is, his worth, and his rank in his tribe. Roy Pascal's dictum (1960:182-183) that the making of autobiography recreates the autobiographer achieves new meaning with the coup tales. The work with Wildschut, then, meant that he could recount his coups for all the world to read. We have seen how White Bull adapted the requirement for witnesses to the medium of writing. Two Leggings made sure that, when he talked with Wildschut, his old friend Bull Does Not Fall Down was usually in attendance, "verifying incidents" (xiii).

There are other ways as well in which *Two Leggings* is shaped by the Indian's sense of what it meant to tell autobiographical stories. In the first place, all of Two Leggings's desires were fixed in his heart as he listened to the old men telling their tales of warfare:

> As a boy I spent my evenings listening to the stories of our warriors and medicine men. I wanted to be just as brave and honored, and the following day would train myself that much harder, running and riding and playing war games with my friends. (6)

He is even able to recite the autobiographical tales of others. He recalls Sees The Living Bull's story of his vision quest, because he has purchased Sees The Living Bull's medicine, and so this story has become his own. And he recites the story of a poor orphan who became a great warrior. "I was excited by this story," he says, "and hoped to make a name for myself in the same way" (60). Although we know little about the kinds of questions that Wildschut urged upon Two Leggings, it does at least seem clear that Two Leggings himself was inclined to relate episodes of tribal history along with his own.

Two Leggings is also shaped by traditional autobiographical conventions in the Crow warrior's concern to tell us exclusively about his adult deeds. And since Two Leggings saw himself as a warrior, there was little question about which deeds he would recount. Despite all the questions Wildschut must have asked him about other aspects of his life, there is little in *Two Leggings* that does not have to do with raids, battles, hunting, and the preparations necessary for these pursuits. The little he has to say about his boyhood has all to do with his yearning to become an honored warrior (as we have seen). His wife is mentioned only in passing, his children not at all.

By the same token, Two Leggings refused to tell any stories about events after his last raid:

> Nothing happened after that. We just lived. There were no more war parties, no capturing of horses from the Piegans and the Sioux, no buffalo to hunt. There is nothing more to tell. (197)

Generally, this passage is understood as a poignant statement that "The Crow way of life . . . was over."[10] But if we recall how White Bull had to work his innovations upon the coup tale form before he could tell about his later achievements at all, we must realize that one of the reasons Two Leggings has "nothing more to tell" is that it has not occurred to him, as it had to White Bull, how he might change the familiar form in order to tell the story of his life in a new kind of way, to recount deeds which were not coups. Put baldly, without the form for telling about his postreservation accomplishments, he has difficulty seeing the content. There are no stories to tell about his life after warfare for the same reasons as there are no stories to tell about his life *before* warfare. His conception of his life is limited by the Crow warrior's conventions for telling about lives.

Sarah Winnemucca

Sarah Winnemucca was born probably in 1844.[11] She was, then, just a few years older than Two Leggings and White Bull, but the circumstances of her life were very different. White Bull and Two Leggings grew up with little white interference; they were trained for the hunt; they were trained for war. The victories Two Leggings remembers with such relish were victories over the Crow's traditional enemies; the stories he tells about his exploits (discounting his editors' labors) could have been told nearly word for word by his grandfathers. White Bull's enemies were often dressed in cavalry blue, but his assumptions in fighting these men did not differ in any essential way from those of his grandfathers in their wars with the Crows. White Bull did work some innovations, as we have seen; but—orthography aside—White Bull recounted his deeds in ways that would not have seemed strange to his grandfathers.

The old ways began to crumble earlier among the Paiutes. The Crows and the Sioux had the vast fertility of the Plains and the Rocky Mountain woodlands at their disposal. If an enemy drove them from one valley, they knew of other valleys two hundred miles distant which promised buffalo and water, grass for their horses, and poles for their lodges. The Paiutes were wonderfully adept at winning their sustenance from dry expanses of the Great Basin. They hunted rabbits, dug for roots, gathered pine nuts and seeds, fished, and found insects to eat. Sometimes they hunted the antelope. But they were bound to the few lakes and thin rivers, as desert peoples must be. When the white man came among the Paiutes, he chose for his own use, of course, the banks of those same few rivers and lakes. And so, although her band of the Paiutes had no memory of any white contact before about 1848, white influence on the tribe was immediately and unremittingly disruptive of the old ways. Neither so numerous nor so warlike as the Sioux, the Paiutes, especially those who were led by Winnemucca's grandfather, Captain Truckee, tried to live among the whites by practicing cooperation and, where that failed, appeasement. They took up arms only rarely, and as a desperate last resort.

By the time she reached adulthood, then, Winnemucca had experienced a wide range of what late-nineteenth-century America had to offer. As a young child she had lived with a stone-age, hunter-gatherer people; by the time she was twenty she had made her stage debut, acting in Indian tableaux vivants and interpreting for her father in his attempts to explain the Paiutes to the good burghers of Virginia City. By twenty-four she was a figure of some influence in the Great Basin, serving as the Army's emissary to recalcitrant bands of Paiutes and Bannocks, to win them to the reservations. In 1870, when a letter she had written on the plight of the Paiutes was published by *Harper's Weekly,* she became one of the darlings of the eastern Indian enthusiasts. In 1881 she headed East on a speaking tour, spending most of her time in Boston, where she became the especial friend of Elizabeth Palmer Peabody (the woman who published the works of the Transcendentalists) and her sister, Mrs. Horace Mann. It was Mrs. Mann who edited Winnemucca's autobiography, and Elizabeth Peabody who published it. Winnemucca delivered lectures in the homes of Emerson and John Greenleaf Whittier (Fowler, 1978:38).

When her life is described in this way, we might expect that her autobiography would be like that of the educated Indian autobiographers. In a forthcoming article La Vonne Ruoff, for example, asks us to consider Winnemucca along with two other early, literate Indian autobiographers, William Apes and George Copway.[12] Copway, indeed, was very widely read. Ruoff argues that *Life among the Piutes* should be understood in the light of contemporary literary trends and types, such as the captivity narratives and the slave narratives. She points to a number of features which *Life among the Piutes* has in common with such narratives: some sexual violence, for example, and lots of daring adventures. But probably Ruoff is telling us more about Winnemucca's audience than about what might have influenced Winnemucca in writing her autobiography. I think it is unlikely that Winnemucca herself was familiar with such literature; indeed, aside from the hymns she quotes occasionally, it is unlikely that Winnemucca was much aware of literary influences at all.

In fact, it is not at all clear just how literate Winnemucca was. She was certainly a fluent *speaker* of English, as numerous newspaper accounts of her lectures and interviews attest.[13] She was employed as an interpreter on many occasions. And there is little reason to doubt that she did, herself, write *Life among the Piutes.* But her editor, Mrs. Horace Mann, had this to say in a letter to a friend about Winnemucca's manuscript:

> I wish you could see her manuscript as a matter of curiosity. I don't think the English language ever got such treatment before. I have to recur to her sometimes to know what a word is, as spelling is an unknown quantity to her. . . . She often takes syllables off of words & adds them or rather prefixes them to other words, but the story is heart-breaking, and told with a simplicity & eloquence that cannot be described. (In Canfield, 1983:203)

The book allows us to see some of this for ourselves. As Catherine Fowler has noticed, some of Winnemucca's "pronunciation spellings" slipped past Mann's editorial eye: "Acotrass" for "Alcatraz," "Carochel" for "Churchill," and even "shut off the postles" for "shot off the pistols" (1978:40). Now, this is exactly what we would expect of one who was a fluent speaker, but an infrequent reader—as those of us who read undergraduate writing know to our cost. Winnemucca herself candidly confirms this. She recalls reading a four-line letter: "It took me some time to read it, as I was [at age 24] very poor, indeed, at reading writing; and I assure you, my dear readers, I am not much better now" (82). And what little is known of her education seems to indicate that she had virtually no formal schooling (Canfield, 1983:30-31; Fowler, 1978:35). According to her own account in *Life among the Piutes,* she had just three weeks at a convent school in San Jose before a group of anxious parents convinced the pious sisters that it was unseemly that their white and delightsome daughters be educated in the company of an Indian (70).

One must be careful not to overstate this. Winnemucca could read; and she carried on a remarkable correspondence, some of which, in fact, was published, once in *Harper's,* as we have seen, and more often in local newspapers. And, of course, Canfield and Fowler may just possibly be wrong in their estimation of Winnemucca's education.[14] But given what they tell us, given Mann's letter, and given what Winnemucca herself tells us in *Life among the Piutes,* it does seem that we should not simply *assume* the degree of literacy and the breadth of reading which Ruoff's argument would require of Winnemucca. *Life among the Piutes* probably was not influenced by written captivity or slave narratives.

Winnemucca's autobiography does, on the other hand, seem to owe a good deal to preliterate autobiographical traditions. Consider how different Winnemucca's autobiography is from other early autobiographies by literate Indians. William Apes (1829), George Copway (1847), Charles Alexander Eastman (1902, 1916), and Joseph Griffis (1915) all made the journey Winnemucca made, from the tribal world to the white world. The autobiographies of Apes and Copway have at their center their conversion to Christianity. Eastman and Griffis . . . saw themselves as embodiments of Social Darwinist ideas about the progression of the races. All four of these men wrote autobiography in such a way as to describe an individual self and to account for just how that self came to be. Their autobiographies describe certain clear turning points. Had Eastman not been taken away from the Santee Sioux by his father and sent to school, he would not have become the man he became. Had Apes not found Christianity, he would have remained in a state of sin. In this way, at least, all four are typical modern autobiographers in the Western tradition.

Winnemucca has virtually nothing to say in *Life among the Piutes* about turning points. Her biographer, Canfield, on the other hand, quite reasonably does include a chapter entitled "The Turning Point." The turning points are there for Western eyes to see; Winnemucca saw her life differently.

And she is again unlike modern, Western autobiographers in that she is unconcerned about self-definition. In 1870 a Sacramento reporter sought her out in a Paiute village:

> She said: I am glad to see you, although I have not now a parlor to ask you into except the one made by nature for all. I like this Indian life tolerably well; however, my only object in staying with these people is that I may do them good. I would rather be with my people, but not live as they live. I was not raised so; . . . my happiest life has been spent in Santa Clara while at school and living among the whites. (In Canfield, 1983:65)

The choices here seem to have little to do with the question of self-definition. Winnemuuca enjoys living a comfortable life in the cities; when she can live in a house, she gladly does so. When she must live in a brush nobee, she is not unwilling to do so. She knows how to live in the Paiute way. She stays with her people, however, not because of a fervent love of their ways—she certainly does not stay with them because of her love of the Nevada landscape,[15] say, or roots, or rabbit's flesh. She stays, rather, out of a sense of obligation. Winnemucca did remember some of the Paiute rituals fondly, and she may be exaggerating her altruism a bit. But this passage does seem to suggest that Winnemucca did not see the choice between the Paiute and the white way as having to do with self-definition. Eastman, Griffis, and Luther Standing Bear, on the other hand, were concerned to work out an explicit sense of who they were in relation to the two worlds they knew. Their autobiographies suggest in many that, in moving from prereservation Indian life to the white world, they were passing over a great divide. They speak as from a great distance of the "superstitions" of their people. Eastman and Standing Bear, especially, describe the prereservation Sioux as being simple and "childlike."

Winnemucca does not seem to see any such fundamental difference between her Indian people and the whites. Certainly she is aware of different customs; she is outraged at how dishonest the whites are, and she contrasts this with the honesty of her own people; she realizes that her people have to learn a great deal in order to become self-supporting farmers, but she nowhere suggests that there are *essential* differences. Indeed, the point of her chapter on "Domestic and Social Moralities" would seem to be that the Paiutes are *not* essentially different from whites: they are "taught to love everybody"; their women are *not* allowed to marry "until they have come to womanhood"; and, says Winnemucca, "We have a republic as well as you. The council-tent is our Congress." All of this is a part of the book's argument that the Paiutes ought to be granted land in severalty and full rights of citizenship.

Quite aside from this line of argument, Winnemucca just does not seem to see differences beyond differences in customs. Indian agent Henry Douglas wrote of Winnemucca that "She conforms readily to civilized customs, and will as readily join in an Indian dance" (Canfield, 1983:62). He would probably not have been surprised to find that she has nothing to say in *Life among the Piutes* about her conversion to Christianity; nothing, either, about a moment when she decided that, really, she preferred the white to the Paiute way. She spent time among whites; she spent time among the Paiutes. In reading her book *we* may see implicit in some of her experiences features of a cultural identity crisis, but she seems herself not to have thought about her life in this way.

In many ways she is like White Bull and Two Leggings. Like those two warriors, she seems mainly concerned to set down her *deeds*. And I think she is like them, too, in conceiving of herself as something like the sum total of her deeds. Like White Bull and Two Leggings, she assumes that she may rise in the regard of her tribe by telling her deeds; and like Two Leggings she realizes that the written word may allow her to rise in the regard of a much larger tribe. At one point Winnemucca is explaining the position of women in the tribe:

> [The women] are always interested in what their husbands are doing and thinking about. And they take some part even in the wars. They are always near at hand when fighting is going on, ready to snatch their husbands up and carry them off if wounded or killed. One splendid woman . . . went out on the battle-field after her uncle was killed, and went into the front ranks and cheered the men on. Her uncle's horse was dressed in a splendid robe made of eagles' feathers and she snatched it off and swung it in the face of the enemy . . . ; and she staid and took her uncle's place, as brave as any of the men. (53)

Winnemucca wants to be remembered in this way, as a woman who was brave as any man, as a woman who did great things. She recalls leading a detail of soldiers to rescue her father and his band of Paiutes from the hostile Bannocks, for example. Her relish of this memory is nearly palpable: "we have come with you," she remembers the soldiers saying, "and [we] are at your command. Whatever you say we will follow you" (156). She talks about these soldiers as "my men," her "boys" (155). Later she says,

> This was the hardest work I ever did for the government in all my life . . . having been in the saddle night and day; distance about two hundred and twenty-three miles. Yes, I went for the government when the officers could not get an Indian man or white man to go for love or money. I, only an Indian woman, went and saved my father and his people. (164)

Clearly, she is telling something like a coup tale. And she remembers her father's praise of her before the Paiutes:

> Oh, yes! my child's name is so far beyond yours; none of you can ever come up to hers. Her name is everywhere and everyone praises her. Oh! how thankful I feel that it is my own child who has saved so many lives. . . . Now hereafter we will look on her as our chieftain, for none of us are worthy of being chief but her, and all I can say to you is to send her to the wars and you stay and do women's work, and talk as women do. (193)

Bataille and Sands claim that Winnemucca's autobiography is "heavily biased by her acculturated and Christianized point of view" (1984:21). A good Methodist—and Winnemucca was a Methodist—should recognize vanity in such passages, all vanity. White Bull, I think, would be puzzled by such a response. And Two Leggings? Every sinew of his being yearned to hear just such praise. He would—he did—quite literally kill to hear such words. Winnemucca is trying to establish her standing, trying to establish just how it is that she ought to be regarded, just as did Two Leggings and White Bull. In many ways, *Life among the Piutes* assumes an audience with Paiute habits of mind, not Christian. She is what she has accomplished; like White Bull and Two Leggings—and Achilles—she is the sum of her reputation. And so the maintenance of her reputation is of great importance to Winnemucca.

Like White Bull and Two Leggings, her first education was in a shame culture rather than a guilt culture. It should not surprise us, then, that she is concerned with self-vindication. . . . [W]hen Nathaniel accused Don Talayesva of being a Two-Heart, his defense took the form of a detailed recounting of the events related to the charge and a detailed countercharge, urging that his accuser is himself a Two-Heart. Talayesva makes his case persuasive by bringing into his account details and events that it had never occurred to his accuser to mention. Much of *Life among the Piutes* works according to this pattern.[16] Winnemucca remembers many such scenes in her book. At one point, for example, a Captain Jerome bade them come talk with him, since the Indian agent, Newgent, had accused the Paiutes of killing two white men:

> We went like the wind, never stopping until we got there. The officer met us. I told him everything from the first beginning of the trouble. I told him that the agent sold some powder to an Indian, and that his own men had killed the Indian. I told him how brother and I went to him and asked him and his men to go away, as we had heard that our people were going to kill him. I told him that he talked bad to brother and me, because we went to tell him of it. I told this to the officer right before the agent. The agent did not have anything to say, and then the officer asked my brother what he knew about it. (83)

This is typical of Paiute responses to accusations in the book. Does this seem merely "natural," universally human? I think not—at least not in Winnemucca's view. The whites in her book respond to accusations very differently. For example, the Paiutes had a great deal of trouble with another agent, Rinehart. Once they charged him and his cronies with stealing their government-issue clothing: "You are all wearing the clothes that we fools thought belonged to us." Rinehart's response?

> He turned round . . . and said, "If you don't like the way I do, you can all leave here. I am not going to

> be fooled with by you. I never allow a white man to talk to me like that. (126)

Nearly every Paiute answer to an accusation is "autobiographical" or "historical": "No, no—in fact, I (or we) did this, and then this happened, and then I (or we) did thus, whereupon you did such a thing."[16] The white people in the book, on the other hand, never respond to charges "autobiographically." They reply with dismissals, flat denials, and, especially, with assertions of authority. Another agent, Wilbur, simply refused, repeatedly, to speak with a Paiute delegation at all: "You are talking against me all the time, and if you don't look out I will have you put in irons and in prison" (239). Winnemucca's Paiutes even had an explanation for such behavior. After yet another promise had been broken, Winnemucca recalls,

> My uncle, Captain John, rose and spoke, saying, "My dear people, I have lived many years with white people . . . and I have known a great many of them. I have never known one of them to do what they promised. I think they mean it just at the time, but I tell you they are very forgetful. It seems to me, sometimes, that their memory is not good, and since I have understood them, if they say they will do so and so for me, I would say to them, now or never . . . . They are a weak people." (225)

The weakness has to do with memory. Small wonder, then, that all of Winnemucca's Paiutes use autobiographical-historical self-vindications, while the whites, in their weakness, must rely simply upon authority. In this book it is the Indians who have the memory that history requires. Indeed, Winnemucca's whole book may be seen as an extended self-vindication, as an attempt to defend her own reputation and that of her family and her tribe:

1. The Paiutes would have rescued the Donner party (the famous party that tried to make it over the Donner Pass too late in the season; they ended up eating one another) but they were *afraid* to approach too closely, because the members of this same party had wantonly burned the winter stores of the Paiutes on their way to the Donner Pass. (13)

2. She includes a whole chapter on the moral education of the Paiutes, which seems designed to demonstrate that they are not "savages," contrary to white assertions. (45-57)

3. The Paiutes are not "revengeful." (54)

4. "There is nothing cruel about [the Paiutes]. They never scalped a human being." (54)

5. "The chiefs do not live in idleness." They are poor because they feel it is their responsibility to give to the poor. (54)

6. She responds to a particular charge that "bloodthirsty savages" killed "innocent" white men. (71)

Among many other examples that might be adduced are the letters appended to the book, twenty-seven letters (!) bearing witness to Winnemucca's good character and important work. (Witnesses, it seems, are at least as important to Winnemucca as they are to White Bull and Two Leggings.) Just as part of Talayesva's response to Nathaniel was an attack upon his attacker, so Winnemucca sometimes attacks the whites (and other detractors):

1. The Paiutes were "less barbarous" before they fell under the influence of the whites. (10)

2. "There were very bad men there. Sometimes they would throw ropes over our women, and do fearful things to them." (228)

3. The "citizens" who follow the army are forever urging the extermination of the Paiutes, but when a battle is at hand, they fall to the rear, until the battle is over, whereupon they commence their looting. (177)

Examples could be multiplied; the broken promises alone would require a sizable list. But I would not wish to be misunderstood: I am not claiming that only a Paiute could have conceived of autobiography as a way to answer slander. My point is that we do not have to look to contemporary literary models to explain the form of *Life among the Piutes*. Indians of many tribes were answering their accusers with autobiographical narratives long before the Paiutes came into contact with the white man.

This does leave the question of the book's narrative polish. We may talk about ways in which the conception of self implicit in the book is closer to that which we find in White Bull's *Personal Narrative* than it is to the conception of self that is usual in the autobiographies of literate moderns, but these are differences we must teach ourselves to notice. If I am right about the book, Ruoff is wrong not at all because she is an insensitive reader, but rather because Winnemucca was so good at adapting Paiute oral conventions to the uses of the pen and to the entertainment and persuasion of white audiences. In this, of course, she had a good deal of practice before she ever sat down to write *Life among the Piutes*.

Winnemucca first appeared on stage in 1864, in Virginia City.[17] In that same year she appeared at the Metropolitan Theater in San Francisco. In these early performances she acted in tableaux vivants: "The Indian Camp," "The Camp Fire," "The Message of War," "The War Council," "The War Dance," "The Capture of a Bannock Spy," "Scalping the Prisoner," and others. She also interpreted her father's brief speeches on these occasions. Her father evidently undertook these exercises in Indian stereotyping in order to get money for his people (Canfield, 1983:41). But these experiences put Winnemucca before the public eye, and they must have given her an immediate sense of what she might accomplish with an audience. With her command of English, she soon became an important spokesperson for her people not only in their negotiations with agents and army, then, but also on the lecture platform.

She was evidently an effective lecturer. Even a reporter who doubted her personal morality could write that "she speaks with force and decision, and talks eloquently of her people" (Canfield, 1983:163). Another San Francisco reporter described one of her lectures:

> San Francisco was treated to the most novel entertainment it has ever known, last evening, in the shape of an address by Sarah, daughter of Chief Winnemucca. . . . The Princess wore a short buckskin dress, the skirt bordered with fringe and embroidery. . . . On her head she wore a proud head dress of eagle's feathers. . . . The lecture was unlike anything ever before heard in the civilized world—eloquent, pathetic, tragical at times; at others her quaint anecdotes, sarcasms and wonderful mimicry surprised the audience again and again into bursts of laughter and rounds of applause. *There was no set lecture from written manuscript, but a spontaneous flow of eloquence.* Nature's child spoke in natural, unconstrained language, accompanied by gestures that were scarcely ever surpassed by any actress on the stage. . . . [T]he Indian girl walked upon the stage in an easy, unembarrassed manner, and entered at once upon the story of her race. (In Canfield, 1983:163-164)

Perhaps Secretary of the Interior Carl Schurz bore the most convincing testimony as to her power to move an audience: he did everything he could to keep her from lecturing while she was seeking justice in Washington. He knew that her subjects would have been the evils of "the Indian Ring" and the wrongs of the Paiutes.

Much of *Life among the Piutes: Their Wrongs and Claims* must have had its original in one of her lectures. By the time she came to write it down, she would have delivered her tale, in parts, on many occasions, and she would have had a lively sense of how white audiences had responded to this version of a particular episode, and how they had responded to the other version of the same episode. Again, we need not assume that Winnemucca was at all aware of literary models.

Winnemucca's autobiography is far from White Bull's in some ways. She had learned a good deal about her white audience. She also works self-consciously with analogies in ways White Bull does not. For example, she tells a tale from the mythic history of her people. At one time the Paiutes' neighbors were cannibals.

The Paiutes did everything they could to avoid war even with these "barbrians"; when finally they did rise up and smite these neighbors, they did so out of necessity. The tale serves, then, not only as a refutation of the charge that the Paiutes are "bloodthirsty savages"; it also suggests a neat historical analogue for one of the first groups of whites the Paiutes came to know—the Donner party. Winnemucca's work is "connected" in ways that White Bull's certainly is not. But Winnemucca's book is like White Bull's in that it is essentially an oral performance put down in writing.[18]

In her conception of her self, too, and in her conception of what it means to tell the story of one's life, she was not far from White Bull and Two Leggings. Eastman and Griffis felt a great gulf to open up between themselves and the Indians they had "left behind." They became full-time participants in the modern world, however much they may have yearned with a part of their being for the old life. Sarah Winnemucca, however much she may have preferred the comforts of a California house to the dirt and draft of a Paiute reed shelter, never seems to have felt such a distance between herself and her people. For all her acquaintance with the Transcendentalists, for all her Indian activism, Winnemucca retained an essentially tribal sense of self.

> Like the old men Pretty-shield would not talk at any length of the days when her people were readjusting themselves to the changed conditions brought on by the disappearance of the buffalo, so that her story is largely of her youth and early maturity. "There is nothing to tell, because we did nothing," she insisted when pressed for stories of her middle life. "There were no buffalo. We stayed in one place, and grew lazy." (10)

Notes

[9] For the influence of Boasian assumptions on early as-told-to autobiographies, see Langness and Frank (1981:18-20) and Krupat (1985:54-105).

[10] See, e.g., Nabokov's introduction: xxi; see also O'Brien (1973:20). Other Indians expressed a similar reluctance to tell stories about reservation times. See, e.g., *Plenty-coups* (311) and Linderman's foreword to *Pretty-shield:*

[11] Canfield's (1983) biography of Sarah Winnemucca is essential reading for anyone interested in *Life among the Piutes.* Fowler (1978) is also helpful, especially for her arguments about the authorship and style of the book.

[12] While I do take issue with some of what Ruoff has to say about Winnemucca, her essay is a very helpful introduction to three early autobiographers who have

otherwise received scant attention. Ruoff places Apes in relation to early American pietistic autobiography, and she is able to tell us a great deal about the life of Copway, who seems to have been a more deeply troubled man than his autobiographical writings would suggest.

[13] Canfield (1983:88, 164) includes a good sampling of these.

[14] Canfield and Fowler both warn us that it is difficult to know just how literate Winnemucca was. One newspaper man reported in 1891 that Winnemucca "spent a goodly portion of her meager earnings on books" (Fowler, 1978:58). See also the manuscript letter reproduced in Canfield (1983:66) that is virtually free of errors. But it is not at all difficult to imagine Winnemucca seeking out assistance from friendly whites when she had an important letter to write—just as she had Mann's help in writing her book.

[15] N. Scott Momaday has written so evocatively about landscape and self-definition that he has inspired a good deal of nonsense. Bataille and Sands, for example, go so far as to assert that one of the "basic characteristics" oral Indian literature "shares" with American Indian women's autobiography is the "concern with landscape" (1984:3). In fact, of course, one could easily find many autobiographical narratives by Indian men *and* women and hundreds of transcriptions of oral performances by Indians which do not mention landscape at all.

[16] See, e.g., *Life among the Piutes:* 142, 166, 190-191, 235.

[17] All that follows relating to Winnemucca's stage career comes from Canfield (1983).

[18] She probably had already set some of her stories down in writing, in letters to supporters and in letters written to appeal to various authorities. See, e.g., the passage where Bannock Jack, realizing that Winnemucca "can talk on paper," asks her to write down all that he will tell her about certain injustices that his band has suffered. He then asks her to send it to "our Great Father in Washington" (142-143).

Works Cited

The Autobiographies

Eastman, Charles Alexander. *Indian Boyhood.* Boston: Little, Brown and Co., 1922 [1902].

————. *From the Deep Woods to Civilization: Chapters in the Autobiography of an Indian,* with an introduction by Raymond Wilson. Lincoln: Univ. of Nebraska Press, 1977 [1916].

Griffis, Joseph K. *Tahan: Out of Savagery, into Civilization.* New York: George H. Doran, Co., 1915.

Hopkins, Sarah Winnemucca. Mrs. Horace Mann. *Life among the Piutes: Their Wrongs and Claims.* Bishop, Cal.: Sierra Media, Inc., 1969 [1883].

Two Leggings. [Ed.] Peter Nabokov. *Two Leggings: The Making of a Crow Warrior.* New York: Crowell, 1967. . . .

Bibliography of Other Sources Cited

Bataille, Gretchen, and Kathleen Sands (1984). *American Indian Women: Telling their Lives.* Lincoln: Univ. of Nebraska Press.

Canfield, Gae Whitney (1983). *Sarah Winnemucca of the Northern Paiutes.* Norman: Univ. of Oklahoma.

Fowler, Catherine S. (1978). "Sarah Winnemucca, Northern Paiute, ca. 1844-1891." In Liberty (1978):33-44.

[Krupat, Arnold] (1985). *For Those Who Come After: A Study of American Indian Autobiography.* Berkeley, Los Angeles, London: Univ. of California Press.

[Langness, L. L.], and Gelya Frank (1981). *Lives: An Anthropological Approach to Biography.* Novato, Cal.: Chandler and Sharp.

Liberty, Margot (1978). *American Indian Intellectuals.* St. Paul: West Publishing Co.

O'Brien, Lynn Woods (1973). *Plains Indian Autobiographies.* Boise, Idaho: Western Writers Series, no. 10.

Pascal, Roy (1960). *Design and Truth in Autobiography.* Cambridge: Harvard Univ. Press.

Ruoff, A. LaVonne (1985). "Gerald Vizenor: A Selected Bibliography." *American Indian Quarterly,* 9:75-78.

—— (forthcoming). "Nineteenth-Century American Indian Autobiographers: William Apes, George Copway, and Sarah Winnemucca." In Jerry Ward, ed., *The New American Literary History,* New York: MLA.

Vestal, Stanley (1984 [1934]). *Warpath: The True Story of the Fighting Sioux Told in a Biography of Chief White Bull,* with a foreword by Raymond J. DeMallie. Lincoln: Univ. of Nebraska Press.

Wildschut, William (1959). *Crow Indian Bead Work,* ed. John C. Ewers. New York: Museum of the American Indian, Heye Foundation.

—— (1960). *Crow Indian Medicine Bundles,* ed. John C. Ewers. New York: Museum of the American Indian, Heye Foundation. . . .

Erik Peterson (essay date 1992)

SOURCE: "An Indian, An American," in *Studies in American Indian Literature,* Vol. 4, Nos. 2-3, Summer/Fall, 1992, pp. 145-60.

[*In the essay that follows, Peterson claims that autobiographies such as Charles Eastman's exemplify an attempt to reconcile cultural and political tensions between Native American and white societies, and reflect the conflicting responses of Native Americans to Western expansion.*]

> But after the white people came, elements in this world began to shift; and it became necessary to create new ceremonies. I have made changes in the rituals. The people mistrust this greatly, but only this growth keeps the ceremonies strong.
>
> —Leslie Marmon Silko, *Ceremony*

Four centuries after Columbus stumbled onto the "New World" and mistakenly named its inhabitants, over fifty representatives of the newly formed American Indian Association met on his birthday in Columbus, Ohio. Their purpose was to define their "common ground" as Indians and visibly demonstrate their ability to participate fully in American society (Hertzberg 59-78). At this conference, one of the delegates and founders of the new association, Doctor Charles A. Eastman, illustrated the contradictions the conference and many of its delegates faced. On one hand, Eastman sought to dispel the charge of racial inferiority pervasive in nineteenth century anthropology by appealing to the assimilationist metaphor of the "melting pot" and the Spencerian logic of cultural evolution, both of which assumed the inevitable demise of Indian culture. At the same time, however, he recognized who defined the "pot"—and its homogenizing effect—and challenged his listeners to preserve their Indian identity and redefine the "pot." In the confrontation between Euro-American evolutionary progress and the traditions of his Santee Sioux culture, Eastman sought to bridge their divisions and discover their continuities.[1]

His negotiation between "two worlds," of course, is not unique; his autobiographies and other writings share with many ethnic and immigrant autobiographical narratives a preoccupation with cultural differences and a need to reconcile two (often conflicting) experiences. But, as Michael Fischer has recently suggested, it is precisely because they address these cultural tensions that ethnic autobiographies and fiction "can perhaps serve as key forms for explanations of pluralist, post-industrial, late twentieth century society" (195). I suggest that Eastman's intricate "balancing act" parallels our own contemporary attempts to create narratives and critical postures which embrace a pluralistic world and recognize difference without reifying it.[2] His struggle to heal the divisions in his own life still urgently speaks to our contemporary desire to "delight in difference" yet dissolve the boundaries which bind and divide us.

Nowhere do these divisions run more deeply than in Eastman's second autobiography, *From the Deep Woods to Civilization* (1916). When his autobiography came out, most reviewers gave it positive reviews. The reviewer in *The New York Times* wrote that Eastman "never failed to see the wise judgement of his old father's choice of civilized ways" (570), while in *The North American Review* the reviewer declared that Eastman's book was "a record of one who honestly sought to appropriate white man's civilization as the highest good" (949). This last reviewer also celebrated Eastman as an example of an Indian who "in less than half a lifetime . . . [had] traversed the whole path from savagery to civilization" (949).

More recently, scholars have criticized, rather than praised, Eastman's intellectual debt to Social Darwinism and embrace of civilization. H. David Brumble III devotes an entire chapter to Eastman in his study, *American Indian Autobiography,* but dismisses Eastman's first autobiography, *Indian Boyhood* (1902), as simply another example of Spencerian thinking. He gives only the faintest hint that Eastman's position might become more problematic in *From the Deep Woods to Civilization.* Similarly, Marion Copeland argues that Eastman's "role as an apologist superseded his conviction that the Sioux had a viable perspective . . . [and] he fell into the role of functionary to one faction after another whose primary concern was to control and convert the Indian" (8).

Both Eastman's early reviewers and his more recent critics assume his full assimilation and embrace of a dominant Euro-American sensibility even if they disagree on whether to praise or criticize it; in effect, they assume that after leaving his tribe Eastman became somehow less "Indian."

Certainly, as Brumble has argued so convincingly, as a highly educated and Christianized Sioux, Eastman was deeply influenced by the evolutionary racialism of his day (149). But "straight line" interpretations of Eastman's assimilation implicitly assume two mutually exclusive worlds—Anglo or Indian—whose division, like the river Styx, can be crossed in only one direction (113).[3] They define borders but not borderlands. "Borders," Gloria Anzaldua writes, "are set up to define the places that are safe and unsafe, to distinguish us from them. . . . A borderland is a vague and undetermined place created by the emotional residue

of an unnatural boundary. It is in a constant state of transition. The prohibited and forbidden are its inhabitants" (3). Eastman's autobiography represents one such cultural borderland and an interstitial position among other early American Indian autobiographies (Krupat, *For Those* 30-31). As such, it can reveal other ways of understanding ethnicity, assimilation and multiculturalism.

Ethnicity, as a critical category, emerged out of and in dialogic response to the intellectual and social movements of the 1950s and 1960s. It challenged the inherent racialism of the melting pot, which presumed the homogenized blending of diverse cultural ingredients into a unique American "stew," but which denied the institutional, economic and political power exercised in coloring that stew a decidedly Anglo beige. It also challenged a postwar, Cold War liberal consensus, which had reproduced the homogenized stew under the banner of pluralistic tolerance.[4] Out of this scholarship, new descriptive and critical metaphors of assimilation and ethnic literature have also emerged; the most recent one has been that of the multicultural mosaic.

A mosaic is a beautiful metaphor, eliciting images of rich and dazzling pigments. But despite its aesthetic qualifications, as a social and literary metaphor it does raise some disturbing connotations. While acknowledging the brilliance of diversity, a mosaic also metaphorically separates and cements these differences as disparate cultural fragments. As a critical metaphor, it too often privileges the essentialisms of cultural authenticity or ignores differentials in power. This does not mean that we should stop studying the differences which comprise our cultural diversity—as some recent conservative critics suggest that we should do—but rather that we must critically reexamine the borders we draw between different cultural experiences, borders that can delimit diversity rather than accomodate it. By taking another look at Eastman's life and autobiography, without either celebrating his assimilation or demanding of him some standard of authenticity, we can perhaps begin imagining borderlands, rather than positioning borders.[5]

Eastman grew up in a cultural borderland. His father, Ite Wakanhdi Ota, descended from a long line of Wahpeton Sioux leaders. His mother was a mixed-blood: she was the daughter of Captain Seth Eastman, the noted painter of the West, and granddaughter of Chief Cloud Man, one of the first Santee converts to Christianity. In 1862, at the age of four, Eastman fled from United States soldiers into Canada with his uncle and grandmother. There he heard that his father had been executed. This news sparked a hatred in him for all whites. For the next ten years Eastman's uncle and grandmother raised him in the traditions of his tribe to become a successful warrior and avenge his father's death on the warpath. His father, however, had not been executed, and while in prison he had converted to Christianity. Suddenly, when Eastman was fifteen, his father appeared in Canada to bring him back to Flandreau, South Dakota, to learn the ways of the white man. After his initial shock, Eastman stoically dedicated himself to succeeding along his new path. He converted to Christianity and began a very successful education, eventually graduating from Boston Medical School in 1890 as the first American Indian physician. But Eastman only actively practiced medicine for fewer than six years. He left medical practice after his second job (and second controversy) as an agency physician, and for the rest of his life moved among a variety of jobs: YMCA field secretary, summer camp leader, Washington lobbyist for Sioux treaty rights, ethnographer and, at various times, Indian Bureau agent.

Eastman, however, is perhaps best known as an author. As one of the most prolific writers and visible Indian leaders at the turn of the century, he dedicated his energies and education to making Euro-Americans aware of the significant contributions Indians had made to American society and to bettering the conditions of his people.[6] For his efforts, Eastman was hailed by the Commissioner of Indian Affairs, T.J. Morgan, as "one of the finest specimens of Indians . . . [and an] example of what can be done . . . by education" (qtd. in Wilson 72); nevertheless, Eastman himself steadfastly rejected the assimilated label, preferring instead to call himself an acculturated Sioux (Wilson 189).

Yet despite his reluctance to call himself assimilated, there is little doubt that Eastman saw the inevitable technological victory of civilization over traditional tribal ways. Many of his readers—convinced of evolutionary law and dedicated to "kill[ing] the Indian and sav[ing] the man"—understood this victory to mean that Indians must "shed" their identity, as Indians, in order to assimilate into white society.[7] Certainly Eastman's title, *From the Deep Woods to Civilization,* suggests this reading. But Eastman also grew up learning that the transition from the "old" to the "new" is not the same as the Western linear historical narrative.[8] In his autobiography we can see the complexities of these two understandings of history.

Like many early autobiographers, Eastman structures his account as a spiritual journey, whose predictable narrative frames conversion in the "born again" language of a personal separation and spiritual growth away from the sins and failures of an old life.[9] A. LaVonne Brown Ruoff has suggested that later 19th century American Indian autobiographers moved away from making such a spiritual journey the center of their narratives, and instead, increasingly began emphasizing more traditional tribal narratives and adopting a more militant tone ("Three Autobiographers" 265). Eastman does adopt a significantly more critical pos-

ture toward Christian civilization in his second autobiography than in his earlier one, *Indian Boyhood* (1902). He also pays scant attention to his own Christian conversion, although he repeatedly draws comparisons between "true" Christian and Indian beliefs. However, like many immigrant autobiographers who sought to write themselves into American society, Eastman continues to draw on many of the narrative strategies which structure the spiritual confession.[10] Stylistically, he shapes his struggle to become educated in the form of a conventional confession's growing awareness of God: his witness of the Wounded Knee massacre and troubles with government bureaucracy replace the confession's fall from grace; and his role as an emissary between the Indian and white worlds functions to bring them together in some form of reconciliation and recovery. But while he may overtly structure his autobiography as a confessional jeremiad, his emphasis, and hence his goal, is quite different.

Eastman notably departs from the climactic moments of divine inspiration and repentance usually expected in a conventional confessional narrative. The confession's central concern with Christian conversion completely disappears; Eastman does not even mention his baptism. His "conversion" to civilization is similarly understated. On his journey to Reverend Riggs' school, Eastman spends the night with an American family. After offering twice to pay and having his money refused, Eastman suddenly announces: "Then and there I loved civilization and renounced my wild life" (39). There is no intensification of the conflict building toward this "climactic" moment, as one would expect in a conventional confession. And when Eastman's "conversion" actually comes, his description seems so improbable and anticlimactic that it loses all of the moral authority and narrative force traditionally associated with conversion.

Eastman also subverts conventional narrative expectations in his account of the massacre at Wounded Knee. In November 1890, Eastman arrived at Pine Ridge as the agency's new physician. Less than two months later, on December 29, the Seventh Cavalry panicked and attacked an encampment of Sioux. Three days later, Eastman went with a party to search for survivors. For two pages in the center of his book he describes in detail the grim spectacle he found. While Eastman's passage appears to be a prelude to an angry condemnation of white atrocities, his emotional tension does not lead to this expected resolution. Rather, he avoids condemnation altogether, reporting matter-of-factly: ". . . I passed no hasty judgement, and was thankful that I might be of some service and relieve even a small part of the suffering" (114). While his disillusionment at Wounded Knee played a pivotal role in his life, in his autobiography Eastman quickly undercuts any expected climactic condemnation with his hesitancy to make hasty judgments.[11]

Charles Gamage Eastman (1816-1860), engraved by Capewell & Kimmel, New York.

Thus, Eastman's autobiography does not methodically build towards a climactic conversion in the conventional Western sense; in the one case, we saw a "climactic resolution" with no narrative tension, and in the other, narrative tension with no climactic resolution.

Like many of his Progressive readers, Eastman stressed the inevitability of civilization's "victory," yet he does not simply rehearse the inevitable displacement of "inferior" cultures by "superior" ones. "Some people," he wrote, "imagine that we are still wild savages, living on the hunt or on rations; but as a matter of fact, we Sioux are now fully entrenched, for all practical purposes, in the warfare of civilized life" (165).

The ironies in this passage work to subvert Eastman's optimism about the Sioux's transition to civilization. The metaphor of "trench warfare" is antithetical to the nomadic life Eastman experienced in his boyhood and contrary to a Sioux warrior's concept of bravery and battle. It becomes grimmer when read in the context of having being written twenty-five years after Eastman witnessed the literal entrenchment of the Sioux dead following the Wounded Knee massacre—an act he clearly associated with civilization. While stressing the

inevitability of civilization, his passage also implies that the Sioux will not simply be its victims or vanish in the face of its encroachment. Whether consciously ironic and subversive or not, he suggests that within new cultural forms the Sioux will struggle and fight . . . as Sioux.

It is this suggestion of continuity that distinguishes Eastman's account from other spiritual confessions and early American Indian autobiographies. Paula Gunn Allen describes the nature of continuity to mean "bring[ing] those structures and symbols which retain their essential meaning forward into a changed context in such a way that the metaphysical point remains true, in spite of apparently changed circumstances" (573). In Eastman's changed circumstances he struggled to make sense of his new schooling and religion.

> I obeyed my father's wishes, and went regularly to the little day-school, but as yet my mind was in darkness. What has all of this talk of books to do with hunting or even with planting corn? I thought. The subject occupied my thoughts more and more, doubtless owing to my father's decided position on the matter; while on the other hand my grandmother's view of this new life was not encouraging.
>
> I took the situation seriously enough, and I remember I went with it where all my people go when they want light—into the thick woods. . . .
>
> When I came back my heart was strong. I decided to follow the new trail to the end. (25-26)

A few pages later, when he leaves for Santee to go to school, Eastman instructs his neighbor Peter, "Tell my father . . . that I shall not return until I finish my warpath" (34). Eastman demonstrates his continuity with his past by depicting his journey in civilization as his first warpath. He also resolves to "follow the new trail to the end," from darkness into light, a metaphor which is easily accessible to his largely Christian readership. Yet his irony in making the woods the source of light, just as he sets off for school to gain the knowledge that he hopes will dispel his mind's darkness, is striking. Even more striking is the fact that Eastman does not try to resolve the contradictions between his two sympathies through the Western narrative of linear progress available to him.

Once he has decided to follow his new trail with the "undaunted bravery and stoic resignation" he knew was proper for a Sioux warrior, Eastman narratively brings together the two conflicting forces in his life (26).

> It appears remarkable to me now that my father, thorough Indian as he was, should have had such deep and sound conceptions of true civilization. But there is the contrast—my father's mother! whose

faith in her people's philosophy and training could not be superseded by any other allegiance.

To her such a life as we lead to-day would be no less than sacrilege. "It is not a true life," she often said. "It is a sham. I cannot bear to see my boy live a made-up life!"

Ah, Grandmother! you had forgotten one of the first principles of your own teaching, namely: "When you see a new trail, or a footprint you do not know, follow it to the point of knowing."

"All I want to say to you," the old grandmother seems to answer, "is this: Do not get lost on this new trail." (27-28)

Eastman begins the passage juxtaposing his father's "sound conceptions of true civilization" with his grandmother's emphatic declaration, "It is a sham. I cannot bear to see my boy live a made-up life!" His grandmother's declaration takes on particular poignancy for Eastman, who knows that she actually could not bear his decision and died shortly after he had left to go to school. But, interestingly, midway through the passage, Eastman turns from his readers and directly addresses his dead grandmother, reminding her that she had forgotten her own teaching. Eastman's switch in verb tense to past perfect is significant. In effect, it frames the action of his grandmother's "forgetting" before her condemnation of civilization as a "sham," and allows that at some earlier time she "knew" and taught him that a new path must be followed "to the point of knowing." Even more significant is Eastman's having his dead grandmother reply to him by giving a resigned blessing. Through this passage Eastman is able to demonstrate the continuity between his grandmother's and father's wishes, while still retaining, at one level, the contradiction of their views.

Eastman's juxtaposition of two conflicting forces to demonstrate their inclusion, without "resolving" their contradiction, strikingly parallels a similar narrative pattern Elaine Jahner has analyzed in the creation stories written by the Oglala Sioux, George Sword ("Lakota Genesis" 45-56). A holy man who had converted to Christianity, Sword, like Eastman, wished to demonstrate the syncretisms of Lakota and Christian beliefs. Like Eastman's explanation of his new trail within his grandmother's teachings, Sword's tales attempt to demonstrate how the structure of one set of beliefs can be carried on within the other. A suggestive example of this narrative pattern is Sword's story "When the People Laughed at the Moon" (Walker 52-57).[12] Although this story is not directly cited in Eastman's autobiography or collections of Indian tales, it contains narrative tensions similar to those he raised in the passage above.

Sword begins his story by establishing the kinship relations between gods and humans, sun and moon, and children and parents. *Wazi*, chief of the Buffalo People, is married to *Kanka*, the wise woman who can foretell future events. Their beautiful daughter, *Ite*, is married to the god *Tate* and has borne him four sons. By marrying *Tate*, *Ite* establishes a link between humans and gods. Yet her human father, *Wazi*, desires the gods' powers and conspires with the trickster *Iktomi* to obtain them; then with his wife he conspires to trick *Iktomi*. But *Iktomi* overhears their plans and manipulates them into helping him convince *Ite* that she deserves to be honored as a god alongside *Wi*, the sun. When *Ite* takes the moon *Hanwi*'s seat next to *Wi* and shames her, *Ite* irrevocably disrupts the established order.

Jahner describes how Sword structures each character's punishment to demonstrate how oppositions can function together to help establish a new order and set of relationships ("Lakota Genesis" 48-50; introd. *Lakota Myth* 44-46). *Wi*'s forgetfulness of *Hanwi* results in their separation and the creation of a new temporal order; *Ite*'s turning away from her family to become like the gods results in her becoming a wanderer in the world as *Anog Ite*, or the Double Woman; *Kanka*, who helped bring about what she foresaw, is also condemned to wander the world mediating between the present and the future; and *Wazi*, who worked inadvertently to bring about the Third Time, is ordered to help bring about the Fourth Time when the four sons of *Tate* and *Ite* will become the four directions at the edge of the world. All characters assume new mediatory roles through acting out the opposite of their original action or intent.

Sword's tales are neither purely mythic (in the sense of traditional folklore) nor Western; rather they draw on both Christian and Lakota beliefs in order to demonstrate the syncretisms of the two. Sword did this narratively by juxtaposing oppositions in order to show how they might function together. Jahner describes his tales as presenting "oppositions only to show how their development works to create a structure of inclusion," a combination that is not always simple, nor always positive ("Lakota Genesis" 49). Sword's tales demonstrate how disruptions of the cosmic order require the establishment of new relationships to maintain a balance. The rules of reciprocity allow individuals to live within this dynamic and turn the opposing forces into fruitful relationships.

There is probably no way to know whether or not Sword and Eastman collaborated or even talked about their writings. We do know from Eastman's autobiography that they were friends during Eastman's stay at Pine Ridge. We might also never be able to decipher accurately the extent to which each author drew on oral stories and storytelling conventions. Nor, if we could, would it be easy to separate their narrative posture of being caught between two worlds from traditional oral narrative patterns. But without establishing (absolutely) the authentic roots of their stories, we can say that their stories represent a *different* narrative pattern. And there is at least strong circumstantial evidence to suggest that this narrative pattern, used by two Sioux storytellers who had different levels of education, who grew up in different geographical locations and who did not meet one another until well into adulthood, is initially Sioux. Elaine Jahner's work, which argues that Sword's tales contain the ethical and emotional forces that structure traditional Lakota oral narratives, further suggests this probability ("Lakota Genesis" 49; introd. *Lakota Myth* 12-27, 46).[13]

Throughout his autobiography Eastman repeats this narrative pattern of juxtaposing contradictions and opposing forces to demonstrate structures of inclusion. Like Sword, whose characters disrupted the established order and made necessary new roles and relationships to maintain the balance, Eastman demonstrates his father's "true conceptions of civilization" functioning within his grandmother's old teachings. In doing so Eastman appeals to the assimilationist argument that Indians were vanishing in the face of civilization and could only be "saved" if they forgot their past, yet then immediately undercuts this position by stressing his own continuity with that past.

Eastman's juxtaposition of progress and tradition is critical. It suggests that to maintain a balanced life Eastman had to account for the shifting elements of his new world. It also establishes his position in the crossroads of two worlds, where the forces of progress and tradition powerfully shape him in different and often contradictory ways: an Indian, in "civilization" Eastman assumed the role of "Indian"; a Christian, in the "deep woods" he assumed the role of "Christian." Nowhere is this intricate intersection more present and hidden than in Eastman's last chapter—"The Soul of the White Man."

In his closing chapter, Eastman does not recite, as might be expected, his final redemption from the darkness of the "deep woods" into the light of "civilization." And, curiously, he also spends very little time talking about the white man's soul; when he does in the final two pages, his tone is critical.

> Why do we find so much evil and wickedness practised by the nations composed of professedly "Christian" individuals? The pages of history are full of licensed murder and the plundering of weaker and less developed peoples, and obviously the world today has not outgrown this system. Behind the material and intellectual splendour of our civilization, primitive savagery and cruelty and lust hold sway. (194)

Rather than showing civilization's progress out of the darkness of the deep woods, Eastman denounces its savagery. Yet, he continues to employ Social Darwinist language and places himself within "our civilization" and against "primitive savagery." He invokes the moral outrage expected many pages earlier following the massacre at Wounded Knee, but this passage is no less puzzling than the earlier one.

Like his earlier conversion to civilization, his condemnation of it seems to lack any preparatory emotional intensification. Without apparent transition, Eastman launches from describing his involvement in the Boy Scouts, whose "program appealed to [him] strongly," into condemning the "material and intellectual splendour" of civilization. And characteristically, he just as quickly subverts the climactic action with: "Yet in the deep jungles God's own sunlight penetrates and I stand before my own people still as an advocate of civilization"—then asks the obvious question, "Why?" (194). His answer lacks all of the emotional "punch" that his condemnation contained: "First, because there is no chance for our former simple life any more; and second, because I realize that the white man's religion is not responsible for his mistakes" (195).

In distinguishing "true faith" from "practiced faith," while appealing to the simplicity of a former time, Eastman aligns himself with a long Western apocalyptic tradition of "nostalgic innovation" which ties condemnation to communal revitalization.[14] His rhetorical jeremiad parallels what Sacvan Bercovitch has described as the "American jeremiad," the forward-looking rhetorical ritual that laments the distance between the community's ideals and its lived practice, only to prophesy that redemption is possible in the future if the community returns to its original ideals (3-30). Eastman locates his promise of redemption in the "true" Christian and Indian ideals, which he sees as synchronous, then challenges his readers to remember the many civilizations which have "collapsed in physical and moral decadence," warning, "It is for us to avoid their fate if we can" (195).

But Eastman does not end his book apocalyptically or as a progressive jeremiad. Rather, he ends it with a puzzling personal declaration which brings together, for the last time, the two conflicting forces in his life:

> I am an Indian; and while I have learned much from civilization, for which I am grateful, I have never lost my Indian sense of right and justice. I am for development and progress along social and spiritual lines, rather than those of commerce, nationalism, or material efficiency. Nevertheless, so long as I live, I am an American. (195)

Eastman's resolute statement that he is an Indian, and just as certain pledge that he will always be an American, were contradictory statements in assimilationist and Social Darwinist thinking. In a world of borders, it is impossible to be on both sides at once. Either Eastman has assimilated or he has not. But "I am an Indian . . . I am an American" no longer contains the direction of "I was an Indian . . . I am now an American" implicit in his title. In his last chapter, the question shifts from "Who am I—American or Indian?" to "Which side am I most on now?"[15] Knowing who he is, the power Eastman derives from this last paragraph is in boldly bringing together the two public identities of what he has done. In doing so, he also suggests a successful warpath, a path which connects both deep woods and civilization.

Eastman's autobiography creates contexts for re-seeing meanings and possibilities obscured in a world of borders by challenging the lines which enclose and define the world in binary choices of either/or. Like W.E.B. DuBois's "double consciousness" as "an American, a Negro,"[16] Eastman's contradictory roles as "an Indian, an American" challenge simplistic understandings of cultural assimilation and the moralistic charges of "selling out" often directed toward ethnic writers, particularly "successful" ones. Eastman tries to heal divisions—not by "solving" them, or finding them to be unreal or false—but by bringing them together and acknowledging their contradictions. In his autobiography, he brings together "I am an Indian . . . I am an American" to find the balance, the borderlands, where he (and we) might be able to live well within and between their contradictions.

Notes

[1] See Miller; Wilson; Stensland.

[2] Paul Rabinow makes a similar appeal for what he calls "cosmopolitanism." 258.

[3] For a discussion of the "straight line" theory of assimilation, see Sandberg. For a perspective which suggests that assimilation is less a departure from some past than a negotiation with present conditions, see Yancy, Ericksen, and Juliani.

[4] Many postwar liberal intellectuals embraced political and cultural diversity as long as it did not fundamentally challenge the political values of democratic liberalism, the economic values of corporate capitalism and the aesthetic values of the classical works of Western Civilization, values which were considered transcendent of the political, ideological and economic struggles which comprise a multiethnic society. In literary studies New Criticism, with its foregrounding of the isolate text apart from any historical or cultural context, achieved academic ascendancy by the 1940s and early 1950s.

[5] Along similar lines, Werner Sollors has suggested that we must begin developing "a terminology that goes beyond the organicist imagery of roots and come[s] to

the pervasiveness and inventiveness of syncretism" (*Beyond Ethnicity* 15).

Recently, many critics, including Sollors, are challenging the binary divisions often drawn in ethnic studies (us/them or inside/outside) and inherent in most theories of assimilation. See, for example: Sollors, *The Invention of Ethnicity* and "Of Mules and Mares in a Land of Difference"; Hobsbaum; Steinberg; Gans; and Takaki.

[6] History has demonstrated that many of the programs and institutions he embraced often contributed more to his people's plight than to their betterment. For instance, Eastman supported the Dawes Severalty Act (1887) and the Lake Mohonk Conference of Friends of the Indians (1883), both of which worked to destroy tribal identity and sovereignty.

[7] "Kill the Indian and save the man" was the infamous motto of General Pratt's Carlisle Indian School. It drew on the dominant anthropology of the day, which believed that Indians had to lose their presumably archaic tribal identities if they were to evolve culturally and assimilate into American society. See Berkhofer 49-61, 134-75; Bieder. For an overview of the importance of Social Darwinism in Anglo-American intellectual thought, see Bannister; Haller.

[8] Eastman's title *From the Deep Woods to Civilization* parallels a number of "From . . . to" titles of immigrant autobiographies published during the first decades of this century describing the exodus from homelands and successful (if often difficult) assimilation into American society. For example, Mary Antin, *From Plotzk to Boston* (1899); Edward Steiner, *From Alien to Citizen* (1914); Michael Pupin, *From Immigrant to Inventor* (1923); and Richard Bartholdt, *From Steerage to Congress* (1930) (Sollors, *Beyond Ethnicity* 31-32).

[9] See Powers 159-208; Allen; and Martin.

[10] I am using the definition of the spiritual confession provided by A. LaVonne Brown Ruoff ("American Indian Authors" 191-201). Ruoff argues that William Apes (*A Son of the Forest*, 1829) and George Copeway (*Life, History, and Travels of Kah-ge-ga-gah-bowh [George Copway]*, 1847) both structure their autobiographies after a spiritual confession. Arnold Krupat parallels Ruoff's analysis of Apes and extends it to *Black Hawk: An Autobiography* (1833) (*The Voice in the Margin* 141-55).

[11] Brumble also points to the importance of this passage, but argues that it reflects Eastman's "Romantic Racialism and Social Darwinist assumptions" (148). This is no doubt true, but Brumble does not elaborate on the role this passage plays in Eastman's total narrative, and subsequently, misses how it works to subvert precisely the ideological expectations Brumble suggests it represents.

[12] James R. Walker arrived at Pine Ridge in 1896 as the agency physician. Over the next eighteen years he collected Sioux oral stories. George Sword was one of his primary informants. Jahner, introd. *Lakota Myth* 52-57.

[13] To further complicate the problem of determining authenticity, Eastman's non-Indian wife, Elaine, was his chief editor, and it is probably impossible to distinguish his original manuscript from her corrections and additions. We know that they differed in their philosophical approaches to assimilation and that these differences may have contributed to their eventual separation. According to Raymond Wilson, Elaine "stressed total assimilation of Native Americans, while [Charles] favored a more selective process of acculturation" (164-65).

Perhaps there are parallels between Charles and Elaine (as Charles' editor) and Sword and Walker (as Sword's recorder). Jahner reports that Sword's original narratives stressed more "traditional" themes of kinship and the "controlling laws of the cosmos," whereas Walker's final revisions minimized these themes (introd. *Lakota Myth* 15). Whether or not a similar muting of "traditional" themes occurred in Eastman's writings as a result of Elaine's editing we may never know, although Eastman's grandson recalls his grandfather's resentment that Elaine's revisions changed his intended meanings (Wilson 164).

[14] "Nostalgic innovation" is the term Robert Crunden uses to describe the political/artistic projects of Progressive artists and writers. David Levin suggests that the narrative of progress, as a romantic narrative, must constantly be revitalized. Sacvan Bercovitch's work on the American jeremiad suggests a useful way for seeing how such narratives might be revitalized, and a way in which Eastman could prophesy that the corruptions of the present civilization could be overcome by returning to the "true faith" of his Sioux and Christian cultures. For an overview of the importance of this rhetorical convention for the Progressives, see Noble; Danbom; and Conn.

[15] Eastman prepares for the interrogative switch from "Who am I?" to "What am I?" in the "silent" transitions and digressions of his final chapter. He begins the chapter describing his last government job revising the Sioux allotment rolls. One of the main tasks he faced was Anglicizing Sioux names and assigning surnames when necessary. The fact that he rearranged the chronology of his autobiography to begin his final chapter with this particular event suggests its importance for him, but it is significant for cultural reasons as well. Naming is an important and intimate event in Sioux culture, evident in Eastman's own extensive description of his becoming "Ohiyesa" in his earlier autobiography, *Indian Boyhood* (1902). By telling about his work "renaming" the Sioux, in effect, he affirms his identity and declares his "insight into the relationships and intimate history of 30,000 Sioux" (185).

After establishing this relationship, Eastman suddenly begins a lengthy account of his recognitions and honors in both "deep woods" and "civilization." Yet he ties his public accolades with healing the divisions between the Indian and white worlds. Eastman recounts that only after he had established that "the philosophy of the original American was demonstrably on a high plane" did he consent "to appear on stage in [the Sioux] ancestral garb of honor" (188). What is compelling in his last chapter is that only after he intimately established himself as a Sioux did he "boast" of his different mediating roles. In effect, his "boasting" is similar to "coup stories," which were traditionally told by Sioux warriors following a successful warpath.

[16] DuBois 45. James Weldon Johnson described the "dilemma of the Negro author" as the "problem of a double audience" (477). For an excellent discussion of "doubleness" in W.E.B. DuBois's work, see Holt.

Works Cited

Allen, Paula Gunn. "Bringing Home the Fact: Tradition and Continuity in the Imagination." *Recovering the Word: Essays on Native American Literature.* Eds. Brian Swann and Arnold Krupat. Berkeley: U of California P, 1987. 563-579.

Anzaldua, Gloria. *Borderlands, La Frontera: The New Mestiza.* San Francisco: Spinsters/Aunt Lute, 1987.

Bannister, Robert C. *Social Darwinism: Science and Myth in Anglo-American Social Thought.* Philadelphia: Temple U P, 1979.

Berkhofer, Robert F. *The White Man's Indian: Images of the American Indian from Colonialism to the Present.* New York: Knopf, 1978.

Bercovitch, Sacvan. *The American Jeremiad.* Madison: U of Wisconsin P, 1978.

Bieder, Robert. *Science Encounters the Indian, 1820-1880: The Early Years of American Ethnology.* Norman: U of Oklahoma P, 1986.

Brumble, H. David, III. *American Indian Autobiography.* Berkeley: U of California P, 1988.

Conn, Peter. *The Divided Mind: Ideology and Imagination in America, 1898-1917.* Cambridge: Cambridge U P, 1983.

Copeland, Marion W. *Charles Alexander Eastman (Ohiyesa).* Western Writers Series 33. Boise: Boise State U, 1978.

Crunden, Robert. *Ministers of Reform: The Progressive Achievement in American Civilization, 1889-1920.* New York: Basic Books, 1982.

Danbom, David B. *The World of Hope: Progressives and the Struggle for an Ethical Public Life.* Philadelphia: Temple U P, 1987.

DuBois, W.E.B. *The Souls of Black Folk.* New York: New American Library, 1969.

Eastman, Charles Alexander. *From the Deep Woods to Civilization: Chapters in the Autobiography of an Indian.* 1916. Introd. Raymond Wilson. Lincoln: U of Nebraska P, 1977.

————. *Indian Boyhood.* 1902. New York: Dover, 1971.

Fischer, Michael M.J. "Ethnicity and the Post-Modern Arts of Memory." *Writing Culture: The Poetics and Politics of Ethnography.* Eds. James Clifford and George Marcus. Berkeley: U of California P, 1986. 194-233.

Rev. of *From the Deep Woods to Civilization* by Charles A. Eastman. *The New York Times* 24 December, 1916, sec. VI: 570.

Rev. of *From the Deep Woods to Civilization* by Charles A. Eastman. *The North American Review* 204 (December 1916): 948-49.

Gans, Herbert. "Symbolic Ethnicity: The Future of Ethnic Groups and Cultures in America." *On the Making of Americans: Essays in Honor of David Reisman.* Eds. Herbert Gans et al. Philadelphia: U of Pennsylvania P, 1979. 193-220.

Haller, John S. *Outcasts from Evolution: Scientific Attitudes of Racial Inferiority, 1859-1900.* Urbana: U of Illinois P, 1971.

Hertzberg, Hazel. *The Search for an American Indian Identity: Modern Pan-Indian Movements.* Syracuse: Syracuse U P, 1981.

Hobsbaum, Eric. "Introduction: Inventing Traditions." *The Invention of Tradition.* Eds. Eric Hobsbaum and Terrence Ranger. Cambridge: Cambridge U P, 1983. 1-14.

Holt, Thomas C. "The Political Uses of Alienation: W.E.B. Du Bois on Politics, Race, and Culture, 1903-1940." *American Quarterly* 42 (June 1990): 301-23.

Jahner, Elaine A. "Lakota Genesis: The Oral Tradition." *Sioux Indian Religion.* Eds. Raymond DeMallie and Douglas R. Parks. Norman: U of Oklahoma P, 1987. 45-56.

————. Introd. *Lakota Myth,* by James R. Walker. Ed. Elaine A. Jahner. Lincoln: U of Nebraska P, 1983. 1-52.

Johnson, James Weldon. "The Dilemma of the Negro Author." *American Mercury* (December 1928): 477-81.

Krupat, Arnold. *For Those Who Come After: A Study of Native American Autobiography.* Berkeley: U of California P, 1985.

————. *The Voice in the Margin: Native American Literature and the Canon.* Berkeley: U of California P, 1989.

Levin, David. *History as Romantic Art.* New York: Harcourt, Brace, and World, 1959.

Martin, Calvin. *The American Indian and the Problem of History.* New York: Oxford U P, 1987.

Miller, David R. "Charles A. Eastman: One Man's Journey in Two Worlds." MA Thesis. U of North Dakota, 1976.

Noble, David W. *The Progressive Mind, 1890-1917.* Chicago: Rand McNally College Publishing House, 1970.

Powers, William K. *Oglala Religion.* Lincoln: U of Nebraska P, 1975.

Rabinow, Paul. "Representations are Social Facts: Modernity and Post-Modernity in Anthropology." *Writing Culture: The Poetics and Politics of Ethnography.* Eds. James Clifford and George Marcus. Berkeley: U of California P, 1986. 234-61.

Ruoff, A. LaVonne Brown. "American Indian Authors: 1774-1899." *Critical Essays on Native American Literature.* Ed. Andrew Wiget. Boston: G.K. Hall, 1985. 191-201.

————. "Three Nineteenth-Century American Indian Autobiographers." *Redefining American Literary History.* Eds. A. LaVonne Brown Ruoff and Jerry W. Ward, Jr. New York: The Modern Language Association, 1990. 251-69.

Sandberg, Neil. *Ethnic Identity and Assimilation: The Polish American Community.* New York: Praeger, 1974.

Sollors, Werner. *Beyond Ethnicity: Consent and Descent in American Culture.* New York: Oxford U P, 1986.

————, ed. *The Invention of Ethnicity.* New York: Oxford U P, 1989.

————. "Of Mules and Mares in a Land of Difference: Or, Quadrepeds All?" *American Quarterly* 42 (June 1990): 167-90.

Steinberg, Steven. *The Ethnic Myth: Race, Ethnicity, and Class in America.* New York: Atheneum, 1981.

Stensland, Anna Lee. "Charles Alexander Eastman: Sioux Storyteller and Historian." *American Indian Quarterly* 3 (1977): 199-208.

Takaki, Ronald. ed. *From Different Shores: Perspectives on Race and Culture in America.* Oxford: Oxford U P, 1987.

Walker, James R. *Lakota Myth.* Ed. Elaine A. Jahner. Lincoln: U of Nebraska P, 1983.

Wilson, Raymond. *Ohiyesa: Charles Eastman, Santee Sioux.* Urbana: U of Illinois P, 1983.

Yancy, W., E. Ericksen and R. Juliani. "Emergent Ethnicity: A Review and Reformulation." *American Sociological Review* 41 (1976): 391-403.

FURTHER READING

Bibliography

Brumble, H. David III. *An Annotated Bibliography of American Indian and Eskimo Autobiographies.* Lincoln: University of Nebraska Press, 1981, 177 p.

This often-cited reference provides a listing of more than five hundred Native American autobiographies, dating from the eighteenth century to the present.

Ruoff, A. LaVonne Brown. *American Indian Literatures: An Introduction, Bibliographic Review, and Selected Bibliography.* New York: Modern Language Association of America, 1990, 200 p.

An extensive bibliographical listing of Native American literature, including autobiography.

Biography

Brimlow, George F. "The Life of Sarah Winnemucca: The Formative Years." *Oregon Historical Quarterly* 53, No. 2 (June 1952): 103-34.

Provides a detailed account of the cultural origins and early life of Sarah Winnemucca, whose later lectures and autobiography were popularly and politically influential.

Fowler, Catherine S. "Sarah Winnemucca." In *American Indian Intellectuals*, edited by Margot Liberty, pp. 33-42. St. Paul, Minn.: West Publishing Company, 1978.

Offers a brief biography of Sarah Winnemucca and argues that her controversial stance on Native American assimilation has led to the neglect of her complex political views.

Smith, Donald B. "The Life of George Copway or Kah-ge-ga-gah-bowh (1818-1869) and a Review of His Writings." *Journal of Canadian Studies* 23, No. 3 (Fall 1988): 5-38.

Recounts the early life, conversion, and circumstances leading to the writing of the autobiographies of George Copway.

Criticism

Bloodworth, William. "Varieties of American Indian Autobiography." *MELUS* 5, No. 3 (Fall 1978): 67-81.

Develops a general classification of Native American autobiography according to the amount of Western influence each work underwent.

Brumble, H. David III. "Sam Blowsnake's Confessions: *Crashing Thunder* and the History of American Indian Autobiography." In *Recovering the Word: Essays on Native American Literature*, edited by Brian Swann and Arnold Krupat, pp. 537-51. Berkeley: University of California Press, 1987.

Contends that the autobiography of Sam Blowsnake differs significantly from earlier Native American memoirs, insofar as it is organized around a central dramatic experience and expresses a confessional "sense of self."

Carr, Helen. "In Other Words: Native American Women's Autobiography." In *Life/Lines: Theorizing Women's Autobiography*, edited by Bella Brodzki and Celeste Schenck, pp. 131-53. Ithaca, N.Y.: Cornell University Press, 1988.

Criticizes the consideration of Native American autobiography as representative life-experiences, arguing that the literary form is more suited to the expression of individual recollections.

Krupat, Arnold. "The Indian Autobiography: Origins, Type, and Function." *American Literature* 53, No. 1 (March 1981): 22-42.

Examines the political context in which both early white and Native American autobiographies were written.

———. "Monologue and Dialogue in Native American Autobiography." In his *The Voice in the Margin: Native American Literature and the Canon*, pp. 132-201. Berkeley: University of California Press, 1989.

Claims that some Native American autobiographers deliberately adopt a Western model of individual identity, and in so doing suppress a more traditional dialogic understanding of identity.

Sanders, Thomas E., and Walter W. Peek. "Memories Miserable and Magnificent: Biography and Autobiography." In their *Literature of the American Indian*, pp. 409-44. Beverly Hills, Calif.: Glencoe Press, 1973.

Presents excerpts from autobiographical narratives that are indicative of the tension between traditional culture and the increasingly dominant Western influence.

Sands, Kathleen Mullen. "American Indian Autobiography." In *Studies in American Indian Literature: Critical Essays and Course Designs*, edited by Paula Gunn Allen, pp. 55-65. New York: Modern Language Association of America, 1983.

Examines the narrator/editor collaborative relationship in Native American autobiographies.

Walsh, Susan. "'With Them Was My Home': Native American Autobiography and *A Narrative of the Life of Mrs. Mary Jemison*." *American Literature* 64, No. 1 (March 1992): 49-70.

Reviews the context in which the collaborative memoir of Mary Jemison, a white woman who was captured and adopted by Senecas, was composed. The autobiography, the critic argues, is a "bicultural composition" and is "marked by Native American as well as Anglo-European narrative elements."

Wong, Hertha D. "Pictographs as Autobiography: Plains Indian Sketchbooks, Diaries, and Text Construction." In her *Sending My Heart Back Across the Years: Tradition and Innovation in Native American Autobiography*, pp. 57-87. New York: Oxford University Press, 1992.

Studies the marginalized pictorial forms of autobiography and the ways the narratives changed through contact with the Euro-American culture.

————. "Pre-literate Native American Autobiography: Forms of Personal Narrative." *MELUS* 14, No. 1 (Spring 1987): 17-32.

Examines traditional Native American personal narratives—such as oral storytelling and pictorial renditions of events—forms of self-expression that the critic finds are often overlooked in favor of the collaborative and ethnographic autobiographies which dominate scholarly interest.

Nineteenth-Century Literature Criticism

Topics Volume
Cumulative Indexes
Volumes 1-64

How to Use This Index

The main references

Calvino, Italo
1923-1985.....CLC 5, 8, 11, 22, 33, 39,
73; SSC 3

list all author entries in the following Gale Literary Criticism series:

BLC = *Black Literature Criticism*
CLC = *Contemporary Literary Criticism*
CLR = *Children's Literature Review*
CMLC = *Classical and Medieval Literature
      Criticism*
DA = *DISCovering Authors*
DAB = *DISCovering Authors: British*
DAC = *DISCovering Authors: Canadian*
DAM = *DISCovering Authors Modules*
      DRAM: *Dramatists module*
      MST: *Most-studied authors module*
      MULT: *Multicultural authors module*
      NOV: *Novelists module*
      POET: *Poets module*
      POP: *Popular/genre writers module*

DC = *Drama Criticism*
HLC = *Hispanic Literature Criticism*
LC = *Literature Criticism from 1400 to 1800*
NCLC = *Nineteenth-Century Literature Criticism*
PC = *Poetry Criticism*
SSC = *Short Story Criticism*
TCLC = *Twentieth-Century Literary Criticism*
WLC = *World Literature Criticism, 1500 to the
      Present*

The cross-references

See also CANR 23; CA 85-88;
   obituary CA 116

list all author entries in the following Gale biographical and literary sources:

AAYA = *Authors & Artists for Young Adults*
AITN = *Authors in the News*
BEST = *Bestsellers*
BW = *Black Writers*
CA = *Contemporary Authors*
CAAS = *Contemporary Authors
      Autobiography Series*
CABS = *Contemporary Authors
      Bibliographical Series*
CANR = *Contemporary Authors New
      Revision Series*
CAP = *Contemporary Authors Permanent
      Series*
CDALB = *Concise Dictionary of American
      Literary Biography*
CDBLB = *Concise Dictionary of British
      Literary Biography*

DLB = *Dictionary of Literary Biography*
DLBD = *Dictionary of Literary Biography
      Documentary Series*
DLBY = *Dictionary of Literary Biography Yearbook*
HW = *Hispanic Writers*
JRDA = *Junior DISCovering Authors*
MAICYA = *Major Authors and Illustrators for
      Children and Young Adults*
MTCW = *Major 20th-Century Writers*
NNAL = *Native North American Literature*
SAAS = *Something about the Author Autobiography
      Series*
SATA = *Something about the Author*
YABC = *Yesterday's Authors of Books for Children*

Literary Criticism Series
Cumulative Author Index

Abasiyanik, Sait Faik 1906-1954
See Sait Faik
See also CA 123

Abbey, Edward 1927-1989 . . . . . . **CLC 36, 59**
See also CA 45-48; 128; CANR 2, 41

Abbott, Lee K(ittredge) 1947- . . . . . . **CLC 48**
See also CA 124; CANR 51; DLB 130

Abe, Kobo
1924-1993 . . . . **CLC 8, 22, 53, 81;**
DAM NOV
See also CA 65-68; 140; CANR 24, 60;
DLB 182; MTCW

Abelard, Peter c. 1079-c. 1142 . . . **CMLC 11**
See also DLB 115

Abell, Kjeld 1901-1961 . . . . **CLC 15**
See also CA 111

Abish, Walter 1931- . . . . **CLC 22**
See also CA 101; CANR 37; DLB 130

Abrahams, Peter (Henry) 1919- . . . . . **CLC 4**
See also BW 1; CA 57-60; CANR 26;
DLB 117; MTCW

Abrams, M(eyer) H(oward) 1912- . . . **CLC 24**
See also CA 57-60; CANR 13, 33; DLB 67

Abse, Dannie
1923- . . . **CLC 7, 29; DAB; DAM POET**
See also CA 53-56; CAAS 1; CANR 4, 46;
DLB 27

Achebe, (Albert) Chinua(lumogu)
1930- . . . . . **CLC 1, 3, 5, 7, 11, 26, 51, 75;**
BLC; DA; DAB; DAC; DAM MST,
MULT, NOV; WLC
See also AAYA 15; BW 2; CA 1-4R;
CANR 6, 26, 47; CLR 20; DLB 117;
MAICYA; MTCW; SATA 40;
SATA-Brief 38

Acker, Kathy 1948- . . . . **CLC 45**
See also CA 117; 122; CANR 55

Ackroyd, Peter 1949- . . . . **CLC 34, 52**
See also CA 123; 127; CANR 51; DLB 155;
INT 127

Acorn, Milton 1923- . . . . **CLC 15; DAC**
See also CA 103; DLB 53; INT 103

Adamov, Arthur
1908-1970 . . . . **CLC 4, 25; DAM DRAM**
See also CA 17-18; 25-28R; CAP 2; MTCW

Adams, Alice (Boyd)
1926- . . . . **CLC 6, 13, 46; SSC 24**
See also CA 81-84; CANR 26, 53;
DLBY 86; INT CANR-26; MTCW

Adams, Andy 1859-1935 . . . . **TCLC 56**
See also YABC 1

Adams, Douglas (Noel)
1952- . . . . **CLC 27, 60; DAM POP**
See also AAYA 4; BEST 89:3; CA 106;
CANR 34; DLBY 83; JRDA

Adams, Francis 1862-1893 . . . . **NCLC 33**

Adams, Henry (Brooks)
1838-1918 . . . . . . **TCLC 4, 52; DA; DAB;**
DAC; DAM MST
See also CA 104; 133; DLB 12, 47

Adams, Richard (George)
1920- . . . . **CLC 4, 5, 18; DAM NOV**
See also AAYA 16; AITN 1, 2; CA 49-52;
CANR 3, 35; CLR 20; JRDA; MAICYA;
MTCW; SATA 7, 69

Adamson, Joy(-Friederike Victoria)
1910-1980 . . . . **CLC 17**
See also CA 69-72; 93-96; CANR 22;
MTCW; SATA 11; SATA-Obit 22

Adcock, Fleur 1934- . . . . **CLC 41**
See also CA 25-28R; CAAS 23; CANR 11,
34; DLB 40

Addams, Charles (Samuel)
1912-1988 . . . . **CLC 30**
See also CA 61-64; 126; CANR 12

Addison, Joseph 1672-1719 . . . . **LC 18**
See also CDBLB 1660-1789; DLB 101

Adler, Alfred (F.) 1870-1937 . . . . . . **TCLC 61**
See also CA 119; 159

Adler, C(arole) S(chwerdtfeger)
1932- . . . . **CLC 35**
See also AAYA 4; CA 89-92; CANR 19,
40; JRDA; MAICYA; SAAS 15;
SATA 26, 63

Adler, Renata 1938- . . . . **CLC 8, 31**
See also CA 49-52; CANR 5, 22, 52;
MTCW

Ady, Endre 1877-1919 . . . . **TCLC 11**
See also CA 107

Aeschylus
525B.C.-456B.C. . . . . **CMLC 11; DA;**
DAB; DAC; DAM DRAM, MST; WLCS
See also DLB 176

Afton, Effie
See Harper, Frances Ellen Watkins

Agapida, Fray Antonio
See Irving, Washington

Agee, James (Rufus)
1909-1955 . . . . **TCLC 1, 19; DAM NOV**
See also AITN 1; CA 108; 148;
CDALB 1941-1968; DLB 2, 26, 152

Aghill, Gordon
See Silverberg, Robert

Agnon, S(hmuel) Y(osef Halevi)
1888-1970 . . . . **CLC 4, 8, 14; SSC 29**
See also CA 17-18; 25-28R; CANR 60;
CAP 2; MTCW

Agrippa von Nettesheim, Henry Cornelius
1486-1535 . . . . **LC 27**

Aherne, Owen
See Cassill, R(onald) V(erlin)

Ai 1947- . . . . **CLC 4, 14, 69**
See also CA 85-88; CAAS 13; DLB 120

Aickman, Robert (Fordyce)
1914-1981 . . . . **CLC 57**
See also CA 5-8R; CANR 3

Aiken, Conrad (Potter)
1889-1973 . . . . **CLC 1, 3, 5, 10, 52;**
DAM NOV, POET; SSC 9
See also CA 5-8R; 45-48; CANR 4, 60;
CDALB 1929-1941; DLB 9, 45, 102;
MTCW; SATA 3, 30

Aiken, Joan (Delano) 1924- . . . . **CLC 35**
See also AAYA 1; CA 9-12R; CANR 4, 23,
34; CLR 1, 19; DLB 161; JRDA;
MAICYA; MTCW; SAAS 1; SATA 2,
30, 73

Ainsworth, William Harrison
1805-1882 . . . . **NCLC 13**
See also DLB 21; SATA 24

Aitmatov, Chingiz (Torekulovich)
1928- . . . . **CLC 71**
See also CA 103; CANR 38; MTCW;
SATA 56

Akers, Floyd
See Baum, L(yman) Frank

Akhmadulina, Bella Akhatovna
1937- . . . . **CLC 53; DAM POET**
See also CA 65-68

Akhmatova, Anna
1888-1966 . . . . **CLC 11, 25, 64;**
DAM POET; PC 2
See also CA 19-20; 25-28R; CANR 35;
CAP 1; MTCW

Aksakov, Sergei Timofeyvich
1791-1859 . . . . **NCLC 2**

Aksenov, Vassily
See Aksyonov, Vassily (Pavlovich)

Aksyonov, Vassily (Pavlovich)
1932- . . . . **CLC 22, 37, 101**
See also CA 53-56; CANR 12, 48

Akutagawa, Ryunosuke
1892-1927 . . . . **TCLC 16**
See also CA 117; 154

Alain 1868-1951 . . . . **TCLC 41**

Alain-Fournier . . . . **TCLC 6**
See also Fournier, Henri Alban
See also DLB 65

Alarcon, Pedro Antonio de
1833-1891 . . . . **NCLC 1**

Alas (y Urena), Leopoldo (Enrique Garcia)
1852-1901 . . . . **TCLC 29**
See also CA 113; 131; HW

Albee, Edward (Franklin III)
1928- . . . . . . **CLC 1, 2, 3, 5, 9, 11, 13, 25,**
53, 86; DA; DAB; DAC; DAM DRAM,
MST; WLC
See also AITN 1; CA 5-8R; CABS 3;
CANR 8, 54; CDALB 1941-1968; DLB 7;
INT CANR-8; MTCW

Anderson, Maxwell
1888-1959 . . . . . **TCLC 2; DAM DRAM**
See also CA 105; 152; DLB 7

Anderson, Poul (William) 1926- . . . . **CLC 15**
See also AAYA 5; CA 1-4R; CAAS 2;
CANR 2, 15, 34; DLB 8; INT CANR-15;
MTCW; SATA 90; SATA-Brief 39

Anderson, Robert (Woodruff)
1917- . . . . **CLC 23; DAM DRAM**
See also AITN 1; CA 21-24R; CANR 32;
DLB 7

Anderson, Sherwood
1876-1941 . . . . **TCLC 1, 10, 24; DA;**
DAB; DAC; DAM MST, NOV; SSC 1;
WLC
See also CA 104; 121; CANR 61;
CDALB 1917-1929; DLB 4, 9, 86;
DLBD 1; MTCW

Andier, Pierre
See Desnos, Robert

Andouard
See Giraudoux, (Hippolyte) Jean

Andrade, Carlos Drummond de . . . . . . **CLC 18**
See also Drummond de Andrade, Carlos

Andrade, Mario de 1893-1945 . . . . . **TCLC 43**

Andreae, Johann V(alentin)
1586-1654 . . . . **LC 32**
See also DLB 164

Andreas-Salome, Lou 1861-1937 . . . **TCLC 56**
See also DLB 66

Andrewes, Lancelot 1555-1626 . . . . **LC 5**
See also DLB 151, 172

Andrews, Cicily Fairfield
See West, Rebecca

Andrews, Elton V.
See Pohl, Frederik

Andreyev, Leonid (Nikolaevich)
1871-1919 . . . . **TCLC 3**
See also CA 104

Andric, Ivo 1892-1975 . . . . **CLC 8**
See also CA 81-84; 57-60; CANR 43, 60;
DLB 147; MTCW

Angelique, Pierre
See Bataille, Georges

Angell, Roger 1920- . . . . **CLC 26**
See also CA 57-60; CANR 13, 44; DLB 171

Angelou, Maya
1928- . . . . **CLC 12, 35, 64, 77; BLC; DA;**
DAB; DAC; DAM MST, MULT, POET,
POP; WLCS
See also AAYA 7, 20; BW 2; CA 65-68;
CANR 19, 42; DLB 38; MTCW;
SATA 49

Annensky, Innokenty (Fyodorovich)
1856-1909 . . . . **TCLC 14**
See also CA 110; 155

Annunzio, Gabriele d'
See D'Annunzio, Gabriele

Anodos
See Coleridge, Mary E(lizabeth)

Anon, Charles Robert
See Pessoa, Fernando (Antonio Nogueira)

Anouilh, Jean (Marie Lucien Pierre)
1910-1987 . . . . . . **CLC 1, 3, 8, 13, 40, 50;**
DAM DRAM
See also CA 17-20R; 123; CANR 32;
MTCW

Anthony, Florence
See Ai

Anthony, John
See Ciardi, John (Anthony)

Anthony, Peter
See Shaffer, Anthony (Joshua); Shaffer,
Peter (Levin)

Anthony, Piers 1934- . . **CLC 35; DAM POP**
See also AAYA 11; CA 21-24R; CANR 28,
56; DLB 8; MTCW; SAAS 22; SATA 84

Antoine, Marc
See Proust, (Valentin-Louis-George-Eugene-)
Marcel

Antoninus, Brother
See Everson, William (Oliver)

Antonioni, Michelangelo 1912- . . . . . **CLC 20**
See also CA 73-76; CANR 45

Antschel, Paul 1920-1970
See Celan, Paul
See also CA 85-88; CANR 33, 61; MTCW

Anwar, Chairil 1922-1949 . . . . **TCLC 22**
See also CA 121

Apollinaire, Guillaume
1880-1918 . . . . **TCLC 3, 8, 51;**
DAM POET; PC 7
See also Kostrowitzki, Wilhelm Apollinaris
de
See also CA 152

Appelfeld, Aharon 1932- . . . . **CLC 23, 47**
See also CA 112; 133

Apple, Max (Isaac) 1941- . . . . **CLC 9, 33**
See also CA 81-84; CANR 19, 54; DLB 130

Appleman, Philip (Dean) 1926- . . . . . **CLC 51**
See also CA 13-16R; CAAS 18; CANR 6,
29, 56

Appleton, Lawrence
See Lovecraft, H(oward) P(hillips)

Apteryx
See Eliot, T(homas) S(tearns)

Apuleius, (Lucius Madaurensis)
125(?)-175(?) . . . . **CMLC 1**

Aquin, Hubert 1929-1977 . . . . **CLC 15**
See also CA 105; DLB 53

Aragon, Louis
1897-1982 . . . . . **CLC 3, 22; DAM NOV,**
POET
See also CA 69-72; 108; CANR 28;
DLB 72; MTCW

Arany, Janos 1817-1882 . . . . **NCLC 34**

Arbuthnot, John 1667-1735 . . . . **LC 1**
See also DLB 101

Archer, Herbert Winslow
See Mencken, H(enry) L(ouis)

Archer, Jeffrey (Howard)
1940- . . . . **CLC 28; DAM POP**
See also AAYA 16; BEST 89:3; CA 77-80;
CANR 22, 52; INT CANR-22

Archer, Jules 1915- . . . . **CLC 12**
See also CA 9-12R; CANR 6; SAAS 5;
SATA 4, 85

Archer, Lee
See Ellison, Harlan (Jay)

Arden, John
1930- . . . . . **CLC 6, 13, 15; DAM DRAM**
See also CA 13-16R; CAAS 4; CANR 31;
DLB 13; MTCW

Arenas, Reinaldo
1943-1990 . . . . . . **CLC 41; DAM MULT;**
HLC
See also CA 124; 128; 133; DLB 145; HW

Arendt, Hannah 1906-1975 . . . . . **CLC 66, 98**
See also CA 17-20R; 61-64; CANR 26, 60;
MTCW

Aretino, Pietro 1492-1556 . . . . **LC 12**

Arghezi, Tudor . . . . **CLC 80**
See also Theodorescu, Ion N.

Arguedas, Jose Maria
1911-1969 . . . . **CLC 10, 18**
See also CA 89-92; DLB 113; HW

Argueta, Manlio 1936- . . . . **CLC 31**
See also CA 131; DLB 145; HW

Ariosto, Ludovico 1474-1533 . . . . **LC 6**

Aristides
See Epstein, Joseph

Aristophanes
450B.C.-385B.C. . . . . **CMLC 4; DA;**
DAB; DAC; DAM DRAM, MST; DC 2;
WLCS
See also DLB 176

Arlt, Roberto (Godofredo Christophersen)
1900-1942 . . . . . **TCLC 29; DAM MULT;**
HLC
See also CA 123; 131; HW

Armah, Ayi Kwei
1939- . . . . **CLC 5, 33; BLC;**
DAM MULT, POET
See also BW 1; CA 61-64; CANR 21;
DLB 117; MTCW

Armatrading, Joan 1950- . . . . **CLC 17**
See also CA 114

Arnette, Robert
See Silverberg, Robert

Arnim, Achim von (Ludwig Joachim von
Arnim) 1781-1831 . . . **NCLC 5; SSC 29**
See also DLB 90

Arnim, Bettina von 1785-1859 . . . . **NCLC 38**
See also DLB 90

Arnold, Matthew
1822-1888 . . . . . **NCLC 6, 29; DA; DAB;**
DAC; DAM MST, POET; PC 5; WLC
See also CDBLB 1832-1890; DLB 32, 57

Arnold, Thomas 1795-1842 . . . . . . **NCLC 18**
See also DLB 55

Arnow, Harriette (Louisa) Simpson
1908-1986 . . . . **CLC 2, 7, 18**
See also CA 9-12R; 118; CANR 14; DLB 6;
MTCW; SATA 42; SATA-Obit 47

Arp, Hans
See Arp, Jean

Arp, Jean 1887-1966 . . . . **CLC 5**
See also CA 81-84; 25-28R; CANR 42

Arrabal
See Arrabal, Fernando

Arrabal, Fernando 1932- . . . **CLC 2, 9, 18, 58**
See also CA 9-12R; CANR 15

Arrick, Fran. . . . . CLC 30
See also Gaberman, Judie Angell

Artaud, Antonin (Marie Joseph)
1896-1948 . . . TCLC 3, 36; DAM DRAM
See also CA 104; 149

Arthur, Ruth M(abel) 1905-1979. . . . CLC 12
See also CA 9-12R; 85-88; CANR 4;
SATA 7, 26

Artsybashev, Mikhail (Petrovich)
1878-1927 . . . . TCLC 31

Arundel, Honor (Morfydd)
1919-1973 . . . . CLC 17
See also CA 21-22; 41-44R; CAP 2;
CLR 35; SATA 4; SATA-Obit 24

Arzner, Dorothy 1897-1979. . . . . . . CLC 98

Asch, Sholem 1880-1957 . . . . TCLC 3
See also CA 105

Ash, Shalom
See Asch, Sholem

Ashbery, John (Lawrence)
1927- . . . . . . CLC 2, 3, 4, 6, 9, 13, 15, 25,
41, 77; DAM POET
See also CA 5-8R; CANR 9, 37; DLB 5,
165; DLBY 81; INT CANR-9; MTCW

Ashdown, Clifford
See Freeman, R(ichard) Austin

Ashe, Gordon
See Creasey, John

Ashton-Warner, Sylvia (Constance)
1908-1984 . . . . CLC 19
See also CA 69-72; 112; CANR 29; MTCW

Asimov, Isaac
1920-1992 . . . . . . CLC 1, 3, 9, 19, 26, 76,
92; DAM POP
See also AAYA 13; BEST 90:2; CA 1-4R;
137; CANR 2, 19, 36, 60; CLR 12;
DLB 8; DLBY 92; INT CANR-19;
JRDA; MAICYA; MTCW; SATA 1, 26,
74

Assis, Joaquim Maria Machado de
See Machado de Assis, Joaquim Maria

Astley, Thea (Beatrice May)
1925- . . . . CLC 41
See also CA 65-68; CANR 11, 43

Aston, James
See White, T(erence) H(anbury)

Asturias, Miguel Angel
1899-1974 . . . . CLC 3, 8, 13;
DAM MULT, NOV; HLC
See also CA 25-28; 49-52; CANR 32;
CAP 2; DLB 113; HW; MTCW

Atares, Carlos Saura
See Saura (Atares), Carlos

Atheling, William
See Pound, Ezra (Weston Loomis)

Atheling, William, Jr.
See Blish, James (Benjamin)

Atherton, Gertrude (Franklin Horn)
1857-1948 . . . . TCLC 2
See also CA 104; 155; DLB 9, 78

Atherton, Lucius
See Masters, Edgar Lee

Atkins, Jack
See Harris, Mark

Atkinson, Kate. . . . . CLC 99

Attaway, William (Alexander)
1911-1986 . . . . CLC 92; BLC;
DAM MULT
See also BW 2; CA 143; DLB 76

Atticus
See Fleming, Ian (Lancaster)

Atwood, Margaret (Eleanor)
1939- . . . . . CLC 2, 3, 4, 8, 13, 15, 25, 44,
84; DA; DAB; DAC; DAM MST, NOV,
POET; PC 8; SSC 2; WLC
See also AAYA 12; BEST 89:2; CA 49-52;
CANR 3, 24, 33, 59; DLB 53;
INT CANR-24; MTCW; SATA 50

Aubigny, Pierre d'
See Mencken, H(enry) L(ouis)

Aubin, Penelope 1685-1731(?) . . . . LC 9
See also DLB 39

Auchincloss, Louis (Stanton)
1917- . . . . CLC 4, 6, 9, 18, 45;
DAM NOV; SSC 22
See also CA 1-4R; CANR 6, 29, 55; DLB 2;
DLBY 80; INT CANR-29; MTCW

Auden, W(ystan) H(ugh)
1907-1973 . . . . . . CLC 1, 2, 3, 4, 6, 9, 11,
14, 43; DA; DAB; DAC; DAM DRAM,
MST, POET; PC 1; WLC
See also AAYA 18; CA 9-12R; 45-48;
CANR 5, 61; CDBLB 1914-1945;
DLB 10, 20; MTCW

Audiberti, Jacques
1900-1965 . . . . . . CLC 38; DAM DRAM
See also CA 25-28R

Audubon, John James
1785-1851 . . . . NCLC 47

Auel, Jean M(arie)
1936- . . . . CLC 31; DAM POP
See also AAYA 7; BEST 90:4; CA 103;
CANR 21; INT CANR-21; SATA 91

Auerbach, Erich 1892-1957 . . . . . . TCLC 43
See also CA 118; 155

Augier, Emile 1820-1889 . . . . NCLC 31

August, John
See De Voto, Bernard (Augustine)

Augustine, St. 354-430 . . . . . . CMLC 6; DAB

Aurelius
See Bourne, Randolph S(illiman)

Aurobindo, Sri 1872-1950 . . . . TCLC 63

Austen, Jane
1775-1817 . . . . . NCLC 1, 13, 19, 33, 51;
DA; DAB; DAC; DAM MST, NOV;
WLC
See also AAYA 19; CDBLB 1789-1832;
DLB 116

Auster, Paul 1947- . . . . CLC 47
See also CA 69-72; CANR 23, 52

Austin, Frank
See Faust, Frederick (Schiller)

Austin, Mary (Hunter)
1868-1934 . . . . TCLC 25
See also CA 109; DLB 9, 78

Autran Dourado, Waldomiro
See Dourado, (Waldomiro Freitas) Autran

Averroes 1126-1198 . . . . CMLC 7
See also DLB 115

Avicenna 980-1037 . . . . CMLC 16
See also DLB 115

Avison, Margaret
1918- . . . . CLC 2, 4, 97; DAC;
DAM POET
See also CA 17-20R; DLB 53; MTCW

Axton, David
See Koontz, Dean R(ay)

Ayckbourn, Alan
1939- . . . . . . CLC 5, 8, 18, 33, 74; DAB;
DAM DRAM
See also CA 21-24R; CANR 31, 59;
DLB 13; MTCW

Aydy, Catherine
See Tennant, Emma (Christina)

Ayme, Marcel (Andre) 1902-1967. . . CLC 11
See also CA 89-92; CLR 25; DLB 72;
SATA 91

Ayrton, Michael 1921-1975. . . . . CLC 7
See also CA 5-8R; 61-64; CANR 9, 21

Azorin. . . . . CLC 11
See also Martinez Ruiz, Jose

Azuela, Mariano
1873-1952 . . . . . TCLC 3; DAM MULT;
HLC
See also CA 104; 131; HW; MTCW

Baastad, Babbis Friis
See Friis-Baastad, Babbis Ellinor

Bab
See Gilbert, W(illiam) S(chwenck)

Babbis, Eleanor
See Friis-Baastad, Babbis Ellinor

Babel, Isaac
See Babel, Isaak (Emmanuilovich)

Babel, Isaak (Emmanuilovich)
1894-1941(?) . . . . . . TCLC 2, 13; SSC 16
See also CA 104; 155

Babits, Mihaly 1883-1941 . . . . TCLC 14
See also CA 114

Babur 1483-1530. . . . . LC 18

Bacchelli, Riccardo 1891-1985 . . . . . CLC 19
See also CA 29-32R; 117

Bach, Richard (David)
1936- . . . . . . CLC 14; DAM NOV, POP
See also AITN 1; BEST 89:2; CA 9-12R;
CANR 18; MTCW; SATA 13

Bachman, Richard
See King, Stephen (Edwin)

Bachmann, Ingeborg 1926-1973. . . . . CLC 69
See also CA 93-96; 45-48; DLB 85

Bacon, Francis 1561-1626 . . . . LC 18, 32
See also CDBLB Before 1660; DLB 151

Bacon, Roger 1214(?)-1292 . . . . . . CMLC 14
See also DLB 115

Bacovia, George. . . . . TCLC 24
See also Vasiliu, Gheorghe

Badanes, Jerome 1937-. . . . . CLC 59

Bagehot, Walter 1826-1877 . . . . . . NCLC 10
See also DLB 55

Bagnold, Enid
1889-1981 . . . . . . CLC 25; DAM DRAM
See also CA 5-8R; 103; CANR 5, 40;
DLB 13, 160; MAICYA; SATA 1, 25

Bagritsky, Eduard 1895-1934 . . . . . TCLC 60

Bagrjana, Elisaveta
 See Belcheva, Elisaveta

Bagryana, Elisaveta. . . . . **CLC 10**
 See also Belcheva, Elisaveta
 See also DLB 147

Bailey, Paul 1937- . . . . **CLC 45**
 See also CA 21-24R; CANR 16, 62;
 DLB 14

Baillie, Joanna 1762-1851 . . . . **NCLC 2**
 See also DLB 93

Bainbridge, Beryl (Margaret)
 1933- . . . . **CLC 4, 5, 8, 10, 14, 18, 22, 62;**
 DAM NOV
 See also CA 21-24R; CANR 24, 55;
 DLB 14; MTCW

Baker, Elliott 1922- . . . . **CLC 8**
 See also CA 45-48; CANR 2

Baker, Jean H. . . . . **TCLC 3, 10**
 See also Russell, George William

Baker, Nicholson
 1957- . . . . **CLC 61; DAM POP**
 See also CA 135

Baker, Ray Stannard 1870-1946 . . . **TCLC 47**
 See also CA 118

Baker, Russell (Wayne) 1925- . . . . . . **CLC 31**
 See also BEST 89:4; CA 57-60; CANR 11,
 41, 59; MTCW

Bakhtin, M.
 See Bakhtin, Mikhail Mikhailovich

Bakhtin, M. M.
 See Bakhtin, Mikhail Mikhailovich

Bakhtin, Mikhail
 See Bakhtin, Mikhail Mikhailovich

Bakhtin, Mikhail Mikhailovich
 1895-1975 . . . . **CLC 83**
 See also CA 128; 113

Bakshi, Ralph 1938(?)- . . . . **CLC 26**
 See also CA 112; 138

Bakunin, Mikhail (Alexandrovich)
 1814-1876 . . . . **NCLC 25, 58**

Baldwin, James (Arthur)
 1924-1987 . . . . . . **CLC 1, 2, 3, 4, 5, 8, 13,**
 15, 17, 42, 50, 67, 90; BLC; DA; DAB;
 DAC; DAM MST, MULT, NOV, POP;
 DC 1; SSC 10; WLC
 See also AAYA 4; BW 1; CA 1-4R; 124;
 CABS 1; CANR 3, 24;
 CDALB 1941-1968; DLB 2, 7, 33;
 DLBY 87; MTCW; SATA 9;
 SATA-Obit 54

Ballard, J(ames) G(raham)
 1930- . . . . **CLC 3, 6, 14, 36; DAM NOV,**
 POP; SSC 1
 See also AAYA 3; CA 5-8R; CANR 15, 39;
 DLB 14; MTCW; SATA 93

Balmont, Konstantin (Dmitriyevich)
 1867-1943 . . . . **TCLC 11**
 See also CA 109; 155

Balzac, Honore de
 1799-1850 . . . . **NCLC 5, 35, 53; DA;**
 DAB; DAC; DAM MST, NOV; SSC 5;
 WLC
 See also DLB 119

Bambara, Toni Cade
 1939-1995 . . . . . **CLC 19, 88; BLC; DA;**
 DAC; DAM MST, MULT; WLCS
 See also AAYA 5; BW 2; CA 29-32R; 150;
 CANR 24, 49; DLB 38; MTCW

Bamdad, A.
 See Shamlu, Ahmad

Banat, D. R.
 See Bradbury, Ray (Douglas)

Bancroft, Laura
 See Baum, L(yman) Frank

Banim, John 1798-1842 . . . . **NCLC 13**
 See also DLB 116, 158, 159

Banim, Michael 1796-1874 . . . . . . **NCLC 13**
 See also DLB 158, 159

Banjo, The
 See Paterson, A(ndrew) B(arton)

Banks, Iain
 See Banks, Iain M(enzies)

Banks, Iain M(enzies) 1954- . . . . **CLC 34**
 See also CA 123; 128; CANR 61; INT 128

Banks, Lynne Reid . . . . **CLC 23**
 See also Reid Banks, Lynne
 See also AAYA 6

Banks, Russell 1940- . . . . **CLC 37, 72**
 See also CA 65-68; CAAS 15; CANR 19,
 52; DLB 130

Banville, John 1945- . . . . **CLC 46**
 See also CA 117; 128; DLB 14; INT 128

Banville, Theodore (Faullain) de
 1832-1891 . . . . **NCLC 9**

Baraka, Amiri
 1934- . . . . **CLC 1, 2, 3, 5, 10, 14, 33;**
 BLC; DA; DAC; DAM MST, MULT,
 POET, POP; DC 6; PC 4; WLCS
 See also Jones, LeRoi
 See also BW 2; CA 21-24R; CABS 3;
 CANR 27, 38, 61; CDALB 1941-1968;
 DLB 5, 7, 16, 38; DLBD 8; MTCW

Barbauld, Anna Laetitia
 1743-1825 . . . . **NCLC 50**
 See also DLB 107, 109, 142, 158

Barbellion, W. N. P. . . . . **TCLC 24**
 See also Cummings, Bruce F(rederick)

Barbera, Jack (Vincent) 1945- . . . . . . **CLC 44**
 See also CA 110; CANR 45

Barbey d'Aurevilly, Jules Amedee
 1808-1889 . . . . **NCLC 1; SSC 17**
 See also DLB 119

Barbusse, Henri 1873-1935 . . . . **TCLC 5**
 See also CA 105; 154; DLB 65

Barclay, Bill
 See Moorcock, Michael (John)

Barclay, William Ewert
 See Moorcock, Michael (John)

Barea, Arturo 1897-1957 . . . . **TCLC 14**
 See also CA 111

Barfoot, Joan 1946- . . . . **CLC 18**
 See also CA 105

Baring, Maurice 1874-1945 . . . . **TCLC 8**
 See also CA 105; DLB 34

Barker, Clive 1952- . . . **CLC 52; DAM POP**
 See also AAYA 10; BEST 90:3; CA 121;
 129; INT 129; MTCW

Barker, George Granville
 1913-1991 . . . . . **CLC 8, 48; DAM POET**
 See also CA 9-12R; 135; CANR 7, 38;
 DLB 20; MTCW

Barker, Harley Granville
 See Granville-Barker, Harley
 See also DLB 10

Barker, Howard 1946- . . . . **CLC 37**
 See also CA 102; DLB 13

Barker, Pat(ricia) 1943- . . . . **CLC 32, 94**
 See also CA 117; 122; CANR 50; INT 122

Barlow, Joel 1754-1812 . . . . **NCLC 23**
 See also DLB 37

Barnard, Mary (Ethel) 1909- . . . . **CLC 48**
 See also CA 21-22; CAP 2

Barnes, Djuna
 1892-1982 . . . **CLC 3, 4, 8, 11, 29; SSC 3**
 See also CA 9-12R; 107; CANR 16, 55;
 DLB 4, 9, 45; MTCW

Barnes, Julian (Patrick)
 1946- . . . . **CLC 42; DAB**
 See also CA 102; CANR 19, 54; DLBY 93

Barnes, Peter 1931- . . . . **CLC 5, 56**
 See also CA 65-68; CAAS 12; CANR 33,
 34; DLB 13; MTCW

Baroja (y Nessi), Pio
 1872-1956 . . . . **TCLC 8; HLC**
 See also CA 104

Baron, David
 See Pinter, Harold

Baron Corvo
 See Rolfe, Frederick (William Serafino
 Austin Lewis Mary)

Barondess, Sue K(aufman)
 1926-1977 . . . . **CLC 8**
 See also Kaufman, Sue
 See also CA 1-4R; 69-72; CANR 1

Baron de Teive
 See Pessoa, Fernando (Antonio Nogueira)

Barres, Maurice 1862-1923 . . . . **TCLC 47**
 See also DLB 123

Barreto, Afonso Henrique de Lima
 See Lima Barreto, Afonso Henrique de

Barrett, (Roger) Syd 1946- . . . . **CLC 35**

Barrett, William (Christopher)
 1913-1992 . . . . **CLC 27**
 See also CA 13-16R; 139; CANR 11;
 INT CANR-11

Barrie, J(ames) M(atthew)
 1860-1937 . . . . **TCLC 2; DAB;**
 DAM DRAM
 See also CA 104; 136; CDBLB 1890-1914;
 CLR 16; DLB 10, 141, 156; MAICYA;
 YABC 1

Barrington, Michael
 See Moorcock, Michael (John)

Barrol, Grady
 See Bograd, Larry

Barry, Mike
 See Malzberg, Barry N(athaniel)

Barry, Philip 1896-1949 . . . . **TCLC 11**
 See also CA 109; DLB 7

Bart, Andre Schwarz
 See Schwarz-Bart, Andre

Bellin, Edward J.
See Kuttner, Henry

Belloc, (Joseph) Hilaire (Pierre Sebastien Rene Swanton)
1870-1953 . . . **TCLC 7, 18; DAM POET**
See also CA 106; 152; DLB 19, 100, 141, 174; YABC 1

Belloc, Joseph Peter Rene Hilaire
See Belloc, (Joseph) Hilaire (Pierre Sebastien Rene Swanton)

Belloc, Joseph Pierre Hilaire
See Belloc, (Joseph) Hilaire (Pierre Sebastien Rene Swanton)

Belloc, M. A.
See Lowndes, Marie Adelaide (Belloc)

Bellow, Saul
1915- . . . . . . **CLC 1, 2, 3, 6, 8, 10, 13, 15, 25, 33, 34, 63, 79; DA; DAB; DAC; DAM MST, NOV, POP; SSC 14; WLC**
See also AITN 2; BEST 89:3; CA 5-8R; CABS 1; CANR 29, 53; CDALB 1941-1968; DLB 2, 28; DLBD 3; DLBY 82; MTCW

Belser, Reimond Karel Maria de 1929-
See Ruyslinck, Ward
See also CA 152

Bely, Andrey . . . . **TCLC 7; PC 11**
See also Bugayev, Boris Nikolayevich

Benary, Margot
See Benary-Isbert, Margot

Benary-Isbert, Margot 1889-1979 . . . **CLC 12**
See also CA 5-8R; 89-92; CANR 4; CLR 12; MAICYA; SATA 2; SATA-Obit 21

Benavente (y Martinez), Jacinto
1866-1954 . . . . . **TCLC 3; DAM DRAM, MULT**
See also CA 106; 131; HW; MTCW

Benchley, Peter (Bradford)
1940- . . . . . **CLC 4, 8; DAM NOV, POP**
See also AAYA 14; AITN 2; CA 17-20R; CANR 12, 35; MTCW; SATA 3, 89

Benchley, Robert (Charles)
1889-1945 . . . . **TCLC 1, 55**
See also CA 105; 153; DLB 11

Benda, Julien 1867-1956 . . . . **TCLC 60**
See also CA 120; 154

Benedict, Ruth (Fulton)
1887-1948 . . . . **TCLC 60**
See also CA 158

Benedikt, Michael 1935- . . . . **CLC 4, 14**
See also CA 13-16R; CANR 7; DLB 5

Benet, Juan 1927- . . . . **CLC 28**
See also CA 143

Benet, Stephen Vincent
1898-1943 . . . . . . **TCLC 7; DAM POET; SSC 10**
See also CA 104; 152; DLB 4, 48, 102; YABC 1

Benet, William Rose
1886-1950 . . . . . . **TCLC 28; DAM POET**
See also CA 118; 152; DLB 45

Benford, Gregory (Albert) 1941- . . . . **CLC 52**
See also CA 69-72; CAAS 27; CANR 12, 24, 49; DLBY 82

Bengtsson, Frans (Gunnar)
1894-1954 . . . . **TCLC 48**

Benjamin, David
See Slavitt, David R(ytman)

Benjamin, Lois
See Gould, Lois

Benjamin, Walter 1892-1940 . . . . . . **TCLC 39**

Benn, Gottfried 1886-1956 . . . . **TCLC 3**
See also CA 106; 153; DLB 56

Bennett, Alan
1934- . . . **CLC 45, 77; DAB; DAM MST**
See also CA 103; CANR 35, 55; MTCW

Bennett, (Enoch) Arnold
1867-1931 . . . . **TCLC 5, 20**
See also CA 106; 155; CDBLB 1890-1914; DLB 10, 34, 98, 135

Bennett, Elizabeth
See Mitchell, Margaret (Munnerlyn)

Bennett, George Harold 1930-
See Bennett, Hal
See also BW 1; CA 97-100

Bennett, Hal . . . . **CLC 5**
See also Bennett, George Harold
See also DLB 33

Bennett, Jay 1912- . . . . **CLC 35**
See also AAYA 10; CA 69-72; CANR 11, 42; JRDA; SAAS 4; SATA 41, 87; SATA-Brief 27

Bennett, Louise (Simone)
1919- . . . . . **CLC 28; BLC; DAM MULT**
See also BW 2; CA 151; DLB 117

Benson, E(dward) F(rederic)
1867-1940 . . . . **TCLC 27**
See also CA 114; 157; DLB 135, 153

Benson, Jackson J. 1930- . . . . **CLC 34**
See also CA 25-28R; DLB 111

Benson, Sally 1900-1972 . . . . **CLC 17**
See also CA 19-20; 37-40R; CAP 1; SATA 1, 35; SATA-Obit 27

Benson, Stella 1892-1933 . . . . **TCLC 17**
See also CA 117; 155; DLB 36, 162

Bentham, Jeremy 1748-1832 . . . . . **NCLC 38**
See also DLB 107, 158

Bentley, E(dmund) C(lerihew)
1875-1956 . . . . **TCLC 12**
See also CA 108; DLB 70

Bentley, Eric (Russell) 1916- . . . . **CLC 24**
See also CA 5-8R; CANR 6; INT CANR-6

Beranger, Pierre Jean de
1780-1857 . . . . **NCLC 34**

Berdyaev, Nicolas
See Berdyaev, Nikolai (Aleksandrovich)

Berdyaev, Nikolai (Aleksandrovich)
1874-1948 . . . . **TCLC 67**
See also CA 120; 157

Berdyayev, Nikolai (Aleksandrovich)
See Berdyaev, Nikolai (Aleksandrovich)

Berendt, John (Lawrence) 1939- . . . . **CLC 86**
See also CA 146

Berger, Colonel
See Malraux, (Georges-)Andre

Berger, John (Peter) 1926- . . . . . . **CLC 2, 19**
See also CA 81-84; CANR 51; DLB 14

Berger, Melvin H. 1927- . . . . **CLC 12**
See also CA 5-8R; CANR 4; CLR 32; SAAS 2; SATA 5, 88

Berger, Thomas (Louis)
1924- . . . . **CLC 3, 5, 8, 11, 18, 38; DAM NOV**
See also CA 1-4R; CANR 5, 28, 51; DLB 2; DLBY 80; INT CANR-28; MTCW

Bergman, (Ernst) Ingmar
1918- . . . . **CLC 16, 72**
See also CA 81-84; CANR 33

Bergson, Henri 1859-1941 . . . . **TCLC 32**

Bergstein, Eleanor 1938- . . . . **CLC 4**
See also CA 53-56; CANR 5

Berkoff, Steven 1937- . . . . **CLC 56**
See also CA 104

Bermant, Chaim (Icyk) 1929- . . . . . . **CLC 40**
See also CA 57-60; CANR 6, 31, 57

Bern, Victoria
See Fisher, M(ary) F(rances) K(ennedy)

Bernanos, (Paul Louis) Georges
1888-1948 . . . . **TCLC 3**
See also CA 104; 130; DLB 72

Bernard, April 1956- . . . . **CLC 59**
See also CA 131

Berne, Victoria
See Fisher, M(ary) F(rances) K(ennedy)

Bernhard, Thomas
1931-1989 . . . . **CLC 3, 32, 61**
See also CA 85-88; 127; CANR 32, 57; DLB 85, 124; MTCW

Berriault, Gina 1926- . . . . **CLC 54**
See also CA 116; 129; DLB 130

Berrigan, Daniel 1921- . . . . **CLC 4**
See also CA 33-36R; CAAS 1; CANR 11, 43; DLB 5

Berrigan, Edmund Joseph Michael, Jr.
1934-1983
See Berrigan, Ted
See also CA 61-64; 110; CANR 14

Berrigan, Ted . . . . **CLC 37**
See also Berrigan, Edmund Joseph Michael, Jr.
See also DLB 5, 169

Berry, Charles Edward Anderson 1931-
See Berry, Chuck
See also CA 115

Berry, Chuck . . . . **CLC 17**
See also Berry, Charles Edward Anderson

Berry, Jonas
See Ashbery, John (Lawrence)

Berry, Wendell (Erdman)
1934- . . . . **CLC 4, 6, 8, 27, 46; DAM POET**
See also AITN 1; CA 73-76; CANR 50; DLB 5, 6

Berryman, John
1914-1972 . . . . . . **CLC 1, 2, 3, 4, 6, 8, 10, 13, 25, 62; DAM POET**
See also CA 13-16; 33-36R; CABS 2; CANR 35; CAP 1; CDALB 1941-1968; DLB 48; MTCW

Bertolucci, Bernardo 1940- . . . . **CLC 16**
See also CA 106

Boas, Franz 1858-1942 . . . . **TCLC 56**
See also CA 115

Bobette
See Simenon, Georges (Jacques Christian)

Boccaccio, Giovanni
1313-1375 . . . . **CMLC 13; SSC 10**

Bochco, Steven 1943- . . . . **CLC 35**
See also AAYA 11; CA 124; 138

Bodenheim, Maxwell 1892-1954 . . . **TCLC 44**
See also CA 110; DLB 9, 45

Bodker, Cecil 1927- . . . . **CLC 21**
See also CA 73-76; CANR 13, 44; CLR 23;
MAICYA; SATA 14

Boell, Heinrich (Theodor)
1917-1985 . . . . **CLC 2, 3, 6, 9, 11, 15, 27,
32, 72; DA; DAB; DAC; DAM MST,
NOV; SSC 23; WLC**
See also CA 21-24R; 116; CANR 24;
DLB 69; DLBY 85; MTCW

Boerne, Alfred
See Doeblin, Alfred

Boethius 480(?)-524(?) . . . . **CMLC 15**
See also DLB 115

Bogan, Louise
1897-1970 . . . . **CLC 4, 39, 46, 93;
DAM POET; PC 12**
See also CA 73-76; 25-28R; CANR 33;
DLB 45, 169; MTCW

Bogarde, Dirk . . . . **CLC 19**
See also Van Den Bogarde, Derek Jules
Gaspard Ulric Niven
See also DLB 14

Bogosian, Eric 1953- . . . . **CLC 45**
See also CA 138

Bograd, Larry 1953- . . . . **CLC 35**
See also CA 93-96; CANR 57; SAAS 21;
SATA 33, 89

Boiardo, Matteo Maria 1441-1494 . . . . **LC 6**

Boileau-Despreaux, Nicolas
1636-1711 . . . . **LC 3**

Bojer, Johan 1872-1959 . . . . **TCLC 64**

Boland, Eavan (Aisling)
1944- . . . . **CLC 40, 67; DAM POET**
See also CA 143; CANR 61; DLB 40

Bolt, Lee
See Faust, Frederick (Schiller)

Bolt, Robert (Oxton)
1924-1995 . . . . . . **CLC 14; DAM DRAM**
See also CA 17-20R; 147; CANR 35;
DLB 13; MTCW

Bombet, Louis-Alexandre-Cesar
See Stendhal

Bomkauf
See Kaufman, Bob (Garnell)

Bonaventura . . . . **NCLC 35**
See also DLB 90

Bond, Edward
1934- . . . **CLC 4, 6, 13, 23; DAM DRAM**
See also CA 25-28R; CANR 38; DLB 13;
MTCW

Bonham, Frank 1914-1989 . . . . **CLC 12**
See also AAYA 1; CA 9-12R; CANR 4, 36;
JRDA; MAICYA; SAAS 3; SATA 1, 49;
SATA-Obit 62

Bonnefoy, Yves
1923- . . . . . . **CLC 9, 15, 58; DAM MST,
POET**
See also CA 85-88; CANR 33; MTCW

Bontemps, Arna(ud Wendell)
1902-1973 . . . . **CLC 1, 18; BLC;
DAM MULT, NOV, POET**
See also BW 1; CA 1-4R; 41-44R; CANR 4,
35; CLR 6; DLB 48, 51; JRDA;
MAICYA; MTCW; SATA 2, 44;
SATA-Obit 24

Booth, Martin 1944- . . . . **CLC 13**
See also CA 93-96; CAAS 2

Booth, Philip 1925- . . . . **CLC 23**
See also CA 5-8R; CANR 5; DLBY 82

Booth, Wayne C(layson) 1921- . . . . . **CLC 24**
See also CA 1-4R; CAAS 5; CANR 3, 43;
DLB 67

Borchert, Wolfgang 1921-1947 . . . . . **TCLC 5**
See also CA 104; DLB 69, 124

Borel, Petrus 1809-1859 . . . . **NCLC 41**

Borges, Jorge Luis
1899-1986 . . . **CLC 1, 2, 3, 4, 6, 8, 9, 10,
13, 19, 44, 48, 83; DA; DAB; DAC;
DAM MST, MULT; HLC; SSC 4; WLC**
See also AAYA 19; CA 21-24R; CANR 19,
33; DLB 113; DLBY 86; HW; MTCW

Borowski, Tadeusz 1922-1951 . . . . . . **TCLC 9**
See also CA 106; 154

Borrow, George (Henry)
1803-1881 . . . . **NCLC 9**
See also DLB 21, 55, 166

Bosman, Herman Charles
1905-1951 . . . . **TCLC 49**

Bosschere, Jean de 1878(?)-1953 . . . **TCLC 19**
See also CA 115

Boswell, James
1740-1795 . . . . . . **LC 4; DA; DAB; DAC;
DAM MST; WLC**
See also CDBLB 1660-1789; DLB 104, 142

Bottoms, David 1949- . . . . **CLC 53**
See also CA 105; CANR 22; DLB 120;
DLBY 83

Boucicault, Dion 1820-1890 . . . . . . **NCLC 41**

Boucolon, Maryse 1937(?)-
See Conde, Maryse
See also CA 110; CANR 30, 53

Bourget, Paul (Charles Joseph)
1852-1935 . . . . **TCLC 12**
See also CA 107; DLB 123

Bourjaily, Vance (Nye) 1922- . . . . **CLC 8, 62**
See also CA 1-4R; CAAS 1; CANR 2;
DLB 2, 143

Bourne, Randolph S(illiman)
1886-1918 . . . . **TCLC 16**
See also CA 117; 155; DLB 63

Bova, Ben(jamin William) 1932- . . . . **CLC 45**
See also AAYA 16; CA 5-8R; CAAS 18;
CANR 11, 56; CLR 3; DLBY 81;
INT CANR-11; MAICYA; MTCW;
SATA 6, 68

Bowen, Elizabeth (Dorothea Cole)
1899-1973 . . . . . . **CLC 1, 3, 6, 11, 15, 22;
DAM NOV; SSC 3, 28**
See also CA 17-18; 41-44R; CANR 35;
CAP 2; CDBLB 1945-1960; DLB 15, 162;
MTCW

Bowering, George 1935- . . . . **CLC 15, 47**
See also CA 21-24R; CAAS 16; CANR 10;
DLB 53

Bowering, Marilyn R(uthe) 1949- . . . **CLC 32**
See also CA 101; CANR 49

Bowers, Edgar 1924- . . . . **CLC 9**
See also CA 5-8R; CANR 24; DLB 5

Bowie, David . . . . **CLC 17**
See also Jones, David Robert

Bowles, Jane (Sydney)
1917-1973 . . . . **CLC 3, 68**
See also CA 19-20; 41-44R; CAP 2

Bowles, Paul (Frederick)
1910- . . . . **CLC 1, 2, 19, 53; SSC 3**
See also CA 1-4R; CAAS 1; CANR 1, 19,
50; DLB 5, 6; MTCW

Box, Edgar
See Vidal, Gore

Boyd, Nancy
See Millay, Edna St. Vincent

Boyd, William 1952- . . . . **CLC 28, 53, 70**
See also CA 114; 120; CANR 51

Boyle, Kay
1902-1992 . . . . . **CLC 1, 5, 19, 58; SSC 5**
See also CA 13-16R; 140; CAAS 1;
CANR 29, 61; DLB 4, 9, 48, 86;
DLBY 93; MTCW

Boyle, Mark
See Kienzle, William X(avier)

Boyle, Patrick 1905-1982 . . . . **CLC 19**
See also CA 127

Boyle, T. C. 1948-
See Boyle, T(homas) Coraghessan

Boyle, T(homas) Coraghessan
1948- . . . . . **CLC 36, 55, 90; DAM POP;
SSC 16**
See also BEST 90:4; CA 120; CANR 44;
DLBY 86

Boz
See Dickens, Charles (John Huffam)

Brackenridge, Hugh Henry
1748-1816 . . . . **NCLC 7**
See also DLB 11, 37

Bradbury, Edward P.
See Moorcock, Michael (John)

Bradbury, Malcolm (Stanley)
1932- . . . . **CLC 32, 61; DAM NOV**
See also CA 1-4R; CANR 1, 33; DLB 14;
MTCW

Bradbury, Ray (Douglas)
1920- . . . . . **CLC 1, 3, 10, 15, 42, 98; DA;
DAB; DAC; DAM MST, NOV, POP;
SSC 29; WLC**
See also AAYA 15; AITN 1, 2; CA 1-4R;
CANR 2, 30; CDALB 1968-1988; DLB 2,
8; INT CANR-30; MTCW; SATA 11, 64

Bradford, Gamaliel 1863-1932 . . . . . **TCLC 36**
See also DLB 17

Bradley, David (Henry, Jr.)
1950- . . . . . **CLC 23; BLC; DAM MULT**
See also BW 1; CA 104; CANR 26; DLB 33

Bradley, John Ed(mund, Jr.)
1958- . . . . **CLC 55**
See also CA 139

Bradley, Marion Zimmer
1930- . . . . **CLC 30; DAM POP**
See also AAYA 9; CA 57-60; CAAS 10;
CANR 7, 31, 51; DLB 8; MTCW;
SATA 90

Bradstreet, Anne
1612(?)-1672 . . . . . **LC 4, 30; DA; DAC;**
DAM MST, POET; PC 10
See also CDALB 1640-1865; DLB 24

Brady, Joan 1939- . . . . **CLC 86**
See also CA 141

Bragg, Melvyn 1939- . . . . **CLC 10**
See also BEST 89:3; CA 57-60; CANR 10,
48; DLB 14

Braine, John (Gerard)
1922-1986 . . . . **CLC 1, 3, 41**
See also CA 1-4R; 120; CANR 1, 33;
CDBLB 1945-1960; DLB 15; DLBY 86;
MTCW

Bramah, Ernest 1868-1942 . . . . **TCLC 72**
See also CA 156; DLB 70

Brammer, William 1930(?)-1978 . . . . **CLC 31**
See also CA 77-80

Brancati, Vitaliano 1907-1954 . . . . . **TCLC 12**
See also CA 109

Brancato, Robin F(idler) 1936- . . . . . **CLC 35**
See also AAYA 9; CA 69-72; CANR 11,
45; CLR 32; JRDA; SAAS 9; SATA 23

Brand, Max
See Faust, Frederick (Schiller)

Brand, Millen 1906-1980 . . . . **CLC 7**
See also CA 21-24R; 97-100

Branden, Barbara . . . . **CLC 44**
See also CA 148

Brandes, Georg (Morris Cohen)
1842-1927 . . . . **TCLC 10**
See also CA 105

Brandys, Kazimierz 1916- . . . . **CLC 62**

Branley, Franklyn M(ansfield)
1915- . . . . **CLC 21**
See also CA 33-36R; CANR 14, 39;
CLR 13; MAICYA; SAAS 16; SATA 4,
68

Brathwaite, Edward Kamau
1930- . . . . **CLC 11; DAM POET**
See also BW 2; CA 25-28R; CANR 11, 26,
47; DLB 125

Brautigan, Richard (Gary)
1935-1984 . . . . **CLC 1, 3, 5, 9, 12, 34, 42;**
DAM NOV
See also CA 53-56; 113; CANR 34; DLB 2,
5; DLBY 80, 84; MTCW; SATA 56

Brave Bird, Mary 1953-
See Crow Dog, Mary (Ellen)
See also NNAL

Braverman, Kate 1950- . . . . **CLC 67**
See also CA 89-92

Brecht, (Eugen) Bertolt (Friedrich)
1898-1956 . . . . . . **TCLC 1, 6, 13, 35; DA;**
DAB; DAC; DAM DRAM, MST; DC 3;
WLC
See also CA 104; 133; CANR 62; DLB 56,
124; MTCW

Brecht, Eugen Berthold Friedrich
See Brecht, (Eugen) Bertolt (Friedrich)

Bremer, Fredrika 1801-1865 . . . . . **NCLC 11**

Brennan, Christopher John
1870-1932 . . . . **TCLC 17**
See also CA 117

Brennan, Maeve 1917- . . . . **CLC 5**
See also CA 81-84

Brentano, Clemens (Maria)
1778-1842 . . . . **NCLC 1**
See also DLB 90

Brent of Bin Bin
See Franklin, (Stella Maraia Sarah) Miles

Brenton, Howard 1942- . . . . **CLC 31**
See also CA 69-72; CANR 33; DLB 13;
MTCW

Breslin, James 1930-
See Breslin, Jimmy
See also CA 73-76; CANR 31; DAM NOV;
MTCW

Breslin, Jimmy . . . . **CLC 4, 43**
See also Breslin, James
See also AITN 1

Bresson, Robert 1901- . . . . **CLC 16**
See also CA 110; CANR 49

Breton, Andre
1896-1966 . . . . . **CLC 2, 9, 15, 54; PC 15**
See also CA 19-20; 25-28R; CANR 40, 60;
CAP 2; DLB 65; MTCW

Breytenbach, Breyten
1939(?)- . . . . . . **CLC 23, 37; DAM POET**
See also CA 113; 129; CANR 61

Bridgers, Sue Ellen 1942- . . . . **CLC 26**
See also AAYA 8; CA 65-68; CANR 11,
36; CLR 18; DLB 52; JRDA; MAICYA;
SAAS 1; SATA 22, 90

Bridges, Robert (Seymour)
1844-1930 . . . . . . **TCLC 1; DAM POET**
See also CA 104; 152; CDBLB 1890-1914;
DLB 19, 98

Bridie, James . . . . **TCLC 3**
See also Mavor, Osborne Henry
See also DLB 10

Brin, David 1950- . . . . **CLC 34**
See also AAYA 21; CA 102; CANR 24;
INT CANR-24; SATA 65

Brink, Andre (Philippus)
1935- . . . . **CLC 18, 36**
See also CA 104; CANR 39, 62; INT 103;
MTCW

Brinsmead, H(esba) F(ay) 1922- . . . . **CLC 21**
See also CA 21-24R; CANR 10; MAICYA;
SAAS 5; SATA 18, 78

Brittain, Vera (Mary)
1893(?)-1970 . . . . **CLC 23**
See also CA 13-16; 25-28R; CANR 58;
CAP 1; MTCW

Broch, Hermann 1886-1951 . . . . **TCLC 20**
See also CA 117; DLB 85, 124

Brock, Rose
See Hansen, Joseph

Brodkey, Harold (Roy) 1930-1996 . . **CLC 56**
See also CA 111; 151; DLB 130

Brodsky, Iosif Alexandrovich 1940-1996
See Brodsky, Joseph
See also AITN 1; CA 41-44R; 151;
CANR 37; DAM POET; MTCW

Brodsky, Joseph
1940-1996 . . **CLC 4, 6, 13, 36, 100; PC 9**
See also Brodsky, Iosif Alexandrovich

Brodsky, Michael (Mark) 1948- . . . . **CLC 19**
See also CA 102; CANR 18, 41, 58

Bromell, Henry 1947- . . . . **CLC 5**
See also CA 53-56; CANR 9

Bromfield, Louis (Brucker)
1896-1956 . . . . **TCLC 11**
See also CA 107; 155; DLB 4, 9, 86

Broner, E(sther) M(asserman)
1930- . . . . **CLC 19**
See also 17-20R; CANR 8, 25; DLB 28

Bronk, William 1918- . . . . **CLC 10**
See also CA 89-92; CANR 23; DLB 165

Bronstein, Lev Davidovich
See Trotsky, Leon

Bronte, Anne 1820-1849 . . . . **NCLC 4**
See also DLB 21

Bronte, Charlotte
1816-1855 . . . . . **NCLC 3, 8, 33, 58; DA;**
DAB; DAC; DAM MST, NOV; WLC
See also AAYA 17; CDBLB 1832-1890;
DLB 21, 159

Bronte, Emily (Jane)
1818-1848 . . . . **NCLC 16, 35; DA; DAB;**
DAC; DAM MST, NOV, POET; PC 8;
WLC
See also AAYA 17; CDBLB 1832-1890;
DLB 21, 32

Brooke, Frances 1724-1789 . . . . **LC 6**
See also DLB 39, 99

Brooke, Henry 1703(?)-1783 . . . . **LC 1**
See also DLB 39

Brooke, Rupert (Chawner)
1887-1915 . . . . **TCLC 2, 7; DA; DAB;**
DAC; DAM MST, POET; WLC
See also CA 104; 132; CANR 61;
CDBLB 1914-1945; DLB 19; MTCW

Brooke-Haven, P.
See Wodehouse, P(elham) G(renville)

Brooke-Rose, Christine 1926(?)- . . . . **CLC 40**
See also CA 13-16R; CANR 58; DLB 14

Brookner, Anita
1928- . . . . **CLC 32, 34, 51; DAB;**
DAM POP
See also CA 114; 120; CANR 37, 56;
DLBY 87; MTCW

Brooks, Cleanth 1906-1994 . . . . . **CLC 24, 86**
See also CA 17-20R; 145; CANR 33, 35;
DLB 63; DLBY 94; INT CANR-35;
MTCW

Brooks, George
See Baum, L(yman) Frank

Brooks, Gwendolyn
1917- ...... **CLC 1, 2, 4, 5, 15, 49; BLC;
DA; DAC; DAM MST, MULT, POET;
PC 7; WLC**
See also AAYA 20; AITN 1; BW 2;
CA 1-4R; CANR 1, 27, 52;
CDALB 1941-1968; CLR 27; DLB 5, 76,
165; MTCW; SATA 6

Brooks, Mel.................... **CLC 12**
See also Kaminsky, Melvin
See also AAYA 13; DLB 26

Brooks, Peter 1938-.............. **CLC 34**
See also CA 45-48; CANR 1

Brooks, Van Wyck 1886-1963...... **CLC 29**
See also CA 1-4R; CANR 6; DLB 45, 63,
103

Brophy, Brigid (Antonia)
1929-1995 .... **CLC 6, 11, 29**
See also CA 5-8R; 149; CAAS 4; CANR 25,
53; DLB 14; MTCW

Brosman, Catharine Savage 1934-.... **CLC 9**
See also CA 61-64; CANR 21, 46

Brother Antoninus
See Everson, William (Oliver)

Broughton, T(homas) Alan 1936- ... **CLC 19**
See also CA 45-48; CANR 2, 23, 48

Broumas, Olga 1949-.......... **CLC 10, 73**
See also CA 85-88; CANR 20

Brown, Alan 1951-.............. **CLC 99**

Brown, Charles Brockden
1771-1810 .... **NCLC 22**
See also CDALB 1640-1865; DLB 37, 59,
73

Brown, Christy 1932-1981........ **CLC 63**
See also CA 105; 104; DLB 14

Brown, Claude
1937- ..... **CLC 30; BLC; DAM MULT**
See also AAYA 7; BW 1; CA 73-76

Brown, Dee (Alexander)
1908- .... **CLC 18, 47; DAM POP**
See also CA 13-16R; CAAS 6; CANR 11,
45, 60; DLBY 80; MTCW; SATA 5

Brown, George
See Wertmueller, Lina

Brown, George Douglas
1869-1902 .... **TCLC 28**

Brown, George Mackay
1921-1996 .... **CLC 5, 48, 100**
See also CA 21-24R; 151; CAAS 6;
CANR 12, 37, 62; DLB 14, 27, 139;
MTCW; SATA 35

Brown, (William) Larry 1951-...... **CLC 73**
See also CA 130; 134; INT 133

Brown, Moses
See Barrett, William (Christopher)

Brown, Rita Mae
1944- ..... **CLC 18, 43, 79; DAM NOV,
POP**
See also CA 45-48; CANR 2, 11, 35, 62;
INT CANR-11; MTCW

Brown, Roderick (Langmere) Haig-
See Haig-Brown, Roderick (Langmere)

Brown, Rosellen 1939-........... **CLC 32**
See also CA 77-80; CAAS 10; CANR 14, 44

Brown, Sterling Allen
1901-1989 .... **CLC 1, 23, 59; BLC;
DAM MULT, POET**
See also BW 1; CA 85-88; 127; CANR 26;
DLB 48, 51, 63; MTCW

Brown, Will
See Ainsworth, William Harrison

Brown, William Wells
1813-1884 .... **NCLC 2; BLC;
DAM MULT; DC 1**
See also DLB 3, 50

Browne, (Clyde) Jackson 1948(?)-... **CLC 21**
See also CA 120

Browning, Elizabeth Barrett
1806-1861 .... **NCLC 1, 16, 61; DA;
DAB; DAC; DAM MST, POET; PC 6;
WLC**
See also CDBLB 1832-1890; DLB 32

Browning, Robert
1812-1889 ...... **NCLC 19; DA; DAB;
DAC; DAM MST, POET; PC 2; WLCS**
See also CDBLB 1832-1890; DLB 32, 163;
YABC 1

Browning, Tod 1882-1962 .... **CLC 16**
See also CA 141; 117

Brownson, Orestes (Augustus)
1803-1876 .... **NCLC 50**

Bruccoli, Matthew J(oseph) 1931-.. **CLC 34**
See also CA 9-12R; CANR 7; DLB 103

Bruce, Lenny.................... **CLC 21**
See also Schneider, Leonard Alfred

Bruin, John
See Brutus, Dennis

Brulard, Henri
See Stendhal

Brulls, Christian
See Simenon, Georges (Jacques Christian)

Brunner, John (Kilian Houston)
1934-1995 ...... **CLC 8, 10; DAM POP**
See also CA 1-4R; 149; CAAS 8; CANR 2,
37; MTCW

Bruno, Giordano 1548-1600........ **LC 27**

Brutus, Dennis
1924- ..... **CLC 43; BLC; DAM MULT,
POET**
See also BW 2; CA 49-52; CAAS 14;
CANR 2, 27, 42; DLB 117

Bryan, C(ourtlandt) D(ixon) B(arnes)
1936- .... **CLC 29**
See also CA 73-76; CANR 13;
INT CANR-13

Bryan, Michael
See Moore, Brian

Bryant, William Cullen
1794-1878 ..... **NCLC 6, 46; DA; DAB;
DAC; DAM MST, POET**
See also CDALB 1640-1865; DLB 3, 43, 59

Bryusov, Valery Yakovlevich
1873-1924 .... **TCLC 10**
See also CA 107; 155

Buchan, John
1875-1940 .... **TCLC 41; DAB;
DAM POP**
See also CA 108; 145; DLB 34, 70, 156;
YABC 2

Buchanan, George 1506-1582 .... **LC 4**

Buchheim, Lothar-Guenther 1918- ... **CLC 6**
See also CA 85-88

Buchner, (Karl) Georg
1813-1837 .... **NCLC 26**

Buchwald, Art(hur) 1925-......... **CLC 33**
See also AITN 1; CA 5-8R; CANR 21;
MTCW; SATA 10

Buck, Pearl S(ydenstricker)
1892-1973 .... **CLC 7, 11, 18; DA; DAB;
DAC; DAM MST, NOV**
See also AITN 1; CA 1-4R; 41-44R;
CANR 1, 34; DLB 9, 102; MTCW;
SATA 1, 25

Buckler, Ernest
1908-1984 .. **CLC 13; DAC; DAM MST**
See also CA 11-12; 114; CAP 1; DLB 68;
SATA 47

Buckley, Vincent (Thomas)
1925-1988 .... **CLC 57**
See also CA 101

Buckley, William F(rank), Jr.
1925- .... **CLC 7, 18, 37; DAM POP**
See also AITN 1; CA 1-4R; CANR 1, 24,
53; DLB 137; DLBY 80; INT CANR-24;
MTCW

Buechner, (Carl) Frederick
1926- ...... **CLC 2, 4, 6, 9; DAM NOV**
See also CA 13-16R; CANR 11, 39;
DLBY 80; INT CANR-11; MTCW

Buell, John (Edward) 1927-........ **CLC 10**
See also CA 1-4R; DLB 53

Buero Vallejo, Antonio 1916- ... **CLC 15, 46**
See also CA 106; CANR 24, 49; HW;
MTCW

Bufalino, Gesualdo 1920(?)-........ **CLC 74**

Bugayev, Boris Nikolayevich 1880-1934
See Bely, Andrey
See also CA 104

Bukowski, Charles
1920-1994 .... **CLC 2, 5, 9, 41, 82;
DAM NOV, POET; PC 18**
See also CA 17-20R; 144; CANR 40, 62;
DLB 5, 130, 169; MTCW

Bulgakov, Mikhail (Afanas'evich)
1891-1940 .... **TCLC 2, 16;
DAM DRAM, NOV; SSC 18**
See also CA 105; 152

Bulgya, Alexander Alexandrovich
1901-1956 .... **TCLC 53**
See also Fadeyev, Alexander
See also CA 117

Bullins, Ed
1935- .... **CLC 1, 5, 7; BLC;
DAM DRAM, MULT; DC 6**
See also BW 2; CA 49-52; CAAS 16;
CANR 24, 46; DLB 7, 38; MTCW

Bulwer-Lytton, Edward (George Earle Lytton)
1803-1873 .... **NCLC 1, 45**
See also DLB 21

Bunin, Ivan Alexeyevich
1870-1953 .... **TCLC 6; SSC 5**
See also CA 104

Bunting, Basil
1900-1985 . . . . **CLC 10, 39, 47;
DAM POET**
See also CA 53-56; 115; CANR 7; DLB 20

Bunuel, Luis
1900-1983 . . . . **CLC 16, 80;
DAM MULT; HLC**
See also CA 101; 110; CANR 32; HW

Bunyan, John
1628-1688 . . . . . . **LC 4; DA; DAB; DAC;
DAM MST; WLC**
See also CDBLB 1660-1789; DLB 39

Burckhardt, Jacob (Christoph)
1818-1897 . . . . **NCLC 49**

Burford, Eleanor
See Hibbert, Eleanor Alice Burford

Burgess, Anthony
. **CLC 1, 2, 4, 5, 8, 10, 13, 15, 22, 40, 62,
81, 94; DAB**
See also Wilson, John (Anthony) Burgess
See also AITN 1; CDBLB 1960 to Present;
DLB 14

Burke, Edmund
1729(?)-1797 . . . . . . **LC 7, 36; DA; DAB;
DAC; DAM MST; WLC**
See also DLB 104

Burke, Kenneth (Duva)
1897-1993 . . . . **CLC 2, 24**
See also CA 5-8R; 143; CANR 39; DLB 45,
63; MTCW

Burke, Leda
See Garnett, David

Burke, Ralph
See Silverberg, Robert

Burke, Thomas 1886-1945 . . . . **TCLC 63**
See also CA 113; 155

Burney, Fanny 1752-1840 . . . . **NCLC 12, 54**
See also DLB 39

Burns, Robert 1759-1796 . . . . **PC 6**
See also CDBLB 1789-1832; DA; DAB;
DAC; DAM MST, POET; DLB 109;
WLC

Burns, Tex
See L'Amour, Louis (Dearborn)

Burnshaw, Stanley 1906- . . . . . **CLC 3, 13, 44**
See also CA 9-12R; DLB 48

Burr, Anne 1937- . . . . **CLC 6**
See also CA 25-28R

Burroughs, Edgar Rice
1875-1950 . . . . **TCLC 2, 32; DAM NOV**
See also AAYA 11; CA 104; 132; DLB 8;
MTCW; SATA 41

Burroughs, William S(eward)
1914- . . . . **CLC 1, 2, 5, 15, 22, 42, 75;
DA; DAB; DAC; DAM MST, NOV,
POP; WLC**
See also AITN 2; CA 9-12R; CANR 20, 52;
DLB 2, 8, 16, 152; DLBY 81; MTCW

Burton, Richard F. 1821-1890 . . . . **NCLC 42**
See also DLB 55, 184

Busch, Frederick 1941- . . . **CLC 7, 10, 18, 47**
See also CA 33-36R; CAAS 1; CANR 45;
DLB 6

Bush, Ronald 1946- . . . . **CLC 34**
See also CA 136

Bustos, F(rancisco)
See Borges, Jorge Luis

Bustos Domecq, H(onorio)
See Bioy Casares, Adolfo; Borges, Jorge
Luis

Butler, Octavia E(stelle)
1947- . . . . . **CLC 38; DAM MULT, POP**
See also AAYA 18; BW 2; CA 73-76;
CANR 12, 24, 38; DLB 33; MTCW;
SATA 84

Butler, Robert Olen (Jr.)
1945- . . . . **CLC 81; DAM POP**
See also CA 112; DLB 173; INT 112

Butler, Samuel 1612-1680 . . . . **LC 16**
See also DLB 101, 126

Butler, Samuel
1835-1902 . . . . . . **TCLC 1, 33; DA; DAB;
DAC; DAM MST, NOV; WLC**
See also CA 143; CDBLB 1890-1914;
DLB 18, 57, 174

Butler, Walter C.
See Faust, Frederick (Schiller)

Butor, Michel (Marie Francois)
1926- . . . . **CLC 1, 3, 8, 11, 15**
See also CA 9-12R; CANR 33; DLB 83;
MTCW

Buzo, Alexander (John) 1944- . . . . . . **CLC 61**
See also CA 97-100; CANR 17, 39

Buzzati, Dino 1906-1972 . . . . **CLC 36**
See also CA 33-36R; DLB 177

Byars, Betsy (Cromer) 1928- . . . . **CLC 35**
See also AAYA 19; CA 33-36R; CANR 18,
36, 57; CLR 1, 16; DLB 52;
INT CANR-18; JRDA; MAICYA;
MTCW; SAAS 1; SATA 4, 46, 80

Byatt, A(ntonia) S(usan Drabble)
1936- . . . **CLC 19, 65; DAM NOV, POP**
See also CA 13-16R; CANR 13, 33, 50;
DLB 14; MTCW

Byrne, David 1952- . . . . **CLC 26**
See also CA 127

Byrne, John Keyes 1926-
See Leonard, Hugh
See also CA 102; INT 102

Byron, George Gordon (Noel)
1788-1824 . . . . . **NCLC 2, 12; DA; DAB;
DAC; DAM MST, POET; PC 16; WLC**
See also CDBLB 1789-1832; DLB 96, 110

Byron, Robert 1905-1941 . . . . **TCLC 67**

C. 3. 3.
See Wilde, Oscar (Fingal O'Flahertie Wills)

Caballero, Fernan 1796-1877 . . . . . **NCLC 10**

Cabell, Branch
See Cabell, James Branch

Cabell, James Branch 1879-1958 . . . **TCLC 6**
See also CA 105; 152; DLB 9, 78

Cable, George Washington
1844-1925 . . . . **TCLC 4; SSC 4**
See also CA 104; 155; DLB 12, 74;
DLBD 13

Cabral de Melo Neto, Joao
1920- . . . . **CLC 76; DAM MULT**
See also CA 151

Cabrera Infante, G(uillermo)
1929- . . . . . **CLC 5, 25, 45; DAM MULT;
HLC**
See also CA 85-88; CANR 29; DLB 113;
HW; MTCW

Cade, Toni
See Bambara, Toni Cade

Cadmus and Harmonia
See Buchan, John

Caedmon fl. 658-680 . . . . **CMLC 7**
See also DLB 146

Caeiro, Alberto
See Pessoa, Fernando (Antonio Nogueira)

Cage, John (Milton, Jr.) 1912- . . . . . **CLC 41**
See also CA 13-16R; CANR 9;
INT CANR-9

Cahan, Abraham 1860-1951 . . . . . . **TCLC 71**
See also CA 108; 154; DLB 9, 25, 28

Cain, G.
See Cabrera Infante, G(uillermo)

Cain, Guillermo
See Cabrera Infante, G(uillermo)

Cain, James M(allahan)
1892-1977 . . . . **CLC 3, 11, 28**
See also AITN 1; CA 17-20R; 73-76;
CANR 8, 34, 61; MTCW

Caine, Mark
See Raphael, Frederic (Michael)

Calasso, Roberto 1941- . . . . **CLC 81**
See also CA 143

Calderon de la Barca, Pedro
1600-1681 . . . . **LC 23; DC 3**

Caldwell, Erskine (Preston)
1903-1987 . . . . **CLC 1, 8, 14, 50, 60;
DAM NOV; SSC 19**
See also AITN 1; CA 1-4R; 121; CAAS 1;
CANR 2, 33; DLB 9, 86; MTCW

Caldwell, (Janet Miriam) Taylor (Holland)
1900-1985 . . . . **CLC 2, 28, 39;
DAM NOV, POP**
See also CA 5-8R; 116; CANR 5

Calhoun, John Caldwell
1782-1850 . . . . **NCLC 15**
See also DLB 3

Calisher, Hortense
1911- . . . . . **CLC 2, 4, 8, 38; DAM NOV;
SSC 15**
See also CA 1-4R; CANR 1, 22; DLB 2;
INT CANR-22; MTCW

Callaghan, Morley Edward
1903-1990 . . . . . **CLC 3, 14, 41, 65; DAC;
DAM MST**
See also CA 9-12R; 132; CANR 33;
DLB 68; MTCW

Callimachus
c. 305B.C.-c. 240B.C. . . . . **CMLC 18**
See also DLB 176

Calvin, John 1509-1564 . . . . **LC 37**

Calvino, Italo
1923-1985 . . . . . **CLC 5, 8, 11, 22, 33, 39,
73; DAM NOV; SSC 3**
See also CA 85-88; 116; CANR 23, 61;
MTCW

Cameron, Carey 1952- . . . . **CLC 59**
See also CA 135

Cameron, Peter 1959-............ **CLC 44**
See also CA 125; CANR 50

Campana, Dino 1885-1932....... **TCLC 20**
See also CA 117; DLB 114

Campanella, Tommaso 1568-1639.... **LC 32**

Campbell, John W(ood, Jr.)
1910-1971 .... **CLC 32**
See also CA 21-22; 29-32R; CANR 34;
CAP 2; DLB 8; MTCW

Campbell, Joseph 1904-1987...... **CLC 69**
See also AAYA 3; BEST 89:2; CA 1-4R;
124; CANR 3, 28, 61; MTCW

Campbell, Maria 1940-...... **CLC 85; DAC**
See also CA 102; CANR 54; NNAL

Campbell, (John) Ramsey
1946- .... **CLC 42; SSC 19**
See also CA 57-60; CANR 7; INT CANR-7

Campbell, (Ignatius) Roy (Dunnachie)
1901-1957 .... **TCLC 5**
See also CA 104; 155; DLB 20

Campbell, Thomas 1777-1844.... **NCLC 19**
See also DLB 93; 144

Campbell, Wilfred .... **TCLC 9**
See also Campbell, William

Campbell, William 1858(?)-1918
See Campbell, Wilfred
See also CA 106; DLB 92

Campion, Jane .... **CLC 95**
See also CA 138

Campos, Alvaro de
See Pessoa, Fernando (Antonio Nogueira)

Camus, Albert
1913-1960.... **CLC 1, 2, 4, 9, 11, 14, 32,
63, 69; DA; DAB; DAC; DAM DRAM,
MST, NOV; DC 2; SSC 9; WLC**
See also CA 89-92; DLB 72; MTCW

Canby, Vincent 1924-............ **CLC 13**
See also CA 81-84

Cancale
See Desnos, Robert

Canetti, Elias
1905-1994....... **CLC 3, 14, 25, 75, 86**
See also CA 21-24R; 146; CANR 23, 61;
DLB 85, 124; MTCW

Canin, Ethan 1960-.............. **CLC 55**
See also CA 131; 135

Cannon, Curt
See Hunter, Evan

Cape, Judith
See Page, P(atricia) K(athleen)

Capek, Karel
1890-1938...... **TCLC 6, 37; DA; DAB;
DAC; DAM DRAM, MST, NOV; DC 1;
WLC**
See also CA 104; 140

Capote, Truman
1924-1984...... **CLC 1, 3, 8, 13, 19, 34,
38, 58; DA; DAB; DAC; DAM MST,
NOV, POP; SSC 2; WLC**
See also CA 5-8R; 113; CANR 18, 62;
CDALB 1941-1968; DLB 2; DLBY 80,
84; MTCW; SATA 91

Capra, Frank 1897-1991.......... **CLC 16**
See also CA 61-64; 135

Caputo, Philip 1941-............. **CLC 32**
See also CA 73-76; CANR 40

Card, Orson Scott
1951- ...... **CLC 44, 47, 50; DAM POP**
See also AAYA 11; CA 102; CANR 27, 47;
INT CANR-27; MTCW; SATA 83

Cardenal, Ernesto
1925- .... **CLC 31; DAM MULT,
POET; HLC**
See also CA 49-52; CANR 2, 32; HW;
MTCW

Cardozo, Benjamin N(athan)
1870-1938 .... **TCLC 65**
See also CA 117

Carducci, Giosue 1835-1907...... **TCLC 32**

Carew, Thomas 1595(?)-1640....... **LC 13**
See also DLB 126

Carey, Ernestine Gilbreth 1908-.... **CLC 17**
See also CA 5-8R; SATA 2

Carey, Peter 1943-......... **CLC 40, 55, 96**
See also CA 123; 127; CANR 53; INT 127;
MTCW; SATA 94

Carleton, William 1794-1869...... **NCLC 3**
See also DLB 159

Carlisle, Henry (Coffin) 1926-...... **CLC 33**
See also CA 13-16R; CANR 15

Carlsen, Chris
See Holdstock, Robert P.

Carlson, Ron(ald F.) 1947-........ **CLC 54**
See also CA 105; CANR 27

Carlyle, Thomas
1795-1881....... **NCLC 22; DA; DAB;
DAC; DAM MST**
See also CDBLB 1789-1832; DLB 55; 144

Carman, (William) Bliss
1861-1929 .... **TCLC 7; DAC**
See also CA 104; 152; DLB 92

Carnegie, Dale 1888-1955........ **TCLC 53**

Carossa, Hans 1878-1956........ **TCLC 48**
See also DLB 66

Carpenter, Don(ald Richard)
1931-1995 .... **CLC 41**
See also CA 45-48; 149; CANR 1

Carpentier (y Valmont), Alejo
1904-1980 .... **CLC 8, 11, 38;
DAM MULT; HLC**
See also CA 65-68; 97-100; CANR 11;
DLB 113; HW

Carr, Caleb 1955(?)-.............. **CLC 86**
See also CA 147

Carr, Emily 1871-1945.......... **TCLC 32**
See also CA 159; DLB 68

Carr, John Dickson 1906-1977...... **CLC 3**
See also Fairbairn, Roger
See also CA 49-52; 69-72; CANR 3, 33, 60;
MTCW

Carr, Philippa
See Hibbert, Eleanor Alice Burford

Carr, Virginia Spencer 1929-....... **CLC 34**
See also CA 61-64; DLB 111

Carrere, Emmanuel 1957- .... **CLC 89**

Carrier, Roch
1937- ... **CLC 13, 78; DAC; DAM MST**
See also CA 130; CANR 61; DLB 53

Carroll, James P. 1943(?)-........ **CLC 38**
See also CA 81-84

Carroll, Jim 1951- .... **CLC 35**
See also AAYA 17; CA 45-48; CANR 42

Carroll, Lewis .... **NCLC 2, 53; PC 18; WLC**
See also Dodgson, Charles Lutwidge
See also CDBLB 1832-1890; CLR 2, 18;
DLB 18, 163, 178; JRDA

Carroll, Paul Vincent 1900-1968.... **CLC 10**
See also CA 9-12R; 25-28R; DLB 10

Carruth, Hayden
1921- ...... **CLC 4, 7, 10, 18, 84; PC 10**
See also CA 9-12R; CANR 4, 38, 59;
DLB 5, 165; INT CANR-4; MTCW;
SATA 47

Carson, Rachel Louise
1907-1964 .... **CLC 71; DAM POP**
See also CA 77-80; CANR 35; MTCW;
SATA 23

Carter, Angela (Olive)
1940-1992 ...... **CLC 5, 41, 76; SSC 13**
See also CA 53-56; 136; CANR 12, 36, 61;
DLB 14; MTCW; SATA 66;
SATA-Obit 70

Carter, Nick
See Smith, Martin Cruz

Carver, Raymond
1938-1988 .... **CLC 22, 36, 53, 55;
DAM NOV; SSC 8**
See also CA 33-36R; 126; CANR 17, 34, 61;
DLB 130; DLBY 84, 88; MTCW

Cary, Elizabeth, Lady Falkland
1585-1639 .... **LC 30**

Cary, (Arthur) Joyce (Lunel)
1888-1957 .... **TCLC 1, 29**
See also CA 104; CDBLB 1914-1945;
DLB 15, 100

Casanova de Seingalt, Giovanni Jacopo
1725-1798 .... **LC 13**

Casares, Adolfo Bioy
See Bioy Casares, Adolfo

Casely-Hayford, J(oseph) E(phraim)
1866-1930 .... **TCLC 24; BLC;
DAM MULT**
See also BW 2; CA 123; 152

Casey, John (Dudley) 1939-........ **CLC 59**
See also BEST 90:2; CA 69-72; CANR 23

Casey, Michael 1947-.............. **CLC 2**
See also CA 65-68; DLB 5

Casey, Patrick
See Thurman, Wallace (Henry)

Casey, Warren (Peter) 1935-1988... **CLC 12**
See also CA 101; 127; INT 101

Casona, Alejandro................ **CLC 49**
See also Alvarez, Alejandro Rodriguez

Cassavetes, John 1929-1989........ **CLC 20**
See also CA 85-88; 127

Cassian, Nina 1924-.............. **PC 17**

Cassill, R(onald) V(erlin) 1919-... **CLC 4, 23**
See also CA 9-12R; CAAS 1; CANR 7, 45;
DLB 6

Cassirer, Ernst 1874-1945....... **TCLC 61**
See also CA 157

Cassity, (Allen) Turner 1929- .... **CLC 6, 42**
See also CA 17-20R; CAAS 8; CANR 11;
DLB 105

Castaneda, Carlos 1931(?)-......... **CLC 12**
See also CA 25-28R; CANR 32; HW;
MTCW

Castedo, Elena 1937- .... **CLC 65**
See also CA 132

Castedo-Ellerman, Elena
See Castedo, Elena

Castellanos, Rosario
1925-1974 ...... **CLC 66; DAM MULT;**
HLC
See also CA 131; 53-56; CANR 58;
DLB 113; HW

Castelvetro, Lodovico 1505-1571..... **LC 12**

Castiglione, Baldassare 1478-1529 ... **LC 12**

Castle, Robert
See Hamilton, Edmond

Castro, Guillen de 1569-1631........ **LC 19**

Castro, Rosalia de
1837-1885 ...... **NCLC 3; DAM MULT**

Cather, Willa
See Cather, Willa Sibert

Cather, Willa Sibert
1873-1947 .... **TCLC 1, 11, 31; DA;**
DAB; DAC; DAM MST, NOV; SSC 2;
WLC
See also CA 104; 128; CDALB 1865-1917;
DLB 9, 54, 78; DLBD 1; MTCW;
SATA 30

Cato, Marcus Porcius
234B.C.-149B.C............. **CMLC 21**

Catton, (Charles) Bruce
1899-1978 .... **CLC 35**
See also AITN 1; CA 5-8R; 81-84;
CANR 7; DLB 17; SATA 2;
SATA-Obit 24

Catullus c. 84B.C.-c. 54B.C. ..... **CMLC 18**

Cauldwell, Frank
See King, Francis (Henry)

Caunitz, William J. 1933-1996 ..... **CLC 34**
See also BEST 89:3; CA 125; 130; 152;
INT 130

Causley, Charles (Stanley) 1917-..... **CLC 7**
See also CA 9-12R; CANR 5, 35; CLR 30;
DLB 27; MTCW; SATA 3, 66

Caute, David 1936-.... **CLC 29; DAM NOV**
See also CA 1-4R; CAAS 4; CANR 1, 33;
DLB 14

Cavafy, C(onstantine) P(eter)
1863-1933 .... **TCLC 2, 7; DAM POET**
See also Kavafis, Konstantinos Petrou
See also CA 148

Cavallo, Evelyn
See Spark, Muriel (Sarah)

Cavanna, Betty .... **CLC 12**
See also Harrison, Elizabeth Cavanna
See also JRDA; MAICYA; SAAS 4;
SATA 1, 30

Cavendish, Margaret Lucas
1623-1673 .... **LC 30**
See also DLB 131

Caxton, William 1421(?)-1491(?)..... **LC 17**
See also DLB 170

Cayrol, Jean 1911-............... **CLC 11**
See also CA 89-92; DLB 83

Cela, Camilo Jose
1916- ..... **CLC 4, 13, 59; DAM MULT;**
HLC
See also BEST 90:2; CA 21-24R; CAAS 10;
CANR 21, 32; DLBY 89; HW; MTCW

Celan, Paul ..... **CLC 10, 19, 53, 82; PC 10**
See also Antschel, Paul
See also DLB 69

Celine, Louis-Ferdinand
.... **CLC 1, 3, 4, 7, 9, 15, 47**
See also Destouches, Louis-Ferdinand
See also DLB 72

Cellini, Benvenuto 1500-1571 .... **LC 7**

Cendrars, Blaise .... **CLC 18**
See also Sauser-Hall, Frederic

Cernuda (y Bidon), Luis
1902-1963 .... **CLC 54; DAM POET**
See also CA 131; 89-92; DLB 134; HW

Cervantes (Saavedra), Miguel de
1547-1616 .... **LC 6, 23; DA; DAB;**
DAC; DAM MST, NOV; SSC 12; WLC

Cesaire, Aime (Fernand)
1913- .... **CLC 19, 32; BLC;**
DAM MULT, POET
See also BW 2; CA 65-68; CANR 24, 43;
MTCW

Chabon, Michael 1963- .... **CLC 55**
See also CA 139; CANR 57

Chabrol, Claude 1930- .... **CLC 16**
See also CA 110

Challans, Mary 1905-1983
See Renault, Mary
See also CA 81-84; 111; SATA 23;
SATA-Obit 36

Challis, George
See Faust, Frederick (Schiller)

Chambers, Aidan 1934- .... **CLC 35**
See also CA 25-28R; CANR 12, 31, 58;
JRDA; MAICYA; SAAS 12; SATA 1, 69

Chambers, James 1948-
See Cliff, Jimmy
See also CA 124

Chambers, Jessie
See Lawrence, D(avid) H(erbert Richards)

Chambers, Robert W. 1865-1933... **TCLC 41**

Chandler, Raymond (Thornton)
1888-1959 .... **TCLC 1, 7; SSC 23**
See also CA 104; 129; CANR 60;
CDALB 1929-1941; DLBD 6; MTCW

Chang, Jung 1952- .... **CLC 71**
See also CA 142

Channing, William Ellery
1780-1842 .... **NCLC 17**
See also DLB 1, 59

Chaplin, Charles Spencer
1889-1977 .... **CLC 16**
See also Chaplin, Charlie
See also CA 81-84; 73-76

Chaplin, Charlie
See Chaplin, Charles Spencer
See also DLB 44

Chapman, George
1559(?)-1634 ..... **LC 22; DAM DRAM**
See also DLB 62, 121

Chapman, Graham 1941-1989 ...... **CLC 21**
See also Monty Python
See also CA 116; 129; CANR 35

Chapman, John Jay 1862-1933 ..... **TCLC 7**
See also CA 104

Chapman, Lee
See Bradley, Marion Zimmer

Chapman, Walker
See Silverberg, Robert

Chappell, Fred (Davis) 1936-.... **CLC 40, 78**
See also CA 5-8R; CAAS 4; CANR 8, 33;
DLB 6, 105

Char, Rene(-Emile)
1907-1988 .... **CLC 9, 11, 14, 55;**
DAM POET
See also CA 13-16R; 124; CANR 32;
MTCW

Charby, Jay
See Ellison, Harlan (Jay)

Chardin, Pierre Teilhard de
See Teilhard de Chardin, (Marie Joseph)
Pierre

Charles I 1600-1649............... **LC 13**

Charyn, Jerome 1937- .... **CLC 5, 8, 18**
See also CA 5-8R; CAAS 1; CANR 7, 61;
DLBY 83; MTCW

Chase, Mary (Coyle) 1907-1981 ...... **DC 1**
See also CA 77-80; 105; SATA 17;
SATA-Obit 29

Chase, Mary Ellen 1887-1973....... **CLC 2**
See also CA 13-16; 41-44R; CAP 1;
SATA 10

Chase, Nicholas
See Hyde, Anthony

Chateaubriand, Francois Rene de
1768-1848 .... **NCLC 3**
See also DLB 119

Chatterje, Sarat Chandra 1876-1936(?)
See Chatterji, Saratchandra
See also CA 109

Chatterji, Bankim Chandra
1838-1894 .... **NCLC 19**

Chatterji, Saratchandra .... **TCLC 13**
See also Chatterje, Sarat Chandra

Chatterton, Thomas
1752-1770 .... **LC 3; DAM POET**
See also DLB 109

Chatwin, (Charles) Bruce
1940-1989 .. **CLC 28, 57, 59; DAM POP**
See also AAYA 4; BEST 90:1; CA 85-88;
127

Chaucer, Daniel
See Ford, Ford Madox

Chaucer, Geoffrey
1340(?)-1400 .... **LC 17; DA; DAB;**
DAC; DAM MST, POET; PC 19; WLCS
See also CDBLB Before 1660; DLB 146

Chaviaras, Strates 1935-
See Haviaras, Stratis
See also CA 105

Clarke, Austin C(hesterfield)
    1934- .... CLC 8, 53; BLC; DAC;
                                    DAM MULT
    See also BW 1; CA 25-28R; CAAS 16;
    CANR 14, 32; DLB 53, 125

Clarke, Gillian 1937- .... CLC 61
    See also CA 106; DLB 40

Clarke, Marcus (Andrew Hislop)
    1846-1881 .... NCLC 19

Clarke, Shirley 1925- .... CLC 16

Clash, The
    See Headon, (Nicky) Topper; Jones, Mick;
    Simonon, Paul; Strummer, Joe

Claudel, Paul (Louis Charles Marie)
    1868-1955 .... TCLC 2, 10
    See also CA 104

Clavell, James (duMaresq)
    1925-1994 .... CLC 6, 25, 87;
                                    DAM NOV, POP
    See also CA 25-28R; 146; CANR 26, 48;
    MTCW

Cleaver, (Leroy) Eldridge
    1935- ..... CLC 30; BLC; DAM MULT
    See also BW 1; CA 21-24R; CANR 16

Cleese, John (Marwood) 1939- ..... CLC 21
    See also Monty Python
    See also CA 112; 116; CANR 35; MTCW

Cleishbotham, Jebediah
    See Scott, Walter

Cleland, John 1710-1789 .... LC 2
    See also DLB 39

Clemens, Samuel Langhorne 1835-1910
    See Twain, Mark
    See also CA 104; 135; CDALB 1865-1917;
    DA; DAB; DAC; DAM MST, NOV;
    DLB 11, 12, 23, 64, 74; JRDA;
    MAICYA; YABC 2

Cleophil
    See Congreve, William

Clerihew, E.
    See Bentley, E(dmund) C(lerihew)

Clerk, N. W.
    See Lewis, C(live) S(taples)

Cliff, Jimmy .... CLC 21
    See also Chambers, James

Clifton, (Thelma) Lucille
    1936- .... CLC 19, 66; BLC;
                            DAM MULT, POET; PC 17
    See also BW 2; CA 49-52; CANR 2, 24, 42;
    CLR 5; DLB 5, 41; MAICYA; MTCW;
    SATA 20, 69

Clinton, Dirk
    See Silverberg, Robert

Clough, Arthur Hugh 1819-1861.. NCLC 27
    See also DLB 32

Clutha, Janet Paterson Frame 1924-
    See Frame, Janet
    See also CA 1-4R; CANR 2, 36; MTCW

Clyne, Terence
    See Blatty, William Peter

Cobalt, Martin
    See Mayne, William (James Carter)

Cobbett, William 1763-1835 ..... NCLC 49
    See also DLB 43, 107, 158

Coburn, D(onald) L(ee) 1938- ...... CLC 10
    See also CA 89-92

Cocteau, Jean (Maurice Eugene Clement)
    1889-1963 .... CLC 1, 8, 15, 16, 43; DA;
    DAB; DAC; DAM DRAM, MST, NOV;
                                        WLC
    See also CA 25-28; CANR 40; CAP 2;
    DLB 65; MTCW

Codrescu, Andrei
    1946- .... CLC 46; DAM POET
    See also CA 33-36R; CAAS 19; CANR 13,
    34, 53

Coe, Max
    See Bourne, Randolph S(illiman)

Coe, Tucker
    See Westlake, Donald E(dwin)

Coetzee, J(ohn) M(ichael)
    1940- ...... CLC 23, 33, 66; DAM NOV
    See also CA 77-80; CANR 41, 54; MTCW

Coffey, Brian
    See Koontz, Dean R(ay)

Cohan, George M. 1878-1942 ..... TCLC 60
    See also CA 157

Cohen, Arthur A(llen)
    1928-1986 .... CLC 7, 31
    See also CA 1-4R; 120; CANR 1, 17, 42;
    DLB 28

Cohen, Leonard (Norman)
    1934- .... CLC 3, 38; DAC; DAM MST
    See also CA 21-24R; CANR 14; DLB 53;
    MTCW

Cohen, Matt 1942- .... CLC 19; DAC
    See also CA 61-64; CAAS 18; CANR 40;
    DLB 53

Cohen-Solal, Annie 19(?)- .... CLC 50

Colegate, Isabel 1931- .... CLC 36
    See also CA 17-20R; CANR 8, 22; DLB 14;
    INT CANR-22; MTCW

Coleman, Emmett
    See Reed, Ishmael

Coleridge, M. E.
    See Coleridge, Mary E(lizabeth)

Coleridge, Mary E(lizabeth)
    1861-1907 .... TCLC 73
    See also CA 116; DLB 19, 98

Coleridge, Samuel Taylor
    1772-1834 ..... NCLC 9, 54; DA; DAB;
    DAC; DAM MST, POET; PC 11; WLC
    See also CDBLB 1789-1832; DLB 93, 107

Coleridge, Sara 1802-1852 ...... NCLC 31

Coles, Don 1928- .... CLC 46
    See also CA 115; CANR 38

Colette, (Sidonie-Gabrielle)
    1873-1954 .... TCLC 1, 5, 16;
                            DAM NOV; SSC 10
    See also CA 104; 131; DLB 65; MTCW

Collett, (Jacobine) Camilla (Wergeland)
    1813-1895 .... NCLC 22

Collier, Christopher 1930- .... CLC 30
    See also AAYA 13; CA 33-36R; CANR 13,
    33; JRDA; MAICYA; SATA 16, 70

Collier, James L(incoln)
    1928- .... CLC 30; DAM POP
    See also AAYA 13; CA 9-12R; CANR 4,
    33, 60; CLR 3; JRDA; MAICYA;
    SAAS 21; SATA 8, 70

Collier, Jeremy 1650-1726.......... LC 6

Collier, John 1901-1980........... SSC 19
    See also CA 65-68; 97-100; CANR 10;
    DLB 77

Collingwood, R(obin) G(eorge)
    1889(?)-1943 .... TCLC 67
    See also CA 117; 155

Collins, Hunt
    See Hunter, Evan

Collins, Linda 1931- .... CLC 44
    See also CA 125

Collins, (William) Wilkie
    1824-1889 .... NCLC 1, 18
    See also CDBLB 1832-1890; DLB 18, 70,
    159

Collins, William
    1721-1759 .... LC 4; DAM POET
    See also DLB 109

Collodi, Carlo 1826-1890........ NCLC 54
    See also Lorenzini, Carlo
    See also CLR 5

Colman, George
    See Glassco, John

Colt, Winchester Remington
    See Hubbard, L(afayette) Ron(ald)

Colter, Cyrus 1910- .... CLC 58
    See also BW 1; CA 65-68; CANR 10;
    DLB 33

Colton, James
    See Hansen, Joseph

Colum, Padraic 1881-1972........ CLC 28
    See also CA 73-76; 33-36R; CANR 35;
    CLR 36; MAICYA; MTCW; SATA 15

Colvin, James
    See Moorcock, Michael (John)

Colwin, Laurie (E.)
    1944-1992 .... CLC 5, 13, 23, 84
    See also CA 89-92; 139; CANR 20, 46;
    DLBY 80; MTCW

Comfort, Alex(ander)
    1920- .... CLC 7; DAM POP
    See also CA 1-4R; CANR 1, 45

Comfort, Montgomery
    See Campbell, (John) Ramsey

Compton-Burnett, I(vy)
    1884(?)-1969 ...... CLC 1, 3, 10, 15, 34;
                                        DAM NOV
    See also CA 1-4R; 25-28R; CANR 4;
    DLB 36; MTCW

Comstock, Anthony 1844-1915 .... TCLC 13
    See also CA 110

Comte, Auguste 1798-1857....... NCLC 54

Conan Doyle, Arthur
    See Doyle, Arthur Conan

Conde, Maryse
    1937- .... CLC 52, 92; DAM MULT
    See also Boucolon, Maryse
    See also BW 2

Condillac, Etienne Bonnot de
    1714-1780 .... LC 26

Condon, Richard (Thomas)
1915-1996 . . . . . **CLC 4, 6, 8, 10, 45, 100; DAM NOV**
See also BEST 90:3; CA 1-4R; 151;
CAAS 1; CANR 2, 23; INT CANR-23;
MTCW

Confucius
551B.C.-479B.C. . . . . **CMLC 19; DA; DAB; DAC; DAM MST; WLCS**

Congreve, William
1670-1729 . . . . **LC 5, 21; DA; DAB; DAC; DAM DRAM, MST, POET; DC 2; WLC**
See also CDBLB 1660-1789; DLB 39, 84

Connell, Evan S(helby), Jr.
1924- . . . . **CLC 4, 6, 45; DAM NOV**
See also AAYA 7; CA 1-4R; CAAS 2;
CANR 2, 39; DLB 2; DLBY 81; MTCW

Connelly, Marc(us Cook)
1890-1980 . . . . **CLC 7**
See also CA 85-88; 102; CANR 30; DLB 7;
DLBY 80; SATA-Obit 25

Connor, Ralph . . . . **TCLC 31**
See also Gordon, Charles William
See also DLB 92

Conrad, Joseph
1857-1924 . . . . **TCLC 1, 6, 13, 25, 43, 57; DA; DAB; DAC; DAM MST, NOV; SSC 9; WLC**
See also CA 104; 131; CANR 60;
CDBLB 1890-1914; DLB 10, 34, 98, 156;
MTCW; SATA 27

Conrad, Robert Arnold
See Hart, Moss

Conroy, Donald Pat(rick)
1945- . . . **CLC 30, 74; DAM NOV, POP**
See also AAYA 8; AITN 1; CA 85-88;
CANR 24, 53; DLB 6; MTCW

Constant (de Rebecque), (Henri) Benjamin
1767-1830 . . . . **NCLC 6**
See also DLB 119

Conybeare, Charles Augustus
See Eliot, T(homas) S(tearns)

Cook, Michael 1933- . . . . **CLC 58**
See also CA 93-96; DLB 53

Cook, Robin 1940- . . . . **CLC 14; DAM POP**
See also BEST 90:2; CA 108; 111;
CANR 41; INT 111

Cook, Roy
See Silverberg, Robert

Cooke, Elizabeth 1948- . . . . **CLC 55**
See also CA 129

Cooke, John Esten 1830-1886 . . . . . **NCLC 5**
See also DLB 3

Cooke, John Estes
See Baum, L(yman) Frank

Cooke, M. E.
See Creasey, John

Cooke, Margaret
See Creasey, John

Cook-Lynn, Elizabeth
1930- . . . . **CLC 93; DAM MULT**
See also CA 133; DLB 175; NNAL

Cooney, Ray . . . . **CLC 62**

Cooper, Douglas 1960- . . . . **CLC 86**

Cooper, Henry St. John
See Creasey, John

Cooper, J(oan) California
. . . . **CLC 56; DAM MULT**
See also AAYA 12; BW 1; CA 125;
CANR 55

Cooper, James Fenimore
1789-1851 . . . . **NCLC 1, 27, 54**
See also AAYA 22; CDALB 1640-1865;
DLB 3; SATA 19

Coover, Robert (Lowell)
1932- . . . . **CLC 3, 7, 15, 32, 46, 87; DAM NOV; SSC 15**
See also CA 45-48; CANR 3, 37, 58;
DLB 2; DLBY 81; MTCW

Copeland, Stewart (Armstrong)
1952- . . . . **CLC 26**

Coppard, A(lfred) E(dgar)
1878-1957 . . . . **TCLC 5; SSC 21**
See also CA 114; DLB 162; YABC 1

Coppee, Francois 1842-1908 . . . . . . **TCLC 25**

Coppola, Francis Ford 1939- . . . . **CLC 16**
See also CA 77-80; CANR 40; DLB 44

Corbiere, Tristan 1845-1875 . . . . . **NCLC 43**

Corcoran, Barbara 1911- . . . . **CLC 17**
See also AAYA 14; CA 21-24R; CAAS 2;
CANR 11, 28, 48; DLB 52; JRDA;
SAAS 20; SATA 3, 77

Cordelier, Maurice
See Giraudoux, (Hippolyte) Jean

Corelli, Marie 1855-1924 . . . . **TCLC 51**
See also Mackay, Mary
See also DLB 34, 156

Corman, Cid . . . . **CLC 9**
See also Corman, Sidney
See also CAAS 2; DLB 5

Corman, Sidney 1924-
See Corman, Cid
See also CA 85-88; CANR 44; DAM POET

Cormier, Robert (Edmund)
1925- . . . . **CLC 12, 30; DA; DAB; DAC; DAM MST, NOV**
See also AAYA 3, 19; CA 1-4R; CANR 5,
23; CDALB 1968-1988; CLR 12; DLB 52;
INT CANR-23; JRDA; MAICYA;
MTCW; SATA 10, 45, 83

Corn, Alfred (DeWitt III) 1943- . . . . **CLC 33**
See also CA 104; CAAS 25; CANR 44;
DLB 120; DLBY 80

Corneille, Pierre
1606-1684 . . . . **LC 28; DAB; DAM MST**

Cornwell, David (John Moore)
1931- . . . . **CLC 9, 15; DAM POP**
See also le Carre, John
See also CA 5-8R; CANR 13, 33, 59;
MTCW

Corso, (Nunzio) Gregory 1930- . . . **CLC 1, 11**
See also CA 5-8R; CANR 41; DLB 5, 16;
MTCW

Cortazar, Julio
1914-1984 . . . . . . **CLC 2, 3, 5, 10, 13, 15, 33, 34, 92; DAM MULT, NOV; HLC; SSC 7**
See also CA 21-24R; CANR 12, 32;
DLB 113; HW; MTCW

CORTES, HERNAN 1484-1547 . . . . . **LC 31**

Corwin, Cecil
See Kornbluth, C(yril) M.

Cosic, Dobrica 1921- . . . . **CLC 14**
See also CA 122; 138; DLB 181

Costain, Thomas B(ertram)
1885-1965 . . . . **CLC 30**
See also CA 5-8R; 25-28R; DLB 9

Costantini, Humberto
1924(?)-1987 . . . . **CLC 49**
See also CA 131; 122; HW

Costello, Elvis 1955- . . . . **CLC 21**

Cotes, Cecil V.
See Duncan, Sara Jeannette

Cotter, Joseph Seamon Sr.
1861-1949 . . . . **TCLC 28; BLC; DAM MULT**
See also BW 1; CA 124; DLB 50

Couch, Arthur Thomas Quiller
See Quiller-Couch, Arthur Thomas

Coulton, James
See Hansen, Joseph

Couperus, Louis (Marie Anne)
1863-1923 . . . . **TCLC 15**
See also CA 115

Coupland, Douglas
1961- . . . . **CLC 85; DAC; DAM POP**
See also CA 142; CANR 57

Court, Wesli
See Turco, Lewis (Putnam)

Courtenay, Bryce 1933- . . . . **CLC 59**
See also CA 138

Courtney, Robert
See Ellison, Harlan (Jay)

Cousteau, Jacques-Yves
1910-1997 . . . . **CLC 30**
See also CA 65-68; 159; CANR 15; MTCW;
SATA 38

Cowan, Peter (Walkinshaw) 1914- . . **SSC 28**
See also CA 21-24R; CANR 9, 25, 50

Coward, Noel (Peirce)
1899-1973 . . . . **CLC 1, 9, 29, 51; DAM DRAM**
See also AITN 1; CA 17-18; 41-44R;
CANR 35; CAP 2; CDBLB 1914-1945;
DLB 10; MTCW

Cowley, Malcolm 1898-1989 . . . . **CLC 39**
See also CA 5-8R; 128; CANR 3, 55;
DLB 4, 48; DLBY 81, 89; MTCW

Cowper, William
1731-1800 . . . . . . **NCLC 8; DAM POET**
See also DLB 104, 109

Cox, William Trevor
1928- . . . . **CLC 9, 14, 71; DAM NOV**
See also Trevor, William
See also CA 9-12R; CANR 4, 37, 55;
DLB 14; INT CANR-37; MTCW

Coyne, P. J.
See Masters, Hilary

Cozzens, James Gould
1903-1978 . . . . **CLC 1, 4, 11, 92**
See also CA 9-12R; 81-84; CANR 19;
CDALB 1941-1968; DLB 9; DLBD 2;
DLBY 84; MTCW

Crabbe, George 1754-1832 . . . . . . **NCLC 26**
See also DLB 93

Craddock, Charles Egbert
See Murfree, Mary Noailles

Craig, A. A.
See Anderson, Poul (William)

Craik, Dinah Maria (Mulock)
1826-1887 . . . . NCLC 38
See also DLB 35, 163; MAICYA; SATA 34

Cram, Ralph Adams 1863-1942 . . . . TCLC 45

Crane, (Harold) Hart
1899-1932 . . . . TCLC 2, 5; DA; DAB;
DAC; DAM MST, POET; PC 3; WLC
See also CA 104; 127; CDALB 1917-1929;
DLB 4, 48; MTCW

Crane, R(onald) S(almon)
1886-1967 . . . . CLC 27
See also CA 85-88; DLB 63

Crane, Stephen (Townley)
1871-1900 . . . . TCLC 11, 17, 32; DA;
DAB; DAC; DAM MST, NOV, POET;
SSC 7; WLC
See also AAYA 21; CA 109; 140;
CDALB 1865-1917; DLB 12, 54, 78;
YABC 2

Crase, Douglas 1944- . . . . CLC 58
See also CA 106

Crashaw, Richard 1612(?)-1649 . . . . . . LC 24
See also DLB 126

Craven, Margaret
1901-1980 . . . . CLC 17; DAC
See also CA 103

Crawford, F(rancis) Marion
1854-1909 . . . . TCLC 10
See also CA 107; DLB 71

Crawford, Isabella Valancy
1850-1887 . . . . NCLC 12
See also DLB 92

Crayon, Geoffrey
See Irving, Washington

Creasey, John 1908-1973 . . . . CLC 11
See also CA 5-8R; 41-44R; CANR 8, 59;
DLB 77; MTCW

Crebillon, Claude Prosper Jolyot de (fils)
1707-1777 . . . . LC 28

Credo
See Creasey, John

Creeley, Robert (White)
1926- . . . . . CLC 1, 2, 4, 8, 11, 15, 36, 78;
DAM POET
See also CA 1-4R; CAAS 10; CANR 23, 43;
DLB 5, 16, 169; MTCW

Crews, Harry (Eugene)
1935- . . . . CLC 6, 23, 49
See also AITN 1; CA 25-28R; CANR 20,
57; DLB 6, 143; MTCW

Crichton, (John) Michael
1942- . . . . CLC 2, 6, 54, 90; DAM NOV,
POP
See also AAYA 10; AITN 2; CA 25-28R;
CANR 13, 40, 54; DLBY 81;
INT CANR-13; JRDA; MTCW; SATA 9,
88

Crispin, Edmund . . . . CLC 22
See also Montgomery, (Robert) Bruce
See also DLB 87

Cristofer, Michael
1945(?)- . . . . CLC 28; DAM DRAM
See also CA 110; 152; DLB 7

Croce, Benedetto 1866-1952 . . . . . . TCLC 37
See also CA 120; 155

Crockett, David 1786-1836 . . . . NCLC 8
See also DLB 3, 11

Crockett, Davy
See Crockett, David

Crofts, Freeman Wills
1879-1957 . . . . TCLC 55
See also CA 115; DLB 77

Croker, John Wilson 1780-1857 . . NCLC 10
See also DLB 110

Crommelynck, Fernand 1885-1970 . . CLC 75
See also CA 89-92

Cronin, A(rchibald) J(oseph)
1896-1981 . . . . CLC 32
See also CA 1-4R; 102; CANR 5; SATA 47;
SATA-Obit 25

Cross, Amanda
See Heilbrun, Carolyn G(old)

Crothers, Rachel 1878(?)-1958 . . . . . TCLC 19
See also CA 113; DLB 7

Croves, Hal
See Traven, B.

Crow Dog, Mary (Ellen) (?)- . . . . CLC 93
See also Brave Bird, Mary
See also CA 154

Crowfield, Christopher
See Stowe, Harriet (Elizabeth) Beecher

Crowley, Aleister . . . . TCLC 7
See also Crowley, Edward Alexander

Crowley, Edward Alexander 1875-1947
See Crowley, Aleister
See also CA 104

Crowley, John 1942- . . . . CLC 57
See also CA 61-64; CANR 43; DLBY 82;
SATA 65

Crud
See Crumb, R(obert)

Crumarums
See Crumb, R(obert)

Crumb, R(obert) 1943- . . . . CLC 17
See also CA 106

Crumbum
See Crumb, R(obert)

Crumski
See Crumb, R(obert)

Crum the Bum
See Crumb, R(obert)

Crunk
See Crumb, R(obert)

Crustt
See Crumb, R(obert)

Cryer, Gretchen (Kiger) 1935- . . . . . . CLC 21
See also CA 114; 123

Csath, Geza 1887-1919 . . . . TCLC 13
See also CA 111

Cudlip, David 1933- . . . . CLC 34

Cullen, Countee
1903-1946 . . . . . . TCLC 4, 37; BLC; DA;
DAC; DAM MST, MULT, POET;
WLCS
See also BW 1; CA 108; 124;
CDALB 1917-1929; DLB 4, 48, 51;
MTCW; SATA 18

Cum, R.
See Crumb, R(obert)

Cummings, Bruce F(rederick) 1889-1919
See Barbellion, W. N. P.
See also CA 123

Cummings, E(dward) E(stlin)
1894-1962 . . . . . . CLC 1, 3, 8, 12, 15, 68;
DA; DAB; DAC; DAM MST, POET;
PC 5; WLC 2
See also CA 73-76; CANR 31;
CDALB 1929-1941; DLB 4, 48; MTCW

Cunha, Euclides (Rodrigues Pimenta) da
1866-1909 . . . . TCLC 24
See also CA 123

Cunningham, E. V.
See Fast, Howard (Melvin)

Cunningham, J(ames) V(incent)
1911-1985 . . . . CLC 3, 31
See also CA 1-4R; 115; CANR 1; DLB 5

Cunningham, Julia (Woolfolk)
1916- . . . . CLC 12
See also CA 9-12R; CANR 4, 19, 36;
JRDA; MAICYA; SAAS 2; SATA 1, 26

Cunningham, Michael 1952- . . . . CLC 34
See also CA 136

Cunninghame Graham, R(obert) B(ontine)
1852-1936 . . . . TCLC 19
See also Graham, R(obert) B(ontine)
Cunninghame
See also CA 119; DLB 98

Currie, Ellen 19(?)- . . . . CLC 44

Curtin, Philip
See Lowndes, Marie Adelaide (Belloc)

Curtis, Price
See Ellison, Harlan (Jay)

Cutrate, Joe
See Spiegelman, Art

Cynewulf c. 770-c. 840 . . . . CMLC 23

Czaczkes, Shmuel Yosef
See Agnon, S(hmuel) Y(osef Halevi)

Dabrowska, Maria (Szumska)
1889-1965 . . . . CLC 15
See also CA 106

Dabydeen, David 1955- . . . . CLC 34
See also BW 1; CA 125; CANR 56

Dacey, Philip 1939- . . . . CLC 51
See also CA 37-40R; CAAS 17; CANR 14,
32; DLB 105

Dagerman, Stig (Halvard)
1923-1954 . . . . TCLC 17
See also CA 117; 155

Dahl, Roald
1916-1990 . . . . . . CLC 1, 6, 18, 79; DAB;
DAC; DAM MST, NOV, POP
See also AAYA 15; CA 1-4R; 133;
CANR 6, 32, 37, 62; CLR 1, 7, 41;
DLB 139; JRDA; MAICYA; MTCW;
SATA 1, 26, 73; SATA-Obit 65

Dahlberg, Edward 1900-1977... **CLC 1, 7, 14**
  See also CA 9-12R; 69-72; CANR 31, 62;
  DLB 48; MTCW

Daitch, Susan 1954- .... **CLC 103**

Dale, Colin .... **TCLC 18**
  See also Lawrence, T(homas) E(dward)

Dale, George E.
  See Asimov, Isaac

Daly, Elizabeth 1878-1967 .... **CLC 52**
  See also CA 23-24; 25-28R; CANR 60;
  CAP 2

Daly, Maureen 1921- .... **CLC 17**
  See also AAYA 5; CANR 37; JRDA;
  MAICYA; SAAS 1; SATA 2

Damas, Leon-Gontran 1912-1978 ... **CLC 84**
  See also BW 1; CA 125; 73-76

Dana, Richard Henry Sr.
  1787-1879 .... **NCLC 53**

Daniel, Samuel 1562(?)-1619 .... **LC 24**
  See also DLB 62

Daniels, Brett
  See Adler, Renata

Dannay, Frederic
  1905-1982 .... **CLC 11; DAM POP**
  See also Queen, Ellery
  See also CA 1-4R; 107; CANR 1, 39;
  DLB 137; MTCW

D'Annunzio, Gabriele
  1863-1938 .... **TCLC 6, 40**
  See also CA 104; 155

Danois, N. le
  See Gourmont, Remy (-Marie-Charles) de

d'Antibes, Germain
  See Simenon, Georges (Jacques Christian)

Danticat, Edwidge 1969- .... **CLC 94**
  See also CA 152

Danvers, Dennis 1947- .... **CLC 70**

Danziger, Paula 1944- .... **CLC 21**
  See also AAYA 4; CA 112; 115; CANR 37;
  CLR 20; JRDA; MAICYA; SATA 36,
  63; SATA-Brief 30

Da Ponte, Lorenzo 1749-1838 .... **NCLC 50**

Dario, Ruben
  1867-1916 ..... **TCLC 4; DAM MULT;**
                   HLC; PC 15
  See also CA 131; HW; MTCW

Darley, George 1795-1846 .... **NCLC 2**
  See also DLB 96

Darwin, Charles 1809-1882 ...... **NCLC 57**
  See also DLB 57, 166

Daryush, Elizabeth 1887-1977.... **CLC 6, 19**
  See also CA 49-52; CANR 3; DLB 20

Dashwood, Edmee Elizabeth Monica de la
  Pasture 1890-1943
  See Delafield, E. M.
  See also CA 119; 154

Daudet, (Louis Marie) Alphonse
  1840-1897 .... **NCLC 1**
  See also DLB 123

Daumal, Rene 1908-1944 .... **TCLC 14**
  See also CA 114

Davenport, Guy (Mattison, Jr.)
  1927- .... **CLC 6, 14, 38; SSC 16**
  See also CA 33-36R; CANR 23; DLB 130

Davidson, Avram 1923-
  See Queen, Ellery
  See also CA 101; CANR 26; DLB 8

Davidson, Donald (Grady)
  1893-1968 .... **CLC 2, 13, 19**
  See also CA 5-8R; 25-28R; CANR 4;
  DLB 45

Davidson, Hugh
  See Hamilton, Edmond

Davidson, John 1857-1909 .... **TCLC 24**
  See also CA 118; DLB 19

Davidson, Sara 1943- .... **CLC 9**
  See also CA 81-84; CANR 44

Davie, Donald (Alfred)
  1922-1995 .... **CLC 5, 8, 10, 31**
  See also CA 1-4R; 149; CAAS 3; CANR 1,
  44; DLB 27; MTCW

Davies, Ray(mond Douglas) 1944- .. **CLC 21**
  See also CA 116; 146

Davies, Rhys 1903-1978 .... **CLC 23**
  See also CA 9-12R; 81-84; CANR 4;
  DLB 139

Davies, (William) Robertson
  1913-1995 ..... **CLC 2, 7, 13, 25, 42, 75,**
  91; DA; DAB; DAC; DAM MST, NOV,
                    POP; WLC
  See also BEST 89:2; CA 33-36R; 150;
  CANR 17, 42; DLB 68; INT CANR-17;
  MTCW

Davies, W(illiam) H(enry)
  1871-1940 .... **TCLC 5**
  See also CA 104; DLB 19, 174

Davies, Walter C.
  See Kornbluth, C(yril) M.

Davis, Angela (Yvonne)
  1944- .... **CLC 77; DAM MULT**
  See also BW 2; CA 57-60; CANR 10

Davis, B. Lynch
  See Bioy Casares, Adolfo; Borges, Jorge
  Luis

Davis, Gordon
  See Hunt, E(verette) Howard, (Jr.)

Davis, Harold Lenoir 1896-1960.... **CLC 49**
  See also CA 89-92; DLB 9

Davis, Rebecca (Blaine) Harding
  1831-1910 .... **TCLC 6**
  See also CA 104; DLB 74

Davis, Richard Harding
  1864-1916 .... **TCLC 24**
  See also CA 114; DLB 12, 23, 78, 79;
  DLBD 13

Davison, Frank Dalby 1893-1970 ... **CLC 15**
  See also CA 116

Davison, Lawrence H.
  See Lawrence, D(avid) H(erbert Richards)

Davison, Peter (Hubert) 1928- ..... **CLC 28**
  See also CA 9-12R; CAAS 4; CANR 3, 43;
  DLB 5

Davys, Mary 1674-1732............. **LC 1**
  See also DLB 39

Dawson, Fielding 1930- .... **CLC 6**
  See also CA 85-88; DLB 130

Dawson, Peter
  See Faust, Frederick (Schiller)

Day, Clarence (Shepard, Jr.)
  1874-1935 .... **TCLC 25**
  See also CA 108; DLB 11

Day, Thomas 1748-1789............. **LC 1**
  See also DLB 39; YABC 1

Day Lewis, C(ecil)
  1904-1972 .... **CLC 1, 6, 10;**
                DAM POET; PC 11
  See also Blake, Nicholas
  See also CA 13-16; 33-36R; CANR 34;
  CAP 1; DLB 15, 20; MTCW

Dazai, Osamu .... **TCLC 11**
  See also Tsushima, Shuji
  See also DLB 182

de Andrade, Carlos Drummond
  See Drummond de Andrade, Carlos

Deane, Norman
  See Creasey, John

de Beauvoir, Simone (Lucie Ernestine Marie
  Bertrand)
  See Beauvoir, Simone (Lucie Ernestine
  Marie Bertrand) de

de Brissac, Malcolm
  See Dickinson, Peter (Malcolm)

de Chardin, Pierre Teilhard
  See Teilhard de Chardin, (Marie Joseph)
  Pierre

Dee, John 1527-1608 .... **LC 20**

Deer, Sandra 1940- .... **CLC 45**

De Ferrari, Gabriella 1941- .... **CLC 65**
  See also CA 146

Defoe, Daniel
  1660(?)-1731 .... **LC 1; DA; DAB; DAC;**
           DAM MST, NOV; WLC
  See also CDBLB 1660-1789; DLB 39, 95,
  101; JRDA; MAICYA; SATA 22

de Gourmont, Remy(-Marie-Charles)
  See Gourmont, Remy (-Marie-Charles) de

de Hartog, Jan 1914- .... **CLC 19**
  See also CA 1-4R; CANR 1

de Hostos, E. M.
  See Hostos (y Bonilla), Eugenio Maria de

de Hostos, Eugenio M.
  See Hostos (y Bonilla), Eugenio Maria de

Deighton, Len .... **CLC 4, 7, 22, 46**
  See also Deighton, Leonard Cyril
  See also AAYA 6; BEST 89:2;
  CDBLB 1960 to Present; DLB 87

Deighton, Leonard Cyril 1929-
  See Deighton, Len
  See also CA 9-12R; CANR 19, 33;
  DAM NOV, POP; MTCW

Dekker, Thomas
  1572(?)-1632 ..... **LC 22; DAM DRAM**
  See also CDBLB Before 1660; DLB 62, 172

Delafield, E. M. 1890-1943 .... **TCLC 61**
  See also Dashwood, Edmee Elizabeth
  Monica de la Pasture
  See also DLB 34

de la Mare, Walter (John)
  1873-1956 .... **TCLC 4, 53; DAB; DAC;**
       DAM MST, POET; SSC 14; WLC
  See also CDBLB 1914-1945; CLR 23;
  DLB 162; SATA 16

Dickinson, Peter (Malcolm)
　　1927- . . . . **CLC 12, 35**
　　See also AAYA 9; CA 41-44R; CANR 31,
　　58; CLR 29; DLB 87, 161; JRDA;
　　MAICYA; SATA 5, 62, 95

Dickson, Carr
　　See Carr, John Dickson

Dickson, Carter
　　See Carr, John Dickson

Diderot, Denis　1713-1784 . . . . **LC 26**

Didion, Joan
　　1934- . . **CLC 1, 3, 8, 14, 32; DAM NOV**
　　See also AITN 1; CA 5-8R; CANR 14, 52;
　　CDALB 1968-1988; DLB 2, 173;
　　DLBY 81, 86; MTCW

Dietrich, Robert
　　See Hunt, E(verette) Howard, (Jr.)

Dillard, Annie
　　1945- . . . . **CLC 9, 60; DAM NOV**
　　See also AAYA 6; CA 49-52; CANR 3, 43,
　　62; DLBY 80; MTCW; SATA 10

Dillard, R(ichard) H(enry) W(ilde)
　　1937- . . . . **CLC 5**
　　See also CA 21-24R; CAAS 7; CANR 10;
　　DLB 5

Dillon, Eilis　1920-1994 . . . . **CLC 17**
　　See also CA 9-12R; 147; CAAS 3; CANR 4,
　　38; CLR 26; MAICYA; SATA 2, 74;
　　SATA-Obit 83

Dimont, Penelope
　　See Mortimer, Penelope (Ruth)

Dinesen, Isak . . . . **CLC 10, 29, 95; SSC 7**
　　See also Blixen, Karen (Christentze
　　Dinesen)

Ding Ling . . . . **CLC 68**
　　See also Chiang Pin-chin

Disch, Thomas M(ichael)　1940- . . . **CLC 7, 36**
　　See also AAYA 17; CA 21-24R; CAAS 4;
　　CANR 17, 36, 54; CLR 18; DLB 8;
　　MAICYA; MTCW; SAAS 15; SATA 92

Disch, Tom
　　See Disch, Thomas M(ichael)

d'Isly, Georges
　　See Simenon, Georges (Jacques Christian)

Disraeli, Benjamin　1804-1881 . . **NCLC 2, 39**
　　See also DLB 21, 55

Ditcum, Steve
　　See Crumb, R(obert)

Dixon, Paige
　　See Corcoran, Barbara

Dixon, Stephen　1936- . . . . . **CLC 52; SSC 16**
　　See also CA 89-92; CANR 17, 40, 54;
　　DLB 130

Dobell, Sydney Thompson
　　1824-1874 . . . . **NCLC 43**
　　See also DLB 32

Doblin, Alfred . . . . **TCLC 13**
　　See also Doeblin, Alfred

Dobrolyubov, Nikolai Alexandrovich
　　1836-1861 . . . . **NCLC 5**

Dobyns, Stephen　1941- . . . . **CLC 37**
　　See also CA 45-48; CANR 2, 18

Doctorow, E(dgar) L(aurence)
　　1931- . . . . . **CLC 6, 11, 15, 18, 37, 44, 65;**
　　　　　　　　　　　　　　　　DAM NOV, POP
　　See also AAYA 22; AITN 2; BEST 89:3;
　　CA 45-48; CANR 2, 33, 51;
　　CDALB 1968-1988; DLB 2, 28, 173;
　　DLBY 80; MTCW

Dodgson, Charles Lutwidge　1832-1898
　　See Carroll, Lewis
　　See also CLR 2; DA; DAB; DAC;
　　DAM MST, NOV, POET; MAICYA;
　　YABC 2

Dodson, Owen (Vincent)
　　1914-1983 . . . . **CLC 79; BLC;**
　　　　　　　　　　　　　　　　　　DAM MULT
　　See also BW 1; CA 65-68; 110; CANR 24;
　　DLB 76

Doeblin, Alfred　1878-1957 . . . . **TCLC 13**
　　See also Doblin, Alfred
　　See also CA 110; 141; DLB 66

Doerr, Harriet　1910- . . . . **CLC 34**
　　See also CA 117; 122; CANR 47; INT 122

Domecq, H(onorio) Bustos
　　See Bioy Casares, Adolfo; Borges, Jorge
　　Luis

Domini, Rey
　　See Lorde, Audre (Geraldine)

Dominique
　　See Proust, (Valentin-Louis-George-Eugene-)
　　Marcel

Don, A
　　See Stephen, Leslie

Donaldson, Stephen R.
　　1947- . . . . **CLC 46; DAM POP**
　　See also CA 89-92; CANR 13, 55;
　　INT CANR-13

Donleavy, J(ames) P(atrick)
　　1926- . . . . **CLC 1, 4, 6, 10, 45**
　　See also AITN 2; CA 9-12R; CANR 24, 49,
　　62; DLB 6, 173; INT CANR-24; MTCW

Donne, John
　　1572-1631 . . . . **LC 10, 24; DA; DAB;**
　　　　　　　　　DAC; DAM MST, POET; PC 1
　　See also CDBLB Before 1660; DLB 121,
　　151

Donnell, David　1939(?)- . . . . **CLC 34**

Donoghue, P. S.
　　See Hunt, E(verette) Howard, (Jr.)

Donoso (Yanez), Jose
　　1924-1996 . . . . **CLC 4, 8, 11, 32, 99;**
　　　　　　　　　　　　　　　DAM MULT; HLC
　　See also CA 81-84; 155; CANR 32;
　　DLB 113; HW; MTCW

Donovan, John　1928-1992 . . . . **CLC 35**
　　See also AAYA 20; CA 97-100; 137;
　　CLR 3; MAICYA; SATA 72;
　　SATA-Brief 29

Don Roberto
　　See Cunninghame Graham, R(obert)
　　B(ontine)

Doolittle, Hilda
　　1886-1961 . . . . . **CLC 3, 8, 14, 31, 34, 73;**
　　　　　　　DA; DAC; DAM MST, POET; PC 5;
　　　　　　　　　　　　　　　　　　　　　WLC
　　See also H. D.
　　See also CA 97-100; CANR 35; DLB 4, 45;
　　MTCW

Dorfman, Ariel
　　1942- . . . . **CLC 48, 77; DAM MULT;**
　　　　　　　　　　　　　　　　　　　　　HLC
　　See also CA 124; 130; HW; INT 130

Dorn, Edward (Merton)　1929- . . . **CLC 10, 18**
　　See also CA 93-96; CANR 42; DLB 5;
　　INT 93-96

Dorsan, Luc
　　See Simenon, Georges (Jacques Christian)

Dorsange, Jean
　　See Simenon, Georges (Jacques Christian)

Dos Passos, John (Roderigo)
　　1896-1970 . . . . . . **CLC 1, 4, 8, 11, 15, 25,**
　　　　　　34, 82; DA; DAB; DAC; DAM MST,
　　　　　　　　　　　　　　　　　　NOV; WLC
　　See also CA 1-4R; 29-32R; CANR 3;
　　CDALB 1929-1941; DLB 4, 9; DLBD 1,
　　15; DLBY 96; MTCW

Dossage, Jean
　　See Simenon, Georges (Jacques Christian)

Dostoevsky, Fedor Mikhailovich
　　1821-1881 . . . . . . **NCLC 2, 7, 21, 33, 43;**
　　　　　　　DA; DAB; DAC; DAM MST, NOV;
　　　　　　　　　　　　　　　　　SSC 2; WLC

Doughty, Charles M(ontagu)
　　1843-1926 . . . . **TCLC 27**
　　See also CA 115; DLB 19, 57, 174

Douglas, Ellen . . . . **CLC 73**
　　See also Haxton, Josephine Ayres;
　　Williamson, Ellen Douglas

Douglas, Gavin　1475(?)-1522 . . . . **LC 20**

Douglas, Keith　1920-1944 . . . . **TCLC 40**
　　See also DLB 27

Douglas, Leonard
　　See Bradbury, Ray (Douglas)

Douglas, Michael
　　See Crichton, (John) Michael

Douglas, Norman　1868-1952 . . . . . . **TCLC 68**

Douglass, Frederick
　　1817(?)-1895 . . . . **NCLC 7, 55; BLC; DA;**
　　　　　　　　　DAC; DAM MST, MULT; WLC
　　See also CDALB 1640-1865; DLB 1, 43, 50,
　　79; SATA 29

Dourado, (Waldomiro Freitas) Autran
　　1926- . . . . **CLC 23, 60**
　　See also CA 25-28R; CANR 34

Dourado, Waldomiro Autran
　　See Dourado, (Waldomiro Freitas) Autran

Dove, Rita (Frances)
　　1952- . . . . **CLC 50, 81; DAM MULT,**
　　　　　　　　　　　　　　　　POET; PC 6
　　See also BW 2; CA 109; CAAS 19;
　　CANR 27, 42; DLB 120

Dowell, Coleman　1925-1985 . . . . **CLC 60**
　　See also CA 25-28R; 117; CANR 10;
　　DLB 130

Dowson, Ernest (Christopher)
　　1867-1900 . . . . **TCLC 4**
　　See also CA 105; 150; DLB 19, 135

Doyle, A. Conan
　　See Doyle, Arthur Conan

Doyle, Arthur Conan
1859-1930 .... **TCLC 7; DA; DAB;
DAC; DAM MST, NOV; SSC 12; WLC**
See also AAYA 14; CA 104; 122;
CDBLB 1890-1914; DLB 18, 70, 156, 178;
MTCW; SATA 24

Doyle, Conan
See Doyle, Arthur Conan

Doyle, John
See Graves, Robert (von Ranke)

Doyle, Roddy 1958(?)- .... **CLC 81**
See also AAYA 14; CA 143

Doyle, Sir A. Conan
See Doyle, Arthur Conan

Doyle, Sir Arthur Conan
See Doyle, Arthur Conan

Dr. A
See Asimov, Isaac; Silverstein, Alvin

Drabble, Margaret
1939- .... **CLC 2, 3, 5, 8, 10, 22, 53;
DAB; DAC; DAM MST, NOV, POP**
See also CA 13-16R; CANR 18, 35;
CDBLB 1960 to Present; DLB 14, 155;
MTCW; SATA 48

Drapier, M. B.
See Swift, Jonathan

Drayham, James
See Mencken, H(enry) L(ouis)

Drayton, Michael 1563-1631 .... **LC 8**

Dreadstone, Carl
See Campbell, (John) Ramsey

Dreiser, Theodore (Herman Albert)
1871-1945 .... **TCLC 10, 18, 35; DA;
DAC; DAM MST, NOV; WLC**
See also CA 106; 132; CDALB 1865-1917;
DLB 9, 12, 102, 137; DLBD 1; MTCW

Drexler, Rosalyn 1926- .... **CLC 2, 6**
See also CA 81-84

Dreyer, Carl Theodor 1889-1968 .... **CLC 16**
See also CA 116

Drieu la Rochelle, Pierre(-Eugene)
1893-1945 .... **TCLC 21**
See also CA 117; DLB 72

Drinkwater, John 1882-1937 ...... **TCLC 57**
See also CA 109; 149; DLB 10, 19, 149

Drop Shot
See Cable, George Washington

Droste-Hulshoff, Annette Freiin von
1797-1848 .... **NCLC 3**
See also DLB 133

Drummond, Walter
See Silverberg, Robert

Drummond, William Henry
1854-1907 .... **TCLC 25**
See also DLB 92

Drummond de Andrade, Carlos
1902-1987 .... **CLC 18**
See also Andrade, Carlos Drummond de
See also CA 132; 123

Drury, Allen (Stuart) 1918- .... **CLC 37**
See also CA 57-60; CANR 18, 52;
INT CANR-18

Dryden, John
1631-1700 .... **LC 3, 21; DA; DAB;
DAC; DAM DRAM, MST, POET;
DC 3; WLC**
See also CDBLB 1660-1789; DLB 80, 101,
131

Duberman, Martin 1930- .... **CLC 8**
See also CA 1-4R; CANR 2

Dubie, Norman (Evans) 1945- ...... **CLC 36**
See also CA 69-72; CANR 12; DLB 120

Du Bois, W(illiam) E(dward) B(urghardt)
1868-1963 .... **CLC 1, 2, 13, 64, 96;
BLC; DA; DAC; DAM MST, MULT,
NOV; WLC**
See also BW 1; CA 85-88; CANR 34;
CDALB 1865-1917; DLB 47, 50, 91;
MTCW; SATA 42

Dubus, Andre
1936- .... **CLC 13, 36, 97; SSC 15**
See also CA 21-24R; CANR 17; DLB 130;
INT CANR-17

Duca Minimo
See D'Annunzio, Gabriele

Ducharme, Rejean 1941- .... **CLC 74**
See also DLB 60

Duclos, Charles Pinot 1704-1772 ..... **LC 1**

Dudek, Louis 1918- .... **CLC 11, 19**
See also CA 45-48; CAAS 14; CANR 1;
DLB 88

Duerrenmatt, Friedrich
1921-1990 ...... **CLC 1, 4, 8, 11, 15, 43,
102; DAM DRAM**
See also CA 17-20R; CANR 33; DLB 69,
124; MTCW

Duffy, Bruce (?)- .... **CLC 50**

Duffy, Maureen 1933- .... **CLC 37**
See also CA 25-28R; CANR 33; DLB 14;
MTCW

Dugan, Alan 1923- .... **CLC 2, 6**
See also CA 81-84; DLB 5

du Gard, Roger Martin
See Martin du Gard, Roger

Duhamel, Georges 1884-1966 .... **CLC 8**
See also CA 81-84; 25-28R; CANR 35;
DLB 65; MTCW

Dujardin, Edouard (Emile Louis)
1861-1949 .... **TCLC 13**
See also CA 109; DLB 123

Dulles, John Foster 1888-1959 .... **TCLC 72**
See also CA 115; 149

Dumas, Alexandre (Davy de la Pailleterie)
1802-1870 .... **NCLC 11; DA; DAB;
DAC; DAM MST, NOV; WLC**
See also DLB 119; SATA 18

Dumas, Alexandre
1824-1895 .... **NCLC 9; DC 1**
See also AAYA 22

Dumas, Claudine
See Malzberg, Barry N(athaniel)

Dumas, Henry L. 1934-1968 ..... **CLC 6, 62**
See also BW 1; CA 85-88; DLB 41

du Maurier, Daphne
1907-1989 .... **CLC 6, 11, 59; DAB;
DAC; DAM MST, POP; SSC 18**
See also CA 5-8R; 128; CANR 6, 55;
MTCW; SATA 27; SATA-Obit 60

Dunbar, Paul Laurence
1872-1906 ...... **TCLC 2, 12; BLC; DA;
DAC; DAM MST, MULT, POET; PC 5;
SSC 8; WLC**
See also BW 1; CA 104; 124;
CDALB 1865-1917; DLB 50, 54, 78;
SATA 34

Dunbar, William 1460(?)-1530(?) .... **LC 20**
See also DLB 132, 146

Duncan, Dora Angela
See Duncan, Isadora

Duncan, Isadora 1877(?)-1927 ..... **TCLC 68**
See also CA 118; 149

Duncan, Lois 1934- .... **CLC 26**
See also AAYA 4; CA 1-4R; CANR 2, 23,
36; CLR 29; JRDA; MAICYA; SAAS 2;
SATA 1, 36, 75

Duncan, Robert (Edward)
1919-1988 .... **CLC 1, 2, 4, 7, 15, 41, 55;
DAM POET; PC 2**
See also CA 9-12R; 124; CANR 28, 62;
DLB 5, 16; MTCW

Duncan, Sara Jeannette
1861-1922 .... **TCLC 60**
See also CA 157; DLB 92

Dunlap, William 1766-1839 .... **NCLC 2**
See also DLB 30, 37, 59

Dunn, Douglas (Eaglesham)
1942- .... **CLC 6, 40**
See also CA 45-48; CANR 2, 33; DLB 40;
MTCW

Dunn, Katherine (Karen) 1945- ..... **CLC 71**
See also CA 33-36R

Dunn, Stephen 1939- .... **CLC 36**
See also CA 33-36R; CANR 12, 48, 53;
DLB 105

Dunne, Finley Peter 1867-1936 .... **TCLC 28**
See also CA 108; DLB 11, 23

Dunne, John Gregory 1932- .... **CLC 28**
See also CA 25-28R; CANR 14, 50;
DLBY 80

**Dunsany, Edward John Moreton Drax
Plunkett** 1878-1957
See Dunsany, Lord
See also CA 104; 148; DLB 10

Dunsany, Lord .... **TCLC 2, 59**
See also Dunsany, Edward John Moreton
Drax Plunkett
See also DLB 77, 153, 156

du Perry, Jean
See Simenon, Georges (Jacques Christian)

Durang, Christopher (Ferdinand)
1949- .... **CLC 27, 38**
See also CA 105; CANR 50

Duras, Marguerite
1914-1996 ..... **CLC 3, 6, 11, 20, 34, 40,
68, 100**
See also CA 25-28R; 151; CANR 50;
DLB 83; MTCW

Durban, (Rosa) Pam 1947- .... **CLC 39**
See also CA 123

Durcan, Paul
    1944- . . . . **CLC 43, 70; DAM POET**
    See also CA 134

Durkheim, Emile 1858-1917 . . . . . . **TCLC 55**

Durrell, Lawrence (George)
    1912-1990 . . . . **CLC 1, 4, 6, 8, 13, 27, 41;**
                                                      DAM NOV
    See also CA 9-12R; 132; CANR 40;
        CDBLB 1945-1960; DLB 15, 27;
        DLBY 90; MTCW

Durrenmatt, Friedrich
    See Duerrenmatt, Friedrich

Dutt, Toru 1856-1877. . . . . **NCLC 29**

Dwight, Timothy 1752-1817. . . . . . **NCLC 13**
    See also DLB 37

Dworkin, Andrea 1946- . . . . **CLC 43**
    See also CA 77-80; CAAS 21; CANR 16,
        39; INT CANR-16; MTCW

Dwyer, Deanna
    See Koontz, Dean R(ay)

Dwyer, K. R.
    See Koontz, Dean R(ay)

Dylan, Bob 1941- . . . . . . **CLC 3, 4, 6, 12, 77**
    See also CA 41-44R; DLB 16

Eagleton, Terence (Francis) 1943-
    See Eagleton, Terry
    See also CA 57-60; CANR 7, 23; MTCW

Eagleton, Terry . . . . **CLC 63**
    See also Eagleton, Terence (Francis)

Early, Jack
    See Scoppettone, Sandra

East, Michael
    See West, Morris L(anglo)

Eastaway, Edward
    See Thomas, (Philip) Edward

Eastlake, William (Derry)
    1917-1997 . . . . **CLC 8**
    See also CA 5-8R; 158; CAAS 1; CANR 5;
        DLB 6; INT CANR-5

Eastman, Charles A(lexander)
    1858-1939 . . . . . **TCLC 55; DAM MULT**
    See also DLB 175; NNAL; YABC 1

Eberhart, Richard (Ghormley)
    1904- . . **CLC 3, 11, 19, 56; DAM POET**
    See also CA 1-4R; CANR 2;
        CDALB 1941-1968; DLB 48; MTCW

Eberstadt, Fernanda 1960- . . . . **CLC 39**
    See also CA 136

Echegaray (y Eizaguirre), Jose (Maria Waldo)
    1832-1916 . . . . **TCLC 4**
    See also CA 104; CANR 32; HW; MTCW

Echeverria, (Jose) Esteban (Antonino)
    1805-1851 . . . . **NCLC 18**

Echo
    See Proust, (Valentin-Louis-George-Eugene-)
        Marcel

Eckert, Allan W. 1931- . . . . **CLC 17**
    See also AAYA 18; CA 13-16R; CANR 14,
        45; INT CANR-14; SAAS 21; SATA 29,
        91; SATA-Brief 27

Eckhart, Meister 1260(?)-1328(?) . . **CMLC 9**
    See also DLB 115

Eckmar, F. R.
    See de Hartog, Jan

Eco, Umberto
    1932- . . . **CLC 28, 60; DAM NOV, POP**
    See also BEST 90:1; CA 77-80; CANR 12,
        33, 55; MTCW

Eddison, E(ric) R(ucker)
    1882-1945 . . . . **TCLC 15**
    See also CA 109; 156

Eddy, Mary (Morse) Baker
    1821-1910 . . . . **TCLC 71**
    See also CA 113

Edel, (Joseph) Leon 1907- . . . . . . **CLC 29, 34**
    See also CA 1-4R; CANR 1, 22; DLB 103;
        INT CANR-22

Eden, Emily 1797-1869 . . . . **NCLC 10**

Edgar, David
    1948- . . . . **CLC 42; DAM DRAM**
    See also CA 57-60; CANR 12, 61; DLB 13;
        MTCW

Edgerton, Clyde (Carlyle) 1944- . . . . **CLC 39**
    See also AAYA 17; CA 118; 134; INT 134

Edgeworth, Maria 1768-1849. . . **NCLC 1, 51**
    See also DLB 116, 159, 163; SATA 21

Edmonds, Paul
    See Kuttner, Henry

Edmonds, Walter D(umaux) 1903- . . **CLC 35**
    See also CA 5-8R; CANR 2; DLB 9;
        MAICYA; SAAS 4; SATA 1, 27

Edmondson, Wallace
    See Ellison, Harlan (Jay)

Edson, Russell . . . . **CLC 13**
    See also CA 33-36R

Edwards, Bronwen Elizabeth
    See Rose, Wendy

Edwards, G(erald) B(asil)
    1899-1976 . . . . **CLC 25**
    See also CA 110

Edwards, Gus 1939- . . . . **CLC 43**
    See also CA 108; INT 108

Edwards, Jonathan
    1703-1758 . . . . **LC 7; DA; DAC;**
                                                      DAM MST
    See also DLB 24

Efron, Marina Ivanovna Tsvetaeva
    See Tsvetaeva (Efron), Marina (Ivanovna)

Ehle, John (Marsden, Jr.) 1925- . . . . **CLC 27**
    See also CA 9-12R

Ehrenbourg, Ilya (Grigoryevich)
    See Ehrenburg, Ilya (Grigoryevich)

Ehrenburg, Ilya (Grigoryevich)
    1891-1967 . . . . **CLC 18, 34, 62**
    See also CA 102; 25-28R

Ehrenburg, Ilyo (Grigoryevich)
    See Ehrenburg, Ilya (Grigoryevich)

Eich, Guenter 1907-1972 . . . . **CLC 15**
    See also CA 111; 93-96; DLB 69, 124

Eichendorff, Joseph Freiherr von
    1788-1857 . . . . **NCLC 8**
    See also DLB 90

Eigner, Larry . . . . **CLC 9**
    See also Eigner, Laurence (Joel)
    See also CAAS 23; DLB 5

Eigner, Laurence (Joel) 1927-1996
    See Eigner, Larry
    See also CA 9-12R; 151; CANR 6

Einstein, Albert 1879-1955 . . . . **TCLC 65**
    See also CA 121; 133; MTCW

Eiseley, Loren Corey 1907-1977 . . . . . **CLC 7**
    See also AAYA 5; CA 1-4R; 73-76;
        CANR 6

Eisenstadt, Jill 1963- . . . . **CLC 50**
    See also CA 140

Eisenstein, Sergei (Mikhailovich)
    1898-1948 . . . . **TCLC 57**
    See also CA 114; 149

Eisner, Simon
    See Kornbluth, C(yril) M.

Ekeloef, (Bengt) Gunnar
    1907-1968 . . . . **CLC 27; DAM POET**
    See also CA 123; 25-28R

Ekelof, (Bengt) Gunnar
    See Ekeloef, (Bengt) Gunnar

Ekwensi, C. O. D.
    See Ekwensi, Cyprian (Odiatu Duaka)

Ekwensi, Cyprian (Odiatu Duaka)
    1921- . . . . . . **CLC 4; BLC; DAM MULT**
    See also BW 2; CA 29-32R; CANR 18, 42;
        DLB 117; MTCW; SATA 66

Elaine . . . . **TCLC 18**
    See also Leverson, Ada

El Crummo
    See Crumb, R(obert)

Elia
    See Lamb, Charles

Eliade, Mircea 1907-1986 . . . . **CLC 19**
    See also CA 65-68; 119; CANR 30, 62;
        MTCW

Eliot, A. D.
    See Jewett, (Theodora) Sarah Orne

Eliot, Alice
    See Jewett, (Theodora) Sarah Orne

Eliot, Dan
    See Silverberg, Robert

Eliot, George
    1819-1880 . . . . . **NCLC 4, 13, 23, 41, 49;**
                                        DA; DAB; DAC; DAM MST, NOV;
                                                      WLC
    See also CDBLB 1832-1890; DLB 21, 35, 55

Eliot, John 1604-1690 . . . . **LC 5**
    See also DLB 24

Eliot, T(homas) S(tearns)
    1888-1965 . . . . . **CLC 1, 2, 3, 6, 9, 10, 13,**
                          15, 24, 34, 41, 55, 57; DA; DAB; DAC;
                                   DAM DRAM, MST, POET; PC 5;
                                                      WLC 2
    See also CA 5-8R; 25-28R; CANR 41;
        CDALB 1929-1941; DLB 7, 10, 45, 63;
        DLBY 88; MTCW

Elizabeth 1866-1941. . . . . **TCLC 41**

Elkin, Stanley L(awrence)
    1930-1995 . . . . . . **CLC 4, 6, 9, 14, 27, 51,**
                           91; DAM NOV, POP; SSC 12
    See also CA 9-12R; 148; CANR 8, 46;
        DLB 2, 28; DLBY 80; INT CANR-8;
        MTCW

Elledge, Scott. . . . . **CLC 34**

Elliot, Don
    See Silverberg, Robert

Elliott, Don
    See Silverberg, Robert

Eynhardt, Guillermo
　　See Quiroga, Horacio (Sylvestre)

Ezekiel, Nissim　1924-............ **CLC 61**
　　See also CA 61-64

Ezekiel, Tish O'Dowd　1943-....... **CLC 34**
　　See also CA 129

Fadeyev, A.
　　See Bulgya, Alexander Alexandrovich

Fadeyev, Alexander.............. **TCLC 53**
　　See also Bulgya, Alexander Alexandrovich

Fagen, Donald　1948-............ **CLC 26**

Fainzilberg, Ilya Arnoldovich　1897-1937
　　See Ilf, Ilya
　　See also CA 120

Fair, Ronald L.　1932-............ **CLC 18**
　　See also BW 1; CA 69-72; CANR 25;
　　DLB 33

Fairbairn, Roger
　　See Carr, John Dickson

Fairbairns, Zoe (Ann)　1948-....... **CLC 32**
　　See also CA 103; CANR 21

Falco, Gian
　　See Papini, Giovanni

Falconer, James
　　See Kirkup, James

Falconer, Kenneth
　　See Kornbluth, C(yril) M.

Falkland, Samuel
　　See Heijermans, Herman

Fallaci, Oriana　1930-............ **CLC 11**
　　See also CA 77-80; CANR 15, 58; MTCW

Faludy, George　1913-............ **CLC 42**
　　See also CA 21-24R

Faludy, Gyoergy
　　See Faludy, George

Fanon, Frantz
　　1925-1961 .... **CLC 74; BLC;**
　　　　　　　　　　　　　DAM MULT
　　See also BW 1; CA 116; 89-92

Fanshawe, Ann　1625-1680 .... **LC 11**

Fante, John (Thomas)　1911-1983 ... **CLC 60**
　　See also CA 69-72; 109; CANR 23;
　　DLB 130; DLBY 83

Farah, Nuruddin
　　1945- ..... **CLC 53; BLC; DAM MULT**
　　See also BW 2; CA 106; DLB 125

Fargue, Leon-Paul　1876(?)-1947 ... **TCLC 11**
　　See also CA 109

Farigoule, Louis
　　See Romains, Jules

Farina, Richard　1936(?)-1966 .... **CLC 9**
　　See also CA 81-84; 25-28R

Farley, Walter (Lorimer)
　　1915-1989 .... **CLC 17**
　　See also CA 17-20R; CANR 8, 29; DLB 22;
　　JRDA; MAICYA; SATA 2, 43

Farmer, Philip Jose　1918-....... **CLC 1, 19**
　　See also CA 1-4R; CANR 4, 35; DLB 8;
　　MTCW; SATA 93

Farquhar, George
　　1677-1707 .... **LC 21; DAM DRAM**
　　See also DLB 84

Farrell, J(ames) G(ordon)
　　1935-1979 .... **CLC 6**
　　See also CA 73-76; 89-92; CANR 36;
　　DLB 14; MTCW

Farrell, James T(homas)
　　1904-1979 .. **CLC 1, 4, 8, 11, 66; SSC 28**
　　See also CA 5-8R; 89-92; CANR 9, 61;
　　DLB 4, 9, 86; DLBD 2; MTCW

Farren, Richard J.
　　See Betjeman, John

Farren, Richard M.
　　See Betjeman, John

Fassbinder, Rainer Werner
　　1946-1982 .... **CLC 20**
　　See also CA 93-96; 106; CANR 31

Fast, Howard (Melvin)
　　1914- .... **CLC 23; DAM NOV**
　　See also AAYA 16; CA 1-4R; CAAS 18;
　　CANR 1, 33, 54; DLB 9; INT CANR-33;
　　SATA 7

Faulcon, Robert
　　See Holdstock, Robert P.

Faulkner, William (Cuthbert)
　　1897-1962 ..... **CLC 1, 3, 6, 8, 9, 11, 14,**
　　　　　　　　　18, 28, 52, 68; DA; DAB; DAC;
　　　　　　　DAM MST, NOV; SSC 1; WLC
　　See also AAYA 7; CA 81-84; CANR 33;
　　CDALB 1929-1941; DLB 9, 11, 44, 102;
　　DLBD 2; DLBY 86; MTCW

Fauset, Jessie Redmon
　　1884(?)-1961 .... **CLC 19, 54; BLC;**
　　　　　　　　　　　　　DAM MULT
　　See also BW 1; CA 109; DLB 51

Faust, Frederick (Schiller)
　　1892-1944(?) ..... **TCLC 49; DAM POP**
　　See also CA 108; 152

Faust, Irvin　1924-................ **CLC 8**
　　See also CA 33-36R; CANR 28; DLB 2, 28;
　　DLBY 80

Fawkes, Guy
　　See Benchley, Robert (Charles)

Fearing, Kenneth (Flexner)
　　1902-1961 .... **CLC 51**
　　See also CA 93-96; CANR 59; DLB 9

Fecamps, Elise
　　See Creasey, John

Federman, Raymond　1928-...... **CLC 6, 47**
　　See also CA 17-20R; CAAS 8; CANR 10,
　　43; DLBY 80

Federspiel, J(uerg) F.　1931-........ **CLC 42**
　　See also CA 146

Feiffer, Jules (Ralph)
　　1929-...... **CLC 2, 8, 64; DAM DRAM**
　　See also AAYA 3; CA 17-20R; CANR 30,
　　59; DLB 7, 44; INT CANR-30; MTCW;
　　SATA 8, 61

Feige, Hermann Albert Otto Maximilian
　　See Traven, B.

Feinberg, David B.　1956-1994 ...... **CLC 59**
　　See also CA 135; 147

Feinstein, Elaine　1930-............ **CLC 36**
　　See also CA 69-72; CAAS 1; CANR 31;
　　DLB 14, 40; MTCW

Feldman, Irving (Mordecai)　1928-.... **CLC 7**
　　See also CA 1-4R; CANR 1; DLB 169

Felix-Tchicaya, Gerald
　　See Tchicaya, Gerald Felix

Fellini, Federico　1920-1993 ..... **CLC 16, 85**
　　See also CA 65-68; 143; CANR 33

Felsen, Henry Gregor　1916- .... **CLC 17**
　　See also CA 1-4R; CANR 1; SAAS 2;
　　SATA 1

Fenton, James Martin　1949-....... **CLC 32**
　　See also CA 102; DLB 40

Ferber, Edna　1887-1968........ **CLC 18, 93**
　　See also AITN 1; CA 5-8R; 25-28R; DLB 9,
　　28, 86; MTCW; SATA 7

Ferguson, Helen
　　See Kavan, Anna

Ferguson, Samuel　1810-1886..... **NCLC 33**
　　See also DLB 32

Fergusson, Robert　1750-1774 .... **LC 29**
　　See also DLB 109

Ferling, Lawrence
　　See Ferlinghetti, Lawrence (Monsanto)

Ferlinghetti, Lawrence (Monsanto)
　　1919(?)- .... **CLC 2, 6, 10, 27;**
　　　　　　　　　　　　DAM POET; PC 1
　　See also CA 5-8R; CANR 3, 41;
　　CDALB 1941-1968; DLB 5, 16; MTCW

Fernandez, Vicente Garcia Huidobro
　　See Huidobro Fernandez, Vicente Garcia

Ferrer, Gabriel (Francisco Victor) Miro
　　See Miro (Ferrer), Gabriel (Francisco
　　Victor)

Ferrier, Susan (Edmonstone)
　　1782-1854 .... **NCLC 8**
　　See also DLB 116

Ferrigno, Robert　1948(?)-......... **CLC 65**
　　See also CA 140

Ferron, Jacques　1921-1985 ... **CLC 94; DAC**
　　See also CA 117; 129; DLB 60

Feuchtwanger, Lion　1884-1958 ..... **TCLC 3**
　　See also CA 104; DLB 66

Feuillet, Octave　1821-1890 ...... **NCLC 45**

Feydeau, Georges (Leon Jules Marie)
　　1862-1921 ..... **TCLC 22; DAM DRAM**
　　See also CA 113; 152

Fichte, Johann Gottlieb
　　1762-1814 .... **NCLC 62**
　　See also DLB 90

Ficino, Marsilio　1433-1499 .... **LC 12**

Fiedeler, Hans
　　See Doeblin, Alfred

Fiedler, Leslie A(aron)
　　1917- .... **CLC 4, 13, 24**
　　See also CA 9-12R; CANR 7; DLB 28, 67;
　　MTCW

Field, Andrew　1938-.............. **CLC 44**
　　See also CA 97-100; CANR 25

Field, Eugene　1850-1895 .... **NCLC 3**
　　See also DLB 23, 42, 140; DLBD 13;
　　MAICYA; SATA 16

Field, Gans T.
　　See Wellman, Manly Wade

Field, Michael .... **TCLC 43**

Field, Peter
　　See Hobson, Laura Z(ametkin)

Fielding, Henry
1707-1754 . . . . . . **LC 1; DA; DAB; DAC;**
DAM DRAM, MST, NOV; WLC
See also CDBLB 1660-1789; DLB 39, 84,
101

Fielding, Sarah   1710-1768 . . . . **LC 1**
See also DLB 39

Fierstein, Harvey (Forbes)
1954- . . . . . **CLC 33; DAM DRAM, POP**
See also CA 123; 129

Figes, Eva   1932- . . . . **CLC 31**
See also CA 53-56; CANR 4, 44; DLB 14

Finch, Robert (Duer Claydon)
1900- . . . . **CLC 18**
See also CA 57-60; CANR 9, 24, 49;
DLB 88

Findley, Timothy
1930- . . **CLC 27, 102; DAC; DAM MST**
See also CA 25-28R; CANR 12, 42;
DLB 53

Fink, William
See Mencken, H(enry) L(ouis)

Firbank, Louis   1942-
See Reed, Lou
See also CA 117

Firbank, (Arthur Annesley) Ronald
1886-1926 . . . . **TCLC 1**
See also CA 104; DLB 36

Fisher, M(ary) F(rances) K(ennedy)
1908-1992 . . . . **CLC 76, 87**
See also CA 77-80; 138; CANR 44

Fisher, Roy   1930- . . . . **CLC 25**
See also CA 81-84; CAAS 10; CANR 16;
DLB 40

Fisher, Rudolph
1897-1934 . . . . **TCLC 11; BLC;**
DAM MULT; SSC 25
See also BW 1; CA 107; 124; DLB 51, 102

Fisher, Vardis (Alvero)   1895-1968. . . . **CLC 7**
See also CA 5-8R; 25-28R; DLB 9

Fiske, Tarleton
See Bloch, Robert (Albert)

Fitch, Clarke
See Sinclair, Upton (Beall)

Fitch, John IV
See Cormier, Robert (Edmund)

Fitzgerald, Captain Hugh
See Baum, L(yman) Frank

FitzGerald, Edward   1809-1883 . . . . **NCLC 9**
See also DLB 32

Fitzgerald, F(rancis) Scott (Key)
1896-1940 . . . . . . **TCLC 1, 6, 14, 28, 55;**
DA; DAB; DAC; DAM MST, NOV;
SSC 6; WLC
See also AITN 1; CA 110; 123;
CDALB 1917-1929; DLB 4, 9, 86;
DLBD 1, 15, 16; DLBY 81, 96; MTCW

Fitzgerald, Penelope   1916-. . . **CLC 19, 51, 61**
See also CA 85-88; CAAS 10; CANR 56;
DLB 14

Fitzgerald, Robert (Stuart)
1910-1985 . . . . **CLC 39**
See also CA 1-4R; 114; CANR 1; DLBY 80

FitzGerald, Robert D(avid)
1902-1987 . . . . **CLC 19**
See also CA 17-20R

Fitzgerald, Zelda (Sayre)
1900-1948 . . . . **TCLC 52**
See also CA 117; 126; DLBY 84

Flanagan, Thomas (James Bonner)
1923- . . . . **CLC 25, 52**
See also CA 108; CANR 55; DLBY 80;
INT 108; MTCW

Flaubert, Gustave
1821-1880 . . . . **NCLC 2, 10, 19, 62; DA;**
DAB; DAC; DAM MST, NOV; SSC 11;
WLC
See also DLB 119

Flecker, Herman Elroy
See Flecker, (Herman) James Elroy

Flecker, (Herman) James Elroy
1884-1915 . . . . **TCLC 43**
See also CA 109; 150; DLB 10, 19

Fleming, Ian (Lancaster)
1908-1964 . . . . . . **CLC 3, 30; DAM POP**
See also CA 5-8R; CANR 59;
CDBLB 1945-1960; DLB 87; MTCW;
SATA 9

Fleming, Thomas (James)   1927- . . . . **CLC 37**
See also CA 5-8R; CANR 10;
INT CANR-10; SATA 8

Fletcher, John   1579-1625. . . . . . **LC 33; DC 6**
See also CDBLB Before 1660; DLB 58

Fletcher, John Gould   1886-1950 . . . **TCLC 35**
See also CA 107; DLB 4, 45

Fleur, Paul
See Pohl, Frederik

Flooglebuckle, Al
See Spiegelman, Art

Flying Officer X
See Bates, H(erbert) E(rnest)

Fo, Dario   1926-. . . . . **CLC 32; DAM DRAM**
See also CA 116; 128; MTCW

Fogarty, Jonathan Titulescu Esq.
See Farrell, James T(homas)

Folke, Will
See Bloch, Robert (Albert)

Follett, Ken(neth Martin)
1949- . . . . . . **CLC 18; DAM NOV, POP**
See also AAYA 6; BEST 89:4; CA 81-84;
CANR 13, 33, 54; DLB 87; DLBY 81;
INT CANR-33; MTCW

Fontane, Theodor   1819-1898 . . . . . **NCLC 26**
See also DLB 129

Foote, Horton
1916- . . . . **CLC 51, 91; DAM DRAM**
See also CA 73-76; CANR 34, 51; DLB 26;
INT CANR-34

Foote, Shelby
1916- . . . . . . **CLC 75; DAM NOV, POP**
See also CA 5-8R; CANR 3, 45; DLB 2, 17

Forbes, Esther   1891-1967. . . . . **CLC 12**
See also AAYA 17; CA 13-14; 25-28R;
CAP 1; CLR 27; DLB 22; JRDA;
MAICYA; SATA 2

Forche, Carolyn (Louise)
1950- . . . . **CLC 25, 83, 86; DAM POET;**
PC 10
See also CA 109; 117; CANR 50; DLB 5;
INT 117

Ford, Elbur
See Hibbert, Eleanor Alice Burford

Ford, Ford Madox
1873-1939 . . . . **TCLC 1, 15, 39, 57;**
DAM NOV
See also CA 104; 132; CDBLB 1914-1945;
DLB 162; MTCW

Ford, Henry   1863-1947 . . . . **TCLC 73**
See also CA 115; 148

Ford, John   1895-1973. . . . . **CLC 16**
See also CA 45-48

Ford, Richard . . . . **CLC 99**

Ford, Richard   1944-. . . . . **CLC 46**
See also CA 69-72; CANR 11, 47

Ford, Webster
See Masters, Edgar Lee

Foreman, Richard   1937-. . . . . **CLC 50**
See also CA 65-68; CANR 32

Forester, C(ecil) S(cott)
1899-1966 . . . . **CLC 35**
See also CA 73-76; 25-28R; SATA 13

Forez
See Mauriac, Francois (Charles)

Forman, James Douglas   1932-. . . . . . **CLC 21**
See also AAYA 17; CA 9-12R; CANR 4,
19, 42; JRDA; MAICYA; SATA 8, 70

Fornes, Maria Irene   1930-. . . . . . **CLC 39, 61**
See also CA 25-28R; CANR 28; DLB 7;
HW; INT CANR-28; MTCW

Forrest, Leon   1937- . . . . **CLC 4**
See also BW 2; CA 89-92; CAAS 7;
CANR 25, 52; DLB 33

Forster, E(dward) M(organ)
1879-1970 . . . . . **CLC 1, 2, 3, 4, 9, 10, 13,**
15, 22, 45, 77; DA; DAB; DAC;
DAM MST, NOV; SSC 27; WLC
See also AAYA 2; CA 13-14; 25-28R;
CANR 45; CAP 1; CDBLB 1914-1945;
DLB 34, 98, 162, 178; DLBD 10; MTCW;
SATA 57

Forster, John   1812-1876 . . . . **NCLC 11**
See also DLB 144, 184

Forsyth, Frederick
1938- . . **CLC 2, 5, 36; DAM NOV, POP**
See also BEST 89:4; CA 85-88; CANR 38,
62; DLB 87; MTCW

Forten, Charlotte L. . . . . **TCLC 16; BLC**
See also Grimke, Charlotte L(ottie) Forten
See also DLB 50

Foscolo, Ugo   1778-1827. . . . . **NCLC 8**

Fosse, Bob . . . . **CLC 20**
See also Fosse, Robert Louis

Fosse, Robert Louis   1927-1987
See Fosse, Bob
See also CA 110; 123

Foster, Stephen Collins
1826-1864 . . . . **NCLC 26**

Foucault, Michel
1926-1984 . . . . **CLC 31, 34, 69**
See also CA 105; 113; CANR 34; MTCW

Fouque, Friedrich (Heinrich Karl) de la Motte
1777-1843 . . . . **NCLC 2**
See also DLB 90

Fourier, Charles 1772-1837 . . . . . . **NCLC 51**

Fournier, Henri Alban 1886-1914
See Alain-Fournier
See also CA 104

Fournier, Pierre 1916- . . . . **CLC 11**
See also Gascar, Pierre
See also CA 89-92; CANR 16, 40

Fowles, John
1926- . . . . . . **CLC 1, 2, 3, 4, 6, 9, 10, 15,
33, 87; DAB; DAC; DAM MST**
See also CA 5-8R; CANR 25; CDBLB 1960
to Present; DLB 14, 139; MTCW;
SATA 22

Fox, Paula 1923- . . . . **CLC 2, 8**
See also AAYA 3; CA 73-76; CANR 20,
36, 62; CLR 1, 44; DLB 52; JRDA;
MAICYA; MTCW; SATA 17, 60

Fox, William Price (Jr.) 1926- . . . . . **CLC 22**
See also CA 17-20R; CAAS 19; CANR 11;
DLB 2; DLBY 81

Foxe, John 1516(?)-1587 . . . . **LC 14**

Frame, Janet
1924- . . . **CLC 2, 3, 6, 22, 66, 96; SSC 29**
See also Clutha, Janet Paterson Frame

France, Anatole . . . . **TCLC 9**
See also Thibault, Jacques Anatole Francois
See also DLB 123

Francis, Claude 19(?)- . . . . **CLC 50**

Francis, Dick
1920- . . . **CLC 2, 22, 42, 102; DAM POP**
See also AAYA 5, 21; BEST 89:3; CA 5-8R;
CANR 9, 42; CDBLB 1960 to Present;
DLB 87; INT CANR-9; MTCW

Francis, Robert (Churchill)
1901-1987 . . . . **CLC 15**
See also CA 1-4R; 123; CANR 1

Frank, Anne(lies Marie)
1929-1945 . . . . **TCLC 17; DA; DAB;
DAC; DAM MST; WLC**
See also AAYA 12; CA 113; 133; MTCW;
SATA 87; SATA-Brief 42

Frank, Elizabeth 1945- . . . . **CLC 39**
See also CA 121; 126; INT 126

Frankl, Viktor E(mil) 1905- . . . . **CLC 93**
See also CA 65-68

Franklin, Benjamin
See Hasek, Jaroslav (Matej Frantisek)

Franklin, Benjamin
1706-1790 . . . . . **LC 25; DA; DAB; DAC;
DAM MST; WLCS**
See also CDALB 1640-1865; DLB 24, 43,
73

Franklin, (Stella Maraia Sarah) Miles
1879-1954 . . . . **TCLC 7**
See also CA 104

Fraser, (Lady) Antonia (Pakenham)
1932- . . . . **CLC 32**
See also CA 85-88; CANR 44; MTCW;
SATA-Brief 32

Fraser, George MacDonald 1925- . . . . **CLC 7**
See also CA 45-48; CANR 2, 48

Fraser, Sylvia 1935- . . . . **CLC 64**
See also CA 45-48; CANR 1, 16, 60

Frayn, Michael
1933- . . . . **CLC 3, 7, 31, 47;
DAM DRAM, NOV**
See also CA 5-8R; CANR 30; DLB 13, 14;
MTCW

Fraze, Candida (Merrill) 1945- . . . . . **CLC 50**
See also CA 126

Frazer, J(ames) G(eorge)
1854-1941 . . . . **TCLC 32**
See also CA 118

Frazer, Robert Caine
See Creasey, John

Frazer, Sir James George
See Frazer, J(ames) G(eorge)

Frazier, Ian 1951- . . . . **CLC 46**
See also CA 130; CANR 54

Frederic, Harold 1856-1898 . . . . . . **NCLC 10**
See also DLB 12, 23; DLBD 13

Frederick, John
See Faust, Frederick (Schiller)

Frederick the Great 1712-1786 . . . . . . **LC 14**

Fredro, Aleksander 1793-1876 . . . . . **NCLC 8**

Freeling, Nicolas 1927- . . . . **CLC 38**
See also CA 49-52; CAAS 12; CANR 1, 17,
50; DLB 87

Freeman, Douglas Southall
1886-1953 . . . . **TCLC 11**
See also CA 109; DLB 17

Freeman, Judith 1946- . . . . **CLC 55**
See also CA 148

Freeman, Mary Eleanor Wilkins
1852-1930 . . . . **TCLC 9; SSC 1**
See also CA 106; DLB 12, 78

Freeman, R(ichard) Austin
1862-1943 . . . . **TCLC 21**
See also CA 113; DLB 70

French, Albert 1943- . . . . **CLC 86**

French, Marilyn
1929- . . . . **CLC 10, 18, 60;
DAM DRAM, NOV, POP**
See also CA 69-72; CANR 3, 31;
INT CANR-31; MTCW

French, Paul
See Asimov, Isaac

Freneau, Philip Morin 1752-1832 . . **NCLC 1**
See also DLB 37, 43

Freud, Sigmund 1856-1939 . . . . **TCLC 52**
See also CA 115; 133; MTCW

Friedan, Betty (Naomi) 1921- . . . . . . **CLC 74**
See also CA 65-68; CANR 18, 45; MTCW

Friedlander, Saul 1932- . . . . **CLC 90**
See also CA 117; 130

Friedman, B(ernard) H(arper)
1926- . . . . **CLC 7**
See also CA 1-4R; CANR 3, 48

Friedman, Bruce Jay 1930- . . . . **CLC 3, 5, 56**
See also CA 9-12R; CANR 25, 52; DLB 2,
28; INT CANR-25

Friel, Brian 1929- . . . . **CLC 5, 42, 59**
See also CA 21-24R; CANR 33; DLB 13;
MTCW

Friis-Baastad, Babbis Ellinor
1921-1970 . . . . **CLC 12**
See also CA 17-20R; 134; SATA 7

Frisch, Max (Rudolf)
1911-1991 . . . . . **CLC 3, 9, 14, 18, 32, 44;
DAM DRAM, NOV**
See also CA 85-88; 134; CANR 32;
DLB 69, 124; MTCW

Fromentin, Eugene (Samuel Auguste)
1820-1876 . . . . **NCLC 10**
See also DLB 123

Frost, Frederick
See Faust, Frederick (Schiller)

Frost, Robert (Lee)
1874-1963 . . . . **CLC 1, 3, 4, 9, 10, 13, 15,
26, 34, 44; DA; DAB; DAC; DAM MST,
POET; PC 1; WLC**
See also AAYA 21; CA 89-92; CANR 33;
CDALB 1917-1929; DLB 54; DLBD 7;
MTCW; SATA 14

Froude, James Anthony
1818-1894 . . . . **NCLC 43**
See also DLB 18, 57, 144

Froy, Herald
See Waterhouse, Keith (Spencer)

Fry, Christopher
1907- . . . . . **CLC 2, 10, 14; DAM DRAM**
See also CA 17-20R; CAAS 23; CANR 9,
30; DLB 13; MTCW; SATA 66

Frye, (Herman) Northrop
1912-1991 . . . . **CLC 24, 70**
See also CA 5-8R; 133; CANR 8, 37;
DLB 67, 68; MTCW

Fuchs, Daniel 1909-1993 . . . . **CLC 8, 22**
See also CA 81-84; 142; CAAS 5;
CANR 40; DLB 9, 26, 28; DLBY 93

Fuchs, Daniel 1934- . . . . **CLC 34**
See also CA 37-40R; CANR 14, 48

Fuentes, Carlos
1928- . . . . . . **CLC 3, 8, 10, 13, 22, 41, 60;
DA; DAB; DAC; DAM MST, MULT,
NOV; HLC; SSC 24; WLC**
See also AAYA 4; AITN 2; CA 69-72;
CANR 10, 32; DLB 113; HW; MTCW

Fuentes, Gregorio Lopez y
See Lopez y Fuentes, Gregorio

Fugard, (Harold) Athol
1932- . . . . **CLC 5, 9, 14, 25, 40, 80;
DAM DRAM; DC 3**
See also AAYA 17; CA 85-88; CANR 32,
54; MTCW

Fugard, Sheila 1932- . . . . **CLC 48**
See also CA 125

Fuller, Charles (H., Jr.)
1939- . . . . **CLC 25; BLC; DAM DRAM,
MULT; DC 1**
See also BW 2; CA 108; 112; DLB 38;
INT 112; MTCW

Fuller, John (Leopold) 1937- . . . . **CLC 62**
See also CA 21-24R; CANR 9, 44; DLB 40

Fuller, Margaret . . . . **NCLC 5, 50**
See also Ossoli, Sarah Margaret (Fuller
marchesa d')

Fuller, Roy (Broadbent)
  1912-1991 . . . . CLC **4, 28**
  See also CA 5-8R; 135; CAAS 10;
  CANR 53; DLB 15, 20; SATA 87

Fulton, Alice 1952- . . . . CLC **52**
  See also CA 116; CANR 57

Furphy, Joseph 1843-1912 . . . . TCLC **25**

Fussell, Paul 1924- . . . . CLC **74**
  See also BEST 90:1; CA 17-20R; CANR 8,
  21, 35; INT CANR-21; MTCW

Futabatei, Shimei 1864-1909 . . . . . . TCLC **44**
  See also DLB 180

Futrelle, Jacques 1875-1912 . . . . . . TCLC **19**
  See also CA 113; 155

Gaboriau, Emile 1835-1873 . . . . . . NCLC **14**

Gadda, Carlo Emilio 1893-1973 . . . . CLC **11**
  See also CA 89-92; DLB 177

Gaddis, William
  1922- . . . . . CLC **1, 3, 6, 8, 10, 19, 43, 86**
  See also CA 17-20R; CANR 21, 48; DLB 2;
  MTCW

Gage, Walter
  See Inge, William (Motter)

Gaines, Ernest J(ames)
  1933- . . . . CLC **3, 11, 18, 86; BLC;**
                                      DAM MULT
  See also AAYA 18; AITN 1; BW 2;
  CA 9-12R; CANR 6, 24, 42;
  CDALB 1968-1988; DLB 2, 33, 152;
  DLBY 80; MTCW; SATA 86

Gaitskill, Mary 1954- . . . . CLC **69**
  See also CA 128; CANR 61

Galdos, Benito Perez
  See Perez Galdos, Benito

Gale, Zona
  1874-1938 . . . . . . TCLC **7; DAM DRAM**
  See also CA 105; 153; DLB 9, 78

Galeano, Eduardo (Hughes) 1940- . . . CLC **72**
  See also CA 29-32R; CANR 13, 32; HW

Galiano, Juan Valera y Alcala
  See Valera y Alcala-Galiano, Juan

Gallagher, Tess
  1943- . . CLC **18, 63; DAM POET; PC 9**
  See also CA 106; DLB 120

Gallant, Mavis
  1922- . . . . CLC **7, 18, 38; DAC;**
                                    DAM MST; SSC 5
  See also CA 69-72; CANR 29; DLB 53;
  MTCW

Gallant, Roy A(rthur) 1924- . . . . CLC **17**
  See also CA 5-8R; CANR 4, 29, 54;
  CLR 30; MAICYA; SATA 4, 68

Gallico, Paul (William) 1897-1976 . . . CLC **2**
  See also AITN 1; CA 5-8R; 69-72;
  CANR 23; DLB 9, 171; MAICYA;
  SATA 13

Gallo, Max Louis 1932- . . . . CLC **95**
  See also CA 85-88

Gallois, Lucien
  See Desnos, Robert

Gallup, Ralph
  See Whitemore, Hugh (John)

Galsworthy, John
  1867-1933 . . . . . . TCLC **1, 45; DA; DAB;**
                      DAC; DAM DRAM, MST, NOV;
                                        SSC 22; WLC 2
  See also CA 104; 141; CDBLB 1890-1914;
  DLB 10, 34, 98, 162; DLBD 16

Galt, John 1779-1839 . . . . NCLC **1**
  See also DLB 99, 116, 159

Galvin, James 1951- . . . . CLC **38**
  See also CA 108; CANR 26

Gamboa, Federico 1864-1939 . . . . . TCLC **36**

Gandhi, M. K.
  See Gandhi, Mohandas Karamchand

Gandhi, Mahatma
  See Gandhi, Mohandas Karamchand

Gandhi, Mohandas Karamchand
  1869-1948 . . . . . TCLC **59; DAM MULT**
  See also CA 121; 132; MTCW

Gann, Ernest Kellogg 1910-1991 . . . . CLC **23**
  See also AITN 1; CA 1-4R; 136; CANR 1

Garcia, Cristina 1958- . . . . CLC **76**
  See also CA 141

Garcia Lorca, Federico
  1898-1936 . . . TCLC **1, 7, 49; DA; DAB;**
                  DAC; DAM DRAM, MST, MULT,
                          POET; DC 2; HLC; PC 3; WLC
  See also CA 104; 131; DLB 108; HW;
  MTCW

Garcia Marquez, Gabriel (Jose)
  1928- . . . . CLC **2, 3, 8, 10, 15, 27, 47, 55,**
              68; DA; DAB; DAC; DAM MST,
              MULT, NOV, POP; HLC; SSC 8; WLC
  See also AAYA 3; BEST 89:1, 90:4;
  CA 33-36R; CANR 10, 28, 50; DLB 113;
  HW; MTCW

Gard, Janice
  See Latham, Jean Lee

Gard, Roger Martin du
  See Martin du Gard, Roger

Gardam, Jane 1928- . . . . CLC **43**
  See also CA 49-52; CANR 2, 18, 33, 54;
  CLR 12; DLB 14, 161; MAICYA;
  MTCW; SAAS 9; SATA 39, 76;
  SATA-Brief 28

Gardner, Herb(ert) 1934- . . . . CLC **44**
  See also CA 149

Gardner, John (Champlin), Jr.
  1933-1982 . . . . . CLC **2, 3, 5, 7, 8, 10, 18,**
                      28, 34; DAM NOV, POP; SSC 7
  See also AITN 1; CA 65-68; 107;
  CANR 33; DLB 2; DLBY 82; MTCW;
  SATA 40; SATA-Obit 31

Gardner, John (Edmund)
  1926- . . . . CLC **30; DAM POP**
  See also CA 103; CANR 15; MTCW

Gardner, Miriam
  See Bradley, Marion Zimmer

Gardner, Noel
  See Kuttner, Henry

Gardons, S. S.
  See Snodgrass, W(illiam) D(e Witt)

Garfield, Leon 1921-1996 . . . . CLC **12**
  See also AAYA 8; CA 17-20R; 152;
  CANR 38, 41; CLR 21; DLB 161; JRDA;
  MAICYA; SATA 1, 32, 76;
  SATA-Obit 90

Garland, (Hannibal) Hamlin
  1860-1940 . . . . TCLC **3; SSC 18**
  See also CA 104; DLB 12, 71, 78

Garneau, (Hector de) Saint-Denys
  1912-1943 . . . . TCLC **13**
  See also CA 111; DLB 88

Garner, Alan
  1934- . . . . CLC **17; DAB; DAM POP**
  See also AAYA 18; CA 73-76; CANR 15;
  CLR 20; DLB 161; MAICYA; MTCW;
  SATA 18, 69

Garner, Hugh 1913-1979 . . . . CLC **13**
  See also CA 69-72; CANR 31; DLB 68

Garnett, David 1892-1981 . . . . CLC **3**
  See also CA 5-8R; 103; CANR 17; DLB 34

Garos, Stephanie
  See Katz, Steve

Garrett, George (Palmer)
  1929- . . . . CLC **3, 11, 51**
  See also CA 1-4R; CAAS 5; CANR 1, 42;
  DLB 2, 5, 130, 152; DLBY 83

Garrick, David
  1717-1779 . . . . LC **15; DAM DRAM**
  See also DLB 84

Garrigue, Jean 1914-1972 . . . . CLC **2, 8**
  See also CA 5-8R; 37-40R; CANR 20

Garrison, Frederick
  See Sinclair, Upton (Beall)

Garth, Will
  See Hamilton, Edmond; Kuttner, Henry

Garvey, Marcus (Moziah, Jr.)
  1887-1940 . . . . TCLC **41; BLC;**
                                        DAM MULT
  See also BW 1; CA 120; 124

Gary, Romain . . . . CLC **25**
  See also Kacew, Romain
  See also DLB 83

Gascar, Pierre . . . . CLC **11**
  See also Fournier, Pierre

Gascoyne, David (Emery) 1916- . . . . CLC **45**
  See also CA 65-68; CANR 10, 28, 54;
  DLB 20; MTCW

Gaskell, Elizabeth Cleghorn
  1810-1865 . . . . NCLC **5; DAB;**
                                  DAM MST; SSC 25
  See also CDBLB 1832-1890; DLB 21, 144,
  159

Gass, William H(oward)
  1924- . . . CLC **1, 2, 8, 11, 15, 39; SSC 12**
  See also CA 17-20R; CANR 30; DLB 2;
  MTCW

Gasset, Jose Ortega y
  See Ortega y Gasset, Jose

Gates, Henry Louis, Jr.
  1950- . . . . CLC **65; DAM MULT**
  See also BW 2; CA 109; CANR 25, 53;
  DLB 67

Gautier, Theophile
  1811-1872 . . . . NCLC **1, 59;**
                              DAM POET; PC 18; SSC 20
  See also DLB 119

Gawsworth, John
  See Bates, H(erbert) E(rnest)

Gay, Oliver
  See Gogarty, Oliver St. John

Author Index

Gaye, Marvin (Penze) 1939-1984 ... **CLC 26**
See also CA 112

Gebler, Carlo (Ernest) 1954- .... **CLC 39**
See also CA 119; 133

Gee, Maggie (Mary) 1948- .... **CLC 57**
See also CA 130

Gee, Maurice (Gough) 1931- .... **CLC 29**
See also CA 97-100; SATA 46

Gelbart, Larry (Simon) 1923- ... **CLC 21, 61**
See also CA 73-76; CANR 45

Gelber, Jack 1932- .... **CLC 1, 6, 14, 79**
See also CA 1-4R; CANR 2; DLB 7

Gellhorn, Martha (Ellis) 1908- .. **CLC 14, 60**
See also CA 77-80; CANR 44; DLBY 82

Genet, Jean
1910-1986 ...... **CLC 1, 2, 5, 10, 14, 44,
46; DAM DRAM**
See also CA 13-16R; CANR 18; DLB 72;
DLBY 86; MTCW

Gent, Peter 1942- .... **CLC 29**
See also AITN 1; CA 89-92; DLBY 82

Gentlewoman in New England, A
See Bradstreet, Anne

Gentlewoman in Those Parts, A
See Bradstreet, Anne

George, Jean Craighead 1919- ...... **CLC 35**
See also AAYA 8; CA 5-8R; CANR 25;
CLR 1; DLB 52; JRDA; MAICYA;
SATA 2, 68

George, Stefan (Anton)
1868-1933 .... **TCLC 2, 14**
See also CA 104

Georges, Georges Martin
See Simenon, Georges (Jacques Christian)

Gerhardi, William Alexander
See Gerhardie, William Alexander

Gerhardie, William Alexander
1895-1977 .... **CLC 5**
See also CA 25-28R; 73-76; CANR 18;
DLB 36

Gerstler, Amy 1956- .... **CLC 70**
See also CA 146

Gertler, T. .... **CLC 34**
See also CA 116; 121; INT 121

Ghalib .... **NCLC 39**
See also Ghalib, Hsadullah Khan

Ghalib, Hsadullah Khan 1797-1869
See Ghalib
See also DAM POET

Ghelderode, Michel de
1898-1962 .... **CLC 6, 11; DAM DRAM**
See also CA 85-88; CANR 40

Ghiselin, Brewster 1903- .... **CLC 23**
See also CA 13-16R; CAAS 10; CANR 13

Ghose, Zulfikar 1935- .... **CLC 42**
See also CA 65-68

Ghosh, Amitav 1956- .... **CLC 44**
See also CA 147

Giacosa, Giuseppe 1847-1906 ...... **TCLC 7**
See also CA 104

Gibb, Lee
See Waterhouse, Keith (Spencer)

Gibbon, Lewis Grassic .... **TCLC 4**
See also Mitchell, James Leslie

Gibbons, Kaye
1960- .... **CLC 50, 88; DAM POP**
See also CA 151

Gibran, Kahlil
1883-1931 .... **TCLC 1, 9; DAM POET,
POP; PC 9**
See also CA 104; 150

Gibran, Khalil
See Gibran, Kahlil

Gibson, William
1914- .... **CLC 23; DA; DAB; DAC;
DAM DRAM, MST**
See also CA 9-12R; CANR 9, 42; DLB 7;
SATA 66

Gibson, William (Ford)
1948- .... **CLC 39, 63; DAM POP**
See also AAYA 12; CA 126; 133; CANR 52

Gide, Andre (Paul Guillaume)
1869-1951 .... **TCLC 5, 12, 36; DA;
DAB; DAC; DAM MST, NOV; SSC 13;
WLC**
See also CA 104; 124; DLB 65; MTCW

Gifford, Barry (Colby) 1946- .... **CLC 34**
See also CA 65-68; CANR 9, 30, 40

Gilbert, W(illiam) S(chwenck)
1836-1911 ..... **TCLC 3; DAM DRAM,
POET**
See also CA 104; SATA 36

Gilbreth, Frank B., Jr. 1911- .... **CLC 17**
See also CA 9-12R; SATA 2

Gilchrist, Ellen
1935- .... **CLC 34, 48; DAM POP;
SSC 14**
See also CA 113; 116; CANR 41, 61;
DLB 130; MTCW

Giles, Molly 1942- .... **CLC 39**
See also CA 126

Gill, Patrick
See Creasey, John

Gilliam, Terry (Vance) 1940- .... **CLC 21**
See also Monty Python
See also AAYA 19; CA 108; 113;
CANR 35; INT 113

Gillian, Jerry
See Gilliam, Terry (Vance)

Gilliatt, Penelope (Ann Douglass)
1932-1993 .... **CLC 2, 10, 13, 53**
See also AITN 2; CA 13-16R; 141;
CANR 49; DLB 14

Gilman, Charlotte (Anna) Perkins (Stetson)
1860-1935 .... **TCLC 9, 37; SSC 13**
See also CA 106; 150

Gilmour, David 1949- .... **CLC 35**
See also CA 138, 147

Gilpin, William 1724-1804 .... **NCLC 30**

Gilray, J. D.
See Mencken, H(enry) L(ouis)

Gilroy, Frank D(aniel) 1925- .... **CLC 2**
See also CA 81-84; CANR 32; DLB 7

Gilstrap, John 1957(?)- .... **CLC 99**

Ginsberg, Allen (Irwin)
1926-1997 ..... **CLC 1, 2, 3, 4, 6, 13, 36,
69; DA; DAB; DAC; DAM MST, POET;
PC 4; WLC 3**
See also AITN 1; CA 1-4R; 157; CANR 2,
41; CDALB 1941-1968; DLB 5, 16, 169;
MTCW

Ginzburg, Natalia
1916-1991 .... **CLC 5, 11, 54, 70**
See also CA 85-88; 135; CANR 33;
DLB 177; MTCW

Giono, Jean 1895-1970.......... **CLC 4, 11**
See also CA 45-48; 29-32R; CANR 2, 35;
DLB 72; MTCW

Giovanni, Nikki
1943- ...... **CLC 2, 4, 19, 64; BLC; DA;
DAB; DAC; DAM MST, MULT, POET;
PC 19; WLCS**
See also AAYA 22; AITN 1; BW 2;
CA 29-32R; CAAS 6; CANR 18, 41, 60;
CLR 6; DLB 5, 41; INT CANR-18;
MAICYA; MTCW; SATA 24

Giovene, Andrea 1904-............. **CLC 7**
See also CA 85-88

Gippius, Zinaida (Nikolayevna) 1869-1945
See Hippius, Zinaida
See also CA 106

Giraudoux, (Hippolyte) Jean
1882-1944 .... **TCLC 2, 7; DAM DRAM**
See also CA 104; DLB 65

Gironella, Jose Maria 1917- .... **CLC 11**
See also CA 101

Gissing, George (Robert)
1857-1903 .... **TCLC 3, 24, 47**
See also CA 105; DLB 18, 135, 184

Giurlani, Aldo
See Palazzeschi, Aldo

Gladkov, Fyodor (Vasilyevich)
1883-1958 .... **TCLC 27**

Glanville, Brian (Lester) 1931- ...... **CLC 6**
See also CA 5-8R; CAAS 9; CANR 3;
DLB 15, 139; SATA 42

Glasgow, Ellen (Anderson Gholson)
1873(?)-1945 .... **TCLC 2, 7**
See also CA 104; DLB 9, 12

Glaspell, Susan 1882(?)-1948...... **TCLC 55**
See also CA 110; 154; DLB 7, 9, 78;
YABC 2

Glassco, John 1909-1981 .... **CLC 9**
See also CA 13-16R; 102; CANR 15;
DLB 68

Glasscock, Amnesia
See Steinbeck, John (Ernst)

Glasser, Ronald J. 1940(?)- .... **CLC 37**

Glassman, Joyce
See Johnson, Joyce

Glendinning, Victoria 1937- .... **CLC 50**
See also CA 120; 127; CANR 59; DLB 155

Glissant, Edouard
1928- .... **CLC 10, 68; DAM MULT**
See also CA 153

Gloag, Julian 1930- .... **CLC 40**
See also AITN 1; CA 65-68; CANR 10

Glowacki, Aleksander
See Prus, Boleslaw

Gluck, Louise (Elisabeth)
1943- . . . . CLC 7, 22, 44, 81;
DAM POET; PC 16
See also CA 33-36R; CANR 40; DLB 5

Glyn, Elinor 1864-1943 . . . . TCLC 72
See also DLB 153

Gobineau, Joseph Arthur (Comte) de
1816-1882 . . . . NCLC 17
See also DLB 123

Godard, Jean-Luc 1930- . . . . CLC 20
See also CA 93-96

Godden, (Margaret) Rumer 1907- . . . CLC 53
See also AAYA 6; CA 5-8R; CANR 4, 27,
36, 55; CLR 20; DLB 161; MAICYA;
SAAS 12; SATA 3, 36

Godoy Alcayaga, Lucila 1889-1957
See Mistral, Gabriela
See also BW 2; CA 104; 131; DAM MULT;
HW; MTCW

Godwin, Gail (Kathleen)
1937- . . . . CLC 5, 8, 22, 31, 69;
DAM POP
See also CA 29-32R; CANR 15, 43; DLB 6;
INT CANR-15; MTCW

Godwin, William 1756-1836 . . . . . . NCLC 14
See also CDBLB 1789-1832; DLB 39, 104,
142, 158, 163

Goebbels, Josef
See Goebbels, (Paul) Joseph

Goebbels, (Paul) Joseph
1897-1945 . . . . TCLC 68
See also CA 115; 148

Goebbels, Joseph Paul
See Goebbels, (Paul) Joseph

Goethe, Johann Wolfgang von
1749-1832 . . . . NCLC 4, 22, 34; DA;
DAB; DAC; DAM DRAM, MST,
POET; PC 5; WLC 3
See also DLB 94

Gogarty, Oliver St. John
1878-1957 . . . . TCLC 15
See also CA 109; 150; DLB 15, 19

Gogol, Nikolai (Vasilyevich)
1809-1852 . . . . NCLC 5, 15, 31; DA;
DAB; DAC; DAM DRAM, MST, DC 1;
SSC 4, 29; WLC

Goines, Donald
1937(?)-1974 . . . . CLC 80; BLC;
DAM MULT, POP
See also AITN 1; BW 1; CA 124; 114;
DLB 33

Gold, Herbert 1924- . . . . CLC 4, 7, 14, 42
See also CA 9-12R; CANR 17, 45; DLB 2;
DLBY 81

Goldbarth, Albert 1948- . . . . CLC 5, 38
See also CA 53-56; CANR 6, 40; DLB 120

Goldberg, Anatol 1910-1982 . . . . CLC 34
See also CA 131; 117

Goldemberg, Isaac 1945- . . . . CLC 52
See also CA 69-72; CAAS 12; CANR 11,
32; HW

Golding, William (Gerald)
1911-1993 . . . . CLC 1, 2, 3, 8, 10, 17, 27,
58, 81; DA; DAB; DAC; DAM MST,
NOV; WLC
See also AAYA 5; CA 5-8R; 141;
CANR 13, 33, 54; CDBLB 1945-1960;
DLB 15, 100; MTCW

Goldman, Emma 1869-1940 . . . . . . TCLC 13
See also CA 110; 150

Goldman, Francisco 1955- . . . . CLC 76

Goldman, William (W.) 1931- . . . . CLC 1, 48
See also CA 9-12R; CANR 29; DLB 44

Goldmann, Lucien 1913-1970 . . . . . . CLC 24
See also CA 25-28; CAP 2

Goldoni, Carlo
1707-1793 . . . . LC 4; DAM DRAM

Goldsberry, Steven 1949- . . . . CLC 34
See also CA 131

Goldsmith, Oliver
1728-1774 . . . . . . LC 2; DA; DAB; DAC;
DAM DRAM, MST, NOV, POET;
WLC
See also CDBLB 1660-1789; DLB 39, 89,
104, 109, 142; SATA 26

Goldsmith, Peter
See Priestley, J(ohn) B(oynton)

Gombrowicz, Witold
1904-1969 . . . . CLC 4, 7, 11, 49;
DAM DRAM
See also CA 19-20; 25-28R; CAP 2

Gomez de la Serna, Ramon
1888-1963 . . . . CLC 9
See also CA 153; 116; HW

Goncharov, Ivan Alexandrovich
1812-1891 . . . . NCLC 1, 63

Goncourt, Edmond (Louis Antoine Huot) de
1822-1896 . . . . NCLC 7
See also DLB 123

Goncourt, Jules (Alfred Huot) de
1830-1870 . . . . NCLC 7
See also DLB 123

Gontier, Fernande 19(?)- . . . . CLC 50

Gonzalez Martinez, Enrique
1871-1952 . . . . TCLC 72
See also HW

Goodman, Paul 1911-1972 . . . . CLC 1, 2, 4, 7
See also CA 19-20; 37-40R; CANR 34;
CAP 2; DLB 130; MTCW

Gordimer, Nadine
1923- . . . . CLC 3, 5, 7, 10, 18, 33, 51, 70;
DA; DAB; DAC; DAM MST, NOV;
SSC 17; WLCS
See also CA 5-8R; CANR 3, 28, 56;
INT CANR-28; MTCW

Gordon, Adam Lindsay
1833-1870 . . . . NCLC 21

Gordon, Caroline
1895-1981 . . . CLC 6, 13, 29, 83; SSC 15
See also CA 11-12; 103; CANR 36; CAP 1;
DLB 4, 9, 102; DLBY 81; MTCW

Gordon, Charles William 1860-1937
See Connor, Ralph
See also CA 109

Gordon, Mary (Catherine)
1949- . . . . CLC 13, 22
See also CA 102; CANR 44; DLB 6;
DLBY 81; INT 102; MTCW

Gordon, Sol 1923- . . . . CLC 26
See also CA 53-56; CANR 4; SATA 11

Gordone, Charles
1925-1995 . . . . . CLC 1, 4; DAM DRAM
See also BW 1; CA 93-96; 150; CANR 55;
DLB 7; INT 93-96; MTCW

Gorenko, Anna Andreevna
See Akhmatova, Anna

Gorky, Maxim
. . . . TCLC 8; DAB; SSC 28; WLC
See also Peshkov, Alexei Maximovich

Goryan, Sirak
See Saroyan, William

Gosse, Edmund (William)
1849-1928 . . . . TCLC 28
See also CA 117; DLB 57, 144, 184

Gotlieb, Phyllis Fay (Bloom)
1926- . . . . CLC 18
See also CA 13-16R; CANR 7; DLB 88

Gottesman, S. D.
See Kornbluth, C(yril) M.; Pohl, Frederik

Gottfried von Strassburg
fl. c. 1210- . . . . CMLC 10
See also DLB 138

Gould, Lois . . . . CLC 4, 10
See also CA 77-80; CANR 29; MTCW

Gourmont, Remy (-Marie-Charles) de
1858-1915 . . . . TCLC 17
See also CA 109; 150

Govier, Katherine 1948- . . . . CLC 51
See also CA 101; CANR 18, 40

Goyen, (Charles) William
1915-1983 . . . . CLC 5, 8, 14, 40
See also AITN 2; CA 5-8R; 110; CANR 6;
DLB 2; DLBY 83; INT CANR-6

Goytisolo, Juan
1931- . . . . . CLC 5, 10, 23; DAM MULT;
HLC
See also CA 85-88; CANR 32, 61; HW;
MTCW

Gozzano, Guido 1883-1916 . . . . PC 10
See also CA 154; DLB 114

Gozzi, (Conte) Carlo 1720-1806 . . NCLC 23

Grabbe, Christian Dietrich
1801-1836 . . . . NCLC 2
See also DLB 133

Grace, Patricia 1937- . . . . CLC 56

Gracian y Morales, Baltasar
1601-1658 . . . . LC 15

Gracq, Julien . . . . CLC 11, 48
See also Poirier, Louis
See also DLB 83

Grade, Chaim 1910-1982 . . . . CLC 10
See also CA 93-96; 107

Graduate of Oxford, A
See Ruskin, John

Grafton, Garth
See Duncan, Sara Jeannette

Graham, John
See Phillips, David Graham

Graham, Jorie 1951-.............. **CLC 48**
See also CA 111; DLB 120

Graham, R(obert) B(ontine) Cunninghame
See Cunninghame Graham, R(obert)
B(ontine)
See also DLB 98, 135, 174

Graham, Robert
See Haldeman, Joe (William)

Graham, Tom
See Lewis, (Harry) Sinclair

Graham, W(illiam) S(ydney)
1918-1986 .... **CLC 29**
See also CA 73-76; 118; DLB 20

Graham, Winston (Mawdsley)
1910- .... **CLC 23**
See also CA 49-52; CANR 2, 22, 45;
DLB 77

Grahame, Kenneth
1859-1932 .... **TCLC 64; DAB**
See also CA 108; 136; CLR 5; DLB 34, 141,
178; MAICYA; YABC 1

Grant, Skeeter
See Spiegelman, Art

Granville-Barker, Harley
1877-1946 ...... **TCLC 2; DAM DRAM**
See Barker, Harley Granville
See also CA 104

Grass, Guenter (Wilhelm)
1927- ..... **CLC 1, 2, 4, 6, 11, 15, 22, 32,
49, 88; DA; DAB; DAC; DAM MST,
NOV; WLC**
See also CA 13-16R; CANR 20; DLB 75,
124; MTCW

Gratton, Thomas
See Hulme, T(homas) E(rnest)

Grau, Shirley Ann
1929- .... **CLC 4, 9; SSC 15**
See also CA 89-92; CANR 22; DLB 2;
INT CANR-22; MTCW

Gravel, Fern
See Hall, James Norman

Graver, Elizabeth 1964-........... **CLC 70**
See also CA 135

Graves, Richard Perceval 1945- .... **CLC 44**
See also CA 65-68; CANR 9, 26, 51

Graves, Robert (von Ranke)
1895-1985 ...... **CLC 1, 2, 6, 11, 39, 44,
45; DAB; DAC; DAM MST, POET;
PC 6**
See also CA 5-8R; 117; CANR 5, 36;
CDBLB 1914-1945; DLB 20, 100;
DLBY 85; MTCW; SATA 45

Graves, Valerie
See Bradley, Marion Zimmer

Gray, Alasdair (James) 1934- ...... **CLC 41**
See also CA 126; CANR 47; INT 126;
MTCW

Gray, Amlin 1946- .... **CLC 29**
See also CA 138

Gray, Francine du Plessix
1930- .... **CLC 22; DAM NOV**
See also BEST 90:3; CA 61-64; CAAS 2;
CANR 11, 33; INT CANR-11; MTCW

Gray, John (Henry) 1866-1934 .... **TCLC 19**
See also CA 119

Gray, Simon (James Holliday)
1936- .... **CLC 9, 14, 36**
See also AITN 1; CA 21-24R; CAAS 3;
CANR 32; DLB 13; MTCW

Gray, Spalding
1941- ...... **CLC 49; DAM POP; DC 7**
See also CA 128

Gray, Thomas
1716-1771 ...... **LC 4; DA; DAB; DAC;
DAM MST; PC 2; WLC**
See also CDBLB 1660-1789; DLB 109

Grayson, David
See Baker, Ray Stannard

Grayson, Richard (A.) 1951- .... **CLC 38**
See also CA 85-88; CANR 14, 31, 57

Greeley, Andrew M(oran)
1928- .... **CLC 28; DAM POP**
See also CA 5-8R; CAAS 7; CANR 7, 43;
MTCW

Green, Anna Katharine
1846-1935 .... **TCLC 63**
See also CA 112; 159

Green, Brian
See Card, Orson Scott

Green, Hannah
See Greenberg, Joanne (Goldenberg)

Green, Hannah 1927(?)-1996........ **CLC 3**
See also CA 73-76; CANR 59

Green, Henry 1905-1973 ..... **CLC 2, 13, 97**
See also Yorke, Henry Vincent
See also DLB 15

Green, Julian (Hartridge) 1900-
See Green, Julien
See also CA 21-24R; CANR 33; DLB 4, 72;
MTCW

Green, Julien .... **CLC 3, 11, 77**
See also Green, Julian (Hartridge)

Green, Paul (Eliot)
1894-1981 ...... **CLC 25; DAM DRAM**
See also AITN 1; CA 5-8R; 103; CANR 3;
DLB 7, 9; DLBY 81

Greenberg, Ivan 1908-1973
See Rahv, Philip
See also CA 85-88

Greenberg, Joanne (Goldenberg)
1932- .... **CLC 7, 30**
See also AAYA 12; CA 5-8R; CANR 14,
32; SATA 25

Greenberg, Richard 1959(?)- .... **CLC 57**
See also CA 138

Greene, Bette 1934- .... **CLC 30**
See also AAYA 7; CA 53-56; CANR 4;
CLR 2; JRDA; MAICYA; SAAS 16;
SATA 8

Greene, Gael .... **CLC 8**
See also CA 13-16R; CANR 10

Greene, Graham Henry
1904-1991 .... **CLC 1, 3, 6, 9, 14, 18, 27,
37, 70, 72; DA; DAB; DAC; DAM MST,
NOV; SSC 29; WLC**
See also AITN 2; CA 13-16R; 133;
CANR 35, 61; CDBLB 1945-1960;
DLB 13, 15, 77, 100, 162; DLBY 91;
MTCW; SATA 20

Greer, Richard
See Silverberg, Robert

Gregor, Arthur 1923-.............. **CLC 9**
See also CA 25-28R; CAAS 10; CANR 11;
SATA 36

Gregor, Lee
See Pohl, Frederik

Gregory, Isabella Augusta (Persse)
1852-1932 .... **TCLC 1**
See also CA 104; DLB 10

Gregory, J. Dennis
See Williams, John A(lfred)

Grendon, Stephen
See Derleth, August (William)

Grenville, Kate 1950-............. **CLC 61**
See also CA 118; CANR 53

Grenville, Pelham
See Wodehouse, P(elham) G(renville)

Greve, Felix Paul (Berthold Friedrich)
1879-1948
See Grove, Frederick Philip
See also CA 104; 141; DAC; DAM MST

Grey, Zane
1872-1939 .... **TCLC 6; DAM POP**
See also CA 104; 132; DLB 9; MTCW

Grieg, (Johan) Nordahl (Brun)
1902-1943 .... **TCLC 10**
See also CA 107

Grieve, C(hristopher) M(urray)
1892-1978 .... **CLC 11, 19; DAM POET**
See also MacDiarmid, Hugh; Pteleon
See also CA 5-8R; 85-88; CANR 33;
MTCW

Griffin, Gerald 1803-1840 .... **NCLC 7**
See also DLB 159

Griffin, John Howard 1920-1980.... **CLC 68**
See also AITN 1; CA 1-4R; 101; CANR 2

Griffin, Peter 1942- .... **CLC 39**
See also CA 136

Griffith, D(avid Lewelyn) W(ark)
1875(?)-1948 .... **TCLC 68**
See also CA 119; 150

Griffith, Lawrence
See Griffith, D(avid Lewelyn) W(ark)

Griffiths, Trevor 1935-......... **CLC 13, 52**
See also CA 97-100; CANR 45; DLB 13

Grigson, Geoffrey (Edward Harvey)
1905-1985 .... **CLC 7, 39**
See also CA 25-28R; 118; CANR 20, 33;
DLB 27; MTCW

Grillparzer, Franz 1791-1872....... **NCLC 1**
See also DLB 133

Grimble, Reverend Charles James
See Eliot, T(homas) S(tearns)

Grimke, Charlotte L(ottie) Forten
1837(?)-1914
See Forten, Charlotte L.
See also BW 1; CA 117; 124; DAM MULT,
POET

Grimm, Jacob Ludwig Karl
1785-1863 .... **NCLC 3**
See also DLB 90; MAICYA; SATA 22

Grimm, Wilhelm Karl 1786-1859 .. **NCLC 3**
See also DLB 90; MAICYA; SATA 22

Grimmelshausen, Johann Jakob Christoffel
von 1621-1676 .... **LC 6**
See also DLB 168

Hartmann, Sadakichi 1867-1944 . . . **TCLC 73**
See also CA 157; DLB 54

Hartmann von Aue
c. 1160-c. 1205 . . . . **CMLC 15**
See also DLB 138

Hartmann von Aue 1170-1210 . . . . **CMLC 15**

Haruf, Kent 1943- . . . . **CLC 34**
See also CA 149

Harwood, Ronald
1934- . . . . **CLC 32; DAM DRAM, MST**
See also CA 1-4R; CANR 4, 55; DLB 13

Hasek, Jaroslav (Matej Frantisek)
1883-1923 . . . . **TCLC 4**
See also CA 104; 129; MTCW

Hass, Robert
1941- . . . . **CLC 18, 39, 99; PC 16**
See also CA 111; CANR 30, 50; DLB 105;
SATA 94

Hastings, Hudson
See Kuttner, Henry

Hastings, Selina . . . . **CLC 44**

Hathorne, John 1641-1717 . . . . **LC 38**

Hatteras, Amelia
See Mencken, H(enry) L(ouis)

Hatteras, Owen . . . . **TCLC 18**
See also Mencken, H(enry) L(ouis); Nathan,
George Jean

Hauptmann, Gerhart (Johann Robert)
1862-1946 . . . . . . **TCLC 4; DAM DRAM**
See also CA 104; 153; DLB 66, 118

Havel, Vaclav
1936- . . . . **CLC 25, 58, 65;**
DAM DRAM; DC 6
See also CA 104; CANR 36; MTCW

Haviaras, Stratis . . . . **CLC 33**
See also Chaviaras, Strates

Hawes, Stephen 1475(?)-1523(?) . . . . . **LC 17**

Hawkes, John (Clendennin Burne, Jr.)
1925- . . . . . . **CLC 1, 2, 3, 4, 7, 9, 14, 15,**
27, 49
See also CA 1-4R; CANR 2, 47; DLB 2, 7;
DLBY 80; MTCW

Hawking, S. W.
See Hawking, Stephen W(illiam)

Hawking, Stephen W(illiam)
1942- . . . . **CLC 63**
See also AAYA 13; BEST 89:1; CA 126;
129; CANR 48

Hawthorne, Julian 1846-1934 . . . . . **TCLC 25**

Hawthorne, Nathaniel
1804-1864 . . . . **NCLC 39; DA; DAB;**
DAC; DAM MST, NOV; SSC 29; WLC
See also AAYA 18; CDALB 1640-1865;
DLB 1, 74; YABC 2

Haxton, Josephine Ayres 1921-
See Douglas, Ellen
See also CA 115; CANR 41

Hayaseca y Eizaguirre, Jorge
See Echegaray (y Eizaguirre), Jose (Maria
Waldo)

Hayashi Fumiko 1904-1951 . . . . **TCLC 27**
See also DLB 180

Haycraft, Anna
See Ellis, Alice Thomas
See also CA 122

Hayden, Robert E(arl)
1913-1980 . . . . . . **CLC 5, 9, 14, 37; BLC;**
DA; DAC; DAM MST, MULT, POET;
PC 6
See also BW 1; CA 69-72; 97-100; CABS 2;
CANR 24; CDALB 1941-1968; DLB 5,
76; MTCW; SATA 19; SATA-Obit 26

Hayford, J(oseph) E(phraim) Casely
See Casely-Hayford, J(oseph) E(phraim)

Hayman, Ronald 1932- . . . . **CLC 44**
See also CA 25-28R; CANR 18, 50;
DLB 155

Haywood, Eliza (Fowler)
1693(?)-1756 . . . . **LC 1**

Hazlitt, William 1778-1830 . . . . . . **NCLC 29**
See also DLB 110, 158

Hazzard, Shirley 1931- . . . . **CLC 18**
See also CA 9-12R; CANR 4; DLBY 82;
MTCW

Head, Bessie
1937-1986 . . . . **CLC 25, 67; BLC;**
DAM MULT
See also BW 2; CA 29-32R; 119; CANR 25;
DLB 117; MTCW

Headon, (Nicky) Topper 1956(?)- . . . **CLC 30**

Heaney, Seamus (Justin)
1939- . . . . . . **CLC 5, 7, 14, 25, 37, 74, 91;**
DAB; DAM POET; PC 18; WLCS
See also CA 85-88; CANR 25, 48;
CDBLB 1960 to Present; DLB 40;
DLBY 95; MTCW

Hearn, (Patricio) Lafcadio (Tessima Carlos)
1850-1904 . . . . **TCLC 9**
See also CA 105; DLB 12, 78

Hearne, Vicki 1946- . . . . **CLC 56**
See also CA 139

Hearon, Shelby 1931- . . . . **CLC 63**
See also AITN 2; CA 25-28R; CANR 18,
48

Heat-Moon, William Least . . . . **CLC 29**
See also Trogdon, William (Lewis)
See also AAYA 9

Hebbel, Friedrich
1813-1863 . . . . **NCLC 43; DAM DRAM**
See also DLB 129

Hebert, Anne
1916- . . . . **CLC 4, 13, 29; DAC;**
DAM MST, POET
See also CA 85-88; DLB 68; MTCW

Hecht, Anthony (Evan)
1923- . . . . . . **CLC 8, 13, 19; DAM POET**
See also CA 9-12R; CANR 6; DLB 5, 169

Hecht, Ben 1894-1964 . . . . **CLC 8**
See also CA 85-88; DLB 7, 9, 25, 26, 28, 86

Hedayat, Sadeq 1903-1951 . . . . **TCLC 21**
See also CA 120

Hegel, Georg Wilhelm Friedrich
1770-1831 . . . . **NCLC 46**
See also DLB 90

Heidegger, Martin 1889-1976 . . . . . . **CLC 24**
See also CA 81-84; 65-68; CANR 34;
MTCW

Heidenstam, (Carl Gustaf) Verner von
1859-1940 . . . . **TCLC 5**
See also CA 104

Heifner, Jack 1946- . . . . **CLC 11**
See also CA 105; CANR 47

Heijermans, Herman 1864-1924 . . . **TCLC 24**
See also CA 123

Heilbrun, Carolyn G(old) 1926- . . . . . **CLC 25**
See also CA 45-48; CANR 1, 28, 58

Heine, Heinrich 1797-1856 . . . . **NCLC 4, 54**
See also DLB 90

Heinemann, Larry (Curtiss) 1944- . . **CLC 50**
See also CA 110; CAAS 21; CANR 31;
DLBD 9; INT CANR-31

Heiney, Donald (William) 1921-1993
See Harris, MacDonald
See also CA 1-4R; 142; CANR 3, 58

Heinlein, Robert A(nson)
1907-1988 . . . . . . **CLC 1, 3, 8, 14, 26, 55;**
DAM POP
See also AAYA 17; CA 1-4R; 125;
CANR 1, 20, 53; DLB 8; JRDA;
MAICYA; MTCW; SATA 9, 69;
SATA-Obit 56

Helforth, John
See Doolittle, Hilda

Hellenhofferu, Vojtech Kapristian z
See Hasek, Jaroslav (Matej Frantisek)

Heller, Joseph
1923- . . . . **CLC 1, 3, 5, 8, 11, 36, 63; DA;**
DAB; DAC; DAM MST, NOV, POP;
WLC
See also AITN 1; CA 5-8R; CABS 1;
CANR 8, 42; DLB 2, 28; DLBY 80;
INT CANR-8; MTCW

Hellman, Lillian (Florence)
1906-1984 . . . . . . **CLC 2, 4, 8, 14, 18, 34,**
44, 52; DAM DRAM; DC 1
See also AITN 1, 2; CA 13-16R; 112;
CANR 33; DLB 7; DLBY 84; MTCW

Helprin, Mark
1947- . . . . **CLC 7, 10, 22, 32;**
DAM NOV, POP
See also CA 81-84; CANR 47; DLBY 85;
MTCW

Helvetius, Claude-Adrien
1715-1771 . . . . **LC 26**

Helyar, Jane Penelope Josephine 1933-
See Poole, Josephine
See also CA 21-24R; CANR 10, 26;
SATA 82

Hemans, Felicia 1793-1835 . . . . . . **NCLC 29**
See also DLB 96

Hemingway, Ernest (Miller)
1899-1961 . . . . **CLC 1, 3, 6, 8, 10, 13, 19,**
30, 34, 39, 41, 44, 50, 61, 80; DA; DAB;
DAC; DAM MST, NOV; SSC 25; WLC
See also AAYA 19; CA 77-80; CANR 34;
CDALB 1917-1929; DLB 4, 9, 102;
DLBD 1, 15, 16; DLBY 81, 87, 96;
MTCW

Hempel, Amy 1951- . . . . **CLC 39**
See also CA 118; 137

Henderson, F. C.
See Mencken, H(enry) L(ouis)

Henderson, Sylvia
See Ashton-Warner, Sylvia (Constance)

Henderson, Zenna (Chlarson)
1917-1983 .... **SSC 29**
See also CA 1-4R; 133; CANR 1; DLB 8;
SATA 5

Henley, Beth .... **CLC 23; DC 6**
See also Henley, Elizabeth Becker
See also CABS 3; DLBY 86

Henley, Elizabeth Becker 1952-
See Henley, Beth
See also CA 107; CANR 32; DAM DRAM,
MST; MTCW

Henley, William Ernest
1849-1903 .... **TCLC 8**
See also CA 105; DLB 19

Hennissart, Martha
See Lathen, Emma
See also CA 85-88

Henry, O......... **TCLC 1, 19; SSC 5; WLC**
See also Porter, William Sydney

Henry, Patrick 1736-1799 .... **LC 25**

Henryson, Robert 1430(?)-1506(?).... **LC 20**
See also DLB 146

Henry VIII 1491-1547 .... **LC 10**

Henschke, Alfred
See Klabund

Hentoff, Nat(han Irving) 1925- ..... **CLC 26**
See also AAYA 4; CA 1-4R; CAAS 6;
CANR 5, 25; CLR 1; INT CANR-25;
JRDA; MAICYA; SATA 42, 69;
SATA-Brief 27

Heppenstall, (John) Rayner
1911-1981 .... **CLC 10**
See also CA 1-4R; 103; CANR 29

Heraclitus
c. 540B.C.-c. 450B.C......... **CMLC 22**
See also DLB 176

Herbert, Frank (Patrick)
1920-1986 ...... **CLC 12, 23, 35, 44, 85;**
DAM POP
See also AAYA 21; CA 53-56; 118;
CANR 5, 43; DLB 8; INT CANR-5;
MTCW; SATA 9, 37; SATA-Obit 47

Herbert, George
1593-1633 .... **LC 24; DAB;**
DAM POET; PC 4
See also CDBLB Before 1660; DLB 126

Herbert, Zbigniew
1924- .... **CLC 9, 43; DAM POET**
See also CA 89-92; CANR 36; MTCW

Herbst, Josephine (Frey)
1897-1969 .... **CLC 34**
See also CA 5-8R; 25-28R; DLB 9

Hergesheimer, Joseph
1880-1954 .... **TCLC 11**
See also CA 109; DLB 102, 9

Herlihy, James Leo 1927-1993 ...... **CLC 6**
See also CA 1-4R; 143; CANR 2

Hermogenes fl. c. 175- .... **CMLC 6**

Hernandez, Jose 1834-1886 ...... **NCLC 17**

Herodotus c. 484B.C.-429B.C..... **CMLC 17**
See also DLB 176

Herrick, Robert
1591-1674 ..... **LC 13; DA; DAB; DAC;**
DAM MST, POP; PC 9
See also DLB 126

Herring, Guilles
See Somerville, Edith

Herriot, James
1916-1995 .... **CLC 12; DAM POP**
See also Wight, James Alfred
See also AAYA 1; CA 148; CANR 40;
SATA 86

Herrmann, Dorothy 1941- .... **CLC 44**
See also CA 107

Herrmann, Taffy
See Herrmann, Dorothy

Hersey, John (Richard)
1914-1993 .... **CLC 1, 2, 7, 9, 40, 81, 97;**
DAM POP
See also CA 17-20R; 140; CANR 33;
DLB 6; MTCW; SATA 25;
SATA-Obit 76

Herzen, Aleksandr Ivanovich
1812-1870 .... **NCLC 10, 61**

Herzl, Theodor 1860-1904 .... **TCLC 36**

Herzog, Werner 1942- .... **CLC 16**
See also CA 89-92

Hesiod c. 8th cent. B.C.- .... **CMLC 5**
See also DLB 176

Hesse, Hermann
1877-1962 .... **CLC 1, 2, 3, 6, 11, 17, 25,**
69; DA; DAB; DAC; DAM MST, NOV;
SSC 9; WLC
See also CA 17-18; CAP 2; DLB 66;
MTCW; SATA 50

Hewes, Cady
See De Voto, Bernard (Augustine)

Heyen, William 1940- .... **CLC 13, 18**
See also CA 33-36R; CAAS 9; DLB 5

Heyerdahl, Thor 1914- .... **CLC 26**
See also CA 5-8R; CANR 5, 22; MTCW;
SATA 2, 52

Heym, Georg (Theodor Franz Arthur)
1887-1912 .... **TCLC 9**
See also CA 106

Heym, Stefan 1913- .... **CLC 41**
See also CA 9-12R; CANR 4; DLB 69

Heyse, Paul (Johann Ludwig von)
1830-1914 .... **TCLC 8**
See also CA 104; DLB 129

Heyward, (Edwin) DuBose
1885-1940 .... **TCLC 59**
See also CA 108; 157; DLB 7, 9, 45;
SATA 21

Hibbert, Eleanor Alice Burford
1906-1993 .... **CLC 7; DAM POP**
See also BEST 90:4; CA 17-20R; 140;
CANR 9, 28, 59; SATA 2; SATA-Obit 74

Hichens, Robert S. 1864-1950 ..... **TCLC 64**
See also DLB 153

Higgins, George V(incent)
1939- .... **CLC 4, 7, 10, 18**
See also CA 77-80; CAAS 5; CANR 17, 51;
DLB 2; DLBY 81; INT CANR-17;
MTCW

Higginson, Thomas Wentworth
1823-1911 .... **TCLC 36**
See also DLB 1, 64

Highet, Helen
See MacInnes, Helen (Clark)

Highsmith, (Mary) Patricia
1921-1995 .... **CLC 2, 4, 14, 42, 102;**
DAM NOV, POP
See also CA 1-4R; 147; CANR 1, 20, 48,
62; MTCW

Highwater, Jamake (Mamake)
1942(?)- .... **CLC 12**
See also AAYA 7; CA 65-68; CAAS 7;
CANR 10, 34; CLR 17; DLB 52;
DLBY 85; JRDA; MAICYA; SATA 32,
69; SATA-Brief 30

Highway, Tomson
1951- ...... **CLC 92; DAC; DAM MULT**
See also CA 151; NNAL

Higuchi, Ichiyo 1872-1896....... **NCLC 49**

Hijuelos, Oscar
1951- .... **CLC 65; DAM MULT, POP;**
HLC
See also BEST 90:1; CA 123; CANR 50;
DLB 145; HW

Hikmet, Nazim 1902(?)-1963....... **CLC 40**
See also CA 141; 93-96

Hildegard von Bingen
1098-1179 .... **CMLC 20**
See also DLB 148

Hildesheimer, Wolfgang
1916-1991 .... **CLC 49**
See also CA 101; 135; DLB 69, 124

Hill, Geoffrey (William)
1932- ... **CLC 5, 8, 18, 45; DAM POET**
See also CA 81-84; CANR 21;
CDBLB 1960 to Present; DLB 40;
MTCW

Hill, George Roy 1921- .... **CLC 26**
See also CA 110; 122

Hill, John
See Koontz, Dean R(ay)

Hill, Susan (Elizabeth)
1942- .. **CLC 4; DAB; DAM MST, NOV**
See also CA 33-36R; CANR 29; DLB 14,
139; MTCW

Hillerman, Tony
1925- .... **CLC 62; DAM POP**
See also AAYA 6; BEST 89:1; CA 29-32R;
CANR 21, 42; SATA 6

Hillesum, Etty 1914-1943 .... **TCLC 49**
See also CA 137

Hilliard, Noel (Harvey) 1929- ...... **CLC 15**
See also CA 9-12R; CANR 7

Hillis, Rick 1956- .... **CLC 66**
See also CA 134

Hilton, James 1900-1954........ **TCLC 21**
See also CA 108; DLB 34, 77; SATA 34

Himes, Chester (Bomar)
1909-1984 .... **CLC 2, 4, 7, 18, 58; BLC;**
DAM MULT
See also BW 2; CA 25-28R; 114; CANR 22;
DLB 2, 76, 143; MTCW

Hinde, Thomas .... **CLC 6, 11**
See also Chitty, Thomas Willes

Hindin, Nathan
See Bloch, Robert (Albert)

Hine, (William) Daryl 1936- .... **CLC 15**
See also CA 1-4R; CAAS 15; CANR 1, 20;
DLB 60

Hinkson, Katharine Tynan
See Tynan, Katharine

Hinton, S(usan) E(loise)
1950- .... **CLC 30; DA; DAB; DAC;**
DAM MST, NOV
See also AAYA 2; CA 81-84; CANR 32,
62; CLR 3, 23; JRDA; MAICYA;
MTCW; SATA 19, 58

Hippius, Zinaida .... **TCLC 9**
See also Gippius, Zinaida (Nikolayevna)

Hiraoka, Kimitake 1925-1970
See Mishima, Yukio
See also CA 97-100; 29-32R; DAM DRAM;
MTCW

Hirsch, E(ric) D(onald), Jr. 1928- ... **CLC 79**
See also CA 25-28R; CANR 27, 51;
DLB 67; INT CANR-27; MTCW

Hirsch, Edward 1950- .... **CLC 31, 50**
See also CA 104; CANR 20, 42; DLB 120

Hitchcock, Alfred (Joseph)
1899-1980 .... **CLC 16**
See also AAYA 22; CA 159; 97-100;
SATA 27; SATA-Obit 24

Hitler, Adolf 1889-1945 .... **TCLC 53**
See also CA 117; 147

Hoagland, Edward 1932- .... **CLC 28**
See also CA 1-4R; CANR 2, 31, 57; DLB 6;
SATA 51

Hoban, Russell (Conwell)
1925- .... **CLC 7, 25; DAM NOV**
See also CA 5-8R; CANR 23, 37; CLR 3;
DLB 52; MAICYA; MTCW; SATA 1,
40, 78

Hobbes, Thomas 1588-1679 .... **LC 36**
See also DLB 151

Hobbs, Perry
See Blackmur, R(ichard) P(almer)

Hobson, Laura Z(ametkin)
1900-1986 .... **CLC 7, 25**
See also CA 17-20R; 118; CANR 55;
DLB 28; SATA 52

Hochhuth, Rolf
1931- ..... **CLC 4, 11, 18; DAM DRAM**
See also CA 5-8R; CANR 33; DLB 124;
MTCW

Hochman, Sandra 1936- .... **CLC 3, 8**
See also CA 5-8R; DLB 5

Hochwaelder, Fritz
1911-1986 ...... **CLC 36; DAM DRAM**
See also CA 29-32R; 120; CANR 42;
MTCW

Hochwalder, Fritz
See Hochwaelder, Fritz

Hocking, Mary (Eunice) 1921- ..... **CLC 13**
See also CA 101; CANR 18, 40

Hodgins, Jack 1938- .... **CLC 23**
See also CA 93-96; DLB 60

Hodgson, William Hope
1877(?)-1918 .... **TCLC 13**
See also CA 111; DLB 70, 153, 156, 178

Hoeg, Peter 1957- .... **CLC 95**
See also CA 151

Hoffman, Alice
1952- .... **CLC 51; DAM NOV**
See also CA 77-80; CANR 34; MTCW

Hoffman, Daniel (Gerard)
1923- .... **CLC 6, 13, 23**
See also CA 1-4R; CANR 4; DLB 5

Hoffman, Stanley 1944- .... **CLC 5**
See also CA 77-80

Hoffman, William M(oses) 1939- ... **CLC 40**
See also CA 57-60; CANR 11

Hoffmann, E(rnst) T(heodor) A(madeus)
1776-1822 .... **NCLC 2; SSC 13**
See also DLB 90; SATA 27

Hofmann, Gert 1931- .... **CLC 54**
See also CA 128

Hofmannsthal, Hugo von
1874-1929 .... **TCLC 11; DAM DRAM;**
DC 4
See also CA 106; 153; DLB 81, 118

Hogan, Linda
1947- .... **CLC 73; DAM MULT**
See also CA 120; CANR 45; DLB 175;
NNAL

Hogarth, Charles
See Creasey, John

Hogarth, Emmett
See Polonsky, Abraham (Lincoln)

Hogg, James 1770-1835 .... **NCLC 4**
See also DLB 93, 116, 159

Holbach, Paul Henri Thiry Baron
1723-1789 .... **LC 14**

Holberg, Ludvig 1684-1754 .... **LC 6**

Holden, Ursula 1921- .... **CLC 18**
See also CA 101; CAAS 8; CANR 22

Holderlin, (Johann Christian) Friedrich
1770-1843 .... **NCLC 16; PC 4**

Holdstock, Robert
See Holdstock, Robert P.

Holdstock, Robert P. 1948- .... **CLC 39**
See also CA 131

Holland, Isabelle 1920- .... **CLC 21**
See also AAYA 11; CA 21-24R; CANR 10,
25, 47; JRDA; MAICYA; SATA 8, 70

Holland, Marcus
See Caldwell, (Janet Miriam) Taylor
(Holland)

Hollander, John 1929- ...... **CLC 2, 5, 8, 14**
See also CA 1-4R; CANR 1, 52; DLB 5;
SATA 13

Hollander, Paul
See Silverberg, Robert

Holleran, Andrew 1943(?)- .... **CLC 38**
See also CA 144

Hollinghurst, Alan 1954- .... **CLC 55, 91**
See also CA 114

Hollis, Jim
See Summers, Hollis (Spurgeon, Jr.)

Holly, Buddy 1936-1959 .... **TCLC 65**

Holmes, John
See Souster, (Holmes) Raymond

Holmes, John Clellon 1926-1988. ... **CLC 56**
See also CA 9-12R; 125; CANR 4; DLB 16

Holmes, Oliver Wendell
1809-1894 .... **NCLC 14**
See also CDALB 1640-1865; DLB 1;
SATA 34

Holmes, Raymond
See Souster, (Holmes) Raymond

Holt, Victoria
See Hibbert, Eleanor Alice Burford

Holub, Miroslav 1923- .... **CLC 4**
See also CA 21-24R; CANR 10

Homer
c. 8th cent. B.C.- ..... **CMLC 1, 16; DA;**
DAB; DAC; DAM MST, POET; WLCS
See also DLB 176

Honig, Edwin 1919- .... **CLC 33**
See also CA 5-8R; CAAS 8; CANR 4, 45;
DLB 5

Hood, Hugh (John Blagdon)
1928- .... **CLC 15, 28**
See also CA 49-52; CAAS 17; CANR 1, 33;
DLB 53

Hood, Thomas 1799-1845 .... **NCLC 16**
See also DLB 96

Hooker, (Peter) Jeremy 1941- ...... **CLC 43**
See also CA 77-80; CANR 22; DLB 40

hooks, bell .... **CLC 94**
See also Watkins, Gloria

Hope, A(lec) D(erwent) 1907- .... **CLC 3, 51**
See also CA 21-24R; CANR 33; MTCW

Hope, Brian
See Creasey, John

Hope, Christopher (David Tully)
1944- .... **CLC 52**
See also CA 106; CANR 47; SATA 62

Hopkins, Gerard Manley
1844-1889 .... **NCLC 17; DA; DAB;**
DAC; DAM MST, POET; PC 15; WLC
See also CDBLB 1890-1914; DLB 35, 57

Hopkins, John (Richard) 1931- ...... **CLC 4**
See also CA 85-88

Hopkins, Pauline Elizabeth
1859-1930 .... **TCLC 28; BLC;**
DAM MULT
See also BW 2; CA 141; DLB 50

Hopkinson, Francis 1737-1791 ...... **LC 25**
See also DLB 31

Hopley-Woolrich, Cornell George 1903-1968
See Woolrich, Cornell
See also CA 13-14; CANR 58; CAP 1

Horatio
See Proust, (Valentin-Louis-George-Eugene-)
Marcel

Horgan, Paul (George Vincent O'Shaughnessy)
1903-1995 ...... **CLC 9, 53; DAM NOV**
See also CA 13-16R; 147; CANR 9, 35;
DLB 102; DLBY 85; INT CANR-9;
MTCW; SATA 13; SATA-Obit 84

Horn, Peter
See Kuttner, Henry

Hornem, Horace Esq.
See Byron, George Gordon (Noel)

Horney, Karen (Clementine Theodore
    Danielsen) 1885-1952....... **TCLC 71**
    See also CA 114

Hornung, E(rnest) W(illiam)
    1866-1921 .... **TCLC 59**
    See also CA 108; DLB 70

Horovitz, Israel (Arthur)
    1939- .... **CLC 56; DAM DRAM**
    See also CA 33-36R; CANR 46, 59; DLB 7

Horvath, Odon von
    See Horvath, Oedoen von
    See also DLB 85, 124

Horvath, Oedoen von 1901-1938... **TCLC 45**
    See also Horvath, Odon von
    See also CA 118

Horwitz, Julius 1920-1986........ **CLC 14**
    See also CA 9-12R; 119; CANR 12

Hospital, Janette Turner 1942-..... **CLC 42**
    See also CA 108; CANR 48

Hostos, E. M. de
    See Hostos (y Bonilla), Eugenio Maria de

Hostos, Eugenio M. de
    See Hostos (y Bonilla), Eugenio Maria de

Hostos, Eugenio Maria
    See Hostos (y Bonilla), Eugenio Maria de

Hostos (y Bonilla), Eugenio Maria de
    1839-1903 .... **TCLC 24**
    See also CA 123; 131; HW

Houdini
    See Lovecraft, H(oward) P(hillips)

Hougan, Carolyn 1943- .... **CLC 34**
    See also CA 139

Household, Geoffrey (Edward West)
    1900-1988 .... **CLC 11**
    See also CA 77-80; 126; CANR 58;
    DLB 87; SATA 14; SATA-Obit 59

Housman, A(lfred) E(dward)
    1859-1936 ...... **TCLC 1, 10; DA; DAB;**
    DAC; DAM MST, POET; PC 2; WLCS
    See also CA 104; 125; DLB 19; MTCW

Housman, Laurence 1865-1959..... **TCLC 7**
    See also CA 106; 155; DLB 10; SATA 25

Howard, Elizabeth Jane 1923- ... **CLC 7, 29**
    See also CA 5-8R; CANR 8, 62

Howard, Maureen 1930- ..... **CLC 5, 14, 46**
    See also CA 53-56; CANR 31; DLBY 83;
    INT CANR-31; MTCW

Howard, Richard 1929- ...... **CLC 7, 10, 47**
    See also AITN 1; CA 85-88; CANR 25;
    DLB 5; INT CANR-25

Howard, Robert E(rvin)
    1906-1936 .... **TCLC 8**
    See also CA 105; 157

Howard, Warren F.
    See Pohl, Frederik

Howe, Fanny 1940- .... **CLC 47**
    See also CA 117; CAAS 27; SATA-Brief 52

Howe, Irving 1920-1993.......... **CLC 85**
    See also CA 9-12R; 141; CANR 21, 50;
    DLB 67; MTCW

Howe, Julia Ward 1819-1910 ..... **TCLC 21**
    See also CA 117; DLB 1

Howe, Susan 1937-.............. **CLC 72**
    See also DLB 120

Howe, Tina 1937-................ **CLC 48**
    See also CA 109

Howell, James 1594(?)-1666 .... **LC 13**
    See also DLB 151

Howells, W. D.
    See Howells, William Dean

Howells, William D.
    See Howells, William Dean

Howells, William Dean
    1837-1920 .... **TCLC 7, 17, 41**
    See also CA 104; 134; CDALB 1865-1917;
    DLB 12, 64, 74, 79

Howes, Barbara 1914-1996 .... **CLC 15**
    See also CA 9-12R; 151; CAAS 3;
    CANR 53; SATA 5

Hrabal, Bohumil 1914-1997..... **CLC 13, 67**
    See also CA 106; 156; CAAS 12; CANR 57

Hsun, Lu
    See Lu Hsun

Hubbard, L(afayette) Ron(ald)
    1911-1986 .... **CLC 43; DAM POP**
    See also CA 77-80; 118; CANR 52

Huch, Ricarda (Octavia)
    1864-1947 .... **TCLC 13**
    See also CA 111; DLB 66

Huddle, David 1942- .... **CLC 49**
    See also CA 57-60; CAAS 20; DLB 130

Hudson, Jeffrey
    See Crichton, (John) Michael

Hudson, W(illiam) H(enry)
    1841-1922 .... **TCLC 29**
    See also CA 115; DLB 98, 153, 174;
    SATA 35

Hueffer, Ford Madox
    See Ford, Ford Madox

Hughart, Barry 1934-............ **CLC 39**
    See also CA 137

Hughes, Colin
    See Creasey, John

Hughes, David (John) 1930- .... **CLC 48**
    See also CA 116; 129; DLB 14

Hughes, Edward James
    See Hughes, Ted
    See also DAM MST, POET

Hughes, (James) Langston
    1902-1967 ..... **CLC 1, 5, 10, 15, 35, 44;**
    BLC; DA; DAB; DAC; DAM DRAM,
    MST, MULT, POET; DC 3; PC 1;
    SSC 6; WLC
    See also AAYA 12; BW 1; CA 1-4R;
    25-28R; CANR 1, 34; CDALB 1929-1941;
    CLR 17; DLB 4, 7, 48, 51, 86; JRDA;
    MAICYA; MTCW; SATA 4, 33

Hughes, Richard (Arthur Warren)
    1900-1976 ...... **CLC 1, 11; DAM NOV**
    See also CA 5-8R; 65-68; CANR 4;
    DLB 15, 161; MTCW; SATA 8;
    SATA-Obit 25

Hughes, Ted
    1930- .... **CLC 2, 4, 9, 14, 37; DAB;**
    DAC; PC 7
    See also Hughes, Edward James
    See also CA 1-4R; CANR 1, 33; CLR 3;
    DLB 40, 161; MAICYA; MTCW;
    SATA 49; SATA-Brief 27

Hugo, Richard F(ranklin)
    1923-1982 .... **CLC 6, 18, 32;**
    DAM POET
    See also CA 49-52; 108; CANR 3; DLB 5

Hugo, Victor (Marie)
    1802-1885 .... **NCLC 3, 10, 21; DA;**
    DAB; DAC; DAM DRAM, MST, NOV,
    POET; PC 17; WLC
    See also DLB 119; SATA 47

Huidobro, Vicente
    See Huidobro Fernandez, Vicente Garcia

Huidobro Fernandez, Vicente Garcia
    1893-1948 .... **TCLC 31**
    See also CA 131; HW

Hulme, Keri 1947- .... **CLC 39**
    See also CA 125; INT 125

Hulme, T(homas) E(rnest)
    1883-1917 .... **TCLC 21**
    See also CA 117; DLB 19

Hume, David 1711-1776............. **LC 7**
    See also DLB 104

Humphrey, William 1924-......... **CLC 45**
    See also CA 77-80; DLB 6

Humphreys, Emyr Owen 1919-..... **CLC 47**
    See also CA 5-8R; CANR 3, 24; DLB 15

Humphreys, Josephine 1945-.... **CLC 34, 57**
    See also CA 121; 127; INT 127

Huneker, James Gibbons
    1857-1921 .... **TCLC 65**
    See also DLB 71

Hungerford, Pixie
    See Brinsmead, H(esba) F(ay)

Hunt, E(verette) Howard, (Jr.)
    1918- .... **CLC 3**
    See also AITN 1; CA 45-48; CANR 2, 47

Hunt, Kyle
    See Creasey, John

Hunt, (James Henry) Leigh
    1784-1859 ...... **NCLC 1; DAM POET**

Hunt, Marsha 1946-.............. **CLC 70**
    See also BW 2; CA 143

Hunt, Violet 1866-1942 .... **TCLC 53**
    See also DLB 162

Hunter, E. Waldo
    See Sturgeon, Theodore (Hamilton)

Hunter, Evan
    1926- .... **CLC 11, 31; DAM POP**
    See also CA 5-8R; CANR 5, 38, 62;
    DLBY 82; INT CANR-5; MTCW;
    SATA 25

Hunter, Kristin (Eggleston) 1931-... **CLC 35**
    See also AITN 1; BW 1; CA 13-16R;
    CANR 13; CLR 3; DLB 33;
    INT CANR-13; MAICYA; SAAS 10;
    SATA 12

Hunter, Mollie 1922-............ **CLC 21**
    See also McIlwraith, Maureen Mollie
    Hunter
    See also AAYA 13; CANR 37; CLR 25;
    DLB 161; JRDA; MAICYA; SAAS 7;
    SATA 54

Hunter, Robert (?)-1734............ **LC 7**

Hurston, Zora Neale
1903-1960 .... **CLC 7, 30, 61; BLC; DA; DAC; DAM MST, MULT, NOV; SSC 4; WLCS**
See also AAYA 15; BW 1; CA 85-88; CANR 61; DLB 51, 86; MTCW

Huston, John (Marcellus)
1906-1987 .... **CLC 20**
See also CA 73-76; 123; CANR 34; DLB 26

Hustvedt, Siri 1955- .... **CLC 76**
See also CA 137

Hutten, Ulrich von 1488-1523 .... **LC 16**
See also DLB 179

Huxley, Aldous (Leonard)
1894-1963 ..... **CLC 1, 3, 4, 5, 8, 11, 18, 35, 79; DA; DAB; DAC; DAM MST, NOV; WLC**
See also AAYA 11; CA 85-88; CANR 44; CDBLB 1914-1945; DLB 36, 100, 162; MTCW; SATA 63

Huysmans, Charles Marie Georges
1848-1907
See Huysmans, Joris-Karl
See also CA 104

Huysmans, Joris-Karl .... **TCLC 7, 69**
See also Huysmans, Charles Marie Georges
See also DLB 123

Hwang, David Henry
1957- .... **CLC 55; DAM DRAM; DC 4**
See also CA 127; 132; INT 132

Hyde, Anthony 1946- .... **CLC 42**
See also CA 136

Hyde, Margaret O(ldroyd) 1917- ... **CLC 21**
See also CA 1-4R; CANR 1, 36; CLR 23; JRDA; MAICYA; SAAS 8; SATA 1, 42, 76

Hynes, James 1956(?)- .... **CLC 65**

Ian, Janis 1951- .... **CLC 21**
See also CA 105

Ibanez, Vicente Blasco
See Blasco Ibanez, Vicente

Ibarguengoitia, Jorge 1928-1983.... **CLC 37**
See also CA 124; 113; HW

Ibsen, Henrik (Johan)
1828-1906 .... **TCLC 2, 8, 16, 37, 52; DA; DAB; DAC; DAM DRAM, MST; DC 2; WLC**
See also CA 104; 141

Ibuse Masuji 1898-1993.......... **CLC 22**
See also CA 127; 141; DLB 180

Ichikawa, Kon 1915-.............. **CLC 20**
See also CA 121

Idle, Eric 1943-.................. **CLC 21**
See Monty Python
See also CA 116; CANR 35

Ignatow, David 1914-...... **CLC 4, 7, 14, 40**
See also CA 9-12R; CAAS 3; CANR 31, 57; DLB 5

Ihimaera, Witi 1944- .... **CLC 46**
See also CA 77-80

Ilf, Ilya........................ **TCLC 21**
See also Fainzilberg, Ilya Arnoldovich

Illyes, Gyula 1902-1983........... **PC 16**
See also CA 114; 109

Immermann, Karl (Lebrecht)
1796-1840 .... **NCLC 4, 49**
See also DLB 133

Inchbald, Elizabeth 1753-1821 ... **NCLC 62**
See also DLB 39, 89

Inclan, Ramon (Maria) del Valle
See Valle-Inclan, Ramon (Maria) del

Infante, G(uillermo) Cabrera
See Cabrera Infante, G(uillermo)

Ingalls, Rachel (Holmes) 1940-..... **CLC 42**
See also CA 123; 127

Ingamells, Rex 1913-1955 .... **TCLC 35**

Inge, William (Motter)
1913-1973 .. **CLC 1, 8, 19; DAM DRAM**
See also CA 9-12R; CDALB 1941-1968; DLB 7; MTCW

Ingelow, Jean 1820-1897 .... **NCLC 39**
See also DLB 35, 163; SATA 33

Ingram, Willis J.
See Harris, Mark

Innaurato, Albert (F.) 1948(?)- .. **CLC 21, 60**
See also CA 115; 122; INT 122

Innes, Michael
See Stewart, J(ohn) I(nnes) M(ackintosh)

Ionesco, Eugene
1909-1994 .... **CLC 1, 4, 6, 9, 11, 15, 41, 86; DA; DAB; DAC; DAM DRAM, MST; WLC**
See also CA 9-12R; 144; CANR 55; MTCW; SATA 7; SATA-Obit 79

Iqbal, Muhammad 1873-1938 ..... **TCLC 28**

Ireland, Patrick
See O'Doherty, Brian

Iron, Ralph
See Schreiner, Olive (Emilie Albertina)

Irving, John (Winslow)
1942- ..... **CLC 13, 23, 38; DAM NOV, POP**
See also AAYA 8; BEST 89:3; CA 25-28R; CANR 28; DLB 6; DLBY 82; MTCW

Irving, Washington
1783-1859 ..... **NCLC 2, 19; DA; DAB; DAM MST; SSC 2; WLC**
See also CDALB 1640-1865; DLB 3, 11, 30, 59, 73, 74; YABC 2

Irwin, P. K.
See Page, P(atricia) K(athleen)

Isaacs, Susan 1943- ... **CLC 32; DAM POP**
See also BEST 89:1; CA 89-92; CANR 20, 41; INT CANR-20; MTCW

Isherwood, Christopher (William Bradshaw)
1904-1986 .... **CLC 1, 9, 11, 14, 44; DAM DRAM, NOV**
See also CA 13-16R; 117; CANR 35; DLB 15; DLBY 86; MTCW

Ishiguro, Kazuo
1954- ...... **CLC 27, 56, 59; DAM NOV**
See also BEST 90:2; CA 120; CANR 49; MTCW

Ishikawa, Hakuhin
See Ishikawa, Takuboku

Ishikawa, Takuboku
1886(?)-1912 .... **TCLC 15; DAM POET; PC 10**
See also CA 113; 153

Iskander, Fazil 1929- .... **CLC 47**
See also CA 102

Isler, Alan (David) 1934-.......... **CLC 91**
See also CA 156

Ivan IV 1530-1584 .... **LC 17**

Ivanov, Vyacheslav Ivanovich
1866-1949 .... **TCLC 33**
See also CA 122

Ivask, Ivar Vidrik 1927-1992....... **CLC 14**
See also CA 37-40R; 139; CANR 24

Ives, Morgan
See Bradley, Marion Zimmer

J. R. S.
See Gogarty, Oliver St. John

Jabran, Kahlil
See Gibran, Kahlil

Jabran, Khalil
See Gibran, Kahlil

Jackson, Daniel
See Wingrove, David (John)

Jackson, Jesse 1908-1983 .... **CLC 12**
See also BW 1; CA 25-28R; 109; CANR 27; CLR 28; MAICYA; SATA 2, 29; SATA-Obit 48

Jackson, Laura (Riding) 1901-1991
See Riding, Laura
See also CA 65-68; 135; CANR 28; DLB 48

Jackson, Sam
See Trumbo, Dalton

Jackson, Sara
See Wingrove, David (John)

Jackson, Shirley
1919-1965 .... **CLC 11, 60, 87; DA; DAC; DAM MST; SSC 9; WLC**
See also AAYA 9; CA 1-4R; 25-28R; CANR 4, 52; CDALB 1941-1968; DLB 6; SATA 2

Jacob, (Cyprien-)Max 1876-1944 ... **TCLC 6**
See also CA 104

Jacobs, Jim 1942-................. **CLC 12**
See also CA 97-100; INT 97-100

Jacobs, W(illiam) W(ymark)
1863-1943 .... **TCLC 22**
See also CA 121; DLB 135

Jacobsen, Jens Peter 1847-1885 .. **NCLC 34**

Jacobsen, Josephine 1908-..... **CLC 48, 102**
See also CA 33-36R; CAAS 18; CANR 23, 48

Jacobson, Dan 1929- .... **CLC 4, 14**
See also CA 1-4R; CANR 2, 25; DLB 14; MTCW

Jacqueline
See Carpentier (y Valmont), Alejo

Jagger, Mick 1944-.............. **CLC 17**

Jakes, John (William)
1932- ...... **CLC 29; DAM NOV, POP**
See also BEST 89:4; CA 57-60; CANR 10, 43; DLBY 83; INT CANR-10; MTCW; SATA 62

James, Andrew
See Kirkup, James

James, C(yril) L(ionel) R(obert)
1901-1989 .... **CLC 33**
See also BW 2; CA 117; 125; 128;
CANR 62; DLB 125; MTCW

James, Daniel (Lewis) 1911-1988
See Santiago, Danny
See also CA 125

James, Dynely
See Mayne, William (James Carter)

James, Henry Sr. 1811-1882 ..... **NCLC 53**

James, Henry
1843-1916 ...... **TCLC 2, 11, 24, 40, 47,
64; DA; DAB; DAC; DAM MST, NOV;
SSC 8; WLC**
See also CA 104; 132; CDALB 1865-1917;
DLB 12, 71, 74; DLBD 13; MTCW

James, M. R.
See James, Montague (Rhodes)
See also DLB 156

James, Montague (Rhodes)
1862-1936 .... **TCLC 6; SSC 16**
See also CA 104

James, P. D. .... **CLC 18, 46**
See also White, Phyllis Dorothy James
See also BEST 90:2; CDBLB 1960 to
Present; DLB 87

James, Philip
See Moorcock, Michael (John)

James, William 1842-1910 ..... **TCLC 15, 32**
See also CA 109

James I 1394-1437 .... **LC 20**

Jameson, Anna 1794-1860 .... **NCLC 43**
See also DLB 99, 166

Jami, Nur al-Din 'Abd al-Rahman
1414-1492 .... **LC 9**

Jandl, Ernst 1925- .... **CLC 34**

Janowitz, Tama
1957- .... **CLC 43; DAM POP**
See also CA 106; CANR 52

Japrisot, Sebastien 1931- .... **CLC 90**

Jarrell, Randall
1914-1965 .... **CLC 1, 2, 6, 9, 13, 49;
DAM POET**
See also CA 5-8R; 25-28R; CABS 2;
CANR 6, 34; CDALB 1941-1968; CLR 6;
DLB 48, 52; MAICYA; MTCW; SATA 7

Jarry, Alfred
1873-1907 .... **TCLC 2, 14;
DAM DRAM; SSC 20**
See also CA 104; 153

Jarvis, E. K.
See Bloch, Robert (Albert); Ellison, Harlan
(Jay); Silverberg, Robert

Jeake, Samuel, Jr.
See Aiken, Conrad (Potter)

Jean Paul 1763-1825 .... **NCLC 7**

Jefferies, (John) Richard
1848-1887 .... **NCLC 47**
See also DLB 98, 141; SATA 16

Jeffers, (John) Robinson
1887-1962 .... **CLC 2, 3, 11, 15, 54; DA;
DAC; DAM MST, POET; PC 17; WLC**
See also CA 85-88; CANR 35;
CDALB 1917-1929; DLB 45; MTCW

Jefferson, Janet
See Mencken, H(enry) L(ouis)

Jefferson, Thomas 1743-1826 .... **NCLC 11**
See also CDALB 1640-1865; DLB 31

Jeffrey, Francis 1773-1850 ...... **NCLC 33**
See also DLB 107

Jelakowitch, Ivan
See Heijermans, Herman

Jellicoe, (Patricia) Ann 1927- ...... **CLC 27**
See also CA 85-88; DLB 13

Jen, Gish .... **CLC 70**
See also Jen, Lillian

Jen, Lillian 1956(?)-
See Jen, Gish
See also CA 135

Jenkins, (John) Robin 1912- .... **CLC 52**
See also CA 1-4R; CANR 1; DLB 14

Jennings, Elizabeth (Joan)
1926- .... **CLC 5, 14**
See also CA 61-64; CAAS 5; CANR 8, 39;
DLB 27; MTCW; SATA 66

Jennings, Waylon 1937- .... **CLC 21**

Jensen, Johannes V. 1873-1950 .... **TCLC 41**

Jensen, Laura (Linnea) 1948- ...... **CLC 37**
See also CA 103

Jerome, Jerome K(lapka)
1859-1927 .... **TCLC 23**
See also CA 119; DLB 10, 34, 135

Jerrold, Douglas William
1803-1857 .... **NCLC 2**
See also DLB 158, 159

Jewett, (Theodora) Sarah Orne
1849-1909 .... **TCLC 1, 22; SSC 6**
See also CA 108; 127; DLB 12, 74;
SATA 15

Jewsbury, Geraldine (Endsor)
1812-1880 .... **NCLC 22**
See also DLB 21

Jhabvala, Ruth Prawer
1927- .... **CLC 4, 8, 29, 94; DAB;
DAM NOV**
See also CA 1-4R; CANR 2, 29, 51;
DLB 139; INT CANR-29; MTCW

Jibran, Kahlil
See Gibran, Kahlil

Jibran, Khalil
See Gibran, Kahlil

Jiles, Paulette 1943- .... **CLC 13, 58**
See also CA 101

Jimenez (Mantecon), Juan Ramon
1881-1958 ..... **TCLC 4; DAM MULT,
POET; HLC; PC 7**
See also CA 104; 131; DLB 134; HW;
MTCW

Jimenez, Ramon
See Jimenez (Mantecon), Juan Ramon

Jimenez Mantecon, Juan
See Jimenez (Mantecon), Juan Ramon

Joel, Billy .... **CLC 26**
See also Joel, William Martin

Joel, William Martin 1949-
See Joel, Billy
See also CA 108

John of the Cross, St. 1542-1591 .... **LC 18**

Johnson, B(ryan) S(tanley William)
1933-1973 .... **CLC 6, 9**
See also CA 9-12R; 53-56; CANR 9;
DLB 14, 40

Johnson, Benj. F. of Boo
See Riley, James Whitcomb

Johnson, Benjamin F. of Boo
See Riley, James Whitcomb

Johnson, Charles (Richard)
1948- .... **CLC 7, 51, 65; BLC;
DAM MULT**
See also BW 2; CA 116; CAAS 18;
CANR 42; DLB 33

Johnson, Denis 1949- .... **CLC 52**
See also CA 117; 121; DLB 120

Johnson, Diane 1934- .... **CLC 5, 13, 48**
See also CA 41-44R; CANR 17, 40, 62;
DLBY 80; INT CANR-17; MTCW

Johnson, Eyvind (Olof Verner)
1900-1976 .... **CLC 14**
See also CA 73-76; 69-72; CANR 34

Johnson, J. R.
See James, C(yril) L(ionel) R(obert)

Johnson, James Weldon
1871-1938 .... **TCLC 3, 19; BLC;
DAM MULT, POET**
See also BW 1; CA 104; 125;
CDALB 1917-1929; CLR 32; DLB 51;
MTCW; SATA 31

Johnson, Joyce 1935- .... **CLC 58**
See also CA 125; 129

Johnson, Lionel (Pigot)
1867-1902 .... **TCLC 19**
See also CA 117; DLB 19

Johnson, Mel
See Malzberg, Barry N(athaniel)

Johnson, Pamela Hansford
1912-1981 .... **CLC 1, 7, 27**
See also CA 1-4R; 104; CANR 2, 28;
DLB 15; MTCW

Johnson, Robert 1911(?)-1938 ..... **TCLC 69**

Johnson, Samuel
1709-1784 ..... **LC 15; DA; DAB; DAC;
DAM MST; WLC**
See also CDBLB 1660-1789; DLB 39, 95,
104, 142

Johnson, Uwe
1934-1984 .... **CLC 5, 10, 15, 40**
See also CA 1-4R; 112; CANR 1, 39;
DLB 75; MTCW

Johnston, George (Benson) 1913- ... **CLC 51**
See also CA 1-4R; CANR 5, 20; DLB 88

Johnston, Jennifer 1930- .... **CLC 7**
See also CA 85-88; DLB 14

Jolley, (Monica) Elizabeth
1923- .... **CLC 46; SSC 19**
See also CA 127; CAAS 13; CANR 59

Jones, Arthur Llewellyn 1863-1947
See Machen, Arthur
See also CA 104

Jones, D(ouglas) G(ordon) 1929- .... **CLC 10**
See also CA 29-32R; CANR 13; DLB 53

Kavafis, Konstantinos Petrou 1863-1933
See Cavafy, C(onstantine) P(eter)
See also CA 104

Kavan, Anna 1901-1968 . . . . . . **CLC 5, 13, 82**
See also CA 5-8R; CANR 6, 57; MTCW

Kavanagh, Dan
See Barnes, Julian (Patrick)

Kavanagh, Patrick (Joseph)
1904-1967 . . . . **CLC 22**
See also CA 123; 25-28R; DLB 15, 20;
MTCW

Kawabata, Yasunari
1899-1972 . . . . **CLC 2, 5, 9, 18;**
DAM MULT; SSC 17
See also CA 93-96; 33-36R; DLB 180

Kaye, M(ary) M(argaret) 1909- . . . . . **CLC 28**
See also CA 89-92; CANR 24, 60; MTCW;
SATA 62

Kaye, Mollie
See Kaye, M(ary) M(argaret)

Kaye-Smith, Sheila 1887-1956 . . . . . **TCLC 20**
See also CA 118; DLB 36

Kaymor, Patrice Maguilene
See Senghor, Leopold Sedar

Kazan, Elia 1909- . . . . **CLC 6, 16, 63**
See also CA 21-24R; CANR 32

Kazantzakis, Nikos
1883(?)-1957 . . . . **TCLC 2, 5, 33**
See also CA 105; 132; MTCW

Kazin, Alfred 1915- . . . . **CLC 34, 38**
See also CA 1-4R; CAAS 7; CANR 1, 45;
DLB 67

Keane, Mary Nesta (Skrine) 1904-1996
See Keane, Molly
See also CA 108; 114; 151

Keane, Molly . . . . **CLC 31**
See also Keane, Mary Nesta (Skrine)
See also INT 114

Keates, Jonathan 19(?)- . . . . **CLC 34**

Keaton, Buster 1895-1966 . . . . **CLC 20**

Keats, John
1795-1821 . . . . **NCLC 8; DA; DAB;**
DAC; DAM MST, POET; PC 1; WLC
See also CDBLB 1789-1832; DLB 96, 110

Keene, Donald 1922- . . . . **CLC 34**
See also CA 1-4R; CANR 5

Keillor, Garrison . . . . **CLC 40**
See also Keillor, Gary (Edward)
See also AAYA 2; BEST 89:3; DLBY 87;
SATA 58

Keillor, Gary (Edward) 1942-
See Keillor, Garrison
See also CA 111; 117; CANR 36, 59;
DAM POP; MTCW

Keith, Michael
See Hubbard, L(afayette) Ron(ald)

Keller, Gottfried
1819-1890 . . . . **NCLC 2; SSC 26**
See also DLB 129

Kellerman, Jonathan
1949- . . . . **CLC 44; DAM POP**
See also BEST 90:1; CA 106; CANR 29, 51;
INT CANR-29

Kelley, William Melvin 1937- . . . . . . **CLC 22**
See also BW 1; CA 77-80; CANR 27;
DLB 33

Kellogg, Marjorie 1922- . . . . **CLC 2**
See also CA 81-84

Kellow, Kathleen
See Hibbert, Eleanor Alice Burford

Kelly, M(ilton) T(erry) 1947- . . . . . . **CLC 55**
See also CA 97-100; CAAS 22; CANR 19,
43

Kelman, James 1946- . . . . **CLC 58, 86**
See also CA 148

Kemal, Yashar 1923- . . . . **CLC 14, 29**
See also CA 89-92; CANR 44

Kemble, Fanny 1809-1893 . . . . **NCLC 18**
See also DLB 32

Kemelman, Harry 1908-1996 . . . . **CLC 2**
See also AITN 1; CA 9-12R; 155; CANR 6;
DLB 28

Kempe, Margery 1373(?)-1440(?) . . . . . **LC 6**
See also DLB 146

Kempis, Thomas a 1380-1471 . . . . **LC 11**

Kendall, Henry 1839-1882 . . . . **NCLC 12**

Keneally, Thomas (Michael)
1935- . . . . . . **CLC 5, 8, 10, 14, 19, 27, 43;**
DAM NOV
See also CA 85-88; CANR 10, 50; MTCW

Kennedy, Adrienne (Lita)
1931- . . . . . **CLC 66; BLC; DAM MULT;**
DC 5
See also BW 2; CA 103; CAAS 20; CABS 3;
CANR 26, 53; DLB 38

Kennedy, John Pendleton
1795-1870 . . . . **NCLC 2**
See also DLB 3

Kennedy, Joseph Charles 1929-
See Kennedy, X. J.
See also CA 1-4R; CANR 4, 30, 40;
SATA 14, 86

Kennedy, William
1928- . . . **CLC 6, 28, 34, 53; DAM NOV**
See also AAYA 1; CA 85-88; CANR 14,
31; DLB 143; DLBY 85; INT CANR-31;
MTCW; SATA 57

Kennedy, X. J. . . . . **CLC 8, 42**
See also Kennedy, Joseph Charles
See also CAAS 9; CLR 27; DLB 5;
SAAS 22

Kenny, Maurice (Francis)
1929- . . . . **CLC 87; DAM MULT**
See also CA 144; CAAS 22; DLB 175;
NNAL

Kent, Kelvin
See Kuttner, Henry

Kenton, Maxwell
See Southern, Terry

Kenyon, Robert O.
See Kuttner, Henry

Kerouac, Jack . . . . . **CLC 1, 2, 3, 5, 14, 29, 61**
See also Kerouac, Jean-Louis Lebris de
See also CDALB 1941-1968; DLB 2, 16;
DLBD 3; DLBY 95

Kerouac, Jean-Louis Lebris de 1922-1969
See Kerouac, Jack
See also AITN 1; CA 5-8R; 25-28R;
CANR 26, 54; DA; DAB; DAC;
DAM MST, NOV, POET, POP; MTCW;
WLC

Kerr, Jean 1923- . . . . **CLC 22**
See also CA 5-8R; CANR 7; INT CANR-7

Kerr, M. E. . . . . **CLC 12, 35**
See also Meaker, Marijane (Agnes)
See also AAYA 2; CLR 29; SAAS 1

Kerr, Robert . . . . **CLC 55**

Kerrigan, (Thomas) Anthony
1918- . . . . **CLC 4, 6**
See also CA 49-52; CAAS 11; CANR 4

Kerry, Lois
See Duncan, Lois

Kesey, Ken (Elton)
1935- . . . . . . **CLC 1, 3, 6, 11, 46, 64; DA;**
DAB; DAC; DAM MST, NOV, POP;
WLC
See also CA 1-4R; CANR 22, 38;
CDALB 1968-1988; DLB 2, 16; MTCW;
SATA 66

Kesselring, Joseph (Otto)
1902-1967 . . . . . **CLC 45; DAM DRAM,**
MST
See also CA 150

Kessler, Jascha (Frederick) 1929- . . . . **CLC 4**
See also CA 17-20R; CANR 8, 48

Kettelkamp, Larry (Dale) 1933- . . . . **CLC 12**
See also CA 29-32R; CANR 16; SAAS 3;
SATA 2

Key, Ellen 1849-1926 . . . . **TCLC 65**

Keyber, Conny
See Fielding, Henry

Keyes, Daniel
1927- . . . . **CLC 80; DA; DAC;**
DAM MST, NOV
See also CA 17-20R; CANR 10, 26, 54;
SATA 37

Keynes, John Maynard
1883-1946 . . . . **TCLC 64**
See also CA 114; DLBD 10

Khanshendel, Chiron
See Rose, Wendy

Khayyam, Omar
1048-1131 . . . . **CMLC 11; DAM POET;**
PC 8

Kherdian, David 1931- . . . . **CLC 6, 9**
See also CA 21-24R; CAAS 2; CANR 39;
CLR 24; JRDA; MAICYA; SATA 16, 74

Khlebnikov, Velimir . . . . **TCLC 20**
See also Khlebnikov, Viktor Vladimirovich

Khlebnikov, Viktor Vladimirovich 1885-1922
See Khlebnikov, Velimir
See also CA 117

Khodasevich, Vladislav (Felitsianovich)
1886-1939 . . . . **TCLC 15**
See also CA 115

Kielland, Alexander Lange
1849-1906 . . . . **TCLC 5**
See also CA 104

Kiely, Benedict 1919- . . . . **CLC 23, 43**
See also CA 1-4R; CANR 2; DLB 15

Kienzle, William X(avier)
1928- . . . . **CLC 25; DAM POP**
See also CA 93-96; CAAS 1; CANR 9, 31,
59; INT CANR-31; MTCW

Kierkegaard, Soren 1813-1855. . . . **NCLC 34**

Killens, John Oliver 1916-1987. . . . . **CLC 10**
See also BW 2; CA 77-80; 123; CAAS 2;
CANR 26; DLB 33

Killigrew, Anne 1660-1685. . . . . **LC 4**
See also DLB 131

Kim
See Simenon, Georges (Jacques Christian)

Kincaid, Jamaica
1949- . . . . **CLC 43, 68; BLC;**
DAM MULT, NOV
See also AAYA 13; BW 2; CA 125;
CANR 47, 59; DLB 157

King, Francis (Henry)
1923- . . . . **CLC 8, 53; DAM NOV**
See also CA 1-4R; CANR 1, 33; DLB 15,
139; MTCW

King, Martin Luther, Jr.
1929-1968 . . . . **CLC 83; BLC; DA; DAB;**
DAC; DAM MST, MULT; WLCS
See also BW 2; CA 25-28; CANR 27, 44;
CAP 2; MTCW; SATA 14

King, Stephen (Edwin)
1947- . . . . **CLC 12, 26, 37, 61;**
DAM NOV, POP; SSC 17
See also AAYA 1, 17; BEST 90:1;
CA 61-64; CANR 1, 30, 52; DLB 143;
DLBY 80; JRDA; MTCW; SATA 9, 55

King, Steve
See King, Stephen (Edwin)

King, Thomas
1943- . . . . . **CLC 89; DAC; DAM MULT**
See also CA 144; DLB 175; NNAL

Kingman, Lee. . . . . **CLC 17**
See also Natti, (Mary) Lee
See also SAAS 3; SATA 1, 67

Kingsley, Charles 1819-1875 . . . . . **NCLC 35**
See also DLB 21, 32, 163; YABC 2

Kingsley, Sidney 1906-1995. . . . . . . **CLC 44**
See also CA 85-88; 147; DLB 7

Kingsolver, Barbara
1955- . . . . **CLC 55, 81; DAM POP**
See also AAYA 15; CA 129; 134;
CANR 60; INT 134

Kingston, Maxine (Ting Ting) Hong
1940- . . . . **CLC 12, 19, 58; DAM MULT,**
NOV; WLCS
See also AAYA 8; CA 69-72; CANR 13,
38; DLB 173; DLBY 80; INT CANR-13;
MTCW; SATA 53

Kinnell, Galway
1927- . . . . **CLC 1, 2, 3, 5, 13, 29**
See also CA 9-12R; CANR 10, 34; DLB 5;
DLBY 87; INT CANR-34; MTCW

Kinsella, Thomas 1928- . . . . **CLC 4, 19**
See also CA 17-20R; CANR 15; DLB 27;
MTCW

Kinsella, W(illiam) P(atrick)
1935- . . . . **CLC 27, 43; DAC;**
DAM NOV, POP
See also AAYA 7; CA 97-100; CAAS 7;
CANR 21, 35; INT CANR-21; MTCW

Kipling, (Joseph) Rudyard
1865-1936 . . . . . . **TCLC 8, 17; DA; DAB;**
DAC; DAM MST, POET; PC 3; SSC 5;
WLC
See also CA 105; 120; CANR 33;
CDBLB 1890-1914; CLR 39; DLB 19, 34,
141, 156; MAICYA; MTCW; YABC 2

Kirkup, James 1918- . . . . **CLC 1**
See also CA 1-4R; CAAS 4; CANR 2;
DLB 27; SATA 12

Kirkwood, James 1930(?)-1989 . . . . . . **CLC 9**
See also AITN 2; CA 1-4R; 128; CANR 6,
40

Kirshner, Sidney
See Kingsley, Sidney

Kis, Danilo 1935-1989 . . . . **CLC 57**
See also CA 109; 118; 129; CANR 61;
DLB 181; MTCW

Kivi, Aleksis 1834-1872. . . . . **NCLC 30**

Kizer, Carolyn (Ashley)
1925- . . . . . **CLC 15, 39, 80; DAM POET**
See also CA 65-68; CAAS 5; CANR 24;
DLB 5, 169

Klabund 1890-1928. . . . . **TCLC 44**
See also DLB 66

Klappert, Peter 1942-. . . . . **CLC 57**
See also CA 33-36R; DLB 5

Klein, A(braham) M(oses)
1909-1972 . . . . **CLC 19; DAB; DAC;**
DAM MST
See also CA 101; 37-40R; DLB 68

Klein, Norma 1938-1989 . . . . **CLC 30**
See also AAYA 2; CA 41-44R; 128;
CANR 15, 37; CLR 2, 19;
INT CANR-15; JRDA; MAICYA;
SAAS 1; SATA 7, 57

Klein, T(heodore) E(ibon) D(onald)
1947- . . . . **CLC 34**
See also CA 119; CANR 44

Kleist, Heinrich von
1777-1811 . . . . **NCLC 2, 37;**
DAM DRAM; SSC 22
See also DLB 90

Klima, Ivan 1931-. . . . . **CLC 56; DAM NOV**
See also CA 25-28R; CANR 17, 50

Klimentov, Andrei Platonovich 1899-1951
See Platonov, Andrei
See also CA 108

Klinger, Friedrich Maximilian von
1752-1831 . . . . **NCLC 1**
See also DLB 94

Klingsor the Magician
See Hartmann, Sadakichi

Klopstock, Friedrich Gottlieb
1724-1803 . . . . **NCLC 11**
See also DLB 97

Knapp, Caroline 1959-. . . . . **CLC 99**
See also CA 154

Knebel, Fletcher 1911-1993. . . . . **CLC 14**
See also AITN 1; CA 1-4R; 140; CAAS 3;
CANR 1, 36; SATA 36; SATA-Obit 75

Knickerbocker, Diedrich
See Irving, Washington

Knight, Etheridge
1931-1991 . . . . **CLC 40; BLC;**
DAM POET; PC 14
See also BW 1; CA 21-24R; 133; CANR 23;
DLB 41

Knight, Sarah Kemble 1666-1727 . . . . . **LC 7**
See also DLB 24

Knister, Raymond 1899-1932. . . . . . **TCLC 56**
See also DLB 68

Knowles, John
1926- . . . . . . **CLC 1, 4, 10, 26; DA; DAC;**
DAM MST, NOV
See also AAYA 10; CA 17-20R; CANR 40;
CDALB 1968-1988; DLB 6; MTCW;
SATA 8, 89

Knox, Calvin M.
See Silverberg, Robert

Knox, John c. 1505-1572. . . . . **LC 37**
See also DLB 132

Knye, Cassandra
See Disch, Thomas M(ichael)

Koch, C(hristopher) J(ohn) 1932- . . . **CLC 42**
See also CA 127

Koch, Christopher
See Koch, C(hristopher) J(ohn)

Koch, Kenneth
1925- . . . . **CLC 5, 8, 44; DAM POET**
See also CA 1-4R; CANR 6, 36, 57; DLB 5;
INT CANR-36; SATA 65

Kochanowski, Jan 1530-1584. . . . . . . **LC 10**

Kock, Charles Paul de
1794-1871 . . . . **NCLC 16**

Koda Shigeyuki 1867-1947
See Rohan, Koda
See also CA 121

Koestler, Arthur
1905-1983 . . . . **CLC 1, 3, 6, 8, 15, 33**
See also CA 1-4R; 109; CANR 1, 33;
CDBLB 1945-1960; DLBY 83; MTCW

Kogawa, Joy Nozomi
1935- . . . . . . **CLC 78; DAC; DAM MST,**
MULT
See also CA 101; CANR 19, 62

Kohout, Pavel 1928-. . . . . **CLC 13**
See also CA 45-48; CANR 3

Koizumi, Yakumo
See Hearn, (Patricio) Lafcadio (Tessima
Carlos)

Kolmar, Gertrud 1894-1943. . . . . . **TCLC 40**

Komunyakaa, Yusef 1947-. . . . . . **CLC 86, 94**
See also CA 147; DLB 120

Konrad, George
See Konrad, Gyoergy

Konrad, Gyoergy 1933- . . . . . . **CLC 4, 10, 73**
See also CA 85-88

Konwicki, Tadeusz 1926-. . . . . **CLC 8, 28, 54**
See also CA 101; CAAS 9; CANR 39, 59;
MTCW

Koontz, Dean R(ay)
1945- . . . . . . **CLC 78; DAM NOV, POP**
See also AAYA 9; BEST 89:3, 90:2;
CA 108; CANR 19, 36, 52; MTCW;
SATA 92

Kopit, Arthur (Lee)
  1937- ..... **CLC 1, 18, 33; DAM DRAM**
  See also AITN 1; CA 81-84; CABS 3;
  DLB 7; MTCW

Kops, Bernard 1926- .... **CLC 4**
  See also CA 5-8R; DLB 13

Kornbluth, C(yril) M. 1923-1958.... **TCLC 8**
  See also CA 105; DLB 8

Korolenko, V. G.
  See Korolenko, Vladimir Galaktionovich

Korolenko, Vladimir
  See Korolenko, Vladimir Galaktionovich

Korolenko, Vladimir G.
  See Korolenko, Vladimir Galaktionovich

Korolenko, Vladimir Galaktionovich
  1853-1921 .... **TCLC 22**
  See also CA 121

Korzybski, Alfred (Habdank Skarbek)
  1879-1950 .... **TCLC 61**
  See also CA 123

Kosinski, Jerzy (Nikodem)
  1933-1991 .... **CLC 1, 2, 3, 6, 10, 15, 53,**
                    70; DAM NOV
  See also CA 17-20R; 134; CANR 9, 46;
  DLB 2; DLBY 82; MTCW

Kostelanetz, Richard (Cory) 1940- .. **CLC 28**
  See also CA 13-16R; CAAS 8; CANR 38

Kostrowitzki, Wilhelm Apollinaris de
  1880-1918
  See Apollinaire, Guillaume
  See also CA 104

Kotlowitz, Robert 1924- .... **CLC 4**
  See also CA 33-36R; CANR 36

Kotzebue, August (Friedrich Ferdinand) von
  1761-1819 .... **NCLC 25**
  See also DLB 94

Kotzwinkle, William 1938- ... **CLC 5, 14, 35**
  See also CA 45-48; CANR 3, 44; CLR 6;
  DLB 173; MAICYA; SATA 24, 70

Kowna, Stancy
  See Szymborska, Wislawa

Kozol, Jonathan 1936- .... **CLC 17**
  See also CA 61-64; CANR 16, 45

Kozoll, Michael 1940(?)- .... **CLC 35**

Kramer, Kathryn 19(?)- .... **CLC 34**

Kramer, Larry 1935- .. **CLC 42; DAM POP**
  See also CA 124; 126; CANR 60

Krasicki, Ignacy 1735-1801 .... **NCLC 8**

Krasinski, Zygmunt 1812-1859 .... **NCLC 4**

Kraus, Karl 1874-1936............ **TCLC 5**
  See also CA 104; DLB 118

Kreve (Mickevicius), Vincas
  1882-1954 .... **TCLC 27**

Kristeva, Julia 1941- .... **CLC 77**
  See also CA 154

Kristofferson, Kris 1936- .... **CLC 26**
  See also CA 104

Krizanc, John 1956- .... **CLC 57**

Krleza, Miroslav 1893-1981........ **CLC 8**
  See also CA 97-100; 105; CANR 50;
  DLB 147

Kroetsch, Robert
  1927- .... **CLC 5, 23, 57; DAC;**
                    DAM POET
  See also CA 17-20R; CANR 8, 38; DLB 53;
  MTCW

Kroetz, Franz
  See Kroetz, Franz Xaver

Kroetz, Franz Xaver 1946- .... **CLC 41**
  See also CA 130

Kroker, Arthur 1945- .... **CLC 77**

Kropotkin, Peter (Aleksieevich)
  1842-1921 .... **TCLC 36**
  See also CA 119

Krotkov, Yuri 1917- .... **CLC 19**
  See also CA 102

Krumb
  See Crumb, R(obert)

Krumgold, Joseph (Quincy)
  1908-1980 .... **CLC 12**
  See also CA 9-12R; 101; CANR 7;
  MAICYA; SATA 1, 48; SATA-Obit 23

Krumwitz
  See Crumb, R(obert)

Krutch, Joseph Wood 1893-1970.... **CLC 24**
  See also CA 1-4R; 25-28R; CANR 4;
  DLB 63

Krutzch, Gus
  See Eliot, T(homas) S(tearns)

Krylov, Ivan Andreevich
  1768(?)-1844 .... **NCLC 1**
  See also DLB 150

Kubin, Alfred (Leopold Isidor)
  1877-1959 .... **TCLC 23**
  See also CA 112; 149; DLB 81

Kubrick, Stanley 1928- .... **CLC 16**
  See also CA 81-84; CANR 33; DLB 26

Kumin, Maxine (Winokur)
  1925- ..... **CLC 5, 13, 28; DAM POET;**
                    PC 15
  See also AITN 2; CA 1-4R; CAAS 8;
  CANR 1, 21; DLB 5; MTCW; SATA 12

Kundera, Milan
  1929- .... **CLC 4, 9, 19, 32, 68;**
                    DAM NOV; SSC 24
  See also AAYA 2; CA 85-88; CANR 19,
  52; MTCW

Kunene, Mazisi (Raymond) 1930-... **CLC 85**
  See also BW 1; CA 125; DLB 117

Kunitz, Stanley (Jasspon)
  1905- .... **CLC 6, 11, 14; PC 19**
  See also CA 41-44R; CANR 26, 57;
  DLB 48; INT CANR-26; MTCW

Kunze, Reiner 1933- .... **CLC 10**
  See also CA 93-96; DLB 75

Kuprin, Aleksandr Ivanovich
  1870-1938 .... **TCLC 5**
  See also CA 104

Kureishi, Hanif 1954(?)-.......... **CLC 64**
  See also CA 139

Kurosawa, Akira
  1910- .... **CLC 16; DAM MULT**
  See also AAYA 11; CA 101; CANR 46

Kushner, Tony
  1957(?)- .... **CLC 81; DAM DRAM**
  See also CA 144

Kuttner, Henry 1915-1958........ **TCLC 10**
  See also Vance, Jack
  See also CA 107; 157; DLB 8

Kuzma, Greg 1944-................ **CLC 7**
  See also CA 33-36R

Kuzmin, Mikhail 1872(?)-1936 .... **TCLC 40**

Kyd, Thomas
  1558-1594 .... **LC 22; DAM DRAM;**
                    DC 3
  See also DLB 62

Kyprianos, Iossif
  See Samarakis, Antonis

La Bruyere, Jean de 1645-1696...... **LC 17**

Lacan, Jacques (Marie Emile)
  1901-1981 .... **CLC 75**
  See also CA 121; 104

Laclos, Pierre Ambroise Francois Choderlos
  de 1741-1803 .... **NCLC 4**

La Colere, Francois
  See Aragon, Louis

Lacolere, Francois
  See Aragon, Louis

La Deshabilleuse
  See Simenon, Georges (Jacques Christian)

Lady Gregory
  See Gregory, Isabella Augusta (Persse)

Lady of Quality, A
  See Bagnold, Enid

La Fayette, Marie (Madelaine Pioche de la
  Vergne Comtes 1634-1693....... **LC 2**

Lafayette, Rene
  See Hubbard, L(afayette) Ron(ald)

Laforgue, Jules
  1860-1887 .... **NCLC 5, 53; PC 14;**
                    SSC 20

Lagerkvist, Paer (Fabian)
  1891-1974 .... **CLC 7, 10, 13, 54;**
                    DAM DRAM, NOV
  See also Lagerkvist, Par
  See also CA 85-88; 49-52; MTCW

Lagerkvist, Par .... **SSC 12**
  See also Lagerkvist, Paer (Fabian)

Lagerloef, Selma (Ottiliana Lovisa)
  1858-1940 .... **TCLC 4, 36**
  See also Lagerlof, Selma (Ottiliana Lovisa)
  See also CA 108; SATA 15

Lagerlof, Selma (Ottiliana Lovisa)
  See Lagerloef, Selma (Ottiliana Lovisa)
  See also CLR 7; SATA 15

La Guma, (Justin) Alex(ander)
  1925-1985 .... **CLC 19; DAM NOV**
  See also BW 1; CA 49-52; 118; CANR 25;
  DLB 117; MTCW

Laidlaw, A. K.
  See Grieve, C(hristopher) M(urray)

Lainez, Manuel Mujica
  See Mujica Lainez, Manuel
  See also HW

Laing, R(onald) D(avid)
  1927-1989 .... **CLC 95**
  See also CA 107; 129; CANR 34; MTCW

Lamartine, Alphonse (Marie Louis Prat) de
  1790-1869 ..... **NCLC 11; DAM POET;**
                    PC 16

Lear, Edward 1812-1888 . . . . NCLC 3
See also CLR 1; DLB 32, 163, 166;
MAICYA; SATA 18

Lear, Norman (Milton) 1922- . . . . . . CLC 12
See also CA 73-76

Leavis, F(rank) R(aymond)
1895-1978 . . . . CLC 24
See also CA 21-24R; 77-80; CANR 44;
MTCW

Leavitt, David 1961-. . . CLC 34; DAM POP
See also CA 116; 122; CANR 50, 62;
DLB 130; INT 122

Leblanc, Maurice (Marie Emile)
1864-1941 . . . . TCLC 49
See also CA 110

Lebowitz, Fran(ces Ann)
1951(?)- . . . . CLC 11, 36
See also CA 81-84; CANR 14, 60;
INT CANR-14; MTCW

Lebrecht, Peter
See Tieck, (Johann) Ludwig

le Carre, John . . . . CLC 3, 5, 9, 15, 28
See also Cornwell, David (John Moore)
See also BEST 89:4; CDBLB 1960 to
Present; DLB 87

Le Clezio, J(ean) M(arie) G(ustave)
1940- . . . . CLC 31
See also CA 116; 128; DLB 83

Leconte de Lisle, Charles-Marie-Rene
1818-1894 . . . . NCLC 29

Le Coq, Monsieur
See Simenon, Georges (Jacques Christian)

Leduc, Violette 1907-1972 . . . . CLC 22
See also CA 13-14; 33-36R; CAP 1

Ledwidge, Francis 1887(?)-1917 . . . TCLC 23
See also CA 123; DLB 20

Lee, Andrea
1953- . . . . . CLC 36; BLC; DAM MULT
See also BW 1; CA 125

Lee, Andrew
See Auchincloss, Louis (Stanton)

Lee, Chang-rae 1965- . . . . CLC 91
See also CA 148

Lee, Don L. . . . . CLC 2
See also Madhubuti, Haki R.

Lee, George W(ashington)
1894-1976 . . . . CLC 52; BLC;
DAM MULT
See also BW 1; CA 125; DLB 51

Lee, (Nelle) Harper
1926- . . . . CLC 12, 60; DA; DAB; DAC;
DAM MST, NOV; WLC
See also AAYA 13; CA 13-16R; CANR 51;
CDALB 1941-1968; DLB 6; MTCW;
SATA 11

Lee, Helen Elaine 1959(?)- . . . . CLC 86
See also CA 148

Lee, Julian
See Latham, Jean Lee

Lee, Larry
See Lee, Lawrence

Lee, Laurie
1914-1997 . . . CLC 90; DAB; DAM POP
See also CA 77-80; 158; CANR 33;
DLB 27; MTCW

Lee, Lawrence 1941-1990 . . . . CLC 34
See also CA 131; CANR 43

Lee, Manfred B(ennington)
1905-1971 . . . . CLC 11
See also Queen, Ellery
See also CA 1-4R; 29-32R; CANR 2;
DLB 137

Lee, Stan 1922- . . . . CLC 17
See also AAYA 5; CA 108; 111; INT 111

Lee, Tanith 1947- . . . . CLC 46
See also AAYA 15; CA 37-40R; CANR 53;
SATA 8, 88

Lee, Vernon . . . . TCLC 5
See also Paget, Violet
See also DLB 57, 153, 156, 174, 178

Lee, William
See Burroughs, William S(eward)

Lee, Willy
See Burroughs, William S(eward)

Lee-Hamilton, Eugene (Jacob)
1845-1907 . . . . TCLC 22
See also CA 117

Leet, Judith 1935- . . . . CLC 11

Le Fanu, Joseph Sheridan
1814-1873 . . . . NCLC 9, 58; DAM POP;
SSC 14
See also DLB 21, 70, 159, 178

Leffland, Ella 1931- . . . . CLC 19
See also CA 29-32R; CANR 35; DLBY 84;
INT CANR-35; SATA 65

Leger, Alexis
See Leger, (Marie-Rene Auguste) Alexis
Saint-Leger

**Leger, (Marie-Rene Auguste) Alexis
Saint-Leger**
1887-1975 . . . . . . CLC 11; DAM POET
See also Perse, St.-John
See also CA 13-16R; 61-64; CANR 43;
MTCW

Leger, Saintleger
See Leger, (Marie-Rene Auguste) Alexis
Saint-Leger

Le Guin, Ursula K(roeber)
1929- . . . . . . CLC 8, 13, 22, 45, 71; DAB;
DAC; DAM MST, POP; SSC 12
See also AAYA 9; AITN 1; CA 21-24R;
CANR 9, 32, 52; CDALB 1968-1988;
CLR 3, 28; DLB 8, 52; INT CANR-32;
JRDA; MAICYA; MTCW; SATA 4, 52

Lehmann, Rosamond (Nina)
1901-1990 . . . . CLC 5
See also CA 77-80; 131; CANR 8; DLB 15

Leiber, Fritz (Reuter, Jr.)
1910-1992 . . . . CLC 25
See also CA 45-48; 139; CANR 2, 40;
DLB 8; MTCW; SATA 45;
SATA-Obit 73

Leibniz, Gottfried Wilhelm von
1646-1716 . . . . LC 35
See also DLB 168

Leimbach, Martha 1963-
See Leimbach, Marti
See also CA 130

Leimbach, Marti . . . . CLC 65
See also Leimbach, Martha

Leino, Eino . . . . TCLC 24
See also Loennbohm, Armas Eino Leopold

Leiris, Michel (Julien) 1901-1990 . . . CLC 61
See also CA 119; 128; 132

Leithauser, Brad 1953-. . . . . CLC 27
See also CA 107; CANR 27; DLB 120

Lelchuk, Alan 1938-. . . . . CLC 5
See also CA 45-48; CAAS 20; CANR 1

Lem, Stanislaw 1921-. . . . . . . CLC 8, 15, 40
See also CA 105; CAAS 1; CANR 32;
MTCW

Lemann, Nancy 1956-. . . . . CLC 39
See also CA 118; 136

Lemonnier, (Antoine Louis) Camille
1844-1913 . . . . TCLC 22
See also CA 121

Lenau, Nikolaus 1802-1850 . . . . . . NCLC 16

L'Engle, Madeleine (Camp Franklin)
1918- . . . . CLC 12; DAM POP
See also AAYA 1; AITN 2; CA 1-4R;
CANR 3, 21, 39; CLR 1, 14; DLB 52;
JRDA; MAICYA; MTCW; SAAS 15;
SATA 1, 27, 75

Lengyel, Jozsef 1896-1975 . . . . CLC 7
See also CA 85-88; 57-60

Lenin 1870-1924
See Lenin, V. I.
See also CA 121

Lenin, V. I. . . . . TCLC 67
See also Lenin

Lennon, John (Ono)
1940-1980 . . . . CLC 12, 35
See also CA 102

Lennox, Charlotte Ramsay
1729(?)-1804 . . . . NCLC 23
See also DLB 39

Lentricchia, Frank (Jr.) 1940-. . . . . . CLC 34
See also CA 25-28R; CANR 19

Lenz, Siegfried 1926-. . . . . CLC 27
See also CA 89-92; DLB 75

Leonard, Elmore (John, Jr.)
1925- . . . . . . CLC 28, 34, 71; DAM POP
See also AAYA 22; AITN 1; BEST 89:1,
90:4; CA 81-84; CANR 12, 28, 53;
DLB 173; INT CANR-28; MTCW

Leonard, Hugh. . . . . CLC 19
See also Byrne, John Keyes
See also DLB 13

Leonov, Leonid (Maximovich)
1899-1994 . . . . CLC 92; DAM NOV
See also CA 129; MTCW

Leopardi, (Conte) Giacomo
1798-1837 . . . . NCLC 22

Le Reveler
See Artaud, Antonin (Marie Joseph)

Lerman, Eleanor 1952-. . . . . CLC 9
See also CA 85-88

Lerman, Rhoda 1936-. . . . . CLC 56
See also CA 49-52

Lermontov, Mikhail Yuryevich
1814-1841 . . . . NCLC 47; PC 18

Leroux, Gaston 1868-1927. . . . . TCLC 25
See also CA 108; 136; SATA 65

Lesage, Alain-Rene 1668-1747 . . . . . . LC 28

Leskov, Nikolai (Semyonovich)
1831-1895 .... **NCLC 25**

Lessing, Doris (May)
1919- ..... **CLC 1, 2, 3, 6, 10, 15, 22, 40,
94; DA; DAB; DAC; DAM MST, NOV;
SSC 6; WLCS**
See also CA 9-12R; CAAS 14; CANR 33,
54; CDBLB 1960 to Present; DLB 15,
139; DLBY 85; MTCW

Lessing, Gotthold Ephraim
1729-1781 .... **LC 8**
See also DLB 97

Lester, Richard 1932- .... **CLC 20**

Lever, Charles (James)
1806-1872 .... **NCLC 23**
See also DLB 21

Leverson, Ada 1865(?)-1936(?) .... **TCLC 18**
See also Elaine
See also CA 117; DLB 153

Levertov, Denise
1923- ...... **CLC 1, 2, 3, 5, 8, 15, 28, 66;
DAM POET; PC 11**
See also CA 1-4R; CAAS 19; CANR 3, 29,
50; DLB 5, 165; INT CANR-29; MTCW

Levi, Jonathan .... **CLC 76**

Levi, Peter (Chad Tigar) 1931- ..... **CLC 41**
See also CA 5-8R; CANR 34; DLB 40

Levi, Primo
1919-1987 .... **CLC 37, 50; SSC 12**
See also CA 13-16R; 122; CANR 12, 33, 61;
DLB 177; MTCW

Levin, Ira 1929- ..... **CLC 3, 6; DAM POP**
See also CA 21-24R; CANR 17, 44;
MTCW; SATA 66

Levin, Meyer
1905-1981 .... **CLC 7; DAM POP**
See also AITN 1; CA 9-12R; 104;
CANR 15; DLB 9, 28; DLBY 81;
SATA 21; SATA-Obit 27

Levine, Norman 1924- .... **CLC 54**
See also CA 73-76; CAAS 23; CANR 14;
DLB 88

Levine, Philip
1928- .... **CLC 2, 4, 5, 9, 14, 33;
DAM POET**
See also CA 9-12R; CANR 9, 37, 52;
DLB 5

Levinson, Deirdre 1931- .... **CLC 49**
See also CA 73-76

Levi-Strauss, Claude 1908- .... **CLC 38**
See also CA 1-4R; CANR 6, 32, 57; MTCW

Levitin, Sonia (Wolff) 1934- .... **CLC 17**
See also AAYA 13; CA 29-32R; CANR 14,
32; JRDA; MAICYA; SAAS 2; SATA 4,
68

Levon, O. U.
See Kesey, Ken (Elton)

Levy, Amy 1861-1889 .... **NCLC 59**
See also DLB 156

Lewes, George Henry
1817-1878 .... **NCLC 25**
See also DLB 55, 144

Lewis, Alun 1915-1944 .... **TCLC 3**
See also CA 104; DLB 20, 162

Lewis, C. Day
See Day Lewis, C(ecil)

Lewis, C(live) S(taples)
1898-1963 ..... **CLC 1, 3, 6, 14, 27; DA;
DAB; DAC; DAM MST, NOV, POP;
WLC**
See also AAYA 3; CA 81-84; CANR 33;
CDBLB 1945-1960; CLR 3, 27; DLB 15,
100, 160; JRDA; MAICYA; MTCW;
SATA 13

Lewis, Janet 1899- .... **CLC 41**
See also Winters, Janet Lewis
See also CA 9-12R; CANR 29; CAP 1;
DLBY 87

Lewis, Matthew Gregory
1775-1818 .... **NCLC 11, 62**
See also DLB 39, 158, 178

Lewis, (Harry) Sinclair
1885-1951 ..... **TCLC 4, 13, 23, 39; DA;
DAB; DAC; DAM MST, NOV; WLC**
See also CA 104; 133; CDALB 1917-1929;
DLB 9, 102; DLBD 1; MTCW

Lewis, (Percy) Wyndham
1882(?)-1957 .... **TCLC 2, 9**
See also CA 104; 157; DLB 15

Lewisohn, Ludwig 1883-1955 ...... **TCLC 19**
See also CA 107; DLB 4, 9, 28, 102

Leyner, Mark 1956- .... **CLC 92**
See also CA 110; CANR 28, 53

Lezama Lima, Jose
1910-1976 .... **CLC 4, 10, 101;
DAM MULT**
See also CA 77-80; DLB 113; HW

L'Heureux, John (Clarke) 1934- .... **CLC 52**
See also CA 13-16R; CANR 23, 45

Liddell, C. H.
See Kuttner, Henry

Lie, Jonas (Lauritz Idemil)
1833-1908(?) .... **TCLC 5**
See also CA 115

Lieber, Joel 1937-1971 .... **CLC 6**
See also CA 73-76; 29-32R

Lieber, Stanley Martin
See Lee, Stan

Lieberman, Laurence (James)
1935- .... **CLC 4, 36**
See also CA 17-20R; CANR 8, 36

Lieksman, Anders
See Haavikko, Paavo Juhani

Li Fei-kan 1904-
See Pa Chin
See also CA 105

Lifton, Robert Jay 1926- .... **CLC 67**
See also CA 17-20R; CANR 27;
INT CANR-27; SATA 66

Lightfoot, Gordon 1938- .... **CLC 26**
See also CA 109

Lightman, Alan P. 1948- .... **CLC 81**
See also CA 141

Ligotti, Thomas (Robert)
1953- .... **CLC 44; SSC 16**
See also CA 123; CANR 49

Li Ho 791-817 .... **PC 13**

Liliencron, (Friedrich Adolf Axel) Detlev von
1844-1909 .... **TCLC 18**
See also CA 117

Lilly, William 1602-1681 .... **LC 27**

Lima, Jose Lezama
See Lezama Lima, Jose

Lima Barreto, Afonso Henrique de
1881-1922 .... **TCLC 23**
See also CA 117

Limonov, Edward 1944- .... **CLC 67**
See also CA 137

Lin, Frank
See Atherton, Gertrude (Franklin Horn)

Lincoln, Abraham 1809-1865 ..... **NCLC 18**

Lind, Jakov .... **CLC 1, 2, 4, 27, 82**
See also Landwirth, Heinz
See also CAAS 4

Lindbergh, Anne (Spencer) Morrow
1906- .... **CLC 82; DAM NOV**
See also CA 17-20R; CANR 16; MTCW;
SATA 33

Lindsay, David 1878-1945 .... **TCLC 15**
See also CA 113

Lindsay, (Nicholas) Vachel
1879-1931 .... **TCLC 17; DA; DAC;
DAM MST, POET; WLC**
See also CA 114; 135; CDALB 1865-1917;
DLB 54; SATA 40

Linke-Poot
See Doeblin, Alfred

Linney, Romulus 1930- .... **CLC 51**
See also CA 1-4R; CANR 40, 44

Linton, Eliza Lynn 1822-1898 .... **NCLC 41**
See also DLB 18

Li Po 701-763 .... **CMLC 2**

Lipsius, Justus 1547-1606 .... **LC 16**

Lipsyte, Robert (Michael)
1938- .... **CLC 21; DA; DAC;
DAM MST, NOV**
See also AAYA 7; CA 17-20R; CANR 8,
57; CLR 23; JRDA; MAICYA; SATA 5,
68

Lish, Gordon (Jay) 1934- .. **CLC 45; SSC 18**
See also CA 113; 117; DLB 130; INT 117

Lispector, Clarice 1925-1977 .... **CLC 43**
See also CA 139; 116; DLB 113

Littell, Robert 1935(?)- .... **CLC 42**
See also CA 109; 112

Little, Malcolm 1925-1965
See Malcolm X
See also BW 1; CA 125; 111; DA; DAB;
DAC; DAM MST, MULT; MTCW

Littlewit, Humphrey Gent.
See Lovecraft, H(oward) P(hillips)

Litwos
See Sienkiewicz, Henryk (Adam Alexander
Pius)

Liu E 1857-1909 .... **TCLC 15**
See also CA 115

Lively, Penelope (Margaret)
1933- .... **CLC 32, 50; DAM NOV**
See also CA 41-44R; CANR 29; CLR 7;
DLB 14, 161; JRDA; MAICYA; MTCW;
SATA 7, 60

Livesay, Dorothy (Kathleen)
1909- . . . . **CLC 4, 15, 79; DAC; DAM MST, POET**
See also AITN 2; CA 25-28R; CAAS 8; CANR 36; DLB 68; MTCW

Livy   c. 59B.C.-c. 17 . . . . **CMLC 11**

Lizardi, Jose Joaquin Fernandez de
1776-1827 . . . . **NCLC 30**

Llewellyn, Richard
See Llewellyn Lloyd, Richard Dafydd Vivian
See also DLB 15

Llewellyn Lloyd, Richard Dafydd Vivian
1906-1983 . . . . **CLC 7, 80**
See also Llewellyn, Richard
See also CA 53-56; 111; CANR 7; SATA 11; SATA-Obit 37

Llosa, (Jorge) Mario (Pedro) Vargas
See Vargas Llosa, (Jorge) Mario (Pedro)

Lloyd Webber, Andrew   1948-
See Webber, Andrew Lloyd
See also AAYA 1; CA 116; 149; DAM DRAM; SATA 56

Llull, Ramon   c. 1235-c. 1316 . . . . . **CMLC 12**

Locke, Alain (Le Roy)
1886-1954 . . . . **TCLC 43**
See also BW 1; CA 106; 124; DLB 51

Locke, John   1632-1704 . . . . **LC 7, 35**
See also DLB 101

Locke-Elliott, Sumner
See Elliott, Sumner Locke

Lockhart, John Gibson
1794-1854 . . . . **NCLC 6**
See also DLB 110, 116, 144

Lodge, David (John)
1935- . . . . **CLC 36; DAM POP**
See also BEST 90:1; CA 17-20R; CANR 19, 53; DLB 14; INT CANR-19; MTCW

Loennbohm, Armas Eino Leopold   1878-1926
See Leino, Eino
See also CA 123

Loewinsohn, Ron(ald William)
1937- . . . . **CLC 52**
See also CA 25-28R

Logan, Jake
See Smith, Martin Cruz

Logan, John (Burton)   1923-1987 . . . . . **CLC 5**
See also CA 77-80; 124; CANR 45; DLB 5

Lo Kuan-chung   1330(?)-1400(?) . . . . . . **LC 12**

Lombard, Nap
See Johnson, Pamela Hansford

London, Jack . . **TCLC 9, 15, 39; SSC 4; WLC**
See also London, John Griffith
See also AAYA 13; AITN 2; CDALB 1865-1917; DLB 8, 12, 78; SATA 18

London, John Griffith   1876-1916
See London, Jack
See also CA 110; 119; DA; DAB; DAC; DAM MST, NOV; JRDA; MAICYA; MTCW

Long, Emmett
See Leonard, Elmore (John, Jr.)

Longbaugh, Harry
See Goldman, William (W.)

Longfellow, Henry Wadsworth
1807-1882 . . . . . **NCLC 2, 45; DA; DAB; DAC; DAM MST, POET; WLCS**
See also CDALB 1640-1865; DLB 1, 59; SATA 19

Longley, Michael   1939- . . . . **CLC 29**
See also CA 102; DLB 40

Longus   fl. c. 2nd cent. - . . . . **CMLC 7**

Longway, A. Hugh
See Lang, Andrew

Lonnrot, Elias   1802-1884 . . . . **NCLC 53**

Lopate, Phillip   1943- . . . . **CLC 29**
See also CA 97-100; DLBY 80; INT 97-100

Lopez Portillo (y Pacheco), Jose
1920- . . . . **CLC 46**
See also CA 129; HW

Lopez y Fuentes, Gregorio
1897(?)-1966 . . . . **CLC 32**
See also CA 131; HW

Lorca, Federico Garcia
See Garcia Lorca, Federico

Lord, Bette Bao   1938- . . . . **CLC 23**
See also BEST 90:3; CA 107; CANR 41; INT 107; SATA 58

Lord Auch
See Bataille, Georges

Lord Byron
See Byron, George Gordon (Noel)

Lorde, Audre (Geraldine)
1934-1992 . . . . **CLC 18, 71; BLC; DAM MULT, POET; PC 12**
See also BW 1; CA 25-28R; 142; CANR 16, 26, 46; DLB 41; MTCW

Lord Houghton
See Milnes, Richard Monckton

Lord Jeffrey
See Jeffrey, Francis

Lorenzini, Carlo   1826-1890
See Collodi, Carlo
See also MAICYA; SATA 29

Lorenzo, Heberto Padilla
See Padilla (Lorenzo), Heberto

Loris
See Hofmannsthal, Hugo von

Loti, Pierre . . . . **TCLC 11**
See also Viaud, (Louis Marie) Julien
See also DLB 123

Louie, David Wong   1954- . . . . **CLC 70**
See also CA 139

Louis, Father M.
See Merton, Thomas

Lovecraft, H(oward) P(hillips)
1890-1937 . . . . **TCLC 4, 22; DAM POP; SSC 3**
See also AAYA 14; CA 104; 133; MTCW

Lovelace, Earl   1935- . . . . **CLC 51**
See also BW 2; CA 77-80; CANR 41; DLB 125; MTCW

Lovelace, Richard   1618-1657 . . . . **LC 24**
See also DLB 131

Lowell, Amy
1874-1925 . . . . **TCLC 1, 8; DAM POET; PC 13**
See also CA 104; 151; DLB 54, 140

Lowell, James Russell   1819-1891 . . **NCLC 2**
See also CDALB 1640-1865; DLB 1, 11, 64, 79

Lowell, Robert (Traill Spence, Jr.)
1917-1977 . . . **CLC 1, 2, 3, 4, 5, 8, 9, 11, 15, 37; DA; DAB; DAC; DAM MST, NOV; PC 3; WLC**
See also CA 9-12R; 73-76; CABS 2; CANR 26, 60; DLB 5, 169; MTCW

Lowndes, Marie Adelaide (Belloc)
1868-1947 . . . . **TCLC 12**
See also CA 107; DLB 70

Lowry, (Clarence) Malcolm
1909-1957 . . . . **TCLC 6, 40**
See also CA 105; 131; CDBLB 1945-1960; DLB 15; MTCW

Lowry, Mina Gertrude   1882-1966
See Loy, Mina
See also CA 113

Loxsmith, John
See Brunner, John (Kilian Houston)

Loy, Mina . . . . **CLC 28; DAM POET; PC 16**
See also Lowry, Mina Gertrude
See also DLB 4, 54

Loyson-Bridet
See Schwob, (Mayer Andre) Marcel

Lucas, Craig   1951- . . . . **CLC 64**
See also CA 137

Lucas, E(dward) V(errall)
1868-1938 . . . . **TCLC 73**
See also DLB 98, 149, 153; SATA 20

Lucas, George   1944- . . . . **CLC 16**
See also AAYA 1; CA 77-80; CANR 30; SATA 56

Lucas, Hans
See Godard, Jean-Luc

Lucas, Victoria
See Plath, Sylvia

Ludlam, Charles   1943-1987 . . . . . **CLC 46, 50**
See also CA 85-88; 122

Ludlum, Robert
1927- . . . **CLC 22, 43; DAM NOV; POP**
See also AAYA 10; BEST 89:1, 90:3; CA 33-36R; CANR 25, 41; DLBY 82; MTCW

Ludwig, Ken . . . . **CLC 60**

Ludwig, Otto   1813-1865 . . . . **NCLC 4**
See also DLB 129

Lugones, Leopoldo   1874-1938 . . . . . **TCLC 15**
See also CA 116; 131; HW

Lu Hsun   1881-1936 . . . . . . **TCLC 3; SSC 20**
See also Shu-Jen, Chou

Lukacs, George . . . . **CLC 24**
See also Lukacs, Gyorgy (Szegeny von)

Lukacs, Gyorgy (Szegeny von)   1885-1971
See Lukacs, George
See also CA 101; 29-32R

Luke, Peter (Ambrose Cyprian)
1919-1995 . . . . **CLC 38**
See also CA 81-84; 147; DLB 13

Lunar, Dennis
See Mungo, Raymond

Lurie, Alison   1926- . . . . **CLC 4, 5, 18, 39**
See also CA 1-4R; CANR 2, 17, 50; DLB 2; MTCW; SATA 46

Lustig, Arnost 1926-.............. **CLC 56**
See also AAYA 3; CA 69-72; CANR 47;
SATA 56

Luther, Martin 1483-1546....... **LC 9, 37**
See also DLB 179

Luxemburg, Rosa 1870(?)-1919.... **TCLC 63**
See also CA 118

Luzi, Mario 1914-................. **CLC 13**
See also CA 61-64; CANR 9; DLB 128

Lyly, John 1554(?)-1606............. **DC 7**
See also DAM DRAM; DLB 62, 167

L'Ymagier
See Gourmont, Remy (-Marie-Charles) de

Lynch, B. Suarez
See Bioy Casares, Adolfo; Borges, Jorge
Luis

Lynch, David (K.) 1946-.......... **CLC 66**
See also CA 124; 129

Lynch, James
See Andreyev, Leonid (Nikolaevich)

Lynch Davis, B.
See Bioy Casares, Adolfo; Borges, Jorge
Luis

Lyndsay, Sir David 1490-1555 ...... **LC 20**

Lynn, Kenneth S(chuyler) 1923-.... **CLC 50**
See also CA 1-4R; CANR 3, 27

Lynx
See West, Rebecca

Lyons, Marcus
See Blish, James (Benjamin)

Lyre, Pinchbeck
See Sassoon, Siegfried (Lorraine)

Lytle, Andrew (Nelson) 1902-1995 .. **CLC 22**
See also CA 9-12R; 150; DLB 6; DLBY 95

Lyttelton, George 1709-1773........ **LC 10**

Maas, Peter 1929- .... **CLC 29**
See also CA 93-96; INT 93-96

Macaulay, Rose 1881-1958 ..... **TCLC 7, 44**
See also CA 104; DLB 36

Macaulay, Thomas Babington
1800-1859 .... **NCLC 42**
See also CDBLB 1832-1890; DLB 32, 55

MacBeth, George (Mann)
1932-1992 .... **CLC 2, 5, 9**
See also CA 25-28R; 136; CANR 61;
DLB 40; MTCW; SATA 4;
SATA-Obit 70

MacCaig, Norman (Alexander)
1910- ..... **CLC 36; DAB; DAM POET**
See also CA 9-12R; CANR 3, 34; DLB 27

MacCarthy, (Sir Charles Otto) Desmond
1877-1952 .... **TCLC 36**

MacDiarmid, Hugh
.... **CLC 2, 4, 11, 19, 63; PC 9**
See also Grieve, C(hristopher) M(urray)
See also CDBLB 1945-1960; DLB 20

MacDonald, Anson
See Heinlein, Robert A(nson)

Macdonald, Cynthia 1928-...... **CLC 13, 19**
See also CA 49-52; CANR 4, 44; DLB 105

MacDonald, George 1824-1905..... **TCLC 9**
See also CA 106; 137; DLB 18, 163, 178;
MAICYA; SATA 33

Macdonald, John
See Millar, Kenneth

MacDonald, John D(ann)
1916-1986 .... **CLC 3, 27, 44;**
DAM NOV, POP
See also CA 1-4R; 121; CANR 1, 19, 60;
DLB 8; DLBY 86; MTCW

Macdonald, John Ross
See Millar, Kenneth

Macdonald, Ross..... CLC 1, 2, 3, 14, 34, 41
See also Millar, Kenneth
See also DLBD 6

MacDougal, John
See Blish, James (Benjamin)

MacEwen, Gwendolyn (Margaret)
1941-1987 .... **CLC 13, 55**
See also CA 9-12R; 124; CANR 7, 22;
DLB 53; SATA 50; SATA-Obit 55

Macha, Karel Hynek 1810-1846.. **NCLC 46**

Machado (y Ruiz), Antonio
1875-1939 .... **TCLC 3**
See also CA 104; DLB 108

Machado de Assis, Joaquim Maria
1839-1908 ..... **TCLC 10; BLC; SSC 24**
See also CA 107; 153

Machen, Arthur.......... TCLC 4; SSC 20
See also Jones, Arthur Llewellyn
See also DLB 36, 156, 178

Machiavelli, Niccolo
1469-1527 .... **LC 8, 36; DA; DAB;**
DAC; DAM MST; WLCS

MacInnes, Colin 1914-1976...... **CLC 4, 23**
See also CA 69-72; 65-68; CANR 21;
DLB 14; MTCW

MacInnes, Helen (Clark)
1907-1985 ..... **CLC 27, 39; DAM POP**
See also CA 1-4R; 117; CANR 1, 28, 58;
DLB 87; MTCW; SATA 22;
SATA-Obit 44

Mackay, Mary 1855-1924
See Corelli, Marie
See also CA 118

Mackenzie, Compton (Edward Montague)
1883-1972 .... **CLC 18**
See also CA 21-22; 37-40R; CAP 2;
DLB 34, 100

Mackenzie, Henry 1745-1831 .... **NCLC 41**
See also DLB 39

Mackintosh, Elizabeth 1896(?)-1952
See Tey, Josephine
See also CA 110

MacLaren, James
See Grieve, C(hristopher) M(urray)

Mac Laverty, Bernard 1942-....... **CLC 31**
See also CA 116; 118; CANR 43; INT 118

MacLean, Alistair (Stuart)
1922(?)-1987 .... **CLC 3, 13, 50, 63;**
DAM POP
See also CA 57-60; 121; CANR 28, 61;
MTCW; SATA 23; SATA-Obit 50

Maclean, Norman (Fitzroy)
1902-1990 .... **CLC 78; DAM POP;**
SSC 13
See also CA 102; 132; CANR 49

MacLeish, Archibald
1892-1982 .... **CLC 3, 8, 14, 68;**
DAM POET
See also CA 9-12R; 106; CANR 33; DLB 4,
7, 45; DLBY 82; MTCW

MacLennan, (John) Hugh
1907-1990 .... **CLC 2, 14, 92; DAC;**
DAM MST
See also CA 5-8R; 142; CANR 33; DLB 68;
MTCW

MacLeod, Alistair
1936- ...... **CLC 56; DAC; DAM MST**
See also CA 123; DLB 60

MacNeice, (Frederick) Louis
1907-1963 ...... **CLC 1, 4, 10, 53; DAB;**
DAM POET
See also CA 85-88; CANR 61; DLB 10, 20;
MTCW

MacNeill, Dand
See Fraser, George MacDonald

Macpherson, James 1736-1796 ...... **LC 29**
See also DLB 109

Macpherson, (Jean) Jay 1931-...... **CLC 14**
See also CA 5-8R; DLB 53

MacShane, Frank 1927-........... **CLC 39**
See also CA 9-12R; CANR 3, 33; DLB 111

Macumber, Mari
See Sandoz, Mari(e Susette)

Madach, Imre 1823-1864........ **NCLC 19**

Madden, (Jerry) David 1933- .... **CLC 5, 15**
See also CA 1-4R; CAAS 3; CANR 4, 45;
DLB 6; MTCW

Maddern, Al(an)
See Ellison, Harlan (Jay)

Madhubuti, Haki R.
1942- .... **CLC 6, 73; BLC;**
DAM MULT, POET; PC 5
See also Lee, Don L.
See also BW 2; CA 73-76; CANR 24, 51;
DLB 5, 41; DLBD 8

Maepenn, Hugh
See Kuttner, Henry

Maepenn, K. H.
See Kuttner, Henry

Maeterlinck, Maurice
1862-1949 ...... **TCLC 3; DAM DRAM**
See also CA 104; 136; SATA 66

Maginn, William 1794-1842....... **NCLC 8**
See also DLB 110, 159

Mahapatra, Jayanta
1928- .... **CLC 33; DAM MULT**
See also CA 73-76; CAAS 9; CANR 15, 33

Mahfouz, Naguib (Abdel Aziz Al-Sabilgi)
1911(?)-
See Mahfuz, Najib
See also BEST 89:2; CA 128; CANR 55;
DAM NOV; MTCW

Mahfuz, Najib................. CLC 52, 55
See also Mahfouz, Naguib (Abdel Aziz
Al-Sabilgi)
See also DLBY 88

Mahon, Derek 1941-............. **CLC 27**
See also CA 113; 128; DLB 40

Mailer, Norman
1923- . . . . . . **CLC 1, 2, 3, 4, 5, 8, 11, 14,
28, 39, 74; DA; DAB; DAC; DAM MST,
NOV, POP**
See also AITN 2; CA 9-12R; CABS 1;
CANR 28; CDALB 1968-1988; DLB 2,
16, 28; DLBD 3; DLBY 80, 83; MTCW

Maillet, Antonine 1929- . . . . . . **CLC 54; DAC**
See also CA 115; 120; CANR 46; DLB 60;
INT 120

Mais, Roger 1905-1955 . . . . **TCLC 8**
See also BW 1; CA 105; 124; DLB 125;
MTCW

Maistre, Joseph de 1753-1821 . . . . **NCLC 37**

Maitland, Frederic 1850-1906 . . . . . **TCLC 65**

Maitland, Sara (Louise) 1950- . . . . . . **CLC 49**
See also CA 69-72; CANR 13, 59

Major, Clarence
1936- . . . . **CLC 3, 19, 48; BLC;
DAM MULT**
See also BW 2; CA 21-24R; CAAS 6;
CANR 13, 25, 53; DLB 33

Major, Kevin (Gerald)
1949- . . . . **CLC 26; DAC**
See also AAYA 16; CA 97-100; CANR 21,
38; CLR 11; DLB 60; INT CANR-21;
JRDA; MAICYA; SATA 32, 82

Maki, James
See Ozu, Yasujiro

Malabaila, Damiano
See Levi, Primo

Malamud, Bernard
1914-1986 . . . . . . **CLC 1, 2, 3, 5, 8, 9, 11,
18, 27, 44, 78, 85; DA; DAB; DAC;
DAM MST, NOV, POP; SSC 15; WLC**
See also AAYA 16; CA 5-8R; 118; CABS 1;
CANR 28; CDALB 1941-1968; DLB 2,
28, 152; DLBY 80, 86; MTCW

Malaparte, Curzio 1898-1957 . . . . . **TCLC 52**

Malcolm, Dan
See Silverberg, Robert

Malcolm X . . . . **CLC 82; BLC; WLCS**
See also Little, Malcolm

Malherbe, Francois de 1555-1628 . . . . . **LC 5**

Mallarme, Stephane
1842-1898 . . . . **NCLC 4, 41;
DAM POET; PC 4**

Mallet-Joris, Francoise 1930- . . . . . . **CLC 11**
See also CA 65-68; CANR 17; DLB 83

Malley, Ern
See McAuley, James Phillip

Mallowan, Agatha Christie
See Christie, Agatha (Mary Clarissa)

Maloff, Saul 1922- . . . . **CLC 5**
See also CA 33-36R

Malone, Louis
See MacNeice, (Frederick) Louis

Malone, Michael (Christopher)
1942- . . . . **CLC 43**
See also CA 77-80; CANR 14, 32, 57

Malory, (Sir) Thomas
1410(?)-1471(?) . . . . . . **LC 11; DA; DAB;
DAC; DAM MST; WLCS**
See also CDBLB Before 1660; DLB 146;
SATA 59; SATA-Brief 33

Malouf, (George Joseph) David
1934- . . . . **CLC 28, 86**
See also CA 124; CANR 50

Malraux, (Georges-)Andre
1901-1976 . . . . . . **CLC 1, 4, 9, 13, 15, 57;
DAM NOV**
See also CA 21-22; 69-72; CANR 34, 58;
CAP 2; DLB 72; MTCW

Malzberg, Barry N(athaniel) 1939- . . . **CLC 7**
See also CA 61-64; CAAS 4; CANR 16;
DLB 8

Mamet, David (Alan)
1947- . . . . **CLC 9, 15, 34, 46, 91;
DAM DRAM; DC 4**
See also AAYA 3; CA 81-84; CABS 3;
CANR 15, 41; DLB 7; MTCW

Mamoulian, Rouben (Zachary)
1897-1987 . . . . **CLC 16**
See also CA 25-28R; 124

Mandelstam, Osip (Emilievich)
1891(?)-1938(?) . . . . . . **TCLC 2, 6; PC 14**
See also CA 104; 150

Mander, (Mary) Jane 1877-1949 . . . **TCLC 31**

Mandeville, John fl. 1350- . . . . **CMLC 19**
See also DLB 146

Mandiargues, Andre Pieyre de . . . . . . **CLC 41**
See also Pieyre de Mandiargues, Andre
See also DLB 83

Mandrake, Ethel Belle
See Thurman, Wallace (Henry)

Mangan, James Clarence
1803-1849 . . . . **NCLC 27**

Maniere, J.-E.
See Giraudoux, (Hippolyte) Jean

Manley, (Mary) Delariviere
1672(?)-1724 . . . . **LC 1**
See also DLB 39, 80

Mann, Abel
See Creasey, John

Mann, Emily 1952- . . . . **DC 7**
See also CA 130; CANR 55

Mann, (Luiz) Heinrich 1871-1950 . . . **TCLC 9**
See also CA 106; DLB 66

Mann, (Paul) Thomas
1875-1955 . . . . **TCLC 2, 8, 14, 21, 35, 44,
60; DA; DAB; DAC; DAM MST, NOV;
SSC 5; WLC**
See also CA 104; 128; DLB 66; MTCW

Mannheim, Karl 1893-1947 . . . . **TCLC 65**

Manning, David
See Faust, Frederick (Schiller)

Manning, Frederic 1887(?)-1935 . . . **TCLC 25**
See also CA 124

Manning, Olivia 1915-1980 . . . . . . **CLC 5, 19**
See also CA 5-8R; 101; CANR 29; MTCW

Mano, D. Keith 1942- . . . . **CLC 2, 10**
See also CA 25-28R; CAAS 6; CANR 26,
57; DLB 6

Mansfield, Katherine
. . **TCLC 2, 8, 39; DAB; SSC 9, 23; WLC**
See also Beauchamp, Kathleen Mansfield
See also DLB 162

Manso, Peter 1940- . . . . **CLC 39**
See also CA 29-32R; CANR 44

Mantecon, Juan Jimenez
See Jimenez (Mantecon), Juan Ramon

Manton, Peter
See Creasey, John

Man Without a Spleen, A
See Chekhov, Anton (Pavlovich)

Manzoni, Alessandro 1785-1873 . . **NCLC 29**

Mapu, Abraham (ben Jekutiel)
1808-1867 . . . . **NCLC 18**

Mara, Sally
See Queneau, Raymond

Marat, Jean Paul 1743-1793 . . . . **LC 10**

Marcel, Gabriel Honore
1889-1973 . . . . **CLC 15**
See also CA 102; 45-48; MTCW

Marchbanks, Samuel
See Davies, (William) Robertson

Marchi, Giacomo
See Bassani, Giorgio

Margulies, Donald . . . . **CLC 76**

Marie de France c. 12th cent. - . . . . **CMLC 8**

Marie de l'Incarnation 1599-1672 . . . . **LC 10**

Marier, Captain Victor
See Griffith, D(avid Lewelyn) W(ark)

Mariner, Scott
See Pohl, Frederik

Marinetti, Filippo Tommaso
1876-1944 . . . . **TCLC 10**
See also CA 107; DLB 114

Marivaux, Pierre Carlet de Chamblain de
1688-1763 . . . . **LC 4; DC 7**

Markandaya, Kamala . . . . **CLC 8, 38**
See also Taylor, Kamala (Purnaiya)

Markfield, Wallace 1926- . . . . **CLC 8**
See also CA 69-72; CAAS 3; DLB 2, 28

Markham, Edwin 1852-1940 . . . . . . **TCLC 47**
See also DLB 54

Markham, Robert
See Amis, Kingsley (William)

Marks, J
See Highwater, Jamake (Mamake)

Marks-Highwater, J
See Highwater, Jamake (Mamake)

Markson, David M(errill) 1927- . . . . **CLC 67**
See also CA 49-52; CANR 1

Marley, Bob . . . . **CLC 17**
See also Marley, Robert Nesta

Marley, Robert Nesta 1945-1981
See Marley, Bob
See also CA 107; 103

Marlowe, Christopher
1564-1593 . . . . . **LC 22; DA; DAB; DAC;
DAM DRAM, MST; DC 1; WLC**
See also CDBLB Before 1660; DLB 62

Marlowe, Stephen 1928-
See Queen, Ellery
See also CA 13-16R; CANR 6, 55

Marmontel, Jean-Francois
1723-1799 . . . . **LC 2**

Marquand, John P(hillips)
1893-1960 . . . . **CLC 2, 10**
See also CA 85-88; DLB 9, 102

Mavor, Osborne Henry 1888-1951
See Bridie, James
See also CA 104

Maxwell, William (Keepers, Jr.)
1908- . . . . **CLC 19**
See also CA 93-96; CANR 54; DLBY 80;
INT 93-96

May, Elaine 1932- . . . . **CLC 16**
See also CA 124; 142; DLB 44

Mayakovski, Vladimir (Vladimirovich)
1893-1930 . . . . **TCLC 4, 18**
See also CA 104; 158

Mayhew, Henry 1812-1887 . . . . . . **NCLC 31**
See also DLB 18, 55

Mayle, Peter 1939(?)- . . . . **CLC 89**
See also CA 139

Maynard, Joyce 1953- . . . . **CLC 23**
See also CA 111; 129

Mayne, William (James Carter)
1928- . . . . **CLC 12**
See also AAYA 20; CA 9-12R; CANR 37;
CLR 25; JRDA; MAICYA; SAAS 11;
SATA 6, 68

Mayo, Jim
See L'Amour, Louis (Dearborn)

Maysles, Albert 1926- . . . . **CLC 16**
See also CA 29-32R

Maysles, David 1932- . . . . **CLC 16**

Mazer, Norma Fox 1931- . . . . **CLC 26**
See also AAYA 5; CA 69-72; CANR 12,
32; CLR 23; JRDA; MAICYA; SAAS 1;
SATA 24, 67

Mazzini, Guiseppe 1805-1872 . . . . **NCLC 34**

McAuley, James Phillip
1917-1976 . . . . **CLC 45**
See also CA 97-100

McBain, Ed
See Hunter, Evan

McBrien, William Augustine
1930- . . . . **CLC 44**
See also CA 107

McCaffrey, Anne (Inez)
1926- . . . . . . **CLC 17; DAM NOV, POP**
See also AAYA 6; AITN 2; BEST 89:2;
CA 25-28R; CANR 15, 35, 55; DLB 8;
JRDA; MAICYA; MTCW; SAAS 11;
SATA 8, 70

McCall, Nathan 1955(?)- . . . . **CLC 86**
See also CA 146

McCann, Arthur
See Campbell, John W(ood, Jr.)

McCann, Edson
See Pohl, Frederik

McCarthy, Charles, Jr. 1933-
See McCarthy, Cormac
See also CANR 42; DAM POP

McCarthy, Cormac
1933- . . . . **CLC 4, 57, 59, 101**
See also McCarthy, Charles, Jr.
See also DLB 6, 143

McCarthy, Mary (Therese)
1912-1989 . . . . . **CLC 1, 3, 5, 14, 24, 39,
59; SSC 24**
See also CA 5-8R; 129; CANR 16, 50;
DLB 2; DLBY 81; INT CANR-16;
MTCW

McCartney, (James) Paul
1942- . . . . **CLC 12, 35**
See also CA 146

McCauley, Stephen (D.) 1955- . . . . . **CLC 50**
See also CA 141

McClure, Michael (Thomas)
1932- . . . . **CLC 6, 10**
See also CA 21-24R; CANR 17, 46;
DLB 16

McCorkle, Jill (Collins) 1958- . . . . . . **CLC 51**
See also CA 121; DLBY 87

McCourt, James 1941- . . . . **CLC 5**
See also CA 57-60

McCoy, Horace (Stanley)
1897-1955 . . . . **TCLC 28**
See also CA 108; 155; DLB 9

McCrae, John 1872-1918 . . . . **TCLC 12**
See also CA 109; DLB 92

McCreigh, James
See Pohl, Frederik

McCullers, (Lula) Carson (Smith)
1917-1967 . . . . **CLC 1, 4, 10, 12, 48, 100;
DA; DAB; DAC; DAM MST, NOV;
SSC 9, 24; WLC**
See also AAYA 21; CA 5-8R; 25-28R;
CABS 1, 3; CANR 18;
CDALB 1941-1968; DLB 2, 7, 173;
MTCW; SATA 27

McCulloch, John Tyler
See Burroughs, Edgar Rice

McCullough, Colleen
1938(?)- . . . . **CLC 27; DAM NOV, POP**
See also CA 81-84; CANR 17, 46; MTCW

McDermott, Alice 1953- . . . . **CLC 90**
See also CA 109; CANR 40

McElroy, Joseph 1930- . . . . **CLC 5, 47**
See also CA 17-20R

McEwan, Ian (Russell)
1948- . . . . **CLC 13, 66; DAM NOV**
See also BEST 90:4; CA 61-64; CANR 14,
41; DLB 14; MTCW

McFadden, David 1940- . . . . **CLC 48**
See also CA 104; DLB 60; INT 104

McFarland, Dennis 1950- . . . . **CLC 65**

McGahern, John
1934- . . . . **CLC 5, 9, 48; SSC 17**
See also CA 17-20R; CANR 29; DLB 14;
MTCW

McGinley, Patrick (Anthony)
1937- . . . . **CLC 41**
See also CA 120; 127; CANR 56; INT 127

McGinley, Phyllis 1905-1978 . . . . . . **CLC 14**
See also CA 9-12R; 77-80; CANR 19;
DLB 11, 48; SATA 2, 44; SATA-Obit 24

McGinniss, Joe 1942- . . . . **CLC 32**
See also AITN 2; BEST 89:2; CA 25-28R;
CANR 26; INT CANR-26

McGivern, Maureen Daly
See Daly, Maureen

McGrath, Patrick 1950- . . . . **CLC 55**
See also CA 136

McGrath, Thomas (Matthew)
1916-1990 . . . . **CLC 28, 59; DAM POET**
See also CA 9-12R; 132; CANR 6, 33;
MTCW; SATA 41; SATA-Obit 66

McGuane, Thomas (Francis III)
1939- . . . . **CLC 3, 7, 18, 45**
See also AITN 2; CA 49-52; CANR 5, 24,
49; DLB 2; DLBY 80; INT CANR-24;
MTCW

McGuckian, Medbh
1950- . . . . **CLC 48; DAM POET**
See also CA 143; DLB 40

McHale, Tom 1942(?)-1982 . . . . **CLC 3, 5**
See also AITN 1; CA 77-80; 106

McIlvanney, William 1936- . . . . **CLC 42**
See also CA 25-28R; CANR 61; DLB 14

McIlwraith, Maureen Mollie Hunter
See Hunter, Mollie
See also SATA 2

McInerney, Jay
1955- . . . . **CLC 34; DAM POP**
See also AAYA 18; CA 116; 123;
CANR 45; INT 123

McIntyre, Vonda N(eel) 1948- . . . . . **CLC 18**
See also CA 81-84; CANR 17, 34; MTCW

McKay, Claude
. . . . **TCLC 7, 41; BLC; DAB; PC 2**
See also McKay, Festus Claudius
See also DLB 4, 45, 51, 117

McKay, Festus Claudius 1889-1948
See McKay, Claude
See BW 1; CA 104; 124; DA; DAC;
DAM MST, MULT, NOV, POET;
MTCW; WLC

McKuen, Rod 1933- . . . . **CLC 1, 3**
See also AITN 1; CA 41-44R; CANR 40

McLoughlin, R. B.
See Mencken, H(enry) L(ouis)

McLuhan, (Herbert) Marshall
1911-1980 . . . . **CLC 37, 83**
See also CA 9-12R; 102; CANR 12, 34, 61;
DLB 88; INT CANR-12; MTCW

McMillan, Terry (L.)
1951- . . . . **CLC 50, 61; DAM MULT,
NOV, POP**
See also AAYA 21; BW 2; CA 140;
CANR 60

McMurtry, Larry (Jeff)
1936- . . . . **CLC 2, 3, 7, 11, 27, 44;
DAM NOV, POP**
See also AAYA 15; AITN 2; BEST 89:2;
CA 5-8R; CANR 19, 43;
CDALB 1968-1988; DLB 2, 143;
DLBY 80, 87; MTCW

McNally, T. M. 1961- . . . . **CLC 82**

McNally, Terrence
1939- . . . **CLC 4, 7, 41, 91; DAM DRAM**
See also CA 45-48; CANR 2, 56; DLB 7

McNamer, Deirdre 1950- . . . . **CLC 70**

McNeile, Herman Cyril 1888-1937
See Sapper
See also DLB 77

McNickle, (William) D'Arcy
1904-1977 . . . . . **CLC 89; DAM MULT**
See also CA 9-12R; 85-88; CANR 5, 45;
DLB 175; NNAL; SATA-Obit 22

McPhee, John (Angus) 1931- . . . . . . **CLC 36**
See also BEST 90:1; CA 65-68; CANR 20,
46; MTCW

McPherson, James Alan
1943- . . . . **CLC 19, 77**
See also BW 1; CA 25-28R; CAAS 17;
CANR 24; DLB 38; MTCW

McPherson, William (Alexander)
1933- . . . . **CLC 34**
See also CA 69-72; CANR 28;
INT CANR-28

Mead, Margaret 1901-1978 . . . . **CLC 37**
See also AITN 1; CA 1-4R; 81-84;
CANR 4; MTCW; SATA-Obit 20

Meaker, Marijane (Agnes) 1927-
See Kerr, M. E.
See also CA 107; CANR 37; INT 107;
JRDA; MAICYA; MTCW; SATA 20, 61

Medoff, Mark (Howard)
1940- . . . . **CLC 6, 23; DAM DRAM**
See also AITN 1; CA 53-56; CANR 5;
DLB 7; INT CANR-5

Medvedev, P. N.
See Bakhtin, Mikhail Mikhailovich

Meged, Aharon
See Megged, Aharon

Meged, Aron
See Megged, Aharon

Megged, Aharon 1920- . . . . **CLC 9**
See also CA 49-52; CAAS 13; CANR 1

Mehta, Ved (Parkash) 1934- . . . . **CLC 37**
See also CA 1-4R; CANR 2, 23; MTCW

Melanter
See Blackmore, R(ichard) D(oddridge)

Melikow, Loris
See Hofmannsthal, Hugo von

Melmoth, Sebastian
See Wilde, Oscar (Fingal O'Flahertie Wills)

Meltzer, Milton 1915- . . . . **CLC 26**
See also AAYA 8; CA 13-16R; CANR 38;
CLR 13; DLB 61; JRDA; MAICYA;
SAAS 1; SATA 1, 50, 80

Melville, Herman
1819-1891 . . . . . **NCLC 3, 12, 29, 45, 49;**
DA; DAB; DAC; DAM MST, NOV;
SSC 1, 17; WLC
See also CDALB 1640-1865; DLB 3, 74;
SATA 59

Menander
c. 342B.C.-c. 292B.C. . . . . **CMLC 9;**
DAM DRAM; DC 3
See also DLB 176

Mencken, H(enry) L(ouis)
1880-1956 . . . . **TCLC 13**
See also CA 105; 125; CDALB 1917-1929;
DLB 11, 29, 63, 137; MTCW

Mendelsohn, Jane 1965(?)- . . . . **CLC 99**
See also CA 154

Mercer, David
1928-1980 . . . . **CLC 5; DAM DRAM**
See also CA 9-12R; 102; CANR 23;
DLB 13; MTCW

Merchant, Paul
See Ellison, Harlan (Jay)

Meredith, George
1828-1909 . . **TCLC 17, 43; DAM POET**
See also CA 117; 153; CDBLB 1832-1890;
DLB 18, 35, 57, 159

Meredith, William (Morris)
1919- . . **CLC 4, 13, 22, 55; DAM POET**
See also CA 9-12R; CAAS 14; CANR 6, 40;
DLB 5

Merezhkovsky, Dmitry Sergeyevich
1865-1941 . . . . **TCLC 29**

Merimee, Prosper
1803-1870 . . . . **NCLC 6; SSC 7**
See also DLB 119

Merkin, Daphne 1954- . . . . **CLC 44**
See also CA 123

Merlin, Arthur
See Blish, James (Benjamin)

Merrill, James (Ingram)
1926-1995 . . . . **CLC 2, 3, 6, 8, 13, 18, 34,**
91; DAM POET
See also CA 13-16R; 147; CANR 10, 49;
DLB 5, 165; DLBY 85; INT CANR-10;
MTCW

Merriman, Alex
See Silverberg, Robert

Merritt, E. B.
See Waddington, Miriam

Merton, Thomas
1915-1968 . . **CLC 1, 3, 11, 34, 83; PC 10**
See also CA 5-8R; 25-28R; CANR 22, 53;
DLB 48; DLBY 81; MTCW

Merwin, W(illiam) S(tanley)
1927- . . . . . . **CLC 1, 2, 3, 5, 8, 13, 18, 45,**
88; DAM POET
See also CA 13-16R; CANR 15, 51; DLB 5,
169; INT CANR-15; MTCW

Metcalf, John 1938- . . . . **CLC 37**
See also CA 113; DLB 60

Metcalf, Suzanne
See Baum, L(yman) Frank

Mew, Charlotte (Mary)
1870-1928 . . . . **TCLC 8**
See also CA 105; DLB 19, 135

Mewshaw, Michael 1943- . . . . **CLC 9**
See also CA 53-56; CANR 7, 47; DLBY 80

Meyer, June
See Jordan, June

Meyer, Lynn
See Slavitt, David R(ytman)

Meyer-Meyrink, Gustav 1868-1932
See Meyrink, Gustav
See also CA 117

Meyers, Jeffrey 1939- . . . . **CLC 39**
See also CA 73-76; CANR 54; DLB 111

Meynell, Alice (Christina Gertrude Thompson)
1847-1922 . . . . **TCLC 6**
See also CA 104; DLB 19, 98

Meyrink, Gustav . . . . **TCLC 21**
See also Meyer-Meyrink, Gustav
See also DLB 81

Michaels, Leonard
1933- . . . . **CLC 6, 25; SSC 16**
See also CA 61-64; CANR 21; DLB 130;
MTCW

Michaux, Henri 1899-1984 . . . . . . **CLC 8, 19**
See also CA 85-88; 114

Michelangelo 1475-1564 . . . . **LC 12**

Michelet, Jules 1798-1874 . . . . **NCLC 31**

Michener, James A(lbert)
1907(?)- . . . . **CLC 1, 5, 11, 29, 60;**
DAM NOV, POP
See also AITN 1; BEST 90:1; CA 5-8R;
CANR 21, 45; DLB 6; MTCW

Mickiewicz, Adam 1798-1855 . . . . . **NCLC 3**

Middleton, Christopher 1926- . . . . . . **CLC 13**
See also CA 13-16R; CANR 29, 54;
DLB 40

Middleton, Richard (Barham)
1882-1911 . . . . **TCLC 56**
See also DLB 156

Middleton, Stanley 1919- . . . . **CLC 7, 38**
See also CA 25-28R; CAAS 23; CANR 21,
46; DLB 14

Middleton, Thomas
1580-1627 . . . . **LC 33; DAM DRAM,**
MST; DC 5
See also DLB 58

Migueis, Jose Rodrigues 1901- . . . . . **CLC 10**

Mikszath, Kalman 1847-1910 . . . . . **TCLC 31**

Miles, Jack . . . . **CLC 100**

Miles, Josephine (Louise)
1911-1985 . . . . **CLC 1, 2, 14, 34, 39;**
DAM POET
See also CA 1-4R; 116; CANR 2, 55;
DLB 48

Militant
See Sandburg, Carl (August)

Mill, John Stuart 1806-1873 . . **NCLC 11, 58**
See also CDBLB 1832-1890; DLB 55

Millar, Kenneth
1915-1983 . . . . **CLC 14; DAM POP**
See also Macdonald, Ross
See also CA 9-12R; 110; CANR 16; DLB 2;
DLBD 6; DLBY 83; MTCW

Millay, E. Vincent
See Millay, Edna St. Vincent

Millay, Edna St. Vincent
1892-1950 . . . . . . **TCLC 4, 49; DA; DAB;**
DAC; DAM MST, POET; PC 6; WLCS
See also CA 104; 130; CDALB 1917-1929;
DLB 45; MTCW

Miller, Arthur
1915- . . . . **CLC 1, 2, 6, 10, 15, 26, 47, 78;**
DA; DAB; DAC; DAM DRAM, MST;
DC 1; WLC
See also AAYA 15; AITN 1; CA 1-4R;
CABS 3; CANR 2, 30, 54;
CDALB 1941-1968; DLB 7; MTCW

Miller, Henry (Valentine)
1891-1980 . . . . **CLC 1, 2, 4, 9, 14, 43, 84;**
DA; DAB; DAC; DAM MST, NOV;
WLC
See also CA 9-12R; 97-100; CANR 33;
CDALB 1929-1941; DLB 4, 9; DLBY 80;
MTCW

Miller, Jason 1939(?)- .... **CLC 2**
See also AITN 1; CA 73-76; DLB 7

Miller, Sue 1943- ..... **CLC 44; DAM POP**
See also BEST 90:3; CA 139; CANR 59;
DLB 143

Miller, Walter M(ichael, Jr.)
1923- .... **CLC 4, 30**
See also CA 85-88; DLB 8

Millett, Kate 1934- .... **CLC 67**
See also AITN 1; CA 73-76; CANR 32, 53;
MTCW

Millhauser, Steven 1943- .... **CLC 21, 54**
See also CA 110; 111; DLB 2; INT 111

Millin, Sarah Gertrude 1889-1968 .. **CLC 49**
See also CA 102; 93-96

Milne, A(lan) A(lexander)
1882-1956 ...... **TCLC 6; DAB; DAC;**
DAM MST
See also CA 104; 133; CLR 1, 26; DLB 10,
77, 100, 160; MAICYA; MTCW;
YABC 1

Milner, Ron(ald)
1938- ..... **CLC 56; BLC; DAM MULT**
See also AITN 1; BW 1; CA 73-76;
CANR 24; DLB 38; MTCW

Milnes, Richard Monckton
1809-1885 .... **NCLC 61**
See also DLB 32, 184

Milosz, Czeslaw
1911- .... **CLC 5, 11, 22, 31, 56, 82;**
DAM MST, POET; PC 8; WLCS
See also CA 81-84; CANR 23, 51; MTCW

Milton, John
1608-1674 ...... **LC 9; DA; DAB; DAC;**
DAM MST, POET; PC 19; WLC
See also CDBLB 1660-1789; DLB 131, 151

Min, Anchee 1957- .... **CLC 86**
See also CA 146

Minehaha, Cornelius
See Wedekind, (Benjamin) Frank(lin)

Miner, Valerie 1947- .... **CLC 40**
See also CA 97-100; CANR 59

Minimo, Duca
See D'Annunzio, Gabriele

Minot, Susan 1956- .... **CLC 44**
See also CA 134

Minus, Ed 1938- .... **CLC 39**

Miranda, Javier
See Bioy Casares, Adolfo

Mirbeau, Octave 1848-1917 ...... **TCLC 55**
See also DLB 123

Miro (Ferrer), Gabriel (Francisco Victor)
1879-1930 .... **TCLC 5**
See also CA 104

Mishima, Yukio
1925-1970 .... **CLC 2, 4, 6, 9, 27; DC 1;**
SSC 4
See also Hiraoka, Kimitake
See also DLB 182

Mistral, Frederic 1830-1914 ...... **TCLC 51**
See also CA 122

Mistral, Gabriela .... **TCLC 2; HLC**
See also Godoy Alcayaga, Lucila

Mistry, Rohinton 1952- ...... **CLC 71; DAC**
See also CA 141

Mitchell, Clyde
See Ellison, Harlan (Jay); Silverberg, Robert

Mitchell, James Leslie 1901-1935
See Gibbon, Lewis Grassic
See also CA 104; DLB 15

Mitchell, Joni 1943- .... **CLC 12**
See also CA 112

Mitchell, Joseph (Quincy)
1908-1996 .... **CLC 98**
See also CA 77-80; 152; DLBY 96

Mitchell, Margaret (Munnerlyn)
1900-1949 ..... **TCLC 11; DAM NOV,**
POP
See also CA 109; 125; CANR 55; DLB 9;
MTCW

Mitchell, Peggy
See Mitchell, Margaret (Munnerlyn)

Mitchell, S(ilas) Weir 1829-1914 .. **TCLC 36**

Mitchell, W(illiam) O(rmond)
1914- ...... **CLC 25; DAC; DAM MST**
See also CA 77-80; CANR 15, 43; DLB 88

Mitford, Mary Russell 1787-1855.. **NCLC 4**
See also DLB 110, 116

Mitford, Nancy 1904-1973 .... **CLC 44**
See also CA 9-12R

Miyamoto, Yuriko 1899-1951 ..... **TCLC 37**
See also DLB 180

Mizoguchi, Kenji 1898-1956 ...... **TCLC 72**

Mo, Timothy (Peter) 1950(?)- ...... **CLC 46**
See also CA 117; MTCW

Modarressi, Taghi (M.) 1931- ...... **CLC 44**
See also CA 121; 134; INT 134

Modiano, Patrick (Jean) 1945- ..... **CLC 18**
See also CA 85-88; CANR 17, 40; DLB 83

Moerck, Paal
See Roelvaag, O(le) E(dvart)

Mofolo, Thomas (Mokopu)
1875(?)-1948 .... **TCLC 22; BLC;**
DAM MULT
See also CA 121; 153

Mohr, Nicholasa
1935- ..... **CLC 12; DAM MULT; HLC**
See also AAYA 8; CA 49-52; CANR 1, 32;
CLR 22; DLB 145; HW; JRDA; SAAS 8;
SATA 8

Mojtabai, A(nn) G(race)
1938- .... **CLC 5, 9, 15, 29**
See also CA 85-88

Moliere
1622-1673 ..... **LC 28; DA; DAB; DAC;**
DAM DRAM, MST; WLC

Molin, Charles
See Mayne, William (James Carter)

Molnar, Ferenc
1878-1952 ..... **TCLC 20; DAM DRAM**
See also CA 109; 153

Momaday, N(avarre) Scott
1934- ..... **CLC 2, 19, 85, 95; DA; DAB;**
DAC; DAM MST, MULT, NOV, POP;
WLCS
See also AAYA 11; CA 25-28R; CANR 14,
34; DLB 143, 175; INT CANR-14;
MTCW; NNAL; SATA 48;
SATA-Brief 30

Monette, Paul 1945-1995 .... **CLC 82**
See also CA 139; 147

Monroe, Harriet 1860-1936 ...... **TCLC 12**
See also CA 109; DLB 54, 91

Monroe, Lyle
See Heinlein, Robert A(nson)

Montagu, Elizabeth 1917- .... **NCLC 7**
See also CA 9-12R

Montagu, Mary (Pierrepont) Wortley
1689-1762 .... **LC 9; PC 16**
See also DLB 95, 101

Montagu, W. H.
See Coleridge, Samuel Taylor

Montague, John (Patrick)
1929- .... **CLC 13, 46**
See also CA 9-12R; CANR 9; DLB 40;
MTCW

Montaigne, Michel (Eyquem) de
1533-1592 ...... **LC 8; DA; DAB; DAC;**
DAM MST; WLC

Montale, Eugenio
1896-1981 .... **CLC 7, 9, 18; PC 13**
See also CA 17-20R; 104; CANR 30;
DLB 114; MTCW

Montesquieu, Charles-Louis de Secondat
1689-1755 .... **LC 7**

Montgomery, (Robert) Bruce 1921-1978
See Crispin, Edmund
See also CA 104

Montgomery, L(ucy) M(aud)
1874-1942 .... **TCLC 51; DAC;**
DAM MST
See also AAYA 12; CA 108; 137; CLR 8;
DLB 92; DLBD 14; JRDA; MAICYA;
YABC 1

Montgomery, Marion H., Jr. 1925- .. **CLC 7**
See also AITN 1; CA 1-4R; CANR 3, 48;
DLB 6

Montgomery, Max
See Davenport, Guy (Mattison, Jr.)

Montherlant, Henry (Milon) de
1896-1972 .... **CLC 8, 19; DAM DRAM**
See also CA 85-88; 37-40R; DLB 72;
MTCW

Monty Python
See Chapman, Graham; Cleese, John
(Marwood); Gilliam, Terry (Vance); Idle,
Eric; Jones, Terence Graham Parry; Palin,
Michael (Edward)
See also AAYA 7

Moodie, Susanna (Strickland)
1803-1885 .... **NCLC 14**
See also DLB 99

Mooney, Edward 1951-
See Mooney, Ted
See also CA 130

Mooney, Ted .... **CLC 25**
See also Mooney, Edward

Moorcock, Michael (John)
1939- .... **CLC 5, 27, 58**
See also CA 45-48; CAAS 5; CANR 2, 17,
38; DLB 14; MTCW; SATA 93

Moore, Brian
1921- ...... **CLC 1, 3, 5, 7, 8, 19, 32, 90;**
DAB; DAC; DAM MST
See also CA 1-4R; CANR 1, 25, 42; MTCW

Moore, Edward
See Muir, Edwin

Moore, George Augustus
1852-1933 . . . . **TCLC 7; SSC 19**
See also CA 104; DLB 10, 18, 57, 135

Moore, Lorrie . . . . **CLC 39, 45, 68**
See also Moore, Marie Lorena

Moore, Marianne (Craig)
1887-1972 . . . . **CLC 1, 2, 4, 8, 10, 13, 19,
47; DA; DAB; DAC; DAM MST, POET;
PC 4; WLCS**
See also CA 1-4R; 33-36R; CANR 3, 61;
CDALB 1929-1941; DLB 45; DLBD 7;
MTCW; SATA 20

Moore, Marie Lorena 1957-
See Moore, Lorrie
See also CA 116; CANR 39

Moore, Thomas 1779-1852. . . . . . . **NCLC 6**
See also DLB 96, 144

Morand, Paul 1888-1976 . . **CLC 41; SSC 22**
See also CA 69-72; DLB 65

Morante, Elsa 1918-1985. . . . . . . **CLC 8, 47**
See also CA 85-88; 117; CANR 35;
DLB 177; MTCW

Moravia, Alberto
1907-1990 . . . . **CLC 2, 7, 11, 27, 46;
SSC 26**
See also Pincherle, Alberto
See also DLB 177

More, Hannah 1745-1833 . . . . **NCLC 27**
See also DLB 107, 109, 116, 158

More, Henry 1614-1687. . . . . **LC 9**
See also DLB 126

More, Sir Thomas 1478-1535 . . . . **LC 10, 32**

Moreas, Jean. . . . . **TCLC 18**
See also Papadiamantopoulos, Johannes

Morgan, Berry 1919- . . . . **CLC 6**
See also CA 49-52; DLB 6

Morgan, Claire
See Highsmith, (Mary) Patricia

Morgan, Edwin (George) 1920- . . . . **CLC 31**
See also CA 5-8R; CANR 3, 43; DLB 27

Morgan, (George) Frederick
1922- . . . . **CLC 23**
See also CA 17-20R; CANR 21

Morgan, Harriet
See Mencken, H(enry) L(ouis)

Morgan, Jane
See Cooper, James Fenimore

Morgan, Janet 1945- . . . . **CLC 39**
See also CA 65-68

Morgan, Lady 1776(?)-1859. . . . . . **NCLC 29**
See also DLB 116, 158

Morgan, Robin 1941- . . . . **CLC 2**
See also CA 69-72; CANR 29; MTCW;
SATA 80

Morgan, Scott
See Kuttner, Henry

Morgan, Seth 1949(?)-1990 . . . . **CLC 65**
See also CA 132

Morgenstern, Christian
1871-1914 . . . . **TCLC 8**
See also CA 105

Morgenstern, S.
See Goldman, William (W.)

Moricz, Zsigmond 1879-1942 . . . . . **TCLC 33**

Morike, Eduard (Friedrich)
1804-1875 . . . . **NCLC 10**
See also DLB 133

Mori Ogai . . . . **TCLC 14**
See also Mori Rintaro

Mori Rintaro 1862-1922
See Mori Ogai
See also CA 110

Moritz, Karl Philipp 1756-1793 . . . . . . **LC 2**
See also DLB 94

Morland, Peter Henry
See Faust, Frederick (Schiller)

Morren, Theophil
See Hofmannsthal, Hugo von

Morris, Bill 1952- . . . . **CLC 76**

Morris, Julian
See West, Morris L(anglo)

Morris, Steveland Judkins 1950(?)-
See Wonder, Stevie
See also CA 111

Morris, William 1834-1896 . . . . **NCLC 4**
See also CDBLB 1832-1890; DLB 18, 35,
57, 156, 178, 184

Morris, Wright 1910- . . . **CLC 1, 3, 7, 18, 37**
See also CA 9-12R; CANR 21; DLB 2;
DLBY 81; MTCW

Morrison, Arthur 1863-1945 . . . . . . **TCLC 72**
See also CA 120; 157; DLB 70, 135

Morrison, Chloe Anthony Wofford
See Morrison, Toni

Morrison, James Douglas 1943-1971
See Morrison, Jim
See also CA 73-76; CANR 40

Morrison, Jim . . . . **CLC 17**
See also Morrison, James Douglas

Morrison, Toni
1931- . . . . **CLC 4, 10, 22, 55, 81, 87;
BLC; DA; DAB; DAC; DAM MST,
MULT, NOV, POP**
See also AAYA 1, 22; BW 2; CA 29-32R;
CANR 27, 42; CDALB 1968-1988;
DLB 6, 33, 143; DLBY 81; MTCW;
SATA 57

Morrison, Van 1945- . . . . **CLC 21**
See also CA 116

Morrissy, Mary 1958- . . . . **CLC 99**

Mortimer, John (Clifford)
1923- . . . . . . **CLC 28, 43; DAM DRAM,
POP**
See also CA 13-16R; CANR 21;
CDBLB 1960 to Present; DLB 13;
INT CANR-21; MTCW

Mortimer, Penelope (Ruth) 1918- . . . . **CLC 5**
See also CA 57-60; CANR 45

Morton, Anthony
See Creasey, John

Mosher, Howard Frank 1943- . . . . . . **CLC 62**
See also CA 139

Mosley, Nicholas 1923- . . . . **CLC 43, 70**
See also CA 69-72; CANR 41, 60; DLB 14

Mosley, Walter
1952- . . . . . **CLC 97; DAM MULT, POP**
See also AAYA 17; BW 2; CA 142;
CANR 57

Moss, Howard
1922-1987 . . . . **CLC 7, 14, 45, 50;
DAM POET**
See also CA 1-4R; 123; CANR 1, 44;
DLB 5

Mossgiel, Rab
See Burns, Robert

Motion, Andrew (Peter) 1952- . . . . . . **CLC 47**
See also CA 146; DLB 40

Motley, Willard (Francis)
1909-1965 . . . . **CLC 18**
See also BW 1; CA 117; 106; DLB 76, 143

Motoori, Norinaga 1730-1801 . . . . **NCLC 45**

Mott, Michael (Charles Alston)
1930- . . . . **CLC 15, 34**
See also CA 5-8R; CAAS 7; CANR 7, 29

Mountain Wolf Woman
1884-1960 . . . . **CLC 92**
See also CA 144; NNAL

Moure, Erin 1955- . . . . **CLC 88**
See also CA 113; DLB 60

Mowat, Farley (McGill)
1921- . . . . . . **CLC 26; DAC; DAM MST**
See also AAYA 1; CA 1-4R; CANR 4, 24,
42; CLR 20; DLB 68; INT CANAR-24;
JRDA; MAICYA; MTCW; SATA 3, 55

Moyers, Bill 1934- . . . . **CLC 74**
See also AITN 2; CA 61-64; CANR 31, 52

Mphahlele, Es'kia
See Mphahlele, Ezekiel
See also DLB 125

Mphahlele, Ezekiel
1919- . . . . . **CLC 25; BLC; DAM MULT**
See also Mphahlele, Es'kia
See also BW 2; CA 81-84; CANR 26

Mqhayi, S(amuel) E(dward) K(rune Loliwe)
1875-1945 . . . . **TCLC 25; BLC;
DAM MULT**
See also CA 153

Mrozek, Slawomir 1930- . . . . **CLC 3, 13**
See also CA 13-16R; CAAS 10; CANR 29;
MTCW

Mrs. Belloc-Lowndes
See Lowndes, Marie Adelaide (Belloc)

Mtwa, Percy (?)- . . . . **CLC 47**

Mueller, Lisel 1924- . . . . **CLC 13, 51**
See also CA 93-96; DLB 105

Muir, Edwin 1887-1959 . . . . **TCLC 2**
See also CA 104; DLB 20, 100

Muir, John 1838-1914 . . . . **TCLC 28**

Mujica Lainez, Manuel
1910-1984 . . . . **CLC 31**
See also Lainez, Manuel Mujica
See also CA 81-84; 112; CANR 32; HW

Mukherjee, Bharati
1940- . . . . **CLC 53; DAM NOV**
See also BEST 89:2; CA 107; CANR 45;
DLB 60; MTCW

Muldoon, Paul
    1951- . . . . **CLC 32, 72; DAM POET**
    See also CA 113; 129; CANR 52; DLB 40;
    INT 129

Mulisch, Harry   1927- . . . . **CLC 42**
    See also CA 9-12R; CANR 6, 26, 56

Mull, Martin   1943- . . . . **CLC 17**
    See also CA 105

Mulock, Dinah Maria
    See Craik, Dinah Maria (Mulock)

Munford, Robert   1737(?)-1783 . . . . **LC 5**
    See also DLB 31

Mungo, Raymond   1946- . . . . **CLC 72**
    See also CA 49-52; CANR 2

Munro, Alice
    1931- . . . . . . **CLC 6, 10, 19, 50, 95; DAC;**
        DAM MST, NOV; SSC 3; WLCS
    See also AITN 2; CA 33-36R; CANR 33,
    53; DLB 53; MTCW; SATA 29

Munro, H(ector) H(ugh)   1870-1916
    See Saki
    See also CA 104; 130; CDBLB 1890-1914;
    DA; DAB; DAC; DAM MST, NOV;
    DLB 34, 162; MTCW; WLC

Murasaki, Lady . . . . **CMLC 1**

Murdoch, (Jean) Iris
    1919- . . . . . . **CLC 1, 2, 3, 4, 6, 8, 11, 15,**
        22, 31, 51; DAB; DAC; DAM MST,
                                            NOV
    See also CA 13-16R; CANR 8, 43;
    CDBLB 1960 to Present; DLB 14;
    INT CANR-8; MTCW

Murfree, Mary Noailles
    1850-1922 . . . . **SSC 22**
    See also CA 122; DLB 12, 74

Murnau, Friedrich Wilhelm
    See Plumpe, Friedrich Wilhelm

Murphy, Richard   1927- . . . . **CLC 41**
    See also CA 29-32R; DLB 40

Murphy, Sylvia   1937- . . . . **CLC 34**
    See also CA 121

Murphy, Thomas (Bernard)   1935- . . . **CLC 51**
    See also CA 101

Murray, Albert L.   1916- . . . . **CLC 73**
    See also BW 2; CA 49-52; CANR 26, 52;
    DLB 38

Murray, Judith Sargent
    1751-1820 . . . . **NCLC 63**
    See also DLB 37

Murray, Les(lie) A(llan)
    1938- . . . . **CLC 40; DAM POET**
    See also CA 21-24R; CANR 11, 27, 56

Murry, J. Middleton
    See Murry, John Middleton

Murry, John Middleton
    1889-1957 . . . . **TCLC 16**
    See also CA 118; DLB 149

Musgrave, Susan   1951- . . . . **CLC 13, 54**
    See also CA 69-72; CANR 45

Musil, Robert (Edler von)
    1880-1942 . . . . . . **TCLC 12, 68; SSC 18**
    See also CA 109; CANR 55; DLB 81, 124

Muske, Carol   1945- . . . . **CLC 90**
    See also Muske-Dukes, Carol (Anne)

Muske-Dukes, Carol (Anne)   1945-
    See Muske, Carol
    See also CA 65-68; CANR 32

Musset, (Louis Charles) Alfred de
    1810-1857 . . . . **NCLC 7**

My Brother's Brother
    See Chekhov, Anton (Pavlovich)

Myers, L(eopold) H(amilton)
    1881-1944 . . . . **TCLC 59**
    See also CA 157; DLB 15

Myers, Walter Dean
    1937- . . . . . **CLC 35; BLC; DAM MULT,**
                                            NOV
    See also AAYA 4; BW 2; CA 33-36R;
    CANR 20, 42; CLR 4, 16, 35; DLB 33;
    INT CANR-20; JRDA; MAICYA;
    SAAS 2; SATA 41, 71; SATA-Brief 27

Myers, Walter M.
    See Myers, Walter Dean

Myles, Symon
    See Follett, Ken(neth Martin)

Nabokov, Vladimir (Vladimirovich)
    1899-1977 . . . . . **CLC 1, 2, 3, 6, 8, 11, 15,**
        23, 44, 46, 64; DA; DAB; DAC;
        DAM MST, NOV; SSC 11; WLC
    See also CA 5-8R; 69-72; CANR 20;
    CDALB 1941-1968; DLB 2; DLBD 3;
    DLBY 80, 91; MTCW

Nagai Kafu   1879-1959 . . . . **TCLC 51**
    See also Nagai Sokichi
    See also DLB 180

Nagai Sokichi   1879-1959
    See Nagai Kafu
    See also CA 117

Nagy, Laszlo   1925-1978 . . . . **CLC 7**
    See also CA 129; 112

Naipaul, Shiva(dhar Srinivasa)
    1945-1985 . . . . . **CLC 32, 39; DAM NOV**
    See also CA 110; 112; 116; CANR 33;
    DLB 157; DLBY 85; MTCW

Naipaul, V(idiadhar) S(urajprasad)
    1932- . . . . **CLC 4, 7, 9, 13, 18, 37; DAB;**
                    DAC; DAM MST, NOV
    See also CA 1-4R; CANR 1, 33, 51;
    CDBLB 1960 to Present; DLB 125;
    DLBY 85; MTCW

Nakos, Lilika   1899(?)- . . . . **CLC 29**

Narayan, R(asipuram) K(rishnaswami)
    1906- . . . . . . **CLC 7, 28, 47; DAM NOV;**
                                            SSC 25
    See also CA 81-84; CANR 33, 61; MTCW;
    SATA 62

Nash, (Frediric) Ogden
    1902-1971 . . . . . . **CLC 23; DAM POET**
    See also CA 13-14; 29-32R; CANR 34, 61;
    CAP 1; DLB 11; MAICYA; MTCW;
    SATA 2, 46

Nathan, Daniel
    See Dannay, Frederic

Nathan, George Jean   1882-1958 . . . **TCLC 18**
    See also Hatteras, Owen
    See also CA 114; DLB 137

Natsume, Kinnosuke   1867-1916
    See Natsume, Soseki
    See also CA 104

Natsume, Soseki   1867-1916 . . . . . **TCLC 2, 10**
    See also Natsume, Kinnosuke
    See also DLB 180

Natti, (Mary) Lee   1919-
    See Kingman, Lee
    See also CA 5-8R; CANR 2

Naylor, Gloria
    1950- . . . . . **CLC 28, 52; BLC; DA; DAC;**
        DAM MST, MULT, NOV, POP; WLCS
    See also AAYA 6; BW 2; CA 107;
    CANR 27, 51; DLB 173; MTCW

Neihardt, John Gneisenau
    1881-1973 . . . . **CLC 32**
    See also CA 13-14; CAP 1; DLB 9, 54

Nekrasov, Nikolai Alekseevich
    1821-1878 . . . . **NCLC 11**

Nelligan, Emile   1879-1941 . . . . **TCLC 14**
    See also CA 114; DLB 92

Nelson, Willie   1933- . . . . **CLC 17**
    See also CA 107

Nemerov, Howard (Stanley)
    1920-1991 . . . . **CLC 2, 6, 9, 36;**
                                            DAM POET
    See also CA 1-4R; 134; CABS 2; CANR 1,
    27, 53; DLB 5, 6; DLBY 83;
    INT CANR-27; MTCW

Neruda, Pablo
    1904-1973 . . . . . **CLC 1, 2, 5, 7, 9, 28, 62;**
        DA; DAB; DAC; DAM MST, MULT,
                    POET; HLC; PC 4; WLC
    See also CA 19-20; 45-48; CAP 2; HW;
    MTCW

Nerval, Gerard de
    1808-1855 . . . . . **NCLC 1; PC 13; SSC 18**

Nervo, (Jose) Amado (Ruiz de)
    1870-1919 . . . . **TCLC 11**
    See also CA 109; 131; HW

Nessi, Pio Baroja y
    See Baroja (y Nessi), Pio

Nestroy, Johann   1801-1862 . . . . . . **NCLC 42**
    See also DLB 133

Netterville, Luke
    See O'Grady, Standish (James)

Neufeld, John (Arthur)   1938- . . . . . . **CLC 17**
    See also AAYA 11; CA 25-28R; CANR 11,
    37, 56; MAICYA; SAAS 3; SATA 6, 81

Neville, Emily Cheney   1919- . . . . **CLC 12**
    See also CA 5-8R; CANR 3, 37; JRDA;
    MAICYA; SAAS 2; SATA 1

Newbound, Bernard Slade   1930-
    See Slade, Bernard
    See also CA 81-84; CANR 49;
    DAM DRAM

Newby, P(ercy) H(oward)
    1918- . . . . **CLC 2, 13; DAM NOV**
    See also CA 5-8R; CANR 32; DLB 15;
    MTCW

Newlove, Donald   1928- . . . . **CLC 6**
    See also CA 29-32R; CANR 25

Newlove, John (Herbert)   1938- . . . . . **CLC 14**
    See also CA 21-24R; CANR 9, 25

Newman, Charles   1938- . . . . **CLC 2, 8**
    See also CA 21-24R

Newman, Edwin (Harold)   1919- . . . . **CLC 14**
    See also AITN 1; CA 69-72; CANR 5

Newman, John Henry
1801-1890 . . . . NCLC 38
See also DLB 18, 32, 55

Newton, Suzanne 1936- . . . . CLC 35
See also CA 41-44R; CANR 14; JRDA;
SATA 5, 77

Nexo, Martin Andersen
1869-1954 . . . . TCLC 43

Nezval, Vitezslav 1900-1958 . . . . . . TCLC 44
See also CA 123

Ng, Fae Myenne 1957(?)- . . . . CLC 81
See also CA 146

Ngema, Mbongeni 1955- . . . . CLC 57
See also BW 2; CA 143

Ngugi, James T(hiong'o) . . . . CLC 3, 7, 13
See also Ngugi wa Thiong'o

Ngugi wa Thiong'o
1938- . . . . . CLC 36; BLC; DAM MULT,
NOV
See also Ngugi, James T(hiong'o)
See also BW 2; CA 81-84; CANR 27, 58;
DLB 125; MTCW

Nichol, B(arrie) P(hillip)
1944-1988 . . . . CLC 18
See also CA 53-56; DLB 53; SATA 66

Nichols, John (Treadwell) 1940- . . . . CLC 38
See also CA 9-12R; CAAS 2; CANR 6;
DLBY 82

Nichols, Leigh
See Koontz, Dean R(ay)

Nichols, Peter (Richard)
1927- . . . . CLC 5, 36, 65
See also CA 104; CANR 33; DLB 13;
MTCW

Nicolas, F. R. E.
See Freeling, Nicolas

Niedecker, Lorine
1903-1970 . . . . CLC 10, 42; DAM POET
See also CA 25-28; CAP 2; DLB 48

Nietzsche, Friedrich (Wilhelm)
1844-1900 . . . . TCLC 10, 18, 55
See also CA 107; 121; DLB 129

Nievo, Ippolito 1831-1861 . . . . NCLC 22

Nightingale, Anne Redmon 1943-
See Redmon, Anne
See also CA 103

Nik. T. O.
See Annensky, Innokenty (Fyodorovich)

Nin, Anais
1903-1977 . . . . . . CLC 1, 4, 8, 11, 14, 60;
DAM NOV, POP; SSC 10
See also AITN 2; CA 13-16R; 69-72;
CANR 22, 53; DLB 2, 4, 152; MTCW

Nishiwaki, Junzaburo 1894-1982 . . . . PC 15
See also CA 107

Nissenson, Hugh 1933- . . . . CLC 4, 9
See also CA 17-20R; CANR 27; DLB 28

Niven, Larry . . . . CLC 8
See also Niven, Laurence Van Cott
See also DLB 8

Niven, Laurence Van Cott 1938-
See Niven, Larry
See also CA 21-24R; CAAS 12; CANR 14,
44; DAM POP; MTCW; SATA 95

Nixon, Agnes Eckhardt 1927- . . . . . . CLC 21
See also CA 110

Nizan, Paul 1905-1940 . . . . TCLC 40
See also DLB 72

Nkosi, Lewis
1936- . . . . . CLC 45; BLC; DAM MULT
See also BW 1; CA 65-68; CANR 27;
DLB 157

Nodier, (Jean) Charles (Emmanuel)
1780-1844 . . . . NCLC 19
See also DLB 119

Nolan, Christopher 1965- . . . . CLC 58
See also CA 111

Noon, Jeff 1957- . . . . CLC 91
See also CA 148

Norden, Charles
See Durrell, Lawrence (George)

Nordhoff, Charles (Bernard)
1887-1947 . . . . TCLC 23
See also CA 108; DLB 9; SATA 23

Norfolk, Lawrence 1963- . . . . CLC 76
See also CA 144

Norman, Marsha
1947- . . . . CLC 28; DAM DRAM
See also CA 105; CABS 3; CANR 41;
DLBY 84

Norris, Benjamin Franklin, Jr.
1870-1902 . . . . TCLC 24
See also Norris, Frank
See also CA 110

Norris, Frank 1870-1902 . . . . SSC 28
See also Norris, Benjamin Franklin, Jr.
See also CDALB 1865-1917; DLB 12, 71

Norris, Leslie 1921- . . . . CLC 14
See also CA 11-12; CANR 14; CAP 1;
DLB 27

North, Andrew
See Norton, Andre

North, Anthony
See Koontz, Dean R(ay)

North, Captain George
See Stevenson, Robert Louis (Balfour)

North, Milou
See Erdrich, Louise

Northrup, B. A.
See Hubbard, L(afayette) Ron(ald)

North Staffs
See Hulme, T(homas) E(rnest)

Norton, Alice Mary
See Norton, Andre
See also MAICYA; SATA 1, 43

Norton, Andre 1912- . . . . CLC 12
See also Norton, Alice Mary
See also AAYA 14; CA 1-4R; CANR 2, 31;
DLB 8, 52; JRDA; MTCW; SATA 91

Norton, Caroline 1808-1877 . . . . . . NCLC 47
See also DLB 21, 159

Norway, Nevil Shute 1899-1960
See Shute, Nevil
See also CA 102; 93-96

Norwid, Cyprian Kamil
1821-1883 . . . . NCLC 17

Nosille, Nabrah
See Ellison, Harlan (Jay)

Nossack, Hans Erich 1901-1978 . . . . . CLC 6
See also CA 93-96; 85-88; DLB 69

Nostradamus 1503-1566 . . . . LC 27

Nosu, Chuji
See Ozu, Yasujiro

Notenburg, Eleanora (Genrikhovna) von
See Guro, Elena

Nova, Craig 1945- . . . . CLC 7, 31
See also CA 45-48; CANR 2, 53

Novak, Joseph
See Kosinski, Jerzy (Nikodem)

Novalis 1772-1801 . . . . NCLC 13
See also DLB 90

Novis, Emile
See Weil, Simone (Adolphine)

Nowlan, Alden (Albert)
1933-1983 . . CLC 15; DAC; DAM MST
See also CA 9-12R; CANR 5; DLB 53

Noyes, Alfred 1880-1958 . . . . TCLC 7
See also CA 104; DLB 20

Nunn, Kem . . . . CLC 34
See also CA 159

Nye, Robert
1939- . . . . CLC 13, 42; DAM NOV
See also CA 33-36R; CANR 29; DLB 14;
MTCW; SATA 6

Nyro, Laura 1947- . . . . CLC 17

Oates, Joyce Carol
1938- . . . . . . CLC 1, 2, 3, 6, 9, 11, 15, 19,
33, 52; DA; DAB; DAC; DAM MST,
NOV, POP; SSC 6; WLC
See also AAYA 15; AITN 1; BEST 89:2;
CA 5-8R; CANR 25, 45;
CDALB 1968-1988; DLB 2, 5, 130;
DLBY 81; INT CANR-25; MTCW

O'Brien, Darcy 1939- . . . . CLC 11
See also CA 21-24R; CANR 8, 59

O'Brien, E. G.
See Clarke, Arthur C(harles)

O'Brien, Edna
1936- . . . . CLC 3, 5, 8, 13, 36, 65;
DAM NOV; SSC 10
See also CA 1-4R; CANR 6, 41;
CDBLB 1960 to Present; DLB 14;
MTCW

O'Brien, Fitz-James 1828-1862 . . . NCLC 21
See also DLB 74

O'Brien, Flann . . . . CLC 1, 4, 5, 7, 10, 47
See also O Nuallain, Brian

O'Brien, Richard 1942- . . . . CLC 17
See also CA 124

O'Brien, (William) Tim(othy)
1946- . . . CLC 7, 19, 40, 103; DAM POP
See also AAYA 16; CA 85-88; CANR 40,
58; DLB 152; DLBD 9; DLBY 80

Obstfelder, Sigbjoern 1866-1900 . . . TCLC 23
See also CA 123

O'Casey, Sean
1880-1964 . . . . . . CLC 1, 5, 9, 11, 15, 88;
DAB; DAC; DAM DRAM, MST; WLCS
See also CA 89-92; CDBLB 1914-1945;
DLB 10; MTCW

O'Cathasaigh, Sean
See O'Casey, Sean

Ochs, Phil 1940-1976 . . . . **CLC 17**
See also CA 65-68

O'Connor, Edwin (Greene)
1918-1968 . . . . **CLC 14**
See also CA 93-96; 25-28R

O'Connor, (Mary) Flannery
1925-1964 . . . . **CLC 1, 2, 3, 6, 10, 13, 15,**
21, 66, 104; DA; DAB; DAC;
DAM MST, NOV; SSC 1, 23; WLC
See also AAYA 7; CA 1-4R; CANR 3, 41;
CDALB 1941-1968; DLB 2, 152;
DLBD 12; DLBY 80; MTCW

O'Connor, Frank . . . . **CLC 23; SSC 5**
See also O'Donovan, Michael John
See also DLB 162

O'Dell, Scott 1898-1989 . . . . **CLC 30**
See also AAYA 3; CA 61-64; 129;
CANR 12, 30; CLR 1, 16; DLB 52;
JRDA; MAICYA; SATA 12, 60

Odets, Clifford
1906-1963 . . . . **CLC 2, 28, 98;**
DAM DRAM; DC 6
See also CA 85-88; DLB 7, 26; MTCW

O'Doherty, Brian 1934- . . . . **CLC 76**
See also CA 105

O'Donnell, K. M.
See Malzberg, Barry N(athaniel)

O'Donnell, Lawrence
See Kuttner, Henry

O'Donovan, Michael John
1903-1966 . . . . **CLC 14**
See also O'Connor, Frank
See also CA 93-96

Oe, Kenzaburo
1935- . . . . . **CLC 10, 36, 86; DAM NOV;**
SSC 20
See also CA 97-100; CANR 36, 50;
DLB 182; DLBY 94; MTCW

O'Faolain, Julia 1932- . . . . **CLC 6, 19, 47**
See also CA 81-84; CAAS 2; CANR 12, 61;
DLB 14; MTCW

O'Faolain, Sean
1900-1991 . . . . **CLC 1, 7, 14, 32, 70;**
SSC 13
See also CA 61-64; 134; CANR 12;
DLB 15, 162; MTCW

O'Flaherty, Liam
1896-1984 . . . . **CLC 5, 34; SSC 6**
See also CA 101; 113; CANR 35; DLB 36,
162; DLBY 84; MTCW

Ogilvy, Gavin
See Barrie, J(ames) M(atthew)

O'Grady, Standish (James)
1846-1928 . . . . **TCLC 5**
See also CA 104; 157

O'Grady, Timothy 1951- . . . . **CLC 59**
See also CA 138

O'Hara, Frank
1926-1966 . . . . **CLC 2, 5, 13, 78;**
DAM POET
See also CA 9-12R; 25-28R; CANR 33;
DLB 5, 16; MTCW

O'Hara, John (Henry)
1905-1970 . . . . . . **CLC 1, 2, 3, 6, 11, 42;**
DAM NOV; SSC 15
See also CA 5-8R; 25-28R; CANR 31, 60;
CDALB 1929-1941; DLB 9, 86; DLBD 2;
MTCW

O Hehir, Diana 1922- . . . . **CLC 41**
See also CA 93-96

Okigbo, Christopher (Ifenayichukwu)
1932-1967 . . . . **CLC 25, 84; BLC;**
DAM MULT, POET; PC 7
See also BW 1; CA 77-80; DLB 125;
MTCW

Okri, Ben 1959- . . . . **CLC 87**
See also BW 2; CA 130; 138; DLB 157;
INT 138

Olds, Sharon
1942- . . . . . **CLC 32, 39, 85; DAM POET**
See also CA 101; CANR 18, 41; DLB 120

Oldstyle, Jonathan
See Irving, Washington

Olesha, Yuri (Karlovich)
1899-1960 . . . . **CLC 8**
See also CA 85-88

Oliphant, Laurence
1829(?)-1888 . . . . **NCLC 47**
See also DLB 18, 166

Oliphant, Margaret (Oliphant Wilson)
1828-1897 . . . . **NCLC 11, 61; SSC 25**
See also DLB 18, 159

Oliver, Mary 1935- . . . . **CLC 19, 34, 98**
See also CA 21-24R; CANR 9, 43; DLB 5

Olivier, Laurence (Kerr)
1907-1989 . . . . **CLC 20**
See also CA 111; 150; 129

Olsen, Tillie
1913- . . . . . **CLC 4, 13; DA; DAB; DAC;**
DAM MST; SSC 11
See also CA 1-4R; CANR 1, 43; DLB 28;
DLBY 80; MTCW

Olson, Charles (John)
1910-1970 . . . . . **CLC 1, 2, 5, 6, 9, 11, 29;**
DAM POET; PC 19
See also CA 13-16; 25-28R; CABS 2;
CANR 35, 61; CAP 1; DLB 5, 16;
MTCW

Olson, Toby 1937- . . . . **CLC 28**
See also CA 65-68; CANR 9, 31

Olyesha, Yuri
See Olesha, Yuri (Karlovich)

Ondaatje, (Philip) Michael
1943- . . . . **CLC 14, 29, 51, 76; DAB;**
DAC; DAM MST
See also CA 77-80; CANR 42; DLB 60

Oneal, Elizabeth 1934-
See Oneal, Zibby
See also CA 106; CANR 28; MAICYA;
SATA 30, 82

Oneal, Zibby . . . . **CLC 30**
See also Oneal, Elizabeth
See also AAYA 5; CLR 13; JRDA

O'Neill, Eugene (Gladstone)
1888-1953 . . . . . . **TCLC 1, 6, 27, 49; DA;**
DAB; DAC; DAM DRAM, MST; WLC
See also AITN 1; CA 110; 132;
CDALB 1929-1941; DLB 7; MTCW

Onetti, Juan Carlos
1909-1994 . . . . **CLC 7, 10; DAM MULT,**
NOV; SSC 23
See also CA 85-88; 145; CANR 32;
DLB 113; HW; MTCW

O Nuallain, Brian 1911-1966
See O'Brien, Flann
See also CA 21-22; 25-28R; CAP 2

Oppen, George 1908-1984 . . . . **CLC 7, 13, 34**
See also CA 13-16R; 113; CANR 8; DLB 5,
165

Oppenheim, E(dward) Phillips
1866-1946 . . . . **TCLC 45**
See also CA 111; DLB 70

Origen c. 185-c. 254 . . . . **CMLC 19**

Orlovitz, Gil 1918-1973 . . . . **CLC 22**
See also CA 77-80; 45-48; DLB 2, 5

Orris
See Ingelow, Jean

Ortega y Gasset, Jose
1883-1955 . . . . . **TCLC 9; DAM MULT;**
HLC
See also CA 106; 130; HW; MTCW

Ortese, Anna Maria 1914- . . . . **CLC 89**
See also DLB 177

Ortiz, Simon J(oseph)
1941- . . . . **CLC 45; DAM MULT,**
POET; PC 17
See also CA 134; DLB 120, 175; NNAL

Orton, Joe . . . . **CLC 4, 13, 43; DC 3**
See also Orton, John Kingsley
See also CDBLB 1960 to Present; DLB 13

Orton, John Kingsley 1933-1967
See Orton, Joe
See also CA 85-88; CANR 35;
DAM DRAM; MTCW

Orwell, George
. . . . . **TCLC 2, 6, 15, 31, 51; DAB; WLC**
See also Blair, Eric (Arthur)
See also CDBLB 1945-1960; DLB 15, 98

Osborne, David
See Silverberg, Robert

Osborne, George
See Silverberg, Robert

Osborne, John (James)
1929-1994 . . . . . **CLC 1, 2, 5, 11, 45; DA;**
DAB; DAC; DAM DRAM, MST; WLC
See also CA 13-16R; 147; CANR 21, 56;
CDBLB 1945-1960; DLB 13; MTCW

Osborne, Lawrence 1958- . . . . **CLC 50**

Oshima, Nagisa 1932- . . . . **CLC 20**
See also CA 116; 121

Oskison, John Milton
1874-1947 . . . . . **TCLC 35; DAM MULT**
See also CA 144; DLB 175; NNAL

Ossoli, Sarah Margaret (Fuller marchesa d')
1810-1850
See Fuller, Margaret
See also SATA 25

Ostrovsky, Alexander
1823-1886 . . . . **NCLC 30, 57**

Otero, Blas de 1916-1979 . . . . **CLC 11**
See also CA 89-92; DLB 134

Otto, Whitney 1955- . . . . **CLC 70**
See also CA 140

Ouida . . . . **TCLC 43**
See also De La Ramee, (Marie) Louise
See also DLB 18, 156

Ousmane, Sembene 1923- . . . . **CLC 66; BLC**
See also BW 1; CA 117; 125; MTCW

Ovid
43B.C.-18(?) . . . **CMLC 7; DAM POET;**
PC 2

Owen, Hugh
See Faust, Frederick (Schiller)

Owen, Wilfred (Edward Salter)
1893-1918 . . . . . . **TCLC 5, 27; DA; DAB;**
DAC; DAM MST, POET; PC 19; WLC
See also CA 104; 141; CDBLB 1914-1945;
DLB 20

Owens, Rochelle 1936- . . . . **CLC 8**
See also CA 17-20R; CAAS 2; CANR 39

Oz, Amos
1939- . . . . **CLC 5, 8, 11, 27, 33, 54;**
DAM NOV
See also CA 53-56; CANR 27, 47; MTCW

Ozick, Cynthia
1928- . . . . **CLC 3, 7, 28, 62; DAM NOV,**
POP; SSC 15
See also BEST 90:1; CA 17-20R; CANR 23,
58; DLB 28, 152; DLBY 82;
INT CANR-23; MTCW

Ozu, Yasujiro 1903-1963 . . . . **CLC 16**
See also CA 112

Pacheco, C.
See Pessoa, Fernando (Antonio Nogueira)

Pa Chin . . . . **CLC 18**
See also Li Fei-kan

Pack, Robert 1929- . . . . **CLC 13**
See also CA 1-4R; CANR 3, 44; DLB 5

Padgett, Lewis
See Kuttner, Henry

Padilla (Lorenzo), Heberto 1932- . . . **CLC 38**
See also AITN 1; CA 123; 131; HW

Page, Jimmy 1944- . . . . **CLC 12**

Page, Louise 1955- . . . . **CLC 40**
See also CA 140

Page, P(atricia) K(athleen)
1916- . . . . **CLC 7, 18; DAC; DAM MST;**
PC 12
See also CA 53-56; CANR 4, 22; DLB 68;
MTCW

Page, Thomas Nelson 1853-1922 . . . . **SSC 23**
See also CA 118; DLB 12, 78; DLBD 13

Pagels, Elaine Hiesey 1943- . . . . . . **CLC 104**
See also CA 45-48; CANR 2, 24, 51

Paget, Violet 1856-1935
See Lee, Vernon
See also CA 104

Paget-Lowe, Henry
See Lovecraft, H(oward) P(hillips)

Paglia, Camille (Anna) 1947- . . . . . . **CLC 68**
See also CA 140

Paige, Richard
See Koontz, Dean R(ay)

Paine, Thomas 1737-1809 . . . . **NCLC 62**
See also CDALB 1640-1865; DLB 31, 43,
73, 158

Pakenham, Antonia
See Fraser, (Lady) Antonia (Pakenham)

Palamas, Kostes 1859-1943 . . . . **TCLC 5**
See also CA 105

Palazzeschi, Aldo 1885-1974 . . . . **CLC 11**
See also CA 89-92; 53-56; DLB 114

Paley, Grace
1922- . . . . **CLC 4, 6, 37; DAM POP;**
SSC 8
See also CA 25-28R; CANR 13, 46;
DLB 28; INT CANR-13; MTCW

Palin, Michael (Edward) 1943- . . . . . **CLC 21**
See also Monty Python
See also CA 107; CANR 35; SATA 67

Palliser, Charles 1947- . . . . **CLC 65**
See also CA 136

Palma, Ricardo 1833-1919 . . . . **TCLC 29**

Pancake, Breece Dexter 1952-1979
See Pancake, Breece D'J
See also CA 123; 109

Pancake, Breece D'J . . . . **CLC 29**
See also Pancake, Breece Dexter
See also DLB 130

Panko, Rudy
See Gogol, Nikolai (Vasilyevich)

Papadiamantis, Alexandros
1851-1911 . . . . **TCLC 29**

Papadiamantopoulos, Johannes 1856-1910
See Moreas, Jean
See also CA 117

Papini, Giovanni 1881-1956 . . . . . . **TCLC 22**
See also CA 121

Paracelsus 1493-1541 . . . . **LC 14**
See also DLB 179

Parasol, Peter
See Stevens, Wallace

Pareto, Vilfredo 1848-1923 . . . . **TCLC 69**

Parfenie, Maria
See Codrescu, Andrei

Parini, Jay (Lee) 1948- . . . . **CLC 54**
See also CA 97-100; CAAS 16; CANR 32

Park, Jordan
See Kornbluth, C(yril) M.; Pohl, Frederik

Park, Robert E(zra) 1864-1944 . . . . **TCLC 73**
See also CA 122

Parker, Bert
See Ellison, Harlan (Jay)

Parker, Dorothy (Rothschild)
1893-1967 . . . . **CLC 15, 68;**
DAM POET; SSC 2
See also CA 19-20; 25-28R; CAP 2;
DLB 11, 45, 86; MTCW

Parker, Robert B(rown)
1932- . . . . . . **CLC 27; DAM NOV, POP**
See also BEST 89:4; CA 49-52; CANR 1,
26, 52; INT CANR-26; MTCW

Parkin, Frank 1940- . . . . **CLC 43**
See also CA 147

Parkman, Francis, Jr.
1823-1893 . . . . **NCLC 12**
See also DLB 1, 30

Parks, Gordon (Alexander Buchanan)
1912- . . . **CLC 1, 16; BLC; DAM MULT**
See also AITN 2; BW 2; CA 41-44R;
CANR 26; DLB 33; SATA 8

Parmenides
c. 515B.C.-c. 450B.C. . . . . **CMLC 22**
See also DLB 176

Parnell, Thomas 1679-1718 . . . . **LC 3**
See also DLB 94

Parra, Nicanor
1914- . . . . **CLC 2, 102; DAM MULT;**
HLC
See also CA 85-88; CANR 32; HW; MTCW

Parrish, Mary Frances
See Fisher, M(ary) F(rances) K(ennedy)

Parson
See Coleridge, Samuel Taylor

Parson Lot
See Kingsley, Charles

Partridge, Anthony
See Oppenheim, E(dward) Phillips

Pascal, Blaise 1623-1662 . . . . **LC 35**

Pascoli, Giovanni 1855-1912 . . . . . . **TCLC 45**

Pasolini, Pier Paolo
1922-1975 . . . . **CLC 20, 37; PC 17**
See also CA 93-96; 61-64; DLB 128, 177;
MTCW

Pasquini
See Silone, Ignazio

Pastan, Linda (Olenik)
1932- . . . . **CLC 27; DAM POET**
See also CA 61-64; CANR 18, 40, 61;
DLB 5

Pasternak, Boris (Leonidovich)
1890-1960 . . . . . . **CLC 7, 10, 18, 63; DA;**
DAB; DAC; DAM MST, NOV, POET;
PC 6; WLC
See also CA 127; 116; MTCW

Patchen, Kenneth
1911-1972 . . . **CLC 1, 2, 18; DAM POET**
See also CA 1-4R; 33-36R; CANR 3, 35;
DLB 16, 48; MTCW

Pater, Walter (Horatio)
1839-1894 . . . . **NCLC 7**
See also CDBLB 1832-1890; DLB 57, 156

Paterson, A(ndrew) B(arton)
1864-1941 . . . . **TCLC 32**
See also CA 155

Paterson, Katherine (Womeldorf)
1932- . . . . **CLC 12, 30**
See also AAYA 1; CA 21-24R; CANR 28,
59; CLR 7; DLB 52; JRDA; MAICYA;
MTCW; SATA 13, 53, 92

Patmore, Coventry Kersey Dighton
1823-1896 . . . . **NCLC 9**
See also DLB 35, 98

Paton, Alan (Stewart)
1903-1988 . . . . . . **CLC 4, 10, 25, 55; DA;**
DAB; DAC; DAM MST, NOV; WLC
See also CA 13-16; 125; CANR 22; CAP 1;
MTCW; SATA 11; SATA-Obit 56

Paton Walsh, Gillian 1937-
See Walsh, Jill Paton
See also CANR 38; JRDA; MAICYA;
SAAS 3; SATA 4, 72

Paulding, James Kirke 1778-1860.. **NCLC 2**
See also DLB 3, 59, 74

Paulin, Thomas Neilson 1949-
See Paulin, Tom
See also CA 123; 128

Paulin, Tom................... **CLC 37**
See also Paulin, Thomas Neilson
See also DLB 40

Paustovsky, Konstantin (Georgievich)
1892-1968 .... **CLC 40**
See also CA 93-96; 25-28R

Pavese, Cesare
1908-1950 ..... **TCLC 3; PC 13; SSC 19**
See also CA 104; DLB 128, 177

Pavic, Milorad 1929-............. **CLC 60**
See also CA 136; DLB 181

Payne, Alan
See Jakes, John (William)

Paz, Gil
See Lugones, Leopoldo

Paz, Octavio
1914- .... **CLC 3, 4, 6, 10, 19, 51, 65;**
DA; DAB; DAC; DAM MST, MULT,
POET; HLC; PC 1; WLC
See also CA 73-76; CANR 32; DLBY 90;
HW; MTCW

p'Bitek, Okot
1931-1982 .... **CLC 96; BLC;**
DAM MULT
See also BW 2; CA 124; 107; DLB 125;
MTCW

Peacock, Molly 1947-............. **CLC 60**
See also CA 103; CAAS 21; CANR 52;
DLB 120

Peacock, Thomas Love
1785-1866 .... **NCLC 22**
See also DLB 96, 116

Peake, Mervyn 1911-1968....... **CLC 7, 54**
See also CA 5-8R; 25-28R; CANR 3;
DLB 15, 160; MTCW; SATA 23

Pearce, Philippa .... **CLC 21**
See also Christie, (Ann) Philippa
See also CLR 9; DLB 161; MAICYA;
SATA 1, 67

Pearl, Eric
See Elman, Richard

Pearson, T(homas) R(eid) 1956- .... **CLC 39**
See also CA 120; 130; INT 130

Peck, Dale 1967- .... **CLC 81**
See also CA 146

Peck, John 1941- .... **CLC 3**
See also CA 49-52; CANR 3

Peck, Richard (Wayne) 1934- ...... **CLC 21**
See also AAYA 1; CA 85-88; CANR 19,
38; CLR 15; INT CANR-19; JRDA;
MAICYA; SAAS 2; SATA 18, 55

Peck, Robert Newton
1928- .. **CLC 17; DA; DAC; DAM MST**
See also AAYA 3; CA 81-84; CANR 31;
CLR 45; JRDA; MAICYA; SAAS 1;
SATA 21, 62

Peckinpah, (David) Sam(uel)
1925-1984 .... **CLC 20**
See also CA 109; 114

Pedersen, Knut 1859-1952
See Hamsun, Knut
See also CA 104; 119; MTCW

Peeslake, Gaffer
See Durrell, Lawrence (George)

Peguy, Charles Pierre
1873-1914 .... **TCLC 10**
See also CA 107

Pena, Ramon del Valle y
See Valle-Inclan, Ramon (Maria) del

Pendennis, Arthur Esquir
See Thackeray, William Makepeace

Penn, William 1644-1718........... **LC 25**
See also DLB 24

Pepys, Samuel
1633-1703 ..... **LC 11; DA; DAB; DAC;**
DAM MST; WLC
See also CDBLB 1660-1789; DLB 101

Percy, Walker
1916-1990 .... **CLC 2, 3, 6, 8, 14, 18, 47,**
65; DAM NOV, POP
See also CA 1-4R; 131; CANR 1, 23;
DLB 2; DLBY 80, 90; MTCW

Perec, Georges 1936-1982 .... **CLC 56**
See also CA 141; DLB 83

Pereda (y Sanchez de Porrua), Jose Maria de
1833-1906 .... **TCLC 16**
See also CA 117

Pereda y Porrua, Jose Maria de
See Pereda (y Sanchez de Porrua), Jose
Maria de

Peregoy, George Weems
See Mencken, H(enry) L(ouis)

Perelman, S(idney) J(oseph)
1904-1979 ...... **CLC 3, 5, 9, 15, 23, 44,**
49; DAM DRAM
See also AITN 1, 2; CA 73-76; 89-92;
CANR 18; DLB 11, 44; MTCW

Peret, Benjamin 1899-1959 .... **TCLC 20**
See also CA 117

Peretz, Isaac Loeb
1851(?)-1915 .... **TCLC 16; SSC 26**
See also CA 109

Peretz, Yitzkhok Leibush
See Peretz, Isaac Loeb

Perez Galdos, Benito 1843-1920 ... **TCLC 27**
See also CA 125; 153; HW

Perrault, Charles 1628-1703 .... **LC 2**
See also MAICYA; SATA 25

Perry, Brighton
See Sherwood, Robert E(mmet)

Perse, St.-John .... **CLC 4, 11, 46**
See also Leger, (Marie-Rene Auguste) Alexis
Saint-Leger

Perutz, Leo 1882-1957........... **TCLC 60**
See also DLB 81

Peseenz, Tulio F.
See Lopez y Fuentes, Gregorio

Pesetsky, Bette 1932-............. **CLC 28**
See also CA 133; DLB 130

Peshkov, Alexei Maximovich 1868-1936
See Gorky, Maxim
See also CA 105; 141; DA; DAC;
DAM DRAM, MST, NOV

Pessoa, Fernando (Antonio Nogueira)
1888-1935 .... **TCLC 27; HLC**
See also CA 125

Peterkin, Julia Mood 1880-1961.... **CLC 31**
See also CA 102; DLB 9

Peters, Joan K(aren) 1945- .... **CLC 39**
See also CA 158

Peters, Robert L(ouis) 1924-........ **CLC 7**
See also CA 13-16R; CAAS 8; DLB 105

Petofi, Sandor 1823-1849....... **NCLC 21**

Petrakis, Harry Mark 1923-........ **CLC 3**
See also CA 9-12R; CANR 4, 30

Petrarch
1304-1374 .... **CMLC 20; DAM POET;**
PC 8

Petrov, Evgeny .... **TCLC 21**
See also Kataev, Evgeny Petrovich

Petry, Ann (Lane) 1908-1997... **CLC 1, 7, 18**
See also BW 1; CA 5-8R; 157; CAAS 6;
CANR 4, 46; CLR 12; DLB 76; JRDA;
MAICYA; MTCW; SATA 5;
SATA-Obit 94

Petursson, Halligrimur 1614-1674 .... **LC 8**

Philips, Katherine 1632-1664....... **LC 30**
See also DLB 131

Philipson, Morris H. 1926-........ **CLC 53**
See also CA 1-4R; CANR 4

Phillips, Caryl
1958-........... **CLC 96; DAM MULT**
See also BW 2; CA 141; DLB 157

Phillips, David Graham
1867-1911 .... **TCLC 44**
See also CA 108; DLB 9, 12

Phillips, Jack
See Sandburg, Carl (August)

Phillips, Jayne Anne
1952-............. **CLC 15, 33; SSC 16**
See also CA 101; CANR 24, 50; DLBY 80;
INT CANR-24; MTCW

Phillips, Richard
See Dick, Philip K(indred)

Phillips, Robert (Schaeffer) 1938-... **CLC 28**
See also CA 17-20R; CAAS 13; CANR 8;
DLB 105

Phillips, Ward
See Lovecraft, H(oward) P(hillips)

Piccolo, Lucio 1901-1969......... **CLC 13**
See also CA 97-100; DLB 114

Pickthall, Marjorie L(owry) C(hristie)
1883-1922 .... **TCLC 21**
See also CA 107; DLB 92

Pico della Mirandola, Giovanni
1463-1494 .... **LC 15**

Piercy, Marge
1936-........ **CLC 3, 6, 14, 18, 27, 62**
See also CA 21-24R; CAAS 1; CANR 13,
43; DLB 120; MTCW

Piers, Robert
See Anthony, Piers

Pieyre de Mandiargues, Andre 1909-1991
See Mandiargues, Andre Pieyre de
See also CA 103; 136; CANR 22

Pilnyak, Boris .... **TCLC 23**
See also Vogau, Boris Andreyevich

Pincherle, Alberto
    1907-1990 ..... **CLC 11, 18; DAM NOV**
    See also Moravia, Alberto
    See also CA 25-28R; 132; CANR 33;
    MTCW

Pinckney, Darryl 1953- .... **CLC 76**
    See also BW 2; CA 143

Pindar 518B.C.-446B.C.... **CMLC 12; PC 19**
    See also DLB 176

Pineda, Cecile 1942-.............. **CLC 39**
    See also CA 118

Pinero, Arthur Wing
    1855-1934 ..... **TCLC 32; DAM DRAM**
    See also CA 110; 153; DLB 10

Pinero, Miguel (Antonio Gomez)
    1946-1988 .... **CLC 4, 55**
    See also CA 61-64; 125; CANR 29; HW

Pinget, Robert 1919- .... **CLC 7, 13, 37**
    See also CA 85-88; DLB 83

Pink Floyd
    See Barrett, (Roger) Syd; Gilmour, David;
    Mason, Nick; Waters, Roger; Wright,
    Rick

Pinkney, Edward 1802-1828 ..... **NCLC 31**

Pinkwater, Daniel Manus 1941- .... **CLC 35**
    See also Pinkwater, Manus
    See also AAYA 1; CA 29-32R; CANR 12,
    38; CLR 4; JRDA; MAICYA; SAAS 3;
    SATA 46, 76

Pinkwater, Manus
    See Pinkwater, Daniel Manus
    See also SATA 8

Pinsky, Robert
    1940- .. **CLC 9, 19, 38, 94; DAM POET**
    See also CA 29-32R; CAAS 4; CANR 58;
    DLBY 82

Pinta, Harold
    See Pinter, Harold

Pinter, Harold
    1930- ..... **CLC 1, 3, 6, 9, 11, 15, 27, 58,**
        73; DA; DAB; DAC; DAM DRAM,
                        MST; WLC
    See also CA 5-8R; CANR 33; CDBLB 1960
    to Present; DLB 13; MTCW

Piozzi, Hester Lynch (Thrale)
    1741-1821 .... **NCLC 57**
    See also DLB 104, 142

Pirandello, Luigi
    1867-1936 ...... **TCLC 4, 29; DA; DAB;**
        DAC; DAM DRAM, MST; DC 5;
                        SSC 22; WLC
    See also CA 104; 153

Pirsig, Robert M(aynard)
    1928- .... **CLC 4, 6, 73; DAM POP**
    See also CA 53-56; CANR 42; MTCW;
    SATA 39

Pisarev, Dmitry Ivanovich
    1840-1868 .... **NCLC 25**

Pix, Mary (Griffith) 1666-1709 .... **LC 8**
    See also DLB 80

Pixerecourt, Guilbert de
    1773-1844 .... **NCLC 39**

Plaatje, Sol(omon) T(shekisho)
    1876-1932 .... **TCLC 73**
    See also BW 2; CA 141

Plaidy, Jean
    See Hibbert, Eleanor Alice Burford

Planche, James Robinson
    1796-1880 .... **NCLC 42**

Plant, Robert 1948- .... **CLC 12**

Plante, David (Robert)
    1940- .... **CLC 7, 23, 38; DAM NOV**
    See also CA 37-40R; CANR 12, 36, 58;
    DLBY 83; INT CANR-12; MTCW

Plath, Sylvia
    1932-1963 ..... **CLC 1, 2, 3, 5, 9, 11, 14,**
        17, 50, 51, 62; DA; DAB; DAC;
        DAM MST, POET; PC 1; WLC
    See also AAYA 13; CA 19-20; CANR 34;
    CAP 2; CDALB 1941-1968; DLB 5, 6,
    152; MTCW

Plato
    428(?)B.C.-348(?)B.C..... **CMLC 8; DA;**
        DAB; DAC; DAM MST; WLCS
    See also DLB 176

Platonov, Andrei .... **TCLC 14**
    See also Klimentov, Andrei Platonovich

Platt, Kin 1911- .... **CLC 26**
    See also AAYA 11; CA 17-20R; CANR 11;
    JRDA; SAAS 17; SATA 21, 86

Plautus c. 251B.C.-184B.C. .... **DC 6**

Plick et Plock
    See Simenon, Georges (Jacques Christian)

Plimpton, George (Ames) 1927-..... **CLC 36**
    See also AITN 1; CA 21-24R; CANR 32;
    MTCW; SATA 10

Pliny the Elder c. 23-79........ **CMLC 23**

Plomer, William Charles Franklin
    1903-1973 .... **CLC 4, 8**
    See also CA 21-22; CANR 34; CAP 2;
    DLB 20, 162; MTCW; SATA 24

Plowman, Piers
    See Kavanagh, Patrick (Joseph)

Plum, J.
    See Wodehouse, P(elham) G(renville)

Plumly, Stanley (Ross) 1939- ...... **CLC 33**
    See also CA 108; 110; DLB 5; INT 110

Plumpe, Friedrich Wilhelm
    1888-1931 .... **TCLC 53**
    See also CA 112

Poe, Edgar Allan
    1809-1849 .... **NCLC 1, 16, 55; DA;**
        DAB; DAC; DAM MST, POET; PC 1;
                        SSC 1, 22; WLC
    See also AAYA 14; CDALB 1640-1865;
    DLB 3, 59, 73, 74; SATA 23

Poet of Titchfield Street, The
    See Pound, Ezra (Weston Loomis)

Pohl, Frederik 1919- ..... **CLC 18; SSC 25**
    See also CA 61-64; CAAS 1; CANR 11, 37;
    DLB 8; INT CANR-11; MTCW;
    SATA 24

Poirier, Louis 1910-
    See Gracq, Julien
    See also CA 122; 126

Poitier, Sidney 1927-.............. **CLC 26**
    See also BW 1; CA 117

Polanski, Roman 1933- .... **CLC 16**
    See also CA 77-80

Poliakoff, Stephen 1952- .... **CLC 38**
    See also CA 106; DLB 13

Police, The
    See Copeland, Stewart (Armstrong);
    Summers, Andrew James; Sumner,
    Gordon Matthew

Polidori, John William
    1795-1821 .... **NCLC 51**
    See also DLB 116

Pollitt, Katha 1949-............... **CLC 28**
    See also CA 120; 122; MTCW

Pollock, (Mary) Sharon
    1936- .... **CLC 50; DAC; DAM DRAM,**
                        MST
    See also CA 141; DLB 60

Polo, Marco 1254-1324 .... **CMLC 15**

Polonsky, Abraham (Lincoln)
    1910- .... **CLC 92**
    See also CA 104; DLB 26; INT 104

Polybius c. 200B.C.-c. 118B.C.... **CMLC 17**
    See also DLB 176

Pomerance, Bernard
    1940- .... **CLC 13; DAM DRAM**
    See also CA 101; CANR 49

Ponge, Francis (Jean Gaston Alfred)
    1899-1988 ..... **CLC 6, 18; DAM POET**
    See also CA 85-88; 126; CANR 40

Pontoppidan, Henrik 1857-1943 ... **TCLC 29**

Poole, Josephine .... **CLC 17**
    See also Helyar, Jane Penelope Josephine
    See also SAAS 2; SATA 5

Popa, Vasko 1922-1991 .... **CLC 19**
    See also CA 112; 148; DLB 181

Pope, Alexander
    1688-1744 ...... **LC 3; DA; DAB; DAC;**
                DAM MST, POET; WLC
    See also CDBLB 1660-1789; DLB 95, 101

Porter, Connie (Rose) 1959(?)- ..... **CLC 70**
    See also BW 2; CA 142; SATA 81

Porter, Gene(va Grace) Stratton
    1863(?)-1924 .... **TCLC 21**
    See also CA 112

Porter, Katherine Anne
    1890-1980 ...... **CLC 1, 3, 7, 10, 13, 15,**
        27, 101; DA; DAB; DAC; DAM MST,
                        NOV; SSC 4
    See also AITN 2; CA 1-4R; 101; CANR 1;
    DLB 4, 9, 102; DLBD 12; DLBY 80;
    MTCW; SATA 39; SATA-Obit 23

Porter, Peter (Neville Frederick)
    1929- .... **CLC 5, 13, 33**
    See also CA 85-88; DLB 40

Porter, William Sydney 1862-1910
    See Henry, O.
    See also CA 104; 131; CDALB 1865-1917;
    DA; DAB; DAC; DAM MST; DLB 12,
    78, 79; MTCW; YABC 2

Portillo (y Pacheco), Jose Lopez
    See Lopez Portillo (y Pacheco), Jose

Post, Melville Davisson
    1869-1930 .... **TCLC 39**
    See also CA 110

Potok, Chaim
1929- .... **CLC 2, 7, 14, 26; DAM NOV**
See also AAYA 15; AITN 1, 2; CA 17-20R;
CANR 19, 35; DLB 28, 152;
INT CANR-19; MTCW; SATA 33

Potter, (Helen) Beatrix 1866-1943
See Webb, (Martha) Beatrice (Potter)
See also MAICYA

Potter, Dennis (Christopher George)
1935-1994 .... **CLC 58, 86**
See also CA 107; 145; CANR 33, 61;
MTCW

Pound, Ezra (Weston Loomis)
1885-1972 ...... **CLC 1, 2, 3, 4, 5, 7, 10,
13, 18, 34, 48, 50; DA; DAB; DAC;
DAM MST, POET; PC 4; WLC**
See also CA 5-8R; 37-40R; CANR 40;
CDALB 1917-1929; DLB 4, 45, 63;
DLBD 15; MTCW

Povod, Reinaldo 1959-1994 .... **CLC 44**
See also CA 136; 146

Powell, Adam Clayton, Jr.
1908-1972 .... **CLC 89; BLC;
DAM MULT**
See also BW 1; CA 102; 33-36R

Powell, Anthony (Dymoke)
1905- .... **CLC 1, 3, 7, 9, 10, 31**
See also CA 1-4R; CANR 1, 32;
CDBLB 1945-1960; DLB 15; MTCW

Powell, Dawn 1897-1965 .... **CLC 66**
See also CA 5-8R

Powell, Padgett 1952-............ **CLC 34**
See also CA 126

Power, Susan.................... **CLC 91**

Powers, J(ames) F(arl)
1917- .... **CLC 1, 4, 8, 57; SSC 4**
See also CA 1-4R; CANR 2, 61; DLB 130;
MTCW

Powers, John J(ames) 1945-
See Powers, John R.
See also CA 69-72

Powers, John R. .... **CLC 66**
See also Powers, John J(ames)

Powers, Richard (S.) 1957- .... **CLC 93**
See also CA 148

Pownall, David 1938-............. **CLC 10**
See also CA 89-92; CAAS 18; CANR 49;
DLB 14

Powys, John Cowper
1872-1963 .... **CLC 7, 9, 15, 46**
See also CA 85-88; DLB 15; MTCW

Powys, T(heodore) F(rancis)
1875-1953 .... **TCLC 9**
See also CA 106; DLB 36, 162

Prager, Emily 1952-.............. **CLC 56**

Pratt, E(dwin) J(ohn)
1883(?)-1964 .... **CLC 19; DAC;
DAM POET**
See also CA 141; 93-96; DLB 92

Premchand...................... **TCLC 21**
See also Srivastava, Dhanpat Rai

Preussler, Otfried 1923-........... **CLC 17**
See also CA 77-80; SATA 24

Prevert, Jacques (Henri Marie)
1900-1977 .... **CLC 15**
See also CA 77-80; 69-72; CANR 29, 61;
MTCW; SATA-Obit 30

Prevost, Abbe (Antoine Francois)
1697-1763 .... **LC 1**

Price, (Edward) Reynolds
1933- .... **CLC 3, 6, 13, 43, 50, 63;
DAM NOV; SSC 22**
See also CA 1-4R; CANR 1, 37, 57; DLB 2;
INT CANR-37

Price, Richard 1949- .... **CLC 6, 12**
See also CA 49-52; CANR 3; DLBY 81

Prichard, Katharine Susannah
1883-1969 .... **CLC 46**
See also CA 11-12; CANR 33; CAP 1;
MTCW; SATA 66

Priestley, J(ohn) B(oynton)
1894-1984 .... **CLC 2, 5, 9, 34;
DAM DRAM, NOV**
See also CA 9-12R; 113; CANR 33;
CDBLB 1914-1945; DLB 10, 34, 77, 100,
139; DLBY 84; MTCW

Prince 1958(?)- .... **CLC 35**

Prince, F(rank) T(empleton) 1912- ... **CLC 22**
See also CA 101; CANR 43; DLB 20

Prince Kropotkin
See Kropotkin, Peter (Alekseievich)

Prior, Matthew 1664-1721.......... **LC 4**
See also DLB 95

Pritchard, William H(arrison)
1932- .... **CLC 34**
See also CA 65-68; CANR 23; DLB 111

Pritchett, V(ictor) S(awdon)
1900-1997 .... **CLC 5, 13, 15, 41;
DAM NOV; SSC 14**
See also CA 61-64; 157; CANR 31;
DLB 15, 139; MTCW

Private 19022
See Manning, Frederic

Probst, Mark 1925- .... **CLC 59**
See also CA 130

Prokosch, Frederic 1908-1989.... **CLC 4, 48**
See also CA 73-76; 128; DLB 48

Prophet, The
See Dreiser, Theodore (Herman Albert)

Prose, Francine 1947-............. **CLC 45**
See also CA 109; 112; CANR 46

Proudhon
See Cunha, Euclides (Rodrigues Pimenta) da

Proulx, E. Annie 1935- .... **CLC 81**

**Proust, (Valentin-Louis-George-Eugene-)
Marcel**
1871-1922 .... **TCLC 7, 13, 33; DA;
DAB; DAC; DAM MST, NOV; WLC**
See also CA 104; 120; DLB 65; MTCW

Prowler, Harley
See Masters, Edgar Lee

Prus, Boleslaw 1845-1912 .... **TCLC 48**

Pryor, Richard (Franklin Lenox Thomas)
1940- .... **CLC 26**
See also CA 122

Przybyszewski, Stanislaw
1868-1927 .... **TCLC 36**
See also DLB 66

Pteleon
See Grieve, C(hristopher) M(urray)
See also DAM POET

Puckett, Lute
See Masters, Edgar Lee

Puig, Manuel
1932-1990 .... **CLC 3, 5, 10, 28, 65;
DAM MULT; HLC**
See also CA 45-48; CANR 2, 32; DLB 113;
HW; MTCW

Purdy, Al(fred Wellington)
1918- .... **CLC 3, 6, 14, 50; DAC;
DAM MST, POET**
See also CA 81-84; CAAS 17; CANR 42;
DLB 88

Purdy, James (Amos)
1923- .... **CLC 2, 4, 10, 28, 52**
See also CA 33-36R; CAAS 1; CANR 19,
51; DLB 2; INT CANR-19; MTCW

Pure, Simon
See Swinnerton, Frank Arthur

Pushkin, Alexander (Sergeyevich)
1799-1837 ..... **NCLC 3, 27; DA; DAB;
DAC; DAM DRAM, MST, POET;
PC 10; SSC 27; WLC**
See also SATA 61

P'u Sung-ling 1640-1715 .... **LC 3**

Putnam, Arthur Lee
See Alger, Horatio, Jr.

Puzo, Mario
1920- ..... **CLC 1, 2, 6, 36; DAM NOV,
POP**
See also CA 65-68; CANR 4, 42; DLB 6;
MTCW

Pygge, Edward
See Barnes, Julian (Patrick)

Pyle, Ernest Taylor 1900-1945
See Pyle, Ernie
See also CA 115

Pyle, Ernie 1900-1945 .... **TCLC 75**
See also Pyle, Ernest Taylor
See also DLB 29

Pym, Barbara (Mary Crampton)
1913-1980 .... **CLC 13, 19, 37**
See also CA 13-14; 97-100; CANR 13, 34;
CAP 1; DLB 14; DLBY 87; MTCW

Pynchon, Thomas (Ruggles, Jr.)
1937- ..... **CLC 2, 3, 6, 9, 11, 18, 33, 62,
72; DA; DAB; DAC; DAM MST, NOV,
POP; SSC 14; WLC**
See also BEST 90:2; CA 17-20R; CANR 22,
46; DLB 2, 173; MTCW

Pythagoras
c. 570B.C.-c. 500B.C......... **CMLC 22**
See also DLB 176

Qian Zhongshu
See Ch'ien Chung-shu

Qroll
See Dagerman, Stig (Halvard)

Quarrington, Paul (Lewis) 1953-.... **CLC 65**
See also CA 129

Quasimodo, Salvatore 1901-1968 ... **CLC 10**
See also CA 13-16; 25-28R; CAP 1;
DLB 114; MTCW

Quay, Stephen 1947- .... **CLC 95**

Reid, Desmond
See Moorcock, Michael (John)

Reid Banks, Lynne 1929-
See Banks, Lynne Reid
See also CA 1-4R; CANR 6, 22, 38;
CLR 24; JRDA; MAICYA; SATA 22, 75

Reilly, William K.
See Creasey, John

Reiner, Max
See Caldwell, (Janet Miriam) Taylor
(Holland)

Reis, Ricardo
See Pessoa, Fernando (Antonio Nogueira)

Remarque, Erich Maria
1898-1970 .... **CLC 21; DA; DAB; DAC;**
DAM MST, NOV
See also CA 77-80; 29-32R; DLB 56;
MTCW

Remizov, A.
See Remizov, Aleksei (Mikhailovich)

Remizov, A. M.
See Remizov, Aleksei (Mikhailovich)

Remizov, Aleksei (Mikhailovich)
1877-1957 .... **TCLC 27**
See also CA 125; 133

Renan, Joseph Ernest
1823-1892 .... **NCLC 26**

Renard, Jules 1864-1910 .... **TCLC 17**
See also CA 117

Renault, Mary .... **CLC 3, 11, 17**
See also Challans, Mary
See also DLBY 83

Rendell, Ruth (Barbara)
1930- .... **CLC 28, 48; DAM POP**
See also Vine, Barbara
See also CA 109; CANR 32, 52; DLB 87;
INT CANR-32; MTCW

Renoir, Jean 1894-1979 .... **CLC 20**
See also CA 129; 85-88

Resnais, Alain 1922- .... **CLC 16**

Reverdy, Pierre 1889-1960 .... **CLC 53**
See also CA 97-100; 89-92

Rexroth, Kenneth
1905-1982 ...... **CLC 1, 2, 6, 11, 22, 49;**
DAM POET
See also CA 5-8R; 107; CANR 14, 34;
CDALB 1941-1968; DLB 16, 48, 165;
DLBY 82; INT CANR-14; MTCW

Reyes, Alfonso 1889-1959 .... **TCLC 33**
See also CA 131; HW

Reyes y Basoalto, Ricardo Eliecer Neftali
See Neruda, Pablo

Reymont, Wladyslaw (Stanislaw)
1868(?)-1925 .... **TCLC 5**
See also CA 104

Reynolds, Jonathan 1942- .... **CLC 6, 38**
See also CA 65-68; CANR 28

Reynolds, Joshua 1723-1792 .... **LC 15**
See also DLB 104

Reynolds, Michael Shane 1937- .... **CLC 44**
See also CA 65-68; CANR 9

Reznikoff, Charles 1894-1976 .... **CLC 9**
See also CA 33-36; 61-64; CAP 2; DLB 28,
45

Rezzori (d'Arezzo), Gregor von
1914- .... **CLC 25**
See also CA 122; 136

Rhine, Richard
See Silverstein, Alvin

Rhodes, Eugene Manlove
1869-1934 .... **TCLC 53**

R'hoone
See Balzac, Honore de

Rhys, Jean
1890(?)-1979 .... **CLC 2, 4, 6, 14, 19, 51;**
DAM NOV; SSC 21
See also CA 25-28R; 85-88; CANR 35;
CDBLB 1945-1960; DLB 36, 117, 162;
MTCW

Ribeiro, Darcy 1922-1997 .... **CLC 34**
See also CA 33-36R; 156

Ribeiro, Joao Ubaldo (Osorio Pimentel)
1941- .... **CLC 10, 67**
See also CA 81-84

Ribman, Ronald (Burt) 1932- .... **CLC 7**
See also CA 21-24R; CANR 46

Ricci, Nino 1959- .... **CLC 70**
See also CA 137

Rice, Anne 1941- ..... **CLC 41; DAM POP**
See also AAYA 9; BEST 89:2; CA 65-68;
CANR 12, 36, 53

Rice, Elmer (Leopold)
1892-1967 .... **CLC 7, 49; DAM DRAM**
See also CA 21-22; 25-28R; CAP 2; DLB 4,
7; MTCW

Rice, Tim(othy Miles Bindon)
1944- .... **CLC 21**
See also CA 103; CANR 46

Rich, Adrienne (Cecile)
1929- .... **CLC 3, 6, 7, 11, 18, 36, 73, 76;**
DAM POET; PC 5
See also CA 9-12R; CANR 20, 53; DLB 5,
67; MTCW

Rich, Barbara
See Graves, Robert (von Ranke)

Rich, Robert
See Trumbo, Dalton

Richard, Keith .... **CLC 17**
See also Richards, Keith

Richards, David Adams
1950- .... **CLC 59; DAC**
See also CA 93-96; CANR 60; DLB 53

Richards, I(vor) A(rmstrong)
1893-1979 .... **CLC 14, 24**
See also CA 41-44R; 89-92; CANR 34;
DLB 27

Richards, Keith 1943-
See Richard, Keith
See also CA 107

Richardson, Anne
See Roiphe, Anne (Richardson)

Richardson, Dorothy Miller
1873-1957 .... **TCLC 3**
See also CA 104; DLB 36

Richardson, Ethel Florence (Lindesay)
1870-1946
See Richardson, Henry Handel
See also CA 105

Richardson, Henry Handel .... **TCLC 4**
See also Richardson, Ethel Florence
(Lindesay)

Richardson, John
1796-1852 .... **NCLC 55; DAC**
See also DLB 99

Richardson, Samuel
1689-1761 ...... **LC 1; DA; DAB; DAC;**
DAM MST, NOV; WLC
See also CDBLB 1660-1789; DLB 39

Richler, Mordecai
1931- .... **CLC 3, 5, 9, 13, 18, 46, 70;**
DAC; DAM MST, NOV
See also AITN 1; CA 65-68; CANR 31;
CLR 17; DLB 53; MAICYA; MTCW;
SATA 44; SATA-Brief 27

Richter, Conrad (Michael)
1890-1968 .... **CLC 30**
See also AAYA 21; CA 5-8R; 25-28R;
CANR 23; DLB 9; MTCW; SATA 3

Ricostranza, Tom
See Ellis, Trey

Riddell, J. H. 1832-1906 .... **TCLC 40**

Riding, Laura .... **CLC 3, 7**
See also Jackson, Laura (Riding)

Riefenstahl, Berta Helene Amalia 1902-
See Riefenstahl, Leni
See also CA 108

Riefenstahl, Leni .... **CLC 16**
See also Riefenstahl, Berta Helene Amalia

Riffe, Ernest
See Bergman, (Ernst) Ingmar

Riggs, (Rolla) Lynn
1899-1954 ..... **TCLC 56; DAM MULT**
See also CA 144; DLB 175; NNAL

Riley, James Whitcomb
1849-1916 ...... **TCLC 51; DAM POET**
See also CA 118; 137; MAICYA; SATA 17

Riley, Tex
See Creasey, John

Rilke, Rainer Maria
1875-1926 .... **TCLC 1, 6, 19;**
DAM POET; PC 2
See also CA 104; 132; DLB 81; MTCW

Rimbaud, (Jean Nicolas) Arthur
1854-1891 ..... **NCLC 4, 35; DA; DAB;**
DAC; DAM MST, POET; PC 3; WLC

Rinehart, Mary Roberts
1876-1958 .... **TCLC 52**
See also CA 108

Ringmaster, The
See Mencken, H(enry) L(ouis)

Ringwood, Gwen(dolyn Margaret) Pharis
1910-1984 .... **CLC 48**
See also CA 148; 112; DLB 88

Rio, Michel 19(?)- .... **CLC 43**

Ritsos, Giannes
See Ritsos, Yannis

Ritsos, Yannis 1909-1990 ..... **CLC 6, 13, 31**
See also CA 77-80; 133; CANR 39, 61;
MTCW

Ritter, Erika 1948(?)- .... **CLC 52**

Rivera, Jose Eustasio 1889-1928... **TCLC 35**
See also HW

Rivers, Conrad Kent 1933-1968...... **CLC 1**
See also BW 1; CA 85-88; DLB 41

Rivers, Elfrida
See Bradley, Marion Zimmer

Riverside, John
See Heinlein, Robert A(nson)

Rizal, Jose 1861-1896.......... **NCLC 27**

Roa Bastos, Augusto (Antonio)
1917-..... **CLC 45; DAM MULT; HLC**
See also CA 131; DLB 113; HW

Robbe-Grillet, Alain
1922-...... **CLC 1, 2, 4, 6, 8, 10, 14, 43**
See also CA 9-12R; CANR 33; DLB 83;
MTCW

Robbins, Harold
1916-............ **CLC 5; DAM NOV**
See also CA 73-76; CANR 26, 54; MTCW

Robbins, Thomas Eugene 1936-
See Robbins, Tom
See also CA 81-84; CANR 29, 59;
DAM NOV, POP; MTCW

Robbins, Tom................ **CLC 9, 32, 64**
See also Robbins, Thomas Eugene
See also BEST 90:3; DLBY 80

Robbins, Trina 1938-............. **CLC 21**
See also CA 128

Roberts, Charles G(eorge) D(ouglas)
1860-1943 .... **TCLC 8**
See also CA 105; CLR 33; DLB 92;
SATA 88; SATA-Brief 29

Roberts, Elizabeth Madox
1886-1941 .... **TCLC 68**
See also CA 111; DLB 9, 54, 102;
SATA 33; SATA-Brief 27

Roberts, Kate 1891-1985 .... **CLC 15**
See also CA 107; 116

Roberts, Keith (John Kingston)
1935-....................... **CLC 14**
See also CA 25-28R; CANR 46

Roberts, Kenneth (Lewis)
1885-1957 .... **TCLC 23**
See also CA 109; DLB 9

Roberts, Michele (B.) 1949-........ **CLC 48**
See also CA 115; CANR 58

Robertson, Ellis
See Ellison, Harlan (Jay); Silverberg, Robert

Robertson, Thomas William
1829-1871 .... **NCLC 35; DAM DRAM**

Robeson, Kenneth
See Dent, Lester

Robinson, Edwin Arlington
1869-1935 .... **TCLC 5; DA; DAC;**
DAM MST, POET; PC 1
See also CA 104; 133; CDALB 1865-1917;
DLB 54; MTCW

Robinson, Henry Crabb
1775-1867 .... **NCLC 15**
See also DLB 107

Robinson, Jill 1936-............. **CLC 10**
See also CA 102; INT 102

Robinson, Kim Stanley 1952- ...... **CLC 34**
See also CA 126

Robinson, Lloyd
See Silverberg, Robert

Robinson, Marilynne 1944-........ **CLC 25**
See also CA 116

Robinson, Smokey................. **CLC 21**
See also Robinson, William, Jr.

Robinson, William, Jr. 1940-
See Robinson, Smokey
See also CA 116

Robison, Mary 1949-.......... **CLC 42, 98**
See also CA 113; 116; DLB 130; INT 116

Rod, Edouard 1857-1910 .... **TCLC 52**

Roddenberry, Eugene Wesley 1921-1991
See Roddenberry, Gene
See also CA 110; 135; CANR 37; SATA 45;
SATA-Obit 69

Roddenberry, Gene .... **CLC 17**
See also Roddenberry, Eugene Wesley
See also AAYA 5; SATA-Obit 69

Rodgers, Mary 1931-............. **CLC 12**
See also CA 49-52; CANR 8, 55; CLR 20;
INT CANR-8; JRDA; MAICYA;
SATA 8

Rodgers, W(illiam) R(obert)
1909-1969 .... **CLC 7**
See also CA 85-88; DLB 20

Rodman, Eric
See Silverberg, Robert

Rodman, Howard 1920(?)-1985..... **CLC 65**
See also CA 118

Rodman, Maia
See Wojciechowska, Maia (Teresa)

Rodriguez, Claudio 1934-.......... **CLC 10**
See also DLB 134

Roelvaag, O(le) E(dvart)
1876-1931 .... **TCLC 17**
See also CA 117; DLB 9

Roethke, Theodore (Huebner)
1908-1963 ...... **CLC 1, 3, 8, 11, 19, 46,**
101; DAM POET; PC 15
See also CA 81-84; CABS 2;
CDALB 1941-1968; DLB 5; MTCW

Rogers, Thomas Hunter 1927- ..... **CLC 57**
See also CA 89-92; INT 89-92

Rogers, Will(iam Penn Adair)
1879-1935 ... **TCLC 8, 71; DAM MULT**
See also CA 105; 144; DLB 11; NNAL

Rogin, Gilbert 1929-............. **CLC 18**
See also CA 65-68; CANR 15

Rohan, Koda .... **TCLC 22**
See also Koda Shigeyuki

Rohlfs, Anna Katharine Green
See Green, Anna Katharine

Rohmer, Eric..................... **CLC 16**
See also Scherer, Jean-Marie Maurice

Rohmer, Sax .... **TCLC 28**
See also Ward, Arthur Henry Sarsfield
See also DLB 70

Roiphe, Anne (Richardson)
1935-..................... **CLC 3, 9**
See also CA 89-92; CANR 45; DLBY 80;
INT 89-92

Rojas, Fernando de 1465-1541 ..... **LC 23**

Rolfe, Frederick (William Serafino Austin
Lewis Mary) 1860-1913...... **TCLC 12**
See also CA 107; DLB 34, 156

Rolland, Romain 1866-1944....... **TCLC 23**
See also CA 118; DLB 65

Rolle, Richard c. 1300-c. 1349 ... **CMLC 21**
See also DLB 146

Rolvaag, O(le) E(dvart)
See Roelvaag, O(le) E(dvart)

Romain Arnaud, Saint
See Aragon, Louis

Romains, Jules 1885-1972.......... **CLC 7**
See also CA 85-88; CANR 34; DLB 65;
MTCW

Romero, Jose Ruben 1890-1952 ... **TCLC 14**
See also CA 114; 131; HW

Ronsard, Pierre de
1524-1585 .... **LC 6; PC 11**

Rooke, Leon
1934-.......... **CLC 25, 34; DAM POP**
See also CA 25-28R; CANR 23, 53

Roosevelt, Theodore 1858-1919.... **TCLC 69**
See also CA 115; DLB 47

Roper, William 1498-1578.......... **LC 10**

Roquelaure, A. N.
See Rice, Anne

Rosa, Joao Guimaraes 1908-1967... **CLC 23**
See also CA 89-92; DLB 113

Rose, Wendy
1948- .... **CLC 85; DAM MULT; PC 13**
See also CA 53-56; CANR 5, 51; DLB 175;
NNAL; SATA 12

Rosen, Richard (Dean) 1949-....... **CLC 39**
See also CA 77-80; INT CANR-30

Rosenberg, Isaac 1890-1918....... **TCLC 12**
See also CA 107; DLB 20

Rosenblatt, Joe .... **CLC 15**
See also Rosenblatt, Joseph

Rosenblatt, Joseph 1933-
See Rosenblatt, Joe
See also CA 89-92; INT 89-92

Rosenfeld, Samuel 1896-1963
See Tzara, Tristan
See also CA 89-92

Rosenstock, Sami
See Tzara, Tristan

Rosenstock, Samuel
See Tzara, Tristan

Rosenthal, M(acha) L(ouis)
1917-1996 .... **CLC 28**
See also CA 1-4R; 152; CAAS 6; CANR 4,
51; DLB 5; SATA 59

Ross, Barnaby
See Dannay, Frederic

Ross, Bernard L.
See Follett, Ken(neth Martin)

Ross, J. H.
See Lawrence, T(homas) E(dward)

Ross, Martin
See Martin, Violet Florence
See also DLB 135

Ross, (James) Sinclair
1908- ...... **CLC 13; DAC; DAM MST;**
SSC 24
See also CA 73-76; DLB 88

Rossetti, Christina (Georgina)
1830-1894 .... **NCLC 2, 50; DA; DAB; DAC; DAM MST, POET; PC 7; WLC**
See also DLB 35, 163; MAICYA; SATA 20

Rossetti, Dante Gabriel
1828-1882 .... **NCLC 4; DA; DAB; DAC; DAM MST, POET; WLC**
See also CDBLB 1832-1890; DLB 35

Rossner, Judith (Perelman)
1935- .... **CLC 6, 9, 29**
See also AITN 2; BEST 90:3; CA 17-20R; CANR 18, 51; DLB 6; INT CANR-18; MTCW

Rostand, Edmond (Eugene Alexis)
1868-1918 ..... **TCLC 6, 37; DA; DAB; DAC; DAM DRAM, MST**
See also CA 104; 126; MTCW

Roth, Henry 1906-1995 ... **CLC 2, 6, 11, 104**
See also CA 11-12; 149; CANR 38; CAP 1; DLB 28; MTCW

Roth, Philip (Milton)
1933- ...... **CLC 1, 2, 3, 4, 6, 9, 15, 22, 31, 47, 66, 86; DA; DAB; DAC; DAM MST, NOV, POP; SSC 26; WLC**
See also BEST 90:3; CA 1-4R; CANR 1, 22, 36, 55; CDALB 1968-1988; DLB 2, 28, 173; DLBY 82; MTCW

Rothenberg, Jerome 1931- .... **CLC 6, 57**
See also CA 45-48; CANR 1; DLB 5

Roumain, Jacques (Jean Baptiste)
1907-1944 .... **TCLC 19; BLC; DAM MULT**
See also BW 1; CA 117; 125

Rourke, Constance (Mayfield)
1885-1941 .... **TCLC 12**
See also CA 107; YABC 1

Rousseau, Jean-Baptiste 1671-1741 ... **LC 9**

Rousseau, Jean-Jacques
1712-1778 .... **LC 14, 36; DA; DAB; DAC; DAM MST; WLC**

Roussel, Raymond 1877-1933 ..... **TCLC 20**
See also CA 117

Rovit, Earl (Herbert) 1927- .... **CLC 7**
See also CA 5-8R; CANR 12

Rowe, Nicholas 1674-1718 .... **LC 8**
See also DLB 84

Rowley, Ames Dorrance
See Lovecraft, H(oward) P(hillips)

Rowson, Susanna Haswell
1762(?)-1824 .... **NCLC 5**
See also DLB 37

Roy, Gabrielle
1909-1983 .... **CLC 10, 14; DAB; DAC; DAM MST**
See also CA 53-56; 110; CANR 5, 61; DLB 68; MTCW

Rozewicz, Tadeusz
1921- .... **CLC 9, 23; DAM POET**
See also CA 108; CANR 36; MTCW

Ruark, Gibbons 1941- .... **CLC 3**
See also CA 33-36R; CAAS 23; CANR 14, 31, 57; DLB 120

Rubens, Bernice (Ruth) 1923- ... **CLC 19, 31**
See also CA 25-28R; CANR 33; DLB 14; MTCW

Rubin, Harold
See Robbins, Harold

Rudkin, (James) David 1936- ...... **CLC 14**
See also CA 89-92; DLB 13

Rudnik, Raphael 1933- .... **CLC 7**
See also CA 29-32R

Ruffian, M.
See Hasek, Jaroslav (Matej Frantisek)

Ruiz, Jose Martinez .... **CLC 11**
See also Martinez Ruiz, Jose

Rukeyser, Muriel
1913-1980 .... **CLC 6, 10, 15, 27; DAM POET; PC 12**
See also CA 5-8R; 93-96; CANR 26, 60; DLB 48; MTCW; SATA-Obit 22

Rule, Jane (Vance) 1931- .... **CLC 27**
See also CA 25-28R; CAAS 18; CANR 12; DLB 60

Rulfo, Juan
1918-1986 .... **CLC 8, 80; DAM MULT; HLC; SSC 25**
See also CA 85-88; 118; CANR 26; DLB 113; HW; MTCW

Rumi, Jalal al-Din 1297-1373 .... **CMLC 20**

Runeberg, Johan 1804-1877 ...... **NCLC 41**

Runyon, (Alfred) Damon
1884(?)-1946 .... **TCLC 10**
See also CA 107; DLB 11, 86, 171

Rush, Norman 1933- .... **CLC 44**
See also CA 121; 126; INT 126

Rushdie, (Ahmed) Salman
1947- .... **CLC 23, 31, 55, 100; DAB; DAC; DAM MST, NOV, POP; WLCS**
See also BEST 89:3; CA 108; 111; CANR 33, 56; INT 111; MTCW

Rushforth, Peter (Scott) 1945- ..... **CLC 19**
See also CA 101

Ruskin, John 1819-1900 .... **TCLC 63**
See also CA 114; 129; CDBLB 1832-1890; DLB 55, 163; SATA 24

Russ, Joanna 1937- .... **CLC 15**
See also CA 25-28R; CANR 11, 31; DLB 8; MTCW

Russell, George William 1867-1935
See Baker, Jean H.
See also CA 104; 153; CDBLB 1890-1914; DAM POET

Russell, (Henry) Ken(neth Alfred)
1927- .... **CLC 16**
See also CA 105

Russell, Willy 1947- .... **CLC 60**

Rutherford, Mark .... **TCLC 25**
See also White, William Hale
See also DLB 18

Ruyslinck, Ward 1929- .... **CLC 14**
See also Belser, Reimond Karel Maria de

Ryan, Cornelius (John) 1920-1974 ... **CLC 7**
See also CA 69-72; 53-56; CANR 38

Ryan, Michael 1946- .... **CLC 65**
See also CA 49-52; DLBY 82

Ryan, Tim
See Dent, Lester

Rybakov, Anatoli (Naumovich)
1911- .... **CLC 23, 53**
See also CA 126; 135; SATA 79

Ryder, Jonathan
See Ludlum, Robert

Ryga, George
1932-1987 .. **CLC 14; DAC; DAM MST**
See also CA 101; 124; CANR 43; DLB 60

S. H.
See Hartmann, Sadakichi

S. S.
See Sassoon, Siegfried (Lorraine)

Saba, Umberto 1883-1957 .... **TCLC 33**
See also CA 144; DLB 114

Sabatini, Rafael 1875-1950 .... **TCLC 47**

Sabato, Ernesto (R.)
1911- .... **CLC 10, 23; DAM MULT; HLC**
See also CA 97-100; CANR 32; DLB 145; HW; MTCW

Sacastru, Martin
See Bioy Casares, Adolfo

Sacher-Masoch, Leopold von
1836(?)-1895 .... **NCLC 31**

Sachs, Marilyn (Stickle) 1927- ..... **CLC 35**
See also AAYA 2; CA 17-20R; CANR 13, 47; CLR 2; JRDA; MAICYA; SAAS 2; SATA 3, 68

Sachs, Nelly 1891-1970 .... **CLC 14, 98**
See also CA 17-18; 25-28R; CAP 2

Sackler, Howard (Oliver)
1929-1982 .... **CLC 14**
See also CA 61-64; 108; CANR 30; DLB 7

Sacks, Oliver (Wolf) 1933- .... **CLC 67**
See also CA 53-56; CANR 28, 50; INT CANR-28; MTCW

Sadakichi
See Hartmann, Sadakichi

Sade, Donatien Alphonse Francois Comte
1740-1814 .... **NCLC 47**

Sadoff, Ira 1945- .... **CLC 9**
See also CA 53-56; CANR 5, 21; DLB 120

Saetone
See Camus, Albert

Safire, William 1929- .... **CLC 10**
See also CA 17-20R; CANR 31, 54

Sagan, Carl (Edward) 1934-1996.... **CLC 30**
See also AAYA 2; CA 25-28R; 155; CANR 11, 36; MTCW; SATA 58; SATA-Obit 94

Sagan, Francoise .... **CLC 3, 6, 9, 17, 36**
See also Quoirez, Francoise
See also DLB 83

Sahgal, Nayantara (Pandit) 1927-... **CLC 41**
See also CA 9-12R; CANR 11

Saint, H(arry) F. 1941- .... **CLC 50**
See also CA 127

St. Aubin de Teran, Lisa 1953-
See Teran, Lisa St. Aubin de
See also CA 118; 126; INT 126

Sainte-Beuve, Charles Augustin
1804-1869 .... **NCLC 5**

Saint-Exupery, Antoine (Jean Baptiste Marie Roger) de
1900-1944 .... **TCLC 2, 56; DAM NOV; WLC**
See also CA 108; 132; CLR 10; DLB 72; MAICYA; MTCW; SATA 20

St. John, David
See Hunt, E(verette) Howard, (Jr.)

Saint-John Perse
See Leger, (Marie-Rene Auguste) Alexis Saint-Leger

Saintsbury, George (Edward Bateman)
1845-1933 .... **TCLC 31**
See also DLB 57, 149

Sait Faik .... **TCLC 23**
See also Abasiyanik, Sait Faik

Saki .... **TCLC 3; SSC 12**
See also Munro, H(ector) H(ugh)

Sala, George Augustus .... **NCLC 46**

Salama, Hannu 1936- .... **CLC 18**

Salamanca, J(ack) R(ichard)
1922- .... **CLC 4, 15**
See also CA 25-28R

Sale, J. Kirkpatrick
See Sale, Kirkpatrick

Sale, Kirkpatrick 1937- .... **CLC 68**
See also CA 13-16R; CANR 10

Salinas, Luis Omar
1937- ..... **CLC 90; DAM MULT; HLC**
See also CA 131; DLB 82; HW

Salinas (y Serrano), Pedro
1891(?)-1951 .... **TCLC 17**
See also CA 117; DLB 134

Salinger, J(erome) D(avid)
1919- ...... **CLC 1, 3, 8, 12, 55, 56; DA; DAB; DAC; DAM MST, NOV, POP; SSC 2, 28; WLC**
See also AAYA 2; CA 5-8R; CANR 39; CDALB 1941-1968; CLR 18; DLB 2, 102, 173; MAICYA; MTCW; SATA 67

Salisbury, John
See Caute, David

Salter, James 1925- .... **CLC 7, 52, 59**
See also CA 73-76; DLB 130

Saltus, Edgar (Everton)
1855-1921 .... **TCLC 8**
See also CA 105

Saltykov, Mikhail Evgrafovich
1826-1889 .... **NCLC 16**

Samarakis, Antonis 1919- .... **CLC 5**
See also CA 25-28R; CAAS 16; CANR 36

Sanchez, Florencio 1875-1910 ..... **TCLC 37**
See also CA 153; HW

Sanchez, Luis Rafael 1936- .... **CLC 23**
See also CA 128; DLB 145; HW

Sanchez, Sonia
1934- ...... **CLC 5; BLC; DAM MULT; PC 9**
See also BW 2; CA 33-36R; CANR 24, 49; CLR 18; DLB 41; DLBD 8; MAICYA; MTCW; SATA 22

Sand, George
1804-1876 .... **NCLC 2, 42, 57; DA; DAB; DAC; DAM MST, NOV; WLC**
See also DLB 119

Sandburg, Carl (August)
1878-1967 .... **CLC 1, 4, 10, 15, 35; DA; DAB; DAC; DAM MST, POET; PC 2; WLC**
See also CA 5-8R; 25-28R; CANR 35; CDALB 1865-1917; DLB 17, 54; MAICYA; MTCW; SATA 8

Sandburg, Charles
See Sandburg, Carl (August)

Sandburg, Charles A.
See Sandburg, Carl (August)

Sanders, (James) Ed(ward) 1939- ... **CLC 53**
See also CA 13-16R; CAAS 21; CANR 13, 44; DLB 16

Sanders, Lawrence
1920- .... **CLC 41; DAM POP**
See also BEST 89:4; CA 81-84; CANR 33; MTCW

Sanders, Noah
See Blount, Roy (Alton), Jr.

Sanders, Winston P.
See Anderson, Poul (William)

Sandoz, Mari(e Susette)
1896-1966 .... **CLC 28**
See also CA 1-4R; 25-28R; CANR 17; DLB 9; MTCW; SATA 5

Saner, Reg(inald Anthony) 1931- .... **CLC 9**
See also CA 65-68

Sannazaro, Jacopo 1456(?)-1530 ...... **LC 8**

Sansom, William
1912-1976 ...... **CLC 2, 6; DAM NOV; SSC 21**
See also CA 5-8R; 65-68; CANR 42; DLB 139; MTCW

Santayana, George 1863-1952 ..... **TCLC 40**
See also CA 115; DLB 54, 71; DLBD 13

Santiago, Danny .... **CLC 33**
See also James, Daniel (Lewis)
See also DLB 122

Santmyer, Helen Hoover
1895-1986 .... **CLC 33**
See also CA 1-4R; 118; CANR 15, 33; DLBY 84; MTCW

Santoka, Taneda 1882-1940 ...... **TCLC 72**

Santos, Bienvenido N(uqui)
1911-1996 ...... **CLC 22; DAM MULT**
See also CA 101; 151; CANR 19, 46

Sapper .... **TCLC 44**
See also McNeile, Herman Cyril

Sapphire 1950- .... **CLC 99**

Sappho
fl. 6th cent. B.C.- .... **CMLC 3; DAM POET; PC 5**
See also DLB 176

Sarduy, Severo 1937-1993 ...... **CLC 6, 97**
See also CA 89-92; 142; CANR 58; DLB 113; HW

Sargeson, Frank 1903-1982 .... **CLC 31**
See also CA 25-28R; 106; CANR 38

Sarmiento, Felix Ruben Garcia
See Dario, Ruben

Saroyan, William
1908-1981 ..... **CLC 1, 8, 10, 29, 34, 56; DA; DAB; DAC; DAM DRAM, MST, NOV; SSC 21; WLC**
See also CA 5-8R; 103; CANR 30; DLB 7, 9, 86; DLBY 81; MTCW; SATA 23; SATA-Obit 24

Sarraute, Nathalie
1900- .... **CLC 1, 2, 4, 8, 10, 31, 80**
See also CA 9-12R; CANR 23; DLB 83; MTCW

Sarton, (Eleanor) May
1912-1995 .... **CLC 4, 14, 49, 91; DAM POET**
See also CA 1-4R; 149; CANR 1, 34, 55; DLB 48; DLBY 81; INT CANR-34; MTCW; SATA 36; SATA-Obit 86

Sartre, Jean-Paul
1905-1980 .... **CLC 1, 4, 7, 9, 13, 18, 24, 44, 50, 52; DA; DAB; DAC; DAM DRAM, MST, NOV; DC 3; WLC**
See also CA 9-12R; 97-100; CANR 21; DLB 72; MTCW

Sassoon, Siegfried (Lorraine)
1886-1967 .... **CLC 36; DAB; DAM MST, NOV, POET; PC 12**
See also CA 104; 25-28R; CANR 36; DLB 20; MTCW

Satterfield, Charles
See Pohl, Frederik

Saul, John (W. III)
1942- ...... **CLC 46; DAM NOV, POP**
See also AAYA 10; BEST 90:4; CA 81-84; CANR 16, 40

Saunders, Caleb
See Heinlein, Robert A(nson)

Saura (Atares), Carlos 1932- .... **CLC 20**
See also CA 114; 131; HW

Sauser-Hall, Frederic 1887-1961.... **CLC 18**
See also Cendrars, Blaise
See also CA 102; 93-96; CANR 36; MTCW

Saussure, Ferdinand de
1857-1913 .... **TCLC 49**

Savage, Catharine
See Brosman, Catharine Savage

Savage, Thomas 1915- .... **CLC 40**
See also CA 126; 132; CAAS 15; INT 132

Savan, Glenn 19(?)- .... **CLC 50**

Sayers, Dorothy L(eigh)
1893-1957 ..... **TCLC 2, 15; DAM POP**
See also CA 104; 119; CANR 60; CDBLB 1914-1945; DLB 10, 36, 77, 100; MTCW

Sayers, Valerie 1952- .... **CLC 50**
See also CA 134; CANR 61

Sayles, John (Thomas)
1950- .... **CLC 7, 10, 14**
See also CA 57-60; CANR 41; DLB 44

Scammell, Michael 1935- .... **CLC 34**
See also CA 156

Scannell, Vernon 1922- .... **CLC 49**
See also CA 5-8R; CANR 8, 24, 57; DLB 27; SATA 59

Scarlett, Susan
See Streatfeild, (Mary) Noel

Schaeffer, Susan Fromberg
1941- . . . . **CLC 6, 11, 22**
See also CA 49-52; CANR 18; DLB 28;
MTCW; SATA 22

Schary, Jill
See Robinson, Jill

Schell, Jonathan 1943- . . . . **CLC 35**
See also CA 73-76; CANR 12

Schelling, Friedrich Wilhelm Joseph von
1775-1854 . . . . **NCLC 30**
See also DLB 90

Schendel, Arthur van 1874-1946 . . . **TCLC 56**

Scherer, Jean-Marie Maurice 1920-
See Rohmer, Eric
See also CA 110

Schevill, James (Erwin) 1920- . . . . **CLC 7**
See also CA 5-8R; CAAS 12

Schiller, Friedrich
1759-1805 . . . . **NCLC 39; DAM DRAM**
See also DLB 94

Schisgal, Murray (Joseph) 1926- . . . . . **CLC 6**
See also CA 21-24R; CANR 48

Schlee, Ann 1934- . . . . **CLC 35**
See also CA 101; CANR 29; SATA 44;
SATA-Brief 36

Schlegel, August Wilhelm von
1767-1845 . . . . **NCLC 15**
See also DLB 94

Schlegel, Friedrich 1772-1829 . . . . **NCLC 45**
See also DLB 90

Schlegel, Johann Elias (von)
1719(?)-1749 . . . . **LC 5**

Schlesinger, Arthur M(eier), Jr.
1917- . . . . **CLC 84**
See also AITN 1; CA 1-4R; CANR 1, 28,
58; DLB 17; INT CANR-28; MTCW;
SATA 61

Schmidt, Arno (Otto) 1914-1979 . . . . **CLC 56**
See also CA 128; 109; DLB 69

Schmitz, Aron Hector 1861-1928
See Svevo, Italo
See also CA 104; 122; MTCW

Schnackenberg, Gjertrud 1953- . . . . . **CLC 40**
See also CA 116; DLB 120

Schneider, Leonard Alfred 1925-1966
See Bruce, Lenny
See also CA 89-92

Schnitzler, Arthur
1862-1931 . . . . **TCLC 4; SSC 15**
See also CA 104; DLB 81, 118

Schoenberg, Arnold 1874-1951 . . . . **TCLC 75**
See also CA 109

Schonberg, Arnold
See Schoenberg, Arnold

Schopenhauer, Arthur
1788-1860 . . . . **NCLC 51**
See also DLB 90

Schor, Sandra (M.) 1932(?)-1990 . . . **CLC 65**
See also CA 132

Schorer, Mark 1908-1977 . . . . **CLC 9**
See also CA 5-8R; 73-76; CANR 7;
DLB 103

Schrader, Paul (Joseph) 1946- . . . . . . **CLC 26**
See also CA 37-40R; CANR 41; DLB 44

Schreiner, Olive (Emilie Albertina)
1855-1920 . . . . **TCLC 9**
See also CA 105; DLB 18, 156

Schulberg, Budd (Wilson)
1914- . . . . **CLC 7, 48**
See also CA 25-28R; CANR 19; DLB 6, 26,
28; DLBY 81

Schulz, Bruno
1892-1942 . . . . **TCLC 5, 51; SSC 13**
See also CA 115; 123

Schulz, Charles M(onroe) 1922- . . . . **CLC 12**
See also CA 9-12R; CANR 6;
INT CANR-6; SATA 10

Schumacher, E(rnst) F(riedrich)
1911-1977 . . . . **CLC 80**
See also CA 81-84; 73-76; CANR 34

Schuyler, James Marcus
1923-1991 . . . . . **CLC 5, 23; DAM POET**
See also CA 101; 134; DLB 5, 169; INT 101

Schwartz, Delmore (David)
1913-1966 . . . **CLC 2, 4, 10, 45, 87; PC 8**
See also CA 17-18; 25-28R; CANR 35;
CAP 2; DLB 28, 48; MTCW

Schwartz, Ernst
See Ozu, Yasujiro

Schwartz, John Burnham 1965- . . . . **CLC 59**
See also CA 132

Schwartz, Lynne Sharon 1939- . . . . . **CLC 31**
See also CA 103; CANR 44

Schwartz, Muriel A.
See Eliot, T(homas) S(tearns)

Schwarz-Bart, Andre 1928- . . . . **CLC 2, 4**
See also CA 89-92

Schwarz-Bart, Simone 1938- . . . . **CLC 7**
See also BW 2; CA 97-100

Schwob, (Mayer Andre) Marcel
1867-1905 . . . . **TCLC 20**
See also CA 117; DLB 123

Sciascia, Leonardo
1921-1989 . . . . **CLC 8, 9, 41**
See also CA 85-88; 130; CANR 35;
DLB 177; MTCW

Scoppettone, Sandra 1936- . . . . **CLC 26**
See also AAYA 11; CA 5-8R; CANR 41;
SATA 9, 92

Scorsese, Martin 1942- . . . . **CLC 20, 89**
See also CA 110; 114; CANR 46

Scotland, Jay
See Jakes, John (William)

Scott, Duncan Campbell
1862-1947 . . . . **TCLC 6; DAC**
See also CA 104; 153; DLB 92

Scott, Evelyn 1893-1963 . . . . **CLC 43**
See also CA 104; 112; DLB 9, 48

Scott, F(rancis) R(eginald)
1899-1985 . . . . **CLC 22**
See also CA 101; 114; DLB 88; INT 101

Scott, Frank
See Scott, F(rancis) R(eginald)

Scott, Joanna 1960- . . . . **CLC 50**
See also CA 126; CANR 53

Scott, Paul (Mark) 1920-1978 . . . . **CLC 9, 60**
See also CA 81-84; 77-80; CANR 33;
DLB 14; MTCW

Scott, Walter
1771-1832 . . . . . . **NCLC 15; DA; DAB;
DAC; DAM MST, NOV, POET; PC 13;
WLC**
See also AAYA 22; CDBLB 1789-1832;
DLB 93, 107, 116, 144, 159; YABC 2

Scribe, (Augustin) Eugene
1791-1861 . . . . **NCLC 16; DAM DRAM;
DC 5**

Scrum, R.
See Crumb, R(obert)

Scudery, Madeleine de 1607-1701 . . . . . **LC 2**

Scum
See Crumb, R(obert)

Scumbag, Little Bobby
See Crumb, R(obert)

Seabrook, John
See Hubbard, L(afayette) Ron(ald)

Sealy, I. Allan 1951- . . . . **CLC 55**

Search, Alexander
See Pessoa, Fernando (Antonio Nogueira)

Sebastian, Lee
See Silverberg, Robert

Sebastian Owl
See Thompson, Hunter S(tockton)

Sebestyen, Ouida 1924- . . . . **CLC 30**
See also AAYA 8; CA 107; CANR 40;
CLR 17; JRDA; MAICYA; SAAS 10;
SATA 39

Secundus, H. Scriblerus
See Fielding, Henry

Sedges, John
See Buck, Pearl S(ydenstricker)

Sedgwick, Catharine Maria
1789-1867 . . . . **NCLC 19**
See also DLB 1, 74

Seelye, John 1931- . . . . **CLC 7**

Seferiades, Giorgos Stylianou 1900-1971
See Seferis, George
See also CA 5-8R; 33-36R; CANR 5, 36;
MTCW

Seferis, George . . . . **CLC 5, 11**
See also Seferiades, Giorgos Stylianou

Segal, Erich (Wolf)
1937- . . . . **CLC 3, 10; DAM POP**
See also BEST 89:1; CA 25-28R; CANR 20,
36; DLBY 86; INT CANR-20; MTCW

Seger, Bob 1945- . . . . **CLC 35**

Seghers, Anna . . . . **CLC 7**
See also Radvanyi, Netty
See also DLB 69

Seidel, Frederick (Lewis) 1936- . . . . . **CLC 18**
See also CA 13-16R; CANR 8; DLBY 84

Seifert, Jaroslav
1901-1986 . . . . **CLC 34, 44, 93**
See also CA 127; MTCW

Sei Shonagon c. 966-1017(?) . . . . . . **CMLC 6**

Selby, Hubert, Jr.
1928- . . . . **CLC 1, 2, 4, 8; SSC 20**
See also CA 13-16R; CANR 33; DLB 2

Selzer, Richard 1928- . . . . **CLC 74**
See also CA 65-68; CANR 14

Sembene, Ousmane
See Ousmane, Sembene

Shields, David 1956-.............. **CLC 97**
See also CA 124; CANR 48

Shiga, Naoya 1883-1971... **CLC 33; SSC 23**
See also CA 101; 33-36R; DLB 180

Shilts, Randy 1951-1994 .... **CLC 85**
See also AAYA 19; CA 115; 127; 144;
CANR 45; INT 127

Shimazaki, Haruki 1872-1943
See Shimazaki Toson
See also CA 105; 134

Shimazaki Toson 1872-1943 .... **TCLC 5**
See also Shimazaki, Haruki
See also DLB 180

Sholokhov, Mikhail (Aleksandrovich)
1905-1984 .... **CLC 7, 15**
See also CA 101; 112; MTCW;
SATA-Obit 36

Shone, Patric
See Hanley, James

Shreve, Susan Richards 1939-...... **CLC 23**
See also CA 49-52; CAAS 5; CANR 5, 38;
MAICYA; SATA 46, 95; SATA-Brief 41

Shue, Larry
1946-1985 ...... **CLC 52; DAM DRAM**
See also CA 145; 117

Shu-Jen, Chou 1881-1936
See Lu Hsun
See also CA 104

Shulman, Alix Kates 1932- ...... **CLC 2, 10**
See also CA 29-32R; CANR 43; SATA 7

Shuster, Joe 1914- .... **CLC 21**

Shute, Nevil..................... **CLC 30**
See also Norway, Nevil Shute

Shuttle, Penelope (Diane) 1947- ..... **CLC 7**
See also CA 93-96; CANR 39; DLB 14, 40

Sidney, Mary 1561-1621 .... **LC 19, 39**

Sidney, Sir Philip
1554-1586 ...... **LC 19, 39; DA; DAB;**
DAC; DAM MST, POET
See also CDBLB Before 1660; DLB 167

Siegel, Jerome 1914-1996 .... **CLC 21**
See also CA 116; 151

Siegel, Jerry
See Siegel, Jerome

Sienkiewicz, Henryk (Adam Alexander Pius)
1846-1916 .... **TCLC 3**
See also CA 104; 134

Sierra, Gregorio Martinez
See Martinez Sierra, Gregorio

Sierra, Maria (de la O'LeJarraga) Martinez
See Martinez Sierra, Maria (de la
O'LeJarraga)

Sigal, Clancy 1926-................ **CLC 7**
See also CA 1-4R

Sigourney, Lydia Howard (Huntley)
1791-1865 .... **NCLC 21**
See also DLB 1, 42, 73

Siguenza y Gongora, Carlos de
1645-1700 .... **LC 8**

Sigurjonsson, Johann 1880-1919... **TCLC 27**

Sikelianos, Angelos 1884-1951 .... **TCLC 39**

Silkin, Jon 1930- .... **CLC 2, 6, 43**
See also CA 5-8R; CAAS 5; DLB 27

Silko, Leslie (Marmon)
1948-.......... **CLC 23, 74; DA; DAC;**
DAM MST, MULT, POP; WLCS
See also AAYA 14; CA 115; 122;
CANR 45; DLB 143, 175; NNAL

Sillanpaa, Frans Eemil 1888-1964... **CLC 19**
See also CA 129; 93-96; MTCW

Sillitoe, Alan
1928-.......... **CLC 1, 3, 6, 10, 19, 57**
See also AITN 1; CA 9-12R; CAAS 2;
CANR 8, 26, 55; CDBLB 1960 to
Present; DLB 14, 139; MTCW; SATA 61

Silone, Ignazio 1900-1978 .... **CLC 4**
See also CA 25-28; 81-84; CANR 34;
CAP 2; MTCW

Silver, Joan Micklin 1935- .... **CLC 20**
See also CA 114; 121; INT 121

Silver, Nicholas
See Faust, Frederick (Schiller)

Silverberg, Robert
1935-........... **CLC 7; DAM POP**
See also CA 1-4R; CAAS 3; CANR 1, 20,
36; DLB 8; INT CANR-20; MAICYA;
MTCW; SATA 13, 91

Silverstein, Alvin 1933-........... **CLC 17**
See also CA 49-52; CANR 2; CLR 25;
JRDA; MAICYA; SATA 8, 69

Silverstein, Virginia B(arbara Opshelor)
1937-..................... **CLC 17**
See also CA 49-52; CANR 2; CLR 25;
JRDA; MAICYA; SATA 8, 69

Sim, Georges
See Simenon, Georges (Jacques Christian)

Simak, Clifford D(onald)
1904-1988 .... **CLC 1, 55**
See also CA 1-4R; 125; CANR 1, 35;
DLB 8; MTCW; SATA-Obit 56

Simenon, Georges (Jacques Christian)
1903-1989 .... **CLC 1, 2, 3, 8, 18, 47;**
DAM POP
See also CA 85-88; 129; CANR 35;
DLB 72; DLBY 89; MTCW

Simic, Charles
1938-........... **CLC 6, 9, 22, 49, 68;**
DAM POET
See also CA 29-32R; CAAS 4; CANR 12,
33, 52, 61; DLB 105

Simmel, Georg 1858-1918 .... **TCLC 64**
See also CA 157

Simmons, Charles (Paul) 1924-..... **CLC 57**
See also CA 89-92; INT 89-92

Simmons, Dan 1948-... **CLC 44; DAM POP**
See also AAYA 16; CA 138; CANR 53

Simmons, James (Stewart Alexander)
1933-..................... **CLC 43**
See also CA 105; CAAS 21; DLB 40

Simms, William Gilmore
1806-1870 .... **NCLC 3**
See also DLB 3, 30, 59, 73

Simon, Carly 1945-.............. **CLC 26**
See also CA 105

Simon, Claude
1913-.... **CLC 4, 9, 15, 39; DAM NOV**
See also CA 89-92; CANR 33; DLB 83;
MTCW

Simon, (Marvin) Neil
1927-........... **CLC 6, 11, 31, 39, 70;**
DAM DRAM
See also AITN 1; CA 21-24R; CANR 26,
54; DLB 7; MTCW

Simon, Paul (Frederick) 1941(?)- ... **CLC 17**
See also CA 116; 153

Simonon, Paul 1956(?)- .... **CLC 30**

Simpson, Harriette
See Arnow, Harriette (Louisa) Simpson

Simpson, Louis (Aston Marantz)
1923-.... **CLC 4, 7, 9, 32; DAM POET**
See also CA 1-4R; CAAS 4; CANR 1, 61;
DLB 5; MTCW

Simpson, Mona (Elizabeth) 1957-... **CLC 44**
See also CA 122; 135

Simpson, N(orman) F(rederick)
1919-..................... **CLC 29**
See also CA 13-16R; DLB 13

Sinclair, Andrew (Annandale)
1935-..................... **CLC 2, 14**
See also CA 9-12R; CAAS 5; CANR 14, 38;
DLB 14; MTCW

Sinclair, Emil
See Hesse, Hermann

Sinclair, Iain 1943-.............. **CLC 76**
See also CA 132

Sinclair, Iain MacGregor
See Sinclair, Iain

Sinclair, Irene
See Griffith, D(avid Lewelyn) W(ark)

Sinclair, Mary Amelia St. Clair 1865(?)-1946
See Sinclair, May
See also CA 104

Sinclair, May.................. **TCLC 3, 11**
See also Sinclair, Mary Amelia St. Clair
See also DLB 36, 135

Sinclair, Roy
See Griffith, D(avid Lewelyn) W(ark)

Sinclair, Upton (Beall)
1878-1968 ...... **CLC 1, 11, 15, 63; DA;**
DAB; DAC; DAM MST, NOV; WLC
See also CA 5-8R; 25-28R; CANR 7;
CDALB 1929-1941; DLB 9;
INT CANR-7; MTCW; SATA 9

Singer, Isaac
See Singer, Isaac Bashevis

Singer, Isaac Bashevis
1904-1991 .... **CLC 1, 3, 6, 9, 11, 15, 23,**
38, 69; DA; DAB; DAC; DAM MST,
NOV; SSC 3; WLC
See also AITN 1, 2; CA 1-4R; 134;
CANR 1, 39; CDALB 1941-1968; CLR 1;
DLB 6, 28, 52; DLBY 91; JRDA;
MAICYA; MTCW; SATA 3, 27;
SATA-Obit 68

Singer, Israel Joshua 1893-1944... **TCLC 33**

Singh, Khushwant 1915-........... **CLC 11**
See also CA 9-12R; CAAS 9; CANR 6

Singleton, Ann
See Benedict, Ruth (Fulton)

Sinjohn, John
See Galsworthy, John

Sophocles
496(?)B.C.-406(?)B.C..... **CMLC 2; DA; DAB; DAC; DAM DRAM, MST; DC 1; WLCS**
See also DLB 176

Sordello 1189-1269............ **CMLC 15**

Sorel, Julia
See Drexler, Rosalyn

Sorrentino, Gilbert
1929-........... **CLC 3, 7, 14, 22, 40**
See also CA 77-80; CANR 14, 33; DLB 5, 173; DLBY 80; INT CANR-14

Soto, Gary
1952-....... **CLC 32, 80; DAM MULT; HLC**
See also AAYA 10; CA 119; 125; CANR 50; CLR 38; DLB 82; HW; INT 125; JRDA; SATA 80

Soupault, Philippe 1897-1990 ...... **CLC 68**
See also CA 116; 147; 131

Souster, (Holmes) Raymond
1921-... **CLC 5, 14; DAC; DAM POET**
See also CA 13-16R; CAAS 14; CANR 13, 29, 53; DLB 88; SATA 63

Southern, Terry 1924(?)-1995 .... **CLC 7**
See also CA 1-4R; 150; CANR 1, 55; DLB 2

Southey, Robert 1774-1843 .... **NCLC 8**
See also DLB 93, 107, 142; SATA 54

Southworth, Emma Dorothy Eliza Nevitte
1819-1899 .... **NCLC 26**

Souza, Ernest
See Scott, Evelyn

Soyinka, Wole
1934-...... **CLC 3, 5, 14, 36, 44; BLC; DA; DAB; DAC; DAM DRAM, MST, MULT; DC 2; WLC**
See also BW 2; CA 13-16R; CANR 27, 39; DLB 125; MTCW

Spackman, W(illiam) M(ode)
1905-1990 .... **CLC 46**
See also CA 81-84; 132

Spacks, Barry (Bernard) 1931-..... **CLC 14**
See also CA 154; CANR 33; DLB 105

Spanidou, Irini 1946-............. **CLC 44**

Spark, Muriel (Sarah)
1918-..... **CLC 2, 3, 5, 8, 13, 18, 40, 94; DAB; DAC; DAM MST, NOV; SSC 10**
See also CA 5-8R; CANR 12, 36; CDBLB 1945-1960; DLB 15, 139; INT CANR-12; MTCW

Spaulding, Douglas
See Bradbury, Ray (Douglas)

Spaulding, Leonard
See Bradbury, Ray (Douglas)

Spence, J. A. D.
See Eliot, T(homas) S(tearns)

Spencer, Elizabeth 1921-.......... **CLC 22**
See also CA 13-16R; CANR 32; DLB 6; MTCW; SATA 14

Spencer, Leonard G.
See Silverberg, Robert

Spencer, Scott 1945-.............. **CLC 30**
See also CA 113; CANR 51; DLBY 86

Spender, Stephen (Harold)
1909-1995 ...... **CLC 1, 2, 5, 10, 41, 91; DAM POET**
See also CA 9-12R; 149; CANR 31, 54; CDBLB 1945-1960; DLB 20; MTCW

Spengler, Oswald (Arnold Gottfried)
1880-1936 .... **TCLC 25**
See also CA 118

Spenser, Edmund
1552(?)-1599 ...... **LC 5, 39; DA; DAB; DAC; DAM MST, POET; PC 8; WLC**
See also CDBLB Before 1660; DLB 167

Spicer, Jack
1925-1965 .... **CLC 8, 18, 72; DAM POET**
See also CA 85-88; DLB 5, 16

Spiegelman, Art 1948-............ **CLC 76**
See also AAYA 10; CA 125; CANR 41, 55

Spielberg, Peter 1929-............. **CLC 6**
See also CA 5-8R; CANR 4, 48; DLBY 81

Spielberg, Steven 1947-........... **CLC 20**
See also AAYA 8; CA 77-80; CANR 32; SATA 32

Spillane, Frank Morrison 1918-
See Spillane, Mickey
See also CA 25-28R; CANR 28; MTCW; SATA 66

Spillane, Mickey .... **CLC 3, 13**
See also Spillane, Frank Morrison

Spinoza, Benedictus de 1632-1677 .... **LC 9**

Spinrad, Norman (Richard) 1940-... **CLC 46**
See also CA 37-40R; CAAS 19; CANR 20; DLB 8; INT CANR-20

Spitteler, Carl (Friedrich Georg)
1845-1924 .... **TCLC 12**
See also CA 109; DLB 129

Spivack, Kathleen (Romola Drucker)
1938-........................ **CLC 6**
See also CA 49-52

Spoto, Donald 1941-.............. **CLC 39**
See also CA 65-68; CANR 11, 57

Springsteen, Bruce (F.) 1949-...... **CLC 17**
See also CA 111

Spurling, Hilary 1940-............ **CLC 34**
See also CA 104; CANR 25, 52

Spyker, John Howland
See Elman, Richard

Squires, (James) Radcliffe
1917-1993 .... **CLC 51**
See also CA 1-4R; 140; CANR 6, 21

Srivastava, Dhanpat Rai 1880(?)-1936
See Premchand
See also CA 118

Stacy, Donald
See Pohl, Frederik

Stael, Germaine de
See Stael-Holstein, Anne Louise Germaine Necker Baronn
See also DLB 119

Stael-Holstein, Anne Louise Germaine Necker Baronn 1766-1817 .... **NCLC 3**
See also Stael, Germaine de

Stafford, Jean
1915-1979 .... **CLC 4, 7, 19, 68; SSC 26**
See also CA 1-4R; 85-88; CANR 3; DLB 2, 173; MTCW; SATA-Obit 22

Stafford, William (Edgar)
1914-1993 ...**CLC 4, 7, 29; DAM POET**
See also CA 5-8R; 142; CAAS 3; CANR 5, 22; DLB 5; INT CANR-22

Stagnelius, Eric Johan
1793-1823 .... **NCLC 61**

Staines, Trevor
See Brunner, John (Kilian Houston)

Stairs, Gordon
See Austin, Mary (Hunter)

Stannard, Martin 1947-........... **CLC 44**
See also CA 142; DLB 155

Stanton, Elizabeth Cady
1815-1902 .... **TCLC 73**
See also DLB 79

Stanton, Maura 1946-............. **CLC 9**
See also CA 89-92; CANR 15; DLB 120

Stanton, Schuyler
See Baum, L(yman) Frank

Stapledon, (William) Olaf
1886-1950 .... **TCLC 22**
See also CA 111; DLB 15

Starbuck, George (Edwin)
1931-1996 .... **CLC 53; DAM POET**
See also CA 21-24R; 153; CANR 23

Stark, Richard
See Westlake, Donald E(dwin)

Staunton, Schuyler
See Baum, L(yman) Frank

Stead, Christina (Ellen)
1902-1983 .... **CLC 2, 5, 8, 32, 80**
See also CA 13-16R; 109; CANR 33, 40; MTCW

Stead, William Thomas
1849-1912 .... **TCLC 48**

Steele, Richard 1672-1729 .... **LC 18**
See also CDBLB 1660-1789; DLB 84, 101

Steele, Timothy (Reid) 1948-....... **CLC 45**
See also CA 93-96; CANR 16, 50; DLB 120

Steffens, (Joseph) Lincoln
1866-1936 .... **TCLC 20**
See also CA 117

Stegner, Wallace (Earle)
1909-1993 .... **CLC 9, 49, 81; DAM NOV; SSC 27**
See also AITN 1; BEST 90:3; CA 1-4R; 141; CAAS 9; CANR 1, 21, 46; DLB 9; DLBY 93; MTCW

Stein, Gertrude
1874-1946 ...... **TCLC 1, 6, 28, 48; DA; DAB; DAC; DAM MST, NOV, POET; PC 18; WLC**
See also CA 104; 132; CDALB 1917-1929; DLB 4, 54, 86; DLBD 15; MTCW

Steinbeck, John (Ernst)
1902-1968 ...... **CLC 1, 5, 9, 13, 21, 34, 45, 75; DA; DAB; DAC; DAM DRAM, MST, NOV; SSC 11; WLC**
See also AAYA 12; CA 1-4R; 25-28R; CANR 1, 35; CDALB 1929-1941; DLB 7, 9; DLBD 2; MTCW; SATA 9

Steinem, Gloria 1934-. . . . . **CLC 63**
See also CA 53-56; CANR 28, 51; MTCW

Steiner, George
1929- . . . . **CLC 24; DAM NOV**
See also CA 73-76; CANR 31; DLB 67;
MTCW; SATA 62

Steiner, K. Leslie
See Delany, Samuel R(ay, Jr.)

Steiner, Rudolf 1861-1925 . . . . **TCLC 13**
See also CA 107

Stendhal
1783-1842 . . . . **NCLC 23, 46; DA; DAB;**
DAC; DAM MST, NOV; SSC 27; WLC
See also DLB 119

Stephen, Leslie 1832-1904 . . . . **TCLC 23**
See also CA 123; DLB 57, 144

Stephen, Sir Leslie
See Stephen, Leslie

Stephen, Virginia
See Woolf, (Adeline) Virginia

Stephens, James 1882(?)-1950 . . . . . . **TCLC 4**
See also CA 104; DLB 19, 153, 162

Stephens, Reed
See Donaldson, Stephen R.

Steptoe, Lydia
See Barnes, Djuna

Sterchi, Beat 1949- . . . . **CLC 65**

Sterling, Brett
See Bradbury, Ray (Douglas); Hamilton,
Edmond

Sterling, Bruce 1954- . . . . **CLC 72**
See also CA 119; CANR 44

Sterling, George 1869-1926 . . . . **TCLC 20**
See also CA 117; DLB 54

Stern, Gerald 1925- . . . . **CLC 40, 100**
See also CA 81-84; CANR 28; DLB 105

Stern, Richard (Gustave) 1928-. . . **CLC 4, 39**
See also CA 1-4R; CANR 1, 25, 52;
DLBY 87; INT CANR-25

Sternberg, Josef von 1894-1969. . . . . **CLC 20**
See also CA 81-84

Sterne, Laurence
1713-1768 . . . . . . **LC 2; DA; DAB; DAC;**
DAM MST, NOV; WLC
See also CDBLB 1660-1789; DLB 39

Sternheim, (William Adolf) Carl
1878-1942 . . . . **TCLC 8**
See also CA 105; DLB 56, 118

Stevens, Mark 1951- . . . . **CLC 34**
See also CA 122

Stevens, Wallace
1879-1955 . . . . **TCLC 3, 12, 45; DA;**
DAB; DAC; DAM MST, POET; PC 6;
WLC
See also CA 104; 124; CDALB 1929-1941;
DLB 54; MTCW

Stevenson, Anne (Katharine)
1933- . . . . **CLC 7, 33**
See also CA 17-20R; CAAS 9; CANR 9, 33;
DLB 40; MTCW

Stevenson, Robert Louis (Balfour)
1850-1894 . . . . **NCLC 5, 14, 63; DA;**
DAB; DAC; DAM MST, NOV; SSC 11;
WLC
See also CDBLB 1890-1914; CLR 10, 11;
DLB 18, 57, 141, 156, 174; DLBD 13;
JRDA; MAICYA; YABC 2

Stewart, J(ohn) I(nnes) M(ackintosh)
1906-1994 . . . . **CLC 7, 14, 32**
See also CA 85-88; 147; CAAS 3;
CANR 47; MTCW

Stewart, Mary (Florence Elinor)
1916- . . . . **CLC 7, 35; DAB**
See also CA 1-4R; CANR 1, 59; SATA 12

Stewart, Mary Rainbow
See Stewart, Mary (Florence Elinor)

Stifle, June
See Campbell, Maria

Stifter, Adalbert
1805-1868 . . . . **NCLC 41; SSC 28**
See also DLB 133

Still, James 1906- . . . . **CLC 49**
See also CA 65-68; CAAS 17; CANR 10,
26; DLB 9; SATA 29

Sting
See Sumner, Gordon Matthew

Stirling, Arthur
See Sinclair, Upton (Beall)

Stitt, Milan 1941- . . . . **CLC 29**
See also CA 69-72

Stockton, Francis Richard 1834-1902
See Stockton, Frank R.
See also CA 108; 137; MAICYA; SATA 44

Stockton, Frank R. . . . . **TCLC 47**
See also Stockton, Francis Richard
See also DLB 42, 74; DLBD 13;
SATA-Brief 32

Stoddard, Charles
See Kuttner, Henry

Stoker, Abraham 1847-1912
See Stoker, Bram
See also CA 105; DA; DAC; DAM MST,
NOV; SATA 29

Stoker, Bram
1847-1912 . . . . **TCLC 8; DAB; WLC**
See also Stoker, Abraham
See also CA 150; CDBLB 1890-1914;
DLB 36, 70, 178

Stolz, Mary (Slattery) 1920- . . . . **CLC 12**
See also AAYA 8; AITN 1; CA 5-8R;
CANR 13, 41; JRDA; MAICYA;
SAAS 3; SATA 10, 71

Stone, Irving
1903-1989 . . . . **CLC 7; DAM POP**
See also AITN 1; CA 1-4R; 129; CAAS 3;
CANR 1, 23; INT CANR-23; MTCW;
SATA 3; SATA-Obit 64

Stone, Oliver (William) 1946- . . . . . . **CLC 73**
See also AAYA 15; CA 110; CANR 55

Stone, Robert (Anthony)
1937- . . . . **CLC 5, 23, 42**
See also CA 85-88; CANR 23; DLB 152;
INT CANR-23; MTCW

Stone, Zachary
See Follett, Ken(neth Martin)

Stoppard, Tom
1937- . . . . . . **CLC 1, 3, 4, 5, 8, 15, 29, 34,**
63, 91; DA; DAB; DAC; DAM DRAM,
MST; DC 6; WLC
See also CA 81-84; CANR 39;
CDBLB 1960 to Present; DLB 13;
DLBY 85; MTCW

Storey, David (Malcolm)
1933- . . . . . **CLC 2, 4, 5, 8; DAM DRAM**
See also CA 81-84; CANR 36; DLB 13, 14;
MTCW

Storm, Hyemeyohsts
1935- . . . . **CLC 3; DAM MULT**
See also CA 81-84; CANR 45; NNAL

Storm, (Hans) Theodor (Woldsen)
1817-1888 . . . . **NCLC 1; SSC 27**

Storni, Alfonsina
1892-1938 . . . . . **TCLC 5; DAM MULT;**
HLC
See also CA 104; 131; HW

Stoughton, William 1631-1701. . . . . . **LC 38**
See also DLB 24

Stout, Rex (Todhunter) 1886-1975 . . . **CLC 3**
See also AITN 2; CA 61-64

Stow, (Julian) Randolph 1935- . . **CLC 23, 48**
See also CA 13-16R; CANR 33; MTCW

Stowe, Harriet (Elizabeth) Beecher
1811-1896 . . . . . **NCLC 3, 50; DA; DAB;**
DAC; DAM MST, NOV; WLC
See also CDALB 1865-1917; DLB 1, 12, 42,
74; JRDA; MAICYA; YABC 1

Strachey, (Giles) Lytton
1880-1932 . . . . **TCLC 12**
See also CA 110; DLB 149; DLBD 10

Strand, Mark
1934-. . **CLC 6, 18, 41, 71; DAM POET**
See also CA 21-24R; CANR 40; DLB 5;
SATA 41

Straub, Peter (Francis)
1943- . . . . **CLC 28; DAM POP**
See also BEST 89:1; CA 85-88; CANR 28;
DLBY 84; MTCW

Strauss, Botho 1944- . . . . **CLC 22**
See also CA 157; DLB 124

Streatfeild, (Mary) Noel
1895(?)-1986 . . . . **CLC 21**
See also CA 81-84; 120; CANR 31;
CLR 17; DLB 160; MAICYA; SATA 20;
SATA-Obit 48

Stribling, T(homas) S(igismund)
1881-1965 . . . . **CLC 23**
See also CA 107; DLB 9

Strindberg, (Johan) August
1849-1912 . . . . . . **TCLC 1, 8, 21, 47; DA;**
DAB; DAC; DAM DRAM, MST; WLC
See also CA 104; 135

Stringer, Arthur 1874-1950 . . . . **TCLC 37**
See also DLB 92

Stringer, David
See Roberts, Keith (John Kingston)

Stroheim, Erich von 1885-1957. . . . **TCLC 71**

Strugatskii, Arkadii (Natanovich)
1925-1991 . . . . **CLC 27**
See also CA 106; 135

Strugatskii, Boris (Natanovich)
1933- . . . . **CLC 27**
See also CA 106

Strummer, Joe 1953(?)- . . . . **CLC 30**

Stuart, Don A.
See Campbell, John W(ood, Jr.)

Stuart, Ian
See MacLean, Alistair (Stuart)

Stuart, Jesse (Hilton)
1906-1984 . . . . **CLC 1, 8, 11, 14, 34**
See also CA 5-8R; 112; CANR 31; DLB 9,
48, 102; DLBY 84; SATA 2;
SATA-Obit 36

Sturgeon, Theodore (Hamilton)
1918-1985 . . . . **CLC 22, 39**
See also Queen, Ellery
See also CA 81-84; 116; CANR 32; DLB 8;
DLBY 85; MTCW

Sturges, Preston 1898-1959 . . . . . . **TCLC 48**
See also CA 114; 149; DLB 26

Styron, William
1925- . . . . **CLC 1, 3, 5, 11, 15, 60;**
DAM NOV, POP; SSC 25
See also BEST 90:4; CA 5-8R; CANR 6, 33;
CDALB 1968-1988; DLB 2, 143;
DLBY 80; INT CANR-6; MTCW

Suarez Lynch, B.
See Bioy Casares, Adolfo; Borges, Jorge
Luis

Su Chien 1884-1918
See Su Man-shu
See also CA 123

Suckow, Ruth 1892-1960 . . . . **SSC 18**
See also CA 113; DLB 9, 102

Sudermann, Hermann 1857-1928 . . **TCLC 15**
See also CA 107; DLB 118

Sue, Eugene 1804-1857 . . . . **NCLC 1**
See also DLB 119

Sueskind, Patrick 1949- . . . . **CLC 44**
See also Suskind, Patrick

Sukenick, Ronald 1932- . . . . . **CLC 3, 4, 6, 48**
See also CA 25-28R; CAAS 8; CANR 32;
DLB 173; DLBY 81

Suknaski, Andrew 1942- . . . . **CLC 19**
See also CA 101; DLB 53

Sullivan, Vernon
See Vian, Boris

Sully Prudhomme 1839-1907 . . . . . **TCLC 31**

Su Man-shu . . . . **TCLC 24**
See also Su Chien

Summerforest, Ivy B.
See Kirkup, James

Summers, Andrew James 1942- . . . . . **CLC 26**

Summers, Andy
See Summers, Andrew James

Summers, Hollis (Spurgeon, Jr.)
1916- . . . . **CLC 10**
See also CA 5-8R; CANR 3; DLB 6

Summers, (Alphonsus Joseph-Mary Augustus)
Montague 1880-1948 . . . . **TCLC 16**
See also CA 118

Sumner, Gordon Matthew 1951- . . . . **CLC 26**

Surtees, Robert Smith
1803-1864 . . . . **NCLC 14**
See also DLB 21

Susann, Jacqueline 1921-1974 . . . . . . **CLC 3**
See also AITN 1; CA 65-68; 53-56; MTCW

Su Shih 1036-1101 . . . . **CMLC 15**

Suskind, Patrick
See Sueskind, Patrick
See also CA 145

Sutcliff, Rosemary
1920-1992 . . . . **CLC 26; DAB; DAC;**
DAM MST, POP
See also AAYA 10; CA 5-8R; 139;
CANR 37; CLR 1, 37; JRDA; MAICYA;
SATA 6, 44, 78; SATA-Obit 73

Sutro, Alfred 1863-1933 . . . . **TCLC 6**
See also CA 105; DLB 10

Sutton, Henry
See Slavitt, David R(ytman)

Svevo, Italo
1861-1928 . . . . **TCLC 2, 35; SSC 25**
See also Schmitz, Aron Hector

Swados, Elizabeth (A.) 1951- . . . . **CLC 12**
See also CA 97-100; CANR 49; INT 97-100

Swados, Harvey 1920-1972 . . . . **CLC 5**
See also CA 5-8R; 37-40R; CANR 6;
DLB 2

Swan, Gladys 1934- . . . . **CLC 69**
See also CA 101; CANR 17, 39

Swarthout, Glendon (Fred)
1918-1992 . . . . **CLC 35**
See also CA 1-4R; 139; CANR 1, 47;
SATA 26

Sweet, Sarah C.
See Jewett, (Theodora) Sarah Orne

Swenson, May
1919-1989 . . . . **CLC 4, 14, 61; DA; DAB;**
DAC; DAM MST, POET; PC 14
See also CA 5-8R; 130; CANR 36, 61;
DLB 5; MTCW; SATA 15

Swift, Augustus
See Lovecraft, H(oward) P(hillips)

Swift, Graham (Colin) 1949- . . . . **CLC 41, 88**
See also CA 117; 122; CANR 46

Swift, Jonathan
1667-1745 . . . . . . **LC 1; DA; DAB; DAC;**
DAM MST, NOV, POET; PC 9; WLC
See also CDBLB 1660-1789; DLB 39, 95,
101; SATA 19

Swinburne, Algernon Charles
1837-1909 . . . . . . **TCLC 8, 36; DA; DAB;**
DAC; DAM MST, POET; WLC
See also CA 105; 140; CDBLB 1832-1890;
DLB 35, 57

Swinfen, Ann . . . . **CLC 34**

Swinnerton, Frank Arthur
1884-1982 . . . . **CLC 31**
See also CA 108; DLB 34

Swithen, John
See King, Stephen (Edwin)

Sylvia
See Ashton-Warner, Sylvia (Constance)

Symmes, Robert Edward
See Duncan, Robert (Edward)

Symonds, John Addington
1840-1893 . . . . **NCLC 34**
See also DLB 57, 144

Symons, Arthur 1865-1945 . . . . **TCLC 11**
See also CA 107; DLB 19, 57, 149

Symons, Julian (Gustave)
1912-1994 . . . . **CLC 2, 14, 32**
See also CA 49-52; 147; CAAS 3; CANR 3,
33, 59; DLB 87, 155; DLBY 92; MTCW

Synge, (Edmund) J(ohn) M(illington)
1871-1909 . . . . **TCLC 6, 37;**
DAM DRAM; DC 2
See also CA 104; 141; CDBLB 1890-1914;
DLB 10, 19

Syruc, J.
See Milosz, Czeslaw

Szirtes, George 1948- . . . . **CLC 46**
See also CA 109; CANR 27, 61

Szymborska, Wislawa 1923- . . . . **CLC 99**
See also CA 154; DLBY 96

T. O., Nik
See Annensky, Innokenty (Fyodorovich)

Tabori, George 1914- . . . . **CLC 19**
See also CA 49-52; CANR 4

Tagore, Rabindranath
1861-1941 . . . . **TCLC 3, 53;**
DAM DRAM, POET; PC 8
See also CA 104; 120; MTCW

Taine, Hippolyte Adolphe
1828-1893 . . . . **NCLC 15**

Talese, Gay 1932- . . . . **CLC 37**
See also AITN 1; CA 1-4R; CANR 9, 58;
INT CANR-9; MTCW

Tallent, Elizabeth (Ann) 1954- . . . . . **CLC 45**
See also CA 117; DLB 130

Tally, Ted 1952- . . . . **CLC 42**
See also CA 120; 124; INT 124

Tamayo y Baus, Manuel
1829-1898 . . . . **NCLC 1**

Tammsaare, A(nton) H(ansen)
1878-1940 . . . . **TCLC 27**

Tam'si, Tchicaya U
See Tchicaya, Gerald Felix

Tan, Amy (Ruth)
1952- . . . . **CLC 59; DAM MULT, NOV,**
POP
See also AAYA 9; BEST 89:3; CA 136;
CANR 54; DLB 173; SATA 75

Tandem, Felix
See Spitteler, Carl (Friedrich Georg)

Tanizaki, Jun'ichiro
1886-1965 . . . . . . **CLC 8, 14, 28; SSC 21**
See also CA 93-96; 25-28R; DLB 180

Tanner, William
See Amis, Kingsley (William)

Tao Lao
See Storni, Alfonsina

Tarassoff, Lev
See Troyat, Henri

Tarbell, Ida M(inerva)
1857-1944 . . . . **TCLC 40**
See also CA 122; DLB 47

Thomson, James
1700-1748 ..... **LC 16, 29; DAM POET**
See also DLB 95

Thomson, James
1834-1882 ..... **NCLC 18; DAM POET**
See also DLB 35

Thoreau, Henry David
1817-1862 .... **NCLC 7, 21, 61; DA;**
DAB; DAC; DAM MST; WLC
See also CDALB 1640-1865; DLB 1

Thornton, Hall
See Silverberg, Robert

Thucydides c. 455B.C.-399B.C.... **CMLC 17**
See also DLB 176

Thurber, James (Grover)
1894-1961 .... **CLC 5, 11, 25; DA; DAB;**
DAC; DAM DRAM, MST, NOV; SSC 1
See also CA 73-76; CANR 17, 39;
CDALB 1929-1941; DLB 4, 11, 22, 102;
MAICYA; MTCW; SATA 13

Thurman, Wallace (Henry)
1902-1934 .... **TCLC 6; BLC;**
DAM MULT
See also BW 1; CA 104; 124; DLB 51

Ticheburn, Cheviot
See Ainsworth, William Harrison

Tieck, (Johann) Ludwig
1773-1853 .... **NCLC 5, 46**
See also DLB 90

Tiger, Derry
See Ellison, Harlan (Jay)

Tilghman, Christopher 1948(?)-..... **CLC 65**
See also CA 159

Tillinghast, Richard (Williford)
1940- .... **CLC 29**
See also CA 29-32R; CAAS 23; CANR 26,
51

Timrod, Henry 1828-1867 .... **NCLC 25**
See also DLB 3

Tindall, Gillian 1938-............. **CLC 7**
See also CA 21-24R; CANR 11

Tiptree, James, Jr. .... **CLC 48, 50**
See also Sheldon, Alice Hastings Bradley
See also DLB 8

Titmarsh, Michael Angelo
See Thackeray, William Makepeace

**Tocqueville, Alexis (Charles Henri Maurice
Clerel Comte)**
1805-1859 .... **NCLC 7, 63**

Tolkien, J(ohn) R(onald) R(euel)
1892-1973 .... **CLC 1, 2, 3, 8, 12, 38;**
DA; DAB; DAC; DAM MST, NOV,
POP; WLC
See also AAYA 10; AITN 1; CA 17-18;
45-48; CANR 36; CAP 2;
CDBLB 1914-1945; DLB 15, 160; JRDA;
MAICYA; MTCW; SATA 2, 32;
SATA-Obit 24

Toller, Ernst 1893-1939 .... **TCLC 10**
See also CA 107; DLB 124

Tolson, M. B.
See Tolson, Melvin B(eaunorus)

Tolson, Melvin B(eaunorus)
1898(?)-1966 .... **CLC 36; BLC;**
DAM MULT, POET
See also BW 1; CA 124; 89-92; DLB 48, 76

Tolstoi, Aleksei Nikolaevich
See Tolstoy, Alexey Nikolaevich

Tolstoy, Alexey Nikolaevich
1882-1945 .... **TCLC 18**
See also CA 107; 158

Tolstoy, Count Leo
See Tolstoy, Leo (Nikolaevich)

Tolstoy, Leo (Nikolaevich)
1828-1910 ...... **TCLC 4, 11, 17, 28, 44;**
DA; DAB; DAC; DAM MST, NOV;
SSC 9; WLC
See also CA 104; 123; SATA 26

Tomasi di Lampedusa, Giuseppe 1896-1957
See Lampedusa, Giuseppe (Tomasi) di
See also CA 111

Tomlin, Lily.................... CLC 17
See also Tomlin, Mary Jean

Tomlin, Mary Jean 1939(?)-
See Tomlin, Lily
See also CA 117

Tomlinson, (Alfred) Charles
1927- .... **CLC 2, 4, 6, 13, 45;**
DAM POET; PC 17
See also CA 5-8R; CANR 33; DLB 40

Tomlinson, H(enry) M(ajor)
1873-1958 .... **TCLC 71**
See also CA 118; DLB 36, 100

Tonson, Jacob
See Bennett, (Enoch) Arnold

Toole, John Kennedy
1937-1969 .... **CLC 19, 64**
See also CA 104; DLBY 81

Toomer, Jean
1894-1967 ...... **CLC 1, 4, 13, 22; BLC;**
DAM MULT; PC 7; SSC 1; WLCS
See also BW 1; CA 85-88;
CDALB 1917-1929; DLB 45, 51; MTCW

Torley, Luke
See Blish, James (Benjamin)

Tornimparte, Alessandra
See Ginzburg, Natalia

Torre, Raoul della
See Mencken, H(enry) L(ouis)

Torrey, E(dwin) Fuller 1937-....... **CLC 34**
See also CA 119

Torsvan, Ben Traven
See Traven, B.

Torsvan, Benno Traven
See Traven, B.

Torsvan, Berick Traven
See Traven, B.

Torsvan, Berwick Traven
See Traven, B.

Torsvan, Bruno Traven
See Traven, B.

Torsvan, Traven
See Traven, B.

Tournier, Michel (Edouard)
1924- .... **CLC 6, 23, 36, 95**
See also CA 49-52; CANR 3, 36; DLB 83;
MTCW; SATA 23

Tournimparte, Alessandra
See Ginzburg, Natalia

Towers, Ivar
See Kornbluth, C(yril) M.

Towne, Robert (Burton) 1936(?)-.... **CLC 87**
See also CA 108; DLB 44

Townsend, Sue 1946-.. **CLC 61; DAB; DAC**
See also CA 119; 127; INT 127; MTCW;
SATA 55, 93; SATA-Brief 48

Townshend, Peter (Dennis Blandford)
1945- .... **CLC 17, 42**
See also CA 107

Tozzi, Federigo 1883-1920....... **TCLC 31**

Traill, Catharine Parr
1802-1899 .... **NCLC 31**
See also DLB 99

Trakl, Georg 1887-1914.......... **TCLC 5**
See also CA 104

Transtroemer, Tomas (Goesta)
1931- .... **CLC 52, 65; DAM POET**
See also CA 117; 129; CAAS 17

Transtromer, Tomas Gosta
See Transtroemer, Tomas (Goesta)

Traven, B. (?)-1969............. **CLC 8, 11**
See also CA 19-20; 25-28R; CAP 2; DLB 9,
56; MTCW

Treitel, Jonathan 1959- .... **CLC 70**

Tremain, Rose 1943-.............. **CLC 42**
See also CA 97-100; CANR 44; DLB 14

Tremblay, Michel
1942-.. **CLC 29, 102; DAC; DAM MST**
See also CA 116; 128; DLB 60; MTCW

Trevanian.................... CLC 29
See also Whitaker, Rod(ney)

Trevor, Glen
See Hilton, James

Trevor, William
1928- ..... **CLC 7, 9, 14, 25, 71; SSC 21**
See also Cox, William Trevor
See also DLB 14, 139

Trifonov, Yuri (Valentinovich)
1925-1981 .... **CLC 45**
See also CA 126; 103; MTCW

Trilling, Lionel 1905-1975 .... **CLC 9, 11, 24**
See also CA 9-12R; 61-64; CANR 10;
DLB 28, 63; INT CANR-10; MTCW

Trimball, W. H.
See Mencken, H(enry) L(ouis)

Tristan
See Gomez de la Serna, Ramon

Tristram
See Housman, A(lfred) E(dward)

Trogdon, William (Lewis) 1939-
See Heat-Moon, William Least
See also CA 115; 119; CANR 47; INT 119

Trollope, Anthony
1815-1882 ..... **NCLC 6, 33; DA; DAB;**
DAC; DAM MST, NOV; SSC 28; WLC
See also CDBLB 1832-1890; DLB 21, 57,
159; SATA 22

Trollope, Frances 1779-1863 ..... **NCLC 30**
See also DLB 21, 166

Trotsky, Leon 1879-1940........ **TCLC 22**
See also CA 118

Trotter (Cockburn), Catharine
  1679-1749 . . . . **LC 8**
  See also DLB 84

Trout, Kilgore
  See Farmer, Philip Jose

Trow, George W. S. 1943- . . . . **CLC 52**
  See also CA 126

Troyat, Henri 1911- . . . . **CLC 23**
  See also CA 45-48; CANR 2, 33; MTCW

Trudeau, G(arretson) B(eekman) 1948-
  See Trudeau, Garry B.
  See also CA 81-84; CANR 31; SATA 35

Trudeau, Garry B. . . . . **CLC 12**
  See also Trudeau, G(arretson) B(eekman)
  See also AAYA 10; AITN 2

Truffaut, Francois 1932-1984 . . . **CLC 20, 101**
  See also CA 81-84; 113; CANR 34

Trumbo, Dalton 1905-1976 . . . . **CLC 19**
  See also CA 21-24R; 69-72; CANR 10;
  DLB 26

Trumbull, John 1750-1831 . . . . . . **NCLC 30**
  See also DLB 31

Trundlett, Helen B.
  See Eliot, T(homas) S(tearns)

Tryon, Thomas
  1926-1991 . . . . . . **CLC 3, 11; DAM POP**
  See also AITN 1; CA 29-32R; 135;
  CANR 32; MTCW

Tryon, Tom
  See Tryon, Thomas

Ts'ao Hsueh-ch'in 1715(?)-1763 . . . . . . **LC 1**

Tsushima, Shuji 1909-1948
  See Dazai, Osamu
  See also CA 107

Tsvetaeva (Efron), Marina (Ivanovna)
  1892-1941 . . . . **TCLC 7, 35; PC 14**
  See also CA 104; 128; MTCW

Tuck, Lily 1938- . . . . **CLC 70**
  See also CA 139

Tu Fu 712-770 . . . . **PC 9**
  See also DAM MULT

Tunis, John R(oberts) 1889-1975 . . . **CLC 12**
  See also CA 61-64; DLB 22, 171; JRDA;
  MAICYA; SATA 37; SATA-Brief 30

Tuohy, Frank . . . . **CLC 37**
  See also Tuohy, John Francis
  See also DLB 14, 139

Tuohy, John Francis 1925-
  See Tuohy, Frank
  See also CA 5-8R; CANR 3, 47

Turco, Lewis (Putnam) 1934- . . . **CLC 11, 63**
  See also CA 13-16R; CAAS 22; CANR 24,
  51; DLBY 84

Turgenev, Ivan
  1818-1883 . . . . **NCLC 21; DA; DAB;
  DAC; DAM MST, NOV; DC 7; SSC 7;
  WLC**

Turgot, Anne-Robert-Jacques
  1727-1781 . . . . **LC 26**

Turner, Frederick 1943- . . . . **CLC 48**
  See also CA 73-76; CAAS 10; CANR 12,
  30, 56; DLB 40

Tutu, Desmond M(pilo)
  1931- . . . . . **CLC 80; BLC; DAM MULT**
  See also BW 1; CA 125

Tutuola, Amos
  1920-1997 . . . . **CLC 5, 14, 29; BLC;
  DAM MULT**
  See also BW 2; CA 9-12R; 159; CANR 27;
  DLB 125; MTCW

Twain, Mark
  . . . . **TCLC 6, 12, 19, 36, 48, 59; SSC 26;
  WLC**
  See also Clemens, Samuel Langhorne
  See also AAYA 20; DLB 11, 12, 23, 64, 74

Tyler, Anne
  1941- . . . . **CLC 7, 11, 18, 28, 44, 59, 103;
  DAM NOV, POP**
  See also AAYA 18; BEST 89:1; CA 9-12R;
  CANR 11, 33, 53; DLB 6, 143; DLBY 82;
  MTCW; SATA 7, 90

Tyler, Royall 1757-1826 . . . . **NCLC 3**
  See also DLB 37

Tynan, Katharine 1861-1931 . . . . . . **TCLC 3**
  See also CA 104; DLB 153

Tyutchev, Fyodor 1803-1873 . . . . . **NCLC 34**

Tzara, Tristan
  1896-1963 . . . . **CLC 47; DAM POET**
  See also Rosenfeld, Samuel; Rosenstock,
  Sami; Rosenstock, Samuel
  See also CA 153

Uhry, Alfred
  1936- . . . . . **CLC 55; DAM DRAM, POP**
  See also CA 127; 133; INT 133

Ulf, Haerved
  See Strindberg, (Johan) August

Ulf, Harved
  See Strindberg, (Johan) August

Ulibarri, Sabine R(eyes)
  1919- . . . . **CLC 83; DAM MULT**
  See also CA 131; DLB 82; HW

Unamuno (y Jugo), Miguel de
  1864-1936 . . . **TCLC 2, 9; DAM MULT,
  NOV; HLC; SSC 11**
  See also CA 104; 131; DLB 108; HW;
  MTCW

Undercliffe, Errol
  See Campbell, (John) Ramsey

Underwood, Miles
  See Glassco, John

Undset, Sigrid
  1882-1949 . . . . **TCLC 3; DA; DAB;
  DAC; DAM MST, NOV; WLC**
  See also CA 104; 129; MTCW

Ungaretti, Giuseppe
  1888-1970 . . . . **CLC 7, 11, 15**
  See also CA 19-20; 25-28R; CAP 2;
  DLB 114

Unger, Douglas 1952- . . . . **CLC 34**
  See also CA 130

Unsworth, Barry (Forster) 1930- . . . . **CLC 76**
  See also CA 25-28R; CANR 30, 54

Updike, John (Hoyer)
  1932- . . . . . . **CLC 1, 2, 3, 5, 7, 9, 13, 15,
  23, 34, 43, 70; DA; DAB; DAC;
  DAM MST, NOV, POET, POP;
  SSC 13, 27; WLC**
  See also CA 1-4R; CABS 1; CANR 4, 33,
  51; CDALB 1968-1988; DLB 2, 5, 143;
  DLBD 3; DLBY 80, 82; MTCW

Upshaw, Margaret Mitchell
  See Mitchell, Margaret (Munnerlyn)

Upton, Mark
  See Sanders, Lawrence

Urdang, Constance (Henriette)
  1922- . . . . **CLC 47**
  See also CA 21-24R; CANR 9, 24

Uriel, Henry
  See Faust, Frederick (Schiller)

Uris, Leon (Marcus)
  1924- . . . . **CLC 7, 32; DAM NOV, POP**
  See also AITN 1, 2; BEST 89:2; CA 1-4R;
  CANR 1, 40; MTCW; SATA 49

Urmuz
  See Codrescu, Andrei

Urquhart, Jane 1949- . . . . **CLC 90; DAC**
  See also CA 113; CANR 32

Ustinov, Peter (Alexander) 1921- . . . . **CLC 1**
  See also AITN 1; CA 13-16R; CANR 25,
  51; DLB 13

U Tam'si, Gerald Felix Tchicaya
  See Tchicaya, Gerald Felix

U Tam'si, Tchicaya
  See Tchicaya, Gerald Felix

Vaculik, Ludvik 1926- . . . . **CLC 7**
  See also CA 53-56

Vaihinger, Hans 1852-1933 . . . . **TCLC 71**
  See also CA 116

Valdez, Luis (Miguel)
  1940- . . . . . **CLC 84; DAM MULT; HLC**
  See also CA 101; CANR 32; DLB 122; HW

Valenzuela, Luisa
  1938- . . . . . . **CLC 31, 104; DAM MULT;
  SSC 14**
  See also CA 101; CANR 32; DLB 113; HW

Valera y Alcala-Galiano, Juan
  1824-1905 . . . . **TCLC 10**
  See also CA 106

Valery, (Ambroise) Paul (Toussaint Jules)
  1871-1945 . . . . **TCLC 4, 15;
  DAM POET; PC 9**
  See also CA 104; 122; MTCW

Valle-Inclan, Ramon (Maria) del
  1866-1936 . . . . . **TCLC 5; DAM MULT;
  HLC**
  See also CA 106; 153; DLB 134

Vallejo, Antonio Buero
  See Buero Vallejo, Antonio

Vallejo, Cesar (Abraham)
  1892-1938 . . . . **TCLC 3, 56;
  DAM MULT; HLC**
  See also CA 105; 153; HW

Vallette, Marguerite Eymery
  See Rachilde

Valle Y Pena, Ramon del
  See Valle-Inclan, Ramon (Maria) del

Van Ash, Cay 1918- . . . . **CLC 34**

Vanbrugh, Sir John
1664-1726 . . . . . . **LC 21; DAM DRAM**
See also DLB 80

Van Campen, Karl
See Campbell, John W(ood, Jr.)

Vance, Gerald
See Silverberg, Robert

Vance, Jack . . . . **CLC 35**
See also Kuttner, Henry; Vance, John
Holbrook
See also DLB 8

Vance, John Holbrook 1916-
See Queen, Ellery; Vance, Jack
See also CA 29-32R; CANR 17; MTCW

**Van Den Bogarde, Derek Jules Gaspard Ulric
Niven** 1921-
See Bogarde, Dirk
See also CA 77-80

Vandenburgh, Jane . . . . **CLC 59**

Vanderhaeghe, Guy 1951- . . . . **CLC 41**
See also CA 113

van der Post, Laurens (Jan)
1906-1996 . . . . **CLC 5**
See also CA 5-8R; 155; CANR 35

van de Wetering, Janwillem 1931- . . **CLC 47**
See also CA 49-52; CANR 4

Van Dine, S. S. . . . . **TCLC 23**
See also Wright, Willard Huntington

Van Doren, Carl (Clinton)
1885-1950 . . . . **TCLC 18**
See also CA 111

Van Doren, Mark 1894-1972 . . . . . **CLC 6, 10**
See also CA 1-4R; 37-40R; CANR 3;
DLB 45; MTCW

Van Druten, John (William)
1901-1957 . . . . **TCLC 2**
See also CA 104; DLB 10

Van Duyn, Mona (Jane)
1921- . . . . **CLC 3, 7, 63; DAM POET**
See also CA 9-12R; CANR 7, 38, 60;
DLB 5

Van Dyne, Edith
See Baum, L(yman) Frank

van Itallie, Jean-Claude 1936- . . . . **CLC 3**
See also CA 45-48; CAAS 2; CANR 1, 48;
DLB 7

van Ostaijen, Paul 1896-1928 . . . . . **TCLC 33**

Van Peebles, Melvin
1932- . . . . **CLC 2, 20; DAM MULT**
See also BW 2; CA 85-88; CANR 27

Vansittart, Peter 1920- . . . . **CLC 42**
See also CA 1-4R; CANR 3, 49

Van Vechten, Carl 1880-1964 . . . . . . **CLC 33**
See also CA 89-92; DLB 4, 9, 51

Van Vogt, A(lfred) E(lton) 1912- . . . . . **CLC 1**
See also CA 21-24R; CANR 28; DLB 8;
SATA 14

Varda, Agnes 1928- . . . . **CLC 16**
See also CA 116; 122

Vargas Llosa, (Jorge) Mario (Pedro)
1936- . . . . **CLC 3, 6, 9, 10, 15, 31, 42, 85;
DA; DAB; DAC; DAM MST, MULT,
NOV; HLC**
See also CA 73-76; CANR 18, 32, 42;
DLB 145; HW; MTCW

Vasiliu, Gheorghe 1881-1957
See Bacovia, George
See also CA 123

Vassa, Gustavus
See Equiano, Olaudah

Vassilikos, Vassilis 1933- . . . . **CLC 4, 8**
See also CA 81-84

Vaughan, Henry 1621-1695 . . . . **LC 27**
See also DLB 131

Vaughn, Stephanie . . . . **CLC 62**

Vazov, Ivan (Minchov)
1850-1921 . . . . **TCLC 25**
See also CA 121; DLB 147

Veblen, Thorstein (Bunde)
1857-1929 . . . . **TCLC 31**
See also CA 115

Vega, Lope de 1562-1635 . . . . **LC 23**

Venison, Alfred
See Pound, Ezra (Weston Loomis)

Verdi, Marie de
See Mencken, H(enry) L(ouis)

Verdu, Matilde
See Cela, Camilo Jose

Verga, Giovanni (Carmelo)
1840-1922 . . . . **TCLC 3; SSC 21**
See also CA 104; 123

Vergil
70B.C.-19B.C. . . . . . **CMLC 9; DA; DAB;
DAC; DAM MST, POET; PC 12; WLCS**

Verhaeren, Emile (Adolphe Gustave)
1855-1916 . . . . **TCLC 12**
See also CA 109

Verlaine, Paul (Marie)
1844-1896 . . . . **NCLC 2, 51;
DAM POET; PC 2**

Verne, Jules (Gabriel)
1828-1905 . . . . **TCLC 6, 52**
See also AAYA 16; CA 110; 131; DLB 123;
JRDA; MAICYA; SATA 21

Very, Jones 1813-1880 . . . . **NCLC 9**
See also DLB 1

Vesaas, Tarjei 1897-1970 . . . . **CLC 48**
See also CA 29-32R

Vialis, Gaston
See Simenon, Georges (Jacques Christian)

Vian, Boris 1920-1959 . . . . **TCLC 9**
See also CA 106; DLB 72

Viaud, (Louis Marie) Julien 1850-1923
See Loti, Pierre
See also CA 107

Vicar, Henry
See Felsen, Henry Gregor

Vicker, Angus
See Felsen, Henry Gregor

Vidal, Gore
1925- . . . . . **CLC 2, 4, 6, 8, 10, 22, 33, 72;
DAM NOV, POP**
See also AITN 1; BEST 90:2; CA 5-8R;
CANR 13, 45; DLB 6, 152;
INT CANR-13; MTCW

Viereck, Peter (Robert Edwin)
1916- . . . . **CLC 4**
See also CA 1-4R; CANR 1, 47; DLB 5

Vigny, Alfred (Victor) de
1797-1863 . . . . . . **NCLC 7; DAM POET**
See also DLB 119

Vilakazi, Benedict Wallet
1906-1947 . . . . **TCLC 37**

**Villiers de l'Isle Adam, Jean Marie Mathias
Philippe Auguste Comte**
1838-1889 . . . . **NCLC 3; SSC 14**
See also DLB 123

Villon, Francois 1431-1463(?) . . . . **PC 13**

Vinci, Leonardo da 1452-1519 . . . . . . **LC 12**

Vine, Barbara . . . . **CLC 50**
See also Rendell, Ruth (Barbara)
See also BEST 90:4

Vinge, Joan D(ennison)
1948- . . . . **CLC 30; SSC 24**
See also CA 93-96; SATA 36

Violis, G.
See Simenon, Georges (Jacques Christian)

Visconti, Luchino 1906-1976 . . . . **CLC 16**
See also CA 81-84; 65-68; CANR 39

Vittorini, Elio 1908-1966 . . . . . . **CLC 6, 9, 14**
See also CA 133; 25-28R

Vizenor, Gerald Robert
1934- . . . . **CLC 103; DAM MULT**
See also CA 13-16R; CAAS 22; CANR 5,
21, 44; DLB 175; NNAL

Vizinczey, Stephen 1933- . . . . **CLC 40**
See also CA 128; INT 128

Vliet, R(ussell) G(ordon)
1929-1984 . . . . **CLC 22**
See also CA 37-40R; 112; CANR 18

Vogau, Boris Andreyevich 1894-1937(?)
See Pilnyak, Boris
See also CA 123

Vogel, Paula A(nne) 1951- . . . . **CLC 76**
See also CA 108

Voight, Ellen Bryant 1943- . . . . **CLC 54**
See also CA 69-72; CANR 11, 29, 55;
DLB 120

Voigt, Cynthia 1942- . . . . **CLC 30**
See also AAYA 3; CA 106; CANR 18, 37,
40; CLR 13; INT CANR-18; JRDA;
MAICYA; SATA 48, 79; SATA-Brief 33

Voinovich, Vladimir (Nikolaevich)
1932- . . . . **CLC 10, 49**
See also CA 81-84; CAAS 12; CANR 33;
MTCW

Vollmann, William T.
1959- . . . . . . **CLC 89; DAM NOV, POP**
See also CA 134

Voloshinov, V. N.
See Bakhtin, Mikhail Mikhailovich

Voltaire
1694-1778 . . . . . **LC 14; DA; DAB; DAC;
DAM DRAM, MST; SSC 12; WLC**

von Daeniken, Erich 1935- . . . . **CLC 30**
See also AITN 1; CA 37-40R; CANR 17,
44

von Daniken, Erich
See von Daeniken, Erich

von Heidenstam, (Carl Gustaf) Verner
See Heidenstam, (Carl Gustaf) Verner von

von Heyse, Paul (Johann Ludwig)
See Heyse, Paul (Johann Ludwig von)

von Hofmannsthal, Hugo
See Hofmannsthal, Hugo von

von Horvath, Odon
See Horvath, Oedoen von

von Horvath, Oedoen
See Horvath, Oedoen von

von Liliencron, (Friedrich Adolf Axel) Detlev
See Liliencron, (Friedrich Adolf Axel)
Detlev von

Vonnegut, Kurt, Jr.
1922- ...... CLC 1, 2, 3, 4, 5, 8, 12, 22,
40, 60; DA; DAB; DAC; DAM MST,
NOV, POP; SSC 8; WLC
See also AAYA 6; AITN 1; BEST 90:4;
CA 1-4R; CANR 1, 25, 49;
CDALB 1968-1988; DLB 2, 8, 152;
DLBD 3; DLBY 80; MTCW

Von Rachen, Kurt
See Hubbard, L(afayette) Ron(ald)

von Rezzori (d'Arezzo), Gregor
See Rezzori (d'Arezzo), Gregor von

von Sternberg, Josef
See Sternberg, Josef von

Vorster, Gordon 1924- .... CLC 34
See also CA 133

Vosce, Trudie
See Ozick, Cynthia

Voznesensky, Andrei (Andreievich)
1933- ...... CLC 1, 15, 57; DAM POET
See also CA 89-92; CANR 37; MTCW

Waddington, Miriam 1917- .... CLC 28
See also CA 21-24R; CANR 12, 30;
DLB 68

Wagman, Fredrica 1937- .... CLC 7
See also CA 97-100; INT 97-100

Wagner, Linda W.
See Wagner-Martin, Linda (C.)

Wagner, Linda Welshimer
See Wagner-Martin, Linda (C.)

Wagner, Richard 1813-1883....... NCLC 9
See also DLB 129

Wagner-Martin, Linda (C.) 1936- ... CLC 50
See also CA 159

Wagoner, David (Russell)
1926- .... CLC 3, 5, 15
See also CA 1-4R; CAAS 3; CANR 2;
DLB 5; SATA 14

Wah, Fred(erick James) 1939-...... CLC 44
See also CA 107; 141; DLB 60

Wahloo, Per 1926-1975 .... CLC 7
See also CA 61-64

Wahloo, Peter
See Wahloo, Per

Wain, John (Barrington)
1925-1994 .... CLC 2, 11, 15, 46
See also CA 5-8R; 145; CAAS 4; CANR 23,
54; CDBLB 1960 to Present; DLB 15, 27,
139, 155; MTCW

Wajda, Andrzej 1926-............. CLC 16
See also CA 102

Wakefield, Dan 1932-............. CLC 7
See also CA 21-24R; CAAS 7

Wakoski, Diane
1937- .... CLC 2, 4, 7, 9, 11, 40;
DAM POET; PC 15
See also CA 13-16R; CAAS 1; CANR 9, 60;
DLB 5; INT CANR-9

Wakoski-Sherbell, Diane
See Wakoski, Diane

Walcott, Derek (Alton)
1930- .... CLC 2, 4, 9, 14, 25, 42, 67, 76;
BLC; DAB; DAC; DAM MST, MULT,
POET; DC 7
See also BW 2; CA 89-92; CANR 26, 47;
DLB 117; DLBY 81; MTCW

Waldman, Anne 1945- .... CLC 7
See also CA 37-40R; CAAS 17; CANR 34;
DLB 16

Waldo, E. Hunter
See Sturgeon, Theodore (Hamilton)

Waldo, Edward Hamilton
See Sturgeon, Theodore (Hamilton)

Walker, Alice (Malsenior)
1944- .... CLC 5, 6, 9, 19, 27, 46, 58,
103; BLC; DA; DAB; DAC; DAM MST,
MULT, NOV, POET, POP; SSC 5;
WLCS
See also AAYA 3; BEST 89:4; BW 2;
CA 37-40R; CANR 9, 27, 49;
CDALB 1968-1988; DLB 6, 33, 143;
INT CANR-27; MTCW; SATA 31

Walker, David Harry 1911-1992.... CLC 14
See also CA 1-4R; 137; CANR 1; SATA 8;
SATA-Obit 71

Walker, Edward Joseph 1934-
See Walker, Ted
See also CA 21-24R; CANR 12, 28, 53

Walker, George F.
1947- .... CLC 44, 61; DAB; DAC;
DAM MST
See also CA 103; CANR 21, 43, 59;
DLB 60

Walker, Joseph A.
1935- .... CLC 19; DAM DRAM, MST
See also BW 1; CA 89-92; CANR 26;
DLB 38

Walker, Margaret (Abigail)
1915- .... CLC 1, 6; BLC; DAM MULT
See also BW 2; CA 73-76; CANR 26, 54;
DLB 76, 152; MTCW

Walker, Ted..................... CLC 13
See Walker, Edward Joseph
See also DLB 40

Wallace, David Foster 1962-....... CLC 50
See also CA 132; CANR 59

Wallace, Dexter
See Masters, Edgar Lee

Wallace, (Richard Horatio) Edgar
1875-1932................TCLC 57
See also CA 115; DLB 70

Wallace, Irving
1916-1990 ..... CLC 7, 13; DAM NOV,
POP
See also AITN 1; CA 1-4R; 132; CAAS 1;
CANR 1, 27; INT CANR-27; MTCW

Wallant, Edward Lewis
1926-1962 .... CLC 5, 10
See also CA 1-4R; CANR 22; DLB 2, 28,
143; MTCW

Walley, Byron
See Card, Orson Scott

Walpole, Horace 1717-1797......... LC 2
See also DLB 39, 104

Walpole, Hugh (Seymour)
1884-1941 .... TCLC 5
See also CA 104; DLB 34

Walser, Martin 1927-............. CLC 27
See also CA 57-60; CANR 8, 46; DLB 75,
124

Walser, Robert
1878-1956 .... TCLC 18; SSC 20
See also CA 118; DLB 66

Walsh, Jill Paton................. CLC 35
See also Paton Walsh, Gillian
See also AAYA 11; CLR 2; DLB 161;
SAAS 3

Walter, Villiam Christian
See Andersen, Hans Christian

Wambaugh, Joseph (Aloysius, Jr.)
1937- .... CLC 3, 18; DAM NOV, POP
See also AITN 1; BEST 89:3; CA 33-36R;
CANR 42; DLB 6; DLBY 83; MTCW

Wang Wei 699(?)-761(?)............ PC 18

Ward, Arthur Henry Sarsfield 1883-1959
See Rohmer, Sax
See also CA 108

Ward, Douglas Turner 1930-....... CLC 19
See also BW 1; CA 81-84; CANR 27;
DLB 7, 38

Ward, Mary Augusta
See Ward, Mrs. Humphry

Ward, Mrs. Humphry
1851-1920 .... TCLC 55
See also DLB 18

Ward, Peter
See Faust, Frederick (Schiller)

Warhol, Andy 1928(?)-1987........ CLC 20
See also AAYA 12; BEST 89:4; CA 89-92;
121; CANR 34

Warner, Francis (Robert le Plastrier)
1937- .... CLC 14
See also CA 53-56; CANR 11

Warner, Marina 1946-............ CLC 59
See also CA 65-68; CANR 21, 55

Warner, Rex (Ernest) 1905-1986.... CLC 45
See also CA 89-92; 119; DLB 15

Warner, Susan (Bogert)
1819-1885 .... NCLC 31
See also DLB 3, 42

Warner, Sylvia (Constance) Ashton
See Ashton-Warner, Sylvia (Constance)

Warner, Sylvia Townsend
1893-1978 .... CLC 7, 19; SSC 23
See also CA 61-64; 77-80; CANR 16, 60;
DLB 34, 139; MTCW

Warren, Mercy Otis 1728-1814... NCLC 13
See also DLB 31

Warren, Robert Penn
1905-1989 .... **CLC 1, 4, 6, 8, 10, 13, 18, 39, 53, 59; DA; DAB; DAC; DAM MST, NOV, POET; SSC 4; WLC**
See also AITN 1; CA 13-16R; 129; CANR 10, 47; CDALB 1968-1988; DLB 2, 48, 152; DLBY 80, 89; INT CANR-10; MTCW; SATA 46; SATA-Obit 63

Warshofsky, Isaac
See Singer, Isaac Bashevis

Warton, Thomas
1728-1790 .... **LC 15; DAM POET**
See also DLB 104, 109

Waruk, Kona
See Harris, (Theodore) Wilson

Warung, Price 1855-1911........ **TCLC 45**

Warwick, Jarvis
See Garner, Hugh

Washington, Alex
See Harris, Mark

Washington, Booker T(aliaferro)
1856-1915 .... **TCLC 10; BLC; DAM MULT**
See also BW 1; CA 114; 125; SATA 28

Washington, George 1732-1799...... **LC 25**
See also DLB 31

Wassermann, (Karl) Jakob
1873-1934 .... **TCLC 6**
See also CA 104; DLB 66

Wasserstein, Wendy
1950- .... **CLC 32, 59, 90; DAM DRAM; DC 4**
See also CA 121; 129; CABS 3; CANR 53; INT 129; SATA 94

Waterhouse, Keith (Spencer)
1929- .... **CLC 47**
See also CA 5-8R; CANR 38; DLB 13, 15; MTCW

Waters, Frank (Joseph)
1902-1995 .... **CLC 88**
See also CA 5-8R; 149; CAAS 13; CANR 3, 18; DLBY 86

Waters, Roger 1944-.............. **CLC 35**

Watkins, Frances Ellen
See Harper, Frances Ellen Watkins

Watkins, Gerrold
See Malzberg, Barry N(athaniel)

Watkins, Gloria 1955(?)-
See hooks, bell
See also BW 2; CA 143

Watkins, Paul 1964-.............. **CLC 55**
See also CA 132

Watkins, Vernon Phillips
1906-1967 .... **CLC 43**
See also CA 9-10; 25-28R; CAP 1; DLB 20

Watson, Irving S.
See Mencken, H(enry) L(ouis)

Watson, John H.
See Farmer, Philip Jose

Watson, Richard F.
See Silverberg, Robert

Waugh, Auberon (Alexander) 1939-.. **CLC 7**
See also CA 45-48; CANR 6, 22; DLB 14

Waugh, Evelyn (Arthur St. John)
1903-1966 ...... **CLC 1, 3, 8, 13, 19, 27, 44; DA; DAB; DAC; DAM MST, NOV, POP; WLC**
See also CA 85-88; 25-28R; CANR 22; CDBLB 1914-1945; DLB 15, 162; MTCW

Waugh, Harriet 1944- .... **CLC 6**
See also CA 85-88; CANR 22

Ways, C. R.
See Blount, Roy (Alton), Jr.

Waystaff, Simon
See Swift, Jonathan

Webb, (Martha) Beatrice (Potter)
1858-1943 .... **TCLC 22**
See also Potter, (Helen) Beatrix
See also CA 117

Webb, Charles (Richard) 1939-...... **CLC 7**
See also CA 25-28R

Webb, James H(enry), Jr. 1946-.... **CLC 22**
See also CA 81-84

Webb, Mary (Gladys Meredith)
1881-1927 .... **TCLC 24**
See also CA 123; DLB 34

Webb, Mrs. Sidney
See Webb, (Martha) Beatrice (Potter)

Webb, Phyllis 1927-.............. **CLC 18**
See also CA 104; CANR 23; DLB 53

Webb, Sidney (James)
1859-1947 .... **TCLC 22**
See also CA 117

Webber, Andrew Lloyd............. CLC 21
See also Lloyd Webber, Andrew

Weber, Lenora Mattingly
1895-1971 .... **CLC 12**
See also CA 19-20; 29-32R; CAP 1; SATA 2; SATA-Obit 26

Weber, Max 1864-1920 .... **TCLC 69**
See also CA 109

Webster, John
1579(?)-1634(?) ...... **LC 33; DA; DAB; DAC; DAM DRAM, MST; DC 2; WLC**
See also CDBLB Before 1660; DLB 58

Webster, Noah 1758-1843 .... **NCLC 30**

Wedekind, (Benjamin) Frank(lin)
1864-1918 ...... **TCLC 7; DAM DRAM**
See also CA 104; 153; DLB 118

Weidman, Jerome 1913-............ **CLC 7**
See also AITN 2; CA 1-4R; CANR 1; DLB 28

Weil, Simone (Adolphine)
1909-1943 .... **TCLC 23**
See also CA 117; 159

Weinstein, Nathan
See West, Nathanael

Weinstein, Nathan von Wallenstein
See West, Nathanael

Weir, Peter (Lindsay) 1944- .... **CLC 20**
See also CA 113; 123

Weiss, Peter (Ulrich)
1916-1982 .... **CLC 3, 15, 51; DAM DRAM**
See also CA 45-48; 106; CANR 3; DLB 69, 124

Weiss, Theodore (Russell)
1916- .... **CLC 3, 8, 14**
See also CA 9-12R; CAAS 2; CANR 46; DLB 5

Welch, (Maurice) Denton
1915-1948 .... **TCLC 22**
See also CA 121; 148

Welch, James
1940- ..... **CLC 6, 14, 52; DAM MULT, POP**
See also CA 85-88; CANR 42; DLB 175; NNAL

Weldon, Fay
1933- .... **CLC 6, 9, 11, 19, 36, 59; DAM POP**
See also CA 21-24R; CANR 16, 46; CDBLB 1960 to Present; DLB 14; INT CANR-16; MTCW

Wellek, Rene 1903-1995.......... **CLC 28**
See also CA 5-8R; 150; CAAS 7; CANR 8; DLB 63; INT CANR-8

Weller, Michael 1942-........ **CLC 10, 53**
See also CA 85-88

Weller, Paul 1958-............... **CLC 26**

Wellershoff, Dieter 1925-.......... **CLC 46**
See also CA 89-92; CANR 16, 37

Welles, (George) Orson
1915-1985 .... **CLC 20, 80**
See also CA 93-96; 117

Wellman, Mac 1945- .... **CLC 65**

Wellman, Manly Wade 1903-1986 .. **CLC 49**
See also CA 1-4R; 118; CANR 6, 16, 44; SATA 6; SATA-Obit 47

Wells, Carolyn 1869(?)-1942 ...... **TCLC 35**
See also CA 113; DLB 11

Wells, H(erbert) G(eorge)
1866-1946 ...... **TCLC 6, 12, 19; DA; DAB; DAC; DAM MST, NOV; SSC 6; WLC**
See also AAYA 18; CA 110; 121; CDBLB 1914-1945; DLB 34, 70, 156, 178; MTCW; SATA 20

Wells, Rosemary 1943-............ **CLC 12**
See also AAYA 13; CA 85-88; CANR 48; CLR 16; MAICYA; SAAS 1; SATA 18, 69

Welty, Eudora
1909- ...... **CLC 1, 2, 5, 14, 22, 33; DA; DAB; DAC; DAM MST, NOV; SSC 1, 27; WLC**
See also CA 9-12R; CABS 1; CANR 32; CDALB 1941-1968; DLB 2, 102, 143; DLBD 12; DLBY 87; MTCW

Wen I-to 1899-1946 .... **TCLC 28**

Wentworth, Robert
See Hamilton, Edmond

Werfel, Franz (V.) 1890-1945 ...... **TCLC 8**
See also CA 104; DLB 81, 124

Wergeland, Henrik Arnold
1808-1845 .... **NCLC 5**

Wersba, Barbara 1932-............ **CLC 30**
See also AAYA 2; CA 29-32R; CANR 16, 38; CLR 3; DLB 52; JRDA; MAICYA; SAAS 2; SATA 1, 58

Wertmueller, Lina 1928- .... **CLC 16**
See also CA 97-100; CANR 39

Wescott, Glenway 1901-1987....... **CLC 13**
See also CA 13-16R; 121; CANR 23;
DLB 4, 9, 102

Wesker, Arnold
1932- .... **CLC 3, 5, 42; DAB;
DAM DRAM**
See also CA 1-4R; CAAS 7; CANR 1, 33;
CDBLB 1960 to Present; DLB 13;
MTCW

Wesley, Richard (Errol) 1945-....... **CLC 7**
See also BW 1; CA 57-60; CANR 27;
DLB 38

Wessel, Johan Herman 1742-1785 .... **LC 7**

West, Anthony (Panther)
1914-1987 .... **CLC 50**
See also CA 45-48; 124; CANR 3, 19;
DLB 15

West, C. P.
See Wodehouse, P(elham) G(renville)

West, (Mary) Jessamyn
1902-1984 .... **CLC 7, 17**
See also CA 9-12R; 112; CANR 27; DLB 6;
DLBY 84; MTCW; SATA-Obit 37

West, Morris L(anglo) 1916-..... **CLC 6, 33**
See also CA 5-8R; CANR 24, 49; MTCW

West, Nathanael
1903-1940 ..... **TCLC 1, 14, 44; SSC 16**
See also CA 104; 125; CDALB 1929-1941;
DLB 4, 9, 28; MTCW

West, Owen
See Koontz, Dean R(ay)

West, Paul 1930- .... **CLC 7, 14, 96**
See also CA 13-16R; CAAS 7; CANR 22,
53; DLB 14; INT CANR-22

West, Rebecca 1892-1983 .. **CLC 7, 9, 31, 50**
See also CA 5-8R; 109; CANR 19; DLB 36;
DLBY 83; MTCW

Westall, Robert (Atkinson)
1929-1993 .... **CLC 17**
See also AAYA 12; CA 69-72; 141;
CANR 18; CLR 13; JRDA; MAICYA;
SAAS 2; SATA 23, 69; SATA-Obit 75

Westlake, Donald E(dwin)
1933- .... **CLC 7, 33; DAM POP**
See also CA 17-20R; CAAS 13; CANR 16,
44; INT CANR-16

Westmacott, Mary
See Christie, Agatha (Mary Clarissa)

Weston, Allen
See Norton, Andre

Wetcheek, J. L.
See Feuchtwanger, Lion

Wetering, Janwillem van de
See van de Wetering, Janwillem

Wetherell, Elizabeth
See Warner, Susan (Bogert)

Whale, James 1889-1957 .... **TCLC 63**

Whalen, Philip 1923-.......... **CLC 6, 29**
See also CA 9-12R; CANR 5, 39; DLB 16

Wharton, Edith (Newbold Jones)
1862-1937 ...... **TCLC 3, 9, 27, 53; DA;
DAB; DAC; DAM MST, NOV; SSC 6;
WLC**
See also CA 104; 132; CDALB 1865-1917;
DLB 4, 9, 12, 78; DLBD 13; MTCW

Wharton, James
See Mencken, H(enry) L(ouis)

Wharton, William (a pseudonym)
.... **CLC 18, 37**
See also CA 93-96; DLBY 80; INT 93-96

Wheatley (Peters), Phillis
1754(?)-1784 .... **LC 3; BLC; DA; DAC;
DAM MST, MULT, POET; PC 3; WLC**
See also CDALB 1640-1865; DLB 31, 50

Wheelock, John Hall 1886-1978.... **CLC 14**
See also CA 13-16R; 77-80; CANR 14;
DLB 45

White, E(lwyn) B(rooks)
1899-1985 .. **CLC 10, 34, 39; DAM POP**
See also AITN 2; CA 13-16R; 116;
CANR 16, 37; CLR 1, 21; DLB 11, 22;
MAICYA; MTCW; SATA 2, 29;
SATA-Obit 44

White, Edmund (Valentine III)
1940- .... **CLC 27; DAM POP**
See also AAYA 7; CA 45-48; CANR 3, 19,
36; MTCW

White, Patrick (Victor Martindale)
1912-1990 .. **CLC 3, 4, 5, 7, 9, 18, 65, 69**
See also CA 81-84; 132; CANR 43; MTCW

White, Phyllis Dorothy James 1920-
See James, P. D.
See also CA 21-24R; CANR 17, 43;
DAM POP; MTCW

White, T(erence) H(anbury)
1906-1964 .... **CLC 30**
See also AAYA 22; CA 73-76; CANR 37;
DLB 160; JRDA; MAICYA; SATA 12

White, Terence de Vere
1912-1994 .... **CLC 49**
See also CA 49-52; 145; CANR 3

White, Walter F(rancis)
1893-1955 .... **TCLC 15**
See also White, Walter
See also BW 1; CA 115; 124; DLB 51

White, William Hale 1831-1913
See Rutherford, Mark
See also CA 121

Whitehead, E(dward) A(nthony)
1933- .... **CLC 5**
See also CA 65-68; CANR 58

Whitemore, Hugh (John) 1936-..... **CLC 37**
See also CA 132; INT 132

Whitman, Sarah Helen (Power)
1803-1878 .... **NCLC 19**
See also DLB 1

Whitman, Walt(er)
1819-1892 ..... **NCLC 4, 31; DA; DAB;
DAC; DAM MST, POET; PC 3; WLC**
See also CDALB 1640-1865; DLB 3, 64;
SATA 20

Whitney, Phyllis A(yame)
1903- .... **CLC 42; DAM POP**
See also AITN 2; BEST 90:3; CA 1-4R;
CANR 3, 25, 38, 60; JRDA; MAICYA;
SATA 1, 30

Whittemore, (Edward) Reed (Jr.)
1919- .... **CLC 4**
See also CA 9-12R; CAAS 8; CANR 4;
DLB 5

Whittier, John Greenleaf
1807-1892 .... **NCLC 8, 59**
See also DLB 1

Whittlebot, Hernia
See Coward, Noel (Peirce)

Wicker, Thomas Grey 1926-
See Wicker, Tom
See also CA 65-68; CANR 21, 46

Wicker, Tom .... **CLC 7**
See also Wicker, Thomas Grey

Wideman, John Edgar
1941- .... **CLC 5, 34, 36, 67; BLC;
DAM MULT**
See also BW 2; CA 85-88; CANR 14, 42;
DLB 33, 143

Wiebe, Rudy (Henry)
1934- .... **CLC 6, 11, 14; DAC;
DAM MST**
See also CA 37-40R; CANR 42; DLB 60

Wieland, Christoph Martin
1733-1813 .... **NCLC 17**
See also DLB 97

Wiene, Robert 1881-1938........ **TCLC 56**

Wieners, John 1934-............... **CLC 7**
See also CA 13-16R; DLB 16

Wiesel, Elie(zer)
1928-...... **CLC 3, 5, 11, 37; DA; DAB;
DAC; DAM MST, NOV;
WLCS 2:855-57, 854**
See also AAYA 7; AITN 1; CA 5-8R;
CAAS 4; CANR 8, 40; DLB 83;
DLBY 87; INT CANR-8; MTCW;
SATA 56

Wiggins, Marianne 1947-......... **CLC 57**
See also BEST 89:3; CA 130; CANR 60

Wight, James Alfred 1916-
See Herriot, James
See also CA 77-80; SATA 55;
SATA-Brief 44

Wilbur, Richard (Purdy)
1921- ... **CLC 3, 6, 9, 14, 53; DA; DAB;
DAC; DAM MST, POET**
See also CA 1-4R; CABS 2; CANR 2, 29;
DLB 5, 169; INT CANR-29; MTCW;
SATA 9

Wild, Peter 1940-................ **CLC 14**
See also CA 37-40R; DLB 5

Wilde, Oscar (Fingal O'Flahertie Wills)
1854(?)-1900 .... **TCLC 1, 8, 23, 41; DA;
DAB; DAC; DAM DRAM, MST, NOV;
SSC 11; WLC**
See also CA 104; 119; CDBLB 1890-1914;
DLB 10, 19, 34, 57, 141, 156; SATA 24

Wilder, Billy .... **CLC 20**
See also Wilder, Samuel
See also DLB 26

Wilder, Samuel 1906-
See Wilder, Billy
See also CA 89-92

Wilder, Thornton (Niven)
1897-1975 ...... **CLC 1, 5, 6, 10, 15, 35,
82; DA; DAB; DAC; DAM DRAM,
MST, NOV; DC 1; WLC**
See also AITN 2; CA 13-16R; 61-64;
CANR 40; DLB 4, 7, 9; MTCW

Wilding, Michael 1942- . . . . CLC 73
See also CA 104; CANR 24, 49

Wiley, Richard 1944- . . . . CLC 44
See also CA 121; 129

Wilhelm, Kate . . . . CLC 7
See also Wilhelm, Katie Gertrude
See also AAYA 20; CAAS 5; DLB 8;
INT CANR-17

Wilhelm, Katie Gertrude 1928-
See Wilhelm, Kate
See also CA 37-40R; CANR 17, 36, 60;
MTCW

Wilkins, Mary
See Freeman, Mary Eleanor Wilkins

Willard, Nancy 1936- . . . . CLC 7, 37
See also CA 89-92; CANR 10, 39; CLR 5;
DLB 5, 52; MAICYA; MTCW;
SATA 37, 71; SATA-Brief 30

Williams, C(harles) K(enneth)
1936- . . . . CLC 33, 56; DAM POET
See also CA 37-40R; CAAS 26; CANR 57;
DLB 5

Williams, Charles
See Collier, James L(incoln)

Williams, Charles (Walter Stansby)
1886-1945 . . . . TCLC 1, 11
See also CA 104; DLB 100, 153

Williams, (George) Emlyn
1905-1987 . . . . . . CLC 15; DAM DRAM
See also CA 104; 123; CANR 36; DLB 10,
77; MTCW

Williams, Hugo 1942- . . . . CLC 42
See also CA 17-20R; CANR 45; DLB 40

Williams, J. Walker
See Wodehouse, P(elham) G(renville)

Williams, John A(lfred)
1925- . . . CLC 5, 13; BLC; DAM MULT
See also BW 2; CA 53-56; CAAS 3;
CANR 6, 26, 51; DLB 2, 33;
INT CANR-6

Williams, Jonathan (Chamberlain)
1929- . . . . CLC 13
See also CA 9-12R; CAAS 12; CANR 8;
DLB 5

Williams, Joy 1944- . . . . CLC 31
See also CA 41-44R; CANR 22, 48

Williams, Norman 1952- . . . . CLC 39
See also CA 118

Williams, Sherley Anne
1944- . . . . . CLC 89; BLC; DAM MULT,
POET
See also BW 2; CA 73-76; CANR 25;
DLB 41; INT CANR-25; SATA 78

Williams, Shirley
See Williams, Sherley Anne

Williams, Tennessee
1911-1983 . . . . . CLC 1, 2, 5, 7, 8, 11, 15,
19, 30, 39, 45, 71; DA; DAB; DAC;
DAM DRAM, MST; DC 4; WLC
See also AITN 1, 2; CA 5-8R; 108;
CABS 3; CANR 31; CDALB 1941-1968;
DLB 7; DLBD 4; DLBY 83; MTCW

Williams, Thomas (Alonzo)
1926-1990 . . . . CLC 14
See also CA 1-4R; 132; CANR 2

Williams, William C.
See Williams, William Carlos

Williams, William Carlos
1883-1963 . . . . CLC 1, 2, 5, 9, 13, 22, 42,
67; DA; DAB; DAC; DAM MST, POET;
PC 7
See also CA 89-92; CANR 34;
CDALB 1917-1929; DLB 4, 16, 54, 86;
MTCW

Williamson, David (Keith) 1942- . . . . CLC 56
See also CA 103; CANR 41

Williamson, Ellen Douglas 1905-1984
See Douglas, Ellen
See also CA 17-20R; 114; CANR 39

Williamson, Jack . . . . CLC 29
See also Williamson, John Stewart
See also CAAS 8; DLB 8

Williamson, John Stewart 1908-
See Williamson, Jack
See also CA 17-20R; CANR 23

Willie, Frederick
See Lovecraft, H(oward) P(hillips)

Willingham, Calder (Baynard, Jr.)
1922-1995 . . . . CLC 5, 51
See also CA 5-8R; 147; CANR 3; DLB 2,
44; MTCW

Willis, Charles
See Clarke, Arthur C(harles)

Willy
See Colette, (Sidonie-Gabrielle)

Willy, Colette
See Colette, (Sidonie-Gabrielle)

Wilson, A(ndrew) N(orman) 1950- . . CLC 33
See also CA 112; 122; DLB 14, 155

Wilson, Angus (Frank Johnstone)
1913-1991 . . CLC 2, 3, 5, 25, 34; SSC 21
See also CA 5-8R; 134; CANR 21; DLB 15,
139, 155; MTCW

Wilson, August
1945- . . . . CLC 39, 50, 63; BLC; DA;
DAB; DAC; DAM DRAM, MST,
MULT; DC 2; WLCS
See also AAYA 16; BW 2; CA 115; 122;
CANR 42, 54; MTCW

Wilson, Brian 1942- . . . . CLC 12

Wilson, Colin 1931- . . . . CLC 3, 14
See also CA 1-4R; CAAS 5; CANR 1, 22,
33; DLB 14; MTCW

Wilson, Dirk
See Pohl, Frederik

Wilson, Edmund
1895-1972 . . . . CLC 1, 2, 3, 8, 24
See also CA 1-4R; 37-40R; CANR 1, 46;
DLB 63; MTCW

Wilson, Ethel Davis (Bryant)
1888(?)-1980 . . . . CLC 13; DAC;
DAM POET
See also CA 102; DLB 68; MTCW

Wilson, John 1785-1854 . . . . NCLC 5

Wilson, John (Anthony) Burgess 1917-1993
See Burgess, Anthony
See also CA 1-4R; 143; CANR 2, 46; DAC;
DAM NOV; MTCW

Wilson, Lanford
1937- . . . . . CLC 7, 14, 36; DAM DRAM
See also CA 17-20R; CABS 3; CANR 45;
DLB 7

Wilson, Robert M. 1944- . . . . CLC 7, 9
See also CA 49-52; CANR 2, 41; MTCW

Wilson, Robert McLiam 1964- . . . . . CLC 59
See also CA 132

Wilson, Sloan 1920- . . . . CLC 32
See also CA 1-4R; CANR 1, 44

Wilson, Snoo 1948- . . . . CLC 33
See also CA 69-72

Wilson, William S(mith) 1932- . . . . . CLC 49
See also CA 81-84

Wilson, Woodrow 1856-1924 . . . . . . TCLC 73
See also DLB 47

Winchilsea, Anne (Kingsmill) Finch Counte
1661-1720 . . . . LC 3

Windham, Basil
See Wodehouse, P(elham) G(renville)

Wingrove, David (John) 1954- . . . . . . CLC 68
See also CA 133

Wintergreen, Jane
See Duncan, Sara Jeannette

Winters, Janet Lewis . . . . CLC 41
See also Lewis, Janet
See also DLBY 87

Winters, (Arthur) Yvor
1900-1968 . . . . CLC 4, 8, 32
See also CA 11-12; 25-28R; CAP 1;
DLB 48; MTCW

Winterson, Jeanette
1959- . . . . CLC 64; DAM POP
See also CA 136; CANR 58

Winthrop, John 1588-1649 . . . . LC 31
See also DLB 24, 30

Wiseman, Frederick 1930- . . . . CLC 20
See also CA 159

Wister, Owen 1860-1938 . . . . TCLC 21
See also CA 108; DLB 9, 78; SATA 62

Witkacy
See Witkiewicz, Stanislaw Ignacy

Witkiewicz, Stanislaw Ignacy
1885-1939 . . . . TCLC 8
See also CA 105

Wittgenstein, Ludwig (Josef Johann)
1889-1951 . . . . TCLC 59
See also CA 113

Wittig, Monique 1935(?)- . . . . CLC 22
See also CA 116; 135; DLB 83

Wittlin, Jozef 1896-1976 . . . . CLC 25
See also CA 49-52; 65-68; CANR 3

Wodehouse, P(elham) G(renville)
1881-1975 . . . CLC 1, 2, 5, 10, 22; DAB;
DAC; DAM NOV; SSC 2
See also AITN 2; CA 45-48; 57-60;
CANR 3, 33; CDBLB 1914-1945;
DLB 34, 162; MTCW; SATA 22

Woiwode, L.
See Woiwode, Larry (Alfred)

Woiwode, Larry (Alfred) 1941- . . . CLC 6, 10
See also CA 73-76; CANR 16; DLB 6;
INT CANR-16

Wojciechowska, Maia (Teresa)
1927- . . . . **CLC 26**
See also AAYA 8; CA 9-12R; CANR 4, 41;
CLR 1; JRDA; MAICYA; SAAS 1;
SATA 1, 28, 83

Wolf, Christa 1929- . . . . **CLC 14, 29, 58**
See also CA 85-88; CANR 45; DLB 75;
MTCW

Wolfe, Gene (Rodman)
1931- . . . . **CLC 25; DAM POP**
See also CA 57-60; CAAS 9; CANR 6, 32,
60; DLB 8

Wolfe, George C. 1954- . . . . **CLC 49**
See also CA 149

Wolfe, Thomas (Clayton)
1900-1938 . . . . . **TCLC 4, 13, 29, 61; DA;**
DAB; DAC; DAM MST, NOV; WLC
See also CA 104; 132; CDALB 1929-1941;
DLB 9, 102; DLBD 2, 16; DLBY 85;
MTCW

Wolfe, Thomas Kennerly, Jr. 1931-
See Wolfe, Tom
See also CA 13-16R; CANR 9, 33;
DAM POP; INT CANR-9; MTCW

Wolfe, Tom . . . . **CLC 1, 2, 9, 15, 35, 51**
See also Wolfe, Thomas Kennerly, Jr.
See also AAYA 8; AITN 2; BEST 89:1;
DLB 152

Wolff, Geoffrey (Ansell) 1937- . . . . . **CLC 41**
See also CA 29-32R; CANR 29, 43

Wolff, Sonia
See Levitin, Sonia (Wolff)

Wolff, Tobias (Jonathan Ansell)
1945- . . . . **CLC 39, 64**
See also AAYA 16; BEST 90:2; CA 114;
117; CAAS 22; CANR 54; DLB 130;
INT 117

Wolfram von Eschenbach
c. 1170-c. 1220 . . . . **CMLC 5**
See also DLB 138

Wolitzer, Hilma 1930- . . . . **CLC 17**
See also CA 65-68; CANR 18, 40;
INT CANR-18; SATA 31

Wollstonecraft, Mary 1759-1797. . . . . . **LC 5**
See also CDBLB 1789-1832; DLB 39, 104,
158

Wonder, Stevie . . . . **CLC 12**
See also Morris, Steveland Judkins

Wong, Jade Snow 1922-. . . . . **CLC 17**
See also CA 109

Woodberry, George Edward
1855-1930 . . . . **TCLC 73**
See also DLB 71, 103

Woodcott, Keith
See Brunner, John (Kilian Houston)

Woodruff, Robert W.
See Mencken, H(enry) L(ouis)

Woolf, (Adeline) Virginia
1882-1941 . . . . . . **TCLC 1, 5, 20, 43, 56;**
DA; DAB; DAC; DAM MST, NOV;
SSC 7; WLC
See also CA 104; 130; CDBLB 1914-1945;
DLB 36, 100, 162; DLBD 10; MTCW

Woollcott, Alexander (Humphreys)
1887-1943 . . . . **TCLC 5**
See also CA 105; DLB 29

Woolrich, Cornell 1903-1968. . . . . . **CLC 77**
See also Hopley-Woolrich, Cornell George

Wordsworth, Dorothy
1771-1855 . . . . **NCLC 25**
See also DLB 107

Wordsworth, William
1770-1850 . . . . **NCLC 12, 38; DA; DAB;**
DAC; DAM MST, POET; PC 4; WLC
See also CDBLB 1789-1832; DLB 93, 107

Wouk, Herman
1915- . . **CLC 1, 9, 38; DAM NOV, POP**
See also CA 5-8R; CANR 6, 33; DLBY 82;
INT CANR-6; MTCW

Wright, Charles (Penzel, Jr.)
1935- . . . . **CLC 6, 13, 28**
See also CA 29-32R; CAAS 7; CANR 23,
36; DLB 165; DLBY 82; MTCW

Wright, Charles Stevenson
1932- . . . . **CLC 49; BLC 3;**
DAM MULT, POET
See also BW 1; CA 9-12R; CANR 26;
DLB 33

Wright, Jack R.
See Harris, Mark

Wright, James (Arlington)
1927-1980 . . . . **CLC 3, 5, 10, 28;**
DAM POET
See also AITN 2; CA 49-52; 97-100;
CANR 4, 34; DLB 5, 169; MTCW

Wright, Judith (Arundell)
1915- . . . . **CLC 11, 53; PC 14**
See also CA 13-16R; CANR 31; MTCW;
SATA 14

Wright, L(auraii) R. 1939-. . . . . **CLC 44**
See also CA 138

Wright, Richard (Nathaniel)
1908-1960 . . . . **CLC 1, 3, 4, 9, 14, 21, 48,**
74; BLC; DA; DAB; DAC; DAM MST,
MULT, NOV; SSC 2; WLC
See also AAYA 5; BW 1; CA 108;
CDALB 1929-1941; DLB 76, 102;
DLBD 2; MTCW

Wright, Richard B(ruce) 1937- . . . . . . **CLC 6**
See also CA 85-88; DLB 53

Wright, Rick 1945-. . . . . **CLC 35**

Wright, Rowland
See Wells, Carolyn

Wright, Stephen Caldwell 1946- . . . . **CLC 33**
See also BW 2

Wright, Willard Huntington 1888-1939
See Van Dine, S. S.
See also CA 115; DLBD 16

Wright, William 1930- . . . . **CLC 44**
See also CA 53-56; CANR 7, 23

Wroth, LadyMary 1587-1653(?) . . . . . **LC 30**
See also DLB 121

Wu Ch'eng-en 1500(?)-1582(?). . . . . . . **LC 7**

Wu Ching-tzu 1701-1754 . . . . **LC 2**

Wurlitzer, Rudolph 1938(?)- . . . **CLC 2, 4, 15**
See also CA 85-88; DLB 173

Wycherley, William
1641-1715 . . . . . **LC 8, 21; DAM DRAM**
See also CDBLB 1660-1789; DLB 80

Wylie, Elinor (Morton Hoyt)
1885-1928 . . . . **TCLC 8**
See also CA 105; DLB 9, 45

Wylie, Philip (Gordon) 1902-1971. . . **CLC 43**
See also CA 21-22; 33-36R; CAP 2; DLB 9

Wyndham, John. . . . . **CLC 19**
See also Harris, John (Wyndham Parkes
Lucas) Beynon

Wyss, Johann David Von
1743-1818 . . . . **NCLC 10**
See also JRDA; MAICYA; SATA 29;
SATA-Brief 27

Xenophon
c. 430B.C.-c. 354B.C. . . . . **CMLC 17**
See also DLB 176

Yakumo Koizumi
See Hearn, (Patricio) Lafcadio (Tessima
Carlos)

Yanez, Jose Donoso
See Donoso (Yanez), Jose

Yanovsky, Basile S.
See Yanovsky, V(assily) S(emenovich)

Yanovsky, V(assily) S(emenovich)
1906-1989 . . . . **CLC 2, 18**
See also CA 97-100; 129

Yates, Richard 1926-1992 . . . . . **CLC 7, 8, 23**
See also CA 5-8R; 139; CANR 10, 43;
DLB 2; DLBY 81, 92; INT CANR-10

Yeats, W. B.
See Yeats, William Butler

Yeats, William Butler
1865-1939 . . . . . **TCLC 1, 11, 18, 31; DA;**
DAB; DAC; DAM DRAM, MST,
POET; WLC
See also CA 104; 127; CANR 45;
CDBLB 1890-1914; DLB 10, 19, 98, 156;
MTCW

Yehoshua, A(braham) B.
1936- . . . . **CLC 13, 31**
See also CA 33-36R; CANR 43

Yep, Laurence Michael 1948- . . . . . . **CLC 35**
See also AAYA 5; CA 49-52; CANR 1, 46;
CLR 3, 17; DLB 52; JRDA; MAICYA;
SATA 7, 69

Yerby, Frank G(arvin)
1916-1991 . . . . **CLC 1, 7, 22; BLC;**
DAM MULT
See also BW 1; CA 9-12R; 136; CANR 16,
52; DLB 76; INT CANR-16; MTCW

Yesenin, Sergei Alexandrovich
See Esenin, Sergei (Alexandrovich)

Yevtushenko, Yevgeny (Alexandrovich)
1933- . . . . **CLC 1, 3, 13, 26, 51;**
DAM POET
See also CA 81-84; CANR 33, 54; MTCW

Yezierska, Anzia 1885(?)-1970 . . . . . **CLC 46**
See also CA 126; 89-92; DLB 28; MTCW

Yglesias, Helen 1915-. . . . . **CLC 7, 22**
See also CA 37-40R; CAAS 20; CANR 15;
INT CANR-15; MTCW

Yokomitsu Riichi 1898-1947 . . . . . . **TCLC 47**

Yonge, Charlotte (Mary)
1823-1901 . . . . **TCLC 48**
See also CA 109; DLB 18, 163; SATA 17

York, Jeremy
See Creasey, John

York, Simon
See Heinlein, Robert A(nson)

Yorke, Henry Vincent 1905-1974 ... **CLC 13**
See also Green, Henry
See also CA 85-88; 49-52

Yosano Akiko 1878-1942 .. **TCLC 59; PC 11**

Yoshimoto, Banana .... **CLC 84**
See also Yoshimoto, Mahoko

Yoshimoto, Mahoko 1964-
See Yoshimoto, Banana
See also CA 144

Young, Al(bert James)
1939- ..... **CLC 19; BLC; DAM MULT**
See also BW 2; CA 29-32R; CANR 26;
DLB 33

Young, Andrew (John) 1885-1971 .... **CLC 5**
See also CA 5-8R; CANR 7, 29

Young, Collier
See Bloch, Robert (Albert)

Young, Edward 1683-1765 .... **LC 3**
See also DLB 95

Young, Marguerite (Vivian)
1909-1995 .... **CLC 82**
See also CA 13-16; 150; CAP 1

Young, Neil 1945- .... **CLC 17**
See also CA 110

Young Bear, Ray A.
1950- .... **CLC 94; DAM MULT**
See also CA 146; DLB 175; NNAL

Yourcenar, Marguerite
1903-1987 .... **CLC 19, 38, 50, 87;
DAM NOV**
See also CA 69-72; CANR 23, 60; DLB 72;
DLBY 88; MTCW

Yurick, Sol 1925- .... **CLC 6**
See also CA 13-16R; CANR 25

Zabolotskii, Nikolai Alekseevich
1903-1958 .... **TCLC 52**
See also CA 116

Zamiatin, Yevgenii
See Zamyatin, Evgeny Ivanovich

Zamora, Bernice (B. Ortiz)
1938- ..... **CLC 89; DAM MULT; HLC**
See also CA 151; DLB 82; HW

Zamyatin, Evgeny Ivanovich
1884-1937 .... **TCLC 8, 37**
See also CA 105

Zangwill, Israel 1864-1926 .... **TCLC 16**
See also CA 109; DLB 10, 135

Zappa, Francis Vincent, Jr. 1940-1993
See Zappa, Frank
See also CA 108; 143; CANR 57

Zappa, Frank .... **CLC 17**
See also Zappa, Francis Vincent, Jr.

Zaturenska, Marya 1902-1982 .... **CLC 6, 11**
See also CA 13-16R; 105; CANR 22

Zeami 1363-1443 .... **DC 7**

Zelazny, Roger (Joseph)
1937-1995 .... **CLC 21**
See also AAYA 7; CA 21-24R; 148;
CANR 26, 60; DLB 8; MTCW;
SATA 57; SATA-Brief 39

Zhdanov, Andrei A(lexandrovich)
1896-1948 .... **TCLC 18**
See also CA 117

Zhukovsky, Vasily 1783-1852 .... **NCLC 35**

Ziegenhagen, Eric .... **CLC 55**

Zimmer, Jill Schary
See Robinson, Jill

Zimmerman, Robert
See Dylan, Bob

Zindel, Paul
1936- ..... **CLC 6, 26; DA; DAB; DAC;
DAM DRAM, MST, NOV; DC 5**
See also AAYA 2; CA 73-76; CANR 31;
CLR 3, 45; DLB 7, 52; JRDA; MAICYA;
MTCW; SATA 16, 58

Zinov'Ev, A. A.
See Zinoviev, Alexander (Aleksandrovich)

Zinoviev, Alexander (Aleksandrovich)
1922- .... **CLC 19**
See also CA 116; 133; CAAS 10

Zoilus
See Lovecraft, H(oward) P(hillips)

Zola, Emile (Edouard Charles Antoine)
1840-1902 ...... **TCLC 1, 6, 21, 41; DA;
DAB; DAC; DAM MST, NOV; WLC**
See also CA 104; 138; DLB 123

Zoline, Pamela 1941- .... **CLC 62**

Zorrilla y Moral, Jose 1817-1893 .. **NCLC 6**

Zoshchenko, Mikhail (Mikhailovich)
1895-1958 .... **TCLC 15; SSC 15**
See also CA 115

Zuckmayer, Carl 1896-1977 .... **CLC 18**
See also CA 69-72; DLB 56, 124

Zuk, Georges
See Skelton, Robin

Zukofsky, Louis
1904-1978 .... **CLC 1, 2, 4, 7, 11, 18;
DAM POET; PC 11**
See also CA 9-12R; 77-80; CANR 39;
DLB 5, 165; MTCW

Zweig, Paul 1935-1984 .... **CLC 34, 42**
See also CA 85-88; 113

Zweig, Stefan 1881-1942 .... **TCLC 17**
See also CA 112; DLB 81, 118

Zwingli, Huldreich 1484-1531 .... **LC 37**
See also DLB 179

Literary Criticism Series
Cumulative Topic Index

This index lists all topic entries in Gale's *Classical and Medieval Literature Criticism, Contemporary Literary Criticism, Literature Criticism from 1400 to 1800, Nineteenth-Century Literature Criticism,* and *Twentieth-Century Literary Criticism.*

Topic Index

Topic Index

Topic Index

NCLC Cumulative Nationality Index

Nationality Index

ISBN 0-7876-1247-2